D0793592

America Votes™

America Votes™

ELECTION RETURNS BY STATE

RHODES COOK
ALICE V. McGILLIVRAY
RICHARD M. SCAMMON

2005–2006

A Division of Congressional Quarterly Inc.
Washington, D.C.

CQ Press
1255 22nd Street, NW, Suite 400
Washington, DC 20037

Phone: 202-729-1900; toll-free, 1-866-4CQ-PRESS (1-866-427-7737)

Web: www.cqpress.com

Copyright © 2007 by CQ Press, a division of Congressional Quarterly Inc.

All rights reserved. No part of this publication may be reproduced or transmitted in any form or by any means, electronic or mechanical, including photocopy, recording, or any information storage and retrieval system, without permission in writing from the publisher.

Cover design: Anne Masters Design, Inc.
Composition: Aptara, Inc.

♾ The paper used in this publication exceeds the requirements of the American National Standard for Information Sciences–Permanence of Paper for Printed Library Materials, ANSI Z39.48-1992.

Printed and bound in the United States of America

11   10   09   08   07   1   2   3   4   5

ISBN: 978-0-87289-358-0
ISSN: 0065-678X

Contents

Election Returns by State

List of Maps

Introduction

The jury is out on whether the 2006 midterm election should be considered a great victory for the Democrats, but there is little doubt that the results were a stern rebuff for President George W. Bush and the Republican-controlled Congress: Not since 1986 have Republicans lost as many as six Senate seats in a single election, as they did in 2006. Not since 1974 has the GOP lost as many as thirty House seats. Not since 1954 have Republicans lost control of both houses of Congress in the same election.

Moreover, Republican setbacks were not limited to the national level in 2006. The GOP also lost a half dozen governorships, the largest number of gubernatorial losses for the party since 1982. At each of these levels, not a single Democratic incumbent on the November ballot suffered defeat. To be sure, the Republican losses in 2006 were not as great as they were for the Democrats in 1994, when Congress and a majority of governorships went to the GOP. That year, however, the Republican tidal wave caught the political community unaware. Dozens of vulnerable Democratic seats, particularly in the South, were unexpectedly swept away.

This time, Republicans had fewer exposed seats to defend as well as plenty of advance warning that 2006 would be a difficult election for them. President Bush's approval rating stood well below 40 percent much of the year, and the standing of the Republican Congress sat mired at a much lower level than his. Rising public disapproval of the violent, seemingly endless war in Iraq weighed down Bush, keeping his approval rating fully 20 percentage points below where it had been on the eve of the 2002 midterm election and fully 10 points below his standing in fall 2004. The Republican-dominated Congress drew fire for a "culture of corruption," which ended the careers of several ethically tainted GOP members, as well as a reputation as an underperforming rubber stamp of the executive branch. Republicans had hoped to minimize their losses by localizing congressional races, insulating them from the national tide in a way that would allow incumbents to emphasize their own individual records and exploit their large campaign chests. The array of problems facing the GOP blunted that strategy, enabling Democrats

2006: DEMOCRATIC COMEBACK

Twelve years after losing both the House and the Senate, Democrats won back both chambers. They regained the House in 2006 with more than a dozen seats to spare. Their margin in the Senate, however, was razor thin, with control depending on the willingness of two independents—Joseph I. Lieberman of Connecticut and Bernard Sanders of Vermont— to caucus with the Democrats. To complete their comeback, Democrats also reversed the Republican advantage in governorships.

The chart below reflects partisan totals immediately before and after the 2006 general election. The preelection House totals include four vacancies—representing a trio of seats formerly held by the Republicans in Florida, Ohio, and Texas plus a Democratic vacancy in New Jersey—that are credited to the appropriate party in the preelection count.

	Preelection			Postelection		
	Rep.	Dem.	Other	Rep.	Dem.	Other
Governor	28	22	0	22	28	0
Senate	55	44	1	49	49	2
House	232	202	1	202	233	0

to nationalize the congressional races by essentially saying "Had enough? Vote Democratic!"

As such, the 2006 midterm election turned into a referendum on President Bush and Republican leadership—a referendum that the GOP clearly lost: Abruptly ended (at least for the time being) was the Republican era of governance. Put on hold (maybe for good) was talk of a permanent Republican majority in the nation at large. Thrown into doubt was the wisdom of the White House strategy of nurturing the GOP's base rather than appealing to a broader swath of the electorate.

As in 2004, Republican voters cast their ballots virtually en masse for Republican candidates as did Democrats for Democratic candidates. Self-described independents, who had split their presidential ballots almost evenly between the two sides in 2004, broke for the Democrats in

Counting the 2006 Vote

There was no mistaking the dominance of the Democrats in the 2006 midterm election. They rolled up an aggregate advantage of more than 4 million votes in gubernatorial races across the country, more than 6 million votes in House contests, and more than 7 million votes in Senate races. Results are based on official returns from 38 gubernatorial contests (36 held in 2006, 2 in 2005) and 33 Senate races, as well as two versions of the House vote. "All Races" feature the results from the 430 districts in which a vote was taken in 2006. "Contested Races" are those in which both the Democrats and Republicans fielded candidates. In 2006, seats in 380 districts were contested, 55 were not. No blank or void ballots are included in the totals below.

Office	Total Vote	Republican	Democratic	Other	Rep.-Dem. Plurality	Percentage of Total Vote		
						Rep.	Dem.	Other
Governor	70,782,569	31,284,213	35,699,318	3,799,038	4,415,105 D	44.2%	50.4%	5.4%
Senate	62,959,001	26,677,327	33,932,637	2,349,037	7,255,310 D	42.4%	53.9%	3.7%
House								
All Races	80,136,543	35,943,108	42,347,880	1,845,555	6,404,772 D	44.9%	52.8%	2.3%
Contested Races	73,307,166	34,540,353	37,572,689	1,194,124	3,032,336 D	47.1%	51.3%	1.6%

2006: Close House Races

Close House races abounded in 2006, as 42 candidates were elected to a seat in the 110th Congress with less than 52 percent of the total vote in their district. That compares with 25 sub-52 percent winners in 2002 and just 11 in 2004. An asterisk (*) indicates an incumbent.

Republicans (24)	2006 Winning Percentage	Democrats (18)	2006 Winning Percentage
Marilyn Musgrave, Colo. 4*	45.6%	Tim Mahoney, Fla. 16	49.5%
Barbara Cubin, Wyo. AL*	48.3%	Joe Courtney, Conn. 2	50.0%
Jon Porter, Nev. 3*	48.5%	Baron P. Hill, Ind. 9	50.0%
John T. Doolittle, Calif. 4*	49.1%	John Barrow, Ga. 12*	50.3%
Mike Ferguson, N.J. 7*	49.4%	Patrick J. Murphy, Pa. 8	50.3%
Bill Sali, Idaho 1	49.9%	Harry Mitchell, Ariz. 5	50.4%
Tim Walberg, Mich. 7	49.9%	Jim Marshall, Ga. 8*	50.5%
Michele Bachmann, Minn. 6	50.1%	Nancy Boyda, Kan. 2	50.6%
Vern Buchanan, Fla. 13	50.1%	John Yarmuth, Ky. 3	50.6%
Robin Hayes, N.C. 8*	50.1%	Melissa Bean, Ill. 8*	50.9%
Deborah Pryce, Ohio 15*	50.2%	Steven L. Kagen, Wis. 8	50.9%
Heather A. Wilson, N.M. 1*	50.2%	Ron Klein, Fla. 22	50.9%
Dean Heller, Nev. 2	50.3%	John Hall, N.Y. 19	51.2%
Jean Schmidt, Ohio 2*	50.5%	Carol Shea-Porter, N.H. 1	51.3%
Jim Gerlach, Pa. 6*	50.7%	Dave Loebsack, Iowa 2	51.4%
James T. Walsh, N.Y. 25*	50.8%	Leonard L. Boswell, Iowa 3*	51.8%
Christopher Shays, Conn. 4*	51.0%		
Thelma Drake, Va. 2*	51.3%	Nick Lampson, Texas 22	51.8%
Peter J. Roskam, Ill. 6	51.4%	Jason Altmire, Pa. 4	51.9%
John R. "Randy" Kuhl Jr., N.Y. 29*	51.5%		
Dave Reichert, Wash. 8*	51.5%		
Joe Knollenberg, Mich. 9*	51.6%		
Geoff Davis, Ky. 4*	51.7%		
Rick Renzi, Ariz. 1*	51.8%		

2006 by a margin of roughly 20 percentage points. Other important segments of the electorate also moved dramatically toward the Democrats, including self-described moderates, young voters, and the fast-growing Hispanic community, assiduously courted by Bush and Republican leaders in recent years. Hispanics went Democratic by a margin of more than 2-to-1 in 2006, just two years after giving Bush some 40 percent of the vote en route to reelection. As a result, the GOP, which had gained seats in both houses of Congress in every previous election during Bush's presidency, now has fewer seats in both chambers than when Bush was first elected, in 2000. To be fair, this has been the norm for virtually every two-term president since Woodrow Wilson in the early twentieth century, with sixth-year losses so common that they have become known as the "six-year itch."

The "itch," however, is not an immutable law of politics. Democrats defied it during Bill Clinton's sixth-year midterm in 1998, gaining five House seats and maintaining their total in the Senate, even as Clinton staggered under the weight of impeachment. The 2006 vote was more like a traditional sixth-year election, exacerbated by strong personal feelings throughout the electorate toward Bush and his administration. More than half of all voters said they cast their vote, at least in part, as a reflection of their sentiments toward the president, about whom most of these voters had a negative opinion. In another sense, the 2006 midterm voting had the feel of a British parliamentary election, with many voters casting their ballots along party lines rather than for the individual candidates.

The House since 1990: From Democratic to Republican to Democratic

The House of Representatives went from Democratic to Republican control in 1994, fueled in large part by the GOP upsurge in the South. The House reverted to the Democrats in 2006, due in no small measure to the huge Democratic advantage in the East. Regions are defined below. An "I" indicates Independent.

	South				West			Midwest			East				Total House			
	R	D	I		R	D		R	D		R	D	I		R	D	I	
1990	44	85	0	D	37	48	D	45	68	D	41	66	1	D	167	267	1	D
1992	52	85	0	D	38	55	D	44	61	D	42	57	1	D	176	258	1	D
1994	73	64	0	R	53	40	R	59	46	R	45	54	1	D	230	204	1	R
1996	82	55	0	R	51	42	R	55	50	R	39	60	1	D	227	207	1	R
1998	82	55	0	R	49	44	R	54	51	R	38	61	1	D	223	211	1	R
2000	81	55	1	R	43	50	D	57	48	R	40	59	1	D	221	212	2	R
2002	85	57	0	R	46	52	D	61	39	R	37	57	1	D	229	205	1	R
2004	91	51	0	R	45	53	D	60	40	R	36	58	1	D	232	202	1	R
2006	85	57	0	R	41	57	D	51	49	R	25	70	0	D	202	233	0	D
Net Change in GOP Seats, 1994–2006	+12				−12			−8			−20				−28			

EAST—Connecticut, Delaware, Maine, Maryland, Massachusetts, New Hampshire, New Jersey, New York, Pennsylvania, Rhode Island, Vermont, West Virginia.
MIDWEST—Illinois, Indiana, Iowa, Kansas, Michigan, Minnesota, Missouri, Nebraska, North Dakota, Ohio, South Dakota, Wisconsin.
SOUTH—Alabama, Arkansas, Florida, Georgia, Kentucky, Louisiana, Mississippi, North Carolina, Oklahoma, South Carolina, Tennessee, Texas, Virginia.
WEST—Alaska, Arizona, California, Colorado, Hawaii, Idaho, Montana, Nevada, New Mexico, Oregon, Utah, Washington, Wyoming.

In 2004, the GOP had won the presidential and congressional votes by an identical margin of 3 percentage points: 51 to 48 percent for Bush in the presidential balloting (a decrease of 6 points from Bush's share of the 2000 presidential vote) and 50 to 47 percent for Republicans in the House of Representatives. In 2006, the House vote flipped to 53 to 45 percent for the Democrats, representing a decline of 5 percentage points in the Republicans' share of the congressional vote from 2004.

Democrats made significant gains in rural and small-town America compared to their showings in recent elections, but the party's most dramatic gains were in the suburbs, particularly those in the Northeast, Midwest, and upper South. Since 1992, the Democrats had been making visible inroads within this segment of the electorate—reliably Republican a generation ago—helping the party carry major electoral vote prizes, such as California, Illinois, Michigan, New Jersey, and Pennsylvania, with regularity in presidential voting.

In 2006, the suburbs played a primary role in the Democratic takeover of the Senate. In Pennsylvania, Democratic challenger Bob Casey Jr. swamped Republican incumbent Rick Santorum by a margin of 175,000 votes in the suburban Philadelphia counties of Bucks, Chester, Delaware, and Montgomery. In winning reelection six years earlier, Santorum had carried these same four counties by 150,000 votes. In Missouri, Democratic challenger Claire McCaskill overwhelmed GOP incumbent Jim Talent by 50,000 votes in suburban St. Louis County, the state's most populous jurisdiction. Talent had lost the county by only 15,000 votes in his narrow win over Democratic incumbent Jean Carnahan in a 2002 special election. In Virginia, Democratic challenger James Webb bested Republican Senator George Allen by 65,000 votes in the Old Dominion's most populous jurisdiction, suburban Fairfax County. Allen had lost the county by barely 15,000 votes in 2000, when he ousted Democratic incumbent Charles Robb. Whereas, Casey won his Senate race

2006: Defeated Incumbents

In many recent elections, open seats have been the main battleground in congressional voting, as nearly all of the incumbents in both parties have routinely glided to reelection. In 2006, the Democratic congressional takeover was due primarily to the party's success in ousting Republican incumbents. All six Senate seats and 22 of the 30 House seats that Democrats picked up resulted from the defeat of GOP incumbents. Only in gubernatorial contests were open seats the prime source of Democratic gains. There, the party defeated only one Republican governor but captured five open seats for a total gain of six governorships.

The chart below lists the gubernatorial, Senate, and House incumbents defeated in the 2006 primaries and general election, the number of terms they had served in that office at the time of their loss in 2006, the percentage of the total vote they had received in the previous general election (2000 for senators, 2002 for governors, and 2004 for House members), and their percentage of the total vote in the 2006 general election (for those who were not sidelined by the primaries).

	Number of Terms	Previous Election Percentage	2006 Election Percentage
GOVERNORS (2)			
Primaries			
(1 Republican)			
Frank H. Murkowski, R-Alaska	1	55.8%	—
General Election			
(1 Republican)			
Robert L. Ehrlich Jr., R-Md.	1	51.6%	46.2%
SENATOR (7)			
Primaries			
(1 Democrat)			
Joseph I. Lieberman, D-Conn.*	3	63.2%	49.7%
General Election			
(6 Republicans)			
George Allen, R-Va.	1	52.3%	49.2%
Conrad Burns, R-Mont.	3	50.6%	48.3%
Lincoln Chafee, R-R.I.	1	56.8%	46.4%
Mike DeWine, R-Ohio	2	59.9%	43.8%
Rick Santorum, R-Pa.	2	52.4%	41.3%
Jim Talent, R-Mo.#	1	49.8%	47.3%
REPRESENTATIVES (24)			
Primaries			
(1 Democrat, 1 Republican)			
Cynthia A. McKinney, D-Ga. 4	6	63.8%	—
Joe Schwarz, R-Mich. 7	1	58.4%	—
General Election			
(22 Republicans)			
Charles Bass, R-N.H. 2	6	58.3%	45.6%
Henry Bonilla, R-Texas 23@	7	69.3%	45.7%
Jeb Bradley, R-N.H. 1	2	63.3%	48.6%
Chris Chocola, R-Ind. 2	2	54.2%	46.0%
Michael G. Fitzpatrick, R-Pa. 8	1	55.3%	49.7%
Gil Gutknecht, R-Minn. 1	6	59.6%	47.1%
Melissa A. Hart, R-Pa. 4	3	63.1%	48.0%
J. D. Hayworth, R-Ariz. 5	6	59.5%	46.4%
John Hostettler, R-Ind. 8	6	53.4%	39.0%
Nancy L. Johnson, R-Conn. 5	12	59.8%	43.5%
Sue W. Kelly, R-N.Y. 19	6	66.7%	48.8%
Jim Leach, R-Iowa 2	15	58.9%	48.5%
Anne M. Northup, R-Ky. 3	5	60.3%	48.2%
Richard W. Pombo, R-Calif. 11	7	61.2%	46.7%
Jim Ryun, R-Kan. 2	5	56.1%	47.1%
E. Clay Shaw Jr., R-Fla. 22	13	62.8%	47.1%
Don Sherwood, R-Pa. 10	4	92.8%	47.0%
Rob Simmons, R-Conn. 2	3	54.2%	50.0%
Mike Sodrel, R-Ind. 9	1	49.5%	45.5%
John E. Sweeney, R-N.Y. 20	4	65.8%	46.9%
Charles H. Taylor, R-N.C. 11	8	54.9%	46.2%
Curt Weldon, R-Pa. 7	10	58.8%	43.6%

Note: An asterisk (*) indicates that Senator Joseph I. Lieberman lost the Democratic primary in Connecticut, but won reelection in the fall running on the ballot of Connecticut for Lieberman. A pound sign (#) indicates that Senator Jim Talent of Missouri was first elected in a 2002 special election. @ indicates that the 2006 general election percentage for Rep. Henry Bonilla of Texas was from a runoff.

handily over Santorum in November—his victory in the Philadelphia suburbs representing icing on the cake—for McCaskill and Webb, their large margins of victory in St. Louis and Fairfax counties, respectively, were critical, as neither would have won their race without them.

Republicans can argue that the 2006 election was hardly devastating. Remove the liberal bicoastal bookends of California and New York—where Democrats won thirty-two more House seats than the Republicans and all four Senate seats—and the Republicans would have maintained an edge in both chambers of Congress. On the other hand, Democrats can argue that the GOP has been reduced to being the party of the South but little else. In 2002, Republican House candidates won more votes than the Democrats in every region except the Northeast. In 2006, Democratic House candidates won more votes than the Republicans in every region except the South.

Democrats consolidated their hold on the Northeast so firmly in 2006 that it now provides a greater building block for the Democrats in congressional voting than the South provides the GOP. To be sure, the South has more political clout in terms of raw numbers. Its thirteen states (those of the old Confederacy plus Kentucky and Oklahoma) have 142 House seats. The twelve states of the Northeast, stretching from Maine to West Virginia, have just ninety-five seats.

With the rout of Republicans across the Northeast in 2006, the Democratic advantage in the region reached forty-five House seats, while the GOP edge in the South fell to less than thirty seats. Meanwhile, with Webb's victory in Virginia, Democrats controlled five Senate seats from the South. That equals the number of Senate seats the Republicans held in the Northeast after the defeat of Lincoln Chafee of Rhode Island and Santorum. To round out their consolidation of the region, Democrats gained governorships in Maryland, Massachusetts, and New York.

In the category of "how times have changed," once-Republican New England has now become the cornerstone of the Democratic Northeast. Democrats picked up both Republican House seats in New Hampshire, the land of "Live Free or Die," plus two GOP seats in Connecticut. That put the House count for New England at 21 Democrats to 1 Republican. Connecticut's Christopher Shays, a 51 percent winner in 2006, held the distinction of being the lone Republican standing.

Democratic success in 2006 was nationwide, as the party made inroads in all parts of the country. In the Midwest, they picked up a pair of Senate seats (Ohio and Missouri), a governorship (Ohio), and turned a 60–40 GOP House majority in this battleground region into a virtual dead heat. In the Mountain West, Democrats built on inroads made in 2004, gaining a critical Senate seat in Montana, a governorship in Colorado, and a trio of House seats (two in Arizona, one in Colorado). In the South, Democrats made notable gains on the fringes, picking up a House seat in Louisville, two in south Florida, and two in Texas (including one predominantly Hispanic district that stretches along the Mexican border from San Antonio to El Paso). For good measure, Democrats retook the Arkansas governorship and captured a western North Carolina House seat on the home turf of evangelist Billy Graham.

There is little doubt that the 2006 results tarnished the reputation for voter mobilization that the Republicans had built earlier in the Bush presidency. The GOP operation was clearly not strong enough to serve as a firewall in a political environment loaded with bad news for the party. Yet it is also arguable that without their well-calibrated turnout machinery, Republican losses would have been even more severe in 2006, particularly in the House. There, a Republican loss of thirty seats might have approached fifty, if a number of GOP incumbents—from Shays in Connecticut to John Doolittle in California—had not been able to narrowly weather the anti-Republican tide.

Roughly 80 million voters cast ballots in the 2006 midterm congressional election, about two-thirds the number that had participated in the 2004 presidential election. Yet the turnout in 2006 was still high for a midterm election, with the rate for House elections approaching 40 percent of the citizen voting-age population, the highest midterm rate since 1982.

Democrats scored significant gains in the House largely because they were able to expand the playing field, which had shrunk dramatically in recent elections. When Republicans won control of Congress in 1994, there were nearly 100 competitive House races (as measured by a winning percentage of less than 55 percent of the total vote). In 2002, that number was less than 50, and two years later, the total of such competitive House contests fell to just 32. In 2006, the number of sub-55 percent winners rebounded to 68, the highest in a decade. Going into the election, Republicans held virtually all of these seats but Democrats then won many of them, with the result that a number of marginal House seats are now held either by Democratic challengers who won narrowly or Republican incumbents who barely escaped defeat.

Clearly, the 2006 election was a unique one—a sharp rebuke for President Bush and his party, if not a vote of confidence in the Democrats. Yet the pro-Republican elections of 2002 and 2004, with their backdrop of war and terror, were also unusual. Neither the Democrats nor the GOP came out of the 2006 election able to realistically portray themselves as the country's "party of choice"— underscored by the fact that even seemingly decisive elections like 2002, 2004, and 2006 were not determined by landslide margins. Not since 1986 has either party won more than 53 percent of the nationwide House vote. Not since 1988 has either party captured even 51 percent of the popular vote for president. The United States may no longer be a "50–50" nation, but it is not far removed from being so.

The Methodology

The twenty-seventh volume of *America Votes* follows the same general pattern of recent editions in this series. An introduction with text and tables ties together various aspects of the 2006 election cycle. The section that follows presents tables with state-by-state voter turnout and votes for gubernatorial, Senate, and House elections in the 2006 election cycle. Also featured are a summary of special elections held between the general elections of 2004 and 2006 to fill vacancies in the 109th Congress and a list of changes in congressional membership in the 110th Congress that occurred between the 2006 general election and the end of June 2007. The heart of the volume, fifty chapters—one for each state—follows this introductory material.

Each state chapter begins with a profile listing the current governor, senators, and representatives, followed by tables of the statewide vote for president, governor, and senator from 1946 or 1948 to the present. A map of the state shows its counties, major population centers, and congressional districts for members of the House in the 110th Congress. County-by-county tables of gubernatorial and Senate elections follow the maps. All these tables concern the 2006 general election with the exception of the governorships in New Jersey and Virginia, where voting took place in 2005.

The county tables for gubernatorial and Senate elections feature a three-column format of candidates (Republican, Democratic, Other). Exceptions occur where another candidate has received at least 10 percent of the vote, in which case a column for his or her votes is also included. All the county tables include 2000 population figures from the Census Bureau.

A listing of votes cast for candidates for the House of Representatives is arranged by congressional district. The implementation of the 2000 Census for redistricting purposes led to changes in all states with more than one House member before the 2002 election, with the exception of Maine, which drew new congressional district lines after 2002. There were also post-2002 district changes in Pennsylvania and Texas—with those in Texas having major political ramifications—and significant post-2004 changes in Georgia and again in Texas. Votes for House members in Georgia and Texas are for the districts as defined for the 110th Congress alone. House results for elections before 2002 are not included for any state except those with a single member in the House.

The conclusion of each state chapter consists of two parts. The first part is a notes section containing a breakdown of votes cast in the general election for third party, independent, and write-in candidates. For those major party candidates who also ran on a third party ballot line, votes are aggregated as Democratic or Republican. Blank space by a contest indicates that no votes were cast in these categories. The second part provides official results for the primary elections for governor, Senate, and House held in the 2006 election cycle.

In the chapters for New England states, tables list the vote for governor and senator by larger cities and towns as well as by counties. In Rhode Island, the results are listed for all cities and towns.

The America Votes series is compiled from official results obtained from election authorities in each state. Although complete accuracy is always the goal, it can sometimes prove elusive in a work such as this. On occasion, states may belatedly report changes in their vote totals that occur after publication of this volume, and human nature being what it is, there is always an example or two (or three) of self-inflicted errors. The goal is always to keep these to a minimum. In light of the desire to make these reference volumes as useful as possible to readers and researchers, corrections of data are always welcome as are suggestions for new material.

As in the preparation of *America Votes 23, 24, 25*, and *26*, heartfelt thanks are in order to the Federal Election Commission's Eileen J. Canavan, with whom the author consulted in an effort to reconcile discrepancies in vote totals.

Considerable thanks also go to David Arthur and his CQ Press colleagues, who once again shepherded the movement of copy with skill and good humor. His work, with that of others, was invaluable in the completion of this volume.

Rhodes Cook
July 2007

America
Votes™

UNITED STATES

VOTER TURNOUT 2006

State	2006 Voting Age Population	Registration- '06 General Election	Percentage Voting Age Registered	U.S. House Vote	House Vote as Percent of Voting Age Population	House Vote as Percent of Registered Voters	Senate Vote	Governor Vote	Highest Vote	Highest Vote as Percent of Voting Age Pop.	High Race
Alabama	3,482,000	2,717,521	78.0%	1,140,152	32.7%	42.0%	—	1,250,401	G	35.9%	1,250,401
Alaska	458,000	464,620	101.4%	234,645	51.2%	50.5%	—	237,322	G	51.8%	237,322
Arizona	3,936,000	3,061,540	77.8%	1,493,150	37.9%	48.8%	1,526,782	1,533,645	G	39.0%	1,533,645
Arkansas	2,103,000	1,656,863	78.8%	763,011	36.3%	46.1%	—	774,680	G	36.8%	774,680
California	21,091,000	15,837,108	75.1%	8,295,816	39.3%	52.4%	8,541,476	8,679,416	G	41.2%	8,679,416
Colorado	3,400,000	2,975,845	87.5%	1,538,908	45.3%	51.7%	—	1,558,387	G	45.8%	1,558,387
Connecticut	2,386,000	2,046,487	85.8%	1,074,739	45.0%	52.5%	1,134,780	1,123,466	S	47.6%	1,134,780
Delaware	616,000	557,703	90.5%	251,694	40.9%	45.1%	254,099	—	S	41.2%	254,099
Florida	12,680,000	11,614,788	91.6%	3,851,942	30.4%	33.2%	4,793,534	4,829,270	G	38.1%	4,829,270
Georgia	6,337,000	5,132,902	81.0%	2,070,307	32.7%	40.3%	—	2,122,258	G	33.5%	2,122,258
Hawaii	892,000	662,728	74.3%	337,944	37.9%	51.0%	342,842	344,315	G	38.6%	344,315
Idaho	1,026,000	764,880	74.5%	445,306	43.4%	58.2%	—	450,832	G	43.9%	450,832
Illinois	8,615,000	7,320,080	85.0%	3,453,708	40.1%	47.2%	—	3,487,989	G	40.5%	3,487,989
Indiana	4,643,000	4,295,687	92.5%	1,666,922	35.9%	38.8%	1,341,111	—	H	35.9%	1,666,922
Iowa	2,211,000	2,077,239	94.0%	1,033,688	46.8%	49.8%	—	1,053,255	G	47.6%	1,053,255
Kansas	1,977,000	1,663,017	84.1%	845,127	42.7%	50.8%	—	849,700	G	43.0%	849,700
Kentucky	3,191,000	2,766,288	86.7%	1,253,526	39.3%	45.3%	—	—	H	39.3%	1,253,526
Louisiana	3,359,000	2,890,093	86.0%	902,498	26.9%	31.2%	—	—	H	26.9%	902,498
Maine	995,000	1,023,956	102.9%	535,865	53.9%	52.3%	543,981	550,865	G	55.4%	550,865
Maryland	3,851,000	3,348,207	86.9%	1,701,202	44.2%	50.8%	1,781,139	1,788,316	G	46.4%	1,788,316
Massachusetts	4,515,000	3,990,505	88.4%	1,923,657	42.6%	48.2%	2,165,490	2,219,779	G	49.2%	2,219,779
Michigan	7,370,000	7,180,778	97.4%	3,648,502	49.5%	50.8%	3,780,142	3,801,256	G	51.6%	3,801,256
Minnesota	3,727,000	3,118,393	83.7%	2,178,974	58.5%	69.9%	2,202,772	2,202,937	G	59.1%	2,202,937
Mississippi	2,201,000	1,778,119	80.8%	600,697	27.3%	33.8%	610,921	—	S	27.8%	610,921
Missouri	4,307,000	4,007,174	93.0%	2,097,322	48.7%	52.3%	2,128,459	—	S	49.4%	2,128,459
Montana	727,000	645,678	88.8%	406,134	55.9%	62.9%	406,505	—	S	55.9%	406,505
Nebraska	1,272,000	1,138,069	89.5%	596,087	46.9%	52.4%	592,316	593,357	H	46.9%	596,087
Nevada	1,621,000	1,229,229	75.8%	574,827	35.5%	46.8%	582,572	582,158	S	35.9%	582,572
New Hampshire	960,000	848,317	88.4%	402,669	41.9%	47.5%	—	403,679	G	42.0%	403,679
New Jersey	5,729,000	4,861,279	84.9%	2,136,842	37.3%	44.0%	2,250,070	2,290,099	G	40.0%	2,290,099
New Mexico	1,363,000	1,088,928	79.9%	561,084	41.2%	51.5%	558,550	559,170	H	41.2%	561,084
New York	12,511,000	11,677,187	93.3%	4,140,378	33.1%	35.5%	4,490,053	4,437,220	S	35.9%	4,490,053
North Carolina	6,379,000	5,568,981	87.3%	1,940,808	30.4%	34.9%	—	—	H	30.4%	1,940,808
North Dakota	486,000	—		217,621	44.8%	—	218,152	—	S	44.9%	218,152
Ohio	8,559,000	7,905,705	92.4%	3,961,195	46.3%	50.1%	4,019,236	4,022,754	G	47.0%	4,022,754
Oklahoma	2,623,000	2,066,533	78.8%	905,194	34.5%	43.8%	—	926,462	G	35.3%	926,462
Oregon	2,654,000	2,561,428	96.5%	1,357,434	51.1%	53.0%	—	1,379,475	G	52.0%	1,379,475
Pennsylvania	9,268,000	8,182,876	88.3%	4,013,388	43.3%	49.0%	4,081,043	4,096,077	G	44.2%	4,096,077
Rhode Island	754,000	682,344	90.5%	373,382	49.5%	54.7%	385,451	387,010	G	51.3%	387,010
South Carolina	3,199,000	2,593,791	81.1%	1,086,206	34.0%	41.9%	—	1,091,952	G	34.1%	1,091,952
South Dakota	579,000	554,038	95.7%	333,562	57.6%	60.2%	—	335,508	G	57.9%	335,508
Tennessee	4,576,000	3,738,154	81.7%	1,715,426	37.5%	45.9%	1,833,695	1,818,549	S	40.1%	1,833,695
Texas	14,594,000	13,074,279	89.6%	4,179,701	28.6%	32.0%	4,314,663	4,399,116	G	30.1%	4,399,116
Utah	1,658,000	1,507,463	90.9%	569,690	34.4%	37.8%	571,252	—	S	34.5%	571,252
Vermont	478,000	433,576	90.7%	262,726	55.0%	60.6%	262,419	262,524	H	55.0%	262,726
Virginia	5,395,000	4,555,940	84.4%	2,297,236	42.6%	50.4%	2,370,445	1,983,778	S	43.9%	2,370,445
Washington	4,495,000	3,807,857	84.7%	2,054,056	45.7%	53.9%	2,083,734	—	S	46.4%	2,083,734
West Virginia	1,434,000	1,137,371	79.3%	454,813	31.7%	40.0%	459,884	—	S	32.1%	459,884
Wisconsin	4,126,000	3,448,767	83.6%	2,063,413	50.0%	59.8%	2,138,297	2,161,700	G	52.4%	2,161,700
Wyoming	389,000	263,083	67.6%	193,369	49.7%	73.5%	193,136	193,892	G	49.8%	193,892
TOTAL	205,198,000	176,523,394	86.0%	80,136,543	39.1%	45.4%	62,959,001	70,782,569		40.8%	83,750,549

Note: The "Highest Vote" reflects the race among the following with the highest number of votes cast: G - Governor; S - Senate; H - House. The District of Columbia is not included in this midterm election table because it does not elect a governor or voting members of Congress. Nonetheless, the District had an estimated voting age population of 383,000 in 2006, which would bring the national voting age population to 205,581,000, if included. Votes are from the November 2006 general election, with the exception of gubernatorial elections in New Jersey and Virginia, which were held in 2005.

Source: Registration and voting age population figures were provided by the Committee for the Study of the American Electorate (CSAE), a part of the American University Center for Democracy and Election Management. Voting age population figures are based on the estimated citizen voting age population in each state (and nationally) at the time of the November 2006 general election. Registration figures for virtually every state are as of the November 2006 general election. In some cases, the registration totals are suspect as some states include inactive voters in their totals. In Alaska and Wyoming, the number of registered voters was more than 100 percent of the voting age population. North Dakota does not require voter registration.

GUBERNATORIAL ELECTIONS 2005 AND 2006

State	Total Vote	Republican		Democratic		Other Vote	Rep.-Dem. Plurality	Percentage			
								Total Vote		Major Vote	
		Vote	Candidate	Vote	Candidate			Rep.	Dem.	Rep.	Dem.
Alabama	1,250,401	718,327	Riley, Bob	519,827	Baxley, Lucy	12,247	198,500 R	57.4%	41.6%	58.0%	42.0%
Alaska	237,322	114,697	Palin, Sarah H.	97,238	Knowles, Tony	25,387	17,459 R	48.3%	41.0%	54.1%	45.9%
Arizona	1,533,645	543,528	Munsil, Len	959,830	Napolitano, Janet	30,287	416,302 D	35.4%	62.6%	36.2%	63.8%
Arkansas	774,680	315,040	Hutchinson, Asa	430,765	Beebe, Mike D.	28,875	115,725 D	40.7%	55.6%	42.2%	57.8%
California	8,679,416	4,850,157	Schwarzenegger, Arnold	3,376,732	Angelides, Phil	452,527	1,473,425 R	55.9%	38.9%	59.0%	41.0%
Colorado	1,558,387	625,886	Beauprez, Bob	888,096	Ritter, Bill Jr.	44,405	262,210 D	40.2%	57.0%	41.3%	58.7%
Connecticut	1,123,466	710,048	Rell, M. Jodi	398,220	DeStefano, John	15,198	311,828 R	63.2%	35.4%	64.1%	35.9%
Florida	4,829,270	2,519,845	Crist, Charlie	2,178,289	Davis, Jim	131,136	341,556 R	52.2%	45.1%	53.6%	46.4%
Georgia	2,122,258	1,229,724	Perdue, Sonny	811,049	Taylor, Mark	81,485	418,675 R	57.9%	38.2%	60.3%	39.7%
Hawaii	344,315	215,313	Lingle, Linda	121,717	Iwase, Randy	7,285	93,596 R	62.5%	35.4%	63.9%	36.1%
Idaho	450,832	237,437	Otter, C. L. "Butch"	198,845	Brady, Jerry M.	14,550	38,592 R	52.7%	44.1%	54.4%	45.6%
Illinois	3,487,989	1,369,315	Topinka, Judy Baar	1,736,731	Blagojevich, Rod R.	381,943	367,416 D	39.3%	49.8%	44.1%	55.9%
Iowa	1,053,255	467,425	Nussle, Jim	569,021	Culver, Chet	16,809	101,596 D	44.4%	54.0%	45.1%	54.9%
Kansas	849,700	343,586	Barnett, Jim	491,993	Sebelius, Kathleen	14,121	148,407 D	40.4%	57.9%	41.1%	58.9%
Maine	550,865	166,425	Woodcock, Chandler E.	209,927	Baldacci, John	174,513	43,502 D	30.2%	38.1%	44.2%	55.8%
Maryland	1,788,316	825,464	Ehrlich, Robert L. Jr.	942,279	O'Malley, Martin	20,573	116,815 D	46.2%	52.7%	46.7%	53.3%
Massachusetts	2,219,779	784,342	Healey, Kerry	1,234,984	Patrick, Deval	200,453	450,642 D	35.3%	55.6%	38.8%	61.2%
Michigan	3,801,256	1,608,086	DeVos, Dick	2,142,513	Granholm, Jennifer M.	50,657	534,427 D	42.3%	56.4%	42.9%	57.1%
Minnesota	2,202,937	1,028,568	Pawlenty, Tim	1,007,460	Hatch, Mike	166,909	21,108 R	46.7%	45.7%	50.5%	49.5%
Nebraska	593,357	435,507	Heineman, Dave	145,115	Hahn, David	12,735	290,392 R	73.4%	24.5%	75.0%	25.0%
Nevada	582,158	279,003	Gibbons, Jim	255,684	Titus, Dina	47,471	23,319 R	47.9%	43.9%	52.2%	47.8%
New Hampshire	403,679	104,288	Coburn, Jim	298,760	Lynch, John	631	194,472 D	25.8%	74.0%	25.9%	74.1%
New Jersey (1)	2,290,099	985,271	Forrester, Doug	1,224,551	Corzine, Jon	80,277	239,280 D	43.0%	53.5%	44.6%	55.4%
New Mexico	559,170	174,364	Dendahl, John	384,806	Richardson, Bill		210,442 D	31.2%	68.8%	31.2%	68.8%
New York	4,437,220	1,274,335	Faso, John	3,086,709	Spitzer, Eliot	76,176	1,812,374 D	28.7%	69.6%	29.2%	70.8%
Ohio	4,022,754	1,474,285	Blackwell, J. Kenneth	2,435,384	Strickland, Ted	113,085	961,099 D	36.6%	60.5%	37.7%	62.3%
Oklahoma	926,462	310,327	Istook, Ernest	616,135	Henry, Brad		305,808 D	33.5%	66.5%	33.5%	66.5%
Oregon	1,379,475	589,748	Saxton, Ron	699,786	Kulongoski, Theodore R.	89,941	110,038 D	42.8%	50.7%	45.7%	54.3%
Pennsylvania	4,096,077	1,622,135	Swann, Lynn	2,470,517	Rendell, Edward G.	3,425	848,382 D	39.6%	60.3%	39.6%	60.4%
Rhode Island	387,010	197,366	Carcieri, Donald L.	189,562	Fogarty, Charles J.	82	7,804 R	51.0%	49.0%	51.0%	49.0%
South Carolina	1,091,952	601,868	Sanford, Mark	489,076	Moore, Tommy	1,008	112,792 R	55.1%	44.8%	55.2%	44.8%
South Dakota	335,508	206,990	Rounds, Mike	121,226	Billion, Jack	7,292	85,764 R	61.7%	36.1%	63.1%	36.9%
Tennessee	1,818,549	540,853	Bryson, Jim	1,247,491	Bredesen, Phil	30,205	706,638 D	29.7%	68.6%	30.2%	69.8%
Texas	4,399,116	1,716,792	Perry, Rick	1,310,337	Bell, Chris	1,371,987	406,455 R	39.0%	29.8%	56.7%	43.3%
Vermont	262,524	148,014	Douglas, Jim	108,090	Parker, Scudder	6,420	39,924 R	56.4%	41.2%	57.8%	42.2%
Virginia (1)	1,983,778	912,327	Kilgore, Jerry W.	1,025,942	Kaine, Timothy M.	45,509	113,615 D	46.0%	51.7%	47.1%	52.9%
Wisconsin	2,161,700	979,427	Green, Mark	1,139,115	Doyle, James E.	43,158	159,688 D	45.3%	52.7%	46.2%	53.8%
Wyoming	193,892	58,100	Hunkins, Ray	135,516	Freudenthal, Dave	276	77,416 D	30.0%	69.9%	30.0%	70.0%
TOTAL	70,782,569	31,284,213		35,699,318		3,799,038	4,415,105 D	44.2%	50.4%	46.7%	53.3%

(1) 2005 election

SENATE ELECTIONS 2006

State	Total Vote	Republican		Democratic		Other Vote	Rep.-Dem. Plurality	Percentage			
		Vote	Candidate	Vote	Candidate			Total Vote		Major Vote	
								Rep.	Dem.	Rep.	Dem.
Arizona	1,526,782	814,398	Kyl, Jon	664,141	Pederson, Jim	48,243	150,257 R	53.3%	43.5%	55.1%	44.9%
California	8,541,476	2,990,822	Mountjoy, Richard "Dick"	5,076,289	Feinstein, Dianne	474,365	2,085,467 D	35.0%	59.4%	37.1%	62.9%
Connecticut (1)	1,134,780	109,198	Schlesinger, Alan	450,844	Lamont, Ned	574,738	113,251 I	9.6%	39.7%	19.5%	80.5%
Delaware	254,099	69,734	Ting, Jan	170,567	Carper, Thomas R.	13,798	100,833 D	27.4%	67.1%	29.0%	71.0%
Florida	4,793,534	1,826,127	Harris, Katherine	2,890,548	Nelson, Bill	76,859	1,064,421 D	38.1%	60.3%	38.7%	61.3%
Hawaii	342,842	126,097	Thielen, Cynthia	210,330	Akaka, Daniel K.	6,415	84,233 D	36.8%	61.3%	37.5%	62.5%
Indiana	1,341,111	1,171,553	Lugar, Richard G.		—	169,558	1,171,553 R	87.4%		100.0%	
Maine	543,981	402,598	Snowe, Olympia J.	111,984	Hay Bright, Jean	29,399	290,614 R	74.0%	20.6%	78.2%	21.8%
Maryland	1,781,139	787,182	Steele, Michael S.	965,477	Cardin, Benjamin L.	28,480	178,295 D	44.2%	54.2%	44.9%	55.1%
Massachusetts	2,165,490	661,532	Chase, Kenneth G.	1,500,738	Kennedy, Edward M.	3,220	839,206 D	30.5%	69.3%	30.6%	69.4%
Michigan	3,780,142	1,559,597	Bouchard, Michael	2,151,278	Stabenow, Debbie	69,267	591,681 D	41.3%	56.9%	42.0%	58.0%
Minnesota	2,202,772	835,653	Kennedy, Mark	1,278,849	Klobuchar, Amy	88,270	443,196 D	37.9%	58.1%	39.5%	60.5%
Mississippi	610,921	388,399	Lott, Trent	213,000	Fleming, Erik R.	9,522	175,399 R	63.6%	34.9%	64.6%	35.4%
Missouri	2,128,459	1,006,941	Talent, Jim	1,055,255	McCaskill, Claire	66,263	48,314 D	47.3%	49.6%	48.8%	51.2%
Montana	406,505	196,283	Burns, Conrad	199,845	Tester, Jon	10,377	3,562 D	48.3%	49.2%	49.6%	50.4%
Nebraska	592,316	213,928	Ricketts, Pete	378,388	Nelson, Ben		164,460 D	36.1%	63.9%	36.1%	63.9%
Nevada	582,572	322,501	Ensign, John	238,796	Carter, Jack	21,275	83,705 R	55.4%	41.0%	57.5%	42.5%
New Jersey	2,250,070	997,775	Kean, Thomas H. Jr.	1,200,843	Menendez, Robert	51,452	203,068 D	44.3%	53.4%	45.4%	54.6%
New Mexico	558,550	163,826	McCulloch, Allen W.	394,365	Bingaman, Jeff	359	230,539 D	29.3%	70.6%	29.3%	70.7%
New York	4,490,053	1,392,189	Spencer, John	3,008,428	Clinton, Hillary Rodham	89,436	1,616,239 D	31.0%	67.0%	31.6%	68.4%
North Dakota	218,152	64,417	Grotberg, Dwight	150,146	Conrad, Kent	3,589	85,729 D	29.5%	68.8%	30.0%	70.0%
Ohio	4,019,236	1,761,037	DeWine, Mike	2,257,369	Brown, Sherrod	830	496,332 D	43.8%	56.2%	43.8%	56.2%
Pennsylvania	4,081,043	1,684,778	Santorum, Rick	2,392,984	Casey, Bob Jr.	3,281	708,206 D	41.3%	58.6%	41.3%	58.7%
Rhode Island	385,451	179,001	Chafee, Lincoln	206,110	Whitehouse, Sheldon	340	27,109 D	46.4%	53.5%	46.5%	53.5%
Tennessee	1,833,695	929,911	Corker, Bob	879,976	Ford, Harold E. Jr.	23,808	49,935 R	50.7%	48.0%	51.4%	48.6%
Texas	4,314,663	2,661,789	Hutchison, Kay Bailey	1,555,202	Radnofsky, Barbara Ann	97,672	1,106,587 R	61.7%	36.0%	63.1%	36.9%
Utah	571,252	356,238	Hatch, Orrin G.	177,459	Ashdown, Pete	37,555	178,779 R	62.4%	31.1%	66.7%	33.3%
Vermont (2)	262,419	84,924	Tarrant, Rich		—	177,495	86,714 I	32.4%		100.0%	
Virginia	2,370,445	1,166,277	Allen, George	1,175,606	Webb, James	28,562	9,329 D	49.2%	49.6%	49.8%	50.2%
Washington	2,083,734	832,106	McGavick, Mike	1,184,659	Cantwell, Maria	66,969	352,553 D	39.9%	56.9%	41.3%	58.7%
West Virginia	459,884	155,043	Raese, John R.	296,276	Byrd, Robert C.	8,565	141,233 D	33.7%	64.4%	34.4%	65.6%
Wisconsin	2,138,297	630,299	Lorge, Robert Gerald	1,439,214	Kohl, Herb	68,784	808,915 D	29.5%	67.3%	30.5%	69.5%
Wyoming	193,136	135,174	Thomas, Craig	57,671	Groutage, Dale	291	77,503 R	70.0%	29.9%	70.1%	29.9%
TOTAL	62,959,001	26,677,327		33,932,637		2,349,037	7,255,310 D	42.4%	53.9%	44.0%	56.0%

(1) In Connecticut, Joseph I. Lieberman ran on the Connecticut for Lieberman line and won the election with 564,095 votes (49.7 percent of the total vote). The plurality listed is the difference between Lieberman's vote and the vote for the Democratic runner-up.

(2) In Vermont, Bernard Sanders ran as an independent and won the election with 171,638 votes (65.4 percent of the total vote). The plurality listed is the difference between Sanders' vote and the vote for the Republican runner-up.

HOUSE OF REPRESENTATIVES ELECTIONS 2006

State	Seats Won Republican	Seats Won Democratic	Total Vote	Republican	Democratic	Other	Rep.-Dem. Plurality	Total Vote Rep.	Total Vote Dem.	Major Vote Rep.	Major Vote Dem.
Alabama	5	2	1,140,152	627,501	502,046	10,605	125,455 R	55.0%	44.0%	55.6%	44.4%
Alaska	1	0	234,645	132,743	93,879	8,023	38,864 R	56.6%	40.0%	58.6%	41.4%
Arizona	4	4	1,493,150	771,246	627,259	94,645	143,987 R	51.7%	42.0%	55.1%	44.9%
Arkansas	1	3	763,011	306,442	456,569		150,127 D	40.2%	59.8%	40.2%	59.8%
California	19	34	8,295,816	3,314,398	4,720,164	261,254	1,405,766 D	40.0%	56.9%	41.3%	58.7%
Colorado	3	4	1,538,908	623,784	832,888	82,236	209,104 D	40.5%	54.1%	42.8%	57.2%
Connecticut	1	4	1,074,739	419,895	648,653	6,191	228,758 D	39.1%	60.4%	39.3%	60.7%
Delaware	1	0	251,694	143,897	97,565	10,232	46,332 R	57.2%	38.8%	59.6%	40.4%
Florida	16	9	3,851,942	2,182,833	1,599,968	69,141	582,865 R	56.7%	41.5%	57.7%	42.3%
Georgia	7	6	2,070,307	1,138,048	932,143	116	205,905 R	55.0%	45.0%	55.0%	45.0%
Hawaii	0	2	337,944	118,134	219,810		101,676 D	35.0%	65.0%	35.0%	65.0%
Idaho	2	0	445,306	248,105	177,376	19,825	70,729 R	55.7%	39.8%	58.3%	41.7%
Illinois	9	10	3,453,708	1,442,969	1,987,114	23,625	544,145 D	41.8%	57.5%	42.1%	57.9%
Indiana	4	5	1,666,922	831,785	812,496	22,641	19,289 R	49.9%	48.7%	50.6%	49.4%
Iowa	2	3	1,033,688	522,388	492,937	18,363	29,451 R	50.5%	47.7%	51.5%	48.5%
Kansas	2	2	845,127	459,267	369,191	16,669	90,076 R	54.3%	43.7%	55.4%	44.6%
Kentucky	4	2	1,253,526	611,780	601,723	40,023	10,057 R	48.8%	48.0%	50.4%	49.6%
Louisiana	5	2	902,498	579,702	295,762	27,034	283,940 R	64.2%	32.8%	66.2%	33.8%
Maine	0	2	535,865	163,155	350,681	22,029	187,526 D	30.4%	65.4%	31.8%	68.2%
Maryland	2	6	1,701,202	546,862	1,099,441	54,899	552,579 D	32.1%	64.6%	33.2%	66.8%
Massachusetts	0	10	1,923,657	198,550	1,632,307	92,800	1,433,757 D	10.3%	84.9%	10.8%	89.2%
Michigan	9	6	3,648,502	1,624,865	1,923,485	100,152	298,620 D	44.5%	52.7%	45.8%	54.2%
Minnesota	3	5	2,178,974	924,636	1,152,621	101,717	227,985 D	42.4%	52.9%	44.5%	55.5%
Mississippi	2	2	600,697	304,308	260,330	36,059	43,978 R	50.7%	43.3%	53.9%	46.1%
Missouri	5	4	2,097,322	1,049,346	992,258	55,718	57,088 R	50.0%	47.3%	51.4%	48.6%
Montana	1	0	406,134	239,124	158,916	8,094	80,208 R	58.9%	39.1%	60.1%	39.9%
Nebraska	3	0	596,087	334,177	261,910		72,267 R	56.1%	43.9%	56.1%	43.9%
Nevada	2	1	574,827	260,317	287,879	26,631	27,562 D	45.3%	50.1%	47.5%	52.5%
New Hampshire	0	2	402,669	189,615	209,434	3,620	19,819 D	47.1%	52.0%	47.5%	52.5%
New Jersey	6	7	2,136,842	903,176	1,207,784	25,882	304,608 D	42.3%	56.5%	42.8%	57.2%
New Mexico	2	1	561,084	247,825	313,124	135	65,299 D	44.2%	55.8%	44.2%	55.8%
New York	6	23	4,140,378	1,338,518	2,794,262	7,598	1,455,744 D	32.3%	67.5%	32.4%	67.6%
North Carolina	6	7	1,940,808	913,893	1,026,915		113,022 D	47.1%	52.9%	47.1%	52.9%
North Dakota	0	1	217,621	74,687	142,934		68,247 D	34.3%	65.7%	34.3%	65.7%
Ohio	11	7	3,961,195	1,870,390	2,081,737	9,068	211,347 D	47.2%	52.6%	47.3%	52.7%
Oklahoma	4	1	905,194	518,025	372,888	14,281	145,137 R	57.2%	41.2%	58.1%	41.9%
Oregon	1	4	1,357,434	557,491	765,853	34,090	208,362 D	41.1%	56.4%	42.1%	57.9%
Pennsylvania	8	11	4,013,388	1,732,163	2,229,091	52,134	496,928 D	43.2%	55.5%	43.7%	56.3%
Rhode Island	0	2	373,382	41,856	265,028	66,498	223,172 D	11.2%	71.0%	13.6%	86.4%
South Carolina	4	2	1,086,206	599,615	472,719	13,872	126,896 R	55.2%	43.5%	55.9%	44.1%
South Dakota	0	1	333,562	97,864	230,468	5,230	132,604 D	29.3%	69.1%	29.8%	70.2%
Tennessee	4	5	1,715,426	799,547	860,861	55,018	61,314 D	46.6%	50.2%	48.2%	51.8%
Texas	19	13	4,179,701	2,183,833	1,852,613	143,255	331,220 R	52.2%	44.3%	54.1%	45.9%
Utah	2	1	569,690	292,235	244,483	32,972	47,752 R	51.3%	42.9%	54.4%	45.6%
Vermont	0	1	262,726	117,023	139,815	5,888	22,792 D	44.5%	53.2%	45.6%	54.4%
Virginia	8	3	2,297,236	1,222,790	947,103	127,343	275,687 R	53.2%	41.2%	56.4%	43.6%
Washington	3	6	2,054,056	798,005	1,244,095	11,956	446,090 D	38.9%	60.6%	39.1%	60.9%
West Virginia	1	2	454,813	190,893	263,822	98	72,929 D	42.0%	58.0%	42.0%	58.0%
Wisconsin	3	5	2,063,413	1,040,071	1,003,156	20,186	36,915 R	50.4%	48.6%	50.9%	49.1%
Wyoming	1	0	193,369	93,336	92,324	7,709	1,012 R	48.3%	47.7%	50.3%	49.7%
TOTAL	202	233	80,136,543	35,943,108	42,347,880	1,845,555	6,404,772 D	44.9%	52.8%	45.9%	54.1%

UNITED STATES

SPECIAL ELECTIONS TO THE 109TH CONGRESS

From the beginning of 2005 through 2006, one appointment was made to fill a vacancy in the Senate and six special elections were held to fill vacancies in the House of Representatives. In addition, Republican Mark Foley of the Florida 16th District resigned his seat on September 29, 2006, after the disclosure of sexually explicit e-mails he wrote to male congressional pages, and Republican Bob Ney of the Ohio 18th District resigned his seat on November 3, 2006, after pleading guilty to influence peddling on behalf of clients of convicted lobbyist Jack Abramoff. In neither case was there a special election. The Senate appointment and House special elections held to fill vacancies in the 109th Congress are listed below.

SENATOR

NEW JERSEY

Jon Corzine (D) resigned January 17, 2007, to become governor of New Jersey. Rep. Robert Menendez (D) was appointed by Corzine to be his successor and was sworn in as senator on January 18, 2007.

REPRESENTATIVES

CALIFORNIA 5th CD

Robert T. Matsui (D) died January 1, 2005. His widow, Doris Matsui (D), was elected in the first round of voting on March 8, 2005, to fill the remainder of his term in the 109th Congress.

March 8, 2005 Special Primary Election

56,175 Doris Matsui (D); 7,158 Julie Padilla (D); 6,559 John Thomas Flynn (R); 3,742 Serge A. Chernay (R); 2,591 Michael O'Brien (R); 1,753 Shane Singh (R); 1,124 Bruce Robert Stevens (R); 976 Pat Driscoll (Green); 916 Leonard Padilla (Independent); 659 Charles "Carlos" Pineda Jr. (D); 451 Gale Morgan (Libertarian); 286 John C. Reiger (Peace & Freedom); 6 Lara Shapiro (write-in).

CALIFORNIA 48th CD

Christopher Cox (R) resigned August 2, 2005, to become chairman of the Securities and Exchange Commission (SEC). John Campbell (R) was elected December 6, 2005, to fill the remainder of his term in the 109th Congress. The highest vote-getter in each party in the October 4, 2005, special primary election qualified for the December 6 voting.

October 4, 2005 Special Primary Election

41,420 John Campbell (R); 15,595 Marilyn C. Brewer (R); 13,423 Jim Gilchrist (American Independent); 7,941 Steve Young (D); 3,667 John Graham (D); 2,944 Bea Foster (D); 1,417 Don Udall (R); 1,070 John Kelly (R); 790 Bea Tiritilli (Green); 731 Bruce Cohen (Libertarian); 523 David R. Crouch (R); 397 Scott MacCabe (R); 351 Marsha A. Morris (R); 307 Tom Pallow (D); 153 Guy E. Mailly (R); 110 Marshall Samuel Sanders (R); 101 Edward A. Suppe (R); 11 Delecia Holt (R write-in); 2 Steven Wesley Blake (R write-in).

December 6, 2005 Special General Election

46,184 John Campbell (R); 28,853 Steve Young (D); 26,507 Jim Gilchrist (American Independent); 1,430 Bea Tiritilli (Green); 974 Bruce Cohen (Libertarian).

CALIFORNIA 50th CD

Randy "Duke" Cunningham (R) resigned December 1, 2005, after pleading guilty to accepting bribes and tax evasion. Brian P. Bilbray (R) was elected June 6, 2006, to fill the remainder of his term in the 109th Congress. The highest vote-getter in each party in the April 11, 2006, special primary election qualified for the June 6 voting.

April 11, 2006 Special Primary Election

60,010 Francine Busby (D); 20,952 Brian P. Bilbray (R); 19,891 Eric Roach (R); 10,207 Howard Kaloogian (R); 7,369 Bill Morrow (R); 5,477 Alan Uke (R); 2,957 Richard Earnest (R); 2,207 Bill Hauf (R); 2,041 Scott Turner (R); 1,808 Chris Young (D); 1,111 William Griffith (Independent); 912 Victor E. Ramirez (R); 819 Paul King (Libertarian); 574 Jeff Newsome (R); 345 Scott Orren (R); 261 Delicia Holt (R); 204 Bill Boyer (R); 58 Milton Gale (R).

UNITED STATES

SPECIAL ELECTIONS TO THE 109th CONGRESS

June 6, 2006 Special General Election

78,341 Brian P. Bilbray (R); 71,146 Francine Busby (D); 6,027 William Griffith (Independent); 2,519 Libertarian (Paul King).

NEW JERSEY 13th CD

Robert Menendez (D) resigned his seat January 17, 2006, on appointment to the Senate. Albio Sires (D) was elected November 7, 2006, to fill the remainder of his term in the 109th Congress.

November 7, 2006 Special Election

75,403 Albio Sires (D); 2,592 Dick Hester (Pro Life Conservative).

OHIO 2nd CD

Rob Portman (R) resigned his seat April 29, 2005, to become U.S. trade representative in the Bush administration. Jean Schmidt (R) was elected August 2, 2005, to fill the remainder of his term in the 109th Congress.

June 14, 2005 Special Democratic Primary

7,935 Paul Hackett; 3,800 Victoria Wells Wulsin; 1,215 Charles W. Sanders; 663 James John Parker; 268 Jeff Sinnard; 12 Arthur Stanley Katz (write-in).

June 14, 2005 Special Republican Primary

14,331 Jean Schmidt; 11,663 Bob McEwen; 9,320 Tom Brinkman Jr.; 5,467 Pat De wine; 2,113 Eric Minamyer; 1,029 Peter A. Fossett; 687 Tom Bemmes; 403 Jeff Morgan; 362 David R. Smith; 217 Steve Austin; 90 Douglas E. Mink.

August 2, 2005 Special Election

59,671 Jean Schmidt (R); 55,886 Paul Hackett; 15 James J. Condit Jr. (write-in); 4 James E. Constable Jr. (write-in).

TEXAS 22nd CD

Tom DeLay (R) resigned his seat June 9, 2006, after indictment the previous year on money laundering charges. Shelley Sekula Gibbs (R) was elected November 7, 2006, to fill the remainder of his term in the 109th Congress.

November 7, 2006 Special Election

76,924 Shelley Sekula Gibbs (R); 23,425 M. Bob Smither (Libertarian); 13,600 Steve Stockman (R); 7,405 Don Richardson (R); 2,568 Giannibicego Hoa Tran (R).

UNITED STATES

HOUSE SPECIAL ELECTIONS 2005 TO 2006: A SUMMARY

Six special House elections were held to fill vacancies in the 109th Congress. None resulted in a change of party hands, but two of the special elections were won with less than 50 percent of the vote and another with a bare majority. The results below are based on the decisive round of voting in each special election when the new member was elected to Congress. The special elections are listed in the chronological order in which they were held.

District	Former Member	New Member	Date Elected	Winning Percentage	Voter Turnout
California 5th	Robert T. Matsui (D)	Doris Matsui (D)	March 8, 2005	68.2%	82,396
Ohio 2	Rob Portman (R)	Jean Schmidt (R)	August 2, 2005	51.6%	115,576
California 48th	Christopher Cox (R)	John Campbell (R)	December 6, 2005	44.4%	103,948
California 50th	Randy "Duke" Cunningham (R)	Brian P. Bilbray (R)	June 6, 2006	49.6%	158,033
New Jersey 13th	Robert Menendez (D)	Albio Sires (D)	November 7, 2006	96.7%	77,995
Texas 22nd	Tom DeLay (R)	Shelley Sekula Gibbs (R)	November 7, 2006	62.1%	123,922

CHANGES FOLLOWING THE 2006 ELECTION

Following the 2006 general election, and through June 30, 2007, the following changes took place in the membership of the 110th Congress.

REPRESENTATIVES

California, 37th District–Juanita Millender-McDonald (D) died April 22, 2007. A special election was scheduled for August 21, 2007, to fill the seat.

Georgia, 10th District–Charlie Norwood (R) died February 13, 2007. A special election was scheduled for July 17, 2007, to fill the seat.

SENATOR

Wyoming–Craig Thomas (R) died June 4, 2007.

UNITED STATES

POPULAR VOTE FOR PRESIDENT 1920 TO 2004

Year	Total Vote	Republican Vote	Candidate	Democratic Vote	Candidate	Other Vote	Plurality	Percentage Total Vote Rep.	Dem.	Major Vote Rep.	Dem.
2004	122,295,345	62,040,610	Bush, George W.	59,028,439	Kerry, John	1,226,296	3,012,171 R	50.7%	48.3%	51.2%	48.8%
2000	105,396,627	50,455,156	Bush, George W.	50,992,335	Gore, Al	3,949,136	537,179 D	47.9%	48.4%	49.7%	50.3%
1996	96,277,872	39,198,755	Dole, Bob	47,402,357	Clinton, Bill	9,676,760	8,203,602 D	40.7%	49.2%	45.3%	54.7%
1992	104,425,014	39,103,882	Bush, George	44,909,326	Clinton, Bill	20,411,806	5,805,444 D	37.4%	43.0%	46.5%	53.5%
1988	91,594,809	48,886,097	Bush, George	41,809,074	Dukakis, Michael S.	899,638	7,077,023 R	53.4%	45.6%	53.9%	46.1%
1984	92,652,842	54,455,075	Reagan, Ronald	37,577,185	Mondale, Walter F.	620,582	16,877,890 R	58.8%	40.6%	59.2%	40.8%
1980	86,515,221	43,904,153	Reagan, Ronald	35,483,883	Carter, Jimmy	7,127,185	8,420,270 R	50.7%	41.0%	55.3%	44.7%
1976	81,555,889	39,147,793	Ford, Gerald R.	40,830,763	Carter, Jimmy	1,577,333	1,682,970 D	48.0%	50.1%	48.9%	51.1%
1972	77,718,554	47,169,911	Nixon, Richard M.	29,170,383	McGovern, George S.	1,378,260	17,999,528 R	60.7%	37.5%	61.8%	38.2%
1968	73,211,875	31,785,480	Nixon, Richard M.	31,275,166	Humphrey, Hubert H.	10,151,229	510,314 R	43.4%	42.7%	50.4%	49.6%
1964	70,644,592	27,178,188	Goldwater, Barry M.	43,129,566	Johnson, Lyndon B.	336,838	15,951,378 D	38.5%	61.1%	38.7%	61.3%
1960	68,838,219	34,108,157	Nixon, Richard M.	34,226,731	Kennedy, John F.	503,331	118,574 D	49.5%	49.7%	49.9%	50.1%
1956	62,026,908	35,590,472	Eisenhower, Dwight D.	26,022,752	Stevenson, Adlai E.	413,684	9,567,720 R	57.4%	42.0%	57.8%	42.2%
1952	61,550,918	33,936,234	Eisenhower, Dwight D.	27,314,992	Stevenson, Adlai E.	299,692	6,621,242 R	55.1%	44.4%	55.4%	44.6%
1948	48,793,826	21,991,291	Dewey, Thomas E.	24,179,345	Truman, Harry S.	2,623,190	2,188,054 D	45.1%	49.6%	47.6%	52.4%
1944	47,976,670	22,017,617	Dewey, Thomas E.	25,612,610	Roosevelt, Franklin D.	346,443	3,594,993 D	45.9%	53.4%	46.2%	53.8%
1940	49,900,418	22,348,480	Willkie, Wendell	27,313,041	Roosevelt, Franklin D.	238,897	4,964,561 D	44.8%	54.7%	45.0%	55.0%
1936	45,654,763	16,684,231	Landon, Alfred M.	27,757,333	Roosevelt, Franklin D.	1,213,199	11,073,102 D	36.5%	60.8%	37.5%	62.5%
1932	39,758,759	15,760,684	Hoover, Herbert C.	22,829,501	Roosevelt, Franklin D.	1,168,574	7,068,817 D	39.6%	57.4%	40.8%	59.2%
1928	36,805,951	21,437,277	Hoover, Herbert C.	15,007,698	Smith, Alfred E.	360,976	6,429,579 R	58.2%	40.8%	58.8%	41.2%
1924	29,095,023	15,719,921	Coolidge, Calvin	8,386,704	Davis, John W.	4,988,398	7,333,217 R	54.0%	28.8%	65.2%	34.8%
1920	26,768,613	16,153,115	Harding, Warren G.	9,133,092	Cox, James M.	1,482,406	7,020,023 R	60.3%	34.1%	63.9%	36.1%

Note: For detail of other vote see note section included with each U.S. summary table that follows.

ELECTORAL COLLEGE VOTE 1920 TO 2004

Year	Total	Republican	Democratic	Other	
2004	538	286	251	1	EDWARDS
2000	538	271	266	1	(Blank)
1996	538	159	379	—	
1992	538	168	370	—	
1988	538	426	111	1	BENTSEN
1984	538	525	13	—	
1980	538	489	49	—	
1976	538	240	297	1	REAGAN
1972	538	520	17	1	LIBERTARIAN
1968	538	301	191	46	AIP
1964	538	52	486	—	
1960	537	219	303	15	BYRD
1956	531	457	73	1	JONES
1952	531	442	89	—	
1948	531	189	303	39	SR
1944	531	99	432	—	
1940	531	82	449	—	
1936	531	8	523	—	
1932	531	59	472	—	
1928	531	444	87	—	
1924	531	382	136	13	PROGRESSIVE
1920	531	404	127	—	

ALABAMA

Congressional districts first established for elections held in 2002
7 members

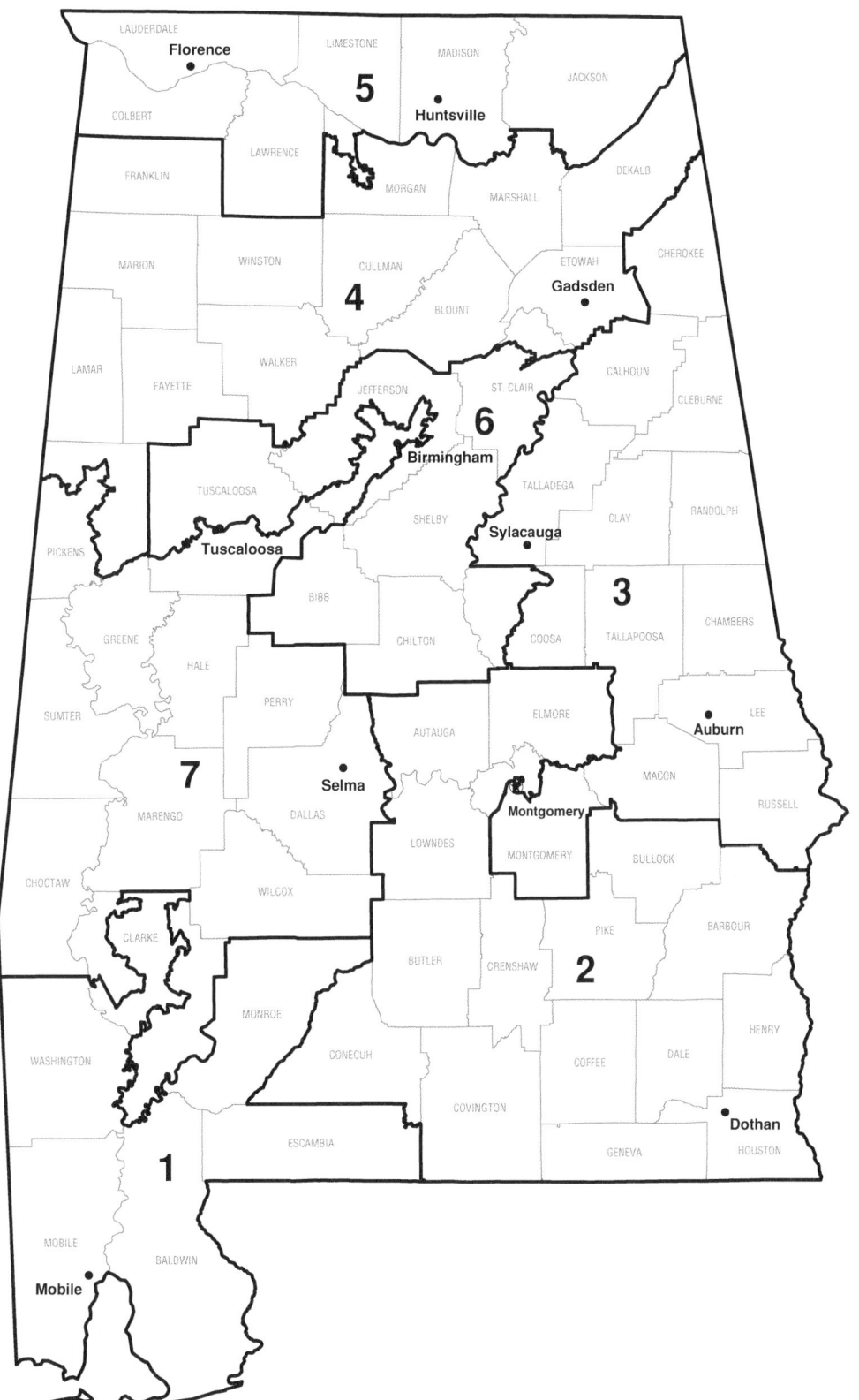

ALABAMA

GOVERNOR
Bob Riley (R). Reelected 2006 to a four-year term. Previously elected 2002.

SENATORS (2 Republicans)
Richard C. Shelby (R). Reelected 2004 to a six-year term. Previously elected 1998, 1992, 1986. Changed party affiliation from Democratic to Republican in November 1994.

Jeff Sessions (R). Reelected 2002 to a six-year term. Previously elected 1996.

REPRESENTATIVES (5 Republicans, 2 Democrats)
1. Jo Bonner (R)
2. Terry Everett (R)
3. Mike D. Rogers (R)
4. Robert B. Aderholt (R)
5. Robert E. "Bud" Cramer (D)
6. Spencer Bachus (R)
7. Artur Davis (D)

POSTWAR VOTE FOR PRESIDENT

Year	Total Vote	Republican Vote	Republican Candidate	Democratic Vote	Democratic Candidate	Other Vote	Plurality	Total Vote Rep.	Total Vote Dem.	Major Vote Rep.	Major Vote Dem.
2004	1,883,415	1,176,394	Bush, George W.	693,933	Kerry, John	13,088	482,461 R	62.5%	36.8%	62.9%	37.1%
2000**	1,666,272	941,173	Bush, George W.	692,611	Gore, Al	32,488	248,562 R	56.5%	41.6%	57.6%	42.4%
1996**	1,534,349	769,044	Dole, Bob	662,165	Clinton, Bill	103,140	106,879 R	50.1%	43.2%	53.7%	46.3%
1992**	1,688,060	804,283	Bush, George	690,080	Clinton, Bill	193,697	114,203 R	47.6%	40.9%	53.8%	46.2%
1988	1,378,476	815,576	Bush, George	549,506	Dukakis, Michael S.	13,394	266,070 R	59.2%	39.9%	59.7%	40.3%
1984	1,441,713	872,849	Reagan, Ronald	551,899	Mondale, Walter F.	16,965	320,950 R	60.5%	38.3%	61.3%	38.7%
1980**	1,341,929	654,192	Reagan, Ronald	636,730	Carter, Jimmy	51,007	17,462 R	48.8%	47.4%	50.7%	49.3%
1976	1,182,850	504,070	Ford, Gerald R.	659,170	Carter, Jimmy	19,610	155,100 D	42.6%	55.7%	43.3%	56.7%
1972	1,006,111	728,701	Nixon, Richard M.	256,923	McGovern, George S.	20,487	471,778 R	72.4%	25.5%	73.9%	26.1%
1968**	1,049,922	146,923	Nixon, Richard M.	196,579	Humphrey, Hubert H.	706,420	494,846 A	14.0%	18.7%	42.8%	57.2%
1964**	689,818	479,085	Goldwater, Barry M.		Johnson, Lyndon B.	210,733	268,353 R	69.5%		100.0%	
1960	570,225	237,981	Nixon, Richard M.	324,050	Kennedy, John F.	8,194	86,069 D	41.7%	56.8%	42.3%	57.7%
1956	496,861	195,694	Eisenhower, Dwight D.	280,844	Stevenson, Adlai E.	20,323	85,150 D	39.4%	56.5%	41.1%	58.9%
1952	426,120	149,231	Eisenhower, Dwight D.	275,075	Stevenson, Adlai E.	1,814	125,844 D	35.0%	64.6%	35.2%	64.8%
1948**	214,980	40,930	Dewey, Thomas E.		Truman, Harry S.	174,050	130,513 SR	19.0%		100.0%	

**In past elections, the other vote included: 2000 - 18,323 Green (Ralph Nader); 1996 - 92,149 Reform (Ross Perot); 1992 - 183,109 Independent (Ross Perot); 1980 - 16,481 Independent (John Anderson); 1968 - 691,425 American Independent (George Wallace); 1964 - 210,732 Unpledged Democratic; 1948 - 171,443 States' Rights (Strom Thurmond). In 1948 and 1964 the national Democratic candidates were not listed on the ballot.

ALABAMA

POSTWAR VOTE FOR GOVERNOR

Year	Total Vote	Republican		Democratic		Other Vote	Rep.-Dem. Plurality	Percentage			
								Total Vote		Major Vote	
		Vote	Candidate	Vote	Candidate			Rep.	Dem.	Rep.	Dem.
2006	1,250,401	718,327	Riley, Bob	519,827	Baxley, Lucy	12,247	198,500 R	57.4%	41.6%	58.0%	42.0%
2002	1,367,053	672,225	Riley, Bob	669,105	Siegelman, Don	25,723	3,120 R	49.2%	48.9%	50.1%	49.9%
1998	1,317,842	554,746	James, Forrest H.	760,155	Siegelman, Don	2,941	205,409 D	42.1%	57.7%	42.2%	57.8%
1994	1,201,969	604,926	James, Forrest H.	594,169	Folsom, James E.	2,874	10,757 R	50.3%	49.4%	50.4%	49.6%
1990	1,216,250	633,519	Hunt, Guy	582,106	Hubbert, Paul R.	625	51,413 R	52.1%	47.9%	52.1%	47.9%
1986	1,236,230	696,203	Hunt, Guy	537,163	Baxley, Bill	2,864	159,040 R	56.3%	43.5%	56.4%	43.6%
1982	1,128,725	440,815	Folmar, Emory	650,538	Wallace, George C.	37,372	209,723 D	39.1%	57.6%	40.4%	59.6%
1978	760,474	196,963	Hunt, Guy	551,886	James, Forrest H.	11,625	354,923 D	25.9%	72.6%	26.3%	73.7%
1974	598,305	88,381	McCary, Elvin	497,574	Wallace, George C.	12,350	409,193 D	14.8%	83.2%	15.1%	84.9%
1970**	854,952		—	637,046	Wallace, George C.	217,906	637,046 D		74.5%		100.0%
1966	848,101	262,943	Martin, James D.	537,505	Wallace, Mrs. George C.	47,653	274,562 D	31.0%	63.4%	32.8%	67.2%
1962	315,776			303,987	Wallace, George C.	11,789	303,987 D		96.3%		100.0%
1958	270,952	30,415	Longshore, W. L.	239,633	Patterson, John	904	209,218 D	11.2%	88.4%	11.3%	88.7%
1954	333,090	88,688	Amernethy, Tom	244,401	Folsom, James E.	1	155,713 D	26.6%	73.4%	26.6%	73.4%
1950	170,541	15,127	Crowder, John S.	155,414	Persons, Gordon		140,287 D	8.9%	91.1%	8.9%	91.1%
1946	197,324	22,362	Ward, Lyman	174,962	Folsom, James E.		152,600 D	11.3%	88.7%	11.3%	88.7%

**In past elections, the other vote included: 1970 - 125,491 National Democratic Party of Alabama (John Logan Cashin); 75,679 Independent (A. C. Shelton).

POSTWAR VOTE FOR SENATOR

Year	Total Vote	Republican		Democratic		Other Vote	Rep.-Dem. Plurality	Percentage			
								Total Vote		Major Vote	
		Vote	Candidate	Vote	Candidate			Rep.	Dem.	Rep.	Dem.
2004	1,839,066	1,242,200	Shelby, Richard C.	595,018	Sowell, Wayne	1,848	647,182 R	67.5%	32.4%	67.6%	32.4%
2002	1,353,023	792,561	Sessions, Jeff	538,878	Parker, Susan	21,584	253,683 R	58.6%	39.8%	59.5%	40.5%
1998	1,293,405	817,973	Shelby, Richard C.	474,568	Suddith, Clayton	864	343,405 R	63.2%	36.7%	63.3%	36.7%
1996	1,499,393	786,436	Sessions, Jeff	681,651	Bedford, Roger	31,306	104,785 R	52.5%	45.5%	53.6%	46.4%
1992	1,577,799	522,015	Sellers, Richard	1,022,698	Shelby, Richard C.	33,086	500,683 D	33.1%	64.8%	33.8%	66.2%
1990	1,185,563	467,190	Cabaniss, Bill	717,814	Heflin, Howell	559	250,624 D	39.4%	60.5%	39.4%	60.6%
1986	1,211,953	602,537	Denton, Jeremiah	609,360	Shelby, Richard C.	56	6,823 D	49.7%	50.3%	49.7%	50.3%
1984	1,371,238	498,508	Smith, Albert L.	860,535	Heflin, Howell	12,195	362,027 D	36.4%	62.8%	36.7%	63.3%
1980	1,296,757	650,362	Denton, Jeremiah	610,175	Folsom, James E. Jr.	36,220	40,187 R	50.2%	47.1%	51.6%	48.4%
1978	582,025		—	547,054	Heflin, Howell	34,971	547,054 D		94.0%		100.0%
1978S	731,614	316,170	Martin, James D.	401,852	Stewart, Donald W.	13,592	85,682 D	43.2%	54.9%	44.0%	56.0%
1974	523,290		—	501,541	Allen, James B.	21,749	501,541 D		95.8%		100.0%
1972	1,051,099	347,523	Blount, Winston M.	654,491	Sparkman, John J.	49,085	306,968 D	33.1%	62.3%	34.7%	65.3%
1968	912,708	201,227	Hooper, Perry	638,774	Allen, James B.	72,707	437,547 D	22.0%	70.0%	24.0%	76.0%
1966	802,608	313,018	Grenier, John	482,138	Sparkman, John J.	7,452	169,120 D	39.0%	60.1%	39.4%	60.6%
1962	397,079	195,134	Martin, James D.	201,937	Hill, Lister	8	6,803 D	49.1%	50.9%	49.1%	50.9%
1960	554,081	164,868	Elgin, Julian	389,196	Sparkman, John J.	17	224,328 D	29.8%	70.2%	29.8%	70.2%
1956	330,191		—	330,182	Hill, Lister	9	330,182 D		100.0%		100.0%
1954	314,459	55,110	Guin, J. Foy	259,348	Sparkman, John J.	1	204,238 D	17.5%	82.5%	17.5%	82.5%
1950	164,011		—	125,534	Hill, Lister	38,477	125,534 D		76.5%		100.0%
1948	220,875	35,341	Parsons, Paul G.	185,534	Sparkman, John J.		150,193 D	16.0%	84.0%	16.0%	84.0%
1946S	163,217		—	163,217	Sparkman, John J.		163,217 D		100.0%		100.0%

The 1946 election and one of the 1978 elections were for short terms to fill vacancies.

ALABAMA

GOVERNOR 2006

2000 Census Population	County	Total Votes	Republican	Democratic	Other	Rep.-Dem. Plurality	Total Vote Rep.	Total Vote Dem.	Major Vote Rep.	Major Vote Dem.
43,671	AUTAUGA	14,032	9,556	4,399	77	5,157 R	68.1%	31.3%	68.5%	31.5%
140,415	BALDWIN	45,783	34,969	10,604	210	24,365 R	76.4%	23.2%	76.7%	23.3%
29,038	BARBOUR	6,229	2,866	3,349	14	483 D	46.0%	53.8%	46.1%	53.9%
20,826	BIBB	5,555	3,263	2,207	85	1,056 R	58.7%	39.7%	59.7%	40.3%
51,024	BLOUNT	14,151	8,877	5,058	216	3,819 R	62.7%	35.7%	63.7%	36.3%
11,714	BULLOCK	3,101	881	2,217	3	1,336 D	28.4%	71.5%	28.4%	71.6%
21,399	BUTLER	6,814	3,615	3,181	18	434 R	53.1%	46.7%	53.2%	46.8%
112,249	CALHOUN	29,697	17,542	11,858	297	5,684 R	59.1%	39.9%	59.7%	40.3%
36,583	CHAMBERS	9,203	4,789	4,414	—	375 R	52.0%	48.0%	52.0%	48.0%
23,988	CHEROKEE	7,072	3,700	3,337	35	363 R	52.3%	47.2%	52.6%	47.4%
39,593	CHILTON	12,163	7,955	4,103	105	3,852 R	65.4%	33.7%	66.0%	34.0%
15,922	CHOCTAW	4,915	2,134	2,775	6	641 D	43.4%	56.5%	43.5%	56.5%
27,867	CLARKE	9,057	4,904	4,134	19	770 R	54.1%	45.6%	54.3%	45.7%
14,254	CLAY	4,850	2,893	1,904	53	989 R	59.6%	39.3%	60.3%	39.7%
14,123	CLEBURNE	4,108	2,662	1,415	31	1,247 R	64.8%	34.4%	65.3%	34.7%
43,615	COFFEE	13,203	8,634	4,526	43	4,108 R	65.4%	34.3%	65.6%	34.4%
54,984	COLBERT	15,778	7,386	8,281	111	895 D	46.8%	52.5%	47.1%	52.9%
14,089	CONECUH	4,237	1,975	2,252	10	277 D	46.6%	53.2%	46.7%	53.3%
12,202	COOSA	4,347	1,915	2,404	28	489 D	44.1%	55.3%	44.3%	55.7%
37,631	COVINGTON	11,291	7,196	4,055	40	3,141 R	63.7%	35.9%	64.0%	36.0%
13,665	CRENSHAW	4,300	2,511	1,775	14	736 R	58.4%	41.3%	58.6%	41.4%
77,483	CULLMAN	25,539	15,081	9,531	927	5,550 R	59.1%	37.3%	61.3%	38.7%
49,129	DALE	12,449	8,287	4,098	64	4,189 R	66.6%	32.9%	66.9%	33.1%
46,365	DALLAS	14,148	5,409	8,698	41	3,289 D	38.2%	61.5%	38.3%	61.7%
64,452	DE KALB	17,663	10,532	6,878	253	3,654 R	59.6%	38.9%	60.5%	39.5%
65,874	ELMORE	20,877	14,594	6,146	137	8,448 R	69.9%	29.4%	70.4%	29.6%
38,440	ESCAMBIA	8,786	5,202	3,547	37	1,655 R	59.2%	40.4%	59.5%	40.5%
103,459	ETOWAH	29,329	14,923	13,984	422	939 R	50.9%	47.7%	51.6%	48.4%
18,495	FAYETTE	6,035	3,127	2,812	96	315 R	51.8%	46.6%	52.7%	47.3%
31,223	FRANKLIN	7,621	3,385	4,122	114	737 D	44.4%	54.1%	45.1%	54.9%
25,764	GENEVA	7,274	4,911	2,335	28	2,576 R	67.5%	32.1%	67.8%	32.2%
9,974	GREENE	4,245	973	3,260	12	2,287 D	22.9%	76.8%	23.0%	77.0%
17,185	HALE	5,303	1,951	3,335	17	1,384 D	36.8%	62.9%	36.9%	63.1%
16,310	HENRY	5,796	3,075	2,706	15	369 R	53.1%	46.7%	53.2%	46.8%
88,787	HOUSTON	26,109	16,253	9,705	151	6,548 R	62.3%	37.2%	62.6%	37.4%
53,926	JACKSON	12,697	6,515	6,077	105	438 R	51.3%	47.9%	51.7%	48.3%
662,047	JEFFERSON	179,391	93,132	84,137	2,122	8,995 R	51.9%	46.9%	52.5%	47.5%
15,904	LAMAR	4,815	2,336	2,429	50	93 D	48.5%	50.4%	49.0%	51.0%
87,966	LAUDERDALE	24,989	13,943	10,831	215	3,112 R	55.8%	43.3%	56.3%	43.7%
34,803	LAWRENCE	10,202	4,450	5,558	194	1,108 D	43.6%	54.5%	44.5%	55.5%
115,092	LEE	27,170	16,490	10,469	211	6,021 R	60.7%	38.5%	61.2%	38.8%
65,676	LIMESTONE	19,373	11,910	7,214	249	4,696 R	61.5%	37.2%	62.3%	37.7%
13,473	LOWNDES	4,310	1,235	3,068	7	1,833 D	28.7%	71.2%	28.7%	71.3%
24,105	MACON	5,824	1,274	4,541	9	3,267 D	21.9%	78.0%	21.9%	78.1%
276,700	MADISON	83,712	53,489	29,398	825	24,091 R	63.9%	35.1%	64.5%	35.5%
22,539	MARENGO	7,219	3,159	4,046	14	887 D	43.8%	56.0%	43.8%	56.2%
31,214	MARION	8,766	4,205	4,397	164	192 D	48.0%	50.2%	48.9%	51.1%
82,231	MARSHALL	23,644	14,599	8,615	430	5,984 R	61.7%	36.4%	62.9%	37.1%
399,843	MOBILE	93,278	58,750	34,221	307	24,529 R	63.0%	36.7%	63.2%	36.8%
24,324	MONROE	8,056	4,841	3,215	—	1,626 R	60.1%	39.9%	60.1%	39.9%
223,510	MONTGOMERY	61,579	30,659	30,589	331	70 R	49.8%	49.7%	50.1%	49.9%
111,064	MORGAN	33,425	21,156	11,717	552	9,439 R	63.3%	35.1%	64.4%	35.6%
11,861	PERRY	4,270	1,237	3,025	8	1,788 D	29.0%	70.8%	29.0%	71.0%
20,949	PICKENS	6,269	3,311	2,920	38	391 R	52.8%	46.6%	53.1%	46.9%
29,605	PIKE	8,043	4,627	3,393	23	1,234 R	57.5%	42.2%	57.7%	42.3%
22,380	RANDOLPH	6,513	3,653	2,829	31	824 R	56.1%	43.4%	56.4%	43.6%
49,756	RUSSELL	9,522	3,955	5,536	31	1,581 D	41.5%	58.1%	41.7%	58.3%
64,742	ST. CLAIR	19,140	12,803	5,882	455	6,921 R	66.9%	30.7%	68.5%	31.5%
143,293	SHELBY	48,555	37,167	10,696	692	26,471 R	76.5%	22.0%	77.7%	22.3%
14,798	SUMTER	5,447	1,614	3,821	12	2,207 D	29.6%	70.1%	29.7%	70.3%

ALABAMA

GOVERNOR 2006

2000 Census Population	County	Total Votes	Republican	Democratic	Other	Rep.-Dem. Plurality	Percentage			
							Total Vote		Major Vote	
							Rep.	Dem.	Rep.	Dem.
80,321	TALLADEGA	19,283	9,399	9,634	250	235 D	48.7%	50.0%	49.4%	50.6%
41,475	TALLAPOOSA	13,174	8,078	5,069	27	3,009 R	61.3%	38.5%	61.4%	38.6%
164,875	TUSCALOOSA	43,768	24,247	19,078	443	5,169 R	55.4%	43.6%	56.0%	44.0%
70,713	WALKER	18,267	8,749	9,014	504	265 D	47.9%	49.3%	49.3%	50.7%
18,097	WASHINGTON	6,064	3,376	2,676	12	700 R	55.7%	44.1%	55.8%	44.2%
13,183	WILCOX	4,533	1,189	3,342	2	2,153 D	26.2%	73.7%	26.2%	73.8%
24,843	WINSTON	8,043	4,853	2,985	205	1,868 R	60.3%	37.1%	61.9%	38.1%
4,447,100	TOTAL	1,250,401	718,327	519,827	12,247	198,500 R	57.4%	41.6%	58.0%	42.0%

ALABAMA

HOUSE OF REPRESENTATIVES

CD	Year	Total Vote	Republican		Democratic		Other Vote	Rep.-Dem. Plurality	Percentage			
			Vote	Candidate	Vote	Candidate			Total Vote		Major Vote	
									Rep.	Dem.	Rep.	Dem.
1	2006	165,841	112,944	BONNER, JO*	52,770	BECKERLE, VIVIAN SHEFFIELD	127	60,174 R	68.1%	31.8%	68.2%	31.8%
1	2004	255,164	161,067	BONNER, JO*	93,938	BELK, JUDY McCAIN	159	67,129 R	63.1%	36.8%	63.2%	36.8%
1	2002	178,687	108,102	BONNER, JO	67,507	BELK, JUDY McCAIN	3,078	40,595 R	60.5%	37.8%	61.6%	38.4%
2	2006	178,919	124,302	EVERETT, TERRY*	54,450	JAMES, CHARLES "CHUCK" DEAN	167	69,852 R	69.5%	30.4%	69.5%	30.5%
2	2004	247,947	177,086	EVERETT, TERRY*	70,562	JAMES, CHARLES "CHUCK" DEAN	299	106,524 R	71.4%	28.5%	71.5%	28.5%
2	2002	187,965	129,233	EVERETT, TERRY*	55,495	WOODS, CHARLES	3,237	73,738 R	68.8%	29.5%	70.0%	30.0%
3	2006	165,301	98,257	ROGERS, MIKE D.*	63,559	PIERCE, GREG A.	3,485	34,698 R	59.4%	38.5%	60.7%	39.3%
3	2004	245,784	150,411	ROGERS, MIKE D.*	95,240	FULLER, BILL	133	55,171 R	61.2%	38.7%	61.2%	38.8%
3	2002	181,223	91,169	ROGERS, MIKE D.	87,351	TURNHAM, JOE	2,703	3,818 R	50.3%	48.2%	51.1%	48.9%
4	2006	183,072	128,484	ADERHOLT, ROBERT B.*	54,382	BOBO, BARBARA	206	74,102 R	70.2%	29.7%	70.3%	29.7%
4	2004	255,724	191,110	ADERHOLT, ROBERT B.*	64,278	COLE, CARL	336	126,832 R	74.7%	25.1%	74.8%	25.2%
4	2002	161,101	139,705	ADERHOLT, ROBERT B.*		—	21,396	139,705 R	86.7%		100.0%	
5	2006	145,555		—	143,015	CRAMER, ROBERT E. "BUD"*	2,540	143,015 D	98.3%		100.0%	
5	2004	275,459	74,145	WALLACE, GERALD "GERRY"	200,999	CRAMER, ROBERT E. "BUD"*	315	126,854 D	26.9%	73.0%	26.9%	73.1%
5	2002	195,171	48,226	ENGEL, STEPHEN P.	143,029	CRAMER, ROBERT E. "BUD"*	3,916	94,803 D	24.7%	73.3%	25.2%	74.8%
6	2006	166,300	163,514	BACHUS, SPENCER*		—	2,786	163,514 R	98.3%		100.0%	
6	2004	268,043	264,819	BACHUS, SPENCER*		—	3,224	264,819 R	98.8%		100.0%	
6	2002	198,346	178,171	BACHUS, SPENCER*		—	20,175	178,171 R	89.8%		100.0%	
7	2006	135,164		—	133,870	DAVIS, ARTUR*	1,294	133,870 D		99.0%		100.0%
7	2004	244,638	61,019	CAMERON, STEVE F.	183,408	DAVIS, ARTUR*	211	122,389 D	24.9%	75.0%	25.0%	75.0%
7	2002	166,309		—	153,735	DAVIS, ARTUR	12,574	153,735 D		92.4%		100.0%
TOTAL	2006	1,140,152	627,501		502,046		10,605	125,455 R	55.0%	44.0%	55.6%	44.4%
TOTAL	2004	1,792,759	1,079,657		708,425		4,677	371,232 R	60.2%	39.5%	60.4%	39.6%
TOTAL	2002	1,268,802	694,606		507,117		67,079	187,489 R	54.7%	40.0%	57.8%	42.2%

An asterisk (*) denotes incumbent.

ALABAMA

GENERAL AND PRIMARY ELECTIONS

2006 GENERAL ELECTIONS

Governor   Other vote was 12,247 scattered write-in.

House   Other vote was:

CD 1:	127 scattered write-in.
CD 2:	167 scattered write-in.
CD 3:	3,414 Independent (Mark Edwin Layfield); 71 scattered write-in.
CD 4:	206 scattered write-in.
CD 5:	2,540 scattered write-in.
CD 6:	2,786 scattered write-in.
CD 7:	1,294 scattered write-in.

2006 PRIMARY ELECTIONS

Primary   June 6, 2006   Registration (as of June 6, 2006)   2,413,279   No Party Registration

Primary Type   Open—Any registered voter could vote in either the Democratic or Republican primary, although any voter that participated in the Republican primary could not vote in the Democratic runoff. There was no such restriction on participation in the Republican runoff. (No runoffs for governor or Congress were held in 2006.)

Note: An asterisk (*) denotes incumbent. The names of unopposed candidates did not appear on the ballot; therefore, no votes were cast for these candidates.

	REPUBLICAN PRIMARIES			DEMOCRATIC PRIMARIES		
Governor	Bob Riley*	306,665	66.7%	Lucy Baxley	279,165	59.8%
	Roy Moore	153,354	33.3%	Don Siegelman	170,016	36.4%
				Joe Copeland	4,141	0.9%
				Nathan Mathis	4,000	0.9%
				Katherine Mack	3,392	0.7%
				James Potts	3,333	0.7%
				Harry Lyon	2,490	0.5%
	TOTAL	460,019		TOTAL	466,537	
Congressional District 1	Jo Bonner*	Unopposed		Vivian Sheffield Beckerle	Unopposed	
Congressional District 2	Terry Everett*	Unopposed		Charles "Chuck" Dean James	36,058	70.6%
				John Morykwas Jr.	15,016	29.4%
				TOTAL	51,074	
Congressional District 3	Mike D. Rogers*	Unopposed		Greg A. Pierce	Unopposed	
Congressional District 4	Robert B. Aderholt*	Unopposed		Barbara Bobo	Unopposed	
Congressional District 5	No Republican candidate			Robert E. "Bud" Cramer*	Unopposed	
Congressional District 6	Spencer Bachus*	Unopposed		No Democratic candidate		
Congressional District 7	No Republican candidate			Artur Davis*	93,586	90.9%
				Eddison T. Walters	9,358	9.1%
				TOTAL	102,944	

ALASKA

One member At Large

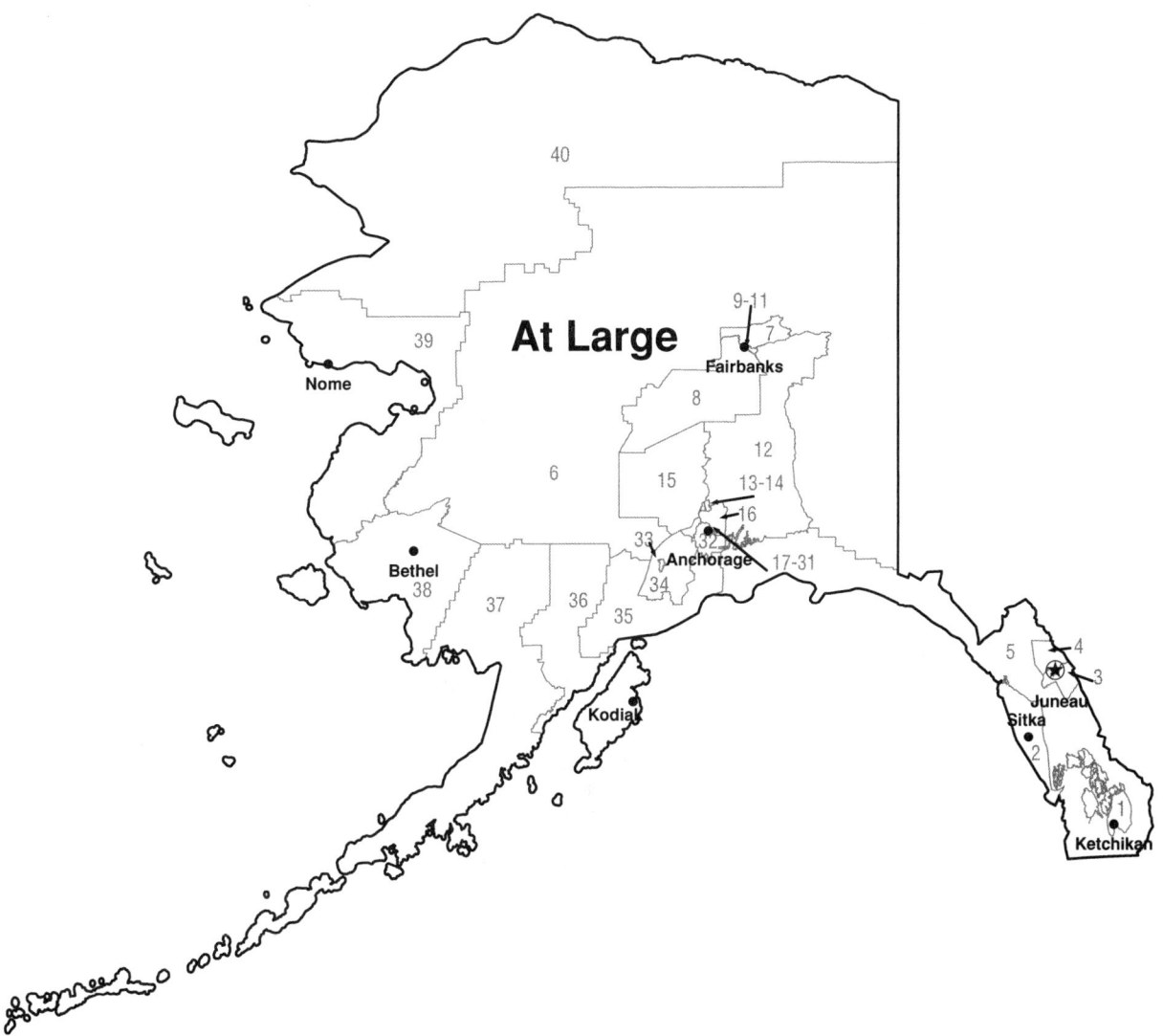

ALASKA

GOVERNOR
Sarah H. Palin (R). Elected 2006 to a four-year term.

SENATORS (2 Republicans)
Lisa Murkowski (R). Elected 2004 to a six-year term. Had been appointed in December 2002 to fill the vacancy created by the resignation of her father, Frank H. Murkowski (R), to become governor of Alaska.

Ted Stevens (R). Reelected 2002 to a six-year term. Previously elected 1996, 1990, 1984, 1978, 1972, and in 1970 to fill the remaining two years of the term vacated by the death of Senator E. L. Bartlett (D). Had been appointed in December 1968 to fill this vacancy.

REPRESENTATIVE (1 Republican)
At Large. Don Young (R)

POSTWAR VOTE FOR PRESIDENT

									Percentage			
									Total Vote		Major Vote	
	Total	Republican		Democratic		Other	Rep.-Dem.					
Year	Vote	Vote	Candidate	Vote	Candidate	Vote	Plurality		Rep.	Dem.	Rep.	Dem.
2004	312,598	190,889	Bush, George W.	111,025	Kerry, John	10,684	79,864	R	61.1%	35.5%	63.2%	36.8%
2000**	285,560	167,398	Bush, George W.	79,004	Gore, Al	39,158	88,394	R	58.6%	27.7%	67.9%	32.1%
1996**	241,620	122,746	Dole, Bob	80,380	Clinton, Bill	38,494	42,366	R	50.8%	33.3%	60.4%	39.6%
1992**	258,506	102,000	Bush, George	78,294	Clinton, Bill	78,212	23,706	R	39.5%	30.3%	56.6%	43.4%
1988	200,116	119,251	Bush, George	72,584	Dukakis, Michael S.	8,281	46,667	R	59.6%	36.3%	62.2%	37.8%
1984	207,605	138,377	Reagan, Ronald	62,007	Mondale, Walter F.	7,221	76,370	R	66.7%	29.9%	69.1%	30.9%
1980**	158,445	86,112	Reagan, Ronald	41,842	Carter, Jimmy	30,491	44,270	R	54.3%	26.4%	67.3%	32.7%
1976	123,574	71,555	Ford, Gerald R.	44,058	Carter, Jimmy	7,961	27,497	R	57.9%	35.7%	61.9%	38.1%
1972	95,219	55,349	Nixon, Richard M.	32,967	McGovern, George S.	6,903	22,382	R	58.1%	34.6%	62.7%	37.3%
1968**	83,035	37,600	Nixon, Richard M.	35,411	Humphrey, Hubert H.	10,024	2,189	R	45.3%	42.6%	51.5%	48.5%
1964	67,259	22,930	Goldwater, Barry M.	44,329	Johnson, Lyndon B.		21,399	D	34.1%	65.9%	34.1%	65.9%
1960	60,762	30,953	Nixon, Richard M.	29,809	Kennedy, John F.		1,144	R	50.9%	49.1%	50.9%	49.1%

**In past elections, the other vote included: 2000 - 28,747 Green (Ralph Nader); 1996 - 26,333 Reform (Ross Perot); 1992 - 73,481 Independent (Ross Perot); 1980 - 18,479 Libertarian (Ed Clark) and 11,155 Independent (John Anderson); 1968 - 10,024 American Independent (George Wallace). Alaska was formally admitted as a state in January 1959.

POSTWAR VOTE FOR GOVERNOR

									Percentage			
									Total Vote		Major Vote	
	Total	Republican		Democratic		Other	Rep.-Dem.					
Year	Vote	Vote	Candidate	Vote	Candidate	Vote	Plurality		Rep.	Dem.	Rep.	Dem.
2006	237,322	114,697	Palin, Sarah H.	97,238	Knowles, Tony	25,387	17,459	R	48.3%	41.0%	54.1%	45.9%
2002	231,484	129,279	Murkowski, Frank H.	94,216	Ulmer, Fran	7,989	35,063	R	55.8%	40.7%	57.8%	42.2%
1998**	220,177	39,331	Lindauer, John	112,879	Knowles, Tony	67,967	73,548	D	17.9%	51.3%	25.8%	74.2%
1994	213,435	87,157	Campbell, James O.	87,693	Knowles, Tony	38,585	536	D	40.8%	41.1%	49.8%	50.2%
1990**	194,750	50,991	Sturgulewski, Arliss	60,201	Knowles, Tony	83,558	15,520	I	26.2%	30.9%	45.9%	54.1%
1986	179,555	76,515	Sturgulewski, Arliss	84,943	Cowper, Steve	18,097	8,428	D	42.6%	47.3%	47.4%	52.6%
1982	194,885	72,291	Fink, Tom	89,918	Sheffield, Bill	32,676	17,627	D	37.1%	46.1%	44.6%	55.4%
1978**	126,910	49,580	Hammond, Jay S.	25,656	Croft, Chancy	51,674	16,025	R	39.1%	20.2%	65.9%	34.1%
1974	96,163	45,840	Hammond, Jay S.	45,553	Egan, William A.	4,770	287	R	47.7%	47.4%	50.2%	49.8%
1970	80,779	37,264	Miller, Keith	42,309	Egan, William A.	1,206	5,045	D	46.1%	52.4%	46.8%	53.2%
1966	66,294	33,145	Hickel, Walter J.	32,065	Egan, William A.	1,084	1,080	R	50.0%	48.4%	50.8%	49.2%
1962	56,681	27,054	Stepovich, Mike	29,627	Egan, William A.		2,573	D	47.7%	52.3%	47.7%	52.3%
1958	48,968	19,299	Butrovich, John	29,189	Egan, William A.	480	9,890	D	39.4%	59.6%	39.8%	60.2%

**In past elections, the other vote included: 1998 - 43,571 scattered write-in (most for Republican Robin Taylor); 1990 - 75,721 Alaskan Independence (Walter J. Hickel); 1978 - 33,555 write-in (Hickel) and 15,656 Alaskans for Kelly (Tom Kelly). Hickel won the 1990 election with 38.9 percent of the total vote, and finished second in 1978.

ALASKA

POSTWAR VOTE FOR SENATOR

Year	Total Vote	Republican Vote	Republican Candidate	Democratic Vote	Democratic Candidate	Other Vote	Plurality	Percentage Total Vote Rep.	Percentage Total Vote Dem.	Percentage Major Vote Rep.	Percentage Major Vote Dem.
2004	308,315	149,773	Murkowski, Lisa	140,424	Knowles, Tony	18,118	9,349 R	48.6%	45.5%	51.6%	48.4%
2002	229,548	179,438	Stevens, Ted	24,133	Vondersaar, Frank	25,977	155,305 R	78.2%	10.5%	88.1%	11.9%
1998	221,807	165,227	Murkowski, Frank H.	43,743	Sonneman, Joseph	12,837	121,484 R	74.5%	19.7%	79.1%	20.9%
1996**	231,916	177,893	Stevens, Ted	23,977	Obermeyer, Theresa	30,046	148,856 R	76.7%	10.3%	88.1%	11.9%
1992	239,714	127,163	Murkowski, Frank H.	92,065	Smith, Tony	20,486	35,098 R	53.0%	38.4%	58.0%	42.0%
1990	189,957	125,806	Stevens, Ted	61,152	Beasley, Michael	2,999	64,654 R	66.2%	32.2%	67.3%	32.7%
1986	180,801	97,674	Murkowski, Frank H.	79,727	Olds, Glenn	3,400	17,947 R	54.0%	44.1%	55.1%	44.9%
1984	206,438	146,919	Stevens, Ted	58,804	Havelock, John E.	715	88,115 R	71.2%	28.5%	71.4%	28.6%
1980	156,762	84,159	Murkowski, Frank H.	72,007	Gruening, Clark S.	596	12,152 R	53.7%	45.9%	53.9%	46.1%
1978	122,741	92,783	Stevens, Ted	29,574	Hobbs, Donald W.	384	63,209 R	75.6%	24.1%	75.8%	24.2%
1974	93,275	38,914	Lewis, C. R.	54,361	Gravel, Mike		15,447 D	41.7%	58.3%	41.7%	58.3%
1972	96,007	74,216	Stevens, Ted	21,791	Guess, Gene		52,425 R	77.3%	22.7%	77.3%	22.7%
1970S	80,364	47,908	Stevens, Ted	32,456	Kay, Wendell P.		15,452 R	59.6%	40.4%	59.6%	40.4%
1968	80,931	30,286	Rasmuson, Elmer	36,527	Gravel, Mike	14,118	6,241 D	37.4%	45.1%	45.3%	54.7%
1966	65,250	15,961	McKinley, Lee L.	49,289	Bartlett, E. L.		33,328 D	24.5%	75.5%	24.5%	75.5%
1962	58,181	24,354	Stevens, Ted	33,827	Gruening, Ernest		9,473 D	41.9%	58.1%	41.9%	58.1%
1960	59,978	21,937	McKinley, Lee L.	38,041	Bartlett, E. L.		16,104 D	36.6%	63.4%	36.6%	63.4%
1958S	49,525	23,462	Stepovich, Mike	26,063	Gruening, Ernest		2,601 D	47.4%	52.6%	47.4%	52.6%
1958S	48,837	7,299	Robertson, R. E.	40,939	Bartlett, E. L.	599	33,640 D	14.9%	83.8%	15.1%	84.9%

**In past elections, the other vote included: 1996 - 29,037 Green (Jed Whittaker). Whittaker finished second, 148,856 votes behind Republican Ted Stevens. The 1970 election was for a short term to fill a vacancy. The two 1958 elections were held to indeterminate terms and the Senate later determined by lot that Senator Gruening would serve four years, Senator Bartlett two.

ALASKA

GOVERNOR 2006

2000 Census Population	District	Total Vote	Republican	Democratic	Other	Rep.-Dem. Plurality		Percentage			
								Total Vote		Major Vote	
								Rep.	Dem.	Rep.	Dem.
15,031	DISTRICT 1	4,956	2,467	1,831	658	636	R	49.8%	36.9%	57.4%	42.6%
14,991	DISTRICT 2	5,660	2,059	3,011	590	952	D	36.4%	53.2%	40.6%	59.4%
15,203	DISTRICT 3	7,222	1,308	5,155	759	3,847	D	18.1%	71.4%	20.2%	79.8%
15,508	DISTRICT 4	6,789	1,859	4,108	822	2,249	D	27.4%	60.5%	31.2%	68.8%
15,048	DISTRICT 5	5,546	2,141	2,845	560	704	D	38.6%	51.3%	42.9%	57.1%
14,905	DISTRICT 6	5,374	2,451	2,453	470	2	D	45.6%	45.6%	50.0%	50.0%
15,494	DISTRICT 7	8,295	4,194	3,202	899	992	R	50.6%	38.6%	56.7%	43.3%
15,552	DISTRICT 8	7,811	3,259	3,586	966	327	D	41.7%	45.9%	47.6%	52.4%
15,723	DISTRICT 9	5,155	2,582	2,054	519	528	R	50.1%	39.8%	55.7%	44.3%
15,599	DISTRICT 10	3,271	1,813	1,152	306	661	R	55.4%	35.2%	61.1%	38.9%
15,904	DISTRICT 11	6,534	4,526	1,361	647	3,165	R	69.3%	20.8%	76.9%	23.1%
16,303	DISTRICT 12	5,089	3,415	1,242	432	2,173	R	67.1%	24.4%	73.3%	26.7%
16,231	DISTRICT 13	8,082	5,374	2,007	701	3,367	R	66.5%	24.8%	72.8%	27.2%
16,119	DISTRICT 14	7,335	5,313	1,428	594	3,885	R	72.4%	19.5%	78.8%	21.2%
16,137	DISTRICT 15	7,571	5,295	1,551	725	3,744	R	69.9%	20.5%	77.3%	22.7%
16,104	DISTRICT 16	8,028	5,180	2,027	821	3,153	R	64.5%	25.2%	71.9%	28.1%
15,819	DISTRICT 17	6,794	4,146	1,992	656	2,154	R	61.0%	29.3%	67.5%	32.5%
15,639	DISTRICT 18	2,640	1,639	793	208	846	R	62.1%	30.0%	67.4%	32.6%
15,841	DISTRICT 19	5,252	2,598	2,114	540	484	R	49.5%	40.3%	55.1%	44.9%
15,837	DISTRICT 20	3,363	1,474	1,568	321	94	D	43.8%	46.6%	48.5%	51.5%
15,850	DISTRICT 21	6,463	3,041	2,828	594	213	R	47.1%	43.8%	51.8%	48.2%
15,831	DISTRICT 22	4,644	1,765	2,379	500	614	D	38.0%	51.2%	42.6%	57.4%
15,847	DISTRICT 23	5,214	1,588	3,034	592	1,446	D	30.5%	58.2%	34.4%	65.6%
15,812	DISTRICT 24	5,408	2,330	2,431	647	101	D	43.1%	45.0%	48.9%	51.1%
15,836	DISTRICT 25	4,656	1,814	2,318	524	504	D	39.0%	49.8%	43.9%	56.1%
15,823	DISTRICT 26	6,873	2,499	3,554	820	1,055	D	36.4%	51.7%	41.3%	58.7%
15,820	DISTRICT 27	6,355	3,121	2,386	848	735	R	49.1%	37.5%	56.7%	43.3%
15,839	DISTRICT 28	7,235	3,515	2,759	961	756	R	48.6%	38.1%	56.0%	44.0%
15,846	DISTRICT 29	4,847	2,422	1,873	552	549	R	50.0%	38.6%	56.4%	43.6%
15,839	DISTRICT 30	6,714	3,283	2,692	739	591	R	48.9%	40.1%	54.9%	45.1%
15,811	DISTRICT 31	7,901	4,105	2,838	958	1,267	R	52.0%	35.9%	59.1%	40.9%
15,329	DISTRICT 32	9,305	4,166	3,928	1,211	238	R	44.8%	42.2%	51.5%	48.5%
16,466	DISTRICT 33	6,306	3,921	1,646	739	2,275	R	62.2%	26.1%	70.4%	29.6%
16,409	DISTRICT 34	6,759	4,690	1,315	754	3,375	R	69.4%	19.5%	78.1%	21.9%
16,436	DISTRICT 35	6,935	3,117	2,983	835	134	R	44.9%	43.0%	51.1%	48.9%
14,928	DISTRICT 36	4,689	2,423	1,625	641	798	R	51.7%	34.7%	59.9%	40.1%
15,150	DISTRICT 37	4,044	1,594	2,084	366	490	D	39.4%	51.5%	43.3%	56.7%
14,921	DISTRICT 38	3,928	539	3,133	256	2,594	D	13.7%	79.8%	14.7%	85.3%
14,996	DISTRICT 39	4,382	843	3,139	400	2,296	D	19.2%	71.6%	21.2%	78.8%
15,155	DISTRICT 40	3,897	828	2,813	256	1,985	D	21.2%	72.2%	22.7%	77.3%
626,932	TOTAL	237,322	114,697	97,238	25,387	17,459	R	48.3%	41.0%	54.1%	45.9%

ALASKA

HOUSE OF REPRESENTATIVES

CD	Year	Total Vote	Republican Vote	Republican Candidate	Democratic Vote	Democratic Candidate	Other Vote	Rep.-Dem. Plurality	Percentage Total Vote Rep.	Total Vote Dem.	Major Vote Rep.	Major Vote Dem.
AL	2006	234,645	132,743	YOUNG, DON*	93,879	BENSON, DIANE E.	8,023	38,864 R	56.6%	40.0%	58.6%	41.4%
AL	2004	299,996	213,216	YOUNG, DON*	67,074	HIGGINS, THOMAS M.	19,706	146,142 R	71.1%	22.4%	76.1%	23.9%
AL	2002	227,725	169,685	YOUNG, DON*	39,357	GREENE, CLIFFORD	18,683	130,328 R	74.5%	17.3%	81.2%	18.8%
AL	2000	274,393	190,862	YOUNG, DON*	45,372	GREENE, CLIFFORD	38,159	145,490 R	69.6%	16.5%	80.8%	19.2%
AL	1998	223,300	139,676	YOUNG, DON*	77,232	DUNCAN, JIM	6,392	62,444 R	62.6%	34.6%	64.4%	35.6%
AL	1996	233,700	138,834	YOUNG, DON*	85,114	LINCOLN, GEORGIANNA	9,752	53,720 R	59.4%	36.4%	62.0%	38.0%
AL	1994	208,240	118,537	YOUNG, DON*	68,172	SMITH, TONY	21,531	50,365 R	56.9%	32.7%	63.5%	36.5%
AL	1992	239,116	111,849	YOUNG, DON*	102,378	DEVENS, JOHN S.	24,889	9,471 R	46.8%	42.8%	52.2%	47.8%
AL	1990	191,647	99,003	YOUNG, DON*	91,677	DEVENS, JOHN S.	967	7,326 R	51.7%	47.8%	51.9%	48.1%
AL	1988	192,955	120,595	YOUNG, DON*	71,881	GRUENSTEIN, PETER	479	48,714 R	62.5%	37.3%	62.7%	37.3%
AL	1986	180,277	101,799	YOUNG, DON*	74,053	BEGICH, PEGGE	4,425	27,746 R	56.5%	41.1%	57.9%	42.1%
AL	1984	206,437	113,582	YOUNG, DON*	86,052	BEGICH, PEGGE	6,803	27,530 R	55.0%	41.7%	56.9%	43.1%
AL	1982	181,084	128,274	YOUNG, DON*	52,011	CARLSON, DAVE	799	76,263 R	70.8%	28.7%	71.2%	28.8%
AL	1980	154,618	114,089	YOUNG, DON*	39,922	PARNELL, KEVIN	607	74,167 R	73.8%	25.8%	74.1%	25.9%
AL	1978	124,187	68,811	YOUNG, DON*	55,176	RODNEY, PATRICK	200	13,635 R	55.4%	44.4%	55.5%	44.5%
AL	1976	118,208	83,722	YOUNG, DON*	34,194	HOPSON, EBEN	292	49,528 R	70.8%	28.9%	71.0%	29.0%
AL	1974	95,921	51,641	YOUNG, DON*	44,280	HENSLEY, WILLIAM L.		7,361 R	53.8%	46.2%	53.8%	46.2%
AL	1972	95,401	41,750	YOUNG, DON	53,651	BEGICH, NICK*		11,901 D	43.8%	56.2%	43.8%	56.2%
AL	1970	80,084	35,947	MURKOWSKI, FRANK H.	44,137	BEGICH, NICK		8,190 D	44.9%	55.1%	44.9%	55.1%
AL	1968	80,362	43,577	POLLOCK, HOWARD W.*	36,785	BEGICH, NICK		6,792 R	54.2%	45.8%	54.2%	45.8%
AL	1966	65,907	34,040	POLLOCK, HOWARD W.	31,867	RIVERS, RALPH J.*		2,173 R	51.6%	48.4%	51.6%	48.4%
AL	1964	67,146	32,556	THOMAS, LOWELL	34,590	RIVERS, RALPH J.*		2,034 D	48.5%	51.5%	48.5%	51.5%
AL	1962	58,591	26,638	THOMAS, LOWELL	31,953	RIVERS, RALPH J.*		5,315 D	45.5%	54.5%	45.5%	54.5%
AL	1960	59,063	25,517	RETTIG, R. L.	33,546	RIVERS, RALPH J.*		8,029 D	43.2%	56.8%	43.2%	56.8%
AL	1958	48,647	20,699	BENSON, HENRY A.	27,948	RIVERS, RALPH J.		7,249 D	42.5%	57.5%	42.5%	57.5%

An asterisk (*) denotes incumbent.

ALASKA

GENERAL AND PRIMARY ELECTIONS

2006 GENERAL ELECTIONS

Governor   Other vote was 22,443 Independent (Andrew J. Halcro); 1,285 Alaskan Independence (Don R. Wright); 682 Libertarian (William S. "Billy" Toien); 593 Green (David M. Massie); 384 scattered write-in.

House   Other vote was:

   At Large   4,029 Libertarian (Alexander Crawford); 1,819 Green (Eva L. Ince); 1,615 Impeach Now! (William Ratigan); 560 scattered write-in.

2006 PRIMARY ELECTIONS

Primary   August 22, 2006   **Registration** (as of August 19, 2006)

Republican	112,793
Democratic	66,307
Alaskan Independence	13,658
Libertarian	9,018
Republican Moderate	5,083
Green	3,684
Veterans	2,227
Other	1,570
Nonpartisan	71,548
Undeclared	174,304
TOTAL	460,192

ALASKA

GENERAL AND PRIMARY ELECTIONS

2006 PRIMARY ELECTIONS

Primary Type Any registered voter could participate in the Democratic primary. The Republican primary was restricted to registered Republican, Undeclared and Nonpartisan voters. (Undeclared voters may be associated with a party but do not wish to declare which one. Nonpartisan voters are not associated with any party.) Democratic candidates were listed on a combined primary ballot with candidates of the Alaskan Independence, Green and Libertarian parties. The high vote-getter of each party went onto the general election ballot. Republican candidates were listed on a primary ballot of their own.

Note: An asterisk (*) denotes incumbent.

	REPUBLICAN PRIMARIES			DEMOCRATIC PRIMARIES		
Governor	Sarah H. Palin	51,443	50.6%	Tony Knowles	37,316	74.6%
	John Binkley	30,349	29.8%	Eric Croft	11,952	23.9%
	Frank H. Murkowski*	19,412	19.1%	Bruce J. Lemke	732	1.5%
	Gerald L. "Jerry" Heikes	280	0.3%			
	Merica Hlatcu	211	0.2%			
	TOTAL	*101,695*		*TOTAL*	*50,000*	
House At Large	Don Young*	81,089	100.0%	Diane E. Benson	19,421	47.9%
				Ray Metcalfe	16,529	40.7%
				Todd Hyde	2,482	6.1%
				Frank Vondersaar	2,141	5.3%
				TOTAL	*40,573*	

ARIZONA

Congressional districts first established for elections held in 2002
8 members

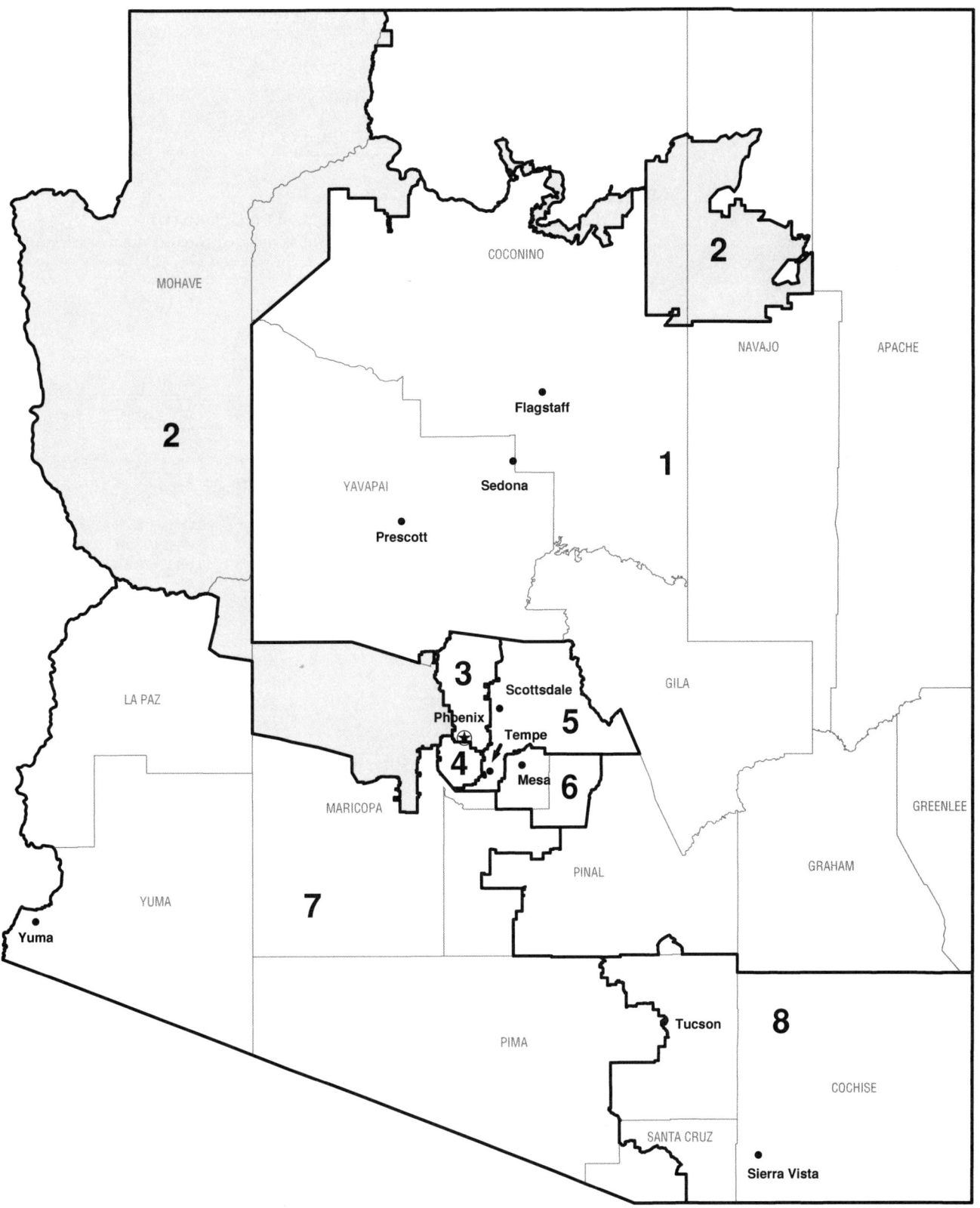

ARIZONA

GOVERNOR
Janet Napolitano (D). Reelected 2006 to a four-year term. Previously elected 2002.

SENATORS (2 Republicans)
Jon Kyl (R). Reelected 2006 to a six-year term. Previously elected 2000, 1994.

John McCain (R). Reelected 2004 to a six-year term. Previously elected 1998, 1992, 1986.

REPRESENTATIVES (4 Democrats, 4 Republicans)
1. Rick Renzi (R)
2. Trent Franks (R)
3. John Shadegg (R)
4. Ed Pastor (D)
5. Harry Mitchell (D)
6. Jeff Flake (R)
7. Raul M. Grijalva (D)
8. Gabrielle Giffords (D)

POSTWAR VOTE FOR PRESIDENT

| | | Republican | | Democratic | | Other | | Percentage | | | |
| | | | | | | | | Total Vote | | Major Vote | |
Year	Total Vote	Vote	Candidate	Vote	Candidate	Vote	Plurality	Rep.	Dem.	Rep.	Dem.
2004	2,012,585	1,104,294	Bush, George W.	893,524	Kerry, John	14,767	210,770 R	54.9%	44.4%	55.3%	44.7%
2000**	1,532,016	781,652	Bush, George W.	685,341	Gore, Al	65,023	96,311 R	51.0%	44.7%	53.3%	46.7%
1996**	1,404,405	622,073	Dole, Bob	653,288	Clinton, Bill	129,044	31,215 D	44.3%	46.5%	48.8%	51.2%
1992**	1,486,975	572,086	Bush, George	543,050	Clinton, Bill	371,839	29,036 R	38.5%	36.5%	51.3%	48.7%
1988	1,171,873	702,541	Bush, George	454,029	Dukakis, Michael S.	15,303	248,512 R	60.0%	38.7%	60.7%	39.3%
1984	1,025,897	681,416	Reagan, Ronald	333,854	Mondale, Walter F.	10,627	347,562 R	66.4%	32.5%	67.1%	32.9%
1980**	873,945	529,688	Reagan, Ronald	246,843	Carter, Jimmy	97,414	282,845 R	60.6%	28.2%	68.2%	31.8%
1976	742,719	418,642	Ford, Gerald R.	295,602	Carter, Jimmy	28,475	123,040 R	56.4%	39.8%	58.6%	41.4%
1972	622,926	402,812	Nixon, Richard M.	198,540	McGovern, George S.	21,574	204,272 R	64.7%	31.9%	67.0%	33.0%
1968**	486,936	266,721	Nixon, Richard M.	170,514	Humphrey, Hubert H.	49,701	96,207 R	54.8%	35.0%	61.0%	39.0%
1964	480,770	242,535	Goldwater, Barry M.	237,753	Johnson, Lyndon B.	482	4,782 R	50.4%	49.5%	50.5%	49.5%
1960	398,491	221,241	Nixon, Richard M.	176,781	Kennedy, John F.	469	44,460 R	55.5%	44.4%	55.6%	44.4%
1956	290,173	176,990	Eisenhower, Dwight D.	112,880	Stevenson, Adlai E.	303	64,110 R	61.0%	38.9%	61.1%	38.9%
1952	260,570	152,042	Eisenhower, Dwight D.	108,528	Stevenson, Adlai E.		43,514 R	58.3%	41.7%	58.3%	41.7%
1948	177,065	77,597	Dewey, Thomas E.	95,251	Truman, Harry S.	4,217	17,654 D	43.8%	53.8%	44.9%	55.1%

**In past elections, the other vote included: 2000 - 45,645 Green (Ralph Nader); 1996 - 112,072 Reform (Ross Perot); 1992 - 353,741 Independent (Ross Perot); 1980 - 76,952 Independent (John Anderson); 1968 - 46,573 American Independent (George Wallace).

ARIZONA

POSTWAR VOTE FOR GOVERNOR

Year	Total Vote	Republican Vote	Republican Candidate	Democratic Vote	Democratic Candidate	Other Vote	Rep.-Dem. Plurality	Total Vote Rep.	Total Vote Dem.	Major Vote Rep.	Major Vote Dem.
2006	1,533,645	543,528	Munsil, Len	959,830	Napolitano, Janet	30,287	416,302 D	35.4%	62.6%	36.2%	63.8%
2002	1,226,111	554,465	Salmon, Matt	566,284	Napolitano, Janet	105,362	11,819 D	45.2%	46.2%	49.5%	50.5%
1998	1,017,616	620,188	Hull, Jane Dee	361,552	Johnson, Paul	35,876	258,636 R	60.9%	35.5%	63.2%	36.8%
1994	1,129,607	593,492	Symington, Fife	500,702	Basha, Eddie	35,413	92,790 R	52.5%	44.3%	54.2%	45.8%
1990**	940,737	492,569	Symington, Fife	448,168	Goddard, Terry		44,401 R	52.4%	47.6%	52.4%	47.6%
1986**	866,984	343,913	Mecham, Evan	298,986	Warner, Carolyn	224,085	44,927 R	39.7%	34.5%	53.5%	46.5%
1982	726,364	235,877	Corbet, Leo	453,795	Babbitt, Bruce	36,692	217,918 D	32.5%	62.5%	34.2%	65.8%
1978	538,556	241,093	Mecham, Evan	282,605	Babbitt, Bruce	14,858	41,512 D	44.8%	52.5%	46.0%	54.0%
1974	552,202	273,674	Williams, Russell	278,375	Castro, Raul H.	153	4,701 D	49.6%	50.4%	49.6%	50.4%
1970**	411,409	209,522	Williams, John R.	201,887	Castro, Raul H.		7,635 R	50.9%	49.1%	50.9%	49.1%
1968	483,998	279,923	Williams, John R.	204,075	Goddard, Sam		75,848 R	57.8%	42.2%	57.8%	42.2%
1966	378,342	203,438	Williams, John R.	174,904	Goddard, Sam		28,534 R	53.8%	46.2%	53.8%	46.2%
1964	473,502	221,404	Kleindienst, Richard	252,098	Goddard, Sam		30,694 D	46.8%	53.2%	46.8%	53.2%
1962	365,841	200,578	Fannin, Paul	165,263	Goddard, Sam		35,315 R	54.8%	45.2%	54.8%	45.2%
1960	397,107	235,502	Fannin, Paul	161,605	Ackerman, Lee		73,897 R	59.3%	40.7%	59.3%	40.7%
1958	290,465	160,136	Fannin, Paul	130,329	Morrison, Robert		29,807 R	55.1%	44.9%	55.1%	44.9%
1956	288,592	116,744	Griffen, Horace B.	171,848	McFarland, Ernest W.		55,104 D	40.5%	59.5%	40.5%	59.5%
1954	243,970	115,866	Pyle, Howard	128,104	McFarland, Ernest W.		12,238 D	47.5%	52.5%	47.5%	52.5%
1952	260,285	156,592	Pyle, Howard	103,693	Haldiman, Joe C.		52,899 R	60.2%	39.8%	60.2%	39.8%
1950	195,227	99,109	Pyle, Howard	96,118	Frohmiller, Ana		2,991 R	50.8%	49.2%	50.8%	49.2%
1948	175,767	70,419	Brockett, Bruce	104,008	Garvey, Dan E.	1,340	33,589 D	40.1%	59.2%	40.4%	59.6%
1946	122,462	48,867	Brockett, Bruce	73,595	Osborn, Sidney P.		24,728 D	39.9%	60.1%	39.9%	60.1%

**In 1990 neither major party candidate won an absolute majority, therefore a runoff election was held February 26, 1991; the vote above is for the February runoff. In the November 1990 election, a total of 1,055,406 votes were cast as follows: 523,984 Republican (49.6 percent); 519,691 Democratic (49.2 percent); 11,731 Other (1.1 percent). In past elections, the other vote included: 1986 - 224,085 Independent (Bill Schulz). The term of office for Arizona's governor was increased from two to four years effective with the 1970 election.

POSTWAR VOTE FOR SENATOR

Year	Total Vote	Republican Vote	Republican Candidate	Democratic Vote	Democratic Candidate	Other Vote	Rep.-Dem. Plurality	Total Vote Rep.	Total Vote Dem.	Major Vote Rep.	Major Vote Dem.
2006	1,526,782	814,398	Kyl, Jon	664,141	Pederson, Jim	48,243	150,257 R	53.3%	43.5%	55.1%	44.9%
2004	1,961,677	1,505,372	McCain, John	404,507	Starky, Stuart	51,798	1,100,865 R	76.7%	20.6%	78.8%	21.2%
2000**	1,397,076	1,108,196	Kyl, Jon	—		288,880	1,108,196 R	79.3%		100.0%	
1998	1,013,280	696,577	McCain, John	275,224	Ranger, Ed	41,479	421,353 R	68.7%	27.2%	71.7%	28.3%
1994	1,119,060	600,999	Kyl, Jon	442,510	Coppersmith, Sam	75,551	158,489 R	53.7%	39.5%	57.6%	42.4%
1992**	1,382,051	771,395	McCain, John	436,321	Sargent, Claire	174,335	335,074 R	55.8%	31.6%	63.9%	36.1%
1988	1,164,539	478,060	DeGreen, Keith	660,403	DeConcini, Dennis	26,076	182,343 D	41.1%	56.7%	42.0%	58.0%
1986	862,921	521,850	McCain, John	340,965	Kimball, Richard	106	180,885 R	60.5%	39.5%	60.5%	39.5%
1982	723,885	291,749	Dunn, Pete	411,970	DeConcini, Dennis	20,166	120,221 D	40.3%	56.9%	41.5%	58.5%
1980	874,238	432,371	Goldwater, Barry M.	422,972	Schulz, Bill	18,895	9,399 R	49.5%	48.4%	50.5%	49.5%
1976	741,210	321,236	Steiger, Sam	400,334	DeConcini, Dennis	19,640	79,098 D	43.3%	54.0%	44.5%	55.5%
1974	549,919	320,396	Goldwater, Barry M.	229,523	Marshall, Jonathan		90,873 R	58.3%	41.7%	58.3%	41.7%
1970	407,796	228,284	Fannin, Paul	179,512	Grossman, Sam		48,772 R	56.0%	44.0%	56.0%	44.0%
1968	479,945	274,607	Goldwater, Barry M.	205,338	Elson, Roy L.		69,269 R	57.2%	42.8%	57.2%	42.8%
1964	468,801	241,089	Fannin, Paul	227,712	Elson, Roy L.		13,377 R	51.4%	48.6%	51.4%	48.6%
1962	362,605	163,388	Mecham, Evan	199,217	Hayden, Carl		35,829 D	45.1%	54.9%	45.1%	54.9%
1958	293,623	164,593	Goldwater, Barry M.	129,030	McFarland, Ernest W.		35,563 R	56.1%	43.9%	56.1%	43.9%
1956	278,263	107,447	Jones, Ross F.	170,816	Hayden, Carl		63,369 D	38.6%	61.4%	38.6%	61.4%
1952	257,401	132,063	Goldwater, Barry M.	125,338	McFarland, Ernest W.		6,725 R	51.3%	48.7%	51.3%	48.7%
1950	185,092	68,846	Brockett, Bruce	116,246	Hayden, Carl		47,400 D	37.2%	62.8%	37.2%	62.8%
1946	116,239	35,022	Powers, Ward S.	80,415	McFarland, Ernest W.	802	45,393 D	30.1%	69.2%	30.3%	69.7%

**The Democratic Party did not run a candidate in the 2000 Senate election. In past elections, the other vote included: 1992 - 145,361 Independent (Evan Mecham).

ARIZONA

GOVERNOR 2006

2000 Census Population	County	Total Vote	Republican	Democratic	Other	Rep.-Dem. Plurality	Percentage Total Vote Rep.	Dem.	Major Vote Rep.	Dem.
69,423	APACHE	18,795	3,627	14,475	693	10,848 D	19.3%	77.0%	20.0%	80.0%
117,755	COCHISE	36,377	14,038	21,416	923	7,378 D	38.6%	58.9%	39.6%	60.4%
116,320	COCONINO	38,304	8,879	28,551	874	19,672 D	23.2%	74.5%	23.7%	76.3%
51,335	GILA	16,747	5,803	10,586	358	4,783 D	34.7%	63.2%	35.4%	64.6%
33,489	GRAHAM	7,815	3,306	4,348	161	1,042 D	42.3%	55.6%	43.2%	56.8%
8,547	GREENLEE	2,132	588	1,486	58	898 D	27.6%	69.7%	28.4%	71.6%
19,715	LA PAZ	3,833	1,342	2,353	138	1,011 D	35.0%	61.4%	36.3%	63.7%
3,072,149	MARICOPA	887,853	332,570	538,383	16,900	205,813 D	37.5%	60.6%	38.2%	61.8%
155,032	MOHAVE	46,118	19,588	25,400	1,130	5,812 D	42.5%	55.1%	43.5%	56.5%
97,470	NAVAJO	26,734	8,708	17,368	658	8,660 D	32.6%	65.0%	33.4%	66.6%
843,746	PIMA	282,151	82,052	195,305	4,794	113,253 D	29.1%	69.2%	29.6%	70.4%
179,727	PINAL	57,261	20,716	35,428	1,117	14,712 D	36.2%	61.9%	36.9%	63.1%
38,381	SANTA CRUZ	8,276	1,634	6,482	160	4,848 D	19.7%	78.3%	20.1%	79.9%
167,517	YAVAPAI	72,639	30,203	40,848	1,588	10,645 D	41.6%	56.2%	42.5%	57.5%
160,026	YUMA	28,610	10,474	17,401	735	6,927 D	36.6%	60.8%	37.6%	62.4%
5,130,632	TOTAL	1,533,645	543,528	959,830	30,287	416,302 D	35.4%	62.6%	36.2%	63.8%

ARIZONA

SENATOR 2006

2000 Census Population	County	Total Vote	Republican	Democratic	Other	Rep.-Dem. Plurality	Percentage Total Vote Rep.	Dem.	Major Vote Rep.	Dem.
69,423	APACHE	18,763	6,530	11,402	831	4,872 D	34.8%	60.8%	36.4%	63.6%
117,755	COCHISE	36,345	20,194	14,849	1,302	5,345 R	55.6%	40.9%	57.6%	42.4%
116,320	COCONINO	38,062	16,003	20,610	1,449	4,607 D	42.0%	54.1%	43.7%	56.3%
51,335	GILA	16,688	9,512	6,643	533	2,869 R	57.0%	39.8%	58.9%	41.1%
33,489	GRAHAM	7,837	5,127	2,194	516	2,933 R	65.4%	28.0%	70.0%	30.0%
8,547	GREENLEE	2,129	1,068	942	119	126 R	50.2%	44.2%	53.1%	46.9%
19,715	LA PAZ	3,833	2,203	1,457	173	746 R	57.5%	38.0%	60.2%	39.8%
3,072,149	MARICOPA	883,119	491,721	364,661	26,737	127,060 R	55.7%	41.3%	57.4%	42.6%
155,032	MOHAVE	45,944	26,964	16,998	1,982	9,966 R	58.7%	37.0%	61.3%	38.7%
97,470	NAVAJO	26,663	13,927	11,785	951	2,142 R	52.2%	44.2%	54.2%	45.8%
843,746	PIMA	281,202	128,987	144,275	7,940	15,288 D	45.9%	51.3%	47.2%	52.8%
179,727	PINAL	57,005	30,379	24,790	1,836	5,589 R	53.3%	43.5%	55.1%	44.9%
38,381	SANTA CRUZ	8,156	3,067	4,892	197	1,825 D	37.6%	60.0%	38.5%	61.5%
167,517	YAVAPAI	72,408	43,219	26,340	2,849	16,879 R	59.7%	36.4%	62.1%	37.9%
160,026	YUMA	28,628	15,497	12,303	828	3,194 R	54.1%	43.0%	55.7%	44.3%
5,130,632	TOTAL	1,526,782	814,398	664,141	48,243	150,257 R	53.3%	43.5%	55.1%	44.9%

ARIZONA

HOUSE OF REPRESENTATIVES

CD	Year	Total Vote	Republican Vote	Republican Candidate	Democratic Vote	Democratic Candidate	Other Vote	Rep.-Dem. Plurality	Percentage Total Vote Rep.	Dem.	Major Vote Rep.	Dem.
1	2006	204,139	105,646	RENZI, RICK*	88,691	SIMON, ELLEN	9,802	16,955 R	51.8%	43.4%	54.4%	45.6%
1	2004	253,351	148,315	RENZI, RICK*	91,776	BABBITT, PAUL	13,260	56,539 R	58.5%	36.2%	61.8%	38.2%
1	2002	174,687	85,967	RENZI, RICK	79,730	CORDOVA, GEORGE	8,990	6,237 R	49.2%	45.6%	51.9%	48.1%
2	2006	230,560	135,150	FRANKS, TRENT*	89,671	THRASHER, JOHN	5,739	45,479 R	58.6%	38.9%	60.1%	39.9%
2	2004	279,303	165,260	FRANKS, TRENT*	107,406	CAMACHO, RANDY	6,637	57,854 R	59.2%	38.5%	60.6%	39.4%
2	2002	167,502	100,359	FRANKS, TRENT	61,217	CAMACHO, RANDY	5,926	39,142 R	59.9%	36.5%	62.1%	37.9%
3	2006	189,849	112,519	SHADEGG, JOHN*	72,586	PAINE, HERB	4,744	39,933 R	59.3%	38.2%	60.8%	39.2%
3	2004	225,974	181,012	SHADEGG, JOHN*		—	44,962	181,012 R	80.1%		100.0%	
3	2002	155,751	104,847	SHADEGG, JOHN*	47,173	HILL, CHARLES	3,731	57,674 R	67.3%	30.3%	69.0%	31.0%
4	2006	77,861	18,627	KARG, DON	56,464	PASTOR, ED*	2,770	37,837 D	23.9%	72.5%	24.8%	75.2%
4	2004	110,027	28,238	KARG, DON	77,150	PASTOR, ED*	4,639	48,912 D	25.7%	70.1%	26.8%	73.2%
4	2002	66,065	18,381	BARNETT, JONATHAN	44,517	PASTOR, ED*	3,167	26,136 D	27.8%	67.4%	29.2%	70.8%
5	2006	202,010	93,815	HAYWORTH, J. D.*	101,838	MITCHELL, HARRY	6,357	8,023 D	46.4%	50.4%	47.9%	52.1%
5	2004	268,007	159,455	HAYWORTH, J. D.*	102,363	ROGERS, ELIZABETH	6,189	57,092 R	59.5%	38.2%	60.9%	39.1%
5	2002	169,812	103,870	HAYWORTH, J. D.*	61,559	COLUMBUS, CRAIG	4,383	42,311 R	61.2%	36.3%	62.8%	37.2%
6	2006	203,486	152,201	FLAKE, JEFF*		—	51,285	152,201 R	74.8%		100.0%	
6	2004	255,577	202,882	FLAKE, JEFF*		—	52,695	202,882 R	79.4%		100.0%	
6	2002	156,337	103,094	FLAKE, JEFF*	49,355	THOMAS, DEBORAH	3,888	53,739 R	65.9%	31.6%	67.6%	32.4%
7	2006	131,525	46,498	DRAKE, RON	80,354	GRIJALVA, RAUL M.*	4,673	33,856 D	35.4%	61.1%	36.7%	63.3%
7	2004	175,437	59,066	SWEENEY, JOSEPH	108,868	GRIJALVA, RAUL M.*	7,503	49,802 D	33.7%	62.1%	35.2%	64.8%
7	2002	103,818	38,474	HIEB, ROSS	61,256	GRIJALVA, RAUL M.	4,088	22,782 D	37.1%	59.0%	38.6%	61.4%
8	2006	253,720	106,790	GRAF, RANDY	137,655	GIFFORDS, GABRIELLE	9,275	30,865 D	42.1%	54.3%	43.7%	56.3%
8	2004	303,769	183,363	KOLBE, JIM*	109,963	BACAL, EVA	10,443	73,400 R	60.4%	36.2%	62.5%	37.5%
8	2002	200,428	126,930	KOLBE, JIM*	67,328	RYAN, MARY JUDGE	6,170	59,602 R	63.3%	33.6%	65.3%	34.7%
TOTAL	2006	1,493,150	771,246		627,259		94,645	143,987 R	51.7%	42.0%	55.1%	44.9%
TOTAL	2004	1,871,445	1,127,591		597,526		146,328	530,065 R	60.3%	31.9%	65.4%	34.6%
TOTAL	2002	1,194,400	681,922		472,135		40,343	209,787 R	57.1%	39.5%	59.1%	40.9%

An asterisk (*) denotes incumbent.

ARIZONA

GENERAL AND PRIMARY ELECTIONS

2006 GENERAL ELECTIONS

Governor   Other vote was 30,268 Libertarian (Barry J. Hess II); 10 write-in (Arthur Ray Arvizu); 6 write-in (Brian Wright); 3 write-in (Robert B. Winn).

Senator   Other vote was 48,231 Libertarian (Richard Mack); 7 write-in (Stephen Baker); 5 write-in (Ray Caplette).

House   Other vote was:

CD 1   9,802 Libertarian (David Schlosser).
CD 2   5,734 Libertarian (Powell Gammill); 5 write-in (William Crum).
CD 3   4,744 Libertarian (Mark Yannone).
CD 4   2,770 Libertarian (Ronald Harders).
CD 5   6,357 Libertarian (Warren Severin).
CD 6   51,285 Libertarian (Jason M. Blair).
CD 7   4,673 Libertarian (Joe Cobb).
CD 8   4,849 Libertarian (David F. Nolan); 4,408 Independent (Jay Quick); 7 write-in (Russ Dove); 7 write-in (Paul Price); 4 write-in (Leo F. Kimminau Sr.).

ARIZONA

GENERAL AND PRIMARY ELECTIONS

2006 PRIMARY ELECTIONS

Primary	September 12, 2006	**Registration** (as of September 12, 2006)	Republican	1,003,977
			Democratic	847,490
			Libertarian	16,529
			Other	665,312
			TOTAL	2,533,308

Primary Type Semi-open—Registered Democrats and Republicans could vote only in their party's primary. Voters not registered with any political party could participate in the primary of their choice.

Note: An asterisk (*) denotes incumbent.

	REPUBLICAN PRIMARIES			DEMOCRATIC PRIMARIES		
Governor	Len Munsil	155,778	50.6%	Janet Napolitano*	230,881	100.0%
	Don Goldwater	122,283	39.7%			
	Mike Harris	18,734	6.1%			
	Gary Tupper	11,250	3.7%			
	Steve Moore (write-in)	49				
	TOTAL	308,094				
Senator	Jon Kyl*	297,636	99.9%	Jim Pederson	214,455	100.0%
	Michael Aloisi (write-in)	155	0.1%			
	TOTAL	297,791				
Congressional District 1	Rick Renzi*	37,664	100.0%	Ellen Simon	20,273	52.8%
				Susan Friedman	7,062	18.4%
				Bob Donahue	5,927	15.4%
				Mike Caccioppoli	3,635	9.5%
				Vic McKerlie	1,512	3.9%
				TOTAL	38,409	
Congressional District 2	Trent Franks*	51,386	100.0%	John Thrasher	11,521	46.7%
				Gene Scharer	8,462	34.3%
				Suchindran "Chat" Chatterjee	4,667	18.9%
				TOTAL	24,650	
Congressional District 3	John Shadegg*	35,763	100.0%	Herb Paine	7,902	50.4%
				Don Chilton	7,759	49.5%
				Jim McCoy (write-in)	12	0.1%
				TOTAL	15,673	
Congressional District 4	Don Karg	7,175	100.0%	Ed Pastor*	14,833	100.0%
Congressional District 5	J. D. Hayworth*	38,275	100.0%	Harry Mitchell	20,852	100.0%
Congressional District 6	Jeff Flake*	43,199	100.0%	No Democratic candidate		
Congressional District 7	Ron Drake	10,022	60.4%	Raul M. Grijalva*	26,604	100.0%
	Joseph Sweeney	6,565	39.6%			
	TOTAL	16,587				
Congressional District 8	Randy Graf	27,063	42.2%	Gabrielle Giffords	33,375	54.3%
	Steve Huffman	24,119	37.6%	Patty Weiss	19,148	31.2%
	Mike Hellon	8,095	12.6%	Jeffrey Lynn "Jeff" Latas	3,687	6.0%
	Frank Antenori	2,724	4.3%	Alex Rodriguez	2,855	4.6%
	Mike "Michael T." Jenkins	2,075	3.2%	William "Bill" Johnson	1,768	2.9%
				Francine Shacter	576	0.9%
	TOTAL	64,076		TOTAL	61,409	

ARKANSAS

Congressional districts first established for elections held in 2002
4 members

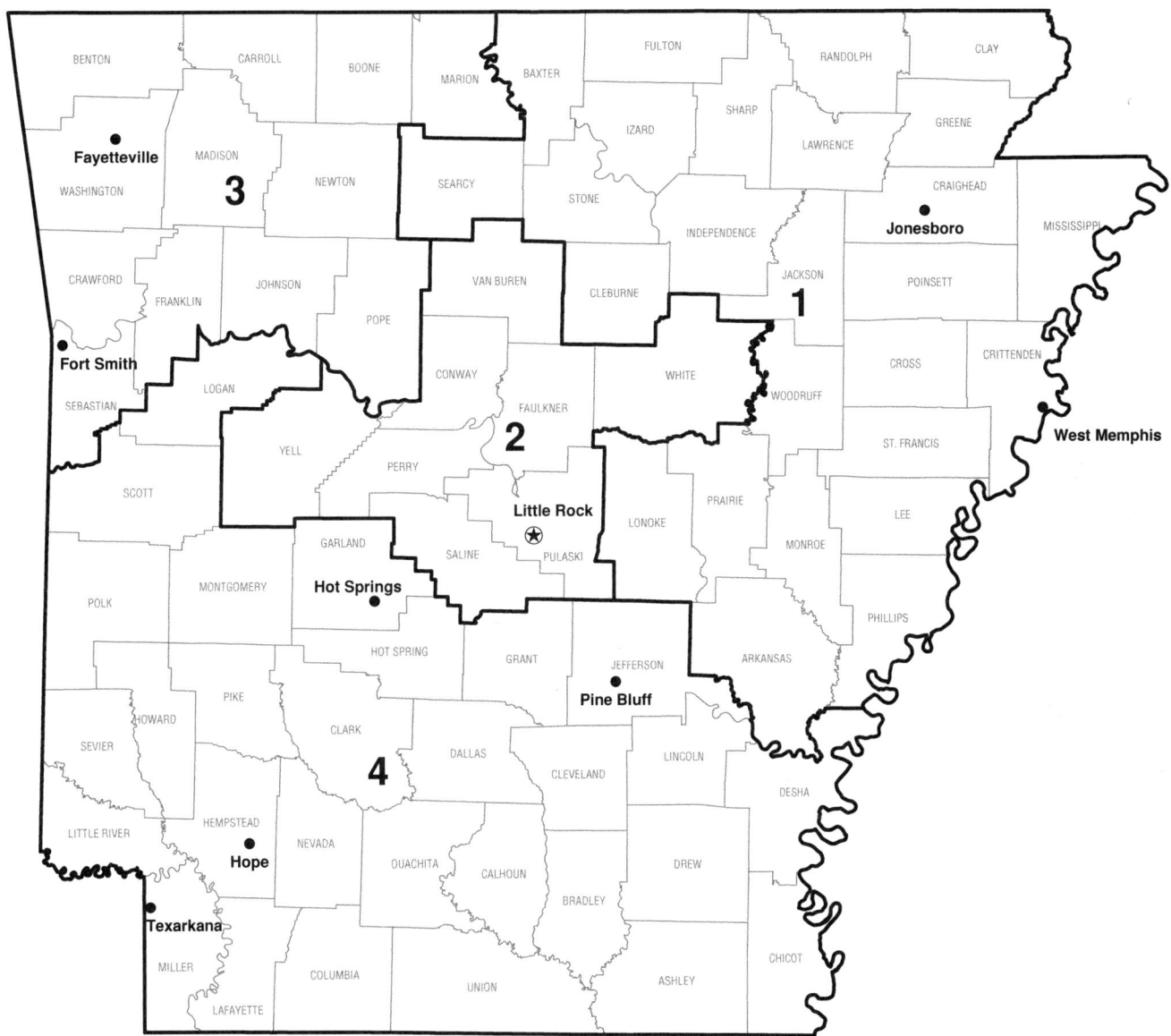

ARKANSAS

GOVERNOR
Mike D. Beebe (D). Elected 2006 to a four-year term.

SENATORS (2 Democrats)
Blanche Lincoln (D). Reelected 2004 to a six-year term. Previously elected 1998.

Mark Pryor (D). Elected 2002 to a six-year term.

REPRESENTATIVES (3 Democrats, 1 Republican)
1. Marion Berry (D)
2. Vic Snyder (D)
3. John Boozman (R)
4. Mike Ross (D)

POSTWAR VOTE FOR PRESIDENT

| | | Republican | | Democratic | | Other | | Percentage | | | |
| | | | | | | | | Total Vote | | Major Vote | |
Year	Total Vote	Vote	Candidate	Vote	Candidate	Vote	Plurality	Rep.	Dem.	Rep.	Dem.
2004	1,054,945	572,898	Bush, George W.	469,953	Kerry, John	12,094	102,945 R	54.3%	44.5%	54.9%	45.1%
2000**	921,781	472,940	Bush, George W.	422,768	Gore, Al	26,073	50,172 R	51.3%	45.9%	52.8%	47.2%
1996**	884,262	325,416	Dole, Bob	475,171	Clinton, Bill	83,675	149,755 D	36.8%	53.7%	40.6%	59.4%
1992**	950,653	337,324	Bush, George	505,823	Clinton, Bill	107,506	168,499 D	35.5%	53.2%	40.0%	60.0%
1988	827,738	466,578	Bush, George	349,237	Dukakis, Michael S.	11,923	117,341 R	56.4%	42.2%	57.2%	42.8%
1984	884,406	534,774	Reagan, Ronald	338,646	Mondale, Walter F.	10,986	196,128 R	60.5%	38.3%	61.2%	38.8%
1980**	837,582	403,164	Reagan, Ronald	398,041	Carter, Jimmy	36,377	5,123 R	48.1%	47.5%	50.3%	49.7%
1976	767,535	267,903	Ford, Gerald R.	498,604	Carter, Jimmy	1,028	230,701 D	34.9%	65.0%	35.0%	65.0%
1972	651,320	448,541	Nixon, Richard M.	199,892	McGovern, George S.	2,887	248,649 R	68.9%	30.7%	69.2%	30.8%
1968**	619,969	190,759	Nixon, Richard M.	188,228	Humphrey, Hubert H.	240,982	50,223 A	30.8%	30.4%	50.3%	49.7%
1964	560,426	243,264	Goldwater, Barry M.	314,197	Johnson, Lyndon B.	2,965	70,933 D	43.4%	56.1%	43.6%	56.4%
1960	428,509	184,508	Nixon, Richard M.	215,049	Kennedy, John F.	28,952	30,541 D	43.1%	50.2%	46.2%	53.8%
1956	406,572	186,287	Eisenhower, Dwight D.	213,277	Stevenson, Adlai E.	7,008	26,990 D	45.8%	52.5%	46.6%	53.4%
1952	404,800	177,155	Eisenhower, Dwight D.	226,300	Stevenson, Adlai E.	1,345	49,145 D	43.8%	55.9%	43.9%	56.1%
1948**	242,475	50,959	Dewey, Thomas E.	149,659	Truman, Harry S.	41,857	98,700 D	21.0%	61.7%	25.4%	74.6%

**In past elections, the other vote included: 2000 - 13,421 Green (Ralph Nader); 1996 - 69,884 Reform (Ross Perot); 1992 - 99,132 Independent (Ross Perot); 1980 - 22,468 Independent (John Anderson); 1968 - 240,982 American Independent (George Wallace); 1948 - 40,068 States' Rights (Strom Thurmond).

ARKANSAS

POSTWAR VOTE FOR GOVERNOR

Year	Total Vote	Republican		Democratic		Other Vote	Rep.-Dem. Plurality	Percentage			
								Total Vote		Major Vote	
		Vote	Candidate	Vote	Candidate			Rep.	Dem.	Rep.	Dem.
2006	774,680	315,040	Hutchinson, Asa	430,765	Beebe, Mike D.	28,875	115,725 D	40.7%	55.6%	42.2%	57.8%
2002	805,696	427,082	Huckabee, Mike	378,250	Fisher, Jimmie Lou	364	48,832 R	53.0%	46.9%	53.0%	47.0%
1998	706,011	421,989	Huckabee, Mike	272,923	Bristow, Bill	11,099	149,066 R	59.8%	38.7%	60.7%	39.3%
1994	716,840	287,904	Nelson, Sheffield	428,936	Tucker, Jim Guy		141,032 D	40.2%	59.8%	40.2%	59.8%
1990	696,412	295,925	Nelson, Sheffield	400,386	Clinton, Bill	101	104,461 D	42.5%	57.5%	42.5%	57.5%
1986**	688,551	248,427	White, Frank D.	439,882	Clinton, Bill	242	191,455 D	36.1%	63.9%	36.1%	63.9%
1984	886,548	331,987	Freeman, Woody	554,561	Clinton, Bill		222,574 D	37.4%	62.6%	37.4%	62.6%
1982	789,351	357,496	White, Frank D.	431,855	Clinton, Bill		74,359 D	45.3%	54.7%	45.3%	54.7%
1980	838,925	435,684	White, Frank D.	403,241	Clinton, Bill		32,443 R	51.9%	48.1%	51.9%	48.1%
1978	528,912	193,746	Lowe, A. Lynn	335,101	Clinton, Bill	65	141,355 D	36.6%	63.4%	36.6%	63.4%
1976	726,949	121,716	Griffith, Leon	605,083	Pryor, David H.	150	483,367 D	16.7%	83.2%	16.7%	83.3%
1974	545,974	187,872	Coon, Ken	358,018	Pryor, David H.	84	170,146 D	34.4%	65.6%	34.4%	65.6%
1972	648,069	159,177	Blaylock, Len E.	488,892	Bumpers, Dale		329,715 D	24.6%	75.4%	24.6%	75.4%
1970	609,198	197,418	Rockefeller, Winthrop	375,648	Bumpers, Dale	36,132	178,230 D	32.4%	61.7%	34.4%	65.6%
1968	615,595	322,782	Rockefeller, Winthrop	292,813	Crank, Marion		29,969 R	52.4%	47.6%	52.4%	47.6%
1966	563,527	306,324	Rockefeller, Winthrop	257,203	Johnson, James D.		49,121 R	54.4%	45.6%	54.4%	45.6%
1964	592,113	254,561	Rockefeller, Winthrop	337,489	Faubus, Orval E.	63	82,928 D	43.0%	57.0%	43.0%	57.0%
1962	308,092	82,349	Ricketts, Willis	225,743	Faubus, Orval E.		143,394 D	26.7%	73.3%	26.7%	73.3%
1960	421,985	129,921	Britt, Henry M.	292,064	Faubus, Orval E.		162,143 D	30.8%	69.2%	30.8%	69.2%
1958	286,886	50,288	Johnson, George W.	236,598	Faubus, Orval E.		186,310 D	17.5%	82.5%	17.5%	82.5%
1956	399,012	77,215	Mitchell, Roy	321,797	Faubus, Orval E.		244,582 D	19.4%	80.6%	19.4%	80.6%
1954	335,176	127,004	Remmel, Pratt C.	208,121	Faubus, Orval E.	51	81,117 D	37.9%	62.1%	37.9%	62.1%
1952	391,592	49,292	Speck, Jefferson W.	342,292	Cherry, Francis	8	293,000 D	12.6%	87.4%	12.6%	87.4%
1950	317,087	50,309	Speck, Jefferson W.	266,778	McMath, Sidney S.		216,469 D	15.9%	84.1%	15.9%	84.1%
1948	249,301	26,500	Black, Charles R.	222,801	McMath, Sidney S.		196,301 D	10.6%	89.4%	10.6%	89.4%
1946	152,162	24,133	Mills, W. T.	128,029	Laney, Ben T.		103,896 D	15.9%	84.1%	15.9%	84.1%

**The term of office for Arkansas' governor was increased from two to four years effective with the 1986 election.

POSTWAR VOTE FOR SENATOR

Year	Total Vote	Republican		Democratic		Other Vote	Rep.-Dem. Plurality	Percentage			
								Total Vote		Major Vote	
		Vote	Candidate	Vote	Candidate			Rep.	Dem.	Rep.	Dem.
2004	1,039,349	458,036	Holt, Jim	580,973	Lincoln, Blanche	340	122,937 D	44.1%	55.9%	44.1%	55.9%
2002	803,959	370,653	Hutchinson, Tim	433,306	Pryor, Mark		62,653 D	46.1%	53.9%	46.1%	53.9%
1998	700,644	295,870	Boozman, Fay	385,878	Lincoln, Blanche	18,896	90,008 D	42.2%	55.1%	43.4%	56.6%
1996	846,183	445,942	Hutchinson, Tim	400,241	Bryant, Winston		45,701 R	52.7%	47.3%	52.7%	47.3%
1992	920,008	366,373	Huckabee, Mike	553,635	Bumpers, Dale		187,262 D	39.8%	60.2%	39.8%	60.2%
1990**	494,735		—	493,910	Pryor, David H.	825	493,910 D		99.8%		100.0%
1986	695,487	262,313	Hutchinson, Asa	433,122	Bumpers, Dale	52	170,809 D	37.7%	62.3%	37.7%	62.3%
1984	875,956	373,615	Bethune, Ed	502,341	Pryor, David H.		128,726 D	42.7%	57.3%	42.7%	57.3%
1980	808,812	330,576	Clark, Bill	477,905	Bumpers, Dale	331	147,329 D	40.9%	59.1%	40.9%	59.1%
1978	522,239	84,722	Kelly, Tom	399,916	Pryor, David H.	37,601	315,194 D	16.2%	76.6%	17.5%	82.5%
1974	543,082	82,026	Jones, John H.	461,056	Bumpers, Dale		379,030 D	15.1%	84.9%	15.1%	84.9%
1972	634,636	248,238	Babbitt, Wayne H.	386,398	McClellan, John L.		138,160 D	39.1%	60.9%	39.1%	60.9%
1968	591,704	241,739	Bernard, Charles T.	349,965	Fulbright, J. W.		108,226 D	40.9%	59.1%	40.9%	59.1%
1966**			—		McClellan, John L.		D				
1962	312,880	98,013	Jones, Kenneth	214,867	Fulbright, J. W.		116,854 D	31.3%	68.7%	31.3%	68.7%
1960**			—		McClellan, John L.		D				
1956	399,695	68,016	Henley, Ben C.	331,679	Fulbright, J. W.		263,663 D	17.0%	83.0%	17.0%	83.0%
1954	291,058		—	291,058	McClellan, John L.		291,058 D		100.0%		100.0%
1950	302,582		—	302,582	Fulbright, J. W.		302,582 D		100.0%		100.0%
1948	216,401		—	216,401	McClellan, John L.		216,401 D		100.0%		100.0%

**In 1990 the vote for Senator David H. Pryor was not canvassed in seven counties because he was unopposed. Senator John L. McClellan was reelected in 1966 and in 1960, but his vote was not canvassed in many counties.

ARKANSAS

GOVERNOR 2006

2000 Census Population	County	Total Vote	Republican	Democratic	Other	Rep.-Dem. Plurality	Percentage Total Vote Rep.	Dem.	Percentage Major Vote Rep.	Dem.
20,749	ARKANSAS	5,729	1,639	3,898	192	2,259 D	28.6%	68.0%	29.6%	70.4%
24,209	ASHLEY	5,564	1,737	3,550	277	1,813 D	31.2%	63.8%	32.9%	67.1%
38,386	BAXTER	13,365	6,440	6,248	677	192 R	48.2%	46.7%	50.8%	49.2%
153,406	BENTON	48,659	28,608	18,811	1,240	9,797 R	58.8%	38.7%	60.3%	39.7%
33,948	BOONE	10,649	5,784	4,362	503	1,422 R	54.3%	41.0%	57.0%	43.0%
12,600	BRADLEY	2,762	862	1,776	124	914 D	31.2%	64.3%	32.7%	67.3%
5,744	CALHOUN	1,754	635	1,001	118	366 D	36.2%	57.1%	38.8%	61.2%
25,357	CARROLL	8,243	3,978	3,881	384	97 R	48.3%	47.1%	50.6%	49.4%
14,117	CHICOT	3,440	791	2,570	79	1,779 D	23.0%	74.7%	23.5%	76.5%
23,546	CLARK	6,446	2,024	4,162	260	2,138 D	31.4%	64.6%	32.7%	67.3%
17,609	CLAY	4,377	1,137	3,010	230	1,873 D	26.0%	68.8%	27.4%	72.6%
24,046	CLEBURNE	9,618	4,370	4,881	367	511 D	45.4%	50.7%	47.2%	52.8%
8,571	CLEVELAND	2,567	982	1,450	135	468 D	38.3%	56.5%	40.4%	59.6%
25,603	COLUMBIA	6,041	2,549	3,379	113	830 D	42.2%	55.9%	43.0%	57.0%
20,336	CONWAY	6,634	2,268	4,125	241	1,857 D	34.2%	62.2%	35.5%	64.5%
82,148	CRAIGHEAD	20,876	7,696	12,753	427	5,057 D	36.9%	61.1%	37.6%	62.4%
53,247	CRAWFORD	15,992	8,139	7,249	604	890 R	50.9%	45.3%	52.9%	47.1%
50,866	CRITTENDEN	18,597	5,023	13,246	328	8,223 D	27.0%	71.2%	27.5%	72.5%
19,526	CROSS	5,395	1,819	3,331	245	1,512 D	33.7%	61.7%	35.3%	64.7%
9,210	DALLAS	2,821	975	1,774	72	799 D	34.6%	62.9%	35.5%	64.5%
15,341	DESHA	3,321	703	2,516	102	1,813 D	21.2%	75.8%	21.8%	78.2%
18,723	DREW	4,130	1,447	2,556	127	1,109 D	35.0%	61.9%	36.1%	63.9%
86,014	FAULKNER	24,883	11,506	12,419	958	913 D	46.2%	49.9%	48.1%	51.9%
17,771	FRANKLIN	5,526	2,452	2,908	166	456 D	44.4%	52.6%	45.7%	54.3%
11,642	FULTON	3,365	1,199	2,002	164	803 D	35.6%	59.5%	37.5%	62.5%
88,068	GARLAND	29,582	12,530	15,482	1,570	2,952 D	42.4%	52.3%	44.7%	55.3%
16,464	GRANT	5,183	2,186	2,798	199	612 D	42.2%	54.0%	43.9%	56.1%
37,331	GREENE	9,203	3,283	5,724	196	2,441 D	35.7%	62.2%	36.4%	63.6%
23,587	HEMPSTEAD	4,896	1,566	3,212	118	1,646 D	32.0%	65.6%	32.8%	67.2%
30,353	HOT SPRING	8,648	3,012	5,312	324	2,300 D	34.8%	61.4%	36.2%	63.8%
14,300	HOWARD	3,255	1,057	2,090	108	1,033 D	32.5%	64.2%	33.6%	66.4%
34,233	INDEPENDENCE	10,002	3,934	5,608	460	1,674 D	39.3%	56.1%	41.2%	58.8%
13,249	IZARD	4,155	1,534	2,412	209	878 D	36.9%	58.1%	38.9%	61.1%
18,418	JACKSON	4,550	1,036	3,189	325	2,153 D	22.8%	70.1%	24.5%	75.5%
84,278	JEFFERSON	20,231	4,955	14,659	617	9,704 D	24.5%	72.5%	25.3%	74.7%
22,781	JOHNSON	6,134	2,410	3,372	352	962 D	39.3%	55.0%	41.7%	58.3%
8,559	LAFAYETTE	2,528	741	1,684	103	943 D	29.3%	66.6%	30.6%	69.4%
17,774	LAWRENCE	4,836	1,400	3,227	209	1,827 D	28.9%	66.7%	30.3%	69.7%
12,580	LEE	2,933	621	2,233	79	1,612 D	21.2%	76.1%	21.8%	78.2%
14,492	LINCOLN	2,807	757	1,960	90	1,203 D	27.0%	69.8%	27.9%	72.1%
13,628	LITTLE RIVER	3,777	1,012	2,552	213	1,540 D	26.8%	67.6%	28.4%	71.6%
22,486	LOGAN	6,540	2,794	3,525	221	731 D	42.7%	53.9%	44.2%	55.8%
52,828	LONOKE	16,065	7,792	7,768	505	24 R	48.5%	48.4%	50.1%	49.9%
14,243	MADISON	5,403	2,650	2,587	166	63 R	49.0%	47.9%	50.6%	49.4%
16,140	MARION	6,049	2,858	2,810	381	48 R	47.2%	46.5%	50.4%	49.6%
40,443	MILLER	9,751	3,933	5,466	352	1,533 D	40.3%	56.1%	41.8%	58.2%
51,979	MISSISSIPPI	10,176	2,677	7,119	380	4,442 D	26.3%	70.0%	27.3%	72.7%
10,254	MONROE	2,757	776	1,914	67	1,138 D	28.1%	69.4%	28.8%	71.2%
9,245	MONTGOMERY	2,888	1,207	1,526	155	319 D	41.8%	52.8%	44.2%	55.8%
9,955	NEVADA	2,621	811	1,694	116	883 D	30.9%	64.6%	32.4%	67.6%
8,608	NEWTON	3,508	1,804	1,519	185	285 R	51.4%	43.3%	54.3%	45.7%
28,790	OUACHITA	7,488	2,647	4,665	176	2,018 D	35.3%	62.3%	36.2%	63.8%
10,209	PERRY	3,644	1,456	1,918	270	462 D	40.0%	52.6%	43.2%	56.8%
26,445	PHILLIPS	6,916	1,563	4,934	419	3,371 D	22.6%	71.3%	24.1%	75.9%
11,303	PIKE	3,183	1,317	1,770	96	453 D	41.4%	55.6%	42.7%	57.3%
25,614	POINSETT	6,258	1,793	4,346	119	2,553 D	28.7%	69.4%	29.2%	70.8%
20,229	POLK	5,599	2,831	2,465	303	366 R	50.6%	44.0%	53.5%	46.5%
54,469	POPE	15,328	7,778	6,847	703	931 R	50.7%	44.7%	53.2%	46.8%
9,539	PRAIRIE	2,879	804	1,901	174	1,097 D	27.9%	66.0%	29.7%	70.3%
361,474	PULASKI	109,928	38,653	66,821	4,454	28,168 D	35.2%	60.8%	36.6%	63.4%

ARKANSAS

GOVERNOR 2006

2000 Census Population	County	Total Vote	Republican	Democratic	Other	Rep.-Dem. Plurality	Percentage			
							Total Vote		Major Vote	
							Rep.	Dem.	Rep.	Dem.
18,195	RANDOLPH	4,619	1,403	2,894	322	1,491 D	30.4%	62.7%	32.7%	67.3%
29,329	ST. FRANCIS	6,905	1,769	4,939	197	3,170 D	25.6%	71.5%	26.4%	73.6%
83,529	SALINE	31,954	15,931	14,754	1,269	1,177 R	49.9%	46.2%	51.9%	48.1%
10,996	SCOTT	2,774	1,230	1,407	137	177 D	44.3%	50.7%	46.6%	53.4%
8,261	SEARCY	3,123	1,629	1,296	198	333 R	52.2%	41.5%	55.7%	44.3%
115,071	SEBASTIAN	31,778	16,142	14,971	665	1,171 R	50.8%	47.1%	51.9%	48.1%
15,757	SEVIER	3,022	956	1,959	107	1,003 D	31.6%	64.8%	32.8%	67.2%
17,119	SHARP	5,586	2,021	3,159	406	1,138 D	36.2%	56.6%	39.0%	61.0%
11,499	STONE	4,462	1,956	2,270	236	314 D	43.8%	50.9%	46.3%	53.7%
45,629	UNION	11,439	5,222	6,057	160	835 D	45.7%	53.0%	46.3%	53.7%
16,192	VAN BUREN	5,523	2,202	3,007	314	805 D	39.9%	54.4%	42.3%	57.7%
157,715	WASHINGTON	45,037	20,930	22,836	1,271	1,906 D	46.5%	50.7%	47.8%	52.2%
67,165	WHITE	20,993	8,653	11,670	670	3,017 D	41.2%	55.6%	42.6%	57.4%
8,741	WOODRUFF	2,496	473	1,907	116	1,434 D	19.0%	76.4%	19.9%	80.1%
21,139	YELL	4,514	1,582	2,672	260	1,090 D	35.0%	59.2%	37.2%	62.8%
2,673,400	TOTAL	774,680	315,040	430,765	28,875	115,725 D	40.7%	55.6%	42.2%	57.8%

ARKANSAS

HOUSE OF REPRESENTATIVES

CD	Year	Total Vote	Republican		Democratic		Other Vote	Rep.-Dem. Plurality	Percentage			
			Vote	Candidate	Vote	Candidate			Total Vote		Major Vote	
									Rep.	Dem.	Rep.	Dem.
1	2006	184,188	56,611	STUMBAUGH, MICKEY	127,577	BERRY, MARION*		70,966 D	30.7%	69.3%	30.7%	69.3%
1	2004	243,944	81,556	HUMPHREY, VERNON	162,388	BERRY, MARION*		80,832 D	33.4%	66.6%	33.4%	66.6%
1	2002	194,058	64,357	ROBINSON, TOMMY F.	129,701	BERRY, MARION*		65,344 D	33.2%	66.8%	33.2%	66.8%
2	2006	206,303	81,432	MAYBERRY, ANDY	124,871	SNYDER, VIC*		43,439 D	39.5%	60.5%	39.5%	60.5%
2	2004	276,493	115,655	PARKS, MARVIN	160,834	SNYDER, VIC*	4	45,179 D	41.8%	58.2%	41.8%	58.2%
2	2002	153,626		—	142,752	SNYDER, VIC*	10,874	142,752 D		92.9%		100.0%
3	2006	200,924	125,039	BOOZMAN, JOHN*	75,885	ANDERSON, WOODROW		49,154 R	62.2%	37.8%	62.2%	37.8%
3	2004	270,803	160,629	BOOZMAN, JOHN*	103,158	JUDY, JAN	7,016	57,471 R	59.3%	38.1%	60.9%	39.1%
3	2002	143,055	141,478	BOOZMAN, JOHN*		—	1,577	141,478 R	98.9%		100.0%	
4	2006	171,596	43,360	ROSS, JOE	128,236	ROSS, MIKE*		84,876 D	25.3%	74.7%	25.3%	74.7%
4	2004			—		ROSS, MIKE*		D				
4	2002	197,537	77,904	DICKEY, JAY	119,633	ROSS, MIKE*		41,729 D	39.4%	60.6%	39.4%	60.6%
TOTAL	2006	763,011	306,442		456,569			150,127 D	40.2%	59.8%	40.2%	59.8%
TOTAL	2004	791,240	357,840		426,380		7,020	68,540 D	45.2%	53.9%	45.6%	54.4%
TOTAL	2002	688,276	283,739		392,086		12,451	108,347 D	41.2%	57.0%	42.0%	58.0%

An asterisk (*) denotes incumbent.

ARKANSAS

GENERAL AND PRIMARY ELECTIONS

2006 GENERAL ELECTIONS

Governor   Other vote was 15,767 Independent (Rod Bryan); 12,774 Green Party of Arkansas (Jim Lendall); 215 write-in (Michael Jones); 119 write-in (Gene Mason).

House   Other vote was:

    CD 1
    CD 2
    CD 3
    CD 4

2006 PRIMARY ELECTIONS

Primary   May 23, 2006   **Registration** (as of April 24, 2006)   1,659,501   No Party Registration

Primary Type   Open—Any registered voter could participate in either the Democratic or Republican primary.

Note: An asterisk (*) denotes incumbent. No votes were tallied in contests where a candidate ran unopposed.

	REPUBLICAN PRIMARIES			DEMOCRATIC PRIMARIES	
Governor	Asa Hutchinson	Unopposed		Mike D. Beebe	Unopposed
Congressional District 1	Mickey Stumbaugh	Unopposed		Marion Berry*	Unopposed
Congressional District 2	Andy Mayberry	12,460	77.3%	Vic Snyder*	Unopposed
	Tom Formicola	3,658	22.7%		
	Total	*16,118*			
Congressional District 3	John Boozman*	Unopposed		Woodrow Anderson	Unopposed
Congressional District 4	Joe Ross	Unopposed		Mike Ross*	Unopposed

CALIFORNIA

Congressional districts first established for elections held in 2002
53 members

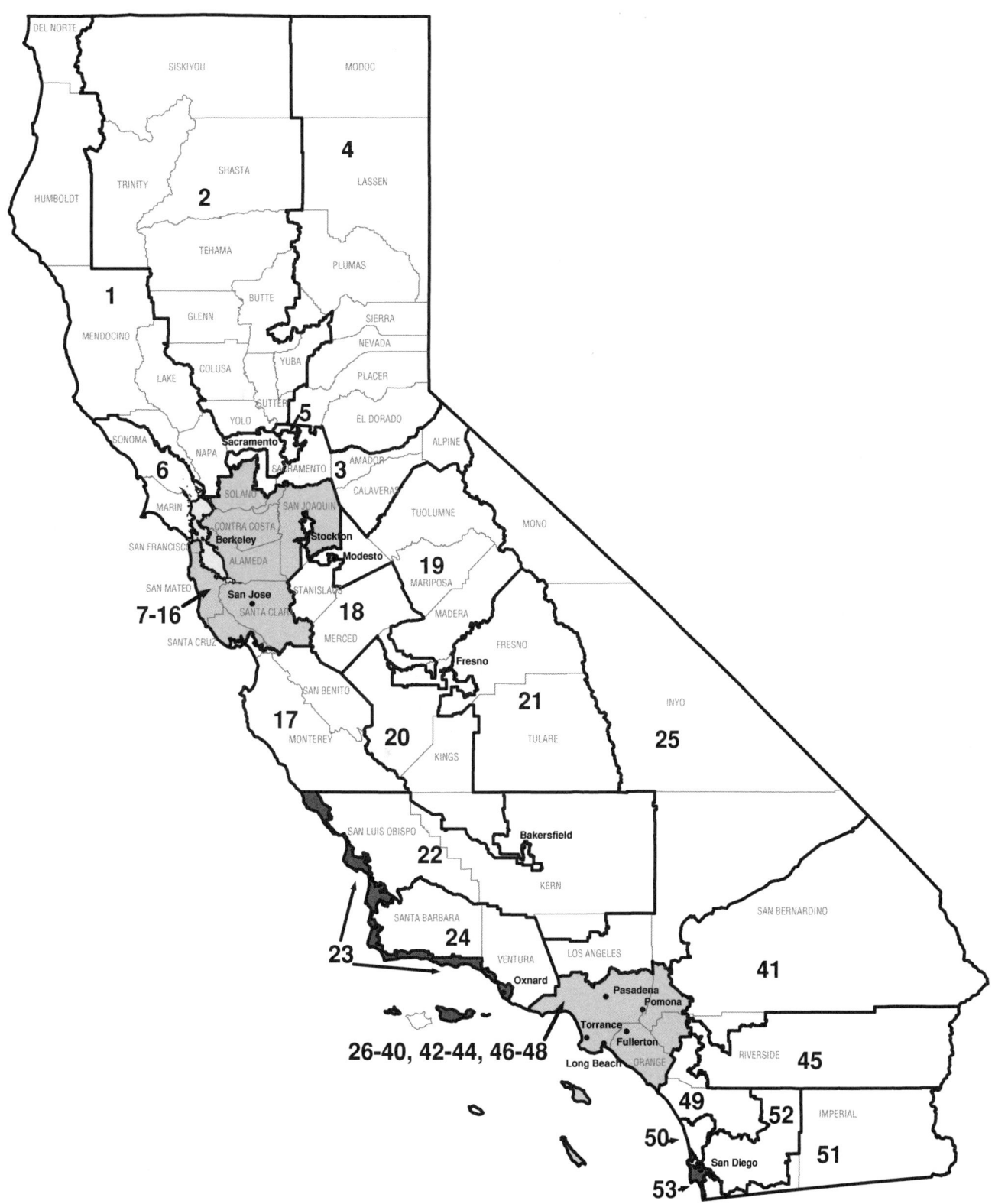

CALIFORNIA

San Francisco Bay Area

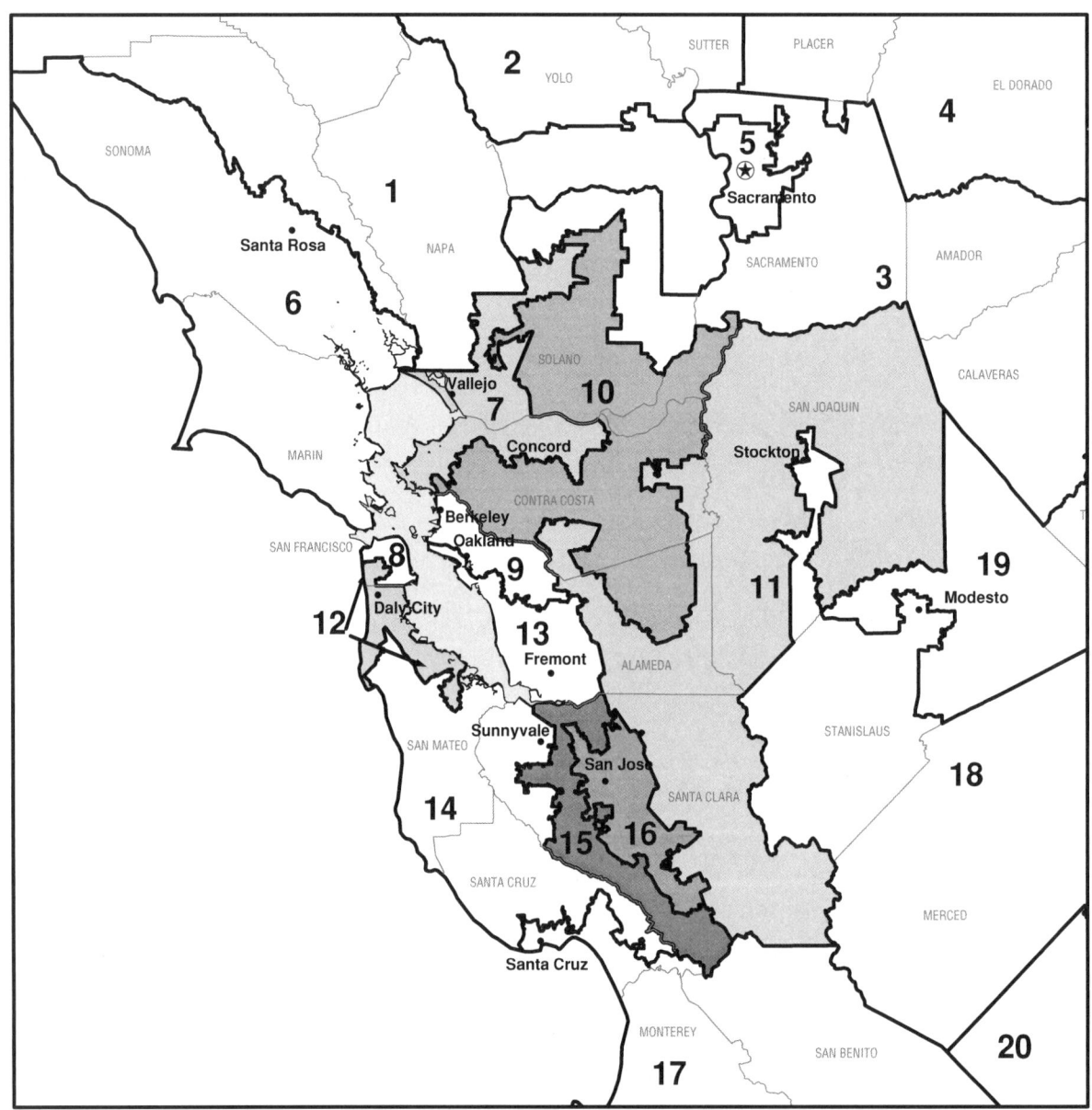

CALIFORNIA

Los Angeles, San Diego Areas

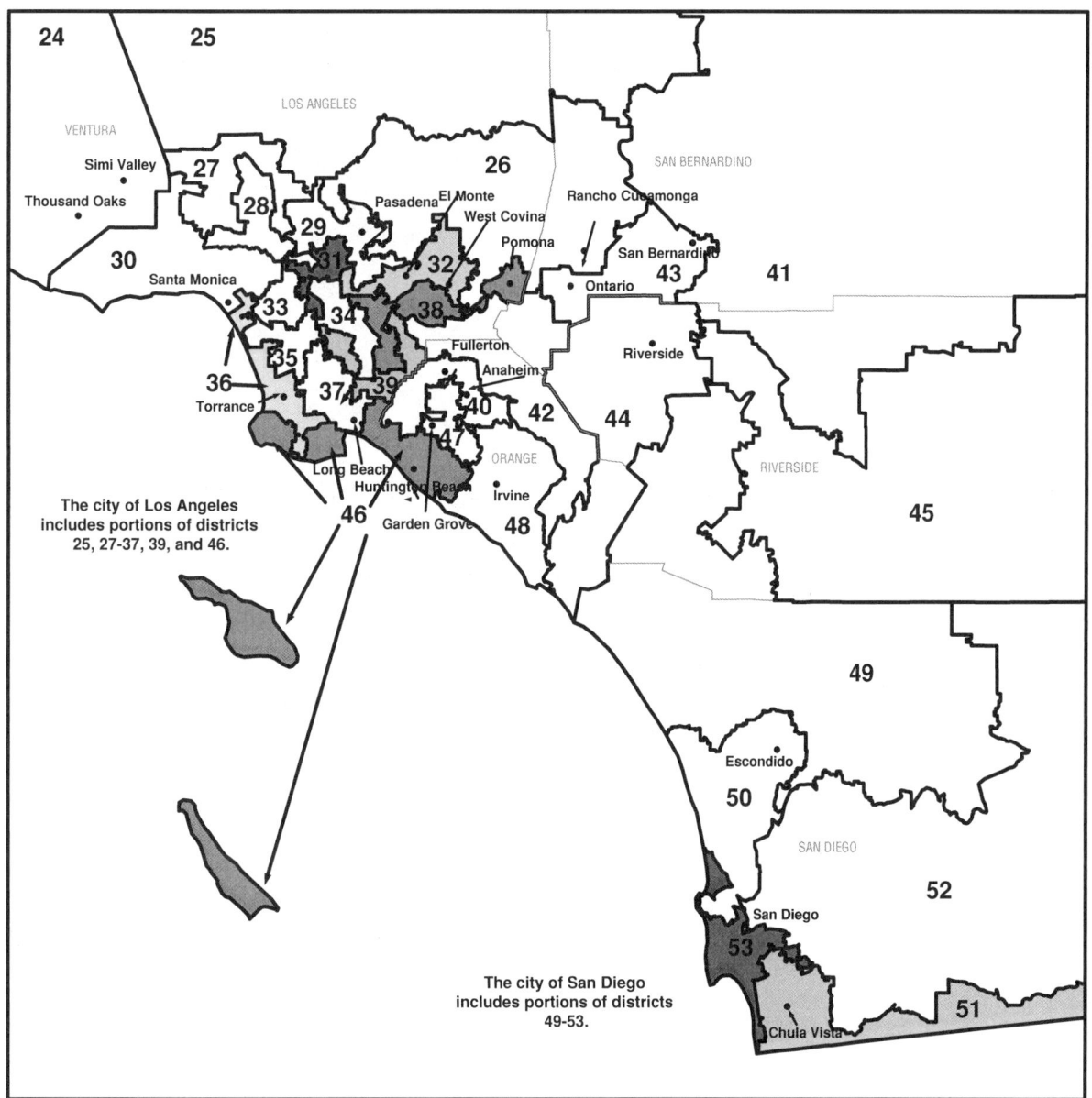

The city of Los Angeles includes portions of districts 25, 27-37, 39, and 46.

The city of San Diego includes portions of districts 49-53.

CALIFORNIA

GOVERNOR

Arnold Schwarzenegger (R). Reelected 2006 to a four-year term. Previously elected in October 2003 to fill the remaining three years of the term vacated when Governor Gray Davis (D) lost a recall vote in the same special election.

SENATORS (2 Democrats)

Dianne Feinstein (D). Reelected 2006 to a six-year term. Previously elected 2000, 1994 and 1992 to fill the remaining two years of the term vacated when Senator Pete Wilson (R) was elected governor in November 1990.

Barbara Boxer (D). Reelected 2004 to a six-year term. Previously elected 1998, 1992.

REPRESENTATIVES (33 Democrats, 19 Republicans, 1 Vacancy)

1. Mike Thompson (D)
2. Wally Herger (R)
3. Dan Lungren (R)
4. John T. Doolittle (R)
5. Doris Matsui (D)
6. Lynn Woolsey (D)
7. George Miller (D)
8. Nancy Pelosi (D)
9. Barbara Lee (D)
10. Ellen O. Tauscher (D)
11. Jerry McNerney (D)
12. Tom Lantos (D)
13. Pete Stark (D)
14. Anna G. Eshoo (D)
15. Michael M. Honda (D)
16. Zoe Lofgren (D)
17. Sam Farr (D)
18. Dennis Cardoza (D)
19. George P. Radanovich (R)
20. Jim Costa (D)
21. Devin Nunes (R)
22. Kevin McCarthy (R)
23. Lois Capps (D)
24. Elton Gallegly (R)
25. Howard P. "Buck" McKeon (R)
26. David Dreier (R)
27. Brad Sherman (D)
28. Howard L. Berman (D)
29. Adam B. Schiff (D)
30. Henry A. Waxman (D)
31. Xavier Becerra (D)
32. Hilda L. Solis (D)
33. Diane Watson (D)
34. Lucille Roybal-Allard (D)
35. Maxine Waters (D)
36. Jane Harman (D)
37. Vacancy
38. Grace F. Napolitano (D)
39. Linda T. Sánchez (D)
40. Ed Royce (R)
41. Jerry Lewis (R)
42. Gary G. Miller (R)
43. Joe Baca (D)
44. Ken Calvert (R)
45. Mary Bono (R)
46. Dana Rohrabacher (R)
47. Loretta Sanchez (D)
48. John Campbell (R)
49. Darrell Issa (R)
50. Brian P. Bilbray (R)
51. Bob Filner (D)
52. Duncan Hunter (R)
53. Susan A. Davis (D)

POSTWAR VOTE FOR PRESIDENT

Year	Total Vote	Republican Vote	Candidate	Democratic Vote	Candidate	Other Vote	Plurality	Total Vote Rep.	Total Vote Dem.	Major Vote Rep.	Major Vote Dem.
2004	12,421,852	5,509,826	Bush, George W.	6,745,485	Kerry, John	166,541	1,235,659 D	44.4%	54.3%	45.0%	55.0%
2000**	10,965,856	4,567,429	Bush, George W.	5,861,203	Gore, Al	537,224	1,293,774 D	41.7%	53.4%	43.8%	56.2%
1996**	10,019,484	3,828,380	Dole, Bob	5,119,835	Clinton, Bill	1,071,269	1,291,455 D	38.2%	51.1%	42.8%	57.2%
1992**	11,131,721	3,630,574	Bush, George	5,121,325	Clinton, Bill	2,379,822	1,490,751 D	32.6%	46.0%	41.5%	58.5%
1988	9,887,065	5,054,917	Bush, George	4,702,233	Dukakis, Michael S.	129,915	352,684 R	51.1%	47.6%	51.8%	48.2%
1984	9,505,423	5,467,009	Reagan, Ronald	3,922,519	Mondale, Walter F.	115,895	1,544,490 R	57.5%	41.3%	58.2%	41.8%
1980**	8,587,063	4,524,858	Reagan, Ronald	3,083,661	Carter, Jimmy	978,544	1,441,197 R	52.7%	35.9%	59.5%	40.5%
1976	7,867,117	3,882,244	Ford, Gerald R.	3,742,284	Carter, Jimmy	242,589	139,960 R	49.3%	47.6%	50.9%	49.1%
1972	8,367,862	4,602,096	Nixon, Richard M.	3,475,847	McGovern, George S.	289,919	1,126,249 R	55.0%	41.5%	57.0%	43.0%
1968**	7,251,587	3,467,664	Nixon, Richard M.	3,244,318	Humphrey, Hubert H.	539,605	223,346 R	47.8%	44.7%	51.7%	48.3%
1964	7,057,586	2,879,108	Goldwater, Barry M.	4,171,877	Johnson, Lyndon B.	6,601	1,292,769 D	40.8%	59.1%	40.8%	59.2%
1960	6,506,578	3,259,722	Nixon, Richard M.	3,224,099	Kennedy, John F.	22,757	35,623 R	50.1%	49.6%	50.3%	49.7%
1956	5,466,355	3,027,668	Eisenhower, Dwight D.	2,420,135	Stevenson, Adlai E.	18,552	607,533 R	55.4%	44.3%	55.6%	44.4%
1952	5,141,849	2,897,310	Eisenhower, Dwight D.	2,197,548	Stevenson, Adlai E.	46,991	699,762 R	56.3%	42.7%	56.9%	43.1%
1948	4,021,538	1,895,269	Dewey, Thomas E.	1,913,134	Truman, Harry S.	213,135	17,865 D	47.1%	47.6%	49.8%	50.2%

**In past elections, the other vote included: 2000 - 418,707 Green (Ralph Nader); 1996 - 697,847 Reform (Ross Perot); 1992 - 2,296,006 Independent (Ross Perot); 1980 - 739,833 Independent (John Anderson); 1968 - 487,270 American Independent (George Wallace).

Note: The vacancy in the California 37th District was created by the death in April 2007 of Juanita Millender-McDonald (D). The vacancy will be filled in a special election to be held in August 2007.

CALIFORNIA

POSTWAR VOTE FOR GOVERNOR

Year	Total Vote	Republican Vote	Republican Candidate	Democratic Vote	Democratic Candidate	Other Vote	Rep.-Dem. Plurality	Percentage Total Vote Rep.	Percentage Total Vote Dem.	Percentage Major Vote Rep.	Percentage Major Vote Dem.
2006	8,679,416	4,850,157	Schwarzenegger, Arnold	3,376,732	Angelides, Phil	452,527	1,473,425 R	55.9%	38.9%	59.0%	41.0%
2003S	8,657,915	4,206,284	Schwarzenegger, Arnold	2,724,874	Bustamante, Cruz	1,726,757	1,481,410 R	48.6%	31.5%	—	—
2002	7,476,311	3,169,801	Simon, Bill	3,533,490	Davis, Gray	773,020	363,689 D	42.4%	47.3%	47.3%	52.7%
1998	8,385,196	3,218,030	Lungren, Dan	4,860,702	Davis, Gray	306,464	1,642,672 D	38.4%	58.0%	39.8%	60.2%
1994	8,665,375	4,781,766	Wilson, Pete	3,519,799	Brown, Kathleen	363,810	1,261,967 R	55.2%	40.6%	57.6%	42.4%
1990	7,699,467	3,791,904	Wilson, Pete	3,525,197	Feinstein, Dianne	382,366	266,707 R	49.2%	45.8%	51.8%	48.2%
1986	7,443,551	4,506,601	Deukmejian, George	2,781,714	Bradley, Tom	155,236	1,724,887 R	60.5%	37.4%	61.8%	38.2%
1982	7,876,698	3,881,014	Deukmejian, George	3,787,669	Bradley, Tom	208,015	93,345 R	49.3%	48.1%	50.6%	49.4%
1978	6,922,378	2,526,534	Younger, Evelle J.	3,878,812	Brown, Edmund G. Jr.	517,032	1,352,278 D	36.5%	56.0%	39.4%	60.6%
1974	6,248,070	2,952,954	Flournoy, Houston I.	3,131,648	Brown, Edmund G. Jr.	163,468	178,694 D	47.3%	50.1%	48.5%	51.5%
1970	6,510,072	3,439,664	Reagan, Ronald	2,938,607	Unruh, Jess	131,801	501,057 R	52.8%	45.1%	53.9%	46.1%
1966	6,503,445	3,742,913	Reagan, Ronald	2,749,174	Brown, Edmund G.	11,358	993,739 R	57.6%	42.3%	57.7%	42.3%
1962	5,853,270	2,740,351	Nixon, Richard M.	3,037,109	Brown, Edmund G.	75,810	296,758 D	46.8%	51.9%	47.4%	52.6%
1958	5,255,777	2,110,911	Knowland, William F.	3,140,076	Brown, Edmund G.	4,790	1,029,165 D	40.2%	59.7%	40.2%	59.8%
1954	4,030,368	2,290,519	Knight, Goodwin J.	1,739,368	Graves, Richard P.	481	551,151 R	56.8%	43.2%	56.8%	43.2%
1950	3,796,090	2,461,754	Warren, Earl	1,333,856	Roosevelt, James	480	1,127,898 R	64.8%	35.1%	64.9%	35.1%
1946**	2,558,399	2,344,542	Warren, Earl	—		213,857	2,344,542 R	91.6%		100.0%	

**The 2003 election was for a short term to fill a vacancy created by voter approval of a measure to remove Governor Gray Davis (D) from office. The measure passed by a vote of 4,976,274 votes (55.4 percent) for recall to 4,007,783 (44.6 percent) against recall. In the same election, more than 100 candidates ran for the right to succeed Davis. No primary election was held to cull the field. All candidates, regardless of party, ran together on the same ballot. The winner, Arnold Schwarzenegger, is listed as the Republican candidate. The leading Democratic vote-getter, Cruz Bustamante, is listed as the Democratic candidate. The percentages given are for Schwarzenegger and Bustamante. The leading "Other" candidate was Republican Tom McClintock, who received 1,161,287 votes (13.4 percent of the total). In 1946 the Republican candidate won both major party nominations.

POSTWAR VOTE FOR SENATOR

Year	Total Vote	Republican Vote	Republican Candidate	Democratic Vote	Democratic Candidate	Other Vote	Rep.-Dem. Plurality	Percentage Total Vote Rep.	Percentage Total Vote Dem.	Percentage Major Vote Rep.	Percentage Major Vote Dem.
2006	8,541,476	2,990,822	Mountjoy, Richard "Dick"	5,076,289	Feinstein, Dianne	474,365	2,085,467 D	35.0%	59.4%	37.1%	62.9%
2004	12,053,295	4,555,922	Jones, Bill	6,955,728	Boxer, Barbara	541,645	2,399,806 D	37.8%	57.7%	39.6%	60.4%
2000	10,623,614	3,886,853	Campbell, Tom	5,932,522	Feinstein, Dianne	804,239	2,045,669 D	36.6%	55.8%	39.6%	60.4%
1998	8,314,953	3,576,351	Fong, Matt	4,411,705	Boxer, Barbara	326,897	835,354 D	43.0%	53.1%	44.8%	55.2%
1994	8,514,089	3,817,025	Huffington, Michael	3,979,152	Feinstein, Dianne	717,912	162,127 D	44.8%	46.7%	49.0%	51.0%
1992	10,799,703	4,644,182	Herschensohn, Bruce	5,173,467	Boxer, Barbara	982,054	529,285 D	43.0%	47.9%	47.3%	52.7%
1992S	10,782,743	4,093,501	Seymour, John	5,853,651	Feinstein, Dianne	835,591	1,760,150 D	38.0%	54.3%	41.2%	58.8%
1988	9,743,598	5,143,409	Wilson, Pete	4,287,253	McCarthy, Leo	312,936	856,156 R	52.8%	44.0%	54.5%	45.5%
1986	7,398,549	3,541,804	Zschau, Ed	3,646,672	Cranston, Alan	210,073	104,868 D	47.9%	49.3%	49.3%	50.7%
1982	7,805,538	4,022,565	Wilson, Pete	3,494,968	Brown, Edmund G. Jr.	288,005	527,597 R	51.5%	44.8%	53.5%	46.5%
1980	8,327,481	3,093,426	Gann, Paul	4,705,399	Cranston, Alan	528,656	1,611,973 D	37.1%	56.5%	39.7%	60.3%
1976	7,472,268	3,748,973	Hayakawa, S. I.	3,502,862	Tunney, John V.	220,433	246,111 R	50.2%	46.9%	51.7%	48.3%
1974	6,102,432	2,210,267	Richardson, H. L.	3,693,160	Cranston, Alan	199,005	1,482,893 D	36.2%	60.5%	37.4%	62.6%
1970	6,492,157	2,877,617	Murphy, George	3,496,558	Tunney, John V.	117,982	618,941 D	44.3%	53.9%	45.1%	54.9%
1968	7,102,465	3,329,148	Rafferty, Max	3,680,352	Cranston, Alan	92,965	351,204 D	46.9%	51.8%	47.5%	52.5%
1964	7,041,821	3,628,555	Murphy, George	3,411,912	Salinger, Pierre	1,354	216,643 R	51.5%	48.5%	51.5%	48.5%
1962	5,647,952	3,180,483	Kuchel, Thomas H.	2,452,839	Richards, Richard	14,630	727,644 R	56.3%	43.4%	56.5%	43.5%
1958	5,135,221	2,204,337	Knight, Goodwin J.	2,927,693	Engle, Clair	3,191	723,356 D	42.9%	57.0%	43.0%	57.0%
1956	5,361,467	2,892,918	Kuchel, Thomas H.	2,445,816	Richards, Richard	22,733	447,102 R	54.0%	45.6%	54.2%	45.8%
1954S	3,929,668	2,090,836	Kuchel, Thomas H.	1,788,071	Yorty, Samuel W.	50,761	302,765 R	53.2%	45.5%	53.9%	46.1%
1952**	4,542,548	3,982,448	Knowland, William F.	—		560,100	3,982,448 R	87.7%		100.0%	
1950	3,686,315	2,183,454	Nixon, Richard M.	1,502,507	Douglas, Helen	354	680,947 R	59.2%	40.8%	59.2%	40.8%
1946	2,639,465	1,428,067	Knowland, William F.	1,167,161	Rogers, Will	44,237	260,906 R	54.1%	44.2%	55.0%	45.0%

**One of the 1992 elections was for a short term to fill a vacancy. The 1954 election was for a short term to fill a vacancy. In 1952 the Republican candidate won both major party nominations.

CALIFORNIA

GOVERNOR 2006

2000 Census Population	County	Total Vote	Republican	Democratic	Other	Rep.-Dem. Plurality	Total Vote Rep.	Total Vote Dem.	Major Vote Rep.	Major Vote Dem.
1,443,741	ALAMEDA	405,378	148,322	229,217	27,839	80,895 D	36.6%	56.5%	39.3%	60.7%
1,208	ALPINE	544	295	218	31	77 R	54.2%	40.1%	57.5%	42.5%
35,100	AMADOR	14,919	10,755	3,354	810	7,401 R	72.1%	22.5%	76.2%	23.8%
203,171	BUTTE	69,268	45,591	18,672	5,005	26,919 R	65.8%	27.0%	70.9%	29.1%
40,554	CALAVERAS	18,016	12,691	4,268	1,057	8,423 R	70.4%	23.7%	74.8%	25.2%
18,804	COLUSA	4,969	3,665	1,104	200	2,561 R	73.8%	22.2%	76.9%	23.1%
948,816	CONTRA COSTA	302,513	158,565	128,578	15,370	29,987 R	52.4%	42.5%	55.2%	44.8%
27,507	DEL NORTE	6,634	3,639	2,531	464	1,108 R	54.9%	38.2%	59.0%	41.0%
156,299	EL DORADO	67,837	49,771	14,535	3,531	35,236 R	73.4%	21.4%	77.4%	22.6%
799,407	FRESNO	176,363	116,534	53,605	6,224	62,929 R	66.1%	30.4%	68.5%	31.5%
26,453	GLENN	7,549	5,775	1,421	353	4,354 R	76.5%	18.8%	80.3%	19.7%
126,518	HUMBOLDT	48,286	23,282	20,070	4,934	3,212 R	48.2%	41.6%	53.7%	46.3%
142,361	IMPERIAL	22,174	10,363	10,024	1,787	339 R	46.7%	45.2%	50.8%	49.2%
17,945	INYO	6,492	4,180	1,892	420	2,288 R	64.4%	29.1%	68.8%	31.2%
661,645	KERN	150,222	108,253	35,512	6,457	72,741 R	72.1%	23.6%	75.3%	24.7%
129,461	KINGS	22,904	15,683	6,344	877	9,339 R	68.5%	27.7%	71.2%	28.8%
58,309	LAKE	19,429	10,930	7,031	1,468	3,899 R	56.3%	36.2%	60.9%	39.1%
33,828	LASSEN	8,580	5,665	2,353	562	3,312 R	66.0%	27.4%	70.7%	29.3%
9,519,338	LOS ANGELES	1,971,076	907,919	967,149	96,008	59,230 D	46.1%	49.1%	48.4%	51.6%
123,109	MADERA	30,113	21,416	7,473	1,224	13,943 R	71.1%	24.8%	74.1%	25.9%
247,289	MARIN	105,743	48,439	50,441	6,863	2,002 D	45.8%	47.7%	49.0%	51.0%
17,130	MARIPOSA	7,593	5,074	1,985	534	3,089 R	66.8%	26.1%	71.9%	28.1%
86,265	MENDOCINO	30,834	14,002	13,790	3,042	212 R	45.4%	44.7%	50.4%	49.6%
210,554	MERCED	41,959	26,231	14,027	1,701	12,204 R	62.5%	33.4%	65.2%	34.8%
9,449	MODOC	3,762	2,829	723	210	2,106 R	75.2%	19.2%	79.6%	20.4%
12,853	MONO	3,744	2,315	1,176	253	1,139 R	61.8%	31.4%	66.3%	33.7%
401,762	MONTEREY	87,906	46,882	35,769	5,255	11,113 R	53.3%	40.7%	56.7%	43.3%
124,279	NAPA	42,488	23,187	16,504	2,797	6,683 R	54.6%	38.8%	58.4%	41.6%
92,033	NEVADA	43,268	28,570	11,833	2,865	16,737 R	66.0%	27.3%	70.7%	29.3%
2,846,289	ORANGE	728,031	507,413	185,388	35,230	322,025 R	69.7%	25.5%	73.2%	26.8%
248,399	PLACER	123,652	91,972	26,723	4,957	65,249 R	74.4%	21.6%	77.5%	22.5%
20,824	PLUMAS	8,860	6,160	2,194	506	3,966 R	69.5%	24.8%	73.7%	26.3%
1,545,387	RIVERSIDE	384,744	251,962	115,803	16,979	136,159 R	65.5%	30.1%	68.5%	31.5%
1,223,499	SACRAMENTO	362,095	218,889	123,685	19,521	95,204 R	60.5%	34.2%	63.9%	36.1%
53,234	SAN BENITO	14,379	8,208	5,400	771	2,808 R	57.1%	37.6%	60.3%	39.7%
1,709,434	SAN BERNARDINO	344,301	212,200	114,388	17,713	97,812 R	61.6%	33.2%	65.0%	35.0%
2,813,833	SAN DIEGO	777,305	509,059	234,938	33,308	274,121 R	65.5%	30.2%	68.4%	31.6%
776,733	SAN FRANCISCO	244,468	72,722	153,335	18,411	80,613 D	29.7%	62.7%	32.2%	67.8%
563,598	SAN JOAQUIN	139,168	83,952	49,868	5,348	34,084 R	60.3%	35.8%	62.7%	37.3%
246,681	SAN LUIS OBISPO	97,292	61,842	30,568	4,882	31,274 R	63.6%	31.4%	66.9%	33.1%
707,161	SAN MATEO	204,764	96,478	97,092	11,194	614 D	47.1%	47.4%	49.8%	50.2%
399,347	SANTA BARBARA	122,781	73,677	42,880	6,224	30,797 R	60.0%	34.9%	63.2%	36.8%
1,682,585	SANTA CLARA	431,655	225,132	185,037	21,486	40,095 R	52.2%	42.9%	54.9%	45.1%
255,602	SANTA CRUZ	90,189	37,866	43,619	8,704	5,753 D	42.0%	48.4%	46.5%	53.5%
163,256	SHASTA	58,763	43,436	12,434	2,893	31,002 R	73.9%	21.2%	77.7%	22.3%
3,555	SIERRA	1,602	1,131	353	118	778 R	70.6%	22.0%	76.2%	23.8%
44,301	SISKIYOU	16,631	10,916	4,615	1,100	6,301 R	65.6%	27.7%	70.3%	29.7%
394,542	SOLANO	103,726	55,130	43,501	5,095	11,629 R	53.1%	41.9%	55.9%	44.1%
458,614	SONOMA	173,514	81,608	77,392	14,514	4,216 R	47.0%	44.6%	51.3%	48.7%
446,997	STANISLAUS	103,872	67,427	31,981	4,464	35,446 R	64.9%	30.8%	67.8%	32.2%
78,930	SUTTER	23,913	17,393	5,487	1,033	11,906 R	72.7%	22.9%	76.0%	24.0%
56,039	TEHAMA	18,005	13,442	3,666	897	9,776 R	74.7%	20.4%	78.6%	21.4%
13,022	TRINITY	5,911	3,819	1,614	478	2,205 R	64.6%	27.3%	70.3%	29.7%
368,021	TULARE	68,730	48,607	17,571	2,552	31,036 R	70.7%	25.6%	73.4%	26.6%
54,501	TUOLUMNE	21,141	14,836	5,105	1,200	9,731 R	70.2%	24.1%	74.4%	25.6%
753,197	VENTURA	220,965	134,862	75,790	10,313	59,072 R	61.0%	34.3%	64.0%	36.0%
168,660	YOLO	54,458	29,073	21,733	3,652	7,340 R	53.4%	39.9%	57.2%	42.8%
60,219	YUBA	13,938	10,122	2,973	843	7,149 R	72.6%	21.3%	77.3%	22.7%
33,871,648	TOTAL	8,679,416	4,850,157	3,376,732	452,527	1,473,425 R	55.9%	38.9%	59.0%	41.0%

CALIFORNIA

SENATOR 2006

2000 Census Population	County	Total Vote	Republican	Democratic	Other	Rep.-Dem. Plurality		Percentage Total Vote		Major Vote	
								Rep.	Dem.	Rep.	Dem.
1,443,741	ALAMEDA	404,218	66,550	307,495	30,173	240,945	D	16.5%	76.1%	17.8%	82.2%
1,208	ALPINE	530	188	303	39	115	D	35.5%	57.2%	38.3%	61.7%
35,100	AMADOR	14,734	7,382	6,534	818	848	R	50.1%	44.3%	53.0%	47.0%
203,171	BUTTE	68,339	31,316	32,131	4,892	815	D	45.8%	47.0%	49.4%	50.6%
40,554	CALAVERAS	17,729	8,642	7,860	1,227	782	R	48.7%	44.3%	52.4%	47.6%
18,804	COLUSA	4,854	2,647	1,994	213	653	R	54.5%	41.1%	57.0%	43.0%
948,816	CONTRA COSTA	300,098	80,764	205,516	13,818	124,752	D	26.9%	68.5%	28.2%	71.8%
27,507	DEL NORTE	6,666	2,955	3,207	504	252	D	44.3%	48.1%	48.0%	52.0%
156,299	EL DORADO	66,859	34,091	28,915	3,853	5,176	R	51.0%	43.2%	54.1%	45.9%
799,407	FRESNO	173,610	76,286	89,331	7,993	13,045	D	43.9%	51.5%	46.1%	53.9%
26,453	GLENN	7,433	4,219	2,813	401	1,406	R	56.8%	37.8%	60.0%	40.0%
126,518	HUMBOLDT	47,619	15,003	27,652	4,964	12,649	D	31.5%	58.1%	35.2%	64.8%
142,361	IMPERIAL	21,962	7,338	13,182	1,442	5,844	D	33.4%	60.0%	35.8%	64.2%
17,945	INYO	6,378	3,281	2,641	456	640	R	51.4%	41.4%	55.4%	44.6%
661,645	KERN	148,479	81,944	58,330	8,205	23,614	R	55.2%	39.3%	58.4%	41.6%
129,461	KINGS	22,673	11,016	10,660	997	356	R	48.6%	47.0%	50.8%	49.2%
58,309	LAKE	19,199	6,691	10,830	1,678	4,139	D	34.9%	56.4%	38.2%	61.8%
33,828	LASSEN	8,466	4,820	2,968	678	1,852	R	56.9%	35.1%	61.9%	38.1%
9,519,338	LOS ANGELES	1,934,666	536,200	1,298,820	99,646	762,620	D	27.7%	67.1%	29.2%	70.8%
123,109	MADERA	29,863	15,609	12,658	1,596	2,951	R	52.3%	42.4%	55.2%	44.8%
247,289	MARIN	105,759	17,788	82,025	5,946	64,237	D	16.8%	77.6%	17.8%	82.2%
17,130	MARIPOSA	7,559	3,842	3,249	468	593	R	50.8%	43.0%	54.2%	45.8%
86,265	MENDOCINO	30,456	7,662	19,645	3,149	11,983	D	25.2%	64.5%	28.1%	71.9%
210,554	MERCED	41,016	16,914	22,081	2,021	5,167	D	41.2%	53.8%	43.4%	56.6%
9,449	MODOC	3,670	2,093	1,264	313	829	R	57.0%	34.4%	62.3%	37.7%
12,853	MONO	3,734	1,657	1,829	248	172	D	44.4%	49.0%	47.5%	52.5%
401,762	MONTEREY	87,139	25,400	56,887	4,852	31,487	D	29.1%	65.3%	30.9%	69.1%
124,279	NAPA	42,379	12,958	27,144	2,277	14,186	D	30.6%	64.1%	32.3%	67.7%
92,033	NEVADA	42,428	18,618	21,204	2,606	2,586	D	43.9%	50.0%	46.8%	53.2%
2,846,289	ORANGE	712,666	353,924	321,646	37,096	32,278	R	49.7%	45.1%	52.4%	47.6%
248,399	PLACER	121,165	61,615	53,956	5,594	7,659	R	50.9%	44.5%	53.3%	46.7%
20,824	PLUMAS	8,749	4,345	3,881	523	464	R	49.7%	44.4%	52.8%	47.2%
1,545,387	RIVERSIDE	378,081	175,543	183,532	19,006	7,989	D	46.4%	48.5%	48.9%	51.1%
1,223,499	SACRAMENTO	355,555	134,887	201,221	19,447	66,334	D	37.9%	56.6%	40.1%	59.9%
53,234	SAN BENITO	14,201	4,768	8,626	807	3,858	D	33.6%	60.7%	35.6%	64.4%
1,709,434	SAN BERNARDINO	339,693	153,430	167,821	18,442	14,391	D	45.2%	49.4%	47.8%	52.2%
2,813,833	SAN DIEGO	761,346	322,760	403,711	34,875	80,951	D	42.4%	53.0%	44.4%	55.6%
776,733	SAN FRANCISCO	233,045	19,374	187,692	25,979	168,318	D	8.3%	80.5%	9.4%	90.6%
563,598	SAN JOAQUIN	137,109	54,874	75,011	7,224	20,137	D	40.0%	54.7%	42.2%	57.8%
246,681	SAN LUIS OBISPO	95,610	42,742	47,891	4,977	5,149	D	44.7%	50.1%	47.2%	52.8%
707,161	SAN MATEO	203,325	41,043	152,082	10,200	111,039	D	20.2%	74.8%	21.3%	78.7%
399,347	SANTA BARBARA	120,991	44,864	68,970	7,157	24,106	D	37.1%	57.0%	39.4%	60.6%
1,682,585	SANTA CLARA	427,355	106,383	298,451	22,521	192,068	D	24.9%	69.8%	26.3%	73.7%
255,602	SANTA CRUZ	89,384	17,279	65,214	6,891	47,935	D	19.3%	73.0%	20.9%	79.1%
163,256	SHASTA	58,240	32,876	22,097	3,267	10,779	R	56.4%	37.9%	59.8%	40.2%
3,555	SIERRA	1,576	814	641	121	173	R	51.6%	40.7%	55.9%	44.1%
44,301	SISKIYOU	16,388	8,433	6,752	1,203	1,681	R	51.5%	41.2%	55.5%	44.5%
394,542	SOLANO	102,809	32,956	64,828	5,025	31,872	D	32.1%	63.1%	33.7%	66.3%
458,614	SONOMA	172,197	39,619	119,672	12,906	80,053	D	23.0%	69.5%	24.9%	75.1%
446,997	STANISLAUS	102,758	47,513	50,656	4,589	3,143	D	46.2%	49.3%	48.4%	51.6%
78,930	SUTTER	23,548	13,113	9,297	1,138	3,816	R	55.7%	39.5%	58.5%	41.5%
56,039	TEHAMA	17,865	9,865	6,914	1,086	2,951	R	55.2%	38.7%	58.8%	41.2%
13,022	TRINITY	5,718	2,356	2,824	538	468	D	41.2%	49.4%	45.5%	54.5%
368,021	TULARE	68,176	36,526	28,694	2,956	7,832	R	53.6%	42.1%	56.0%	44.0%
54,501	TUOLUMNE	20,947	10,228	9,535	1,184	693	R	48.8%	45.5%	51.8%	48.2%
753,197	VENTURA	216,955	91,374	115,471	10,110	24,097	D	42.1%	53.2%	44.2%	55.8%
168,660	YOLO	53,771	16,187	34,548	3,036	18,361	D	30.1%	64.3%	31.9%	68.1%
60,219	YUBA	13,738	7,257	5,487	994	1,770	R	52.8%	39.9%	56.9%	43.1%
33,871,648	TOTAL	8,541,476	2,990,822	5,076,289	474,365	2,085,467	D	35.0%	59.4%	37.1%	62.9%

CALIFORNIA

HOUSE OF REPRESENTATIVES

CD	Year	Total Vote	Republican Vote	Republican Candidate	Democratic Vote	Democratic Candidate	Other Vote	Rep.-Dem. Plurality	Total Vote Rep.	Total Vote Dem.	Major Vote Rep.	Major Vote Dem.
1	2006	218,044	63,194	JONES, JOHN W.	144,409	THOMPSON, MIKE*	10,441	81,215 D	29.0%	66.2%	30.4%	69.6%
1	2004	282,971	79,970	WIESNER, LAWRENCE R.	189,366	THOMPSON, MIKE*	13,635	109,396 D	28.3%	66.9%	29.7%	70.3%
1	2002	185,216	60,013	WIESNER, LAWRENCE R.	118,669	THOMPSON, MIKE*	6,534	58,656 D	32.4%	64.1%	33.6%	66.4%
2	2006	210,202	134,911	HERGER, WALLY*	68,234	SEKHON, A. J.	7,057	66,677 R	64.2%	32.5%	66.4%	33.6%
2	2004	272,429	182,119	HERGER, WALLY*	90,310	JOHNSON, MIKE		91,809 R	66.9%	33.1%	66.9%	33.1%
2	2002	178,985	117,747	HERGER, WALLY*	52,455	JOHNSON, MIKE	8,783	65,292 R	65.8%	29.3%	69.2%	30.8%
3	2006	228,169	135,709	LUNGREN, DAN*	86,318	DURSTON, BILL	6,142	49,391 R	59.5%	37.8%	61.1%	38.9%
3	2004	287,073	177,738	LUNGREN, DAN	100,025	CASTILLO, GABE	9,310	77,713 R	61.9%	34.8%	64.0%	36.0%
3	2002	194,918	121,732	OSE, DOUG*	67,136	BEEMAN, HOWARD	6,050	54,596 R	62.5%	34.4%	64.5%	35.5%
4	2006	276,893	135,818	DOOLITTLE, JOHN T.*	126,999	BROWN, CHARLIE	14,076	8,819 R	49.1%	45.9%	51.7%	48.3%
4	2004	339,369	221,926	DOOLITTLE, JOHN T.*	117,443	WINTERS, DAVID I.		104,483 R	65.4%	34.6%	65.4%	34.6%
4	2002	228,506	147,997	DOOLITTLE, JOHN T.*	72,860	NORBERG, MARK A.	7,649	75,137 R	64.8%	31.9%	67.0%	33.0%
5	2006	149,266	35,106	YAN, CLAIRE	105,676	MATSUI, DORIS*	8,484	70,570 D	23.5%	70.8%	24.9%	75.1%
5	2004	193,387	45,120	DUGAS, MIKE	138,004	MATSUI, ROBERT T.*	10,263	92,884 D	23.3%	71.4%	24.6%	75.4%
5	2002	131,578	34,749	FRANKHUIZEN, RICHARD	92,726	MATSUI, ROBERT T.*	4,103	57,977 D	26.4%	70.5%	27.3%	72.7%
6	2006	246,628	64,405	HOOPER, TODD	173,190	WOOLSEY, LYNN*	9,033	108,785 D	26.1%	70.2%	27.1%	72.9%
6	2004	311,667	85,244	ERICKSON, PAUL L.	226,423	WOOLSEY, LYNN*		141,179 D	27.4%	72.6%	27.4%	72.6%
6	2002	209,563	62,052	ERICKSON, PAUL L.	139,750	WOOLSEY, LYNN*	7,761	77,698 D	29.6%	66.7%	30.7%	69.3%
7	2006	140,486		—	118,000	MILLER, GEORGE*	22,486	118,000 D		84.0%		100.0%
7	2004	219,277	52,446	HARGRAVE, CHARLES	166,831	MILLER, GEORGE*		114,385 D	23.9%	76.1%	23.9%	76.1%
7	2002	138,376	36,584	HARGRAVE, CHARLES	97,849	MILLER, GEORGE*	3,943	61,265 D	26.4%	70.7%	27.2%	72.8%
8	2006	184,639	19,800	DeNUNZIO, MIKE	148,435	PELOSI, NANCY*	16,404	128,635 D	10.7%	80.4%	11.8%	88.2%
8	2004	270,064	31,074	DEPALMA, JENNIFER	224,017	PELOSI, NANCY*	14,973	192,943 D	11.5%	82.9%	12.2%	87.8%
8	2002	160,441	20,063	GERMAN, G. MICHAEL	127,684	PELOSI, NANCY*	12,694	107,621 D	12.5%	79.6%	13.6%	86.4%
9	2006	193,686	20,786	denDULK, JOHN "J. D."	167,245	LEE, BARBARA*	5,655	146,459 D	10.7%	86.3%	11.1%	88.9%
9	2004	255,039	31,278	BERMUDEZ, CLAUDIA	215,630	LEE, BARBARA*	8,131	184,352 D	12.3%	84.5%	12.7%	87.3%
9	2002	166,917	25,333	UDINSKY, JERRY	135,893	LEE, BARBARA*	5,691	110,560 D	15.2%	81.4%	15.7%	84.3%
10	2006	196,978	66,069	LINN, DARCY	130,859	TAUSCHER, ELLEN O.*	50	64,790 D	33.5%	66.4%	33.5%	66.5%
10	2004	278,099	95,349	KETELSON, JEFF	182,750	TAUSCHER, ELLEN O.*		87,401 D	34.3%	65.7%	34.3%	65.7%
10	2002	167,197		—	126,390	TAUSCHER, ELLEN O.*	40,807	126,390 D		75.6%		100.0%
11	2006	206,264	96,396	POMBO, RICHARD W.*	109,868	McNERNEY, JERRY		13,472 D	46.7%	53.3%	46.7%	53.3%
11	2004	267,169	163,582	POMBO, RICHARD W.*	103,587	McNERNEY, JERRY		59,995 R	61.2%	38.8%	61.2%	38.8%
11	2002	173,956	104,921	POMBO, RICHARD W.*	69,035	SHAW, ELAINE DUGGER		35,886 R	60.3%	39.7%	60.3%	39.7%
12	2006	182,324	43,674	MOLONEY, MIKE	138,650	LANTOS, TOM*		94,976 D	24.0%	76.0%	24.0%	76.0%
12	2004	252,599	52,593	GARZA, MIKE	171,852	LANTOS, TOM*	28,154	119,259 D	20.8%	68.0%	23.4%	76.6%
12	2002	154,984	38,381	MOLONEY, MIKE	105,597	LANTOS, TOM*	11,006	67,216 D	24.8%	68.1%	26.7%	73.3%
13	2006	147,897	37,141	BRUNO, GEORGE I.	110,756	STARK, PETE*		73,615 D	25.1%	74.9%	25.1%	74.9%
13	2004	201,921	48,439	BRUNO, GEORGE I.	144,605	STARK, PETE*	8,877	96,166 D	24.0%	71.6%	25.1%	74.9%
13	2002	121,723	26,852	MAHMOOD, SYED R.	86,495	STARK, PETE*	8,376	59,643 D	22.1%	71.1%	23.7%	76.3%
14	2006	198,575	48,097	SMITH, ROB	141,153	ESHOO, ANNA G.*	9,325	93,056 D	24.2%	71.1%	25.4%	74.6%
14	2004	261,888	69,564	HAUGEN, CHRIS	182,712	ESHOO, ANNA G.*	9,612	113,148 D	26.6%	69.8%	27.6%	72.4%
14	2002	171,678	48,346	NIXON, JOSEPH H.	117,055	ESHOO, ANNA G.*	6,277	68,709 D	28.2%	68.2%	29.2%	70.8%
15	2006	159,718	44,186	CHUKWU, RAYMOND L.	115,532	HONDA, MICHAEL M.*		71,346 D	27.7%	72.3%	27.7%	72.3%
15	2004	214,338	59,953	CHUKWU, RAYMOND L.	154,385	HONDA, MICHAEL M.*		94,432 D	28.0%	72.0%	28.0%	72.0%
15	2002	133,022	41,251	HERMANN, LINDA RAE	87,482	HONDA, MICHAEL M.*	4,289	46,231 D	31.0%	65.8%	32.0%	68.0%
16	2006	136,059	37,130	WINSTON, CHAREL	98,929	LOFGREN, ZOE*		61,799 D	27.3%	72.7%	27.3%	72.7%
16	2004	182,281	47,992	McNEA, DOUGLAS ADAMS	129,222	LOFGREN, ZOE*	5,067	81,230 D	26.3%	70.9%	27.1%	72.9%
16	2002	107,986	32,182	McNEA, DOUGLAS ADAMS	72,370	LOFGREN, ZOE*	3,434	40,188 D	29.8%	67.0%	30.8%	69.2%

CALIFORNIA

HOUSE OF REPRESENTATIVES

CD	Year	Total Vote	Republican		Democratic		Other Vote	Rep.-Dem. Plurality	Percentage			
									Total Vote		Major Vote	
			Vote	Candidate	Vote	Candidate			Rep.	Dem.	Rep.	Dem.
17	2006	159,293	35,932	De MAIO, ANTHONY R.	120,750	FARR, SAM*	2,611	84,818 D	22.6%	75.8%	22.9%	77.1%
17	2004	223,225	65,117	RISLEY, MARK	148,958	FARR, SAM*	9,150	83,841 D	29.2%	66.7%	30.4%	69.6%
17	2002	149,296	40,334	ENGLER, CLINT C.	101,632	FARR, SAM*	7,330	61,298 D	27.0%	68.1%	28.4%	71.6%
18	2006	108,713	37,531	KANNO, JOHN A.	71,182	CARDOZA, DENNIS*		33,651 D	34.5%	65.5%	34.5%	65.5%
18	2004	153,705	49,973	PRINGLE, CHARLES F.	103,732	CARDOZA, DENNIS*		53,759 D	32.5%	67.5%	32.5%	67.5%
18	2002	109,593	47,528	MONTEITH, DICK	56,181	CARDOZA, DENNIS	5,884	8,653 D	43.4%	51.3%	45.8%	54.2%
19	2006	181,994	110,246	RADANOVICH, GEORGE P.*	71,748	COX, T. J.		38,498 R	60.6%	39.4%	60.6%	39.4%
19	2004	235,264	155,354	RADANOVICH, GEORGE P.*	64,047	BUFFORD, JAMES LEX	15,863	91,307 R	66.0%	27.2%	70.8%	29.2%
19	2002	157,802	106,209	RADANOVICH, GEORGE P.*	47,403	VEEN, JOHN	4,190	58,806 R	67.3%	30.0%	69.1%	30.9%
20	2006	61,120		—	61,120	COSTA, JIM*		61,120 D		100.0%		100.0%
20	2004	114,236	53,231	ASHBURN, ROY	61,005	COSTA, JIM		7,774 D	46.6%	53.4%	46.6%	53.4%
20	2002	74,770	25,628	MINUTH, ANDRE	47,627	DOOLEY, CAL*	1,515	21,999 D	34.3%	63.7%	35.0%	65.0%
21	2006	142,661	95,214	NUNES, DEVIN*	42,718	HAZE, STEVEN	4,729	52,496 R	66.7%	29.9%	69.0%	31.0%
21	2004	192,315	140,721	NUNES, DEVIN*	51,594	DAVIS, FRED B.		89,127 R	73.2%	26.8%	73.2%	26.8%
21	2002	124,198	87,544	NUNES, DEVIN	32,584	LaPERE, DAVID G.	4,070	54,960 R	70.5%	26.2%	72.9%	27.1%
22	2006	188,504	133,278	McCARTHY, KEVIN	55,226	BEERY, SHARON M.		78,052 R	70.7%	29.3%	70.7%	29.3%
22	2004	209,384	209,384	THOMAS, BILL*		—		209,384 R	100.0%		100.0%	
22	2002	164,285	120,473	THOMAS, BILL*	38,988	CORVERA, JAIME	4,824	81,485 R	73.3%	23.7%	75.6%	24.4%
23	2006	175,951	61,272	TOGNAZZINI, VICTOR D.	114,661	CAPPS, LOIS*	18	53,389 D	34.8%	65.2%	34.8%	65.2%
23	2004	244,297	83,926	REGAN, DON	153,980	CAPPS, LOIS*	6,391	70,054 D	34.4%	63.0%	35.3%	64.7%
23	2002	162,222	62,604	ROGERS, BETH	95,752	CAPPS, LOIS*	3,866	33,148 D	38.6%	59.0%	39.5%	60.5%
24	2006	209,292	129,812	GALLEGLY, ELTON*	79,461	MARTINEZ, JILL M.	19	50,351 R	62.0%	38.0%	62.0%	38.0%
24	2004	284,378	178,660	GALLEGLY, ELTON*	96,397	WAGNER, BRETT	9,321	82,263 R	62.8%	33.9%	65.0%	35.0%
24	2002	185,006	120,585	GALLEGLY, ELTON*	58,755	RUDIN, FERN	5,666	61,830 R	65.2%	31.8%	67.2%	32.8%
25	2006	156,773	93,987	McKEON, HOWARD P. "BUCK"*	55,913	RODRIGUEZ, ROBERT	6,873	38,074 R	60.0%	35.7%	62.7%	37.3%
25	2004	225,970	145,575	McKEON, HOWARD P. "BUCK"*	80,395	WILLOUGHBY, FRED "TIM"		65,180 R	64.4%	35.6%	64.4%	35.6%
25	2002	124,336	80,775	McKEON, HOWARD P. "BUCK"*	38,674	CONAWAY, BOB	4,887	42,101 R	65.0%	31.1%	67.6%	32.4%
26	2006	179,144	102,028	DREIER, DAVID*	67,878	MATTHEWS, CYNTHIA	9,238	34,150 R	57.0%	37.9%	60.0%	40.0%
26	2004	251,207	134,596	DREIER, DAVID*	107,522	MATTHEWS, CYNTHIA	9,089	27,074 R	53.6%	42.8%	55.6%	44.4%
26	2002	149,530	95,360	DREIER, DAVID*	50,081	MIKELS, MARJORIE MUSSER	4,089	45,279 R	63.8%	33.5%	65.6%	34.4%
27	2006	134,724	42,074	HANKWITZ, PETER	92,650	SHERMAN, BRAD*		50,576 D	31.2%	68.8%	31.2%	68.8%
27	2004	201,198	66,946	LEVY, ROBERT M.	125,296	SHERMAN, BRAD*	8,956	58,350 D	33.3%	62.3%	34.8%	65.2%
27	2002	128,811	48,996	LEVY, ROBERT M.	79,815	SHERMAN, BRAD*		30,819 D	38.0%	62.0%	38.0%	62.0%
28	2006	108,042	20,629	KESSELMAN, STANLEY KIMMEL	79,866	BERMAN, HOWARD L.*	7,547	59,237 D	19.1%	73.9%	20.5%	79.5%
28	2004	162,510	37,868	HERNANDEZ, DAVID	115,303	BERMAN, HOWARD L.*	9,339	77,435 D	23.3%	71.0%	24.7%	75.3%
28	2002	103,326	23,926	HERNANDEZ, DAVID	73,771	BERMAN, HOWARD L.*	5,629	49,845 D	23.2%	71.4%	24.5%	75.5%
29	2006	143,404	39,321	BODELL, WILLIAM J.	91,014	SCHIFF, ADAM B.*	13,069	51,693 D	27.4%	63.5%	30.2%	69.8%
29	2004	206,832	62,871	SCOLINOS, HARRY FRANK	133,670	SCHIFF, ADAM B.*	10,291	70,799 D	30.4%	64.6%	32.0%	68.0%
29	2002	121,541	40,616	SCILEPPI, JIM	76,036	SCHIFF, ADAM B.*	4,889	35,420 D	33.4%	62.6%	34.8%	65.2%
30	2006	211,734	55,904	JONES, DAVID NELSON	151,284	WAXMAN, HENRY A.*	4,546	95,380 D	26.4%	71.5%	27.0%	73.0%
30	2004	304,147	87,465	ELIZALDE, VICTOR	216,682	WAXMAN, HENRY A.*		129,217 D	28.8%	71.2%	28.8%	71.2%
30	2002	185,593	54,989	GOSS, TONY D.	130,604	WAXMAN, HENRY A.*		75,615 D	29.6%	70.4%	29.6%	70.4%
31	2006	64,952		—	64,952	BECERRA, XAVIER*		64,952 D		100.0%		100.0%
31	2004	111,411	22,048	VEGA, LUIS	89,363	BECERRA, XAVIER*		67,315 D	19.8%	80.2%	19.8%	80.2%
31	2002	67,243	12,674	VEGA, LUIS	54,569	BECERRA, XAVIER*		41,895 D	18.8%	81.2%	18.8%	81.2%
32	2006	91,686		—	76,059	SOLIS, HILDA L.*	15,627	76,059 D		83.0%		100.0%
32	2004	140,146		—	119,144	SOLIS, HILDA L.*	21,002	119,144 D		85.0%		100.0%
32	2002	85,079	23,366	FISCHBECK, EMMA E.	58,530	SOLIS, HILDA L.*	3,183	35,164 D	27.5%	68.8%	28.5%	71.5%

CALIFORNIA

HOUSE OF REPRESENTATIVES

CD	Year	Total Vote	Republican Vote	Candidate	Democratic Vote	Candidate	Other Vote	Rep.-Dem. Plurality	Total Vote Rep.	Total Vote Dem.	Major Vote Rep.	Major Vote Dem.
33	2004	113,715		—	113,715	WATSON, DIANE*		113,715 D		100.0%		100.0%
33	2004	188,314		—	166,801	WATSON, DIANE*	21,513	166,801 D		88.6%		100.0%
33	2002	118,449	16,699	KIM, ANDREW	97,779	WATSON, DIANE*	3,971	81,080 D	14.1%	82.5%	14.6%	85.4%
34	2006	74,819	17,359	MILLER, WAYNE	57,459	ROYBAL-ALLARD, LUCILLE*	1	40,100 D	23.2%	76.8%	23.2%	76.8%
34	2004	110,457	28,175	MILLER, WAYNE	82,282	ROYBAL-ALLARD, LUCILLE*		54,107 D	25.5%	74.5%	25.5%	74.5%
34	2002	65,824	17,090	MILLER, WAYNE	48,734	ROYBAL-ALLARD, LUCILLE*		31,644 D	26.0%	74.0%	26.0%	74.0%
35	2006	98,506		—	82,498	WATERS, MAXINE*	16,008	82,498 D		83.7%		100.0%
35	2004	156,407	23,591	MOEN, ROSS	125,949	WATERS, MAXINE*	6,867	102,358 D	15.1%	80.5%	15.8%	84.2%
35	2002	93,407	18,094	MOEN, ROSS	72,401	WATERS, MAXINE*	2,912	54,307 D	19.4%	77.5%	20.0%	80.0%
36	2006	166,153	53,068	GIBSON, BRIAN	105,323	HARMAN, JANE*	7,762	52,255 D	31.9%	63.4%	33.5%	66.5%
36	2004	244,044	81,666	WHITEHEAD, PAUL	151,208	HARMAN, JANE*	11,170	69,542 D	33.5%	62.0%	35.1%	64.9%
36	2002	143,751	50,328	JOHNSON, STUART	88,198	HARMAN, JANE*	5,225	37,870 D	35.0%	61.4%	36.3%	63.7%
37	2006	97,962		—	80,716	MILLENDER-McDONALD, JUANITA*	17,246	80,716 D		82.4%		100.0%
37	2004	158,318	31,960	VAN, VERNON	118,823	MILLENDER-McDONALD, JUANITA*	7,535	86,863 D	20.2%	75.1%	21.2%	78.8%
37	2002	87,012	20,154	VELASCO, OSCAR A.	63,445	MILLENDER-McDONALD, JUANITA*	3,413	43,291 D	23.2%	72.9%	24.1%	75.9%
38	2006	99,801	24,620	STREET, SIDNEY W.	75,181	NAPOLITANO, GRACE F.*		50,561 D	24.7%	75.3%	24.7%	75.3%
38	2004	116,851		—	116,851	NAPOLITANO, GRACE F.*		116,851 D		100.0%		100.0%
38	2002	88,027	23,126	BURROLA, ALEX A.	62,600	NAPOLITANO, GRACE F.*	2,301	39,474 D	26.3%	71.1%	27.0%	73.0%
39	2006	109,533	37,384	ANDION, JAMES L.	72,149	SÁNCHEZ, LINDA T.*		34,765 D	34.1%	65.9%	34.1%	65.9%
39	2004	164,964	64,832	ESCOBAR, TIM	100,132	SÁNCHEZ, LINDA T.*		35,300 D	39.3%	60.7%	39.3%	60.7%
39	2002	95,346	38,925	ESCOBAR, TIM	52,256	SÁNCHEZ, LINDA T.	4,165	13,331 D	40.8%	54.8%	42.7%	57.3%
40	2006	151,289	100,995	ROYCE, ED*	46,418	HOFFMAN, FLORICE OREA	3,876	54,577 R	66.8%	30.7%	68.5%	31.5%
40	2004	217,301	147,617	ROYCE, ED*	69,684	WILLIAMS, J. TILMAN		77,933 R	67.9%	32.1%	67.9%	32.1%
40	2002	136,642	92,422	ROYCE, ED*	40,265	AVALOS, CHRISTINA	3,955	52,157 R	67.6%	29.5%	69.7%	30.3%
41	2006	164,044	109,761	LEWIS, JERRY*	54,235	CONTRERAS, LOUIE A.	48	55,526 R	66.9%	33.1%	66.9%	33.1%
41	2004	218,937	181,605	LEWIS, JERRY*		—	37,332	181,605 R	82.9%		100.0%	
41	2002	135,533	91,326	LEWIS, JERRY*	40,155	JOHNSON, KEITH A.	4,052	51,171 R	67.4%	29.6%	69.5%	30.5%
42	2006	129,720	129,720	MILLER, GARY G.*		—		129,720 R	100.0%		100.0%	
42	2004	246,025	167,632	MILLER, GARY G.*	78,393	MYERS, LEWIS		89,239 R	68.1%	31.9%	68.1%	31.9%
42	2002	145,246	98,476	MILLER, GARY G.*	42,090	WALDRON, RICHARD	4,680	56,386 R	67.8%	29.0%	70.1%	29.9%
43	2006	81,860	29,069	FOLKENS, SCOTT	52,791	BACA, JOE*		23,722 D	35.5%	64.5%	35.5%	64.5%
43	2004	130,834	44,004	LANING, ED	86,830	BACA, JOE*		42,826 D	33.6%	66.4%	33.6%	66.4%
43	2002	68,340	20,821	NEIGHBOR, WENDY C.	45,374	BACA, JOE*	2,145	24,553 D	30.5%	66.4%	31.5%	68.5%
44	2006	149,316	89,555	CALVERT, KEN*	55,275	VANDENBERG, LOUIS	4,486	34,280 R	60.0%	37.0%	61.8%	38.2%
44	2004	225,123	138,768	CALVERT, KEN*	78,796	VANDENBERG, LOUIS	7,559	59,972 R	61.6%	35.0%	63.8%	36.2%
44	2002	120,463	76,686	CALVERT, KEN*	38,021	VANDENBERG, LOUIS	5,756	38,665 R	63.7%	31.6%	66.9%	33.1%
45	2006	164,251	99,638	BONO, MARY*	64,613	ROTH, DAVID		35,025 R	60.7%	39.3%	60.7%	39.3%
45	2004	230,490	153,523	BONO, MARY*	76,967	MEYER, RICHARD J.		76,556 R	66.6%	33.4%	66.6%	33.4%
45	2002	133,533	87,101	BONO, MARY*	43,692	KURPIEWSKI, ELLE K.	2,740	43,409 R	65.2%	32.7%	66.6%	33.4%
46	2006	195,052	116,176	ROHRABACHER, DANA*	71,573	BRANDT, JIM	7,303	44,603 R	59.6%	36.7%	61.9%	38.1%
46	2004	276,690	171,318	ROHRABACHER, DANA*	90,129	BRANDT, JIM	15,243	81,189 R	61.9%	32.6%	65.5%	34.5%
46	2002	176,265	108,807	ROHRABACHER, DANA*	60,890	SCHIPSKE, GERRIE	6,568	47,917 R	61.7%	34.5%	64.1%	35.9%
47	2006	75,619	28,485	NGUYEN, TAN	47,134	SANCHEZ, LORETTA*		18,649 D	37.7%	62.3%	37.7%	62.3%
47	2004	108,783	43,099	CORONADO, ALEXANDRIA A. "ALEX"	65,684	SANCHEZ, LORETTA*		22,585 D	39.6%	60.4%	39.6%	60.4%
47	2002	70,178	24,346	CHAVEZ, JEFF	42,501	SANCHEZ, LORETTA*	3,331	18,155 D	34.7%	60.6%	36.4%	63.6%
48	2006	200,527	120,130	CAMPBELL, JOHN*	74,647	YOUNG, STEVE	5,750	45,483 R	59.9%	37.2%	61.7%	38.3%
48	2004	290,872	189,004	COX, CHRISTOPHER*	93,525	GRAHAM, JOHN	8,343	95,479 R	65.0%	32.2%	66.9%	33.1%
48	2002	179,549	122,884	COX, CHRISTOPHER*	51,058	GRAHAM, JOHN	5,607	71,826 R	68.4%	28.4%	70.6%	29.4%

CALIFORNIA

HOUSE OF REPRESENTATIVES

CD	Year	Total Vote	Republican			Democratic			Other Vote	Rep.-Dem. Plurality	Percentage			
			Vote		Candidate	Vote		Candidate			Total Vote		Major Vote	
											Rep.	Dem.	Rep.	Dem.
49	2006	156,137	98,831		ISSA, DARRELL*	52,227		CRISCENZO, JEENI	5,079	46,604 R	63.3%	33.4%	65.4%	34.6%
49	2004	226,466	141,658		ISSA, DARRELL*	79,057		BYRON, MIKE	5,751	62,601 R	62.6%	34.9%	64.2%	35.8%
49	2002	122,497	94,594		ISSA, DARRELL*			—	27,903	94,594 R	77.2%		100.0%	
50	2006	222,102	118,018		BILBRAY, BRIAN P.	96,612		BUSBY, FRANCINE	7,472	21,406 R	53.1%	43.5%	55.0%	45.0%
50	2004	289,328	169,025		CUNNINGHAM, RANDY "DUKE"*	105,590		BUSBY, FRANCINE	14,713	63,435 R	58.4%	36.5%	61.5%	38.5%
50	2002	172,701	111,095		CUNNINGHAM, RANDY "DUKE"*	55,855		STEWART, DEL G.	5,751	55,240 R	64.3%	32.3%	66.5%	33.5%
51	2006	115,839	34,931		MILES, BLAKE L.	78,114		FILNER, BOB*	2,794	43,183 D	30.2%	67.4%	30.9%	69.1%
51	2004	180,879	63,526		GIORGINO, MICHAEL	111,441		FILNER, BOB*	5,912	47,915 D	35.1%	61.6%	36.3%	63.7%
51	2002	102,787	40,430		GARCIA, MARIA GUADALUPE	59,541		FILNER, BOB*	2,816	19,111 D	39.3%	57.9%	40.4%	59.6%
52	2006	191,369	123,696		HUNTER, DUNCAN*	61,208		RINALDI, JOHN	6,465	62,488 R	64.6%	32.0%	66.9%	33.1%
52	2004	271,438	187,799		HUNTER, DUNCAN*	74,857		KELIHER, BRIAN S.	8,782	112,942 R	69.2%	27.6%	71.5%	28.5%
52	2002	169,010	118,561		HUNTER, DUNCAN*	43,526		MOORE-KOCHLACS, PETER	6,923	75,035 R	70.2%	25.8%	73.1%	26.9%
53	2006	144,387	43,312		WOODRUM, JOHN "WOODY"	97,541		DAVIS, SUSAN A.*	3,534	54,229 D	30.0%	67.6%	30.7%	69.3%
53	2004	221,436	63,897		HUNZEKER, DARIN	146,449		DAVIS, SUSAN A.*	11,090	82,552 D	28.9%	66.1%	30.4%	69.6%
53	2002	116,180	43,891		VanDeWEGHE, BILL	72,252		DAVIS, SUSAN A.*	37	28,361 D	37.8%	62.2%	37.8%	62.2%
TOTAL	2006	8,295,816	3,314,398			4,720,164			261,254	1,405,766 D	40.0%	56.9%	41.3%	58.7%
TOTAL	2004	11,623,753	5,030,821			6,223,698			369,234	1,192,877 D	43.3%	53.5%	44.7%	55.3%
TOTAL	2002	7,258,417	3,225,666			3,731,081			301,670	505,415 D	44.4%	51.4%	46.4%	53.6%

Note: An asterisk (*) denotes incumbent.

44

CALIFORNIA

GENERAL AND PRIMARY ELECTIONS

2006 GENERAL ELECTIONS

Governor Other vote was 205,995 Green (Peter Miguel Camejo); 114,329 Libertarian (Art Olivier); 69,934 Peace and Freedom (Janice Jordan); 61,901 American Independent (Edward C. Noonan); 219 Republican write-in (Robert C. Newman II); 46 Independent write-in (James Harris); 43 Independent write-in (Donald "Dr. Don" Etkes); 36 Independent write-in (Elisha Shapiro); 18 Independent write-in (Vibert Greene); 6 Independent write-in (Dealphria Christina Tarver).

Senator Other vote was 147,074 Green (Todd Chretien); 133,851 Libertarian (Michael S. Metti); 117,764 Peace and Freedom (Marsha Feinland); 75,350 American Independent (Don J. Grundmann); 160 Green write-in (Kent P. Mesplay); 108 Independent write-in (Jeffrey Mackler); 47 Independent write-in (Lea Sherman); 11 Independent write-in (Connor Vlakancic).

House Other vote was:

CD 1 6,899 Green (Pamela Elizondo); 3,503 Peace and Freedom (Timothy J. Stock); 39 Independent write-in (Carol Wolman).
CD 2 7,057 Libertarian (E. Kent Hinesley).
CD 3 3,772 Libertarian (Douglas Arthur Tuma); 2,370 Peace and Freedom (Michael Roskey).
CD 4 14,076 Libertarian (Dan Warren).
CD 5 6,466 Green (Jeff Kravitz); 2,018 Peace and Freedom (John C. Reiger).
CD 6 9,028 Libertarian (Richard W. Friesen); 5 Republican write-in (Michael Halliwell).
CD 7 22,486 Libertarian (Camden McConnell).
CD 8 13,653 Green (Krissy Keefer); 2,751 Libertarian (Philip Zimt Berg).
CD 9 5,655 Libertarian (James Eyer).
CD 10 50 Republican write-in (Jeff Ketelson).
CD 11
CD 12
CD 13
CD 14 4,692 Libertarian (Brian Holtz); 4,633 Green (Carol Brouillet).
CD 15
CD 16
CD 17 2,611 Independent write-in (Jeff Edward Taylor).
CD 18
CD 19
CD 20
CD 21 4,729 Green (John Roger Miller).
CD 22
CD 23 18 Independent write-in (H. A. Gardner Jr.).
CD 24 16 Independent write-in (Michael Kurt Stettler); 3 Independent write-in (Henry Nicolle).
CD 25 6,873 Libertarian (David W. Erickson).
CD 26 5,887 Libertarian (Ted Brown); 3,351 American Independent (Elliott Graham).
CD 27
CD 28 3,868 Green (Byron De Lear); 3,679 Libertarian (Kelley L. Ross).
CD 29 8,197 Green (William M. Paparian); 2,599 Peace and Freedom (Lynda L. Llamas); 2,258 Libertarian (Jim Keller); 15 Independent write-in (John Burton).
CD 30 4,546 Peace and Freedom (Adele M. Cannon).
CD 31
CD 32 15,627 Libertarian (Leland Faegre).
CD 33
CD 34 1 Independent write-in (Naomi Craine).
CD 35 8,343 American Independent (Gordon Michael Mego); 7,665 Libertarian (Paul T. Ireland).
CD 36 4,592 Peace and Freedom (James R. Smith); 3,170 Libertarian (Mike Binkley).
CD 37 17,246 Libertarian (Herb Peters).
CD 38
CD 39

CALIFORNIA

GENERAL AND PRIMARY ELECTIONS

CD 40   3,876 Libertarian (Philip H. Inman).
CD 41   48 Independent write-in (Carol Petersen).
CD 42
CD 43
CD 44   4,486 Peace and Freedom (Kevin Akin).
CD 45
CD 46   7,303 Libertarian (Dennis Chang).
CD 47
CD 48   5,750 Libertarian (Bruce Cohen).
CD 49   4,952 Libertarian (Lars R. Grossmith); 127 Democratic write-in (Frank Ford).
CD 50   4,119 Libertarian (Paul King); 3,353 Peace and Freedom (Miriam E. Clark).
CD 51   2,790 Libertarian (Dan Litwin); 4 Independent write-in (David Arguello).
CD 52   6,465 Libertarian (Michael Benoit).
CD 53   3,534 Libertarian (Ernie Lippe).

2006 PRIMARY ELECTIONS

Primary	June 6, 2006	**Registration** (as of May 22, 2006)	Democratic	6,685,288
			Republican	5,387,865
			American Independent	311,481
			Green	143,573
			Libertarian	83,132
			Peace and Freedom	59,545
			Natural Law	22,892
			Other	83,690
			Decline to State	2,890,973
			TOTAL	15,668,439

Primary Type   Semi-open—Voters registered with a recognized party in California could vote only in their party's primary. Other voters not registered with a recognized party (i.e., Decline to State) could participate in the primary of either the Democratic, Republican or American Independent Party.

CALIFORNIA

GENERAL AND PRIMARY ELECTIONS

Note: An asterisk (*) denotes incumbent.

	REPUBLICAN PRIMARIES			DEMOCRATIC PRIMARIES		
Governor	Arnold Schwarzenegger*	1,724,296	90.0%	Phil Angelides	1,202,884	48.0%
	Robert C. Newman II	68,663	3.6%	Steve Westly	1,081,971	43.2%
	Bill Chambers	65,488	3.4%	Barbara Becnel	66,550	2.7%
	Jeffrey R. Burns	57,652	3.0%	Joe Brouillette	42,077	1.7%
				Michael Strimling	35,122	1.4%
				Frank A. Macaluso Jr.	30,871	1.2%
				Vibert Greene	25,747	1.0%
				Jerald Robert Gerst	21,039	0.8%
	TOTAL	*1,916,099*		*TOTAL*	*2,506,261*	
Senator	Richard "Dick" Mountjoy	1,560,472	100.0%	Dianne Feinstein*	2,176,888	87.0%
				Colleen Fernald	199,180	8.0%
				Martin Luther Church	127,301	5.1%
				TOTAL	*2,503,369*	
Congressional District 1	John W. Jones	41,953	100.0%	Mike Thompson*	79,138	100.0%
Congressional District 2	Wally Herger*	69,669	100.0%	A. J. Sekhon	23,663	55.0%
				Bill Falzett	19,311	44.9%
				Robert Seals (write-in)	43	0.1%
				TOTAL	*43,017*	
Congressional District 3	Dan Lungren*	56,968	100.0%	Bill Durston	42,980	100.0%
Congressional District 4	John T. Doolittle*	63,731	67.2%	Charlie Brown	26,241	46.3%
	J. M. "Mike" Holmes	31,162	32.8%	Lisa Rea	19,038	33.6%
				Michael Hamersley	11,405	20.1%
	TOTAL	*94,893*		*TOTAL*	*56,684*	
Congressional District 5	Claire Yan	19,005	100.0%	Doris Matsui*	52,951	100.0%
Congressional District 6	Todd Hooper	19,448	57.4%	Lynn Woolsey*	72,058	66.2%
	Mike Halliwell	14,445	42.6%	Joe Nation	36,845	33.8%
				Michael Halliwell (write-in)	11	
	TOTAL	*33,893*		*TOTAL*	*108,914*	
Congressional District 7	No Republican candidate			George Miller*	57,308	100.0%
Congressional District 8	Mike DeNunzio	7,260	75.8%	Nancy Pelosi*	77,976	100.0%
	Eve Del Castello	2,319	24.2%			
	TOTAL	*9,579*				
Congressional District 9	John "J. D." denDulk	9,350	100.0%	Barbara Lee*	97,874	100.0%
Congressional District 10	Darcy Linn	33,198	100.0%	Ellen O. Tauscher*	60,669	100.0%
Congressional District 11	Richard W. Pombo*	35,493	62.4%	Jerry McNerney	23,598	52.8%
	Paul N. "Pete" McCloskey Jr.	18,132	31.9%	Steve Filson	12,744	28.5%
	Thomas "Tom" A. Benigno	3,263	5.7%	Steve Thomas	8,390	18.8%
	TOTAL	*56,888*		*TOTAL*	*44,732*	
Congressional District 12	Mike Moloney	8,068	42.1%	Tom Lantos*	61,510	83.3%
	Mike Garza	7,098	37.0%	Kevin Hearle	6,973	9.4%
	Chris Huskins	4,002	20.9%	Robert M. Barrows	5,401	7.3%
	TOTAL	*19,168*		*TOTAL*	*73,884*	
Congressional District 13	George I. Bruno	15,788	100.0%	Pete Stark*	54,654	100.0%
Congressional District 14	Rob Smith	28,011	100.0%	Anna G. Eshoo*	65,255	100.0%
Congressional District 15	Raymond L. Chukwu	23,693	100.0%	Michael M. Honda*	49,400	100.0%
Congressional District 16	Charel Winston	19,886	100.0%	Zoe Lofgren*	46,286	100.0%

CALIFORNIA

GENERAL AND PRIMARY ELECTIONS

	REPUBLICAN PRIMARIES			DEMOCRATIC PRIMARIES		
Congressional District 17	Anthony R. De Maio	23,703	100.0%	Sam Farr*	54,998	100.0%
Congressional District 18	John A. Kanno	19,851	100.0%	Dennis Cardoza*	31,088	100.0%
Congressional District 19	George P. Radanovich*	54,722	100.0%	T. J. Cox	35,278	100.0%
Congressional District 20	Jim Lopez (write-in)	472	100.0%	Jim Costa*	24,356	100.0%
	Jim Lopez did not qualify for the general election ballot. As a write-in candidate, he needed to receive in the vicinity of 1,142 votes in the primary, or 1 percent of the number cast for the House in the 20th District in the previous general election.					
Congressional District 21	Devin Nunes*	43,364	100.0%	Steven Haze	24,927	100.0%
Congressional District 22	Kevin McCarthy Steve W. Nichols David W. Evans TOTAL	63,399 5,995 4,637 74,031	85.6% 8.1% 6.3%	Sharon M. Beery	31,966	100.0%
Congressional District 23	Victor D. Tognazzini Will Levison TOTAL	21,444 14,512 35,956	59.6% 40.4%	Lois Capps*	53,503	100.0%
Congressional District 24	Elton Gallegly* Michael Tenenbaum Total	51,923 12,903 64,826	80.0% 19.9%	Jill M. Martinez	36,619	100.0%
Congressional District 25	Howard P. "Buck" McKeon*	36,291	100.0%	Robert Rodriguez	23,203	100.0%
Congressional District 26	David Dreier* Sonny Sardo Melvin C. "Mel" Milton TOTAL	29,569 12,186 3,826 45,581	64.9% 26.7% 8.4%	Cynthia Matthews Russ Warner Hoyt Hilsman TOTAL	14,380 11,498 4,695 30,573	47.0% 37.6% 15.4%
Congressional District 27	Peter Hankwitz	17,065	100.0%	Brad Sherman*	35,563	100.0%
Congressional District 28	Stanley Kimmel Kesselman	8,632	100.0%	Howard L. Berman* Charles R. Coleman Jr. TOTAL	31,048 7,547 38,595	80.4% 19.6%
Congressional District 29	William J. Bodell	19,281	100.0%	Adam B. Schiff* Bob McCloskey TOTAL	33,750 7,102 40,852	82.6% 17.4%
Congressional District 30	David Nelson Jones	20,660	100.0%	Henry A. Waxman*	59,955	100.0%
Congressional District 31	No Republican candidate			Xavier Becerra* Sal Genovese TOTAL	26,904 3,227 30,131	89.3% 10.7%
Congressional District 32	No Republican candidate			Hilda L. Solis*	30,355	100.0%
Congressional District 33	No Republican candidate			Diane Watson* Mervin L. Evans TOTAL	47,461 4,774 52,235	90.9% 9.1%
Congressional District 34	Wayne Miller	5,927	100.0%	Lucille Roybal-Allard*	22,173	100.0%
Congressional District 35	No Republican candidate	7,573	100.0%	Maxine Waters* Carl McGill TOTAL	34,338 5,538 39,876	86.1% 13.9%
Congressional District 36	Brian Gibson	23,881	100.0%	Jane Harman* Marcy Winograd TOTAL	30,333 18,227 48,560	62.5% 37.5%

CALIFORNIA

GENERAL AND PRIMARY ELECTIONS

	REPUBLICAN PRIMARIES			DEMOCRATIC PRIMARIES		
Congressional District 37	No Republican candidate		100.0%	Juanita Millender-McDonald*	28,480	75.8%
				Peter Mathews	9,094	24.2%
				TOTAL	37,574	
Congressional District 38	Sidney W. Street	8,427	100.0%	Grace F. Napolitano*	31,123	100.0%
Congressional District 39	James L. Andion	12,870	100.0%	Linda T. Sánchez*	23,893	77.8%
				Kenneth L. Graham	5,083	16.5%
				Frank Amador	1,738	5.7%
				TOTAL	30,714	
Congressional District 40	Ed Royce*	44,038	100.0%	Florice Orea Hoffman	13,229	52.2%
				Christina Avalos	12,116	47.8%
				TOTAL	25,345	
Congressional District 41	Jerry Lewis*	45,119	100.0%	Louie A. Contreras	26,466	100.0%
Congressional District 42	Gary G. Miller*	43,813	100.0%	Mark Hull-Richter (write-in)	273	100.0%
				Mark Hull-Richter did not qualify for the general election ballot. As a write-in candidate, he needed to receive in the vicinity of 2,460 votes in the primary, or 1 percent of the number of votes cast for the House in the 42nd District in the previous general election.		
Congressional District 43	Scott Folkens	10,119	100.0%	Joe Baca*	20,959	100.0%
Congressional District 44	Ken Calvert*	35,444	100.0%	Louis Vandenberg	23,592	100.0%
Congressional District 45	Mary Bono*	42,080	99.6%	David Roth	22,776	68.1%
	John C. Barker (write-in)	183	0.4%	Marty Schwimmer	10,679	31.9%
	TOTAL	42,263		TOTAL	33,455	
Congressional District 46	Dana Rohrabacher*	53,239	100.0%	Jim Brandt	31,292	100.0%
Congressional District 47	Tan Nguyen	9,473	55.4%	Loretta Sanchez*	19,179	100.0%
	Rosemarie "Rosie" Avila	6,453	37.7%			
	Angelita J. Campos	1,175	6.9%			
	TOTAL	17,101				
Congressional District 48	John Campbell*	55,483	100.0%	Steve Young	27,812	100.0%
Congressional District 49	Darrell Issa*	47,693	100.0%	Jeeni Criscenzo	24,004	100.0%
Congressional District 50	Brian P. Bilbray	41,545	54.0%	Francine Busby	52,039	89.8%
	Eric Roach	10,617	13.8%	Chris Young	5,881	10.2%
	Bill Hauf	9,952	12.9%			
	Bill Morrow	4,788	6.2%			
	Howard Kaloogian	3,689	4.8%			
	Alan Uke	1,866	2.4%			
	Victor E. Ramirez	1,425	1.9%			
	Richard Lee Earnest	1,081	1.4%			
	Scott Orren	973	1.3%			
	Scott Turner	960	1.2%			
	TOTAL	76,896		TOTAL	57,920	
Congressional District 51	Blake L. Miles	13,942	62.0%	Bob Filner*	23,312	51.2%
	Jim Galley	8,558	38.0%	Juan Vargas	19,364	42.5%
				Daniel C. "Danny" Ramirez	2,862	6.3%
	TOTAL	22,500		TOTAL	45,538	
Congressional District 52	Duncan Hunter*	60,772	100.0%	John Rinaldi	12,386	38.7%
				Derek Casady	6,214	19.4%
				Karen Marie Otter	5,063	15.8%
				Connie Frankowiak	4,805	15.0%
				Peter Moore-Kochlacs	3,535	11.0%
				TOTAL	32,003	
Congressional District 53	John "Woody" Woodrum	14,651	61.2%	Susan A. Davis*	41,231	100.0%
	Bryan Barton	9,304	38.8%			
	TOTAL	23,955				

COLORADO

Congressional districts first established for elections held in 2002
7 members

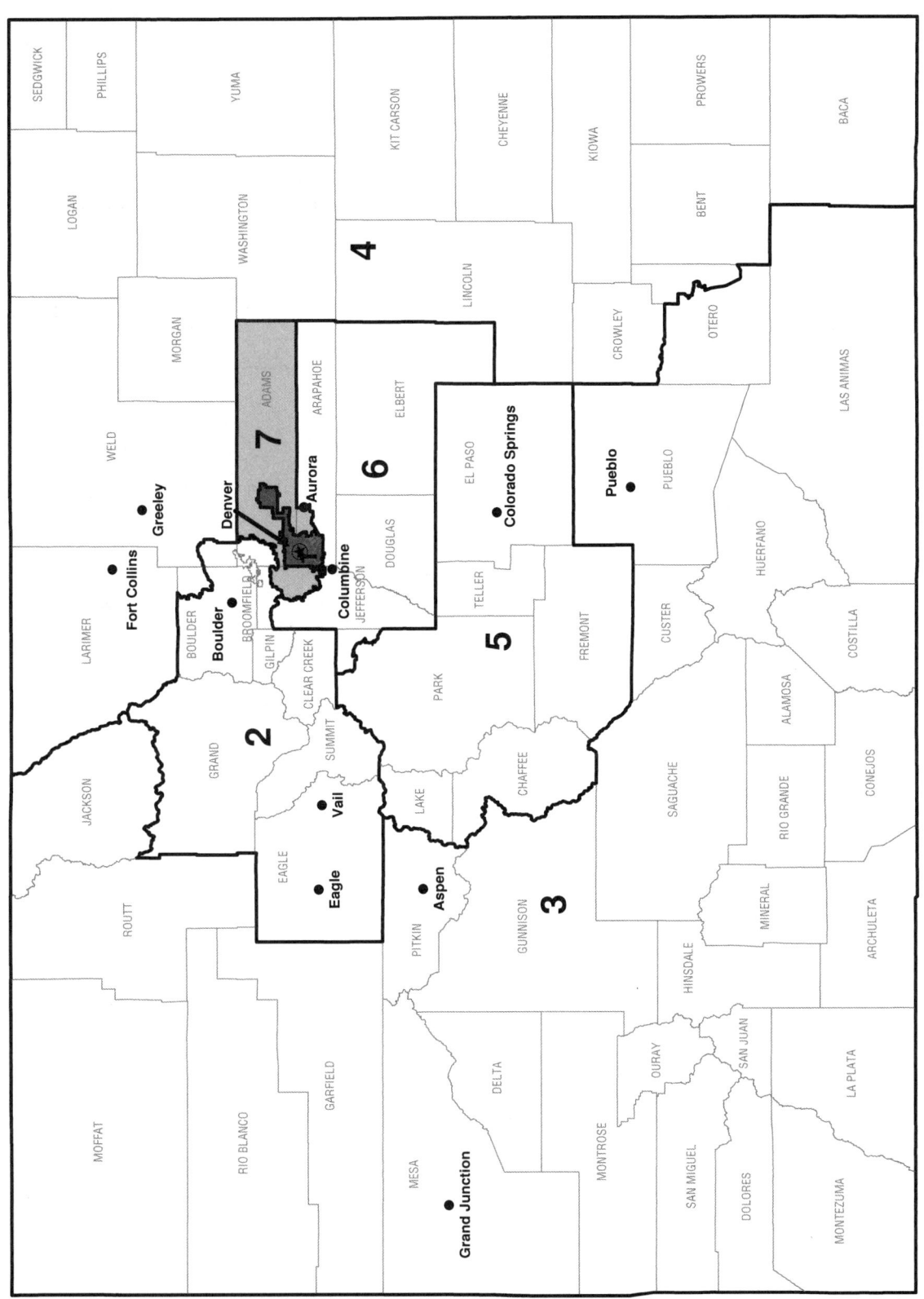

COLORADO

Denver Area

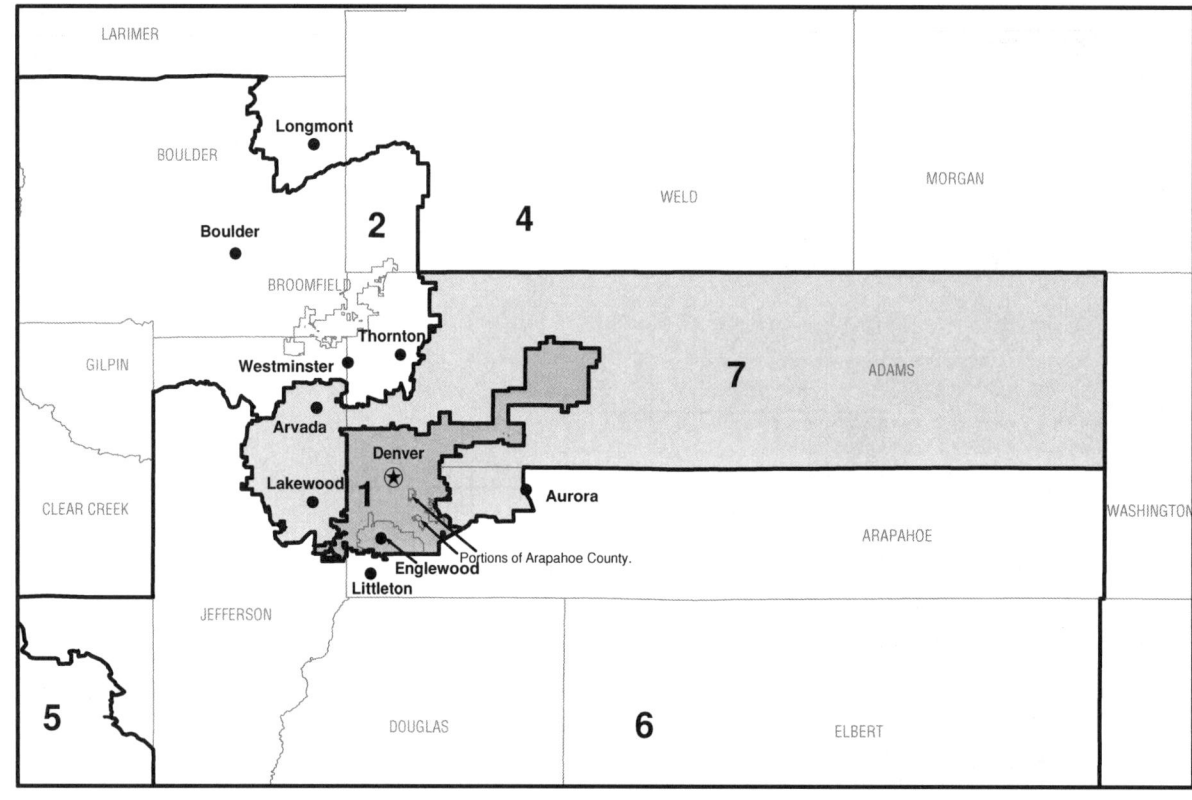

COLORADO

GOVERNOR
Bill Ritter Jr. (D). Elected 2006 to a four-year term.

SENATORS (1 Democrat, 1 Republican)
Ken Salazar (D). Elected 2004 to a six-year term.

Wayne Allard (R). Reelected 2002 to a six-year term. Previously elected 1996.

REPRESENTATIVES (4 Democrats, 3 Republicans)
1. Diana DeGette (D)
2. Mark Udall (D)
3. John Salazar (D)
4. Marilyn Musgrave (R)
5. Doug Lamborn (R)
6. Tom Tancredo (R)
7. Ed Perlmutter (D)

POSTWAR VOTE FOR PRESIDENT

Year	Total Vote	Republican Vote	Candidate	Democratic Vote	Candidate	Other Vote	Plurality	Total Vote Rep.	Dem.	Major Vote Rep.	Dem.
2004	2,130,330	1,101,255	Bush, George W.	1,001,732	Kerry, John	27,343	99,523 R	51.7%	47.0%	52.4%	47.6%
2000**	1,741,368	883,748	Bush, George W.	738,227	Gore, Al	119,393	145,521 R	50.8%	42.4%	54.5%	45.5%
1996**	1,510,704	691,848	Dole, Bob	671,152	Clinton, Bill	147,704	20,696 R	45.8%	44.4%	50.8%	49.2%
1992**	1,569,180	562,850	Bush, George	629,681	Clinton, Bill	376,649	66,831 D	35.9%	40.1%	47.2%	52.8%
1988	1,372,394	728,177	Bush, George	621,453	Dukakis, Michael S.	22,764	106,724 R	53.1%	45.3%	54.0%	46.0%
1984	1,295,380	821,817	Reagan, Ronald	454,975	Mondale, Walter F.	18,588	366,842 R	63.4%	35.1%	64.4%	35.6%
1980**	1,184,415	652,264	Reagan, Ronald	367,973	Carter, Jimmy	164,178	284,291 R	55.1%	31.1%	63.9%	36.1%
1976	1,081,554	584,367	Ford, Gerald R.	460,353	Carter, Jimmy	36,834	124,014 R	54.0%	42.6%	55.9%	44.1%
1972	953,884	597,189	Nixon, Richard M.	329,980	McGovern, George S.	26,715	267,209 R	62.6%	34.6%	64.4%	35.6%
1968**	811,199	409,345	Nixon, Richard M.	335,174	Humphrey, Hubert H.	66,680	74,171 R	50.5%	41.3%	55.0%	45.0%
1964	776,986	296,767	Goldwater, Barry M.	476,024	Johnson, Lyndon B.	4,195	179,257 D	38.2%	61.3%	38.4%	61.6%
1960	736,236	402,242	Nixon, Richard M.	330,629	Kennedy, John F.	3,365	71,613 R	54.6%	44.9%	54.9%	45.1%
1956	657,074	394,479	Eisenhower, Dwight D.	257,997	Stevenson, Adlai E.	4,598	136,482 R	60.0%	39.3%	60.5%	39.5%
1952	630,103	379,782	Eisenhower, Dwight D.	245,504	Stevenson, Adlai E.	4,817	134,278 R	60.3%	39.0%	60.7%	39.3%
1948	515,237	239,714	Dewey, Thomas E.	267,288	Truman, Harry S.	8,235	27,574 D	46.5%	51.9%	47.3%	52.7%

**In past elections, the other vote included: 2000 - 91,434 Green (Ralph Nader); 1996 - 99,629 Reform (Ross Perot); 1992 - 366,010 Independent (Ross Perot); 1980 - 130,633 Independent (John Anderson); 1968 - 60,813 American Independent (George Wallace).

COLORADO

POSTWAR VOTE FOR GOVERNOR

Year	Total Vote	Republican Vote	Republican Candidate	Democratic Vote	Democratic Candidate	Other Vote	Rep.-Dem. Plurality	Total Vote Rep.	Total Vote Dem.	Major Vote Rep.	Major Vote Dem.
2006	1,558,387	625,886	Beauprez, Bob	888,096	Ritter, Bill Jr.	44,405	262,210 D	40.2%	57.0%	41.3%	58.7%
2002	1,412,602	884,583	Owens, Bill	475,373	Heath, Rollie	52,646	409,210 R	62.6%	33.7%	65.0%	35.0%
1998	1,321,307	648,202	Owens, Bill	639,905	Schoettler, Gail	33,200	8,297 R	49.1%	48.4%	50.3%	49.7%
1994	1,116,307	432,042	Benson, Bruce	619,205	Romer, Roy	65,060	187,163 D	38.7%	55.5%	41.1%	58.9%
1990	1,011,272	358,403	Andrews, John	626,032	Romer, Roy	26,837	267,629 D	35.4%	61.9%	36.4%	63.6%
1986	1,058,928	434,420	Strickland, Ted	616,325	Romer, Roy	8,183	181,905 D	41.0%	58.2%	41.3%	58.7%
1982	956,021	302,740	Fuhr, John D.	627,960	Lamm, Richard D.	25,321	325,220 D	31.7%	65.7%	32.5%	67.5%
1978	823,807	317,292	Strickland, Ted	483,985	Lamm, Richard D.	22,530	166,693 D	38.5%	58.7%	39.6%	60.4%
1974	828,968	378,698	Vanderhoof, John D.	441,408	Lamm, Richard D.	8,862	62,710 D	45.7%	53.2%	46.2%	53.8%
1970	668,496	350,690	Love, John A.	302,432	Hogan, Mark	15,374	48,258 R	52.5%	45.2%	53.7%	46.3%
1966	660,063	356,730	Love, John A.	287,132	Knous, Robert L.	16,201	69,598 R	54.0%	43.5%	55.4%	44.6%
1962	616,481	349,342	Love, John A.	262,890	McNichols, Stephen	4,249	86,452 R	56.7%	42.6%	57.1%	42.9%
1958**	549,808	228,643	Burch, Palmer L.	321,165	McNichols, Stephen		92,522 D	41.6%	58.4%	41.6%	58.4%
1956	645,233	313,950	Brotzman, Donald G.	331,283	McNichols, Stephen		17,333 D	48.7%	51.3%	48.7%	51.3%
1954	489,540	227,335	Brotzman, Donald G.	262,205	Johnson, Ed C.		34,870 D	46.4%	53.6%	46.4%	53.6%
1952	613,034	349,924	Thornton, Dan	260,044	Metzger, John W.	3,066	89,880 R	57.1%	42.4%	57.4%	42.6%
1950	450,994	236,472	Thornton, Dan	212,976	Johnson, Walter	1,546	23,496 R	52.4%	47.2%	52.6%	47.4%
1948	501,680	168,928	Hamil, David A.	332,752	Knous, William Lee		163,824 D	33.7%	66.3%	33.7%	66.3%
1946	335,087	160,483	Lavington, Leon E.	174,604	Knous, William Lee		14,121 D	47.9%	52.1%	47.9%	52.1%

**The term of office of Colorado's governor was increased from two to four years effective with the 1958 election.

POSTWAR VOTE FOR SENATOR

Year	Total Vote	Republican Vote	Republican Candidate	Democratic Vote	Democratic Candidate	Other Vote	Rep.-Dem. Plurality	Total Vote Rep.	Total Vote Dem.	Major Vote Rep.	Major Vote Dem.
2004	2,107,554	980,668	Coors, Pete	1,081,188	Salazar, Ken	45,698	100,520 D	46.5%	51.3%	47.6%	52.4%
2002	1,416,082	717,893	Allard, Wayne	648,130	Strickland, Tom	50,059	69,763 R	50.7%	45.8%	52.6%	47.4%
1998	1,327,235	829,370	Campbell, Ben Nighthorse	464,754	Lamm, Dottie	33,111	364,616 R	62.5%	35.0%	64.1%	35.9%
1996	1,469,611	750,325	Allard, Wayne	677,600	Strickland, Tom	41,686	72,725 R	51.1%	46.1%	52.5%	47.5%
1992	1,552,289	662,893	Considine, Terry	803,725	Campbell, Ben Nighthorse	85,671	140,832 D	42.7%	51.8%	45.2%	54.8%
1990	1,022,027	569,048	Brown, Hank	425,746	Heath, Josie	27,233	143,302 R	55.7%	41.7%	57.2%	42.8%
1986	1,060,765	512,994	Kramer, Ken	529,449	Wirth, Timothy E.	18,322	16,455 D	48.4%	49.9%	49.2%	50.8%
1984	1,297,809	833,821	Armstrong, William L.	449,327	Dick, Nancy	14,661	384,494 R	64.2%	34.6%	65.0%	35.0%
1980	1,173,646	571,295	Buchanan, Mary E.	590,501	Hart, Gary W.	11,850	19,206 D	48.7%	50.3%	49.2%	50.8%
1978	819,150	480,596	Armstrong, William L.	330,247	Haskell, Floyd K.	8,307	150,349 R	58.7%	40.3%	59.3%	40.7%
1974	824,166	325,508	Dominick, Peter H.	471,691	Hart, Gary W.	26,967	146,183 D	39.5%	57.2%	40.8%	59.2%
1972	926,093	447,957	Allott, Gordon	457,545	Haskell, Floyd K.	20,591	9,588 D	48.4%	49.4%	49.5%	50.5%
1968	785,536	459,952	Dominick, Peter H.	325,584	McNichols, Stephen		134,368 R	58.6%	41.4%	58.6%	41.4%
1966	634,898	368,307	Allott, Gordon	266,259	Romer, Roy	332	102,048 R	58.0%	41.9%	58.0%	42.0%
1962	613,444	328,655	Dominick, Peter H.	279,586	Carroll, John A.	5,203	49,069 R	53.6%	45.6%	54.0%	46.0%
1960	727,633	389,428	Allott, Gordon	334,854	Knous, Robert L.	3,351	54,574 R	53.5%	46.0%	53.8%	46.2%
1956	636,974	317,102	Thornton, Dan	319,872	Carroll, John A.		2,770 D	49.8%	50.2%	49.8%	50.2%
1954	484,188	248,502	Allott, Gordon	235,686	Carroll, John A.		12,816 R	51.3%	48.7%	51.3%	48.7%
1950	450,176	239,734	Millikin, Eugene D.	210,442	Carroll, John A.		29,292 R	53.3%	46.7%	53.3%	46.7%
1948	510,121	165,069	Nicholson, W. F.	340,719	Johnson, Ed C.	4,333	175,650 D	32.4%	66.8%	32.6%	67.4%

COLORADO

GOVERNOR 2006

2000 Census Population	County	Total Vote	Republican	Democratic	Other	Rep.-Dem. Plurality	Percentage Total Vote Rep.	Dem.	Major Vote Rep.	Dem.
348,618	ADAMS	93,148	34,607	55,930	2,611	21,323 D	37.2%	60.0%	38.2%	61.8%
14,966	ALAMOSA	4,778	1,589	3,098	91	1,509 D	33.3%	64.8%	33.9%	66.1%
487,967	ARAPAHOE	169,322	66,907	98,203	4,212	31,296 D	39.5%	58.0%	40.5%	59.5%
9,898	ARCHULETA	4,623	2,227	2,274	122	47 D	48.2%	49.2%	49.5%	50.5%
4,517	BACA	1,869	1,022	783	64	239 R	54.7%	41.9%	56.6%	43.4%
5,998	BENT	1,607	657	910	40	253 D	40.9%	56.6%	41.9%	58.1%
269,814	BOULDER	118,331	30,974	84,235	3,122	53,261 D	26.2%	71.2%	26.9%	73.1%
38,272	BROOMFIELD*	18,531	7,544	10,517	470	2,973 D	40.7%	56.8%	41.8%	58.2%
16,242	CHAFFEE	7,440	2,940	4,298	202	1,358 D	39.5%	57.8%	40.6%	59.4%
2,231	CHEYENNE	956	598	339	19	259 R	62.6%	35.5%	63.8%	36.2%
9,322	CLEAR CREEK	4,416	1,516	2,708	192	1,192 D	34.3%	61.3%	35.9%	64.1%
8,400	CONEJOS	3,193	1,055	2,063	75	1,008 D	33.0%	64.6%	33.8%	66.2%
3,663	COSTILLA	1,472	293	1,146	33	853 D	19.9%	77.9%	20.4%	79.6%
5,518	CROWLEY	1,262	625	594	43	31 R	49.5%	47.1%	51.3%	48.7%
3,503	CUSTER	1,871	1,042	788	41	254 R	55.7%	42.1%	56.9%	43.1%
27,834	DELTA	11,324	5,748	5,078	498	670 R	50.8%	44.8%	53.1%	46.9%
554,636	DENVER	157,454	31,851	121,494	4,109	89,643 D	20.2%	77.2%	20.8%	79.2%
1,844	DOLORES	990	432	527	31	95 D	43.6%	53.2%	45.0%	55.0%
175,766	DOUGLAS	80,366	42,493	36,364	1,509	6,129 R	52.9%	45.2%	53.9%	46.1%
41,659	EAGLE	13,015	4,492	8,158	365	3,666 D	34.5%	62.7%	35.5%	64.5%
19,872	ELBERT	8,820	5,463	3,134	223	2,329 R	61.9%	35.5%	63.5%	36.5%
516,929	EL PASO	174,098	99,613	69,237	5,248	30,376 R	57.2%	39.8%	59.0%	41.0%
46,145	FREMONT	14,063	6,872	6,768	423	104 R	48.9%	48.1%	50.4%	49.6%
43,791	GARFIELD	15,171	6,043	8,602	526	2,559 D	39.8%	56.7%	41.3%	58.7%
4,757	GILPIN	2,455	769	1,551	135	782 D	31.3%	63.2%	33.1%	66.9%
12,442	GRAND	5,939	2,620	3,149	170	529 D	44.1%	53.0%	45.4%	54.6%
13,956	GUNNISON	6,305	1,793	4,154	358	2,361 D	28.4%	65.9%	30.1%	69.9%
790	HINSDALE	500	220	252	28	32 D	44.0%	50.4%	46.6%	53.4%
7,862	HUERFANO	2,906	921	1,910	75	989 D	31.7%	65.7%	32.5%	67.5%
1,577	JACKSON	754	406	302	46	104 R	53.8%	40.1%	57.3%	42.7%
525,507	JEFFERSON	207,559	82,314	119,420	5,825	37,106 D	39.7%	57.5%	40.8%	59.2%
1,622	KIOWA	805	478	313	14	165 R	59.4%	38.9%	60.4%	39.6%
8,011	KIT CARSON	2,787	1,582	1,131	74	451 R	56.8%	40.6%	58.3%	41.7%
7,812	LAKE	2,337	709	1,517	111	808 D	30.3%	64.9%	31.9%	68.1%
43,941	LA PLATA	19,146	6,666	11,962	518	5,296 D	34.8%	62.5%	35.8%	64.2%
251,494	LARIMER	112,929	45,700	63,297	3,932	17,597 D	40.5%	56.1%	41.9%	58.1%
15,207	LAS ANIMAS	4,868	1,501	3,243	124	1,742 D	30.8%	66.6%	31.6%	68.4%
6,087	LINCOLN	1,831	1,030	737	64	293 R	56.3%	40.3%	58.3%	41.7%
20,504	LOGAN	7,567	3,821	3,559	187	262 R	50.5%	47.0%	51.8%	48.2%
116,255	MESA	46,699	23,444	21,475	1,780	1,969 R	50.2%	46.0%	52.2%	47.8%
831	MINERAL	583	235	338	10	103 D	40.3%	58.0%	41.0%	59.0%
13,184	MOFFAT	4,160	2,216	1,750	194	466 R	53.3%	42.1%	55.9%	44.1%
23,830	MONTEZUMA	8,606	4,263	4,146	197	117 R	49.5%	48.2%	50.7%	49.3%
33,432	MONTROSE	12,241	6,067	5,639	535	428 R	49.6%	46.1%	51.8%	48.2%
27,171	MORGAN	7,612	3,997	3,419	196	578 R	52.5%	44.9%	53.9%	46.1%
20,311	OTERO	6,181	2,603	3,432	146	829 D	42.1%	55.5%	43.1%	56.9%
3,742	OURAY	2,279	916	1,289	74	373 D	40.2%	56.6%	41.5%	58.5%
14,523	PARK	6,792	3,293	3,208	291	85 R	48.5%	47.2%	50.7%	49.3%
4,480	PHILLIPS	1,801	998	773	30	225 R	55.4%	42.9%	56.4%	43.6%
14,872	PITKIN	6,692	1,428	5,095	169	3,667 D	21.3%	76.1%	21.9%	78.1%
14,483	PROWERS	3,306	1,688	1,549	69	139 R	51.1%	46.9%	52.1%	47.9%
141,472	PUEBLO	52,041	16,094	34,968	979	18,874 D	30.9%	67.2%	31.5%	68.5%
5,986	RIO BLANCO	2,152	1,305	773	74	532 R	60.6%	35.9%	62.8%	37.2%
12,413	RIO GRANDE	4,262	1,884	2,284	94	400 D	44.2%	53.6%	45.2%	54.8%
19,690	ROUTT	7,814	2,452	5,172	190	2,720 D	31.4%	66.2%	32.2%	67.8%
5,917	SAGUACHE	2,188	632	1,466	90	834 D	28.9%	67.0%	30.1%	69.9%
558	SAN JUAN	388	114	255	19	141 D	29.4%	65.7%	30.9%	69.1%
6,594	SAN MIGUEL	2,704	594	1,991	119	1,397 D	22.0%	73.6%	23.0%	77.0%
2,747	SEDGWICK	1,167	568	575	24	7 D	48.7%	49.3%	49.7%	50.3%
23,548	SUMMIT	9,922	2,939	6,683	300	3,744 D	29.6%	67.4%	30.5%	69.5%

COLORADO

GOVERNOR 2006

2000 Census Population	County	Total Vote	Republican	Democratic	Other	Rep.-Dem. Plurality	Percentage			
							Total Vote		Major Vote	
							Rep.	Dem.	Rep.	Dem.
20,555	TELLER	8,655	4,981	3,383	291	1,598 R	57.6%	39.1%	59.6%	40.4%
4,926	WASHINGTON	2,083	1,359	672	52	687 R	65.2%	32.3%	66.9%	33.1%
180,926	WELD	67,557	32,398	32,677	2,482	279 D	48.0%	48.4%	49.8%	50.2%
9,841	YUMA	3,694	2,285	1,339	70	946 R	61.9%	36.2%	63.1%	36.9%
4,301,261	TOTAL	1,558,387	625,886	888,096	44,405	262,210 D	40.2%	57.0%	41.3%	58.7%

Note: Broomfield County was created effective 2001 out of portions of Adams, Boulder, Jefferson, and Weld counties. The population figures in this table have been adjusted for each county using 2000 census data.

COLORADO

HOUSE OF REPRESENTATIVES

CD	Year	Total Vote	Republican		Democratic		Other Vote	Rep.-Dem. Plurality	Percentage			
			Vote	Candidate	Vote	Candidate			Total Vote		Major Vote	
									Rep.	Dem.	Rep.	Dem.
1	2006	162,271		—	129,446	DeGETTE, DIANA*	32,825	129,446 D		79.8%		100.0%
1	2004	240,929	58,659	CHICAS, ROLAND	177,077	DeGETTE, DIANA*	5,193	118,418 D	24.3%	73.5%	24.9%	75.1%
1	2002	168,564	49,884	CHLOUBER, KEN	111,718	DeGETTE, DIANA*	6,962	61,834 D	29.6%	66.3%	30.9%	69.1%
2	2006	231,307	65,481	MANCUSO, RICH	157,850	UDALL, MARK*	7,976	92,369 D	28.3%	68.2%	29.3%	70.7%
2	2004	309,364	94,160	HACKMAN, STEPHEN M.	207,900	UDALL, MARK*	7,304	113,740 D	30.4%	67.2%	31.2%	68.8%
2	2002	205,522	75,564	HUME, SANDY	123,504	UDALL, MARK*	6,454	47,940 D	36.8%	60.1%	38.0%	62.0%
3	2006	237,858	86,930	TIPTON, SCOTT	146,488	SALAZAR, JOHN*	4,440	59,558 D	36.5%	61.6%	37.2%	62.8%
3	2004	303,646	141,376	WALCHER, GREG	153,500	SALAZAR, JOHN	8,770	12,124 D	46.6%	50.6%	47.9%	52.1%
3	2002	217,972	143,433	McINNIS, SCOTT*	68,160	BERCKEFELDT, DENIS	6,379	75,273 R	65.8%	31.3%	67.8%	32.2%
4	2006	240,613	109,732	MUSGRAVE, MARILYN*	103,748	PACCIONE, ANGIE	27,133	5,984 R	45.6%	43.1%	51.4%	48.6%
4	2004	305,509	155,958	MUSGRAVE, MARILYN*	136,812	MATSUNAKA, STAN	12,739	19,146 R	51.0%	44.8%	53.3%	46.7%
4	2002	209,955	115,359	MUSGRAVE, MARILYN	87,499	MATSUNAKA, STAN	7,097	27,860 R	54.9%	41.7%	56.9%	43.1%
5	2006	206,756	123,264	LAMBORN, DOUG	83,431	FAWCETT, JAY	61	39,833 R	59.6%	40.4%	59.6%	40.4%
5	2004	274,058	193,333	HEFLEY, JOEL*	74,098	HARDEE, FRED	6,627	119,235 R	70.5%	27.0%	72.3%	27.7%
5	2002	184,677	128,118	HEFLEY, JOEL*	45,587	IMRIE, CURTIS	10,972	82,531 R	69.4%	24.7%	73.8%	26.2%
6	2006	270,931	158,806	TANCREDO, TOM*	108,007	WINTER, BILL	4,118	50,799 R	58.6%	39.9%	59.5%	40.5%
6	2004	357,741	212,778	TANCREDO, TOM*	139,870	CONTI, JOANNA L.	5,093	72,908 R	59.5%	39.1%	60.3%	39.7%
6	2002	237,501	158,851	TANCREDO, TOM*	71,327	WRIGHT, LANCE	7,323	87,524 R	66.9%	30.0%	69.0%	31.0%
7	2006	189,172	79,571	O'DONNELL, RICK	103,918	PERLMUTTER, ED	5,683	24,347 D	42.1%	54.9%	43.4%	56.6%
7	2004	247,764	135,571	BEAUPREZ, BOB*	106,026	THOMAS, DAVE	6,167	29,545 R	54.7%	42.8%	56.1%	43.9%
7	2002	172,879	81,789	BEAUPREZ, BOB	81,668	FEELEY, MIKE	9,422	121 R	47.3%	47.2%	50.0%	50.0%
TOTAL	2006	1,538,908	623,784		832,888		82,236	209,104 D	40.5%	54.1%	42.8%	57.2%
TOTAL	2004	2,039,011	991,835		995,283		51,893	3,448 D	48.6%	48.8%	49.9%	50.1%
TOTAL	2002	1,397,070	752,998		589,463		54,609	163,535 R	53.9%	42.2%	56.1%	43.9%

An asterisk (*) denotes incumbent.

COLORADO

GENERAL AND PRIMARY ELECTIONS

2006 GENERAL ELECTIONS

Governor Other vote was 23,323 Libertarian (Dawn Winkler-Kinateder); 10,996 Unaffiliated (Paul Noel Fiorino); 9,716 American Constitution (Clyde J. Harkins); 370 Republican write-in (Charles Walter Sylvester Jr.).

House Other vote was:

CD 1 32,825 Green (Thomas D. Kelly).
CD 2 5,025 Libertarian (Norm Olsen); 2,951 Green (J. A. Calhoun).
CD 3 4,417 Libertarian (Bert L. Sargent); 23 Green write-in (Bruce E. Lohmiller).
CD 4 27,133 Reform (Eric Eidsness).
CD 5 41 Republican write-in (Richard D. Hand); 12 Democratic write-in (Brian X. Scott); 8 Republican write-in (Gregory S. Hollister).
CD 6 4,093 Libertarian (Jack J. Woehr); 25 Republican write-in (Juan B. Botero).
CD 7 3,073 Green (Dave Chandler); 2,605 American Constitution (Roger McCarville); 2 Concerns of the People write-in (John Heckman); 2 Democratic write-in (Steve Moore); 1 Unaffiliated write-in (John David Sexton).

2006 PRIMARY ELECTIONS

Primary August 8, 2006

Registration
(as of July 14, 2006)

Republican	1,050,766
Democratic	880,627
Libertarian	6,273
Green	4,866
Natural Law	439
American Constitution	332
Reform	279
Gun Owners' Rights	99
Pro Life	57
Unaffiliated	985,489
TOTAL	2,929,227

Primary Type Semi-open—Registered Democrats and Republicans could vote only in their party's primary. "Unaffiliated" voters could participate in either primary but in the process had to declare their affiliation with that party.

COLORADO

GENERAL AND PRIMARY ELECTIONS

Note: An asterisk (*) denotes incumbent. The July 2006 party registration figures add to 2,929,227, but Colorado election officials listed the total as 2,929,278.

	REPUBLICAN PRIMARIES			DEMOCRATIC PRIMARIES		
Governor	Bob Beauprez	193,804	100.0%	Bill Ritter Jr.	142,586	100.0%
Congressional District 1	No Republican candidate			Diana DeGette*	26,000	100.0%
Congressional District 2	Rich Mancuso	15,396	100.0%	Mark Udall*	23,725	100.0%
Congressional District 3	Scott Tipton	28,482	100.0%	John Salazar*	21,871	100.0%
Congressional District 4	Marilyn Musgrave*	32,205	100.0%	Angie Paccione	16,398	100.0%
Congressional District 5	Doug Lamborn	15,126	27.0%	Jay Fawcett	10,238	100.0%
	Jeff Crank	14,234	25.4%			
	Bentley B. Rayburn	9,735	17.4%			
	Lionel Rivera	7,213	12.9%			
	John Wesley Anderson	6,474	11.5%			
	Duncan Bremer	3,310	5.9%			
	TOTAL	56,092				
Congressional District 6	Tom Tancredo*	44,039	100.0%	Bill Winter	18,673	100.0%
Congressional District 7	Rick O'Donnell	20,535	100.0%	Ed Perlmutter	15,598	53.3%
				Peggy Lamm	11,047	37.7%
				Herb Rubenstein	2,625	9.0%
				TOTAL	29,270	

CONNECTICUT

Congressional districts first established for elections held in 2002
5 members

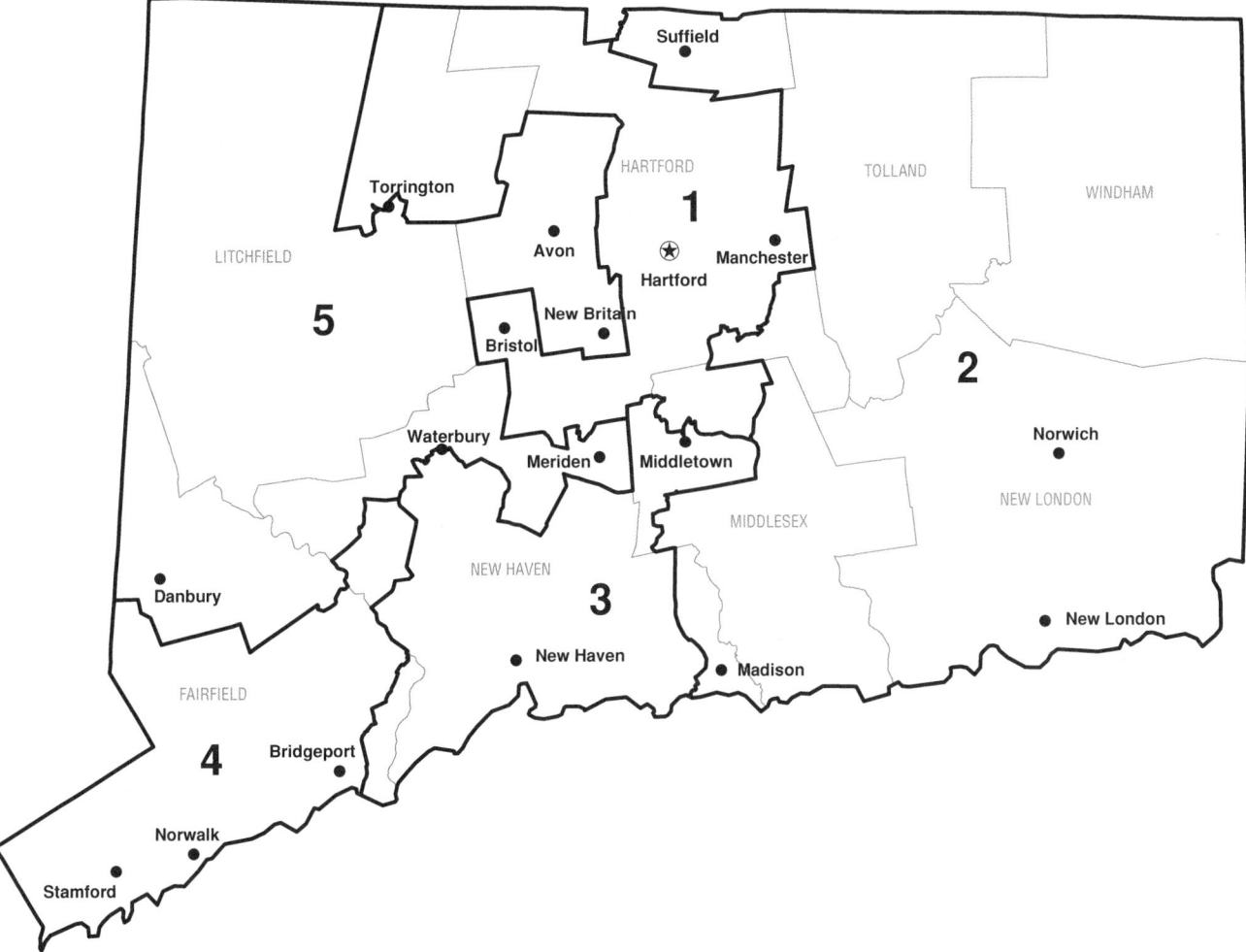

CONNECTICUT

GOVERNOR

M. Jodi Rell (R). Elected 2006 to a four-year term. Assumed office July 1, 2004, following the resignation of John Rowland (R), who was under threat of impeachment for accepting gifts from state employees and contractors.

SENATORS (1 Democrat, 1 Independent Democrat)

Joseph I. Lieberman (ID). Reelected 2006 to a six-year term on the Connecticut for Lieberman ballot line. Previously elected 2000, 1994, and 1988 as a Democrat.

Christopher J. Dodd (D). Reelected 2004 to a six-year term. Previously elected 1998, 1992, 1986, 1980.

REPRESENTATIVES (4 Democrats, 1 Republican)

1. John B. Larson (D)
2. Joe Courtney (D)
3. Rosa DeLauro (D)
4. Christopher Shays (R)
5. Chris Murphy (D)

POSTWAR VOTE FOR PRESIDENT

| Year | Total Vote | Republican | | Democratic | | Other Vote | Plurality | Percentage | | | |
| | | Vote | Candidate | Vote | Candidate | | | Total Vote | | Major Vote | |
								Rep.	Dem.	Rep.	Dem.
2004	1,578,769	693,826	Bush, George W.	857,488	Kerry, John	27,455	163,662 D	43.9%	54.3%	44.7%	55.3%
2000**	1,459,525	561,094	Bush, George W.	816,015	Gore, Al	82,416	254,921 D	38.4%	55.9%	40.7%	59.3%
1996**	1,392,614	483,109	Dole, Bob	735,740	Clinton, Bill	173,765	252,631 D	34.7%	52.8%	39.6%	60.4%
1992**	1,616,332	578,313	Bush, George	682,318	Clinton, Bill	355,701	104,005 D	35.8%	42.2%	45.9%	54.1%
1988	1,443,394	750,241	Bush, George	676,584	Dukakis, Michael S.	16,569	73,657 R	52.0%	46.9%	52.6%	47.4%
1984	1,466,900	890,877	Reagan, Ronald	569,597	Mondale, Walter F.	6,426	321,280 R	60.7%	38.8%	61.0%	39.0%
1980**	1,406,285	677,210	Reagan, Ronald	541,732	Carter, Jimmy	187,343	135,478 R	48.2%	38.5%	55.6%	44.4%
1976	1,381,526	719,261	Ford, Gerald R.	647,895	Carter, Jimmy	14,370	71,366 R	52.1%	46.9%	52.6%	47.4%
1972	1,384,277	810,763	Nixon, Richard M.	555,498	McGovern, George S.	18,016	255,265 R	58.6%	40.1%	59.3%	40.7%
1968**	1,256,232	556,721	Nixon, Richard M.	621,561	Humphrey, Hubert H.	77,950	64,840 D	44.3%	49.5%	47.2%	52.8%
1964	1,218,578	390,996	Goldwater, Barry M.	826,269	Johnson, Lyndon B.	1,313	435,273 D	32.1%	67.8%	32.1%	67.9%
1960	1,222,883	565,813	Nixon, Richard M.	657,055	Kennedy, John F.	15	91,242 D	46.3%	53.7%	46.3%	53.7%
1956	1,117,121	711,837	Eisenhower, Dwight D.	405,079	Stevenson, Adlai E.	205	306,758 R	63.7%	36.3%	63.7%	36.3%
1952	1,096,911	611,012	Eisenhower, Dwight D.	481,649	Stevenson, Adlai E.	4,250	129,363 R	55.7%	43.9%	55.9%	44.1%
1948	883,518	437,754	Dewey, Thomas E.	423,297	Truman, Harry S.	22,467	14,457 R	49.5%	47.9%	50.8%	49.2%

**In past elections, the other vote included: 2000 - 64,452 Green (Ralph Nader); 1996 - 139,523 Reform (Ross Perot); 1992 - 348,771 Independent (Ross Perot); 1980 - 171,807 Independent (John Anderson); 1968 - 76,650 American Independent (George Wallace).

CONNECTICUT

POSTWAR VOTE FOR GOVERNOR

Year	Total Vote	Republican Vote	Republican Candidate	Democratic Vote	Democratic Candidate	Other Vote	Plurality	Total Vote Rep.	Total Vote Dem.	Major Vote Rep.	Major Vote Dem.
2006	1,123,466	710,048	Rell, M. Jodi	398,220	DeStefano, John	15,198	311,828 R	63.2%	35.4%	64.1%	35.9%
2002	1,022,998	573,958	Rowland, John G.	448,984	Curry, Bill	56	124,974 R	56.1%	43.9%	56.1%	43.9%
1998	999,537	628,707	Rowland, John G.	354,187	Kennelly, Barbara B.	16,643	274,520 R	62.9%	35.4%	64.0%	36.0%
1994**	1,147,084	415,201	Rowland, John G.	375,133	Curry, Bill	356,750	40,068 R	36.2%	32.7%	52.5%	47.5%
1990**	1,141,122	427,840	Rowland, John G.	236,641	Morrison, Bruce A.	476,641	32,736 C	37.5%	20.7%	64.4%	35.6%
1986	993,692	408,489	Belaga, Julie D.	575,638	O'Neill, William A.	9,565	167,149 D	41.1%	57.9%	41.5%	58.5%
1982	1,084,156	497,773	Rome, Lewis B.	578,264	O'Neill, William A.	8,119	80,491 D	45.9%	53.3%	46.3%	53.7%
1978	1,036,608	422,316	Sarasin, Ronald A.	613,109	Grasso, Ella T.	1,183	190,793 D	40.7%	59.1%	40.8%	59.2%
1974	1,102,773	440,169	Steele, Robert H.	643,490	Grasso, Ella T.	19,114	203,321 D	39.9%	58.4%	40.6%	59.4%
1970	1,082,797	582,160	Meskill, Thomas J.	500,561	Daddario, Emilio	76	81,599 R	53.8%	46.2%	53.8%	46.2%
1966	1,008,557	446,536	Gengras, E. Clayton	561,599	Dempsey, John N.	422	115,063 D	44.3%	55.7%	44.3%	55.7%
1962	1,031,902	482,852	Alsop, John	549,027	Dempsey, John N.	23	66,175 D	46.8%	53.2%	46.8%	53.2%
1958	974,509	360,644	Zeller, Fred R.	607,012	Ribicoff, Abraham A.	6,853	246,368 D	37.0%	62.3%	37.3%	62.7%
1954	936,753	460,528	Lodge, John D.	463,643	Ribicoff, Abraham A.	12,582	3,115 D	49.2%	49.5%	49.8%	50.2%
1950**	878,735	436,418	Lodge, John D.	419,404	Bowles, Chester	22,913	17,014 R	49.7%	47.7%	51.0%	49.0%
1948	875,170	429,071	Shannon, James C.	431,296	Bowles, Chester	14,803	2,225 D	49.0%	49.3%	49.9%	50.1%
1946	683,831	371,852	McConaughy, J. L.	276,335	Snow, Wilbert	35,644	95,517 R	54.4%	40.4%	57.4%	42.6%

**In past elections, the other vote included: 1994 - 216,585 A Connecticut Party (Elaine Strong Groark); 130,128 Independent (Tom Scott); 1990 - 460,576 A Connecticut Party (Lowell P. Weicker Jr.). Weicker won the 1990 election with 40.4 percent of the total vote. The term of office for Connecticut's governor was increased from two to four years effective with the 1950 election.

POSTWAR VOTE FOR SENATOR

Year	Total Vote	Republican Vote	Republican Candidate	Democratic Vote	Democratic Candidate	Other Vote	Plurality	Total Vote Rep.	Total Vote Dem.	Major Vote Rep.	Major Vote Dem.
2006**	1,134,780	109,198	Schlesinger, Alan	450,844	Lamont, Ned	574,738	113,251 I	9.6%	39.7%	19.5%	80.5%
2004	1,424,726	457,749	Orchulli, Jack	945,347	Dodd, Christopher J.	21,630	487,598 D	32.1%	66.4%	32.6%	67.4%
2000	1,311,261	448,077	Giordano, Philip A.	828,902	Lieberman, Joseph I.	34,282	380,825 D	34.2%	63.2%	35.1%	64.9%
1998	964,457	312,177	Franks, Gary A.	628,306	Dodd, Christopher J.	23,974	316,129 D	32.4%	65.1%	33.2%	66.8%
1994	1,079,767	334,833	Labriola, Jerry	723,842	Lieberman, Joseph I.	21,092	389,009 D	31.0%	67.0%	31.6%	68.4%
1992	1,500,709	572,036	Johnson, Brook	882,569	Dodd, Christopher J.	46,104	310,533 D	38.1%	58.8%	39.3%	60.7%
1988	1,383,526	678,454	Weicker, Lowell P. Jr.	688,499	Lieberman, Joseph I.	16,573	10,045 D	49.0%	49.8%	49.6%	50.4%
1986	976,933	340,438	Eddy, Roger W.	632,695	Dodd, Christopher J.	3,800	292,257 D	34.8%	64.8%	35.0%	65.0%
1982	1,083,613	545,987	Weicker, Lowell P. Jr.	499,146	Moffett, Anthony T.	38,480	46,841 R	50.4%	46.1%	52.2%	47.8%
1980	1,356,075	581,884	Buckley, James L.	763,969	Dodd, Christopher J.	10,222	182,085 D	42.9%	56.3%	43.2%	56.8%
1976	1,361,666	785,683	Weicker, Lowell P. Jr.	561,018	Schaffer, Gloria	14,965	224,665 R	57.7%	41.2%	58.3%	41.7%
1974	1,084,918	372,055	Brannen, James H.	690,820	Ribicoff, Abraham A.	22,043	318,765 D	34.3%	63.7%	35.0%	65.0%
1970**	1,089,353	454,721	Weicker, Lowell P. Jr.	368,111	Duffey, Joseph D.	266,521	86,610 R	41.7%	33.8%	55.3%	44.7%
1968	1,206,537	551,455	May, Edwin H.	655,043	Ribicoff, Abraham A.	39	103,588 D	45.7%	54.3%	45.7%	54.3%
1964	1,208,163	426,939	Lodge, John D.	781,008	Dodd, Thomas J.	216	354,069 D	35.3%	64.6%	35.3%	64.7%
1962	1,029,301	501,694	Seely-Brown, Horace	527,522	Ribicoff, Abraham A.	85	25,828 D	48.7%	51.3%	48.7%	51.3%
1958	965,463	410,622	Purtell, William A.	554,841	Dodd, Thomas J.		144,219 D	42.5%	57.5%	42.5%	57.5%
1956	1,113,819	610,829	Bush, Prescott	479,460	Dodd, Thomas J.	23,530	131,369 R	54.8%	43.0%	56.0%	44.0%
1952	1,093,467	573,854	Purtell, William A.	485,066	Benton, William	34,547	88,788 R	52.5%	44.4%	54.2%	45.8%
1952S	1,093,268	559,465	Bush, Prescott	530,505	Ribicoff, Abraham A.	3,298	28,960 R	51.2%	48.5%	51.3%	48.7%
1950	877,827	409,053	Talbot, Joseph E.	453,646	McMahon, Brien	15,128	44,593 D	46.6%	51.7%	47.4%	52.6%
1950S	877,135	430,311	Bush, Prescott	431,413	Benton, William	15,411	1,102 D	49.1%	49.2%	49.9%	50.1%
1946	682,921	381,328	Baldwin, Raymond	276,424	Tone, Joseph M.	25,169	104,904 R	55.8%	40.5%	58.0%	42.0%

**In past elections, the other vote included: 2006 - 564,095 Connecticut for Lieberman (Joseph I. Lieberman); 1970 - 266,497 Independent (Thomas J. Dodd). Lieberman won the 2006 election with 49.7 percent of the total vote. One each of the 1952 and 1950 elections was for a short term to fill a vacancy.

CONNECTICUT

GOVERNOR 2006

2000 Census Population	County	Total Vote	Republican	Democratic	Other	Rep.-Dem. Plurality	Percentage			
							Total Vote		Major Vote	
							Rep.	Dem.	Rep.	Dem.
882,567	FAIRFIELD	269,293	185,037	81,676	2,580	103,361 R	68.7%	30.3%	69.4%	30.6%
857,183	HARTFORD	284,448	165,660	114,824	3,964	50,836 R	58.2%	40.4%	59.1%	40.9%
182,193	LITCHFIELD	70,764	49,368	20,358	1,038	29,010 R	69.8%	28.8%	70.8%	29.2%
155,071	MIDDLESEX	64,210	39,509	23,783	918	15,726 R	61.5%	37.0%	62.4%	37.6%
824,008	NEW HAVEN	258,685	161,350	93,822	3,513	67,528 R	62.4%	36.3%	63.2%	36.8%
259,088	NEW LONDON	87,416	54,469	31,623	1,324	22,846 R	62.3%	36.2%	63.3%	36.7%
136,364	TOLLAND	53,792	33,648	19,172	972	14,476 R	62.6%	35.6%	63.7%	36.3%
109,091	WINDHAM	34,804	21,007	12,962	835	8,045 R	60.4%	37.2%	61.8%	38.2%
3,405,565	TOTAL	1,123,466	710,048	398,220	15,198	311,828 R	63.2%	35.4%	64.1%	35.9%

Note: There were 54 write-in votes for John M. Joy that were not broken down by county but are included in the statewide totals.

	City/Town									
18,554	ANSONIA	5,258	3,441	1,766	51	1,675 R	65.4%	33.6%	66.1%	33.9%
19,587	BLOOMFIELD	7,796	3,358	4,329	109	971 D	43.1%	55.5%	43.7%	56.3%
28,683	BRANFORD	10,939	7,068	3,758	113	3,310 R	64.6%	34.4%	65.3%	34.7%
139,529	BRIDGEPORT	19,954	8,366	11,267	321	2,901 D	41.9%	56.5%	42.6%	57.4%
60,062	BRISTOL	18,081	11,129	6,741	211	4,388 R	61.6%	37.3%	62.3%	37.7%
28,543	CHESHIRE	11,747	8,149	3,483	115	4,666 R	69.4%	29.7%	70.1%	29.9%
74,848	DANBURY	15,858	10,954	4,715	189	6,239 R	69.1%	29.7%	69.9%	30.1%
19,607	DARIEN	7,693	6,299	1,344	50	4,955 R	81.9%	17.5%	82.4%	17.6%
49,575	EAST HARTFORD	12,368	6,517	5,690	161	827 R	52.7%	46.0%	53.4%	46.6%
28,289	EAST HAVEN	8,353	5,703	2,582	68	3,121 R	68.3%	30.9%	68.8%	31.2%
45,212	ENFIELD	14,039	8,889	4,950	200	3,939 R	63.3%	35.3%	64.2%	35.8%
57,340	FAIRFIELD	21,839	15,684	5,977	178	9,707 R	71.8%	27.4%	72.4%	27.6%
23,641	FARMINGTON	10,628	6,806	3,708	114	3,098 R	64.0%	34.9%	64.7%	35.3%
31,876	GLASTONBURY	14,999	9,728	5,048	223	4,680 R	64.9%	33.7%	65.8%	34.2%
61,101	GREENWICH	20,427	14,552	5,693	182	8,859 R	71.2%	27.9%	71.9%	28.1%
39,907	GROTON	10,255	6,443	3,673	139	2,770 R	62.8%	35.8%	63.7%	36.3%
21,398	GUILFORD	9,767	6,551	3,107	109	3,444 R	67.1%	31.8%	67.8%	32.2%
56,913	HAMDEN	19,701	10,940	8,509	252	2,431 R	55.5%	43.2%	56.2%	43.8%
121,578	HARTFORD	15,163	4,477	10,263	423	5,786 D	29.5%	67.7%	30.4%	69.6%
54,740	MANCHESTER	17,841	10,839	6,685	317	4,154 R	60.8%	37.5%	61.9%	38.1%
20,720	MANSFIELD	6,184	2,669	3,248	267	579 D	43.2%	52.5%	45.1%	54.9%
58,244	MERIDEN	15,178	8,514	6,403	261	2,111 R	56.1%	42.2%	57.1%	42.9%
43,167	MIDDLETOWN	14,082	7,378	6,374	330	1,004 R	52.4%	45.3%	53.7%	46.3%
52,305	MILFORD	18,962	13,171	5,586	205	7,585 R	69.5%	29.5%	70.2%	29.8%
30,989	NAUGATUCK	8,380	5,833	2,430	117	3,403 R	69.6%	29.0%	70.6%	29.4%
71,538	NEW BRITAIN	13,570	6,332	6,975	263	643 D	46.7%	51.4%	47.6%	52.4%
123,626	NEW HAVEN	25,538	8,274	16,589	675	8,315 D	32.4%	65.0%	33.3%	66.7%
25,671	NEW LONDON	5,346	2,324	2,775	247	451 D	43.5%	51.9%	45.6%	54.4%
27,121	NEW MILFORD	9,119	7,012	2,019	88	4,993 R	76.9%	22.1%	77.6%	22.4%
29,306	NEWINGTON	11,783	6,801	4,849	133	1,952 R	57.7%	41.2%	58.4%	41.6%
25,031	NEWTOWN	10,626	8,133	2,382	111	5,751 R	76.5%	22.4%	77.3%	22.7%
23,035	NORTH HAVEN	9,981	6,861	3,029	91	3,832 R	68.7%	30.3%	69.4%	30.6%
82,951	NORWALK	22,634	13,967	8,442	225	5,525 R	61.7%	37.3%	62.3%	37.7%
36,117	NORWICH	9,052	5,210	3,712	130	1,498 R	57.6%	41.0%	58.4%	41.6%
23,643	RIDGEFIELD	9,689	7,105	2,513	71	4,592 R	73.3%	25.9%	73.9%	26.1%
38,101	SHELTON	14,064	10,470	3,457	137	7,013 R	74.4%	24.6%	75.2%	24.8%
23,234	SIMSBURY	11,171	7,112	3,949	110	3,163 R	63.7%	35.4%	64.3%	35.7%
24,412	SOUTH WINDSOR	10,592	6,752	3,739	101	3,013 R	63.7%	35.3%	64.4%	35.6%
39,728	SOUTHINGTON	16,883	11,249	5,433	201	5,816 R	66.6%	32.2%	67.4%	32.6%
117,083	STAMFORD	30,947	19,524	11,081	342	8,443 R	63.1%	35.8%	63.8%	36.2%
49,976	STRATFORD	15,752	11,053	4,555	144	6,498 R	70.2%	28.9%	70.8%	29.2%
35,202	TORRINGTON	10,999	7,586	3,247	166	4,339 R	69.0%	29.5%	70.0%	30.0%
34,243	TRUMBULL	14,076	10,538	3,428	110	7,110 R	74.9%	24.4%	75.5%	24.5%
28,063	VERNON	10,093	6,573	3,385	135	3,188 R	65.1%	33.5%	66.0%	34.0%
43,026	WALLINGFORD	15,857	10,589	5,097	171	5,492 R	66.8%	32.1%	67.5%	32.5%

CONNECTICUT

GOVERNOR 2006

2000 Census Population	City/Town	Total Vote	Republican	Democratic	Other	Rep.-Dem. Plurality	Percentage			
							Total Vote		Major Vote	
							Rep.	Dem.	Rep.	Dem.
107,271	WATERBURY	20,938	12,468	8,019	451	4,449 R	59.5%	38.3%	60.9%	39.1%
21,661	WATERTOWN	8,029	5,731	2,166	132	3,565 R	71.4%	27.0%	72.6%	27.4%
63,589	WEST HARTFORD	25,588	13,535	11,650	403	1,885 R	52.9%	45.5%	53.7%	46.3%
52,360	WEST HAVEN	14,343	8,265	5,916	162	2,349 R	57.6%	41.2%	58.3%	41.7%
25,749	WESTPORT	11,747	7,531	4,151	65	3,380 R	64.1%	35.3%	64.5%	35.5%
26,271	WETHERSFIELD	11,409	6,597	4,679	133	1,918 R	57.8%	41.0%	58.5%	41.5%
22,857	WINDHAM	5,667	2,872	2,449	346	423 R	50.7%	43.2%	54.0%	46.0%
28,237	WINDSOR	10,620	5,685	4,770	165	915 R	53.5%	44.9%	54.4%	45.6%

CONNECTICUT

SENATOR 2006

2000 Census Population	County	Total Vote	Republican	Democratic	Independent (Lieberman)	Other	Plurality	Percentage of Total Vote		
								Rep.	Dem.	Ind.
882,567	FAIRFIELD	272,592	24,659	105,792	140,174	1,967	34,382 I	9.0%	38.8%	51.4%
857,183	HARTFORD	287,097	27,456	124,914	131,950	2,777	7,036 I	9.6%	43.5%	46.0%
182,193	LITCHFIELD	71,699	9,139	25,877	35,864	819	9,987 I	12.7%	36.1%	50.0%
155,071	MIDDLESEX	64,519	6,147	26,768	31,012	592	4,244 I	9.5%	41.5%	48.1%
824,008	NEW HAVEN	261,491	24,650	94,848	139,481	2,512	44,633 I	9.4%	36.3%	53.3%
259,088	NEW LONDON	88,321	7,830	34,713	44,943	835	10,230 I	8.9%	39.3%	50.9%
136,364	TOLLAND	53,944	5,733	23,390	24,187	634	797 I	10.6%	43.4%	44.8%
109,091	WINDHAM	35,034	3,584	14,542	16,484	424	1,942 I	10.2%	41.5%	47.1%
3,405,565	TOTAL	1,134,780	109,198	450,844	564,095	10,643	113,251 I	9.6%	39.7%	49.7%

Note: There were 80 write-in votes for Carl E. Vassar and 3 write-in votes for John M. Joy that were not broken down by county but are included in the statewide totals.

	City/Town									
18,554	ANSONIA	5,247	658	1,729	2,811	49	1,082 I	12.5%	33.0%	53.6%
19,587	BLOOMFIELD	8,040	474	4,270	3,228	68	1,042 D	5.9%	53.1%	40.1%
28,683	BRANFORD	11,053	927	4,151	5,908	67	1,757 I	8.4%	37.6%	53.5%
139,529	BRIDGEPORT	20,676	1,476	12,038	6,935	227	5,103 D	7.1%	58.2%	33.5%
60,062	BRISTOL	18,200	1,929	7,396	8,687	188	1,291 I	10.6%	40.6%	47.7%
28,543	CHESHIRE	11,832	1,199	3,780	6,772	81	2,992 I	10.1%	31.9%	57.2%
74,848	DANBURY	15,907	1,820	6,655	7,234	198	579 I	11.4%	41.8%	45.5%
19,607	DARIEN	7,840	858	2,225	4,723	34	2,498 I	10.9%	28.4%	60.2%
49,575	EAST HARTFORD	12,398	1,012	5,858	5,400	128	458 D	8.2%	47.2%	43.6%
28,289	EAST HAVEN	8,511	753	2,664	5,026	68	2,362 I	8.8%	31.3%	59.1%
45,212	ENFIELD	14,251	1,584	5,961	6,532	174	571 I	11.1%	41.8%	45.8%
57,340	FAIRFIELD	22,091	1,731	8,041	12,158	161	4,117 I	7.8%	36.4%	55.0%
23,641	FARMINGTON	10,754	1,158	4,378	5,117	101	739 I	10.8%	40.7%	47.6%
31,876	GLASTONBURY	15,028	1,453	6,056	7,414	105	1,358 I	9.7%	40.3%	49.3%
61,101	GREENWICH	21,307	1,817	8,258	11,160	72	2,902 I	8.5%	38.8%	52.4%
39,907	GROTON	10,404	887	3,989	5,452	76	1,463 I	8.5%	38.3%	52.4%
21,398	GUILFORD	9,887	731	3,909	5,170	77	1,261 I	7.4%	39.5%	52.3%
56,913	HAMDEN	19,904	1,276	8,294	10,170	164	1,876 I	6.4%	41.7%	51.1%
121,578	HARTFORD	15,704	567	10,521	4,456	160	6,065 D	3.6%	67.0%	28.4%
54,740	MANCHESTER	18,003	1,786	7,970	8,042	205	72 I	9.9%	44.3%	44.7%
20,720	MANSFIELD	6,227	319	3,806	2,017	85	1,789 D	5.1%	61.1%	32.4%
58,244	MERIDEN	15,790	1,376	6,915	7,315	184	400 I	8.7%	43.8%	46.3%
43,167	MIDDLETOWN	14,072	1,149	7,067	5,678	178	1,389 D	8.2%	50.2%	40.3%
52,305	MILFORD	18,789	1,897	6,134	10,577	181	4,443 I	10.1%	32.6%	56.3%
30,989	NAUGATUCK	8,483	1,045	2,507	4,825	106	2,318 I	12.3%	29.6%	56.9%

CONNECTICUT

SENATOR 2006

2000 Census Population	City/Town	Total Vote	Republican	Democratic	Independent (Lieberman)	Other	Plurality	Percentage of Total Vote		
								Rep.	Dem.	Ind.
71,538	NEW BRITAIN	13,866	1,126	7,344	5,224	172	2,120 D	8.1%	53.0%	37.7%
123,626	NEW HAVEN	25,453	861	14,331	9,937	324	4,394 D	3.4%	56.3%	39.0%
25,671	NEW LONDON	5,504	390	2,787	2,228	99	559 D	7.1%	50.6%	40.5%
27,121	NEW MILFORD	9,126	1,051	3,220	4,756	99	1,536 I	11.5%	35.3%	52.1%
29,306	NEWINGTON	11,812	1,128	4,961	5,596	127	635 I	9.5%	42.0%	47.4%
25,031	NEWTOWN	10,654	946	3,531	6,083	94	2,552 I	8.9%	33.1%	57.1%
23,035	NORTH HAVEN	10,025	1,037	3,056	5,837	95	2,781 I	10.3%	30.5%	58.2%
82,951	NORWALK	22,815	2,079	10,341	10,223	172	118 D	9.1%	45.3%	44.8%
36,117	NORWICH	9,210	617	3,680	4,813	100	1,133 I	6.7%	40.0%	52.3%
23,643	RIDGEFIELD	9,890	859	3,666	5,320	45	1,654 I	8.7%	37.1%	53.8%
38,101	SHELTON	14,047	1,808	4,105	8,018	116	3,913 I	12.9%	29.2%	57.1%
23,234	SIMSBURY	11,190	1,202	4,134	5,760	94	1,626 I	10.7%	36.9%	51.5%
24,412	SOUTH WINDSOR	10,613	959	4,436	5,138	80	702 I	9.0%	41.8%	48.4%
39,728	SOUTHINGTON	16,797	1,700	6,101	8,806	190	2,705 I	10.1%	36.3%	52.4%
117,083	STAMFORD	31,387	2,241	13,409	15,514	223	2,105 I	7.1%	42.7%	49.4%
49,976	STRATFORD	15,380	1,646	5,546	8,049	139	2,503 I	10.7%	36.1%	52.3%
35,202	TORRINGTON	11,577	1,681	3,850	5,904	142	2,054 I	14.5%	33.3%	51.0%
34,243	TRUMBULL	14,174	1,449	4,349	8,265	111	3,916 I	10.2%	30.7%	58.3%
28,063	VERNON	10,086	1,079	4,185	4,717	105	532 I	10.7%	41.5%	46.8%
43,026	WALLINGFORD	15,962	1,463	5,577	8,769	153	3,192 I	9.2%	34.9%	54.9%
107,271	WATERBURY	21,639	2,682	7,354	11,296	307	3,942 I	12.4%	34.0%	52.2%
21,661	WATERTOWN	8,029	1,252	2,269	4,408	100	2,139 I	15.6%	28.3%	54.9%
63,589	WEST HARTFORD	25,928	2,096	11,316	12,324	192	1,008 I	8.1%	43.6%	47.5%
52,360	WEST HAVEN	14,530	1,242	5,136	8,033	119	2,897 I	8.5%	35.3%	55.3%
25,749	WESTPORT	12,042	694	5,081	6,229	38	1,148 I	5.8%	42.2%	51.7%
26,271	WETHERSFIELD	11,422	1,147	4,689	5,484	102	795 I	10.0%	41.1%	48.0%
22,857	WINDHAM	5,662	475	2,839	2,258	90	581 D	8.4%	50.1%	39.9%
28,237	WINDSOR	10,808	1,012	5,185	4,490	121	695 D	9.4%	48.0%	41.5%

CONNECTICUT

HOUSE OF REPRESENTATIVES

| CD | Year | Total Vote | Republican | | Democratic | | Other Vote | Rep.-Dem. Plurality | Percentage | | | |
| | | | Vote | Candidate | Vote | Candidate | | | Total Vote | | Major Vote | |
									Rep.	Dem.	Rep.	Dem.
1	2006	207,592	53,010	MacLEAN, SCOTT	154,539	LARSON, JOHN B.*	43	101,529 D	25.5%	74.4%	25.5%	74.5%
1	2004	272,403	73,601	HALSTEAD, JOHN M.	198,802	LARSON, JOHN B.*		125,201 D	27.0%	73.0%	27.0%	73.0%
1	2002	201,688	66,968	STEELE, PHIL	134,698	LARSON, JOHN B.*	22	67,730 D	33.2%	66.8%	33.2%	66.8%
2	2006	242,413	121,165	SIMMONS, ROB*	121,248	COURTNEY, JOE		83 D	50.0%	50.0%	50.0%	50.0%
2	2004	307,078	166,412	SIMMONS, ROB*	140,536	SULLIVAN, JIM	130	25,876 R	54.2%	45.8%	54.2%	45.8%
2	2002	217,108	117,434	SIMMONS, ROB*	99,674	COURTNEY, JOE		17,760 R	54.1%	45.9%	54.1%	45.9%
3	2006	197,911	44,386	VOLLANO, JOSEPH	150,436	DeLAURO, ROSA*	3,089	106,050 D	22.4%	76.0%	22.8%	77.2%
3	2004	276,980	69,160	ELSER, RICHTER	200,638	DeLAURO, ROSA*	7,182	131,478 D	25.0%	72.4%	25.6%	74.4%
3	2002	185,364	54,757	ELSER, RICHTER	121,557	DeLAURO, ROSA*	9,050	66,800 D	29.5%	65.6%	31.1%	68.9%
4	2006	209,019	106,510	SHAYS, CHRISTOPHER*	99,450	FARRELL, DIANE	3,059	7,060 R	51.0%	47.6%	51.7%	48.3%
4	2004	290,830	152,493	SHAYS, CHRISTOPHER*	138,333	FARRELL, DIANE	4	14,160 R	52.4%	47.6%	52.4%	47.6%
4	2002	175,695	113,197	SHAYS, CHRISTOPHER*	62,491	SANCHEZ, STEPHANIE H.	7	50,706 R	64.4%	35.6%	64.4%	35.6%
5	2006	217,804	94,824	JOHNSON, NANCY L.*	122,980	MURPHY, CHRIS		28,156 D	43.5%	56.5%	43.5%	56.5%
5	2004	281,447	168,268	JOHNSON, NANCY L.*	107,438	GERRATANA, THERESA B.	5,741	60,830 R	59.8%	38.2%	61.0%	39.0%
5	2002	209,454	113,626	JOHNSON, NANCY L.*	90,616	MALONEY, JIM*	5,212	23,010 R	54.2%	43.3%	55.6%	44.4%
TOTAL	2006	1,074,739	419,895		648,653		6,191	228,758 D	39.1%	60.4%	39.3%	60.7%
TOTAL	2004	1,428,738	629,934		785,747			155,813 D	44.1%	55.0%	44.5%	55.5%
TOTAL	2002	989,309	465,982		509,036		14,291	43,054 D	47.1%	51.5%	47.8%	52.2%

An asterisk (*) denotes incumbent.

CONNECTICUT

GENERAL AND PRIMARY ELECTIONS

2006 GENERAL ELECTIONS

Governor Other vote was 9,584 Green (Clifford W. Thornton); 5,560 Concerned Citizens (Joseph A. Zdonczyk); 54 write-in (John M. Joy).

Senator Other vote was 5,922 Green (Ralph A. Ferrucci); 4,638 Concerned Citizens (Timothy A. Knibbs); 80 write-in (Carl E. Vassar); 3 write-in (John M. Joy). Joseph I. Lieberman with 564,095 votes ran and won as an independent on the ballot line, Connecticut for Lieberman.

House Other vote was:

CD 1 43 write-in (Stephen Fournier).
CD 2
CD 3 3,089 Green (Daniel A. Sumrall).
CD 4 3,058 Libertarian (Philip Z. Maymin); 1 Green (Vacancy in Nomination).
CD 5 Democrat Chris Murphy received 5,794 votes on the Working Families ballot line that was included in his total vote.

CONNECTICUT

GENERAL AND PRIMARY ELECTIONS

2006 PRIMARY ELECTIONS

Primary   August 8, 2006   **Registration**
(active registrants as of February 2006)

Democratic	652,048
Republican	428,639
Other Parties	6,066
Unaffiliated	870,725
TOTAL	1,957,478

Primary Type   Closed—Only registered Democrats and Republicans could vote in their party's primary.

Note: An asterisk (*) denotes incumbent. A Senate or House candidate had to receive at least 15 percent of the vote in a pre-primary convention to force a primary or petition to appear on the primary ballot.

	REPUBLICAN PRIMARIES			DEMOCRATIC PRIMARIES		
Governor	M. Jodi Rell*	Nominated by convention		John DeStefano	135,431	50.8%
				Dan Malloy	131,258	49.2%
				TOTAL	266,689	
Senator	Alan Schlesinger	Nominated by convention		Ned Lamont	146,404	51.8%
				Joseph I. Lieberman*	136,490	48.2%
				TOTAL	282,894	
Congressional District 1	Scott MacLean	1,998	63.5%	John B. Larson*	Nominated by convention	
	Miriam J. Masullo	1,148	36.5%			
	TOTAL	3,146				
Congressional District 2	Rob Simmons*	Nominated by convention		Joe Courtney	Nominated by convention	
Congressional District 3	Joseph Vollano	Nominated by convention		Rosa DeLauro*	Nominated by convention	
Congressional District 4	Christopher Shays*	Nominated by convention		Diane Farrell	Nominated by convention	
Congressional District 5	Nancy L. Johnson*	Nominated by convention		Chris Murphy	Nominated by convention	

DELAWARE

One member At Large

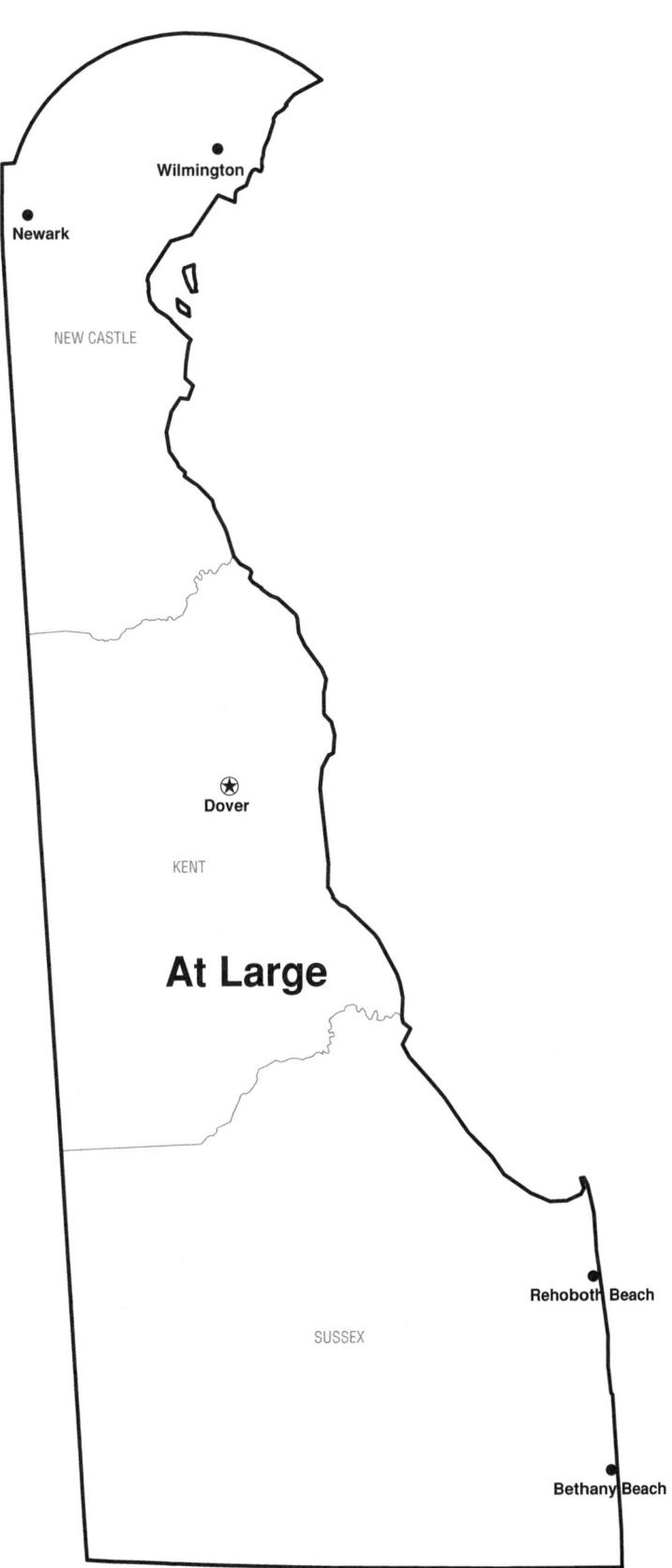

Wilmington

Newark

NEW CASTLE

Dover

KENT

At Large

Rehoboth Beach

SUSSEX

Bethany Beach

DELAWARE

GOVERNOR
Ruth Ann Minner (D). Reelected 2004 to a four-year term. Previously elected 2000.

SENATORS (2 Democrats)
Thomas R. Carper (D). Reelected 2006 to a six-year term. Previously elected 2000.

Joseph R. Biden Jr. (D). Reelected 2002 to a six-year term. Previously elected 1996, 1990, 1984, 1978, 1972.

REPRESENTATIVE (1 Republican)
At Large. Michael N. Castle (R)

POSTWAR VOTE FOR PRESIDENT

| | | Republican | | Democratic | | Other | | Percentage | | | |
| | Total | | | | | | | Total Vote | | Major Vote | |
Year	Vote	Vote	Candidate	Vote	Candidate	Vote	Plurality	Rep.	Dem.	Rep.	Dem.
2004	375,190	171,660	Bush, George W.	200,152	Kerry, John	3,378	28,492 D	45.8%	53.3%	46.2%	53.8%
2000**	327,622	137,288	Bush, George W.	180,068	Gore, Al	10,266	42,780 D	41.9%	55.0%	43.3%	56.7%
1996**	271,084	99,062	Dole, Bob	140,355	Clinton, Bill	31,667	41,293 D	36.5%	51.8%	41.4%	58.6%
1992**	289,735	102,313	Bush, George	126,054	Clinton, Bill	61,368	23,741 D	35.3%	43.5%	44.8%	55.2%
1988	249,891	139,639	Bush, George	108,647	Dukakis, Michael S.	1,605	30,992 R	55.9%	43.5%	56.2%	43.8%
1984	254,572	152,190	Reagan, Ronald	101,656	Mondale, Walter F.	726	50,534 R	59.8%	39.9%	60.0%	40.0%
1980**	235,900	111,252	Reagan, Ronald	105,754	Carter, Jimmy	18,894	5,498 R	47.2%	44.8%	51.3%	48.7%
1976	235,834	109,831	Ford, Gerald R.	122,596	Carter, Jimmy	3,407	12,765 D	46.6%	52.0%	47.3%	52.7%
1972	235,516	140,357	Nixon, Richard M.	92,283	McGovern, George S.	2,876	48,074 R	59.6%	39.2%	60.3%	39.7%
1968**	214,367	96,714	Nixon, Richard M.	89,194	Humphrey, Hubert H.	28,459	7,520 R	45.1%	41.6%	52.0%	48.0%
1964	201,320	78,078	Goldwater, Barry M.	122,704	Johnson, Lyndon B.	538	44,626 D	38.8%	60.9%	38.9%	61.1%
1960	196,683	96,373	Nixon, Richard M.	99,590	Kennedy, John F.	720	3,217 D	49.0%	50.6%	49.2%	50.8%
1956	177,988	98,057	Eisenhower, Dwight D.	79,421	Stevenson, Adlai E.	510	18,636 R	55.1%	44.6%	55.3%	44.7%
1952	174,025	90,059	Eisenhower, Dwight D.	83,315	Stevenson, Adlai E.	651	6,744 R	51.8%	47.9%	51.9%	48.1%
1948	139,073	69,588	Dewey, Thomas E.	67,813	Truman, Harry S.	1,672	1,775 R	50.0%	48.8%	50.6%	49.4%

**In past elections, the other vote included: 2000 - 8,307 Green (Ralph Nader); 1996 - 28,719 Reform (Ross Perot); 1992 - 59,213 Independent (Ross Perot); 1980 - 16,288 Independent (John Anderson); 1968 - 28,459 American Independent (George Wallace).

POSTWAR VOTE FOR GOVERNOR

| | | Republican | | Democratic | | Other | Rep.-Dem. | Percentage | | | |
| | Total | | | | | | | Total Vote | | Major Vote | |
Year	Vote	Vote	Candidate	Vote	Candidate	Vote	Plurality	Rep.	Dem.	Rep.	Dem.
2004	365,008	167,115	Lee, William Swain	185,687	Minner, Ruth Ann	12,206	18,572 D	45.8%	50.9%	47.4%	52.6%
2000	323,688	128,603	Burris, John M.	191,695	Minner, Ruth Ann	3,390	63,092 D	39.7%	59.2%	40.2%	59.8%
1996	271,122	82,654	Rzewnicki, Janet	188,300	Carper, Thomas R.	168	105,646 D	30.5%	69.5%	30.5%	69.5%
1992	277,058	90,725	Scott, B. Gary	179,365	Carper, Thomas R.	6,968	88,640 D	32.7%	64.7%	33.6%	66.4%
1988	239,969	169,733	Castle, Michael N.	70,236	Kreshtoll, Jacob		99,497 R	70.7%	29.3%	70.7%	29.3%
1984	243,565	135,250	Castle, Michael N.	108,315	Quillen, William T.		26,935 R	55.5%	44.5%	55.5%	44.5%
1980	225,081	159,004	duPont, Pierre	64,217	Gordy, William J.	1,860	94,787 R	70.6%	28.5%	71.2%	28.8%
1976	229,563	130,531	duPont, Pierre	97,480	Tribbitt, Sherman W.	1,552	33,051 R	56.9%	42.5%	57.2%	42.8%
1972	228,722	109,583	Peterson, Russell W.	117,274	Tribbitt, Sherman W.	1,865	7,691 D	47.9%	51.3%	48.3%	51.7%
1968	206,834	104,474	Peterson, Russell W.	102,360	Terry, Charles L.		2,114 R	50.5%	49.5%	50.5%	49.5%
1964	200,171	97,374	Buckson, David P.	102,797	Terry, Charles L.		5,423 D	48.6%	51.4%	48.6%	51.4%
1960	194,835	94,043	Rollins, John W.	100,792	Carvel, Elbert N.		6,749 D	48.3%	51.7%	48.3%	51.7%
1956	177,012	91,965	Boggs, J. Caleb	85,047	McConnell, J. H. T.		6,918 R	52.0%	48.0%	52.0%	48.0%
1952	170,749	88,977	Boggs, J. Caleb	81,772	Carvel, Elbert N.		7,205 R	52.1%	47.9%	52.1%	47.9%
1948	140,335	64,996	George, Hyland P.	75,339	Carvel, Elbert N.		10,343 D	46.3%	53.7%	46.3%	53.7%

DELAWARE

POSTWAR VOTE FOR SENATOR

Year	Total Vote	Republican Vote	Republican Candidate	Democratic Vote	Democratic Candidate	Other Vote	Rep.-Dem. Plurality	Total Vote Rep.	Total Vote Dem.	Major Vote Rep.	Major Vote Dem.
2006	254,099	69,734	Ting, Jan	170,567	Carper, Thomas R.	13,798	100,833 D	27.4%	67.1%	29.0%	71.0%
2002	232,314	94,793	Clatworthy, Raymond J.	135,253	Biden, Joseph R. Jr.	2,268	40,460 D	40.8%	58.2%	41.2%	58.8%
2000	327,017	142,891	Roth, William V.	181,566	Carper, Thomas R.	2,560	38,675 D	43.7%	55.5%	44.0%	56.0%
1996	275,605	105,088	Clatworthy, Raymond J.	165,465	Biden, Joseph R. Jr.	5,052	60,377 D	38.1%	60.0%	38.8%	61.2%
1994	199,029	111,088	Roth, William V.	84,554	Oberly, Charles M.	3,387	26,534 R	55.8%	42.5%	56.8%	43.2%
1990	180,152	64,554	Brady, M. Jane	112,918	Biden, Joseph R. Jr.	2,680	48,364 D	35.8%	62.7%	36.4%	63.6%
1988	243,493	151,115	Roth, William V.	92,378	Woo, S. B.		58,737 R	62.1%	37.9%	62.1%	37.9%
1984	245,932	98,101	Burris, John M.	147,831	Biden, Joseph R. Jr.		49,730 D	39.9%	60.1%	39.9%	60.1%
1982	190,960	105,357	Roth, William V.	84,413	Levinson, David N.	1,190	20,944 R	55.2%	44.2%	55.5%	44.5%
1978	162,072	66,479	Baxter, James H.	93,930	Biden, Joseph R. Jr.	1,663	27,451 D	41.0%	58.0%	41.4%	58.6%
1976	224,859	125,502	Roth, William V.	98,055	Maloney, Thomas C.	1,302	27,447 R	55.8%	43.6%	56.1%	43.9%
1972	229,828	112,844	Boggs, J. Caleb	116,006	Biden, Joseph R. Jr.	978	3,162 D	49.1%	50.5%	49.3%	50.7%
1970	161,439	94,979	Roth, William V.	64,740	Zimmerman, Jacob	1,720	30,239 R	58.8%	40.1%	59.5%	40.5%
1966	164,549	97,268	Boggs, J. Caleb	67,281	Tunnell, James M. Jr.		29,987 R	59.1%	40.9%	59.1%	40.9%
1964	200,703	103,782	Williams, John J.	96,850	Carvel, Elbert N.	71	6,932 R	51.7%	48.3%	51.7%	48.3%
1960	194,964	98,874	Boggs, J. Caleb	96,090	Frear, J. Allen		2,784 R	50.7%	49.3%	50.7%	49.3%
1958	154,432	82,280	Williams, John J.	72,152	Carvel, Elbert N.		10,128 R	53.3%	46.7%	53.3%	46.7%
1954	144,900	62,389	Warburton, H. B.	82,511	Frear, J. Allen		20,122 D	43.1%	56.9%	43.1%	56.9%
1952	170,705	93,020	Williams, John J.	77,685	Bayard, A. I. duP.		15,335 R	54.5%	45.5%	54.5%	45.5%
1948	141,362	68,246	Buck, C. Douglas	71,888	Frear, J. Allen	1,228	3,642 D	48.3%	50.9%	48.7%	51.3%
1946	113,513	62,603	Williams, John J.	50,910	Tunnell, James M.		11,693 R	55.2%	44.8%	55.2%	44.8%

DELAWARE

SENATOR 2006

2000 Census Population	County	Total Vote	Republican	Democratic	Other	Rep.-Dem. Plurality	Total Vote Rep.	Total Vote Dem.	Major Vote Rep.	Major Vote Dem.
126,697	KENT	38,427	13,191	23,492	1,744	10,301 D	34.3%	61.1%	36.0%	64.0%
500,265	NEW CASTLE	159,459	39,655	115,769	4,035	76,114 D	24.9%	72.6%	25.5%	74.5%
156,638	SUSSEX	56,213	16,888	31,306	8,019	14,418 D	30.0%	55.7%	35.0%	65.0%
783,600	TOTAL	254,099	69,734	170,567	13,798	100,833 D	27.4%	67.1%	29.0%	71.0%

DELAWARE

HOUSE OF REPRESENTATIVES

CD	Year	Total Vote	Republican Vote	Republican Candidate	Democratic Vote	Democratic Candidate	Other Vote	Rep.-Dem. Plurality	Percentage Total Vote Rep.	Total Vote Dem.	Major Vote Rep.	Major Vote Dem.
AL	2006	251,694	143,897	CASTLE, MICHAEL N.*	97,565	SPIVACK, DENNIS	10,232	46,332 R	57.2%	38.8%	59.6%	40.4%
AL	2004	356,045	245,978	CASTLE, MICHAEL N.*	105,716	DONNELLY, PAUL	4,351	140,262 R	69.1%	29.7%	69.9%	30.1%
AL	2002	228,405	164,605	CASTLE, MICHAEL N.*	61,011	MILLER, MICHEAL C.	2,789	103,594 R	72.1%	26.7%	73.0%	27.0%
AL	2000	313,126	211,797	CASTLE, MICHAEL N.*	96,488	MILLER, MICHEAL C.	4,841	115,309 R	67.6%	30.8%	68.7%	31.3%
AL	1998	180,527	119,811	CASTLE, MICHAEL N.*	57,446	WILLIAMS, DENNIS E.	3,270	62,365 R	66.4%	31.8%	67.6%	32.4%
AL	1996	266,836	185,576	CASTLE, MICHAEL N.*	73,253	WILLIAMS, DENNIS E.	8,007	112,323 R	69.5%	27.5%	71.7%	28.3%
AL	1994	195,037	137,960	CASTLE, MICHAEL N.*	51,803	DESANTIS, CAROL ANN	5,274	86,157 R	70.7%	26.6%	72.7%	27.3%
AL	1992	276,157	153,037	CASTLE, MICHAEL N.	117,426	WOO, S. B.	5,694	35,611 R	55.4%	42.5%	56.6%	43.4%
AL	1990	177,432	58,037	WILLIAMS, RALPH O.	116,274	CARPER, THOMAS R.*	3,121	58,237 D	32.7%	65.5%	33.3%	66.7%
AL	1988	234,517	76,179	KRAPF, JAMES P.	158,338	CARPER, THOMAS R.*		82,159 D	32.5%	67.5%	32.5%	67.5%
AL	1986	160,757	53,767	NEUBERGER, THOMAS S.	106,351	CARPER, THOMAS R.*	639	52,584 D	33.4%	66.2%	33.6%	66.4%
AL	1984	243,014	100,650	duPONT, ELISE	142,070	CARPER, THOMAS R.*	294	41,420 D	41.4%	58.5%	41.5%	58.5%
AL	1982	188,064	87,153	EVANS, THOMAS B.*	98,533	CARPER, THOMAS R.	2,378	11,380 D	46.3%	52.4%	46.9%	53.1%
AL	1980	216,629	133,842	EVANS, THOMAS B.*	81,227	MAXWELL, ROBERT L.	1,560	52,615 R	61.8%	37.5%	62.2%	37.8%
AL	1978	157,566	91,689	EVANS, THOMAS B.*	64,863	HINDES, GARY E.	1,014	26,826 R	58.2%	41.2%	58.6%	41.4%
AL	1976	214,799	110,677	EVANS, THOMAS B.	102,431	SHIPLEY, SAMUEL L.	1,691	8,246 R	51.5%	47.7%	51.9%	48.1%
AL	1974	160,328	93,826	duPONT, PIERRE*	63,490	SOLES, JAMES	3,012	30,336 R	58.5%	39.6%	59.6%	40.4%
AL	1972	225,851	141,237	duPONT, PIERRE*	83,230	HANDLOFF, NORMA	1,384	58,007 R	62.5%	36.9%	62.9%	37.1%
AL	1970	160,313	86,125	duPONT, PIERRE	71,429	DANIELLO, JOHN D.	2,759	14,696 R	53.7%	44.6%	54.7%	45.3%
AL	1968	200,820	117,827	ROTH, WILLIAM V.*	82,993	McDOWELL, HARRIS B.		34,834 R	58.7%	41.3%	58.7%	41.3%
AL	1966	163,103	90,961	ROTH, WILLIAM V.	72,142	McDOWELL, HARRIS B.*		18,819 R	55.8%	44.2%	55.8%	44.2%
AL	1964	198,691	86,254	SNOWDEN, JAMES H.	112,361	McDOWELL, HARRIS B.*	76	26,107 D	43.4%	56.6%	43.4%	56.6%
AL	1962	153,356	71,934	WILLIAMS, WILMER F.	81,166	McDOWELL, HARRIS B.*	256	9,232 D	46.9%	52.9%	47.0%	53.0%
AL	1960	194,564	96,337	McKINSTRY, JAMES T.	98,227	McDOWELL, HARRIS B.*		1,890 D	49.5%	50.5%	49.5%	50.5%
AL	1958	152,896	76,099	HASKELL, HARRY G.*	76,797	McDOWELL, HARRIS B.		698 D	49.8%	50.2%	49.8%	50.2%
AL	1956	176,182	91,538	HASKELL, HARRY G.	84,644	McDOWELL, HARRIS B.*		6,894 R	52.0%	48.0%	52.0%	48.0%
AL	1954	144,236	65,035	MARTIN, LILLIAN	79,201	McDOWELL, HARRIS B.		14,166 D	45.1%	54.9%	45.1%	54.9%
AL	1952	170,015	88,285	WARBURTON, H. B.	81,730	SCANNELL, JOSEPH S.		6,555 R	51.9%	48.1%	51.9%	48.1%
AL	1950	129,404	73,313	BOGGS, J. CALEB*	56,091	WINCHESTER, H. M.		17,222 R	56.7%	43.3%	56.7%	43.3%
AL	1948	140,535	71,127	BOGGS, J. CALEB*	68,909	McGUIGAN, J. CARL	499	2,218 R	50.6%	49.0%	50.8%	49.2%
AL	1946	112,621	63,516	BOGGS, J. CALEB	49,105	TRAYNOR, PHILIP A.*		14,411 R	56.4%	43.6%	56.4%	43.6%

An asterisk (*) denotes incumbent.

DELAWARE

GENERAL AND PRIMARY ELECTIONS

2006 GENERAL ELECTIONS

Senator   Other vote was 11,127 write-in (Christine O'Donnell); 2,671 Libertarian (William E. Morris).

House   Other vote was:

  At Large   5,769 Independent Party of Delaware (Karen M. Hartley-Nagle); 4,463 Green (Michael Berg).

2006 PRIMARY ELECTIONS

Primary	September 12, 2006	**Registration** (as of August 1, 2006)	Democratic	244,308
			Republican	177,973
			Others	131,014
			TOTAL	553,295

Primary Type   Closed—Only registered Democrats and Republicans could vote in their party's primary.

Note: An asterisk (*) denotes incumbent. The names of unopposed candidates did not appear on the primary ballot; therefore, no votes were cast for these candidates.

	REPUBLICAN PRIMARIES			DEMOCRATIC PRIMARIES		
Senator	Jan Ting	6,110	42.5%	Thomas R. Carper*	Unopposed	
	Michael D. Protack	5,771	40.1%			
	Christine O'Donnell	2,505	17.4%			
	TOTAL	*14,386*				
House **At Large**	Michael N. Castle*	Unopposed		Dennis Spivack	9,515	60.3%
				Karen M. Hartley-Nagle	6,253	39.7%
				TOTAL	*15,768*	

FLORIDA

Congressional districts first established for elections held in 2002
25 members

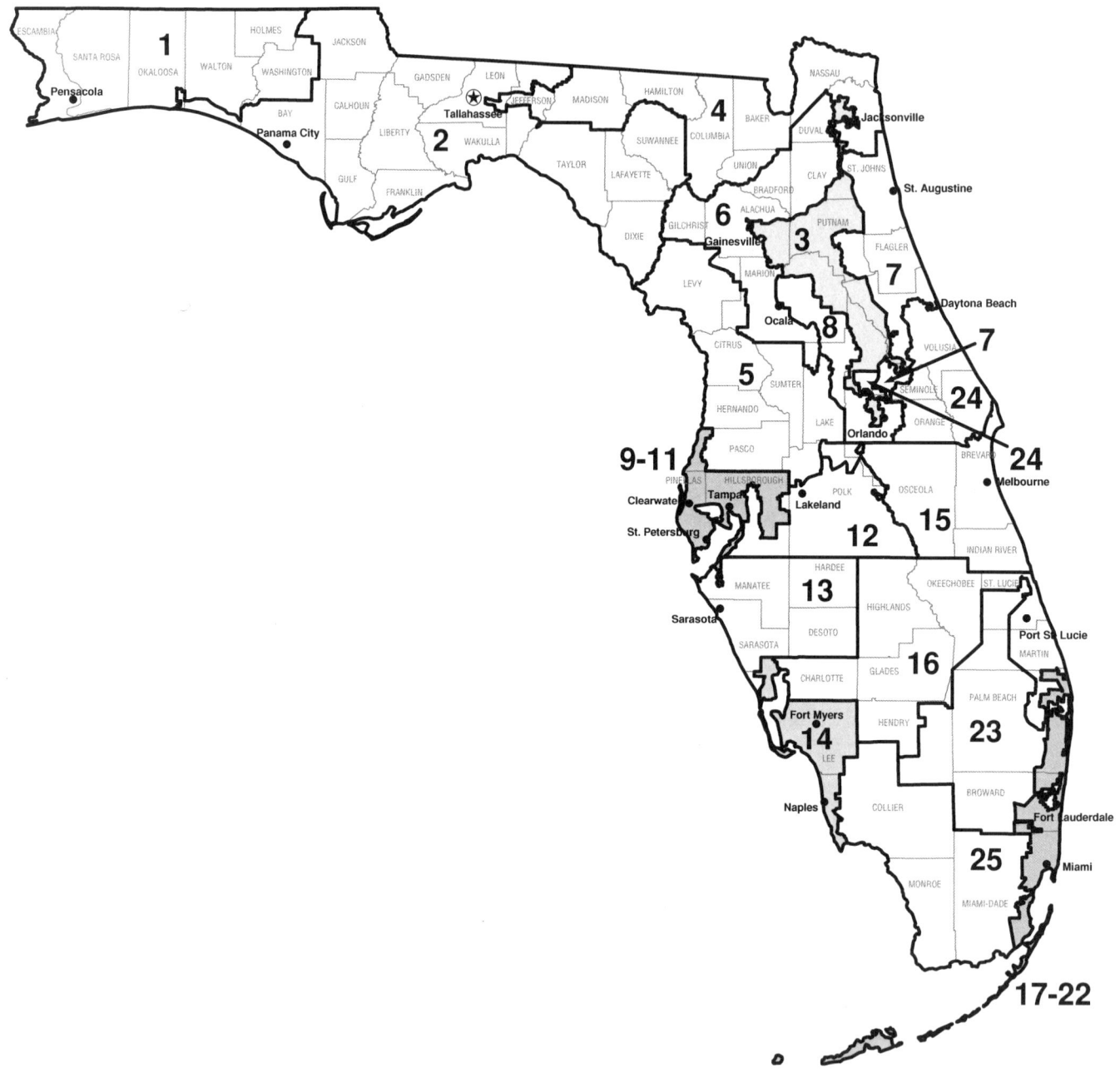

FLORIDA

St. Petersburg, Tampa, Fort Myers Areas

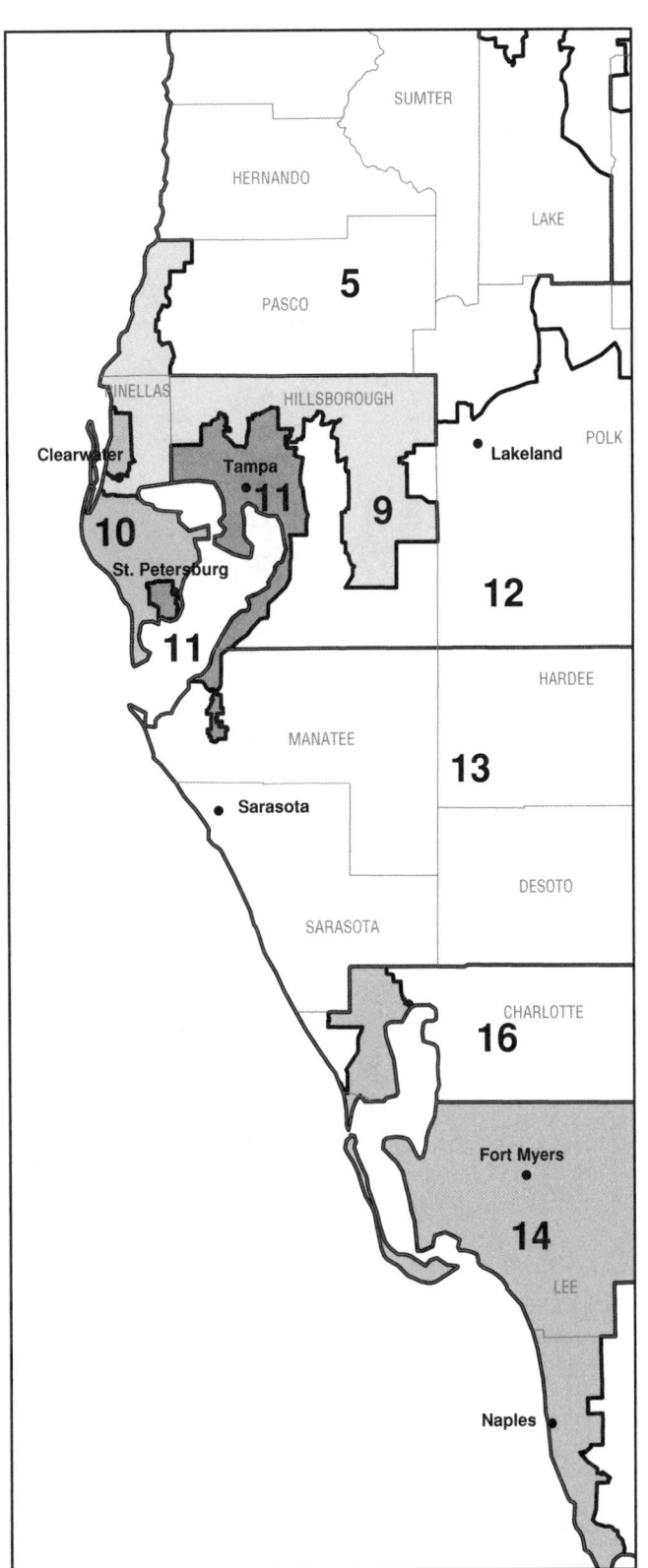

FLORIDA

Miami, Fort Lauderdale Areas

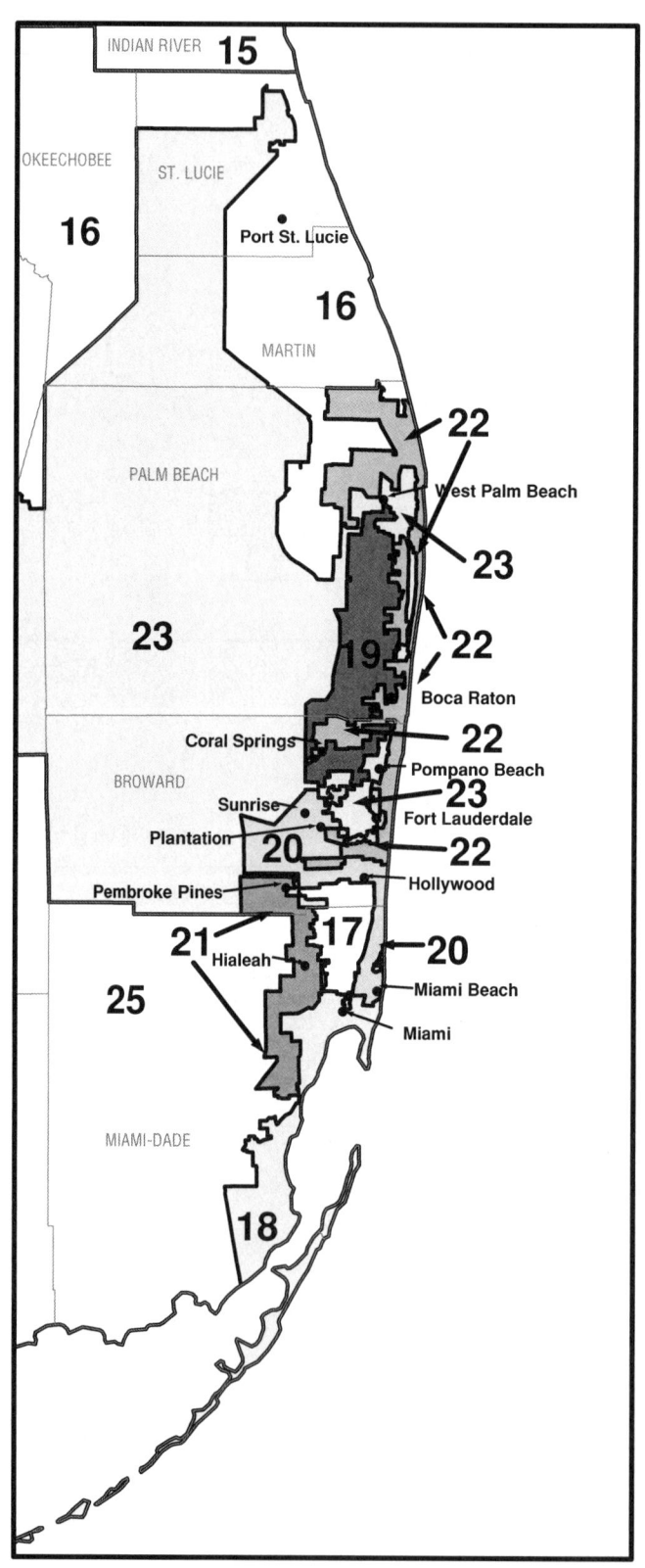

FLORIDA

GOVERNOR
Charlie Crist (R). Elected 2006 to a four-year term.

SENATORS (1 Democrat, 1 Republican)
Bill Nelson (D). Reelected 2006 to a six-year term. Previously elected 2000.

Mel Martinez (R). Elected 2004 to a six-year term.

REPRESENTATIVES (16 Republicans, 9 Democrats)
1. Jeff Miller (R)
2. Allen Boyd (D)
3. Corrine Brown (D)
4. Ander Crenshaw (R)
5. Ginny Brown-Waite (R)
6. Cliff Stearns (R)
7. John L. Mica (R)
8. Ric Keller (R)
9. Gus Michael Bilirakis (R)
10. C. W. Bill Young (R)
11. Kathy Castor (D)
12. Adam H. Putnam (R)
13. Vern Buchanan (R)
14. Connie Mack (R)
15. Dave Weldon (R)
16. Tim Mahoney (D)
17. Kendrick B. Meek (D)
18. Ileana Ros-Lehtinen (R)
19. Robert Wexler (D)
20. Debbie Wasserman Schultz (D)
21. Lincoln Diaz-Balart (R)
22. Ron Klein (D)
23. Alcee L. Hastings (D)
24. Tom Feeney (R)
25. Mario Diaz-Balart (R)

POSTWAR VOTE FOR PRESIDENT

| | | Republican | | Democratic | | | | | Percentage | | | |
| | | | | | | Other | | | Total Vote | | Major Vote | |
Year	Total Vote	Vote	Candidate	Vote	Candidate	Vote	Plurality		Rep.	Dem.	Rep.	Dem.
2004	7,609,810	3,964,522	Bush, George W.	3,583,544	Kerry, John	61,744	380,978	R	52.1%	47.1%	52.5%	47.5%
2000**	5,963,110	2,912,790	Bush, George W.	2,912,253	Gore, Al	138,067	537	R	48.8%	48.8%	50.0%	50.0%
1996**	5,303,794	2,244,536	Dole, Bob	2,546,870	Clinton, Bill	512,388	302,334	D	42.3%	48.0%	46.8%	53.2%
1992**	5,314,392	2,173,310	Bush, George	2,072,698	Clinton, Bill	1,068,384	100,612	R	40.9%	39.0%	51.2%	48.8%
1988	4,302,313	2,618,885	Bush, George	1,656,701	Dukakis, Michael S.	26,727	962,184	R	60.9%	38.5%	61.3%	38.7%
1984	4,180,051	2,730,350	Reagan, Ronald	1,448,816	Mondale, Walter F.	885	1,281,534	R	65.3%	34.7%	65.3%	34.7%
1980**	3,686,930	2,046,951	Reagan, Ronald	1,419,475	Carter, Jimmy	220,504	627,476	R	55.5%	38.5%	59.1%	40.9%
1976	3,150,631	1,469,531	Ford, Gerald R.	1,636,000	Carter, Jimmy	45,100	166,469	D	46.6%	51.9%	47.3%	52.7%
1972	2,583,283	1,857,759	Nixon, Richard M.	718,117	McGovern, George S.	7,407	1,139,642	R	71.9%	27.8%	72.1%	27.9%
1968**	2,187,805	886,804	Nixon, Richard M.	676,794	Humphrey, Hubert H.	624,207	210,010	R	40.5%	30.9%	56.7%	43.3%
1964	1,854,481	905,941	Goldwater, Barry M.	948,540	Johnson, Lyndon B.		42,599	D	48.9%	51.1%	48.9%	51.1%
1960	1,544,176	795,476	Nixon, Richard M.	748,700	Kennedy, John F.		46,776	R	51.5%	48.5%	51.5%	48.5%
1956	1,125,762	643,849	Eisenhower, Dwight D.	480,371	Stevenson, Adlai E.	1,542	163,478	R	57.2%	42.7%	57.3%	42.7%
1952	989,337	544,036	Eisenhower, Dwight D.	444,950	Stevenson, Adlai E.	351	99,086	R	55.0%	45.0%	55.0%	45.0%
1948**	577,643	194,280	Dewey, Thomas E.	281,988	Truman, Harry S.	101,375	87,708	D	33.6%	48.8%	40.8%	59.2%

**In past elections, the other vote included: 2000 - 97,488 Green (Ralph Nader); 1996 - 483,870 Reform (Ross Perot); 1992 - 1,053,067 Independent (Ross Perot); 1980 - 189,692 Independent (John Anderson); 1968 - 624,207 American Independent (George Wallace); 1948 - 89,755 States' Rights (Strom Thurmond).

FLORIDA

POSTWAR VOTE FOR GOVERNOR

Year	Total Vote	Republican Vote	Republican Candidate	Democratic Vote	Democratic Candidate	Other Vote	Rep.-Dem. Plurality	Total Vote Rep.	Total Vote Dem.	Major Vote Rep.	Major Vote Dem.
2006	4,829,270	2,519,845	Crist, Charlie	2,178,289	Davis, Jim	131,136	341,556 R	52.2%	45.1%	53.6%	46.4%
2002	5,100,581	2,856,845	Bush, Jeb	2,201,427	McBride, Bill	42,309	655,418 R	56.0%	43.2%	56.5%	43.5%
1998	3,964,441	2,191,105	Bush, Jeb	1,773,054	MacKay, Buddy	282	418,051 R	55.3%	44.7%	55.3%	44.7%
1994	4,206,659	2,071,068	Bush, Jeb	2,135,008	Chiles, Lawton	583	63,940 D	49.2%	50.8%	49.2%	50.8%
1990	3,530,871	1,535,068	Martinez, Bob	1,995,206	Chiles, Lawton	597	460,138 D	43.5%	56.5%	43.5%	56.5%
1986	3,386,171	1,847,525	Martinez, Bob	1,538,620	Pajcic, Steve	26	308,905 R	54.6%	45.4%	54.6%	45.4%
1982	2,688,566	949,013	Bafalis, L. A.	1,739,553	Graham, Bob		790,540 D	35.3%	64.7%	35.3%	64.7%
1978	2,530,468	1,123,888	Eckerd, Jack M.	1,406,580	Graham, Bob		282,692 D	44.4%	55.6%	44.4%	55.6%
1974	1,828,392	709,438	Thomas, Jerry	1,118,954	Askew, Reubin		409,516 D	38.8%	61.2%	38.8%	61.2%
1970	1,730,813	746,243	Kirk, Claude R.	984,305	Askew, Reubin	265	238,062 D	43.1%	56.9%	43.1%	56.9%
1966	1,489,661	821,190	Kirk, Claude R.	668,233	High, Robert King	238	152,957 R	55.1%	44.9%	55.1%	44.9%
1964S	1,663,481	686,297	Holley, Charles R.	933,554	Burns, Haydon	43,630	247,257 D	41.3%	56.1%	42.4%	57.6%
1960	1,419,343	569,936	Petersen, George C.	849,407	Bryant, Farris		279,471 D	40.2%	59.8%	40.2%	59.8%
1956	1,014,733	266,980	Washburne, W. A.	747,753	Collins, LeRoy		480,773 D	26.3%	73.7%	26.3%	73.7%
1954S	357,783	69,852	Watson, J. Tom	287,769	Collins, LeRoy	162	217,917 D	19.5%	80.4%	19.5%	80.5%
1952	834,518	210,009	Swan, Harry S.	624,463	McCarty, Dan	46	414,454 D	25.2%	74.8%	25.2%	74.8%
1948	457,638	76,153	Acker, Bert Lee	381,459	Warren, Fuller	26	305,306 D	16.6%	83.4%	16.6%	83.4%

The 1964 election was for a two-year term to permit shifting the vote for governor to non-presidential years. The 1954 election was for a short term to fill a vacancy.

POSTWAR VOTE FOR SENATOR

Year	Total Vote	Republican Vote	Republican Candidate	Democratic Vote	Democratic Candidate	Other Vote	Rep.-Dem. Plurality	Total Vote Rep.	Total Vote Dem.	Major Vote Rep.	Major Vote Dem.
2006	4,793,534	1,826,127	Harris, Katherine	2,890,548	Nelson, Bill	76,859	1,064,421 D	38.1%	60.3%	38.7%	61.3%
2004	7,429,894	3,672,864	Martinez, Mel	3,590,201	Castor, Betty	166,829	82,663 R	49.4%	48.3%	50.6%	49.4%
2000	5,856,731	2,705,348	McCollum, Bill	2,989,487	Nelson, Bill	161,896	284,139 D	46.2%	51.0%	47.5%	52.5%
1998	3,900,162	1,463,755	Crist, Charlie	2,436,407	Graham, Bob		972,652 D	37.5%	62.5%	37.5%	62.5%
1994	4,106,176	2,894,726	Mack, Connie	1,210,412	Rodham, Hugh E.	1,038	1,684,314 R	70.5%	29.5%	70.5%	29.5%
1992	4,962,290	1,716,505	Grant, Bill	3,245,565	Graham, Bob	220	1,529,060 D	34.6%	65.4%	34.6%	65.4%
1988	4,068,209	2,051,071	Mack, Connie	2,016,553	MacKay, Buddy	585	34,518 R	50.4%	49.6%	50.4%	49.6%
1986	3,429,996	1,552,376	Hawkins, Paula	1,877,543	Graham, Bob	77	325,167 D	45.3%	54.7%	45.3%	54.7%
1982	2,653,419	1,015,330	Poole, Van B.	1,637,667	Chiles, Lawton	422	622,337 D	38.3%	61.7%	38.3%	61.7%
1980	3,528,028	1,822,460	Hawkins, Paula	1,705,409	Gunter, Bill	159	117,051 R	51.7%	48.3%	51.7%	48.3%
1976	2,857,534	1,057,886	Grady, John	1,799,518	Chiles, Lawton	130	741,632 D	37.0%	63.0%	37.0%	63.0%
1974**	1,800,539	736,674	Eckerd, Jack M.	781,031	Stone, Richard	282,834	44,357 D	40.9%	43.4%	48.5%	51.5%
1970	1,675,378	772,817	Cramer, William C.	902,438	Chiles, Lawton	123	129,621 D	46.1%	53.9%	46.1%	53.9%
1968	2,024,136	1,131,499	Gurney, Edward J.	892,637	Collins, LeRoy		238,862 R	55.9%	44.1%	55.9%	44.1%
1964	1,560,337	562,212	Kirk, Claude R.	997,585	Holland, Spessard L.	540	435,373 D	36.0%	63.9%	36.0%	64.0%
1962	939,207	281,381	Rupert, Emerson H.	657,633	Smathers, George A.	193	376,252 D	30.0%	70.0%	30.0%	70.0%
1958	542,069	155,956	Hyzer, Leland	386,113	Holland, Spessard L.		230,157 D	28.8%	71.2%	28.8%	71.2%
1956	655,418		—	655,418	Smathers, George A.		655,418 D		100.0%		100.0%
1952	617,800		—	616,665	Holland, Spessard L.	1,135	616,665 D		99.8%		100.0%
1950	313,487	74,228	Booth, John P.	238,987	Smathers, George A.	272	164,759 D	23.7%	76.2%	23.7%	76.3%
1946	198,640	42,408	Schad, J. Harry	156,232	Holland, Spessard L.		113,824 D	21.3%	78.7%	21.3%	78.7%

**In past elections, the other vote included: 1974 - 282,659 American (John Grady).

FLORIDA

GOVERNOR 2006

2000 Census Population	County	Total Vote	Republican	Democratic	Other	Rep.-Dem. Plurality	Percentage Total Vote Rep.	Dem.	Major Vote Rep.	Dem.
217,955	ALACHUA	70,516	30,139	38,741	1,636	8,602 D	42.7%	54.9%	43.8%	56.2%
22,259	BAKER	6,247	4,335	1,738	174	2,597 R	69.4%	27.8%	71.4%	28.6%
148,217	BAY	48,091	31,382	14,802	1,907	16,580 R	65.3%	30.8%	67.9%	32.1%
26,088	BRADFORD	7,123	4,458	2,438	227	2,020 R	62.6%	34.2%	64.6%	35.4%
476,230	BREVARD	186,765	100,148	79,854	6,763	20,294 R	53.6%	42.8%	55.6%	44.4%
1,623,018	BROWARD	407,673	143,043	256,072	8,558	113,029 D	35.1%	62.8%	35.8%	64.2%
13,017	CALHOUN	3,420	1,737	1,563	120	174 R	50.8%	45.7%	52.6%	47.4%
141,627	CHARLOTTE	55,286	32,377	21,621	1,288	10,756 R	58.6%	39.1%	60.0%	40.0%
118,085	CITRUS	51,634	29,038	19,905	2,691	9,133 R	56.2%	38.6%	59.3%	40.7%
140,814	CLAY	51,551	37,632	12,610	1,309	25,022 R	73.0%	24.5%	74.9%	25.1%
251,377	COLLIER	86,946	59,821	25,303	1,822	34,518 R	68.8%	29.1%	70.3%	29.7%
56,513	COLUMBIA	15,590	9,313	5,763	514	3,550 R	59.7%	37.0%	61.8%	38.2%
32,209	DESOTO	6,593	3,785	2,603	205	1,182 R	57.4%	39.5%	59.3%	40.7%
13,827	DIXIE	5,031	2,651	2,109	271	542 R	52.7%	41.9%	55.7%	44.3%
778,879	DUVAL	225,297	132,607	87,718	4,972	44,889 R	58.9%	38.9%	60.2%	39.8%
294,410	ESCAMBIA	86,646	51,195	33,777	1,674	17,418 R	59.1%	39.0%	60.2%	39.8%
49,832	FLAGLER	29,679	15,376	13,589	714	1,787 R	51.8%	45.8%	53.1%	46.9%
11,057	FRANKLIN	3,971	1,981	1,854	136	127 R	49.9%	46.7%	51.7%	48.3%
45,087	GADSDEN	14,042	4,557	9,303	182	4,746 D	32.5%	66.3%	32.9%	67.1%
14,437	GILCHRIST	5,303	3,160	1,906	237	1,254 R	59.6%	35.9%	62.4%	37.6%
10,576	GLADES	2,958	1,572	1,292	94	280 R	53.1%	43.7%	54.9%	45.1%
13,332	GULF	4,858	2,702	1,985	171	717 R	55.6%	40.9%	57.6%	42.4%
13,327	HAMILTON	3,511	1,766	1,637	108	129 R	50.3%	46.6%	51.9%	48.1%
26,938	HARDEE	4,536	2,580	1,720	236	860 R	56.9%	37.9%	60.0%	40.0%
36,210	HENDRY	5,463	3,056	2,273	134	783 R	55.9%	41.6%	57.3%	42.7%
130,802	HERNANDO	57,035	29,907	24,412	2,716	5,495 R	52.4%	42.8%	55.1%	44.9%
87,366	HIGHLANDS	30,325	17,426	11,128	1,771	6,298 R	57.5%	36.7%	61.0%	39.0%
998,948	HILLSBOROUGH	289,921	153,134	128,946	7,841	24,188 R	52.8%	44.5%	54.3%	45.7%
18,564	HOLMES	5,460	3,417	1,897	146	1,520 R	62.6%	34.7%	64.3%	35.7%
112,947	INDIAN RIVER	43,336	26,812	15,529	995	11,283 R	61.9%	35.8%	63.3%	36.7%
46,755	JACKSON	13,084	6,835	5,900	349	935 R	52.2%	45.1%	53.7%	46.3%
12,902	JEFFERSON	6,012	2,602	3,275	135	673 D	43.3%	54.5%	44.3%	55.7%
7,022	LAFAYETTE	2,158	1,346	771	41	575 R	62.4%	35.7%	63.6%	36.4%
210,528	LAKE	86,104	53,055	30,419	2,630	22,636 R	61.6%	35.3%	63.6%	36.4%
440,888	LEE	154,567	97,221	53,426	3,920	43,795 R	62.9%	34.6%	64.5%	35.5%
239,452	LEON	90,533	38,296	50,540	1,697	12,244 D	42.3%	55.8%	43.1%	56.9%
34,450	LEVY	11,316	6,317	4,558	441	1,759 R	55.8%	40.3%	58.1%	41.9%
7,021	LIBERTY	1,816	907	850	59	57 R	49.9%	46.8%	51.6%	48.4%
18,733	MADISON	5,921	2,854	2,915	152	61 D	48.2%	49.2%	49.5%	50.5%
264,002	MANATEE	99,977	58,035	38,547	3,395	19,488 R	58.0%	38.6%	60.1%	39.9%
258,916	MARION	100,614	57,111	39,744	3,759	17,367 R	56.8%	39.5%	59.0%	41.0%
126,731	MARTIN	52,869	31,071	20,570	1,228	10,501 R	58.8%	38.9%	60.2%	39.8%
2,253,362	MIAMI-DADE	404,945	183,457	215,930	5,558	32,473 D	45.3%	53.3%	45.9%	54.1%
79,589	MONROE	23,935	11,882	11,390	663	492 R	49.6%	47.6%	51.1%	48.9%
57,663	NASSAU	22,439	15,454	6,378	607	9,076 R	68.9%	28.4%	70.8%	29.2%
170,498	OKALOOSA	55,900	42,686	12,117	1,097	30,569 R	76.4%	21.7%	77.9%	22.1%
35,910	OKEECHOBEE	8,295	4,227	3,853	215	374 R	51.0%	46.4%	52.3%	47.7%
896,344	ORANGE	218,298	116,412	96,795	5,091	19,617 R	53.3%	44.3%	54.6%	45.4%
172,493	OSCEOLA	45,010	23,945	19,864	1,201	4,081 R	53.2%	44.1%	54.7%	45.3%
1,131,184	PALM BEACH	366,970	140,531	219,199	7,240	78,668 D	38.3%	59.7%	39.1%	60.9%
344,765	PASCO	129,081	68,530	54,479	6,072	14,051 R	53.1%	42.2%	55.7%	44.3%
921,482	PINELLAS	291,730	148,257	131,046	12,427	17,211 R	50.8%	44.9%	53.1%	46.9%
483,924	POLK	142,006	79,071	57,018	5,917	22,053 R	55.7%	40.2%	58.1%	41.9%
70,423	PUTNAM	19,744	10,960	8,140	644	2,820 R	55.5%	41.2%	57.4%	42.6%
123,135	ST. JOHNS	60,916	40,979	18,554	1,383	22,425 R	67.3%	30.5%	68.8%	31.2%
192,695	ST. LUCIE	70,298	34,787	33,860	1,651	927 R	49.5%	48.2%	50.7%	49.3%
117,743	SANTA ROSA	42,224	29,041	12,361	822	16,680 R	68.8%	29.3%	70.1%	29.9%
325,957	SARASOTA	140,557	76,198	60,214	4,145	15,984 R	54.2%	42.8%	55.9%	44.1%
365,196	SEMINOLE	111,477	68,149	40,724	2,604	27,425 R	61.1%	36.5%	62.6%	37.4%
53,345	SUMTER	30,298	19,771	9,668	859	10,103 R	65.3%	31.9%	67.2%	32.8%

FLORIDA

GOVERNOR 2006

2000 Census Population	County	Total Vote	Republican	Democratic	Other	Rep.-Dem. Plurality	Percentage			
							Total Vote		Major Vote	
							Rep.	Dem.	Rep.	Dem.
34,844	SUWANNEE	10,982	6,995	3,716	271	3,279 R	63.7%	33.8%	65.3%	34.7%
19,256	TAYLOR	5,610	3,172	2,327	111	845 R	56.5%	41.5%	57.7%	42.3%
13,442	UNION	2,895	1,723	1,086	86	637 R	59.5%	37.5%	61.3%	38.7%
443,343	VOLUSIA	152,912	76,618	72,216	4,078	4,402 R	50.1%	47.2%	51.5%	48.5%
22,863	WAKULLA	9,566	4,837	4,421	308	416 R	50.6%	46.2%	52.2%	47.8%
40,601	WALTON	16,180	10,971	4,835	374	6,136 R	67.8%	29.9%	69.4%	30.6%
20,973	WASHINGTON	7,224	4,435	2,495	294	1,940 R	61.4%	34.5%	64.0%	36.0%
15,982,378	TOTAL	4,829,270	2,519,845	2,178,289	131,136	341,556 R	52.2%	45.1%	53.6%	46.4%

FLORIDA

SENATOR 2006

2000 Census Population	County	Total Vote	Republican	Democratic	Other	Rep.-Dem. Plurality	Percentage			
							Total Vote		Major Vote	
							Rep.	Dem.	Rep.	Dem.
217,955	ALACHUA	70,344	20,887	48,125	1,332	27,238 D	29.7%	68.4%	30.3%	69.7%
22,259	BAKER	6,262	3,420	2,771	71	649 R	54.6%	44.3%	55.2%	44.8%
148,217	BAY	48,085	23,821	23,526	738	295 R	49.5%	48.9%	50.3%	49.7%
26,088	BRADFORD	7,134	3,486	3,539	109	53 D	48.9%	49.6%	49.6%	50.4%
476,230	BREVARD	186,680	72,787	111,031	2,862	38,244 D	39.0%	59.5%	39.6%	60.4%
1,623,018	BROWARD	403,596	102,847	293,758	6,991	190,911 D	25.5%	72.8%	25.9%	74.1%
13,017	CALHOUN	3,415	1,146	2,207	62	1,061 D	33.6%	64.6%	34.2%	65.8%
141,627	CHARLOTTE	55,027	22,836	31,192	999	8,356 D	41.5%	56.7%	42.3%	57.7%
118,085	CITRUS	51,441	20,332	29,741	1,368	9,409 D	39.5%	57.8%	40.6%	59.4%
140,814	CLAY	51,373	30,697	19,871	805	10,826 R	59.8%	38.7%	60.7%	39.3%
251,377	COLLIER	86,093	44,988	39,741	1,364	5,247 R	52.3%	46.2%	53.1%	46.9%
56,513	COLUMBIA	15,599	7,393	7,965	241	572 D	47.4%	51.1%	48.1%	51.9%
32,209	DESOTO	6,613	2,869	3,656	88	787 D	43.4%	55.3%	44.0%	56.0%
13,827	DIXIE	4,992	2,030	2,802	160	772 D	40.7%	56.1%	42.0%	58.0%
778,879	DUVAL	224,118	101,107	120,044	2,967	18,937 D	45.1%	53.6%	45.7%	54.3%
294,410	ESCAMBIA	86,890	42,573	42,964	1,353	391 D	49.0%	49.4%	49.8%	50.2%
49,832	FLAGLER	29,613	11,278	17,957	378	6,679 D	38.1%	60.6%	38.6%	61.4%
11,057	FRANKLIN	3,943	1,349	2,529	65	1,180 D	34.2%	64.1%	34.8%	65.2%
45,087	GADSDEN	14,005	2,527	11,320	158	8,793 D	18.0%	80.8%	18.2%	81.8%
14,437	GILCHRIST	5,307	2,338	2,843	126	505 D	44.1%	53.6%	45.1%	54.9%
10,576	GLADES	2,953	1,081	1,826	46	745 D	36.6%	61.8%	37.2%	62.8%
13,332	GULF	4,875	1,898	2,916	61	1,018 D	38.9%	59.8%	39.4%	60.6%
13,327	HAMILTON	3,510	1,241	2,187	82	946 D	35.4%	62.3%	36.2%	63.8%
26,938	HARDEE	4,536	2,157	2,328	51	171 D	47.6%	51.3%	48.1%	51.9%
36,210	HENDRY	5,419	2,230	3,096	93	866 D	41.2%	57.1%	41.9%	58.1%
130,802	HERNANDO	56,626	20,975	34,316	1,335	13,341 D	37.0%	60.6%	37.9%	62.1%
87,366	HIGHLANDS	30,241	13,053	16,710	478	3,657 D	43.2%	55.3%	43.9%	56.1%
998,948	HILLSBOROUGH	286,868	105,813	176,114	4,941	70,301 D	36.9%	61.4%	37.5%	62.5%
18,564	HOLMES	5,442	2,700	2,641	101	59 R	49.6%	48.5%	50.6%	49.4%
112,947	INDIAN RIVER	42,994	18,696	23,704	594	5,008 D	43.5%	55.1%	44.1%	55.9%
46,755	JACKSON	13,045	4,866	7,994	185	3,128 D	37.3%	61.3%	37.8%	62.2%
12,902	JEFFERSON	5,998	1,485	4,438	75	2,953 D	24.8%	74.0%	25.1%	74.9%
7,022	LAFAYETTE	2,177	894	1,247	36	353 D	41.1%	57.3%	41.8%	58.2%
210,528	LAKE	85,932	36,773	47,749	1,410	10,976 D	42.8%	55.6%	43.5%	56.5%
440,888	LEE	153,447	69,955	80,749	2,743	10,794 D	45.6%	52.6%	46.4%	53.6%
239,452	LEON	89,944	21,959	66,776	1,209	44,817 D	24.4%	74.2%	24.7%	75.3%
34,450	LEVY	11,332	4,848	6,298	186	1,450 D	42.8%	55.6%	43.5%	56.5%
7,021	LIBERTY	1,811	549	1,243	19	694 D	30.3%	68.6%	30.6%	69.4%
18,733	MADISON	5,910	1,769	4,040	101	2,271 D	29.9%	68.4%	30.5%	69.5%
264,002	MANATEE	99,481	42,713	55,168	1,600	12,455 D	42.9%	55.5%	43.6%	56.4%

FLORIDA

SENATOR 2006

2000 Census Population	County	Total Vote	Republican	Democratic	Other	Rep.-Dem. Plurality	Percentage			
							Total Vote		Major Vote	
							Rep.	Dem.	Rep.	Dem.
258,916	MARION	100,573	42,965	55,933	1,675	12,968 D	42.7%	55.6%	43.4%	56.6%
126,731	MARTIN	52,614	22,465	29,448	701	6,983 D	42.7%	56.0%	43.3%	56.7%
2,253,362	MIAMI-DADE	392,744	143,162	243,075	6,507	99,913 D	36.5%	61.9%	37.1%	62.9%
79,589	MONROE	23,821	8,893	14,534	394	5,641 D	37.3%	61.0%	38.0%	62.0%
57,663	NASSAU	22,337	11,955	9,985	397	1,970 R	53.5%	44.7%	54.5%	45.5%
170,498	OKALOOSA	55,772	33,895	20,882	995	13,013 R	60.8%	37.4%	61.9%	38.1%
35,910	OKEECHOBEE	8,270	2,917	5,243	110	2,326 D	35.3%	63.4%	35.7%	64.3%
896,344	ORANGE	217,862	78,409	136,547	2,906	58,138 D	36.0%	62.7%	36.5%	63.5%
172,493	OSCEOLA	44,924	17,223	27,050	651	9,827 D	38.3%	60.2%	38.9%	61.1%
1,131,184	PALM BEACH	365,064	96,176	264,962	3,926	168,786 D	26.3%	72.6%	26.6%	73.4%
344,765	PASCO	127,975	48,124	76,957	2,894	28,833 D	37.6%	60.1%	38.5%	61.5%
921,482	PINELLAS	287,721	99,572	182,572	5,577	83,000 D	34.6%	63.5%	35.3%	64.7%
483,924	POLK	141,325	58,584	80,403	2,338	21,819 D	41.5%	56.9%	42.2%	57.8%
70,423	PUTNAM	19,726	8,303	11,117	306	2,814 D	42.1%	56.4%	42.8%	57.2%
123,135	ST. JOHNS	60,609	32,311	27,329	969	4,982 R	53.3%	45.1%	54.2%	45.8%
192,695	ST. LUCIE	70,146	23,310	45,911	925	22,601 D	33.2%	65.5%	33.7%	66.3%
117,743	SANTA ROSA	42,327	24,298	17,268	761	7,030 R	57.4%	40.8%	58.5%	41.5%
325,957	SARASOTA	140,787	58,339	80,177	2,271	21,838 D	41.4%	56.9%	42.1%	57.9%
365,196	SEMINOLE	111,031	47,119	62,454	1,458	15,335 D	42.4%	56.2%	43.0%	57.0%
53,345	SUMTER	30,178	14,485	15,167	526	682 D	48.0%	50.3%	48.8%	51.2%
34,844	SUWANNEE	10,960	5,146	5,646	168	500 D	47.0%	51.5%	47.7%	52.3%
19,256	TAYLOR	5,590	2,139	3,375	76	1,236 D	38.3%	60.4%	38.8%	61.2%
13,442	UNION	2,902	1,351	1,510	41	159 D	46.6%	52.0%	47.2%	52.8%
443,343	VOLUSIA	152,325	53,817	96,406	2,102	42,589 D	35.3%	63.3%	35.8%	64.2%
22,863	WAKULLA	9,500	2,802	6,517	181	3,715 D	29.5%	68.6%	30.1%	69.9%
40,601	WALTON	16,114	8,685	7,145	284	1,540 R	53.9%	44.3%	54.9%	45.1%
20,973	WASHINGTON	7,266	3,316	3,813	137	497 D	45.6%	52.5%	46.5%	53.5%
15,982,378	TOTAL	4,793,534	1,826,127	2,890,548	76,859	1,064,421 D	38.1%	60.3%	38.7%	61.3%

FLORIDA

HOUSE OF REPRESENTATIVES

CD	Year	Total Vote	Republican		Democratic		Other Vote	Rep.-Dem. Plurality	Percentage			
			Vote	Candidate	Vote	Candidate			Total Vote		Major Vote	
									Rep.	Dem.	Rep.	Dem.
1	2006	198,126	135,786	MILLER, JEFF*	62,340	ROBERTS, JOE		73,446 R	68.5%	31.5%	68.5%	31.5%
1	2004	309,110	236,604	MILLER, JEFF*	72,506	COUTO, MARK S.		164,098 R	76.5%	23.5%	76.5%	23.5%
1	2002	204,626	152,635	MILLER, JEFF*	51,972	ORAM, BERT	19	100,663 R	74.6%	25.4%	74.6%	25.4%
2	2006			—		BOYD, ALLEN*		D				
2	2004	326,987	125,399	KILMER, BEV	201,577	BOYD, ALLEN*	11	76,178 D	38.3%	61.6%	38.4%	61.6%
2	2002	227,439	75,275	McGURK, TOM	152,164	BOYD, ALLEN*		76,889 D	33.1%	66.9%	33.1%	66.9%
3	2006			—		BROWN, CORRINE*		D				
3	2004	174,156		—	172,833	BROWN, CORRINE*	1,323	172,833 D		99.2%		100.0%
3	2002	149,213	60,747	CARROLL, JENIFER	88,462	BROWN, CORRINE*	4	27,715 D	40.7%	59.3%	40.7%	59.3%
4	2006	203,479	141,759	CRENSHAW, ANDER*	61,704	HARMS, ROBERT J.	16	80,055 R	69.7%	30.3%	69.7%	30.3%
4	2004	257,327	256,157	CRENSHAW, ANDER*		—	1,170	256,157 R	99.5%		100.0%	
4	2002	171,661	171,152	CRENSHAW, ANDER*		—	509	171,152 R	99.7%		100.0%	
5	2006	271,380	162,421	BROWN-WAITE, GINNY*	108,959	RUSSELL, JOHN T.		53,462 R	59.9%	40.1%	59.9%	40.1%
5	2004	364,488	240,315	BROWN-WAITE, GINNY*	124,140	WHITTEL, ROBERT G.	33	116,175 R	65.9%	34.1%	65.9%	34.1%
5	2002	254,671	121,998	BROWN-WAITE, GINNY	117,758	THURMAN, KAREN L.*	14,915	4,240 R	47.9%	46.2%	50.9%	49.1%

FLORIDA

HOUSE OF REPRESENTATIVES

		Total	Republican		Democratic		Other	Rep.-Dem.	Percentage			
									Total Vote		Major Vote	
CD	Year	Vote	Vote	Candidate	Vote	Candidate	Vote	Plurality	Rep.	Dem.	Rep.	Dem.
6	2006	228,129	136,601	STEARNS, CLIFF*	91,528	BRUDERLY, DAVID E.		45,073 R	59.9%	40.1%	59.9%	40.1%
6	2004	327,853	211,137	STEARNS, CLIFF*	116,680	BRUDERLY, DAVID E.	36	94,457 R	64.4%	35.6%	64.4%	35.6%
6	2002	216,616	141,570	STEARNS, CLIFF*	75,046	BRUDERLY, DAVID E.		66,524 R	65.4%	34.6%	65.4%	34.6%
7	2006	237,240	149,656	MICA, JOHN L.*	87,584	CHAGNON, JOHN F.		62,072 R	63.1%	36.9%	63.1%	36.9%
7	2004			MICA, JOHN L.*	—			R				
7	2002	238,591	142,147	MICA, JOHN L.*	96,444	HOGAN, WAYNE		45,703 R	59.6%	40.4%	59.6%	40.4%
8	2006	180,444	95,258	KELLER, RIC*	82,526	STUART, CHARLIE	2,660	12,732 R	52.8%	45.7%	53.6%	46.4%
8	2004	284,575	172,232	KELLER, RIC*	112,343	MURRAY, STEPHEN		59,889 R	60.5%	39.5%	60.5%	39.5%
8	2002	189,596	123,497	KELLER, RIC*	66,099	DIAZ, EDDIE		57,398 R	65.1%	34.9%	65.1%	34.9%
9	2006	220,013	123,016	BILIRAKIS, GUS MICHAEL	96,978	BUSANSKY, PHYLLIS	19	26,038 R	55.9%	44.1%	55.9%	44.1%
9	2004	284,278	284,035	BILIRAKIS, MICHAEL*	—		243	284,035 R	99.9%		100.0%	
9	2002	237,008	169,369	BILIRAKIS, MICHAEL*	67,623	KALOGIANIS, CHUCK	16	101,746 R	71.5%	28.5%	71.5%	28.5%
10	2006	199,445	131,488	YOUNG, C. W. BILL*	67,950	SIMPSON, SAMM	7	63,538 R	65.9%	34.1%	65.9%	34.1%
10	2004	298,833	207,175	YOUNG, C. W. BILL*	91,658	DERRY, ROBERT D. "BOB"		115,517 R	69.3%	30.7%	69.3%	30.7%
10	2002			YOUNG, C. W. BILL*	—			R				
11	2006	139,942	42,454	ADAMS, EDDIE JR.	97,470	CASTOR, KATHY	18	55,016 D	30.3%	69.7%	30.3%	69.7%
11	2004	223,481		—	191,780	DAVIS, JIM*	31,701	191,780 D		85.8%		100.0%
11	2002			—		DAVIS, JIM*		D				
12	2006	180,064	124,452	PUTNAM, ADAM H.*	—		55,612	124,452 R	69.1%		100.0%	
12	2004	276,169	179,204	PUTNAM, ADAM H.*	96,965	HAGENMAIER, BOB		82,239 R	64.9%	35.1%	64.9%	35.1%
12	2002			PUTNAM, ADAM H.*	—			R				
13	2006	238,249	119,309	BUCHANAN, VERN	118,940	JENNINGS, CHRISTINE		369 R	50.1%	49.9%	50.1%	49.9%
13	2004	344,438	190,477	HARRIS, KATHERINE*	153,961	SCHNEIDER, JAN		36,516 R	55.3%	44.7%	55.3%	44.7%
13	2002	253,809	139,048	HARRIS, KATHERINE	114,739	SCHNEIDER, JAN	22	24,309 R	54.8%	45.2%	54.8%	45.2%
14	2006	235,539	151,615	MACK, CONNIE*	83,920	NEELD, ROBERT M.	4	67,695 R	64.4%	35.6%	64.4%	35.6%
14	2004	335,334	226,662	MACK, CONNIE	108,672	NEELD, ROBERT M.		117,990 R	67.6%	32.4%	67.6%	32.4%
14	2002			GOSS, PORTER J.*	—			R				
15	2006	223,799	125,965	WELDON, DAVE*	97,834	BOWMAN, BOB		28,131 R	56.3%	43.7%	56.3%	43.7%
15	2004	321,926	210,388	WELDON, DAVE*	111,538	PRISTOOP, SIMON		98,850 R	65.4%	34.6%	65.4%	34.6%
15	2002	231,857	146,414	WELDON, DAVE*	85,433	TSO, JIM	10	60,981 R	63.1%	36.8%	63.2%	36.8%
16	2006	233,773	111,415	NEGRON, JOE#	115,832	MAHONEY, TIM	6,526	4,417 D	47.7%	49.5%	49.0%	51.0%
16	2004	316,810	215,563	FOLEY, MARK#	101,247	FISHER, JEFF		114,316 R	68.0%	32.0%	68.0%	32.0%
16	2002	223,340	176,171	FOLEY, MARK#		—	47,169	176,171 R	78.9%		100.0%	
17	2006	90,686		—	90,663	MEEK, KENDRICK B.*	23	90,663 D		100.0%		100.0%
17	2004	179,424		—	178,690	MEEK, KENDRICK B.*	734	178,690 D		99.6%		100.0%
17	2002	113,822		—	113,749	MEEK, KENDRICK B.	73	113,749 D		99.9%		100.0%
18	2006	128,132	79,631	ROS-LEHTINEN, ILEANA*	48,499	PATLAK, DAVID "BIG DAVE"	2	31,132 R	62.1%	37.9%	62.1%	37.9%
18	2004	221,928	143,647	ROS-LEHTINEN, ILEANA*	78,281	SHELDON, SAM		65,366 R	64.7%	35.3%	64.7%	35.3%
18	2002	149,787	103,512	ROS-LEHTINEN, ILEANA*	42,852	CHOTE, RAY	3,423	60,660 R	69.1%	28.6%	70.7%	29.3%
19	2006			—		WEXLER, ROBERT*		D				
19	2004			—		WEXLER, ROBERT*		D				
19	2002	217,224	60,477	MERKL, JACK	156,747	WEXLER, ROBERT*		96,270 D	27.8%	72.2%	27.8%	72.2%
20	2006			—		WASSERMAN SCHULTZ, DEBBIE*		D				
20	2004	272,408	81,213	HOSTETTER, MARGARET	191,195	WASSERMAN-SCHULTZ, DEBBIE		109,982 D	29.8%	70.2%	29.8%	70.2%
20	2002			—		DEUTSCH, PETER*		D				
21	2006	112,306	66,784	DIAZ-BALART, LINCOLN*	45,522	GONZALEZ, FRANK J.		21,262 R	59.5%	40.5%	59.5%	40.5%
21	2004	201,243	146,507	DIAZ-BALART, LINCOLN*	—		54,736	146,507 R	72.8%		100.0%	
21	2002			DIAZ-BALART, LINCOLN*	—			R				

FLORIDA

HOUSE OF REPRESENTATIVES

CD	Year	Total Vote	Republican		Democratic		Other Vote	Rep.-Dem. Plurality		Percentage			
			Vote	Candidate	Vote	Candidate				Total Vote		Major Vote	
										Rep.	Dem.	Rep.	Dem.
22	2006	213,605	100,663	SHAW, E. CLAY JR.*	108,688	KLEIN, RON	4,254	8,025	D	47.1%	50.9%	48.1%	51.9%
22	2004	306,726	192,581	SHAW, E. CLAY JR.*	108,258	RORAPAUGH, ROBIN	5,887	84,323	R	62.8%	35.3%	64.0%	36.0%
22	2002	217,115	131,930	SHAW, E. CLAY JR.*	83,265	ROBERTS, CAROL A.	1,920	48,665	R	60.8%	38.4%	61.3%	38.7%
23	2006			—		HASTINGS, ALCEE L.*			D				
23	2004			—		HASTINGS, ALCEE L.*			D				
23	2002	124,338	27,986	LAURIE, CHARLES	96,347	HASTINGS, ALCEE L.*	5	68,361	D	22.5%	77.5%	22.5%	77.5%
24	2006	213,658	123,795	FEENEY, TOM*	89,863	CURTIS, CLINT		33,932	R	57.9%	42.1%	57.9%	42.1%
24	2004			FEENEY, TOM*		—			R				
24	2002	219,243	135,576	FEENEY, TOM	83,667	JACOBS, HARRY		51,909	R	61.8%	38.2%	61.8%	38.2%
25	2006	103,933	60,765	DIAZ-BALART, MARIO*	43,168	CALDERIN, MICHAEL		17,597	R	58.5%	41.5%	58.5%	41.5%
25	2004			DIAZ-BALART, MARIO*		—			R				
25	2002	126,602	81,845	DIAZ-BALART, MARIO	44,757	BETANCOURT, ANNIE		37,088	R	64.6%	35.4%	64.6%	35.4%
TOTAL	2006	3,851,942	2,182,833		1,599,968		69,141	582,865	R	56.7%	41.5%	57.7%	42.3%
TOTAL	2004	5,627,494	3,319,296		2,212,324		95,874	1,106,972	R	59.0%	39.3%	60.0%	40.0%
TOTAL	2002	3,766,558	2,161,349		1,537,124		68,085	624,225	R	57.4%	40.8%	58.4%	41.6%

An asterisk (*) denotes incumbent. A pound sign (#) indicates that Republican Rep. Mark Foley resigned from the House in late September 2006, too late to have his name removed from the general election ballot. Votes cast for Foley were credited to Joe Negron, the candidate selected by the Republican Party to replace Foley. In Florida districts where a candidate had no opposition, including write-ins, no vote was taken.

FLORIDA

GENERAL AND PRIMARY ELECTIONS

2006 GENERAL ELECTIONS

Governor   Other vote was 92,595 Reform (Max Linn); 15,987 No Party Affiliation (John Wayne Smith); 11,921 No Party Affiliation (Richard Paul Dembinsky); 10,486 No Party Affiliation (Karl C. C. Behm); 76 write-in (Omari Musa); 53 write-in (C. C. Reed); 18 write-in (Piotr Blass).

Senator   Other vote was 24,880 No Party Affiliation (Belinda Noah); 19,695 No Party Affiliation (Brian Moore); 16,628 No Party Affiliation (Floyd Ray Frazier); 15,562 No Party Affiliation (Roy Tanner); 78 write-in (Lawrence Scott); 16 write-in (Bernard Senter).

House   Other vote was:

CD 1
CD 2
CD 3
CD 4   16 write-in (John Blade).
CD 5
CD 6
CD 7
CD 8   2,640 No Party Affiliation (Wes Hoaglund); 17 write-in (D. J. Mauro); 3 write-in (Larry Sapp).
CD 9   19 write-in (Andrew Pasayan).
CD 10   7 write-in (Salvatore A. Fiorella).
CD 11   13 write-in (Jim Greenwald); 5 write-in (R. J. Spencer).
CD 12   34,976 No Party Affiliation (Joe Viscusi); 20,636 No Party Affiliation (Ed Bowlin).
CD 13
CD 14   3 write-in (Richard Grayson); 1 write-in (Dan).
CD 15
CD 16   6,526 No Party Affiliation (Emmie Ross).
CD 17   23 write-in (Eric Simpson).
CD 18   2 write-in (Margaret Trowe).
CD 19
CD 20
CD 21
CD 22   4,254 No Party Affiliation (Neil Evangelista).
CD 23
CD 24
CD 25

2006 PRIMARY ELECTIONS

Primary   September 5, 2006   **Registration** (as of August 7, 2006)

Democratic	4,230,478
Republican	3,930,602
Independent Party of Florida	238,842
Independence Party of Florida	36,448
Libertarian	15,317
Green	6,611
Other Parties	13,985
No Party Affiliation	1,957,283
TOTAL	10,429,566

Primary Type   Closed—Only registered Democrats and Republicans could vote in their party's primary, with the exception of races where there were to be no other candidates (including write-ins) on the general election ballot. Then, the contested primary would be open to all voters.

FLORIDA

GENERAL AND PRIMARY ELECTIONS

Note: An asterisk (*) denotes incumbent. The names of unopposed candidates did not appear on the primary ballot; therefore, no votes were cast for these candidates.

	REPUBLICAN PRIMARIES			DEMOCRATIC PRIMARIES		
Governor	Charlie Crist	630,816	64.0%	Jim Davis	405,879	47.3%
	Tom Gallagher	330,165	33.5%	Rod Smith	353,161	41.2%
	Vernon Palmer	13,547	1.4%	Carol Castagnero	45,161	5.3%
	Michael W. St. Jean	11,458	1.2%	Glenn Burkett	32,984	3.8%
				John M. Crotty	20,629	2.4%
	TOTAL	985,986		TOTAL	857,814	
Senator	Katherine Harris	474,871	49.4%	Bill Nelson*	Unopposed	
	William "Will" McBride	287,741	30.0%			
	LeRoy Collins Jr.	146,712	15.3%			
	Peter Monroe	51,330	5.3%			
	TOTAL	960,654				
Congressional District 1	Jeff Miller*	Unopposed		Joe Roberts	Unopposed	
Congressional District 2	No Republican candidate			Allen Boyd*	Unopposed	
Congressional District 3	No Republican candidate			Corrine Brown*	Unopposed	
Congressional District 4	Ander Crenshaw*	Unopposed		Robert J. Harms	Unopposed	
Congressional District 5	Ginny Brown-Waite*	Unopposed		John T. Russell	20,521	48.8%
				Rick Penberthy	16,393	39.0%
				H. "David" Werder	5,141	12.2%
				TOTAL	42,055	
Congressional District 6	Cliff Stearns*	Unopposed		David E. Bruderly	Unopposed	
Congressional District 7	John L. Mica*	Unopposed		John F. Chagnon	Unopposed	
Congressional District 8	Ric Keller*	30,707	72.5%	Charlie Stuart	12,728	47.7%
	Elizabeth Doran	11,661	27.5%	Alan Grayson	9,691	36.3%
				Homer Hartage	4,250	15.9%
	TOTAL	42,368		TOTAL	26,669	
Congressional District 9	Gus Michael Bilirakis	40,603	82.0%	Phyllis Busansky	Unopposed	
	David Domenic Langheier	8,915	18.0%			
	TOTAL	49,518				
Congressional District 10	C. W. Bill Young*	Unopposed		Samm Simpson	Unopposed	
Congressional District 11	Eddie Adams Jr.	Unopposed		Kathy Castor	21,310	54.0%
				Lesley "Les" Miller	13,474	34.1%
				Scott Farrell	1,721	4.4%
				Al Fox	1,653	4.2%
				Michael A. Steinberg	1,336	3.4%
				TOTAL	39,494	
Congressional District 12	Adam H. Putnam*	Unopposed		No Democratic candidate		
Congressional District 13	Vern Buchanan	20,918	32.3%	Christine Jennings	23,768	61.8%
	Nancy Carroll Detert	15,804	24.4%	Jan Schneider	14,699	38.2%
	Tramm Hudson	15,535	24.0%			
	Mark G. Flanagan	6,465	10.0%			
	Donna Clarke	5,972	9.2%			
	TOTAL	64,694		TOTAL	38,467	
Congressional District 14	Connie Mack*	Unopposed		Robert M. Neeld	Unopposed	

FLORIDA

GENERAL AND PRIMARY ELECTIONS

	REPUBLICAN PRIMARIES		DEMOCRATIC PRIMARIES		
Congressional District 15	Dave Weldon*	Unopposed	Bob Bowman John M. Kennedy *TOTAL*	14,965 12,520 *27,485*	54.4% 45.6%
Congressional District 16	Mark Foley*	Unopposed	Tim Mahoney	Unopposed	
	Mark Foley withdrew from the race in late September and was replaced as the Republican candidate by Joe Negron.				
Congressional District 17	No Republican candidate		Kendrick B. Meek* Dufirstson Neree *TOTAL*	32,426 3,850 *36,276*	89.4% 10.6%
Congressional District 18	Ileana Ros-Lehtinen*	Unopposed	David "Big Dave" Patlak	Unopposed	
Congressional District 19	No Republican candidate		Robert Wexler*	Unopposed	
Congressional District 20	No Republican candidate		Debbie Wasserman Schultz*	Unopposed	
Congressional District 21	Lincoln Diaz-Balart*	Unopposed	Frank J. Gonzalez	Unopposed	
Congressional District 22	E. Clay Shaw Jr.*	Unopposed	Ron Klein	Unopposed	
Congressional District 23	No Republican candidate		Alcee L. Hastings*	Unopposed	
Congressional District 24	Tom Feeney*	Unopposed	Clint Curtis "Dr. Andy" Michaud *TOTAL*	15,464 9,816 *25,280*	61.2% 38.8%
Congressional District 25	Mario Diaz-Balart*	Unopposed	Michael Calderin	Unopposed	

GEORGIA

Congressional districts first established for elections held in 2002
13 members

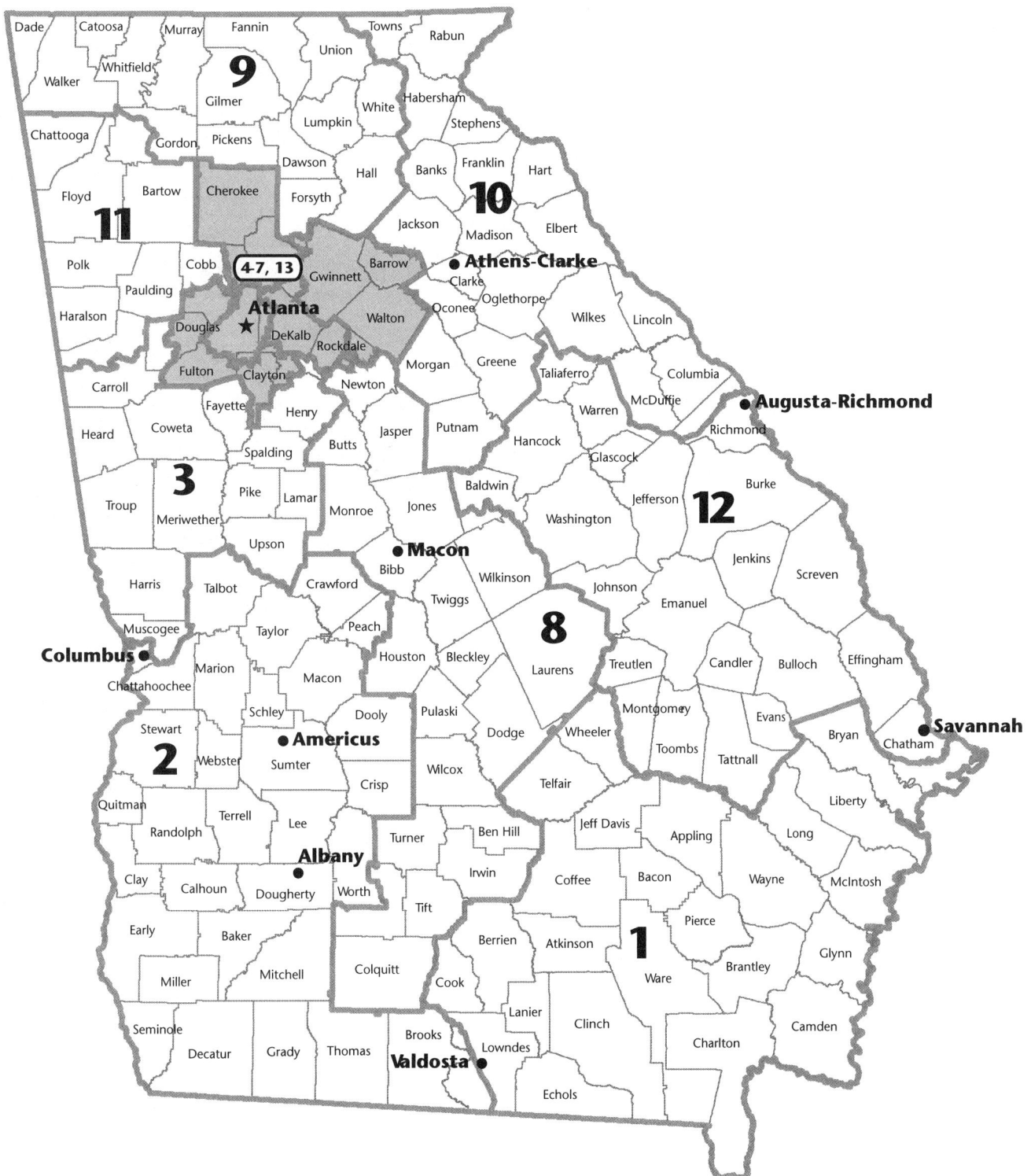

GEORGIA

Atlanta Area

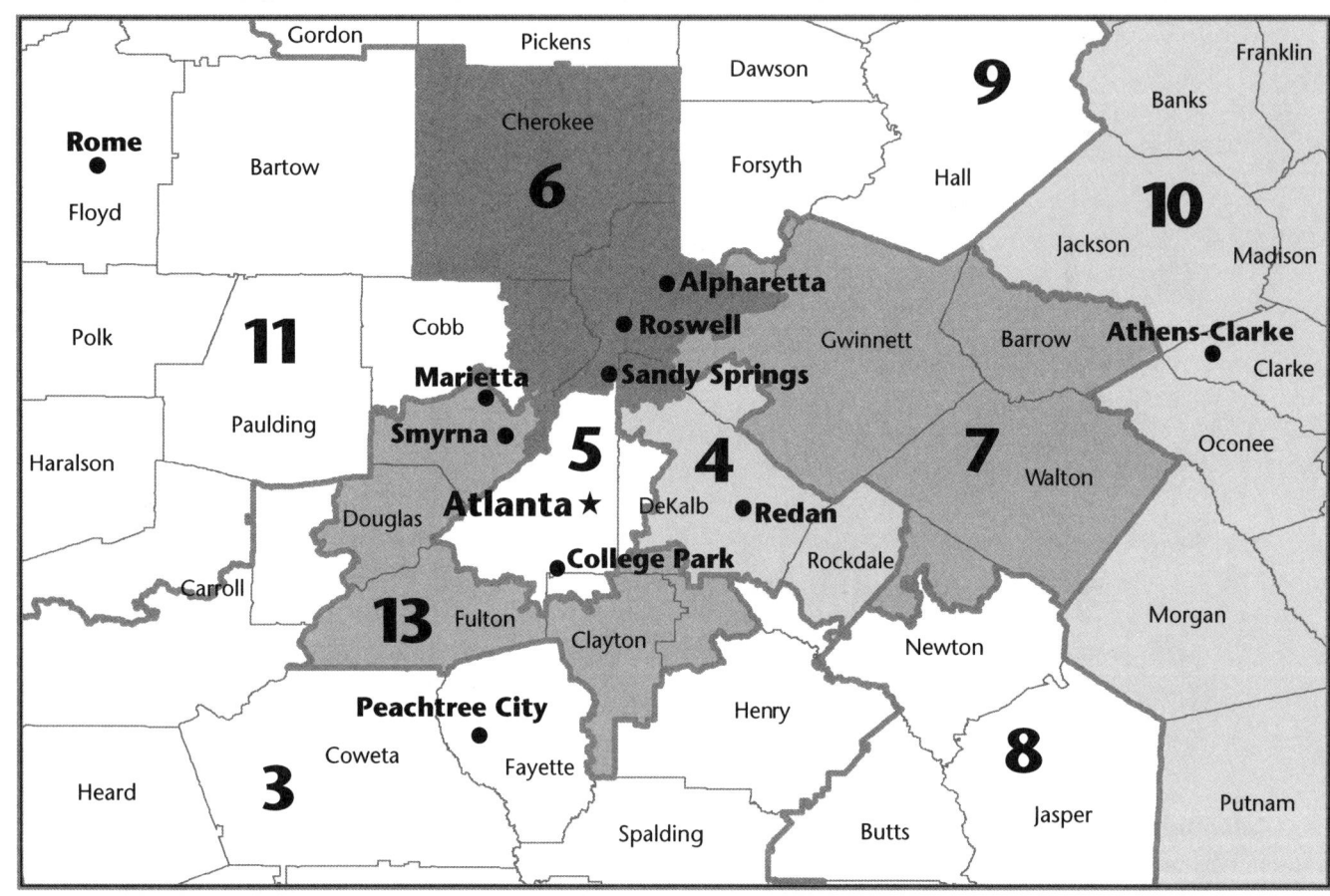

GEORGIA

GOVERNOR
Sonny Perdue (R). Reelected 2006 to a four-year term. Previously elected 2002.

SENATORS (2 Republicans)
Johnny Isakson (R). Elected 2004 to a six-year term.

Saxby Chambliss (R). Elected 2002 to a six-year term.

REPRESENTATIVES (6 Republicans, 6 Democrats, 1 Vacancy)
1. Jack Kingston (R)
2. Sanford D. Bishop Jr. (D)
3. Lynn Westmoreland (R)
4. Henry C. "Hank" Johnson Jr. (D)
5. John Lewis (D)
6. Tom Price (R)
7. John Linder (R)
8. Jim Marshall (D)
9. Nathan Deal (R)
10. Vacancy
11. Phil Gingrey (R)
12. John Barrow (D)
13. David Scott (D)

POSTWAR VOTE FOR PRESIDENT

Year	Total Vote	Republican Vote	Republican Candidate	Democratic Vote	Democratic Candidate	Other Vote	Plurality	Total Vote Rep.	Total Vote Dem.	Major Vote Rep.	Major Vote Dem.
2004	3,301,875	1,914,254	Bush, George W.	1,366,149	Kerry, John	21,472	548,105 R	58.0%	41.4%	58.4%	41.6%
2000**	2,596,645	1,419,720	Bush, George W.	1,116,230	Gore, Al	60,695	303,490 R	54.7%	43.0%	56.0%	44.0%
1996**	2,299,071	1,080,843	Dole, Bob	1,053,849	Clinton, Bill	164,379	26,994 R	47.0%	45.8%	50.6%	49.4%
1992**	2,321,125	995,252	Bush, George	1,008,966	Clinton, Bill	316,907	13,714 D	42.9%	43.5%	49.7%	50.3%
1988	1,809,672	1,081,331	Bush, George	714,792	Dukakis, Michael S.	13,549	366,539 R	59.8%	39.5%	60.2%	39.8%
1984	1,776,120	1,068,722	Reagan, Ronald	706,628	Mondale, Walter F.	770	362,094 R	60.2%	39.8%	60.2%	39.8%
1980**	1,596,695	654,168	Reagan, Ronald	890,733	Carter, Jimmy	51,794	236,565 D	41.0%	55.8%	42.3%	57.7%
1976	1,467,458	483,743	Ford, Gerald R.	979,409	Carter, Jimmy	4,306	495,666 D	33.0%	66.7%	33.1%	66.9%
1972	1,174,772	881,496	Nixon, Richard M.	289,529	McGovern, George S.	3,747	591,967 R	75.0%	24.6%	75.3%	24.7%
1968**	1,250,266	380,111	Nixon, Richard M.	334,440	Humphrey, Hubert H.	535,715	155,439 A	30.4%	26.7%	53.2%	46.8%
1964	1,139,335	616,584	Goldwater, Barry M.	522,556	Johnson, Lyndon B.	195	94,028 R	54.1%	45.9%	54.1%	45.9%
1960	733,349	274,472	Nixon, Richard M.	458,638	Kennedy, John F.	239	184,166 D	37.4%	62.5%	37.4%	62.6%
1956	669,655	222,778	Eisenhower, Dwight D.	444,688	Stevenson, Adlai E.	2,189	221,910 D	33.3%	66.4%	33.4%	66.6%
1952	655,785	198,961	Eisenhower, Dwight D.	456,823	Stevenson, Adlai E.	1	257,862 D	30.3%	69.7%	30.3%	69.7%
1948**	418,844	76,691	Dewey, Thomas E.	254,646	Truman, Harry S.	87,507	169,511 D	18.3%	60.8%	23.1%	76.9%

**In past elections, the other vote included: 2000 - 13,273 Green (Ralph Nader); 1996 - 146,337 Reform (Ross Perot); 1992 - 309,657 Independent (Ross Perot); 1980 - 36,055 Independent (John Anderson); 1968 - 535,550 American Independent (George Wallace); 1948 - 85,135 States' Rights (Strom Thurmond).

GEORGIA

POSTWAR VOTE FOR GOVERNOR

Year	Total Vote	Republican Vote	Republican Candidate	Democratic Vote	Democratic Candidate	Other Vote	Rep.-Dem. Plurality	Percentage Total Vote Rep.	Dem.	Major Vote Rep.	Dem.
2006	2,122,258	1,229,724	Perdue, Sonny	811,049	Taylor, Mark	81,485	418,675 R	57.9%	38.2%	60.3%	39.7%
2002	2,027,177	1,041,700	Perdue, Sonny	937,070	Barnes, Roy	48,407	104,630 R	51.4%	46.2%	52.6%	47.4%
1998	1,792,808	790,201	Millner, Guy	941,076	Barnes, Roy	61,531	150,875 D	44.1%	52.5%	45.6%	54.4%
1994	1,545,328	756,371	Millner, Guy	788,926	Miller, Zell	31	32,555 D	48.9%	51.1%	48.9%	51.1%
1990	1,449,682	645,625	Isakson, Johnny	766,662	Miller, Zell	37,395	121,037 D	44.5%	52.9%	45.7%	54.3%
1986	1,175,114	346,512	Davis, Guy	828,465	Harris, Joe Frank	137	481,953 D	29.5%	70.5%	29.5%	70.5%
1982	1,169,041	434,496	Bell, Robert H.	734,090	Harris, Joe Frank	455	299,594 D	37.2%	62.8%	37.2%	62.8%
1978	662,862	128,139	Cook, Rodney M.	534,572	Busbee, George	151	406,433 D	19.3%	80.6%	19.3%	80.7%
1974	936,438	289,113	Thompson, Ronnie	646,777	Busbee, George	548	357,664 D	30.9%	69.1%	30.9%	69.1%
1970	1,046,663	424,983	Suit, Hal	620,419	Carter, Jimmy	1,261	195,436 D	40.6%	59.3%	40.7%	59.3%
1966**	975,019	453,665	Callaway, Howard H.	450,626	Maddox, Lester	70,728	3,039 R	46.5%	46.2%	50.2%	49.8%
1962	311,691		—	311,524	Sanders, Carl E.	167	311,524 D		99.9%		100.0%
1958	168,497		—	168,414	Vandiver, Ernest	83	168,414 D		100.0%		100.0%
1954	331,966		—	331,899	Griffin, Marvin	67	331,899 D		100.0%		100.0%
1950	234,430		—	230,771	Talmadge, Herman	3,659	230,771 D		98.4%		100.0%
1948S	363,763		—	354,711	Talmadge, Herman	9,052	354,711 D		97.5%		100.0%
1946	145,403		—	143,279	Talmadge, Eugene	2,124	143,279 D		98.5%		100.0%

**In 1966 in the absence of a majority for any candidate, the State Legislature elected Democrat Lester Maddox to a four-year term. The 1948 election was for a short term to fill a vacancy.

POSTWAR VOTE FOR SENATOR

Year	Total Vote	Republican Vote	Republican Candidate	Democratic Vote	Democratic Candidate	Other Vote	Rep.-Dem. Plurality	Percentage Total Vote Rep.	Dem.	Major Vote Rep.	Dem.
2004	3,220,981	1,864,202	Isakson, Johnny	1,287,690	Majette, Denise L.	69,089	576,512 R	57.9%	40.0%	59.1%	40.9%
2002	2,030,608	1,071,464	Chambliss, Saxby	932,156	Cleland, Max	26,988	139,308 R	52.8%	45.9%	53.5%	46.5%
2000S	2,428,510	920,478	Mattingly, Mack	1,413,224	Miller, Zell	94,808	492,746 D	37.9%	58.2%	39.4%	60.6%
1998	1,753,911	918,540	Coverdell, Paul	791,904	Coles, Michael	43,467	126,636 R	52.4%	45.2%	53.7%	46.3%
1996	2,259,232	1,073,969	Millner, Guy	1,103,993	Cleland, Max	81,270	30,024 D	47.5%	48.9%	49.3%	50.7%
1992**	1,253,991	635,114	Coverdell, Paul	618,877	Fowler, Wyche		16,237 R	50.6%	49.4%	50.6%	49.4%
1990	1,033,517		—	1,033,439	Nunn, Sam	78	1,033,439 D		100.0%		100.0%
1986	1,225,008	601,241	Mattingly, Mack	623,707	Fowler, Wyche	60	22,466 D	49.1%	50.9%	49.1%	50.9%
1984	1,681,344	337,196	Hicks, Jon Michael	1,344,104	Nunn, Sam	44	1,006,908 D	20.1%	79.9%	20.1%	79.9%
1980	1,580,340	803,686	Mattingly, Mack	776,143	Talmadge, Herman	511	27,543 R	50.9%	49.1%	50.9%	49.1%
1978	645,164	108,808	Stokes, John W.	536,320	Nunn, Sam	36	427,512 D	16.9%	83.1%	16.9%	83.1%
1974	874,555	246,866	Johnson, Jerry R.	627,376	Talmadge, Herman	313	380,510 D	28.2%	71.7%	28.2%	71.8%
1972	1,178,708	542,331	Thompson, Fletcher	635,970	Nunn, Sam	407	93,639 D	46.0%	54.0%	46.0%	54.0%
1968	1,141,889	256,796	Patton, E. Earl	885,093	Talmadge, Herman		628,297 D	22.5%	77.5%	22.5%	77.5%
1966	622,371		—	622,043	Russell, Richard B.	328	622,043 D		99.9%		100.0%
1962	306,250		—	306,250	Talmadge, Herman		306,250 D		100.0%		100.0%
1960	576,495		—	576,140	Russell, Richard B.	355	576,140 D		99.9%		100.0%
1956	541,267		—	541,094	Talmadge, Herman	173	541,094 D		100.0%		100.0%
1954	333,936		—	333,917	Russell, Richard B.	19	333,917 D		100.0%		100.0%
1950	261,293		—	261,290	George, Walter F.	3	261,290 D		100.0%		100.0%
1948	362,504		—	362,104	Russell, Richard B.	400	362,104 D		99.9%		100.0%

**The 2000 election was for a short term to fill a vacancy. In 1992 the figures in the table are for the runoff election held November 24, as no candidate received a majority of the vote in the November 3 General Election. The vote in the November 3 election was 1,073,282 (47.7%) Republican (Paul Coverdell); 1,108,416 (49.2%) Democratic (Wyche Fowler); and 69,889 (3.1%) Other.

GEORGIA

GOVERNOR 2006

2000 Census Population	County	Total Vote	Republican	Democratic	Other	Rep.-Dem. Plurality	Percentage			
							Total Vote		Major Vote	
							Rep.	Dem.	Rep.	Dem.
17,419	APPLING	4,106	2,698	1,330	78	1,368 R	65.7%	32.4%	67.0%	33.0%
7,609	ATKINSON	1,476	827	614	35	213 R	56.0%	41.6%	57.4%	42.6%
10,103	BACON	2,349	1,216	1,097	36	119 R	51.8%	46.7%	52.6%	47.4%
4,074	BAKER	996	391	589	16	198 D	39.3%	59.1%	39.9%	60.1%
44,700	BALDWIN	10,032	4,843	4,857	332	14 D	48.3%	48.4%	49.9%	50.1%
14,422	BANKS	3,966	2,890	935	141	1,955 R	72.9%	23.6%	75.6%	24.4%
46,144	BARROW	11,613	8,537	2,513	563	6,024 R	73.5%	21.6%	77.3%	22.7%
76,019	BARTOW	19,132	13,412	4,825	895	8,587 R	70.1%	25.2%	73.5%	26.5%
17,484	BEN HILL	3,316	1,739	1,512	65	227 R	52.4%	45.6%	53.5%	46.5%
16,235	BERRIEN	3,617	2,045	1,469	103	576 R	56.5%	40.6%	58.2%	41.8%
153,887	BIBB	37,320	18,954	17,073	1,293	1,881 R	50.8%	45.7%	52.6%	47.4%
11,666	BLECKLEY	3,113	2,130	870	113	1,260 R	68.4%	27.9%	71.0%	29.0%
14,629	BRANTLEY	2,916	1,826	1,017	73	809 R	62.6%	34.9%	64.2%	35.8%
16,450	BROOKS	3,350	1,762	1,506	82	256 R	52.6%	45.0%	53.9%	46.1%
23,417	BRYAN	6,688	4,720	1,822	146	2,898 R	70.6%	27.2%	72.1%	27.9%
55,983	BULLOCH	12,672	8,225	4,131	316	4,094 R	64.9%	32.6%	66.6%	33.4%
22,243	BURKE	5,165	2,679	2,410	76	269 R	51.9%	46.7%	52.6%	47.4%
19,522	BUTTS	5,056	3,245	1,621	190	1,624 R	64.2%	32.1%	66.7%	33.3%
6,320	CALHOUN	1,232	450	761	21	311 D	36.5%	61.8%	37.2%	62.8%
43,664	CAMDEN	7,986	5,202	2,620	164	2,582 R	65.1%	32.8%	66.5%	33.5%
9,577	CANDLER	2,037	1,270	723	44	547 R	62.3%	35.5%	63.7%	36.3%
87,268	CARROLL	22,018	14,885	6,132	1,001	8,753 R	67.6%	27.8%	70.8%	29.2%
53,282	CATOOSA	12,918	10,299	2,475	144	7,824 R	79.7%	19.2%	80.6%	19.4%
10,282	CHARLTON	1,651	967	640	44	327 R	58.6%	38.8%	60.2%	39.8%
232,048	CHATHAM	58,187	32,322	24,646	1,219	7,676 R	55.5%	42.4%	56.7%	43.3%
14,882	CHATTAHOOCHEE	923	443	463	17	20 D	48.0%	50.2%	48.9%	51.1%
25,470	CHATTOOGA	5,186	2,770	2,275	141	495 R	53.4%	43.9%	54.9%	45.1%
141,903	CHEROKEE	49,256	37,886	8,565	2,805	29,321 R	76.9%	17.4%	81.6%	18.4%
101,489	CLARKE	23,384	9,283	12,599	1,502	3,316 D	39.7%	53.9%	42.4%	57.6%
3,357	CLAY	815	316	487	12	171 D	38.8%	59.8%	39.4%	60.6%
236,517	CLAYTON	46,389	13,542	31,586	1,261	18,044 D	29.2%	68.1%	30.0%	70.0%
6,878	CLINCH	1,070	408	645	17	237 D	38.1%	60.3%	38.7%	61.3%
607,751	COBB	178,829	112,527	56,784	9,518	55,743 R	62.9%	31.8%	66.5%	33.5%
37,413	COFFEE	7,437	4,606	2,655	176	1,951 R	61.9%	35.7%	63.4%	36.6%
42,053	COLQUITT	7,689	4,563	2,902	224	1,661 R	59.3%	37.7%	61.1%	38.9%
89,288	COLUMBIA	31,470	23,972	6,872	626	17,100 R	76.2%	21.8%	77.7%	22.3%
15,771	COOK	2,772	1,572	1,133	67	439 R	56.7%	40.9%	58.1%	41.9%
89,215	COWETA	28,462	20,712	6,525	1,225	14,187 R	72.8%	22.9%	76.0%	24.0%
12,495	CRAWFORD	2,987	1,766	1,095	126	671 R	59.1%	36.7%	61.7%	38.3%
21,996	CRISP	4,124	2,558	1,459	107	1,099 R	62.0%	35.4%	63.7%	36.3%
15,154	DADE	3,264	2,361	849	54	1,512 R	72.3%	26.0%	73.6%	26.4%
15,999	DAWSON	5,525	4,373	846	306	3,527 R	79.1%	15.3%	83.8%	16.2%
28,240	DECATUR	5,588	3,361	2,141	86	1,220 R	60.1%	38.3%	61.1%	38.9%
665,865	DEKALB	173,653	52,807	112,119	8,727	59,312 D	30.4%	64.6%	32.0%	68.0%
19,171	DODGE	5,079	2,802	2,138	139	664 R	55.2%	42.1%	56.7%	43.3%
11,525	DOOLY	2,642	1,281	1,298	63	17 D	48.5%	49.1%	49.7%	50.3%
96,065	DOUGHERTY	22,136	7,441	14,371	324	6,930 D	33.6%	64.9%	34.1%	65.9%
92,174	DOUGLAS	26,977	15,930	9,900	1,147	6,030 R	59.1%	36.7%	61.7%	38.3%
12,354	EARLY	2,775	1,463	1,277	35	186 R	52.7%	46.0%	53.4%	46.6%
3,754	ECHOLS	573	323	233	17	90 R	56.4%	40.7%	58.1%	41.9%
37,535	EFFINGHAM	10,938	8,162	2,570	206	5,592 R	74.6%	23.5%	76.1%	23.9%
20,511	ELBERT	4,609	2,575	1,925	109	650 R	55.9%	41.8%	57.2%	42.8%
21,837	EMANUEL	4,747	2,838	1,818	91	1,020 R	59.8%	38.3%	61.0%	39.0%
10,495	EVANS	2,640	1,535	1,071	34	464 R	58.1%	40.6%	58.9%	41.1%
19,798	FANNIN	7,290	5,109	1,921	260	3,188 R	70.1%	26.4%	72.7%	27.3%
91,263	FAYETTE	35,971	25,069	9,329	1,573	15,740 R	69.7%	25.9%	72.9%	27.1%
90,565	FLOYD	20,252	12,803	6,557	892	6,246 R	63.2%	32.4%	66.1%	33.9%
98,407	FORSYTH	40,198	32,969	5,351	1,878	27,618 R	82.0%	13.3%	86.0%	14.0%
20,285	FRANKLIN	4,925	3,027	1,739	159	1,288 R	61.5%	35.3%	63.5%	36.5%
816,006	FULTON	206,160	90,262	106,180	9,718	15,918 D	43.8%	51.5%	45.9%	54.1%

GEORGIA

GOVERNOR 2006

2000 Census Population	County	Total Vote	Republican	Democratic	Other	Rep.-Dem. Plurality		Percentage			
								Total Vote		Major Vote	
								Rep.	Dem.	Rep.	Dem.
23,456	GILMER	7,342	5,234	1,771	337	3,463 R		71.3%	24.1%	74.7%	25.3%
2,556	GLASCOCK	844	628	197	19	431 R		74.4%	23.3%	76.1%	23.9%
67,568	GLYNN	16,998	11,197	5,359	442	5,838 R		65.9%	31.5%	67.6%	32.4%
44,104	GORDON	9,537	6,637	2,521	379	4,116 R		69.6%	26.4%	72.5%	27.5%
23,659	GRADY	5,153	3,029	2,046	78	983 R		58.8%	39.7%	59.7%	40.3%
14,406	GREENE	4,817	2,999	1,675	143	1,324 R		62.3%	34.8%	64.2%	35.8%
588,448	GWINNETT	153,333	101,485	44,498	7,350	56,987 R		66.2%	29.0%	69.5%	30.5%
35,902	HABERSHAM	8,856	6,633	1,863	360	4,770 R		74.9%	21.0%	78.1%	21.9%
139,277	HALL	34,139	26,027	6,570	1,542	19,457 R		76.2%	19.2%	79.8%	20.2%
10,076	HANCOCK	2,230	550	1,631	49	1,081 D		24.7%	73.1%	25.2%	74.8%
25,690	HARALSON	6,066	4,107	1,678	281	2,429 R		67.7%	27.7%	71.0%	29.0%
23,695	HARRIS	7,704	5,365	2,153	186	3,212 R		69.6%	27.9%	71.4%	28.6%
22,997	HART	6,641	3,433	3,012	196	421 R		51.7%	45.4%	53.3%	46.7%
11,012	HEARD	2,380	1,593	690	97	903 R		66.9%	29.0%	69.8%	30.2%
119,341	HENRY	44,128	27,414	14,996	1,718	12,418 R		62.1%	34.0%	64.6%	35.4%
110,765	HOUSTON	31,042	21,395	8,697	950	12,698 R		68.9%	28.0%	71.1%	28.9%
9,931	IRWIN	2,170	1,259	863	48	396 R		58.0%	39.8%	59.3%	40.7%
41,589	JACKSON	11,554	8,727	2,357	470	6,370 R		75.5%	20.4%	78.7%	21.3%
11,426	JASPER	3,351	2,126	1,089	136	1,037 R		63.4%	32.5%	66.1%	33.9%
12,684	JEFF DAVIS	2,863	1,763	1,054	46	709 R		61.6%	36.8%	62.6%	37.4%
17,266	JEFFERSON	4,781	2,366	2,349	66	17 R		49.5%	49.1%	50.2%	49.8%
8,575	JENKINS	1,966	1,173	764	29	409 R		59.7%	38.9%	60.6%	39.4%
8,560	JOHNSON	2,075	1,259	763	53	496 R		60.7%	36.8%	62.3%	37.7%
23,639	JONES	7,217	4,252	2,690	275	1,562 R		58.9%	37.3%	61.3%	38.7%
15,912	LAMAR	4,602	2,900	1,552	150	1,348 R		63.0%	33.7%	65.1%	34.9%
7,241	LANIER	1,279	664	598	17	66 R		51.9%	46.8%	52.6%	47.4%
44,874	LAURENS	10,965	6,199	4,411	355	1,788 R		56.5%	40.2%	58.4%	41.6%
24,757	LEE	7,046	4,570	2,322	154	2,248 R		64.9%	33.0%	66.3%	33.7%
61,610	LIBERTY	7,471	3,509	3,794	168	285 D		47.0%	50.8%	48.0%	52.0%
8,348	LINCOLN	2,536	1,661	839	36	822 R		65.5%	33.1%	66.4%	33.6%
10,304	LONG	1,604	955	615	34	340 R		59.5%	38.3%	60.8%	39.2%
92,115	LOWNDES	20,025	11,036	8,565	424	2,471 R		55.1%	42.8%	56.3%	43.7%
21,016	LUMPKIN	6,046	4,237	1,454	355	2,783 R		70.1%	24.0%	74.5%	25.5%
21,231	MCDUFFIE	5,023	3,285	1,651	87	1,634 R		65.4%	32.9%	66.6%	33.4%
10,847	MCINTOSH	4,052	2,148	1,797	107	351 R		53.0%	44.3%	54.4%	45.6%
14,074	MACON	2,918	1,212	1,656	50	444 D		41.5%	56.8%	42.3%	57.7%
25,730	MADISON	6,288	4,214	1,805	269	2,409 R		67.0%	28.7%	70.0%	30.0%
7,144	MARION	1,999	975	990	34	15 D		48.8%	49.5%	49.6%	50.4%
22,534	MERIWETHER	5,427	3,072	2,179	176	893 R		56.6%	40.2%	58.5%	41.5%
6,383	MILLER	1,293	777	494	22	283 R		60.1%	38.2%	61.1%	38.9%
23,932	MITCHELL	4,869	2,366	2,417	86	51 D		48.6%	49.6%	49.5%	50.5%
21,757	MONROE	7,331	4,717	2,331	283	2,386 R		64.3%	31.8%	66.9%	33.1%
8,270	MONTGOMERY	2,085	1,243	786	56	457 R		59.6%	37.7%	61.3%	38.7%
15,457	MORGAN	5,408	3,680	1,505	223	2,175 R		68.0%	27.8%	71.0%	29.0%
36,506	MURRAY	6,131	4,431	1,557	143	2,874 R		72.3%	25.4%	74.0%	26.0%
186,291	MUSCOGEE	39,247	19,500	19,028	719	472 R		49.7%	48.5%	50.6%	49.4%
62,001	NEWTON	19,748	11,554	7,459	735	4,095 R		58.5%	37.8%	60.8%	39.2%
26,225	OCONEE	10,569	7,335	2,642	592	4,693 R		69.4%	25.0%	73.5%	26.5%
12,635	OGLETHORPE	3,592	2,143	1,259	190	884 R		59.7%	35.1%	63.0%	37.0%
81,678	PAULDING	26,350	18,766	6,389	1,195	12,377 R		71.2%	24.2%	74.6%	25.4%
23,668	PEACH	6,015	3,324	2,471	220	853 R		55.3%	41.1%	57.4%	42.6%
22,983	PICKENS	7,375	5,508	1,489	378	4,019 R		74.7%	20.2%	78.7%	21.3%
15,636	PIERCE	3,727	2,676	1,001	50	1,675 R		71.8%	26.9%	72.8%	27.2%
13,688	PIKE	4,783	3,486	1,094	203	2,392 R		72.9%	22.9%	76.1%	23.9%
38,127	POLK	8,145	5,034	2,766	345	2,268 R		61.8%	34.0%	64.5%	35.5%
9,588	PULASKI	2,307	1,437	774	96	663 R		62.3%	33.6%	65.0%	35.0%
18,812	PUTNAM	5,400	3,577	1,648	175	1,929 R		66.2%	30.5%	68.5%	31.5%
2,598	QUITMAN	624	301	310	13	9 D		48.2%	49.7%	49.3%	50.7%
15,050	RABUN	4,951	3,483	1,270	198	2,213 R		70.3%	25.7%	73.3%	26.7%
7,791	RANDOLPH	1,918	863	1,035	20	172 D		45.0%	54.0%	45.5%	54.5%

GEORGIA

GOVERNOR 2006

2000 Census Population	County	Total Vote	Republican	Democratic	Other	Rep.-Dem. Plurality		Percentage			
								Total Vote		Major Vote	
								Rep.	Dem.	Rep.	Dem.
199,775	RICHMOND	46,782	22,614	23,363	805	749 D		48.3%	49.9%	49.2%	50.8%
70,111	ROCKDALE	19,869	11,089	7,881	899	3,208 R		55.8%	39.7%	58.5%	41.5%
3,766	SCHLEY	911	583	315	13	268 R		64.0%	34.6%	64.9%	35.1%
15,374	SCREVEN	3,933	2,359	1,513	61	846 R		60.0%	38.5%	60.9%	39.1%
9,369	SEMINOLE	1,983	1,048	895	40	153 R		52.8%	45.1%	53.9%	46.1%
58,417	SPALDING	13,450	8,539	4,412	499	4,127 R		63.5%	32.8%	65.9%	34.1%
25,435	STEPHENS	6,776	4,251	2,344	181	1,907 R		62.7%	34.6%	64.5%	35.5%
5,252	STEWART	1,102	395	693	14	298 D		35.8%	62.9%	36.3%	63.7%
33,200	SUMTER	6,948	3,439	3,345	164	94 R		49.5%	48.1%	50.7%	49.3%
6,498	TALBOT	1,848	738	1,061	49	323 D		39.9%	57.4%	41.0%	59.0%
2,077	TALIAFERRO	544	199	334	11	135 D		36.6%	61.4%	37.3%	62.7%
22,305	TATTNALL	4,387	2,896	1,415	76	1,481 R		66.0%	32.3%	67.2%	32.8%
8,815	TAYLOR	1,990	1,087	852	51	235 R		54.6%	42.8%	56.1%	43.9%
11,794	TELFAIR	2,292	1,001	1,233	58	232 D		43.7%	53.8%	44.8%	55.2%
10,970	TERRELL	2,655	1,160	1,454	41	294 D		43.7%	54.8%	44.4%	55.6%
42,737	THOMAS	9,728	5,867	3,649	212	2,218 R		60.3%	37.5%	61.7%	38.3%
38,407	TIFT	8,500	5,580	2,680	240	2,900 R		65.6%	31.5%	67.6%	32.4%
26,067	TOOMBS	6,289	3,914	2,228	147	1,686 R		62.2%	35.4%	63.7%	36.3%
9,319	TOWNS	3,859	2,775	965	119	1,810 R		71.9%	25.0%	74.2%	25.8%
6,854	TREUTLEN	1,494	760	700	34	60 R		50.9%	46.9%	52.1%	47.9%
58,779	TROUP	13,516	9,080	4,096	340	4,984 R		67.2%	30.3%	68.9%	31.1%
9,504	TURNER	2,040	1,099	893	48	206 R		53.9%	43.8%	55.2%	44.8%
10,590	TWIGGS	2,649	1,161	1,395	93	234 D		43.8%	52.7%	45.4%	54.6%
17,289	UNION	6,923	4,915	1,747	261	3,168 R		71.0%	25.2%	73.8%	26.2%
27,597	UPSON	5,812	3,653	1,989	170	1,664 R		62.9%	34.2%	64.7%	35.3%
61,053	WALKER	12,766	9,473	3,052	241	6,421 R		74.2%	23.9%	75.6%	24.4%
60,687	WALTON	19,251	14,765	3,680	806	11,085 R		76.7%	19.1%	80.0%	20.0%
35,483	WARE	6,587	4,055	2,423	109	1,632 R		61.6%	36.8%	62.6%	37.4%
6,336	WARREN	1,559	785	739	35	46 R		50.4%	47.4%	51.5%	48.5%
21,176	WASHINGTON	5,411	2,697	2,616	98	81 R		49.8%	48.3%	50.8%	49.2%
26,565	WAYNE	6,511	3,896	2,444	171	1,452 R		59.8%	37.5%	61.5%	38.5%
2,390	WEBSTER	638	300	327	11	27 D		47.0%	51.3%	47.8%	52.2%
6,179	WHEELER	1,123	547	551	25	4 D		48.7%	49.1%	49.8%	50.2%
19,944	WHITE	6,709	5,039	1,421	249	3,618 R		75.1%	21.2%	78.0%	22.0%
83,525	WHITFIELD	16,869	12,563	3,924	382	8,639 R		74.5%	23.3%	76.2%	23.8%
8,577	WILCOX	1,971	1,138	789	44	349 R		57.7%	40.0%	59.1%	40.9%
10,687	WILKES	2,744	1,561	1,117	66	444 R		56.9%	40.7%	58.3%	41.7%
10,220	WILKINSON	2,846	1,279	1,483	84	204 D		44.9%	52.1%	46.3%	53.7%
21,967	WORTH	5,010	2,986	1,926	98	1,060 R		59.6%	38.4%	60.8%	39.2%
8,186,453	TOTAL	2,122,258	1,229,724	811,049	81,485	418,675 R		57.9%	38.2%	60.3%	39.7%

GEORGIA

HOUSE OF REPRESENTATIVES

CD	Year	Total Vote	Republican Vote	Republican Candidate	Democratic Vote	Democratic Candidate	Other Vote	Rep.-Dem. Plurality	Total Vote Rep.	Total Vote Dem.	Major Vote Rep.	Major Vote Dem.
1	2006	138,629	94,961	KINGSTON, JACK*	43,668	NELSON, JIM		51,293 R	68.5%	31.5%	68.5%	31.5%
2	2006	130,629	41,967	HUGHES, BRADLEY C.	88,662	BISHOP, SANFORD D. JR.*		46,695 D	32.1%	67.9%	32.1%	67.9%
3	2006	192,799	130,428	WESTMORELAND, LYNN*	62,371	McGRAW, MIKE		68,057 R	67.6%	32.4%	67.6%	32.4%
4	2006	141,194	34,778	DAVIS, CATHERINE	106,352	JOHNSON, HENRY C. "HANK" JR.	64	71,574 D	24.6%	75.3%	24.6%	75.4%
5	2006	122,428		—	122,380	LEWIS, JOHN*	48	122,380 D		100.0%		100.0%
6	2006	200,252	144,958	PRICE, TOM*	55,294	SINTON, STEVE		89,664 R	72.4%	27.6%	72.4%	27.6%
7	2006	184,114	130,561	LINDER, JOHN*	53,553	BURNS, ALLAN		77,008 R	70.9%	29.1%	70.9%	29.1%
8	2006	159,568	78,908	COLLINS, MAC	80,660	MARSHALL, JIM*		1,752 D	49.5%	50.5%	49.5%	50.5%
9	2006	167,926	128,685	DEAL, NATHAN*	39,240	BRADBURY, JOHN D.	1	89,445 R	76.6%	23.4%	76.6%	23.4%
10	2006	174,753	117,721	NORWOOD, CHARLIE*	57,032	HOLLEY, TERRY		60,689 R	67.4%	32.6%	67.4%	32.6%
11	2006	166,788	118,524	GINGREY, PHIL*	48,261	PILLION, PATRICK SAMUEL	3	70,263 R	71.1%	28.9%	71.1%	28.9%
12	2006	142,438	70,787	BURNS, MAX	71,651	BARROW, JOHN*		864 D	49.7%	50.3%	49.7%	50.3%
13	2006	148,789	45,770	HONEYCUTT, DEBORAH TRAVIS	103,019	SCOTT, DAVID*		57,249 D	30.8%	69.2%	30.8%	69.2%
TOTAL	2006	2,070,307	1,138,048		932,143		116	205,905 R	55.0%	45.0%	55.0%	45.0%
TOTAL	2004	2,960,763	1,819,817		1,140,869		77	678,948 R	61.5%	38.5%	61.5%	38.5%
TOTAL	2002	1,918,297	1,104,162		814,024		111	290,138 R	57.6%	42.4%	57.6%	42.4%

An asterisk (*) denotes incumbent. Georgia's congressional district lines were changed between the 2004 and 2006 elections. For general election results for 2002 and 2004, see *America Votes 26,* p. 139.

GEORGIA

GENERAL AND PRIMARY ELECTIONS

2006 GENERAL ELECTIONS

Governor	Other vote was 81,412 Libertarian (Garrett Michael Hayes); 52 write-in (William Arth); 21 write-in (David C. Bryne).
House	Other vote was:
CD 1	
CD 2	
CD 3	
CD 4	64 write-in (Loren Collins).
CD 5	48 write-in (Eleanor Garcia).
CD 6	
CD 7	
CD 8	
CD 9	1 write-in (Brian Russell Brown).
CD 10	
CD 11	3 write-in (William Satterwhite).
CD 12	
CD 13	

2006 PRIMARY ELECTIONS

Primary	July 18, 2006	**Registration** (active registrants as of June 2006)	4,260,269 No Party Registration
Primary Runoff	August 8, 2006		

Primary Type Open—Any registered voter could participate in either the Democratic or Republican primary, although if they voted in one party's primary they could not participate in a primary runoff of the other party. Voters who did not participate in the primary could vote in either party's runoff.

GEORGIA

GENERAL AND PRIMARY ELECTIONS

Note: An asterisk (*) denotes incumbent.

	REPUBLICAN PRIMARIES			DEMOCRATIC PRIMARIES		
Governor	Sonny Perdue*	370,756	88.4%	Mark Taylor	249,188	51.7%
	Ray McBerry	48,498	11.6%	Cathy Cox	211,978	44.0%
				Bill Bolton	10,552	2.2%
				Mac McCarley	10,399	2.2%
	TOTAL	419,254		TOTAL	482,117	
Congressional District 1	Jack Kingston*	27,043	100.0%	Jim Nelson	20,722	100.0%
Congressional District 2	Bradley C. Hughes	11,755	100.0%	Sanford D. Bishop Jr.*	46,059	100.0%
Congressional District 3	Lynn Westmoreland*	39,572	100.0%	Mike McGraw	24,197	100.0%
Congressional District 4	Catherine Davis	8,832	100.0%	Cynthia A. McKinney*	27,529	44.4%
				Henry C. "Hank" Johnson Jr.	29,216	47.1%
				John Coyne	5,253	8.5%
				TOTAL	61,998	
				PRIMARY RUNOFF		
				Henry C. "Hank" Johnson Jr.	41,281	58.8%
				Cynthia A. McKinney*	28,915	41.2%
				TOTAL	70,196	
Congressional District 5	No Republican candidate	—		John Lewis*	49,993	100.0%
Congressional District 6	Tom Price*	47,925	82.3%	Steve Sinton	15,989	100.0%
	John Konop	10,322	17.7%			
	TOTAL	58,247				
Congressional District 7	John Linder*	40,940	100.0%	Allan Burns	15,987	100.0%
Congressional District 8	Mac Collins	25,065	81.5%	Jim Marshall*	33,133	100.0%
	James Harris	5,684	18.5%			
	TOTAL	30,749				
Congressional District 9	Nathan Deal*	47,682	100.0%	John D. Bradbury	10,354	69.2%
				Bob Longwith	4,618	30.8%
				TOTAL	14,972	
Congressional District 10	Charlie Norwood*	30,845	100.0%	Terry Holley	23,110	100.0%
Congressional District 11	Phil Gingrey*	30,291	100.0%	Patrick Samuel Pillion	18,881	100.0%
Congressional District 12	Max Burns	14,540	100.0%	John Barrow*	26,257	100.0%
Congressional District 13	Deborah Travis Honeycutt	13,712	100.0%	David Scott*	29,179	67.3%
				Donzella James	14,157	32.7%
				TOTAL	43,336	

HAWAII

Congressional districts first established for elections held in 2002
2 members

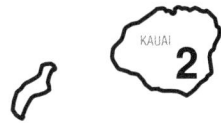

HAWAII

GOVERNOR

Linda Lingle (R). Reelected 2006 to a four-year term. Previously elected 2002.

SENATORS (2 Democrats)

Daniel K. Akaka (D). Reelected 2006 to a six-year term. Previously elected 2000, 1994, and 1990 to fill out the remaining four years of the term vacated by the death of Senator Spark M. Matsunaga (D); had been appointed May 1990 to fill this vacancy.

Daniel K. Inouye (D). Reelected 2004 to a six-year term. Previously elected 1998, 1992, 1986, 1980, 1974, 1968, 1962.

REPRESENTATIVES (2 Democrats)

1. Neil Abercrombie (D)
2. Mazie K. Hirono (D)

POSTWAR VOTE FOR PRESIDENT

| | | Republican | | Democratic | | Other | | Percentage | | | |
| | Total | | | | | | | Total Vote | | Major Vote | |
Year	Vote	Vote	Candidate	Vote	Candidate	Vote	Plurality	Rep.	Dem.	Rep.	Dem.
2004	429,013	194,191	Bush, George W.	231,708	Kerry, John	3,114	37,517 D	45.3%	54.0%	45.6%	54.4%
2000**	367,951	137,845	Bush, George W.	205,286	Gore, Al	24,820	67,441 D	37.5%	55.8%	40.2%	59.8%
1996**	360,120	113,943	Dole, Bob	205,012	Clinton, Bill	41,165	91,069 D	31.6%	56.9%	35.7%	64.3%
1992**	372,842	136,822	Bush, George	179,310	Clinton, Bill	56,710	42,488 D	36.7%	48.1%	43.3%	56.7%
1988	354,461	158,625	Bush, George	192,364	Dukakis, Michael S.	3,472	33,739 D	44.8%	54.3%	45.2%	54.8%
1984	335,846	185,050	Reagan, Ronald	147,154	Mondale, Walter F.	3,642	37,896 R	55.1%	43.8%	55.7%	44.3%
1980**	303,287	130,112	Reagan, Ronald	135,879	Carter, Jimmy	37,296	5,767 D	42.9%	44.8%	48.9%	51.1%
1976	291,301	140,003	Ford, Gerald R.	147,375	Carter, Jimmy	3,923	7,372 D	48.1%	50.6%	48.7%	51.3%
1972	270,274	168,865	Nixon, Richard M.	101,409	McGovern, George S.		67,456 R	62.5%	37.5%	62.5%	37.5%
1968**	236,218	91,425	Nixon, Richard M.	141,324	Humphrey, Hubert H.	3,469	49,899 D	38.7%	59.8%	39.3%	60.7%
1964	207,271	44,022	Goldwater, Barry M.	163,249	Johnson, Lyndon B.		119,227 D	21.2%	78.8%	21.2%	78.8%
1960	184,705	92,295	Nixon, Richard M.	92,410	Kennedy, John F.		115 D	50.0%	50.0%	50.0%	50.0%

**In past elections, the other vote included: 2000 - 21,623 Green (Ralph Nader); 1996 - 27,358 Reform (Ross Perot); 1992 - 53,003 Independent (Ross Perot); 1980 - 32,021 Independent (John Anderson); 1968 - 3,469 American Independent (George Wallace). Hawaii was formally admitted as a state in August 1959.

HAWAII

POSTWAR VOTE FOR GOVERNOR

Year	Total Vote	Republican Vote	Republican Candidate	Democratic Vote	Democratic Candidate	Other Vote	Plurality	Percentage Total Vote Rep.	Percentage Total Vote Dem.	Percentage Major Vote Rep.	Percentage Major Vote Dem.
2006	344,315	215,313	Lingle, Linda	121,717	Iwase, Randy	7,285	93,596 R	62.5%	35.4%	63.9%	36.1%
2002	382,110	197,009	Lingle, Linda	179,647	Hirono, Mazie K.	5,454	17,362 R	51.6%	47.0%	52.3%	47.7%
1998	407,556	198,952	Lingle, Linda	204,206	Cayetano, Benjamin J.	4,398	5,254 D	48.8%	50.1%	49.3%	50.7%
1994**	369,013	107,908	Saiki, Patricia	134,978	Cayetano, Benjamin J.	126,127	21,820 D	29.2%	36.6%	44.4%	55.6%
1990	340,132	131,310	Hemmings, Fred	203,491	Waihee, John	5,331	72,181 D	38.6%	59.8%	39.2%	60.8%
1986	334,115	160,460	Anderson, D.G.	173,655	Waihee, John		13,195 D	48.0%	52.0%	48.0%	52.0%
1982**	311,853	81,507	Anderson, D.G.	141,043	Ariyoshi, George R.	89,303	51,740 D	26.1%	45.2%	36.6%	63.4%
1978	281,587	124,610	Leopold, John	153,394	Ariyoshi, George R.	3,583	28,784 D	44.3%	54.5%	44.8%	55.2%
1974	249,650	113,388	Crossley, Randolph	136,262	Ariyoshi, George R.		22,874 D	45.4%	54.6%	45.4%	54.6%
1970	239,061	101,249	King, Samuel P.	137,812	Burns, John A.		36,563 D	42.4%	57.6%	42.4%	57.6%
1966	213,164	104,324	Crossley, Randolph	108,840	Burns, John A.		4,516 D	48.9%	51.1%	48.9%	51.1%
1962	196,015	81,707	Quinn, William F.	114,308	Burns, John A.		32,601 D	41.7%	58.3%	41.7%	58.3%
1959S	168,662	86,213	Quinn, William F.	82,074	Burns, John A.	375	4,139 R	51.1%	48.7%	51.2%	48.8%

**In past elections, the other vote included: 1994 - 113,158 Best Party (Frank F. Fasi); 1982 - 89,303 Independent Democrat (Fasi). In both 1982 and 1994, Fasi finished second. The 1959 election was for a short term pending the regular vote in 1962.

POSTWAR VOTE FOR SENATOR

Year	Total Vote	Republican Vote	Republican Candidate	Democratic Vote	Democratic Candidate	Other Vote	Rep.-Dem. Plurality	Percentage Total Vote Rep.	Percentage Total Vote Dem.	Percentage Major Vote Rep.	Percentage Major Vote Dem.
2006	342,842	126,097	Thielen, Cynthia	210,330	Akaka, Daniel K.	6,415	84,233 D	36.8%	61.3%	37.5%	62.5%
2004	415,347	87,172	Cavasso, Cam	313,629	Inouye, Daniel K.	14,546	226,457 D	21.0%	75.5%	21.7%	78.3%
2000	345,623	84,701	Carroll, John S.	251,215	Akaka, Daniel K.	9,707	166,514 D	24.5%	72.7%	25.2%	74.8%
1998	398,124	70,964	Young, Crystal	315,252	Inouye, Daniel K.	11,908	244,288 D	17.8%	79.2%	18.4%	81.6%
1994	356,902	86,320	Hustace, Maria M.	256,189	Akaka, Daniel K.	14,393	169,869 D	24.2%	71.8%	25.2%	74.8%
1992	363,662	97,928	Reed, Rick	208,266	Inouye, Daniel K.	57,468	110,338 D	26.9%	57.3%	32.0%	68.0%
1990S	349,666	155,978	Saiki, Patricia	188,901	Akaka, Daniel K.	4,787	32,923 D	44.6%	54.0%	45.2%	54.8%
1988	323,876	66,987	Hustace, Maria M.	247,941	Matsunaga, Spark M.	8,948	180,954 D	20.7%	76.6%	21.3%	78.7%
1986	328,797	86,910	Hutchinson, Frank	241,887	Inouye, Daniel K.		154,977 D	26.4%	73.6%	26.4%	73.6%
1982	306,410	52,071	Brown, Clarence J.	245,386	Matsunaga, Spark M.	8,953	193,315 D	17.0%	80.1%	17.5%	82.5%
1980	288,006	53,068	Brown, Cooper	224,485	Inouye, Daniel K.	10,453	171,417 D	18.4%	77.9%	19.1%	80.9%
1976	302,092	122,724	Quinn, William F.	162,305	Matsunaga, Spark M.	17,063	39,581 D	40.6%	53.7%	43.1%	56.9%
1974	250,221		—	207,454	Inouye, Daniel K.	42,767	207,454 D		82.9%		100.0%
1970	240,760	124,163	Fong, Hiram L.	116,597	Heftel, Cecil		7,566 R	51.6%	48.4%	51.6%	48.4%
1968	226,927	34,008	Thiessen, Wayne C.	189,248	Inouye, Daniel K.	3,671	155,240 D	15.0%	83.4%	15.2%	84.8%
1964	208,814	110,747	Fong, Hiram L.	96,789	Gill, Thomas P.	1,278	13,958 R	53.0%	46.4%	53.4%	46.6%
1962	196,361	60,067	Dillingham, Ben F.	136,294	Inouye, Daniel K.		76,227 D	30.6%	69.4%	30.6%	69.4%
1959**	164,808	87,161	Fong, Hiram L.	77,647	Fasi, Frank F.		9,514 R	52.9%	47.1%	52.9%	47.1%
1959S	163,875	79,123	Tsukiyama, W.C.	83,700	Long, Oren E.	1,052	4,577 D	48.3%	51.1%	48.6%	51.4%

**The 1990 election was for a short term to fill a vacancy. The two 1959 elections were held to indeterminate terms and the Senate later determined by lot that Senator Long would serve a short term, Senator Fong a long term.

HAWAII

GOVERNOR 2006

2000 Census Population	County	Total Vote	Republican	Democratic	Other	Rep.-Dem. Plurality	Percentage Total Vote Rep.	Total Vote Dem.	Major Vote Rep.	Major Vote Dem.
148,677	HAWAII	48,113	27,438	19,388	1,287	8,050 R	57.0%	40.3%	58.6%	41.4%
876,156	HONOLULU	236,756	155,288	76,894	4,574	78,394 R	65.6%	32.5%	66.9%	33.1%
58,463	KAUAI	20,917	10,814	9,505	598	1,309 R	51.7%	45.4%	53.2%	46.8%
128,094	MAUI	38,529	21,773	15,930	826	5,843 R	56.5%	41.3%	57.7%	42.3%
1,211,537	TOTAL	344,315	215,313	121,717	7,285	93,596 R	62.5%	35.4%	63.9%	36.1%

Note: The 2000 Census includes 147 people in Kalawao county; their votes are part of the Maui county returns.

HAWAII

SENATOR 2006

2000 Census Population	County	Total Vote	Republican	Democratic	Other	Rep.-Dem. Plurality	Percentage Total Vote Rep.	Total Vote Dem.	Major Vote Rep.	Major Vote Dem.
148,677	HAWAII	47,797	16,115	30,387	1,295	14,272 D	33.7%	63.6%	34.7%	65.3%
876,156	HONOLULU	235,894	92,762	139,330	3,802	46,568 D	39.3%	59.1%	40.0%	60.0%
58,463	KAUAI	20,698	5,817	14,505	376	8,688 D	28.1%	70.1%	28.6%	71.4%
128,094	MAUI	38,217	11,369	25,916	932	14,547 D	29.7%	67.8%	30.5%	69.5%
	Overseas Ballots	236	34	192	10	158 D	14.4%	81.4%	15.0%	85.0%
1,211,537	TOTAL	342,842	126,097	210,330	6,415	84,233 D	36.8%	61.3%	37.5%	62.5%

Note: The 2000 Census includes 147 people in Kalawao county; their votes are part of the Maui county returns.

HAWAII

HOUSE OF REPRESENTATIVES

CD	Year	Total Vote	Republican Vote	Republican Candidate	Democratic Vote	Democratic Candidate	Other Vote	Rep.-Dem. Plurality	Percentage Total Vote Rep.	Total Vote Dem.	Major Vote Rep.	Major Vote Dem.
1	2006	162,794	49,890	HOUGH, RICHARD "NOAH"	112,904	ABERCROMBIE, NEIL*		63,014 D	30.6%	69.4%	30.6%	69.4%
1	2004	204,181	69,371	TANONAKA, DALTON	128,567	ABERCROMBIE, NEIL*	6,243	59,196 D	34.0%	63.0%	35.0%	65.0%
1	2002	180,733	45,032	TERRY, MARK	131,673	ABERCROMBIE, NEIL*	4,028	86,641 D	24.9%	72.9%	25.5%	74.5%
2	2006	175,150	68,244	HOGUE, BOB	106,906	HIRONO, MAZIE K.		38,662 D	39.0%	61.0%	39.0%	61.0%
2	2004	212,389	79,072	GABBARD, MIKE	133,317	CASE, ED*		54,245 D	37.2%	62.8%	37.2%	62.8%
2	2002	179,251	71,661	McDERMOTT, BOB	100,671	MINK, PATSY T.*	6,919	29,010 D	40.0%	56.2%	41.6%	58.4%
TOTAL	2006	337,944	118,134		219,810			101,676 D	35.0%	65.0%	35.0%	65.0%
TOTAL	2004	416,570	148,443		261,884		6,243	113,441 D	35.6%	62.9%	36.2%	63.8%
TOTAL	2002	359,984	116,693		232,344		10,947	115,651 D	32.4%	64.5%	33.4%	66.6%

An asterisk (*) denotes incumbent.

HAWAII

GENERAL AND PRIMARY ELECTIONS

2006 GENERAL ELECTIONS

Governor Other vote was 5,435 Green (Jim Brewer); 1,850 Libertarian (Ozell Daniel).

Senator Other vote was 6,415 Libertarian (Lloyd Jeffrey Mallan).

House Other vote was:

CD 1
CD 2

2006 PRIMARY ELECTIONS

Primary September 23, 2006 **Registration** 655,741 No Party Registration
(as of September 23, 2006)

Primary Type Open—Any registered voter could participate in the party primary of their choice.

Note: An asterisk (*) denotes incumbent.

	REPUBLICAN PRIMARIES			DEMOCRATIC PRIMARIES		
Governor	Linda Lingle*	31,275	97.4%	Randy Iwase	119,058	66.4%
	George Peabody	322	1.0%	William J. Aila Jr.	43,845	24.5%
	George L. Berish	295	0.9%	Van K. Tanabe	16,317	9.1%
	Paul Manner	211	0.7%			
	TOTAL	*32,103*		*TOTAL*	*179,220*	
Senator	Jerry Coffee	10,139	41.0%	Daniel K. Akaka*	129,158	54.7%
	Mark Beatty	6,057	24.5%	Ed Case	107,163	45.3%
	Charles "Akacase" Collins	3,146	12.7%			
	Jay Friedheim	2,299	9.3%			
	Steve Tataii	1,601	6.5%			
	Edward "Eddie" Pirkowski	1,482	6.0%			
	TOTAL	*24,724*		*TOTAL*	*236,321*	
	Jerry Coffee withdrew from the race before the primary election but too late to have his name removed from the ballot. Cynthia Thielen was subsequently named to fill the vacancy on the general election ballot.					
Congressional District 1	Richard "Noah" Hough	5,652	57.5%	Neil Abercrombie*	82,169	79.1%
	Mark Terry	4,180	42.5%	Alexandra Kaan	21,667	20.9%
	TOTAL	*9,832*		*TOTAL*	*103,836*	
Congressional District 2	Bob Hogue	8,420	50.6%	Mazie K. Hirono	24,487	21.8%
	Quentin Kuhio Kawananakoa	8,226	49.4%	Colleen Hanabusa	23,643	21.1%
				Matt Matsunaga	16,001	14.3%
				Clayton Hee	12,649	11.3%
				Gary L. Hooser	10,730	9.6%
				Brian Schatz	8,254	7.4%
				Ron Menor	8,030	7.2%
				Nestor R. Garcia	4,479	4.0%
				Hanalei Y. Aipoalani	2,688	2.4%
				Joe Zuiker	1,174	1.0%
	TOTAL	*16,646*		*TOTAL*	*112,135*	

IDAHO

Congressional districts first established for elections held in 2002
2 members

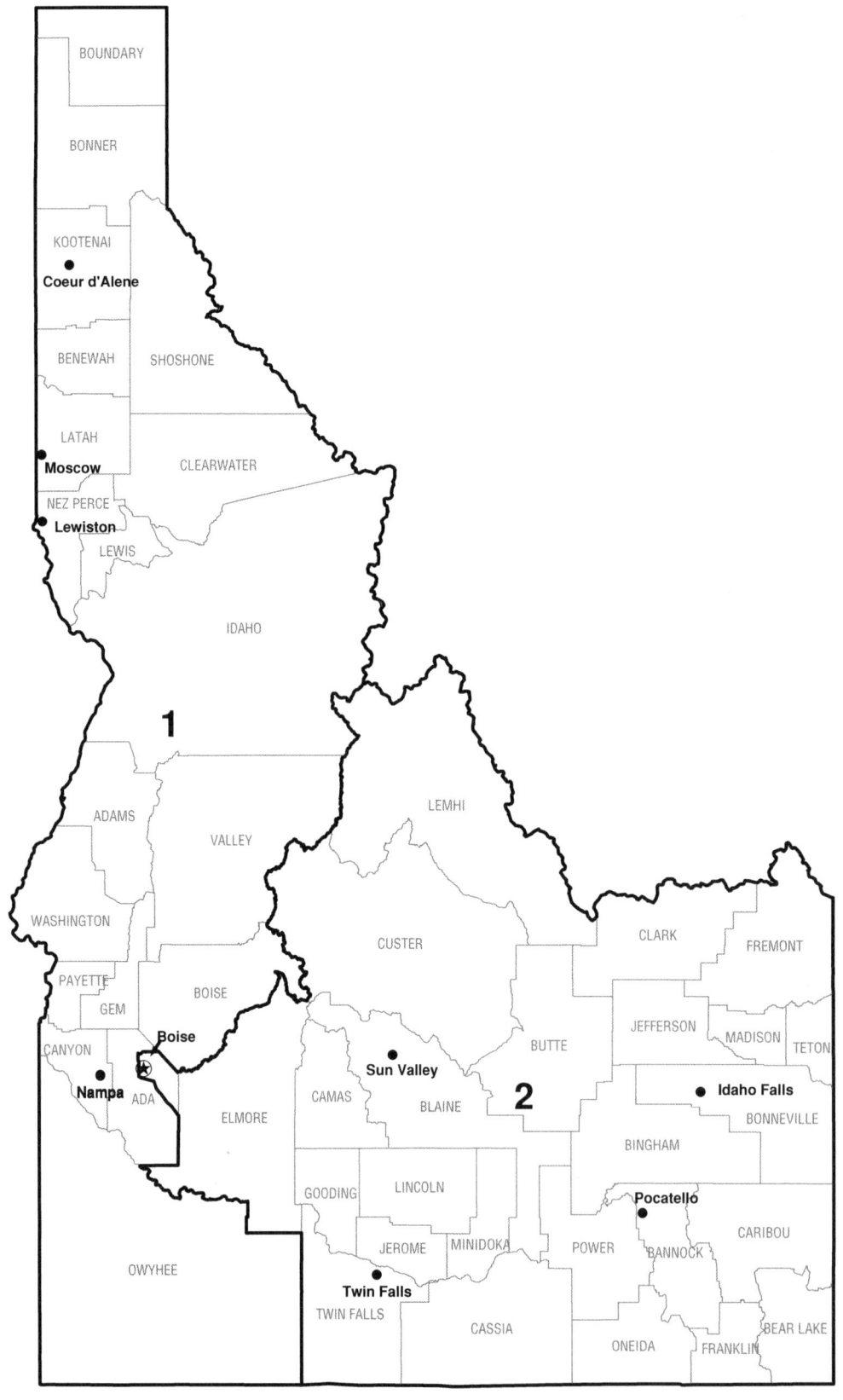

IDAHO

GOVERNOR
C. L. "Butch" Otter (R). Elected 2006 to a four-year term.

SENATORS (2 Republicans)
Michael D. Crapo (R). Reelected 2004 to a six-year term. Previously elected 1998.

Larry E. Craig (R). Reelected 2002 to a six-year term. Previously elected 1996, 1990.

REPRESENTATIVES (2 Republicans)
1. Bill Sali (R)

2. Mike Simpson (R)

POSTWAR VOTE FOR PRESIDENT

| Year | Total Vote | Republican | | Democratic | | Other Vote | Plurality | Percentage | | | |
| | | Vote | Candidate | Vote | Candidate | | | Total Vote | | Major Vote | |
								Rep.	Dem.	Rep.	Dem.
2004	598,447	409,235	Bush, George W.	181,098	Kerry, John	8,114	228,137 R	68.4%	30.3%	69.3%	30.7%
2000**	501,621	336,937	Bush, George W.	138,637	Gore, Al	26,047	198,300 R	67.2%	27.6%	70.8%	29.2%
1996**	491,719	256,595	Dole, Bob	165,443	Clinton, Bill	69,681	91,152 R	52.2%	33.6%	60.8%	39.2%
1992**	482,142	202,645	Bush, George	137,013	Clinton, Bill	142,484	65,632 R	42.0%	28.4%	59.7%	40.3%
1988	408,968	253,881	Bush, George	147,272	Dukakis, Michael S.	7,815	106,609 R	62.1%	36.0%	63.3%	36.7%
1984	411,144	297,523	Reagan, Ronald	108,510	Mondale, Walter F.	5,111	189,013 R	72.4%	26.4%	73.3%	26.7%
1980**	437,431	290,699	Reagan, Ronald	110,192	Carter, Jimmy	36,540	180,507 R	66.5%	25.2%	72.5%	27.5%
1976	344,071	204,151	Ford, Gerald R.	126,549	Carter, Jimmy	13,371	77,602 R	59.3%	36.8%	61.7%	38.3%
1972**	310,379	199,384	Nixon, Richard M.	80,826	McGovern, George S.	30,169	118,558 R	64.2%	26.0%	71.2%	28.8%
1968**	291,183	165,369	Nixon, Richard M.	89,273	Humphrey, Hubert H.	36,541	76,096 R	56.8%	30.7%	64.9%	35.1%
1964	292,477	143,557	Goldwater, Barry M.	148,920	Johnson, Lyndon B.		5,363 D	49.1%	50.9%	49.1%	50.9%
1960	300,450	161,597	Nixon, Richard M.	138,853	Kennedy, John F.		22,744 R	53.8%	46.2%	53.8%	46.2%
1956	272,989	166,979	Eisenhower, Dwight D.	105,868	Stevenson, Adlai E.	142	61,111 R	61.2%	38.8%	61.2%	38.8%
1952	276,254	180,707	Eisenhower, Dwight D.	95,081	Stevenson, Adlai E.	466	85,626 R	65.4%	34.4%	65.5%	34.5%
1948	214,816	101,514	Dewey, Thomas E.	107,370	Truman, Harry S.	5,932	5,856 D	47.3%	50.0%	48.6%	51.4%

**In past elections, the other vote included: 12,292 - Green (Ralph Nader); 1996 - 62,518 Reform (Ross Perot); 1992 - 130,395 Independent (Ross Perot); 1980 - 27,058 Independent (John Anderson); 1972 - 28,869 American (John Schmitz); 1968 - 36,541 American Independent (George Wallace).

IDAHO

POSTWAR VOTE FOR GOVERNOR

Year	Total Vote	Republican Vote	Republican Candidate	Democratic Vote	Democratic Candidate	Other Vote	Rep.-Dem. Plurality	Total Vote Rep.	Total Vote Dem.	Major Vote Rep.	Major Vote Dem.
2006	450,850	237,437	Otter, C. L. "Butch"	198,845	Brady, Jerry M.	14,568	38,592 R	52.7%	44.1%	54.4%	45.6%
2002	411,477	231,566	Kempthorne, Dirk	171,711	Brady, Jerry M.	8,200	59,855 R	56.3%	41.7%	57.4%	42.6%
1998	381,248	258,095	Kempthorne, Dirk	110,815	Huntley, Robert C.	12,338	147,280 R	67.7%	29.1%	70.0%	30.0%
1994	413,346	216,123	Batt, Phil	181,363	EchoHawk, Larry	15,860	34,760 R	52.3%	43.9%	54.4%	45.6%
1990	320,610	101,937	Fairchild, Roger	218,673	Andrus, Cecil D.		116,736 D	31.8%	68.2%	31.8%	68.2%
1986	387,426	189,794	Leroy, David H.	193,429	Andrus, Cecil D.	4,203	3,635 D	49.0%	49.9%	49.5%	50.5%
1982	326,522	161,157	Batt, Phil	165,365	Evans, John V.		4,208 D	49.4%	50.6%	49.4%	50.6%
1978	288,566	114,149	Larsen, Allan	169,540	Evans, John V.	4,877	55,391 D	39.6%	58.8%	40.2%	59.8%
1974	259,632	68,731	Murphy, Jack M.	184,142	Andrus, Cecil D.	6,759	115,411 D	26.5%	70.9%	27.2%	72.8%
1970	245,112	117,108	Samuelson, Don	128,004	Andrus, Cecil D.		10,896 D	47.8%	52.2%	47.8%	52.2%
1966**	252,593	104,586	Samuelson, Don	93,744	Andrus, Cecil D.	54,263	10,842 R	41.4%	37.1%	52.7%	47.3%
1962	255,454	139,578	Smylie, Robert E.	115,876	Smith, Vernon K.		23,702 R	54.6%	45.4%	54.6%	45.4%
1958	239,046	121,810	Smylie, Robert E.	117,236	Derr, A. M.	4,574	4,574 R	51.0%	49.0%	51.0%	49.0%
1954	228,685	124,038	Smylie, Robert E.	104,647	Hamilton, Clark		19,391 R	54.2%	45.8%	54.2%	45.8%
1950	204,792	107,642	Jordan, Len B.	97,150	Wright, Calvin E.		10,492 R	52.6%	47.4%	52.6%	47.4%
1946	181,364	102,233	Robins, C. A.	79,131	Williams, Arnold		23,102 R	56.4%	43.6%	56.4%	43.6%

**In past elections, the other vote included: 1966 - 30,913 Independent (Perry Swisher).

POSTWAR VOTE FOR SENATOR

Year	Total Vote	Republican Vote	Republican Candidate	Democratic Vote	Democratic Candidate	Other Vote	Rep.-Dem. Plurality	Total Vote Rep.	Total Vote Dem.	Major Vote Rep.	Major Vote Dem.
2004**	503,932	499,796	Crapo, Michael D.	—		4,136	499,796 R	99.2%		100.0%	
2002	408,544	266,215	Craig, Larry E.	132,975	Blinken, Alan	9,354	133,240 R	65.2%	32.5%	66.7%	33.3%
1998	378,174	262,966	Crapo, Michael D.	107,375	Mauk, Bill	7,833	155,591 R	69.5%	28.4%	71.0%	29.0%
1996	497,233	283,532	Craig, Larry E.	198,422	Minnick, Walt	15,279	85,110 R	57.0%	39.9%	58.8%	41.2%
1992	478,522	270,468	Kempthorne, Dirk	208,036	Stallings, Richard	18	62,432 R	56.5%	43.5%	56.5%	43.5%
1990	315,936	193,641	Craig, Larry E.	122,295	Twilegar, Ron J.		71,346 R	61.3%	38.7%	61.3%	38.7%
1986	382,024	196,958	Symms, Steven D.	185,066	Evans, John V.		11,892 R	51.6%	48.4%	51.6%	48.4%
1984	406,168	293,193	McClure, James A.	105,591	Busch, Peter M.	7,384	187,602 R	72.2%	26.0%	73.5%	26.5%
1980	439,647	218,701	Symms, Steven D.	214,439	Church, Frank	6,507	4,262 R	49.7%	48.8%	50.5%	49.5%
1978	284,047	194,412	McClure, James A.	89,635	Jensen, Dwight		104,777 R	68.4%	31.6%	68.4%	31.6%
1974	258,847	109,072	Smith, Robert L.	145,140	Church, Frank	4,635	36,068 D	42.1%	56.1%	42.9%	57.1%
1972	309,602	161,804	McClure, James A.	140,913	Davis, William E.	6,885	20,891 R	52.3%	45.5%	53.5%	46.5%
1968	287,876	114,394	Hansen, George V.	173,482	Church, Frank		59,088 D	39.7%	60.3%	39.7%	60.3%
1966	252,456	139,819	Jordan, Len B.	112,637	Harding, Ralph R.		27,182 R	55.4%	44.6%	55.4%	44.6%
1962	258,786	117,129	Hawley, Jack	141,657	Church, Frank		24,528 D	45.3%	54.7%	45.3%	54.7%
1962S	257,677	131,279	Jordan, Len B.	126,398	Pfost, Gracie		4,881 R	50.9%	49.1%	50.9%	49.1%
1960	292,096	152,648	Dworshak, Henry C.	139,448	McLaughlin, Bob		13,200 R	52.3%	47.7%	52.3%	47.7%
1956	265,292	102,781	Welker, Herman	149,096	Church, Frank	13,415	46,315 D	38.7%	56.2%	40.8%	59.2%
1954	226,408	142,269	Dworshak, Henry C.	84,139	Taylor, Glen H.		58,130 R	62.8%	37.2%	62.8%	37.2%
1950	201,417	124,237	Welker, Herman	77,180	Clark, D. Worth		47,057 R	61.7%	38.3%	61.7%	38.3%
1950S	201,970	104,068	Dworshak, Henry C.	97,902	Burtenshaw, Claude		6,166 R	51.5%	48.5%	51.5%	48.5%
1948	214,188	103,868	Dworshak, Henry C.	107,000	Miller, Bert H.	3,320	3,132 D	48.5%	50.0%	49.3%	50.7%
1946S	180,152	105,523	Dworshak, Henry C.	74,629	Donart, George E.		30,894 R	58.6%	41.4%	58.6%	41.4%

In 2004 there was no candidate on the Democratic line. A write-in candidate, who was a Democrat, received 4,136 votes, which are listed in the other vote column. One each of the 1962 and 1950 elections and the 1946 election were for short terms to fill vacancies.

IDAHO

GOVERNOR 2006

2000 Census Population	County	Total Vote	Republican	Democratic	Other	Rep.-Dem. Plurality	Total Vote Rep.	Dem.	Major Vote Rep.	Dem.
300,904	ADA	121,066	55,272	62,632	3,162	7,360 D	45.7%	51.7%	46.9%	53.1%
3,476	ADAMS	1,695	994	635	66	359 R	58.6%	37.5%	61.0%	39.0%
75,565	BANNOCK	25,214	10,912	13,287	1,015	2,375 D	43.3%	52.7%	45.1%	54.9%
6,411	BEAR LAKE	2,219	1,505	621	93	884 R	67.8%	28.0%	70.8%	29.2%
9,171	BENEWAH	2,870	1,631	1,125	114	506 R	56.8%	39.2%	59.2%	40.8%
41,735	BINGHAM	12,725	7,387	4,801	537	2,586 R	58.1%	37.7%	60.6%	39.4%
18,991	BLAINE	7,340	2,061	5,123	156	3,062 D	28.1%	69.8%	28.7%	71.3%
6,670	BOISE	2,875	1,626	1,132	117	494 R	56.6%	39.4%	59.0%	41.0%
36,835	BONNER	13,850	6,933	6,505	412	428 R	50.1%	47.0%	51.6%	48.4%
82,522	BONNEVILLE	30,459	16,900	12,447	1,112	4,453 R	55.5%	40.9%	57.6%	42.4%
9,871	BOUNDARY	3,175	1,781	1,279	115	502 R	56.1%	40.3%	58.2%	41.8%
2,899	BUTTE	1,106	652	402	52	250 R	59.0%	36.3%	61.9%	38.1%
991	CAMAS	441	272	153	16	119 R	61.7%	34.7%	64.0%	36.0%
131,441	CANYON	42,652	25,897	15,237	1,518	10,660 R	60.7%	35.7%	63.0%	37.0%
7,304	CARIBOU	2,507	1,637	765	105	872 R	65.3%	30.5%	68.2%	31.8%
21,416	CASSIA	5,737	3,912	1,576	249	2,336 R	68.2%	27.5%	71.3%	28.7%
1,022	CLARK	337	229	92	16	137 R	68.0%	27.3%	71.3%	28.7%
8,930	CLEARWATER	3,017	1,562	1,346	109	216 R	51.8%	44.6%	53.7%	46.3%
4,342	CUSTER	1,901	1,228	602	71	626 R	64.6%	31.7%	67.1%	32.9%
29,130	ELMORE	5,624	3,282	2,177	165	1,105 R	58.4%	38.7%	60.1%	39.9%
11,329	FRANKLIN	3,949	2,859	899	191	1,960 R	72.4%	22.8%	76.1%	23.9%
11,819	FREMONT	4,392	3,007	1,221	164	1,786 R	68.5%	27.8%	71.1%	28.9%
15,181	GEM	5,688	3,450	2,041	197	1,409 R	60.7%	35.9%	62.8%	37.2%
14,155	GOODING	4,152	2,267	1,740	145	527 R	54.6%	41.9%	56.6%	43.4%
15,511	IDAHO	6,355	3,892	2,251	212	1,641 R	61.2%	35.4%	63.4%	36.6%
19,155	JEFFERSON	7,389	5,220	1,880	289	3,340 R	70.6%	25.4%	73.5%	26.5%
18,342	JEROME	4,897	2,876	1,849	172	1,027 R	58.7%	37.8%	60.9%	39.1%
108,685	KOOTENAI	37,496	20,154	16,246	1,096	3,908 R	53.7%	43.3%	55.4%	44.6%
34,935	LATAH	12,062	4,461	7,155	446	2,694 D	37.0%	59.3%	38.4%	61.6%
7,806	LEMHI	3,193	1,928	1,162	103	766 R	60.4%	36.4%	62.4%	37.6%
3,747	LEWIS	1,387	773	578	36	195 R	55.7%	41.7%	57.2%	42.8%
4,044	LINCOLN	1,422	769	599	54	170 R	54.1%	42.1%	56.2%	43.8%
27,467	MADISON	7,956	5,554	2,118	284	3,436 R	69.8%	26.6%	72.4%	27.6%
20,174	MINIDOKA	5,138	3,217	1,688	233	1,529 R	62.6%	32.9%	65.6%	34.4%
37,410	NEZ PERCE	12,230	5,583	6,355	292	772 D	45.7%	52.0%	46.8%	53.2%
4,125	ONEIDA	1,547	1,030	448	69	582 R	66.6%	29.0%	69.7%	30.3%
10,644	OWYHEE	2,858	1,972	780	106	1,192 R	69.0%	27.3%	71.7%	28.3%
20,578	PAYETTE	5,858	3,723	1,946	189	1,777 R	63.6%	33.2%	65.7%	34.3%
7,538	POWER	2,182	1,229	884	69	345 R	56.3%	40.5%	58.2%	41.8%
13,771	SHOSHONE	3,778	1,434	2,225	119	791 D	38.0%	58.9%	39.2%	60.8%
5,999	TETON	3,036	1,286	1,653	97	367 D	42.4%	54.4%	43.8%	56.2%
64,284	TWIN FALLS	19,754	11,049	8,071	634	2,978 R	55.9%	40.9%	57.8%	42.2%
7,651	VALLEY	3,914	1,889	1,934	91	45 D	48.3%	49.4%	49.4%	50.6%
9,977	WASHINGTON	3,407	2,142	1,185	80	957 R	62.9%	34.8%	64.4%	35.6%
1,293,953	TOTAL	450,850	237,437	198,845	14,568	38,592 R	52.7%	44.1%	54.4%	45.6%

IDAHO

HOUSE OF REPRESENTATIVES

CD	Year	Total Vote	Republican		Democratic		Other Vote	Rep.-Dem. Plurality	Percentage			
									Total Vote		Major Vote	
			Vote	Candidate	Vote	Candidate			Rep.	Dem.	Rep.	Dem.
1	2006	231,974	115,843	SALI, BILL	103,935	GRANT, LARRY	12,196	11,908 R	49.9%	44.8%	52.7%	47.3%
1	2004	298,589	207,662	OTTER, C. L. "BUTCH"*	90,927	PRESTON, NAOMI		116,735 R	69.5%	30.5%	69.5%	30.5%
1	2002	206,141	120,743	OTTER, C. L. "BUTCH"*	80,269	RICHARDSON, BETTY	5,129	40,474 R	58.6%	38.9%	60.1%	39.9%
2	2006	213,332	132,262	SIMPSON, MIKE*	73,441	HANSEN, JIM	7,629	58,821 R	62.0%	34.4%	64.3%	35.7%
2	2004	273,837	193,704	SIMPSON, MIKE*	80,133	WITWORTH, LIN		113,571 R	70.7%	29.3%	70.7%	29.3%
2	2002	198,882	135,605	SIMPSON, MIKE*	57,769	KINGHORN, EDWARD	5,508	77,836 R	68.2%	29.0%	70.1%	29.9%
TOTAL	2006	445,306	248,105		177,376		19,825	70,729 R	55.7%	39.8%	58.3%	41.7%
TOTAL	2004	572,426	401,366		171,060			230,306 R	70.1%	29.9%	70.1%	29.9%
TOTAL	2002	405,023	256,348		138,038		10,637	118,310 R	63.3%	34.1%	65.0%	35.0%

An asterisk (*) denotes incumbent.

IDAHO

GENERAL AND PRIMARY ELECTIONS

2006 GENERAL ELECTIONS

Governor   Other vote was 7,309 Constitution (Marvin Richardson); 7,241 Libertarian (Ted Dunlap); 11 write-in (Glen F. Allen); 7 write-in (Bill Rigoli).

House   Other vote was:

CD 1   6,857 Independent (Dave Olson); 2,882 United (Andy Hedden-Nicely); 2,457 Constitution (Paul Smith).
CD 2   5,113 Independent (Cameron Forth); 2,516 Constitution (Travis J. Hedrick).

2006 PRIMARY ELECTIONS

Primary   May 23, 2006   **Registration**   713,535   No Party Registration
(as of May 23, 2006)

Primary Type   Open—Any registered voter could participate in either the Democratic or Republican primary.

Note: An asterisk (*) denotes incumbent.

	REPUBLICAN PRIMARIES			DEMOCRATIC PRIMARIES		
Governor	C. L. "Butch" Otter	96,045	70.0%	Jerry M. Brady	25,261	83.0%
	Dan Adamson	29,093	21.2%	Lee Chaney Sr.	5,182	17.0%
	Jack Alan Johnson	7,652	5.6%			
	Walt Bayes	4,385	3.2%			
	TOTAL	*137,175*		*TOTAL*	*30,443*	
Congressional District 1	Bill Sali	18,985	25.8%	Larry Grant	10,885	74.8%
	Robert Vasquez	13,624	18.5%	Cecil Kelly III	3,671	25.2%
	Sheila Sorensen	13,472	18.3%			
	Keith Johnson	13,186	17.9%			
	Norman M. "Norm" Semanko	7,976	10.8%			
	R. Skipper "Skip" Brandt	6,289	8.6%			
	TOTAL	*73,532*		*TOTAL*	*14,556*	
Congressional District 2	Mike Simpson*	58,955	100.0%	Jim Hansen	13,300	100.0%

ILLINOIS

Congressional districts first established for elections held in 2002
19 members

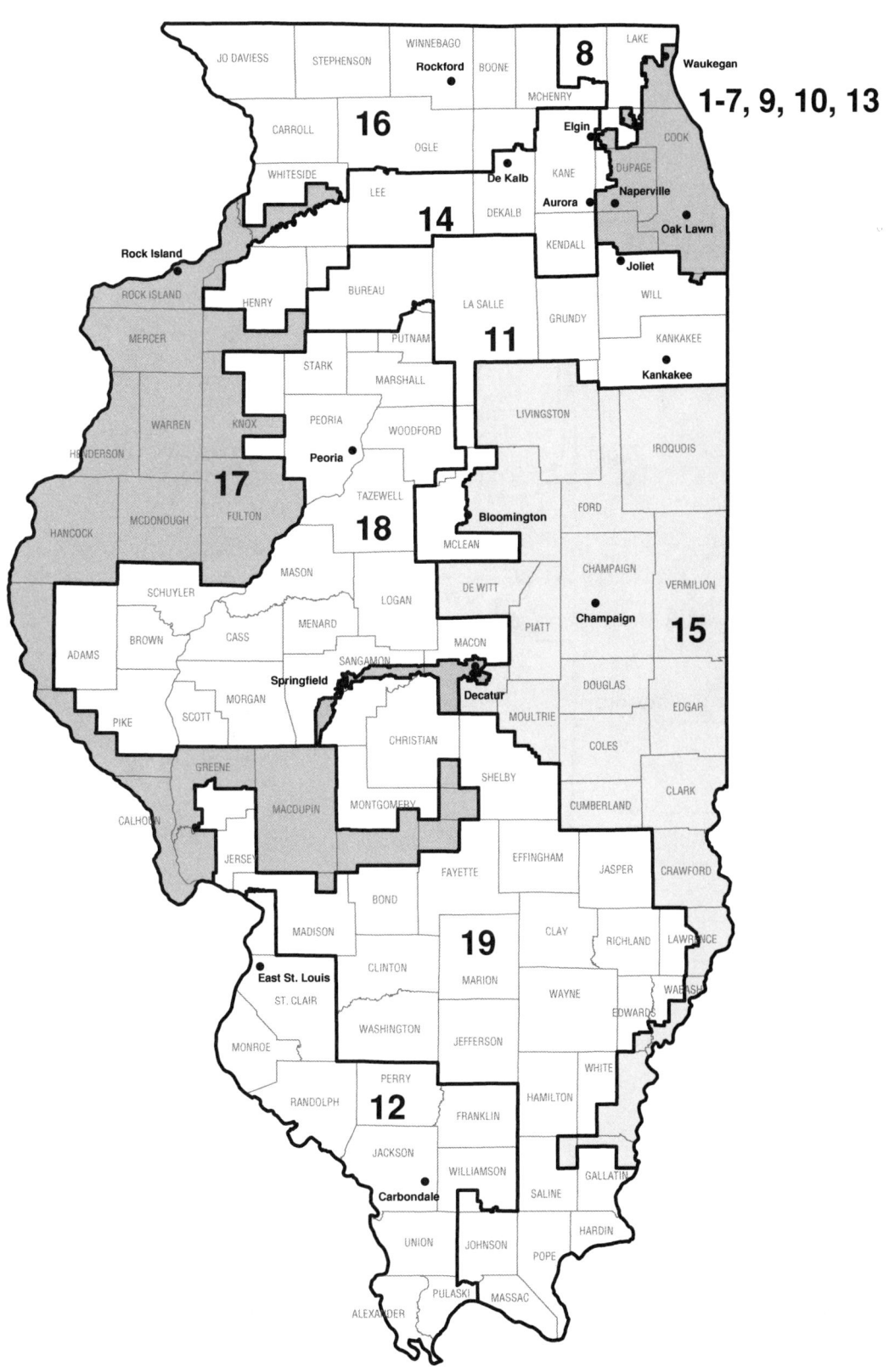

1-7, 9, 10, 13

ILLINOIS

Chicago Area

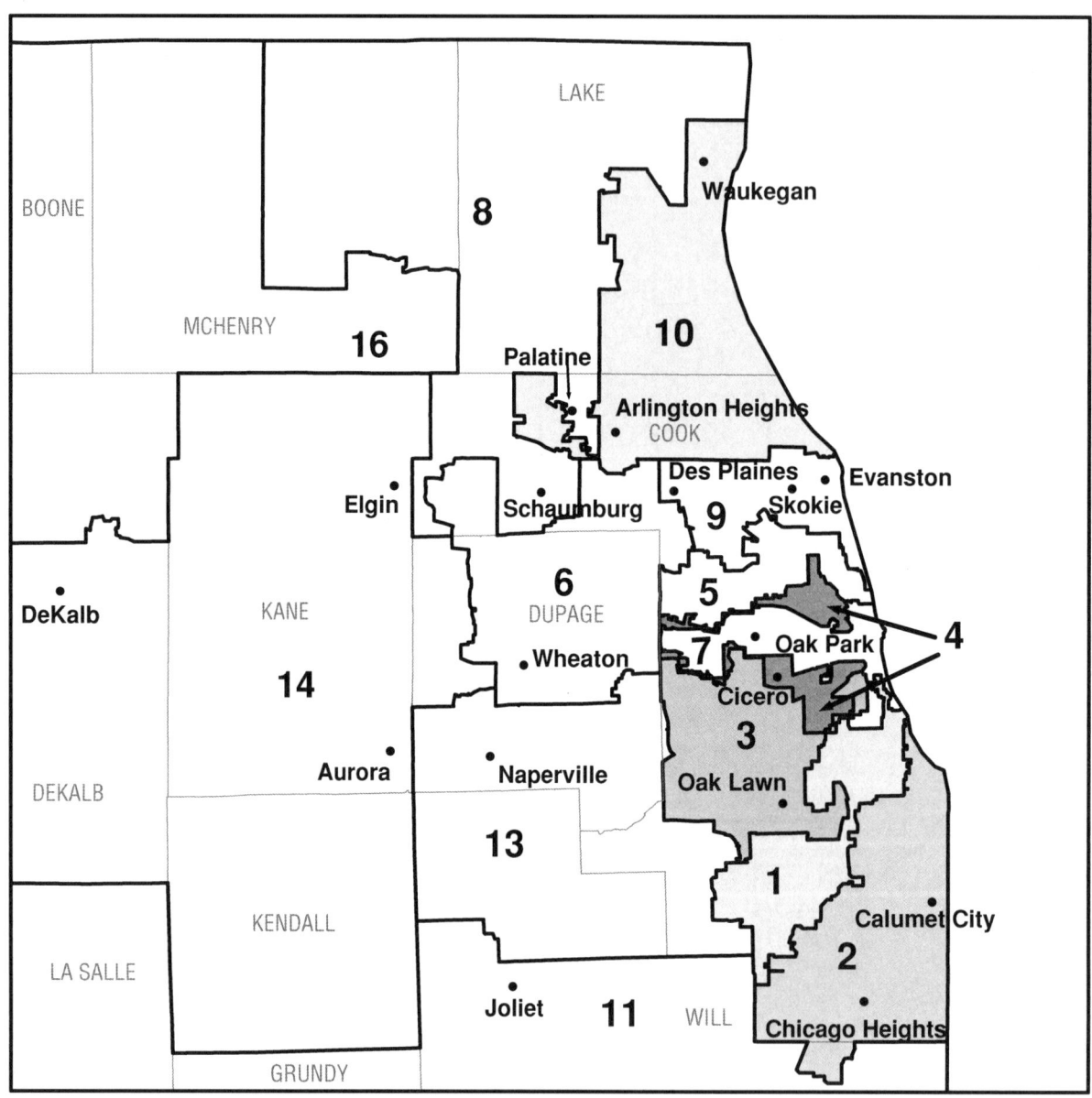

ILLINOIS

GOVERNOR

Rod R. Blagojevich (D). Reelected 2006 to a four-year term. Previously elected 2002.

SENATORS (2 Democrats)

Barack Obama (D). Elected 2004 to a six-year term.

Richard J. Durbin (D). Reelected 2002 to a six-year term. Previously elected 1996.

REPRESENTATIVES (10 Democrats, 9 Republicans)

1. Bobby L. Rush (D)	8. Melissa Bean (D)	15. Timothy V. Johnson (R)
2. Jesse L. Jackson Jr. (D)	9. Jan Schakowsky (D)	16. Donald Manzullo (R)
3. Daniel Lipinski (D)	10. Mark Steven Kirk (R)	17. Phil Hare (D)
4. Luis V. Gutierrez (D)	11. Jerry Weller (R)	18. Ray LaHood (R)
5. Rahm Emanuel (D)	12. Jerry F. Costello (D)	19. John Shimkus (R)
6. Peter J. Roskam (R)	13. Judy Biggert (R)	
7. Danny K. Davis (D)	14. J. Dennis Hastert (R)	

POSTWAR VOTE FOR PRESIDENT

Year	Total Vote	Republican		Democratic		Other Vote	Plurality	Percentage			
								Total Vote		Major Vote	
		Vote	Candidate	Vote	Candidate			Rep.	Dem.	Rep.	Dem.
2004	5,274,322	2,345,946	Bush, George W.	2,891,550	Kerry, John	36,826	545,604 D	44.5%	54.8%	44.8%	55.2%
2000**	4,742,123	2,019,421	Bush, George W.	2,589,026	Gore, Al	133,676	569,605 D	42.6%	54.6%	43.8%	56.2%
1996**	4,311,391	1,587,021	Dole, Bob	2,341,744	Clinton, Bill	382,626	754,723 D	36.8%	54.3%	40.4%	59.6%
1992**	5,050,157	1,734,096	Bush, George	2,453,350	Clinton, Bill	862,711	719,254 D	34.3%	48.6%	41.4%	58.6%
1988	4,559,120	2,310,939	Bush, George	2,215,940	Dukakis, Michael S.	32,241	94,999 R	50.7%	48.6%	51.0%	49.0%
1984	4,819,088	2,707,103	Reagan, Ronald	2,086,499	Mondale, Walter F.	25,486	620,604 R	56.2%	43.3%	56.5%	43.5%
1980**	4,749,721	2,358,049	Reagan, Ronald	1,981,413	Carter, Jimmy	410,259	376,636 R	49.6%	41.7%	54.3%	45.7%
1976	4,718,914	2,364,269	Ford, Gerald R.	2,271,295	Carter, Jimmy	83,350	92,974 R	50.1%	48.1%	51.0%	49.0%
1972	4,723,236	2,788,179	Nixon, Richard M.	1,913,472	McGovern, George S.	21,585	874,707 R	59.0%	40.5%	59.3%	40.7%
1968**	4,619,749	2,174,774	Nixon, Richard M.	2,039,814	Humphrey, Hubert H.	405,161	134,960 R	47.1%	44.2%	51.6%	48.4%
1964	4,702,841	1,905,946	Goldwater, Barry M.	2,796,833	Johnson, Lyndon B.	62	890,887 D	40.5%	59.5%	40.5%	59.5%
1960	4,757,409	2,368,988	Nixon, Richard M.	2,377,846	Kennedy, John F.	10,575	8,858 D	49.8%	50.0%	49.9%	50.1%
1956	4,407,407	2,623,327	Eisenhower, Dwight D.	1,775,682	Stevenson, Adlai E.	8,398	847,645 R	59.5%	40.3%	59.6%	40.4%
1952	4,481,058	2,457,327	Eisenhower, Dwight D.	2,013,920	Stevenson, Adlai E.	9,811	443,407 R	54.8%	44.9%	55.0%	45.0%
1948	3,984,046	1,961,103	Dewey, Thomas E.	1,994,715	Truman, Harry S.	28,228	33,612 D	49.2%	50.1%	49.6%	50.4%

**In past elections, the other vote included: 2000 - 103,759 Green (Ralph Nader); 1996 - 346,408 Reform (Ross Perot); 1992 - 840,515 Independent (Ross Perot); 1980 - 346,754 Independent (John Anderson); 1968 - 390,958 American Independent (George Wallace).

ILLINOIS

POSTWAR VOTE FOR GOVERNOR

Year	Total Vote	Republican Vote	Republican Candidate	Democratic Vote	Democratic Candidate	Other Vote	Plurality	Total Vote Rep.	Total Vote Dem.	Major Vote Rep.	Major Vote Dem.
2006**	3,487,989	1,369,315	Topinka, Judy Baar	1,736,731	Blagojevich, Rod R.	381,943	367,416 D	39.3%	49.8%	44.1%	55.9%
2002	3,538,891	1,594,960	Ryan, Jim	1,847,040	Blagojevich, Rod R.	96,891	252,080 D	45.1%	52.2%	46.3%	53.7%
1998	3,358,705	1,714,094	Ryan, George H.	1,594,191	Poshard, Glenn	50,420	119,903 R	51.0%	47.5%	51.8%	48.2%
1994	3,106,566	1,984,318	Edgar, Jim	1,069,850	Netsch, Dawn C.	52,398	914,468 R	63.9%	34.4%	65.0%	35.0%
1990	3,257,410	1,653,126	Edgar, Jim	1,569,217	Hartigan, Neil F.	35,067	83,909 R	50.7%	48.2%	51.3%	48.7%
1986**	3,143,978	1,655,849	Thompson, James R.	208,830	[See note below]	1,279,299	399,223 R	52.7%	6.6%	88.8%	11.2%
1982	3,673,681	1,816,101	Thompson, James R.	1,811,027	Stevenson, Adlai E. III	46,553	5,074 R	49.4%	49.3%	50.1%	49.9%
1978	3,150,095	1,859,684	Thompson, James R.	1,263,134	Bakalis, Michael	27,277	596,550 R	59.0%	40.1%	59.6%	40.4%
1976S	4,638,997	3,000,395	Thompson, James R.	1,610,258	Howlett, Michael J.	28,344	1,390,137 R	64.7%	34.7%	65.1%	34.9%
1972	4,678,804	2,293,809	Ogilvie, Richard B.	2,371,303	Walker, Daniel	13,692	77,494 D	49.0%	50.7%	49.2%	50.8%
1968	4,506,000	2,307,295	Ogilvie, Richard B.	2,179,501	Shapiro, Samuel H.	19,204	127,794 R	51.2%	48.4%	51.4%	48.6%
1964	4,657,500	2,239,095	Percy, Charles H.	2,418,394	Kerner, Otto	11	179,299 D	48.1%	51.9%	48.1%	51.9%
1960	4,674,187	2,070,479	Stratton, William G.	2,594,731	Kerner, Otto	8,977	524,252 D	44.3%	55.5%	44.4%	55.6%
1956	4,314,611	2,171,786	Stratton, William G.	2,134,909	Austin, Richard B.	7,916	36,877 R	50.3%	49.5%	50.4%	49.6%
1952	4,415,864	2,317,363	Stratton, William G.	2,089,721	Dixon, Sherwood	8,780	227,642 R	52.5%	47.3%	52.6%	47.4%
1948	3,940,257	1,678,007	Green, Dwight H.	2,250,074	Stevenson, Adlai E.	12,176	572,067 D	42.6%	57.1%	42.7%	57.3%

**In past elections, the other vote included: 2006 - 361,336 Green (Rich Whitney); 1986 - 1,256,626 Illinois Solidarity (Adlai E. Stevenson III). In 1986 there was no Democratic candidate for governor on the ballot. Mark Fairchild, a supporter of Lyndon H. LaRouche Jr., was the "paired" Democratic candidate for lieutenant governor and the Democratic vote above was cast for this ticket of "no name" and Fairchild. Running on the Illinois Solidarity line, Stevenson finished second with 40.0 percent of the vote. The 1976 vote was for a two-year term to permit shifting the election for governor to non-presidential years.

POSTWAR VOTE FOR SENATOR

Year	Total Vote	Republican Vote	Republican Candidate	Democratic Vote	Democratic Candidate	Other Vote	Rep.-Dem. Plurality	Total Vote Rep.	Total Vote Dem.	Major Vote Rep.	Major Vote Dem.
2004	5,141,520	1,390,690	Keyes, Alan	3,597,456	Obama, Barack	153,374	2,206,766 D	27.0%	70.0%	27.9%	72.1%
2002	3,486,851	1,325,703	Durkin, Jim	2,103,766	Durbin, Richard J.	57,382	778,063 D	38.0%	60.3%	38.7%	61.3%
1998	3,394,521	1,709,041	Fitzgerald, Peter G.	1,610,496	Moseley-Braun, Carol	74,984	98,545 R	50.3%	47.4%	51.5%	48.5%
1996	4,250,722	1,728,824	Salvi, Al	2,384,028	Durbin, Richard J.	137,870	655,204 D	40.7%	56.1%	42.0%	58.0%
1992	4,939,558	2,126,833	Williamson, Richard S.	2,631,229	Moseley-Braun, Carol	181,496	504,396 D	43.1%	53.3%	44.7%	55.3%
1990	3,251,005	1,135,628	Martin, Lynn	2,115,377	Simon, Paul		979,749 D	34.9%	65.1%	34.9%	65.1%
1986	3,122,883	1,053,734	Koehler, Judy	2,033,783	Dixon, Alan J.	35,366	980,049 D	33.7%	65.1%	34.1%	65.9%
1984	4,787,473	2,308,039	Percy, Charles H.	2,397,303	Simon, Paul	82,131	89,264 D	48.2%	50.1%	49.1%	50.9%
1980	4,580,029	1,946,296	O'Neal, David C.	2,565,302	Dixon, Alan J.	68,431	619,006 D	42.5%	56.0%	43.1%	56.9%
1978	3,184,764	1,698,711	Percy, Charles H.	1,448,187	Seith, Alex	37,866	250,524 R	53.3%	45.5%	54.0%	46.0%
1974	2,914,666	1,084,884	Burditt, George M.	1,811,496	Stevenson, Adlai E. III	18,286	726,612 D	37.2%	62.2%	37.5%	62.5%
1972	4,608,380	2,867,078	Percy, Charles H.	1,721,031	Pucinski, Roman C.	20,271	1,146,047 R	62.2%	37.3%	62.5%	37.5%
1970S	3,599,272	1,519,718	Smith, Ralph T.	2,065,054	Stevenson, Adlai E. III	14,500	545,336 D	42.2%	57.4%	42.4%	57.6%
1968	4,449,757	2,358,947	Dirksen, Everett M.	2,073,242	Clark, William G.	17,568	285,705 R	53.0%	46.6%	53.2%	46.8%
1966	3,822,725	2,100,449	Percy, Charles H.	1,678,147	Douglas, Paul H.	44,129	422,302 R	54.9%	43.9%	55.6%	44.4%
1962	3,709,216	1,961,202	Dirksen, Everett M.	1,748,007	Yates, Sidney R.	7	213,195 R	52.9%	47.1%	52.9%	47.1%
1960	4,632,796	2,093,846	Witwer, Samuel W.	2,530,943	Douglas, Paul H.	8,007	437,097 D	45.2%	54.6%	45.3%	54.7%
1956	4,264,830	2,307,352	Dirksen, Everett M.	1,949,883	Stengel, Richard	7,595	357,469 R	54.1%	45.7%	54.2%	45.8%
1954	3,368,025	1,563,683	Meek, Joseph T.	1,804,338	Douglas, Paul H.	4	240,655 D	46.4%	53.6%	46.4%	53.6%
1950	3,622,673	1,951,984	Dirksen, Everett M.	1,657,630	Lucas, Scott W.	13,059	294,354 R	53.9%	45.8%	54.1%	45.9%
1948	3,900,285	1,740,026	Brooks, C. Wayland	2,147,754	Douglas, Paul H.	12,505	407,728 D	44.6%	55.1%	44.8%	55.2%

The 1970 election was for a short term to fill a vacancy.

ILLINOIS

GOVERNOR 2006

2000 Census Population	County	Total Vote	Republican	Democratic	Green (Whitney)	Other	Rep.-Dem. Plurality	Percentage of Total Vote		
								Rep.	Dem.	Green
68,277	ADAMS	21,849	11,855	7,546	2,155	293	4,309 R	54.3%	34.5%	9.9%
9,590	ALEXANDER	2,973	719	2,005	245	4	1,286 D	24.2%	67.4%	8.2%
17,633	BOND	5,841	3,057	2,341	305	138	716 R	52.3%	40.1%	5.2%
41,786	BOONE	15,210	5,775	5,899	3,392	144	124 D	38.0%	38.8%	22.3%
6,950	BROWN	2,063	1,174	697	160	32	477 R	56.9%	33.8%	7.8%
35,503	BUREAU	12,033	5,384	4,877	1,734	38	507 R	44.7%	40.5%	14.4%
5,084	CALHOUN	2,385	1,018	1,280	86	1	262 D	42.7%	53.7%	3.6%
16,674	CARROLL	5,966	2,997	2,372	534	63	625 R	50.2%	39.8%	9.0%
13,695	CASS	4,507	2,374	1,635	424	74	739 R	52.7%	36.3%	9.4%
179,669	CHAMPAIGN	52,155	27,878	15,141	8,855	281	12,737 R	53.5%	29.0%	17.0%
35,372	CHRISTIAN	11,585	6,111	4,162	1,224	88	1,949 R	52.7%	35.9%	10.6%
17,008	CLARK	5,656	3,372	1,917	318	49	1,455 R	59.6%	33.9%	5.6%
14,560	CLAY	4,829	2,880	1,553	338	58	1,327 R	59.6%	32.2%	7.0%
35,535	CLINTON	12,331	6,708	4,840	708	75	1,868 R	54.4%	39.3%	5.7%
53,196	COLES	13,983	7,596	4,294	1,989	104	3,302 R	54.3%	30.7%	14.2%
5,376,741	COOK	1,310,371	345,528	854,133	109,121	1,589	508,605 D	26.4%	65.2%	8.3%
20,452	CRAWFORD	6,967	4,605	1,884	416	62	2,721 R	66.1%	27.0%	6.0%
11,253	CUMBERLAND	3,902	2,196	1,179	498	29	1,017 R	56.3%	30.2%	12.8%
88,969	DE KALB	25,508	11,870	8,755	4,660	223	3,115 R	46.5%	34.3%	18.3%
16,798	DE WITT	5,821	2,930	1,878	924	89	1,052 R	50.3%	32.3%	15.9%
19,922	DOUGLAS	5,907	3,569	1,566	735	37	2,003 R	60.4%	26.5%	12.4%
904,161	DU PAGE	263,190	132,938	101,859	26,330	2,063	31,079 R	50.5%	38.7%	10.0%
19,704	EDGAR	6,259	3,551	2,079	593	36	1,472 R	56.7%	33.2%	9.5%
6,971	EDWARDS	2,628	1,832	592	137	67	1,240 R	69.7%	22.5%	5.2%
34,264	EFFINGHAM	12,438	8,215	2,960	1,123	140	5,255 R	66.0%	23.8%	9.0%
21,802	FAYETTE	7,704	4,796	2,265	597	46	2,531 R	62.3%	29.4%	7.7%
14,241	FORD	4,386	2,759	1,060	491	76	1,699 R	62.9%	24.2%	11.2%
39,018	FRANKLIN	13,368	4,280	6,803	2,214	71	2,523 D	32.0%	50.9%	16.6%
38,250	FULTON	12,878	4,923	5,903	1,931	121	980 D	38.2%	45.8%	15.0%
6,445	GALLATIN	2,515	770	1,561	173	11	791 D	30.6%	62.1%	6.9%
14,761	GREENE	4,854	2,481	2,033	325	15	448 R	51.1%	41.9%	6.7%
37,535	GRUNDY	14,119	6,139	5,958	1,785	237	181 R	43.5%	42.2%	12.6%
8,621	HAMILTON	3,779	1,421	1,897	436	25	476 D	37.6%	50.2%	11.5%
20,121	HANCOCK	7,442	3,464	2,979	732	267	485 R	46.5%	40.0%	9.8%
4,800	HARDIN	2,157	727	1,280	132	18	553 D	33.7%	59.3%	6.1%
8,213	HENDERSON	2,955	1,179	1,616	140	20	437 D	39.9%	54.7%	4.7%
51,020	HENRY	17,919	8,376	8,159	1,274	110	217 R	46.7%	45.5%	7.1%
31,334	IROQUOIS	9,256	5,613	2,192	1,329	122	3,421 R	60.6%	23.7%	14.4%
59,612	JACKSON	15,733	5,893	5,782	3,941	117	111 R	37.5%	36.8%	25.0%
10,117	JASPER	3,951	2,553	1,073	246	79	1,480 R	64.6%	27.2%	6.2%
40,045	JEFFERSON	12,419	5,279	5,781	1,263	96	502 D	42.5%	46.5%	10.2%
21,668	JERSEY	7,610	3,469	3,624	418	99	155 D	45.6%	47.6%	5.5%
22,289	JO DAVIESS	7,989	3,829	3,365	703	92	464 R	47.9%	42.1%	8.8%
12,878	JOHNSON	4,408	2,090	1,695	617	6	395 R	47.4%	38.5%	14.0%
404,119	KANE	113,125	51,359	45,498	14,528	1,740	5,861 R	45.4%	40.2%	12.8%
103,833	KANKAKEE	30,607	14,285	12,326	3,890	106	1,959 R	46.7%	40.3%	12.7%
54,544	KENDALL	25,771	12,174	10,143	3,283	171	2,031 R	47.2%	39.4%	12.7%
55,836	KNOX	17,523	7,831	8,249	1,394	49	418 D	44.7%	47.1%	8.0%
644,356	LAKE	186,305	79,056	85,430	20,617	1,202	6,374 D	42.4%	45.9%	11.1%
111,509	LA SALLE	33,260	13,488	15,137	4,452	183	1,649 D	40.6%	45.5%	13.4%
15,452	LAWRENCE	5,129	2,790	2,052	203	84	738 R	54.4%	40.0%	4.0%
36,062	LEE	10,854	5,591	3,764	1,406	93	1,827 R	51.5%	34.7%	13.0%
39,678	LIVINGSTON	10,665	6,426	2,984	1,193	62	3,442 R	60.3%	28.0%	11.2%
31,183	LOGAN	9,911	6,244	2,268	1,323	76	3,976 R	63.0%	22.9%	13.3%
32,913	MCDONOUGH	9,827	5,313	3,076	1,310	128	2,237 R	54.1%	31.3%	13.3%
260,077	MCHENRY	80,983	39,113	30,317	10,750	803	8,796 R	48.3%	37.4%	13.3%
150,433	MCLEAN	42,947	23,471	12,895	6,276	305	10,576 R	54.7%	30.0%	14.6%
114,706	MACON	34,646	16,366	14,131	3,961	188	2,235 R	47.2%	40.8%	11.4%
49,019	MACOUPIN	17,226	8,101	7,782	1,257	86	319 R	47.0%	45.2%	7.3%
258,941	MADISON	78,865	31,008	43,620	3,716	521	12,612 D	39.3%	55.3%	4.7%

ILLINOIS

GOVERNOR 2006

2000 Census Population	County	Total Vote	Republican	Democratic	Green (Whitney)	Other	Rep.-Dem. Plurality	Percentage of Total Vote		
								Rep.	Dem.	Green
41,691	MARION	12,277	6,281	5,090	822	84	1,191 R	51.2%	41.5%	6.7%
13,180	MARSHALL	4,550	2,205	1,607	720	18	598 R	48.5%	35.3%	15.8%
16,038	MASON	4,997	2,405	1,895	653	44	510 R	48.1%	37.9%	13.1%
15,161	MASSAC	5,200	1,888	2,882	366	64	994 D	36.3%	55.4%	7.0%
12,486	MENARD	5,090	3,608	882	561	39	2,726 R	70.9%	17.3%	11.0%
16,957	MERCER	6,232	2,668	3,206	339	19	538 D	42.8%	51.4%	5.4%
27,619	MONROE	10,937	4,993	5,410	459	75	417 D	45.7%	49.5%	4.2%
30,652	MONTGOMERY	10,858	5,794	3,991	948	125	1,803 R	53.4%	36.8%	8.7%
36,616	MORGAN	11,808	7,057	3,349	1,312	90	3,708 R	59.8%	28.4%	11.1%
14,287	MOULTRIE	4,762	2,397	1,668	656	41	729 R	50.3%	35.0%	13.8%
51,032	OGLE	15,737	7,034	4,965	3,385	353	2,069 R	44.7%	31.5%	21.5%
183,433	PEORIA	53,748	23,662	21,387	8,216	483	2,275 R	44.0%	39.8%	15.3%
23,094	PERRY	7,722	2,777	3,709	1,206	30	932 D	36.0%	48.0%	15.6%
16,365	PIATT	6,541	3,760	1,725	997	59	2,035 R	57.5%	26.4%	15.2%
17,384	PIKE	6,049	3,118	2,243	502	186	875 R	51.5%	37.1%	8.3%
4,413	POPE	2,023	784	1,045	179	15	261 D	38.8%	51.7%	8.8%
7,348	PULASKI	2,772	950	1,587	235		637 D	34.3%	57.3%	8.5%
6,086	PUTNAM	2,263	948	1,039	263	13	91 D	41.9%	45.9%	11.6%
33,893	RANDOLPH	11,606	4,661	5,889	1,017	39	1,228 D	40.2%	50.7%	8.8%
16,149	RICHLAND	6,040	3,598	1,690	330	422	1,908 R	59.6%	28.0%	5.5%
149,374	ROCK ISLAND	46,229	17,168	26,201	2,720	140	9,033 D	37.1%	56.7%	5.9%
256,082	ST. CLAIR	69,148	27,318	38,441	2,784	605	11,123 D	39.5%	55.6%	4.0%
26,733	SALINE	8,937	3,215	4,618	1,065	39	1,403 D	36.0%	51.7%	11.9%
188,951	SANGAMON	74,322	50,332	15,625	8,064	301	34,707 R	67.7%	21.0%	10.9%
7,189	SCHUYLER	3,080	1,577	1,101	359	43	476 R	51.2%	35.7%	11.7%
5,537	SCOTT	2,020	1,197	627	173	23	570 R	59.3%	31.0%	8.6%
22,893	SHELBY	7,675	4,238	2,271	1,076	90	1,967 R	55.2%	29.6%	14.0%
6,332	STARK	2,158	1,138	705	306	9	433 R	52.7%	32.7%	14.2%
48,979	STEPHENSON	13,310	5,773	5,163	2,134	240	610 R	43.4%	38.8%	16.0%
128,485	TAZEWELL	42,826	19,826	16,062	6,330	608	3,764 R	46.3%	37.5%	14.8%
18,293	UNION	6,757	2,624	2,961	1,142	30	337 D	38.8%	43.8%	16.9%
83,919	VERMILION	23,021	11,054	9,360	2,469	138	1,694 R	48.0%	40.7%	10.7%
12,937	WABASH	4,538	2,958	1,398	160	22	1,560 R	65.2%	30.8%	3.5%
18,735	WARREN	5,909	3,127	2,405	360	17	722 R	52.9%	40.7%	6.1%
15,148	WASHINGTON	6,255	3,328	2,433	455	39	895 R	53.2%	38.9%	7.3%
17,151	WAYNE	7,234	5,051	1,714	397	72	3,337 R	69.8%	23.7%	5.5%
15,371	WHITE	6,061	3,655	2,021	335	50	1,634 R	60.3%	33.3%	5.5%
60,653	WHITESIDE	17,571	7,649	8,258	1,575	89	609 D	43.5%	47.0%	9.0%
502,266	WILL	159,098	67,066	73,944	16,955	1,133	6,878 D	42.2%	46.5%	10.7%
61,296	WILLIAMSON	20,412	8,198	8,493	3,476	245	295 D	40.2%	41.6%	17.0%
278,418	WINNEBAGO	78,116	26,147	32,383	18,539	1,047	6,236 D	33.5%	41.5%	23.7%
35,469	WOODFORD	12,657	7,299	3,146	1,986	226	4,153 R	57.7%	24.9%	15.7%
12,419,293	TOTAL	3,487,989	1,369,315	1,736,731	361,336	20,607	367,416 D	39.3%	49.8%	10.4%

ILLINOIS

HOUSE OF REPRESENTATIVES

CD	Year	Total Vote	Republican Vote	Republican Candidate	Democratic Vote	Democratic Candidate	Other Vote	Rep.-Dem. Plurality	Total Vote Rep.	Total Vote Dem.	Major Vote Rep.	Major Vote Dem.
1	2006	174,427	27,804	TABOUR, JASON E.	146,623	RUSH, BOBBY L.*		118,819 D	15.9%	84.1%	15.9%	84.1%
1	2004	249,949	37,840	WARDINGLEY, RAYMOND G.	212,109	RUSH, BOBBY L.*		174,269 D	15.1%	84.9%	15.1%	84.9%
1	2002	183,656	29,776	WARDINGLEY, RAYMOND G.	149,068	RUSH, BOBBY L.*	4,812	119,292 D	16.2%	81.2%	16.6%	83.4%
2	2006	172,490	20,395	BELIN, ROBERT	146,347	JACKSON, JESSE L. JR*	5,748	125,952 D	11.8%	84.8%	12.2%	87.8%
2	2004	234,525	—		207,535	JACKSON, JESSE L. JR*	26,990	207,535 D		88.5%		100.0%
2	2002	184,010	32,567	NELSON, DOUG	151,443	JACKSON, JESSE L. JR*		118,876 D	17.7%	82.3%	17.7%	82.3%
3	2006	165,722	37,954	WARDINGLEY, RAYMOND G.	127,768	LIPINSKI, DANIEL*		89,814 D	22.9%	77.1%	22.9%	77.1%
3	2004	229,956	57,845	CHLADA, RYAN	167,034	LIPINSKI, DANIEL	5,077	109,189 D	25.2%	72.6%	25.7%	74.3%
3	2002	156,042		—	156,042	LIPINSKI, WILLIAM O.*		156,042 D		100.0%		100.0%
4	2006	81,442	11,532	MELICHAR, ANN	69,910	GUTIERREZ, LUIS V.*		58,378 D	14.2%	85.8%	14.2%	85.8%
4	2004	125,142	15,536	CISNEROS, TONY	104,761	GUTIERREZ, LUIS V.*	4,845	89,225 D	12.4%	83.7%	12.9%	87.1%
4	2002	84,513	12,778	LOPEZ-CISNEROS, ANTHONY J. "TONY"	67,339	GUTIERREZ, LUIS V.*	4,396	54,561 D	15.1%	79.7%	15.9%	84.1%
5	2006	146,581	32,250	WHITE, KEVIN EDWARD	114,319	EMANUEL, RAHM*	12	82,069 D	22.0%	78.0%	22.0%	78.0%
5	2004	207,930	49,530	BEST, BRUCE	158,400	EMANUEL, RAHM*		108,870 D	23.8%	76.2%	23.8%	76.2%
5	2002	159,435	46,008	AUGUSTI, MARK A.	106,514	EMANUEL, RAHM	6,913	60,506 D	28.9%	66.8%	30.2%	69.8%
6	2006	177,957	91,382	ROSKAM, PETER J.	86,572	DUCKWORTH, L. TAMMY	3	4,810 R	51.4%	48.6%	51.4%	48.6%
6	2004	250,097	139,627	HYDE, HENRY J.*	110,470	CEGELIS, CHRISTINE		29,157 R	55.8%	44.2%	55.8%	44.2%
6	2002	173,872	113,174	HYDE, HENRY J.*	60,698	BERRY, TOM		52,476 R	65.1%	34.9%	65.1%	34.9%
7	2006	165,011	21,939	HUTCHINSON, CHARLES	143,071	DAVIS, DANNY K.*	1	121,132 D	13.3%	86.7%	13.3%	86.7%
7	2004	256,736	35,603	DAVIS-FAIRMAN, ANTONIO	221,133	DAVIS, DANNY K.*		185,530 D	13.9%	86.1%	13.9%	86.1%
7	2002	165,756	25,280	TUNNEY, MARK	137,933	DAVIS, DANNY K.*	2,543	112,653 D	15.3%	83.2%	15.5%	84.5%
8	2006	183,394	80,720	McSWEENEY, DAVID	93,355	BEAN, MELISSA*	9,319	12,635 D	44.0%	50.9%	46.4%	53.6%
8	2004	270,393	130,601	CRANE, PHILIP M.*	139,792	BEAN, MELISSA		9,191 D	48.3%	51.7%	48.3%	51.7%
8	2002	165,926	95,275	CRANE, PHILIP M.*	70,626	BEAN, MELISSA	25	24,649 R	57.4%	42.6%	57.4%	42.6%
9	2006	164,713	41,858	SHANNON, MICHAEL P.	122,852	SCHAKOWSKY, JAN*	3	80,994 D	25.4%	74.6%	25.4%	74.6%
9	2004	231,417	56,135	ECKHARDT, KURT J.	175,282	SCHAKOWSKY, JAN*		119,147 D	24.3%	75.7%	24.3%	75.7%
9	2002	168,836	45,307	DURIC, NICHOLAS M.	118,642	SCHAKOWSKY, JAN*	4,887	73,335 D	26.8%	70.3%	27.6%	72.4%
10	2006	202,208	107,929	KIRK, MARK STEVEN*	94,278	SEALS, DANIEL J.	1	13,651 R	53.4%	46.6%	53.4%	46.6%
10	2004	276,711	177,493	KIRK, MARK STEVEN*	99,218	GOODMAN, LEE		78,275 R	64.1%	35.9%	64.1%	35.9%
10	2002	186,911	128,611	KIRK, MARK STEVEN*	58,300	PERRITT, HENRY H. "HANK"		70,311 R	68.8%	31.2%	68.8%	31.2%
11	2006	197,856	109,009	WELLER, JERRY*	88,846	PAVICH, JOHN	1	20,163 R	55.1%	44.9%	55.1%	44.9%
11	2004	294,960	173,057	WELLER, JERRY*	121,903	RENNER, TARI		51,154 R	58.7%	41.3%	58.7%	41.3%
11	2002	193,085	124,192	WELLER, JERRY*	68,893	VAN DUYNE, KEITH S.		55,299 R	64.3%	35.7%	64.3%	35.7%
12	2006	157,809		—	157,802	COSTELLO, JERRY F.*	7	157,802 D		100.0%		100.0%
12	2004	286,435	82,677	ZWEIGART, ERIN R.	198,962	COSTELLO, JERRY F.*	4,796	116,285 D	28.9%	69.5%	29.4%	70.6%
12	2002	190,020	58,440	SADLER, DAVID	131,580	COSTELLO, JERRY F.*		73,140 D	30.8%	69.2%	30.8%	69.2%
13	2006	205,234	119,720	BIGGERT, JUDY*	85,507	SHANNON, JOSEPH	7	34,213 R	58.3%	41.7%	58.3%	41.7%
13	2004	308,312	200,472	BIGGERT, JUDY*	107,836	ANDERSEN, GLORIA SCHOR	4	92,636 R	65.0%	35.0%	65.0%	35.0%
13	2002	198,615	139,546	BIGGERT, JUDY*	59,069	MASON, TOM		80,477 R	70.3%	29.7%	70.3%	29.7%
14	2006	197,144	117,870	HASTERT, J. DENNIS*	79,274	LAESCH, JONATHAN "JOHN"		38,596 R	59.8%	40.2%	59.8%	40.2%
14	2004	279,208	191,618	HASTERT, J. DENNIS*	87,590	ZAMORA, RUBEN		104,028 R	68.6%	31.4%	68.6%	31.4%
14	2002	182,363	135,198	HASTERT, J. DENNIS*	47,165	QUICK, LAURENCE J.		88,033 R	74.1%	25.9%	74.1%	25.9%
15	2006	202,835	116,810	JOHNSON, TIMOTHY V.*	86,025	GILL, DAVID		30,785 R	57.6%	42.4%	57.6%	42.4%
15	2004	291,739	178,114	JOHNSON, TIMOTHY V.*	113,625	GILL, DAVID		64,489 R	61.1%	38.9%	61.1%	38.9%
15	2002	206,617	134,650	JOHNSON, TIMOTHY V.*	64,131	HARTKE, JOSHUA T.	7,836	70,519 R	65.2%	31.0%	67.7%	32.3%
16	2006	198,101	125,951	MANZULLO, DONALD*	63,627	AUMAN, RICHARD D.	8,523	62,324 R	63.6%	32.1%	66.4%	33.6%
16	2004	295,806	204,350	MANZULLO, DONALD*	91,452	KUTSCH, JOHN H.	4	112,898 R	69.1%	30.9%	69.1%	30.9%
16	2002	188,827	133,339	MANZULLO, DONALD*	55,488	KUTSCH, JOHN H.		77,851 R	70.6%	29.4%	70.6%	29.4%

ILLINOIS

HOUSE OF REPRESENTATIVES

			Republican		Democratic				Percentage			
									Total Vote		Major Vote	
CD	Year	Total Vote	Vote	Candidate	Vote	Candidate	Other Vote	Rep.-Dem. Plurality	Rep.	Dem.	Rep.	Dem.
17	2006	201,186	86,161	ZINGA, ANDREA	115,025	HARE, PHIL		28,864 D	42.8%	57.2%	42.8%	57.2%
17	2004	284,000	111,680	ZINGA, ANDREA	172,320	EVANS, LANE*		60,640 D	39.3%	60.7%	39.3%	60.7%
17	2002	203,612	76,519	CALDERONE, PETER	127,093	EVANS, LANE*		50,574 D	37.6%	62.4%	37.6%	62.4%
18	2006	223,246	150,194	LaHOOD, RAY*	73,052	WATERWORTH, STEVE		77,142 R	67.3%	32.7%	67.3%	32.7%
18	2004	307,595	216,047	LaHOOD, RAY*	91,548	WATERWORTH, STEVE		124,499 R	70.2%	29.8%	70.2%	29.8%
18	2002	192,567	192,567	LaHOOD, RAY*		—		192,567 R	100.0%		100.0%	
19	2006	236,352	143,491	SHIMKUS, JOHN*	92,861	STOVER, DANNY L.		50,630 R	60.7%	39.3%	60.7%	39.3%
19	2004	307,754	213,451	SHIMKUS, JOHN*	94,303	BAGWELL, TIM		119,148 R	69.4%	30.6%	69.4%	30.6%
19	2002	244,473	133,956	SHIMKUS, JOHN*	110,517	PHELPS, DAVID*		23,439 R	54.8%	45.2%	54.8%	45.2%
TOTAL	2006	3,453,708	1,442,969		1,987,114		23,625	544,145 D	41.8%	57.5%	42.1%	57.9%
TOTAL	2004	4,988,665	2,271,676		2,675,273		41,716	403,597 D	45.5%	53.6%	45.9%	54.1%
TOTAL	2002	3,429,136	1,657,183		1,740,541		31,412	83,358 D	48.3%	50.8%	48.8%	51.2%

ILLINOIS

GENERAL AND PRIMARY ELECTIONS

2006 GENERAL ELECTIONS

Governor   Other vote was 19,020 write-in (Randall C. "Randy" Stufflebeam); 476 write-in (Mark Robert McCoy); 252 write-in (No Candidate/Randy A. White); 241 write-in (Timothy Ross Nieukirk); 134 write-in (Angel L. Rivera); 129 write-in (Albert "Barney" Sloan); 98 write-in (Mike Shorten); 81 write-in (Jack L. "Captain" Spani); 76 write-in (Kevin J. Bognar); 39 write-in (Marvin J. Koch Jr.); 29 write-in (Joseph S. Krug); 16 write-in (David Louis the Christ Sito); 8 write-in (No Candidate/Garrett Casey DeFauw); 6 write-in (Barry Newman); 2 write-in (William Miller). The Stufflebeam vote included 13,247 votes for the Stufflebeam-White ticket and 5,773 votes for Stufflebeam alone. The Nieukirk vote included 89 votes for the Nieukirk-DeFauw ticket and 152 votes for Nieukirk alone. (The Green Party candidate, Rich Whitney, received 361,336 votes, 10.4 percent of the total vote. The Green Party vote is listed in the county table for the 2006 gubernatorial election in Illinois.)

House   Other vote was:

CD 1
CD 2   5,748 Libertarian (Anthony W. Williams).
CD 3
CD 4
CD 5   12 write-in (John Houlihan).
CD 6   3 write-in (Patricia Elaine Beard).
CD 7   1 write-in (Lowell M. Seida).
CD 8   9,312 Moderate (Bill Scheurer); 7 write-in (Jonathan Farnick).
CD 9   3 write-in (Simon Michael Ribeiro).
CD 10   1 write-in (Arthur C. Brumfield).
CD 11   1 write-in (Alaka Waikar).
CD 12   7 write-in (W. K. Siglar).
CD 13   7 write-in (Mark Alan Mastrogiovanni).
CD 14
CD 15
CD 16   8,523 write-in (General John Borling).
CD 17
CD 18
CD 19

2006 PRIMARY ELECTIONS

Primary   March 21, 2006   **Registration**   7,263,969   No Party Registration
                                        (as of March 21, 2006)

Primary Type   Open—Any registered voter could participate in the primary of either party.

ILLINOIS

GENERAL AND PRIMARY ELECTIONS

Note: An asterisk (*) denotes incumbent.

	REPUBLICAN PRIMARIES			DEMOCRATIC PRIMARIES		
Governor	Judy Baar Topinka	280,701	38.1%	Rod R. Blagojevich*	669,006	70.8%
	Jim Oberweis	233,576	31.7%	Edwin Eisendrath	275,375	29.2%
	Bill Brady	135,370	18.4%	James R. Davis (write-in)	16	
	Ron Gidwitz	80,068	10.9%			
	Andy Martin	6,095	0.8%			
	TOTAL	735,810		TOTAL	944,397	
Congressional District 1	Jason E. Tabour	6,494	100.0%	Bobby L. Rush*	81,593	81.6%
				Phillip Jackson	18,427	18.4%
				TOTAL	100,020	
Congressional District 2	Robert Belin	3,829	58.4%	Jesse L. Jackson Jr.*	90,656	100.0%
	Howard Schug	2,729	41.6%			
	TOTAL	6,558				
Congressional District 3	Raymond G. Wardingley	12,603	70.6%	Daniel Lipinksi*	44,401	54.4%
	Arthur J. Jones	5,242	29.4%	John T. Kelly	20,918	25.7%
	Richard Benedict Mayers (write-in)	2		John P. Sullivan	16,231	19.9%
	TOTAL	17,847		TOTAL	81,550	
Congressional District 4	Ann Melichar	3,102	100.0%	Luis V. Gutierrez*	36,915	100.0%
Congressional District 5	Kevin Edward White	9,567	100.0%	Rahm Emanuel*	53,727	83.1%
				Mark Arnold Fredrickson	6,050	9.4%
				John Haptonstall "Johnny Hap"	4,876	7.5%
				TOTAL	64,653	
Congressional District 6	Peter J. Roskam	50,794	100.0%	L. Tammy Duckworth	14,283	43.8%
				Christine Cegelis	13,159	40.4%
				Lindy Scott	5,133	15.8%
				TOTAL	32,575	
Congressional District 7	Charles Hutchinson	6,586	100.0%	Danny K. Davis*	77,287	89.0%
				Jim Ascot	6,646	7.7%
				Robert Dallas	2,921	3.4%
				TOTAL	86,854	
Congressional District 8	David McSweeney	25,085	42.9%	Melissa Bean*	23,375	100.0%
	Kathy Salvi	19,370	33.1%			
	Robert W. Churchill	9,169	15.7%			
	Aaron B. Lincoln	2,630	4.5%			
	Ken Arnold	1,275	2.2%			
	James Creighton Mitchell Jr.	921	1.6%			
	TOTAL	58,450				
Congressional District 9	Michael P. Shannon	13,482	85.0%	Jan Schakowsky*	57,490	100.0%
	Simon M. Ribeiro	2,385	15.0%			
	TOTAL	15,867				
Congressional District 10	Mark Steven Kirk*	36,115	100.0%	Daniel J. Seals	23,462	70.8%
	Phil Collins (write-in)	13		Zane Smith	9,694	29.2%
	TOTAL	36,128		TOTAL	33,156	
Congressional District 11	Jerry Weller*	45,954	100.0%	John Pavich	29,436	100.0%
Congressional District 12	No Republican candidate			Jerry F. Costello*	45,600	90.1%
				Kenneth Charles Wiezer	4,991	9.9%
				TOTAL	50,591	
Congressional District 13	Judy Biggert*	52,900	79.6%	Joseph Shannon	17,919	56.5%
	Bob Hart	13,564	20.4%	Bill Reedy	13,789	43.5%
	TOTAL	66,464		TOTAL	31,708	
Congressional District 14	J. Dennis Hastert*	69,198	100.0%	Jonathan "John" Laesch	15,022	65.8%
				Ruben Kanhai-Zamora	7,809	34.2%
				TOTAL	22,831	
Congressional District 15	Timothy V. Johnson*	55,833	100.0%	David Gill	17,571	100.0%

ILLINOIS

GENERAL AND PRIMARY ELECTIONS

Note: An asterisk (*) denotes incumbent.

	REPUBLICAN PRIMARIES			DEMOCRATIC PRIMARIES		
Congressional District 16	Donald Manzullo*	60,440	100.0%	Richard D. Auman	27,749	100.0%
Congressional District 17	Andrea Zinga	13,287	42.2%	Lane Evans*	38,780	100.0%
	Jim Mowen	12,962	41.2%			
	Brian S. Gilliland	5,241	16.6%	*Lane Evans subsequently withdrew from the race and was replaced on*		
	TOTAL	31,490		*the general election ballot by Phil Hare.*		
Congressional District 18	Ray LaHood*	49,400	100.0%	Steve Waterworth	21,798	100.0%
Congressional District 19	John Shimkus*	42,588	99.8%	Danny L. Stover	20,555	61.6%
	Don Grimes (write-in)	74	0.2%	Vic Roberts	12,835	38.4%
	TOTAL	42,662		TOTAL	33,390	

INDIANA

Congressional districts first established for elections held in 2002
9 members

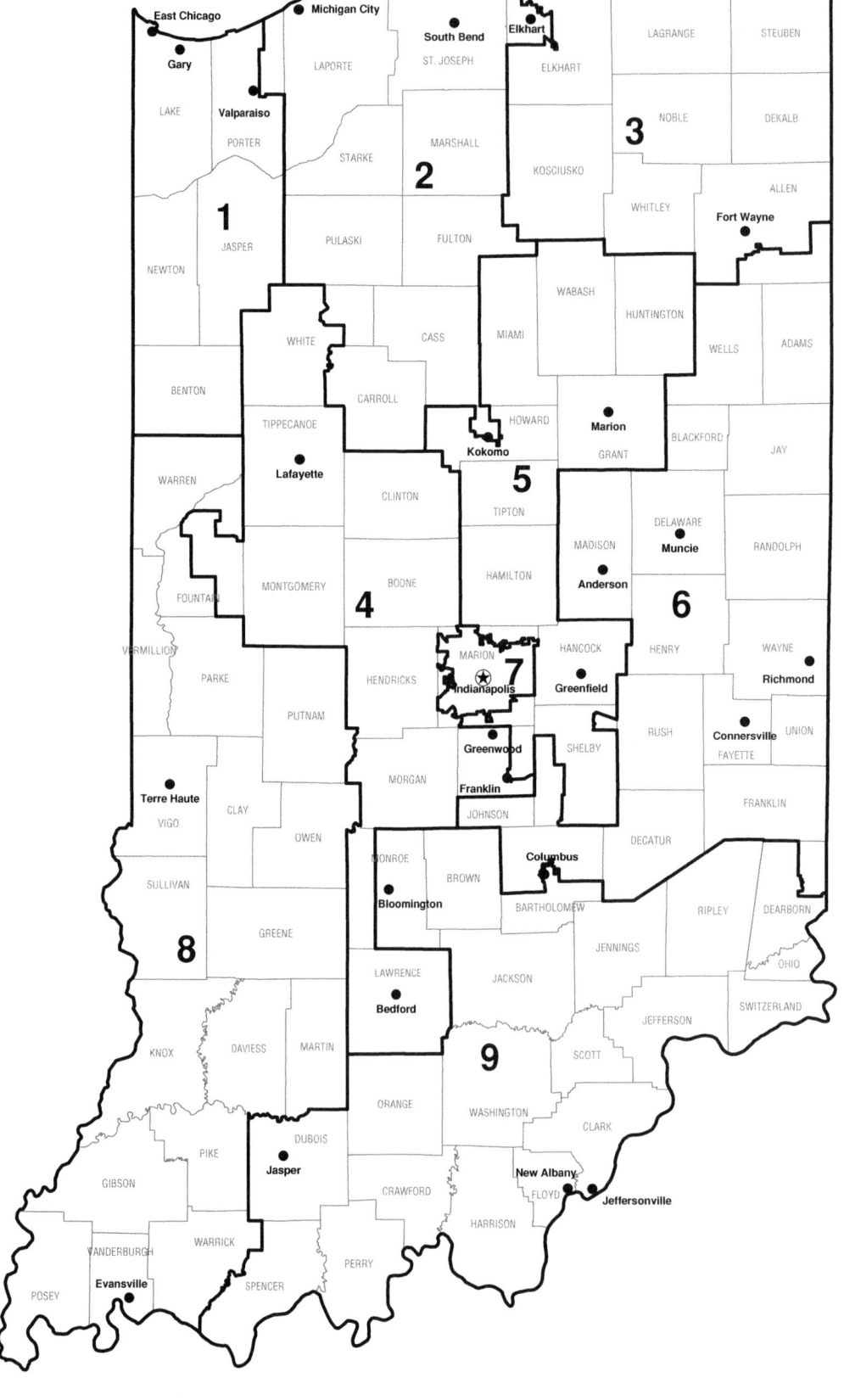

INDIANA

GOVERNOR
Mitch Daniels (R). Elected 2004 to a four-year term.

SENATORS (1 Democrat, 1 Republican)
Richard G. Lugar (R). Reelected 2006 to a six-year term. Previously elected 2000, 1994, 1988, 1982, 1976.

Evan Bayh (D). Reelected 2004 to a six-year term. Previously elected 1998.

REPRESENTATIVES (5 Democrats, 4 Republicans)
1. Peter J. Visclosky (D)
2. Joseph S. Donnelly (D)
3. Mark Souder (R)
4. Steve Buyer (R)
5. Dan Burton (R)
6. Mike Pence (R)
7. Julia Carson (D)
8. Brad Ellsworth (D)
9. Baron P. Hill (D)

POSTWAR VOTE FOR PRESIDENT

Year	Total Vote	Republican Vote	Republican Candidate	Democratic Vote	Democratic Candidate	Other Vote	Plurality	Total Vote Rep.	Total Vote Dem.	Major Vote Rep.	Major Vote Dem.
2004	2,468,002	1,479,438	Bush, George W.	969,011	Kerry, John	19,553	510,427 R	59.9%	39.3%	60.4%	39.6%
2000**	2,199,302	1,245,836	Bush, George W.	901,980	Gore, Al	51,486	343,856 R	56.6%	41.0%	58.0%	42.0%
1996**	2,135,842	1,006,693	Dole, Bob	887,424	Clinton, Bill	241,725	119,269 R	47.1%	41.5%	53.1%	46.9%
1992**	2,305,871	989,375	Bush, George	848,420	Clinton, Bill	468,076	140,955 R	42.9%	36.8%	53.8%	46.2%
1988	2,168,621	1,297,763	Bush, George	860,643	Dukakis, Michael S.	10,215	437,120 R	59.8%	39.7%	60.1%	39.9%
1984	2,233,069	1,377,230	Reagan, Ronald	841,481	Mondale, Walter F.	14,358	535,749 R	61.7%	37.7%	62.1%	37.9%
1980**	2,242,033	1,255,656	Reagan, Ronald	844,197	Carter, Jimmy	142,180	411,459 R	56.0%	37.7%	59.8%	40.2%
1976	2,220,362	1,183,958	Ford, Gerald R.	1,014,714	Carter, Jimmy	21,690	169,244 R	53.3%	45.7%	53.8%	46.2%
1972	2,125,529	1,405,154	Nixon, Richard M.	708,568	McGovern, George S.	11,807	696,586 R	66.1%	33.3%	66.5%	33.5%
1968**	2,123,597	1,067,885	Nixon, Richard M.	806,659	Humphrey, Hubert H.	249,053	261,226 R	50.3%	38.0%	57.0%	43.0%
1964	2,091,606	911,118	Goldwater, Barry M.	1,170,848	Johnson, Lyndon B.	9,640	259,730 D	43.6%	56.0%	43.8%	56.2%
1960	2,135,360	1,175,120	Nixon, Richard M.	952,358	Kennedy, John F.	7,882	222,762 R	55.0%	44.6%	55.2%	44.8%
1956	1,974,607	1,182,811	Eisenhower, Dwight D.	783,908	Stevenson, Adlai E.	7,888	398,903 R	59.9%	39.7%	60.1%	39.9%
1952	1,955,049	1,136,259	Eisenhower, Dwight D.	801,530	Stevenson, Adlai E.	17,260	334,729 R	58.1%	41.0%	58.6%	41.4%
1948	1,656,212	821,079	Dewey, Thomas E.	807,831	Truman, Harry S.	27,302	13,248 R	49.6%	48.8%	50.4%	49.6%

**In past elections, the other vote included: 2000 - 18,531 Green (Ralph Nader); 1996 - 224,299 Reform (Ross Perot); 1992 - 455,934 Independent (Ross Perot); 1980 - 111,639 Independent (John Anderson); 1968 - 243,108 American Independent (George Wallace).

INDIANA

POSTWAR VOTE FOR GOVERNOR

Year	Total Vote	Republican		Democratic		Other Vote	Rep.-Dem. Plurality	Percentage			
		Vote	Candidate	Vote	Candidate			Total Vote		Major Vote	
								Rep.	Dem.	Rep.	Dem.
2004	2,448,498	1,302,912	Daniels, Mitch	1,113,900	Kernan, Joseph E.	31,686	189,012 R	53.2%	45.5%	53.9%	46.1%
2000	2,179,413	908,285	McIntosh, David M.	1,232,525	O'Bannon, Frank L.	38,603	324,240 D	41.7%	56.6%	42.4%	57.6%
1996	2,110,047	986,982	Goldsmith, Stephen	1,087,128	O'Bannon, Frank L.	35,937	100,146 D	46.8%	51.5%	47.6%	52.4%
1992	2,229,116	822,533	Pearson, Linley E.	1,382,151	Bayh, Evan	24,432	559,618 D	36.9%	62.0%	37.3%	62.7%
1988	2,140,781	1,002,207	Mutz, John M.	1,138,574	Bayh, Evan		136,367 D	46.8%	53.2%	46.8%	53.2%
1984	2,197,988	1,146,497	Orr, Robert D.	1,036,922	Townsend, W. Wayne	14,569	109,575 R	52.2%	47.2%	52.5%	47.5%
1980	2,178,403	1,257,383	Orr, Robert D.	913,116	Hillenbrand, John A.	7,904	344,267 R	57.7%	41.9%	57.9%	42.1%
1976	2,175,324	1,236,555	Bowen, Otis R.	927,243	Conrad, Larry A.	11,526	309,312 R	56.8%	42.6%	57.1%	42.9%
1972	2,120,847	1,203,903	Bowen, Otis R.	900,489	Welsh, Matthew E.	16,455	303,414 R	56.8%	42.5%	57.2%	42.8%
1968	2,049,072	1,080,271	Whitcomb, Edgar D.	965,816	Rock, Robert L.	2,985	114,455 R	52.7%	47.1%	52.8%	47.2%
1964	2,072,915	901,342	Ristine, Richard O.	1,164,620	Branigin, Roger D.	6,953	263,278 D	43.5%	56.2%	43.6%	56.4%
1960	2,128,965	1,049,540	Parker, Crawford F.	1,072,717	Welsh, Matthew E.	6,708	23,177 D	49.3%	50.4%	49.5%	50.5%
1956	1,954,290	1,086,868	Handley, Harold W.	859,393	Tucker, Ralph	8,029	227,475 R	55.6%	44.0%	55.8%	44.2%
1952	1,931,869	1,075,685	Craig, George N.	841,984	Watkins, John A.	14,200	233,701 R	55.7%	43.6%	56.1%	43.9%
1948	1,652,321	745,892	Creighton, Hobart	884,995	Schricker, Henry F.	21,434	139,103 D	45.1%	53.6%	45.7%	54.3%

POSTWAR VOTE FOR SENATOR

Year	Total Vote	Republican		Democratic		Other Vote	Rep.-Dem. Plurality	Percentage			
		Vote	Candidate	Vote	Candidate			Total Vote		Major Vote	
								Rep.	Dem.	Rep.	Dem.
2006	1,341,111	1,171,553	Lugar, Richard G.		—	169,558	1,171,553 R	87.4%		100.0%	
2004	2,428,233	903,913	Scott, Marvin	1,496,976	Bayh, Evan	27,344	593,063 D	37.2%	61.6%	37.6%	62.4%
2000	2,145,209	1,427,944	Lugar, Richard G.	683,273	Johnson, David L.	33,992	744,671 R	66.6%	31.9%	67.6%	32.4%
1998	1,588,617	552,732	Helmke, Paul	1,012,244	Bayh, Evan	23,641	459,512 D	34.8%	63.7%	35.3%	64.7%
1994	1,543,568	1,039,625	Lugar, Richard G.	470,799	Jontz, Jim	33,144	568,826 R	67.4%	30.5%	68.8%	31.2%
1992	2,211,426	1,267,972	Coats, Daniel R.	900,148	Hogsett, Joseph H.	43,306	367,824 R	57.3%	40.7%	58.5%	41.5%
1990S	1,504,302	806,048	Coats, Daniel R.	696,639	Hill, Baron P.	1,615	109,409 R	53.6%	46.3%	53.6%	46.4%
1988	2,099,303	1,430,525	Lugar, Richard G.	668,778	Wickes, Jack		761,747 R	68.1%	31.9%	68.1%	31.9%
1986	1,545,563	936,143	Quayle, J. Danforth	595,192	Long, Jill L.	14,228	340,951 R	60.6%	38.5%	61.1%	38.9%
1982	1,817,287	978,301	Lugar, Richard G.	828,400	Fithian, Floyd	10,586	149,901 R	53.8%	45.6%	54.1%	45.9%
1980	2,198,376	1,182,414	Quayle, J. Danforth	1,015,962	Bayh, Birch		166,452 R	53.8%	46.2%	53.8%	46.2%
1976	2,171,187	1,275,833	Lugar, Richard G.	878,522	Hartke, R. Vance	16,832	397,311 R	58.8%	40.5%	59.2%	40.8%
1974	1,752,978	814,117	Lugar, Richard G.	889,269	Bayh, Birch	49,592	75,152 D	46.4%	50.7%	47.8%	52.2%
1970	1,737,697	866,707	Roudebush, Richard	870,990	Hartke, R. Vance		4,283 D	49.9%	50.1%	49.9%	50.1%
1968	2,053,118	988,571	Ruckelshaus, William	1,060,456	Bayh, Birch	4,091	71,885 D	48.1%	51.7%	48.2%	51.8%
1964	2,076,963	941,519	Bontrager, D. Russell	1,128,505	Hartke, R. Vance	6,939	186,986 D	45.3%	54.3%	45.5%	54.5%
1962	1,800,038	894,547	Capehart, Homer E.	905,491	Bayh, Birch		10,944 D	49.7%	50.3%	49.7%	50.3%
1958	1,724,598	731,635	Handley, Harold W.	973,636	Hartke, R. Vance	19,327	242,001 D	42.4%	56.5%	42.9%	57.1%
1956	1,963,986	1,084,262	Capehart, Homer E.	871,781	Wickard, Claude	7,943	212,481 R	55.2%	44.4%	55.4%	44.6%
1952	1,946,118	1,020,605	Jenner, William E.	911,169	Schricker, Henry F.	14,344	109,436 R	52.4%	46.8%	52.8%	47.2%
1950	1,598,724	844,303	Capehart, Homer E.	741,025	Campbell, Alex M.	13,396	103,278 R	52.8%	46.4%	53.3%	46.7%
1946	1,347,434	739,809	Jenner, William E.	584,288	Townsend, M. Clifford	23,337	155,521 R	54.9%	43.4%	55.9%	44.1%

In past elections, the other vote included: 2006 - 168,820 Libertarian (Steve Osborn). The 1990 election was for a short term to fill a vacancy.

INDIANA

SENATOR 2006

2000 Census Population	County	Total Vote	Republican	Democratic	Other	Rep.-Dem. Plurality	Percentage Total Vote Rep.	Dem.	Percentage Major Vote Rep.	Dem.
33,625	ADAMS	7,889	7,143		746	7,143 R	90.5%		100.0%	
331,849	ALLEN	73,658	65,782		7,876	65,782 R	89.3%		100.0%	
71,435	BARTHOLOMEW	18,387	16,544		1,843	16,544 R	90.0%		100.0%	
9,421	BENTON	2,396	2,086		310	2,086 R	87.1%		100.0%	
14,048	BLACKFORD	3,385	2,902		483	2,902 R	85.7%		100.0%	
46,107	BOONE	12,486	11,428		1,058	11,428 R	91.5%		100.0%	
14,957	BROWN	4,925	4,181		744	4,181 R	84.9%		100.0%	
20,165	CARROLL	5,630	4,859		771	4,859 R	86.3%		100.0%	
40,930	CASS	9,161	8,066		1,095	8,066 R	88.0%		100.0%	
96,472	CLARK	25,048	21,690		3,358	21,690 R	86.6%		100.0%	
26,556	CLAY	7,588	6,597		991	6,597 R	86.9%		100.0%	
33,866	CLINTON	6,939	6,076		863	6,076 R	87.6%		100.0%	
10,743	CRAWFORD	2,806	2,318		488	2,318 R	82.6%		100.0%	
29,820	DAVIESS	6,780	6,193		587	6,193 R	91.3%		100.0%	
46,109	DEARBORN	10,861	9,091		1,770	9,091 R	83.7%		100.0%	
24,555	DECATUR	6,415	5,755		660	5,755 R	89.7%		100.0%	
40,285	DE KALB	9,225	7,967		1,258	7,967 R	86.4%		100.0%	
118,769	DELAWARE	24,311	21,571		2,740	21,571 R	88.7%		100.0%	
39,674	DUBOIS	10,441	9,432		1,009	9,432 R	90.3%		100.0%	
182,791	ELKHART	38,214	34,342		3,872	34,342 R	89.9%		100.0%	
25,588	FAYETTE	5,655	4,704		951	4,704 R	83.2%		100.0%	
70,823	FLOYD	19,241	16,941		2,300	16,941 R	88.0%		100.0%	
17,954	FOUNTAIN	4,938	4,267		671	4,267 R	86.4%		100.0%	
22,151	FRANKLIN	6,057	5,061		996	5,061 R	83.6%		100.0%	
20,511	FULTON	6,191	5,493		698	5,493 R	88.7%		100.0%	
32,500	GIBSON	9,366	8,395		971	8,395 R	89.6%		100.0%	
73,403	GRANT	15,396	13,758		1,638	13,758 R	89.4%		100.0%	
33,157	GREENE	8,816	7,757		1,059	7,757 R	88.0%		100.0%	
182,740	HAMILTON	53,350	49,077		4,273	49,077 R	92.0%		100.0%	
55,391	HANCOCK	15,415	13,810		1,605	13,810 R	89.6%		100.0%	
34,325	HARRISON	11,109	9,484		1,625	9,484 R	85.4%		100.0%	
104,093	HENDRICKS	28,072	25,216		2,856	25,216 R	89.8%		100.0%	
48,508	HENRY	12,151	10,375		1,776	10,375 R	85.4%		100.0%	
84,964	HOWARD	20,489	17,660		2,829	17,660 R	86.2%		100.0%	
38,075	HUNTINGTON	8,496	7,392		1,104	7,392 R	87.0%		100.0%	
41,335	JACKSON	11,095	9,887		1,208	9,887 R	89.1%		100.0%	
30,043	JASPER	6,005	5,122		883	5,122 R	85.3%		100.0%	
21,806	JAY	5,645	4,850		795	4,850 R	85.9%		100.0%	
31,705	JEFFERSON	7,988	6,838		1,150	6,838 R	85.6%		100.0%	
27,554	JENNINGS	7,699	6,751		948	6,751 R	87.7%		100.0%	
115,209	JOHNSON	26,803	24,333		2,470	24,333 R	90.8%		100.0%	
39,256	KNOX	10,054	8,764		1,290	8,764 R	87.2%		100.0%	
74,057	KOSCIUSKO	17,246	15,231		2,015	15,231 R	88.3%		100.0%	
34,909	LAGRANGE	5,793	5,063		730	5,063 R	87.4%		100.0%	
484,564	LAKE	58,504	47,868		10,636	47,868 R	81.8%		100.0%	
110,106	LA PORTE	23,740	18,967		4,773	18,967 R	79.9%		100.0%	
45,922	LAWRENCE	10,775	9,404		1,371	9,404 R	87.3%		100.0%	
133,358	MADISON	30,268	25,963		4,305	25,963 R	85.8%		100.0%	
860,454	MARION	143,764	127,898		15,866	127,898 R	89.0%		100.0%	
45,128	MARSHALL	12,211	10,958		1,253	10,958 R	89.7%		100.0%	
10,369	MARTIN	3,200	2,765		435	2,765 R	86.4%		100.0%	
36,082	MIAMI	7,984	6,771		1,213	6,771 R	84.8%		100.0%	
120,563	MONROE	26,449	21,998		4,451	21,998 R	83.2%		100.0%	
37,629	MONTGOMERY	8,591	7,639		952	7,639 R	88.9%		100.0%	
66,689	MORGAN	13,974	12,254		1,720	12,254 R	87.7%		100.0%	
14,566	NEWTON	3,562	2,915		647	2,915 R	81.8%		100.0%	
46,275	NOBLE	10,009	8,800		1,209	8,800 R	87.9%		100.0%	
5,623	OHIO	1,901	1,523		378	1,523 R	80.1%		100.0%	
19,306	ORANGE	5,108	4,503		605	4,503 R	88.2%		100.0%	
21,786	OWEN	5,068	4,418		650	4,418 R	87.2%		100.0%	

INDIANA

SENATOR 2006

2000 Census Population	County	Total Vote	Republican	Democratic	Other	Rep.-Dem. Plurality	Percentage Total Vote Rep.	Dem.	Percentage Major Vote Rep.	Dem.
17,241	PARKE	4,695	4,182		513	4,182 R	89.1%		100.0%	
18,899	PERRY	4,556	3,916		640	3,916 R	86.0%		100.0%	
12,837	PIKE	4,163	3,649		514	3,649 R	87.7%		100.0%	
146,798	PORTER	31,133	25,385		5,748	25,385 R	81.5%		100.0%	
27,061	POSEY	8,513	7,636		877	7,636 R	89.7%		100.0%	
13,755	PULASKI	4,222	3,625		597	3,625 R	85.9%		100.0%	
36,019	PUTNAM	8,186	7,352		834	7,352 R	89.8%		100.0%	
27,401	RANDOLPH	6,388	5,587		801	5,587 R	87.5%		100.0%	
26,523	RIPLEY	7,348	6,224		1,124	6,224 R	84.7%		100.0%	
18,261	RUSH	4,848	4,340		508	4,340 R	89.5%		100.0%	
265,559	ST. JOSEPH	59,024	52,437		6,587	52,437 R	88.8%		100.0%	
22,960	SCOTT	5,059	4,267		792	4,267 R	84.3%		100.0%	
43,445	SHELBY	10,131	9,070		1,061	9,070 R	89.5%		100.0%	
20,391	SPENCER	6,190	5,483		707	5,483 R	88.6%		100.0%	
23,556	STARKE	5,975	4,560		1,415	4,560 R	76.3%		100.0%	
33,214	STEUBEN	8,044	6,728		1,316	6,728 R	83.6%		100.0%	
21,751	SULLIVAN	5,272	4,489		783	4,489 R	85.1%		100.0%	
9,065	SWITZERLAND	2,078	1,615		463	1,615 R	77.7%		100.0%	
148,955	TIPPECANOE	30,281	25,707		4,574	25,707 R	84.9%		100.0%	
16,577	TIPTON	5,170	4,554		616	4,554 R	88.1%		100.0%	
7,349	UNION	2,249	1,913		336	1,913 R	85.1%		100.0%	
171,922	VANDERBURGH	45,372	39,898		5,474	39,898 R	87.9%		100.0%	
16,788	VERMILLION	4,076	3,380		696	3,380 R	82.9%		100.0%	
105,848	VIGO	22,277	19,242		3,035	19,242 R	86.4%		100.0%	
34,960	WABASH	6,508	5,653		855	5,653 R	86.9%		100.0%	
8,419	WARREN	2,536	2,211		325	2,211 R	87.2%		100.0%	
52,383	WARRICK	16,797	15,038		1,759	15,038 R	89.5%		100.0%	
27,223	WASHINGTON	7,575	6,496		1,079	6,496 R	85.8%		100.0%	
71,097	WAYNE	13,477	10,846		2,631	10,846 R	80.5%		100.0%	
27,600	WELLS	8,402	7,389		1,013	7,389 R	87.9%		100.0%	
25,267	WHITE	6,865	5,930		935	5,930 R	86.4%		100.0%	
30,707	WHITLEY	8,978	7,855		1,123	7,855 R	87.5%		100.0%	
6,080,485	TOTAL	1,341,111	1,171,553		169,558	1,171,553 R	87.4%		100.0%	

INDIANA

HOUSE OF REPRESENTATIVES

CD	Year	Total Vote	Republican		Democratic		Other Vote	Rep.-Dem. Plurality	Percentage			
									Total Vote		Major Vote	
			Vote	Candidate	Vote	Candidate			Rep.	Dem.	Rep.	Dem.
1	2006	149,607	40,146	LEYVA, MARK J.	104,195	VISCLOSKY, PETER J.*	5,266	64,049 D	26.8%	69.6%	27.8%	72.2%
1	2004	261,264	82,858	LEYVA, MARK J.	178,406	VISCLOSKY, PETER J.*		95,548 D	31.7%	68.3%	31.7%	68.3%
1	2002	135,111	41,909	LEYVA, MARK J.	90,443	VISCLOSKY, PETER J.*	2,759	48,534 D	31.0%	66.9%	31.7%	68.3%
2	2006	191,861	88,300	CHOCOLA, CHRIS*	103,561	DONNELLY, JOSEPH S.		15,261 D	46.0%	54.0%	46.0%	54.0%
2	2004	259,355	140,496	CHOCOLA, CHRIS*	115,513	DONNELLY, JOSEPH S.	3,346	24,983 R	54.2%	44.5%	54.9%	45.1%
2	2002	188,458	95,081	CHOCOLA, CHRIS	86,253	THOMPSON, JILL LONG	7,124	8,828 R	50.5%	45.8%	52.4%	47.6%
3	2006	175,778	95,421	SOUDER, MARK*	80,357	HAYHURST, THOMAS E.		15,064 R	54.3%	45.7%	54.3%	45.7%
3	2004	247,621	171,389	SOUDER, MARK*	76,232	PARRA, MARIA M.		95,157 R	69.2%	30.8%	69.2%	30.8%
3	2002	146,606	92,566	SOUDER, MARK*	50,509	RIGDON, JAY	3,531	42,057 R	63.1%	34.5%	64.7%	35.3%
4	2006	178,043	111,057	BUYER, STEVE*	66,986	SANDERS, DAVID AVRAM		44,071 R	62.4%	37.6%	62.4%	37.6%
4	2004	274,136	190,445	BUYER, STEVE*	77,574	SANDERS, DAVID AVRAM	6,117	112,871 R	69.5%	28.3%	71.1%	28.9%
4	2002	158,008	112,760	BUYER, STEVE*	41,314	ABBOTT, BILL	3,934	71,446 R	71.4%	26.1%	73.2%	26.8%
5	2006	204,929	133,118	BURTON, DAN*	64,362	CARR, KATHERINE FOX	7,449	68,756 R	65.0%	31.4%	67.4%	32.6%
5	2004	318,363	228,718	BURTON, DAN*	82,637	CARR, KATHERINE FOX	7,008	146,081 R	71.8%	26.0%	73.5%	26.5%
5	2002	179,855	129,442	BURTON, DAN*	45,283	CARR, KATHERINE FOX	5,130	84,159 R	72.0%	25.2%	74.1%	25.9%
6	2006	192,078	115,266	PENCE, MIKE*	76,812	WELSH, BARRY A.		38,454 R	60.0%	40.0%	60.0%	40.0%
6	2004	272,049	182,529	PENCE, MIKE*	85,123	FOX, MELINA ANN	4,397	97,406 R	67.1%	31.3%	68.2%	31.8%
6	2002	185,653	118,436	PENCE, MIKE*	63,871	FOX, MELINA ANN	3,346	54,565 R	63.8%	34.4%	65.0%	35.0%
7	2006	139,054	64,304	DICKERSON, ERIC	74,750	CARSON, JULIA*		10,446 D	46.2%	53.8%	46.2%	53.8%
7	2004	223,175	97,491	HORNING, ANDREW	121,303	CARSON, JULIA*	4,381	23,812 D	43.7%	54.4%	44.6%	55.4%
7	2002	145,840	64,379	McVEY, BROSE A.	77,478	CARSON, JULIA*	3,983	13,099 D	44.1%	53.1%	45.4%	54.6%
8	2006	214,723	83,704	HOSTETTLER, JOHN*	131,019	ELLSWORTH, BRAD		47,315 D	39.0%	61.0%	39.0%	61.0%
8	2004	272,778	145,576	HOSTETTLER, JOHN*	121,522	JENNINGS, JON P.	5,680	24,054 R	53.4%	44.5%	54.5%	45.5%
8	2002	192,865	98,952	HOSTETTLER, JOHN*	88,763	HARTKE, BRYAN L.	5,150	10,189 R	51.3%	46.0%	52.7%	47.3%
9	2006	220,849	100,469	SODREL, MIKE*	110,454	HILL, BARON P.	9,926	9,985 D	45.5%	50.0%	47.6%	52.4%
9	2004	287,510	142,197	SODREL, MIKE	140,772	HILL, BARON P.*	4,541	1,425 R	49.5%	49.0%	50.3%	49.7%
9	2002	188,957	87,169	SODREL, MIKE	96,654	HILL, BARON P.*	5,134	9,485 D	46.1%	51.2%	47.4%	52.6%
TOTAL	2006	1,666,922	831,785		812,496		22,641	19,289 R	49.9%	48.7%	50.6%	49.4%
TOTAL	2004	2,416,251	1,381,699		999,082		35,470	382,617 R	57.2%	41.3%	58.0%	42.0%
TOTAL	2002	1,521,353	840,694		640,568		40,091	200,126 R	55.3%	42.1%	56.8%	43.2%

An asterisk (*) denotes incumbent.

INDIANA

GENERAL AND PRIMARY ELECTIONS

2006 GENERAL ELECTIONS

Senator Other vote was 168,820 Libertarian (Steve Osborn); 444 Independent write-in (Mark Pool); 294 Democratic write-in (Jack H. Baldwin).

House Other vote was:

CD 1 5,266 Independent (Charles E. Barman).
CD 2
CD 3
CD 4
CD 5 7,431 Libertarian (Sheri Conover Sharlow); 18 Independent write-in (John Miller).
CD 6
CD 7
CD 8
CD 9 9,893 Libertarian (D. Eric Schansberg); 33 Republican write-in (Donald W. Mantooth).

2006 PRIMARY ELECTIONS

Primary	May 2, 2006	**Registration** (as of May 2, 2006)	4,375,238	No Party Registration

Primary Type Open—Any registered voter could participate in the primary of either party.

Note: An asterisk (*) denotes incumbent.

	REPUBLICAN PRIMARIES			DEMOCRATIC PRIMARIES		
Senator	Richard G. Lugar*	393,960	100.0%	No Democratic candidate		
Congressional District 1	Mark J. Leyva	8,416	43.8%	Peter J. Visclosky*	55,144	100.0%
	Richard "Ric" Holtz	4,761	24.8%			
	Lewis "149 Farmer" Haas	3,576	18.6%			
	Jayson Reeves	2,457	12.8%			
	TOTAL	19,210				
Congressional District 2	Chris Chocola*	25,139	70.1%	Joseph S. Donnelly	30,589	83.0%
	Tony Zirkle	10,716	29.9%	Steve Francis	6,280	17.0%
	TOTAL	35,855		TOTAL	36,869	
Congressional District 3	Mark Souder*	39,449	71.3%	Thomas E. Hayhurst	12,556	66.4%
	William Larsen	15,845	28.7%	Kevin Boyd	2,494	13.2%
				Thomas Allen Schrader	1,979	10.5%
				Edward W. Smith	1,881	9.9%
	TOTAL	55,294		TOTAL	18,910	
Congressional District 4	Steve Buyer*	50,695	72.9%	David Avram Sanders	7,522	50.9%
	Mike Campbell	18,799	27.1%	Rick Cornstuble	3,828	25.9%
				Darin S. Kinser	3,433	23.2%
	TOTAL	69,494		TOTAL	14,783	
Congressional District 5	Dan Burton*	61,150	83.9%	Katherine Fox Carr	7,039	38.4%
	Clayton L. "C. L. Jim" Alfred	6,869	9.4%	Michael Clements	4,742	25.9%
	Victor D. Wakley	4,822	6.6%	Mike Brown	4,590	25.0%
				Thomas E. Williams	1,953	10.7%
	TOTAL	72,841		TOTAL	18,324	

INDIANA

GENERAL AND PRIMARY ELECTIONS

	REPUBLICAN PRIMARIES			DEMOCRATIC PRIMARIES		
Congressional	Mike Pence*	52,188	86.1%	Barry A. Welsh	23,525	69.5%
District 6	George T. Holland	8,406	13.9%	Ralph Spelbring	10,324	30.5%
	TOTAL	*60,594*		*TOTAL*	*33,849*	
Congressional	Eric Dickerson	11,336	54.1%	Julia Carson*	29,503	81.3%
District 7	Ronald V. Franklin	4,516	21.5%	Kris Kiser	4,052	11.2%
	John Bauer	3,834	18.3%	Bob Hidalgo	1,690	4.7%
	Michael A. Simpson	1,273	6.1%	Joseph Charles "Hippie Joe" Stockett III	730	2.0%
				Pierre Quincy Pullins	306	0.8%
	TOTAL	*20,959*		*TOTAL*	*36,281*	
Congressional	John Hostettler*	32,018	100.0%	Brad Ellsworth	45,765	100.0%
District 8						
Congressional	Mike Sodrel*	30,273	80.4%	Baron P. Hill	53,883	79.2%
District 9	Sam Schultz	7,363	19.6%	Gretchen Clearwater	9,415	13.8%
				Lendall B. Terry	2,501	3.7%
				John "Cosmo" Hockersmith	2,267	3.3%
	TOTAL	*37,636*		*TOTAL*	*68,066*	

IOWA

Congressional districts first established for elections held in 2002
5 members

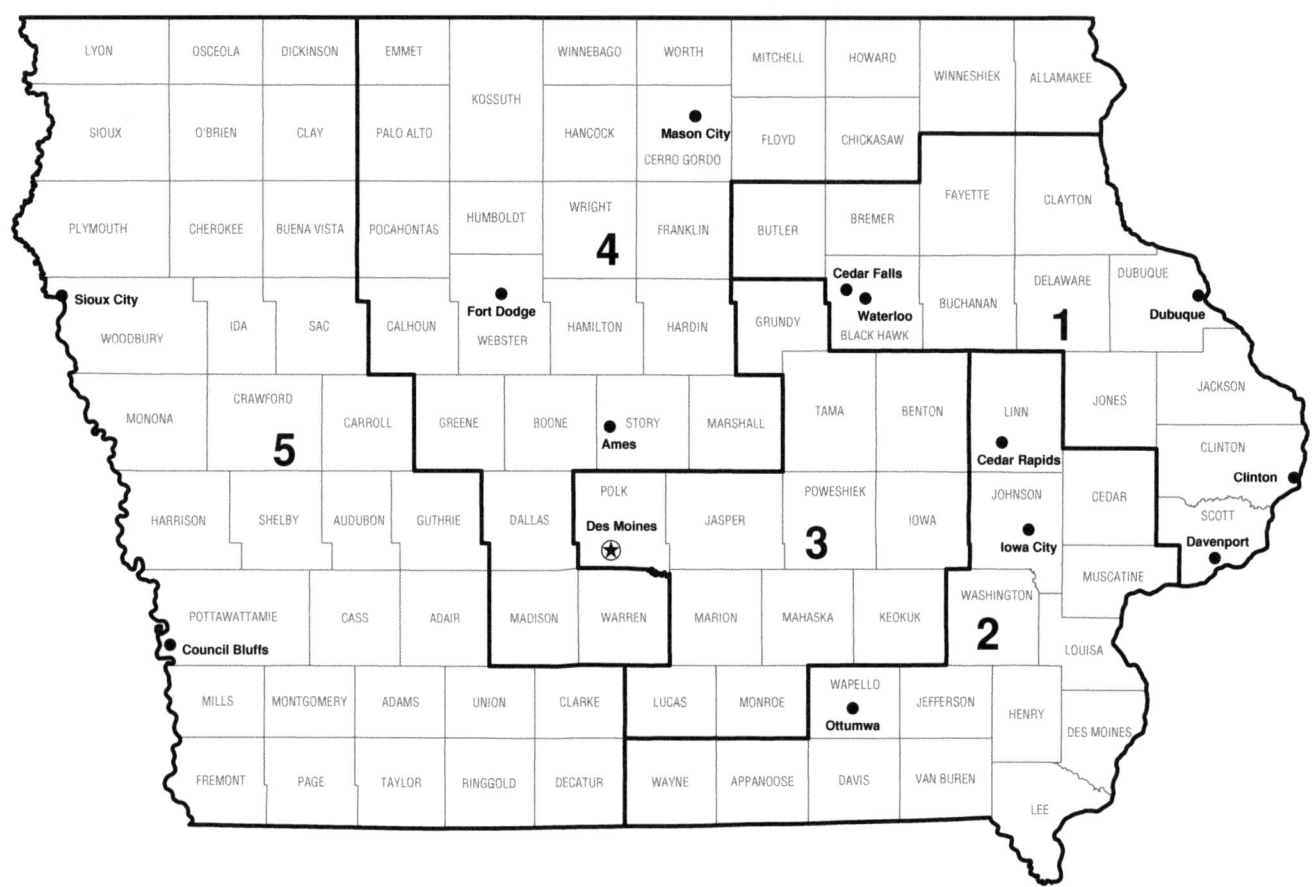

IOWA

GOVERNOR
Chet Culver (D). Elected 2006 to a four-year term.

SENATORS (1 Democrat, 1 Republican)
Charles E. Grassley (R). Reelected 2004 to a six-year term. Previously elected 1998, 1992, 1986, 1980.

Tom Harkin (D). Reelected 2002 to a six-year term. Previously elected 1996, 1990, 1984.

REPRESENTATIVES (3 Democrats, 2 Republicans)
1. Bruce Braley (D)
2. Dave Loebsack (D)
3. Leonard L. Boswell (D)
4. Tom Latham (R)
5. Steve King (R)

POSTWAR VOTE FOR PRESIDENT

Year	Total Vote	Republican Vote	Republican Candidate	Democratic Vote	Democratic Candidate	Other Vote	Plurality	Total Vote Rep.	Total Vote Dem.	Major Vote Rep.	Major Vote Dem.
2004	1,506,908	751,957	Bush, George W.	741,898	Kerry, John	13,053	10,059 R	49.9%	49.2%	50.3%	49.7%
2000**	1,315,563	634,373	Bush, George W.	638,517	Gore, Al	42,673	4,144 D	48.2%	48.5%	49.8%	50.2%
1996**	1,234,075	492,644	Dole, Bob	620,258	Clinton, Bill	121,173	127,614 D	39.9%	50.3%	44.3%	55.7%
1992**	1,354,607	504,891	Bush, George	586,353	Clinton, Bill	263,363	81,462 D	37.3%	43.3%	46.3%	53.7%
1988	1,225,614	545,355	Bush, George	670,557	Dukakis, Michael S.	9,702	125,202 D	44.5%	54.7%	44.9%	55.1%
1984	1,319,805	703,088	Reagan, Ronald	605,620	Mondale, Walter F.	11,097	97,468 R	53.3%	45.9%	53.7%	46.3%
1980**	1,317,661	676,026	Reagan, Ronald	508,672	Carter, Jimmy	132,963	167,354 R	51.3%	38.6%	57.1%	42.9%
1976	1,279,306	632,863	Ford, Gerald R.	619,931	Carter, Jimmy	26,512	12,932 R	49.5%	48.5%	50.5%	49.5%
1972	1,225,944	706,207	Nixon, Richard M.	496,206	McGovern, George S.	23,531	210,001 R	57.6%	40.5%	58.7%	41.3%
1968**	1,167,931	619,106	Nixon, Richard M.	476,699	Humphrey, Hubert H.	72,126	142,407 R	53.0%	40.8%	56.5%	43.5%
1964	1,184,539	449,148	Goldwater, Barry M.	733,030	Johnson, Lyndon B.	2,361	283,882 D	37.9%	61.9%	38.0%	62.0%
1960	1,273,810	722,381	Nixon, Richard M.	550,565	Kennedy, John F.	864	171,816 R	56.7%	43.2%	56.7%	43.3%
1956	1,234,564	729,187	Eisenhower, Dwight D.	501,858	Stevenson, Adlai E.	3,519	227,329 R	59.1%	40.7%	59.2%	40.8%
1952	1,268,773	808,906	Eisenhower, Dwight D.	451,513	Stevenson, Adlai E.	8,354	357,393 R	63.8%	35.6%	64.2%	35.8%
1948	1,038,264	494,018	Dewey, Thomas E.	522,380	Truman, Harry S.	21,866	28,362 D	47.6%	50.3%	48.6%	51.4%

**In past elections, the other vote included: 2000 - 29,374 Green (Ralph Nader); 1996 - 105,159 Reform (Ross Perot); 1992 - 253,468 Independent (Ross Perot); 1980 - 115,633 Independent (John Anderson); 1968 - 66,422 American Independent (George Wallace).

IOWA

POSTWAR VOTE FOR GOVERNOR

Year	Total Vote	Republican Vote	Republican Candidate	Democratic Vote	Democratic Candidate	Other Vote	Rep.-Dem. Plurality	Percentage Total Vote Rep.	Percentage Total Vote Dem.	Percentage Major Vote Rep.	Percentage Major Vote Dem.
2006	1,053,255	467,425	Nussle, Jim	569,021	Culver, Chet	16,809	101,596 D	44.4%	54.0%	45.1%	54.9%
2002	1,025,802	456,612	Gross, Doug	540,449	Vilsack, Tom	28,741	83,837 D	44.5%	52.7%	45.8%	54.2%
1998	956,418	444,787	Lightfoot, Jim Ross	500,231	Vilsack, Tom	11,400	55,444 D	46.5%	52.3%	47.1%	52.9%
1994	997,248	566,395	Branstad, Terry E.	414,453	Campbell, Bonnie J.	16,400	151,942 R	56.8%	41.6%	57.7%	42.3%
1990	976,483	591,852	Branstad, Terry E.	379,372	Avenson, Donald D.	5,259	212,480 R	60.6%	38.9%	60.9%	39.1%
1986	910,623	472,712	Branstad, Terry E.	436,987	Junkins, Lowell L.	924	35,725 R	51.9%	48.0%	52.0%	48.0%
1982	1,038,229	548,313	Branstad, Terry E.	483,291	Conlin, Roxanne	6,625	65,022 R	52.8%	46.5%	53.2%	46.8%
1978	843,190	491,713	Ray, Robert	345,519	Fitzgerald, Jerome D.	5,958	146,194 R	58.3%	41.0%	58.7%	41.3%
1974**	920,458	534,518	Ray, Robert	377,553	Schaben, James, F.	8,387	156,965 R	58.1%	41.0%	58.6%	41.4%
1972	1,210,222	707,177	Ray, Robert	487,282	Franzenburg, Paul	15,763	219,895 R	58.4%	40.3%	59.2%	40.8%
1970	791,241	403,394	Ray, Robert	368,911	Fulton, Robert	18,936	34,483 R	51.0%	46.6%	52.2%	47.8%
1968	1,136,489	614,328	Ray, Robert	521,216	Franzenburg, Paul	945	93,112 R	54.1%	45.9%	54.1%	45.9%
1966	893,175	394,518	Murray, William G.	494,259	Hughes, Harold E.	4,398	99,741 D	44.2%	55.3%	44.4%	55.6%
1964	1,167,734	365,131	Hultman, Evan	794,610	Hughes, Harold E.	7,993	429,479 D	31.3%	68.0%	31.5%	68.5%
1962	819,854	388,955	Erbe, Norman A.	430,899	Hughes, Harold E.		41,944 D	47.4%	52.6%	47.4%	52.6%
1960	1,237,089	645,026	Erbe, Norman A.	592,063	McManus, E. J.		52,963 R	52.1%	47.9%	52.1%	47.9%
1958	859,095	394,071	Murray, William G.	465,024	Loveless, Herschel C.		70,953 D	45.9%	54.1%	45.9%	54.1%
1956	1,204,235	587,383	Hoegh, Leo A.	616,852	Loveless, Herschel C.		29,469 D	48.8%	51.2%	48.8%	51.2%
1954	848,592	435,944	Hoegh, Leo A.	410,255	Herring, Clyde E.	2,393	25,689 R	51.4%	48.3%	51.5%	48.5%
1952	1,230,045	638,388	Beardsley, William	587,671	Loveless, Herschel C.	3,986	50,717 R	51.9%	47.8%	52.1%	47.9%
1950	857,213	506,642	Beardsley, William	347,176	Gillette, Lester S.	3,395	159,466 R	59.1%	40.5%	59.3%	40.7%
1948	994,833	553,900	Beardsley, William	434,432	Switzer, Carroll O.	6,501	119,468 R	55.7%	43.7%	56.0%	44.0%
1946	631,681	362,592	Blue, Robert D.	266,190	Miles, Frank	2,899	96,402 R	57.4%	42.1%	57.7%	42.3%

**The term of office of Iowa's governor was increased from two to four years effective with the 1974 election.

POSTWAR VOTE FOR SENATOR

Year	Total Vote	Republican Vote	Republican Candidate	Democratic Vote	Democratic Candidate	Other Vote	Rep.-Dem. Plurality	Percentage Total Vote Rep.	Percentage Total Vote Dem.	Percentage Major Vote Rep.	Percentage Major Vote Dem.
2004	1,479,228	1,038,175	Grassley, Charles E.	412,365	Small, Arthur	28,688	625,810 R	70.2%	27.9%	71.6%	28.4%
2002	1,023,075	447,892	Ganske, Greg	554,278	Harkin, Tom	20,905	106,386 D	43.8%	54.2%	44.7%	55.3%
1998	947,907	648,480	Grassley, Charles E.	289,049	Osterberg, David	10,378	359,431 R	68.4%	30.5%	69.2%	30.8%
1996	1,224,054	571,807	Lightfoot, Jim Ross	634,166	Harkin, Tom	18,081	62,359 D	46.7%	51.8%	47.4%	52.6%
1992	1,292,494	899,761	Grassley, Charles E.	351,561	Lloyd-Jones, Jean	41,172	548,200 R	69.6%	27.2%	71.9%	28.1%
1990	983,933	446,869	Tauke, Tom	535,975	Harkin, Tom	1,089	89,106 D	45.4%	54.5%	45.5%	54.5%
1986	891,762	588,880	Grassley, Charles E.	299,406	Roehrick, John P.	3,476	289,474 R	66.0%	33.6%	66.3%	33.7%
1984	1,292,700	564,381	Jepsen, Roger W.	716,883	Harkin, Tom	11,436	152,502 D	43.7%	55.5%	44.0%	56.0%
1980	1,277,034	683,014	Grassley, Charles E.	581,545	Culver, John C.	12,475	101,469 R	53.5%	45.5%	54.0%	46.0%
1978	824,654	421,598	Jepsen, Roger W.	395,066	Clark, Richard	7,990	26,532 R	51.1%	47.9%	51.6%	48.4%
1974	889,561	420,546	Stanley, David M.	462,947	Culver, John C.	6,068	42,401 D	47.3%	52.0%	47.6%	52.4%
1972	1,203,333	530,525	Miller, Jack	662,637	Clark, Richard	10,171	132,112 D	44.1%	55.1%	44.5%	55.5%
1968	1,144,086	568,469	Stanley, David M.	574,884	Hughes, Harold E.	733	6,415 D	49.7%	50.2%	49.7%	50.3%
1966	857,496	522,339	Miller, Jack	324,114	Smith, E. B.	11,043	198,225 R	60.9%	37.8%	61.7%	38.3%
1962	807,972	431,364	Hickenlooper, Bourke B.	376,602	Smith, E. B.	6	54,762 R	53.4%	46.6%	53.4%	46.6%
1960	1,237,582	642,463	Miller, Jack	595,119	Loveless, Herschel C.		47,344 R	51.9%	48.1%	51.9%	48.1%
1956	1,178,655	635,499	Hickenlooper, Bourke B.	543,156	Evans, R. M.		92,343 R	53.9%	46.1%	53.9%	46.1%
1954	847,355	442,409	Martin, Thomas E.	402,712	Gillette, Guy	2,234	39,697 R	52.2%	47.5%	52.3%	47.7%
1950	858,523	470,613	Hickenlooper, Bourke B.	383,766	Loveland, A. J.	4,144	86,847 R	54.8%	44.7%	55.1%	44.9%
1948	1,000,412	415,778	Wilson, George A.	578,226	Gillette, Guy	6,408	162,448 D	41.6%	57.8%	41.8%	58.2%

IOWA

GOVERNOR 2006

2000 Census Population	County	Total Vote	Republican	Democratic	Other	Rep.-Dem. Plurality	Total Vote Rep.	Dem.	Major Vote Rep.	Dem.
8,243	ADAIR	3,037	1,430	1,557	50	127 D	47.1%	51.3%	47.9%	52.1%
4,482	ADAMS	1,665	797	825	43	28 D	47.9%	49.5%	49.1%	50.9%
14,675	ALLAMAKEE	4,850	2,128	2,639	83	511 D	43.9%	54.4%	44.6%	55.4%
13,721	APPANOOSE	4,477	1,931	2,466	80	535 D	43.1%	55.1%	43.9%	56.1%
6,830	AUDUBON	2,467	1,159	1,274	34	115 D	47.0%	51.6%	47.6%	52.4%
25,308	BENTON	9,785	4,398	5,286	101	888 D	44.9%	54.0%	45.4%	54.6%
128,012	BLACK HAWK	44,410	17,758	26,080	572	8,322 D	40.0%	58.7%	40.5%	59.5%
26,224	BOONE	9,949	4,295	5,506	148	1,211 D	43.2%	55.3%	43.8%	56.2%
23,325	BREMER	9,603	4,372	5,132	99	760 D	45.5%	53.4%	46.0%	54.0%
21,093	BUCHANAN	7,995	3,263	4,635	97	1,372 D	40.8%	58.0%	41.3%	58.7%
20,411	BUENA VISTA	6,307	3,446	2,743	118	703 R	54.6%	43.5%	55.7%	44.3%
15,305	BUTLER	5,736	2,960	2,686	90	274 R	51.6%	46.8%	52.4%	47.6%
11,115	CALHOUN	4,006	2,036	1,916	54	120 R	50.8%	47.8%	51.5%	48.5%
21,421	CARROLL	7,173	3,553	3,518	102	35 R	49.5%	49.0%	50.2%	49.8%
14,684	CASS	5,029	2,838	2,110	81	728 R	56.4%	42.0%	57.4%	42.6%
18,187	CEDAR	6,858	3,037	3,739	82	702 D	44.3%	54.5%	44.8%	55.2%
46,447	CERRO GORDO	17,215	6,356	10,660	199	4,304 D	36.9%	61.9%	37.4%	62.6%
13,035	CHEROKEE	4,519	2,437	2,016	66	421 R	53.9%	44.6%	54.7%	45.3%
13,095	CHICKASAW	5,021	1,915	3,037	69	1,122 D	38.1%	60.5%	38.7%	61.3%
9,133	CLARKE	3,386	1,449	1,887	50	438 D	42.8%	55.7%	43.4%	56.6%
17,372	CLAY	5,935	3,224	2,611	100	613 R	54.3%	44.0%	55.3%	44.7%
18,678	CLAYTON	6,805	2,936	3,728	141	792 D	43.1%	54.8%	44.1%	55.9%
50,149	CLINTON	16,755	6,239	10,268	248	4,029 D	37.2%	61.3%	37.8%	62.2%
16,942	CRAWFORD	4,642	2,333	2,167	142	166 R	50.3%	46.7%	51.8%	48.2%
40,750	DALLAS	19,707	10,031	9,327	349	704 R	50.9%	47.3%	51.8%	48.2%
8,541	DAVIS	2,838	1,283	1,512	43	229 D	45.2%	53.3%	45.9%	54.1%
8,689	DECATUR	2,918	1,335	1,526	57	191 D	45.8%	52.3%	46.7%	53.3%
18,404	DELAWARE	7,067	3,521	3,471	75	50 R	49.8%	49.1%	50.4%	49.6%
42,351	DES MOINES	14,002	4,634	9,162	206	4,528 D	33.1%	65.4%	33.6%	66.4%
16,424	DICKINSON	6,873	3,468	3,308	97	160 R	50.5%	48.1%	51.2%	48.8%
89,143	DUBUQUE	33,815	12,989	20,420	406	7,431 D	38.4%	60.4%	38.9%	61.1%
11,027	EMMET	3,101	1,420	1,640	41	220 D	45.8%	52.9%	46.4%	53.6%
22,008	FAYETTE	7,904	3,361	4,401	142	1,040 D	42.5%	55.7%	43.3%	56.7%
16,900	FLOYD	6,157	2,288	3,777	92	1,489 D	37.2%	61.3%	37.7%	62.3%
10,704	FRANKLIN	3,790	1,984	1,760	46	224 R	52.3%	46.4%	53.0%	47.0%
8,010	FREMONT	2,568	1,297	1,184	87	113 R	50.5%	46.1%	52.3%	47.7%
10,366	GREENE	3,603	1,668	1,890	45	222 D	46.3%	52.5%	46.9%	53.1%
12,369	GRUNDY	4,947	2,906	1,998	43	908 R	58.7%	40.4%	59.3%	40.7%
11,353	GUTHRIE	4,167	2,061	2,038	68	23 R	49.5%	48.9%	50.3%	49.7%
16,438	HAMILTON	6,318	2,956	3,261	101	305 D	46.8%	51.6%	47.5%	52.5%
12,100	HANCOCK	4,254	2,077	2,112	65	35 D	48.8%	49.6%	49.6%	50.4%
18,812	HARDIN	6,815	3,312	3,384	119	72 D	48.6%	49.7%	49.5%	50.5%
15,666	HARRISON	5,016	2,566	2,342	108	224 R	51.2%	46.7%	52.3%	47.7%
20,336	HENRY	6,482	3,101	3,288	93	187 D	47.8%	50.7%	48.5%	51.5%
9,932	HOWARD	3,358	1,282	2,020	56	738 D	38.2%	60.2%	38.8%	61.2%
10,381	HUMBOLDT	3,750	1,953	1,738	59	215 R	52.1%	46.3%	52.9%	47.1%
7,837	IDA	2,443	1,442	972	29	470 R	59.0%	39.8%	59.7%	40.3%
15,671	IOWA	6,276	3,013	3,167	96	154 D	48.0%	50.5%	48.8%	51.2%
20,296	JACKSON	7,238	2,558	4,596	84	2,038 D	35.3%	63.5%	35.8%	64.2%
37,213	JASPER	14,846	6,494	8,112	240	1,618 D	43.7%	54.6%	44.5%	55.5%
16,181	JEFFERSON	6,065	2,350	3,418	297	1,068 D	38.7%	56.4%	40.7%	59.3%
111,006	JOHNSON	44,064	12,948	30,083	1,033	17,135 D	29.4%	68.3%	30.1%	69.9%
20,221	JONES	7,392	3,049	4,222	121	1,173 D	41.2%	57.1%	41.9%	58.1%
11,400	KEOKUK	3,798	1,901	1,840	57	61 R	50.1%	48.4%	50.8%	49.2%
17,163	KOSSUTH	6,403	3,096	3,219	88	123 D	48.4%	50.3%	49.0%	51.0%
38,052	LEE	11,905	4,073	7,577	255	3,504 D	34.2%	63.6%	35.0%	65.0%
191,701	LINN	77,889	31,112	45,622	1,155	14,510 D	39.9%	58.6%	40.5%	59.5%
12,183	LOUISA	3,438	1,562	1,825	51	263 D	45.4%	53.1%	46.1%	53.9%
9,422	LUCAS	3,388	1,659	1,687	42	28 D	49.0%	49.8%	49.6%	50.4%
11,763	LYON	4,017	3,015	975	27	2,040 R	75.1%	24.3%	75.6%	24.4%

IOWA

GOVERNOR 2006

2000 Census Population	County	Total Vote	Republican	Democratic	Other	Rep.-Dem. Plurality	Percentage Total Vote Rep.	Dem.	Major Vote Rep.	Dem.
14,019	MADISON	6,167	3,118	2,939	110	179 R	50.6%	47.7%	51.5%	48.5%
22,335	MAHASKA	7,473	4,432	2,925	116	1,507 R	59.3%	39.1%	60.2%	39.8%
32,052	MARION	12,103	6,696	5,241	166	1,455 R	55.3%	43.3%	56.1%	43.9%
39,311	MARSHALL	13,698	6,155	7,322	221	1,167 D	44.9%	53.5%	45.7%	54.3%
14,547	MILLS	3,972	2,319	1,587	66	732 R	58.4%	40.0%	59.4%	40.6%
10,874	MITCHELL	3,921	1,638	2,220	63	582 D	41.8%	56.6%	42.5%	57.5%
10,020	MONONA	3,268	1,589	1,616	63	27 D	48.6%	49.4%	49.6%	50.4%
8,016	MONROE	2,647	1,071	1,542	34	471 D	40.5%	58.3%	41.0%	59.0%
11,771	MONTGOMERY	3,174	1,877	1,250	47	627 R	59.1%	39.4%	60.0%	40.0%
41,722	MUSCATINE	12,291	5,119	6,984	188	1,865 D	41.6%	56.8%	42.3%	57.7%
15,102	O'BRIEN	5,161	3,595	1,513	53	2,082 R	69.7%	29.3%	70.4%	29.6%
7,003	OSCEOLA	2,333	1,609	683	41	926 R	69.0%	29.3%	70.2%	29.8%
16,976	PAGE	4,608	2,860	1,692	56	1,168 R	62.1%	36.7%	62.8%	37.2%
10,147	PALO ALTO	3,712	1,744	1,909	59	165 D	47.0%	51.4%	47.7%	52.3%
24,849	PLYMOUTH	8,131	5,275	2,775	81	2,500 R	64.9%	34.1%	65.5%	34.5%
8,662	POCAHONTAS	2,864	1,488	1,322	54	166 R	52.0%	46.2%	53.0%	47.0%
374,601	POLK	145,975	61,268	82,343	2,364	21,075 D	42.0%	56.4%	42.7%	57.3%
87,704	POTTAWATTAMIE	24,889	12,510	11,812	567	698 R	50.3%	47.5%	51.4%	48.6%
18,815	POWESHIEK	7,388	3,134	4,114	140	980 D	42.4%	55.7%	43.2%	56.8%
5,469	RINGGOLD	2,072	946	1,095	31	149 D	45.7%	52.8%	46.3%	53.7%
11,529	SAC	3,617	1,991	1,576	50	415 R	55.0%	43.6%	55.8%	44.2%
158,668	SCOTT	56,146	23,335	32,089	722	8,754 D	41.6%	57.2%	42.1%	57.9%
13,173	SHELBY	4,216	2,352	1,807	57	545 R	55.8%	42.9%	56.6%	43.4%
31,589	SIOUX	11,982	10,251	1,657	74	8,594 R	85.6%	13.8%	86.1%	13.9%
79,981	STORY	29,947	12,369	16,886	692	4,517 D	41.3%	56.4%	42.3%	57.7%
18,103	TAMA	6,771	2,900	3,765	106	865 D	42.8%	55.6%	43.5%	56.5%
6,958	TAYLOR	2,417	1,170	1,185	62	15 D	48.4%	49.0%	49.7%	50.3%
12,309	UNION	3,879	1,893	1,924	62	31 D	48.8%	49.6%	49.6%	50.4%
7,809	VAN BUREN	2,693	1,353	1,272	68	81 R	50.2%	47.2%	51.5%	48.5%
36,051	WAPELLO	11,402	4,011	7,178	213	3,167 D	35.2%	63.0%	35.8%	64.2%
40,671	WARREN	17,421	8,103	9,051	267	948 D	46.5%	52.0%	47.2%	52.8%
20,670	WASHINGTON	7,470	3,737	3,605	128	132 R	50.0%	48.3%	50.9%	49.1%
6,730	WAYNE	2,149	1,044	1,073	32	29 D	48.6%	49.9%	49.3%	50.7%
40,235	WEBSTER	13,213	5,635	7,408	170	1,773 D	42.6%	56.1%	43.2%	56.8%
11,723	WINNEBAGO	4,022	1,816	2,163	43	347 D	45.2%	53.8%	45.6%	54.4%
21,310	WINNESHIEK	7,248	3,275	3,826	147	551 D	45.2%	52.8%	46.1%	53.9%
103,877	WOODBURY	28,631	14,155	14,020	456	135 R	49.4%	49.0%	50.2%	49.8%
7,909	WORTH	3,122	1,169	1,908	45	739 D	37.4%	61.1%	38.0%	62.0%
14,334	WRIGHT	4,825	2,368	2,384	73	16 D	49.1%	49.4%	49.8%	50.2%
2,926,324	TOTAL	1,053,255	467,425	569,021	16,809	101,596 D	44.4%	54.0%	45.1%	54.9%

IOWA

HOUSE OF REPRESENTATIVES

CD	Year	Total Vote	Republican		Democratic		Other Vote	Rep.-Dem. Plurality	Percentage			
									Total Vote		Major Vote	
			Vote	Candidate	Vote	Candidate			Rep.	Dem.	Rep.	Dem.
1	2006	207,621	89,729	WHALEN, MIKE	114,322	BRALEY, BRUCE	3,570	24,593 D	43.2%	55.1%	44.0%	56.0%
1	2004	290,054	159,993	NUSSLE, JIM*	125,490	GLUBA, BILL	4,571	34,503 R	55.2%	43.3%	56.0%	44.0%
1	2002	196,455	112,280	NUSSLE, JIM*	83,779	HUTCHINSON, ANN	396	28,501 R	57.2%	42.6%	57.3%	42.7%
2	2006	209,586	101,707	LEACH, JIM*	107,683	LOEBSACK, DAVE	196	5,976 D	48.5%	51.4%	48.6%	51.4%
2	2004	299,881	176,684	LEACH, JIM*	117,405	FRANKER, DAVE	5,792	59,279 R	58.9%	39.2%	60.1%	39.9%
2	2002	207,171	108,130	LEACH, JIM*	94,767	THOMAS, JULIE	4,274	13,363 R	52.2%	45.7%	53.3%	46.7%
3	2006	223,287	103,722	LAMBERTI, JEFF	115,769	BOSWELL, LEONARD L.*	3,796	12,047 D	46.5%	51.8%	47.3%	52.7%
3	2004	304,319	136,099	THOMPSON, STAN	168,007	BOSWELL, LEONARD L.*	213	31,908 D	44.7%	55.2%	44.8%	55.2%
3	2002	215,985	97,285	THOMPSON, STAN	115,367	BOSWELL, LEONARD L.*	3,333	18,082 D	45.0%	53.4%	45.7%	54.3%
4	2006	212,730	121,650	LATHAM, TOM*	90,982	SPENCER, SELDEN E.	98	30,668 R	57.2%	42.8%	57.2%	42.8%
4	2004	297,566	181,294	LATHAM, TOM*	116,121	JOHNSON, PAUL W.	151	65,173 R	60.9%	39.0%	61.0%	39.0%
4	2002	210,774	115,430	LATHAM, TOM*	90,784	NORRIS, JOHN	4,560	24,646 R	54.8%	43.1%	56.0%	44.0%
5	2006	180,464	105,580	KING, STEVE*	64,181	SCHULTE, JOYCE	10,703	41,399 R	58.5%	35.6%	62.2%	37.8%
5	2004	266,341	168,583	KING, STEVE*	97,597	SCHULTE, JOYCE	161	70,986 R	63.3%	36.6%	63.3%	36.7%
5	2002	182,237	113,257	KING, STEVE	68,853	SHOMSHOR, PAUL	127	44,404 R	62.1%	37.8%	62.2%	37.8%
TOTAL	2006	1,033,688	522,388		492,937		18,363	29,451 R	50.5%	47.7%	51.5%	48.5%
TOTAL	2004	1,458,161	822,653		624,620		10,888	198,033 R	56.4%	42.8%	56.8%	43.2%
TOTAL	2002	1,012,622	546,382		453,550		12,690	92,832 R	54.0%	44.8%	54.6%	45.4%

An asterisk (*) denotes incumbent.

IOWA

GENERAL AND PRIMARY ELECTIONS

2006 GENERAL ELECTIONS

Governor   Other vote was 7,850 Iowa Green (Wendy Barth); 5,735 Libertarian (Kevin Litten); 1,974 Socialist Workers (Mary J. Martin); 1,250 scattered write-in.

House   Other vote was:

CD 1   2,201 Pirate (James F. Hill); 1,226 Nominated by Petition (Albert W. Schoeman); 143 scattered write-in.
CD 2   196 scattered write-in.
CD 3   3,591 Socialist Workers (Helen Meyers); 205 scattered write-in.
CD 4   98 scattered write-in.
CD 5   8,159 Nominated by Petition (Roy Nielsen); 2,479 Nominated by Petition (Cheryl L. Brodersen); 65 scattered write-in.

2006 PRIMARY ELECTIONS

Primary   June 6, 2006

Registration
(as of May 27, 2006—
does not include 165,599
inactive registrants)

Republican	592,434
Democratic	587,909
No Party	742,109
TOTAL	1,922,452

Primary Type   Semi-open—Registered Democrats and Republicans could vote only in their party's primary, although any registered voter could participate in either party's primary by changing their registration to that party on primary day.

IOWA

GENERAL AND PRIMARY ELECTIONS

Note: An asterisk (*) denotes incumbent.

	REPUBLICAN PRIMARIES			**DEMOCRATIC PRIMARIES**		
Governor	Jim Nussle	73,975	99.2%	Chet Culver	58,131	39.1%
	Scattered write-in	579	0.8%	Mike Blouin	50,728	34.1%
				Ed Fallon	38,253	25.7%
				Sal Mohamed	1,545	1.0%
				Scattered write-in	94	0.1%
	TOTAL	74,554		TOTAL	148,751	
Congressional	Mike Whalen	10,977	48.5%	Bruce Braley	10,489	36.0%
District 1	Bill Dix	8,483	37.4%	Rick Dickinson	9,971	34.3%
	Brian Kennedy	3,172	14.0%	Bill Gluba	7,453	25.6%
	Scattered write-in	22	0.1%	Denny Heath	1,161	4.0%
				Scattered write-in	23	0.1%
	TOTAL	22,654		TOTAL	29,097	
Congressional	Jim Leach*	8,430	99.0%	No candidates were listed on the Democratic primary ballot.		
District 2	Scattered write-in	88	1.0%	Dave Loebsack received 501 of the 1,437 write-in votes cast,		
	TOTAL	8,518		with the remaining 936 scattered.		
Congressional	Jeff Lamberti	8,713	99.4%	Leonard L. Boswell*	31,602	98.8%
District 3	Scattered write-in	50	0.6%	Scattered write-in	391	1.2%
	TOTAL	8,763		TOTAL	31,993	
Congressional	Tom Latham*	14,899	99.7%	Selden E. Spencer	20,597	99.6%
District 4	Scattered write-in	45	0.3%	Scattered write-in	77	0.4%
	TOTAL	14,944		TOTAL	20,674	
Congressional	Steve King*	21,512	99.5%	Joyce Schulte	8,874	62.5%
District 5	Scattered write-in	101	0.5%	Robert L. Chambers	5,286	37.3%
				Scattered write-in	28	0.2%
	TOTAL	21,613		TOTAL	14,188	

KANSAS

Congressional districts first established for elections held in 2002
4 members

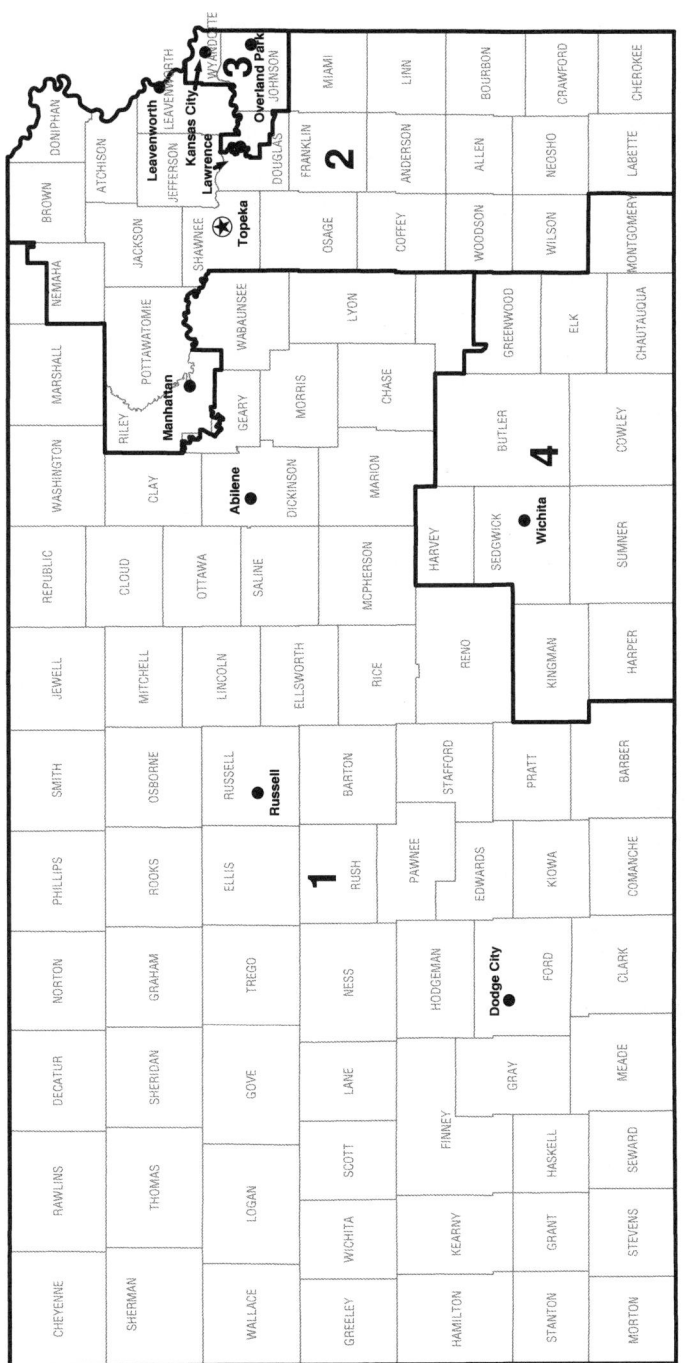

KANSAS

GOVERNOR
Kathleen Sebelius (D). Reelected 2006 to a four-year term. Previously elected 2002.

SENATORS (2 Republicans)
Sam Brownback (R). Reelected 2004 to a six-year term. Previously elected 1998 and 1996 to fill out the remaining two years of the term vacated when Senator Robert Dole (R) resigned to run for president.

Pat Roberts (R). Reelected 2002 to a six-year term. Previously elected 1996.

REPRESENTATIVES (2 Democrats, 2 Republicans)
1. Jerry Moran (R)
2. Nancy Boyda (D)
3. Dennis Moore (D)
4. Todd Tiahrt (R)

POSTWAR VOTE FOR PRESIDENT

Year	Total Vote	Republican Vote	Candidate	Democratic Vote	Candidate	Other Vote	Plurality	Total Vote Rep.	Total Vote Dem.	Major Vote Rep.	Major Vote Dem.
2004	1,187,756	736,456	Bush, George W.	434,993	Kerry, John	16,307	301,463 R	62.0%	36.6%	62.9%	37.1%
2000**	1,072,218	622,332	Bush, George W.	399,276	Gore, Al	50,610	223,056 R	58.0%	37.2%	60.9%	39.1%
1996**	1,074,300	583,245	Dole, Bob	387,659	Clinton, Bill	103,396	195,586 R	54.3%	36.1%	60.1%	39.9%
1992**	1,157,335	449,951	Bush, George	390,434	Clinton, Bill	316,950	59,517 R	38.9%	33.7%	53.5%	46.5%
1988	993,044	554,049	Bush, George	422,636	Dukakis, Michael S.	16,359	131,413 R	55.8%	42.6%	56.7%	43.3%
1984	1,021,991	677,296	Reagan, Ronald	333,149	Mondale, Walter F.	11,546	344,147 R	66.3%	32.6%	67.0%	33.0%
1980**	979,795	566,812	Reagan, Ronald	326,150	Carter, Jimmy	86,833	240,662 R	57.9%	33.3%	63.5%	36.5%
1976	957,845	502,752	Ford, Gerald R.	430,421	Carter, Jimmy	24,672	72,331 R	52.5%	44.9%	53.9%	46.1%
1972	916,095	619,812	Nixon, Richard M.	270,287	McGovern, George S.	25,996	349,525 R	67.7%	29.5%	69.6%	30.4%
1968**	872,783	478,674	Nixon, Richard M.	302,996	Humphrey, Hubert H.	91,113	175,678 R	54.8%	34.7%	61.2%	38.8%
1964	857,901	386,579	Goldwater, Barry M.	464,028	Johnson, Lyndon B.	7,294	77,449 D	45.1%	54.1%	45.4%	54.6%
1960	928,825	561,474	Nixon, Richard M.	363,213	Kennedy, John F.	4,138	198,261 R	60.4%	39.1%	60.7%	39.3%
1956	866,243	566,878	Eisenhower, Dwight D.	296,317	Stevenson, Adlai E.	3,048	270,561 R	65.4%	34.2%	65.7%	34.3%
1952	896,166	616,302	Eisenhower, Dwight D.	273,296	Stevenson, Adlai E.	6,568	343,006 R	68.8%	30.5%	69.3%	30.7%
1948	788,819	423,039	Dewey, Thomas E.	351,902	Truman, Harry S.	13,878	71,137 R	53.6%	44.6%	54.6%	45.4%

**In past elections, the other vote included: 2000 - 36,086 Green (Ralph Nader); 1996 - 92,639 Reform (Ross Perot); 1992 - 312,358 Independent (Ross Perot); 1980 - 68,231 Independent (John Anderson); 1968 - 88,921 American Independent (George Wallace).

KANSAS

POSTWAR VOTE FOR GOVERNOR

Year	Total Vote	Republican		Democratic		Other Vote	Rep.-Dem. Plurality	Percentage			
								Total Vote		Major Vote	
		Vote	Candidate	Vote	Candidate			Rep.	Dem.	Rep.	Dem.
2006	849,700	343,586	Barnett, Jim	491,993	Sebelius, Kathleen	14,121	148,407 D	40.4%	57.9%	41.1%	58.9%
2002	835,692	376,830	Shallenburger, Tim	441,858	Sebelius, Kathleen	17,004	65,028 D	45.1%	52.9%	46.0%	54.0%
1998	742,665	544,882	Graves, Bill	168,243	Sawyer, Tom	29,540	376,639 R	73.4%	22.7%	76.4%	23.6%
1994	821,030	526,113	Graves, Bill	294,733	Slattery, Jim	184	231,380 R	64.1%	35.9%	64.1%	35.9%
1990	783,325	333,589	Hayden, Mike	380,609	Finney, Joan	69,127	47,020 D	42.6%	48.6%	46.7%	53.3%
1986	840,605	436,267	Hayden, Mike	404,338	Docking, Thomas R.		31,929 R	51.9%	48.1%	51.9%	48.1%
1982	763,263	339,356	Hardage, Sam	405,772	Carlin, John	18,135	66,416 D	44.5%	53.2%	45.5%	54.5%
1978	736,246	348,015	Bennett, Robert F.	363,835	Carlin, John	24,396	15,820 D	47.3%	49.4%	48.9%	51.1%
1974**	783,875	387,792	Bennett, Robert F.	384,115	Miller, Vern	11,968	3,677 R	49.5%	49.0%	50.2%	49.8%
1972	921,552	341,440	Kay, Morris	571,256	Docking, Robert	8,856	229,816 D	37.1%	62.0%	37.4%	62.6%
1970	745,196	333,227	Frizzell, Kent	404,611	Docking, Robert	7,358	71,384 D	44.7%	54.3%	45.2%	54.8%
1968	862,473	410,673	Harman, Rick	447,269	Docking, Robert	4,531	36,596 D	47.6%	51.9%	47.9%	52.1%
1966	692,955	304,325	Avery, William H.	380,030	Docking, Robert	8,600	75,705 D	43.9%	54.8%	44.5%	55.5%
1964	850,414	432,667	Avery, William H.	400,264	Wiles, Harry G.	17,483	32,403 R	50.9%	47.1%	51.9%	48.1%
1962	638,798	341,257	Anderson, John	291,285	Saffels, Dale E.	6,256	49,972 R	53.4%	45.6%	54.0%	46.0%
1960	922,522	511,534	Anderson, John	402,261	Docking, George	8,727	109,273 R	55.4%	43.6%	56.0%	44.0%
1958	735,939	313,036	Reed, Clyde M.	415,506	Docking, George	7,397	102,470 D	42.5%	56.5%	43.0%	57.0%
1956	864,935	364,340	Shaw, Warren W.	479,701	Docking, George	20,894	115,361 D	42.1%	55.5%	43.2%	56.8%
1954	622,633	329,868	Hall, Fred	286,218	Docking, George	6,547	43,650 R	53.0%	46.0%	53.5%	46.5%
1952	872,139	491,338	Arn, Edward F.	363,482	Rooney, Charles	17,319	127,856 R	56.3%	41.7%	57.5%	42.5%
1950	619,310	333,001	Arn, Edward F.	275,494	Anderson, Kenneth	10,815	57,507 R	53.8%	44.5%	54.7%	45.3%
1948	760,407	433,396	Carlson, Frank	307,485	Carpenter, Randolph	19,526	125,911 R	57.0%	40.4%	58.5%	41.5%
1946	577,694	309,064	Carlson, Frank	254,283	Woodring, Harry H.	14,347	54,781 R	53.5%	44.0%	54.9%	45.1%

**The term of office of Kansas' governor was increased from two to four years effective with the 1974 election.

POSTWAR VOTE FOR SENATOR

Year	Total Vote	Republican		Democratic		Other Vote	Rep.-Dem. Plurality	Percentage			
								Total Vote		Major Vote	
		Vote	Candidate	Vote	Candidate			Rep.	Dem.	Rep.	Dem.
2004	1,129,022	780,863	Brownback, Sam	310,337	Jones, Lee	37,822	470,526 R	69.2%	27.5%	71.6%	28.4%
2002	776,850	641,075	Roberts, Pat	—		135,775	641,075 R	82.5%		100.0%	
1998	727,236	474,639	Brownback, Sam	229,718	Feleciano, Paul Jr.	22,879	244,921 R	65.3%	31.6%	67.4%	32.6%
1996	1,052,300	652,677	Roberts, Pat	362,380	Thompson, Sally	37,243	290,297 R	62.0%	34.4%	64.3%	35.7%
1996S	1,064,716	574,021	Brownback, Sam	461,344	Docking, Jill	29,351	112,677 R	53.9%	43.3%	55.4%	44.6%
1992	1,126,447	706,246	Dole, Robert	349,525	O'Dell, Gloria	70,676	356,721 R	62.7%	31.0%	66.9%	33.1%
1990	786,235	578,605	Kassebaum, Nancy Landon	207,491	Williams, Dick	139	371,114 R	73.6%	26.4%	73.6%	26.4%
1986	823,566	576,902	Dole, Robert	246,664	MacDonald, Guy		330,238 R	70.0%	30.0%	70.0%	30.0%
1984	996,729	757,402	Kassebaum, Nancy Landon	211,664	Maher, James	27,663	545,738 R	76.0%	21.2%	78.2%	21.8%
1980	938,957	598,686	Dole, Robert	340,271	Simpson, John		258,415 R	63.8%	36.2%	63.8%	36.2%
1978	748,839	403,354	Kassebaum, Nancy Landon	317,602	Roy, William R.	27,883	85,752 R	53.9%	42.4%	55.9%	44.1%
1974	794,437	403,983	Dole, Robert	390,451	Roy, William R.	3	13,532 R	50.9%	49.1%	50.9%	49.1%
1972	871,722	622,591	Pearson, James B.	200,764	Tetzlaff, Arch O.	48,367	421,827 R	71.4%	23.0%	75.6%	24.4%
1968	817,096	490,911	Dole, Robert	315,911	Robinson, William I.	10,274	175,000 R	60.1%	38.7%	60.8%	39.2%
1966	671,345	350,077	Pearson, James B.	303,223	Breeding, J. Floyd	18,045	46,854 R	52.1%	45.2%	53.6%	46.4%
1962	622,232	388,500	Carlson, Frank	223,630	Smith, K. L.	10,102	164,870 R	62.4%	35.9%	63.5%	36.5%
1962S	613,250	344,689	Pearson, James B.	260,756	Aylward, Paul L.	7,805	83,933 R	56.2%	42.5%	56.9%	43.1%
1960	888,592	485,499	Schoeppel, Andrew F.	388,895	Theis, Frank	14,198	96,604 R	54.6%	43.8%	55.5%	44.5%
1956	825,280	477,822	Carlson, Frank	333,939	Hart, George	13,519	143,883 R	57.9%	40.5%	58.9%	41.1%
1954	618,063	348,144	Schoeppel, Andrew F.	258,575	McGill, George	11,344	89,569 R	56.3%	41.8%	57.4%	42.6%
1950	619,104	335,880	Carlson, Frank	271,365	Aiken, Paul	11,859	64,515 R	54.3%	43.8%	55.3%	44.7%
1948	716,342	393,412	Schoeppel, Andrew F.	305,987	McGill, George	16,943	87,425 R	54.9%	42.7%	56.3%	43.7%

One of the 1996 and 1962 elections were for short terms to fill vacancies.

KANSAS

GOVERNOR 2006

2000 Census Population	County	Total Vote	Republican	Democratic	Other	Rep.-Dem. Plurality	Percentage			
							Total Vote		Major Vote	
							Rep.	Dem.	Rep.	Dem.
14,385	ALLEN	4,336	1,571	2,690	75	1,119 D	36.2%	62.0%	36.9%	63.1%
8,110	ANDERSON	2,781	1,040	1,681	60	641 D	37.4%	60.4%	38.2%	61.8%
16,774	ATCHISON	5,008	1,592	3,327	89	1,735 D	31.8%	66.4%	32.4%	67.6%
5,307	BARBER	1,783	889	855	39	34 R	49.9%	48.0%	51.0%	49.0%
28,205	BARTON	8,079	3,525	4,447	107	922 D	43.6%	55.0%	44.2%	55.8%
15,379	BOURBON	4,806	2,236	2,474	96	238 D	46.5%	51.5%	47.5%	52.5%
10,724	BROWN	3,427	1,432	1,948	47	516 D	41.8%	56.8%	42.4%	57.6%
59,482	BUTLER	19,335	9,767	9,166	402	601 R	50.5%	47.4%	51.6%	48.4%
3,030	CHASE	1,182	682	487	13	195 R	57.7%	41.2%	58.3%	41.7%
4,359	CHAUTAUQUA	1,163	686	450	27	236 R	59.0%	38.7%	60.4%	39.6%
22,605	CHEROKEE	6,796	2,676	3,929	191	1,253 D	39.4%	57.8%	40.5%	59.5%
3,165	CHEYENNE	1,060	603	443	14	160 R	56.9%	41.8%	57.6%	42.4%
2,390	CLARK	832	416	400	16	16 R	50.0%	48.1%	51.0%	49.0%
8,822	CLAY	3,143	1,553	1,560	30	7 D	49.4%	49.6%	49.9%	50.1%
10,268	CLOUD	3,218	1,424	1,751	43	327 D	44.3%	54.4%	44.9%	55.1%
8,865	COFFEY	3,447	1,834	1,562	51	272 R	53.2%	45.3%	54.0%	46.0%
1,967	COMANCHE	839	438	385	16	53 R	52.2%	45.9%	53.2%	46.8%
36,291	COWLEY	10,469	4,555	5,689	225	1,134 D	43.5%	54.3%	44.5%	55.5%
38,242	CRAWFORD	11,960	3,872	7,838	250	3,966 D	32.4%	65.5%	33.1%	66.9%
3,472	DECATUR	1,313	622	677	14	55 D	47.4%	51.6%	47.9%	52.1%
19,344	DICKINSON	6,599	3,094	3,424	81	330 D	46.9%	51.9%	47.5%	52.5%
8,249	DONIPHAN	2,406	1,085	1,283	38	198 D	45.1%	53.3%	45.8%	54.2%
99,962	DOUGLAS	34,872	7,544	26,784	544	19,240 D	21.6%	76.8%	22.0%	78.0%
3,449	EDWARDS	1,215	574	629	12	55 D	47.2%	51.8%	47.7%	52.3%
3,261	ELK	1,089	548	524	17	24 R	50.3%	48.1%	51.1%	48.9%
27,507	ELLIS	8,510	3,067	5,312	131	2,245 D	36.0%	62.4%	36.6%	63.4%
6,525	ELLSWORTH	2,190	887	1,270	33	383 D	40.5%	58.0%	41.1%	58.9%
40,523	FINNEY	6,734	3,447	3,190	97	257 R	51.2%	47.4%	51.9%	48.1%
32,458	FORD	5,846	2,840	2,909	97	69 D	48.6%	49.8%	49.4%	50.6%
24,784	FRANKLIN	8,296	3,212	4,930	154	1,718 D	38.7%	59.4%	39.4%	60.6%
27,947	GEARY	4,946	1,743	3,111	92	1,368 D	35.2%	62.9%	35.9%	64.1%
3,068	GOVE	1,198	608	577	13	31 R	50.8%	48.2%	51.3%	48.7%
2,946	GRAHAM	1,003	462	525	16	63 D	46.1%	52.3%	46.8%	53.2%
7,909	GRANT	1,902	1,030	850	22	180 R	54.2%	44.7%	54.8%	45.2%
5,904	GRAY	1,566	895	645	26	250 R	57.2%	41.2%	58.1%	41.9%
1,534	GREELEY	539	293	235	11	58 R	54.4%	43.6%	55.5%	44.5%
7,673	GREENWOOD	2,745	1,394	1,305	46	89 R	50.8%	47.5%	51.6%	48.4%
2,670	HAMILTON	697	350	332	15	18 R	50.2%	47.6%	51.3%	48.7%
6,536	HARPER	2,173	1,073	1,055	45	18 R	49.4%	48.6%	50.4%	49.6%
32,869	HARVEY	11,628	5,231	6,184	213	953 D	45.0%	53.2%	45.8%	54.2%
4,307	HASKELL	1,065	639	411	15	228 R	60.0%	38.6%	60.9%	39.1%
2,085	HODGEMAN	973	539	417	17	122 R	55.4%	42.9%	56.4%	43.6%
12,657	JACKSON	4,739	1,983	2,680	76	697 D	41.8%	56.6%	42.5%	57.5%
18,426	JEFFERSON	7,244	2,906	4,231	107	1,325 D	40.1%	58.4%	40.7%	59.3%
3,791	JEWELL	1,184	574	573	37	1 R	48.5%	48.4%	50.0%	50.0%
451,086	JOHNSON	185,692	67,946	115,251	2,495	47,305 D	36.6%	62.1%	37.1%	62.9%
4,531	KEARNY	1,074	571	484	19	87 R	53.2%	45.1%	54.1%	45.9%
8,673	KINGMAN	2,588	1,229	1,287	72	58 D	47.5%	49.7%	48.8%	51.2%
3,278	KIOWA	1,368	699	627	42	72 R	51.1%	45.8%	52.7%	47.3%
22,835	LABETTE	6,557	2,372	4,077	108	1,705 D	36.2%	62.2%	36.8%	63.2%
2,155	LANE	750	357	385	8	28 D	47.6%	51.3%	48.1%	51.9%
68,691	LEAVENWORTH	18,644	6,570	11,705	369	5,135 D	35.2%	62.8%	36.0%	64.0%
3,578	LINCOLN	1,201	584	598	19	14 D	48.6%	49.8%	49.4%	50.6%
9,570	LINN	3,359	1,291	1,984	84	693 D	38.4%	59.1%	39.4%	60.6%
3,046	LOGAN	1,088	577	493	18	84 R	53.0%	45.3%	53.9%	46.1%
35,935	LYON	10,167	4,981	5,066	120	85 D	49.0%	49.8%	49.6%	50.4%
29,554	MCPHERSON	10,405	5,127	5,151	127	24 D	49.3%	49.5%	49.9%	50.1%
13,361	MARION	4,581	2,611	1,897	73	714 R	57.0%	41.4%	57.9%	42.1%
10,965	MARSHALL	3,750	1,459	2,247	44	788 D	38.9%	59.9%	39.4%	60.6%
4,631	MEADE	1,539	866	619	54	247 R	56.3%	40.2%	58.3%	41.7%

KANSAS

GOVERNOR 2006

2000 Census Population	County	Total Vote	Republican	Democratic	Other	Rep.-Dem. Plurality	Percentage			
							Total Vote		Major Vote	
							Rep.	Dem.	Rep.	Dem.
28,351	MIAMI	10,750	4,391	6,149	210	1,758 D	40.8%	57.2%	41.7%	58.3%
6,932	MITCHELL	2,509	1,132	1,335	42	203 D	45.1%	53.2%	45.9%	54.1%
36,252	MONTGOMERY	9,256	4,729	4,327	200	402 R	51.1%	46.7%	52.2%	47.8%
6,104	MORRIS	2,285	1,059	1,198	28	139 D	46.3%	52.4%	46.9%	53.1%
3,496	MORTON	1,216	617	566	33	51 R	50.7%	46.5%	52.2%	47.8%
10,717	NEMAHA	4,729	2,037	2,631	61	594 D	43.1%	55.6%	43.6%	56.4%
16,997	NEOSHO	5,752	2,292	3,343	117	1,051 D	39.8%	58.1%	40.7%	59.3%
3,454	NESS	1,182	592	577	13	15 R	50.1%	48.8%	50.6%	49.4%
5,953	NORTON	1,896	950	923	23	27 R	50.1%	48.7%	50.7%	49.3%
16,712	OSAGE	6,350	2,751	3,499	100	748 D	43.3%	55.1%	44.0%	56.0%
4,452	OSBORNE	1,520	695	802	23	107 D	45.7%	52.8%	46.4%	53.6%
6,163	OTTAWA	2,712	1,299	1,360	53	61 D	47.9%	50.1%	48.9%	51.1%
7,233	PAWNEE	2,130	870	1,238	22	368 D	40.8%	58.1%	41.3%	58.7%
6,001	PHILLIPS	1,867	862	982	23	120 D	46.2%	52.6%	46.7%	53.3%
18,209	POTTAWATOMIE	7,165	3,541	3,516	108	25 R	49.4%	49.1%	50.2%	49.8%
9,647	PRATT	3,449	1,419	1,987	43	568 D	41.1%	57.6%	41.7%	58.3%
2,966	RAWLINS	1,169	700	448	21	252 R	59.9%	38.3%	61.0%	39.0%
64,790	RENO	20,440	9,290	10,870	280	1,580 D	45.5%	53.2%	46.1%	53.9%
5,835	REPUBLIC	2,054	1,063	971	20	92 R	51.8%	47.3%	52.3%	47.7%
10,761	RICE	3,055	1,371	1,627	57	256 D	44.9%	53.3%	45.7%	54.3%
62,843	RILEY	14,386	5,403	8,825	158	3,422 D	37.6%	61.3%	38.0%	62.0%
5,685	ROOKS	2,064	936	1,104	24	168 D	45.3%	53.5%	45.9%	54.1%
3,551	RUSH	1,209	485	701	23	216 D	40.1%	58.0%	40.9%	59.1%
7,370	RUSSELL	2,500	1,047	1,419	34	372 D	41.9%	56.8%	42.5%	57.5%
53,597	SALINE	17,248	6,793	10,182	273	3,389 D	39.4%	59.0%	40.0%	60.0%
5,120	SCOTT	1,713	983	712	18	271 R	57.4%	41.6%	58.0%	42.0%
452,869	SEDGWICK	117,388	54,278	60,453	2,657	6,175 D	46.2%	51.5%	47.3%	52.7%
22,510	SEWARD	3,310	1,842	1,390	78	452 R	55.6%	42.0%	57.0%	43.0%
169,871	SHAWNEE	65,914	24,331	40,781	802	16,450 D	36.9%	61.9%	37.4%	62.6%
2,813	SHERIDAN	1,002	458	537	7	79 D	45.7%	53.6%	46.0%	54.0%
6,760	SHERMAN	1,948	900	1,018	30	118 D	46.2%	52.3%	46.9%	53.1%
4,536	SMITH	1,677	689	970	18	281 D	41.1%	57.8%	41.5%	58.5%
4,789	STAFFORD	1,657	761	874	22	113 D	45.9%	52.7%	46.5%	53.5%
2,406	STANTON	628	336	282	10	54 R	53.5%	44.9%	54.4%	45.6%
5,463	STEVENS	1,498	884	593	21	291 R	59.0%	39.6%	59.9%	40.1%
25,946	SUMNER	7,837	3,560	4,046	231	486 D	45.4%	51.6%	46.8%	53.2%
8,180	THOMAS	2,534	1,403	1,097	34	306 R	55.4%	43.3%	56.1%	43.9%
3,319	TREGO	1,167	478	676	13	198 D	41.0%	57.9%	41.4%	58.6%
6,885	WABAUNSEE	2,851	1,464	1,333	54	131 R	51.4%	46.8%	52.3%	47.7%
1,749	WALLACE	622	369	246	7	123 R	59.3%	39.5%	60.0%	40.0%
6,483	WASHINGTON	2,150	1,171	948	31	223 R	54.5%	44.1%	55.3%	44.7%
2,531	WICHITA	739	413	318	8	95 R	55.9%	43.0%	56.5%	43.5%
10,332	WILSON	3,088	1,460	1,561	67	101 D	47.3%	50.6%	48.3%	51.7%
3,788	WOODSON	1,237	564	648	25	84 D	45.6%	52.4%	46.5%	53.5%
157,882	WYANDOTTE	32,741	6,242	25,913	586	19,671 D	19.1%	79.1%	19.4%	80.6%
2,688,418	TOTAL	849,693	343,581	491,992	14,120	148,411 D	40.4%	57.9%	41.1%	58.9%
	Certified Totals	849,700	343,586	491,993	14,121	148,407 D	40.4%	57.9%	41.1%	58.9%

KANSAS

HOUSE OF REPRESENTATIVES

			Republican		Democratic				Percentage			
		Total					Other	Rep.-Dem.	Total Vote		Major Vote	
CD	Year	Vote	Vote	Candidate	Vote	Candidate	Vote	Plurality	Rep.	Dem.	Rep.	Dem.
1	2006	199,378	156,728	MORAN, JERRY*	39,781	DOLL, JOHN	2,869	116,947 R	78.6%	20.0%	79.8%	20.2%
1	2004	264,293	239,776	MORAN, JERRY*		—	24,517	239,776 R	90.7%		100.0%	
1	2002	208,561	189,976	MORAN, JERRY*		—	18,585	189,976 R	91.1%		100.0%	
2	2006	225,562	106,329	RYUN, JIM*	114,139	BOYDA, NANCY	5,094	7,810 D	47.1%	50.6%	48.2%	51.8%
2	2004	294,436	165,325	RYUN, JIM*	121,532	BOYDA, NANCY	7,579	43,793 R	56.1%	41.3%	57.6%	42.4%
2	2002	210,977	127,477	RYUN, JIM*	79,160	LYKINS, DAN	4,340	48,317 R	60.4%	37.5%	61.7%	38.3%
3	2006	236,980	79,824	AHNER, CHUCK	153,105	MOORE, DENNIS*	4,051	73,281 D	33.7%	64.6%	34.3%	65.7%
3	2004	335,739	145,542	KOBACH, KRIS	184,050	MOORE, DENNIS*	6,147	38,508 D	43.3%	54.8%	44.2%	55.8%
3	2002	219,389	102,882	TAFF, ADAM	110,095	MOORE, DENNIS*	6,412	7,213 D	46.9%	50.2%	48.3%	51.7%
4	2006	183,207	116,386	TIAHRT, TODD*	62,166	McGINN, GARTH J.	4,655	54,220 R	63.5%	33.9%	65.2%	34.8%
4	2004	261,915	173,151	TIAHRT, TODD*	81,388	KINARD, MICHAEL	7,376	91,763 R	66.1%	31.1%	68.0%	32.0%
4	2002	190,963	115,691	TIAHRT, TODD*	70,656	NOLLA, CARLOS	4,616	45,035 R	60.6%	37.0%	62.1%	37.9%
TOTAL	2006	845,127	459,267		369,191		16,669	90,076 R	54.3%	43.7%	55.4%	44.6%
TOTAL	2004	1,156,383	723,794		386,970		45,619	336,824 R	62.6%	33.5%	65.2%	34.8%
TOTAL	2002	829,890	536,026		259,911		33,953	276,115 R	64.6%	31.3%	67.3%	32.7%

An asterisk (*) denotes incumbent.

KANSAS

GENERAL AND PRIMARY ELECTIONS

2006 GENERAL ELECTIONS

Governor Other vote was 8,896 Libertarian (Carl Kramer); 5,221 Reform (Richard Lee Ranzau); 4 write-in (Randal G. Trackwell).

House Other vote was:

CD 1 2,869 Reform (Sylvester Cain).
CD 2 5,094 Reform (Roger D. Tucker).
CD 3 4,051 Reform (Robert A. Conroy).
CD 4 4,655 Reform (Joy R. Holt).

2006 PRIMARY ELECTIONS

Primary August 1, 2006

Registration (as of July 2006)

Republican	755,725
Democratic	437,854
Libertarian	9,047
Reform	1,503
Unaffiliated	447,205
TOTAL	1,651,334

Primary Type Semi-open—Registered Democrats and Republicans could vote only in their party's primary. "Unaffiliated" voters could participate in either primary, although if they voted in the Republican primary they had to change their registration to Republican on primary day.

KANSAS

GENERAL AND PRIMARY ELECTIONS

Note: An asterisk (*) denotes incumbent.

	REPUBLICAN PRIMARIES			DEMOCRATIC PRIMARIES		
Governor	Jim Barnett	70,299	36.2%	Kathleen Sebelius*	76,046	100.0%
	Ken R. Canfield	51,365	26.4%			
	Robin Jennison	42,678	22.0%			
	Timothy V. Pickell	10,473	5.4%			
	Rex Crowell	8,677	4.5%			
	Dennis Hawver	6,661	3.4%			
	Richard "Rode" Rodewald	4,142	2.1%			
	TOTAL	*194,295*				
Congressional District 1	Jerry Moran*	60,840	100.0%	John Doll	14,109	100.0%
Congressional District 2	Jim Ryun*	41,941	100.0%	Nancy Boyda	21,335	100.0%
Congressional District 3	Chuck Ahner	21,716	51.9%	Dennis Moore*	19,492	100.0%
	Scott Schwab	13,602	32.5%			
	Thomas Scherer	3,610	8.6%			
	Paul V. Showen	2,888	6.9%			
	TOTAL	*41,816*				
Congressional District 4	Todd Tiahrt*	36,844	100.0%	Garth J. McGinn	4,382	27.6%
				Ronald Voth	4,348	27.4%
				Marty Mork	3,848	24.2%
				Patrick Quaney	3,317	20.9%
				TOTAL	*15,895*	

KENTUCKY

Congressional districts first established for elections held in 2002
6 members

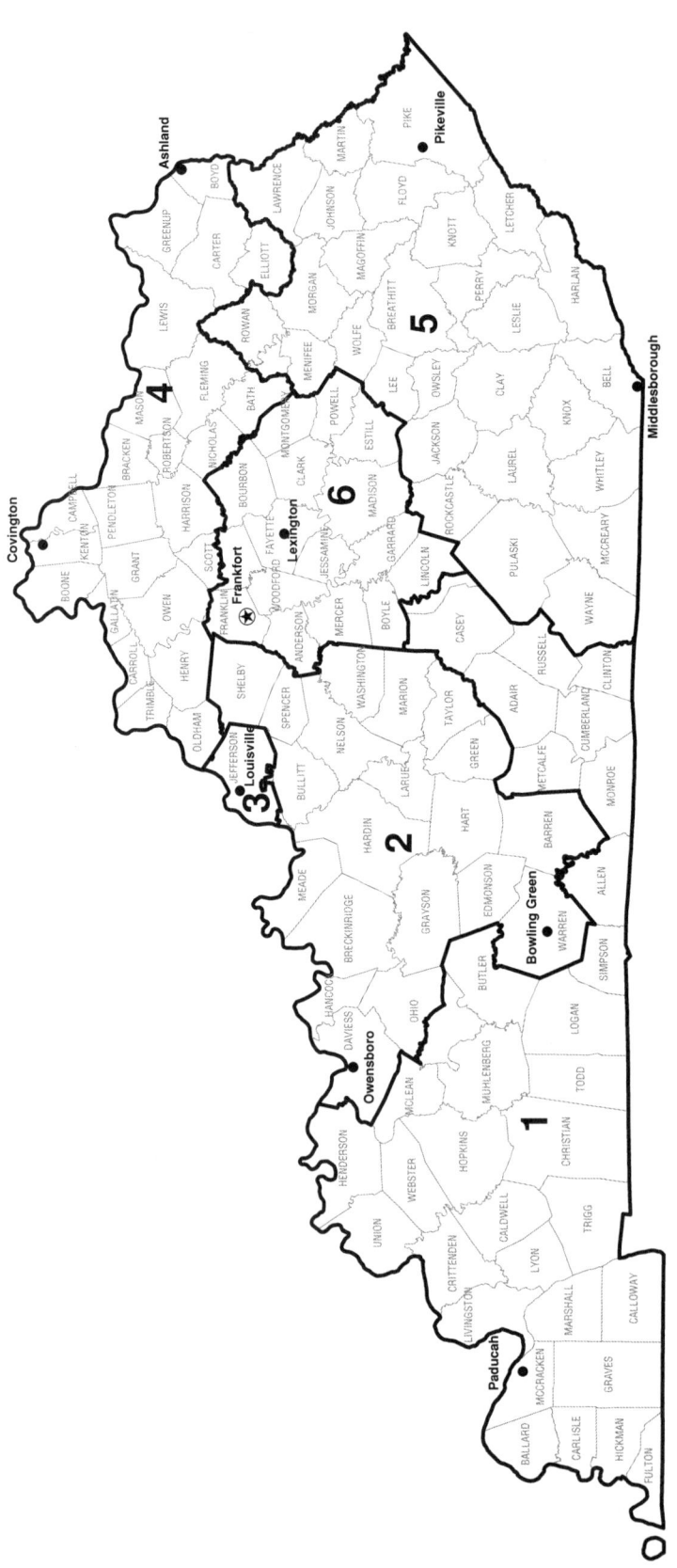

KENTUCKY

GOVERNOR
Ernie Fletcher (R). Elected 2003 to a four-year term.

SENATORS (2 Republicans)
Jim Bunning (R). Reelected 2004 to a six-year term. Previously elected 1998.

Mitch McConnell (R). Reelected 2002 to a six-year term. Previously elected 1996, 1990, 1984.

REPRESENTATIVES (4 Republicans, 2 Democrats)
1. Edward Whitfield (R)
2. Ron Lewis (R)
3. John Yarmuth (D)
4. Geoff Davis (R)
5. Harold Rogers (R)
6. Ben Chandler (D)

POSTWAR VOTE FOR PRESIDENT

Year	Total Vote	Republican Vote	Candidate	Democratic Vote	Candidate	Other Vote	Plurality	Total Vote Rep.	Total Vote Dem.	Major Vote Rep.	Major Vote Dem.
2004	1,795,882	1,069,439	Bush, George W.	712,733	Kerry, John	13,710	356,706 R	59.5%	39.7%	60.0%	40.0%
2000**	1,544,187	872,492	Bush, George W.	638,898	Gore, Al	32,797	233,594 R	56.5%	41.4%	57.7%	42.3%
1996**	1,388,708	623,283	Dole, Bob	636,614	Clinton, Bill	128,811	13,331 D	44.9%	45.8%	49.5%	50.5%
1992**	1,492,900	617,178	Bush, George	665,104	Clinton, Bill	210,618	47,926 D	41.3%	44.6%	48.1%	51.9%
1988	1,322,517	734,281	Bush, George	580,368	Dukakis, Michael S.	7,868	153,913 R	55.5%	43.9%	55.9%	44.1%
1984	1,369,345	821,702	Reagan, Ronald	539,539	Mondale, Walter F.	8,104	282,163 R	60.0%	39.4%	60.4%	39.6%
1980**	1,294,627	635,274	Reagan, Ronald	616,417	Carter, Jimmy	42,936	18,857 R	49.1%	47.6%	50.8%	49.2%
1976	1,167,142	531,852	Ford, Gerald R.	615,717	Carter, Jimmy	19,573	83,865 D	45.6%	52.8%	46.3%	53.7%
1972	1,067,499	676,446	Nixon, Richard M.	371,159	McGovern, George S.	19,894	305,287 R	63.4%	34.8%	64.6%	35.4%
1968**	1,055,893	462,411	Nixon, Richard M.	397,541	Humphrey, Hubert H.	195,941	64,870 R	43.8%	37.6%	53.8%	46.2%
1964	1,046,105	372,977	Goldwater, Barry M.	669,659	Johnson, Lyndon B.	3,469	296,682 D	35.7%	64.0%	35.8%	64.2%
1960	1,124,462	602,607	Nixon, Richard M.	521,855	Kennedy, John F.		80,752 R	53.6%	46.4%	53.6%	46.4%
1956	1,053,805	572,192	Eisenhower, Dwight D.	476,453	Stevenson, Adlai E.	5,160	95,739 R	54.3%	45.2%	54.6%	45.4%
1952	993,148	495,029	Eisenhower, Dwight D.	495,729	Stevenson, Adlai E.	2,390	700 D	49.8%	49.9%	50.0%	50.0%
1948	822,658	341,210	Dewey, Thomas E.	466,756	Truman, Harry S.	14,692	125,546 D	41.5%	56.7%	42.2%	57.8%

**In past elections, the other vote included: 2000 - 23,192 Green (Ralph Nader); 1996 - 120,396 Reform (Ross Perot); 1992 - 203,944 Independent (Ross Perot); 1980 - 31,127 Independent (John Anderson); 1968 - 193,098 American Independent (George Wallace).

KENTUCKY

POSTWAR VOTE FOR GOVERNOR

Year	Total Vote	Republican Vote	Republican Candidate	Democratic Vote	Democratic Candidate	Other Vote	Rep.-Dem. Plurality	Total Vote Rep.	Total Vote Dem.	Major Vote Rep.	Major Vote Dem.
2003	1,083,443	596,284	Fletcher, Ernie	487,159	Chandler, Ben		109,125 R	55.0%	45.0%	55.0%	45.0%
1999**	580,074	128,788	Martin, Peppy	352,099	Patton, Paul E.	99,187	223,311 D	22.2%	60.7%	26.8%	73.2%
1995	983,979	479,227	Forgy, Larry	500,787	Patton, Paul E.	3,965	21,560 D	48.7%	50.9%	48.9%	51.1%
1991	834,920	294,452	Hopkins, Larry J.	540,468	Jones, Brereton C.		246,016 D	35.3%	64.7%	35.3%	64.7%
1987	777,815	273,141	Harper, John	504,674	Wilkinson, Wallace G.		231,533 D	35.1%	64.9%	35.1%	64.9%
1983	1,030,671	454,650	Bunning, Jim	561,674	Collins, Martha Layne	14,347	107,024 D	44.1%	54.5%	44.7%	55.3%
1979	939,366	381,278	Nunn, Louie B.	558,088	Brown, J. Y. Jr.		176,810 D	40.6%	59.4%	40.6%	59.4%
1975	748,157	277,998	Gable, Robert E.	470,159	Carroll, Julian		192,161 D	37.2%	62.8%	37.2%	62.8%
1971	930,790	412,653	Emberton, Thomas	470,720	Ford, Wendell H.	47,417	58,067 D	44.3%	50.6%	46.7%	53.3%
1967	886,946	454,123	Nunn, Louie B.	425,674	Ward, Henry	7,149	28,449 R	51.2%	48.0%	51.6%	48.4%
1963	886,047	436,496	Nunn, Louie B.	449,551	Breathitt, Edward T.		13,055 D	49.3%	50.7%	49.3%	50.7%
1959	853,005	336,456	Robsion, John M.	516,549	Combs, Bert T.		180,093 D	39.4%	60.6%	39.4%	60.6%
1955	778,488	322,671	Denney, Edwin R.	451,647	Chandler, Albert B.	4,170	128,976 D	41.4%	58.0%	41.7%	58.3%
1951	634,359	288,014	Siler, Eugene	346,345	Wetherby, Lawrence		58,331 D	45.4%	54.6%	45.4%	54.6%
1947	672,372	287,130	Dummit, Eldon S.	385,242	Clements, Earle C.		98,112 D	42.7%	57.3%	42.7%	57.3%

**In past elections, the other vote included: 1999 - 88,930 Reform (Gatewood Galbraith).

POSTWAR VOTE FOR SENATOR

Year	Total Vote	Republican Vote	Republican Candidate	Democratic Vote	Democratic Candidate	Other Vote	Rep.-Dem. Plurality	Total Vote Rep.	Total Vote Dem.	Major Vote Rep.	Major Vote Dem.
2004	1,724,362	873,507	Bunning, Jim	850,855	Mongiardo, Daniel		22,652 R	50.7%	49.3%	50.7%	49.3%
2002	1,131,475	731,679	McConnell, Mitch	399,634	Weinberg, Lois Combs	162	332,045 R	64.7%	35.3%	64.7%	35.3%
1998	1,145,414	569,817	Bunning, Jim	563,051	Baesler, Scotty	12,546	6,766 R	49.7%	49.2%	50.3%	49.7%
1996	1,307,046	724,794	McConnell, Mitch	560,012	Beshear, Steven L.	22,240	164,782 R	55.5%	42.8%	56.4%	43.6%
1992	1,330,858	476,604	Williams, David L.	836,888	Ford, Wendell H.	17,366	360,284 D	35.8%	62.9%	36.3%	63.7%
1990	916,010	478,034	McConnell, Mitch	437,976	Sloane, Harvey		40,058 R	52.2%	47.8%	52.2%	47.8%
1986	677,280	173,330	Andrews, Jackson M.	503,775	Ford, Wendell H.	175	330,445 D	25.6%	74.4%	25.6%	74.4%
1984	1,292,407	644,990	McConnell, Mitch	639,721	Huddleston, Walter	7,696	5,269 R	49.9%	49.5%	50.2%	49.8%
1980	1,106,890	386,029	Foust, Mary Louise	720,861	Ford, Wendell H.		334,832 D	34.9%	65.1%	34.9%	65.1%
1978	476,783	175,766	Guenthner, Louie	290,730	Huddleston, Walter	10,287	114,964 D	36.9%	61.0%	37.7%	62.3%
1974	745,994	328,982	Cook, Marlow W.	399,406	Ford, Wendell H.	17,606	70,424 D	44.1%	53.5%	45.2%	54.8%
1972	1,037,861	494,337	Nunn, Louie B.	528,550	Huddleston, Walter	14,974	34,213 D	47.6%	50.9%	48.3%	51.7%
1968	942,865	484,260	Cook, Marlow W.	448,960	Peden, Katherine	9,645	35,300 R	51.4%	47.6%	51.9%	48.1%
1966	749,884	483,805	Cooper, John Sherman	266,079	Brown, J. Y.		217,726 R	64.5%	35.5%	64.5%	35.5%
1962	820,088	432,648	Morton, Thruston B.	387,440	Wyatt, Wilson W.		45,208 R	52.8%	47.2%	52.8%	47.2%
1960	1,088,377	644,087	Cooper, John Sherman	444,290	Johnson, Keen		199,797 R	59.2%	40.8%	59.2%	40.8%
1956	1,006,825	506,903	Morton, Thruston B.	499,922	Clements, Earle C.		6,981 R	50.3%	49.7%	50.3%	49.7%
1956S	1,011,645	538,505	Cooper, John Sherman	473,140	Wetherby, Lawrence		65,365 R	53.2%	46.8%	53.2%	46.8%
1954	797,057	362,948	Cooper, John Sherman	434,109	Barkley, Alben W.		71,161 D	45.5%	54.5%	45.5%	54.5%
1952S	960,228	494,576	Cooper, John Sherman	465,652	Underwood, Thomas R.		28,924 R	51.5%	48.5%	51.5%	48.5%
1950	612,617	278,368	Dawson, Charles L.	334,249	Clements, Earle C.		55,881 D	45.4%	54.6%	45.4%	54.6%
1948	794,469	383,776	Cooper, John Sherman	408,256	Chapman, Virgil	2,437	24,480 D	48.3%	51.4%	48.5%	51.5%
1946S	615,119	327,652	Cooper, John Sherman	285,829	Brown, J. Y.	1,638	41,823 R	53.3%	46.5%	53.4%	46.6%

One of the 1956 elections and those in 1952 and 1946 were for short terms to fill vacancies.

KENTUCKY

HOUSE OF REPRESENTATIVES

| CD | Year | Total Vote | Republican | | Democratic | | Other Vote | Rep.-Dem. Plurality | Percentage | | | |
| | | | Vote | Candidate | Vote | Candidate | | | Total Vote | | Major Vote | |
									Rep.	Dem.	Rep.	Dem.
1	2006	207,483	123,618	WHITFIELD, EDWARD*	83,865	BARLOW, TOM		39,753 R	59.6%	40.4%	59.6%	40.4%
1	2004	261,201	175,972	WHITFIELD, EDWARD*	85,229	CARTWRIGHT, BILLY R.		90,743 R	67.4%	32.6%	67.4%	32.6%
1	2002	180,217	117,600	WHITFIELD, EDWARD*	62,617	ALEXANDER, KLINT		54,983 R	65.3%	34.7%	65.3%	34.7%
2	2006	213,963	118,548	LEWIS, RON*	95,415	WEAVER, MIKE		23,133 R	55.4%	44.6%	55.4%	44.6%
2	2004	272,979	185,394	LEWIS, RON*	87,585	SMITH, ADAM		97,809 R	67.9%	32.1%	67.9%	32.1%
2	2002	176,288	122,773	LEWIS, RON*	51,431	WILLIAMS, DAVID L.	2,084	71,342 R	69.6%	29.2%	70.5%	29.5%
3	2006	241,965	116,568	NORTHUP, ANNE M.*	122,489	YARMUTH, JOHN	2,908	5,921 D	48.2%	50.6%	48.8%	51.2%
3	2004	328,139	197,736	NORTHUP, ANNE M.*	124,040	MILLER, TONY	6,363	73,696 R	60.3%	37.8%	61.5%	38.5%
3	2002	229,074	118,228	NORTHUP, ANNE M.*	110,846	CONWAY, JACK		7,382 R	51.6%	48.4%	51.6%	48.4%
4	2006	204,767	105,845	DAVIS, GEOFF*	88,822	LUCAS, KEN	10,100	17,023 R	51.7%	43.4%	54.4%	45.6%
4	2004	295,927	160,982	DAVIS, GEOFF	129,876	CLOONEY, NICK	5,069	31,106 R	54.4%	43.9%	55.3%	44.7%
4	2002	171,735	81,651	DAVIS, GEOFF	87,776	LUCAS, KEN*	2,308	6,125 D	47.5%	51.1%	48.2%	51.8%
5	2006	199,568	147,201	ROGERS, HAROLD*	52,367	STEPP, KENNETH		94,834 R	73.8%	26.2%	73.8%	26.2%
5	2004	177,579	177,579	ROGERS, HAROLD*		—		177,579 R	100.0%		100.0%	
5	2002	176,240	137,986	ROGERS, HAROLD*	38,254	BAILEY, SIDNEY JANE		99,732 R	78.3%	21.7%	78.3%	21.7%
6	2006	185,780		—	158,765	CHANDLER, BEN*	27,015	158,765 D		85.5%		100.0%
6	2004	299,217	119,716	BUFORD, TOM	175,355	CHANDLER, BEN*	4,146	55,639 D	40.0%	58.6%	40.6%	59.4%
6	2002	160,688	115,622	FLETCHER, ERNIE*		—	45,066	115,622 R	72.0%		100.0%	
TOTAL	2006	1,253,526	611,780		601,723		40,023	10,057 R	48.8%	48.0%	50.4%	49.6%
TOTAL	2004	1,635,042	1,017,379		602,085		15,578	415,294 R	62.2%	36.8%	62.8%	37.2%
TOTAL	2002	1,094,242	693,860		350,924		49,458	342,936 R	63.4%	32.1%	66.4%	33.6%

An asterisk (*) denotes incumbent.

KENTUCKY

GENERAL AND PRIMARY ELECTIONS

2006 GENERAL ELECTIONS

House   Other vote was:

CD 1
CD 2
CD 3   2,134 Libertarian (Donna Walker Mancini); 774 Constitution (W. Ed Parker).
CD 4   10,100 Libertarian (Brian Houillion).
CD 5
CD 6   27,015 Libertarian (Paul Ard).

KENTUCKY

GENERAL AND PRIMARY ELECTIONS

2006 PRIMARY ELECTIONS

Primary	May 16, 2006	**Registration** (as of May 16, 2006)	Democratic Republican Other	1,548,443 989,499 172,017
			TOTAL	2,709,959

Primary Type   Closed—Only registered Democrats and Republicans could vote in their party's primary.

Note: An asterisk (*) denotes incumbent. The names of unopposed candidates did not appear on the primary ballot; therefore, no votes were cast for these candidates.

REPUBLICAN PRIMARIES			DEMOCRATIC PRIMARIES		
Congressional District 1	Edward Whitfield*	Unopposed	Tom Barlow Eric Streit Jim Bloink *TOTAL*	80,594 16,320 7,668 *104,582*	77.1% 15.6% 7.3%
Congressional District 2	Ron Lewis*	Unopposed	Mike Weaver James E. Rice *TOTAL*	49,067 18,470 *67,537*	72.7% 27.3%
Congressional District 3	Anne M. Northup*	Unopposed	John Yarmuth Andrew Horne James Walter Moore Burrel Charles Farnsley *TOTAL*	30,962 18,662 4,582 3,322 *57,528*	53.8% 32.4% 8.0% 5.8%
Congressional District 4	Geoff Davis*	Unopposed	Ken Lucas	Unopposed	
Congressional District 5	Harold Rogers*	Unopposed	Kenneth Stepp James W. Tapley *TOTAL*	47,362 19,928 *67,290*	70.4% 29.6%
Congressional District 6	No Republican candidate		Ben Chandler*	Unopposed	

LOUISIANA

Congressional districts first established for elections held in 2002
7 members

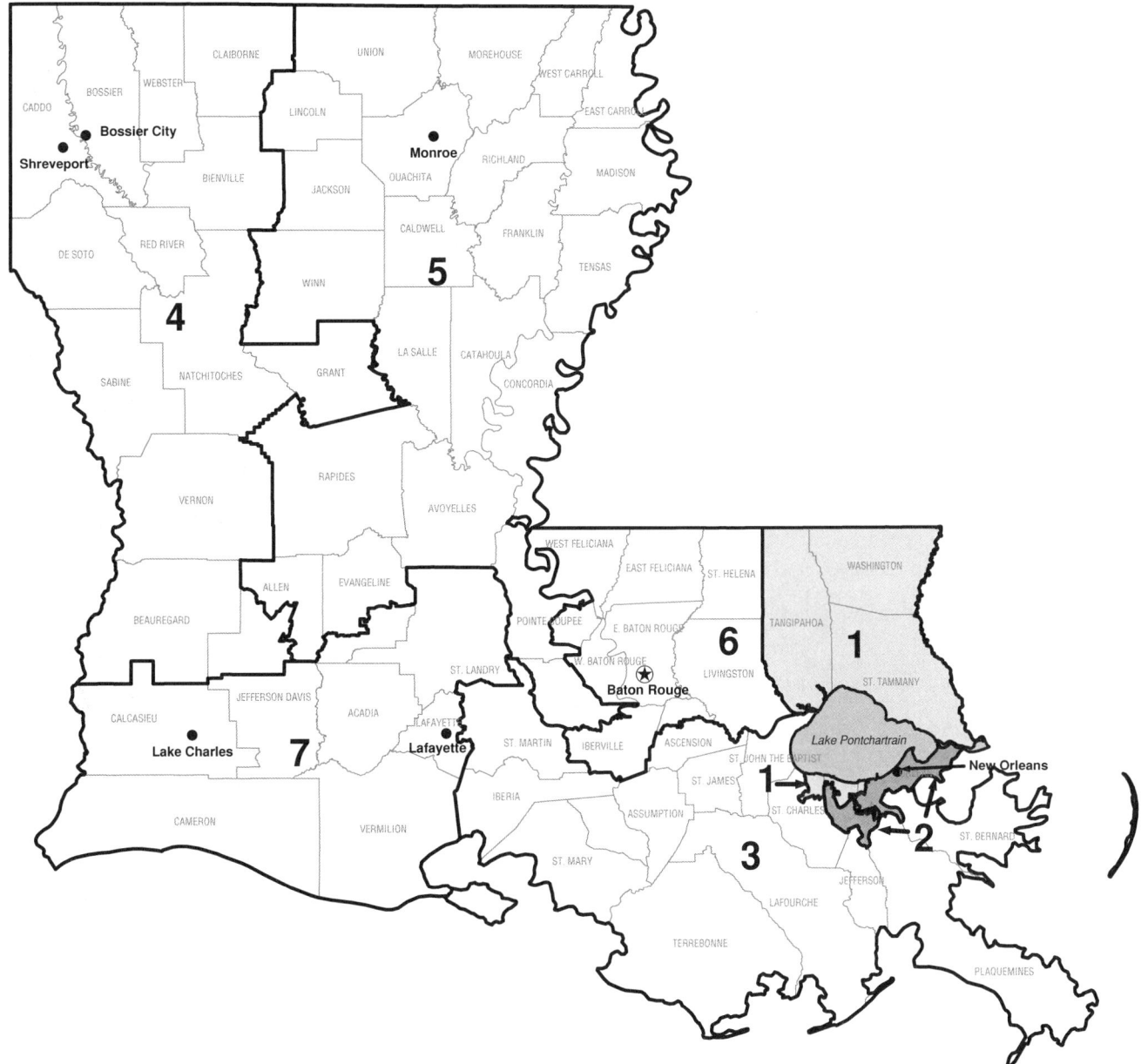

LOUISIANA

GOVERNOR
Kathleen Babineaux Blanco (D). Elected 2003 to a four-year term.

SENATORS (1 Democrat, 1 Republican)
David Vitter (R). Elected 2004 to a six-year term.

Mary L. Landrieu (D). Reelected 2002 to a six-year term. Previously elected 1996.

REPRESENTATIVES (5 Republicans, 2 Democrats)
1. Bobby Jindal (R)
2. William J. Jefferson (D)
3. Charlie Melancon (D)
4. Jim McCrery (R)
5. Rodney Alexander (R)
6. Richard H. Baker (R)
7. Charles Boustany Jr. (R)

POSTWAR VOTE FOR PRESIDENT

		Republican		Democratic		Other		Total Vote		Major Vote	
Year	Total Vote	Vote	Candidate	Vote	Candidate	Vote	Plurality	Rep.	Dem.	Rep.	Dem.
2004	1,943,106	1,102,169	Bush, George W.	820,299	Kerry, John	20,638	281,870 R	56.7%	42.2%	57.3%	42.7%
2000**	1,765,656	927,871	Bush, George W.	792,344	Gore, Al	45,441	135,527 R	52.6%	44.9%	53.9%	46.1%
1996**	1,783,959	712,586	Dole, Bob	927,837	Clinton, Bill	143,536	215,251 D	39.9%	52.0%	43.4%	56.6%
1992**	1,790,017	733,386	Bush, George	815,971	Clinton, Bill	240,660	82,585 D	41.0%	45.6%	47.3%	52.7%
1988	1,628,202	883,702	Bush, George	717,460	Dukakis, Michael S.	27,040	166,242 R	54.3%	44.1%	55.2%	44.8%
1984	1,706,822	1,037,299	Reagan, Ronald	651,586	Mondale, Walter F.	17,937	385,713 R	60.8%	38.2%	61.4%	38.6%
1980**	1,548,591	792,853	Reagan, Ronald	708,453	Carter, Jimmy	47,285	84,400 R	51.2%	45.7%	52.8%	47.2%
1976	1,278,439	587,446	Ford, Gerald R.	661,365	Carter, Jimmy	29,628	73,919 D	46.0%	51.7%	47.0%	53.0%
1972	1,051,491	686,852	Nixon, Richard M.	298,142	McGovern, George S.	66,497	388,710 R	65.3%	28.4%	69.7%	30.3%
1968**	1,097,450	257,535	Nixon, Richard M.	309,615	Humphrey, Hubert H.	530,300	220,685 A	23.5%	28.2%	45.4%	54.6%
1964	896,293	509,225	Goldwater, Barry M.	387,068	Johnson, Lyndon B.		122,157 R	56.8%	43.2%	56.8%	43.2%
1960**	807,891	230,980	Nixon, Richard M.	407,339	Kennedy, John F.	169,572	176,359 D	28.6%	50.4%	36.2%	63.8%
1956	617,544	329,047	Eisenhower, Dwight D.	243,977	Stevenson, Adlai E.	44,520	85,070 R	53.3%	39.5%	57.4%	42.6%
1952	651,952	306,925	Eisenhower, Dwight D.	345,027	Stevenson, Adlai E.		38,102 D	47.1%	52.9%	47.1%	52.9%
1948**	416,336	72,657	Dewey, Thomas E.	136,344	Truman, Harry S.	207,335	67,946 SR	17.5%	32.7%	34.8%	65.2%

**In past elections, the other vote included: 20,473 Green (Ralph Nader); 1996 - 123,293 Reform (Ross Perot); 1992 - 211,478 Independent (Ross Perot); 1980 - 26,345 Independent (John Anderson); 1968 - 530,300 American Independent (George Wallace); 1960 - 169,572 Unpledged Independent Electors; 1948 - 204,290 States' Rights (Strom Thurmond).

LOUISIANA

POSTWAR VOTE FOR GOVERNOR

Year	Total Vote	Republican		Democratic		Other Vote	Plurality	Percentage			
								Total Vote		Major Vote	
		Vote	Candidate	Vote	Candidate			Rep.	Dem.	Rep.	Dem.
2003*	1,407,842	676,484	Jindal, Bobby	731,358	Blanco, Kathleen Babineaux		54,874 D	48.1%	51.9%	48.1%	51.9%
1999	1,295,205	805,203	Foster, Mike	382,445	Jefferson, William J.	107,557	422,758 R	62.2%	29.5%		
1995*	1,550,360	984,499	Foster, Mike	565,861	Fields, Cleo		418,638 R	63.5%	36.5%	63.5%	36.5%
1991*	1,728,040	671,009	Duke, David E.	1,057,031	Edwards, Edwin W.		386,022 D	38.8%	61.2%	38.8%	61.2%
1987**	1,558,730	287,780	Livingston, Robert L.	516,078	Roemer, Charles	754,872	78,277 D	18.5%	33.1%		
1983	1,615,905	588,508	Treen, David C.	1,006,561	Edwards, Edwin W.	20,836	418,053 D	36.4%	62.3%		
1979*	1,371,825	690,691	Treen, David C.	681,134	Lambert, Louis		9,557 R	50.3%	49.7%	50.3%	49.7%
1975	430,095		—	430,095	Edwards, Edwin W.		430,095 D		100.0%		100.0%
1972	1,121,570	480,424	Treen, David C.	641,146	Edwards, Edwin W.		160,722 D	42.8%	57.2%	42.8%	57.2%
1968	372,762		—	372,762	McKeithen, John J.		372,762 D		100.0%		100.0%
1964	773,390	297,753	Lyons, C. H.	469,589	McKeithen, John J.	6,048	171,836 D	38.5%	60.7%	38.8%	61.2%
1960	506,562	86,135	Grevemberg, F. C.	407,907	Davis, Jimmie H.	12,520	321,772 D	17.0%	80.5%	17.4%	82.6%
1956	172,291		—	172,291	Long, Earl K.		172,291 D		100.0%		100.0%
1952	123,681	4,958	Bagwell, Harrison G.	118,723	Kennon, Robert F.		113,765 D	4.0%	96.0%	4.0%	96.0%
1948	76,566		—	76,566	Long, Earl K.		76,566 D		100.0%		100.0%

**Since 1978 Louisiana has had a two-tier election system in which all candidates, regardless of party, run together in a first round, open primary. A candidate that wins a majority of the vote in the first round is elected. If no candidate receives 50 percent, a runoff is held between the top two finishers. An asterisk (*) indicates gubernatorial elections that were decided in a runoff, with the runoff results listed. In elections that did not require a runoff, the leading Democratic and Republican candidates are listed with their first round votes. The votes for other candidates are listed in the "Other" column, regardless of whether they were Democratic, Republican, or Independent. In 1987, Democrat Edwin W. Edwards withdrew after finishing second in the initial round of voting. Democrat Charles Roemer finished first with 33.1 percent and with Edwards' withdrawal, no runoff was held. The major party vote percentages are given for those elections where there was no more than one Democratic and one Republican candidate.

POSTWAR VOTE FOR SENATOR

Year	Total Vote	Republican		Democratic		Other Vote	Plurality	Percentage			
								Total Vote		Major Vote	
		Vote	Candidate	Vote	Candidate			Rep.	Dem.	Rep.	Dem.
2004	1,848,056	943,014	Vitter, David	542,150	John, Chris	362,892	400,864 R	51.0%	29.3%		
2002*	1,235,296	596,642	Terrell, Suzanne Haik	638,654	Landrieu, Mary L.		42,012 D	48.3%	51.7%	48.3%	51.7%
1998	969,165	306,616	Donelon, Jim	620,502	Breaux, John B.	42,047	313,886 D	31.6%	64.0%		
1996*	1,700,102	847,157	Jenkins, Louis	852,945	Landrieu, Mary L.		5,788 D	49.8%	50.2%	49.8%	50.2%
1992	843,037	69,986	Stockstill, Lyle	616,021	Breaux, John B.	157,030	541,236 D	8.3%	73.1%		
1990	1,396,113	607,391	Duke, David E.	752,902	Johnston, J. Bennett	35,820	145,511 D	43.5%	53.9%		
1986*	1,369,897	646,311	Moore, W. Henson	723,586	Breaux, John B.		77,275 D	47.2%	52.8%	47.2%	52.8%
1984	977,473	86,546	Ross, Robert M.	838,181	Johnston, J. Bennett	52,746	751,635 D	8.9%	85.7%		
1980	841,013	13,739	Bardwell, Jerry C.	484,770	Long, Russell B.	342,504	158,848 D	1.6%	57.6%		
1978	839,669		—	498,773	Johnston, J. Bennett	340,896	157,877 D		59.4%		
1974	434,643		—	434,643	Long, Russell B.		434,643 D		100.0%		100.0%
1972**	1,084,904	206,846	Toledano, Ben C.	598,987	Johnston, J. Bennett	279,071	348,826 D	19.1%	55.2%	25.7%	74.3%
1968	518,586		—	518,586	Long, Russell B.		518,586 D		100.0%		100.0%
1966	437,695		—	437,695	Ellender, Allen J.		437,695 D		100.0%		100.0%
1962	421,904	103,066	O'Hearn, Taylor W.	318,838	Long, Russell B.		215,772 D	24.4%	75.6%	24.4%	75.6%
1960	541,928	109,698	Reese, George W.	432,228	Ellender, Allen J.	2	322,530 D	20.2%	79.8%	20.2%	79.8%
1956	335,564		—	335,564	Long, Russell B.		335,564 D		100.0%		100.0%
1954	207,115		—	207,115	Ellender, Allen J.		207,115 D		100.0%		100.0%
1950	251,838	30,931	Gerth, Charles S.	220,907	Long, Russell B.		189,976 D	12.3%	87.7%	12.3%	87.7%
1948	330,124		—	330,115	Ellender, Allen J.	9	330,115 D		100.0%		100.0%
1948S	408,667	102,331	Clarke, Clem S.	306,336	Long, Russell B.		204,005 D	25.0%	75.0%	25.0%	75.0%

An asterisk (*) indicates Senate elections since 1978 that have been decided in a runoff, with the runoff results listed. In elections that did not require a runoff, the leading Democratic and Republican candidates are listed with their first round votes. The votes for other candidates are listed in the "Other" column, regardless of whether they were Democratic, Republican, or Independent. In 1972 the other vote included 250,161 votes for John J. McKeithen (Independent). One of the 1948 elections was for a short term to fill a vacancy. The major party vote percentages are given for those elections where there was no more than one Democratic and one Republican candidate.

LOUISIANA

HOUSE OF REPRESENTATIVES

CD	Year	Total Vote	Republican		Democratic		Other Vote	Rep.-Dem. Plurality	Percentage			
									Total Vote		Major Vote	
			Vote	Candidate	Vote	Candidate			Rep.	Dem.	Rep.	Dem.
1	2006	148,128	130,508	JINDAL, BOBBY*	10,919	GEREIGHTY, DAVID	6,701	119,589 R	88.1%	7.4%		
1	2004	287,897	225,708	JINDAL, BOBBY	19,266	ARMSTRONG, ROY	42,923	206,442 R	78.4%	6.7%		
1	2002	180,570	147,117	VITTER, DAVID*	—		33,453	147,117 R	81.5%			
2	2006#	62,164		—	62,164	JEFFERSON, WILLIAM J.*		8,142 D		100.0%		100.0%
2	2004	219,607	46,097	SCHWERTZ, ARTHUR L. "ART"	173,510	JEFFERSON, WILLIAM J.*		127,413 D	21.0%	79.0%	21.0%	79.0%
2	2002	142,156	15,440	SULLIVAN, "SILKY"	90,310	JEFFERSON, WILLIAM J.*	36,406	74,870 D	10.9%	63.5%		
3	2006	136,331	54,950	ROMERO, CRAIG	75,023	MELANCON, CHARLIE*	6,358	20,073 D	40.3%	55.0%		
3	2004#	114,653	57,042	TAUZIN, W.J. "BILLY" III	57,611	MELANCON, CHARLIE		569 D	49.8%	50.2%	49.8%	50.2%
3	2002	150,342	130,323	TAUZIN, BILLY*	—		20,019	130,323 R	86.7%		100.0%	
4	2006	134,272	77,078	McCRERY, JIM*	22,757	CASH, ARTIS R. SR.	34,437	54,321 R	57.4%	16.9%		
4	2004			McCRERY, JIM*	—			R				
4	2002	160,093	114,649	McCRERY, JIM*	42,340	MILKOVICH, JOHN	3,104	72,309 R	71.6%	26.4%	73.0%	27.0%
5	2006	114,582	78,211	ALEXANDER, RODNEY*	33,233	HEARN, GLORIA WILLIAMS	3,138	44,978 R	68.3%	29.0%	70.2%	29.8%
5	2004	238,057	141,495	ALEXANDER, RODNEY*	58,591	BLAKES, ZELMA "TISA"	37,971	82,904 R	59.4%	24.6%		
5	2002#	172,462	85,744	FLETCHER, LEE	86,718	ALEXANDER, RODNEY		974 D	49.7%	50.3%	49.7%	50.3%
6	2006	114,306	94,658	BAKER, RICHARD H.*	—		19,648	94,658 R	82.8%		100.0%	
6	2004	261,869	189,106	BAKER, RICHARD H.*	50,732	CRAIG, RUFUS HOLT JR.	22,031	138,374 R	72.2%		100.0%	
6	2002	174,830	146,932	BAKER, RICHARD H.*	—		27,898	146,932 R	84.0%		100.0%	
7	2006	160,853	113,720	BOUSTANY, CHARLES JR.*	47,133	STAGG, MIKE		66,587 R	70.7%	29.3%	70.7%	29.3%
7	2004#	136,532	75,039	BOUSTANY, CHARLES JR.	61,493	MOUNT, WILLIE LANDRY		13,546 R	55.0%	45.0%	55.0%	45.0%
7	2002	159,710		—	138,659	JOHN, CHRIS*	21,051	138,659 D		86.8%		100.0%
TOTAL	2006	902,498	579,702		295,762		27,034	283,940 R	64.2%	32.8%	66.2%	33.8%
TOTAL	2004	1,545,982	936,801		609,181			327,620 R	60.6%	39.4%	60.6%	39.4%
TOTAL	2002	1,152,358	707,923		361,473		82,962	346,450 R	61.4%	31.4%	66.2%	33.8%

Note: Louisiana has a unique two-tier electoral system, with a first round of voting that features candidates from all parties running together on the same ballot. A candidate who wins a majority of the vote in the first round is elected. Otherwise, the top two finishers meet in a runoff. In 2002 and again in 2006, one runoff for the House of Representatives was required; in 2004 there were two runoffs. In elections that did not require a runoff, the leading Democratic and Republican candidates are listed with their first-round votes. The votes for other candidates are listed in the "Other" column, regardless of whether they were Democratic, Republican, or unaffiliated with either party. However, the statewide vote totals represent the aggregate vote for all House candidates of each party in the November balloting, not just the top finishers. The major party vote percentages are given for those individual House elections where there was no more than one Democratic and one Republican candidate.

An asterisk (*) denotes incumbent. A pound sign (#) indicates the election was decided in a runoff. In 2006, the runoff in the Louisiana 2nd District featured two Democrats, with their vote as follows: William J. Jefferson 35,153 (56.5 percent); Karen Carter 27,011 (43.5 percent), resulting in a Jefferson plurality of 8,142 votes. First-round election results for the Louisiana 2nd can be found in the primary elections section.

LOUISIANA

GENERAL AND PRIMARY ELECTIONS

2006 GENERAL ELECTIONS

Note: Louisiana has a unique two-tier election system that governs contests for governor and other federal offices besides president. Listed below are candidates who did not finish among the top two vote-getters in races that were decided in the first round of voting. The complete first-round results for contests that were eventually decided in runoffs are presented in the primary elections section. In 2006, the race in the Louisiana 2nd was the only one that required a runoff.

House	Other vote was:
CD 1	5,025 Democrat (Stacey Tallitsch); 1,676 Libertarian (Peter Beary).
CD 2	
CD 3	4,190 Democrat (Olangee "OJ" Breech); 2,168 Libertarian (James Lee Blake Jr.).
CD 4	17,788 Democrat (Patti Cox); 16,649 Republican (Chester T. Kelley).
CD 5	1,876 Libertarian (Brent Sanders); 1,262 Other (John Watts).
CD 6	19,648 Libertarian (Richard M. Fontanesi).
CD 7	

2006 PRIMARY ELECTIONS

Open Election	November 7, 2006	**Registration**	Democratic	1,554,877
Runoff Election	December 9, 2006	(as of November 7, 2006— includes active and inactive registrants)	Republican	708,752
			Other	627,262
			TOTAL	2,890,891

Primary Type   For governor and other federal offices, Louisiana has a two-tier electoral system open to all voters, with a first round of voting (sometimes called an open primary) that features candidates from all parties running together on the same ballot. A candidate that wins a majority of the vote in the first round is elected. Otherwise, there is a runoff held several weeks later between the top two finishers. A runoff was necessary in the Louisiana 2nd District in 2006.

Note: An asterisk (*) denotes incumbent. A pound sign (#) indicates the candidate qualified for a runoff.

	FIRST ROUND VOTE (November 7)		
Congressional	William J. Jefferson (D)*#	28,283	30.1%
District 2	Karen Carter (D)#	20,364	21.7%
	Derrick Shepherd (D)	16,799	17.9%
	Joseph "Joe" Lavigne (R)	12,511	13.3%
	Troy "C" Carter (D)	11,304	12.0%
	Eric T. Bradley (R)	1,159	1.2%
	Regina Bartholomew (D)	1,125	1.2%
	John Edwards (D)	675	0.7%
	Scott Barron (D)	621	0.7%
	Gregory W. "Rhumbline" Kahn (Libertarian)	404	0.4%
	M. V. "Vinny" Mendoza (D)	402	0.4%
	Lawrence William "Lance" von Uhde III (R)	258	0.3%
	Deven "D. C." Collins (D)	121	0.1%
	TOTAL	*94,026*	

MAINE

Congressional districts first established for elections held in 2004
2 members

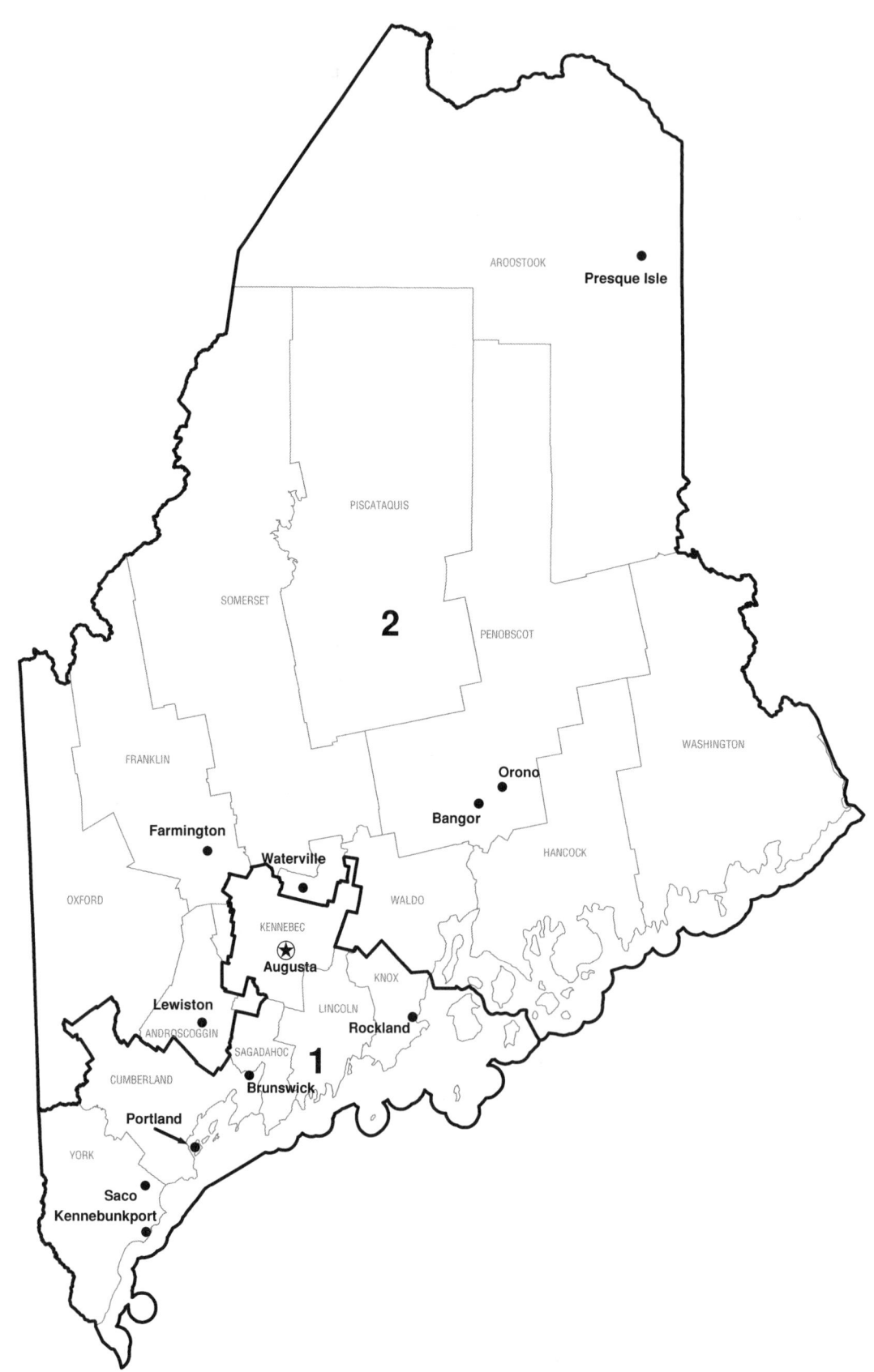

MAINE

GOVERNOR
John Baldacci (D). Reelected 2006 to a four-year term. Previously elected 2002.

SENATORS (2 Republicans)
Olympia J. Snowe (R). Reelected 2006 to a six-year term. Previously elected 2000, 1994.

Susan Collins (R). Reelected 2002 to a six-year term. Previously elected 1996.

REPRESENTATIVES (2 Democrats)
1. Tom Allen (D)   2. Michael H. Michaud (D)

POSTWAR VOTE FOR PRESIDENT

Year	Total Vote	Republican		Democratic		Other Vote	Plurality	Percentage			
								Total Vote		Major Vote	
		Vote	Candidate	Vote	Candidate			Rep.	Dem.	Rep.	Dem.
2004	740,752	330,201	Bush, George W.	396,842	Kerry, John	13,709	66,641 D	44.6%	53.6%	45.4%	54.6%
2000**	651,817	286,616	Bush, George W.	319,951	Gore, Al	45,250	33,335 D	44.0%	49.1%	47.3%	52.7%
1996**	605,897	186,378	Dole, Bob	312,788	Clinton, Bill	106,731	126,410 D	30.8%	51.6%	37.3%	62.7%
1992**	679,499	206,504	Bush, George	263,420	Clinton, Bill	209,575	56,600 D	30.4%	38.8%	43.9%	56.1%
1988	555,035	307,131	Bush, George	243,569	Dukakis, Michael S.	4,335	63,562 R	55.3%	43.9%	55.8%	44.2%
1984	553,144	336,500	Reagan, Ronald	214,515	Mondale, Walter F.	2,129	121,985 R	60.8%	38.8%	61.1%	38.9%
1980**	523,011	238,522	Reagan, Ronald	220,974	Carter, Jimmy	63,515	17,548 R	45.6%	42.3%	51.9%	48.1%
1976	483,216	236,320	Ford, Gerald R.	232,279	Carter, Jimmy	14,617	4,041 R	48.9%	48.1%	50.4%	49.6%
1972	417,042	256,458	Nixon, Richard M.	160,584	McGovern, George S.		95,874 R	61.5%	38.5%	61.5%	38.5%
1968**	392,936	169,254	Nixon, Richard M.	217,312	Humphrey, Hubert H.	6,370	48,058 D	43.1%	55.3%	43.8%	56.2%
1964	380,965	118,701	Goldwater, Barry M.	262,264	Johnson, Lyndon B.		143,563 D	31.2%	68.8%	31.2%	68.8%
1960	421,767	240,608	Nixon, Richard M.	181,159	Kennedy, John F.		59,449 R	57.0%	43.0%	57.0%	43.0%
1956	351,706	249,238	Eisenhower, Dwight D.	102,468	Stevenson, Adlai E.		146,770 R	70.9%	29.1%	70.9%	29.1%
1952	351,786	232,353	Eisenhower, Dwight D.	118,806	Stevenson, Adlai E.	627	113,547 R	66.0%	33.8%	66.2%	33.8%
1948	264,787	150,234	Dewey, Thomas E.	111,916	Truman, Harry S.	2,637	38,318 R	56.7%	42.3%	57.3%	42.7%

**In past elections, the other vote included: 2000 - 37,127 Green (Ralph Nader); 1996 - 85,970 Reform (Ross Perot); 1992 - 206,820 Independent (Ross Perot), who placed second statewide; 1980 - 53,327 Independent (John Anderson); 1968 - 6,370 American Independent (George Wallace).

MAINE

POSTWAR VOTE FOR GOVERNOR

Year	Total Vote	Republican		Democratic		Other Vote	Plurality	Percentage			
								Total Vote		Major Vote	
		Vote	Candidate	Vote	Candidate			Rep.	Dem.	Rep.	Dem.
2006**	550,865	166,425	Woodcock, Chandler E.	209,927	Baldacci, John	174,513	43,502 D	30.2%	38.1%	44.2%	55.8%
2002	505,190	209,496	Cianchette, Peter E.	238,179	Baldacci, John	57,515	28,683 D	41.5%	47.1%	46.8%	53.2%
1998**	421,009	79,716	Longley, James B. Jr.	50,506	Connolly, Thomas J.	290,787	167,056 I	18.9%	12.0%	61.2%	38.8%
1994**	511,308	117,990	Collins, Susan	172,951	Brennan, Joseph E.	220,367	7,878 I	23.1%	33.8%	40.6%	59.4%
1990	522,492	243,766	McKernan, John R.	230,038	Brennan, Joseph E.	48,688	13,728 R	46.7%	44.0%	51.4%	48.6%
1986**	426,861	170,312	McKernan, John R.	128,744	Tierney, James	127,805	41,568 R	39.9%	30.2%	56.9%	43.1%
1982	460,295	172,949	Cragin, Charles L.	281,066	Brennan, Joseph E.	6,280	108,117 D	37.6%	61.1%	38.1%	61.9%
1978	370,258	126,862	Palmer, Linwood E.	176,493	Brennan, Joseph E.	66,903	49,631 D	34.3%	47.7%	41.8%	58.2%
1974**	363,945	84,176	Erwin, James S.	132,219	Mitchell, George J.	147,550	10,245 I	23.1%	36.3%	38.9%	61.1%
1970	325,386	162,248	Erwin, James S.	163,138	Curtis, Kenneth M.		890 D	49.9%	50.1%	49.9%	50.1%
1966	323,838	151,802	Reed, John H.	172,036	Curtis, Kenneth M.		20,234 D	46.9%	53.1%	46.9%	53.1%
1962	292,725	146,604	Reed, John H.	146,121	Dolloff, Maynard C.		483 R	50.1%	49.9%	50.1%	49.9%
1960S	417,315	219,768	Reed, John H.	197,547	Coffin, Frank M.		22,221 R	52.7%	47.3%	52.7%	47.3%
1958**	280,295	134,572	Hildreth, Horace A.	145,723	Clauson, Clinton A.		11,151 D	48.0%	52.0%	48.0%	52.0%
1956	304,649	124,395	Trafton, Willis A.	180,254	Muskie, Edmund S.		55,859 D	40.8%	59.2%	40.8%	59.2%
1954	248,971	113,298	Cross, Burton M.	135,673	Muskie, Edmund S.		22,375 D	45.5%	54.5%	45.5%	54.5%
1952	248,441	128,532	Cross, Burton M.	82,538	Oliver, James C.	37,371	45,994 R	51.7%	33.2%	60.9%	39.1%
1950	241,177	145,823	Payne, Frederick G.	94,304	Grant, Earl S.	1,050	51,519 R	60.5%	39.1%	60.7%	39.3%
1948	222,500	145,956	Payne, Frederick G.	76,544	Lausier, Louis B.		69,412 R	65.6%	34.4%	65.6%	34.4%
1946	179,951	110,327	Hildreth, Horace A.	69,624	Clark, F. Davis		40,703 R	61.3%	38.7%	61.3%	38.7%

**In past elections, the other vote included: 2006 - 118,715 Independent Maine Course (Barbara Merrill); 1998 - 246,772 Independent (Angus King), who was reelected with 58.6 percent of the total vote; 1994 - 180,829 Independent (King), who was elected with 35.4 percent of the total vote; 1986 - 64,317 Independent (Sherry F. Huber), 63,474 Independent (John E. Menario); 1974 - 142,464 Independent (James B. Longley), who was elected with 39.1 percent of the total vote. The 1960 election was for a short term to fill a vacancy. The term of office of Maine's governor was increased from two to four years effective with the 1958 election.

POSTWAR VOTE FOR SENATOR

Year	Total Vote	Republican		Democratic		Other Vote	Rep.-Dem. Plurality	Percentage			
								Total Vote		Major Vote	
		Vote	Candidate	Vote	Candidate			Rep.	Dem.	Rep.	Dem.
2006	543,981	402,598	Snowe, Olympia J.	111,984	Bright, Jean Hay	29,399	290,614 R	74.0%	20.6%	78.2%	21.8%
2002	504,899	295,041	Collins, Susan	209,858	Pingree, Chellie		85,183 R	58.4%	41.6%	58.4%	41.6%
2000	634,872	437,689	Snowe, Olympia J.	197,183	Lawrence, Mark		240,506 R	68.9%	31.1%	68.9%	31.1%
1996	606,777	298,422	Collins, Susan	266,226	Brennan, Joseph E.	42,129	32,196 R	49.2%	43.9%	52.9%	47.1%
1994	511,733	308,244	Snowe, Olympia J.	186,042	Andrews, Thomas H.	17,447	122,202 R	60.2%	36.4%	62.4%	37.6%
1990	520,320	319,167	Cohen, William S.	201,053	Rolde, Neil	100	118,114 R	61.3%	38.6%	61.4%	38.6%
1988	557,375	104,758	Wyman, Jasper S.	452,590	Mitchell, George J.	27	347,832 D	18.8%	81.2%	18.8%	81.2%
1984	551,406	404,414	Cohen, William S.	142,626	Mitchell, Elizabeth H.	4,366	261,788 R	73.3%	25.9%	73.9%	26.1%
1982	459,715	179,882	Emery, David F.	279,819	Mitchell, George J.	14	99,937 D	39.1%	60.9%	39.1%	60.9%
1978	375,172	212,294	Cohen, William S.	127,327	Hathaway, William D.	35,551	84,967 R	56.6%	33.9%	62.5%	37.5%
1976	486,254	193,489	Monks, Robert A. G.	292,704	Muskie, Edmund S.	61	99,215 D	39.8%	60.2%	39.8%	60.2%
1972	421,310	197,040	Smith, Margaret Chase	224,270	Hathaway, William D.		27,230 D	46.8%	53.2%	46.8%	53.2%
1970	323,860	123,906	Bishop, Neil S.	199,954	Muskie, Edmund S.		76,048 D	38.3%	61.7%	38.3%	61.7%
1966	319,535	188,291	Smith, Margaret Chase	131,136	Violette, Elmer H.	108	57,155 R	58.9%	41.0%	58.9%	41.1%
1964	380,551	127,040	McIntire, Clifford	253,511	Muskie, Edmund S.		126,471 D	33.4%	66.6%	33.4%	66.6%
1960	416,699	256,890	Smith, Margaret Chase	159,809	Cormier, Lucia M.		97,081 R	61.6%	38.4%	61.6%	38.4%
1958	284,226	111,522	Payne, Frederick G.	172,704	Muskie, Edmund S.		61,182 D	39.2%	60.8%	39.2%	60.8%
1954	246,605	144,530	Smith, Margaret Chase	102,075	Fullam, Paul A.		42,455 R	58.6%	41.4%	58.6%	41.4%
1952	237,164	139,205	Payne, Frederick G.	82,665	Dube, Roger P.	15,294	56,540 R	58.7%	34.9%	62.7%	37.3%
1948	223,256	159,182	Smith, Margaret Chase	64,074	Scolten, Adrian H.		95,108 R	71.3%	28.7%	71.3%	28.7%
1946	175,014	111,215	Brewster, Owen	63,799	MacDonald, Peter		47,416 R	63.5%	36.5%	63.5%	36.5%

MAINE

GOVERNOR 2006

2000 Census Population	County	Total Vote	Republican	Democratic	Independent (Merrill)	Other	Plurality	Percentage Total Vote		
								Rep.	Dem.	Ind.
103,793	ANDROSCOGGIN	40,916	13,362	13,631	9,805	4,118	269 D	32.7%	33.3%	24.0%
73,938	AROOSTOOK	26,331	7,188	12,752	3,803	2,588	5,564 D	27.3%	48.4%	14.4%
265,612	CUMBERLAND	121,647	31,835	48,449	27,613	13,750	16,614 D	26.2%	39.8%	22.7%
29,467	FRANKLIN	14,421	5,920	4,613	2,521	1,367	1,307 R	41.1%	32.0%	17.5%
51,791	HANCOCK	25,155	7,231	10,138	5,319	2,467	2,907 D	28.7%	40.3%	21.1%
117,114	KENNEBEC	51,424	16,178	18,765	10,748	5,733	2,587 D	31.5%	36.5%	20.9%
39,618	KNOX	18,529	5,019	6,506	5,056	1,948	1,450 D	27.1%	35.1%	27.3%
33,616	LINCOLN	17,631	5,494	5,825	4,537	1,775	331 D	31.2%	33.0%	25.7%
54,755	OXFORD	24,332	7,771	8,281	6,117	2,163	510 D	31.9%	34.0%	25.1%
144,919	PENOBSCOT	58,755	19,100	24,015	10,643	4,997	4,915 D	32.5%	40.9%	18.1%
17,235	PISCATAQUIS	7,502	2,829	2,591	1,476	606	238 R	37.7%	34.5%	19.7%
35,214	SAGADAHOC	16,968	4,829	5,962	4,316	1,861	1,133 D	28.5%	35.1%	25.4%
50,888	SOMERSET	20,141	7,393	6,500	4,025	2,223	893 R	36.7%	32.3%	20.0%
36,280	WALDO	16,938	5,329	5,678	4,143	1,788	349 D	31.5%	33.5%	24.5%
33,941	WASHINGTON	13,279	5,057	3,897	3,002	1,323	1,160 R	38.1%	29.3%	22.6%
186,742	YORK	76,896	21,890	32,324	15,591	7,091	10,434 D	28.5%	42.0%	20.3%
1,274,923	TOTAL	550,865	166,425	209,927	118,715	55,798	43,502 D	30.2%	38.1%	21.6%

Note: In the gubernatorial tables, the plurality is based on the margin of victory of the winner over the runner-up.

MAINE

GOVERNOR 2006

2000 Census Population	City/Town	Total Vote	Republican	Democratic	Independent (Merrill)	Other	Plurality		Percentage Total Vote		
									Rep.	Dem.	Ind.
23,203	AUBURN	9,008	2,840	3,025	2,194	949	185	D	31.5%	33.6%	24.4%
18,560	AUGUSTA	7,653	2,097	3,327	1,403	826	1,230	D	27.4%	43.5%	18.3%
31,473	BANGOR	11,169	3,042	5,548	1,658	921	2,506	D	27.2%	49.7%	14.8%
9,266	BATH	3,773	934	1,585	847	407	651	D	24.8%	42.0%	22.4%
6,381	BELFAST	3,012	799	1,193	732	288	394	D	26.5%	39.6%	24.3%
6,353	BERWICK	2,282	787	1,057	284	154	270	D	34.5%	46.3%	12.4%
20,942	BIDDEFORD	6,918	1,511	3,156	1,508	743	1,645	D	21.8%	45.6%	21.8%
8,987	BREWER	3,903	1,286	1,586	732	299	300	D	32.9%	40.6%	18.8%
21,172	BRUNSWICK	8,729	1,975	4,017	1,823	914	2,042	D	22.6%	46.0%	20.9%
7,452	BUXTON	3,226	1,021	996	897	312	25	R	31.6%	30.9%	27.8%
5,254	CAMDEN	2,807	581	1,257	716	253	541	D	20.7%	44.8%	25.5%
9,068	CAPE ELIZABETH	5,378	1,378	2,312	1,206	482	934	D	25.6%	43.0%	22.4%
8,312	CARIBOU	2,732	732	1,294	420	286	562	D	26.8%	47.4%	15.4%
7,159	CUMBERLAND TOWN	4,189	1,284	1,470	1,063	372	186	D	30.7%	35.1%	25.4%
5,954	ELIOT	2,694	771	1,346	358	219	575	D	28.6%	50.0%	13.3%
6,456	ELLSWORTH	3,105	1,089	1,093	660	263	4	D	35.1%	35.2%	21.3%
6,573	FAIRFIELD	2,495	761	851	511	372	90	D	30.5%	34.1%	20.5%
10,310	FALMOUTH	5,649	1,670	2,100	1,397	482	430	D	29.6%	37.2%	24.7%
7,410	FARMINGTON	3,600	1,526	1,189	462	423	337	R	42.4%	33.0%	12.8%
7,800	FREEPORT	3,943	922	1,532	922	567	610	D	23.4%	38.9%	23.4%
6,198	GARDINER	2,414	729	845	536	304	116	D	30.2%	35.0%	22.2%
14,141	GORHAM	6,170	1,962	2,107	1,504	597	145	D	31.8%	34.1%	24.4%
6,820	GRAY	3,205	1,042	986	901	276	56	R	32.5%	30.8%	28.1%
6,327	HAMPDEN	3,322	1,107	1,251	714	250	144	D	33.3%	37.7%	21.5%
5,239	HARPSWELL	2,837	766	1,049	753	269	283	D	27.0%	37.0%	26.5%
6,476	HOULTON	2,097	624	916	404	153	292	D	29.8%	43.7%	19.3%
4,985	JAY	2,279	772	935	422	150	163	D	33.9%	41.0%	18.5%
10,476	KENNEBUNK	5,282	1,539	2,111	1,145	487	572	D	29.1%	40.0%	21.7%
9,543	KITTERY	3,628	800	2,212	350	266	1,412	D	22.1%	61.0%	9.6%
35,690	LEWISTON	12,172	3,292	5,121	2,579	1,180	1,829	D	27.0%	42.1%	21.2%
2,361	LIMESTONE	697	173	339	112	73	166	D	24.8%	48.6%	16.1%
5,221	LINCOLN TOWN	1,868	630	883	251	104	253	D	33.7%	47.3%	13.4%
9,077	LISBON	3,645	1,185	1,087	978	395	98	R	32.5%	29.8%	26.8%
5,203	MILLINOCKET	2,202	525	1,102	455	120	577	D	23.8%	50.0%	20.7%
5,959	OAKLAND	2,539	829	837	574	299	8	D	32.7%	33.0%	22.6%
8,856	OLD ORCHARD BEACH	3,861	900	1,708	830	423	808	D	23.3%	44.2%	21.5%
8,130	OLD TOWN	3,027	736	1,454	535	302	718	D	24.3%	48.0%	17.7%
9,112	ORONO	3,365	630	1,776	460	499	1,146	D	18.7%	52.8%	13.7%
62,249	PORTLAND	25,711	4,236	12,965	4,682	3,828	8,283	D	16.5%	50.4%	18.2%
9,511	PRESQUE ISLE	3,171	934	1,379	507	351	445	D	29.5%	43.5%	16.0%
7,609	ROCKLAND	2,771	746	1,090	616	319	344	D	26.9%	39.3%	22.2%
6,472	RUMFORD	2,576	618	1,177	559	222	559	D	24.0%	45.7%	21.7%
16,822	SACO	7,181	1,714	3,038	1,782	647	1,256	D	23.9%	42.3%	24.8%
20,806	SANFORD	6,760	1,908	2,962	1,238	652	1,054	D	28.2%	43.8%	18.3%
16,970	SCARBOROUGH	8,827	2,886	3,205	2,016	720	319	D	32.7%	36.3%	22.8%
8,824	SKOWHEGAN	3,180	1,029	1,192	656	303	163	D	32.4%	37.5%	20.6%
6,671	SOUTH BERWICK	2,785	812	1,353	359	261	541	D	29.2%	48.6%	12.9%
23,324	SOUTH PORTLAND	10,476	2,182	4,850	2,191	1,253	2,659	D	20.8%	46.3%	20.9%
9,285	STANDISH	3,625	1,198	1,018	1,024	385	174	R	33.0%	28.1%	28.2%
9,100	TOPSHAM	4,295	1,198	1,553	1,121	423	355	D	27.9%	36.2%	26.1%
15,605	WATERVILLE	5,147	1,118	2,550	883	596	1,432	D	21.7%	49.5%	17.2%
9,400	WELLS	4,187	1,273	1,719	825	370	446	D	30.4%	41.1%	19.7%
16,142	WESTBROOK	6,357	1,638	2,538	1,493	688	900	D	25.8%	39.9%	23.5%
14,904	WINDHAM	6,662	2,195	2,126	1,642	699	69	R	32.9%	31.9%	24.6%
7,743	WINSLOW	3,431	1,065	1,295	706	365	230	D	31.0%	37.7%	20.6%
6,232	WINTHROP	2,902	977	1,005	659	261	28	D	33.7%	34.6%	22.7%
8,360	YARMOUTH	4,432	1,195	1,588	1,058	591	393	D	27.0%	35.8%	23.9%
12,854	YORK TOWN	5,896	1,679	2,965	887	365	1,286	D	28.5%	50.3%	15.0%

MAINE

SENATOR 2006

2000 Census Population	County	Total Vote	Republican	Democratic	Other	Rep.-Dem. Plurality	Percentage			
							Total Vote		Major Vote	
							Rep.	Dem.	Rep.	Dem.
103,793	ANDROSCOGGIN	40,425	31,465	6,690	2,270	24,775 R	77.8%	16.5%	82.5%	17.5%
73,938	AROOSTOOK	25,983	19,845	5,221	917	14,624 R	76.4%	20.1%	79.2%	20.8%
265,612	CUMBERLAND	119,883	83,490	28,270	8,123	55,220 R	69.6%	23.6%	74.7%	25.3%
29,467	FRANKLIN	14,082	10,777	2,640	665	8,137 R	76.5%	18.7%	80.3%	19.7%
51,791	HANCOCK	24,822	16,792	6,752	1,278	10,040 R	67.6%	27.2%	71.3%	28.7%
117,114	KENNEBEC	50,890	39,687	8,958	2,245	30,729 R	78.0%	17.6%	81.6%	18.4%
39,618	KNOX	18,355	13,070	4,423	862	8,647 R	71.2%	24.1%	74.7%	25.3%
33,616	LINCOLN	17,501	13,274	3,427	800	9,847 R	75.8%	19.6%	79.5%	20.5%
54,755	OXFORD	24,036	19,055	3,804	1,177	15,251 R	79.3%	15.8%	83.4%	16.6%
144,919	PENOBSCOT	57,948	42,700	11,507	3,741	31,193 R	73.7%	19.9%	78.8%	21.2%
17,235	PISCATAQUIS	7,376	5,564	1,244	568	4,320 R	75.4%	16.9%	81.7%	18.3%
35,214	SAGADAHOC	16,802	12,704	3,267	831	9,437 R	75.6%	19.4%	79.5%	20.5%
50,888	SOMERSET	19,916	15,053	3,934	929	11,119 R	75.6%	19.8%	79.3%	20.7%
36,280	WALDO	16,704	11,626	4,292	786	7,334 R	69.6%	25.7%	73.0%	27.0%
33,941	WASHINGTON	13,048	9,691	2,623	734	7,068 R	74.3%	20.1%	78.7%	21.3%
186,742	YORK	76,210	57,805	14,932	3,473	42,873 R	75.8%	19.6%	79.5%	20.5%
1,274,923	TOTAL	543,981	402,598	111,984	29,399	290,614 R	74.0%	20.6%	78.2%	21.8%

MAINE

SENATOR 2006

2000 Census Population	City/Town	Total Vote	Republican	Democratic	Other	Rep.-Dem. Plurality	Percentage			
							Total Vote		Major Vote	
							Rep.	Dem.	Rep.	Dem.
23,203	AUBURN	8,960	6,975	1,472	513	5,503 R	77.8%	16.4%	82.6%	17.4%
18,560	AUGUSTA	7,566	5,931	1,300	335	4,631 R	78.4%	17.2%	82.0%	18.0%
31,473	BANGOR	11,015	7,978	2,576	461	5,402 R	72.4%	23.4%	75.6%	24.4%
9,266	BATH	3,738	2,756	809	173	1,947 R	73.7%	21.6%	77.3%	22.7%
6,381	BELFAST	2,976	1,941	906	129	1,035 R	65.2%	30.4%	68.2%	31.8%
6,353	BERWICK	2,263	1,751	418	94	1,333 R	77.4%	18.5%	80.7%	19.3%
20,942	BIDDEFORD	6,863	5,186	1,356	321	3,830 R	75.6%	19.8%	79.3%	20.7%
8,987	BREWER	3,881	3,077	672	132	2,405 R	79.3%	17.3%	82.1%	17.9%
21,172	BRUNSWICK	8,647	5,851	2,358	438	3,493 R	67.7%	27.3%	71.3%	28.7%
7,452	BUXTON	3,175	2,474	533	168	1,941 R	77.9%	16.8%	82.3%	17.7%
5,254	CAMDEN	2,771	1,780	868	123	912 R	64.2%	31.3%	67.2%	32.8%
9,068	CAPE ELIZABETH	5,358	3,742	1,417	199	2,325 R	69.8%	26.4%	72.5%	27.5%
8,312	CARIBOU	2,743	2,255	415	73	1,840 R	82.2%	15.1%	84.5%	15.5%
7,159	CUMBERLAND TOWN	4,175	3,272	744	159	2,528 R	78.4%	17.8%	81.5%	18.5%
5,954	ELIOT	2,662	1,929	625	108	1,304 R	72.5%	23.5%	75.5%	24.5%
6,456	ELLSWORTH	3,078	2,227	699	152	1,528 R	72.4%	22.7%	76.1%	23.9%
6,573	FAIRFIELD	2,477	1,893	463	121	1,430 R	76.4%	18.7%	80.3%	19.7%
10,310	FALMOUTH	5,590	4,219	1,126	245	3,093 R	75.5%	20.1%	78.9%	21.1%
7,410	FARMINGTON	3,492	2,580	715	197	1,865 R	73.9%	20.5%	78.3%	21.7%
7,800	FREEPORT	3,923	2,712	979	232	1,733 R	69.1%	25.0%	73.5%	26.5%
6,198	GARDINER	2,398	1,891	368	139	1,523 R	78.9%	15.3%	83.7%	16.3%
14,141	GORHAM	6,133	4,736	1,109	288	3,627 R	77.2%	18.1%	81.0%	19.0%
6,820	GRAY	3,175	2,536	497	142	2,039 R	79.9%	15.7%	83.6%	16.4%
6,327	HAMPDEN	3,296	2,489	686	121	1,803 R	75.5%	20.8%	78.4%	21.6%
5,239	HARPSWELL	2,816	2,049	619	148	1,430 R	72.8%	22.0%	76.8%	23.2%
6,476	HOULTON	2,082	1,696	304	82	1,392 R	81.5%	14.6%	84.8%	15.2%
4,985	JAY	2,245	1,644	508	93	1,136 R	73.2%	22.6%	76.4%	23.6%
10,476	KENNEBUNK	5,227	3,935	1,065	227	2,870 R	75.3%	20.4%	78.7%	21.3%
9,543	KITTERY	3,596	2,427	1,042	127	1,385 R	67.5%	29.0%	70.0%	30.0%
35,690	LEWISTON	11,960	9,027	2,296	637	6,731 R	75.5%	19.2%	79.7%	20.3%
2,361	LIMESTONE	695	564	107	24	457 R	81.2%	15.4%	84.1%	15.9%
5,221	LINCOLN TOWN	1,832	1,498	273	61	1,225 R	81.8%	14.9%	84.6%	15.4%
9,077	LISBON	3,608	2,908	502	198	2,406 R	80.6%	13.9%	85.3%	14.7%
5,203	MILLINOCKET	2,171	1,694	374	103	1,320 R	78.0%	17.2%	81.9%	18.1%
5,959	OAKLAND	2,526	2,006	407	113	1,599 R	79.4%	16.1%	83.1%	16.9%
8,856	OLD ORCHARD BEACH	3,831	2,906	752	173	2,154 R	75.9%	19.6%	79.4%	20.6%
8,130	OLD TOWN	2,998	2,188	694	116	1,494 R	73.0%	23.1%	75.9%	24.1%
9,112	ORONO	3,310	2,077	1,054	179	1,023 R	62.7%	31.8%	66.3%	33.7%
62,249	PORTLAND	25,490	14,616	9,003	1871	5,613 R	57.3%	35.3%	61.9%	38.1%
9,511	PRESQUE ISLE	3,161	2,567	482	112	2,085 R	81.2%	15.2%	84.2%	15.8%
7,609	ROCKLAND	2,754	1,943	663	148	1,280 R	70.6%	24.1%	74.6%	25.4%
6,472	RUMFORD	2,561	1,968	475	118	1,493 R	76.8%	18.5%	80.6%	19.4%
16,822	SACO	7,115	5,398	1,400	317	3,998 R	75.9%	19.7%	79.4%	20.6%
20,806	SANFORD	6,685	5,156	1,187	342	3,969 R	77.1%	17.8%	81.3%	18.7%
16,970	SCARBOROUGH	8,038	5,937	1,428	673	4,509 R	73.9%	17.8%	80.6%	19.4%
8,824	SKOWHEGAN	3,142	2,407	608	127	1,799 R	76.6%	19.4%	79.8%	20.2%
6,671	SOUTH BERWICK	2,764	2,012	621	131	1,391 R	72.8%	22.5%	76.4%	23.6%
23,324	SOUTH PORTLAND	10,409	7,032	2,833	544	4,199 R	67.6%	27.2%	71.3%	28.7%
9,285	STANDISH	3,587	2,811	559	217	2,252 R	78.4%	15.6%	83.4%	16.6%
9,100	TOPSHAM	4,248	3,234	807	207	2,427 R	76.1%	19.0%	80.0%	20.0%
15,605	WATERVILLE	5,095	3,482	1,390	223	2,092 R	68.3%	27.3%	71.5%	28.5%
9,400	WELLS	4,174	3,189	826	159	2,363 R	76.4%	19.8%	79.4%	20.6%
16,142	WESTBROOK	6,308	4,724	1,262	322	3,462 R	74.9%	20.0%	78.9%	21.1%
14,904	WINDHAM	6,618	5,310	989	319	4,321 R	80.2%	14.9%	84.3%	15.7%
7,743	WINSLOW	3,402	2,653	601	148	2,052 R	78.0%	17.7%	81.5%	18.5%
6,232	WINTHROP	2,876	2,333	437	106	1,896 R	81.1%	15.2%	84.2%	15.8%
8,360	YARMOUTH	4,407	3,342	864	201	2,478 R	75.8%	19.6%	79.5%	20.5%
12,854	YORK TOWN	5,860	4,281	1,351	228	2,930 R	73.1%	23.1%	76.0%	24.0%

MAINE

HOUSE OF REPRESENTATIVES

CD	Year	Total Vote	Republican		Democratic		Other Vote	Rep.-Dem. Plurality	Percentage			
									Total Vote		Major Vote	
			Vote	Candidate	Vote	Candidate			Rep.	Dem.	Rep.	Dem.
1	2006	280,987	88,009	CURLEY, DARLENE J.	170,949	ALLEN, TOM*	22,029	82,940 D	31.3%	60.8%	34.0%	66.0%
1	2004	366,740	147,663	SUMMERS, CHARLES E. JR.	219,077	ALLEN, TOM*		71,414 D	40.3%	59.7%	40.3%	59.7%
1	2002	270,577	97,931	JOYCE, STEVEN	172,646	ALLEN, TOM*		74,715 D	36.2%	63.8%	36.2%	63.8%
2	2006	254,878	75,146	D'AMBOISE, LAURENCE S.	179,732	MICHAUD, MICHAEL H.*		104,586 D	29.5%	70.5%	29.5%	70.5%
2	2004	343,436	135,547	HAMEL, BRIAN N.	199,303	MICHAUD, MICHAEL H.*	8,586	63,756 D	39.5%	58.0%	40.5%	59.5%
2	2002	224,717	107,849	RAYE, KEVIN L.	116,868	MICHAUD, MICHAEL H.		9,019 D	48.0%	52.0%	48.0%	52.0%
TOTAL	2006	535,865	163,155		350,681		22,029	187,526 D	30.4%	65.4%	31.8%	68.2%
TOTAL	2004	710,176	283,210		418,380		8,586	135,170 D	39.9%	58.9%	40.4%	59.6%
TOTAL	2002	495,294	205,780		289,514			83,734 D	41.5%	58.5%	41.5%	58.5%

An asterisk (*) denotes incumbent.

MAINE

GENERAL AND PRIMARY ELECTIONS

2006 GENERAL ELECTIONS

Governor Other vote was 52,690 Green Independent (Patricia H. LaMarche); 3,108 Tax Equality Rebellion (Phillip Morris Napier). (The Independent Maine Course candidate, Barbara Merrill, received 118,715 votes, 21.6 percent of the total vote. Her vote is listed in the county and city/town tables for the 2006 gubernatorial election in Maine.)

Senator Other vote was 29,220 Independent (William H. Slavick); 179 write-in (Michael A. Beardsley).

House Other vote was:

CD 1 22,029 Independent (Dexter Kamilewicz).
CD 2

2006 PRIMARY ELECTIONS

Primary June 13, 2006 **Registration** (as of November 2004)

Democratic	319,198
Republican	287,452
Green Independent	24,155
Unenrolled	393,151
TOTAL	1,023,956

Primary Type Semi-open—Registered voters in a political party could participate only in their party's primary. "Unenrolled" and new voters could vote in either party's primary by enrolling in that party on primary day.

MAINE

GENERAL AND PRIMARY ELECTIONS

Note: An asterisk (*) denotes incumbent.

	REPUBLICAN PRIMARIES			DEMOCRATIC PRIMARIES		
Governor	Chandler E. Woodcock	27,025	38.6%	John Baldacci*	40,314	75.8%
	S. Peter Mills	24,631	35.2%	Christopher F. Miller	12,861	24.2%
	David F. Emery	18,388	26.3%			
	TOTAL	*70,044*		*TOTAL*	*53,175*	
Senator	Olympia J. Snowe*	58,979	98.9%	Jean Hay Bright	22,582	50.6%
	Edward M. Libby (write-in)	673	1.1%	Eric M. Mehnert	22,019	49.4%
	TOTAL	*59,652*		*TOTAL*	*44,601*	
Congressional District 1	Darlene J. Curley	28,172	100.0%	Tom Allen*	26,801	100.0%
Congressional District 2	Laurence S. D'Amboise	24,139	100.0%	Michael H. Michaud*	23,242	100.0%

MARYLAND

Congressional districts first established for elections held in 2002
8 members

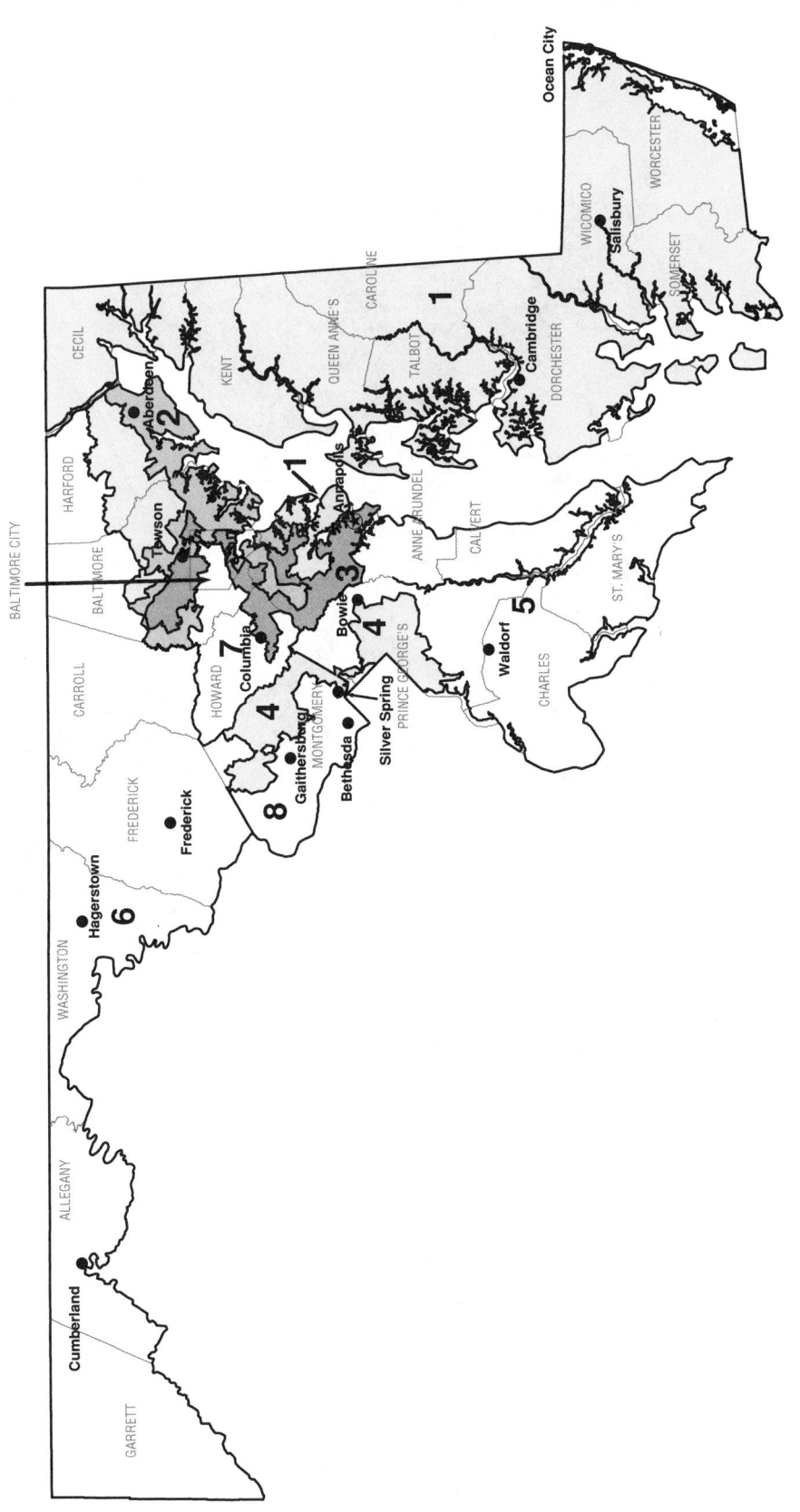

MARYLAND

Baltimore, Washington, D.C., Area

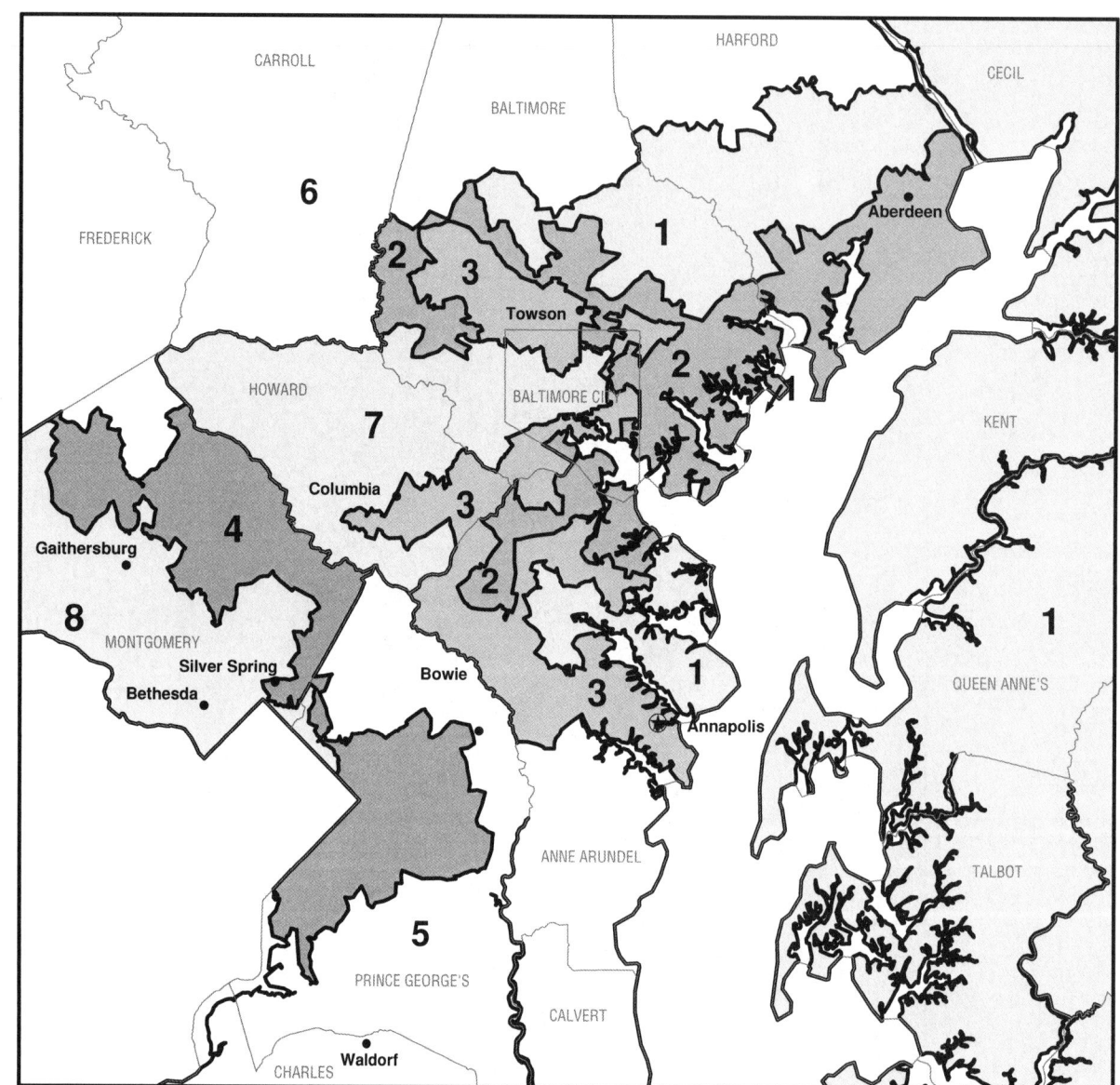

MARYLAND

GOVERNOR
Martin O'Malley (D). Elected 2006 to a four-year term.

SENATORS (2 Democrats)
Benjamin L. Cardin (D). Elected 2006 to a six-year term.

Barbara A. Mikulski (D). Reelected 2004 to a six-year term. Previously elected 1998, 1992, 1986.

REPRESENTATIVES (6 Democrats, 2 Republicans)
1. Wayne T. Gilchrest (R)
2. C. A. Dutch Ruppersberger (D)
3. John P. Sarbanes (D)
4. Albert R. Wynn (D)
5. Steny H. Hoyer (D)
6. Roscoe G. Bartlett (R)
7. Elijah E. Cummings (D)
8. Chris Van Hollen (D)

POSTWAR VOTE FOR PRESIDENT

Year	Total Vote	Republican Vote	Republican Candidate	Democratic Vote	Democratic Candidate	Other Vote	Plurality	Total Vote Rep.	Total Vote Dem.	Major Vote Rep.	Major Vote Dem.
2004	2,386,678	1,024,703	Bush, George W.	1,334,493	Kerry, John	27,482	309,790 D	42.9%	55.9%	43.4%	56.6%
2000**	2,020,480	813,797	Bush, George W.	1,140,782	Gore, Al	65,901	326,985 D	40.3%	56.5%	41.6%	58.4%
1996**	1,780,870	681,530	Dole, Bob	966,207	Clinton, Bill	133,133	284,677 D	38.3%	54.3%	41.4%	58.6%
1992**	1,985,046	707,094	Bush, George	988,571	Clinton, Bill	289,381	281,477 D	35.6%	49.8%	41.7%	58.3%
1988	1,714,358	876,167	Bush, George	826,304	Dukakis, Michael S.	11,887	49,863 R	51.1%	48.2%	51.5%	48.5%
1984	1,675,873	879,918	Reagan, Ronald	787,935	Mondale, Walter F.	8,020	91,983 R	52.5%	47.0%	52.8%	47.2%
1980**	1,540,496	680,606	Reagan, Ronald	726,161	Carter, Jimmy	133,729	45,555 D	44.2%	47.1%	48.4%	51.6%
1976	1,439,897	672,661	Ford, Gerald R.	759,612	Carter, Jimmy	7,624	86,951 D	46.7%	52.8%	47.0%	53.0%
1972	1,353,812	829,305	Nixon, Richard M.	505,781	McGovern, George S.	18,726	323,524 R	61.3%	37.4%	62.1%	37.9%
1968**	1,235,039	517,995	Nixon, Richard M.	538,310	Humphrey, Hubert H.	178,734	20,315 D	41.9%	43.6%	49.0%	51.0%
1964	1,116,457	385,495	Goldwater, Barry M.	730,912	Johnson, Lyndon B.	50	345,417 D	34.5%	65.5%	34.5%	65.5%
1960	1,055,349	489,538	Nixon, Richard M.	565,808	Kennedy, John F.	3	76,270 D	46.4%	53.6%	46.4%	53.6%
1956	932,827	559,738	Eisenhower, Dwight D.	372,613	Stevenson, Adlai E.	476	187,125 R	60.0%	39.9%	60.0%	40.0%
1952	902,074	499,424	Eisenhower, Dwight D.	395,337	Stevenson, Adlai E.	7,313	104,087 R	55.4%	43.8%	55.8%	44.2%
1948	596,748	294,814	Dewey, Thomas E.	286,521	Truman, Harry S.	15,413	8,293 R	49.4%	48.0%	50.7%	49.3%

**In past elections, the other vote included: 2000 - 53,768 Green (Ralph Nader); 1996 - 115,812 Reform (Ross Perot); 1992 - 281,414 Independent (Ross Perot); 1980 - 119,537 Independent (John Anderson); 1968 - 178,734 American Independent (George Wallace).

MARYLAND

POSTWAR VOTE FOR GOVERNOR

Year	Total Vote	Republican Vote	Candidate	Democratic Vote	Candidate	Other Vote	Rep.-Dem. Plurality	Total Vote Rep.	Total Vote Dem.	Major Vote Rep.	Major Vote Dem.
2006	1,788,316	825,464	Ehrlich, Robert L. Jr.	942,279	O'Malley, Martin	20,573	116,815 D	46.2%	52.7%	46.7%	53.3%
2002	1,706,179	879,592	Ehrlich, Robert L. Jr.	813,422	Townsend, Kathleen Kennedy	13,165	66,170 R	51.6%	47.7%	52.0%	48.0%
1998	1,535,978	688,357	Sauerbrey, Ellen R.	846,972	Glendening, Parris N.	649	158,615 D	44.8%	55.1%	44.8%	55.2%
1994	1,410,300	702,101	Sauerbrey, Ellen R.	708,094	Glendening, Parris N.	105	5,993 D	49.8%	50.2%	49.8%	50.2%
1990	1,111,088	446,980	Shepard, William S.	664,015	Schaefer, William D.	93	217,035 D	40.2%	59.8%	40.2%	59.8%
1986	1,101,476	194,185	Mooney, Thomas J.	907,291	Schaefer, William D.		713,106 D	17.6%	82.4%	17.6%	82.4%
1982	1,139,149	432,826	Pascal, Robert A.	705,910	Hughes, Harry	413	273,084 D	38.0%	62.0%	38.0%	62.0%
1978	1,011,963	293,635	Beall, J. Glenn Jr.	718,328	Hughes, Harry		424,693 D	29.0%	71.0%	29.0%	71.0%
1974	949,097	346,449	Gore, Louise	602,648	Mandel, Marvin		256,199 D	36.5%	63.5%	36.5%	63.5%
1970	973,099	314,336	Blain, C. Stanley	639,579	Mandel, Marvin	19,184	325,243 D	32.3%	65.7%	33.0%	67.0%
1966	918,761	455,318	Agnew, Spiro T.	373,543	Mahoney, George P.	89,900	81,775 R	49.6%	40.7%	54.9%	45.1%
1962	775,101	343,051	Small, Frank	432,045	Tawes, J. Millard	5	88,994 D	44.3%	55.7%	44.3%	55.7%
1958	763,234	278,173	Devereux, James	485,061	Tawes, J. Millard		206,888 D	36.4%	63.6%	36.4%	63.6%
1954	700,484	381,451	McKeldin, Theodore	319,033	Byrd, Harry C.		62,418 R	54.5%	45.5%	54.5%	45.5%
1950	645,631	369,807	McKeldin, Theodore	275,824	Lane, William P.		93,983 R	57.3%	42.7%	57.3%	42.7%
1946	489,836	221,752	McKeldin, Theodore	268,084	Lane, William P.		46,332 D	45.3%	54.7%	45.3%	54.7%

POSTWAR VOTE FOR SENATOR

Year	Total Vote	Republican Vote	Candidate	Democratic Vote	Candidate	Other Vote	Rep.-Dem. Plurality	Total Vote Rep.	Total Vote Dem.	Major Vote Rep.	Major Vote Dem.
2006	1,781,139	787,182	Steele, Michael S.	965,477	Cardin, Benjamin L.	28,480	178,295 D	44.2%	54.2%	44.9%	55.1%
2004	2,323,183	783,055	Pipkin, E. J.	1,504,691	Mikulski, Barbara A.	35,437	721,636 D	33.7%	64.8%	34.2%	65.8%
2000	1,946,898	715,178	Rappaport, Paul	1,230,013	Sarbanes, Paul S.	1,707	514,835 D	36.7%	63.2%	36.8%	63.2%
1998	1,507,447	444,637	Pierpont, Ross Z.	1,062,810	Mikulski, Barbara A.		618,173 D	29.5%	70.5%	29.5%	70.5%
1994	1,369,104	559,908	Brock, William E.	809,125	Sarbanes, Paul S.	71	249,217 D	40.9%	59.1%	40.9%	59.1%
1992	1,841,735	533,688	Keyes, Alan L.	1,307,610	Mikulski, Barbara A.	437	773,922 D	29.0%	71.0%	29.0%	71.0%
1988	1,617,065	617,537	Keyes, Alan L.	999,166	Sarbanes, Paul S.	362	381,629 D	38.2%	61.8%	38.2%	61.8%
1986	1,112,637	437,411	Chavez, Linda	675,225	Mikulski, Barbara A.	1	237,814 D	39.3%	60.7%	39.3%	60.7%
1982	1,114,690	407,334	Hogan, Lawrence J.	707,356	Sarbanes, Paul S.		300,022 D	36.5%	63.5%	36.5%	63.5%
1980	1,286,088	850,970	Mathias, Charles	435,118	Conroy, Edward T.		415,852 R	66.2%	33.8%	66.2%	33.8%
1976	1,365,568	530,439	Beall, J. Glenn Jr.	772,101	Sarbanes, Paul S.	63,028	241,662 D	38.8%	56.5%	40.7%	59.3%
1974	877,786	503,223	Mathias, Charles	374,563	Mikulski, Barbara A.		128,660 R	57.3%	42.7%	57.3%	42.7%
1970	956,370	484,960	Beall, J. Glenn Jr.	460,422	Tydings, Joseph D.	10,988	24,538 R	50.7%	48.1%	51.3%	48.7%
1968**	1,133,727	541,893	Mathias, Charles	443,367	Brewster, Daniel B.	148,467	98,526 R	47.8%	39.1%	55.0%	45.0%
1964	1,081,049	402,393	Beall, J. Glenn Jr.	678,649	Tydings, Joseph D.	7	276,256 D	37.2%	62.8%	37.2%	62.8%
1962	714,248	270,312	Miller, Edward T.	443,935	Brewster, Daniel B.	1	173,623 D	37.8%	62.2%	37.8%	62.2%
1958	749,291	382,021	Beall, J. Glenn Jr.	367,270	D'Alesandro, Thomas		14,751 R	51.0%	49.0%	51.0%	49.0%
1956	892,167	473,059	Butler, John Marshall	419,108	Mahoney, George P.		53,951 R	53.0%	47.0%	53.0%	47.0%
1952	856,193	449,823	Beall, J. Glenn Jr.	406,370	Mahoney, George P.		43,453 R	52.5%	47.5%	52.5%	47.5%
1950	615,614	326,291	Butler, John Marshall	283,180	Tydings, Millard E.	6,143	43,111 R	53.0%	46.0%	53.5%	46.5%
1946	472,232	235,000	Markey, David John	237,232	O'Conor, Herbert R.		2,232 D	49.8%	50.2%	49.8%	50.2%

**In past elections, the other vote included: 1968 - 148,467 Independent (George P. Mahoney).

MARYLAND

GOVERNOR 2006

2000 Census Population	County	Total Vote	Republican	Democratic	Other	Rep.-Dem. Plurality	Total Vote Rep.	Total Vote Dem.	Major Vote Rep.	Major Vote Dem.
74,930	ALLEGANY	21,756	12,424	9,033	299	3,391 R	57.1%	41.5%	57.9%	42.1%
489,656	ANNE ARUNDEL	187,923	106,897	78,909	2,117	27,988 R	56.9%	42.0%	57.5%	42.5%
651,154	BALTIMORE CITY	152,934	34,554	115,136	3,244	80,582 D	22.6%	75.3%	23.1%	76.9%
754,292	BALTIMORE COUNTY	282,928	143,970	135,567	3,391	8,403 R	50.9%	47.9%	51.5%	48.5%
74,563	CALVERT	30,001	17,163	12,519	319	4,644 R	57.2%	41.7%	57.8%	42.2%
29,772	CAROLINE	9,074	5,994	2,947	133	3,047 R	66.1%	32.5%	67.0%	33.0%
150,897	CARROLL	62,801	43,921	18,227	653	25,694 R	69.9%	29.0%	70.7%	29.3%
85,951	CECIL	28,675	16,559	11,750	366	4,809 R	57.7%	41.0%	58.5%	41.5%
120,546	CHARLES	41,405	19,757	21,237	411	1,480 D	47.7%	51.3%	48.2%	51.8%
30,674	DORCHESTER	10,759	6,529	4,126	104	2,403 R	60.7%	38.3%	61.3%	38.7%
195,277	FREDERICK	73,088	43,536	28,644	908	14,892 R	59.6%	39.2%	60.3%	39.7%
29,846	GARRETT	9,877	6,642	3,108	127	3,534 R	67.2%	31.5%	68.1%	31.9%
218,590	HARFORD	91,337	57,882	32,490	965	25,392 R	63.4%	35.6%	64.0%	36.0%
247,842	HOWARD	105,750	51,974	52,651	1,125	677 D	49.1%	49.8%	49.7%	50.3%
19,197	KENT	7,942	4,369	3,484	89	885 R	55.0%	43.9%	55.6%	44.4%
873,341	MONTGOMERY	305,731	112,071	190,873	2,787	78,802 D	36.7%	62.4%	37.0%	63.0%
801,515	PRINCE GEORGES	207,126	42,514	162,899	1,713	120,385 D	20.5%	78.6%	20.7%	79.3%
40,563	QUEEN ANNES	18,059	12,054	5,859	146	6,195 R	66.7%	32.4%	67.3%	32.7%
86,211	ST. MARYS	28,633	16,683	11,516	434	5,167 R	58.3%	40.2%	59.2%	40.8%
24,747	SOMERSET	6,755	3,999	2,691	65	1,308 R	59.2%	39.8%	59.8%	40.2%
33,812	TALBOT	15,833	10,062	5,669	102	4,393 R	63.6%	35.8%	64.0%	36.0%
131,923	WASHINGTON	41,457	25,157	15,722	578	9,435 R	60.7%	37.9%	61.5%	38.5%
84,644	WICOMICO	28,209	17,678	10,214	317	7,464 R	62.7%	36.2%	63.4%	36.6%
46,543	WORCESTER	20,263	13,075	7,008	180	6,067 R	64.5%	34.6%	65.1%	34.9%
5,296,486	TOTAL	1,788,316	825,464	942,279	20,573	116,815 D	46.2%	52.7%	46.7%	53.3%

SENATOR 2006

2000 Census Population	County	Total Vote	Republican	Democratic	Other	Rep.-Dem. Plurality	Total Vote Rep.	Total Vote Dem.	Major Vote Rep.	Major Vote Dem.
74,930	ALLEGANY	21,599	12,892	8,396	311	4,496 R	59.7%	38.9%	60.6%	39.4%
489,656	ANNE ARUNDEL	187,207	101,110	82,687	3,410	18,423 R	54.0%	44.2%	55.0%	45.0%
651,154	BALTIMORE CITY	151,338	35,185	112,805	3,348	77,620 D	23.2%	74.5%	23.8%	76.2%
754,292	BALTIMORE COUNTY	281,810	131,291	145,262	5,257	13,971 D	46.6%	51.5%	47.5%	52.5%
74,563	CALVERT	29,881	16,703	12,687	491	4,016 R	55.9%	42.5%	56.8%	43.2%
29,772	CAROLINE	9,010	5,957	2,860	193	3,097 R	66.1%	31.7%	67.6%	32.4%
150,897	CARROLL	62,583	42,550	18,893	1,140	23,657 R	68.0%	30.2%	69.3%	30.7%
85,951	CECIL	28,483	16,296	11,600	587	4,696 R	57.2%	40.7%	58.4%	41.6%
120,546	CHARLES	41,242	19,743	20,938	561	1,195 D	47.9%	50.8%	48.5%	51.5%
30,674	DORCHESTER	10,650	6,326	4,183	141	2,143 R	59.4%	39.3%	60.2%	39.8%
195,277	FREDERICK	72,800	42,174	29,398	1,228	12,776 R	57.9%	40.4%	58.9%	41.1%
29,846	GARRETT	9,794	6,995	2,686	113	4,309 R	71.4%	27.4%	72.3%	27.7%
218,590	HARFORD	90,994	56,703	32,590	1,701	24,113 R	62.3%	35.8%	63.5%	36.5%
247,842	HOWARD	105,524	47,015	56,873	1,636	9,858 D	44.6%	53.9%	45.3%	54.7%
19,197	KENT	7,858	4,239	3,484	135	755 R	53.9%	44.3%	54.9%	45.1%
873,341	MONTGOMERY	305,610	96,616	205,264	3,730	108,648 D	31.6%	67.2%	32.0%	68.0%
801,515	PRINCE GEORGES	206,380	49,484	154,798	2,098	105,314 D	24.0%	75.0%	24.2%	75.8%
40,563	QUEEN ANNES	17,969	11,710	5,935	324	5,775 R	65.2%	33.0%	66.4%	33.6%
86,211	ST. MARYS	28,488	16,381	11,614	493	4,767 R	57.5%	40.8%	58.5%	41.5%
24,747	SOMERSET	6,706	3,953	2,651	102	1,302 R	58.9%	39.5%	59.9%	40.1%
33,812	TALBOT	15,738	9,686	5,844	208	3,842 R	61.5%	37.1%	62.4%	37.6%
131,923	WASHINGTON	41,293	24,773	15,921	599	8,852 R	60.0%	38.6%	60.9%	39.1%
84,644	WICOMICO	28,067	17,074	10,571	422	6,503 R	60.8%	37.7%	61.8%	38.2%
46,543	WORCESTER	20,115	12,326	7,537	252	4,789 R	61.3%	37.5%	62.1%	37.9%
5,296,486	TOTAL	1,781,139	787,182	965,477	28,480	178,295 D	44.2%	54.2%	44.9%	55.1%

MARYLAND

HOUSE OF REPRESENTATIVES

CD	Year	Total Vote	Republican		Democratic		Other Vote	Rep.-Dem. Plurality	Percentage Total Vote		Percentage Major Vote	
			Vote	Candidate	Vote	Candidate			Rep.	Dem.	Rep.	Dem.
1	2006	269,147	185,177	GILCHREST, WAYNE T.*	83,738	CORWIN, JIM	232	101,439 R	68.8%	31.1%	68.9%	31.1%
1	2004	323,526	245,149	GILCHREST, WAYNE T.*	77,872	ALEXAKIS, KOSTAS	505	167,277 R	75.8%	24.1%	75.9%	24.1%
1	2002	250,413	192,004	GILCHREST, WAYNE T.*	57,986	TAMLYN, ANN D.	423	134,018 R	76.7%	23.2%	76.8%	23.2%
2	2006	196,228	60,195	MATHIS, JIMMY	135,818	RUPPERSBERGER, C. A. DUTCH*	215	75,623 D	30.7%	69.2%	30.7%	69.3%
2	2004	247,295	75,812	BROOKS, JANE	164,751	RUPPERSBERGER, C. A. DUTCH*	6,732	88,939 D	30.7%	66.6%	31.5%	68.5%
2	2002	195,202	88,954	BENTLEY, HELEN DELICH	105,718	RUPPERSBERGER, C. A. DUTCH	530	16,764 D	45.6%	54.2%	45.7%	54.3%
3	2006	234,486	79,174	WHITE, JOHN	150,142	SARBANES, JOHN P.	5,170	70,968 D	33.8%	64.0%	34.5%	65.5%
3	2004	287,219	97,008	DUCKWORTH, ROBERT P.	182,066	CARDIN, BENJAMIN L.*	8,145	85,058 D	33.8%	63.4%	34.8%	65.2%
3	2002	221,543	75,721	CONWELL, SCOTT	145,589	CARDIN, BENJAMIN L.*	233	69,868 D	34.2%	65.7%	34.2%	65.8%
4	2006	175,903	32,792	STARKMAN, MICHAEL MOSHE	141,897	WYNN, ALBERT R.*	1,214	109,105 D	18.6%	80.7%	18.8%	81.2%
4	2004	261,860	52,907	McKINNIS, JOHN	196,809	WYNN, ALBERT R.*	12,144	143,902 D	20.2%	75.2%	21.2%	78.8%
4	2002	167,555	34,890	KIMBLE, JOHN B.	131,644	WYNN, ALBERT R.*	1,021	96,754 D	20.8%	78.6%	21.0%	79.0%
5	2006	203,323		—	168,114	HOYER, STENY H.*	35,209	168,114 D		82.7%		100.0%
5	2004	298,335	87,189	JEWITT, BRAD	204,867	HOYER, STENY H.*	6,279	117,678 D	29.2%	68.7%	29.9%	70.1%
5	2002	199,087	60,758	CRAWFORD, JOSEPH T.	137,903	HOYER, STENY H.*	426	77,145 D	30.5%	69.3%	30.6%	69.4%
6	2006	239,453	141,200	BARTLETT, ROSCOE G.*	92,030	DUCK, ANDREW	6,223	49,170 R	59.0%	38.4%	60.5%	39.5%
6	2004	305,857	206,076	BARTLETT, ROSCOE G.*	90,108	BOSLEY, KENNETH T.	9,673	115,968 R	67.4%	29.5%	69.6%	30.4%
6	2002	223,611	147,825	BARTLETT, ROSCOE G.*	75,575	DeARMON, DONALD M.	211	72,250 R	66.1%	33.8%	66.2%	33.8%
7	2006	161,977		—	158,830	CUMMINGS, ELIJAH E.*	3,147	158,830 D		98.1%		100.0%
7	2004	244,183	60,102	SALAZAR, TONY	179,189	CUMMINGS, ELIJAH E.*	4,892	119,087 D	24.6%	73.4%	25.1%	74.9%
7	2002	186,394	49,172	WARD, JOSEPH E.	137,047	CUMMINGS, ELIJAH E.*	175	87,875 D	26.4%	73.5%	26.4%	73.6%
8	2006	220,685	48,324	STEIN, JEFFREY M.	168,872	VAN HOLLEN, CHRIS*	3,489	120,548 D	21.9%	76.5%	22.2%	77.8%
8	2004	287,680	71,989	FLOYD, CHUCK	215,129	VAN HOLLEN, CHRIS*	562	143,140 D	25.0%	74.8%	25.1%	74.9%
8	2002	218,113	103,587	MORELLA, CONSTANCE A.*	112,788	VAN HOLLEN, CHRIS	1,738	9,201 D	47.5%	51.7%	47.9%	52.1%
TOTAL	2006	1,701,202	546,862		1,099,441		54,899	552,579 D	32.1%	64.6%	33.2%	66.8%
TOTAL	2004	2,255,955	896,232		1,310,791		48,932	414,559 D	39.7%	58.1%	40.6%	59.4%
TOTAL	2002	1,661,918	752,911		904,250		4,757	151,339 D	45.3%	54.4%	45.4%	54.6%

An asterisk (*) denotes incumbent.

MARYLAND

GENERAL AND PRIMARY ELECTIONS

2006 GENERAL ELECTIONS

Governor Other vote was 15,551 Green (Ed Boyd); 3,481 Populist (Christopher A. Driscoll); 258 Republican write-in (John J. Simmins); 61 Democratic write-in (Charles Ulysses Smith); 16 Democratic write-in (Ralph Jaffe); 1,206 scattered write-in.

Senator Other vote was 27,564 Green (Kevin Zeese); 120 Democratic write-in (Lih Young); 796 scattered write-in.

House Other vote was:

CD 1   232 scattered write-in.
CD 2   215 scattered write-in.
CD 3   4,941 Libertarian (Charles Curtis McPeek Sr.); 229 scattered write-in.
CD 4   1,214 scattered write-in.
CD 5   33,464 Green (Steve Warner); 635 Constitution write-in (Peter Kuhnert); 1,110 scattered write-in.
CD 6   6,095 Green (Robert E. Kozak); 128 scattered write-in.
CD 7   3,147 scattered write-in.
CD 8   3,298 Green (Gerard P. Giblin); 191 scattered write-in.

MARYLAND

GENERAL AND PRIMARY ELECTIONS

2006 PRIMARY ELECTIONS

Primary	September 12, 2006	**Registration** (as of August 22, 2006)	Democratic	1,805,225
			Republican	958,798
			Green	8,344
			Libertarian	4,427
			Constitution	544
			Populist	99
			Unaffiliated & Other	517,909
			TOTAL	3,295,346

Primary Type Closed—Only registered Democrats and Republicans could vote in their party's primary.

Note: An asterisk (*) denotes incumbent.

	REPUBLICAN PRIMARIES			DEMOCRATIC PRIMARIES		
Governor	Robert L. Ehrlich Jr.*	213,744	100.0%	Martin O'Malley	524,671	100.0%
Senator	Michael S. Steele	190,790	87.0%	Benjamin L. Cardin	257,545	43.7%
	John Kimble	6,280	2.9%	Kweisi Mfume	238,957	40.5%
	Earl S. Gordon	4,110	1.9%	Josh Rales	30,737	5.2%
	Daniel "Wig Man" Vovak	4,063	1.9%	Dennis F. Rasmussen	10,997	1.9%
	Thomas J. Hampton	3,946	1.8%	Mike Schaefer	7,773	1.3%
	Corrogan R. Vaughn	2,565	1.2%	Allan Lichtman	6,919	1.2%
	Daniel Muffoletto	2,335	1.1%	Theresa C. Scaldaferri	5,081	0.9%
	Richard Shawver	2,298	1.0%	James H. Hutchinson	4,949	0.8%
	Ray Bly	2,114	1.0%	David Dickerson	3,950	0.7%
	Edward Raymond Madej	902	0.4%	A. Robert Kaufman	3,908	0.7%
				Anthony Jaworksi	3,486	0.6%
				Thomas McCaskill	3,459	0.6%
				George T. English	2,305	0.4%
				Bob Robinson	2,208	0.4%
				Lih Young	2,039	0.3%
				Blaine Taylor	1,848	0.3%
				Joseph Werner	1,832	0.3%
				Charles Ulysses Smith	1,702	0.3%
	TOTAL	*219,403*		*TOTAL*	*589,695*	
Congressional District 1	Wayne T. Gilchrest*	47,165	100.0%	Jim Corwin	22,021	43.5%
				Christopher R. Robinson	16,848	33.3%
				Kostas Alexakis	11,737	23.2%
				TOTAL	*50,606*	
Congressional District 2	Jimmy Mathis	6,858	40.7%	C. A. Dutch Ruppersberger*	56,450	82.3%
	Dee Hodges	6,437	38.2%	Christopher C. Boardman	12,118	17.7%
	J. D. Urbach	3,551	21.1%			
	TOTAL	*16,846*		*TOTAL*	*68,568*	
Congressional District 3	John White	8,969	37.9%	John P. Sarbanes	26,954	31.9%
	Gary Applebaum	7,886	33.3%	Peter Beilenson	21,481	25.4%
	Scott Smith	1,921	8.1%	Paula C. Hollinger	18,008	21.3%
	Eugenia Korsak Ordynsky	1,596	6.7%	Andy Barth	7,561	9.0%
	Bruce Robert Altschuler	1,322	5.6%	Kevin O'Keeffe	4,084	4.8%
	Rick Hoover	939	4.0%	Oz Bengur	3,774	4.5%
	Paul Spause	579	2.4%	Mishonda Baldwin	2,202	2.6%
	David P. Trudil	462	2.0%	John Rea	390	0.5%
	TOTAL	*23,674*		*TOTAL*	*84,454*	

MARYLAND

GENERAL AND PRIMARY ELECTIONS

	REPUBLICAN PRIMARIES			DEMOCRATIC PRIMARIES		
Congressional District 4	Michael Moshe Starkman	6,407	100.0%	Albert R. Wynn*	40,857	49.7%
				Donna Edwards	38,126	46.4%
				George Edward McDermott	3,200	3.9%
				TOTAL	*82,183*	
Congressional District 5	No Republican candidate			Steny H. Hoyer*	67,698	100.0%
Congressional District 6	Roscoe G. Bartlett*	45,474	79.3%	Andrew Duck	22,903	59.2%
	Joseph T. Krysztoforski	11,889	20.7%	Barry J. C. Kissin	15,780	40.8%
	TOTAL	*57,363*		*TOTAL*	*38,683*	
Congressional District 7	No Republican candidate			Elijah E. Cummings*	73,335	100.0%
Congressional District 8	Jeffrey M. Stein	5,980	45.4%	Chris Van Hollen*	73,544	91.3%
	Daniel F. Zubairi	4,201	31.9%	Deborah A. Vollmer	6,989	8.7%
	Gus Alzona	2,990	22.7%			
	TOTAL	*13,171*		*TOTAL*	*80,533*	

MASSACHUSETTS

Congressional districts first established for elections held in 2002
10 members

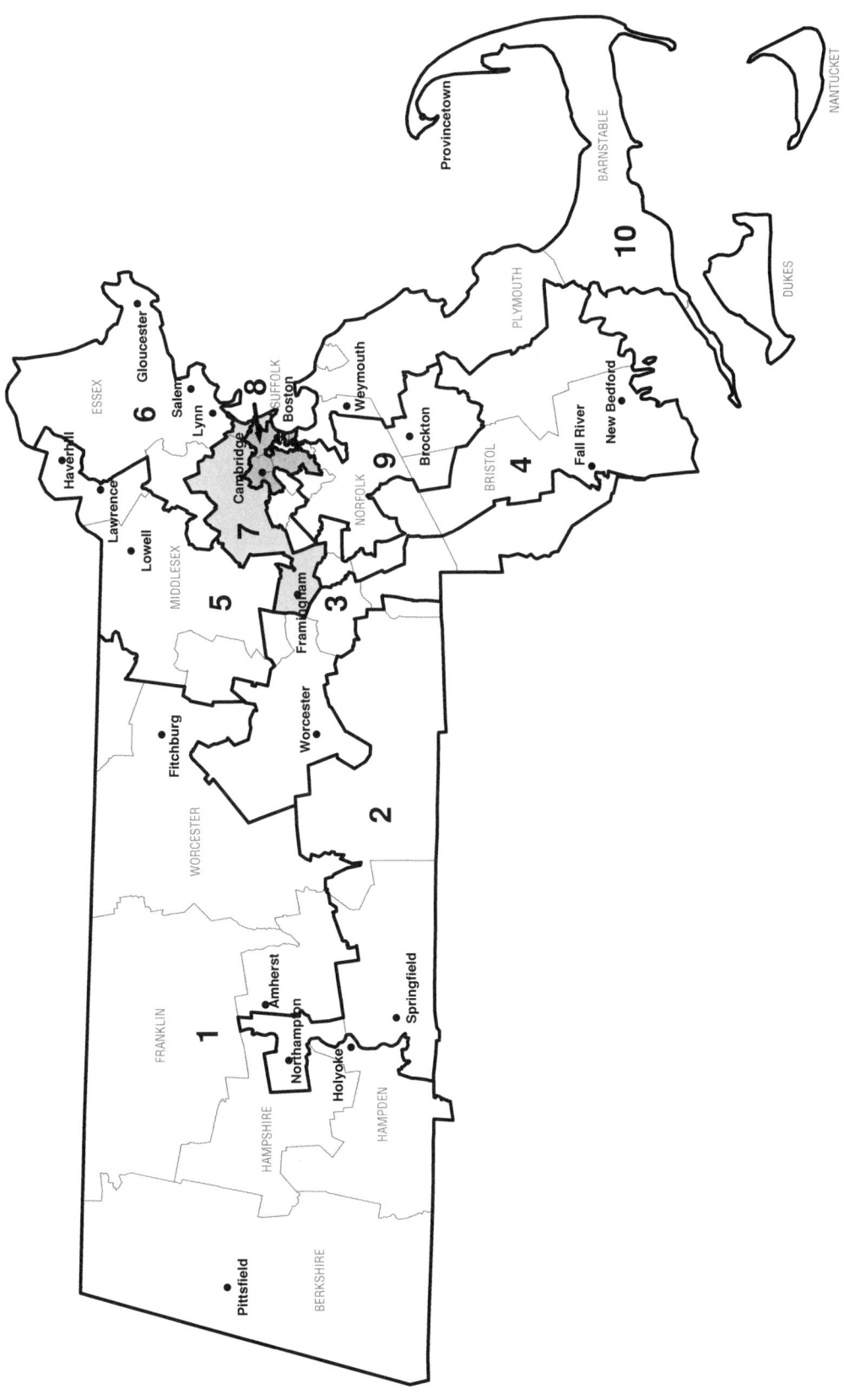

MASSACHUSETTS

Boston Area

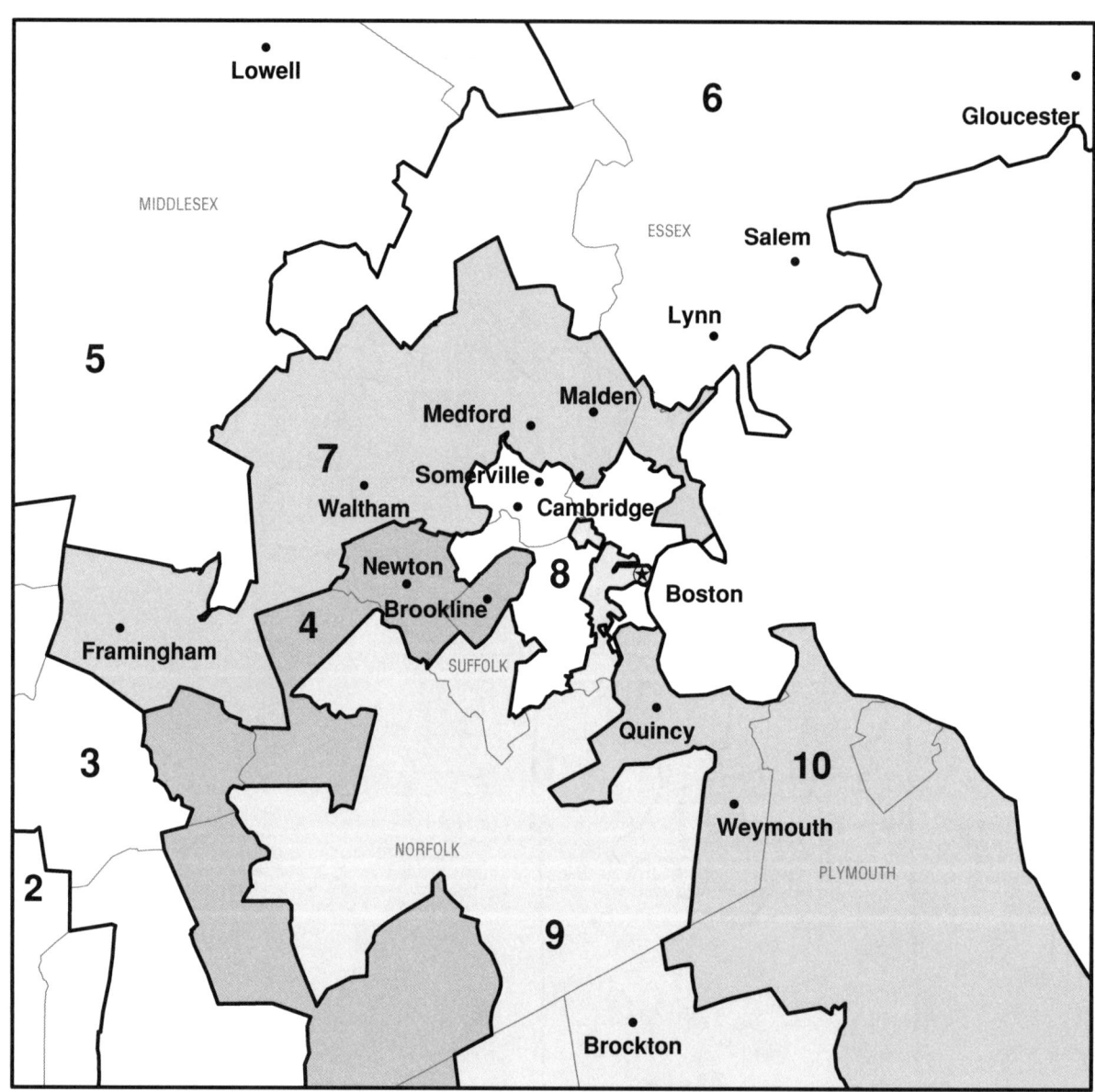

Lowell

6

Gloucester

MIDDLESEX

ESSEX

Salem

5

Lynn

Medford

Malden

7

Somerville

Cambridge

Waltham

Newton

8

Boston

Brookline

Framingham

4

SUFFOLK

3

Quincy

10

NORFOLK

Weymouth

2

PLYMOUTH

9

Brockton

MASSACHUSETTS

GOVERNOR
Deval L. Patrick (D). Elected 2006 to a four-year term.

SENATORS (2 Democrats)
Edward M. Kennedy (D). Reelected 2006 to a six-year term. Previously elected 2000, 1994, 1988, 1982, 1976, 1970, 1964 and in 1962 to fill out the term vacated by the December 1960 resignation of Senator John F. Kennedy, who was elected President in November 1960.

John Kerry (D). Reelected 2002 to a six-year term. Previously elected 1996, 1990, 1984.

REPRESENTATIVES (10 Democrats)
1. John W. Olver (D)
2. Richard E. Neal (D)
3. Jim McGovern (D)
4. Barney Frank (D)
5. Martin T. Meehan (D)
6. John F. Tierney (D)
7. Edward J. Markey (D)
8. Michael E. Capuano (D)
9. Stephen F. Lynch (D)
10. Bill Delahunt (D)

POSTWAR VOTE FOR PRESIDENT

| | | Republican | | Democratic | | Other | | Percentage | | | |
| | | | | | | | | Total Vote | | Major Vote | |
Year	Total Vote	Vote	Candidate	Vote	Candidate	Vote	Plurality	Rep.	Dem.	Rep.	Dem.
2004	2,912,388	1,071,109	Bush, George W.	1,803,800	Kerry, John	37,479	732,691 D	36.8%	61.9%	37.3%	62.7%
2000**	2,702,984	878,502	Bush, George W.	1,616,487	Gore, Al	207,995	737,985 D	32.5%	59.8%	35.2%	64.8%
1996**	2,556,785	718,107	Dole, Bob	1,571,763	Clinton, Bill	266,915	853,656 D	28.1%	61.5%	31.4%	68.6%
1992**	2,773,700	805,049	Bush, George	1,318,662	Clinton, Bill	649,989	513,613 D	29.0%	47.5%	37.9%	62.1%
1988	2,632,805	1,194,635	Bush, George	1,401,415	Dukakis, Michael S.	36,755	206,780 D	45.4%	53.2%	46.0%	54.0%
1984	2,559,453	1,310,936	Reagan, Ronald	1,239,606	Mondale, Walter F.	8,911	71,330 R	51.2%	48.4%	51.4%	48.6%
1980**	2,524,298	1,057,631	Reagan, Ronald	1,053,802	Carter, Jimmy	412,865	3,829 R	41.9%	41.7%	50.1%	49.9%
1976	2,547,558	1,030,276	Ford, Gerald R.	1,429,475	Carter, Jimmy	87,807	399,199 D	40.4%	56.1%	41.9%	58.1%
1972	2,458,756	1,112,078	Nixon, Richard M.	1,332,540	McGovern, George S.	14,138	220,462 D	45.2%	54.2%	45.5%	54.5%
1968**	2,331,752	766,844	Nixon, Richard M.	1,469,218	Humphrey, Hubert H.	95,690	702,374 D	32.9%	63.0%	34.3%	65.7%
1964	2,344,798	549,727	Goldwater, Barry M.	1,786,422	Johnson, Lyndon B.	8,649	1,236,695 D	23.4%	76.2%	23.5%	76.5%
1960	2,469,480	976,750	Nixon, Richard M.	1,487,174	Kennedy, John F.	5,556	510,424 D	39.6%	60.2%	39.6%	60.4%
1956	2,348,506	1,393,197	Eisenhower, Dwight D.	948,190	Stevenson, Adlai E.	7,119	445,007 R	59.3%	40.4%	59.5%	40.5%
1952	2,383,398	1,292,325	Eisenhower, Dwight D.	1,083,525	Stevenson, Adlai E.	7,548	208,800 R	54.2%	45.5%	54.4%	45.6%
1948	2,107,146	909,370	Dewey, Thomas E.	1,151,788	Truman, Harry S.	45,988	242,418 D	43.2%	54.7%	44.1%	55.9%

**In past elections, the other vote included: 173,564 - Green (Ralph Nader); 1996 - 227,217 Reform (Ross Perot); 1992 - 630,731 Independent (Ross Perot); 1980 - 382,539 Independent (John Anderson); 1968 - 87,088 American Independent (George Wallace).

MASSACHUSETTS

POSTWAR VOTE FOR GOVERNOR

Year	Total Vote	Republican Vote	Republican Candidate	Democratic Vote	Democratic Candidate	Other Vote	Rep.-Dem. Plurality	Total Vote Rep.	Total Vote Dem.	Major Vote Rep.	Major Vote Dem.
2006	2,219,779	784,342	Healey, Kerry	1,234,984	Patrick, Deval L.	200,453	450,642 D	35.3%	55.6%	38.8%	61.2%
2002	2,194,179	1,091,988	Romney, Mitt	985,981	O'Brien, Shannon P.	116,210	106,007 R	49.8%	44.9%	52.6%	47.4%
1998	1,903,336	967,160	Cellucci, Paul	901,843	Harshbarger, Scott	34,333	65,317 R	50.8%	47.4%	51.7%	48.3%
1994	2,164,318	1,533,430	Weld, William F.	611,650	Roosevelt, Mark	19,238	921,780 R	70.9%	28.3%	71.5%	28.5%
1990	2,342,927	1,175,817	Weld, William F.	1,099,878	Silber, John	67,232	75,939 R	50.2%	46.9%	51.7%	48.3%
1986	1,684,079	525,364	Kariotis, George	1,157,786	Dukakis, Michael S.	929	632,422 D	31.2%	68.7%	31.2%	68.8%
1982	2,050,254	749,679	Sears, John W.	1,219,109	Dukakis, Michael S.	81,466	469,430 D	36.6%	59.5%	38.1%	61.9%
1978	1,962,251	926,072	Hatch, Francis W.	1,030,294	King, Edward J.	5,885	104,222 D	47.2%	52.5%	47.3%	52.7%
1974	1,854,798	784,353	Sargent, Francis W.	992,284	Dukakis, Michael S.	78,161	207,931 D	42.3%	53.5%	44.1%	55.9%
1970	1,867,906	1,058,623	Sargent, Francis W.	799,269	White, Kevin H.	10,014	259,354 R	56.7%	42.8%	57.0%	43.0%
1966**	2,041,177	1,277,358	Volpe, John A.	752,720	McCormack, Edward J.	11,099	524,638 R	62.6%	36.9%	62.9%	37.1%
1964	2,340,130	1,176,462	Volpe, John A.	1,153,416	Bellotti, Francis X.	10,252	23,046 R	50.3%	49.3%	50.5%	49.5%
1962	2,109,089	1,047,891	Volpe, John A.	1,053,322	Peabody, Endicott	7,876	5,431 D	49.7%	49.9%	49.9%	50.1%
1960	2,417,133	1,269,295	Volpe, John A.	1,130,810	Ward, Joseph D.	17,028	138,485 R	52.5%	46.8%	52.9%	47.1%
1958	1,899,117	818,463	Gibbons, Charles	1,067,020	Furcolo, Foster	13,634	248,557 D	43.1%	56.2%	43.4%	56.6%
1956	2,339,884	1,096,759	Whittier, Sumner G.	1,234,618	Furcolo, Foster	8,507	137,859 D	46.9%	52.8%	47.0%	53.0%
1954	1,903,774	985,339	Herter, Christian A.	910,087	Murphy, Robert F.	8,348	75,252 R	51.8%	47.8%	52.0%	48.0%
1952	2,356,298	1,175,955	Herter, Christian A.	1,161,499	Dever, Paul A.	18,844	14,456 R	49.9%	49.3%	50.3%	49.7%
1950	1,910,180	824,069	Coolidge, Arthur W.	1,074,570	Dever, Paul A.	11,541	250,501 D	43.1%	56.3%	43.4%	56.6%
1948	2,099,250	849,895	Bradford, Robert F.	1,239,247	Dever, Paul A.	10,108	389,352 D	40.5%	59.0%	40.7%	59.3%
1946	1,683,452	911,152	Bradford, Robert F.	762,743	Tobin, Maurice	9,557	148,409 R	54.1%	45.3%	54.4%	45.6%

**The term of office of Massachusetts' governor was increased from two to four years effective with the 1966 election.

POSTWAR VOTE FOR SENATOR

Year	Total Vote	Republican Vote	Republican Candidate	Democratic Vote	Democratic Candidate	Other Vote	Rep.-Dem. Plurality	Total Vote Rep.	Total Vote Dem.	Major Vote Rep.	Major Vote Dem.
2006	2,165,490	661,532	Chase, Kenneth G.	1,500,738	Kennedy, Edward M.	3,220	839,206 D	30.5%	69.3%	30.6%	69.4%
2002	2,006,758		—	1,605,976	Kerry, John	400,782	1,605,976 D		80.0%		100.0%
2000**	2,599,420	334,341	Robinson, Jack E.	1,889,494	Kennedy, Edward M.	375,585	1,555,153 D	12.9%	72.7%	15.0%	85.0%
1996	2,555,886	1,142,837	Weld, William F.	1,334,345	Kerry, John	78,704	191,508 D	44.7%	52.2%	46.1%	53.9%
1994	2,179,964	894,005	Romney, Mitt	1,266,011	Kennedy, Edward M.	19,948	372,006 D	41.0%	58.1%	41.4%	58.6%
1990	2,316,212	992,917	Rappaport, Jim	1,321,712	Kerry, John	1,583	328,795 D	42.9%	57.1%	42.9%	57.1%
1988	2,606,225	884,267	Malone, Joseph	1,693,344	Kennedy, Edward M.	28,614	809,077 D	33.9%	65.0%	34.3%	65.7%
1984	2,530,195	1,136,806	Shamie, Raymond	1,392,981	Kerry, John	408	256,175 D	44.9%	55.1%	44.9%	55.1%
1982	2,050,769	784,602	Shamie, Raymond	1,247,084	Kennedy, Edward M.	19,083	462,482 D	38.3%	60.8%	38.6%	61.4%
1978	1,985,700	890,584	Brooke, Edward W.	1,093,283	Tsongas, Paul E.	1,833	202,699 D	44.8%	55.1%	44.9%	55.1%
1976	2,491,255	722,641	Robertson, Michael	1,726,657	Kennedy, Edward M.	41,957	1,004,016 D	29.0%	69.3%	29.5%	70.5%
1972	2,370,676	1,505,932	Brooke, Edward W.	823,278	Droney, John J.	41,466	682,654 R	63.5%	34.7%	64.7%	35.3%
1970	1,935,607	715,978	Spaulding, Josiah E.	1,202,856	Kennedy, Edward M.	16,773	486,878 D	37.0%	62.1%	37.3%	62.7%
1966	1,999,949	1,213,473	Brooke, Edward W.	774,761	Peabody, Endicott	11,715	438,712 R	60.7%	38.7%	61.0%	39.0%
1964	2,312,028	587,663	Whitmore, Howard	1,716,907	Kennedy, Edward M.	7,458	1,129,244 D	25.4%	74.3%	25.5%	74.5%
1962S	2,097,085	877,669	Lodge, George C.	1,162,611	Kennedy, Edward M.	56,805	284,942 D	41.9%	55.4%	43.0%	57.0%
1960	2,417,813	1,358,556	Saltonstall, Leverett	1,050,725	O'Connor, Thomas J.	8,532	307,831 R	56.2%	43.5%	56.4%	43.6%
1958	1,862,041	488,318	Celeste, Vincent J.	1,362,926	Kennedy, John F.	10,797	874,608 D	26.2%	73.2%	26.4%	73.6%
1954	1,892,710	956,605	Saltonstall, Leverett	927,899	Furcolo, Foster	8,206	28,706 R	50.5%	49.0%	50.8%	49.2%
1952	2,360,425	1,141,247	Lodge, Henry Cabot	1,211,984	Kennedy, John F.	7,194	70,737 D	48.3%	51.3%	48.5%	51.5%
1948	2,055,798	1,088,475	Saltonstall, Leverett	954,398	Fitzgerald, John I.	12,925	134,077 R	52.9%	46.4%	53.3%	46.7%
1946	1,662,063	989,736	Lodge, Henry Cabot	660,200	Walsh, David I.	12,127	329,536 R	59.5%	39.7%	60.0%	40.0%

**In past elections, the other vote included: 2000 - 308,748 Libertarian (Carla Howell). The 1962 election was for a short term to fill a vacancy.

MASSACHUSETTS

GOVERNOR 2006

2000 Census Population	County	Total Vote	Republican	Democratic	Other	Rep.-Dem. Plurality	Percentage Total Vote Rep.	Dem.	Major Vote Rep.	Dem.
222,230	BARNSTABLE	104,295	44,986	47,713	11,596	2,727 D	43.1%	45.7%	48.5%	51.5%
134,953	BERKSHIRE	46,119	9,339	35,035	1,745	25,696 D	20.2%	76.0%	21.0%	79.0%
534,678	BRISTOL	166,781	57,233	95,623	13,925	38,390 D	34.3%	57.3%	37.4%	62.6%
14,987	DUKES	7,620	2,143	4,817	660	2,674 D	28.1%	63.2%	30.8%	69.2%
723,419	ESSEX	257,028	102,584	131,376	23,068	28,792 D	39.9%	51.1%	43.8%	56.2%
71,535	FRANKLIN	28,553	6,212	20,204	2,137	13,992 D	21.8%	70.8%	23.5%	76.5%
456,228	HAMPDEN	135,339	48,511	74,899	11,929	26,388 D	35.8%	55.3%	39.3%	60.7%
152,251	HAMPSHIRE	56,460	14,232	38,025	4,203	23,793 D	25.2%	67.3%	27.2%	72.8%
1,465,396	MIDDLESEX	533,239	185,738	299,749	47,752	114,011 D	34.8%	56.2%	38.3%	61.7%
9,520	NANTUCKET	3,994	1,402	2,244	348	842 D	35.1%	56.2%	38.5%	61.5%
650,308	NORFOLK	259,050	99,995	134,916	24,139	34,921 D	38.6%	52.1%	42.6%	57.4%
472,822	PLYMOUTH	181,658	74,933	84,296	22,429	9,363 D	41.2%	46.4%	47.1%	52.9%
689,807	SUFFOLK	179,233	41,316	126,242	11,675	84,926 D	23.1%	70.4%	24.7%	75.3%
750,963	WORCESTER	260,410	95,718	139,845	24,847	44,127 D	36.8%	53.7%	40.6%	59.4%
6,349,097	TOTAL	2,219,779	784,342	1,234,984	200,453	450,642 D	35.3%	55.6%	38.8%	61.2%
	City/Town									
20,331	ACTON	8,504	2,765	5,074	665	2,309 D	32.5%	59.7%	35.3%	64.7%
28,144	AGAWAM	10,434	4,235	5,147	1,052	912 D	40.6%	49.3%	45.1%	54.9%
34,874	AMHERST	8,186	904	6,877	405	5,973 D	11.0%	84.0%	11.6%	88.4%
31,247	ANDOVER	13,419	6,154	6,395	870	241 D	45.9%	47.7%	49.0%	51.0%
42,389	ARLINGTON	20,036	5,403	12,875	1,758	7,472 D	27.0%	64.3%	29.6%	70.4%
42,068	ATTLEBORO	12,900	5,492	6,343	1,065	851 D	42.6%	49.2%	46.4%	53.6%
47,821	BARNSTABLE	19,790	9,380	7,868	2,542	1,512 R	47.4%	39.8%	54.4%	45.6%
24,194	BELMONT	10,950	3,741	6,334	875	2,593 D	34.2%	57.8%	37.1%	62.9%
39,862	BEVERLY	15,515	6,350	7,916	1,249	1,566 D	40.9%	51.0%	44.5%	55.5%
38,981	BILLERICA	13,606	6,226	5,756	1,624	470 R	45.8%	42.3%	52.0%	48.0%
589,141	BOSTON	155,577	32,920	113,288	9,369	80,368 D	21.2%	72.8%	22.5%	77.5%
33,828	BRAINTREE	14,236	6,289	6,356	1,591	67 D	44.2%	44.6%	49.7%	50.3%
94,304	BROCKTON	22,458	6,236	12,573	3,649	6,337 D	27.8%	56.0%	33.2%	66.8%
57,107	BROOKLINE	20,055	3,924	15,054	1,077	11,130 D	19.6%	75.1%	20.7%	79.3%
22,876	BURLINGTON	9,389	4,097	4,392	900	295 D	43.6%	46.8%	48.3%	51.7%
101,355	CAMBRIDGE	32,369	3,895	26,378	2,096	22,483 D	12.0%	81.5%	12.9%	87.1%
20,775	CANTON	8,930	3,714	4,333	883	619 D	41.6%	48.5%	46.2%	53.8%
33,858	CHELMSFORD	14,665	6,717	6,557	1,391	160 R	45.8%	44.7%	50.6%	49.4%
54,653	CHICOPEE	16,578	5,708	9,046	1,824	3,338 D	34.4%	54.6%	38.7%	61.3%
16,993	CONCORD	8,425	2,616	5,330	479	2,714 D	31.1%	63.3%	32.9%	67.1%
25,212	DANVERS	10,448	4,638	4,820	990	182 D	44.4%	46.1%	49.0%	51.0%
30,666	DARTMOUTH	10,916	3,415	6,738	763	3,323 D	31.3%	61.7%	33.6%	66.4%
23,464	DEDHAM	9,932	4,111	4,874	947	763 D	41.4%	49.1%	45.8%	54.2%
28,562	DRACUT	10,257	4,811	4,319	1,127	492 R	46.9%	42.1%	52.7%	47.3%
22,299	EASTON	8,802	3,832	3,879	1,091	47 D	43.5%	44.1%	49.7%	50.3%
38,037	EVERETT	9,625	3,279	5,235	1,111	1,956 D	34.1%	54.4%	38.5%	61.5%
91,938	FALL RIVER	21,160	4,866	14,845	1,449	9,979 D	23.0%	70.2%	24.7%	75.3%
32,660	FALMOUTH	15,243	5,815	7,887	1,541	2,072 D	38.1%	51.7%	42.4%	57.6%
39,102	FITCHBURG	10,301	3,421	5,770	1,110	2,349 D	33.2%	56.0%	37.2%	62.8%
66,910	FRAMINGHAM	20,140	6,843	11,441	1,856	4,598 D	34.0%	56.8%	37.4%	62.6%
29,560	FRANKLIN	11,477	5,202	5,272	1,003	70 D	45.3%	45.9%	49.7%	50.3%
30,273	GLOUCESTER	11,845	4,272	6,498	1,075	2,226 D	36.1%	54.9%	39.7%	60.3%
58,969	HAVERHILL	17,979	7,222	9,015	1,742	1,793 D	40.2%	50.1%	44.5%	55.5%
19,882	HINGHAM	10,088	4,555	4,668	865	113 D	45.2%	46.3%	49.4%	50.6%
39,838	HOLYOKE	10,362	2,716	6,752	894	4,036 D	26.2%	65.2%	28.7%	71.3%
72,043	LAWRENCE	11,493	2,876	7,911	706	5,035 D	25.0%	68.8%	26.7%	73.3%
41,303	LEOMINSTER	13,375	5,086	7,033	1,256	1,947 D	38.0%	52.6%	42.0%	58.0%
30,355	LEXINGTON	14,062	4,063	9,097	902	5,034 D	28.9%	64.7%	30.9%	69.1%
105,167	LOWELL	21,062	7,217	11,626	2,219	4,409 D	34.3%	55.2%	38.3%	61.7%
89,050	LYNN	20,462	5,849	12,309	2,304	6,460 D	28.6%	60.2%	32.2%	67.8%

MASSACHUSETTS

GOVERNOR 2006

2000 Census Population	City/Town	Total Vote	Republican	Democratic	Other	Rep.-Dem. Plurality		Percentage			
								Total Vote		Major Vote	
								Rep.	Dem.	Rep.	Dem.
56,340	MALDEN	13,978	4,323	8,207	1,448	3,884	D	30.9%	58.7%	34.5%	65.5%
20,377	MARBLEHEAD	9,822	4,032	5,165	625	1,133	D	41.1%	52.6%	43.8%	56.2%
36,255	MARLBOROUGH	11,686	4,675	5,825	1,186	1,150	D	40.0%	49.8%	44.5%	55.5%
24,324	MARSHFIELD	10,700	4,770	4,767	1,163	3	R	44.6%	44.6%	50.0%	50.0%
55,765	MEDFORD	19,419	6,259	11,246	1,914	4,987	D	32.2%	57.9%	35.8%	64.2%
27,134	MELROSE	11,881	4,517	6,247	1,117	1,730	D	38.0%	52.6%	42.0%	58.0%
43,789	METHUEN	14,206	6,505	6,466	1,235	39	R	45.8%	45.5%	50.2%	49.8%
26,799	MILFORD	8,795	3,486	4,456	853	970	D	39.6%	50.7%	43.9%	56.1%
26,062	MILTON	12,720	4,321	7,543	856	3,222	D	34.0%	59.3%	36.4%	63.6%
32,170	NATICK	13,487	4,705	7,554	1,228	2,849	D	34.9%	56.0%	38.4%	61.6%
28,911	NEEDHAM	13,794	4,777	8,089	928	3,312	D	34.6%	58.6%	37.1%	62.9%
93,768	NEW BEDFORD	23,579	5,142	16,704	1,733	11,562	D	21.8%	70.8%	23.5%	76.5%
83,829	NEWTON	33,625	7,937	23,556	2,132	15,619	D	23.6%	70.1%	25.2%	74.8%
27,202	NORTH ANDOVER	10,544	5,059	4,767	718	292	R	48.0%	45.2%	51.5%	48.5%
27,143	NORTH ATTLEBOROUGH	9,326	4,411	3,984	931	427	R	47.3%	42.7%	52.5%	47.5%
28,978	NORTHAMPTON	11,970	1,795	9,419	756	7,624	D	15.0%	78.7%	16.0%	84.0%
28,587	NORWOOD	11,089	4,610	5,309	1,170	699	D	41.6%	47.9%	46.5%	53.5%
48,129	PEABODY	20,208	7,989	10,033	2,186	2,044	D	39.5%	49.6%	44.3%	55.7%
45,793	PITTSFIELD	14,180	2,849	10,826	505	7,977	D	20.1%	76.3%	20.8%	79.2%
51,701	PLYMOUTH	21,097	8,630	10,012	2,455	1,382	D	40.9%	47.5%	46.3%	53.7%
88,025	QUINCY	28,846	10,690	14,918	3,238	4,228	D	37.1%	51.7%	41.7%	58.3%
30,963	RANDOLPH	10,386	2,771	6,699	916	3,928	D	26.7%	64.5%	29.3%	70.7%
23,708	READING	10,125	4,421	4,934	770	513	D	43.7%	48.7%	47.3%	52.7%
47,283	REVERE	11,996	4,551	6,267	1,178	1,716	D	37.9%	52.2%	42.1%	57.9%
40,407	SALEM	13,759	4,260	8,169	1,330	3,909	D	31.0%	59.4%	34.3%	65.7%
26,078	SAUGUS	10,030	4,304	4,512	1,214	208	D	42.9%	45.0%	48.8%	51.2%
17,863	SCITUATE	8,597	3,690	4,002	905	312	D	42.9%	46.6%	48.0%	52.0%
31,640	SHREWSBURY	12,982	5,111	6,933	938	1,822	D	39.4%	53.4%	42.4%	57.6%
77,478	SOMERVILLE	21,991	4,104	16,024	1,863	11,920	D	18.7%	72.9%	20.4%	79.6%
152,082	SPRINGFIELD	32,068	7,665	21,944	2,459	14,279	D	23.9%	68.4%	25.9%	74.1%
22,219	STONEHAM	9,071	3,736	4,387	948	651	D	41.2%	48.4%	46.0%	54.0%
27,149	STOUGHTON	10,055	3,620	5,257	1,178	1,637	D	36.0%	52.3%	40.8%	59.2%
55,976	TAUNTON	15,263	5,044	8,637	1,582	3,593	D	33.0%	56.6%	36.9%	63.1%
28,851	TEWKSBURY	11,433	5,236	4,925	1,272	311	R	45.8%	43.1%	51.5%	48.5%
24,804	WAKEFIELD	10,991	4,719	5,285	987	566	D	42.9%	48.1%	47.2%	52.8%
22,824	WALPOLE	10,154	4,720	4,432	1,002	288	R	46.5%	43.6%	51.6%	48.4%
59,226	WALTHAM	16,591	5,955	9,082	1,554	3,127	D	35.9%	54.7%	39.6%	60.4%
32,986	WATERTOWN	11,995	3,381	7,410	1,204	4,029	D	28.2%	61.8%	31.3%	68.7%
26,613	WELLESLEY	11,306	4,337	6,360	609	2,023	D	38.4%	56.3%	40.5%	59.5%
27,899	WEST SPRINGFIELD	8,429	3,471	4,180	778	709	D	41.2%	49.6%	45.4%	54.6%
40,072	WESTFIELD	12,215	4,894	6,143	1,178	1,249	D	40.1%	50.3%	44.3%	55.7%
53,988	WEYMOUTH	20,712	8,517	9,785	2,410	1,268	D	41.1%	47.2%	46.5%	53.5%
20,810	WINCHESTER	9,996	4,044	5,022	930	978	D	40.5%	50.2%	44.6%	55.4%
37,258	WOBURN	14,287	6,018	6,615	1,654	597	D	42.1%	46.3%	47.6%	52.4%
172,648	WORCESTER	41,809	9,701	28,797	3,311	19,096	D	23.2%	68.9%	25.2%	74.8%
24,807	YARMOUTH	11,159	4,982	4,776	1,401	206	R	44.6%	42.8%	51.1%	48.9%

MASSACHUSETTS

SENATOR 2006

2000 Census Population	County	Total Vote	Republican	Democratic	Other	Rep.-Dem. Plurality	Percentage Total Vote Rep.	Total Vote Dem.	Major Vote Rep.	Major Vote Dem.
222,230	BARNSTABLE	103,032	39,471	63,412	149	23,941 D	38.3%	61.5%	38.4%	61.6%
134,953	BERKSHIRE	45,542	9,382	36,135	25	26,753 D	20.6%	79.3%	20.6%	79.4%
534,678	BRISTOL	163,465	48,204	115,125	136	66,921 D	29.5%	70.4%	29.5%	70.5%
14,987	DUKES	7,479	1,734	5,735	10	4,001 D	23.2%	76.7%	23.2%	76.8%
723,419	ESSEX	250,508	84,150	166,003	355	81,853 D	33.6%	66.3%	33.6%	66.4%
71,535	FRANKLIN	28,119	6,570	21,517	32	14,947 D	23.4%	76.5%	23.4%	76.6%
456,228	HAMPDEN	131,705	44,040	87,430	235	43,390 D	33.4%	66.4%	33.5%	66.5%
152,251	HAMPSHIRE	55,442	13,496	41,867	79	28,371 D	24.3%	75.5%	24.4%	75.6%
1,465,396	MIDDLESEX	520,881	150,257	369,685	939	219,428 D	28.8%	71.0%	28.9%	71.1%
9,520	NANTUCKET	3,940	1,172	2,759	9	1,587 D	29.7%	70.0%	29.8%	70.2%
650,308	NORFOLK	252,225	79,087	172,766	372	93,679 D	31.4%	68.5%	31.4%	68.6%
472,822	PLYMOUTH	177,723	66,274	111,198	251	44,924 D	37.3%	62.6%	37.3%	62.7%
689,807	SUFFOLK	171,104	28,753	142,018	333	113,265 D	16.8%	83.0%	16.8%	83.2%
750,963	WORCESTER	254,325	88,942	165,088	295	76,146 D	35.0%	64.9%	35.0%	65.0%
6,349,097	TOTAL	2,165,490	661,532	1,500,738	3,220	839,206 D	30.5%	69.3%	30.6%	69.4%
	City/Town									
20,331	ACTON	8,298	2,430	5,856	12	3,426 D	29.3%	70.6%	29.3%	70.7%
28,144	AGAWAM	10,155	3,808	6,329	18	2,521 D	37.5%	62.3%	37.6%	62.4%
34,874	AMHERST	8,027	864	7,151	12	6,287 D	10.8%	89.1%	10.8%	89.2%
31,247	ANDOVER	13,047	5,193	7,835	19	2,642 D	39.8%	60.1%	39.9%	60.1%
42,389	ARLINGTON	19,635	4,241	15,345	49	11,104 D	21.6%	78.2%	21.7%	78.3%
42,068	ATTLEBORO	12,704	4,685	8,019		3,334 D	36.9%	63.1%	36.9%	63.1%
47,821	BARNSTABLE	19,554	7,733	11,795	26	4,062 D	39.5%	60.3%	39.6%	60.4%
24,194	BELMONT	10,738	3,086	7,638	14	4,552 D	28.7%	71.1%	28.8%	71.2%
39,862	BEVERLY	15,106	4,938	10,168		5,230 D	32.7%	67.3%	32.7%	67.3%
38,981	BILLERICA	13,342	5,221	8,100	21	2,879 D	39.1%	60.7%	39.2%	60.8%
589,141	BOSTON	148,410	23,152	124,946	312	101,794 D	15.6%	84.2%	15.6%	84.4%
33,828	BRAINTREE	13,843	4,803	9,020	20	4,217 D	34.7%	65.2%	34.7%	65.3%
94,304	BROCKTON	21,767	5,599	16,151	17	10,552 D	25.7%	74.2%	25.7%	74.3%
57,107	BROOKLINE	19,594	2,999	16,578	17	13,579 D	15.3%	84.6%	15.3%	84.7%
22,876	BURLINGTON	9,186	3,290	5,880	16	2,590 D	35.8%	64.0%	35.9%	64.1%
101,355	CAMBRIDGE	31,784	3,321	28,391	72	25,070 D	10.4%	89.3%	10.5%	89.5%
20,775	CANTON	8,643	2,863	5,773	7	2,910 D	33.1%	66.8%	33.2%	66.8%
33,858	CHELMSFORD	14,232	5,621	8,579	32	2,958 D	39.5%	60.3%	39.6%	60.4%
54,653	CHICOPEE	16,291	5,006	11,262	23	6,256 D	30.7%	69.1%	30.8%	69.2%
16,993	CONCORD	8,254	2,315	5,932	7	3,617 D	28.0%	71.9%	28.1%	71.9%
25,212	DANVERS	10,275	3,793	6,464	18	2,671 D	36.9%	62.9%	37.0%	63.0%
30,666	DARTMOUTH	10,372	2,984	7,371	17	4,387 D	28.8%	71.1%	28.8%	71.2%
23,464	DEDHAM	9,649	3,048	6,587	14	3,539 D	31.6%	68.3%	31.6%	68.4%
28,562	DRACUT	10,014	3,839	6,155	20	2,316 D	38.3%	61.5%	38.4%	61.6%
22,299	EASTON	8,572	3,307	5,259	6	1,952 D	38.6%	61.4%	38.6%	61.4%
38,037	EVERETT	9,201	2,068	7,115	18	5,047 D	22.5%	77.3%	22.5%	77.5%
91,938	FALL RIVER	20,795	3,945	16,842	8	12,897 D	19.0%	81.0%	19.0%	81.0%
32,660	FALMOUTH	15,059	5,134	9,856	69	4,722 D	34.1%	65.4%	34.2%	65.8%
39,102	FITCHBURG	10,053	3,085	6,954	14	3,869 D	30.7%	69.2%	30.7%	69.3%
66,910	FRAMINGHAM	19,726	5,410	14,281	35	8,871 D	27.4%	72.4%	27.5%	72.5%
29,560	FRANKLIN	11,192	4,165	7,009	18	2,844 D	37.2%	62.6%	37.3%	62.7%
30,273	GLOUCESTER	11,560	3,267	8,280	13	5,013 D	28.3%	71.6%	28.3%	71.7%
58,969	HAVERHILL	17,507	6,175	11,310	22	5,135 D	35.3%	64.6%	35.3%	64.7%
19,882	HINGHAM	9,836	3,786	6,050		2,264 D	38.5%	61.5%	38.5%	61.5%
39,838	HOLYOKE	9,991	2,524	7,444	23	4,920 D	25.3%	74.5%	25.3%	74.7%
72,043	LAWRENCE	11,011	2,238	8,758	15	6,520 D	20.3%	79.5%	20.4%	79.6%
41,303	LEOMINSTER	13,020	4,344	8,662	14	4,318 D	33.4%	66.5%	33.4%	66.6%
30,355	LEXINGTON	13,709	3,362	10,326	21	6,964 D	24.5%	75.3%	24.6%	75.4%
105,167	LOWELL	20,388	5,416	14,923	49	9,507 D	26.6%	73.2%	26.6%	73.4%
89,050	LYNN	19,843	4,382	15,414	47	11,032 D	22.1%	77.7%	22.1%	77.9%

MASSACHUSETTS

SENATOR 2006

2000 Census Population	City/Town	Total Vote	Republican	Democratic	Other	Rep.-Dem. Plurality	Percentage			
							Total Vote		Major Vote	
							Rep.	Dem.	Rep.	Dem.
56,340	MALDEN	13,645	3,123	10,495	27	7,372 D	22.9%	76.9%	22.9%	77.1%
20,377	MARBLEHEAD	9,558	3,271	6,270	17	2,999 D	34.2%	65.6%	34.3%	65.7%
36,255	MARLBOROUGH	11,442	3,885	7,531	26	3,646 D	34.0%	65.8%	34.0%	66.0%
24,324	MARSHFIELD	10,428	3,971	6,437	20	2,466 D	38.1%	61.7%	38.2%	61.8%
55,765	MEDFORD	18,992	5,239	13,705	48	8,466 D	27.6%	72.2%	27.7%	72.3%
27,134	MELROSE	11,594	3,576	7,994	24	4,418 D	30.8%	68.9%	30.9%	69.1%
43,789	METHUEN	13,849	5,374	8,470	5	3,096 D	38.8%	61.2%	38.8%	61.2%
26,799	MILFORD	8,537	2,673	5,854	10	3,181 D	31.3%	68.6%	31.3%	68.7%
26,062	MILTON	12,179	3,304	8,862	13	5,558 D	27.1%	72.8%	27.2%	72.8%
32,170	NATICK	13,223	3,888	9,321	14	5,433 D	29.4%	70.5%	29.4%	70.6%
28,911	NEEDHAM	13,423	3,854	9,545	24	5,691 D	28.7%	71.1%	28.8%	71.2%
93,768	NEW BEDFORD	23,255	4,023	19,204	28	15,181 D	17.3%	82.6%	17.3%	82.7%
83,829	NEWTON	32,920	5,834	27,037	49	21,203 D	17.7%	82.1%	17.7%	82.3%
27,202	NORTH ANDOVER	10,287	4,430	5,846	11	1,416 D	43.1%	56.8%	43.1%	56.9%
27,143	NORTH ATTLEBOROUGH	9,167	3,808	5,346	13	1,538 D	41.5%	58.3%	41.6%	58.4%
28,978	NORTHAMPTON	11,758	1,670	10,068	20	8,398 D	14.2%	85.6%	14.2%	85.8%
28,587	NORWOOD	10,799	3,460	7,322	17	3,862 D	32.0%	67.8%	32.1%	67.9%
48,129	PEABODY	19,767	5,953	13,775	39	7,822 D	30.1%	69.7%	30.2%	69.8%
45,793	PITTSFIELD	13,952	2,644	11,301	7	8,657 D	19.0%	81.0%	19.0%	81.0%
51,701	PLYMOUTH	20,712	7,847	12,834	31	4,987 D	37.9%	62.0%	37.9%	62.1%
88,025	QUINCY	27,962	7,906	19,995	61	12,089 D	28.3%	71.5%	28.3%	71.7%
30,963	RANDOLPH	10,103	2,117	7,973	13	5,856 D	21.0%	78.9%	21.0%	79.0%
23,708	READING	9,883	3,519	6,353	11	2,834 D	35.6%	64.3%	35.6%	64.4%
47,283	REVERE	11,484	2,911	8,557	16	5,646 D	25.3%	74.5%	25.4%	74.6%
40,407	SALEM	13,416	3,285	10,112	19	6,827 D	24.5%	75.4%	24.5%	75.5%
26,078	SAUGUS	9,752	3,284	6,460	8	3,176 D	33.7%	66.2%	33.7%	66.3%
17,863	SCITUATE	8,384	3,312	5,062	10	1,750 D	39.5%	60.4%	39.6%	60.4%
31,640	SHREWSBURY	12,681	4,495	8,171	15	3,676 D	35.4%	64.4%	35.5%	64.5%
77,478	SOMERVILLE	21,527	3,013	18,439	75	15,426 D	14.0%	85.7%	14.0%	86.0%
152,082	SPRINGFIELD	31,004	6,800	24,142	62	17,342 D	21.9%	77.9%	22.0%	78.0%
22,219	STONEHAM	8,844	2,918	5,912	14	2,994 D	33.0%	66.8%	33.0%	67.0%
27,149	STOUGHTON	9,856	2,846	7,004	6	4,158 D	28.9%	71.1%	28.9%	71.1%
55,976	TAUNTON	14,860	4,198	10,646	16	6,448 D	28.3%	71.6%	28.3%	71.7%
28,851	TEWKSBURY	11,159	4,189	6,960	10	2,771 D	37.5%	62.4%	37.6%	62.4%
24,804	WAKEFIELD	10,735	3,717	6,997	21	3,280 D	34.6%	65.2%	34.7%	65.3%
22,824	WALPOLE	9,896	3,801	6,077	18	2,276 D	38.4%	61.4%	38.5%	61.5%
59,226	WALTHAM	16,066	4,488	11,554	24	7,066 D	27.9%	71.9%	28.0%	72.0%
32,986	WATERTOWN	11,788	2,656	9,098	34	6,442 D	22.5%	77.2%	22.6%	77.4%
26,613	WELLESLEY	11,016	3,629	7,380	7	3,751 D	32.9%	67.0%	33.0%	67.0%
27,899	WEST SPRINGFIELD	8,225	3,144	5,074	7	1,930 D	38.2%	61.7%	38.3%	61.7%
40,072	WESTFIELD	11,888	4,787	7,084	17	2,297 D	40.3%	59.6%	40.3%	59.7%
53,988	WEYMOUTH	20,278	6,757	13,481	40	6,724 D	33.3%	66.5%	33.4%	66.6%
20,810	WINCHESTER	9,706	3,433	6,253	20	2,820 D	35.4%	64.4%	35.4%	64.6%
37,258	WOBURN	13,908	4,654	9,242	12	4,588 D	33.5%	66.5%	33.5%	66.5%
172,648	WORCESTER	40,695	9,478	31,155	62	21,677 D	23.3%	76.6%	23.3%	76.7%
24,807	YARMOUTH	11,016	4,355	6,655	6	2,300 D	39.5%	60.4%	39.6%	60.4%

MASSACHUSETTS

HOUSE OF REPRESENTATIVES

CD	Year	Total Vote	Republican		Democratic		Other Vote	Rep.-Dem. Plurality	Percentage			
									Total Vote		Major Vote	
			Vote	Candidate	Vote	Candidate			Rep.	Dem.	Rep.	Dem.
1	2006	206,884		—	158,057	OLVER, JOHN W.*	48,827	158,057 D		76.4%		100.0%
1	2004	231,747		—	229,465	OLVER, JOHN W.*	2,282	229,465 D		99.0%		100.0%
1	2002	204,019	66,061	KINNAMAN, MATTHEW W.	137,841	OLVER, JOHN W.*	117	71,780 D	32.4%	67.6%	32.4%	67.6%
2	2006	167,193		—	164,939	NEAL, RICHARD E.*	2,254	164,939 D		98.7%		100.0%
2	2004	220,484		—	217,682	NEAL, RICHARD E.*	2,802	217,682 D		98.7%		100.0%
2	2002	154,728		—	153,387	NEAL, RICHARD E.*	1,341	153,387 D		99.1%		100.0%
3	2006	168,956		—	166,973	McGOVERN, JIM*	1,983	166,973 D		98.8%		100.0%
3	2004	272,412	80,197	CREWS, RONALD A.	192,036	McGOVERN, JIM*	179	111,839 D	29.4%	70.5%	29.5%	70.5%
3	2002	157,545		—	155,697	McGOVERN, JIM*	1,848	155,697 D		98.8%		100.0%
4	2006	179,243		—	176,513	FRANK, BARNEY*	2,730	176,513 D		98.5%		100.0%
4	2004	282,039		—	219,260	FRANK, BARNEY*	62,779	219,260 D		77.7%		100.0%
4	2002	167,816		—	166,125	FRANK, BARNEY*	1,691	166,125 D		99.0%		100.0%
5	2006	162,272		—	159,120	MEEHAN, MARTIN T.*	3,152	159,120 D		98.1%		100.0%
5	2004	268,189	88,232	TIERNEY, THOMAS P.	179,652	MEEHAN, MARTIN T.*	305	91,420 D	32.9%	67.0%	32.9%	67.1%
5	2002	203,777	69,337	McCARTHY, CHARLES	122,562	MEEHAN, MARTIN T.*	11,878	53,225 D	34.0%	60.1%	36.1%	63.9%
6	2006	241,625	72,997	BARTON, RICHARD W.	168,056	TIERNEY, JOHN F.*	572	95,059 D	30.2%	69.6%	30.3%	69.7%
6	2004	305,522	91,597	O'MALLEY, STEPHEN P., JR.	213,458	TIERNEY, JOHN F.*	467	121,861 D	30.0%	69.9%	30.0%	70.0%
6	2002	238,615	75,462	SMITH, MARK C.	162,900	TIERNEY, JOHN F.*	253	87,438 D	31.6%	68.3%	31.7%	68.3%
7	2006	174,791		—	171,902	MARKEY, EDWARD J.*	2,889	171,902 D		98.3%		100.0%
7	2004	275,099	60,334	CHASE, KENNETH G.	202,399	MARKEY, EDWARD J.*	12,366	142,065 D	21.9%	73.6%	23.0%	77.0%
7	2002	174,037		—	170,968	MARKEY, EDWARD J.*	3,069	170,968 D		98.2%		100.0%
8	2006	138,455		—	125,515	CAPUANO, MICHAEL E.*	12,940	125,515 D		90.7%		100.0%
8	2004	168,081		—	165,852	CAPUANO, MICHAEL E.*	2,229	165,852 D		98.7%		100.0%
8	2002	112,356		—	111,861	CAPUANO, MICHAEL E.*	495	111,861 D		99.6%		100.0%
9	2006	217,036	47,114	ROBINSON, JACK E.	169,420	LYNCH, STEPHEN F.*	502	122,306 D	21.7%	78.1%	21.8%	78.2%
9	2004	220,312		—	218,167	LYNCH, STEPHEN F.*	2,145	218,167 D		99.0%		100.0%
9	2002	168,976		—	168,055	LYNCH, STEPHEN F.*	921	168,055 D		99.5%		100.0%
10	2006	267,202	78,439	BEATTY, JEFFREY K.	171,812	DELAHUNT, BILL*	16,951	93,373 D	29.4%	64.3%	31.3%	68.7%
10	2004	337,070	114,879	JONES, MICHAEL J.	222,013	DELAHUNT, BILL*	178	107,134 D	34.1%	65.9%	34.1%	65.9%
10	2002	259,002	79,624	GONZAGA, LUIS	179,238	DELAHUNT, BILL*	140	99,614 D	30.7%	69.2%	30.8%	69.2%
TOTAL	2006	1,923,657	198,550		1,632,307		92,800	1,433,757 D	10.3%	84.9%	10.8%	89.2%
TOTAL	2004	2,580,955	435,239		2,059,984		85,732	1,624,745 D	16.9%	79.8%	17.4%	82.6%
TOTAL	2002	1,840,871	290,484		1,528,634		21,753	1,238,150 D	15.8%	83.0%	16.0%	84.0%

An asterisk (*) denotes incumbent.

MASSACHUSETTS

GENERAL AND PRIMARY ELECTIONS

2006 GENERAL ELECTIONS

Governor   Other vote was 154,628 Independent (Christy Mihos); 43,193 Green-Rainbow (Grace Ross); 2,632 scattered write-in.

Senator   Other vote was 3,220 scattered write-in.

House   Other vote was:

CD 1	48,574 Unenrolled (William H. Szych); 253 scattered write-in.
CD 2	2,254 scattered write-in.
CD 3	1,983 scattered write-in.
CD 4	2,730 scattered write-in.
CD 5	3,152 scattered write-in.
CD 6	572 scattered write-in.
CD 7	2,889 scattered write-in.
CD 8	12,449 Socialist Workers (Laura Garza); 491 scattered write-in.
CD 9	502 scattered write-in.
CD 10	16,808 Independent (Peter A. White); 143 scattered write-in.

2006 PRIMARY ELECTIONS

Primary   September 19, 2006

Registration
(as of August 30, 2006)

Democratic	1,453,689
Republican	499,641
Other Parties	33,279
Unenrolled	1,948,063
TOTAL	3,934,672

Primary Type   Semi-open—Registered Democrats and Republican could vote only in their party's primary. "Unenrolled" voters could participate in either party's primary.

MASSACHUSETTS

GENERAL AND PRIMARY ELECTIONS

Note: An asterisk (*) denotes incumbent.

	REPUBLICAN PRIMARIES			DEMOCRATIC PRIMARIES		
Governor	Kerry Healey	68,799	96.3%	Deval L. Patrick	452,229	49.6%
	Scattered write-in	2,631	3.7%	Christopher F. Gabrieli	248,301	27.2%
				Thomas F. Reilly	211,031	23.1%
				Scattered write-in	787	0.1%
	TOTAL	71,430		TOTAL	912,348	
Senator	Kenneth G. Chase	35,595	50.6%	Edward M. Kennedy*	729,137	98.6%
	Kevin P. Scott	34,262	48.7%	Scattered write-in	10,149	1.4%
	Scattered write-in	550	0.8%			
	TOTAL	70,407		TOTAL	739,286	
Congressional District 1	No Republican candidate filed for the primary. There were 135 scattered write-in votes.			John W. Olver*	63,875	99.7%
				Scattered write-in	211	0.3%
				TOTAL	64,086	
Congressional District 2	No Republican candidate filed for the primary. There were 395 scattered write-in votes.			Richard E. Neal*	60,953	99.3%
				Scattered write-in	446	0.7%
				TOTAL	61,399	
Congressional District 3	No Republican candidate filed for the primary. There were 222 scattered write-in votes.			Jim McGovern*	64,756	99.4%
				Scattered write-in	370	0.6%
				TOTAL	65,126	
Congressional District 4	No Republican candidate filed for the primary. There were 145 write-in votes cast for Charles A. Morse, as well as 300 scattered write-in votes.			Barney Frank*	80,066	99.5%
				Scattered write-in	373	0.5%
				TOTAL	80,439	
Congressional District 5	No Republican candidate filed for the primary. There were 753 scattered write-in votes.			Martin T. Meehan*	62,052	99.3%
				Scattered write-in	422	0.7%
				TOTAL	62,474	
Congressional District 6	Richard W. Barton	6,051	98.7%	John F. Tierney*	71,530	98.8%
	Scattered write-in	80	1.3%	Scattered write-in	884	1.2%
	TOTAL	6,131		TOTAL	72,414	
Congressional District 7	No Republican candidate filed for the primary. There were 350 scattered write-in votes.			Edward J. Markey*	80,901	99.3%
				Scattered write-in	560	0.7%
				TOTAL	81,461	
Congressional District 8	No Republican candidate filed for the primary. There were 201 scattered write-in votes.			Michael E. Capuano*	56,482	98.9%
				Scattered write-in	645	1.1%
				TOTAL	57,127	
Congressional District 9	Jack E. Robinson	4,409	98.8%	Stephen F. Lynch*	75,323	77.1%
	Scattered write-in	52	1.2%	Philip Dunkelbarger	22,048	22.6%
				Scattered write-in	287	0.3%
	TOTAL	4,461		TOTAL	97,658	
Congressional District 10	Jeffrey K. Beatty	13,542	98.2%	Bill Delahunt*	82,020	99.5%
	Scattered write-in	255	1.8%	Scattered write-in	450	0.5%
	TOTAL	13,797		TOTAL	82,470	

MICHIGAN

Congressional districts first established for elections held in 2002
15 members

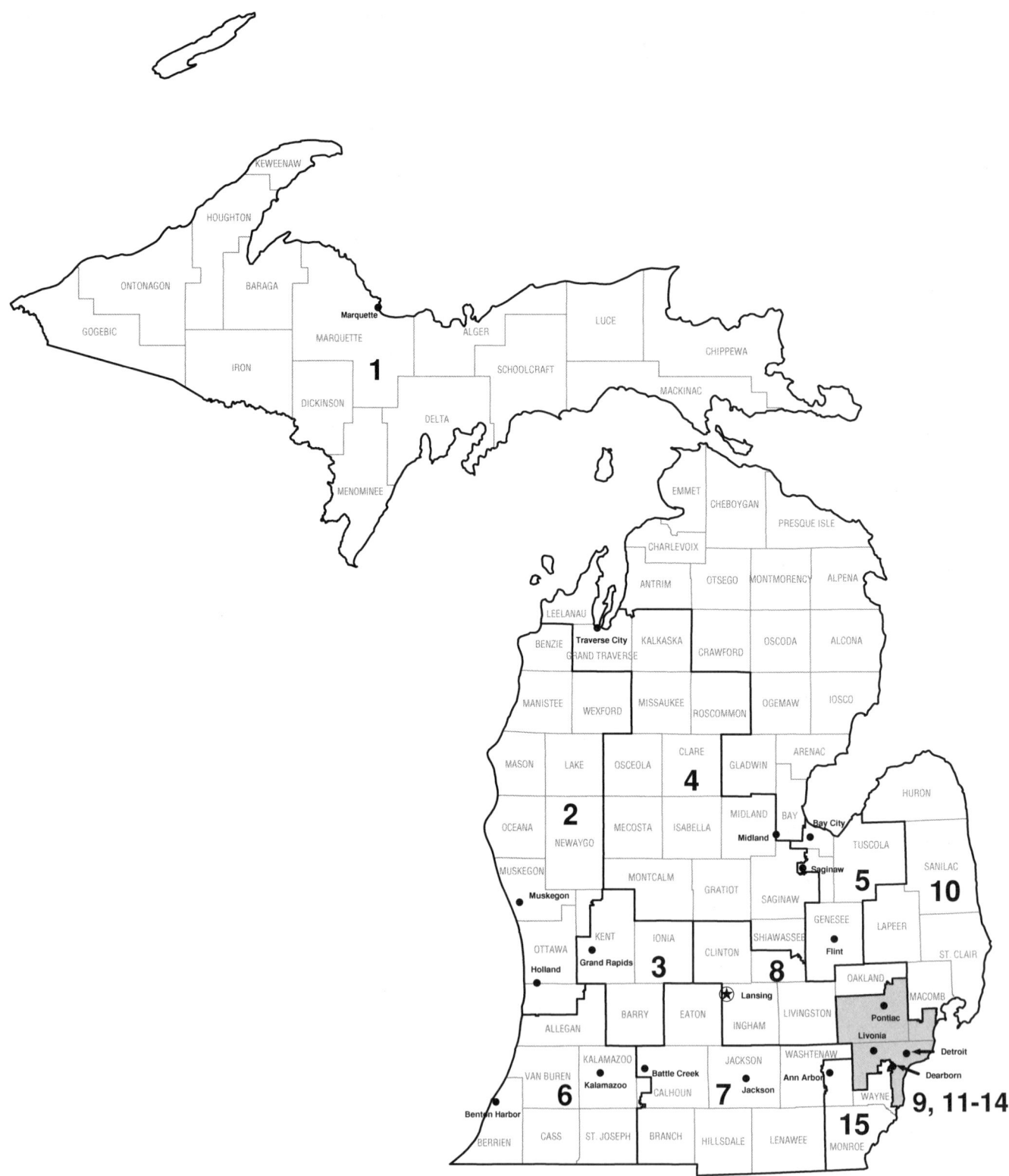

MICHIGAN

Detroit Area

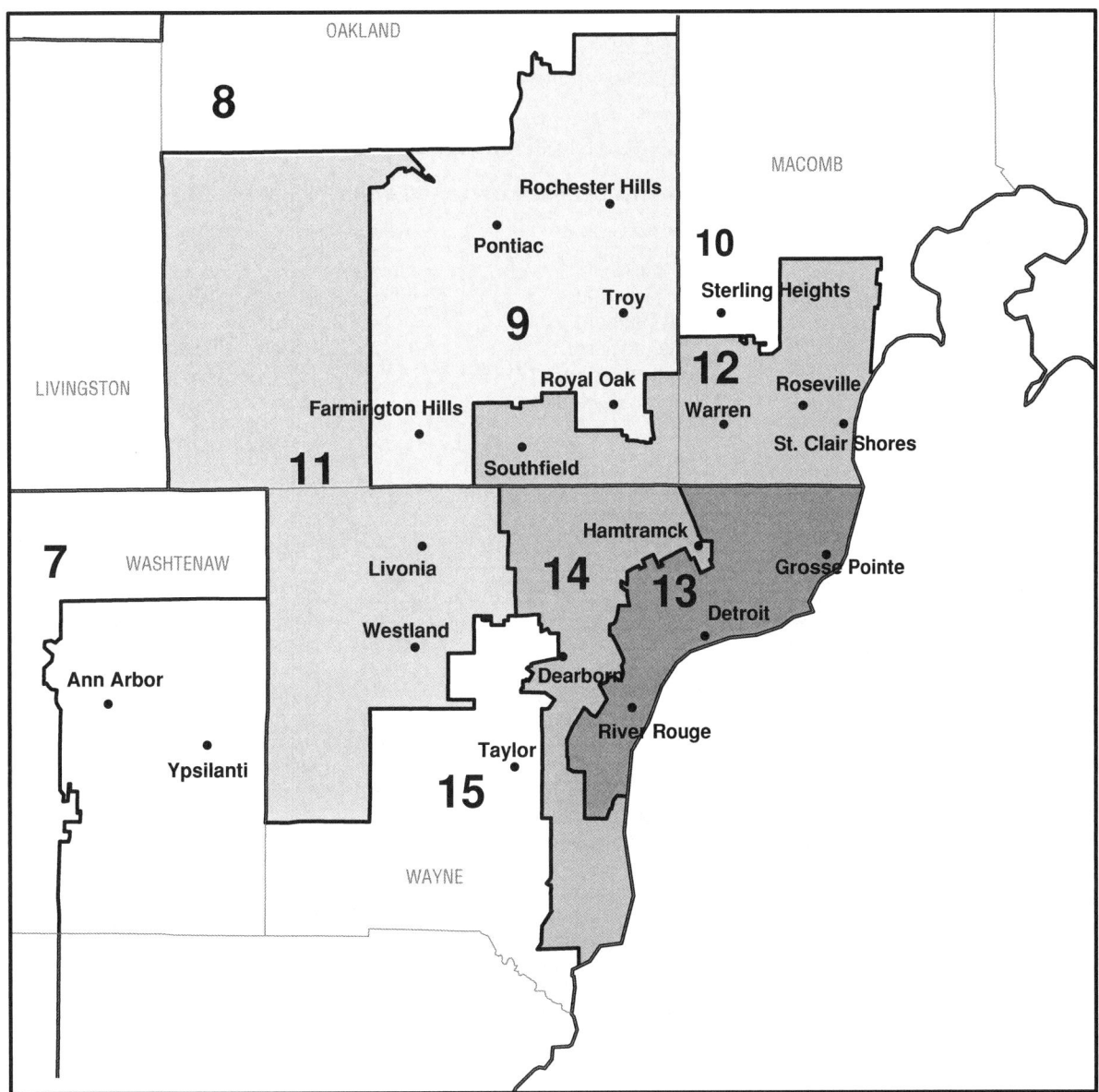

MICHIGAN

GOVERNOR

Jennifer M. Granholm (D). Reelected 2006 to a four-year term. Previously elected 2002.

SENATORS (2 Democrats)

Debbie Stabenow (D). Reelected 2006 to a six-year term. Previously elected 2000.

Carl Levin (D). Reelected 2002 to a six-year term. Previously elected 1996, 1990, 1984, 1978.

REPRESENTATIVES (9 Republicans, 6 Democrats)

1. Bart Stupak (D)	6. Fred Upton (R)	11. Thaddeus McCotter (R)
2. Peter Hoekstra (R)	7. Tim Walberg (R)	12. Sander M. Levin (D)
3. Vernon J. Ehlers (R)	8. Mike Rogers (R)	13. Carolyn Cheeks Kilpatrick (D)
4. Dave Camp (R)	9. Joe Knollenberg (R)	14. John Conyers Jr. (D)
5. Dale E. Kildee (D)	10. Candice S. Miller (R)	15. John D. Dingell (D)

POSTWAR VOTE FOR PRESIDENT

Year	Total Vote	Republican Vote	Republican Candidate	Democratic Vote	Democratic Candidate	Other Vote	Plurality	Total Vote Rep.	Total Vote Dem.	Major Vote Rep.	Major Vote Dem.
2004	4,839,252	2,313,746	Bush, George W.	2,479,183	Kerry, John	46,323	165,437 D	47.8%	51.2%	48.3%	51.7%
2000**	4,232,711	1,953,139	Bush, George W.	2,170,418	Gore, Al	109,154	217,279 D	46.1%	51.3%	47.4%	52.6%
1996**	3,848,844	1,481,212	Dole, Bob	1,989,653	Clinton, Bill	377,979	508,441 D	38.5%	51.7%	42.7%	57.3%
1992**	4,274,673	1,554,940	Bush, George	1,871,182	Clinton, Bill	848,551	316,242 D	36.4%	43.8%	45.4%	54.6%
1988	3,669,163	1,965,486	Bush, George	1,675,783	Dukakis, Michael S.	27,894	289,703 R	53.6%	45.7%	54.0%	46.0%
1984	3,801,658	2,251,571	Reagan, Ronald	1,529,638	Mondale, Walter F.	20,449	721,933 R	59.2%	40.2%	59.5%	40.5%
1980**	3,909,725	1,915,225	Reagan, Ronald	1,661,532	Carter, Jimmy	332,968	253,693 R	49.0%	42.5%	53.5%	46.5%
1976	3,653,749	1,893,742	Ford, Gerald R.	1,696,714	Carter, Jimmy	63,293	197,028 R	51.8%	46.4%	52.7%	47.3%
1972	3,489,727	1,961,721	Nixon, Richard M.	1,459,435	McGovern, George S.	68,571	502,286 R	56.2%	41.8%	57.3%	42.7%
1968**	3,306,250	1,370,665	Nixon, Richard M.	1,593,082	Humphrey, Hubert H.	342,503	222,417 D	41.5%	48.2%	46.2%	53.8%
1964	3,203,102	1,060,152	Goldwater, Barry M.	2,136,615	Johnson, Lyndon B.	6,335	1,076,463 D	33.1%	66.7%	33.2%	66.8%
1960	3,318,097	1,620,428	Nixon, Richard M.	1,687,269	Kennedy, John F.	10,400	66,841 D	48.8%	50.9%	49.0%	51.0%
1956	3,080,468	1,713,647	Eisenhower, Dwight D.	1,359,898	Stevenson, Adlai E.	6,923	353,749 R	55.6%	44.1%	55.8%	44.2%
1952	2,798,592	1,551,529	Eisenhower, Dwight D.	1,230,657	Stevenson, Adlai E.	16,406	320,872 R	55.4%	44.0%	55.8%	44.2%
1948	2,109,609	1,038,595	Dewey, Thomas E.	1,003,448	Truman, Harry S.	67,566	35,147 R	49.2%	47.6%	50.9%	49.1%

**In past elections, the other vote included: 2000 - 84,165 Green (Ralph Nader); 1996 - 336,670 Reform (Ross Perot); 1992 - 824,813 Independent (Ross Perot); 1980 - 275,223 Independent (John Anderson); 1968 - 331,968 American Independent (George Wallace).

MICHIGAN

POSTWAR VOTE FOR GOVERNOR

Year	Total Vote	Republican Vote	Republican Candidate	Democratic Vote	Democratic Candidate	Other Vote	Rep.-Dem. Plurality	Percentage Total Vote Rep.	Percentage Total Vote Dem.	Percentage Major Vote Rep.	Percentage Major Vote Dem.
2006	3,801,256	1,608,086	DeVos, Dick	2,142,513	Granholm, Jennifer M.	50,657	534,427 D	42.3%	56.4%	42.9%	57.1%
2002	3,177,565	1,506,104	Posthumus, Dick	1,633,796	Granholm, Jennifer M.	37,665	127,692 D	47.4%	51.4%	48.0%	52.0%
1998	3,027,104	1,883,005	Engler, John	1,143,574	Fieger, Geoffrey	525	739,431 R	62.2%	37.8%	62.2%	37.8%
1994	3,089,077	1,899,101	Engler, John	1,188,438	Wolpe, Howard	1,538	710,663 R	61.5%	38.5%	61.5%	38.5%
1990	2,564,563	1,276,134	Engler, John	1,258,539	Blanchard, James J.	29,890	17,595 R	49.8%	49.1%	50.3%	49.7%
1986	2,396,564	753,647	Lucas, William	1,632,138	Blanchard, James J.	10,779	878,491 D	31.4%	68.1%	31.6%	68.4%
1982	3,040,008	1,369,582	Headlee, Richard H.	1,561,291	Blanchard, James J.	109,135	191,709 D	45.1%	51.4%	46.7%	53.3%
1978	2,867,212	1,628,485	Milliken, William G.	1,237,256	Fitzgerald, William	1,471	391,229 R	56.8%	43.2%	56.8%	43.2%
1974	2,657,017	1,356,865	Milliken, William G.	1,242,247	Levin, Sander M.	57,905	114,618 R	51.1%	46.8%	52.2%	47.8%
1970	2,656,162	1,339,047	Milliken, William G.	1,294,638	Levin, Sander M.	22,477	44,409 R	50.4%	48.7%	50.8%	49.2%
1966**	2,461,909	1,490,430	Romney, George W.	963,383	Ferency, Zolton A.	8,096	527,047 R	60.5%	39.1%	60.7%	39.3%
1964	3,158,102	1,764,355	Romney, George W.	1,381,442	Staebler, Neil	12,305	382,913 R	55.9%	43.7%	56.1%	43.9%
1962	2,764,839	1,420,086	Romney, George W.	1,339,513	Swainson, John B.	5,240	80,573 R	51.4%	48.4%	51.5%	48.5%
1960	3,255,991	1,602,022	Bagwell, Paul D.	1,643,634	Swainson, John B.	10,335	41,612 D	49.2%	50.5%	49.4%	50.6%
1958	2,312,184	1,078,089	Bagwell, Paul D.	1,225,533	Williams, G. Mennen	8,562	147,444 D	46.6%	53.0%	46.8%	53.2%
1956	3,049,651	1,376,376	Cobo, Albert E.	1,666,689	Williams, G. Mennen	6,586	290,313 D	45.1%	54.7%	45.2%	54.8%
1954	2,187,027	963,300	Leonard, Donald S.	1,216,308	Williams, G. Mennen	7,419	253,008 D	44.0%	55.6%	44.2%	55.8%
1952	2,865,980	1,423,275	Alger, Fred M.	1,431,893	Williams, G. Mennen	10,812	8,618 D	49.7%	50.0%	49.8%	50.2%
1950	1,879,382	933,998	Kelly, Harry F.	935,152	Williams, G. Mennen	10,232	1,154 D	49.7%	49.8%	50.0%	50.0%
1948	2,113,122	964,810	Sigler, Kim	1,128,664	Williams, G. Mennen	19,648	163,854 D	45.7%	53.4%	46.1%	53.9%
1946	1,665,475	1,003,878	Sigler, Kim	644,540	Van Wagoner, Murray	17,057	359,338 R	60.3%	38.7%	60.9%	39.1%

**The term of office of Michigan's governor was increased from two to four years effective with the 1966 election.

POSTWAR VOTE FOR SENATOR

Year	Total Vote	Republican Vote	Republican Candidate	Democratic Vote	Democratic Candidate	Other Vote	Rep.-Dem. Plurality	Percentage Total Vote Rep.	Percentage Total Vote Dem.	Percentage Major Vote Rep.	Percentage Major Vote Dem.
2006	3,780,142	1,559,597	Bouchard, Michael	2,151,278	Stabenow, Debbie	69,267	591,681 D	41.3%	56.9%	42.0%	58.0%
2002	3,129,287	1,185,545	Raczkowski, Andrew	1,896,614	Levin, Carl	47,128	711,069 D	37.9%	60.6%	38.5%	61.5%
2000	4,167,685	1,994,693	Abraham, Spencer	2,061,952	Stabenow, Debbie	111,040	67,259 D	47.9%	49.5%	49.2%	50.8%
1996	3,762,575	1,500,106	Romney, Ronna	2,195,738	Levin, Carl	66,731	695,632 D	39.9%	58.4%	40.6%	59.4%
1994	3,043,385	1,578,770	Abraham, Spencer	1,300,960	Carr, M. Robert	163,655	277,810 R	51.9%	42.7%	54.8%	45.2%
1990	2,560,494	1,055,695	Schuette, Bill	1,471,753	Levin, Carl	33,046	416,058 D	41.2%	57.5%	41.8%	58.2%
1988	3,505,985	1,348,219	Dunn, Jim	2,116,865	Riegle, Donald W.	40,901	768,646 D	38.5%	60.4%	38.9%	61.1%
1984	3,700,938	1,745,302	Lousma, Jack	1,915,831	Levin, Carl	39,805	170,529 D	47.2%	51.8%	47.7%	52.3%
1982	2,994,334	1,223,288	Ruppe, Philip E.	1,728,793	Riegle, Donald W.	42,253	505,505 D	40.9%	57.7%	41.4%	58.6%
1978	2,846,630	1,362,165	Griffin, Robert P.	1,484,193	Levin, Carl	272	122,028 D	47.9%	52.1%	47.9%	52.1%
1976	3,490,664	1,635,087	Esch, Marvin L.	1,831,031	Riegle, Donald W.	24,546	195,944 D	46.8%	52.5%	47.2%	52.8%
1972	3,406,906	1,781,065	Griffin, Robert P.	1,577,178	Kelley, Frank J.	48,663	203,887 R	52.3%	46.3%	53.0%	47.0%
1970	2,610,839	858,470	Romney, Lenore	1,744,716	Hart, Philip A.	7,653	886,246 D	32.9%	66.8%	33.0%	67.0%
1966	2,439,365	1,363,530	Griffin, Robert P.	1,069,484	Williams, G. Mennen	6,351	294,046 R	55.9%	43.8%	56.0%	44.0%
1964	3,101,667	1,096,272	Peterson, Elly M.	1,996,912	Hart, Philip A.	8,483	900,640 D	35.3%	64.4%	35.4%	64.6%
1960	3,226,647	1,548,873	Bentley, Alvin M.	1,669,179	McNamara, Patrick V.	8,595	120,306 D	48.0%	51.7%	48.1%	51.9%
1958	2,271,644	1,046,963	Potter, Charles E.	1,216,966	Hart, Philip A.	7,715	170,003 D	46.1%	53.6%	46.2%	53.8%
1954	2,144,840	1,049,420	Ferguson, Homer	1,088,550	McNamara, Patrick V.	6,870	39,130 D	48.9%	50.8%	49.1%	50.9%
1952	2,821,133	1,428,352	Potter, Charles E.	1,383,416	Moody, Blair	9,365	44,936 R	50.6%	49.0%	50.8%	49.2%
1948	2,062,097	1,045,156	Ferguson, Homer	1,000,329	Hook, Frank E.	16,612	44,827 R	50.7%	48.5%	51.1%	48.9%
1946	1,618,720	1,085,570	Vandenberg, Arthur	517,923	Lee, James H.	15,227	567,647 R	67.1%	32.0%	67.7%	32.3%

MICHIGAN

GOVERNOR 2006

2000 Census Population	County	Total Vote	Republican	Democratic	Other	Rep.-Dem. Plurality	Percentage Total Vote Rep.	Dem.	Major Vote Rep.	Dem.
11,719	ALCONA	5,464	2,583	2,793	88	210 D	47.3%	51.1%	48.0%	52.0%
9,862	ALGER	3,766	1,422	2,285	59	863 D	37.8%	60.7%	38.4%	61.6%
105,665	ALLEGAN	44,715	24,571	19,586	558	4,985 R	55.0%	43.8%	55.6%	44.4%
31,314	ALPENA	12,030	4,689	7,187	154	2,498 D	39.0%	59.7%	39.5%	60.5%
23,110	ANTRIM	11,388	6,115	5,103	170	1,012 R	53.7%	44.8%	54.5%	45.5%
17,269	ARENAC	6,644	2,805	3,737	102	932 D	42.2%	56.2%	42.9%	57.1%
8,746	BARAGA	3,231	1,220	1,952	59	732 D	37.8%	60.4%	38.5%	61.5%
56,755	BARRY	25,306	12,826	12,086	394	740 R	50.7%	47.8%	51.5%	48.5%
110,157	BAY	46,466	17,502	28,286	678	10,784 D	37.7%	60.9%	38.2%	61.8%
15,998	BENZIE	8,247	3,764	4,352	131	588 D	45.6%	52.8%	46.4%	53.6%
162,453	BERRIEN	52,897	27,588	24,606	703	2,982 R	52.2%	46.5%	52.9%	47.1%
45,787	BRANCH	14,383	7,248	6,901	234	347 R	50.4%	48.0%	51.2%	48.8%
137,985	CALHOUN	47,094	19,725	26,674	695	6,949 D	41.9%	56.6%	42.5%	57.5%
51,104	CASS	16,520	7,994	8,302	224	308 D	48.4%	50.3%	49.1%	50.9%
26,090	CHARLEVOIX	11,126	5,621	5,237	268	384 R	50.5%	47.1%	51.8%	48.2%
26,448	CHEBOYGAN	11,560	5,891	5,457	212	434 R	51.0%	47.2%	51.9%	48.1%
38,543	CHIPPEWA	13,211	5,564	7,463	184	1,899 D	42.1%	56.5%	42.7%	57.3%
31,252	CLARE	11,743	5,456	6,068	219	612 D	46.5%	51.7%	47.3%	52.7%
64,753	CLINTON	32,362	14,459	17,528	375	3,069 D	44.7%	54.2%	45.2%	54.8%
14,273	CRAWFORD	5,803	2,765	2,932	106	167 D	47.6%	50.5%	48.5%	51.5%
38,520	DELTA	14,947	5,973	8,792	182	2,819 D	40.0%	58.8%	40.5%	59.5%
27,472	DICKINSON	9,768	4,372	5,251	145	879 D	44.8%	53.8%	45.4%	54.6%
103,655	EATON	46,161	18,977	26,611	573	7,634 D	41.1%	57.6%	41.6%	58.4%
31,437	EMMET	14,071	7,442	6,401	228	1,041 R	52.9%	45.5%	53.8%	46.2%
436,141	GENESEE	163,978	54,089	107,848	2,041	53,759 D	33.0%	65.8%	33.4%	66.6%
26,023	GLADWIN	10,761	4,962	5,588	211	626 D	46.1%	51.9%	47.0%	53.0%
17,370	GOGEBIC	6,161	2,216	3,821	124	1,605 D	36.0%	62.0%	36.7%	63.3%
77,654	GRAND TRAVERSE	36,685	18,711	17,416	558	1,295 R	51.0%	47.5%	51.8%	48.2%
42,285	GRATIOT	13,877	6,156	7,548	173	1,392 D	44.4%	54.4%	44.9%	55.1%
46,527	HILLSDALE	15,694	9,005	6,408	281	2,597 R	57.4%	40.8%	58.4%	41.6%
36,016	HOUGHTON	11,972	5,275	6,497	200	1,222 D	44.1%	54.3%	44.8%	55.2%
36,079	HURON	14,221	7,037	7,002	182	35 R	49.5%	49.2%	50.1%	49.9%
279,320	INGHAM	105,085	34,037	69,820	1,228	35,783 D	32.4%	66.4%	32.8%	67.2%
61,518	IONIA	22,456	10,470	11,700	286	1,230 D	46.6%	52.1%	47.2%	52.8%
27,339	IOSCO	11,221	5,006	6,043	172	1,037 D	44.6%	53.9%	45.3%	54.7%
13,138	IRON	4,838	1,914	2,843	81	929 D	39.6%	58.8%	40.2%	59.8%
63,351	ISABELLA	18,887	7,916	10,676	295	2,760 D	41.9%	56.5%	42.6%	57.4%
158,422	JACKSON	56,828	27,536	28,450	842	914 D	48.5%	50.1%	49.2%	50.8%
238,603	KALAMAZOO	94,204	36,942	56,044	1,218	19,102 D	39.2%	59.5%	39.7%	60.3%
16,571	KALKASKA	6,686	3,614	2,945	127	669 R	54.1%	44.0%	55.1%	44.9%
574,335	KENT	240,782	128,471	109,940	2,371	18,531 R	53.4%	45.7%	53.9%	46.1%
2,301	KEWEENAW	1,161	507	632	22	125 D	43.7%	54.4%	44.5%	55.5%
11,333	LAKE	4,520	2,203	2,228	89	25 D	48.7%	49.3%	49.7%	50.3%
87,904	LAPEER	36,217	18,951	16,580	686	2,371 R	52.3%	45.8%	53.3%	46.7%
21,119	LEELANAU	12,081	5,708	6,212	161	504 D	47.2%	51.4%	47.9%	52.1%
98,890	LENAWEE	34,590	17,662	16,295	633	1,367 R	51.1%	47.1%	52.0%	48.0%
156,951	LIVINGSTON	77,988	44,495	32,406	1,087	12,089 R	57.1%	41.6%	57.9%	42.1%
7,024	LUCE	2,312	789	1,495	28	706 D	34.1%	64.7%	34.5%	65.5%
11,943	MACKINAC	5,483	2,540	2,879	64	339 D	46.3%	52.5%	46.9%	53.1%
788,149	MACOMB	315,433	145,968	164,515	4,950	18,547 D	46.3%	52.2%	47.0%	53.0%
24,527	MANISTEE	10,599	4,672	5,765	162	1,093 D	44.1%	54.4%	44.8%	55.2%
64,634	MARQUETTE	24,405	7,773	16,341	291	8,568 D	31.9%	67.0%	32.2%	67.8%
28,274	MASON	12,227	5,913	6,173	141	260 D	48.4%	50.5%	48.9%	51.1%
40,553	MECOSTA	14,779	7,547	7,045	187	502 R	51.1%	47.7%	51.7%	48.3%
25,326	MENOMINEE	7,668	3,397	4,114	157	717 D	44.3%	53.7%	45.2%	54.8%
82,874	MIDLAND	34,751	17,007	17,218	526	211 D	48.9%	49.5%	49.7%	50.3%
14,478	MISSAUKEE	6,202	3,902	2,211	89	1,691 R	62.9%	35.6%	63.8%	36.2%
145,945	MONROE	55,627	24,828	29,975	824	5,147 D	44.6%	53.9%	45.3%	54.7%
61,266	MONTCALM	22,442	10,178	11,967	297	1,789 D	45.4%	53.3%	46.0%	54.0%
10,315	MONTMORENCY	4,611	2,394	2,128	89	266 R	51.9%	46.2%	52.9%	47.1%

MICHIGAN

GOVERNOR 2006

2000 Census Population	County	Total Vote	Republican	Democratic	Other	Rep.-Dem. Plurality	Percentage			
							Total Vote		Major Vote	
							Rep.	Dem.	Rep.	Dem.
170,200	MUSKEGON	63,167	22,403	40,142	622	17,739 D	35.5%	63.5%	35.8%	64.2%
47,874	NEWAYGO	19,006	9,847	8,932	227	915 R	51.8%	47.0%	52.4%	47.6%
1,194,156	OAKLAND	510,328	227,708	275,757	6,863	48,049 D	44.6%	54.0%	45.2%	54.8%
26,873	OCEANA	10,373	4,835	5,413	125	578 D	46.6%	52.2%	47.2%	52.8%
21,645	OGEMAW	8,813	4,109	4,561	143	452 D	46.6%	51.8%	47.4%	52.6%
7,818	ONTONAGON	3,148	1,318	1,782	48	464 D	41.9%	56.6%	42.5%	57.5%
23,197	OSCEOLA	9,304	5,274	3,884	146	1,390 R	56.7%	41.7%	57.6%	42.4%
9,418	OSCODA	3,553	1,850	1,638	65	212 R	52.1%	46.1%	53.0%	47.0%
23,301	OTSEGO	10,277	5,644	4,465	168	1,179 R	54.9%	43.4%	55.8%	44.2%
238,314	OTTAWA	109,351	71,220	37,055	1,076	34,165 R	65.1%	33.9%	65.8%	34.2%
14,411	PRESQUE ISLE	6,381	2,775	3,515	91	740 D	43.5%	55.1%	44.1%	55.9%
25,469	ROSCOMMON	11,656	5,294	6,139	223	845 D	45.4%	52.7%	46.3%	53.7%
210,039	SAGINAW	81,250	30,702	49,567	981	18,865 D	37.8%	61.0%	38.2%	61.8%
164,235	ST. CLAIR	62,635	31,170	30,369	1,096	801 R	49.8%	48.5%	50.7%	49.3%
62,422	ST. JOSEPH	19,075	9,972	8,818	285	1,154 R	52.3%	46.2%	53.1%	46.9%
44,547	SANILAC	16,430	9,290	6,897	243	2,393 R	56.5%	42.0%	57.4%	42.6%
8,903	SCHOOLCRAFT	3,426	1,395	1,973	58	578 D	40.7%	57.6%	41.4%	58.6%
71,687	SHIAWASSEE	29,484	12,357	16,682	445	4,325 D	41.9%	56.6%	42.6%	57.4%
58,266	TUSCOLA	22,577	10,592	11,634	351	1,042 D	46.9%	51.5%	47.7%	52.3%
76,263	VAN BUREN	26,369	11,403	14,582	384	3,179 D	43.2%	55.3%	43.9%	56.1%
322,895	WASHTENAW	134,140	41,080	91,219	1,841	50,139 D	30.6%	68.0%	31.1%	68.9%
2,061,162	WAYNE	641,965	175,037	459,558	7,370	284,521 D	27.3%	71.6%	27.6%	72.4%
30,484	WEXFORD	12,213	6,448	5,573	192	875 R	52.8%	45.6%	53.6%	46.4%
9,938,444	TOTAL	3,801,256	1,608,086	2,142,513	50,657	534,427 D	42.3%	56.4%	42.9%	57.1%

MICHIGAN

SENATOR 2006

2000 Census Population	County	Total Vote	Republican	Democratic	Other	Rep.-Dem. Plurality		Percentage			
								Total Vote		Major Vote	
								Rep.	Dem.	Rep.	Dem.
11,719	ALCONA	5,442	2,196	3,158	88	962	D	40.4%	58.0%	41.0%	59.0%
9,862	ALGER	3,742	1,407	2,257	78	850	D	37.6%	60.3%	38.4%	61.6%
105,665	ALLEGAN	44,456	24,675	18,854	927	5,821	R	55.5%	42.4%	56.7%	43.3%
31,314	ALPENA	11,978	3,971	7,832	175	3,861	D	33.2%	65.4%	33.6%	66.4%
23,110	ANTRIM	11,353	5,884	5,224	245	660	R	51.8%	46.0%	53.0%	47.0%
17,269	ARENAC	6,642	2,588	3,913	141	1,325	D	39.0%	58.9%	39.8%	60.2%
8,746	BARAGA	3,207	1,211	1,928	68	717	D	37.8%	60.1%	38.6%	61.4%
56,755	BARRY	25,186	12,949	11,626	611	1,323	R	51.4%	46.2%	52.7%	47.3%
110,157	BAY	46,273	16,540	28,992	741	12,452	D	35.7%	62.7%	36.3%	63.7%
15,998	BENZIE	8,217	3,715	4,323	179	608	D	45.2%	52.6%	46.2%	53.8%
162,453	BERRIEN	52,196	26,719	24,351	1,126	2,368	R	51.2%	46.7%	52.3%	47.7%
45,787	BRANCH	14,285	6,872	7,014	399	142	D	48.1%	49.1%	49.5%	50.5%
137,985	CALHOUN	46,667	19,238	26,306	1,123	7,068	D	41.2%	56.4%	42.2%	57.8%
51,104	CASS	16,324	7,765	8,147	412	382	D	47.6%	49.9%	48.8%	51.2%
26,090	CHARLEVOIX	11,303	5,427	5,577	299	150	D	48.0%	49.3%	49.3%	50.7%
26,448	CHEBOYGAN	11,513	5,216	6,051	246	835	D	45.3%	52.6%	46.3%	53.7%
38,543	CHIPPEWA	13,199	5,247	7,740	212	2,493	D	39.8%	58.6%	40.4%	59.6%
31,252	CLARE	11,719	4,595	6,883	241	2,288	D	39.2%	58.7%	40.0%	60.0%
64,753	CLINTON	32,129	15,267	16,345	517	1,078	D	47.5%	50.9%	48.3%	51.7%
14,273	CRAWFORD	5,768	2,507	3,113	148	606	D	43.5%	54.0%	44.6%	55.4%
38,520	DELTA	14,883	5,784	8,916	183	3,132	D	38.9%	59.9%	39.3%	60.7%
27,472	DICKINSON	9,828	4,177	5,484	167	1,307	D	42.5%	55.8%	43.2%	56.8%
103,655	EATON	45,874	19,762	25,227	885	5,465	D	43.1%	55.0%	43.9%	56.1%
31,437	EMMET	14,025	7,037	6,691	297	346	R	50.2%	47.7%	51.3%	48.7%
436,141	GENESEE	163,493	51,612	109,424	2,457	57,812	D	31.6%	66.9%	32.0%	68.0%
26,023	GLADWIN	10,918	4,433	6,288	197	1,855	D	40.6%	57.6%	41.3%	58.7%
17,370	GOGEBIC	6,126	2,054	3,952	120	1,898	D	33.5%	64.5%	34.2%	65.8%
77,654	GRAND TRAVERSE	36,415	18,655	16,989	771	1,666	R	51.2%	46.7%	52.3%	47.7%
42,285	GRATIOT	13,798	6,159	7,405	234	1,246	D	44.6%	53.7%	45.4%	54.6%
46,527	HILLSDALE	15,496	8,310	6,746	440	1,564	R	53.6%	43.5%	55.2%	44.8%
36,016	HOUGHTON	11,951	5,286	6,398	267	1,112	D	44.2%	53.5%	45.2%	54.8%
36,079	HURON	14,130	6,155	7,785	190	1,630	D	43.6%	55.1%	44.2%	55.8%
279,320	INGHAM	104,572	34,811	67,756	2,005	32,945	D	33.3%	64.8%	33.9%	66.1%
61,518	IONIA	22,304	10,562	11,259	483	697	D	47.4%	50.5%	48.4%	51.6%
27,339	IOSCO	11,151	4,523	6,405	223	1,882	D	40.6%	57.4%	41.4%	58.6%
13,138	IRON	4,824	1,790	2,941	93	1,151	D	37.1%	61.0%	37.8%	62.2%
63,351	ISABELLA	18,792	7,364	11,035	393	3,671	D	39.2%	58.7%	40.0%	60.0%
158,422	JACKSON	56,432	25,559	29,507	1,366	3,948	D	45.3%	52.3%	46.4%	53.6%
238,603	KALAMAZOO	93,548	39,516	52,189	1,843	12,673	D	42.2%	55.8%	43.1%	56.9%
16,571	KALKASKA	6,634	3,283	3,180	171	103	R	49.5%	47.9%	50.8%	49.2%
574,335	KENT	239,253	127,313	108,089	3,851	19,224	R	53.2%	45.2%	54.1%	45.9%
2,301	KEWEENAW	1,151	487	631	33	144	D	42.3%	54.8%	43.6%	56.4%
11,333	LAKE	4,500	1,885	2,509	106	624	D	41.9%	55.8%	42.9%	57.1%
87,904	LAPEER	35,965	17,297	17,810	858	513	D	48.1%	49.5%	49.3%	50.7%
21,119	LEELANAU	12,081	5,818	5,984	279	166	D	48.2%	49.5%	49.3%	50.7%
98,890	LENAWEE	34,206	16,317	17,100	789	783	D	47.7%	50.0%	48.8%	51.2%
156,951	LIVINGSTON	77,650	42,292	34,026	1,332	8,266	R	54.5%	43.8%	55.4%	44.6%
7,024	LUCE	2,287	885	1,349	53	464	D	38.7%	59.0%	39.6%	60.4%
11,943	MACKINAC	5,473	2,367	3,031	75	664	D	43.2%	55.4%	43.8%	56.2%
788,149	MACOMB	313,730	135,676	171,971	6,083	36,295	D	43.2%	54.8%	44.1%	55.9%
24,527	MANISTEE	10,576	4,335	6,036	205	1,701	D	41.0%	57.1%	41.8%	58.2%
64,634	MARQUETTE	24,354	7,971	15,970	413	7,999	D	32.7%	65.6%	33.3%	66.7%
28,274	MASON	12,161	5,562	6,376	223	814	D	45.7%	52.4%	46.6%	53.4%
40,553	MECOSTA	14,731	6,915	7,550	266	635	D	46.9%	51.3%	47.8%	52.2%
25,326	MENOMINEE	7,531	3,050	4,306	175	1,256	D	40.5%	57.2%	41.5%	58.5%
82,874	MIDLAND	34,641	16,757	17,366	518	609	D	48.4%	50.1%	49.1%	50.9%
14,478	MISSAUKEE	6,185	3,564	2,504	117	1,060	R	57.6%	40.5%	58.7%	41.3%
145,945	MONROE	54,829	22,347	31,431	1,051	9,084	D	40.8%	57.3%	41.6%	58.4%
61,266	MONTCALM	22,342	10,080	11,784	478	1,704	D	45.1%	52.7%	46.1%	53.9%
10,315	MONTMORENCY	4,578	2,105	2,361	112	256	D	46.0%	51.6%	47.1%	52.9%

MICHIGAN

SENATOR 2006

2000 Census Population	County	Total Vote	Republican	Democratic	Other	Rep.-Dem. Plurality	Percentage			
							Total Vote		Major Vote	
							Rep.	Dem.	Rep.	Dem.
170,200	MUSKEGON	62,693	22,670	39,060	963	16,390 D	36.2%	62.3%	36.7%	63.3%
47,874	NEWAYGO	18,926	9,647	8,879	400	768 R	51.0%	46.9%	52.1%	47.9%
1,194,156	OAKLAND	507,911	228,358	270,623	8,930	42,265 D	45.0%	53.3%	45.8%	54.2%
26,873	OCEANA	10,292	4,837	5,250	205	413 D	47.0%	51.0%	48.0%	52.0%
21,645	OGEMAW	8,753	3,524	5,063	166	1,539 D	40.3%	57.8%	41.0%	59.0%
7,818	ONTONAGON	3,140	1,175	1,876	89	701 D	37.4%	59.7%	38.5%	61.5%
23,197	OSCEOLA	9,278	4,692	4,390	196	302 R	50.6%	47.3%	51.7%	48.3%
9,418	OSCODA	3,537	1,691	1,777	69	86 D	47.8%	50.2%	48.8%	51.2%
23,301	OTSEGO	10,218	5,027	4,989	202	38 R	49.2%	48.8%	50.2%	49.8%
238,314	OTTAWA	108,845	71,706	35,511	1,628	36,195 R	65.9%	32.6%	66.9%	33.1%
14,411	PRESQUE ISLE	6,378	2,532	3,737	109	1,205 D	39.7%	58.6%	40.4%	59.6%
25,469	ROSCOMMON	11,650	4,692	6,723	235	2,031 D	40.3%	57.7%	41.1%	58.9%
210,039	SAGINAW	80,746	30,520	49,232	994	18,712 D	37.8%	61.0%	38.3%	61.7%
164,235	ST. CLAIR	62,299	27,262	33,791	1,246	6,529 D	43.8%	54.2%	44.7%	55.3%
62,422	ST. JOSEPH	18,885	9,604	8,855	426	749 R	50.9%	46.9%	52.0%	48.0%
44,547	SANILAC	16,352	8,132	7,918	302	214 R	49.7%	48.4%	50.7%	49.3%
8,903	SCHOOLCRAFT	3,415	1,309	2,042	64	733 D	38.3%	59.8%	39.1%	60.9%
71,687	SHIAWASSEE	29,381	12,486	16,358	537	3,872 D	42.5%	55.7%	43.3%	56.7%
58,266	TUSCOLA	22,496	9,959	12,100	437	2,141 D	44.3%	53.8%	45.1%	54.9%
76,263	VAN BUREN	26,207	11,479	14,201	527	2,722 D	43.8%	54.2%	44.7%	55.3%
322,895	WASHTENAW	133,521	40,919	89,788	2,814	48,869 D	30.6%	67.2%	31.3%	68.7%
2,061,162	WAYNE	638,034	167,500	459,843	10,691	292,343 D	26.3%	72.1%	26.7%	73.3%
30,484	WEXFORD	12,168	6,032	5,877	259	155 R	49.6%	48.3%	50.7%	49.3%
9,938,444	TOTAL	3,780,142	1,559,597	2,151,278	69,267	591,681 D	41.3%	56.9%	42.0%	58.0%

MICHIGAN

HOUSE OF REPRESENTATIVES

CD	Year	Total Vote	Republican Vote	Republican Candidate	Democratic Vote	Democratic Candidate	Other Vote	Rep.-Dem. Plurality	Total Vote Rep.	Total Vote Dem.	Major Vote Rep.	Major Vote Dem.
1	2006	259,927	72,753	HOOPER, DON	180,448	STUPAK, BART*	6,726	107,695 D	28.0%	69.4%	28.7%	71.3%
1	2004	322,674	105,706	HOOPER, DON	211,571	STUPAK, BART*	5,397	105,865 D	32.8%	65.6%	33.3%	66.7%
1	2002	222,687	69,254	HOOPER, DON	150,701	STUPAK, BART*	2,732	81,447 D	31.1%	67.7%	31.5%	68.5%
2	2006	275,394	183,006	HOEKSTRA, PETER*	86,950	KOTOS, KIMON	5,438	96,056 R	66.5%	31.6%	67.8%	32.2%
2	2004	325,005	225,343	HOEKSTRA, PETER*	94,040	KOTOS, KIMON	5,622	131,303 R	69.3%	28.9%	70.6%	29.4%
2	2002	222,907	156,937	HOEKSTRA, PETER*	61,749	WRISLEY, JEFF	4,221	95,188 R	70.4%	27.7%	71.8%	28.2%
3	2006	271,352	171,212	EHLERS, VERNON J.*	93,846	RINCK, JAMES	6,294	77,366 R	63.1%	34.6%	64.6%	35.4%
3	2004	322,103	214,465	EHLERS, VERNON J.*	101,395	HICKEY, PETER	6,243	113,070 R	66.6%	31.5%	67.9%	32.1%
3	2002	218,855	153,131	EHLERS, VERNON J.*	61,987	LYNNES, KATHRYN	3,737	91,144 R	70.0%	28.3%	71.2%	28.8%
4	2006	264,245	160,041	CAMP, DAVE*	100,260	HUCKLEBERRY, MIKE	3,944	59,781 R	60.6%	37.9%	61.5%	38.5%
4	2004	318,924	205,274	CAMP, DAVE*	110,885	HUCKLEBERRY, MIKE	2,765	94,389 R	64.4%	34.8%	64.9%	35.1%
4	2002	218,573	149,090	CAMP, DAVE*	65,950	HOLLENBECK, LAWRENCE	3,533	83,140 R	68.2%	30.2%	69.3%	30.7%
5	2006	241,691	60,967	KLAMMER, ERIC	176,171	KILDEE, DALE E.*	4,553	115,204 D	25.2%	72.9%	25.7%	74.3%
5	2004	309,915	96,934	KIRKWOOD, MYRAH	208,163	KILDEE, DALE E.*	4,818	111,229 D	31.3%	67.2%	31.8%	68.2%
5	2002	173,339		—	158,709	KILDEE, DALE E.*	14,630	158,709 D		91.6%		100.0%
6	2006	234,583	142,125	UPTON, FRED*	88,978	CLARK, KIM	3,480	53,147 R	60.6%	37.9%	61.5%	38.5%
6	2004	302,158	197,425	UPTON, FRED*	97,978	ELLIOTT, SCOTT	6,755	99,447 R	65.3%	32.4%	66.8%	33.2%
6	2002	183,517	126,936	UPTON, FRED*	53,793	GIGUERE, GARY JR.	2,788	73,143 R	69.2%	29.3%	70.2%	29.8%
7	2006	245,026	122,348	WALBERG, TIM	112,665	RENIER, SHARON	10,013	9,683 R	49.9%	46.0%	52.1%	47.9%
7	2004	301,642	176,053	SCHWARZ, JOE	109,527	RENIER, SHARON	16,062	66,526 R	58.4%	36.3%	61.6%	38.4%
7	2002	203,069	121,142	SMITH, NICK*	78,412	SIMPSON, MIKE	3,515	42,730 R	59.7%	38.6%	60.7%	39.3%
8	2006	284,471	157,237	ROGERS, MIKE*	122,107	MARCINKOWSKI, JIM	5,127	35,130 R	55.3%	42.9%	56.3%	43.7%
8	2004	340,423	207,925	ROGERS, MIKE*	125,619	ALEXANDER, ROBERT	6,879	82,306 R	61.1%	36.9%	62.3%	37.7%
8	2002	230,597	156,525	ROGERS, MIKE*	70,920	McALPINE, FRANK	3,152	85,605 R	67.9%	30.8%	68.8%	31.2%
9	2006	276,180	142,390	KNOLLENBERG, JOE*	127,620	SKINNER, NANCY	6,170	14,770 R	51.6%	46.2%	52.7%	47.3%
9	2004	340,799	199,210	KNOLLENBERG, JOE*	134,764	REIFMAN, STEVEN	6,825	64,446 R	58.5%	39.5%	59.6%	40.4%
9	2002	242,880	141,102	KNOLLENBERG, JOE*	96,856	FINK, DAVID	4,922	44,246 R	58.1%	39.9%	59.3%	40.7%
10	2006	270,421	179,072	MILLER, CANDICE S.*	84,689	DENISON, ROBERT	6,660	94,383 R	66.2%	31.3%	67.9%	32.1%
10	2004	331,868	227,720	MILLER, CANDICE S.*	98,029	CASEY, ROB	6,119	129,691 R	68.6%	29.5%	69.9%	30.1%
10	2002	216,928	137,339	MILLER, CANDICE S.	77,053	MARLINGA, CARL	2,536	60,286 R	63.3%	35.5%	64.1%	35.9%
11	2006	265,784	143,658	McCOTTER, THADDEUS*	114,248	TRUPIANO, TONY	7,878	29,410 R	54.1%	43.0%	55.7%	44.3%
11	2004	327,216	186,431	McCOTTER, THADDEUS*	134,301	TRURAN, PHILLIP	6,484	52,130 R	57.0%	41.0%	58.1%	41.9%
11	2002	220,405	126,050	McCOTTER, THADDEUS	87,402	KELLEY, KEVIN	6,953	38,648 R	57.2%	39.7%	59.1%	40.9%
12	2006	240,115	62,689	SHAFER, RANDELL	168,494	LEVIN, SANDER M.*	8,932	105,805 D	26.1%	70.2%	27.1%	72.9%
12	2004	304,134	88,256	SHAFER, RANDELL	210,827	LEVIN, SANDER M.*	5,051	122,571 D	29.0%	69.3%	29.5%	70.5%
12	2002	206,528	61,502	DEAN, HARVEY	140,970	LEVIN, SANDER M.*	4,056	79,468 D	29.8%	68.3%	30.4%	69.6%
13	2006	126,323		—	126,308	KILPATRICK, CAROLYN CHEEKS*	15	126,308 D		100.0%		100.0%
13	2004	221,654	40,935	CASSELL, CYNTHIA	173,246	KILPATRICK, CAROLYN CHEEKS*	7,473	132,311 D	18.5%	78.2%	19.1%	80.9%
13	2002	131,941		—	120,869	KILPATRICK, CAROLYN CHEEKS*	11,072	120,869 D		91.6%		100.0%
14	2006	186,122	27,367	MILES, CHAD	158,755	CONYERS, JOHN JR.*		131,388 D	14.7%	85.3%	14.7%	85.3%
14	2004	254,580	35,089	PEDRAZA, VERONICA	213,681	CONYERS, JOHN JR.*	5,810	178,592 D	13.8%	83.9%	14.1%	85.9%
14	2002	174,608	26,544	STONE, DAVE	145,285	CONYERS, JOHN JR.*	2,779	118,741 D	15.2%	83.2%	15.4%	84.6%
15	2006	206,868		—	181,946	DINGELL, JOHN D.*	24,922	181,946 D		88.0%		100.0%
15	2004	307,963	81,828	REAMER, DAWN	218,409	DINGELL, JOHN D.*	7,726	136,581 D	26.6%	70.9%	27.3%	72.7%
15	2002	189,063	48,626	KALTENBACH, MARTIN	136,518	DINGELL, JOHN D.*	3,919	87,892 D	25.7%	72.2%	26.3%	73.7%
TOTAL	2006	3,648,502	1,624,865		1,923,485		100,152	298,620 D	44.5%	52.7%	45.8%	54.2%
TOTAL	2004	4,631,058	2,288,594		2,242,435		100,029	46,159 R	49.4%	48.4%	50.5%	49.5%
TOTAL	2002	3,055,897	1,474,178		1,507,174		74,545	32,996 D	48.2%	49.3%	49.4%	50.6%

An asterisk (*) denotes incumbent.

MICHIGAN

GENERAL AND PRIMARY ELECTIONS

2006 GENERAL ELECTIONS

Governor   Other vote was 23,524 Libertarian (Gregory Creswell); 20,009 Green (Douglas Campbell); 7,087 U.S. Taxpayers (Bhagwan Dashairya); 29 write-in (Angelo Brown); 7 write-in (Bob Jones); 1 write-in (Timothy Wellsted).

Senator   Other vote was 27,012 Libertarian (Leonard Schwartz); 23,890 Green (David Sole); 18,341 U.S. Taxpayers (W. FitzSimons); 24 write-in (Bret McAtee).

House   Other vote was:

CD 1	2,278 U.S. Taxpayers (Joshua Warren); 2,252 Green (David Newland); 2,196 Libertarian (Ken Proctor).
CD 2	2,720 U.S. Taxpayers (Ronald Graeser); 2,718 Libertarian (Steven Van Til).
CD 3	3,702 Libertarian (Jeff Steinport); 2,592 Green (Rodger Gurk).
CD 4	2,003 U.S. Taxpayers (John Emerick); 1,941 Libertarian (Allitta Hren).
CD 5	2,294 Green (Ken Mathenia); 2,259 Libertarian (Steve Samoranski II).
CD 6	3,480 Libertarian (Kenneth Howe).
CD 7	3,788 Libertarian (Robert Hutchinson); 3,611 U.S. Taxpayers (David Horn); 2,614 write-in (Joe Schwarz).
CD 8	2,765 Libertarian (Dick Gach); 2,362 Green (Aaron Stuttman).
CD 9	3,702 Libertarian (Adam Goodman); 2,468 Green (Matthew Abel).
CD 10	2,875 Libertarian (Mark Byrne); 1,897 Green (Candace Caveny); 1,888 U.S. Taxpayers (F. Gualdoni).
CD 11	4,340 Libertarian (John Tatar); 3,538 U.S. Taxpayers (Charles Tackett).
CD 12	3,259 Libertarian (Andy Lecureaux); 2,076 U.S. Taxpayers (Les Townsend); 1,862 No Party Affiliation (Jerome White); 1,735 Green (Art Myatt).
CD 13	15 write-in (John Davenport).
CD 14	
CD 15	9,447 Green (Aimee Smith); 8,410 Libertarian (Gregory Stempfle); 7,064 U.S. Taxpayers (Robert Czak); 1 write-in (Mario Fundarski).

2006 PRIMARY ELECTIONS

Primary	August 8, 2006	**Registration** (as of July 10, 2006)	7,113,246	No Party Registration

Primary Type   Open—Any registered voter could participate in the primary of either party.

MICHIGAN

GENERAL AND PRIMARY ELECTIONS

Note: An asterisk (*) denotes incumbent.

	REPUBLICAN PRIMARIES			DEMOCRATIC PRIMARIES		
Governor	Dick DeVos	581,404	100.0%	Jennifer M. Granholm*	531,322	100.0%
	Louis Boven (write-in)	119				
	TOTAL	581,523				
Senator	Michael Bouchard	360,409	60.5%	Debbie Stabenow*	513,438	100.0%
	Keith Butler	235,072	39.5%			
	Randal White (write-in)	18				
	TOTAL	595,499				
Congressional District 1	Don Hooper	31,512	100.0%	Bart Stupak*	44,869	100.0%
Congressional District 2	Peter Hoekstra*	48,946	100.0%	Kimon Kotos	21,350	100.0%
Congressional District 3	Vernon J. Ehlers*	51,401	100.0%	James Rinck	11,797	51.1%
				Peter Hickey	11,287	48.9%
				TOTAL	23,084	
Congressional District 4	Dave Camp*	50,841	100.0%	Mike Huckleberry	32,186	100.0%
Congressional District 5	Eric Klammer	22,832	100.0%	Dale E. Kildee*	55,412	100.0%
Congressional District 6	Fred Upton*	40,425	100.0%	Kim Clark	21,586	100.0%
Congressional District 7	Tim Walberg	33,245	53.1%	Sharon Renier	10,402	52.7%
	Joe Schwarz*	29,330	46.9%	Fred Strack	3,447	17.5%
				Daryl Campbell	3,003	15.2%
				Chuck Ream	2,901	14.7%
	TOTAL	62,575		TOTAL	19,753	
Congressional District 8	Mike Rogers*	41,839	84.3%	Jim Marcinkowski	30,897	100.0%
	Patrick Flynn	7,784	15.7%			
	TOTAL	49,623				
Congressional District 9	Joe Knollenberg*	46,713	69.8%	Nancy Skinner	26,022	100.0%
	Patricia Godchaux	20,211	30.2%			
	TOTAL	66,924				
Congressional District 10	Candice S. Miller*	52,433	100.0%	Robert Denison	8,349	33.9%
				Rob Casey	7,657	31.1%
				Paul Kuligowski	5,686	23.1%
				Anthony America	2,910	11.8%
				TOTAL	24,602	
Congressional District 11	Thaddeus McCotter*	40,241	100.0%	Tony Trupiano	26,484	100.0%
Congressional District 12	Randell Shafer	23,178	100.0%	Sander M. Levin*	40,264	100.0%
Congressional District 13	No Republican candidate			Carolyn Cheeks Kilpatrick*	30,367	100.0%
Congressional District 14	Chad Miles	7,372	100.0%	John Conyers Jr.*	47,579	100.0%
				Alfred Patterson (write-in)	2	
				TOTAL	47,581	
Congressional District 15	No Republican candidate filed for the primary ballot. F. Vernuccio received 842 write-in votes, which was not enough to qualify for the general election ballot.			John D. Dingell*	38,769	100.0%

MINNESOTA

Congressional districts first established for elections held in 2002
8 members

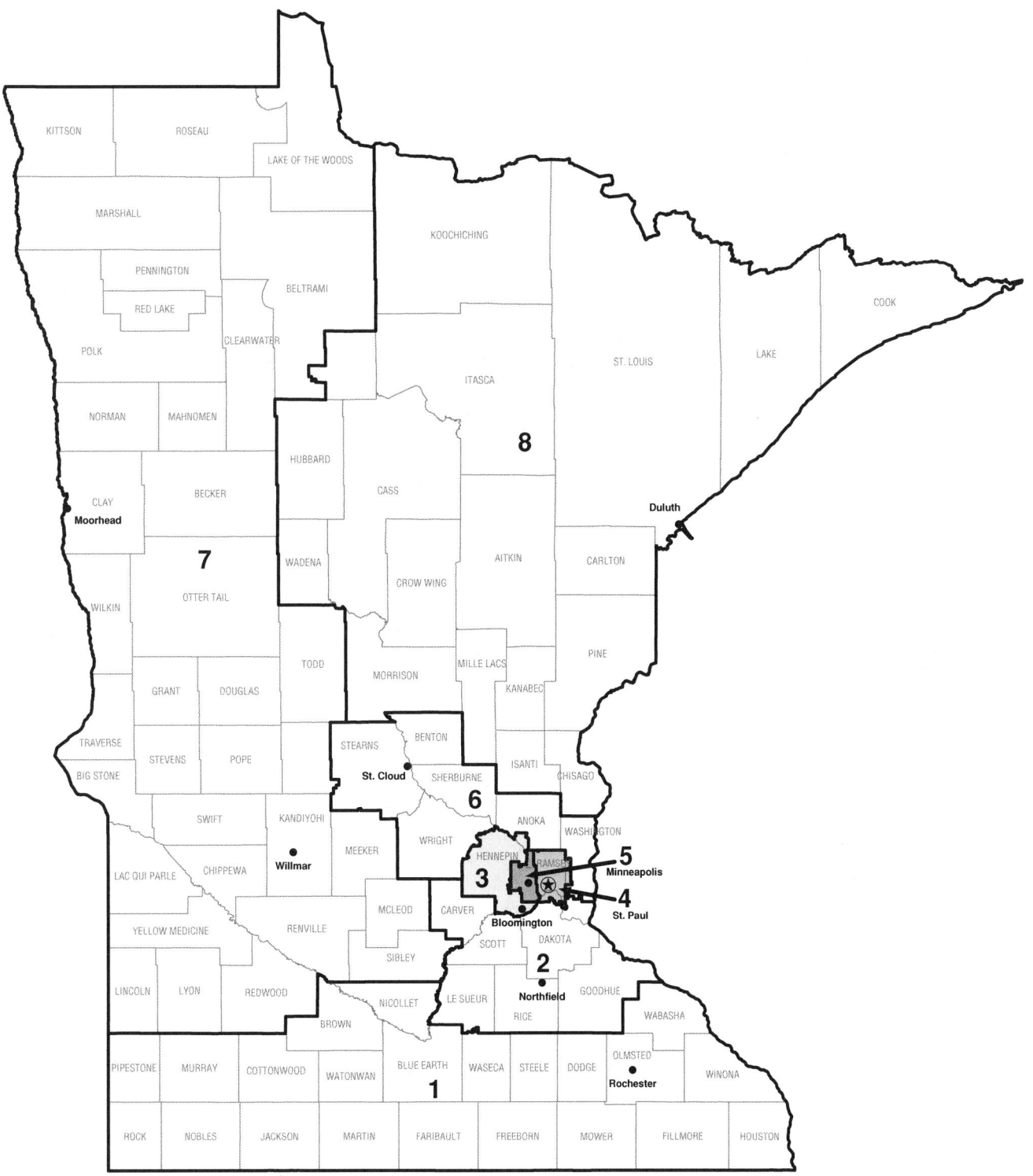

MINNESOTA

Minneapolis–St. Paul Area

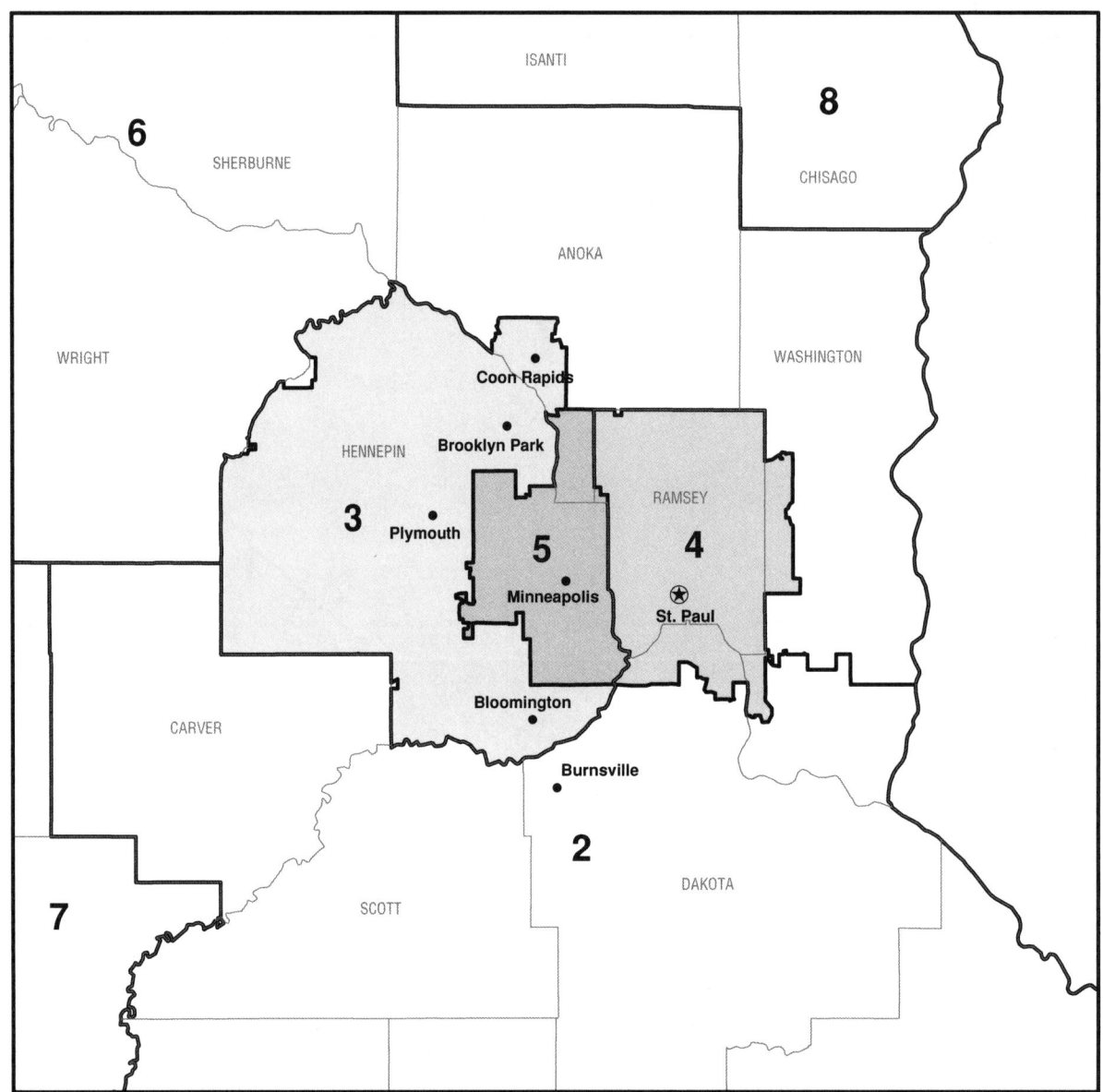

MINNESOTA

GOVERNOR
Tim Pawlenty (R). Reelected 2006 to a four-year term. Previously elected 2002.

SENATORS (1 Democrat, 1 Republican)
Amy Klobuchar (D). Elected 2006 to a six-year term.

Norm Coleman (R). Elected 2002 to a six-year term.

REPRESENTATIVES (5 Democrats, 3 Republicans)
1. Tim Walz (D)
2. John Kline (R)
3. Jim Ramstad (R)
4. Betty McCollum (D)
5. Keith Ellison (D)
6. Michele Bachmann (R)
7. Collin C. Peterson (D)
8. James L. Oberstar (D)

POSTWAR VOTE FOR PRESIDENT

Year	Total Vote	Republican Vote	Republican Candidate	Democratic Vote	Democratic Candidate	Other Vote	Plurality	Total Vote Rep.	Total Vote Dem.	Major Vote Rep.	Major Vote Dem.
2004	2,828,387	1,346,695	Bush, George W.	1,445,014	Kerry, John	36,678	98,319 D	47.6%	51.1%	48.2%	51.8%
2000**	2,438,685	1,109,659	Bush, George W.	1,168,266	Gore, Al	160,760	58,607 D	45.5%	47.9%	48.7%	51.3%
1996**	2,192,640	766,476	Dole, Bob	1,120,438	Clinton, Bill	305,726	353,962 D	35.0%	51.1%	40.6%	59.4%
1992**	2,347,948	747,841	Bush, George	1,020,997	Clinton, Bill	579,110	273,156 D	31.9%	43.5%	42.3%	57.7%
1988	2,096,790	962,337	Bush, George	1,109,471	Dukakis, Michael S.	24,982	147,134 D	45.9%	52.9%	46.4%	53.6%
1984	2,084,449	1,032,603	Reagan, Ronald	1,036,364	Mondale, Walter F.	15,482	3,761 D	49.5%	49.7%	49.9%	50.1%
1980**	2,051,980	873,268	Reagan, Ronald	954,174	Carter, Jimmy	224,538	80,906 D	42.6%	46.5%	47.8%	52.2%
1976	1,949,931	819,395	Ford, Gerald R.	1,070,440	Carter, Jimmy	60,096	251,045 D	42.0%	54.9%	43.4%	56.6%
1972	1,741,652	898,269	Nixon, Richard M.	802,346	McGovern, George S.	41,037	95,923 R	51.6%	46.1%	52.8%	47.2%
1968**	1,588,506	658,643	Nixon, Richard M.	857,738	Humphrey, Hubert H.	72,125	199,095 D	41.5%	54.0%	43.4%	56.6%
1964	1,554,462	559,624	Goldwater, Barry M.	991,117	Johnson, Lyndon B.	3,721	431,493 D	36.0%	63.8%	36.1%	63.9%
1960	1,541,887	757,915	Nixon, Richard M.	779,933	Kennedy, John F.	4,039	22,018 D	49.2%	50.6%	49.3%	50.7%
1956	1,340,005	719,302	Eisenhower, Dwight D.	617,525	Stevenson, Adlai E.	3,178	101,777 R	53.7%	46.1%	53.8%	46.2%
1952	1,379,483	763,211	Eisenhower, Dwight D.	608,458	Stevenson, Adlai E.	7,814	154,753 R	55.3%	44.1%	55.6%	44.4%
1948	1,212,226	483,617	Dewey, Thomas E.	692,966	Truman, Harry S.	35,643	209,349 D	39.9%	57.2%	41.1%	58.9%

**In past elections, the other vote included: 2000 - 126,696 Green (Ralph Nader); 1996 - 257,704 Reform (Ross Perot); 1992 - 562,506 Independent (Ross Perot); 1980 - 174,990 Independent (John Anderson); 1968 - 68,931 American Independent (George Wallace).

MINNESOTA

POSTWAR VOTE FOR GOVERNOR

Year	Total Vote	Republican Vote	Republican Candidate	Democratic Vote	Democratic Candidate	Other Vote	Rep.-Dem. Plurality	Total Vote Rep.	Total Vote Dem.	Major Vote Rep.	Major Vote Dem.
2006	2,202,937	1,028,568	Pawlenty, Tim	1,007,460	Hatch, Mike	166,909	21,108 R	46.7%	45.7%	50.5%	49.5%
2002**	2,252,473	999,473	Pawlenty, Tim	821,268	Moe, Roger D.	431,732	178,205 R	44.4%	36.5%	54.9%	45.1%
1998**	2,090,518	716,880	Coleman, Norm	587,060	Humphrey, Hubert H., III	786,578	56,523 V	34.3%	28.1%	55.0%	45.0%
1994	1,765,590	1,094,165	Carlson, Arne	589,344	Marty, John	82,081	504,821 R	62.0%	33.4%	65.0%	35.0%
1990	1,806,777	895,988	Carlson, Arne	836,218	Perpich, Rudy	74,571	59,770 R	49.6%	46.3%	51.7%	48.3%
1986	1,415,989	606,755	Ludeman, Cal R.	790,138	Perpich, Rudy	19,096	183,383 D	42.9%	55.8%	43.4%	56.6%
1982	1,789,539	715,796	Whitney, Wheelock	1,049,104	Perpich, Rudy	24,639	333,308 D	40.0%	58.6%	40.6%	59.4%
1978	1,585,702	830,019	Quie, Albert H.	718,244	Perpich, Rudy	37,439	111,775 R	52.3%	45.3%	53.6%	46.4%
1974	1,252,898	367,722	Johnson, John W.	786,787	Anderson, Wendell R.	98,389	419,065 D	29.3%	62.8%	31.9%	68.1%
1970	1,365,443	621,780	Head, Douglas M.	737,921	Anderson, Wendell R.	5,742	116,141 D	45.5%	54.0%	45.7%	54.3%
1966	1,295,058	680,593	LeVander, Harold	607,943	Rolvaag, Karl F.	6,522	72,650 R	52.6%	46.9%	52.8%	47.2%
1962**	1,246,904	619,751	Andersen, Elmer L.	619,842	Rolvaag, Karl F.	7,311	91 D	49.7%	49.7%	50.0%	50.0%
1960	1,550,265	783,813	Andersen, Elmer L.	760,934	Freeman, Orville L.	5,518	22,879 R	50.6%	49.1%	50.7%	49.3%
1958	1,159,915	490,731	MacKinnon, George	658,326	Freeman, Orville L.	10,858	167,595 D	42.3%	56.8%	42.7%	57.3%
1956	1,422,161	685,196	Nelsen, Ancher	731,180	Freeman, Orville L.	5,785	45,984 D	48.2%	51.4%	48.4%	51.6%
1954	1,151,417	538,865	Anderson, C. Elmer	607,099	Freeman, Orville L.	5,453	68,234 D	46.8%	52.7%	47.0%	53.0%
1952	1,418,869	785,125	Anderson, C. Elmer	624,480	Freeman, Orville L.	9,264	160,645 R	55.3%	44.0%	55.7%	44.3%
1950	1,046,632	635,800	Youngdahl, Luther	400,637	Peterson, Harry H.	10,195	235,163 R	60.7%	38.3%	61.3%	38.7%
1948	1,210,894	643,572	Youngdahl, Luther	545,766	Halsted, Charles L.	21,556	97,806 R	53.1%	45.1%	54.1%	45.9%
1946	880,348	519,067	Youngdahl, Luther	349,565	Barker, Harold H.	11,716	169,502 R	59.0%	39.7%	59.8%	40.2%

**In past elections, the other vote included: 2002 - 364,534 Independence (Timothy J. Penny); 1998 - 773,403 Reform (Jesse Ventura), who was elected with 37.0 percent of the total vote. The term of office of Minnesota's governor was increased from two to four years effective with the 1962 election.

POSTWAR VOTE FOR SENATOR

Year	Total Vote	Republican Vote	Republican Candidate	Democratic Vote	Democratic Candidate	Other Vote	Rep.-Dem. Plurality	Total Vote Rep.	Total Vote Dem.	Major Vote Rep.	Major Vote Dem.
2006	2,202,772	835,653	Kennedy, Mark	1,278,849	Klobuchar, Amy	88,270	443,196 D	37.9%	58.1%	39.5%	60.5%
2002**	2,254,639	1,116,697	Coleman, Norm	1,067,246	Mondale, Walter F.	70,696	49,451 R	49.5%	47.3%	51.1%	48.9%
2000	2,419,520	1,047,474	Grams, Rod	1,181,553	Dayton, Mark	190,493	134,079 D	43.3%	48.8%	47.0%	53.0%
1996	2,183,062	901,282	Boschwitz, Rudy	1,098,493	Wellstone, Paul	183,287	197,211 D	41.3%	50.3%	45.1%	54.9%
1994	1,772,929	869,653	Grams, Rod	781,860	Wynia, Ann	121,416	87,793 R	49.1%	44.1%	52.7%	47.3%
1990	1,808,045	864,375	Boschwitz, Rudy	911,999	Wellstone, Paul	31,671	47,624 D	47.8%	50.4%	48.7%	51.3%
1988	2,093,953	1,176,210	Durenberger, David	856,694	Humphrey, Hubert H. III	61,049	319,516 R	56.2%	40.9%	57.9%	42.1%
1984	2,066,143	1,199,926	Boschwitz, Rudy	852,844	Growe, Joan Anderson	13,373	347,082 R	58.1%	41.3%	58.5%	41.5%
1982	1,804,675	949,207	Durenberger, David	840,401	Dayton, Mark	15,067	108,806 R	52.6%	46.6%	53.0%	47.0%
1978	1,580,778	894,092	Boschwitz, Rudy	638,375	Anderson, Wendell R.	48,311	255,717 R	56.6%	40.4%	58.3%	41.7%
1978S	1,560,724	957,908	Durenberger, David	538,675	Short, Robert E.	64,141	419,233 R	61.4%	34.5%	64.0%	36.0%
1976	1,912,068	478,611	Brekke, Gerald W.	1,290,736	Humphrey, Hubert H.	142,721	812,125 D	25.0%	67.5%	27.1%	72.9%
1972	1,731,653	742,121	Hansen, Philip	981,340	Mondale, Walter F.	8,192	239,219 D	42.9%	56.7%	43.1%	56.9%
1970	1,364,887	568,025	MacGregor, Clark	788,256	Humphrey, Hubert H.	8,606	220,231 D	41.6%	57.8%	41.9%	58.1%
1966	1,271,426	574,868	Forsythe, Robert A.	685,840	Mondale, Walter F.	10,718	110,972 D	45.2%	53.9%	45.6%	54.4%
1964	1,543,590	605,933	Whitney, Wheelock	931,353	McCarthy, Eugene J.	6,304	325,420 D	39.3%	60.3%	39.4%	60.6%
1960	1,536,839	648,586	Peterson, P.K.	884,168	Humphrey, Hubert H.	4,085	235,582 D	42.2%	57.5%	42.3%	57.7%
1958	1,150,883	536,629	Thye, Edward J.	608,847	McCarthy, Eugene J.	5,407	72,218 D	46.6%	52.9%	46.8%	53.2%
1954	1,138,952	479,619	Bjornson, Val	642,193	Humphrey, Hubert H.	17,140	162,574 D	42.1%	56.4%	42.8%	57.2%
1952	1,387,419	785,649	Thye, Edward J.	590,011	Carlson, William E.	11,759	195,638 R	56.6%	42.5%	57.1%	42.9%
1948	1,220,250	485,801	Ball, Joseph H.	729,494	Humphrey, Hubert H.	4,955	243,693 D	39.8%	59.8%	40.0%	60.0%
1946	878,731	517,775	Thye, Edward J.	349,520	Jorgenson, Theodore	11,436	168,255 R	58.9%	39.8%	59.7%	40.3%

**In 2002 the Democratic incumbent, Paul Wellstone, was killed in an airplane crash in October. Walter F. Mondale was named to replace him on the general election ballot. One of the 1978 elections was for a short term to fill a vacancy.

MINNESOTA

GOVERNOR 2006

2000 Census Population	County	Total Vote	Republican	Democratic	Other	Rep.-Dem. Plurality		Percentage			
								Total Vote		Major Vote	
								Rep.	Dem.	Rep.	Dem.
15,301	AITKIN	8,104	3,473	3,992	639	519	D	42.9%	49.3%	46.5%	53.5%
298,084	ANOKA	133,461	68,422	55,989	9,050	12,433	R	51.3%	42.0%	55.0%	45.0%
30,000	BECKER	13,345	6,959	5,588	798	1,371	R	52.1%	41.9%	55.5%	44.5%
39,650	BELTRAMI	16,914	7,270	8,603	1,041	1,333	D	43.0%	50.9%	45.8%	54.2%
34,226	BENTON	14,243	7,712	5,625	906	2,087	R	54.1%	39.5%	57.8%	42.2%
5,820	BIG STONE	2,713	1,190	1,353	170	163	D	43.9%	49.9%	46.8%	53.2%
55,941	BLUE EARTH	25,455	11,231	12,137	2,087	906	D	44.1%	47.7%	48.1%	51.9%
26,911	BROWN	11,632	6,350	4,357	925	1,993	R	54.6%	37.5%	59.3%	40.7%
31,671	CARLTON	14,177	4,561	8,721	895	4,160	D	32.2%	61.5%	34.3%	65.7%
70,205	CARVER	36,317	23,082	10,932	2,303	12,150	R	63.6%	30.1%	67.9%	32.1%
27,150	CASS	12,513	6,483	5,231	799	1,252	R	51.8%	41.8%	55.3%	44.7%
13,088	CHIPPEWA	5,503	2,378	2,787	338	409	D	43.2%	50.6%	46.0%	54.0%
41,101	CHISAGO	21,881	11,437	8,940	1,504	2,497	R	52.3%	40.9%	56.1%	43.9%
51,229	CLAY	19,562	10,065	8,527	970	1,538	R	51.5%	43.6%	54.1%	45.9%
8,423	CLEARWATER	3,760	1,718	1,795	247	77	D	45.7%	47.7%	48.9%	51.1%
5,168	COOK	2,877	1,051	1,519	307	468	D	36.5%	52.8%	40.9%	59.1%
12,167	COTTONWOOD	5,355	2,700	2,320	335	380	R	50.4%	43.3%	53.8%	46.2%
55,099	CROW WING	27,527	14,113	11,651	1,763	2,462	R	51.3%	42.3%	54.8%	45.2%
355,904	DAKOTA	166,924	87,039	67,939	11,946	19,100	R	52.1%	40.7%	56.2%	43.8%
17,731	DODGE	7,637	4,182	2,925	530	1,257	R	54.8%	38.3%	58.8%	41.2%
32,821	DOUGLAS	16,550	9,233	6,222	1,095	3,011	R	55.8%	37.6%	59.7%	40.3%
16,181	FARIBAULT	7,223	3,558	3,117	548	441	R	49.3%	43.2%	53.3%	46.7%
21,122	FILLMORE	9,313	4,245	4,475	593	230	D	45.6%	48.1%	48.7%	51.3%
32,584	FREEBORN	15,089	5,980	8,155	954	2,175	D	39.6%	54.0%	42.3%	57.7%
44,127	GOODHUE	20,211	10,541	8,115	1,555	2,426	R	52.2%	40.2%	56.5%	43.5%
6,289	GRANT	3,155	1,460	1,497	198	37	D	46.3%	47.4%	49.4%	50.6%
1,116,200	HENNEPIN	491,786	199,867	249,244	42,675	49,377	D	40.6%	50.7%	44.5%	55.5%
19,718	HOUSTON	8,931	4,379	4,009	543	370	R	49.0%	44.9%	52.2%	47.8%
18,376	HUBBARD	9,855	4,834	4,371	650	463	R	49.1%	44.4%	52.5%	47.5%
31,287	ISANTI	14,672	7,829	5,859	984	1,970	R	53.4%	39.9%	57.2%	42.8%
43,992	ITASCA	19,422	7,270	10,976	1,176	3,706	D	37.4%	56.5%	39.8%	60.2%
11,268	JACKSON	4,987	2,374	2,312	301	62	R	47.6%	46.4%	50.7%	49.3%
14,996	KANABEC	6,544	3,190	2,842	512	348	R	48.7%	43.4%	52.9%	47.1%
41,203	KANDIYOHI	17,938	9,248	7,555	1,135	1,693	R	51.6%	42.1%	55.0%	45.0%
5,285	KITTSON	2,178	846	1,229	103	383	D	38.8%	56.4%	40.8%	59.2%
14,355	KOOCHICHING	5,649	1,989	3,309	351	1,320	D	35.2%	58.6%	37.5%	62.5%
8,067	LAC QUI PARLE	3,901	1,748	1,905	248	157	D	44.8%	48.8%	47.9%	52.1%
11,058	LAKE	5,983	1,901	3,632	450	1,731	D	31.8%	60.7%	34.4%	65.6%
4,522	LAKE OF THE WOODS	1,924	953	847	124	106	R	49.5%	44.0%	52.9%	47.1%
25,426	LE SUEUR	11,489	5,874	4,752	863	1,122	R	51.1%	41.4%	55.3%	44.7%
6,429	LINCOLN	2,687	1,234	1,287	166	53	D	45.9%	47.9%	48.9%	51.1%
25,425	LYON	9,470	5,243	3,673	554	1,570	R	55.4%	38.8%	58.8%	41.2%
34,898	MCLEOD	14,663	8,580	4,868	1,215	3,712	R	58.5%	33.2%	63.8%	36.2%
5,190	MAHNOMEN	2,225	852	1,231	142	379	D	38.3%	55.3%	40.9%	59.1%
10,155	MARSHALL	4,400	2,060	2,096	244	36	D	46.8%	47.6%	49.6%	50.4%
21,802	MARTIN	8,997	5,047	3,386	564	1,661	R	56.1%	37.6%	59.8%	40.2%
22,644	MEEKER	10,440	5,576	3,976	888	1,600	R	53.4%	38.1%	58.4%	41.6%
22,330	MILLE LACS	10,337	5,180	4,508	649	672	R	50.1%	43.6%	53.5%	46.5%
31,712	MORRISON	13,754	7,302	5,577	875	1,725	R	53.1%	40.5%	56.7%	43.3%
38,603	MOWER	16,029	6,028	9,014	987	2,986	D	37.6%	56.2%	40.1%	59.9%
9,165	MURRAY	4,295	2,084	2,018	193	66	R	48.5%	47.0%	50.8%	49.2%
29,771	NICOLLET	14,385	6,725	6,468	1,192	257	R	46.8%	45.0%	51.0%	49.0%
20,832	NOBLES	7,546	3,692	3,475	379	217	R	48.9%	46.1%	51.5%	48.5%
7,442	NORMAN	2,865	1,124	1,577	164	453	D	39.2%	55.0%	41.6%	58.4%
124,277	OLMSTED	56,332	30,874	21,833	3,625	9,041	R	54.8%	38.8%	58.6%	41.4%
57,159	OTTER TAIL	25,106	14,017	9,679	1,410	4,338	R	55.8%	38.6%	59.2%	40.8%
13,584	PENNINGTON	5,171	2,320	2,501	350	181	D	44.9%	48.4%	48.1%	51.9%
26,530	PINE	11,191	4,894	5,531	766	637	D	43.7%	49.4%	46.9%	53.1%
9,895	PIPESTONE	4,144	2,329	1,629	186	700	R	56.2%	39.3%	58.8%	41.2%
31,369	POLK	12,052	5,678	5,776	598	98	D	47.1%	47.9%	49.6%	50.4%

MINNESOTA

GOVERNOR 2006

2000 Census Population	County	Total Vote	Republican	Democratic	Other	Rep.-Dem. Plurality		Percentage			
								Total Vote		Major Vote	
								Rep.	Dem.	Rep.	Dem.
11,236	POPE	5,883	2,762	2,698	423	64	R	46.9%	45.9%	50.6%	49.4%
511,035	RAMSEY	207,891	75,171	110,653	22,067	35,482	D	36.2%	53.2%	40.5%	59.5%
4,299	RED LAKE	1,895	769	1,007	119	238	D	40.6%	53.1%	43.3%	56.7%
16,815	REDWOOD	6,545	3,725	2,334	486	1,391	R	56.9%	35.7%	61.5%	38.5%
17,154	RENVILLE	6,763	3,337	2,843	583	494	R	49.3%	42.0%	54.0%	46.0%
56,665	RICE	24,419	10,773	11,681	1,965	908	D	44.1%	47.8%	48.0%	52.0%
9,721	ROCK	4,158	2,318	1,585	255	733	R	55.7%	38.1%	59.4%	40.6%
16,338	ROSEAU	6,362	3,573	2,469	320	1,104	R	56.2%	38.8%	59.1%	40.9%
200,528	ST. LOUIS	89,811	26,351	58,037	5,423	31,686	D	29.3%	64.6%	31.2%	68.8%
89,498	SCOTT	46,970	28,001	16,046	2,923	11,955	R	59.6%	34.2%	63.6%	36.4%
64,417	SHERBURNE	31,903	18,944	11,110	1,849	7,834	R	59.4%	34.8%	63.0%	37.0%
15,356	SIBLEY	6,353	3,549	2,290	514	1,259	R	55.9%	36.0%	60.8%	39.2%
133,166	STEARNS	57,174	31,964	21,557	3,653	10,407	R	55.9%	37.7%	59.7%	40.3%
33,680	STEELE	15,241	8,576	5,599	1,066	2,977	R	56.3%	36.7%	60.5%	39.5%
10,053	STEVENS	4,797	2,375	2,115	307	260	R	49.5%	44.1%	52.9%	47.1%
11,956	SWIFT	4,707	2,030	2,373	304	343	D	43.1%	50.4%	46.1%	53.9%
24,426	TODD	10,211	5,357	4,183	671	1,174	R	52.5%	41.0%	56.2%	43.8%
4,134	TRAVERSE	1,871	852	916	103	64	D	45.5%	49.0%	48.2%	51.8%
21,610	WABASHA	9,407	4,797	3,979	631	818	R	51.0%	42.3%	54.7%	45.3%
13,713	WADENA	5,873	3,130	2,378	365	752	R	53.3%	40.5%	56.8%	43.2%
19,526	WASECA	8,108	4,207	3,070	831	1,137	R	51.9%	37.9%	57.8%	42.2%
201,130	WASHINGTON	104,393	53,879	41,692	8,822	12,187	R	51.6%	39.9%	56.4%	43.6%
11,876	WATONWAN	4,573	2,197	2,026	350	171	R	48.0%	44.3%	52.0%	48.0%
7,138	WILKIN	2,807	1,603	1,037	167	566	R	57.1%	36.9%	60.7%	39.3%
49,985	WINONA	19,714	8,430	9,670	1,614	1,240	D	42.8%	49.1%	46.6%	53.4%
89,986	WRIGHT	47,468	28,065	16,397	3,006	11,668	R	59.1%	34.5%	63.1%	36.9%
11,080	YELLOW MEDICINE	4,851	2,259	2,258	334	1	R	46.6%	46.5%	50.0%	50.0%
4,919,479	TOTAL	2,202,937	1,028,568	1,007,460	166,909	21,108	R	46.7%	45.7%	50.5%	49.5%

MINNESOTA

SENATOR 2006

2000 Census Population	County	Total Vote	Republican	Democratic	Other	Rep.-Dem. Plurality	Percentage Total Vote Rep.	Dem.	Major Vote Rep.	Dem.
15,301	AITKIN	8,106	3,047	4,701	358	1,654 D	37.6%	58.0%	39.3%	60.7%
298,084	ANOKA	133,318	55,399	72,660	5,259	17,261 D	41.6%	54.5%	43.3%	56.7%
30,000	BECKER	13,328	6,016	6,816	496	800 D	45.1%	51.1%	46.9%	53.1%
39,650	BELTRAMI	16,909	6,511	9,714	684	3,203 D	38.5%	57.4%	40.1%	59.9%
34,226	BENTON	14,214	6,314	7,295	605	981 D	44.4%	51.3%	46.4%	53.6%
5,820	BIG STONE	2,711	1,049	1,558	104	509 D	38.7%	57.5%	40.2%	59.8%
55,941	BLUE EARTH	25,474	9,411	14,955	1,108	5,544 D	36.9%	58.7%	38.6%	61.4%
26,911	BROWN	11,639	5,292	5,852	495	560 D	45.5%	50.3%	47.5%	52.5%
31,671	CARLTON	14,179	4,015	9,701	463	5,686 D	28.3%	68.4%	29.3%	70.7%
70,205	CARVER	36,287	18,585	16,476	1,226	2,109 R	51.2%	45.4%	53.0%	47.0%
27,150	CASS	12,530	5,695	6,356	479	661 D	45.5%	50.7%	47.3%	52.7%
13,088	CHIPPEWA	5,503	1,988	3,353	162	1,365 D	36.1%	60.9%	37.2%	62.8%
41,101	CHISAGO	21,867	9,451	11,535	881	2,084 D	43.2%	52.8%	45.0%	55.0%
51,229	CLAY	19,554	7,741	11,086	727	3,345 D	39.6%	56.7%	41.1%	58.9%
8,423	CLEARWATER	3,757	1,675	1,927	155	252 D	44.6%	51.3%	46.5%	53.5%
5,168	COOK	2,877	889	1,835	153	946 D	30.9%	63.8%	32.6%	67.4%
12,167	COTTONWOOD	5,362	2,402	2,771	189	369 D	44.8%	51.7%	46.4%	53.6%
55,099	CROW WING	27,513	12,624	13,775	1,114	1,151 D	45.9%	50.1%	47.8%	52.2%
355,904	DAKOTA	166,709	67,289	93,247	6,173	25,958 D	40.4%	55.9%	41.9%	58.1%
17,731	DODGE	7,640	3,342	3,909	389	567 D	43.7%	51.2%	46.1%	53.9%
32,821	DOUGLAS	16,524	7,474	8,429	621	955 D	45.2%	51.0%	47.0%	53.0%
16,181	FARIBAULT	7,239	3,044	3,877	318	833 D	42.1%	53.6%	44.0%	56.0%
21,122	FILLMORE	9,305	3,531	5,329	445	1,798 D	37.9%	57.3%	39.9%	60.1%
32,584	FREEBORN	15,142	5,180	9,417	545	4,237 D	34.2%	62.2%	35.5%	64.5%
44,127	GOODHUE	20,208	8,353	11,031	824	2,678 D	41.3%	54.6%	43.1%	56.9%
6,289	GRANT	3,149	1,195	1,827	127	632 D	37.9%	58.0%	39.5%	60.5%
1,116,200	HENNEPIN	492,142	155,374	317,234	19,534	161,860 D	31.6%	64.5%	32.9%	67.1%
19,718	HOUSTON	8,882	3,727	4,642	513	915 D	42.0%	52.3%	44.5%	55.5%
18,376	HUBBARD	9,837	4,562	4,895	380	333 D	46.4%	49.8%	48.2%	51.8%
31,287	ISANTI	14,662	6,620	7,468	574	848 D	45.2%	50.9%	47.0%	53.0%
43,992	ITASCA	19,433	6,630	12,082	721	5,452 D	34.1%	62.2%	35.4%	64.6%
11,268	JACKSON	5,002	2,113	2,675	214	562 D	42.2%	53.5%	44.1%	55.9%
14,996	KANABEC	6,550	2,794	3,499	257	705 D	42.7%	53.4%	44.4%	55.6%
41,203	KANDIYOHI	17,944	7,913	9,483	548	1,570 D	44.1%	52.8%	45.5%	54.5%
5,285	KITTSON	2,185	693	1,438	54	745 D	31.7%	65.8%	32.5%	67.5%
14,355	KOOCHICHING	5,657	1,817	3,635	205	1,818 D	32.1%	64.3%	33.3%	66.7%
8,067	LAC QUI PARLE	3,905	1,455	2,313	137	858 D	37.3%	59.2%	38.6%	61.4%
11,058	LAKE	6,002	1,714	4,061	227	2,347 D	28.6%	67.7%	29.7%	70.3%
4,522	LAKE OF THE WOODS	1,936	815	1,032	89	217 D	42.1%	53.3%	44.1%	55.9%
25,426	LE SUEUR	11,498	4,638	6,328	532	1,690 D	40.3%	55.0%	42.3%	57.7%
6,429	LINCOLN	2,682	1,092	1,471	119	379 D	40.7%	54.8%	42.6%	57.4%
25,425	LYON	9,481	4,414	4,718	349	304 D	46.6%	49.8%	48.3%	51.7%
34,898	MCLEOD	14,652	6,988	7,016	648	28 D	47.7%	47.9%	49.9%	50.1%
5,190	MAHNOMEN	2,234	721	1,435	78	714 D	32.3%	64.2%	33.4%	66.6%
10,155	MARSHALL	4,411	1,684	2,571	156	887 D	38.2%	58.3%	39.6%	60.4%
21,802	MARTIN	9,010	4,315	4,344	351	29 D	47.9%	48.2%	49.8%	50.2%
22,644	MEEKER	10,464	4,638	5,396	430	758 D	44.3%	51.6%	46.2%	53.8%
22,330	MILLE LACS	10,338	4,291	5,581	466	1,290 D	41.5%	54.0%	43.5%	56.5%
31,712	MORRISON	13,729	6,229	6,941	559	712 D	45.4%	50.6%	47.3%	52.7%
38,603	MOWER	16,025	4,906	10,450	669	5,544 D	30.6%	65.2%	31.9%	68.1%
9,165	MURRAY	4,306	1,804	2,331	171	527 D	41.9%	54.1%	43.6%	56.4%
29,771	NICOLLET	14,400	5,337	8,511	552	3,174 D	37.1%	59.1%	38.5%	61.5%
20,832	NOBLES	7,532	3,531	3,697	304	166 D	46.9%	49.1%	48.9%	51.1%
7,442	NORMAN	2,882	937	1,827	118	890 D	32.5%	63.4%	33.9%	66.1%
124,277	OLMSTED	56,304	24,054	30,102	2,148	6,048 D	42.7%	53.5%	44.4%	55.6%
57,159	OTTER TAIL	25,099	12,041	11,754	1,304	287 R	48.0%	46.8%	50.6%	49.4%
13,584	PENNINGTON	5,161	1,908	3,074	179	1,166 D	37.0%	59.6%	38.3%	61.7%
26,530	PINE	11,200	4,268	6,420	512	2,152 D	38.1%	57.3%	39.9%	60.1%
9,895	PIPESTONE	4,145	2,146	1,827	172	319 R	51.8%	44.1%	54.0%	46.0%
31,369	POLK	12,058	4,857	6,806	395	1,949 D	40.3%	56.4%	41.6%	58.4%

MINNESOTA

SENATOR 2006

2000 Census Population	County	Total Vote	Republican	Democratic	Other	Rep.-Dem. Plurality	Percentage			
							Total Vote		Major Vote	
							Rep.	Dem.	Rep.	Dem.
11,236	POPE	5,870	2,273	3,359	238	1,086 D	38.7%	57.2%	40.4%	59.6%
511,035	RAMSEY	207,681	60,290	137,558	9,833	77,268 D	29.0%	66.2%	30.5%	69.5%
4,299	RED LAKE	1,903	657	1,166	80	509 D	34.5%	61.3%	36.0%	64.0%
16,815	REDWOOD	6,549	3,181	3,098	270	83 R	48.6%	47.3%	50.7%	49.3%
17,154	RENVILLE	6,768	2,660	3,824	284	1,164 D	39.3%	56.5%	41.0%	59.0%
56,665	RICE	24,412	8,461	14,943	1,008	6,482 D	34.7%	61.2%	36.2%	63.8%
9,721	ROCK	4,150	2,144	1,806	200	338 R	51.7%	43.5%	54.3%	45.7%
16,338	ROSEAU	6,354	2,967	3,140	247	173 D	46.7%	49.4%	48.6%	51.4%
200,528	ST. LOUIS	89,949	23,281	63,750	2,918	40,469 D	25.9%	70.9%	26.8%	73.2%
89,498	SCOTT	46,917	22,023	23,135	1,759	1,112 D	46.9%	49.3%	48.8%	51.2%
64,417	SHERBURNE	31,920	15,737	15,049	1,134	688 R	49.3%	47.1%	51.1%	48.9%
15,356	SIBLEY	6,344	2,835	3,199	310	364 D	44.7%	50.4%	47.0%	53.0%
133,166	STEARNS	57,249	26,358	28,630	2,261	2,272 D	46.0%	50.0%	47.9%	52.1%
33,680	STEELE	15,245	6,434	8,107	704	1,673 D	42.2%	53.2%	44.2%	55.8%
10,053	STEVENS	4,780	1,936	2,588	256	652 D	40.5%	54.1%	42.8%	57.2%
11,956	SWIFT	4,702	1,661	2,864	177	1,203 D	35.3%	60.9%	36.7%	63.3%
24,426	TODD	10,199	4,494	5,230	475	736 D	44.1%	51.3%	46.2%	53.8%
4,134	TRAVERSE	1,881	770	1,052	59	282 D	40.9%	55.9%	42.3%	57.7%
21,610	WABASHA	9,402	3,787	5,204	411	1,417 D	40.3%	55.3%	42.1%	57.9%
13,713	WADENA	5,856	2,890	2,746	220	144 R	49.4%	46.9%	51.3%	48.7%
19,526	WASECA	8,112	3,371	4,307	434	936 D	41.6%	53.1%	43.9%	56.1%
201,130	WASHINGTON	104,346	42,910	57,563	3,873	14,653 D	41.1%	55.2%	42.7%	57.3%
11,876	WATONWAN	4,572	1,878	2,495	199	617 D	41.1%	54.6%	42.9%	57.1%
7,138	WILKIN	2,807	1,238	1,407	162	169 D	44.1%	50.1%	46.8%	53.2%
49,985	WINONA	19,684	7,493	11,183	1,008	3,690 D	38.1%	56.8%	40.1%	59.9%
89,986	WRIGHT	47,478	23,518	22,162	1,798	1,356 R	49.5%	46.7%	51.5%	48.5%
11,080	YELLOW MEDICINE	4,850	1,868	2,795	187	927 D	38.5%	57.6%	40.1%	59.9%
4,919,479	TOTAL	2,202,772	835,653	1,278,849	88,270	443,196 D	37.9%	58.1%	39.5%	60.5%

MINNESOTA

HOUSE OF REPRESENTATIVES

CD	Year	Total Vote	Republican		Democratic		Other Vote	Rep.-Dem. Plurality	Percentage			
									Total Vote		Major Vote	
			Vote	Candidate	Vote	Candidate			Rep.	Dem.	Rep.	Dem.
1	2006	268,421	126,486	GUTKNECHT, GIL*	141,556	WALZ, TIM	379	15,070 D	47.1%	52.7%	47.2%	52.8%
1	2004	324,055	193,132	GUTKNECHT, GIL*	115,088	POMEROY, LEIGH	15,835	78,044 R	59.6%	35.5%	62.7%	37.3%
1	2002	265,982	163,570	GUTKNECHT, GIL*	92,165	ANDREASEN, STEVE	10,247	71,405 R	61.5%	34.7%	64.0%	36.0%
2	2006	290,540	163,269	KLINE, JOHN*	116,343	ROWLEY, COLEEN	10,928	46,926 R	56.2%	40.0%	58.4%	41.6%
2	2004	365,945	206,313	KLINE, JOHN*	147,527	DALY, TERESA	12,105	58,786 R	56.4%	40.3%	58.3%	41.7%
2	2002	286,860	152,970	KLINE, JOHN	121,121	LUTHER, BILL*	12,769	31,849 R	53.3%	42.2%	55.8%	44.2%
3	2006	284,244	184,333	RAMSTAD, JIM*	99,588	WILDE, WENDY	323	84,745 R	64.9%	35.0%	64.9%	35.1%
3	2004	358,892	231,871	RAMSTAD, JIM*	126,665	WATTS, DEBORAH	356	105,206 R	64.6%	35.3%	64.7%	35.3%
3	2002	296,218	213,334	RAMSTAD, JIM*	82,575	STANTON, DARRYL	309	130,759 R	72.0%	27.9%	72.1%	27.9%
4	2006	247,466	74,797	SIUM, OBI	172,096	McCOLLUM, BETTY*	573	97,299 D	30.2%	69.5%	30.3%	69.7%
4	2004	317,299	105,467	BATAGLIA, PATRICE	182,387	McCOLLUM, BETTY*	29,445	76,920 D	33.2%	57.5%	36.6%	63.4%
4	2002	264,540	89,705	BILLINGTON, CLYDE	164,597	McCOLLUM, BETTY*	10,238	74,892 D	33.9%	62.2%	35.3%	64.7%
5	2006	244,905	52,263	FINE, ALAN	136,060	ELLISON, KEITH	56,582	83,797 D	21.3%	55.6%	27.8%	72.2%
5	2004	313,526	76,600	MATHIAS, DANIEL	218,434	SABO, MARTIN OLAV*	18,492	141,834 D	24.4%	69.7%	26.0%	74.0%
5	2002	255,982	66,271	MATHIAS, DANIEL	171,572	SABO, MARTIN OLAV*	18,139	105,301 D	25.9%	67.0%	27.9%	72.1%
6	2006	302,188	151,248	BACHMANN, MICHELE	127,144	WETTERLING, PATTY	23,796	24,104 R	50.1%	42.1%	54.3%	45.7%
6	2004	377,224	203,669	KENNEDY, MARK*	173,309	WETTERLING, PATTY	246	30,360 R	54.0%	45.9%	54.0%	46.0%
6	2002	287,312	164,747	KENNEDY, MARK*	100,738	ROBERT, JANET	21,827	64,009 R	57.3%	35.1%	62.1%	37.9%
7	2006	257,194	74,557	BARRETT, MICHAEL J.	179,164	PETERSON, COLLIN C.*	3,473	104,607 D	29.0%	69.7%	29.4%	70.6%
7	2004	314,257	106,349	STURROCK, DAVID E.	207,628	PETERSON, COLLIN C.*	280	101,279 D	33.8%	66.1%	33.9%	66.1%
7	2002	260,813	90,342	STEVENS, DAN	170,234	PETERSON, COLLIN C.*	237	79,892 D	34.6%	65.3%	34.7%	65.3%
8	2006	284,016	97,683	GRAMS, ROD	180,670	OBERSTAR, JAMES L.*	5,663	82,987 D	34.4%	63.6%	35.1%	64.9%
8	2004	350,483	112,693	GROETTUM, MARK	228,586	OBERSTAR, JAMES L.*	9,204	115,893 D	32.2%	65.2%	33.0%	67.0%
8	2002	283,931	88,673	LEMEN, BOB	194,909	OBERSTAR, JAMES L.*	349	106,236 D	31.2%	68.6%	31.3%	68.7%
TOTAL	2006	2,178,974	924,636		1,152,621		101,717	227,985 D	42.4%	52.9%	44.5%	55.5%
TOTAL	2004	2,721,681	1,236,094		1,399,624		85,963	163,530 D	45.4%	51.4%	46.9%	53.1%
TOTAL	2002	2,201,638	1,029,612		1,097,911		74,115	68,299 D	46.8%	49.9%	48.4%	51.6%

An asterisk (*) denotes incumbent.

MINNESOTA

GENERAL AND PRIMARY ELECTIONS

2006 GENERAL ELECTIONS

Governor Other vote was 141,735 Independence (Peter Hutchinson); 10,800 Green (Ken Pentel); 9,649 Quit Raising Taxes (Walt E. Brown); 3,776 American (Leslie Davis); 2 write-in (Nelson F. Gonzalez); 2 write-in (David W. Hinkley); 1 write-in (Murphy Wentworth); 944 scattered write-in.

Senator Other vote was 71,194 Independence (Robert Fitzgerald); 10,714 Green (Michael James Cavlan); 5,408 Constitution (Ben Powers); 29 write-in (Peter Idusogie); 15 write-in (Charles Aldrich); 5 write-in (Rebecca Williamson); 4 write-in (John Uldrich), 901 scattered write-in.

House Other vote was:

CD 1 4 write-in (Stephen Williams); 375 scattered write-in.
CD 2 10,802 Independence (Douglas Williams); 126 scattered write-in.
CD 3 323 scattered write-in.
CD 4 1 write-in (Tom Fiske); 572 scattered write-in.
CD 5 51,456 Independence (Tammy Lee); 4,792 Green (Jay Pond); 334 scattered write-in.
CD 6 23,557 Independence (John Paul Binkowski); 239 scattered write-in.
CD 7 3,303 Constitution (Ken Lucier); 170 scattered write-in.
CD 8 5,508 Unity (Harry Welty); 155 scattered write-in.

2006 PRIMARY ELECTIONS

Primary September 12, 2006 **Registration** 3,090,135 No Party Registration
(as of August 31, 2006)

Primary Type Open—Any registered voter could participate in the party primary of their choice.

MINNESOTA

GENERAL AND PRIMARY ELECTIONS

Note: An asterisk (*) denotes incumbent. No votes were tallied for unopposed candidates in districts where none of the parties had a contested race.

	REPUBLICAN PRIMARIES			DEMOCRATIC PRIMARIES		
Governor	Tim Pawlenty*	147,622	88.9%	Mike Hatch	231,643	73.2%
	Sue Jeffers	18,490	11.1%	Becky Lourey	77,430	24.5%
				Ole Savior	7,397	2.3%
	TOTAL	166,112		TOTAL	316,470	
Senator	Mark Kennedy	147,091	90.2%	Amy Klobuchar	294,671	92.5%
	John Uldrich	10,025	6.1%	Darryl Stanton	23,872	7.5%
	Harold Shudlick	5,941	3.6%			
	TOTAL	163,057		TOTAL	318,543	
Congressional District 1	Gil Gutknecht*	24,725	87.3%	Tim Walz	26,475	100.0%
	Gregory Mikkelson	3,600	12.7%			
	TOTAL	28,325				
Congressional District 2	John Kline*	Unopposed		Coleen Rowley	Unopposed	
Congressional District 3	Jim Ramstad*	17,579	100.0%	Wendy Wilde	19,259	76.8%
				Kevin Ray Smith	2,911	11.6%
				Gavin Sullivan	2,894	11.5%
				TOTAL	25,064	
Congressional District 4	Obi Sium	8,802	64.2%	Betty McCollum*	37,397	100.0%
	Jack Shepard	4,908	35.8%			
	TOTAL	13,710				
Congressional District 5	Alan Fine	7,352	100.0%	Keith Ellison	29,003	41.2%
				Mike Erlandson	21,857	31.1%
				Ember Reichgott Junge	14,454	20.5%
				Paul Ostrow	3,795	5.4%
				Andrew Vincent Favorite	470	0.7%
				Gregg A. Iverson	448	0.6%
				Patrick J. Wiles	347	0.5%
				TOTAL	70,374	
Congressional District 6	Michele Bachmann	Unopposed		Patty Wetterling	Unopposed	
Congressional District 7	Michael J. Barrett	20,475	100.0%	Collin C. Peterson*	33,732	86.0%
				Erik Thompson	5,476	14.0%
				TOTAL	39,208	
Congressional District 8	Rod Grams	Unopposed		James L. Oberstar*	Unopposed	

MISSISSIPPI

Congressional districts first established for elections held in 2002
4 members

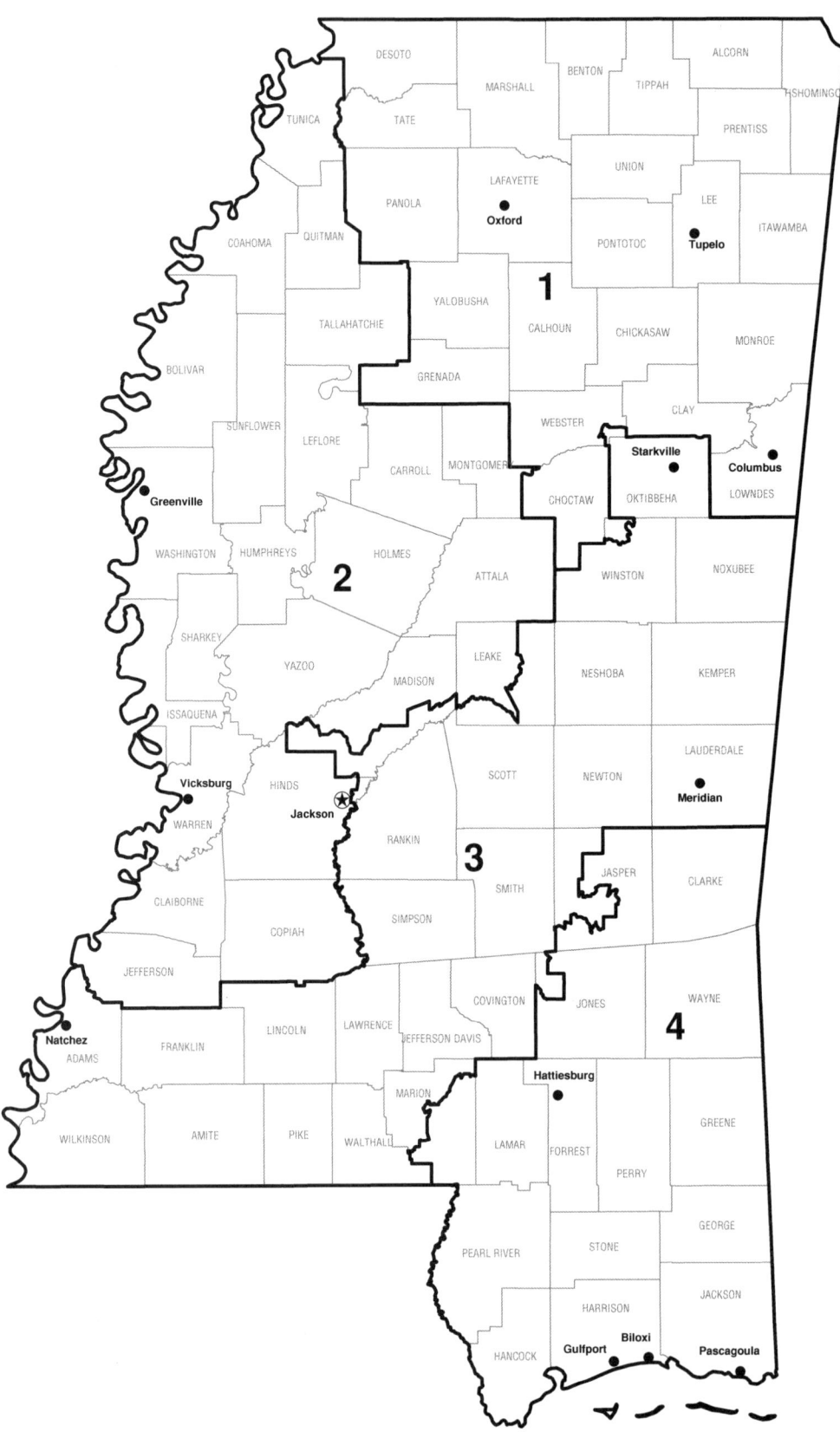

MISSISSIPPI

GOVERNOR
Haley Barbour (R). Elected 2003 to a four-year term.

SENATORS (2 Republicans)
Trent Lott (R). Reelected 2006 to a six-year term. Previously elected 2000, 1994, 1988.

Thad Cochran (R). Reelected 2002 to a six-year term. Previously elected 1996, 1990, 1984, 1978.

REPRESENTATIVES (2 Democrats, 2 Republicans)
1. Roger Wicker (R)
2. Bennie Thompson (D)
3. Charles W. "Chip" Pickering Jr. (R)
4. Gene Taylor (D)

POSTWAR VOTE FOR PRESIDENT

Year	Total Vote	Republican		Democratic		Other Vote	Plurality	Percentage			
								Total Vote		Major Vote	
		Vote	Candidate	Vote	Candidate	Vote		Rep.	Dem.	Rep.	Dem.
2004	1,152,145	684,981	Bush, George W.	458,094	Kerry, John	9,070	226,887 R	59.5%	39.8%	59.9%	40.1%
2000**	994,184	572,844	Bush, George W.	404,614	Gore, Al	16,726	168,230 R	57.6%	40.7%	58.6%	41.4%
1996**	893,857	439,838	Dole, Bob	394,022	Clinton, Bill	59,997	45,816 R	49.2%	44.1%	52.7%	47.3%
1992**	981,793	487,793	Bush, George	400,258	Clinton, Bill	93,742	87,535 R	49.7%	40.8%	54.9%	45.1%
1988	931,527	557,890	Bush, George	363,921	Dukakis, Michael S.	9,716	193,969 R	59.9%	39.1%	60.5%	39.5%
1984	941,104	582,377	Reagan, Ronald	352,192	Mondale, Walter F.	6,535	230,185 R	61.9%	37.4%	62.3%	37.7%
1980**	892,620	441,089	Reagan, Ronald	429,281	Carter, Jimmy	22,250	11,808 R	49.4%	48.1%	50.7%	49.3%
1976	769,361	366,846	Ford, Gerald R.	381,309	Carter, Jimmy	21,206	14,463 D	47.7%	49.6%	49.0%	51.0%
1972	645,963	505,125	Nixon, Richard M.	126,782	McGovern, George S.	14,056	378,343 R	78.2%	19.6%	79.9%	20.1%
1968**	654,509	88,516	Nixon, Richard M.	150,644	Humphrey, Hubert H.	415,349	264,705 A	13.5%	23.0%	37.0%	63.0%
1964	409,146	356,528	Goldwater, Barry M.	52,618	Johnson, Lyndon B.		303,910 R	87.1%	12.9%	87.1%	12.9%
1960**	298,171	73,561	Nixon, Richard M.	108,362	Kennedy, John F.	116,248	7,886 U	24.7%	36.3%	40.4%	59.6%
1956	248,104	60,685	Eisenhower, Dwight D.	144,453	Stevenson, Adlai E.	42,966	83,768 D	24.5%	58.2%	29.6%	70.4%
1952	285,532	112,966	Eisenhower, Dwight D.	172,566	Stevenson, Adlai E.		59,600 D	39.6%	60.4%	39.6%	60.4%
1948**	192,190	5,043	Dewey, Thomas E.	19,384	Truman, Harry S.	167,763	148,154 SR	2.6%	10.1%	20.6%	79.4%

**In past elections, the other vote included: 2000 - 8,122 Green (Ralph Nader); 1996 - 52,222 Reform (Ross Perot); 1992 - 85,626 Independent (Ross Perot); 1980 - 12,036 Independent (John Anderson); 1968 - 415,349 American Independent (George Wallace); 1960 - 116,248 Unpledged Independent Democratic Electors; 1948 - 167,538 States' Rights (Strom Thurmond).

MISSISSIPPI

POSTWAR VOTE FOR GOVERNOR

Year	Total Vote	Republican Vote	Republican Candidate	Democratic Vote	Democratic Candidate	Other Vote	Rep.-Dem. Plurality	Total Vote Rep.	Total Vote Dem.	Major Vote Rep.	Major Vote Dem.
2003	894,487	470,404	Barbour, Haley	409,787	Musgrove, Ronnie	14,296	60,617 R	52.6%	45.8%	53.4%	46.6%
1999**	763,938	370,691	Parker, Mike	379,034	Musgrove, Ronnie	14,213	8,343 D	48.5%	49.6%	49.4%	50.6%
1995	819,471	455,261	Fordice, Kirk	364,210	Molpus, Dick		91,051 R	55.6%	44.4%	55.6%	44.4%
1991	711,188	361,500	Fordice, Kirk	338,435	Mabus, Ray	11,253	23,065 R	50.8%	47.6%	51.6%	48.4%
1987	721,695	336,006	Reed, Jack	385,689	Mabus, Ray		49,683 D	46.6%	53.4%	46.6%	53.4%
1983	742,737	288,764	Bramlett, Leon	409,209	Allain, William A.	44,764	120,445 D	38.9%	55.1%	41.4%	58.6%
1979	677,322	263,702	Carmichael, Gil	413,620	Winter, William F.		149,918 D	38.9%	61.1%	38.9%	61.1%
1975	708,033	319,632	Carmichael, Gil	369,568	Finch, Cliff	18,833	49,936 D	45.1%	52.2%	46.4%	53.6%
1971	780,537		—	601,122	Waller, William L.	179,415	601,122 D		77.0%		100.0%
1967	448,697	133,379	Phillips, Rubel L.	315,318	Williams, John Bell		181,939 D	29.7%	70.3%	29.7%	70.3%
1963	363,971	138,515	Phillips, Rubel L.	225,456	Johnson, Paul B.		86,941 D	38.1%	61.9%	38.1%	61.9%
1959	57,671		—	57,671	Barnett, Ross R.		57,671 D		100.0%		100.0%
1955	40,707		—	40,707	Coleman, James P.		40,707 D		100.0%		100.0%
1951	43,422		—	43,422	White, Hugh		43,422 D		100.0%		100.0%
1947	166,095		—	161,993	Wright, Fielding L.	4,102	161,993 D		97.5%		100.0%

**In 1999 no candidate received a majority of the vote. Democrat Ronnie Musgrove was elected in January 2000 by the Mississippi House of Representatives.

POSTWAR VOTE FOR SENATOR

Year	Total Vote	Republican Vote	Republican Candidate	Democratic Vote	Democratic Candidate	Other Vote	Rep.-Dem. Plurality	Total Vote Rep.	Total Vote Dem.	Major Vote Rep.	Major Vote Dem.
2006	610,921	388,399	Lott, Trent	213,000	Fleming, Erik R.	9,522	175,399 R	63.6%	34.9%	64.6%	35.4%
2002	630,495	533,269	Cochran, Thad		—	97,226	533,269 R	84.6%		100.0%	
2000	994,144	654,941	Lott, Trent	314,090	Brown, Troy	25,113	340,851 R	65.9%	31.6%	67.6%	32.4%
1996	878,662	624,154	Cochran, Thad	240,647	Hunt, James W.	13,861	383,507 R	71.0%	27.4%	72.2%	27.8%
1994	608,085	418,333	Lott, Trent	189,752	Harper, Ken		228,581 R	68.8%	31.2%	68.8%	31.2%
1990	274,244	274,244	Cochran, Thad		—		274,244 R	100.0%		100.0%	
1988	946,719	510,380	Lott, Trent	436,339	Dowdy, Wayne		74,041 R	53.9%	46.1%	53.9%	46.1%
1984	952,240	580,314	Cochran, Thad	371,926	Winter, William F.		208,388 R	60.9%	39.1%	60.9%	39.1%
1982	645,026	230,927	Barbour, Haley	414,099	Stennis, John		183,172 D	35.8%	64.2%	35.8%	64.2%
1978**	583,936	263,089	Cochran, Thad	185,454	Dantin, Maurice	135,393	77,635 R	45.1%	31.8%	58.7%	41.3%
1976	554,433		—	554,433	Stennis, John		554,433 D		100.0%		100.0%
1972	645,746	249,779	Carmichael, Gil	375,102	Eastland, James O.	20,865	125,323 D	38.7%	58.1%	40.0%	60.0%
1970	324,215		—	286,622	Stennis, John	37,593	286,622 D		88.4%		100.0%
1966	393,900	105,150	Walker, Prentiss	258,248	Eastland, James O.	30,502	153,098 D	26.7%	65.6%	28.9%	71.1%
1964	343,364		—	343,364	Stennis, John		343,364 D		100.0%		100.0%
1960	266,148	21,807	Moore, Joe A.	244,341	Eastland, James O.		222,534 D	8.2%	91.8%	8.2%	91.8%
1958	61,039		—	61,039	Stennis, John		61,039 D		100.0%		100.0%
1954	105,526	4,678	White, James A.	100,848	Eastland, James O.		96,170 D	4.4%	95.6%	4.4%	95.6%
1952	233,919		—	233,919	Stennis, John		233,919 D		100.0%		100.0%
1948	151,478		—	151,478	Eastland, James O.		151,478 D		100.0%		100.0%
1947S	193,709		[See note below]				D				
1946	46,747		—	46,747	Bilbo, Theodore		46,747 D		100.0%		100.0%

**In past elections, the other vote included: 1978 - 133,646 Independent (Charles Evers). The 1947 election was for a short term to fill a vacancy and was held without party designation or nomination; John Stennis received 52,068 votes (26.9 percent of the total vote) and won the election with a 6,343 vote plurality. Other candidates included: 45,725 W. M. Colmer; 43,642 Forrest B. Jackson; 27,159 Paul B. Johnson; 24,492 John E. Rankin.

MISSISSIPPI

SENATOR 2006

2000 Census Population	County	Total Vote	Republican	Democratic	Other	Rep.-Dem. Plurality	Total Vote Rep.	Total Vote Dem.	Major Vote Rep.	Major Vote Dem.
34,340	ADAMS	7,054	3,512	3,470	72	42 R	49.8%	49.2%	50.3%	49.7%
34,558	ALCORN	7,821	5,240	2,417	164	2,823 R	67.0%	30.9%	68.4%	31.6%
13,599	AMITE	4,415	2,625	1,705	85	920 R	59.5%	38.6%	60.6%	39.4%
19,661	ATTALA	4,910	3,048	1,817	45	1,231 R	62.1%	37.0%	62.7%	37.3%
8,026	BENTON	2,088	1,085	960	43	125 R	52.0%	46.0%	53.1%	46.9%
40,633	BOLIVAR	7,840	3,436	4,302	102	866 D	43.8%	54.9%	44.4%	55.6%
15,069	CALHOUN	2,913	1,978	903	32	1,075 R	67.9%	31.0%	68.7%	31.3%
10,769	CARROLL	3,482	2,421	1,022	39	1,399 R	69.5%	29.4%	70.3%	29.7%
19,440	CHICKASAW	3,675	1,947	1,678	50	269 R	53.0%	45.7%	53.7%	46.3%
9,758	CHOCTAW	2,251	1,517	696	38	821 R	67.4%	30.9%	68.5%	31.5%
11,831	CLAIBORNE	3,092	798	2,256	38	1,458 D	25.8%	73.0%	26.1%	73.9%
17,955	CLARKE	4,355	2,907	1,372	76	1,535 R	66.8%	31.5%	67.9%	32.1%
21,979	CLAY	5,893	3,002	2,787	104	215 R	50.9%	47.3%	51.9%	48.1%
30,622	COAHOMA	5,720	2,685	2,921	114	236 D	46.9%	51.1%	47.9%	52.1%
28,757	COPIAH	8,105	4,654	3,342	109	1,312 R	57.4%	41.2%	58.2%	41.8%
19,407	COVINGTON	4,863	3,264	1,510	89	1,754 R	67.1%	31.1%	68.4%	31.6%
107,199	DE SOTO	18,981	14,165	4,457	359	9,708 R	74.6%	23.5%	76.1%	23.9%
72,604	FORREST	14,029	9,752	4,031	246	5,721 R	69.5%	28.7%	70.8%	29.2%
8,448	FRANKLIN	2,828	1,944	850	34	1,094 R	68.7%	30.1%	69.6%	30.4%
19,144	GEORGE	3,676	3,076	537	63	2,539 R	83.7%	14.6%	85.1%	14.9%
13,299	GREENE	3,551	2,807	666	78	2,141 R	79.0%	18.8%	80.8%	19.2%
23,263	GRENADA	5,385	3,498	1,816	71	1,682 R	65.0%	33.7%	65.8%	34.2%
42,967	HANCOCK	7,655	6,166	1,329	160	4,837 R	80.5%	17.4%	82.3%	17.7%
189,601	HARRISON	27,245	20,722	6,066	457	14,656 R	76.1%	22.3%	77.4%	22.6%
250,800	HINDS	58,672	24,478	33,343	851	8,865 D	41.7%	56.8%	42.3%	57.7%
21,609	HOLMES	4,919	1,400	3,405	114	2,005 D	28.5%	69.2%	29.1%	70.9%
11,206	HUMPHREYS	2,564	975	1,546	43	571 D	38.0%	60.3%	38.7%	61.3%
2,274	ISSAQUENA	615	275	334	6	59 D	44.7%	54.3%	45.2%	54.8%
22,770	ITAWAMBA	4,555	3,265	1,217	73	2,048 R	71.7%	26.7%	72.8%	27.2%
131,420	JACKSON	22,624	18,029	4,250	345	13,779 R	79.7%	18.8%	80.9%	19.1%
18,149	JASPER	3,783	1,952	1,777	54	175 R	51.6%	47.0%	52.3%	47.7%
9,740	JEFFERSON	2,842	682	2,117	43	1,435 D	24.0%	74.5%	24.4%	75.6%
13,962	JEFFERSON DAVIS	4,006	1,954	1,993	59	39 D	48.8%	49.8%	49.5%	50.5%
64,958	JONES	14,578	10,979	3,375	224	7,604 R	75.3%	23.2%	76.5%	23.5%
10,453	KEMPER	2,931	1,568	1,286	77	282 R	53.5%	43.9%	54.9%	45.1%
38,744	LAFAYETTE	7,406	4,502	2,742	162	1,760 R	60.8%	37.0%	62.1%	37.9%
39,070	LAMAR	12,219	10,346	1,694	179	8,652 R	84.7%	13.9%	85.9%	14.1%
78,161	LAUDERDALE	16,722	12,275	4,205	242	8,070 R	73.4%	25.1%	74.5%	25.5%
13,258	LAWRENCE	3,777	2,493	1,230	54	1,263 R	66.0%	32.6%	67.0%	33.0%
20,940	LEAKE	4,644	2,752	1,840	52	912 R	59.3%	39.6%	59.9%	40.1%
75,755	LEE	13,151	9,063	3,859	229	5,204 R	68.9%	29.3%	70.1%	29.9%
37,947	LEFLORE	6,647	3,410	3,176	61	234 R	51.3%	47.8%	51.8%	48.2%
33,166	LINCOLN	7,283	5,173	2,034	76	3,139 R	71.0%	27.9%	71.8%	28.2%
61,586	LOWNDES	13,286	8,800	4,338	148	4,462 R	66.2%	32.7%	67.0%	33.0%
74,674	MADISON	20,689	13,544	6,895	250	6,649 R	65.5%	33.3%	66.3%	33.7%
25,595	MARION	6,547	4,661	1,773	113	2,888 R	71.2%	27.1%	72.4%	27.6%
34,993	MARSHALL	7,576	3,382	3,999	195	617 D	44.6%	52.8%	45.8%	54.2%
38,014	MONROE	7,197	4,548	2,567	82	1,981 R	63.2%	35.7%	63.9%	36.1%
12,189	MONTGOMERY	3,428	2,106	1,284	38	822 R	61.4%	37.5%	62.1%	37.9%
28,684	NESHOBA	4,938	3,879	996	63	2,883 R	78.6%	20.2%	79.6%	20.4%
21,838	NEWTON	4,121	3,158	920	43	2,238 R	76.6%	22.3%	77.4%	22.6%
12,548	NOXUBEE	3,523	1,432	2,008	83	576 D	40.6%	57.0%	41.6%	58.4%
42,902	OKTIBBEHA	9,462	5,234	4,092	136	1,142 R	55.3%	43.2%	56.1%	43.9%
34,274	PANOLA	6,690	3,747	2,858	85	889 R	56.0%	42.7%	56.7%	43.3%
48,621	PEARL RIVER	14,131	11,318	2,525	288	8,793 R	80.1%	17.9%	81.8%	18.2%
12,138	PERRY	2,662	2,093	512	57	1,581 R	78.6%	19.2%	80.3%	19.7%
38,940	PIKE	9,235	5,396	3,708	131	1,688 R	58.4%	40.2%	59.3%	40.7%
26,726	PONTOTOC	5,646	4,411	1,164	71	3,247 R	78.1%	20.6%	79.1%	20.9%
25,556	PRENTISS	5,952	4,168	1,676	108	2,492 R	70.0%	28.2%	71.3%	28.7%
10,117	QUITMAN	2,056	834	1,182	40	348 D	40.6%	57.5%	41.4%	58.6%

MISSISSIPPI

SENATOR 2006

2000 Census Population	County	Total Vote	Republican	Democratic	Other	Rep.-Dem. Plurality	Total Vote Rep.	Total Vote Dem.	Major Vote Rep.	Major Vote Dem.
115,327	RANKIN	27,843	22,456	4,927	460	17,529 R	80.7%	17.7%	82.0%	18.0%
28,423	SCOTT	4,624	3,035	1,547	42	1,488 R	65.6%	33.5%	66.2%	33.8%
6,580	SHARKEY	1,627	707	900	20	193 D	43.5%	55.3%	44.0%	56.0%
27,639	SIMPSON	5,804	4,027	1,703	74	2,324 R	69.4%	29.3%	70.3%	29.7%
16,182	SMITH	3,977	3,200	720	57	2,480 R	80.5%	18.1%	81.6%	18.4%
13,622	STONE	3,219	2,492	669	58	1,823 R	77.4%	20.8%	78.8%	21.2%
34,369	SUNFLOWER	5,653	2,514	3,073	66	559 D	44.5%	54.4%	45.0%	55.0%
14,903	TALLAHATCHIE	4,435	2,352	1,991	92	361 R	53.0%	44.9%	54.2%	45.8%
25,370	TATE	5,447	3,495	1,845	107	1,650 R	64.2%	33.9%	65.4%	34.6%
20,826	TIPPAH	4,975	3,625	1,255	95	2,370 R	72.9%	25.2%	74.3%	25.7%
19,163	TISHOMINGO	4,327	2,636	1,598	93	1,038 R	60.9%	36.9%	62.3%	37.7%
9,227	TUNICA	1,712	642	1,009	61	367 D	37.5%	58.9%	38.9%	61.1%
25,362	UNION	4,817	3,541	1,203	73	2,338 R	73.5%	25.0%	74.6%	25.4%
15,156	WALTHALL	3,805	2,483	1,248	74	1,235 R	65.3%	32.8%	66.6%	33.4%
49,644	WARREN	12,205	7,650	4,421	134	3,229 R	62.7%	36.2%	63.4%	36.6%
62,977	WASHINGTON	9,421	4,246	5,039	136	793 D	45.1%	53.5%	45.7%	54.3%
21,216	WAYNE	4,643	3,192	1,393	58	1,799 R	68.7%	30.0%	69.6%	30.4%
10,294	WEBSTER	2,786	2,186	562	38	1,624 R	78.5%	20.2%	79.5%	20.5%
10,312	WILKINSON	2,768	1,026	1,688	54	662 D	37.1%	61.0%	37.8%	62.2%
20,160	WINSTON	5,002	3,142	1,783	77	1,359 R	62.8%	35.6%	63.8%	36.2%
13,051	YALOBUSHA	2,986	1,738	1,205	43	533 R	58.2%	40.4%	59.1%	40.9%
28,149	YAZOO	5,941	3,483	2,391	67	1,092 R	58.6%	40.2%	59.3%	40.7%
2,844,658	TOTAL	610,921	388,399	213,000	9,522	175,399 R	63.6%	34.9%	64.6%	35.4%

MISSISSIPPI

HOUSE OF REPRESENTATIVES

CD	Year	Total Vote	Republican Vote	Republican Candidate	Democratic Vote	Democratic Candidate	Other Vote	Rep.-Dem. Plurality	Total Vote Rep.	Total Vote Dem.	Major Vote Rep.	Major Vote Dem.
1	2006	144,272	95,098	WICKER, ROGER*	49,174	HURT, JAMES K. "KEN"		45,924 R	65.9%	34.1%	65.9%	34.1%
1	2004	277,584	219,328	WICKER, ROGER*	—		58,256	219,328 R	79.0%		100.0%	
1	2002	133,567	95,404	WICKER, ROGER*	32,318	WEATHERS, REX N.	5,845	63,086 R	71.4%	24.2%	74.7%	25.3%
2	2006	155,832	55,672	BROWN, YVONNE R.	100,160	THOMPSON, BENNIE*		44,488 D	35.7%	64.3%	35.7%	64.3%
2	2004	264,869	107,647	LeSUEUR, CLINTON B.	154,626	THOMPSON, BENNIE*	2,596	46,979 D	40.6%	58.4%	41.0%	59.0%
2	2002	163,050	69,711	LeSUEUR, CLINTON B.	89,913	THOMPSON, BENNIE*	3,426	20,202 D	42.8%	55.1%	43.7%	56.3%
3	2006	161,480	125,421	PICKERING, CHARLES W. "CHIP" JR.*	—		36,059	125,421 R	77.7%		100.0%	
3	2004	293,368	234,874	PICKERING, CHARLES W. "CHIP" JR.*	—		58,494	234,874 R	80.1%		100.0%	
3	2002	219,151	139,329	PICKERING, CHARLES W. "CHIP" JR.*	76,184	SHOWS, RONNIE*	3,638	63,145 R	63.6%	34.8%	64.6%	35.4%
4	2006	139,113	28,117	McDONNELL, RANDY	110,996	TAYLOR, GENE*		82,879 D	20.2%	79.8%	20.2%	79.8%
4	2004	280,382	96,740	LOTT, MICHAEL	181,614	TAYLOR, GENE*	2,028	84,874 D	34.5%	64.8%	34.8%	65.2%
4	2002	161,868	34,373	MERTZ, KARL CLEVELAND	121,742	TAYLOR, GENE*	5,753	87,369 D	21.2%	75.2%	22.0%	78.0%
TOTAL	2006	600,697	304,308		260,330		36,059	43,978 R	50.7%	43.3%	53.9%	46.1%
TOTAL	2004	1,116,203	658,589		336,240		121,374	322,349 R	59.0%	30.1%	66.2%	33.8%
TOTAL	2002	677,636	338,817		320,157		18,662	18,660 R	50.0%	47.2%	51.4%	48.6%

An asterisk (*) denotes incumbent.

MISSISSIPPI

GENERAL AND PRIMARY ELECTIONS

2006 GENERAL ELECTIONS

Senator	Other vote was 9,522 Libertarian (Harold M. Taylor).
House	Other vote was:
CD 1	
CD 2	
CD 3	25,999 Independent (Jim Giles); 10,060 Reform (Lamonica L. Magee).
CD 4	

2006 PRIMARY ELECTIONS

Primary	June 6, 2006	**Registration**	1,715,348 No Party Registration
Primary Runoff	June 27, 2006	(as of May 6, 2006)	

Primary Type   Open—Any registered voter could participate in the primary of either party. Any voter that participated in the primary of one party could not participate in the runoff of the other party.

Note: An asterisk (*) denotes incumbent. If no candidate received a majority of the primary vote, a runoff was held between the top two finishers. The names of unopposed candidates do not have to appear on the primary ballot; therefore, no votes were cast for these candidates.

	REPUBLICAN PRIMARIES		DEMOCRATIC PRIMARIES		
Senator	Trent Lott*	Unopposed	Erik R. Fleming	46,185	44.1%
			Bill Bowlin	23,175	22.1%
			James O'Keefe	20,815	19.9%
			Catherine M. Starr	14,629	14.0%
			Scattered write-in	42	
			TOTAL	*104,846*	
			PRIMARY RUNOFF		
			Erik R. Fleming	19,477	65.0%
			Bill Bowlin	10,490	35.0%
			TOTAL	*29,967*	
Congressional District 1	Roger Wicker*	Unopposed	James K. "Ken" Hurt	4,159	37.1%
			William Bambach	2,788	24.9%
			Ron Shapiro	2,514	22.4%
			James Forsythe	1,740	15.5%
			TOTAL	*11,201*	
			PRIMARY RUNOFF		
			James K. "Ken" Hurt	5,063	67.4%
			William Bambach	2,446	32.6%
			TOTAL	*7,509*	
Congressional District 2	Yvonne R. Brown	Unopposed	Bennie Thompson*	58,941	64.4%
			Chuck Espy	31,906	34.8%
			Dorothy "Dot" Benford	743	0.8%
			TOTAL	*91,590*	
Congressional District 3	Charles W. "Chip" Pickering Jr.*	Unopposed	No Democratic candidate		
Congressional District 4	Randy McDonnell	Unopposed	Gene Taylor*	6,761	99.9%
			Scattered write-in	8	0.1%
			TOTAL	*6,769*	

MISSOURI

Congressional districts first established for elections held in 2002
9 members

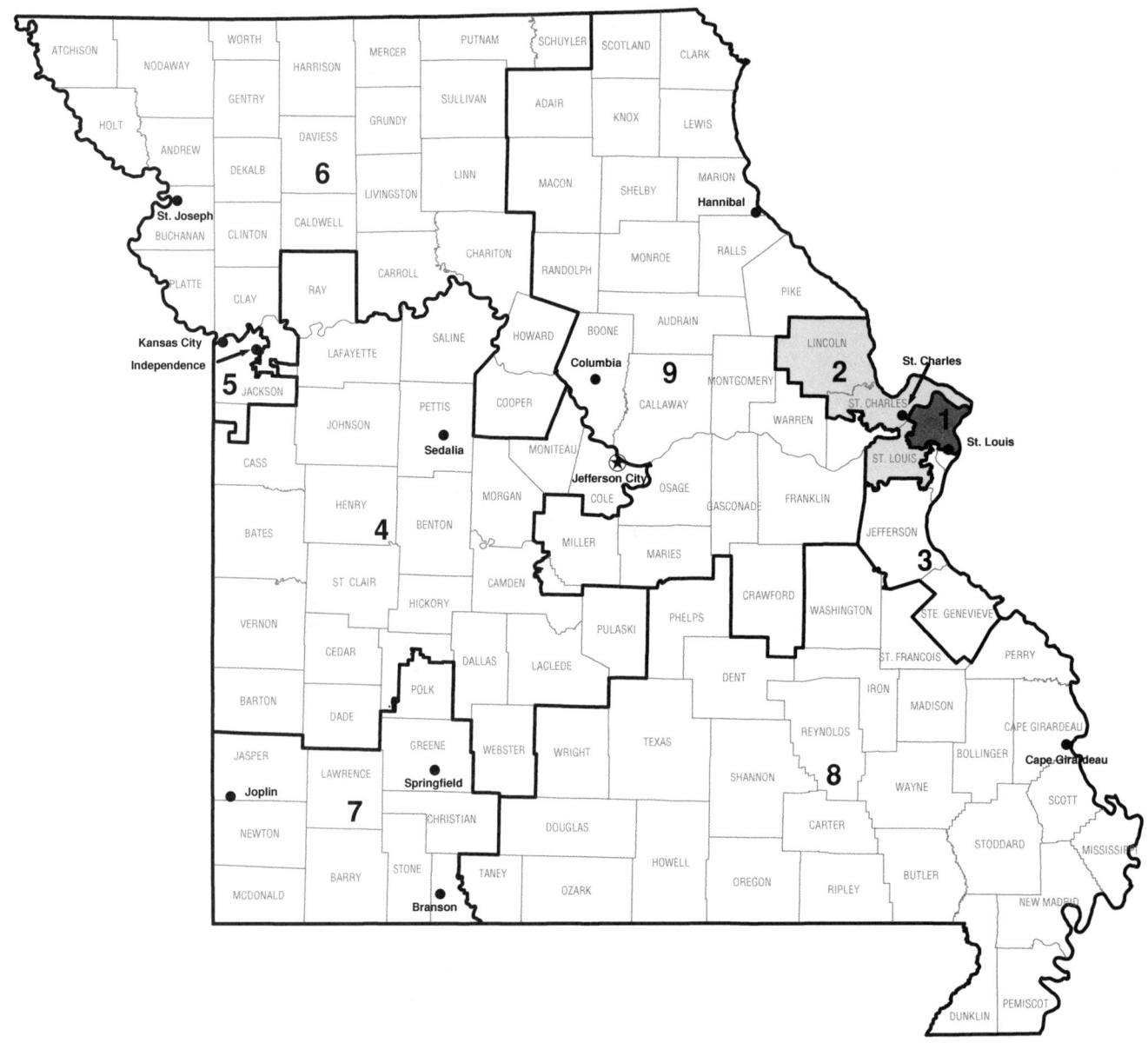

MISSOURI

GOVERNOR
Matt Blunt (R). Elected 2004 to a four-year term.

SENATORS (1 Democrat, 1 Republican)
Claire McCaskill (D). Elected 2006 to a six-year term.

Christopher S. Bond (R). Reelected 2004 to a six-year term. Previously elected 1998, 1992, 1986.

REPRESENTATIVES (5 Republicans, 4 Democrats)
1. William Lacy Clay (D)
2. Todd Akin (R)
3. Russ Carnahan (D)
4. Ike Skelton (D)
5. Emanuel Cleaver II (D)
6. Sam Graves (R)
7. Roy Blunt (R)
8. Jo Ann Emerson (R)
9. Kenny Hulshof (R)

POSTWAR VOTE FOR PRESIDENT

| | | Republican | | Democratic | | Other | | Percentage | | | |
| | | | | | | | | Total Vote | | Major Vote | |
Year	Total Vote	Vote	Candidate	Vote	Candidate	Vote	Plurality	Rep.	Dem.	Rep.	Dem.
2004	2,731,364	1,455,713	Bush, George W.	1,259,171	Kerry, John	16,480	196,542 R	53.3%	46.1%	53.6%	46.4%
2000**	2,359,892	1,189,924	Bush, George W.	1,111,138	Gore, Al	58,830	78,786 R	50.4%	47.1%	51.7%	48.3%
1996**	2,158,065	890,016	Dole, Bob	1,025,935	Clinton, Bill	242,114	135,919 D	41.2%	47.5%	46.5%	53.5%
1992**	2,391,565	811,159	Bush, George	1,053,873	Clinton, Bill	526,533	242,714 D	33.9%	44.1%	43.5%	56.5%
1988	2,093,713	1,084,953	Bush, George	1,001,619	Dukakis, Michael S.	7,141	83,334 R	51.8%	47.8%	52.0%	48.0%
1984	2,122,783	1,274,188	Reagan, Ronald	848,583	Mondale, Walter F.	12	425,605 R	60.0%	40.0%	60.0%	40.0%
1980**	2,099,824	1,074,181	Reagan, Ronald	931,182	Carter, Jimmy	94,461	142,999 R	51.2%	44.3%	53.6%	46.4%
1976	1,953,600	927,443	Ford, Gerald R.	998,387	Carter, Jimmy	27,770	70,944 D	47.5%	51.1%	48.2%	51.8%
1972	1,855,803	1,153,852	Nixon, Richard M.	697,147	McGovern, George S.	4,804	456,705 R	62.2%	37.6%	62.3%	37.7%
1968**	1,809,502	811,932	Nixon, Richard M.	791,444	Humphrey, Hubert H.	206,126	20,488 R	44.9%	43.7%	50.6%	49.4%
1964	1,817,879	653,535	Goldwater, Barry M.	1,164,344	Johnson, Lyndon B.		510,809 D	36.0%	64.0%	36.0%	64.0%
1960	1,934,422	962,221	Nixon, Richard M.	972,201	Kennedy, John F.		9,980 D	49.7%	50.3%	49.7%	50.3%
1956	1,832,562	914,289	Eisenhower, Dwight D.	918,273	Stevenson, Adlai E.		3,984 D	49.9%	50.1%	49.9%	50.1%
1952	1,892,062	959,429	Eisenhower, Dwight D.	929,830	Stevenson, Adlai E.	2,803	29,599 R	50.7%	49.1%	50.8%	49.2%
1948	1,578,628	655,039	Dewey, Thomas E.	917,315	Truman, Harry S.	6,274	262,276 D	41.5%	58.1%	41.7%	58.3%

**In past elections, the other vote included: 2000 - 38,515 Green (Ralph Nader); 1996 - 217,188 Reform (Ross Perot); 1992 - 518,741 Independent (Ross Perot); 1980 - 77,920 Independent (John Anderson); 1968 - 206,126 American Independent (George Wallace).

MISSOURI

POSTWAR VOTE FOR GOVERNOR

Year	Total Vote	Republican Vote	Republican Candidate	Democratic Vote	Democratic Candidate	Other Vote	Rep.-Dem. Plurality	Total Vote Rep.	Total Vote Dem.	Major Vote Rep.	Major Vote Dem.
2004	2,719,599	1,382,419	Blunt, Matt	1,301,442	McCaskill, Claire	35,738	80,977 R	50.8%	47.9%	51.5%	48.5%
2000	2,346,830	1,131,307	Talent, Jim	1,152,752	Holden, Bob	62,771	21,445 D	48.2%	49.1%	49.5%	50.5%
1996	2,142,518	866,268	Kelly, Margaret	1,224,801	Carnahan, Mel	51,449	358,533 D	40.4%	57.2%	41.4%	58.6%
1992	2,344,121	968,574	Webster, William L.	1,375,425	Carnahan, Mel	122	406,851 D	41.3%	58.7%	41.3%	58.7%
1988	2,085,928	1,339,531	Ashcroft, John	724,919	Hearnes, Betty C.	21,478	614,612 R	64.2%	34.8%	64.9%	35.1%
1984	2,108,210	1,194,506	Ashcroft, John	913,700	Rothman, Kenneth J.	4	280,806 R	56.7%	43.3%	56.7%	43.3%
1980	2,088,028	1,098,950	Bond, Christopher S.	981,884	Teasdale, Joseph P.	7,194	117,066 R	52.6%	47.0%	52.8%	47.2%
1976	1,933,575	958,110	Bond, Christopher S.	971,184	Teasdale, Joseph P.	4,281	13,074 D	49.6%	50.2%	49.7%	50.3%
1972	1,865,683	1,029,451	Bond, Christopher S.	832,751	Dowd, Edward L.	3,481	196,700 R	55.2%	44.6%	55.3%	44.7%
1968	1,764,602	691,797	Roos, Lawrence K.	1,072,805	Hearnes, Warren E.		381,008 D	39.2%	60.8%	39.2%	60.8%
1964	1,789,600	678,949	Shepley, Ethan	1,110,651	Hearnes, Warren E.		431,702 D	37.9%	62.1%	37.9%	62.1%
1960	1,887,331	792,131	Farmer, Edward G.	1,095,200	Dalton, John M.		303,069 D	42.0%	58.0%	42.0%	58.0%
1956	1,808,338	866,810	Hocker, Lon	941,528	Blair, James T.		74,718 D	47.9%	52.1%	47.9%	52.1%
1952	1,871,095	886,370	Elliott, Howard	983,166	Donnelly, Phil M.	1,559	96,796 D	47.4%	52.5%	47.4%	52.6%
1948	1,567,338	670,064	Thompson, Murray	893,092	Smith, Forrest	4,182	223,028 D	42.8%	57.0%	42.9%	57.1%

POSTWAR VOTE FOR SENATOR

Year	Total Vote	Republican Vote	Republican Candidate	Democratic Vote	Democratic Candidate	Other Vote	Rep.-Dem. Plurality	Total Vote Rep.	Total Vote Dem.	Major Vote Rep.	Major Vote Dem.
2006	2,128,459	1,006,941	Talent, Jim	1,055,255	McCaskill, Claire	66,263	48,314 D	47.3%	49.6%	48.8%	51.2%
2004	2,706,402	1,518,089	Bond, Christopher S.	1,158,261	Farmer, Nancy	30,052	359,828 R	56.1%	42.8%	56.7%	43.3%
2002S	1,877,620	935,032	Talent, Jim	913,778	Carnahan, Jean	28,810	21,254 R	49.8%	48.7%	50.6%	49.4%
2000**	2,361,586	1,142,852	Ashcroft, John	1,191,812	Carnahan, Mel	26,922	48,960 D	48.4%	50.5%	49.0%	51.0%
1998	1,576,857	830,625	Bond, Christopher S.	690,208	Nixon, Jeremiah W.	56,024	140,417 R	52.7%	43.8%	54.6%	45.4%
1994	1,775,116	1,060,149	Ashcroft, John	633,697	Wheat, Alan	81,270	426,452 R	59.7%	35.7%	62.6%	37.4%
1992	2,354,925	1,221,901	Bond, Christopher S.	1,057,967	Rothman-Serot, Geri	75,057	163,934 R	51.9%	44.9%	53.6%	46.4%
1988	2,078,875	1,407,416	Danforth, John C.	660,045	Nixon, Jeremiah W.	11,414	747,371 R	67.7%	31.8%	68.1%	31.9%
1986	1,477,327	777,612	Bond, Christopher S.	699,624	Woods, Harriett	91	77,988 R	52.6%	47.4%	52.6%	47.4%
1982	1,543,521	784,876	Danforth, John C.	758,629	Woods, Harriett	16	26,247 R	50.8%	49.1%	50.9%	49.1%
1980	2,066,965	985,399	McNary, Gene	1,074,859	Eagleton, Thomas F.	6,707	89,460 D	47.7%	52.0%	47.8%	52.2%
1976	1,914,777	1,090,067	Danforth, John C.	813,571	Hearnes, Warren E.	11,139	276,496 R	56.9%	42.5%	57.3%	42.7%
1974	1,224,303	480,900	Curtis, Thomas B.	735,433	Eagleton, Thomas F.	7,970	254,533 D	39.3%	60.1%	39.5%	60.5%
1970	1,283,912	617,903	Danforth, John C.	655,431	Symington, Stuart	10,578	37,528 D	48.1%	51.0%	48.5%	51.5%
1968	1,737,958	850,544	Curtis, Thomas B.	887,414	Eagleton, Thomas F.		36,870 D	48.9%	51.1%	48.9%	51.1%
1964	1,783,043	596,377	Bradshaw, Jean P.	1,186,666	Symington, Stuart		590,289 D	33.4%	66.6%	33.4%	66.6%
1962	1,222,259	555,330	Kemper, Crosby	666,929	Long, Edward V.		111,599 D	45.4%	54.6%	45.4%	54.6%
1960S	1,880,232	880,576	Hocker, Lon	999,656	Long, Edward V.		119,080 D	46.8%	53.2%	46.8%	53.2%
1958	1,173,903	393,847	Palmer, Hazel	780,056	Symington, Stuart		386,209 D	33.6%	66.4%	33.6%	66.4%
1956	1,800,984	785,048	Douglas, Herbert	1,015,936	Hennings, Thomas C.		230,888 D	43.6%	56.4%	43.6%	56.4%
1952	1,868,083	858,170	Kem, James P.	1,008,523	Symington, Stuart	1,390	150,353 D	45.9%	54.0%	46.0%	54.0%
1950	1,279,414	592,922	Donnell, Forrest C.	685,732	Hennings, Thomas C.	760	92,810 D	46.3%	53.6%	46.4%	53.6%
1946	1,084,100	572,556	Kem, James P.	511,544	Briggs, Frank P.		61,012 R	52.8%	47.2%	52.8%	47.2%

**In 2000 the Democratic candidate, Mel Carnahan, was killed in an airplane crash in October but his name remained on the ballot and he won the election in November. Subsequently, his widow, Jean Carnahan, was appointed to fill the seat until an election could be held in 2002 for the remaining four years of the term. The 1960 election was for a short term to fill a vacancy.

MISSOURI
SENATOR 2006

2000 Census Population	County	Total Vote	Republican	Democratic	Other	Rep.-Dem. Plurality	Total Vote Rep.	Total Vote Dem.	Major Vote Rep.	Major Vote Dem.
24,977	ADAIR	8,144	4,297	3,651	196	646 R	52.8%	44.8%	54.1%	45.9%
16,492	ANDREW	6,685	3,556	2,915	214	641 R	53.2%	43.6%	55.0%	45.0%
6,430	ATCHISON	2,518	1,479	969	70	510 R	58.7%	38.5%	60.4%	39.6%
25,853	AUDRAIN	8,350	4,362	3,695	293	667 R	52.2%	44.3%	54.1%	45.9%
34,010	BARRY	10,997	6,510	3,903	584	2,607 R	59.2%	35.5%	62.5%	37.5%
12,541	BARTON	4,894	3,460	1,235	199	2,225 R	70.7%	25.2%	73.7%	26.3%
16,653	BATES	7,035	3,374	3,326	335	48 R	48.0%	47.3%	50.4%	49.6%
17,180	BENTON	7,581	3,637	3,457	487	180 R	48.0%	45.6%	51.3%	48.7%
12,029	BOLLINGER	4,871	2,961	1,718	192	1,243 R	60.8%	35.3%	63.3%	36.7%
135,454	BOONE	57,666	25,369	30,306	1,991	4,937 D	44.0%	52.6%	45.6%	54.4%
85,998	BUCHANAN	29,397	12,579	15,734	1,084	3,155 D	42.8%	53.5%	44.4%	55.6%
40,867	BUTLER	12,632	7,692	4,521	419	3,171 R	60.9%	35.8%	63.0%	37.0%
8,969	CALDWELL	3,753	1,802	1,740	211	62 R	48.0%	46.4%	50.9%	49.1%
40,766	CALLAWAY	14,466	7,683	6,081	702	1,602 R	53.1%	42.0%	55.8%	44.2%
37,051	CAMDEN	16,352	9,095	6,448	809	2,647 R	55.6%	39.4%	58.5%	41.5%
68,693	CAPE GIRARDEAU	28,077	18,070	9,220	787	8,850 R	64.4%	32.8%	66.2%	33.8%
10,285	CARROLL	3,595	2,001	1,469	125	532 R	55.7%	40.9%	57.7%	42.3%
5,941	CARTER	2,264	1,233	935	96	298 R	54.5%	41.3%	56.9%	43.1%
82,092	CASS	35,609	18,027	16,253	1,329	1,774 R	50.6%	45.6%	52.6%	47.4%
13,733	CEDAR	5,170	2,883	1,973	314	910 R	55.8%	38.2%	59.4%	40.6%
8,438	CHARITON	3,567	1,781	1,646	140	135 R	49.9%	46.1%	52.0%	48.0%
54,285	CHRISTIAN	26,663	16,129	9,407	1,127	6,722 R	60.5%	35.3%	63.2%	36.8%
7,416	CLARK	2,870	1,471	1,326	73	145 R	51.3%	46.2%	52.6%	47.4%
184,006	CLAY	75,035	33,014	39,630	2,391	6,616 D	44.0%	52.8%	45.4%	54.6%
18,979	CLINTON	7,893	3,558	4,045	290	487 D	45.1%	51.2%	46.8%	53.2%
71,397	COLE	30,019	18,185	10,610	1,224	7,575 R	60.6%	35.3%	63.2%	36.8%
16,670	COOPER	6,495	3,607	2,559	329	1,048 R	55.5%	39.4%	58.5%	41.5%
22,804	CRAWFORD	8,107	4,078	3,761	268	317 R	50.3%	46.4%	52.0%	48.0%
7,923	DADE	3,319	2,014	1,120	185	894 R	60.7%	33.7%	64.3%	35.7%
15,661	DALLAS	5,908	3,189	2,358	361	831 R	54.0%	39.9%	57.5%	42.5%
8,016	DAVIESS	3,258	1,628	1,440	190	188 R	50.0%	44.2%	53.1%	46.9%
11,597	DE KALB	3,874	2,021	1,693	160	328 R	52.2%	43.7%	54.4%	45.6%
14,927	DENT	5,865	3,343	2,215	307	1,128 R	57.0%	37.8%	60.1%	39.9%
13,084	DOUGLAS	5,502	3,197	1,996	309	1,201 R	58.1%	36.3%	61.6%	38.4%
33,155	DUNKLIN	8,327	4,138	3,984	205	154 R	49.7%	47.8%	50.9%	49.1%
93,807	FRANKLIN	37,795	19,746	16,890	1,159	2,856 R	52.2%	44.7%	53.9%	46.1%
15,342	GASCONADE	6,019	3,503	2,309	207	1,194 R	58.2%	38.4%	60.3%	39.7%
6,861	GENTRY	2,851	1,427	1,237	187	190 R	50.1%	43.4%	53.6%	46.4%
240,391	GREENE	101,365	54,335	43,219	3,811	11,116 R	53.6%	42.6%	55.7%	44.3%
10,432	GRUNDY	3,954	2,045	1,574	335	471 R	51.7%	39.8%	56.5%	43.5%
8,850	HARRISON	3,222	1,769	1,250	203	519 R	54.9%	38.8%	58.6%	41.4%
21,997	HENRY	9,022	4,014	4,580	428	566 D	44.5%	50.8%	46.7%	53.3%
8,940	HICKORY	4,217	1,876	2,042	299	166 D	44.5%	48.4%	47.9%	52.1%
5,351	HOLT	2,165	1,313	788	64	525 R	60.6%	36.4%	62.5%	37.5%
10,212	HOWARD	4,009	1,952	1,877	180	75 R	48.7%	46.8%	51.0%	49.0%
37,238	HOWELL	12,877	7,157	5,032	688	2,125 R	55.6%	39.1%	58.7%	41.3%
10,697	IRON	3,822	1,563	2,081	178	518 D	40.9%	54.4%	42.9%	57.1%
654,880	JACKSON	133,939	59,818	69,859	4,262	10,041 D	44.7%	52.2%	46.1%	53.9%
104,686	JASPER	34,427	22,790	10,692	945	12,098 R	66.2%	31.1%	68.1%	31.9%
198,099	JEFFERSON	73,656	32,232	39,271	2,153	7,039 D	43.8%	53.3%	45.1%	54.9%
48,258	JOHNSON	15,321	7,467	7,099	755	368 R	48.7%	46.3%	51.3%	48.7%
See Note	KANSAS CITY	96,979	21,512	73,556	1,911	52,044 D	22.2%	75.8%	22.6%	77.4%
4,361	KNOX	1,789	1,029	717	43	312 R	57.5%	40.1%	58.9%	41.1%
32,513	LACLEDE	12,450	7,160	4,558	732	2,602 R	57.5%	36.6%	61.1%	38.9%
32,960	LAFAYETTE	12,838	6,360	6,017	461	343 R	49.5%	46.9%	51.4%	48.6%
35,204	LAWRENCE	12,945	7,729	4,557	659	3,172 R	59.7%	35.2%	62.9%	37.1%
10,494	LEWIS	3,619	1,963	1,571	85	392 R	54.2%	43.4%	55.5%	44.5%
38,944	LINCOLN	17,014	8,373	8,112	529	261 R	49.2%	47.7%	50.8%	49.2%
13,754	LINN	4,708	2,231	2,291	186	60 D	47.4%	48.7%	49.3%	50.7%
14,558	LIVINGSTON	5,415	2,863	2,353	199	510 R	52.9%	43.5%	54.9%	45.1%

Note: Kansas City has established its own election board and reports its results separately from Jackson County.

MISSOURI

SENATOR 2006

2000 Census Population	County	Total Vote	Republican	Democratic	Other	Rep.-Dem. Plurality	Percentage Total Vote		Percentage Major Vote	
							Rep.	Dem.	Rep.	Dem.
21,681	MCDONALD	6,017	3,796	1,949	272	1,847 R	63.1%	32.4%	66.1%	33.9%
15,762	MACON	6,000	3,321	2,526	153	795 R	55.4%	42.1%	56.8%	43.2%
11,800	MADISON	4,227	2,278	1,761	188	517 R	53.9%	41.7%	56.4%	43.6%
8,903	MARIES	3,777	2,049	1,530	198	519 R	54.2%	40.5%	57.3%	42.7%
28,289	MARION	9,599	5,593	3,804	202	1,789 R	58.3%	39.6%	59.5%	40.5%
3,757	MERCER	1,426	837	503	86	334 R	58.7%	35.3%	62.5%	37.5%
23,564	MILLER	8,844	5,308	3,000	536	2,308 R	60.0%	33.9%	63.9%	36.1%
13,427	MISSISSIPPI	4,098	1,983	2,050	65	67 D	48.4%	50.0%	49.2%	50.8%
14,827	MONITEAU	5,343	3,156	1,867	320	1,289 R	59.1%	34.9%	62.8%	37.2%
9,311	MONROE	3,508	1,841	1,569	98	272 R	52.5%	44.7%	54.0%	46.0%
12,136	MONTGOMERY	4,635	2,540	1,898	197	642 R	54.8%	40.9%	57.2%	42.8%
19,309	MORGAN	7,379	3,939	2,993	447	946 R	53.4%	40.6%	56.8%	43.2%
19,760	NEW MADRID	6,099	2,727	3,236	136	509 D	44.7%	53.1%	45.7%	54.3%
52,636	NEWTON	19,214	12,901	5,781	532	7,120 R	67.1%	30.1%	69.1%	30.9%
21,912	NODAWAY	7,502	3,850	3,309	343	541 R	51.3%	44.1%	53.8%	46.2%
10,344	OREGON	3,752	1,785	1,815	152	30 D	47.6%	48.4%	49.6%	50.4%
13,062	OSAGE	5,846	3,738	1,750	358	1,988 R	63.9%	29.9%	68.1%	31.9%
9,542	OZARK	3,677	1,979	1,497	201	482 R	53.8%	40.7%	56.9%	43.1%
20,047	PEMISCOT	4,235	1,992	2,157	86	165 D	47.0%	50.9%	48.0%	52.0%
18,132	PERRY	6,648	4,227	2,208	213	2,019 R	63.6%	33.2%	65.7%	34.3%
39,403	PETTIS	14,170	7,331	6,028	811	1,303 R	51.7%	42.5%	54.9%	45.1%
39,825	PHELPS	15,243	8,183	6,520	540	1,663 R	53.7%	42.8%	55.7%	44.3%
18,351	PIKE	6,286	2,978	3,125	183	147 D	47.4%	49.7%	48.8%	51.2%
73,781	PLATTE	33,072	15,398	16,687	987	1,289 D	46.6%	50.5%	48.0%	52.0%
26,992	POLK	10,293	6,040	3,759	494	2,281 R	58.7%	36.5%	61.6%	38.4%
41,165	PULASKI	9,141	5,150	3,530	461	1,620 R	56.3%	38.6%	59.3%	40.7%
5,223	PUTNAM	1,843	1,151	628	64	523 R	62.5%	34.1%	64.7%	35.3%
9,626	RALLS	3,985	2,069	1,811	105	258 R	51.9%	45.4%	53.3%	46.7%
24,663	RANDOLPH	8,184	4,272	3,494	418	778 R	52.2%	42.7%	55.0%	45.0%
23,354	RAY	8,676	3,459	4,850	367	1,391 D	39.9%	55.9%	41.6%	58.4%
6,689	REYNOLDS	2,872	1,219	1,529	124	310 D	42.4%	53.2%	44.4%	55.6%
13,509	RIPLEY	4,707	2,623	1,905	179	718 R	55.7%	40.5%	57.9%	42.1%
283,883	ST. CHARLES	133,831	71,771	59,408	2,652	12,363 R	53.6%	44.4%	54.7%	45.3%
9,652	ST. CLAIR	4,232	2,041	1,924	267	117 R	48.2%	45.5%	51.5%	48.5%
55,641	ST. FRANCOIS	18,478	8,094	9,781	603	1,687 D	43.8%	52.9%	45.3%	54.7%
1,016,315	ST. LOUIS COUNTY	415,144	178,720	229,264	7,160	50,544 D	43.1%	55.2%	43.8%	56.2%
348,189	ST. LOUIS CITY	95,046	18,135	75,183	1,728	57,048 D	19.1%	79.1%	19.4%	80.6%
17,842	STE. GENEVIEVE	6,838	2,834	3,800	204	966 D	41.4%	55.6%	42.7%	57.3%
23,756	SALINE	7,806	3,547	3,846	413	299 D	45.4%	49.3%	48.0%	52.0%
4,170	SCHUYLER	1,506	754	703	49	51 R	50.1%	46.7%	51.8%	48.2%
4,983	SCOTLAND	1,756	971	732	53	239 R	55.3%	41.7%	57.0%	43.0%
40,422	SCOTT	13,293	7,733	5,211	349	2,522 R	58.2%	39.2%	59.7%	40.3%
8,324	SHANNON	3,287	1,412	1,673	202	261 D	43.0%	50.9%	45.8%	54.2%
6,799	SHELBY	3,004	1,748	1,208	48	540 R	58.2%	40.2%	59.1%	40.9%
29,705	STODDARD	10,163	5,874	3,962	327	1,912 R	57.8%	39.0%	59.7%	40.3%
28,658	STONE	12,429	7,295	4,533	601	2,762 R	58.7%	36.5%	61.7%	38.3%
7,219	SULLIVAN	2,403	1,273	1,026	104	247 R	53.0%	42.7%	55.4%	44.6%
39,703	TANEY	14,915	9,032	5,187	696	3,845 R	60.6%	34.8%	63.5%	36.5%
23,003	TEXAS	9,020	4,749	3,786	485	963 R	52.6%	42.0%	55.6%	44.4%
20,454	VERNON	7,138	4,131	2,738	269	1,393 R	57.9%	38.4%	60.1%	39.9%
24,525	WARREN	11,339	5,931	5,118	290	813 R	52.3%	45.1%	53.7%	46.3%
23,344	WASHINGTON	7,432	2,942	4,223	267	1,281 D	39.6%	56.8%	41.1%	58.9%
13,259	WAYNE	5,263	2,678	2,394	191	284 R	50.9%	45.5%	52.8%	47.2%
31,045	WEBSTER	12,699	7,107	4,862	730	2,245 R	56.0%	38.3%	59.4%	40.6%
2,382	WORTH	1,020	533	415	72	118 R	52.3%	40.7%	56.2%	43.8%
17,955	WRIGHT	6,943	4,273	2,338	332	1,935 R	61.5%	33.7%	64.6%	35.4%
5,595,211	TOTAL	2,128,459	1,006,941	1,055,255	66,263	48,314 D	47.3%	49.6%	48.8%	51.2%

MISSOURI

HOUSE OF REPRESENTATIVES

CD	Year	Total Vote	Republican Vote	Republican Candidate	Democratic Vote	Democratic Candidate	Other Vote	Rep.-Dem. Plurality	Total Vote Rep.	Total Vote Dem.	Major Vote Rep.	Major Vote Dem.
1	2006	194,235	47,893	BYRNE, MARK J.	141,574	CLAY, WILLIAM LACY*	4,768	93,681 D	24.7%	72.9%	25.3%	74.7%
1	2004	283,771	64,791	FARR, LESLIE L. II	213,658	CLAY, WILLIAM LACY*	5,322	148,867 D	22.8%	75.3%	23.3%	76.7%
1	2002	191,055	51,755	SCHWADRON, RICHARD	133,946	CLAY, WILLIAM LACY*	5,354	82,191 D	27.1%	70.1%	27.9%	72.1%
2	2006	287,617	176,452	AKIN, TODD*	105,242	WEBER, GEORGE D.	5,923	71,210 R	61.3%	36.6%	62.6%	37.4%
2	2004	349,867	228,725	AKIN, TODD*	115,366	WEBER, GEORGE D.	5,776	113,359 R	65.4%	33.0%	66.5%	33.5%
2	2002	248,828	167,057	AKIN, TODD*	77,223	HOGAN, JOHN	4,548	89,834 R	67.1%	31.0%	68.4%	31.6%
3	2006	221,448	70,189	BERTELSEN, DAVID	145,219	CARNAHAN, RUSS*	6,040	75,030 D	31.7%	65.6%	32.6%	67.4%
3	2004	277,916	125,422	FEDERER, BILL	146,894	CARNAHAN, RUSS	5,600	21,472 D	45.1%	52.9%	46.1%	53.9%
3	2002	206,878	80,551	ENZ, CATHERINE S.	122,181	GEPHARDT, RICHARD A.*	4,146	41,630 D	38.9%	59.1%	39.7%	60.3%
4	2006	235,525	69,254	NOLAND, JAMES A. "JIM"	159,303	SKELTON, IKE*	6,968	90,049 D	29.4%	67.6%	30.3%	69.7%
4	2004	288,226	93,334	NOLAND, JAMES A. "JIM"	190,800	SKELTON, IKE*	4,092	97,466 D	32.4%	66.2%	32.8%	67.2%
4	2002	210,238	64,451	NOLAND, JAMES A. "JIM"	142,204	SKELTON, IKE*	3,583	77,753 D	30.7%	67.6%	31.2%	68.8%
5	2006	211,919	68,456	TURK, JACOB	136,149	CLEAVER, EMANUEL II*	7,314	67,693 D	32.3%	64.2%	33.5%	66.5%
5	2004	293,025	123,431	PATTERSON, JEANNE	161,727	CLEAVER, EMANUEL II	7,867	38,296 D	42.1%	55.2%	43.3%	56.7%
5	2002	186,167	60,245	GORDON, STEVE	122,645	McCARTHY, KAREN*	3,277	62,400 D	32.4%	65.9%	32.9%	67.1%
6	2006	244,795	150,882	GRAVES, SAM*	87,477	SHETTLES, SARA JO	6,436	63,405 R	61.6%	35.7%	63.3%	36.7%
6	2004	307,855	196,516	GRAVES, SAM*	106,987	BROOMFIELD, CHARLES S.	4,352	89,529 R	63.8%	34.8%	64.7%	35.3%
6	2002	208,088	131,151	GRAVES, SAM*	73,202	RINEHART, CATHY	3,735	57,949 R	63.0%	35.2%	64.2%	35.8%
7	2006	241,123	160,942	BLUNT, ROY*	72,592	TRUMAN, JACK	7,589	88,350 R	66.7%	30.1%	68.9%	31.1%
7	2004	298,205	210,080	BLUNT, ROY*	84,356	NEWBERRY, JIM	3,769	125,724 R	70.4%	28.3%	71.3%	28.7%
7	2002	199,863	149,519	BLUNT, ROY*	45,964	LAPHAM, RON	4,380	103,555 R	74.8%	23.0%	76.5%	23.5%
8	2006	217,989	156,164	EMERSON, JO ANN*	57,557	HAMBACKER, VERONICA J.	4,268	98,607 R	71.6%	26.4%	73.1%	26.9%
8	2004	268,711	194,039	EMERSON, JO ANN*	71,543	HENDERSON, DEAN	3,129	122,496 R	72.2%	26.6%	73.1%	26.9%
8	2002	188,321	135,144	EMERSON, JO ANN*	50,686	CURTIS, GENE	2,491	84,458 R	71.8%	26.9%	72.7%	27.3%
9	2006	242,671	149,114	HULSHOF, KENNY*	87,145	BURGHARD, DUANE N.	6,412	61,969 R	61.4%	35.9%	63.1%	36.9%
9	2004	299,447	193,429	HULSHOF, KENNY*	101,343	JACOBSEN, LINDA	4,675	92,086 R	64.6%	33.8%	65.6%	34.4%
9	2002	214,125	146,032	HULSHOF, KENNY*	61,126	DEICHMAN, DONALD M. "DON"	6,967	84,906 R	68.2%	28.5%	70.5%	29.5%
TOTAL	2006	2,097,322	1,049,346		992,258		55,718	57,088 R	50.0%	47.3%	51.4%	48.6%
TOTAL	2004	2,667,023	1,429,767		1,192,674		44,582	237,093 R	53.6%	44.7%	54.5%	45.5%
TOTAL	2002	1,853,563	985,905		829,177		38,481	156,728 R	53.2%	44.7%	54.3%	45.7%

An asterisk (*) denotes incumbent.

MISSOURI

GENERAL AND PRIMARY ELECTIONS

2006 GENERAL ELECTIONS

Senator   Other vote was 47,792 Libertarian (Frank Gilmour); 18,383 Progressive (Lydia Lewis); 72 write-in (Don Barrett); 16 write-in (Arthur W. Shortland).

House   Other vote was:

CD 1   4,768 Libertarian (Robb E. Cunningham).
CD 2   5,923 Libertarian (Tamara A. Millay).
CD 3   4,213 Libertarian (R. Christophel); 1,827 Progressive (David Sladky).
CD 4   4,479 Libertarian (Bryce A. Holthouse); 2,459 Progressive (Melinda "Mel" Ivey); 30 write-in (Jerry L. Palmer).
CD 5   7,314 Libertarian (Randall David "Randy" Langkraehr).
CD 6   4,757 Libertarian (Erik Buck); 1,679 Progressive (Shirley A. Yurkonis).
CD 7   7,566 Libertarian (Kevin Craig); 23 write-in (Glenn Miller).
CD 8   4,268 Libertarian (Branden C. McCullough).
CD 9   3,925 Libertarian (Steven R. Hedrick); 2,487 Progressive (Bill Hastings).

MISSOURI

GENERAL AND PRIMARY ELECTIONS

2006 PRIMARY ELECTIONS

| Primary | August 8, 2006 | Registration (as of October 2004) | 4,194,146 | No Party Registration |

Primary Type   Open—Any registered voter could participate in the party primary of their choice.

Note: An asterisk (*) denotes incumbent.

	REPUBLICAN PRIMARIES			DEMOCRATIC PRIMARIES		
Senator	Jim Talent*	289,573	88.9%	Claire McCaskill	282,767	80.8%
	Scott Babbitt	13,189	4.0%	Bill Clinton Young	67,173	19.2%
	Joyce P. Lea	11,705	3.6%			
	Isaiah Hair Jr.	6,415	2.0%			
	Roxie L. Fausnaught	4,900	1.5%			
	TOTAL	325,782		TOTAL	349,940	
Congressional District 1	Mark J. Byrne	6,822	72.5%	William Lacy Clay*	33,358	100.0%
	Leslie La Vantres Farr II	1,388	14.7%			
	Lou Mansfield	1,206	12.8%			
	TOTAL	9,416				
Congressional District 2	Todd Akin*	41,464	88.1%	George D. Weber	6,973	29.6%
	Sherman Parker	5,597	11.9%	Charles Karam	6,327	26.9%
				Rich Lesh	5,646	24.0%
				John Hogan	4,576	19.5%
	TOTAL	47,061		TOTAL	23,522	
Congressional District 3	David Bertelsen	11,890	100.0%	Russ Carnahan*	37,200	76.4%
				Jeff Smith	11,517	23.6%
				TOTAL	48,717	
Congressional District 4	James A. "Jim" Noland	22,233	49.7%	Ike Skelton*	36,799	100.0%
	Alan Conner	12,114	27.1%			
	Jeff Parnell	5,781	12.9%			
	Lloyd D. Sanders Sr.	4,605	10.3%			
	TOTAL	44,733				
Congressional District 5	Jacob Turk	14,186	100.0%	Emanuel Cleaver II*	38,734	100.0%
Congressional District 6	Sam Graves*	33,129	100.0%	Sara Jo Shettles	29,473	100.0%
Congressional District 7	Roy Blunt*	47,758	79.9%	Jack Truman	6,896	45.9%
	Clendon L. Kinder	5,197	8.7%	Ron Lapham	4,370	29.1%
	Midge Potts	4,294	7.2%	Charles Christrup	3,772	25.1%
	Bernard F. Kennetz Jr.	2,498	4.2%			
	TOTAL	59,747		TOTAL	15,038	
Congressional District 8	Jo Ann Emerson*	43,527	100.0%	Veronica J. Hambacker	15,279	39.5%
				Gene Curtis	13,305	34.4%
				E. Earl Durnell	10,053	26.0%
				TOTAL	38,637	
Congressional District 9	Kenny Hulshof*	36,036	100.0%	Duane N. Burghard	38,426	100.0%

MONTANA

One member At Large

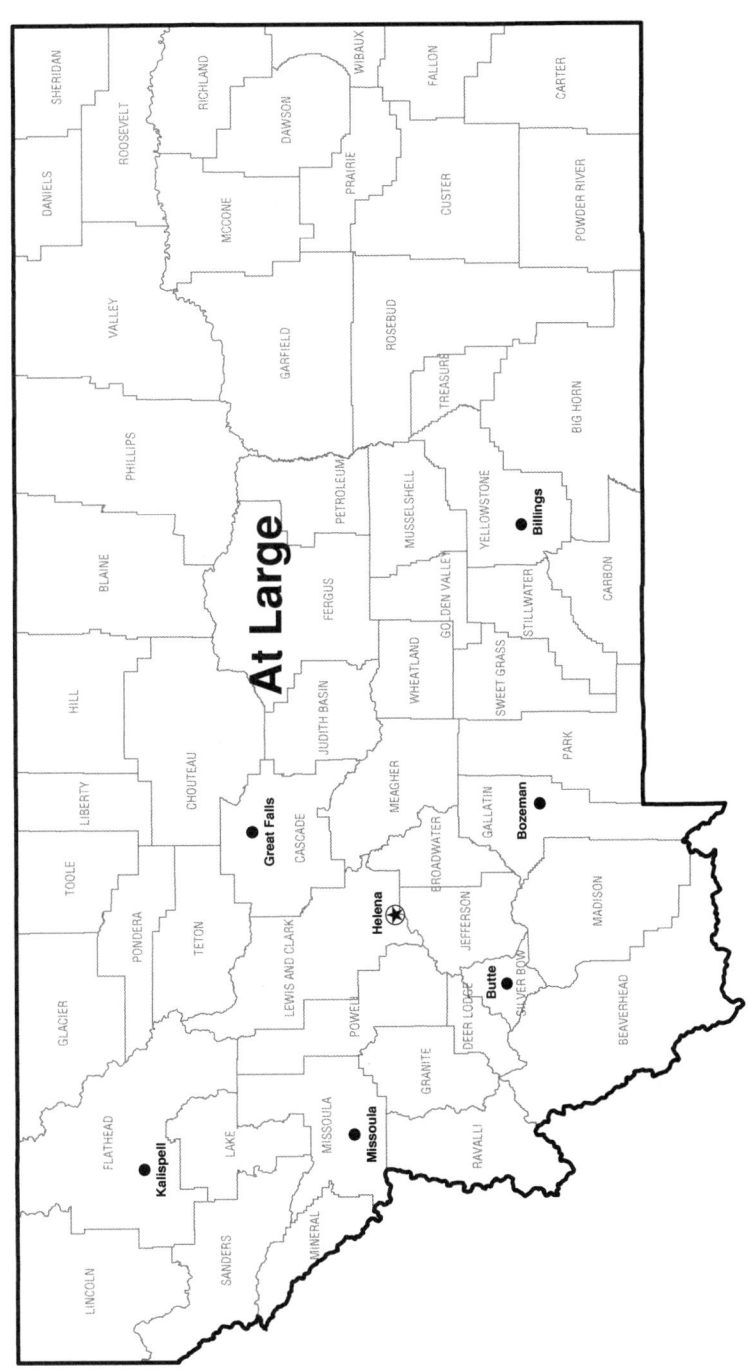

MONTANA

GOVERNOR
Brian Schweitzer (D). Elected 2004 to a four-year term.

SENATORS (2 Democrats)
Jon Tester (D). Elected 2006 to a six-year term.

Max Baucus (D). Reelected 2002 to a six-year term. Previously elected 1996, 1990, 1984, 1978.

REPRESENTATIVE (1 Republican)
At Large. Denny Rehberg (R)

POSTWAR VOTE FOR PRESIDENT

| | | Republican | | Democratic | | Other | | Percentage | | | |
| | Total | | | | | | | Total Vote | | Major Vote | |
Year	Vote	Vote	Candidate	Vote	Candidate	Vote	Plurality	Rep.	Dem.	Rep.	Dem.
2004	450,445	266,063	Bush, George W.	173,710	Kerry, John	10,672	92,353 R	59.1%	38.6%	60.5%	39.5%
2000**	410,997	240,178	Bush, George W.	137,126	Gore, Al	33,693	103,052 R	58.4%	33.4%	63.7%	36.3%
1996**	407,261	179,652	Dole, Bob	167,922	Clinton, Bill	59,687	11,730 R	44.1%	41.2%	51.7%	48.3%
1992**	410,611	144,207	Bush, George	154,507	Clinton, Bill	111,897	10,300 D	35.1%	37.6%	48.3%	51.7%
1988	365,674	190,412	Bush, George	168,936	Dukakis, Michael S.	6,326	21,476 R	52.1%	46.2%	53.0%	47.0%
1984	384,377	232,450	Reagan, Ronald	146,742	Mondale, Walter F.	5,185	85,708 R	60.5%	38.2%	61.3%	38.7%
1980**	363,952	206,814	Reagan, Ronald	118,032	Carter, Jimmy	39,106	88,782 R	56.8%	32.4%	63.7%	36.3%
1976	328,734	173,703	Ford, Gerald R.	149,259	Carter, Jimmy	5,772	24,444 R	52.8%	45.4%	53.8%	46.2%
1972	317,603	183,976	Nixon, Richard M.	120,197	McGovern, George S.	13,430	63,779 R	57.9%	37.8%	60.5%	39.5%
1968**	274,404	138,835	Nixon, Richard M.	114,117	Humphrey, Hubert H.	21,452	24,718 R	50.6%	41.6%	54.9%	45.1%
1964	278,628	113,032	Goldwater, Barry M.	164,246	Johnson, Lyndon B.	1,350	51,214 D	40.6%	58.9%	40.8%	59.2%
1960	277,579	141,841	Nixon, Richard M.	134,891	Kennedy, John F.	847	6,950 R	51.1%	48.6%	51.3%	48.7%
1956	271,171	154,933	Eisenhower, Dwight D.	116,238	Stevenson, Adlai E.		38,695 R	57.1%	42.9%	57.1%	42.9%
1952	265,037	157,394	Eisenhower, Dwight D.	106,213	Stevenson, Adlai E.	1,430	51,181 R	59.4%	40.1%	59.7%	40.3%
1948	224,278	96,770	Dewey, Thomas E.	119,071	Truman, Harry S.	8,437	22,301 D	43.1%	53.1%	44.8%	55.2%

**In past elections, the other vote included: 2000 - 24,437 Green (Ralph Nader); 1996 - 55,229 Reform (Ross Perot); 1992 - 107,225 Independent (Ross Perot); 1980 - 29,281 Independent (John Anderson); 1968 - 20,015 American Independent (George Wallace).

MONTANA

POSTWAR VOTE FOR GOVERNOR

Year	Total Vote	Republican Vote	Candidate	Democratic Vote	Candidate	Other Vote	Rep.-Dem. Plurality	Percentage Total Vote Rep.	Dem.	Major Vote Rep.	Dem.
2004	446,146	205,313	Brown, Bob	225,016	Schweitzer, Brian	15,817	19,703 D	46.0%	50.4%	47.7%	52.3%
2000	410,192	209,135	Martz, Judy	193,131	O'Keefe, Mark	7,926	16,004 R	51.0%	47.1%	52.0%	48.0%
1996**	405,175	320,768	Racicot, Marc	84,407	Jacobson, Judy		236,361 R	79.2%	20.8%	79.2%	20.8%
1992	407,842	209,401	Racicot, Marc	198,421	Bradley, Dorothy	20	10,980 R	51.3%	48.7%	51.3%	48.7%
1988	367,021	190,604	Stephens, Stan	169,313	Judge, Thomas L.	7,104	21,291 R	51.9%	46.1%	53.0%	47.0%
1984	378,970	100,070	Goodover, Pat M.	266,578	Schwinden, Ted	12,322	166,508 D	26.4%	70.3%	27.3%	72.7%
1980	360,466	160,892	Ramirez, Jack	199,574	Schwinden, Ted		38,682 D	44.6%	55.4%	44.6%	55.4%
1976	316,720	115,848	Woodahl, Robert	195,420	Judge, Thomas L.	5,452	79,572 D	36.6%	61.7%	37.2%	62.8%
1972	318,754	146,231	Smith, Ed	172,523	Judge, Thomas L.		26,292 D	45.9%	54.1%	45.9%	54.1%
1968	278,112	116,432	Babcock, Tim M.	150,481	Anderson, Forrest H.	11,199	34,049 D	41.9%	54.1%	43.6%	56.4%
1964	280,975	144,113	Babcock, Tim M.	136,862	Renne, Roland		7,251 R	51.3%	48.7%	51.3%	48.7%
1960	279,881	154,230	Nutter, Donald G.	125,651	Cannon, Paul		28,579 R	55.1%	44.9%	55.1%	44.9%
1956	270,366	138,878	Aronson, J. Hugo	131,488	Olsen, Arnold H.		7,390 R	51.4%	48.6%	51.4%	48.6%
1952	263,792	134,423	Aronson, J. Hugo	129,369	Bonner, John W.		5,054 R	51.0%	49.0%	51.0%	49.0%
1948	222,964	97,792	Ford, Sam C.	124,267	Bonner, John W.	905	26,475 D	43.9%	55.7%	44.0%	56.0%

**In 1996 the Democratic vote total included 7,936 absentee ballots cast for the party's initial gubernatorial candidate, Chet Blaylock, who died that October.

POSTWAR VOTE FOR SENATOR

Year	Total Vote	Republican Vote	Candidate	Democratic Vote	Candidate	Other Vote	Rep.-Dem. Plurality	Percentage Total Vote Rep.	Dem.	Major Vote Rep.	Dem.
2006	406,505	196,283	Burns, Conrad	199,845	Tester, Jon	10,377	3,562 D	48.3%	49.2%	49.6%	50.4%
2002	326,537	103,611	Taylor, Mike	204,853	Baucus, Max	18,073	101,242 D	31.7%	62.7%	33.6%	66.4%
2000	411,601	208,082	Burns, Conrad	194,430	Schweitzer, Brian	9,089	13,652 R	50.6%	47.2%	51.7%	48.3%
1996	407,490	182,111	Rehberg, Denny	201,935	Baucus, Max	23,444	19,824 D	44.7%	49.6%	47.4%	52.6%
1994	350,409	218,542	Burns, Conrad	131,845	Mudd, Jack	22	86,697 R	62.4%	37.6%	62.4%	37.6%
1990	319,336	93,836	Kolstad, Allen C.	217,563	Baucus, Max	7,937	123,727 D	29.4%	68.1%	30.1%	69.9%
1988	365,254	189,445	Burns, Conrad	175,809	Melcher, John		13,636 R	51.9%	48.1%	51.9%	48.1%
1984	379,155	154,308	Cozzens, Chuck	215,704	Baucus, Max	9,143	61,396 D	40.7%	56.9%	41.7%	58.3%
1982	321,062	133,789	Williams, Larry	174,861	Melcher, John	12,412	41,072 D	41.7%	54.5%	43.3%	56.7%
1978	287,942	127,589	Williams, Larry	160,353	Baucus, Max		32,764 D	44.3%	55.7%	44.3%	55.7%
1976	321,445	115,213	Burger, Stanley C.	206,232	Melcher, John		91,019 D	35.8%	64.2%	35.8%	64.2%
1972	314,925	151,316	Hibbard, Henry S.	163,609	Metcalf, Lee		12,293 D	48.0%	52.0%	48.0%	52.0%
1970	247,869	97,809	Wallace, Harold E.	150,060	Mansfield, Mike		52,251 D	39.5%	60.5%	39.5%	60.5%
1966	259,863	121,697	Babcock, Tim M.	138,166	Metcalf, Lee		16,469 D	46.8%	53.2%	46.8%	53.2%
1964	280,010	99,367	Blewett, Alex	180,643	Mansfield, Mike		81,276 D	35.5%	64.5%	35.5%	64.5%
1960	276,612	136,281	Fjare, Orvin B.	140,331	Metcalf, Lee		4,050 D	49.3%	50.7%	49.3%	50.7%
1958	229,483	54,573	Welch, Lou W.	174,910	Mansfield, Mike		120,337 D	23.8%	76.2%	23.8%	76.2%
1954	227,454	112,863	D'Ewart, Wesley A.	114,591	Murray, James E.		1,728 D	49.6%	50.4%	49.6%	50.4%
1952	262,297	127,360	Ecton, Zales N.	133,109	Mansfield, Mike	1,828	5,749 D	48.6%	50.7%	48.9%	51.1%
1948	221,003	94,458	David, Tom J.	125,193	Murray, James E.	1,352	30,735 D	42.7%	56.6%	43.0%	57.0%
1946	190,566	101,901	Ecton, Zales N.	86,476	Erickson, Leif	2,189	15,425 R	53.5%	45.4%	54.1%	45.9%

MONTANA

SENATOR 2006

2000 Census Population	County	Total Vote	Republican	Democratic	Other	Rep.-Dem. Plurality	Percentage Total Vote Rep.	Dem.	Major Vote Rep.	Dem.
9,202	BEAVERHEAD	4,035	2,555	1,377	103	1,178 R	63.3%	34.1%	65.0%	35.0%
12,671	BIG HORN	4,676	1,556	3,036	84	1,480 D	33.3%	64.9%	33.9%	66.1%
7,009	BLAINE	2,688	1,229	1,397	62	168 D	45.7%	52.0%	46.8%	53.2%
4,385	BROADWATER	2,404	1,474	842	88	632 R	61.3%	35.0%	63.6%	36.4%
9,552	CARBON	4,915	2,519	2,258	138	261 R	51.3%	45.9%	52.7%	47.3%
1,360	CARTER	666	554	98	14	456 R	83.2%	14.7%	85.0%	15.0%
80,357	CASCADE	30,461	14,850	15,068	543	218 D	48.8%	49.5%	49.6%	50.4%
5,970	CHOUTEAU	2,672	1,345	1,288	39	57 R	50.3%	48.2%	51.1%	48.9%
11,696	CUSTER	4,700	2,581	1,991	128	590 R	54.9%	42.4%	56.5%	43.5%
2,017	DANIELS	1,040	594	424	22	170 R	57.1%	40.8%	58.3%	41.7%
9,059	DAWSON	3,966	2,254	1,597	115	657 R	56.8%	40.3%	58.5%	41.5%
9,417	DEER LODGE	4,121	1,002	3,016	103	2,014 D	24.3%	73.2%	24.9%	75.1%
2,837	FALLON	1,319	951	347	21	604 R	72.1%	26.3%	73.3%	26.7%
11,893	FERGUS	5,632	3,474	1,985	173	1,489 R	61.7%	35.2%	63.6%	36.4%
74,471	FLATHEAD	33,576	18,784	13,570	1,222	5,214 R	55.9%	40.4%	58.1%	41.9%
67,831	GALLATIN	34,436	16,917	16,789	730	128 R	49.1%	48.8%	50.2%	49.8%
1,279	GARFIELD	601	490	100	11	390 R	81.5%	16.6%	83.1%	16.9%
13,247	GLACIER	4,434	1,572	2,768	94	1,196 D	35.5%	62.4%	36.2%	63.8%
1,042	GOLDEN VALLEY	486	298	181	7	117 R	61.3%	37.2%	62.2%	37.8%
2,830	GRANITE	1,523	864	597	62	267 R	56.7%	39.2%	59.1%	40.9%
16,673	HILL	5,879	2,331	3,431	117	1,100 D	39.6%	58.4%	40.5%	59.5%
10,049	JEFFERSON	5,300	2,730	2,421	149	309 R	51.5%	45.7%	53.0%	47.0%
2,329	JUDITH BASIN	1,192	785	377	30	408 R	65.9%	31.6%	67.6%	32.4%
26,507	LAKE	11,260	5,295	5,552	413	257 D	47.0%	49.3%	48.8%	51.2%
55,716	LEWIS AND CLARK	27,321	11,763	14,950	608	3,187 D	43.1%	54.7%	44.0%	56.0%
2,158	LIBERTY	1,011	596	401	14	195 R	59.0%	39.7%	59.8%	40.2%
18,837	LINCOLN	7,301	4,105	2,860	336	1,245 R	56.2%	39.2%	58.9%	41.1%
1,977	MCCONE	1,040	624	394	22	230 R	60.0%	37.9%	61.3%	38.7%
6,851	MADISON	3,640	2,315	1,225	100	1,090 R	63.6%	33.7%	65.4%	34.6%
1,932	MEAGHER	845	552	272	21	280 R	65.3%	32.2%	67.0%	33.0%
3,884	MINERAL	1,632	782	800	50	18 D	47.9%	49.0%	49.4%	50.6%
95,802	MISSOULA	46,775	15,742	30,069	964	14,327 D	33.7%	64.3%	34.4%	65.6%
4,497	MUSSELSHELL	2,150	1,382	670	98	712 R	64.3%	31.2%	67.3%	32.7%
15,694	PARK	7,399	3,454	3,744	201	290 D	46.7%	50.6%	48.0%	52.0%
493	PETROLEUM	265	180	74	11	106 R	67.9%	27.9%	70.9%	29.1%
4,601	PHILLIPS	1,984	1,366	579	39	787 R	68.9%	29.2%	70.2%	29.8%
6,424	PONDERA	2,638	1,502	1,081	55	421 R	56.9%	41.0%	58.1%	41.9%
1,858	POWDER RIVER	1,010	734	248	28	486 R	72.7%	24.6%	74.7%	25.3%
7,180	POWELL	2,599	1,454	1,052	93	402 R	55.9%	40.5%	58.0%	42.0%
1,199	PRAIRIE	686	456	213	17	243 R	66.5%	31.0%	68.2%	31.8%
36,070	RAVALLI	18,512	10,172	7,880	460	2,292 R	54.9%	42.6%	56.3%	43.7%
9,667	RICHLAND	3,856	2,388	1,359	109	1,029 R	61.9%	35.2%	63.7%	36.3%
10,620	ROOSEVELT	3,856	1,581	2,218	57	637 D	41.0%	57.5%	41.6%	58.4%
9,383	ROSEBUD	3,446	1,432	1,907	107	475 D	41.6%	55.3%	42.9%	57.1%
10,227	SANDERS	4,985	2,581	2,168	236	413 R	51.8%	43.5%	54.3%	45.7%
4,105	SHERIDAN	1,922	887	989	46	102 D	46.1%	51.5%	47.3%	52.7%
34,606	SILVER BOW	14,427	4,462	9,604	361	5,142 D	30.9%	66.6%	31.7%	68.3%
8,195	STILLWATER	3,961	2,262	1,556	143	706 R	57.1%	39.3%	59.2%	40.8%
3,609	SWEET GRASS	1,749	1,124	565	60	559 R	64.3%	32.3%	66.5%	33.5%
6,445	TETON	3,078	1,760	1,256	62	504 R	57.2%	40.8%	58.4%	41.6%
5,267	TOOLE	2,023	1,195	759	69	436 R	59.1%	37.5%	61.2%	38.8%
861	TREASURE	437	260	162	15	98 R	59.5%	37.1%	61.6%	38.4%
7,675	VALLEY	3,635	1,987	1,560	88	427 R	54.7%	42.9%	56.0%	44.0%
2,259	WHEATLAND	858	503	330	25	173 R	58.6%	38.5%	60.4%	39.6%
1,068	WIBAUX	488	317	165	6	152 R	65.0%	33.8%	65.8%	34.2%
129,352	YELLOWSTONE	58,994	29,361	28,225	1,408	1,136 R	49.8%	47.8%	51.0%	49.0%
902,195	TOTAL	406,505	196,283	199,845	10,377	3,562 D	48.3%	49.2%	49.6%	50.4%

MONTANA

HOUSE OF REPRESENTATIVES

CD	Year	Total Vote	Republican Vote	Republican Candidate	Democratic Vote	Democratic Candidate	Other Vote	Rep.-Dem. Plurality	Total Vote Rep.	Total Vote Dem.	Major Vote Rep.	Major Vote Dem.
AL	2006	406,134	239,124	REHBERG, DENNY*	158,916	LINDEEN, MONICA	8,094	80,208 R	58.9%	39.1%	60.1%	39.9%
AL	2004	444,230	286,076	REHBERG, DENNY*	145,606	VELAZQUEZ, TRACY	12,548	140,470 R	64.4%	32.8%	66.3%	33.7%
AL	2002	331,321	214,100	REHBERG, DENNY*	108,233	KELLY, STEVE	8,988	105,867 R	64.6%	32.7%	66.4%	33.6%
AL	2000	410,523	211,418	REHBERG, DENNY	189,971	KEENAN, NANCY	9,134	21,447 R	51.5%	46.3%	52.7%	47.3%
AL	1998	331,551	175,748	HILL, RICK*	147,073	DESCHAMPS, DUSTY	8,730	28,675 R	53.0%	44.4%	54.4%	45.6%
AL	1996	404,426	211,975	HILL, RICK	174,516	YELLOWTAIL, BILL	17,935	37,459 R	52.4%	43.2%	54.8%	45.2%
AL	1994	352,133	148,715	JAMISON, CY	171,372	WILLIAMS, PAT*	32,046	22,657 D	42.2%	48.7%	46.5%	53.5%
AL	1992	403,735	189,570	MARLENEE, RON*	203,711	WILLIAMS, PAT*	10,454	14,141 D	47.0%	50.5%	48.2%	51.8%

An asterisk (*) denotes incumbent.

MONTANA

GENERAL AND PRIMARY ELECTIONS

2006 GENERAL ELECTIONS

Senator   Other vote was 10,377 Libertarian (Stan Jones).

House   Other vote was:

    At Large   8,085 Libertarian (Mike Fellows); 9 write-in (Walter Michael Wlaysewski).

2006 PRIMARY ELECTIONS

Primary   June 6, 2006   **Registration** (as of June 6, 2006)   626,853   No Party Registration

Primary Type   Open—Any registered voter could participate in the primary of either party.

Note: An asterisk (*) denotes incumbent.

	REPUBLICAN PRIMARIES			DEMOCRATIC PRIMARIES		
Senator	Conrad Burns*	70,434	72.3%	Jon Tester	65,757	60.8%
	Bob Keenan	21,754	22.3%	John Morrison	38,394	35.5%
	Bob Kelleher	4,082	4.2%	Paul Richards	1,636	1.5%
	Daniel Lloyd Neste Huffman	1,203	1.2%	Robert Candee	1,471	1.4%
				Kenneth Marcure	940	0.9%
	TOTAL	*97,473*		*TOTAL*	*108,198*	
House **At Large**	Denny Rehberg*	91,836	100.0%	Monica Lindeen	66,364	71.1%
				Eric Jon Gunderson	26,990	28.9%
				TOTAL	*93,354*	

NEBRASKA

Congressional districts first established for elections held in 2002
3 members

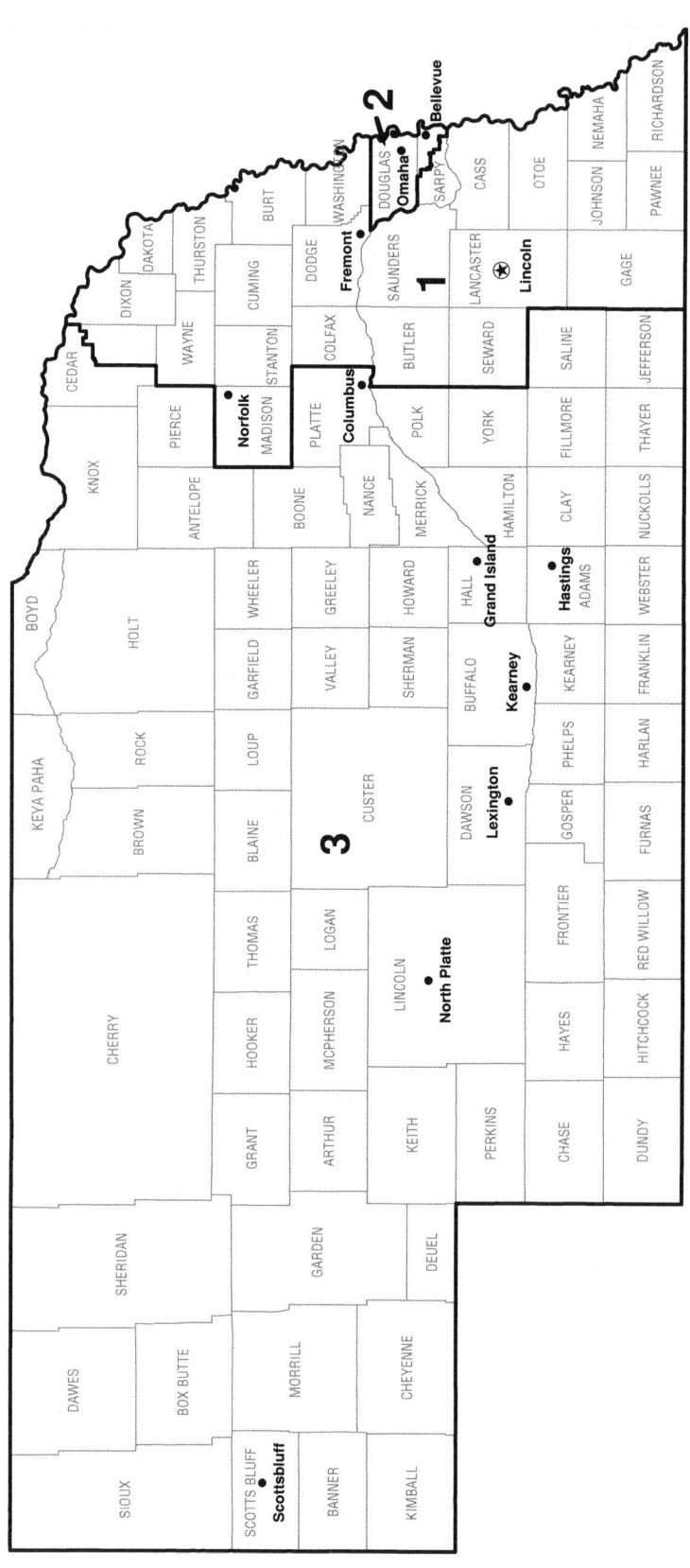

NEBRASKA

GOVERNOR
Dave Heineman (R). Elected 2006 to a six-year term. Became Governor Jan. 21, 2005, upon the resignation of Mike Johanns (R) to become U.S. Secretary of Agriculture.

SENATORS (1 Democrat, 1 Republican)
Ben Nelson (D). Reelected 2006 to a six-year term. Previously elected 2000.

Chuck Hagel (R). Reelected 2002 to a six-year term. Previously elected 1996.

REPRESENTATIVES (3 Republicans)
1. Jeff Fortenberry (R)
2. Lee Terry (R)
3. Adrian Smith (R)

POSTWAR VOTE FOR PRESIDENT

Year	Total Vote	Republican Vote	Candidate	Democratic Vote	Candidate	Other Vote	Plurality	Total Vote Rep.	Dem.	Major Vote Rep.	Dem.
2004	778,186	512,814	Bush, George W.	254,328	Kerry, John	11,044	258,486 R	65.9%	32.7%	66.8%	33.2%
2000**	697,019	433,862	Bush, George W.	231,780	Gore, Al	31,377	202,082 R	62.2%	33.3%	65.2%	34.8%
1996**	677,415	363,467	Dole, Bob	236,761	Clinton, Bill	77,187	126,706 R	53.7%	35.0%	60.6%	39.4%
1992**	737,546	343,678	Bush, George	216,864	Clinton, Bill	177,004	126,814 R	46.6%	29.4%	61.3%	38.7%
1988	661,465	397,956	Bush, George	259,235	Dukakis, Michael S.	4,274	138,721 R	60.2%	39.2%	60.6%	39.4%
1984	652,090	460,054	Reagan, Ronald	187,866	Mondale, Walter F.	4,170	272,188 R	70.6%	28.8%	71.0%	29.0%
1980**	640,854	419,937	Reagan, Ronald	166,851	Carter, Jimmy	54,066	253,086 R	65.5%	26.0%	71.6%	28.4%
1976	607,668	359,705	Ford, Gerald R.	233,692	Carter, Jimmy	14,271	126,013 R	59.2%	38.5%	60.6%	39.4%
1972	576,289	406,298	Nixon, Richard M.	169,991	McGovern, George S.		236,307 R	70.5%	29.5%	70.5%	29.5%
1968**	536,851	321,163	Nixon, Richard M.	170,784	Humphrey, Hubert H.	44,904	150,379 R	59.8%	31.8%	65.3%	34.7%
1964	584,154	276,847	Goldwater, Barry M.	307,307	Johnson, Lyndon B.		30,460 D	47.4%	52.6%	47.4%	52.6%
1960	613,095	380,553	Nixon, Richard M.	232,542	Kennedy, John F.		148,011 R	62.1%	37.9%	62.1%	37.9%
1956	577,137	378,108	Eisenhower, Dwight D.	199,029	Stevenson, Adlai E.		179,079 R	65.5%	34.5%	65.5%	34.5%
1952	609,660	421,603	Eisenhower, Dwight D.	188,057	Stevenson, Adlai E.		233,546 R	69.2%	30.8%	69.2%	30.8%
1948	488,940	264,774	Dewey, Thomas E.	224,165	Truman, Harry S.	1	40,609 R	54.2%	45.8%	54.2%	45.8%

**In past elections, the other vote included: 2000 - 24,540 Green (Ralph Nader); 1996 - 71,278 Reform (Ross Perot); 1992 - 174,104 Independent (Ross Perot); 1980 - 44,993 Independent (John Anderson); 1968 - 44,904 American Independent (George Wallace).

NEBRASKA

POSTWAR VOTE FOR GOVERNOR

Year	Total Vote	Republican Vote	Republican Candidate	Democratic Vote	Democratic Candidate	Other Vote	Rep.-Dem. Plurality	Total Vote Rep.	Total Vote Dem.	Major Vote Rep.	Major Vote Dem.
2006	593,357	435,507	Heineman, Dave	145,115	Hahn, David	12,735	290,392 R	73.4%	24.5%	75.0%	25.0%
2002	480,991	330,349	Johanns, Mike	132,348	Dean, Stormy	18,294	198,001 R	68.7%	27.5%	71.4%	28.6%
1998	545,238	293,910	Johanns, Mike	250,678	Hoppner, Bill	650	43,232 R	53.9%	46.0%	54.0%	46.0%
1994	579,561	148,230	Spence, Gene	423,270	Nelson, Ben	8,061	275,040 D	25.6%	73.0%	25.9%	74.1%
1990	586,542	288,741	Orr, Kay	292,771	Nelson, Ben	5,030	4,030 D	49.2%	49.9%	49.7%	50.3%
1986	564,422	298,325	Orr, Kay	265,156	Boosalis, Helen	941	33,169 R	52.9%	47.0%	52.9%	47.1%
1982	547,902	270,203	Thone, Charles	277,436	Kerrey, Bob	263	7,233 D	49.3%	50.6%	49.3%	50.7%
1978	492,423	275,473	Thone, Charles	216,754	Whelan, Gerald T.	196	58,719 R	55.9%	44.0%	56.0%	44.0%
1974	451,306	159,780	Marvel, Richard D.	267,012	Exon, J. J.	24,514	107,232 D	35.4%	59.2%	37.4%	62.6%
1970	461,619	201,994	Tiemann, Norbert T.	248,552	Exon, J. J.	11,073	46,558 D	43.8%	53.8%	44.8%	55.2%
1966**	486,396	299,245	Tiemann, Norbert T.	186,985	Sorensen, Philip C.	166	112,260 R	61.5%	38.4%	61.5%	38.5%
1964	578,090	231,029	Burney, Dwight W.	347,026	Morrison, Frank B.	35	115,997 D	40.0%	60.0%	40.0%	60.0%
1962	464,585	221,885	Seaton, Fred A.	242,669	Morrison, Frank B.	31	20,784 D	47.8%	52.2%	47.8%	52.2%
1960	598,971	287,302	Cooper, John R.	311,344	Morrison, Frank B.	325	24,042 D	48.0%	52.0%	48.0%	52.0%
1958	421,067	209,705	Anderson, Victor E.	211,345	Brooks, Ralph G.	17	1,640 D	49.8%	50.2%	49.8%	50.2%
1956	567,933	308,293	Anderson, Victor E.	228,048	Sorrell, Frank	31,592	80,245 R	54.3%	40.2%	57.5%	42.5%
1954	414,841	250,080	Anderson, Victor E.	164,753	Ritchie, William	8	85,327 R	60.3%	39.7%	60.3%	39.7%
1952	595,714	366,009	Crosby, Robert B.	229,700	Raecke, Walter R.	5	136,309 R	61.4%	38.6%	61.4%	38.6%
1950	449,720	247,081	Peterson, Val	202,638	Raecke, Walter R.	1	44,443 R	54.9%	45.1%	54.9%	45.1%
1948	476,352	286,119	Peterson, Val	190,214	Sorrell, Frank	19	95,905 R	60.1%	39.9%	60.1%	39.9%
1946	380,835	249,468	Peterson, Val	131,367	Sorrell, Frank		118,101 R	65.5%	34.5%	65.5%	34.5%

**The term of office of Nebraska's governor was increased from two to four years effective with the 1966 election.

POSTWAR VOTE FOR SENATOR

Year	Total Vote	Republican Vote	Republican Candidate	Democratic Vote	Democratic Candidate	Other Vote	Rep.-Dem. Plurality	Total Vote Rep.	Total Vote Dem.	Major Vote Rep.	Major Vote Dem.
2006	592,316	213,928	Ricketts, Pete	378,388	Nelson, Ben		164,460 D	36.1%	63.9%	36.1%	63.9%
2002	480,217	397,438	Hagel, Chuck	70,290	Matulka, Charlie A.	12,489	327,148 R	82.8%	14.6%	85.0%	15.0%
2000	692,344	337,967	Stenberg, Don	353,097	Nelson, Ben	1,280	15,130 D	48.8%	51.0%	48.9%	51.1%
1996	676,789	379,933	Hagel, Chuck	281,904	Nelson, Ben	14,952	98,029 R	56.1%	41.7%	57.4%	42.6%
1994	579,205	260,668	Stoney, Jan	317,297	Kerrey, Bob	1,240	56,629 D	45.0%	54.8%	45.1%	54.9%
1990	593,828	243,013	Daub, Harold J.	349,779	Exon, J. J.	1,036	106,766 D	40.9%	58.9%	41.0%	59.0%
1988	667,860	278,250	Karnes, David	378,717	Kerrey, Bob	10,893	100,467 D	41.7%	56.7%	42.4%	57.6%
1984	639,668	307,147	Hoch, Nancy	332,217	Exon, J. J.	304	25,070 D	48.0%	51.9%	48.0%	52.0%
1982	545,647	155,760	Keck, Jim	363,350	Zorinsky, Edward	26,537	207,590 D	28.5%	66.6%	30.0%	70.0%
1978	494,368	159,806	Shasteen, Donald	334,276	Exon, J. J.	286	174,470 D	32.3%	67.6%	32.3%	67.7%
1976	598,314	284,284	McCollister, John Y.	313,809	Zorinsky, Edward	221	29,525 D	47.5%	52.4%	47.5%	52.5%
1972	568,580	301,841	Curtis, Carl T.	265,922	Carpenter, Terry	817	35,919 R	53.1%	46.8%	53.2%	46.8%
1970	458,966	240,894	Hruska, Roman L.	217,681	Morrison, Frank B.	391	23,213 R	52.5%	47.4%	52.5%	47.5%
1966	485,101	296,116	Curtis, Carl T.	187,950	Morrison, Frank B.	1,035	108,166 R	61.0%	38.7%	61.2%	38.8%
1964	563,401	345,772	Hruska, Roman L.	217,605	Arndt, Raymond W.	24	128,167 R	61.4%	38.6%	61.4%	38.6%
1960	598,743	352,748	Curtis, Carl T.	245,837	Conrad, Robert	158	106,911 R	58.9%	41.1%	58.9%	41.1%
1958	417,385	232,227	Hruska, Roman L.	185,152	Morrison, Frank B.	6	47,075 R	55.6%	44.4%	55.6%	44.4%
1954	418,691	255,695	Curtis, Carl T.	162,990	Neville, Keith	6	92,705 R	61.1%	38.9%	61.1%	38.9%
1954S	411,225	250,341	Hruska, Roman L.	160,881	Green, James F.	3	89,460 R	60.9%	39.1%	60.9%	39.1%
1952	591,749	408,971	Butler, Hugh	164,660	Long, Stanley D.	18,118	244,311 R	69.1%	27.8%	71.3%	28.7%
1952S	581,750	369,841	Griswold, Dwight	211,898	Ritchie, William	11	157,943 R	63.6%	36.4%	63.6%	36.4%
1948	471,895	267,575	Wherry, Kenneth S.	204,320	Carpenter, Terry		63,255 R	56.7%	43.3%	56.7%	43.3%
1946	382,958	271,208	Butler, Hugh	111,750	Mekota, John E.		159,458 R	70.8%	29.2%	70.8%	29.2%

One each of the 1954 and 1952 elections was for a short term to fill a vacancy.

NEBRASKA

GOVERNOR 2006

2000 Census Population	County	Total Vote	Republican	Democratic	Other	Rep.-Dem. Plurality	Percentage Total Vote Rep.	Dem.	Major Vote Rep.	Dem.
31,151	ADAMS	10,656	8,374	2,052	230	6,322 R	78.6%	19.3%	80.3%	19.7%
7,452	ANTELOPE	2,768	2,386	328	54	2,058 R	86.2%	11.8%	87.9%	12.1%
444	ARTHUR	231	202	21	8	181 R	87.4%	9.1%	90.6%	9.4%
819	BANNER	330	291	30	9	261 R	88.2%	9.1%	90.7%	9.3%
583	BLAINE	273	231	33	9	198 R	84.6%	12.1%	87.5%	12.5%
6,259	BOONE	2,563	2,202	329	32	1,873 R	85.9%	12.8%	87.0%	13.0%
12,158	BOX BUTTE	3,995	3,002	881	112	2,121 R	75.1%	22.1%	77.3%	22.7%
2,438	BOYD	972	804	150	18	654 R	82.7%	15.4%	84.3%	15.7%
3,525	BROWN	1,396	1,194	139	63	1,055 R	85.5%	10.0%	89.6%	10.4%
42,259	BUFFALO	15,185	12,445	2,517	223	9,928 R	82.0%	16.6%	83.2%	16.8%
7,791	BURT	2,924	2,148	703	73	1,445 R	73.5%	24.0%	75.3%	24.7%
8,767	BUTLER	3,501	2,722	695	84	2,027 R	77.7%	19.9%	79.7%	20.3%
24,334	CASS	9,339	6,938	2,174	227	4,764 R	74.3%	23.3%	76.1%	23.9%
9,615	CEDAR	3,724	3,088	553	83	2,535 R	82.9%	14.8%	84.8%	15.2%
4,068	CHASE	1,633	1,398	172	63	1,226 R	85.6%	10.5%	89.0%	11.0%
6,148	CHERRY	2,744	2,310	363	71	1,947 R	84.2%	13.2%	86.4%	13.6%
9,830	CHEYENNE	3,289	2,633	547	109	2,086 R	80.1%	16.6%	82.8%	17.2%
7,039	CLAY	2,636	2,250	343	43	1,907 R	85.4%	13.0%	86.8%	13.2%
10,441	COLFAX	2,887	2,322	527	38	1,795 R	80.4%	18.3%	81.5%	18.5%
10,203	CUMING	3,149	2,665	452	32	2,213 R	84.6%	14.4%	85.5%	14.5%
11,793	CUSTER	5,024	4,311	621	92	3,690 R	85.8%	12.4%	87.4%	12.6%
20,253	DAKOTA	4,737	3,018	1,525	194	1,493 R	63.7%	32.2%	66.4%	33.6%
9,060	DAWES	2,913	2,177	652	84	1,525 R	74.7%	22.4%	77.0%	23.0%
24,365	DAWSON	6,795	5,687	966	142	4,721 R	83.7%	14.2%	85.5%	14.5%
2,098	DEUEL	802	642	135	25	507 R	80.0%	16.8%	82.6%	17.4%
6,339	DIXON	2,361	1,776	511	74	1,265 R	75.2%	21.6%	77.7%	22.3%
36,160	DODGE	12,182	9,903	2,105	174	7,798 R	81.3%	17.3%	82.5%	17.5%
463,585	DOUGLAS	146,395	96,427	46,509	3,459	49,918 R	65.9%	31.8%	67.5%	32.5%
2,292	DUNDY	912	719	135	58	584 R	78.8%	14.8%	84.2%	15.8%
6,634	FILLMORE	2,542	2,071	428	43	1,643 R	81.5%	16.8%	82.9%	17.1%
3,574	FRANKLIN	1,488	1,141	323	24	818 R	76.7%	21.7%	77.9%	22.1%
3,099	FRONTIER	1,285	1,070	166	49	904 R	83.3%	12.9%	86.6%	13.4%
5,324	FURNAS	2,079	1,734	291	54	1,443 R	83.4%	14.0%	85.6%	14.4%
22,993	GAGE	8,991	6,649	2,182	160	4,467 R	74.0%	24.3%	75.3%	24.7%
2,292	GARDEN	1,016	829	154	33	675 R	81.6%	15.2%	84.3%	15.7%
1,902	GARFIELD	926	810	105	11	705 R	87.5%	11.3%	88.5%	11.5%
2,143	GOSPER	1,001	875	115	11	760 R	87.4%	11.5%	88.4%	11.6%
747	GRANT	324	297	21	6	276 R	91.7%	6.5%	93.4%	6.6%
2,714	GREELEY	1,053	837	202	14	635 R	79.5%	19.2%	80.6%	19.4%
53,534	HALL	17,592	13,910	3,353	329	10,557 R	79.1%	19.1%	80.6%	19.4%
9,403	HAMILTON	4,600	3,938	573	89	3,365 R	85.6%	12.5%	87.3%	12.7%
3,786	HARLAN	1,752	1,417	305	30	1,112 R	80.9%	17.4%	82.3%	17.7%
1,068	HAYES	496	333	49	114	221 R	67.1%	9.9%	87.2%	12.8%
3,111	HITCHCOCK	1,194	898	223	73	675 R	75.2%	18.7%	80.1%	19.9%
11,551	HOLT	4,518	3,839	555	124	3,284 R	85.0%	12.3%	87.4%	12.6%
783	HOOKER	327	260	53	14	207 R	79.5%	16.2%	83.1%	16.9%
6,567	HOWARD	2,580	2,063	472	45	1,591 R	80.0%	18.3%	81.4%	18.6%
8,333	JEFFERSON	3,215	2,484	693	38	1,791 R	77.3%	21.6%	78.2%	21.8%
4,488	JOHNSON	1,835	1,342	448	45	894 R	73.1%	24.4%	75.0%	25.0%
6,882	KEARNEY	2,779	2,284	449	46	1,835 R	82.2%	16.2%	83.6%	16.4%
8,875	KEITH	3,269	2,682	520	67	2,162 R	82.0%	15.9%	83.8%	16.2%
983	KEYA PAHA	536	464	58	14	406 R	86.6%	10.8%	88.9%	11.1%
4,089	KIMBALL	1,595	1,246	275	74	971 R	78.1%	17.2%	81.9%	18.1%
9,374	KNOX	3,202	2,462	646	94	1,816 R	76.9%	20.2%	79.2%	20.8%
250,291	LANCASTER	91,577	58,256	31,921	1,400	26,335 R	63.6%	34.9%	64.6%	35.4%
34,632	LINCOLN	12,840	9,480	2,948	412	6,532 R	73.8%	23.0%	76.3%	23.7%
774	LOGAN	377	316	48	13	268 R	83.8%	12.7%	86.8%	13.2%
712	LOUP	376	314	54	8	260 R	83.5%	14.4%	85.3%	14.7%
533	MCPHERSON	264	218	35	11	183 R	82.6%	13.3%	86.2%	13.8%
35,226	MADISON	10,802	8,980	1,604	218	7,376 R	83.1%	14.8%	84.8%	15.2%

NEBRASKA
GOVERNOR 2006

2000 Census Population	County	Total Vote	Republican	Democratic	Other	Rep.-Dem. Plurality	Percentage			
							Total Vote		Major Vote	
							Rep.	Dem.	Rep.	Dem.
8,204	MERRICK	3,073	2,517	507	49	2,010 R	81.9%	16.5%	83.2%	16.8%
5,440	MORRILL	1,896	1,553	294	49	1,259 R	81.9%	15.5%	84.1%	15.9%
4,038	NANCE	1,652	1,306	304	42	1,002 R	79.1%	18.4%	81.1%	18.9%
7,576	NEMAHA	2,880	2,215	604	61	1,611 R	76.9%	21.0%	78.6%	21.4%
5,057	NUCKOLLS	2,057	1,609	406	42	1,203 R	78.2%	19.7%	79.9%	20.1%
15,396	OTOE	5,747	4,396	1,230	121	3,166 R	76.5%	21.4%	78.1%	21.9%
3,087	PAWNEE	1,268	995	245	28	750 R	78.5%	19.3%	80.2%	19.8%
3,200	PERKINS	1,284	1,084	174	26	910 R	84.4%	13.6%	86.2%	13.8%
9,747	PHELPS	4,038	3,380	605	53	2,775 R	83.7%	15.0%	84.8%	15.2%
7,857	PIERCE	2,475	2,154	277	44	1,877 R	87.0%	11.2%	88.6%	11.4%
31,662	PLATTE	10,832	9,121	1,546	165	7,575 R	84.2%	14.3%	85.5%	14.5%
5,639	POLK	2,323	1,923	372	28	1,551 R	82.8%	16.0%	83.8%	16.2%
11,448	RED WILLOW	4,287	3,301	772	214	2,529 R	77.0%	18.0%	81.0%	19.0%
9,531	RICHARDSON	3,564	2,876	608	80	2,268 R	80.7%	17.1%	82.5%	17.5%
1,756	ROCK	766	689	66	11	623 R	89.9%	8.6%	91.3%	8.7%
13,843	SALINE	4,633	3,128	1,432	73	1,696 R	67.5%	30.9%	68.6%	31.4%
122,595	SARPY	41,759	31,181	9,619	959	21,562 R	74.7%	23.0%	76.4%	23.6%
19,830	SAUNDERS	8,136	6,263	1,727	146	4,536 R	77.0%	21.2%	78.4%	21.6%
36,951	SCOTTS BLUFF	11,089	8,776	2,103	210	6,673 R	79.1%	19.0%	80.7%	19.3%
16,496	SEWARD	5,946	4,520	1,313	113	3,207 R	76.0%	22.1%	77.5%	22.5%
6,198	SHERIDAN	1,858	1,539	256	63	1,283 R	82.8%	13.8%	85.7%	14.3%
3,318	SHERMAN	1,440	1,121	289	30	832 R	77.8%	20.1%	79.5%	20.5%
1,475	SIOUX	629	548	75	6	473 R	87.1%	11.9%	88.0%	12.0%
6,455	STANTON	1,986	1,659	263	64	1,396 R	83.5%	13.2%	86.3%	13.7%
6,055	THAYER	2,406	1,932	440	34	1,492 R	80.3%	18.3%	81.5%	18.5%
729	THOMAS	332	291	33	8	258 R	87.7%	9.9%	89.8%	10.2%
7,171	THURSTON	1,712	931	667	114	264 R	54.4%	39.0%	58.3%	41.7%
4,647	VALLEY	2,094	1,761	304	29	1,457 R	84.1%	14.5%	85.3%	14.7%
18,780	WASHINGTON	7,645	5,902	1,581	162	4,321 R	77.2%	20.7%	78.9%	21.1%
9,851	WAYNE	3,111	2,621	450	40	2,171 R	84.2%	14.5%	85.3%	14.7%
4,061	WEBSTER	1,747	1,401	318	28	1,083 R	80.2%	18.2%	81.5%	18.5%
886	WHEELER	388	333	49	6	284 R	85.8%	12.6%	87.2%	12.8%
14,598	YORK	5,557	4,717	749	91	3,968 R	84.9%	13.5%	86.3%	13.7%
1,711,263	TOTAL	593,357	435,507	145,115	12,735	290,392 R	73.4%	24.5%	75.0%	25.0%

NEBRASKA

SENATOR 2006

2000 Census Population	County	Total Vote	Republican	Democratic	Other	Rep.-Dem. Plurality	Percentage			
							Total Vote		Major Vote	
							Rep.	Dem.	Rep.	Dem.
31,151	ADAMS	10,543	3,730	6,813		3,083 D	35.4%	64.6%	35.4%	64.6%
7,452	ANTELOPE	2,720	1,157	1,563		406 D	42.5%	57.5%	42.5%	57.5%
444	ARTHUR	234	139	95		44 R	59.4%	40.6%	59.4%	40.6%
819	BANNER	331	173	158		15 R	52.3%	47.7%	52.3%	47.7%
583	BLAINE	273	123	150		27 D	45.1%	54.9%	45.1%	54.9%
6,259	BOONE	2,554	887	1,667		780 D	34.7%	65.3%	34.7%	65.3%
12,158	BOX BUTTE	4,066	1,567	2,499		932 D	38.5%	61.5%	38.5%	61.5%
2,438	BOYD	982	359	623		264 D	36.6%	63.4%	36.6%	63.4%
3,525	BROWN	1,386	679	707		28 D	49.0%	51.0%	49.0%	51.0%
42,259	BUFFALO	15,053	6,551	8,502		1,951 D	43.5%	56.5%	43.5%	56.5%
7,791	BURT	2,933	893	2,040		1,147 D	30.4%	69.6%	30.4%	69.6%
8,767	BUTLER	3,484	936	2,548		1,612 D	26.9%	73.1%	26.9%	73.1%
24,334	CASS	9,311	3,455	5,856		2,401 D	37.1%	62.9%	37.1%	62.9%
9,615	CEDAR	3,855	1,306	2,549		1,243 D	33.9%	66.1%	33.9%	66.1%
4,068	CHASE	1,639	838	801		37 R	51.1%	48.9%	51.1%	48.9%
6,148	CHERRY	2,704	1,267	1,437		170 D	46.9%	53.1%	46.9%	53.1%
9,830	CHEYENNE	3,334	1,780	1,554		226 R	53.4%	46.6%	53.4%	46.6%
7,039	CLAY	2,494	922	1,572		650 D	37.0%	63.0%	37.0%	63.0%
10,441	COLFAX	2,805	858	1,947		1,089 D	30.6%	69.4%	30.6%	69.4%
10,203	CUMING	3,097	1,132	1,965		833 D	36.6%	63.4%	36.6%	63.4%
11,793	CUSTER	4,964	2,047	2,917		870 D	41.2%	58.8%	41.2%	58.8%
20,253	DAKOTA	4,789	1,459	3,330		1,871 D	30.5%	69.5%	30.5%	69.5%
9,060	DAWES	2,997	1,277	1,720		443 D	42.6%	57.4%	42.6%	57.4%
24,365	DAWSON	6,768	2,801	3,967		1,166 D	41.4%	58.6%	41.4%	58.6%
2,098	DEUEL	805	413	392		21 R	51.3%	48.7%	51.3%	48.7%
6,339	DIXON	2,399	802	1,597		795 D	33.4%	66.6%	33.4%	66.6%
36,160	DODGE	12,031	4,003	8,028		4,025 D	33.3%	66.7%	33.3%	66.7%
463,585	DOUGLAS	146,438	50,765	95,673		44,908 D	34.7%	65.3%	34.7%	65.3%
2,292	DUNDY	932	362	570		208 D	38.8%	61.2%	38.8%	61.2%
6,634	FILLMORE	2,507	715	1,792		1,077 D	28.5%	71.5%	28.5%	71.5%
3,574	FRANKLIN	1,462	515	947		432 D	35.2%	64.8%	35.2%	64.8%
3,099	FRONTIER	1,259	435	824		389 D	34.6%	65.4%	34.6%	65.4%
5,324	FURNAS	2,055	708	1,347		639 D	34.5%	65.5%	34.5%	65.5%
22,993	GAGE	8,890	2,404	6,486		4,082 D	27.0%	73.0%	27.0%	73.0%
2,292	GARDEN	1,032	532	500		32 R	51.6%	48.4%	51.6%	48.4%
1,902	GARFIELD	913	370	543		173 D	40.5%	59.5%	40.5%	59.5%
2,143	GOSPER	993	369	624		255 D	37.2%	62.8%	37.2%	62.8%
747	GRANT	327	194	133		61 R	59.3%	40.7%	59.3%	40.7%
2,714	GREELEY	1,063	255	808		553 D	24.0%	76.0%	24.0%	76.0%
53,534	HALL	17,482	6,648	10,834		4,186 D	38.0%	62.0%	38.0%	62.0%
9,403	HAMILTON	4,495	1,828	2,667		839 D	40.7%	59.3%	40.7%	59.3%
3,786	HARLAN	1,747	618	1,129		511 D	35.4%	64.6%	35.4%	64.6%
1,068	HAYES	494	212	282		70 D	42.9%	57.1%	42.9%	57.1%
3,111	HITCHCOCK	1,211	386	825		439 D	31.9%	68.1%	31.9%	68.1%
11,551	HOLT	4,466	2,166	2,300		134 D	48.5%	51.5%	48.5%	51.5%
783	HOOKER	329	144	185		41 D	43.8%	56.2%	43.8%	56.2%
6,567	HOWARD	2,609	804	1,805		1,001 D	30.8%	69.2%	30.8%	69.2%
8,333	JEFFERSON	3,180	908	2,272		1,364 D	28.6%	71.4%	28.6%	71.4%
4,488	JOHNSON	1,831	452	1,379		927 D	24.7%	75.3%	24.7%	75.3%
6,882	KEARNEY	2,759	1,138	1,621		483 D	41.2%	58.8%	41.2%	58.8%
8,875	KEITH	3,289	1,685	1,604		81 R	51.2%	48.8%	51.2%	48.8%
983	KEYA PAHA	557	254	303		49 D	45.6%	54.4%	45.6%	54.4%
4,089	KIMBALL	1,633	876	757		119 R	53.6%	46.4%	53.6%	46.4%
9,374	KNOX	3,234	1,176	2,058		882 D	36.4%	63.6%	36.4%	63.6%
250,291	LANCASTER	91,779	27,115	64,664		37,549 D	29.5%	70.5%	29.5%	70.5%
34,632	LINCOLN	12,725	4,935	7,790		2,855 D	38.8%	61.2%	38.8%	61.2%
774	LOGAN	379	180	199		19 D	47.5%	52.5%	47.5%	52.5%
712	LOUP	376	134	242		108 D	35.6%	64.4%	35.6%	64.4%
533	MCPHERSON	261	144	117		27 R	55.2%	44.8%	55.2%	44.8%
35,226	MADISON	10,768	4,868	5,900		1,032 D	45.2%	54.8%	45.2%	54.8%

NEBRASKA

SENATOR 2006

2000 Census Population	County	Total Vote	Republican	Democratic	Other	Rep.-Dem. Plurality	Percentage			
							Total Vote		Major Vote	
							Rep.	Dem.	Rep.	Dem.
8,204	MERRICK	3,047	1,118	1,929		811 D	36.7%	63.3%	36.7%	63.3%
5,440	MORRILL	1,910	986	924		62 R	51.6%	48.4%	51.6%	48.4%
4,038	NANCE	1,686	478	1,208		730 D	28.4%	71.6%	28.4%	71.6%
7,576	NEMAHA	2,849	1,090	1,759		669 D	38.3%	61.7%	38.3%	61.7%
5,057	NUCKOLLS	2,060	678	1,382		704 D	32.9%	67.1%	32.9%	67.1%
15,396	OTOE	5,708	2,139	3,569		1,430 D	37.5%	62.5%	37.5%	62.5%
3,087	PAWNEE	1,243	405	838		433 D	32.6%	67.4%	32.6%	67.4%
3,200	PERKINS	1,274	599	675		76 D	47.0%	53.0%	47.0%	53.0%
9,747	PHELPS	3,944	1,659	2,285		626 D	42.1%	57.9%	42.1%	57.9%
7,857	PIERCE	2,462	1,083	1,379		296 D	44.0%	56.0%	44.0%	56.0%
31,662	PLATTE	10,725	3,971	6,754		2,783 D	37.0%	63.0%	37.0%	63.0%
5,639	POLK	2,277	844	1,433		589 D	37.1%	62.9%	37.1%	62.9%
11,448	RED WILLOW	4,317	1,267	3,050		1,783 D	29.3%	70.7%	29.3%	70.7%
9,531	RICHARDSON	3,507	1,238	2,269		1,031 D	35.3%	64.7%	35.3%	64.7%
1,756	ROCK	789	338	451		113 D	42.8%	57.2%	42.8%	57.2%
13,843	SALINE	4,629	985	3,644		2,659 D	21.3%	78.7%	21.3%	78.7%
122,595	SARPY	41,906	17,050	24,856		7,806 D	40.7%	59.3%	40.7%	59.3%
19,830	SAUNDERS	8,018	2,594	5,424		2,830 D	32.4%	67.6%	32.4%	67.6%
36,951	SCOTTS BLUFF	11,318	5,436	5,882		446 D	48.0%	52.0%	48.0%	52.0%
16,496	SEWARD	5,894	1,928	3,966		2,038 D	32.7%	67.3%	32.7%	67.3%
6,198	SHERIDAN	1,890	1,067	823		244 R	56.5%	43.5%	56.5%	43.5%
3,318	SHERMAN	1,440	419	1,021		602 D	29.1%	70.9%	29.1%	70.9%
1,475	SIOUX	628	362	266		96 R	57.6%	42.4%	57.6%	42.4%
6,455	STANTON	1,980	912	1,068		156 D	46.1%	53.9%	46.1%	53.9%
6,055	THAYER	2,342	694	1,648		954 D	29.6%	70.4%	29.6%	70.4%
729	THOMAS	336	158	178		20 D	47.0%	53.0%	47.0%	53.0%
7,171	THURSTON	1,778	463	1,315		852 D	26.0%	74.0%	26.0%	74.0%
4,647	VALLEY	2,089	796	1,293		497 D	38.1%	61.9%	38.1%	61.9%
18,780	WASHINGTON	7,621	3,204	4,417		1,213 D	42.0%	58.0%	42.0%	58.0%
9,851	WAYNE	3,072	1,109	1,963		854 D	36.1%	63.9%	36.1%	63.9%
4,061	WEBSTER	1,731	565	1,166		601 D	32.6%	67.4%	32.6%	67.4%
886	WHEELER	392	135	257		122 D	34.4%	65.6%	34.4%	65.6%
14,598	YORK	5,428	2,309	3,119		810 D	42.5%	57.5%	42.5%	57.5%
1,711,263	TOTAL	592,316	213,928	378,388		164,460 D	36.1%	63.9%	36.1%	63.9%

NEBRASKA

HOUSE OF REPRESENTATIVES

CD	Year	Total Vote	Republican Vote	Republican Candidate	Democratic Vote	Democratic Candidate	Other Vote	Rep.-Dem. Plurality		Total Vote Rep.	Total Vote Dem.	Major Vote Rep.	Major Vote Dem.
1	2006	207,375	121,015	FORTENBERRY, JEFF*	86,360	MOUL, MAXINE B.		34,655	R	58.4%	41.6%	58.4%	41.6%
1	2004	265,072	143,756	FORTENBERRY, JEFF	113,971	CONNEALY, MATT	7,345	29,785	R	54.2%	43.0%	55.8%	44.2%
1	2002	155,844	133,013	BEREUTER, DOUG*	—		22,831	133,013	R	85.4%		100.0%	
2	2006	181,979	99,475	TERRY, LEE*	82,504	ESCH, JIM		16,971	R	54.7%	45.3%	54.7%	45.3%
2	2004	249,764	152,608	TERRY, LEE*	90,292	THOMPSON, NANCY	6,864	62,316	R	61.1%	36.2%	62.8%	37.2%
2	2002	142,014	89,917	TERRY, LEE*	46,843	SIMON, JIM	5,254	43,074	R	63.3%	33.0%	65.7%	34.3%
3	2006	206,733	113,687	SMITH, ADRIAN	93,046	KLEEB, SCOTT		20,641	R	55.0%	45.0%	55.0%	45.0%
3	2004	250,136	218,751	OSBORNE, TOM*	26,434	ANDERSON, DONNA J.	4,951	192,317	R	87.5%	10.6%	89.2%	10.8%
3	2002	175,956	163,939	OSBORNE, TOM*	—		12,017	163,939	R	93.2%		100.0%	
TOTAL	2006	596,087	334,177		261,910			72,267	R	56.1%	43.9%	56.1%	43.9%
TOTAL	2004	764,972	515,115		230,697		19,160	284,418	R	67.3%	30.2%	69.1%	30.9%
TOTAL	2002	473,814	386,869		46,843		40,102	340,026	R	81.6%	9.9%	89.2%	10.8%

An asterisk (*) denotes incumbent.

NEBRASKA

GENERAL AND PRIMARY ELECTIONS

2006 GENERAL ELECTIONS

Governor Other vote was 8,953 Nebraska (Barry Richards); 3,782 By Petition (Mort Sullivan).

Senator

House Other vote was:

CD 1
CD 2
CD 3

2006 PRIMARY ELECTIONS

Primary May 9, 2006

Registration
(as of May 9, 2006)

Republican	578,916
Democratic	371,037
Nebraska	6,308
Green	361
Nonpartisan	184,119
TOTAL	1,140,741

Primary Type Semi-open—Registered Democrats and Republicans could vote only in their party's primary. Voters registered as nonpartisan could participate in either party's primary for the Senate and House (but not governor).

NEBRASKA

GENERAL AND PRIMARY ELECTIONS

Note: An asterisk (*) denotes incumbent. Ballots cast by nonpartisan voters in primaries for the House and Senate were tallied separately but were included in the overall totals, which are listed below.

	REPUBLICAN PRIMARIES			DEMOCRATIC PRIMARIES		
Governor	Dave Heineman*	138,216	50.3%	David Hahn	68,004	91.6%
	Tom Osborne	121,973	44.4%	Glenn R. Boot Jr.	6,259	8.4%
	Dave Nabity	14,786	5.4%			
	TOTAL	274,975		TOTAL	74,263	
Senator	Pete Ricketts	129,643	48.0%	Ben Nelson*	92,501	100.0%
	Don Stenberg	96,496	35.7%			
	David J. Kramer	43,815	16.2%			
	TOTAL	269,954				
Congressional District 1	Jeff Fortenberry*	81,188	100.0%	Maxine B. Moul	23,338	71.0%
				James Wilson	9,528	29.0%
				TOTAL	32,866	
Congressional District 2	Lee Terry*	52,890	83.6%	Jim Esch	21,352	100.0%
	Steven Laird	10,380	16.4%			
	TOTAL	63,270				
Congressional District 3	Adrian Smith	42,218	39.5%	Scott Kleeb	23,929	100.0%
	John Hanson	30,501	28.5%			
	Jay Vavricek	29,224	27.3%			
	David Harris	2,934	2.7%			
	Douglas Polk	2,020	1.9%			
	TOTAL	106,897				

NEVADA

Congressional districts first established for elections held in 2002
3 members

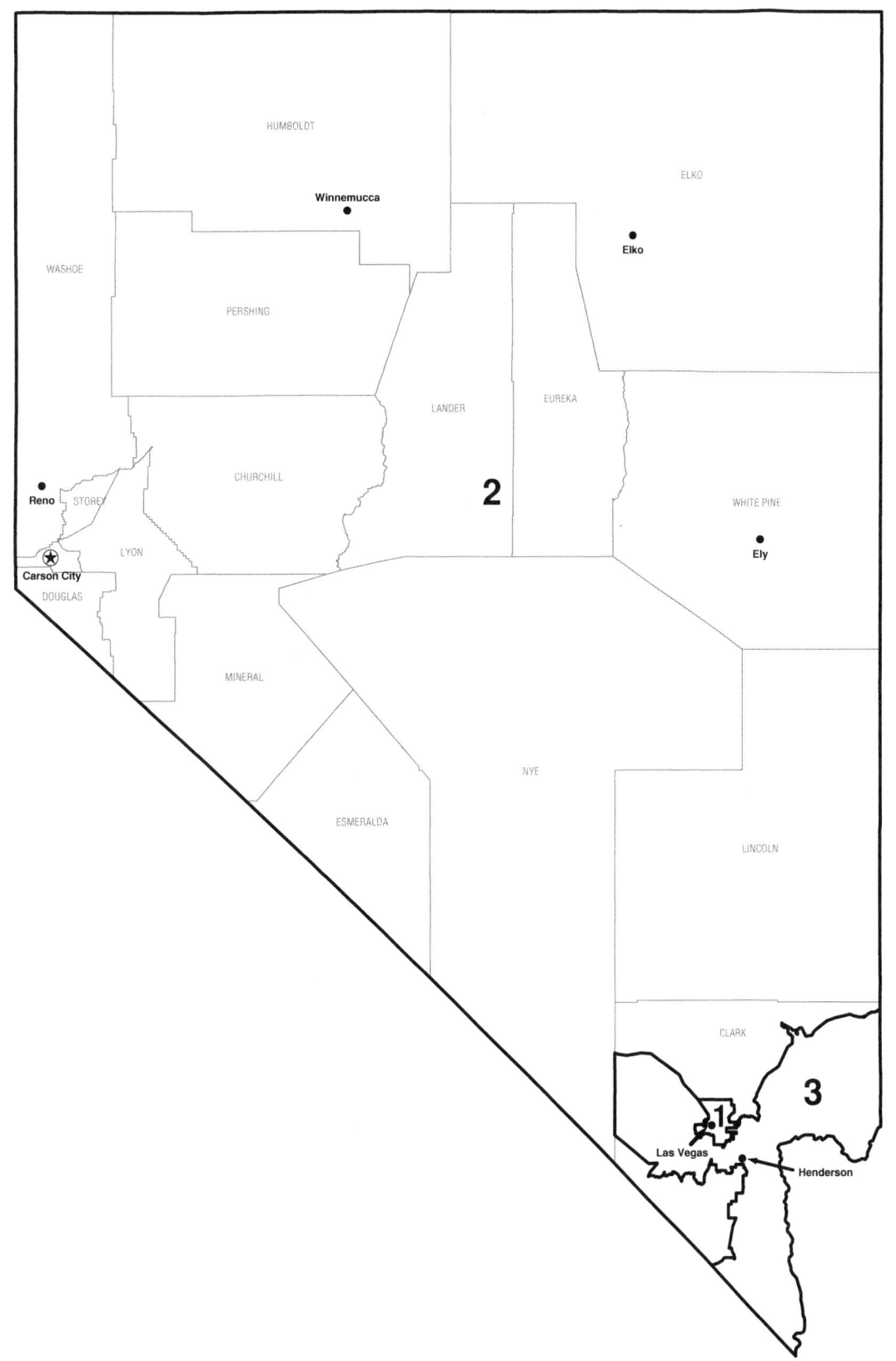

NEVADA

GOVERNOR
Jim Gibbons (R). Elected 2006 to a four-year term.

SENATORS (1 Democrat, 1 Republican)
John Ensign (R). Reelected 2006 to a six-year term. Previously elected 2000.

Harry Reid (D). Reelected 2004 to a six-year term. Previously elected 1998, 1992, 1986.

REPRESENTATIVES (2 Republicans, 1 Democrat)
1. Shelley Berkley (D)   2. Dean Heller (R)   3. Jon Porter (R)

POSTWAR VOTE FOR PRESIDENT

| | | Republican | | Democratic | | Other | | Percentage | | | |
| | | | | | | | | Total Vote | | Major Vote | |
Year	Total Vote	Vote	Candidate	Vote	Candidate	Vote	Plurality	Rep.	Dem.	Rep.	Dem.
2004	829,587	418,690	Bush, George W.	397,190	Kerry, John	13,707	21,500 R	50.5%	47.9%	51.3%	48.7%
2000**	608,970	301,575	Bush, George W.	279,978	Gore, Al	27,417	21,597 R	49.5%	46.0%	51.9%	48.1%
1996**	464,279	199,244	Dole, Bob	203,974	Clinton, Bill	61,061	4,730 D	42.9%	43.9%	49.4%	50.6%
1992**	506,318	175,828	Bush, George	189,148	Clinton, Bill	141,342	13,320 D	34.7%	37.4%	48.2%	51.8%
1988	350,067	206,040	Bush, George	132,738	Dukakis, Michael S.	11,289	73,302 R	58.9%	37.9%	60.8%	39.2%
1984	286,667	188,770	Reagan, Ronald	91,655	Mondale, Walter F.	6,242	97,115 R	65.8%	32.0%	67.3%	32.7%
1980**	247,885	155,017	Reagan, Ronald	66,666	Carter, Jimmy	26,202	88,351 R	62.5%	26.9%	69.9%	30.1%
1976	201,876	101,273	Ford, Gerald R.	92,479	Carter, Jimmy	8,124	8,794 R	50.2%	45.8%	52.3%	47.7%
1972	181,766	115,750	Nixon, Richard M.	66,016	McGovern, George S.		49,734 R	63.7%	36.3%	63.7%	36.3%
1968**	154,218	73,188	Nixon, Richard M.	60,598	Humphrey, Hubert H.	20,432	12,590 R	47.5%	39.3%	54.7%	45.3%
1964	135,433	56,094	Goldwater, Barry M.	79,339	Johnson, Lyndon B.		23,245 D	41.4%	58.6%	41.4%	58.6%
1960	107,267	52,387	Nixon, Richard M.	54,880	Kennedy, John F.		2,493 D	48.8%	51.2%	48.8%	51.2%
1956	96,689	56,049	Eisenhower, Dwight D.	40,640	Stevenson, Adlai E.		15,409 R	58.0%	42.0%	58.0%	42.0%
1952	82,190	50,502	Eisenhower, Dwight D.	31,688	Stevenson, Adlai E.		18,814 R	61.4%	38.6%	61.4%	38.6%
1948	62,117	29,357	Dewey, Thomas E.	31,291	Truman, Harry S.	1,469	1,934 D	47.3%	50.4%	48.4%	51.6%

**In past elections, the other vote included: 2000 - 15,008 Green (Ralph Nader); 1996 - 43,986 Reform (Ross Perot); 1992 - 132,580 Independent (Ross Perot); 1980 - 17,651 Independent (John Anderson); 1968 - 20,432 American Independent (George Wallace).

NEVADA

POSTWAR VOTE FOR GOVERNOR

Year	Total Vote	Republican Vote	Republican Candidate	Democratic Vote	Democratic Candidate	Other Vote	Rep.-Dem. Plurality	Total Vote Rep.	Total Vote Dem.	Major Vote Rep.	Major Vote Dem.
2006	582,158	279,003	Gibbons, Jim	255,684	Titus, Dina	47,471	23,319 R	47.9%	43.9%	52.2%	47.8%
2002	504,079	344,001	Guinn, Kenny	110,935	Neal, Joe	49,143	233,066 R	68.2%	22.0%	75.6%	24.4%
1998	433,630	223,892	Guinn, Kenny	182,281	Jones, Jan Laverty	27,457	41,611 R	51.6%	42.0%	55.1%	44.9%
1994	379,676	156,875	Gibbons, Jim	200,026	Miller, Robert J.	22,775	43,151 D	41.3%	52.7%	44.0%	56.0%
1990	320,743	95,789	Gallaway, Jim	207,878	Miller, Robert J.	17,076	112,089 D	29.9%	64.8%	31.5%	68.5%
1986	260,375	65,081	Cafferata, Patty	187,268	Bryan, Richard H.	8,026	122,187 D	25.0%	71.9%	25.8%	74.2%
1982	239,751	100,104	List, Robert F.	128,132	Bryan, Richard H.	11,515	28,028 D	41.8%	53.4%	43.9%	56.1%
1978	192,445	108,097	List, Robert F.	76,361	Rose, Robert E.	7,987	31,736 R	56.2%	39.7%	58.6%	41.4%
1974**	169,358	28,959	Crumpler, Shirley	114,114	O'Callaghan, Mike	26,285	85,155 D	17.1%	67.4%	20.2%	79.8%
1970	146,991	64,400	Fike, Ed	70,697	O'Callaghan, Mike	11,894	6,297 D	43.8%	48.1%	47.7%	52.3%
1966	137,677	71,807	Laxalt, Paul	65,870	Sawyer, Grant		5,937 R	52.2%	47.8%	52.2%	47.8%
1962	96,929	32,145	Gragson, Oran K.	64,784	Sawyer, Grant		32,639 D	33.2%	66.8%	33.2%	66.8%
1958	84,889	34,025	Russell, Charles H.	50,864	Sawyer, Grant		16,839 D	40.1%	59.9%	40.1%	59.9%
1954	78,462	41,665	Russell, Charles H.	36,797	Pittman, Vail		4,868 R	53.1%	46.9%	53.1%	46.9%
1950	61,773	35,609	Russell, Charles H.	26,164	Pittman, Vail		9,445 R	57.6%	42.4%	57.6%	42.4%
1946	49,902	21,247	Jepson, Melvin E.	28,655	Pittman, Vail		7,408 D	42.6%	57.4%	42.6%	57.4%

**In past elections, the other vote included: 1974 - 26,285 Independent American (James Ray Houston).

POSTWAR VOTE FOR SENATOR

Year	Total Vote	Republican Vote	Republican Candidate	Democratic Vote	Democratic Candidate	Other Vote	Rep.-Dem. Plurality	Total Vote Rep.	Total Vote Dem.	Major Vote Rep.	Major Vote Dem.
2006	582,572	322,501	Ensign, John	238,796	Carter, Jack	21,275	83,705 R	55.4%	41.0%	57.5%	42.5%
2004	810,068	284,640	Ziser, Richard	494,805	Reid, Harry	30,623	210,165 D	35.1%	61.1%	36.5%	63.5%
2000	600,250	330,687	Ensign, John	238,260	Bernstein, Ed	31,303	92,427 R	55.1%	39.7%	58.1%	41.9%
1998	435,790	208,222	Ensign, John	208,650	Reid, Harry	18,918	428 D	47.8%	47.9%	49.9%	50.1%
1994	380,530	156,020	Furman, Hal	193,804	Bryan, Richard H.	30,706	37,784 D	41.0%	50.9%	44.6%	55.4%
1992	495,887	199,413	Dahl, Demar	253,150	Reid, Harry	43,324	53,737 D	40.2%	51.0%	44.1%	55.9%
1988	349,649	161,336	Hecht, Chic	175,548	Bryan, Richard H.	12,765	14,212 D	46.1%	50.2%	47.9%	52.1%
1986	261,932	116,606	Santini, James	130,955	Reid, Harry	14,371	14,349 D	44.5%	50.0%	47.1%	52.9%
1982	240,394	120,377	Hecht, Chic	114,720	Cannon, Howard W.	5,297	5,657 R	50.1%	47.7%	51.2%	48.8%
1980	246,436	144,224	Laxalt, Paul	92,129	Gojack, Mary	10,083	52,095 R	58.5%	37.4%	61.0%	39.0%
1976	201,980	63,471	Towell, David	127,295	Cannon, Howard W.	11,214	63,824 D	31.4%	63.0%	33.3%	66.7%
1974	169,473	79,605	Laxalt, Paul	78,981	Reid, Harry	10,887	624 R	47.0%	46.6%	50.2%	49.8%
1970	147,768	60,838	Raggio, William J.	85,187	Cannon, Howard W.	1,743	24,349 D	41.2%	57.6%	41.7%	58.3%
1968	152,690	69,068	Fike, Ed	83,622	Bible, Alan		14,554 D	45.2%	54.8%	45.2%	54.8%
1964	134,624	67,288	Laxalt, Paul	67,336	Cannon, Howard W.		48 D	50.0%	50.0%	50.0%	50.0%
1962	97,192	33,749	Wright, William B.	63,443	Bible, Alan		29,694 D	34.7%	65.3%	34.7%	65.3%
1958	84,492	35,760	Malone, George W.	48,732	Cannon, Howard W.		12,972 D	42.3%	57.7%	42.3%	57.7%
1956	96,389	45,712	Young, Clifton	50,677	Bible, Alan		4,965 D	47.4%	52.6%	47.4%	52.6%
1954S	77,513	32,470	Brown, Ernest S.	45,043	Bible, Alan		12,573 D	41.9%	58.1%	41.9%	58.1%
1952	81,090	41,906	Malone, George W.	39,184	Mechling, Thomas B.		2,722 R	51.7%	48.3%	51.7%	48.3%
1950	61,762	25,933	Marshall, George E.	35,829	McCarran, Pat		9,896 D	42.0%	58.0%	42.0%	58.0%
1946	50,354	27,801	Malone, George W.	22,553	Bunker, Berkeley		5,248 R	55.2%	44.8%	55.2%	44.8%

The 1954 election was for a short term to fill a vacancy.

NEVADA

GOVERNOR 2006

2000 Census Population	County	Total Vote	Republican	Democratic	Other	Rep.-Dem. Plurality	Total Vote Rep.	Dem.	Major Vote Rep.	Dem.
52,457	CARSON CITY	18,173	9,716	6,989	1,468	2,727 R	53.5%	38.5%	58.2%	41.8%
23,982	CHURCHILL	8,112	5,627	1,806	679	3,821 R	69.4%	22.3%	75.7%	24.3%
1,375,765	CLARK	359,702	153,876	177,300	28,526	23,424 D	42.8%	49.3%	46.5%	53.5%
41,259	DOUGLAS	19,333	11,918	5,929	1,486	5,989 R	61.6%	30.7%	66.8%	33.2%
45,291	ELKO	11,811	7,938	2,873	1,000	5,065 R	67.2%	24.3%	73.4%	26.6%
971	ESMERALDA	434	297	92	45	205 R	68.4%	21.2%	76.3%	23.7%
1,651	EUREKA	721	515	121	85	394 R	71.4%	16.8%	81.0%	19.0%
16,106	HUMBOLDT	4,503	3,119	987	397	2,132 R	69.3%	21.9%	76.0%	24.0%
5,794	LANDER	1,792	1,291	369	132	922 R	72.0%	20.6%	77.8%	22.2%
4,165	LINCOLN	1,847	1,165	465	217	700 R	63.1%	25.2%	71.5%	28.5%
34,501	LYON	15,076	9,329	4,310	1,437	5,019 R	61.9%	28.6%	68.4%	31.6%
5,071	MINERAL	2,104	1,188	676	240	512 R	56.5%	32.1%	63.7%	36.3%
32,485	NYE	11,842	5,950	4,446	1,446	1,504 R	50.2%	37.5%	57.2%	42.8%
6,693	PERSHING	1,533	976	404	153	572 R	63.7%	26.4%	70.7%	29.3%
3,399	STOREY	1,874	1,070	626	178	444 R	57.1%	33.4%	63.1%	36.9%
339,486	WASHOE	119,971	63,057	47,296	9,618	15,761 R	52.6%	39.4%	57.1%	42.9%
9,181	WHITE PINE	3,330	1,971	995	364	976 R	59.2%	29.9%	66.5%	33.5%
1,998,257	TOTAL	582,158	279,003	255,684	47,471	23,319 R	47.9%	43.9%	52.2%	47.8%

NEVADA

SENATOR 2006

2000 Census Population	County	Total Vote	Republican	Democratic	Other	Rep.-Dem. Plurality	Total Vote Rep.	Dem.	Major Vote Rep.	Dem.
52,457	CARSON CITY	18,165	11,002	6,461	702	4,541 R	60.6%	35.6%	63.0%	37.0%
23,982	CHURCHILL	8,104	5,777	2,000	327	3,777 R	71.3%	24.7%	74.3%	25.7%
1,375,765	CLARK	360,040	188,847	159,214	11,979	29,633 R	52.5%	44.2%	54.3%	45.7%
41,259	DOUGLAS	19,333	12,822	5,795	716	7,027 R	66.3%	30.0%	68.9%	31.1%
45,291	ELKO	11,811	8,218	2,941	652	5,277 R	69.6%	24.9%	73.6%	26.4%
971	ESMERALDA	432	289	91	52	198 R	66.9%	21.1%	76.1%	23.9%
1,651	EUREKA	720	510	128	82	382 R	70.8%	17.8%	79.9%	20.1%
16,106	HUMBOLDT	4,490	3,145	1,129	216	2,016 R	70.0%	25.1%	73.6%	26.4%
5,794	LANDER	1,785	1,252	450	83	802 R	70.1%	25.2%	73.6%	26.4%
4,165	LINCOLN	1,853	1,323	415	115	908 R	71.4%	22.4%	76.1%	23.9%
34,501	LYON	15,067	9,876	4,522	669	5,354 R	65.5%	30.0%	68.6%	31.4%
5,071	MINERAL	2,100	1,237	728	135	509 R	58.9%	34.7%	63.0%	37.0%
32,485	NYE	11,837	6,855	4,294	688	2,561 R	57.9%	36.3%	61.5%	38.5%
6,693	PERSHING	1,538	983	462	93	521 R	63.9%	30.0%	68.0%	32.0%
3,399	STOREY	1,880	1,151	635	94	516 R	61.2%	33.8%	64.4%	35.6%
339,486	WASHOE	120,087	67,262	48,385	4,440	18,877 R	56.0%	40.3%	58.2%	41.8%
9,181	WHITE PINE	3,330	1,952	1,146	232	806 R	58.6%	34.4%	63.0%	37.0%
1,998,257	TOTAL	582,572	322,501	238,796	21,275	83,705 R	55.4%	41.0%	57.5%	42.5%

NEVADA

HOUSE OF REPRESENTATIVES

CD	Year	Total Vote	Republican Vote	Republican Candidate	Democratic Vote	Democratic Candidate	Other Vote	Rep.-Dem. Plurality		Total Vote Rep.	Total Vote Dem.	Major Vote Rep.	Major Vote Dem.
1	2006	131,124	40,917	WEGNER, KENNETH	85,025	BERKLEY, SHELLEY*	5,182	44,108	D	31.2%	64.8%	32.5%	67.5%
1	2004	202,436	63,005	MICKELSON, RUSS	133,569	BERKLEY, SHELLEY*	5,862	70,564	D	31.1%	66.0%	32.1%	67.9%
1	2002	119,714	51,148	BOGGS-McDONALD, LYNETTE MARIA	64,312	BERKLEY, SHELLEY*	4,254	13,164	D	42.7%	53.7%	44.3%	55.7%
2	2006	232,724	117,168	HELLER, DEAN	104,593	DERBY, JILL	10,963	12,575	R	50.3%	44.9%	52.8%	47.2%
2	2004	291,079	195,466	GIBBONS, JIM*	79,978	COCHRAN, ANGIE G.	15,635	115,488	R	67.2%	27.5%	71.0%	29.0%
2	2002	201,200	149,574	GIBBONS, JIM*	40,189	SOUZA, TRAVIS O.	11,437	109,385	R	74.3%	20.0%	78.8%	21.2%
3	2006	210,979	102,232	PORTER, JON*	98,261	HAFEN, TESSA M.	10,486	3,971	R	48.5%	46.6%	51.0%	49.0%
3	2004	297,918	162,240	PORTER, JON*	120,365	GALLAGHER, TOM	15,313	41,875	R	54.5%	40.4%	57.4%	42.6%
3	2002	178,994	100,378	PORTER, JON	66,659	HERRERA, DARIO	11,957	33,719	R	56.1%	37.2%	60.1%	39.9%
TOTAL	2006	574,827	260,317		287,879		26,631	27,562	D	45.3%	50.1%	47.5%	52.5%
TOTAL	2004	791,433	420,711		333,912		36,810	86,799	R	53.2%	42.2%	55.8%	44.2%
TOTAL	2002	499,908	301,100		171,160		27,648	129,940	R	60.2%	34.2%	63.8%	36.2%

An asterisk (*) denotes incumbent.

NEVADA

GENERAL AND PRIMARY ELECTIONS

2006 GENERAL ELECTIONS

Governor Other vote was 20,699 "None of these Candidates"; 20,019 Independent American (Christopher H. Hansen); 6,753 Green (Craig O. Bergland).

Senator Other vote was 8,232 "None of these Candidates"; 7,774 Independent American (David K. Schumann); 5,269 Libertarian (Brendan Trainor).

House Other vote was:

CD 1 2,843 Libertarian (Jim Duensing); 2,339 Independent American (Darnell Roberts).
CD 2 5,524 Independent (Daniel Rosen); 5,439 Independent American (James C. Kroshus).
CD 3 5,329 Independent American (Joshua Hansen); 5,157 Libertarian (Joseph P. Silvestri).

2006 PRIMARY ELECTIONS

Primary August 15, 2006 **Registration** (active registrants as of August 15, 2006)

Republican	391,322
Democratic	382,862
Independent American	32,062
Libertarian	5,733
Green	2,705
Natural Law	837
Reform	266
Other	2,560
Nonpartisan	139,059
TOTAL	957,406

Primary Type Closed—Only registered Democrats and Republicans could vote in their party's primary.

NEVADA

GENERAL AND PRIMARY ELECTIONS

Note: An asterisk (*) denotes incumbent. The names of unopposed candidates did not appear on the primary ballot; therefore, no votes were cast for these candidates.

	REPUBLICAN PRIMARIES			DEMOCRATIC PRIMARIES		
Governor	Jim Gibbons	67,717	48.2%	Dina Titus	63,999	53.8%
	Bob Beers	40,876	29.1%	James B. Gibson	42,966	36.1%
	Lorraine T. Hunt	25,161	17.9%	"None of these Candidates"	7,062	5.9%
	"None of these Candidates"	4,316	3.1%	Leola McConnell	5,019	4.2%
	Melody "Mimi Miyagi" Damayo	1,651	1.2%			
	Stanleigh Harold Lusak	794	0.6%			
	TOTAL	140,515		TOTAL	119,046	
Senator	John Ensign*	127,023	90.5%	Jack Carter	92,270	78.3%
	"None of these Candidates"	6,754	4.8%	"None of these Candidates"	14,425	12.2%
	Edward "Fast Eddie" Hamilton	6,649	4.7%	Ruby Jee Tun	11,147	9.5%
	TOTAL	140,426		TOTAL	117,842	
Congressional District 1	Kenneth Wegner	10,615	51.2%	Shelley Berkley*	29,655	90.1%
	Russ Mickelson	7,907	38.2%	Asimo Sondra "Silver" Lawlor	3,267	9.9%
	Michael "Ace" Monroe	2,193	10.6%			
	TOTAL	20,715		TOTAL	32,922	
Congressional District 2	Dean Heller	24,770	35.9%	Jill Derby	Unopposed	
	Sharron E. Angle	24,349	35.3%			
	Dawn Gibbons	17,317	25.1%			
	Glenn Thomas	1,835	2.7%			
	Richard Gilster	721	1.0%			
	TOTAL	68,992				
Congressional District 3	Jon Porter*	Unopposed		Tessa M. Hafen	22,118	57.6%
				Barry Michaels	6,005	15.6%
				Anna Nevenic	4,832	12.6%
				Mark Budetich	3,885	10.1%
				Freddie L. Warman	1,578	4.1%
				TOTAL	38,418	

NEW HAMPSHIRE

Congressional districts first established for elections held in 2002
2 members

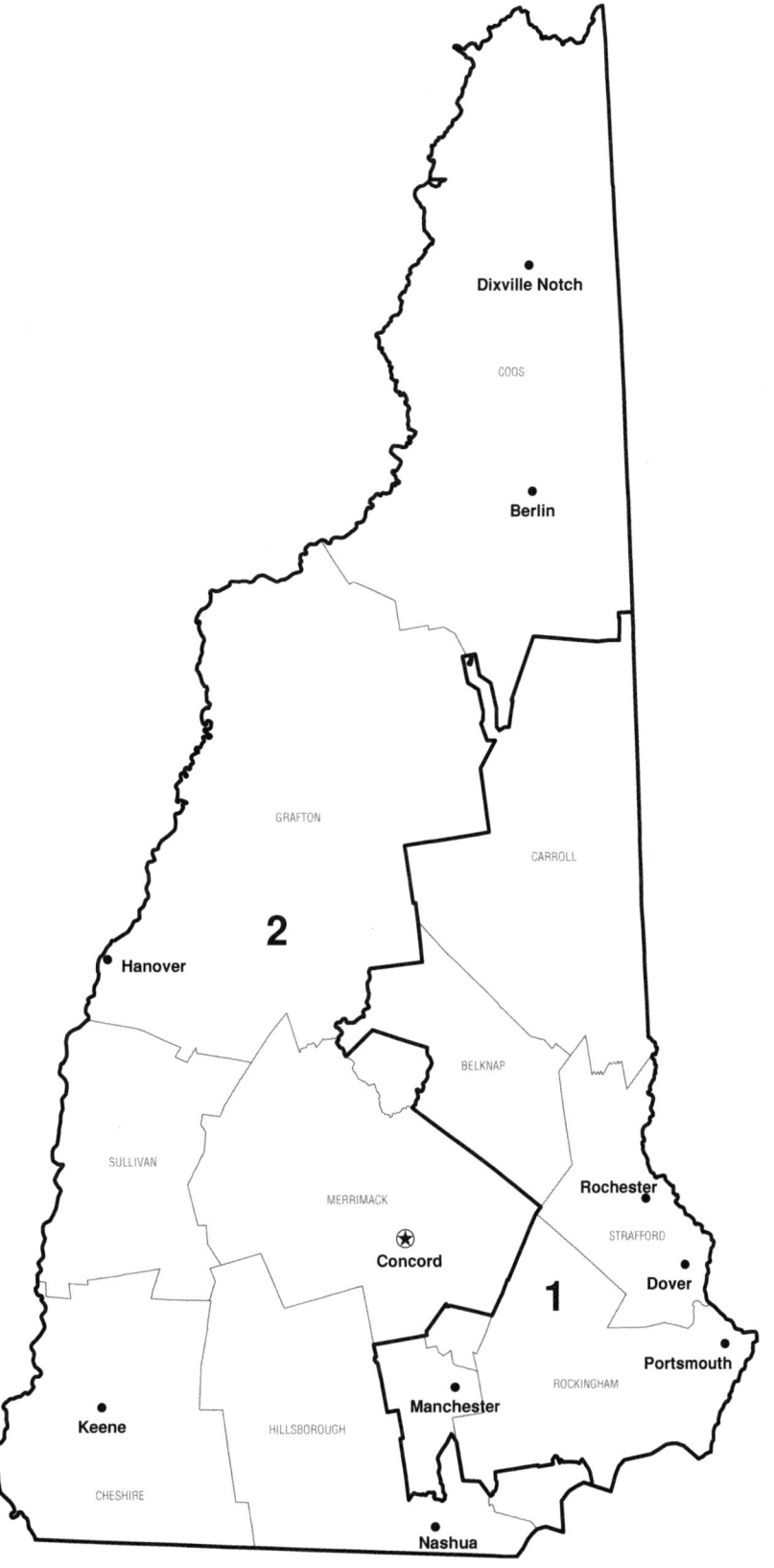

NEW HAMPSHIRE

GOVERNOR

John Lynch (D). Reelected 2006 to a two-year term. Previously elected 2004.

SENATORS (2 Republicans)

Judd Gregg (R). Reelected 2004 to a six-year term. Previously elected 1998, 1992.

John E. Sununu (R). Elected 2002 to a six-year term.

REPRESENTATIVES (2 Democrats)

1. Carol Shea-Porter (D)   2. Paul W. Hodes (D)

POSTWAR VOTE FOR PRESIDENT

| Year | Total Vote | Republican | | Democratic | | Other Vote | Plurality | Percentage | | | |
| | | Vote | Candidate | Vote | Candidate | | | Total Vote | | Major Vote | |
								Rep.	Dem.	Rep.	Dem.
2004	677,738	331,237	Bush, George W.	340,511	Kerry, John	5,990	9,274 D	48.9%	50.2%	49.3%	50.7%
2000**	569,081	273,559	Bush, George W.	266,348	Gore, Al	29,174	7,211 R	48.1%	46.8%	50.7%	49.3%
1996**	499,175	196,532	Dole, Bob	246,214	Clinton, Bill	56,429	49,682 D	39.4%	49.3%	44.4%	55.6%
1992**	537,943	202,484	Bush, George	209,040	Clinton, Bill	126,419	6,556 D	37.6%	38.9%	49.2%	50.8%
1988	451,074	281,537	Bush, George	163,696	Dukakis, Michael S.	5,841	117,841 R	62.4%	36.3%	63.2%	36.8%
1984	389,066	267,051	Reagan, Ronald	120,395	Mondale, Walter F.	1,620	146,656 R	68.6%	30.9%	68.9%	31.1%
1980**	383,990	221,705	Reagan, Ronald	108,864	Carter, Jimmy	53,421	112,841 R	57.7%	28.4%	67.1%	32.9%
1976	339,618	185,935	Ford, Gerald R.	147,635	Carter, Jimmy	6,048	38,300 R	54.7%	43.5%	55.7%	44.3%
1972	334,055	213,724	Nixon, Richard M.	116,435	McGovern, George S.	3,896	97,289 R	64.0%	34.9%	64.7%	35.3%
1968**	297,298	154,903	Nixon, Richard M.	130,589	Humphrey, Hubert H.	11,806	24,314 R	52.1%	43.9%	54.3%	45.7%
1964	288,093	104,029	Goldwater, Barry M.	184,064	Johnson, Lyndon B.		80,035 D	36.1%	63.9%	36.1%	63.9%
1960	295,761	157,989	Nixon, Richard M.	137,772	Kennedy, John F.		20,217 R	53.4%	46.6%	53.4%	46.6%
1956	266,994	176,519	Eisenhower, Dwight D.	90,364	Stevenson, Adlai E.	111	86,155 R	66.1%	33.8%	66.1%	33.9%
1952	272,950	166,287	Eisenhower, Dwight D.	106,663	Stevenson, Adlai E.		59,624 R	60.9%	39.1%	60.9%	39.1%
1948	231,440	121,299	Dewey, Thomas E.	107,995	Truman, Harry S.	2,146	13,304 R	52.4%	46.7%	52.9%	47.1%

**In past elections, the other included: 2000 - 22,198 Green (Ralph Nader); 1996 - 48,390 Reform (Ross Perot); 1992 - 121,337 Independent (Ross Perot); 1980 - 49,693 Independent (John Anderson); 1968 - 11,173 American Independent (George Wallace).

NEW HAMPSHIRE

POSTWAR VOTE FOR GOVERNOR

Year	Total Vote	Republican Vote	Candidate	Democratic Vote	Candidate	Other Vote	Rep.-Dem. Plurality	Total Vote Rep.	Total Vote Dem.	Major Vote Rep.	Major Vote Dem.
2006	403,679	104,288	Coburn, Jim	298,760	Lynch, John	631	194,472 D	25.8%	74.0%	25.9%	74.1%
2004	667,020	325,981	Benson, Craig	340,299	Lynch, John	740	14,318 D	48.9%	51.0%	48.9%	51.1%
2002	442,976	259,663	Benson, Craig	169,277	Fernald, Mark	14,036	90,386 R	58.6%	38.2%	60.5%	39.5%
2000	564,953	246,952	Humphrey, Gordon J.	275,038	Shaheen, Jeanne	42,963	28,086 D	43.7%	48.7%	47.3%	52.7%
1998	318,940	98,473	Lucas, Jay	210,769	Shaheen, Jeanne	9,698	112,296 D	30.9%	66.1%	31.8%	68.2%
1996	497,040	196,321	Lamontagne, Ovide	284,175	Shaheen, Jeanne	16,544	87,854 D	39.5%	57.2%	40.9%	59.1%
1994	311,882	218,134	Merrill, Steve	79,686	King, Wayne D.	14,062	138,448 R	69.9%	25.6%	73.2%	26.8%
1992	516,170	289,170	Merrill, Steve	206,232	Arnesen, Deborah A.	20,768	82,938 R	56.0%	40.0%	58.4%	41.6%
1990	295,018	177,773	Gregg, Judd	101,923	Grandmaison, J. Joseph	15,322	75,850 R	60.3%	34.5%	63.6%	36.4%
1988	441,923	267,064	Gregg, Judd	172,543	McEachern, Paul	2,316	94,521 R	60.4%	39.0%	60.8%	39.2%
1986	251,107	134,824	Sununu, John H.	116,142	McEachern, Paul	141	18,682 R	53.7%	46.3%	53.7%	46.3%
1984	383,910	256,574	Sununu, John H.	127,156	Spirou, Chris	180	129,418 R	66.8%	33.1%	66.9%	33.1%
1982	282,588	145,389	Sununu, John H.	132,317	Gallen, Hugh J.	4,882	13,072 R	51.4%	46.8%	52.4%	47.6%
1980	384,031	156,178	Thomson, Meldrim	226,436	Gallen, Hugh J.	1,417	70,258 D	40.7%	59.0%	40.8%	59.2%
1978	269,587	122,464	Thomson, Meldrim	133,133	Gallen, Hugh J.	13,990	10,669 D	45.4%	49.4%	47.9%	52.1%
1976	342,669	197,589	Thomson, Meldrim	145,015	Spanos, Harry V.	65	52,574 R	57.7%	42.3%	57.7%	42.3%
1974	226,665	115,933	Thomson, Meldrim	110,591	Leonard, Richard W.	141	5,342 R	51.1%	48.8%	51.2%	48.8%
1972**	323,102	133,702	Thomson, Meldrim	126,107	Crowley, Roger J.	63,293	7,595 R	41.4%	39.0%	51.5%	48.5%
1970	222,441	102,298	Peterson, Walter R.	98,098	Crowley, Roger J.	22,045	4,200 R	46.0%	44.1%	51.0%	49.0%
1968	285,342	149,902	Peterson, Walter R.	135,378	Bussiere, Emile R.	62	14,524 R	52.5%	47.4%	52.5%	47.5%
1966	233,642	107,259	Gregg, Hugh	125,882	King, John W.	501	18,623 D	45.9%	53.9%	46.0%	54.0%
1964	285,863	94,824	Pillsbury, John	190,863	King, John W.	176	96,039 D	33.2%	66.8%	33.2%	66.8%
1962	230,048	94,567	Pillsbury, John	135,481	King, John W.		40,914 D	41.1%	58.9%	41.1%	58.9%
1960	290,527	161,123	Powell, Wesley	129,404	Boutin, Bernard L.		31,719 R	55.5%	44.5%	55.5%	44.5%
1958	206,745	106,790	Powell, Wesley	99,955	Boutin, Bernard L.		6,835 R	51.7%	48.3%	51.7%	48.3%
1956	258,695	141,578	Dwinell, Lane	117,117	Shaw, John		24,461 R	54.7%	45.3%	54.7%	45.3%
1954	194,631	107,287	Dwinell, Lane	87,344	Shaw, John		19,943 R	55.1%	44.9%	55.1%	44.9%
1952	265,715	167,791	Gregg, Hugh	97,924	Craig, William H.		69,867 R	63.1%	36.9%	63.1%	36.9%
1950	191,239	108,907	Adams, Sherman	82,258	Bingham, Robert P.	74	26,649 R	56.9%	43.0%	57.0%	43.0%
1948	222,571	116,212	Adams, Sherman	105,207	Hill, Herbert W.	1,152	11,005 R	52.2%	47.3%	52.5%	47.5%
1946	163,451	103,204	Dale, Charles M.	60,247	Keefe, F. Clyde		42,957 R	63.1%	36.9%	63.1%	36.9%

**In past elections, the other vote included: 1972 - 63,199 Independent (Malcolm McLane).

NEW HAMPSHIRE

POSTWAR VOTE FOR SENATOR

Year	Total Vote	Republican Vote	Republican Candidate	Democratic Vote	Democratic Candidate	Other Vote	Rep.-Dem. Plurality	Total Vote Rep.	Total Vote Dem.	Major Vote Rep.	Major Vote Dem.
2004	657,086	434,847	Gregg, Judd	221,549	Haddock, Doris "Granny D."	690	213,298 R	66.2%	33.7%	66.2%	33.8%
2002	447,135	227,229	Sununu, John E.	207,478	Shaheen, Jeanne	12,428	19,751 R	50.8%	46.4%	52.3%	47.7%
1998	314,956	213,477	Gregg, Judd	88,883	Condodemetraky, George	12,596	124,594 R	67.8%	28.2%	70.6%	29.4%
1996	492,598	242,304	Smith, Robert C.	227,397	Swett, Dick	22,897	14,907 R	49.2%	46.2%	51.6%	48.4%
1992	518,416	249,591	Gregg, Judd	234,982	Rauh, John	33,843	14,609 R	48.1%	45.3%	51.5%	48.5%
1990	291,393	189,792	Smith, Robert C.	91,299	Durkin, John A.	10,302	98,493 R	65.1%	31.3%	67.5%	32.5%
1986	244,797	154,090	Rudman, Warren	79,225	Peabody, Endicott	11,482	74,865 R	62.9%	32.4%	66.0%	34.0%
1984	384,406	225,828	Humphrey, Gordon J.	157,447	D'Amours, Norman E.	1,131	68,381 R	58.7%	41.0%	58.9%	41.1%
1980	375,064	195,563	Rudman, Warren	179,455	Durkin, John A.	46	16,108 R	52.1%	47.8%	52.1%	47.9%
1978	263,779	133,745	Humphrey, Gordon J.	127,945	McIntyre, Thomas J.	2,089	5,800 R	50.7%	48.5%	51.1%	48.9%
1975S	262,682	113,007	Wyman, Louis C.	140,778	Durkin, John A.	8,897	27,771 D	43.0%	53.6%	44.5%	55.5%
1974**	223,363	110,926	Wyman, Louis C.	110,924	Durkin, John A.	1,513	2 R	49.7%	49.7%	50.0%	50.0%
1972	324,354	139,852	Powell, Wesley	184,495	McIntyre, Thomas J.	7	44,643 D	43.1%	56.9%	43.1%	56.9%
1968	286,989	170,163	Cotton, Norris	116,816	King, John W.	10	53,347 R	59.3%	40.7%	59.3%	40.7%
1966	229,305	105,241	Thyng, Harrison R.	123,888	McIntyre, Thomas J.	176	18,647 D	45.9%	54.0%	45.9%	54.1%
1962	224,479	134,035	Cotton, Norris	90,444	Catalfo, Alfred		43,591 R	59.7%	40.3%	59.7%	40.3%
1962S	224,811	107,199	Bass, Perkins	117,612	McIntyre, Thomas J.		10,413 D	47.7%	52.3%	47.7%	52.3%
1960	287,545	173,521	Bridges, Styles	114,024	Hill, Herbert W.		59,497 R	60.3%	39.7%	60.3%	39.7%
1956	251,943	161,424	Cotton, Norris	90,519	Pickett, Laurence M.		70,905 R	64.1%	35.9%	64.1%	35.9%
1954	194,536	117,150	Bridges, Styles	77,386	Morin, Gerard L.		39,764 R	60.2%	39.8%	60.2%	39.8%
1954S	189,558	114,068	Cotton, Norris	75,490	Bentley, Stanley J.		38,578 R	60.2%	39.8%	60.2%	39.8%
1950	190,573	106,142	Tobey, Charles W.	72,473	Kelley, Emmet J.	11,958	33,669 R	55.7%	38.0%	59.4%	40.6%
1948	222,898	129,600	Bridges, Styles	91,760	Fortin, Alfred E.	1,538	37,840 R	58.1%	41.2%	58.5%	41.5%

**Following the closely contested 1974 election, neither candidate was seated and the 1975 special election was held for the remaining years of that term. One each of the 1962 and 1954 elections were for short terms to fill vacancies.

NEW HAMPSHIRE

GOVERNOR 2006

2000 Census Population	County	Total Vote	Republican	Democratic	Other	Rep.-Dem. Plurality	Total Vote Rep.	Total Vote Dem.	Major Vote Rep.	Major Vote Dem.
56,325	BELKNAP	20,538	5,050	15,467	21	10,417 D	24.6%	75.3%	24.6%	75.4%
43,666	CARROLL	18,648	5,225	13,403	20	8,178 D	28.0%	71.9%	28.0%	72.0%
73,825	CHESHIRE	25,786	5,278	20,459	49	15,181 D	20.5%	79.3%	20.5%	79.5%
33,111	COOS	9,973	2,216	7,746	11	5,530 D	22.2%	77.7%	22.2%	77.8%
81,743	GRAFTON	29,077	6,573	22,451	53	15,878 D	22.6%	77.2%	22.6%	77.4%
380,841	HILLSBOROUGH	113,914	32,478	81,222	214	48,744 D	28.5%	71.3%	28.6%	71.4%
136,225	MERRIMACK	49,841	10,412	39,351	78	28,939 D	20.9%	79.0%	20.9%	79.1%
277,359	ROCKINGHAM	88,228	26,998	61,102	128	34,104 D	30.6%	69.3%	30.6%	69.4%
112,233	STRAFFORD	33,986	6,776	27,168	42	20,392 D	19.9%	79.9%	20.0%	80.0%
40,458	SULLIVAN	13,688	3,282	10,391	15	7,109 D	24.0%	75.9%	24.0%	76.0%
1,235,786	TOTAL	403,679	104,288	298,760	631	194,472 D	25.8%	74.0%	25.9%	74.1%

NEW HAMPSHIRE

GOVERNOR 2006

2000 Census Population	City/Town	Total Vote	Republican	Democratic	Other	Rep.-Dem. Plurality	Percentage Total Vote Rep.	Dem.	Major Vote Rep.	Dem.
10,769	AMHERST	4,601	1,442	3,151	8	1,709 D	31.3%	68.5%	31.4%	68.6%
6,178	ATKINSON	2,425	912	1,509	4	597 D	37.6%	62.2%	37.7%	62.3%
7,475	BARRINGTON	2,733	608	2,122	3	1,514 D	22.2%	77.6%	22.3%	77.7%
18,274	BEDFORD	7,206	2,661	4,536	9	1,875 D	36.9%	62.9%	37.0%	63.0%
6,716	BELMONT	1,913	469	1,443	1	974 D	24.5%	75.4%	24.5%	75.5%
10,331	BERLIN	2,817	420	2,394	3	1,974 D	14.9%	85.0%	14.9%	85.1%
7,138	BOW	3,423	743	2,672	8	1,929 D	21.7%	78.1%	21.8%	78.2%
13,151	CLAREMONT	3,360	780	2,576	4	1,796 D	23.2%	76.7%	23.2%	76.8%
40,687	CONCORD	13,667	2,154	11,470	43	9,316 D	15.8%	83.9%	15.8%	84.2%
8,604	CONWAY	2,994	731	2,257	6	1,526 D	24.4%	75.4%	24.5%	75.5%
34,021	DERRY	5,898	2,407	3,491		1,084 D	40.8%	59.2%	40.8%	59.2%
26,884	DOVER	8,775	1,579	7,190	6	5,611 D	18.0%	81.9%	18.0%	82.0%
12,664	DURHAM	3,030	432	2,589	9	2,157 D	14.3%	85.4%	14.3%	85.7%
5,476	EPPING	1,615	411	1,202	2	791 D	25.4%	74.4%	25.5%	74.5%
14,058	EXETER	5,222	1,249	3,968	5	2,719 D	23.9%	76.0%	23.9%	76.1%
5,774	FARMINGTON	1,516	390	1,126		736 D	25.7%	74.3%	25.7%	74.3%
8,405	FRANKLIN	2,312	475	1,836	1	1,361 D	20.5%	79.4%	20.6%	79.4%
6,803	GILFORD	2,958	716	2,241	1	1,525 D	24.2%	75.8%	24.2%	75.8%
16,929	GOFFSTOWN	5,107	1,479	3,617	11	2,138 D	29.0%	70.8%	29.0%	71.0%
8,297	HAMPSTEAD	2,610	878	1,727	5	849 D	33.6%	66.2%	33.7%	66.3%
14,937	HAMPTON	5,714	1,520	4,190	4	2,670 D	26.6%	73.3%	26.6%	73.4%
10,850	HANOVER	4,055	550	3,501	4	2,951 D	13.6%	86.3%	13.6%	86.4%
7,015	HOLLIS	3,319	1,068	2,249	2	1,181 D	32.2%	67.8%	32.2%	67.8%
11,721	HOOKSETT	3,767	1,108	2,658	1	1,550 D	29.4%	70.6%	29.4%	70.6%
22,928	HUDSON	5,928	1,880	4,024	24	2,144 D	31.7%	67.9%	31.8%	68.2%
5,476	JAFFREY	1,862	480	1,380	2	900 D	25.8%	74.1%	25.8%	74.2%
22,563	KEENE	7,489	1,191	6,281	17	5,090 D	15.9%	83.9%	15.9%	84.1%
5,862	KINGSTON	1,744	574	1,170		596 D	32.9%	67.1%	32.9%	67.1%
16,411	LACONIA	4,898	1,108	3,783	7	2,675 D	22.6%	77.2%	22.7%	77.3%
12,568	LEBANON	3,999	817	3,178	4	2,361 D	20.4%	79.5%	20.5%	79.5%
7,360	LITCHFIELD	2,290	736	1,547	7	811 D	32.1%	67.6%	32.2%	67.8%
5,845	LITTLETON	1,823	472	1,346	5	874 D	25.9%	73.8%	26.0%	74.0%
23,236	LONDONDERRY	6,592	2,488	4,073	31	1,585 D	37.7%	61.8%	37.9%	62.1%
107,006	MANCHESTER	26,938	6,580	20,299	59	13,719 D	24.4%	75.4%	24.5%	75.5%
25,119	MERRIMACK TOWN	7,961	2,573	5,374	14	2,801 D	32.3%	67.5%	32.4%	67.6%
13,535	MILFORD	4,301	1,203	3,092	6	1,889 D	28.0%	71.9%	28.0%	72.0%
86,605	NASHUA	22,173	5,687	16,457	29	10,770 D	25.6%	74.2%	25.7%	74.3%
8,027	NEWMARKET	2,771	473	2,294	4	1,821 D	17.1%	82.8%	17.1%	82.9%
6,269	NEWPORT	1,717	423	1,290	4	867 D	24.6%	75.1%	24.7%	75.3%
10,914	PELHAM	3,157	1,243	1,909	5	666 D	39.4%	60.5%	39.4%	60.6%
6,897	PEMBROKE	2,156	446	1,704	6	1,258 D	20.7%	79.0%	20.7%	79.3%
5,883	PETERBOROUGH	2,682	525	2,148	9	1,623 D	19.6%	80.1%	19.6%	80.4%
7,747	PLAISTOW	1,852	674	1,177	1	503 D	36.4%	63.6%	36.4%	63.6%
5,892	PLYMOUTH	1,558	274	1,282	2	1,008 D	17.6%	82.3%	17.6%	82.4%
20,784	PORTSMOUTH	7,598	1,185	6,402	11	5,217 D	15.6%	84.3%	15.6%	84.4%
9,674	RAYMOND	2,414	730	1,683	1	953 D	30.2%	69.7%	30.3%	69.7%
28,461	ROCHESTER	7,805	1,699	6,093	13	4,394 D	21.8%	78.1%	21.8%	78.2%
28,112	SALEM	7,712	2,723	4,979	10	2,256 D	35.3%	64.6%	35.4%	64.6%
7,934	SEABROOK	2,034	653	1,378	3	725 D	32.1%	67.7%	32.2%	67.8%
11,477	SOMERSWORTH	2,933	515	2,413	5	1,898 D	17.6%	82.3%	17.6%	82.4%
6,800	SWANZEY	2,151	432	1,715	4	1,283 D	20.1%	79.7%	20.1%	79.9%
7,776	WEARE	2,494	753	1,737	4	984 D	30.2%	69.6%	30.2%	69.8%
10,709	WINDHAM	4,018	1,612	2,401	5	789 D	40.1%	59.8%	40.2%	59.8%

NEW HAMPSHIRE

HOUSE OF REPRESENTATIVES

CD	Year	Total Vote	Republican Vote	Republican Candidate	Democratic Vote	Democratic Candidate	Other Vote	Rep.-Dem. Plurality	Total Vote Rep.	Total Vote Dem.	Major Vote Rep.	Major Vote Dem.
1	2006	196,377	95,527	BRADLEY, JEB*	100,691	SHEA-PORTER, CAROL	159	5,164 D	48.6%	51.3%	48.7%	51.3%
1	2004	323,372	204,836	BRADLEY, JEB*	118,226	NADEAU, JUSTIN	310	86,610 R	63.3%	36.6%	63.4%	36.6%
1	2002	221,987	128,993	BRADLEY, JEB	85,426	CLARK, MARTHA FULLER	7,568	43,567 R	58.1%	38.5%	60.2%	39.8%
2	2006	206,292	94,088	BASS, CHARLES*	108,743	HODES, PAUL W.	3,461	14,655 D	45.6%	52.7%	46.4%	53.6%
2	2004	328,194	191,188	BASS, CHARLES*	125,280	HODES, PAUL W.	11,726	65,908 R	58.3%	38.2%	60.4%	39.6%
2	2002	221,456	125,804	BASS, CHARLES*	90,479	SWETT, KATRINA	5,173	35,325 R	56.8%	40.9%	58.2%	41.8%
TOTAL	2006	402,669	189,615		209,434		3,620	19,819 D	47.1%	52.0%	47.5%	52.5%
TOTAL	2004	651,566	396,024		243,506		12,036	152,518 R	60.8%	37.4%	61.9%	38.1%
TOTAL	2002	443,443	254,797		175,905		12,741	78,892 R	57.5%	39.7%	59.2%	40.8%

An asterisk (*) denotes incumbent.

NEW HAMPSHIRE

GENERAL AND PRIMARY ELECTIONS

2006 GENERAL ELECTIONS

Governor   Other vote was 323 Libertarian write-in (Richard Kahn); 308 scattered write-in.

House   Other vote was:

CD 1   159 scattered write-in.
CD 2   3,305 Libertarian (Ken Blevens); 156 scattered write-in.

2006 PRIMARY ELECTIONS

Primary	September 12, 2006	**Registration** (as of September 12, 2006)	Republican	253,736
			Democratic	216,005
			Undeclared	356,897
			TOTAL	826,638

Primary Type   Semi-open—Registered Democrats and Republicans could vote only in their party's primary. "Undeclared" voters could participate in either party's primary.

NEW HAMPSHIRE

GENERAL AND PRIMARY ELECTIONS

Note: An asterisk (*) denotes incumbent.

	REPUBLICAN PRIMARIES			DEMOCRATIC PRIMARIES		
Governor	Jim Coburn	30,352	85.4%	John Lynch*	43,442	99.5%
	John Lynch (D, write-in)	4,794	13.5%	Jim Coburn (R, write-in)	40	0.1%
	Scattered write-in	396	1.1%	Scattered write-in	174	0.4%
	TOTAL	35,542		TOTAL	43,656	
Congressional	Jeb Bradley*	20,329	85.9%	Carol Shea-Porter	12,497	54.0%
District 1	Michael Callis	3,128	13.2%	Jim Craig	7,944	34.3%
	Carol Shea-Porter (D, write-in)	74	0.3%	Gary Dodds	1,125	4.9%
	Jim Craig (D, write-in)	72	0.3%	Peter M. Sullivan	1,021	4.4%
	Gary Dodds (D, write-in)	10		Dave Jarvis	422	1.8%
	Dave Jarvis (D, write-in)	1		Jeb Bradley (R, write-in)	80	0.3%
	Peter M. Sullivan (D, write-in)	1		Michael Callis (R, write-in)	4	
	Scattered write-in	58	0.2%	Scattered write-in	57	0.2%
	TOTAL	23,673		TOTAL	23,150	
Congressional	Charles Bass*	18,068	75.3%	Paul W. Hodes	18,002	98.5%
District 2	Robert A. Danderson	3,239	13.5%	Charles Bass (R, write-in)	111	0.6%
	Mary Maxwell	2,557	10.7%	Robert A. Danderson (R, write-in)	25	0.1%
	Paul W. Hodes (D, write-in)	46	0.2%	Mary Maxwell (R, write-in)	6	
	Scattered write-in	93	0.4%	Scattered write-in	134	0.7%
	TOTAL	24,003		TOTAL	18,278	

NEW JERSEY

Congressional districts first established for elections held in 2002
13 members

NEW JERSEY

Northern New Jersey Gateway Area

NEW JERSEY

GOVERNOR
Jon Corzine (D). Elected 2005 to a four-year term.

SENATORS (2 Democrats)
Robert Menendez (D). Elected 2006 to a six-year term.

Frank R. Lautenberg (D). Elected 2002 to a six-year term. Previously elected 1994, 1988, 1982.

REPRESENTATIVES (7 Democrats, 6 Republicans)
1. Robert E. Andrews (D)
2. Frank A. LoBiondo (R)
3. H. James Saxton (R)
4. Christopher H. Smith (R)
5. Scott Garrett (R)
6. Frank Pallone Jr. (D)
7. Mike Ferguson (R)
8. Bill Pascrell Jr. (D)
9. Steven R. Rothman (D)
10. Donald M. Payne (D)
11. Rodney Frelinghuysen (R)
12. Rush D. Holt (D)
13. Albio Sires (D)

POSTWAR VOTE FOR PRESIDENT

Year	Total Vote	Republican Vote	Republican Candidate	Democratic Vote	Democratic Candidate	Other Vote	Plurality	Total Vote Rep.	Total Vote Dem.	Major Vote Rep.	Major Vote Dem.
2004	3,611,691	1,670,003	Bush, George W.	1,911,430	Kerry, John	30,258	241,427 D	46.2%	52.9%	46.6%	53.4%
2000**	3,187,226	1,284,173	Bush, George W.	1,788,850	Gore, Al	114,203	504,677 D	40.3%	56.1%	41.8%	58.2%
1996**	3,075,807	1,103,078	Dole, Bob	1,652,329	Clinton, Bill	320,400	549,251 D	35.9%	53.7%	40.0%	60.0%
1992**	3,343,594	1,356,865	Bush, George	1,436,206	Clinton, Bill	550,523	79,341 D	40.6%	43.0%	48.6%	51.4%
1988	3,099,553	1,743,192	Bush, George	1,320,352	Dukakis, Michael S.	36,009	422,840 R	56.2%	42.6%	56.9%	43.1%
1984	3,217,862	1,933,630	Reagan, Ronald	1,261,323	Mondale, Walter F.	22,909	672,307 R	60.1%	39.2%	60.5%	39.5%
1980**	2,975,684	1,546,557	Reagan, Ronald	1,147,364	Carter, Jimmy	281,763	399,193 R	52.0%	38.6%	57.4%	42.6%
1976	3,014,472	1,509,688	Ford, Gerald R.	1,444,653	Carter, Jimmy	60,131	65,035 R	50.1%	47.9%	51.1%	48.9%
1972	2,997,229	1,845,502	Nixon, Richard M.	1,102,211	McGovern, George S.	49,516	743,291 R	61.6%	36.8%	62.6%	37.4%
1968**	2,875,395	1,325,467	Nixon, Richard M.	1,264,206	Humphrey, Hubert H.	285,722	61,261 R	46.1%	44.0%	51.2%	48.8%
1964	2,847,663	964,174	Goldwater, Barry M.	1,868,231	Johnson, Lyndon B.	15,258	904,057 D	33.9%	65.6%	34.0%	66.0%
1960	2,773,111	1,363,324	Nixon, Richard M.	1,385,415	Kennedy, John F.	24,372	22,091 D	49.2%	50.0%	49.6%	50.4%
1956	2,484,312	1,606,942	Eisenhower, Dwight D.	850,337	Stevenson, Adlai E.	27,033	756,605 R	64.7%	34.2%	65.4%	34.6%
1952	2,418,554	1,373,613	Eisenhower, Dwight D.	1,015,902	Stevenson, Adlai E.	29,039	357,711 R	56.8%	42.0%	57.5%	42.5%
1948	1,949,555	981,124	Dewey, Thomas E.	895,455	Truman, Harry S.	72,976	85,669 R	50.3%	45.9%	52.3%	47.7%

**In past elections, the other vote included: 2000 - 94,554 Green (Ralph Nader); 1996 - 262,134 Reform (Ross Perot); 1992 - 521,829 Independent (Ross Perot); 1980 - 234,632 Independent (John Anderson); 1968 - 262,187 American Independent (George Wallace).

NEW JERSEY

POSTWAR VOTE FOR GOVERNOR

Year	Total Vote	Republican		Democratic		Other Vote	Rep.-Dem. Plurality	Percentage			
								Total Vote		Major Vote	
		Vote	Candidate	Vote	Candidate			Rep.	Dem.	Rep.	Dem.
2005	2,290,099	985,271	Forrester, Doug	1,224,551	Corzine, Jon	80,277	239,280 D	43.0%	53.5%	44.6%	55.4%
2001	2,227,165	928,174	Schundler, Bret D.	1,256,853	McGreevey, James E.	42,138	328,679 D	41.7%	56.4%	42.5%	57.5%
1997	2,418,344	1,133,394	Whitman, Christine T.	1,107,968	McGreevey, James E.	176,982	25,426 R	46.9%	45.8%	50.6%	49.4%
1993	2,505,964	1,236,124	Whitman, Christine T.	1,210,031	Florio, James J.	59,809	26,093 R	49.3%	48.3%	50.5%	49.5%
1989	2,253,764	838,553	Courter, James A.	1,379,937	Florio, James J.	35,274	541,384 D	37.2%	61.2%	37.8%	62.2%
1985	1,972,624	1,372,631	Kean, Thomas H.	578,402	Shapiro, Peter	21,591	794,229 R	69.6%	29.3%	70.4%	29.6%
1981	2,317,239	1,145,999	Kean, Thomas H.	1,144,202	Florio, James J.	27,038	1,797 R	49.5%	49.4%	50.0%	50.0%
1977	2,126,264	888,880	Bateman, Raymond H.	1,184,564	Byrne, Brendan T.	52,820	295,684 D	41.8%	55.7%	42.9%	57.1%
1973	2,122,009	676,235	Sandman, Charles W.	1,414,613	Byrne, Brendan T.	31,161	738,378 D	31.9%	66.7%	32.3%	67.7%
1969	2,366,606	1,411,905	Cahill, William T.	911,003	Meyner, Robert B.	43,698	500,902 R	59.7%	38.5%	60.8%	39.2%
1965	2,229,583	915,996	Dumont, Wayne	1,279,568	Hughes, Richard J.	34,019	363,572 D	41.1%	57.4%	41.7%	58.3%
1961	2,152,662	1,049,274	Mitchell, James P.	1,084,194	Hughes, Richard J.	19,194	34,920 D	48.7%	50.4%	49.2%	50.8%
1957	2,018,488	897,321	Forbes, Malcolm S.	1,101,130	Meyner, Robert B.	20,037	203,809 D	44.5%	54.6%	44.9%	55.1%
1953	1,810,812	809,068	Troast, Paul L.	962,710	Meyner, Robert B.	39,034	153,642 D	44.7%	53.2%	45.7%	54.3%
1949**	1,718,788	885,882	Driscoll, Alfred	810,022	Wene, Elmer H.	22,884	75,860 R	51.5%	47.1%	52.2%	47.8%
1946	1,414,527	807,378	Driscoll, Alfred	585,960	Hansen, Lewis G.	21,189	221,418 R	57.1%	41.4%	57.9%	42.1%

**The term of office of New Jersey's governor was increased from three to four years effective with the 1949 election.

POSTWAR VOTE FOR SENATOR

Year	Total Vote	Republican		Democratic		Other Vote	Rep.-Dem. Plurality	Percentage			
								Total Vote		Major Vote	
		Vote	Candidate	Vote	Candidate			Rep.	Dem.	Rep.	Dem.
2006	2,250,070	997,775	Kean, Thomas H., Jr.	1,200,843	Menendez, Robert	51,452	203,068 D	44.3%	53.4%	45.4%	54.6%
2002	2,112,604	928,439	Forrester, Doug	1,138,193	Lautenberg, Frank R.	45,972	209,754 D	43.9%	53.9%	44.9%	55.1%
2000	3,015,662	1,420,267	Franks, Bob	1,511,237	Corzine, Jon	84,158	90,970 D	47.1%	50.1%	48.4%	51.6%
1996	2,884,106	1,227,817	Zimmer, Dick	1,519,328	Torricelli, Robert G.	136,961	291,511 D	42.6%	52.7%	44.7%	55.3%
1994	2,054,887	966,244	Haytaian, Garabed	1,033,487	Lautenberg, Frank R.	55,156	67,243 D	47.0%	50.3%	48.3%	51.7%
1990	1,938,454	918,874	Whitman, Christine T.	977,810	Bradley, Bill	41,770	58,936 D	47.4%	50.4%	48.4%	51.6%
1988	2,987,634	1,349,937	Dawkins, Peter M.	1,599,905	Lautenberg, Frank R.	37,792	249,968 D	45.2%	53.6%	45.8%	54.2%
1984	3,096,456	1,080,100	Mochary, Mary V.	1,986,644	Bradley, Bill	29,712	906,544 D	34.9%	64.2%	35.2%	64.8%
1982	2,193,945	1,047,626	Fenwick, Millicent	1,117,549	Lautenberg, Frank R.	28,770	69,923 D	47.8%	50.9%	48.4%	51.6%
1978	1,957,515	844,200	Bell, Jeffrey	1,082,960	Bradley, Bill	30,355	238,760 D	43.1%	55.3%	43.8%	56.2%
1976	2,771,390	1,054,508	Norcross, David F.	1,681,140	Williams, Harrison	35,742	626,632 D	38.0%	60.7%	38.5%	61.5%
1972	2,791,907	1,743,854	Case, Clifford P.	963,573	Krebs, Paul J.	84,480	780,281 R	62.5%	34.5%	64.4%	35.6%
1970	2,142,105	903,026	Gross, Nelson G.	1,157,074	Williams, Harrison	82,005	254,048 D	42.2%	54.0%	43.8%	56.2%
1966	2,131,188	1,279,343	Case, Clifford P.	788,021	Wilentz, Warren W.	63,824	491,322 R	60.0%	37.0%	61.9%	38.1%
1964	2,710,441	1,011,610	Shanley, Bernard M.	1,678,051	Williams, Harrison	20,780	666,441 D	37.3%	61.9%	37.6%	62.4%
1960	2,664,556	1,483,832	Case, Clifford P.	1,151,385	Lord, Thorn	29,339	332,447 R	55.7%	43.2%	56.3%	43.7%
1958	1,881,329	882,201	Kean, Robert W.	966,832	Williams, Harrison	32,210	84,545 D	46.9%	51.4%	47.7%	52.3%
1954	1,770,557	861,528	Case, Clifford P.	858,158	Howell, Charles R.	50,871	3,370 R	48.7%	48.5%	50.1%	49.9%
1952	2,318,232	1,286,782	Smith, H. Alexander	1,011,187	Alexander, Archibald	20,263	275,595 R	55.5%	43.6%	56.0%	44.0%
1948	1,869,882	934,720	Hendrickson, Robert	884,414	Alexander, Archibald	50,748	50,306 R	50.0%	47.3%	51.4%	48.6%
1946	1,367,155	799,808	Smith, H. Alexander	548,458	Brunner, George E.	18,889	251,350 R	58.5%	40.1%	59.3%	40.7%

NEW JERSEY

GOVERNOR 2005

2000 Census Population	County	Total Vote	Republican	Democratic	Other	Rep.-Dem. Plurality	Percentage			
							Total Vote		Major Vote	
							Rep.	Dem.	Rep.	Dem.
252,552	ATLANTIC	64,781	28,004	34,539	2,238	6,535 D	43.2%	53.3%	44.8%	55.2%
884,118	BERGEN	256,019	108,017	142,319	5,683	34,302 D	42.2%	55.6%	43.1%	56.9%
423,394	BURLINGTON	127,532	57,908	64,421	5,203	6,513 D	45.4%	50.5%	47.3%	52.7%
508,932	CAMDEN	127,492	45,079	76,955	5,458	31,876 D	35.4%	60.4%	36.9%	63.1%
102,326	CAPE MAY	31,797	16,179	14,375	1,243	1,804 R	50.9%	45.2%	53.0%	47.0%
146,438	CUMBERLAND	32,503	12,692	18,580	1,231	5,888 D	39.0%	57.2%	40.6%	59.4%
793,633	ESSEX	180,557	45,789	131,312	3,456	85,523 D	25.4%	72.7%	25.9%	74.1%
254,673	GLOUCESTER	77,357	33,225	41,128	3,004	7,903 D	43.0%	53.2%	44.7%	55.3%
608,975	HUDSON	115,869	25,769	87,409	2,691	61,640 D	22.2%	75.4%	22.8%	77.2%
121,989	HUNTERDON	44,704	27,521	15,004	2,179	12,517 R	61.6%	33.6%	64.7%	35.3%
350,761	MERCER	99,059	38,871	56,592	3,596	17,721 D	39.2%	57.1%	40.7%	59.3%
750,162	MIDDLESEX	191,282	75,021	107,176	9,085	32,155 D	39.2%	56.0%	41.2%	58.8%
615,301	MONMOUTH	194,648	101,085	85,187	8,376	15,898 R	51.9%	43.8%	54.3%	45.7%
470,212	MORRIS	147,533	82,550	60,986	3,997	21,564 R	56.0%	41.3%	57.5%	42.5%
510,916	OCEAN	172,888	93,693	71,953	7,242	21,740 R	54.2%	41.6%	56.6%	43.4%
489,049	PASSAIC	106,748	41,532	61,803	3,413	20,271 D	38.9%	57.9%	40.2%	59.8%
64,285	SALEM	20,673	9,608	10,057	1,008	449 D	46.5%	48.6%	48.9%	51.1%
297,490	SOMERSET	93,526	49,406	40,459	3,661	8,947 R	52.8%	43.3%	55.0%	45.0%
144,166	SUSSEX	42,319	25,283	14,854	2,182	10,429 R	59.7%	35.1%	63.0%	37.0%
522,541	UNION	131,695	50,036	77,982	3,677	27,946 D	38.0%	59.2%	39.1%	60.9%
102,437	WARREN	31,117	18,003	11,460	1,654	6,543 R	57.9%	36.8%	61.1%	38.9%
8,414,350	TOTAL	2,290,099	985,271	1,224,551	80,277	239,280 D	43.0%	53.5%	44.6%	55.4%

NEW JERSEY

SENATOR 2006

2000 Census Population	County	Total Vote	Republican	Democratic	Other	Rep.-Dem. Plurality	Percentage			
							Total Vote		Major Vote	
							Rep.	Dem.	Rep.	Dem.
252,552	ATLANTIC	67,547	31,784	34,251	1,512	2,467 D	47.1%	50.7%	48.1%	51.9%
884,118	BERGEN	261,151	118,199	139,564	3,388	21,365 D	45.3%	53.4%	45.9%	54.1%
423,394	BURLINGTON	127,090	58,725	65,788	2,577	7,063 D	46.2%	51.8%	47.2%	52.8%
508,932	CAMDEN	132,269	47,732	81,577	2,960	33,845 D	36.1%	61.7%	36.9%	63.1%
102,326	CAPE MAY	34,301	19,506	14,038	757	5,468 R	56.9%	40.9%	58.2%	41.8%
146,438	CUMBERLAND	30,640	13,537	16,243	860	2,706 D	44.2%	53.0%	45.5%	54.5%
793,633	ESSEX	170,350	45,266	122,751	2,333	77,485 D	26.6%	72.1%	26.9%	73.1%
254,673	GLOUCESTER	81,442	36,559	42,766	2,117	6,207 D	44.9%	52.5%	46.1%	53.9%
608,975	HUDSON	118,064	27,536	88,696	1,832	61,160 D	23.3%	75.1%	23.7%	76.3%
121,989	HUNTERDON	44,227	25,531	16,873	1,823	8,658 R	57.7%	38.2%	60.2%	39.8%
350,761	MERCER	93,504	34,958	56,111	2,435	21,153 D	37.4%	60.0%	38.4%	61.6%
750,162	MIDDLESEX	177,444	68,734	103,198	5,512	34,464 D	38.7%	58.2%	40.0%	60.0%
615,301	MONMOUTH	182,801	96,247	81,672	4,882	14,575 R	52.7%	44.7%	54.1%	45.9%
470,212	MORRIS	149,825	85,656	61,431	2,738	24,225 R	57.2%	41.0%	58.2%	41.8%
510,916	OCEAN	162,170	92,819	64,621	4,730	28,198 R	57.2%	39.8%	59.0%	41.0%
489,049	PASSAIC	101,973	41,998	58,333	1,642	16,335 D	41.2%	57.2%	41.9%	58.1%
64,285	SALEM	21,276	10,576	9,898	802	678 R	49.7%	46.5%	51.7%	48.3%
297,490	SOMERSET	91,801	46,720	42,242	2,839	4,478 R	50.9%	46.0%	52.5%	47.5%
144,166	SUSSEX	42,793	26,185	14,839	1,769	11,346 R	61.2%	34.7%	63.8%	36.2%
522,541	UNION	130,394	52,496	75,166	2,732	22,670 D	40.3%	57.6%	41.1%	58.9%
102,437	WARREN	29,008	17,011	10,785	1,212	6,226 R	58.6%	37.2%	61.2%	38.8%
8,414,350	TOTAL	2,250,070	997,775	1,200,843	51,452	203,068 D	44.3%	53.4%	45.4%	54.6%

NEW JERSEY

HOUSE OF REPRESENTATIVES

CD	Year	Total Vote	Republican		Democratic		Other Vote	Rep.-Dem. Plurality	Percentage Total Vote		Major Vote	
			Vote	Candidate	Vote	Candidate			Rep.	Dem.	Rep.	Dem.
1	2006	140,110		—	140,110	ANDREWS, ROBERT E.*		140,110 D		100.0%		100.0%
1	2004	268,203	66,109	HUTCHISON, S. DANIEL	201,163	ANDREWS, ROBERT E.*	931	135,054 D	24.6%	75.0%	24.7%	75.3%
1	2002	131,389		—	121,846	ANDREWS, ROBERT E.*	9,543	121,846 D		92.7%		100.0%
2	2006	180,575	111,245	LoBIONDO, FRANK A.*	64,279	THOMAS-HUGHES, VIOLA	5,051	46,966 R	61.6%	35.6%	63.4%	36.6%
2	2004	265,442	172,779	LoBIONDO, FRANK A.*	86,792	ROBB, TIMOTHY J.	5,871	85,987 R	65.1%	32.7%	66.6%	33.4%
2	2002	168,799	116,834	LoBIONDO, FRANK A.*	47,735	FARKAS, STEVEN A.	4,230	69,099 R	69.2%	28.3%	71.0%	29.0%
3	2006	209,851	122,559	SAXTON, H. JAMES*	86,113	SEXTON, RICH	1,179	36,446 R	58.4%	41.0%	58.7%	41.3%
3	2004	308,862	195,938	SAXTON, H. JAMES*	107,034	CONAWAY, HERB	5,890	88,904 R	63.4%	34.7%	64.7%	35.3%
3	2002	189,739	123,375	SAXTON, H. JAMES*	64,364	STRADA, RICHARD	2,000	59,011 R	65.0%	33.9%	65.7%	34.3%
4	2006	189,540	124,482	SMITH, CHRISTOPHER H.*	62,905	GAY, CAROL E.	2,153	61,577 R	65.7%	33.2%	66.4%	33.6%
4	2004	287,553	192,671	SMITH, CHRISTOPHER H.*	92,826	VASQUEZ, AMY	2,056	99,845 R	67.0%	32.3%	67.5%	32.5%
4	2002	174,301	115,293	SMITH, CHRISTOPHER H.*	55,967	BRENNAN, MARY	3,041	59,326 R	66.1%	32.1%	67.3%	32.7%
5	2006	204,242	112,142	GARRETT, SCOTT*	89,503	ARONSOHN, PAUL	2,597	22,639 R	54.9%	43.8%	55.6%	44.4%
5	2004	297,425	171,220	GARRETT, SCOTT*	122,259	WOLFE, DOROTHEA ANNE	3,946	48,961 R	57.6%	41.1%	58.3%	41.7%
5	2002	199,851	118,881	GARRETT, SCOTT	76,504	SUMERS, ANNE	4,466	42,377 R	59.5%	38.3%	60.8%	39.2%
6	2006	143,773	43,539	BELLEW, LEIGH-ANN	98,615	PALLONE, FRANK JR.*	1,619	55,076 D	30.3%	68.6%	30.6%	69.4%
6	2004	230,151	70,942	FERNANDEZ, SYLVESTER	153,981	PALLONE, FRANK JR.*	5,228	83,039 D	30.8%	66.9%	31.5%	68.5%
6	2002	137,495	42,479	MEDROW, RIC	91,379	PALLONE, FRANK JR.*	3,637	48,900 D	30.9%	66.5%	31.7%	68.3%
7	2006	199,075	98,399	FERGUSON, MIKE*	95,454	STENDER, LINDA	5,222	2,945 R	49.4%	47.9%	50.8%	49.2%
7	2004	285,847	162,597	FERGUSON, MIKE*	119,081	BROZAK, STEVE	4,169	43,516 R	56.9%	41.7%	57.7%	42.3%
7	2002	183,002	106,055	FERGUSON, MIKE*	74,879	CARDEN, TIM	2,068	31,176 R	58.0%	40.9%	58.6%	41.4%
8	2006	137,639	39,053	SANDOVAL, JOSE M.	97,568	PASCRELL, BILL JR.*	1,018	58,515 D	28.4%	70.9%	28.6%	71.4%
8	2004	218,820	62,747	AJJAN, GEORGE	152,001	PASCRELL, BILL JR.*	4,072	89,254 D	28.7%	69.5%	29.2%	70.8%
8	2002	131,819	40,318	SILVERMAN, JARED	88,101	PASCRELL, BILL JR.*	3,400	47,783 D	30.6%	66.8%	31.4%	68.6%
9	2006	148,095	40,879	MICCO, VINCENT	105,853	ROTHMAN, STEVEN R.*	1,363	64,974 D	27.6%	71.5%	27.9%	72.1%
9	2004	216,251	68,564	TRAWINSKI, EDWARD	146,038	ROTHMAN, STEVEN R.*	1,649	77,474 D	31.7%	67.5%	31.9%	68.1%
9	2002	139,196	42,088	GLASS, JOSEPH	97,108	ROTHMAN, STEVEN R.*		55,020 D	30.2%	69.8%	30.2%	69.8%
10	2006	90,264		—	90,264	PAYNE, DONALD M.*		90,264 D		100.0%		100.0%
10	2004	160,713		—	155,697	PAYNE, DONALD M.*	5,016	155,697 D		96.9%		100.0%
10	2002	102,346	15,913	WIRTZ, ANDREW	86,433	PAYNE, DONALD M.*		70,520 D	15.5%	84.5%	15.5%	84.5%
11	2006	203,071	126,085	FRELINGHUYSEN, RODNEY*	74,414	WYKA, TOM	2,572	51,671 R	62.1%	36.6%	62.9%	37.1%
11	2004	296,002	200,915	FRELINGHUYSEN, RODNEY*	91,811	BUELL, JAMES W.	3,276	109,104 R	67.9%	31.0%	68.6%	31.4%
11	2002	183,678	132,938	FRELINGHUYSEN, RODNEY*	48,477	PAWAR, VIJ	2,263	84,461 R	72.4%	26.4%	73.3%	26.7%
12	2006	190,977	65,509	SINAGRA, JOSEPH S.	125,468	HOLT, RUSH D.*		59,959 D	34.3%	65.7%	34.3%	65.7%
12	2004	289,785	115,014	SPADEA, BILL	171,691	HOLT, RUSH D.*	3,080	56,677 D	39.7%	59.2%	40.1%	59.9%
12	2002	171,713	62,938	SOARIES, DeFOREST "BUSTER"	104,806	HOLT, RUSH D.*	3,969	41,868 D	36.7%	61.0%	37.5%	62.5%
13	2006	99,630	19,284	GUARINI, JOHN J.	77,238	SIRES, ALBIO	3,108	57,954 D	19.4%	77.5%	20.0%	80.0%
13	2004	159,541	35,288	PIATKOWSKI, RICHARD W.	121,018	MENENDEZ, ROBERT*	3,235	85,730 D	22.1%	75.9%	22.6%	77.4%
13	2002	92,731	16,852	GERON, JAMES	72,605	MENENDEZ, ROBERT*	3,274	55,753 D	18.2%	78.3%	18.8%	81.2%
TOTAL	2006	2,136,842	903,176		1,207,784		25,882	304,608 D	42.3%	56.5%	42.8%	57.2%
TOTAL	2004	3,284,595	1,514,784		1,721,392		48,419	206,608 D	46.1%	52.4%	46.8%	53.2%
TOTAL	2002	2,006,059	933,964		1,030,204		41,891	96,240 D	46.6%	51.4%	47.6%	52.4%

An asterisk (*) denotes incumbent.

NEW JERSEY

GENERAL AND PRIMARY ELECTIONS

2006 GENERAL ELECTIONS

Governor (2005)
Other vote was 29,452 Education Not Corruption (Hector L. Castillo); 15,417 Libertarian (Jeffrey Pawlowski); 12,315 Green (Matthew J. Thieke); 9,137 Legalize Marijuana (G.R.I.P.) (Edward Forchion); 5,169 ONE NEW JERSEY (Michael Latigona); 4,178 various designations by county, most frequent being "Restore Rebates" and "Shake Up Trenton" (Wesley K. "Wes" Bell); 2,531 Socialist Workers (Angela L. Lariscy); 2,078 Socialist (Constantino Rozzo).

Senator
Other vote was 14,637 Libertarian (Len Flynn); 11,593 Legalize Marijuana (G.R.I.P.) (Edward Forchion); 7,918 God We Trust (J. M. Carter); 6,243 Solidarity, Defend Life (N. Leonard Smith); 5,138 Poor People's Campaign (Daryl Mikell Brooks); 3,433 Socialist Workers (Angela L. Lariscy); 2,490 Socialist (Gregory Pason).

House
Other vote was:

CD 1

CD 2   3,071 Preserve Green Space (Robert E. Mullock); 992 A New Direction (Lynn Merle); 603 We The People (Thomas Fanslau); 385 Socialist (Willie Norwood).

CD 3   1,179 The Patriot Movement (Ken Feduniewicz).

CD 4   1,539 Libertarian (Richard Edgar); 614 Remove Medical Negligence (Louis B. Wary Jr.).

CD 5   2,597 An Independent Voice (R. Matthew Fretz).

CD 6   1,619 Diversity Is Strength (Herbert L. Tarbous).

CD 7   3,176 Withdraw Troops Now (Thomas D. Abrams); 2,046 Libertarian (Darren Young).

CD 8   1,018 Libertarian (Lou Jasikoff).

CD 9   1,363 The Moderate Choice (Michael Jarvis).

CD 10

CD 11   1,730 Libertarian (Richard S. Roth); 842 Constitution (John Mele).

CD 12

CD 13   1,049 Socialist Workers (Brian Williams); 998 Politicians Are Crooks (Herbert H. Shaw); 586 Pro Life Conservative (Dick Hester); 475 American (Esmat Zaklama).

2006 PRIMARY ELECTIONS

Primary	June 7, 2005 (Governor) June 6, 2006	**Registration** (as of June 6, 2006)		
		Democratic	1,137,312
		Republican	878,906
		Green	735
		Libertarian	519
		Constitution	132
		Reform	106
		Natural Law	50
		Unaffiliated	2,820,183
		TOTAL	4,837,943

Primary Type   Semi-open—Registered Democrats and Republicans could vote only in their party's primary. "Unaffiliated" voters could participate in either party's primary if they were willing to become a member of that party.

NEW JERSEY

GENERAL AND PRIMARY ELECTIONS

Note: An asterisk (*) denotes incumbent.

	REPUBLICAN PRIMARIES			DEMOCRATIC PRIMARIES		
Governor (2005)	Doug Forrester	108,941	36.0%	Jon Corzine	207,670	88.1%
	Bret D. Schundler	94,417	31.2%	James D. Kelly Jr.	19,512	8.3%
	John Murphy	33,800	11.2%	Francis X. Tenaglio	8,596	3.6%
	Steven M. Lonegan	24,433	8.1%			
	Robert Schroeder	16,763	5.5%			
	Paul DiGaetano	16,684	5.5%			
	Todd Caliguire	7,463	2.5%			
	TOTAL	302,501		TOTAL	235,778	
Senator	Thomas H. Kean Jr.	129,794	75.6%	Robert Menendez	159,604	84.0%
	John P. Ginty	41,828	24.4%	James D. Kelly Jr.	30,340	16.0%
	TOTAL	171,622		TOTAL	189,944	
Congressional District 1	No Republican candidate			Robert E. Andrews*	18,418	100.0%
Congressional District 2	Frank A. LoBiondo*	14,440	100.0%	Viola Thomas-Hughes	8,268	82.9%
				Henry David Marcus	1,703	17.1%
				TOTAL	9,971	
Congressional District 3	H. James Saxton*	16,228	100.0%	Rich Sexton	9,960	100.0%
Congressional District 4	Christopher H. Smith*	16,109	100.0%	Carol E. Gay	8,368	100.0%
Congressional District 5	Scott Garrett*	23,760	86.4%	Paul Aronsohn	6,857	66.3%
	Michael J. Cino	3,747	13.6%	Camille M. Abate	3,484	33.7%
	TOTAL	27,507		TOTAL	10,341	
Congressional District 6	Leigh-Ann Bellew	5,309	100.0%	Frank Pallone Jr.*	10,934	100.0%
Congressional District 7	Mike Ferguson*	16,423	100.0%	Linda Stender	8,631	100.0%
Congressional District 8	Jose M. Sandoval	3,982	100.0%	Bill Pascrell Jr.*	11,083	100.0%
Congressional District 9	Vincent Micco	6,169	100.0%	Steven R. Rothman*	18,513	100.0%
Congressional District 10	No Republican candidate			Donald M. Payne*	22,361	100.0%
Congressional District 11	Rodney Frelinghuysen*	26,461	100.0%	Tom Wyka	8,235	100.0%
Congressional District 12	Joseph S. Sinagra	9,383	100.0%	Rush D. Holt*	13,315	100.0%
Congressional District 13	John J. Guarini	2,769	100.0%	Albio Sires	24,661	72.2%
				Joseph Vas	9,486	27.8%
				TOTAL	34,147	

NEW MEXICO

Congressional districts first established for elections held in 2002
3 members

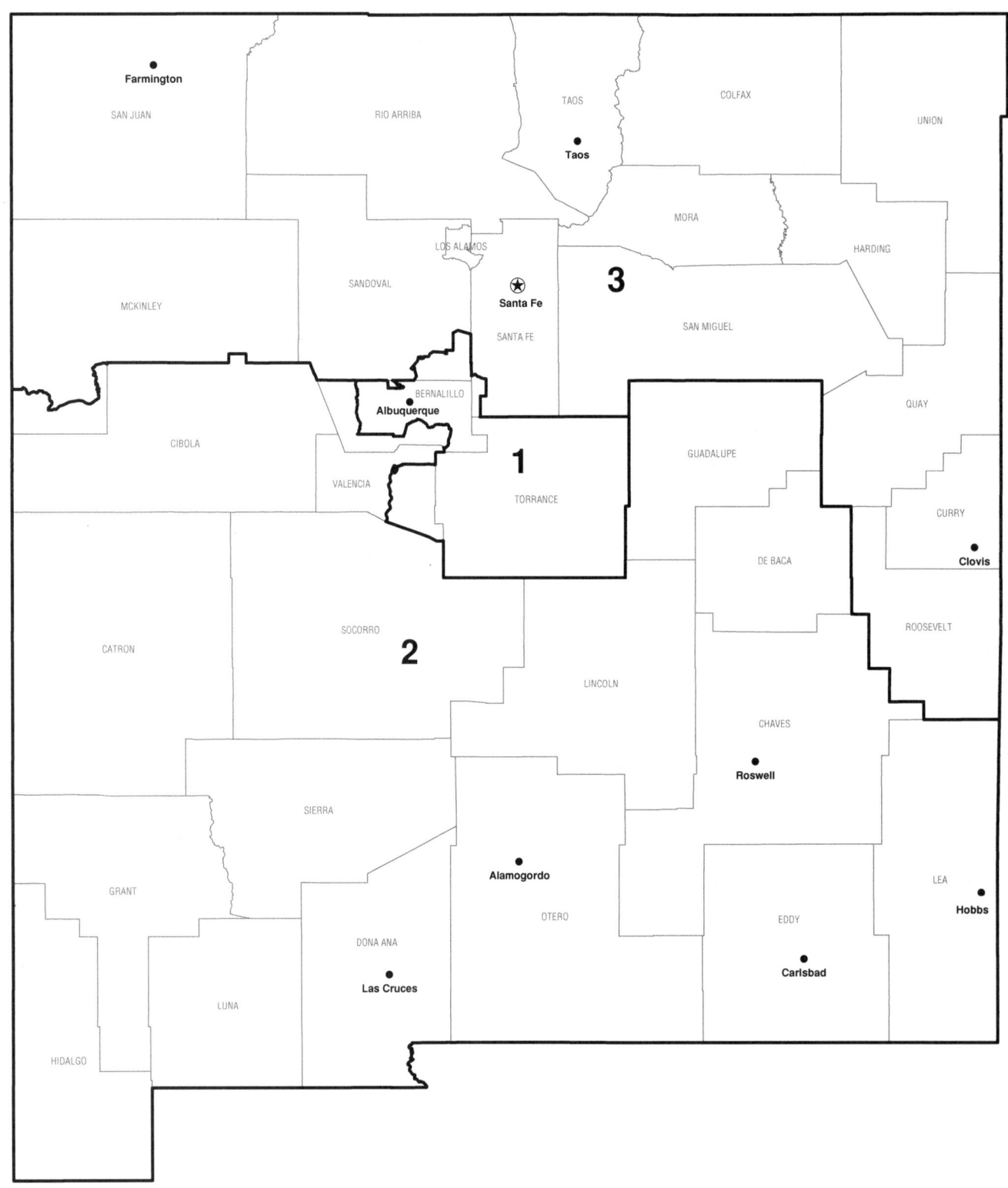

NEW MEXICO

GOVERNOR
Bill Richardson (D). Reelected 2006 to a four-year term. Previously elected 2002.

SENATORS (1 Democrat, 1 Republican)
Jeff Bingaman (D). Reelected 2006 to a six-year term. Previously elected 2000, 1994, 1988, 1982.

Pete V. Domenici (R). Reelected 2002 to a six-year term. Previously elected 1996, 1990, 1984, 1978, 1972.

REPRESENTATIVES (2 Republicans, 1 Democrat)
1. Heather A. Wilson (R) 2. Steve Pearce (R) 3. Tom Udall (D)

POSTWAR VOTE FOR PRESIDENT

Year	Total Vote	Republican Vote	Candidate	Democratic Vote	Candidate	Other Vote	Plurality	Total Vote Rep.	Dem.	Major Vote Rep.	Dem.
2004	756,304	376,930	Bush, George W.	370,942	Kerry, John	8,432	5,988 R	49.8%	49.0%	50.4%	49.6%
2000**	598,605	286,417	Bush, George W.	286,783	Gore, Al	25,405	366 D	47.8%	47.9%	50.0%	50.0%
1996**	556,074	232,751	Dole, Bob	273,495	Clinton, Bill	49,828	40,744 D	41.9%	49.2%	46.0%	54.0%
1992**	569,986	212,824	Bush, George	261,617	Clinton, Bill	95,545	48,793 D	37.3%	45.9%	44.9%	55.1%
1988	521,287	270,341	Bush, George	244,497	Dukakis, Michael S.	6,449	25,844 R	51.9%	46.9%	52.5%	47.5%
1984	514,370	307,101	Reagan, Ronald	201,769	Mondale, Walter F.	5,500	105,332 R	59.7%	39.2%	60.3%	39.7%
1980**	456,971	250,779	Reagan, Ronald	167,826	Carter, Jimmy	38,366	82,953 R	54.9%	36.7%	59.9%	40.1%
1976	418,409	211,419	Ford, Gerald R.	201,148	Carter, Jimmy	5,842	10,271 R	50.5%	48.1%	51.2%	48.8%
1972	386,241	235,606	Nixon, Richard M.	141,084	McGovern, George S.	9,551	94,522 R	61.0%	36.5%	62.5%	37.5%
1968**	327,350	169,692	Nixon, Richard M.	130,081	Humphrey, Hubert H.	27,577	39,611 R	51.8%	39.7%	56.6%	43.4%
1964	328,645	132,838	Goldwater, Barry M.	194,015	Johnson, Lyndon B.	1,792	61,177 D	40.4%	59.0%	40.6%	59.4%
1960	311,107	153,733	Nixon, Richard M.	156,027	Kennedy, John F.	1,347	2,294 D	49.4%	50.2%	49.6%	50.4%
1956	253,926	146,788	Eisenhower, Dwight D.	106,098	Stevenson, Adlai E.	1,040	40,690 R	57.8%	41.8%	58.0%	42.0%
1952	238,608	132,170	Eisenhower, Dwight D.	105,661	Stevenson, Adlai E.	777	26,509 R	55.4%	44.3%	55.6%	44.4%
1948	187,063	80,303	Dewey, Thomas E.	105,464	Truman, Harry S.	1,296	25,161 D	42.9%	56.4%	43.2%	56.8%

**In past elections, the other vote included: 2000 - 21,251 Green (Ralph Nader); 1996 - 32,257 Reform (Ross Perot); 1992 - 91,895 Independent (Ross Perot); 1980 - 29,459 Independent (John Anderson); 1968 - 25,737 American Independent (George Wallace).

NEW MEXICO

POSTWAR VOTE FOR GOVERNOR

Year	Total Vote	Republican Vote	Republican Candidate	Democratic Vote	Democratic Candidate	Other Vote	Rep.-Dem. Plurality	Total Vote Rep.	Total Vote Dem.	Major Vote Rep.	Major Vote Dem.
2006	559,170	174,364	Dendahl, John	384,806	Richardson, Bill		210,442 D	31.2%	68.8%	31.2%	68.8%
2002	484,233	189,074	Sanchez, John A.	268,693	Richardson, Bill	26,466	79,619 D	39.0%	55.5%	41.3%	58.7%
1998	498,703	271,948	Johnson, Gary E.	226,755	Chavez, Martin J.		45,193 R	54.5%	45.5%	54.5%	45.5%
1994**	467,621	232,945	Johnson, Gary E.	186,686	King, Bruce	47,990	46,259 R	49.8%	39.9%	55.5%	44.5%
1990	411,236	185,692	Bond, Frank M.	224,564	King, Bruce	980	38,872 D	45.2%	54.6%	45.3%	54.7%
1986	394,833	209,455	Carruthers, Garrey E.	185,378	Powell, Ray B.		24,077 R	53.0%	47.0%	53.0%	47.0%
1982	407,466	191,626	Irick, John B.	215,840	Anaya, Toney		24,214 D	47.0%	53.0%	47.0%	53.0%
1978	345,577	170,848	Skeen, Joseph R.	174,631	King, Bruce	98	3,783 D	49.4%	50.5%	49.5%	50.5%
1974	328,742	160,430	Skeen, Joseph R.	164,172	Apodaca, Jerry	4,140	3,742 D	48.8%	49.9%	49.4%	50.6%
1970**	290,375	134,640	Domenici, Pete V.	148,835	King, Bruce	6,900	14,195 D	46.4%	51.3%	47.5%	52.5%
1968	318,975	160,140	Cargo, David F.	157,230	Chavez, Fabian	1,605	2,910 R	50.2%	49.3%	50.5%	49.5%
1966	260,232	134,625	Cargo, David F.	125,587	Lusk, Thomas E.	20	9,038 R	51.7%	48.3%	51.7%	48.3%
1964	318,042	126,540	Tucker, Merle H.	191,497	Campbell, Jack M.	5	64,957 D	39.8%	60.2%	39.8%	60.2%
1962	247,135	116,184	Mechem, Edwin L.	130,933	Campbell, Jack M.	18	14,749 D	47.0%	53.0%	47.0%	53.0%
1960	305,542	153,765	Mechem, Edwin L.	151,777	Burroughs, John		1,988 R	50.3%	49.7%	50.3%	49.7%
1958	205,048	101,567	Mechem, Edwin L.	103,481	Burroughs, John		1,914 D	49.5%	50.5%	49.5%	50.5%
1956	251,751	131,488	Mechem, Edwin L.	120,263	Simms, John F.		11,225 R	52.2%	47.8%	52.2%	47.8%
1954	193,956	83,373	Stockton, Alvin	110,583	Simms, John F.		27,210 D	43.0%	57.0%	43.0%	57.0%
1952	240,150	129,116	Mechem, Edwin L.	111,034	Grantham, Everett		18,082 R	53.8%	46.2%	53.8%	46.2%
1950	180,205	96,846	Mechem, Edwin L.	83,359	Miles, John E.		13,487 R	53.7%	46.3%	53.7%	46.3%
1948	189,992	86,023	Lujan, Manuel	103,969	Mabry, Thomas J.		17,946 D	45.3%	54.7%	45.3%	54.7%
1946	132,930	62,875	Safford, Edward L.	70,055	Mabry, Thomas J.		7,180 D	47.3%	52.7%	47.3%	52.7%

**In past elections, the other vote included: 1994 - 47,990 Green (Roberto Mondragon). The term of New Mexico's governor was increased from two to four years effective with the 1970 election.

POSTWAR VOTE FOR SENATOR

Year	Total Vote	Republican Vote	Republican Candidate	Democratic Vote	Democratic Candidate	Other Vote	Rep.-Dem. Plurality	Total Vote Rep.	Total Vote Dem.	Major Vote Rep.	Major Vote Dem.
2006	558,550	163,826	McCulloch, Allen W.	394,365	Bingaman, Jeff	359	230,539 D	29.3%	70.6%	29.3%	70.7%
2002	483,340	314,301	Domenici, Pete V.	169,039	Tristani, Gloria		145,262 R	65.0%	35.0%	65.0%	35.0%
2000	589,526	225,517	Redmond, Bill	363,744	Bingaman, Jeff	265	138,227 D	38.3%	61.7%	38.3%	61.7%
1996	551,821	357,171	Domenici, Pete V.	164,356	Trujillo, Art	30,294	192,815 R	64.7%	29.8%	68.5%	31.5%
1994	463,196	213,025	McMillan, Colin R.	249,989	Bingaman, Jeff	182	36,964 D	46.0%	54.0%	46.0%	54.0%
1990	406,938	296,712	Domenici, Pete V.	110,033	Benavides, Tom R.	193	186,679 R	72.9%	27.0%	72.9%	27.1%
1988	508,598	186,579	Valentine, William	321,983	Bingaman, Jeff	36	135,404 D	36.7%	63.3%	36.7%	63.3%
1984	502,634	361,371	Domenici, Pete V.	141,253	Pratt, Judith A.	10	220,118 R	71.9%	28.1%	71.9%	28.1%
1982	404,810	187,128	Schmitt, Harrison	217,682	Bingaman, Jeff		30,554 D	46.2%	53.8%	46.2%	53.8%
1978	343,554	183,442	Domenici, Pete V.	160,045	Anaya, Toney	67	23,397 R	53.4%	46.6%	53.4%	46.6%
1976	413,141	234,681	Schmitt, Harrison	176,382	Montoya, Joseph M.	2,078	58,299 R	56.8%	42.7%	57.1%	42.9%
1972	378,330	204,253	Domenici, Pete V.	173,815	Daniels, Jack	262	30,438 R	54.0%	45.9%	54.0%	46.0%
1970	289,906	135,004	Carter, Anderson	151,486	Montoya, Joseph M.	3,416	16,482 D	46.6%	52.3%	47.1%	52.9%
1966	258,203	120,988	Carter, Anderson	137,205	Anderson, Clinton P.	10	16,217 D	46.9%	53.1%	46.9%	53.1%
1964	325,774	147,562	Mechem, Edwin L.	178,209	Montoya, Joseph M.	3	30,647 D	45.3%	54.7%	45.3%	54.7%
1960	300,551	109,897	Colwes, William F.	190,654	Anderson, Clinton P.		80,757 D	36.6%	63.4%	36.6%	63.4%
1958	203,323	75,827	Atchley, Forrest S.	127,496	Chavez, Dennis		51,669 D	37.3%	62.7%	37.3%	62.7%
1954	194,422	83,071	Mechem, Edwin L.	111,351	Anderson, Clinton P.		28,280 D	42.7%	57.3%	42.7%	57.3%
1952	239,711	117,168	Hurley, Patrick J.	122,543	Chavez, Dennis		5,375 D	48.9%	51.1%	48.9%	51.1%
1948	188,495	80,226	Hurley, Patrick J.	108,269	Anderson, Clinton P.		28,043 D	42.6%	57.4%	42.6%	57.4%
1946	133,282	64,632	Hurley, Patrick J.	68,650	Chavez, Dennis		4,018 D	48.5%	51.5%	48.5%	51.5%

NEW MEXICO
GOVERNOR 2006

2000 Census Population	County	Total Vote	Republican	Democratic	Other	Rep.-Dem. Plurality	Percentage			
							Total Vote		Major Vote	
							Rep.	Dem.	Rep.	Dem.
556,678	BERNALILLO	195,400	62,205	133,195		70,990 D	31.8%	68.2%	31.8%	68.2%
3,543	CATRON	1,720	863	857		6 R	50.2%	49.8%	50.2%	49.8%
61,382	CHAVES	15,760	6,700	9,060		2,360 D	42.5%	57.5%	42.5%	57.5%
25,595	CIBOLA	6,184	1,486	4,698		3,212 D	24.0%	76.0%	24.0%	76.0%
14,189	COLFAX	4,853	1,728	3,125		1,397 D	35.6%	64.4%	35.6%	64.4%
45,044	CURRY	9,110	3,339	5,771		2,432 D	36.7%	63.3%	36.7%	63.3%
2,240	DE BACA	892	333	559		226 D	37.3%	62.7%	37.3%	62.7%
174,682	DONA ANA	38,845	11,335	27,510		16,175 D	29.2%	70.8%	29.2%	70.8%
51,658	EDDY	14,172	5,633	8,539		2,906 D	39.7%	60.3%	39.7%	60.3%
31,002	GRANT	10,340	2,838	7,502		4,664 D	27.4%	72.6%	27.4%	72.6%
4,680	GUADALUPE	1,834	288	1,546		1,258 D	15.7%	84.3%	15.7%	84.3%
810	HARDING	596	163	433		270 D	27.3%	72.7%	27.3%	72.7%
5,932	HIDALGO	1,458	421	1,037		616 D	28.9%	71.1%	28.9%	71.1%
55,511	LEA	11,741	5,268	6,473		1,205 D	44.9%	55.1%	44.9%	55.1%
19,411	LINCOLN	6,705	2,688	4,017		1,329 D	40.1%	59.9%	40.1%	59.9%
18,343	LOS ALAMOS	8,599	2,929	5,670		2,741 D	34.1%	65.9%	34.1%	65.9%
25,016	LUNA	6,091	1,807	4,284		2,477 D	29.7%	70.3%	29.7%	70.3%
74,798	MCKINLEY	17,400	2,427	14,973		12,546 D	13.9%	86.1%	13.9%	86.1%
5,180	MORA	2,355	617	1,738		1,121 D	26.2%	73.8%	26.2%	73.8%
62,298	OTERO	14,310	6,039	8,271		2,232 D	42.2%	57.8%	42.2%	57.8%
10,155	QUAY	3,240	1,106	2,134		1,028 D	34.1%	65.9%	34.1%	65.9%
41,190	RIO ARRIBA	10,583	1,962	8,621		6,659 D	18.5%	81.5%	18.5%	81.5%
18,018	ROOSEVELT	4,100	1,750	2,350		600 D	42.7%	57.3%	42.7%	57.3%
89,908	SANDOVAL	36,525	11,803	24,722		12,919 D	32.3%	67.7%	32.3%	67.7%
113,801	SAN JUAN	31,367	12,521	18,846		6,325 D	39.9%	60.1%	39.9%	60.1%
30,126	SAN MIGUEL	8,731	1,847	6,884		5,037 D	21.2%	78.8%	21.2%	78.8%
129,292	SANTA FE	47,614	9,965	37,649		27,684 D	20.9%	79.1%	20.9%	79.1%
13,270	SIERRA	4,253	1,808	2,445		637 D	42.5%	57.5%	42.5%	57.5%
18,078	SOCORRO	6,253	1,702	4,551		2,849 D	27.2%	72.8%	27.2%	72.8%
29,979	TAOS	11,461	1,524	9,937		8,413 D	13.3%	86.7%	13.3%	86.7%
16,911	TORRANCE	5,406	2,126	3,280		1,154 D	39.3%	60.7%	39.3%	60.7%
4,174	UNION	1,453	546	907		361 D	37.6%	62.4%	37.6%	62.4%
66,152	VALENCIA	19,819	6,597	13,222		6,625 D	33.3%	66.7%	33.3%	66.7%
1,819,046	TOTAL	559,170	174,364	384,806		210,442 D	31.2%	68.8%	31.2%	68.8%

NEW MEXICO
SENATOR 2006

2000 Census Population	County	Total Vote	Republican	Democratic	Other	Rep.-Dem. Plurality	Percentage			
							Total Vote		Major Vote	
							Rep.	Dem.	Rep.	Dem.
556,678	BERNALILLO	193,989	57,046	136,747	196	79,701 D	29.4%	70.5%	29.4%	70.6%
3,543	CATRON	1,707	786	919	2	133 D	46.0%	53.8%	46.1%	53.9%
61,382	CHAVES	15,787	6,209	9,562	16	3,353 D	39.3%	60.6%	39.4%	60.6%
25,595	CIBOLA	6,175	1,276	4,888	11	3,612 D	20.7%	79.2%	20.7%	79.3%
14,189	COLFAX	4,889	1,222	3,667		2,445 D	25.0%	75.0%	25.0%	75.0%
45,044	CURRY	9,099	3,891	5,203	5	1,312 D	42.8%	57.2%	42.8%	57.2%
2,240	DE BACA	882	271	611		340 D	30.7%	69.3%	30.7%	69.3%
174,682	DONA ANA	38,655	12,188	26,434	33	14,246 D	31.5%	68.4%	31.6%	68.4%
51,658	EDDY	14,167	4,670	9,497		4,827 D	33.0%	67.0%	33.0%	67.0%
31,002	GRANT	10,366	2,537	7,823	6	5,286 D	24.5%	75.5%	24.5%	75.5%
4,680	GUADALUPE	1,822	228	1,594		1,366 D	12.5%	87.5%	12.5%	87.5%
810	HARDING	587	160	427		267 D	27.3%	72.7%	27.3%	72.7%
5,932	HIDALGO	1,449	394	1,055		661 D	27.2%	72.8%	27.2%	72.8%
55,511	LEA	11,740	5,173	6,567		1,394 D	44.1%	55.9%	44.1%	55.9%
19,411	LINCOLN	6,669	2,841	3,826	2	985 D	42.6%	57.4%	42.6%	57.4%
18,343	LOS ALAMOS	8,571	2,548	6,022	1	3,474 D	29.7%	70.3%	29.7%	70.3%
25,016	LUNA	6,020	1,843	4,175	2	2,332 D	30.6%	69.4%	30.6%	69.4%
74,798	MCKINLEY	17,350	2,376	14,962	12	12,586 D	13.7%	86.2%	13.7%	86.3%
5,180	MORA	2,376	349	2,026	1	1,677 D	14.7%	85.3%	14.7%	85.3%
62,298	OTERO	14,274	5,865	8,409		2,544 D	41.1%	58.9%	41.1%	58.9%
10,155	QUAY	3,220	984	2,236		1,252 D	30.6%	69.4%	30.6%	69.4%
41,190	RIO ARRIBA	10,640	1,341	9,298	1	7,957 D	12.6%	87.4%	12.6%	87.4%
18,018	ROOSEVELT	4,109	1,527	2,578	4	1,051 D	37.2%	62.7%	37.2%	62.8%
89,908	SANDOVAL	36,553	11,511	25,008	34	13,497 D	31.5%	68.4%	31.5%	68.5%
113,801	SAN JUAN	31,542	15,351	16,189	2	838 D	48.7%	51.3%	48.7%	51.3%
30,126	SAN MIGUEL	8,887	1,069	7,816	2	6,747 D	12.0%	87.9%	12.0%	88.0%
129,292	SANTA FE	48,401	7,503	40,885	13	33,382 D	15.5%	84.5%	15.5%	84.5%
13,270	SIERRA	4,236	1,507	2,729		1,222 D	35.6%	64.4%	35.6%	64.4%
18,078	SOCORRO	6,233	1,557	4,676		3,119 D	25.0%	75.0%	25.0%	75.0%
29,979	TAOS	11,453	1,246	10,207		8,961 D	10.9%	89.1%	10.9%	89.1%
16,911	TORRANCE	5,392	1,861	3,529	2	1,668 D	34.5%	65.4%	34.5%	65.5%
4,174	UNION	1,420	572	848		276 D	40.3%	59.7%	40.3%	59.7%
66,152	VALENCIA	19,890	5,924	13,952	14	8,028 D	29.8%	70.1%	29.8%	70.2%
1,819,046	TOTAL	558,550	163,826	394,365	359	230,539 D	29.3%	70.6%	29.3%	70.7%

NEW MEXICO

HOUSE OF REPRESENTATIVES

CD	Year	Total Vote	Republican		Democratic		Other Vote	Rep.-Dem. Plurality	Percentage			
									Total Vote		Major Vote	
			Vote	Candidate	Vote	Candidate			Rep.	Dem.	Rep.	Dem.
1	2006	211,111	105,986	WILSON, HEATHER A.*	105,125	MADRID, PATRICIA A.		861 R	50.2%	49.8%	50.2%	49.8%
1	2004	270,905	147,372	WILSON, HEATHER A.*	123,339	ROMERO, RICHARD M.	194	24,033 R	54.4%	45.5%	54.4%	45.6%
1	2002	172,945	95,711	WILSON, HEATHER A.*	77,234	ROMERO, RICHARD M.		18,477 R	55.3%	44.7%	55.3%	44.7%
2	2006	155,874	92,620	PEARCE, STEVE*	63,119	KISSLING, ALBERT D.	135	29,501 R	59.4%	40.5%	59.5%	40.5%
2	2004	216,790	130,498	PEARCE, STEVE*	86,292	KING, GARY K.		44,206 R	60.2%	39.8%	60.2%	39.8%
2	2002	141,629	79,631	PEARCE, STEVE	61,916	SMITH, JOHN ARTHUR	82	17,715 R	56.2%	43.7%	56.3%	43.7%
3	2006	194,099	49,219	DOLIN, RONALD M.	144,880	UDALL, TOM*		95,661 D	25.4%	74.6%	25.4%	74.6%
3	2004	255,204	79,935	TUCKER, GREGORY M.	175,269	UDALL, TOM*		95,334 D	31.3%	68.7%	31.3%	68.7%
3	2002	122,950		—	122,950	UDALL, TOM*		122,950 D		100.0%		100.0%
TOTAL	2006	561,084	247,825		313,124		135	65,299 D	44.2%	55.8%	44.2%	55.8%
TOTAL	2004	742,899	357,805		384,900		194	27,095 D	48.2%	51.8%	48.2%	51.8%
TOTAL	2002	437,524	175,342		262,100		82	86,758 D	40.1%	59.9%	40.1%	59.9%

An asterisk (*) denotes incumbent.

NEW MEXICO

GENERAL AND PRIMARY ELECTIONS

2006 GENERAL ELECTIONS

Governor

Senator Other vote was 359 write-in (Orlin G. Cole).

House Other vote was:

 CD 1
 CD 2 135 write-in (C. Dean Burk).
 CD 3

2006 PRIMARY ELECTIONS

Primary	June 6, 2006	**Registration** (as of June 1, 2006)	Democratic	532,578
			Republican	353,462
			Other Parties	26,380
			Declined to State	161,787
			TOTAL	1,074,207

Primary Type Closed—Only registered Democrats and Republicans could vote in their party's primary.

NEW MEXICO

GENERAL AND PRIMARY ELECTIONS

Note: An asterisk (*) denotes incumbent.

	REPUBLICAN PRIMARIES			DEMOCRATIC PRIMARIES		
Governor	J. R. Damron	52,888	99.6%	Bill Richardson*	107,720	99.6%
	George Brent Bailey Jr. (write-in)	225	0.4%	Anselmo A. Chavez (write-in)	388	0.4%
	TOTAL	53,113		TOTAL	108,108	
	J. R. Damron withdrew from the race after the primary and was replaced on the general election ballot by John Dendahl.					
Senator	Allen W. McCulloch	29,592	51.0%	Jeff Bingaman*	115,198	100.0%
	Joseph J. Carraro	18,312	31.6%			
	David Pfeffer	10,070	17.4%			
	TOTAL	57,974				
Congressional District 1	Heather A. Wilson*	17,035	100.0%	Patricia A. Madrid	30,732	100.0%
Congressional District 2	Steve Pearce*	22,086	100.0%	Albert D. Kissling	23,655	100.0%
Congressional District 3	Ronald M. Dolin	15,654	100.0%	Tom Udall*	50,472	100.0%

NEW YORK

Congressional districts first established for elections held in 2002
29 members

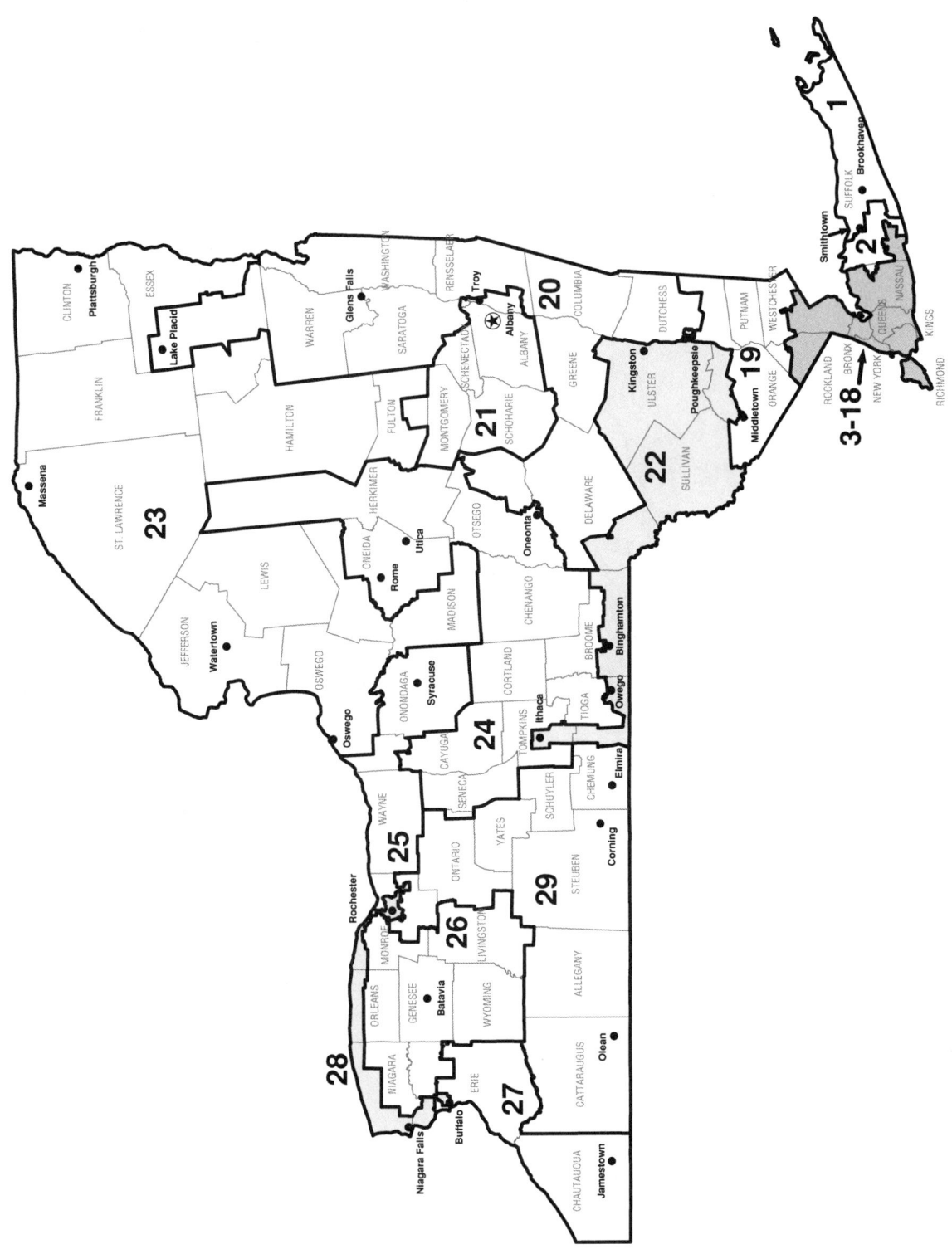

NEW YORK

New York City Area

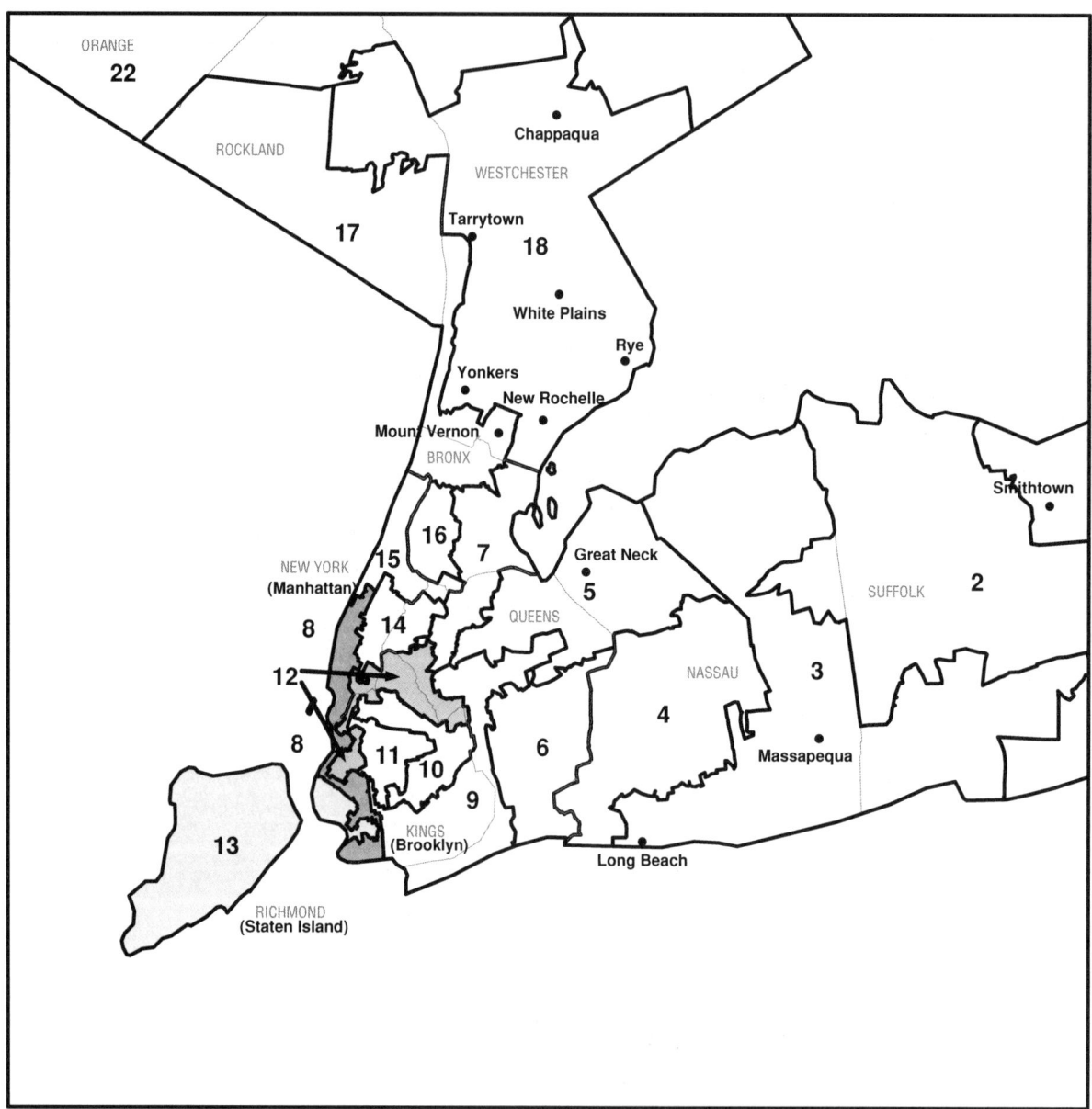

NEW YORK

GOVERNOR
Eliot Spitzer (D). Elected 2006 to a four-year term.

SENATORS (2 Democrats)
Hillary Rodham Clinton (D). Reelected 2006 to a six-year term. Previously elected 2000.

Charles E. Schumer (D). Reelected 2004 to a six-year term. Previously elected 1998.

REPRESENTATIVES (23 Democrats, 6 Republicans)
1. Timothy H. Bishop (D)
2. Steve Israel (D)
3. Peter T. King (R)
4. Carolyn McCarthy (D)
5. Gary L. Ackerman (D)
6. Gregory W. Meeks (D)
7. Joseph Crowley (D)
8. Jerrold Nadler (D)
9. Anthony Weiner (D)
10. Edolphus Towns (D)
11. Yvette D. Clarke (D)
12. Nydia M. Velázquez (D)
13. Vito J. Fossella (R)
14. Carolyn B. Maloney (D)
15. Charles B. Rangel (D)
16. Jose E. Serrano (D)
17. Eliot L. Engel (D)
18. Nita M. Lowey (D)
19. John Hall (D)
20. Kirsten E. Gillibrand (D)
21. Michael R. McNulty (D)
22. Maurice D. Hinchey (D)
23. John M. McHugh (R)
24. Michael A. Arcuri (D)
25. James T. Walsh (R)
26. Thomas M. Reynolds (R)
27. Brian Higgins (D)
28. Louise M. Slaughter (D)
29. John R. "Randy" Kuhl Jr. (R)

POSTWAR VOTE FOR PRESIDENT

Year	Total Vote	Republican Vote	Republican Candidate	Democratic Vote	Democratic Candidate	Other Vote	Plurality	Total Vote Rep.	Total Vote Dem.	Major Vote Rep.	Major Vote Dem.
2004	7,391,036	2,962,567	Bush, George W.	4,314,280	Kerry, John	114,189	1,351,713 D	40.1%	58.4%	40.7%	59.3%
2000**	6,821,999	2,403,374	Bush, George W.	4,107,697	Gore, Al	310,928	1,704,323 D	35.2%	60.2%	36.9%	63.1%
1996**	6,316,129	1,933,492	Dole, Bob	3,756,177	Clinton, Bill	626,460	1,822,685 D	30.6%	59.5%	34.0%	66.0%
1992**	6,926,925	2,346,649	Bush, George	3,444,450	Clinton, Bill	1,135,826	1,097,801 D	33.9%	49.7%	40.5%	59.5%
1988	6,485,683	3,081,871	Bush, George	3,347,882	Dukakis, Michael S.	55,930	266,011 D	47.5%	51.6%	47.9%	52.1%
1984	6,806,810	3,664,763	Reagan, Ronald	3,119,609	Mondale, Walter F.	22,438	545,154 R	53.8%	45.8%	54.0%	46.0%
1980**	6,201,959	2,893,831	Reagan, Ronald	2,728,372	Carter, Jimmy	579,756	165,459 R	46.7%	44.0%	51.5%	48.5%
1976	6,534,170	3,100,791	Ford, Gerald R.	3,389,558	Carter, Jimmy	43,821	288,767 D	47.5%	51.9%	47.8%	52.2%
1972	7,165,919	4,192,778	Nixon, Richard M.	2,951,084	McGovern, George S.	22,057	1,241,694 R	58.5%	41.2%	58.7%	41.3%
1968**	6,791,688	3,007,932	Nixon, Richard M.	3,378,470	Humphrey, Hubert H.	405,286	370,538 D	44.3%	49.7%	47.1%	52.9%
1964	7,166,275	2,243,559	Goldwater, Barry M.	4,913,102	Johnson, Lyndon B.	9,614	2,669,543 D	31.3%	68.6%	31.3%	68.7%
1960	7,291,079	3,446,419	Nixon, Richard M.	3,830,085	Kennedy, John F.	14,575	383,666 D	47.3%	52.5%	47.4%	52.6%
1956	7,095,971	4,345,506	Eisenhower, Dwight D.	2,747,944	Stevenson, Adlai E.	2,521	1,597,562 R	61.2%	38.7%	61.3%	38.7%
1952	7,128,239	3,952,813	Eisenhower, Dwight D.	3,104,601	Stevenson, Adlai E.	70,825	848,212 R	55.5%	43.6%	56.0%	44.0%
1948**	6,177,337	2,841,163	Dewey, Thomas E.	2,780,204	Truman, Harry S.	555,970	60,959 R	46.0%	45.0%	50.5%	49.5%

**In past elections, the other vote included: 2000 - 244,030 Green (Ralph Nader); 1996 - 503,458 Reform (Ross Perot); 1992 - 1,090,721 Independent (Ross Perot); 1980 - 467,801 Independent (John Anderson); 1968 - 358,864 American Independent (George Wallace); 1948 - 509,559 Progressive (Henry Wallace).

NEW YORK

POSTWAR VOTE FOR GOVERNOR

Year	Total Vote	Republican Vote	Candidate	Democratic Vote	Candidate	Other Vote	Rep.-Dem. Plurality	Percentage Total Vote Rep.	Dem.	Major Vote Rep.	Dem.
2006	4,437,220	1,274,335	Faso, John J.	3,086,709	Spitzer, Eliot	76,176	1,812,374 D	28.7%	69.6%	29.2%	70.8%
2002**	4,579,078	2,262,255	Pataki, George E.	1,534,064	McCall, H. Carl	782,759	728,191 R	49.4%	33.5%	59.6%	40.4%
1998	4,735,236	2,571,991	Pataki, George E.	1,570,317	Vallone, Peter F.	592,928	1,001,674 R	54.3%	33.2%	62.1%	37.9%
1994	5,208,762	2,538,702	Pataki, George E.	2,364,904	Cuomo, Mario M.	305,156	173,798 R	48.7%	45.4%	51.8%	48.2%
1990**	4,056,896	865,948	Rinfret, Pierre A.	2,157,087	Cuomo, Mario M.	1,033,861	1,291,139 D	21.3%	53.2%	28.6%	71.4%
1986	4,294,124	1,363,810	O'Rourke, Andrew P.	2,775,229	Cuomo, Mario M.	155,085	1,411,419 D	31.8%	64.6%	32.9%	67.1%
1982	5,254,891	2,494,827	Lehrman, Lew	2,675,213	Cuomo, Mario M.	84,851	180,386 D	47.5%	50.9%	48.3%	51.7%
1978	4,768,820	2,156,404	Duryea, Perry B.	2,429,272	Carey, Hugh L.	183,144	272,868 D	45.2%	50.9%	47.0%	53.0%
1974	5,293,176	2,219,667	Wilson, Malcolm	3,028,503	Carey, Hugh L.	45,006	808,836 D	41.9%	57.2%	42.3%	57.7%
1970	6,013,064	3,151,432	Rockefeller, Nelson A.	2,421,426	Goldberg, Arthur	440,206	730,006 R	52.4%	40.3%	56.5%	43.5%
1966**	6,031,585	2,690,626	Rockefeller, Nelson A.	2,298,363	O'Connor, Frank D.	1,042,596	392,263 R	44.6%	38.1%	53.9%	46.1%
1962	5,805,631	3,081,587	Rockefeller, Nelson A.	2,552,418	Morgenthau, Robert M.	171,626	529,169 R	53.1%	44.0%	54.7%	45.3%
1958	5,712,665	3,126,929	Rockefeller, Nelson A.	2,553,895	Harriman, Averell	31,841	573,034 R	54.7%	44.7%	55.0%	45.0%
1954	5,161,942	2,549,613	Ives, Irving M.	2,560,738	Harriman, Averell	51,591	11,125 D	49.4%	49.6%	49.9%	50.1%
1950	5,308,889	2,819,523	Dewey, Thomas E.	2,246,855	Lynch, Walter A.	242,511	572,668 R	53.1%	42.3%	55.7%	44.3%
1946	4,964,552	2,825,633	Dewey, Thomas E.	2,138,482	Mead, James M.	437	687,151 R	56.9%	43.1%	56.9%	43.1%

**In past elections, the other vote included: 2002 - 654,016 Independence (B. Thomas Golisano); 1990 - 827,614 Conservative (Herbert I. London); 1966 - 510,023 Conservative (Paul L. Adams); 507,234 Liberal (Franklin Roosevelt Jr.).

POSTWAR VOTE FOR SENATOR

Year	Total Vote	Republican Vote	Candidate	Democratic Vote	Candidate	Other Vote	Rep.-Dem. Plurality	Percentage Total Vote Rep.	Dem.	Major Vote Rep.	Dem.
2006	4,490,053	1,392,189	Spencer, John	3,008,428	Clinton, Hillary Rodham	89,436	1,616,239 D	31.0%	67.0%	31.6%	68.4%
2004	6,702,875	1,625,069	Mills, Howard	4,769,824	Schumer, Charles E.	307,982	3,144,755 D	24.2%	71.2%	25.4%	74.6%
2000	6,779,839	2,915,730	Lazio, Rick A.	3,747,310	Clinton, Hillary Rodham	116,799	831,580 D	43.0%	55.3%	43.8%	56.2%
1998	4,670,805	2,058,988	D'Amato, Alfonse M.	2,551,065	Schumer, Charles E.	60,752	492,077 D	44.1%	54.6%	44.7%	55.3%
1994	4,794,601	1,988,308	Castro, Bernadette	2,646,541	Moynihan, Daniel P.	159,752	658,233 D	41.5%	55.2%	42.9%	57.1%
1992	6,458,826	3,166,994	D'Amato, Alfonse M.	3,086,200	Abrams, Robert	205,632	80,794 R	49.0%	47.8%	50.6%	49.4%
1988	6,040,980	1,875,784	McMillan, Robert	4,048,649	Moynihan, Daniel P.	116,547	2,172,865 D	31.1%	67.0%	31.7%	68.3%
1986	4,179,447	2,378,197	D'Amato, Alfonse M.	1,723,216	Green, Mark	78,034	654,981 R	56.9%	41.2%	58.0%	42.0%
1982	4,967,729	1,696,766	Sullivan, Florence M.	3,232,146	Moynihan, Daniel P.	38,817	1,535,380 D	34.2%	65.1%	34.4%	65.6%
1980**	6,014,914	2,699,652	D'Amato, Alfonse M.	2,618,661	Holtzman, Elizabeth	696,601	80,991 R	44.9%	43.5%	50.8%	49.2%
1976	6,319,755	2,836,633	Buckley, James L.	3,422,594	Moynihan, Daniel P.	60,528	585,961 D	44.9%	54.2%	45.3%	54.7%
1974	5,163,600	2,340,188	Javits, Jacob K.	1,973,781	Clark, Ramsey	849,631	366,407 R	45.3%	38.2%	54.2%	45.8%
1970**	5,904,782	1,434,472	Goodell, Charles	2,171,232	Ottinger, Richard L.	2,299,078	116,958 C	24.3%	36.8%	39.8%	60.2%
1968**	6,581,587	3,269,772	Javits, Jacob K.	2,150,695	O'Dwyer, Paul	1,161,120	1,119,077 R	49.7%	32.7%	60.3%	39.7%
1964	7,151,686	3,104,056	Keating, Kenneth B.	3,823,749	Kennedy, Robert F.	223,881	719,693 D	43.4%	53.5%	44.8%	55.2%
1962	5,700,186	3,269,417	Javits, Jacob K.	2,289,341	Donovan, James B.	141,428	980,076 R	57.4%	40.2%	58.8%	41.2%
1958	5,602,088	2,842,942	Keating, Kenneth B.	2,709,950	Hogan, Frank S.	49,196	132,992 R	50.7%	48.4%	51.2%	48.8%
1956	6,991,136	3,723,933	Javits, Jacob K.	3,265,159	Wagner, Robert F.	2,044	458,774 R	53.3%	46.7%	53.3%	46.7%
1952	6,980,259	3,853,934	Ives, Irving M.	2,521,736	Cashmore, John	604,589	1,332,198 R	55.2%	36.1%	60.4%	39.6%
1950	5,228,403	2,367,353	Hanley, Joe R.	2,632,313	Lehman, Herbert H.	228,737	264,960 D	45.3%	50.3%	47.4%	52.6%
1949S	4,966,878	2,384,381	Dulles, John Foster	2,582,438	Lehman, Herbert H.	59	198,057 D	48.0%	52.0%	48.0%	52.0%
1946	4,867,564	2,559,365	Ives, Irving M.	2,308,112	Lehman, Herbert H.	87	251,253 R	52.6%	47.4%	52.6%	47.4%

**In past elections, the other vote included: 1980 - 664,544 Liberal (Jacob K. Javits); 1974 - 822,584 Conservative (Barbara A. Keating); 1970 - 2,288,190 Conservative (James L. Buckley), who won the election with 38.8 percent of the total vote; 1968 - 1,139,402 Conservative (Buckley). The 1949 election was for a short term to fill a vacancy.

NEW YORK

GOVERNOR 2006

2000 Census Population	County	Total Vote	Republican	Democratic	Other	Plurality	Percentage Total Vote Rep.	Dem.	Major Vote Rep.	Dem.
294,565	ALBANY	108,912	26,848	80,210	1,854	53,362 D	24.7%	73.6%	25.1%	74.9%
49,927	ALLEGANY	13,409	6,575	6,568	266	7 R	49.0%	49.0%	50.0%	50.0%
1,332,650	BRONX	165,518	16,118	146,941	2,459	130,823 D	9.7%	88.8%	9.9%	90.1%
200,536	BROOME	62,686	20,944	40,683	1,059	19,739 D	33.4%	64.9%	34.0%	66.0%
83,955	CATTARAUGUS	22,202	10,803	10,981	418	178 D	48.7%	49.5%	49.6%	50.4%
81,963	CAYUGA	26,778	8,900	17,449	429	8,549 D	33.2%	65.2%	33.8%	66.2%
139,750	CHAUTAUQUA	36,878	16,610	19,690	578	3,080 D	45.0%	53.4%	45.8%	54.2%
91,070	CHEMUNG	26,212	9,501	16,341	370	6,840 D	36.2%	62.3%	36.8%	63.2%
51,401	CHENANGO	14,914	6,028	8,521	365	2,493 D	40.4%	57.1%	41.4%	58.6%
79,894	CLINTON	22,969	7,659	14,922	388	7,263 D	33.3%	65.0%	33.9%	66.1%
63,094	COLUMBIA	24,211	9,647	14,182	382	4,535 D	39.8%	58.6%	40.5%	59.5%
48,599	CORTLAND	14,750	5,287	9,180	283	3,893 D	35.8%	62.2%	36.5%	63.5%
48,055	DELAWARE	14,521	6,173	8,041	307	1,868 D	42.5%	55.4%	43.4%	56.6%
280,150	DUTCHESS	81,447	29,095	50,682	1,670	21,587 D	35.7%	62.2%	36.5%	63.5%
950,265	ERIE	278,557	95,819	177,926	4,812	82,107 D	34.4%	63.9%	35.0%	65.0%
38,851	ESSEX	12,737	5,161	7,366	210	2,205 D	40.5%	57.8%	41.2%	58.8%
51,134	FRANKLIN	12,002	4,188	7,635	179	3,447 D	34.9%	63.6%	35.4%	64.6%
55,073	FULTON	14,796	5,840	8,753	203	2,913 D	39.5%	59.2%	40.0%	60.0%
60,370	GENESEE	18,303	8,979	9,038	286	59 D	49.1%	49.4%	49.8%	50.2%
48,195	GREENE	16,967	8,206	8,458	303	252 D	48.4%	49.8%	49.2%	50.8%
5,379	HAMILTON	2,671	1,403	1,217	51	186 R	52.5%	45.6%	53.5%	46.5%
64,427	HERKIMER	19,328	7,611	11,410	307	3,799 D	39.4%	59.0%	40.0%	60.0%
111,738	JEFFERSON	24,724	8,721	15,648	355	6,927 D	35.3%	63.3%	35.8%	64.2%
2,465,326	KINGS	334,618	40,199	287,262	7,157	247,063 D	12.0%	85.8%	12.3%	87.7%
26,944	LEWIS	7,298	3,139	4,059	100	920 D	43.0%	55.6%	43.6%	56.4%
64,328	LIVINGSTON	19,904	8,448	11,068	388	2,620 D	42.4%	55.6%	43.3%	56.7%
69,441	MADISON	21,525	7,696	13,470	359	5,774 D	35.8%	62.6%	36.4%	63.6%
735,343	MONROE	228,088	75,014	149,683	3,391	74,669 D	32.9%	65.6%	33.4%	66.6%
49,708	MONTGOMERY	13,912	4,995	8,699	218	3,704 D	35.9%	62.5%	36.5%	63.5%
1,334,544	NASSAU	361,368	122,567	234,452	4,349	111,885 D	33.9%	64.9%	34.3%	65.7%
1,537,195	NEW YORK	356,982	34,438	313,396	9,148	278,958 D	9.6%	87.8%	9.9%	90.1%
219,846	NIAGARA	63,354	25,060	37,477	817	12,417 D	39.6%	59.2%	40.1%	59.9%
235,469	ONEIDA	71,037	25,332	44,743	962	19,411 D	35.7%	63.0%	36.1%	63.9%
458,336	ONONDAGA	152,594	45,280	104,649	2,665	59,369 D	29.7%	68.6%	30.2%	69.8%
100,224	ONTARIO	33,883	13,207	20,199	477	6,992 D	39.0%	59.6%	39.5%	60.5%
341,367	ORANGE	88,151	29,994	56,770	1,387	26,776 D	34.0%	64.4%	34.6%	65.4%
44,171	ORLEANS	10,774	5,331	5,241	202	90 R	49.5%	48.6%	50.4%	49.6%
122,377	OSWEGO	31,957	11,342	19,975	640	8,633 D	35.5%	62.5%	36.2%	63.8%
61,676	OTSEGO	18,573	6,681	11,467	425	4,786 D	36.0%	61.7%	36.8%	63.2%
95,745	PUTNAM	30,007	11,871	17,542	594	5,671 D	39.6%	58.5%	40.4%	59.6%
2,229,379	QUEENS	305,814	50,284	251,070	4,460	200,786 D	16.4%	82.1%	16.7%	83.3%
152,538	RENSSELAER	54,058	17,207	35,970	881	18,763 D	31.8%	66.5%	32.4%	67.6%
443,728	RICHMOND	81,712	29,348	51,257	1,107	21,909 D	35.9%	62.7%	36.4%	63.6%
286,753	ROCKLAND	79,540	28,857	49,524	1,159	20,667 D	36.3%	62.3%	36.8%	63.2%
111,931	ST. LAWRENCE	28,084	8,744	18,887	453	10,143 D	31.1%	67.3%	31.6%	68.4%
200,635	SARATOGA	80,657	29,266	50,236	1,155	20,970 D	36.3%	62.3%	36.8%	63.2%
146,555	SCHENECTADY	50,579	15,839	33,949	791	18,110 D	31.3%	67.1%	31.8%	68.2%
31,582	SCHOHARIE	10,897	5,181	5,529	187	348 D	47.5%	50.7%	48.4%	51.6%
19,224	SCHUYLER	5,946	2,514	3,317	115	803 D	42.3%	55.8%	43.1%	56.9%
33,342	SENECA	10,312	3,623	6,511	178	2,888 D	35.1%	63.1%	35.8%	64.2%
98,726	STEUBEN	28,079	12,858	14,794	427	1,936 D	45.8%	52.7%	46.5%	53.5%
1,419,369	SUFFOLK	353,271	124,571	223,453	5,247	98,882 D	35.3%	63.3%	35.8%	64.2%
73,966	SULLIVAN	19,675	6,060	13,205	410	7,145 D	30.8%	67.1%	31.5%	68.5%
51,784	TIOGA	15,826	6,841	8,743	242	1,902 D	43.2%	55.2%	43.9%	56.1%
96,501	TOMPKINS	29,124	7,117	21,213	794	14,096 D	24.4%	72.8%	25.1%	74.9%
177,749	ULSTER	60,023	17,315	40,841	1,867	23,526 D	28.8%	68.0%	29.8%	70.2%
63,303	WARREN	22,806	8,457	13,923	426	5,466 D	37.1%	61.0%	37.8%	62.2%
61,042	WASHINGTON	18,186	7,024	10,822	340	3,798 D	38.6%	59.5%	39.4%	60.6%
93,765	WAYNE	26,031	11,651	13,992	388	2,341 D	44.8%	53.8%	45.4%	54.6%
923,459	WESTCHESTER	256,763	75,083	177,246	4,434	102,163 D	29.2%	69.0%	29.8%	70.2%
43,424	WYOMING	12,798	6,659	5,950	189	709 R	52.0%	46.5%	52.8%	47.2%
24,621	YATES	7,522	3,126	4,283	113	1,157 D	41.6%	56.9%	42.2%	57.8%
18,976,457	TOTAL	4,437,220	1,274,335	3,086,709	76,176	1,812,374 D	28.7%	69.6%	29.2%	70.8%

NEW YORK CITY

GOVERNOR 2006

2000 Census Population	County	Total Vote	Republican	Democratic	Other	Plurality	Percentage			
							Total Vote		Major Vote	
							Rep.	Dem.	Rep.	Dem.
1,332,650	BRONX	165,518	16,118	146,941	2,459	130,823 D	9.7%	88.8%	9.9%	90.1%
2,465,326	KINGS	334,618	40,199	287,262	7,157	247,063 D	12.0%	85.8%	12.3%	87.7%
1,537,195	NEW YORK	356,982	34,438	313,396	9,148	278,958 D	9.6%	87.8%	9.9%	90.1%
2,229,379	QUEENS	305,814	50,284	251,070	4,460	200,786 D	16.4%	82.1%	16.7%	83.3%
443,728	RICHMOND	81,712	29,348	51,257	1,107	21,909 D	35.9%	62.7%	36.4%	63.6%
8,008,278	TOTAL	1,244,644	170,387	1,049,926	24,331	879,539 D	13.7%	84.4%	14.0%	86.0%

NEW YORK

SENATOR 2006

2000 Census Population	County	Total Vote	Republican	Democratic	Other	Rep.-Dem. Plurality	Percentage			
							Total Vote		Major Vote	
							Rep.	Dem.	Rep.	Dem.
294,565	ALBANY	108,071	28,709	76,494	2,868	47,785 D	26.6%	70.8%	27.3%	72.7%
49,927	ALLEGANY	13,310	6,739	6,334	237	405 R	50.6%	47.6%	51.5%	48.5%
1,332,650	BRONX	178,572	17,086	159,792	1,694	142,706 D	9.6%	89.5%	9.7%	90.3%
200,536	BROOME	62,588	24,291	36,848	1,449	12,557 D	38.8%	58.9%	39.7%	60.3%
83,955	CATTARAUGUS	22,125	10,031	11,742	352	1,711 D	45.3%	53.1%	46.1%	53.9%
81,963	CAYUGA	27,063	9,348	17,207	508	7,859 D	34.5%	63.6%	35.2%	64.8%
139,750	CHAUTAUQUA	36,886	16,171	20,126	589	3,955 D	43.8%	54.6%	44.6%	55.4%
91,070	CHEMUNG	26,182	10,669	15,179	334	4,510 D	40.7%	58.0%	41.3%	58.7%
51,401	CHENANGO	14,922	6,422	8,071	429	1,649 D	43.0%	54.1%	44.3%	55.7%
79,894	CLINTON	23,163	7,902	14,788	473	6,886 D	34.1%	63.8%	34.8%	65.2%
63,094	COLUMBIA	23,583	8,577	14,353	653	5,776 D	36.4%	60.9%	37.4%	62.6%
48,599	CORTLAND	14,722	5,727	8,622	373	2,895 D	38.9%	58.6%	39.9%	60.1%
48,055	DELAWARE	14,436	6,701	7,376	359	675 D	46.4%	51.1%	47.6%	52.4%
280,150	DUTCHESS	81,269	33,790	45,536	1,943	11,746 D	41.6%	56.0%	42.6%	57.4%
950,265	ERIE	278,404	95,848	177,051	5,505	81,203 D	34.4%	63.6%	35.1%	64.9%
38,851	ESSEX	12,485	5,198	7,007	280	1,809 D	41.6%	56.1%	42.6%	57.4%
51,134	FRANKLIN	11,976	3,973	7,798	205	3,825 D	33.2%	65.1%	33.8%	66.2%
55,073	FULTON	14,555	6,030	8,262	263	2,232 D	41.4%	56.8%	42.2%	57.8%
60,370	GENESEE	18,256	8,700	9,272	284	572 D	47.7%	50.8%	48.4%	51.6%
48,195	GREENE	16,528	7,641	8,477	410	836 D	46.2%	51.3%	47.4%	52.6%
5,379	HAMILTON	2,603	1,445	1,097	61	348 R	55.5%	42.1%	56.8%	43.2%
64,427	HERKIMER	19,145	8,177	10,600	368	2,423 D	42.7%	55.4%	43.5%	56.5%
111,738	JEFFERSON	24,972	9,237	15,384	351	6,147 D	37.0%	61.6%	37.5%	62.5%
2,465,326	KINGS	350,504	48,295	294,625	7,584	246,330 D	13.8%	84.1%	14.1%	85.9%
26,944	LEWIS	7,221	3,168	3,909	144	741 D	43.9%	54.1%	44.8%	55.2%
64,328	LIVINGSTON	19,665	9,103	10,149	413	1,046 D	46.3%	51.6%	47.3%	52.7%
69,441	MADISON	21,407	8,783	12,128	496	3,345 D	41.0%	56.7%	42.0%	58.0%
735,343	MONROE	228,565	83,134	141,823	3,608	58,689 D	36.4%	62.0%	37.0%	63.0%
49,708	MONTGOMERY	13,674	5,088	8,335	251	3,247 D	37.2%	61.0%	37.9%	62.1%
1,334,544	NASSAU	365,636	139,775	221,110	4,751	81,335 D	38.2%	60.5%	38.7%	61.3%
1,537,195	NEW YORK	368,072	40,471	316,367	11,234	275,896 D	11.0%	86.0%	11.3%	88.7%
219,846	NIAGARA	63,265	24,535	37,852	878	13,317 D	38.8%	59.8%	39.3%	60.7%
235,469	ONEIDA	71,459	28,710	41,582	1,167	12,872 D	40.2%	58.2%	40.8%	59.2%
458,336	ONONDAGA	152,860	50,643	98,116	4,101	47,473 D	33.1%	64.2%	34.0%	66.0%
100,224	ONTARIO	33,630	13,847	19,264	519	5,417 D	41.2%	57.3%	41.8%	58.2%
341,367	ORANGE	87,945	36,065	50,280	1,600	14,215 D	41.0%	57.2%	41.8%	58.2%
44,171	ORLEANS	10,709	5,119	5,415	175	296 D	47.8%	50.6%	48.6%	51.4%
122,377	OSWEGO	31,660	12,272	18,612	776	6,340 D	38.8%	58.8%	39.7%	60.3%
61,676	OTSEGO	18,469	7,379	10,467	623	3,088 D	40.0%	56.7%	41.3%	58.7%
95,745	PUTNAM	30,181	13,834	15,690	657	1,856 D	45.8%	52.0%	46.9%	53.1%

NEW YORK

SENATOR 2006

2000 Census Population	County	Total Vote	Republican	Democratic	Other	Rep.-Dem. Plurality	Total Vote		Major Vote	
							Rep.	Dem.	Rep.	Dem.
2,229,379	QUEENS	316,187	57,352	254,267	4,568	196,915 D	18.1%	80.4%	18.4%	81.6%
152,538	RENSSELAER	54,022	18,769	33,986	1,267	15,217 D	34.7%	62.9%	35.6%	64.4%
443,728	RICHMOND	81,102	33,356	46,666	1,080	13,310 D	41.1%	57.5%	41.7%	58.3%
286,753	ROCKLAND	79,215	30,100	47,738	1,377	17,638 D	38.0%	60.3%	38.7%	61.3%
111,931	ST. LAWRENCE	28,091	8,525	19,085	481	10,560 D	30.3%	67.9%	30.9%	69.1%
200,635	SARATOGA	79,354	32,151	45,485	1,718	13,334 D	40.5%	57.3%	41.4%	58.6%
146,555	SCHENECTADY	50,213	16,980	32,131	1,102	15,151 D	33.8%	64.0%	34.6%	65.4%
31,582	SCHOHARIE	10,827	4,965	5,589	273	624 D	45.9%	51.6%	47.0%	53.0%
19,224	SCHUYLER	5,983	2,617	3,187	179	570 D	43.7%	53.3%	45.1%	54.9%
33,342	SENECA	10,317	3,747	6,377	193	2,630 D	36.3%	61.8%	37.0%	63.0%
98,726	STEUBEN	27,641	13,602	13,561	478	41 R	49.2%	49.1%	50.1%	49.9%
1,419,369	SUFFOLK	353,791	137,964	210,104	5,723	72,140 D	39.0%	59.4%	39.6%	60.4%
73,966	SULLIVAN	19,875	7,309	12,094	472	4,785 D	36.8%	60.9%	37.7%	62.3%
51,784	TIOGA	15,806	7,478	8,025	303	547 D	47.3%	50.8%	48.2%	51.8%
96,501	TOMPKINS	29,374	7,946	19,813	1,615	11,867 D	27.1%	67.5%	28.6%	71.4%
177,749	ULSTER	59,607	20,580	36,538	2,489	15,958 D	34.5%	61.3%	36.0%	64.0%
63,303	WARREN	22,246	8,851	12,930	465	4,079 D	39.8%	58.1%	40.6%	59.4%
61,042	WASHINGTON	17,664	7,216	9,990	458	2,774 D	40.9%	56.6%	41.9%	58.1%
93,765	WAYNE	25,916	12,146	13,337	433	1,191 D	46.9%	51.5%	47.7%	52.3%
923,459	WESTCHESTER	261,991	82,273	174,217	5,501	91,944 D	31.4%	66.5%	32.1%	67.9%
43,424	WYOMING	12,683	6,504	5,992	187	512 R	51.3%	47.2%	52.0%	48.0%
24,621	YATES	7,410	3,125	4,176	109	1,051 D	42.2%	56.4%	42.8%	57.2%
18,976,457	TOTAL	4,490,053	1,392,189	3,008,428	89,436	1,616,239 D	31.0%	67.0%	31.6%	68.4%

NEW YORK CITY

SENATOR 2006

2000 Census Population	County	Total Vote	Republican	Democratic	Other	Rep.-Dem. Plurality	Total Vote		Major Vote	
							Rep.	Dem.	Rep.	Dem.
1,332,650	BRONX	178,572	17,086	159,792	1,694	142,706 D	9.6%	89.5%	9.7%	90.3%
2,465,326	KINGS	350,504	48,295	294,625	7,584	246,330 D	13.8%	84.1%	14.1%	85.9%
1,537,195	NEW YORK	368,072	40,471	316,367	11,234	275,896 D	11.0%	86.0%	11.3%	88.7%
2,229,379	QUEENS	316,187	57,352	254,267	4,568	196,915 D	18.1%	80.4%	18.4%	81.6%
443,728	RICHMOND	81,102	33,356	46,666	1,080	13,310 D	41.1%	57.5%	41.7%	58.3%
8,008,278	TOTAL	1,294,437	196,560	1,071,717	26,160	875,157 D	15.2%	82.8%	15.5%	84.5%

NEW YORK

HOUSE OF REPRESENTATIVES

CD	Year	Total Vote	Republican		Democratic		Other Vote	Rep.-Dem. Plurality	Percentage			
			Vote	Candidate	Vote	Candidate			Total Vote		Major Vote	
									Rep.	Dem.	Rep.	Dem.
1	2006	167,688	63,328	# ZANZI, ITALO A.	104,360	# BISHOP, TIMOTHY H.*		41,032 D	37.8%	62.2%	37.8%	62.2%
1	2004	278,209	121,855	# MANGER, WILLIAM M. JR.	156,354	# BISHOP, TIMOTHY H.*		34,499 D	43.8%	56.2%	43.8%	56.2%
1	2002	167,791	81,524	# GRUCCI, FELIX J. JR.*	84,276	# BISHOP, TIMOTHY H.	1,991	2,752 D	48.6%	50.2%	49.2%	50.8%
2	2006	149,488	44,212	# BUGLER, JOHN W.	105,276	# ISRAEL, STEVE*		61,064 D	29.6%	70.4%	29.6%	70.4%
2	2004	242,543	80,950	# HOFFMANN, RICHARD	161,593	# ISRAEL, STEVE*		80,643 D	33.4%	66.6%	33.4%	66.6%
2	2002	146,126	59,117	# FINLEY, JOSEPH P.	85,451	# ISRAEL, STEVE*	1,558	26,334 D	40.5%	58.5%	40.9%	59.1%
3	2006	181,630	101,787	# KING, PETER T.*	79,843	# MEJIAS, DAVID L.		21,944 R	56.0%	44.0%	56.0%	44.0%
3	2004	271,996	171,259	# KING, PETER T.*	100,737	MATHIES, BLAIR H. JR.		70,522 R	63.0%	37.0%	63.0%	37.0%
3	2002	169,072	121,537	# KING, PETER T.*	46,022	FINZ, STUART L.	1,513	75,515 R	71.9%	27.2%	72.5%	27.5%
4	2006	156,911	55,050	# BLESSINGER, MARTIN W.	101,861	# McCARTHY, CAROLYN*		46,811 D	35.1%	64.9%	35.1%	64.9%
4	2004	254,110	94,141	# GARNER, JAMES A.	159,969	# McCARTHY, CAROLYN*		65,828 D	37.0%	63.0%	37.0%	63.0%
4	2002	168,540	72,882	# O'GRADY, MARILYN F.	94,806	# McCARTHY, CAROLYN*	852	21,924 D	43.2%	56.3%	43.5%	56.5%
5	2006	77,190		—	77,190	# ACKERMAN, GARY L.*		77,190 D		100.0%		100.0%
5	2004	167,841	46,867	# GRAVES, STEPHEN	119,726	# ACKERMAN, GARY L.*	1,248	72,859 D	27.9%	71.3%	28.1%	71.9%
5	2002	74,491		—	68,773	# ACKERMAN, GARY L.*	5,718	68,773 D		92.3%		100.0%
6	2006	69,405		—	69,405	MEEKS, GREGORY W.*		69,405 D		100.0%		100.0%
6	2004	129,688		—	129,688	# MEEKS, GREGORY W.*		129,688 D		100.0%		100.0%
6	2002	75,431		—	72,799	# MEEKS, GREGORY W.*	2,632	72,799 D		96.5%		100.0%
7	2006	76,217	12,220	# BRAWLEY, KEVIN	63,997	# CROWLEY, JOSEPH*		51,777 D	16.0%	84.0%	16.0%	84.0%
7	2004	128,823	24,548	# CINQUEMAIN, JOSEPH	104,275	# CROWLEY, JOSEPH*		79,727 D	19.1%	80.9%	19.1%	80.9%
7	2002	69,539	18,572	# BRAWLEY, KEVIN	50,967	# CROWLEY, JOSEPH*		32,395 D	26.7%	73.3%	26.7%	73.3%
8	2006	127,622	17,413	FRIEDMAN, ELEANOR	108,536	# NADLER, JERROLD*	1,673	91,123 D	13.6%	85.0%	13.8%	86.2%
8	2004	201,322	39,240	# HORT, PETER	162,082	# NADLER, JERROLD*		122,842 D	19.5%	80.5%	19.5%	80.5%
8	2002	106,481	19,674	# FARRIN, JIM	81,002	# NADLER, JERROLD*	5,805	61,328 D	18.5%	76.1%	19.5%	80.5%
9	2006	71,762		—	71,762	# WEINER, ANTHONY*		71,762 D		100.0%		100.0%
9	2004	158,476	45,451	# CRONIN, GERARD J.	113,025	# WEINER, ANTHONY*		67,574 D	28.7%	71.3%	28.7%	71.3%
9	2002	92,435	31,698	# DONOHUE, ALFRED F.	60,737	# WEINER, ANTHONY*		29,039 D	34.3%	65.7%	34.3%	65.7%
10	2006	78,307	4,666	ANDERSON, JONATHAN H.	72,171	TOWNS, EDOLPHUS*	1,470	67,505 D	6.0%	92.2%	6.1%	93.9%
10	2004	148,766	11,099	CLARKE, HARVEY R.	136,113	# TOWNS, EDOLPHUS*	1,554	125,014 D	7.5%	91.5%	7.5%	92.5%
10	2002	75,498		—	73,859	# TOWNS, EDOLPHUS*	1,639	73,859 D		97.8%		100.0%
11	2006	98,102	7,447	# FINGER, STEPHEN	88,334	# CLARKE, YVETTE D.	2,321	80,887 D	7.6%	90.0%	7.8%	92.2%
11	2004	154,198		—	144,999	# OWENS, MAJOR R.*	9,199	144,999 D		94.0%		100.0%
11	2002	88,864	11,149	# CLEARY, SUSAN	76,917	# OWENS, MAJOR R.*	798	65,768 D	12.5%	86.6%	12.7%	87.3%
12	2006	70,029	7,182	# ROMAGUERA, ALLAN	62,847	# VELÁZQUEZ, NYDIA M.*		55,665 D	10.3%	89.7%	10.3%	89.7%
12	2004	124,962	17,166	# RODRIGUEZ, PAUL A.	107,796	# VELÁZQUEZ, NYDIA M.*		90,630 D	13.7%	86.3%	13.7%	86.3%
12	2002	50,527		—	48,408	# VELÁZQUEZ, NYDIA M.*	2,119	48,408 D		95.8%		100.0%
13	2006	104,465	59,334	# FOSSELLA, VITO J.*	45,131	# HARRISON, STEPHEN A.		14,203 R	56.8%	43.2%	56.8%	43.2%
13	2004	191,434	112,934	# FOSSELLA, VITO J.*	78,500	# BARBARO, FRANK J.		34,434 R	59.0%	41.0%	59.0%	41.0%
13	2002	103,693	72,204	# FOSSELLA, VITO J.*	29,366	# MATTSSON, ARNE M.	2,123	42,838 R	69.6%	28.3%	71.1%	28.9%
14	2006	141,551	21,969	MAIO, DANNIEL	119,582	# MALONEY, CAROLYN B.*		97,613 D	15.5%	84.5%	15.5%	84.5%
14	2004	230,311	43,623	# SRDANOVIC, ANTON	186,688	# MALONEY, CAROLYN B.*		143,065 D	18.9%	81.1%	18.9%	81.1%
14	2002	127,479	31,548	# SRDANOVIC, ANTON	95,931	# MALONEY, CAROLYN B.*		64,383 D	24.7%	75.3%	24.7%	75.3%
15	2006	110,508	6,592	DANIELS, EDWARD	103,916	# RANGEL, CHARLES B.*		97,324 D	6.0%	94.0%	6.0%	94.0%
15	2004	177,051	12,355	JEFFERSON, KENNETH P. JR.	161,351	# RANGEL, CHARLES B.*	3,345	148,996 D	7.0%	91.1%	7.1%	92.9%
15	2002	95,375	11,008	# FIELDS, JESSIE A.	84,367	# RANGEL, CHARLES B.*		73,359 D	11.5%	88.5%	11.5%	88.5%
16	2006	58,883	2,759	# MOHAMED, ALI	56,124	# SERRANO, JOSE E.*		53,365 D	4.7%	95.3%	4.7%	95.3%
16	2004	117,248	5,610	# MOHAMED, ALI	111,638	# SERRANO, JOSE E.*		106,028 D	4.8%	95.2%	4.8%	95.2%
16	2002	55,082	4,366	# DELLAVALLE, FRANK	50,716	# SERRANO, JOSE E.*		46,350 D	7.9%	92.1%	7.9%	92.1%

NEW YORK

HOUSE OF REPRESENTATIVES

| | | | Republican | | Democratic | | | | Percentage | | | |
| | | | | | | | | | Total Vote | | Major Vote | |
CD	Year	Total Vote	Vote	Candidate	Vote	Candidate	Other Vote	Rep.-Dem. Plurality	Rep.	Dem.	Rep.	Dem.
17	2006	122,456	28,842	# FAULKNER, JIM	93,614	# ENGEL, ELIOT L.*		64,772 D	23.6%	76.4%	23.6%	76.4%
17	2004	184,536	40,524	BRENNAN, MATT I.	140,530	# ENGEL, ELIOT L.*	3,482	100,006 D	22.0%	76.2%	22.4%	77.6%
17	2002	123,843	42,634	# VANDERHOEF, C. SCOTT	77,535	# ENGEL, ELIOT L.*	3,674	34,901 D	34.4%	62.6%	35.5%	64.5%
18	2006	175,706	51,450	# HOFFMAN, RICHARD A.	124,256	# LOWEY, NITA M.*		72,806 D	29.3%	70.7%	29.3%	70.7%
18	2004	244,690	73,975	HOFFMAN, RICHARD A.	170,715	# LOWEY, NITA M.*		96,740 D	30.2%	69.8%	30.2%	69.8%
18	2002	107,515		—	98,957	# LOWEY, NITA M.*	8,558	98,957 D		92.0%		100.0%
19	2006	195,478	95,359	# KELLY, SUE W.*	100,119	HALL, JOHN		4,760 D	48.8%	51.2%	48.8%	51.2%
19	2004	262,830	175,401	# KELLY, SUE W.*	87,429	JALIMAN, MICHAEL		87,972 R	66.7%	33.3%	66.7%	33.3%
19	2002	173,112	121,129	# KELLY, SUE W.*	44,967	SELENDY, JANINE M. H.	7,016	76,162 R	70.0%	26.0%	72.9%	27.1%
20	2006	235,722	110,554	# SWEENEY, JOHN E.*	125,168	# GILLIBRAND, KIRSTEN E.		14,614 D	46.9%	53.1%	46.9%	53.1%
20	2004	286,736	188,753	# SWEENEY, JOHN E.*	96,630	KELLY, DORIS F.	1,353	92,123 R	65.8%	33.7%	66.1%	33.9%
20	2002	191,278	140,238	# SWEENEY, JOHN E.*	45,878	STOPPENBACH, FRANK	5,162	94,360 R	73.3%	24.0%	75.3%	24.7%
21	2006	214,356	46,752	REDLICH, WARREN	167,604	# McNULTY, MICHAEL R.*		120,852 D	21.8%	78.2%	21.8%	78.2%
21	2004	274,154	80,121	REDLICH, WARREN	194,033	# McNULTY, MICHAEL R.*		113,912 D	29.2%	70.8%	29.2%	70.8%
21	2002	214,854	53,525	ROSENSTEIN, CHARLES B.	161,329	# McNULTY, MICHAEL R.*		107,804 D	24.9%	75.1%	24.9%	75.1%
22	2006	121,683		—	121,683	# HINCHEY, MAURICE D.*		121,683 D		100.0%		100.0%
22	2004	249,370	81,881	BRENNER, WILLIAM A.	167,489	# HINCHEY, MAURICE D.*		85,608 D	32.8%	67.2%	32.8%	67.2%
22	2002	176,484	58,008	# HALL, ERIC	113,280	# HINCHEY, MAURICE D.*	5,196	55,272 D	32.9%	64.2%	33.9%	66.1%
23	2006	169,099	106,781	# McHUGH, JOHN M.*	62,318	JOHNSON, ROBERT J.		44,463 R	63.1%	36.9%	63.1%	36.9%
23	2004	226,527	160,079	# McHUGH, JOHN M.*	66,448	JOHNSON, ROBERT J.		93,631 R	70.7%	29.3%	70.7%	29.3%
23	2002	124,682	124,682	# McHUGH, JOHN M.*		—		124,682 R	100.0%		100.0%	
24	2006	203,324	91,504	# MEIER, RAYMOND A.	109,686	# ARCURI, MICHAEL A.	2,134	18,182 D	45.0%	53.9%	45.5%	54.5%
24	2004	251,368	143,000	# BOEHLERT, SHERWOOD*	85,140	MILLER, JEFFREY A.	23,228	57,860 R	56.9%	33.9%	62.7%	37.3%
24	2002	152,777	108,017	BOEHLERT, SHERWOOD*		—	44,760	108,017 R	70.7%		100.0%	
25	2006	217,633	110,525	# WALSH, JAMES T.*	107,108	# MAFFEI, DAN		3,417 R	50.8%	49.2%	50.8%	49.2%
25	2004	209,169	189,063	# WALSH, JAMES T.*		—	20,106	189,063 R	90.4%		100.0%	
25	2002	200,031	144,610	# WALSH, JAMES T.*	53,290	ALDERSLEY, STEPHANIE	2,131	91,320 R	72.3%	26.6%	73.1%	26.9%
26	2006	210,171	109,257	# REYNOLDS, THOMAS M.*	100,914	# DAVIS, JACK		8,343 R	52.0%	48.0%	52.0%	48.0%
26	2004	283,079	157,466	# REYNOLDS. THOMAS M.*	125,613	# DAVIS, JACK		31,853 R	55.6%	44.4%	55.6%	44.4%
26	2002	183,459	135,089	# REYNOLDS. THOMAS M.*	41,140	NARIMAN, AYESHA F.	7,230	93,949 R	73.6%	22.4%	76.7%	23.3%
27	2006	176,641	36,614	McHALE, MICHAEL J.	140,027	# HIGGINS, BRIAN*		103,413 D	20.7%	79.3%	20.7%	79.3%
27	2004	282,890	139,558	# NAPLES, NANCY A.	143,332	# HIGGINS, BRIAN		3,774 D	49.3%	50.7%	49.3%	50.7%
27	2002	173,919	120,117	# QUINN, JACK*	47,811	# CROTTY, PETER	5,991	72,306 R	69.1%	27.5%	71.5%	28.5%
28	2006	152,230	40,844	# DONNELLY, JOHN E.	111,386	# SLAUGHTER, LOUISE M.*		70,542 D	26.8%	73.2%	26.8%	73.2%
28	2004	219,876	54,543	# LABA, MICHAEL D.	159,655	# SLAUGHTER, LOUISE M.*	5,678	105,112 D	24.8%	72.6%	25.5%	74.5%
28	2002	158,604	59,547	# WOJTASZEK, HENRY F.	99,057	# SLAUGHTER, LOUISE M.*		39,510 D	37.5%	62.5%	37.5%	62.5%
29	2006	206,121	106,077	# KUHL, JOHN R. "RANDY" JR.*	100,044	# MASSA, ERIC J.		6,033 R	51.5%	48.5%	51.5%	48.5%
29	2004	270,215	136,883	KUHL, JOHN R. "RANDY" JR.	110,241	# BAREND, SAMARA	23,091	26,642 R	50.7%	40.8%	55.4%	44.6%
29	2002	174,631	127,657	# HOUGHTON, AMO*	37,128	PETERS, KISUN J.	9,846	90,529 R	73.1%	21.3%	77.5%	22.5%
TOTAL	2006	4,140,378	1,338,518		2,794,262		7,598	1,455,744 D	32.3%	67.5%	32.4%	67.6%
TOTAL	2004	6,222,418	2,448,345		3,681,789		92,284	1,233,444 D	39.3%	59.2%	39.9%	60.1%
TOTAL	2002	3,821,613	1,770,532		1,924,769		126,312	154,237 D	46.3%	50.4%	47.9%	52.1%

A pound sign (#) indicates that the candidate received votes on the ballot line of one or more other parties. Each candidate's total vote is listed above. An asterisk (*) denotes incumbent.

NEW YORK

GENERAL AND PRIMARY ELECTIONS

2006 GENERAL ELECTIONS

Note: Candidates in New York can appear on the ballot line of more than one party. In the gubernatorial election, Eliot Spitzer received 2,740,864 votes on the Democratic line, 190,661 votes on the Independence line, and 155,184 votes on the Working Families line, for a total of 3,086,709 votes. John J. Faso received 1,105,681 votes on the Republican line and another 168,654 votes on the Conservative line, for a total of 1,274,335 votes. In the Senate race, Hillary Rodham Clinton received 2,698,931 votes on the Democratic line, 160,705 votes on the Independence line, and 148,792 votes on the Working Families line, for a total of 3,008,428 votes. John Spencer received 1,212,902 votes on the Republican line and another 179,287 votes on the Conservative line, for a total of 1,392,189 votes. In the New York tables, votes received by each Democratic and Republican candidate on the ballot lines of other parties are combined into one overall vote, which is credited to the major party of which they are a member.

Governor Other vote was 42,166 Green (Malachy McCourt); 14,736 Libertarian (John Clifton); 13,355 Rent Is Too High (Jimmy McMillan); 5,919 Socialist Workers (Maura DeLuca).

Senator Other vote was 55,469 Green (Howie Hawkins); 20,996 Libertarian (Jeffrey T. Russell); 6,967 Socialist Workers (Roger Calero); 6,004 Socialist Equality (William Van Auken).

House Other vote was:

CD 1
CD 2
CD 3
CD 4
CD 5
CD 6
CD 7
CD 8 1,673 Conservative (Dennis E. Adornato).
CD 9
CD 10 1,470 Conservative (Ernest Johnson).
CD 11 1,325 Conservative (Marianna Blume); 996 Freedom (Ollie M. McClean).
CD 12
CD 13
CD 14
CD 15
CD 16
CD 17
CD 18
CD 19
CD 20
CD 21
CD 22
CD 23
CD 24 2,134 Libertarian (Michael J. Sylvia III).
CD 25
CD 26
CD 27
CD 28
CD 29

NEW YORK

GENERAL AND PRIMARY ELECTIONS

2006 PRIMARY ELECTIONS

Primary	September 12, 2006	**Registration** (as of April 1, 2006)	Democratic	5,489,521
			Republican	3,143,233
			Independence	339,382
			Conservative	154,614
			Liberal	68,242
			Right to Life	39,594
			Green	36,141
			Working Families	32,723
			Libertarian	798
			Marijuana Reform	171
			Other	7,417
			Unaffiliated	2,315,549
			TOTAL	11,627,385

Primary Type   Closed—Only registered Democrats and Republicans could vote in their party's primary.

NEW YORK

GENERAL AND PRIMARY ELECTIONS

Note: An asterisk (*) denotes incumbent. Write-in votes were broken out separately in the official tally from New York City districts but not those in the rest of the state. Names of unopposed candidates did not appear on the primary ballot; therefore, no votes were cast for these candidates.

	REPUBLICAN PRIMARIES			DEMOCRATIC PRIMARIES		
Governor	John J. Faso	Unopposed		Eliot Spitzer	624,684	81.9%
				Thomas R. Suozzi	138,263	18.1%
				TOTAL	762,947	
Senator	John Spencer	114,914	60.8%	Hillary Rodham Clinton*	640,955	83.7%
	K.T. McFarland	74,108	39.2%	Jonathan B. Tasini	124,999	16.3%
	TOTAL	189,022		TOTAL	765,954	
Congressional District 1	Italo A. Zanzi	Unopposed		Timothy H. Bishop*	Unopposed	
Congressional District 2	John W. Bugler	Unopposed		Steve Israel*	Unopposed	
Congressional District 3	Peter T. King*	11,077	84.0%	David L. Mejias	Unopposed	
	Robert Previdi	2,110	16.0%			
	TOTAL	13,187				
Congressional District 4	Martin W. Blessinger	Unopposed		Carolyn McCarthy*	Unopposed	
Congressional District 5	No Republican candidate			Gary L. Ackerman*	Unopposed	
Congressional District 6	No Republican candidate			Gregory W. Meeks*	Unopposed	
Congressional District 7	Kevin Brawley	Unopposed		Joseph Crowley*	Unopposed	
Congressional District 8	Eleanor Friedman	Unopposed		Jerrold Nadler*	Unopposed	
Congressional District 9	No Republican candidate			Anthony Weiner*	Unopposed	

NEW YORK

GENERAL AND PRIMARY ELECTIONS

	REPUBLICAN PRIMARIES			DEMOCRATIC PRIMARIES		
Congressional District 10	Jonathan H. Anderson	Unopposed		Edolphus Towns*	19,469	47.4%
				Charles Barron	15,345	37.4%
				Roger L. Green	6,237	15.2%
				Scattered write-in	8	
				TOTAL	41,059	
Congressional District 11	Stephen Finger	Unopposed		Yvette D. Clarke	15,711	30.6%
				David S. Yassky	13,928	27.2%
				Carl Andrews	11,685	22.8%
				Chris Owens	9,971	19.4%
				Scattered write-in	1	
				TOTAL	51,296	
Congressional District 12	Allan Romaguera	Unopposed		Nydia M. Velázquez*	Unopposed	
Congressional District 13	Vito J. Fossella*	Unopposed		Stephen A. Harrison	Unopposed	
Congressional District 14	Danniel Maio	Unopposed		Carolyn B. Maloney*	Unopposed	
Congressional District 15	Edward Daniels	Unopposed		Charles B. Rangel*	Unopposed	
Congressional District 16	Ali Mohamed	Unopposed		Jose E. Serrano*	Unopposed	
Congressional District 17	Jim Faulkner	Unopposed		Eliot L. Engel*	26,564	83.0%
				Jessica Flagg	5,430	17.0%
				Scattered write-in	3	
				TOTAL	31,997	
Congressional District 18	Richard A. Hoffman	3,239	52.7%	Nita M. Lowey*	Unopposed	
	Jim Russell	2,908	47.3%			
	TOTAL	6,147				
Congressional District 19	Sue W. Kelly*	Unopposed		John Hall	11,231	49.5%
				Judith Aydelott	6,110	26.9%
				Ben Shuldiner	3,568	15.7%
				Darren J. Rigger	1,799	7.9%
				TOTAL	22,708	
Congressional District 20	John E. Sweeney*	Unopposed		Kirsten E. Gillibrand	Unopposed	
Congressional District 21	Warren Redlich	Unopposed		Michael R. McNulty*	26,246	85.8%
				Thomas J. Raleigh	4,341	14.2%
				TOTAL	30,587	
Congressional District 22	No Republican candidate			Maurice D. Hinchey*	Unopposed	
Congressional District 23	John M. McHugh*	Unopposed		Robert J. Johnson	Unopposed	
Congressional District 24	Raymond A. Meier	Unopposed		Michael A. Arcuri	Unopposed	
Congressional District 25	James T. Walsh*	Unopposed		Dan Maffei	Unopposed	
Congressional District 26	Thomas M. Reynolds*	Unopposed		Jack Davis	Unopposed	
Congressional District 27	Michael J. McHale	Unopposed		Brian Higgins*	Unopposed	
Congressional District 28	John E. Donnelly	Unopposed		Louise M. Slaughter*	Unopposed	
Congressional District 29	John R. "Randy" Kuhl Jr.*	Unopposed		Eric J. Massa	Unopposed	

NORTH CAROLINA

Congressional districts first established for elections held in 2002
13 members

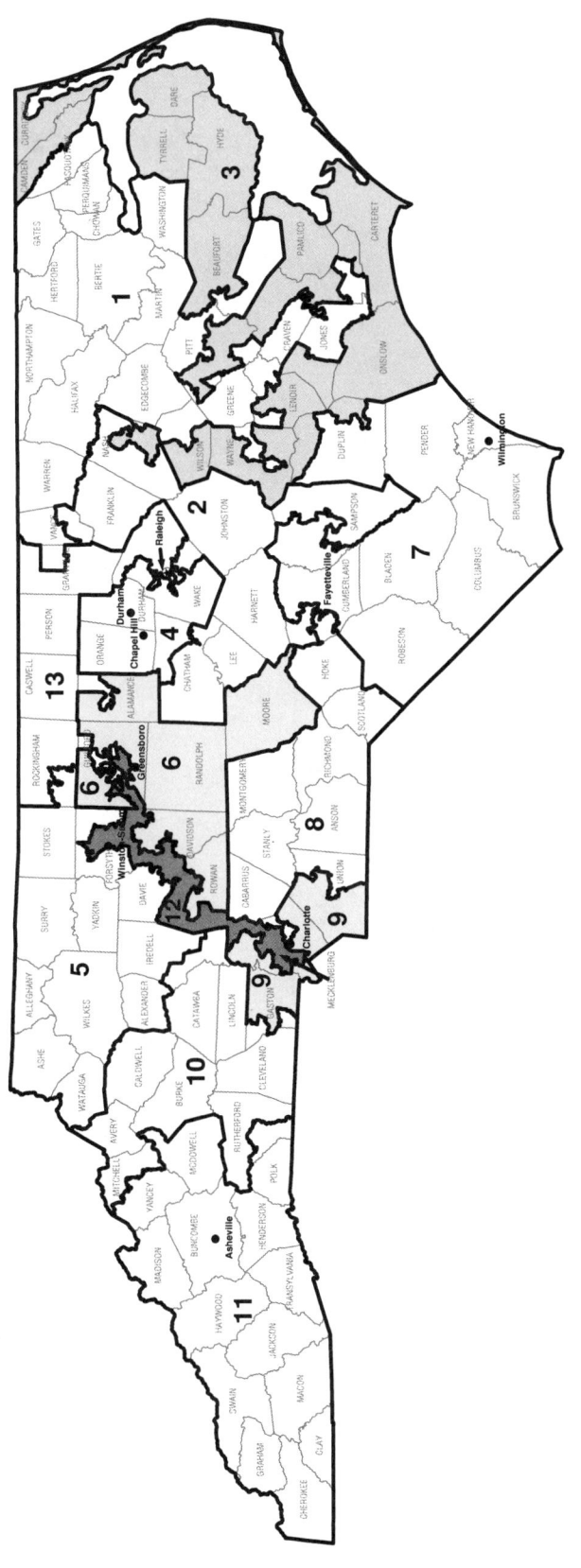

NORTH CAROLINA

Central North Carolina Area

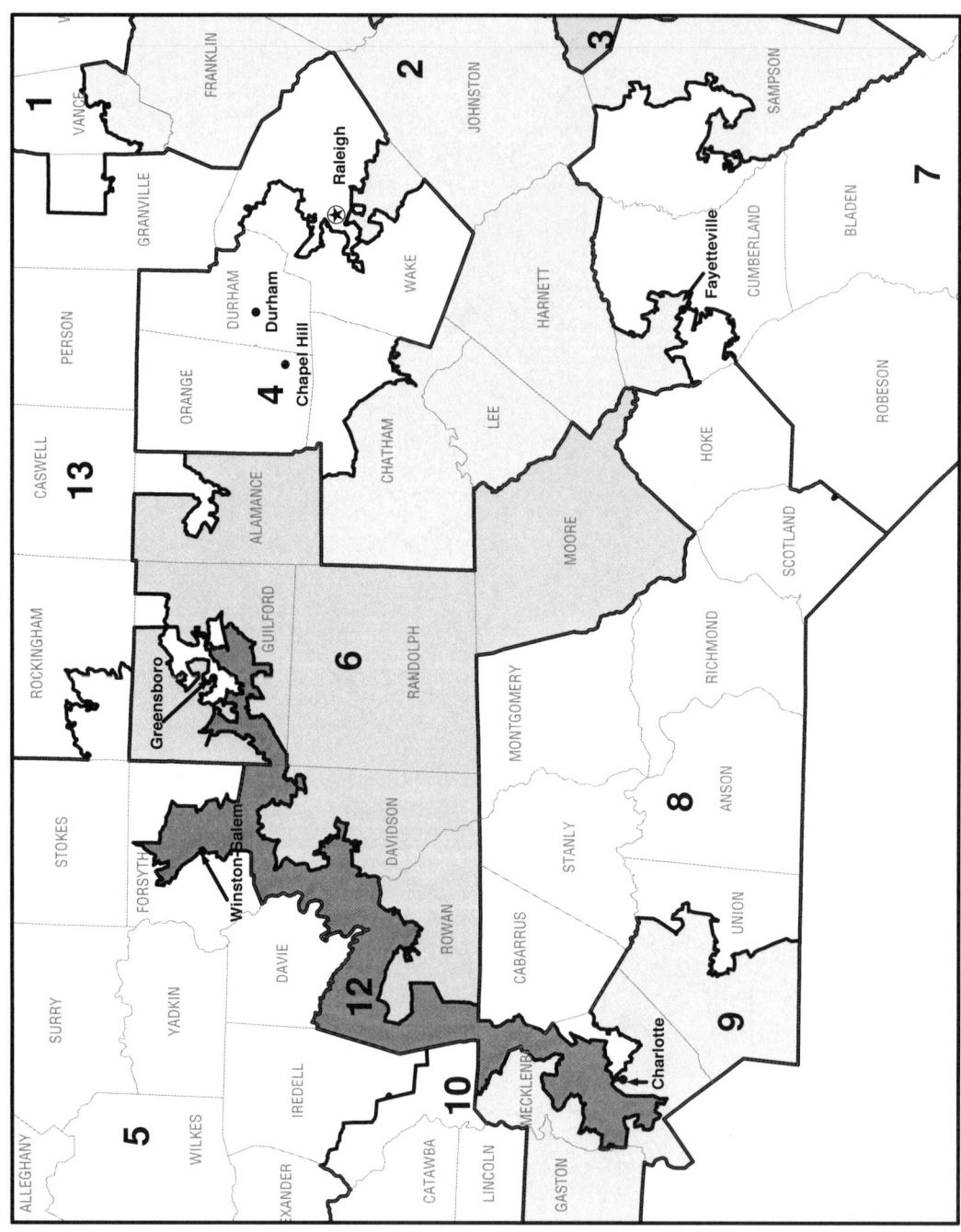

NORTH CAROLINA

GOVERNOR

Michael F. Easley (D). Reelected 2004 to a four-year term. Previously elected 2000.

SENATORS (2 Republicans)

Richard M. Burr (R). Elected 2004 to a six-year term.

Elizabeth Dole (R). Elected 2002 to a six-year term.

REPRESENTATIVES (7 Democrats, 6 Republicans)

1. G. K. Butterfield (D)
2. Bob Etheridge (D)
3. Walter B. Jones (R)
4. David E. Price (D)
5. Virginia Foxx (R)
6. Howard Coble (R)
7. Mike McIntyre (D)
8. Robin Hayes (R)
9. Sue Myrick (R)
10. Patrick T. McHenry (R)
11. Heath Shuler (D)
12. Melvin Watt (D)
13. Brad Miller (D)

POSTWAR VOTE FOR PRESIDENT

Year	Total Vote	Republican		Democratic		Other Vote	Plurality	Percentage			
								Total Vote		Major Vote	
		Vote	Candidate	Vote	Candidate			Rep.	Dem.	Rep.	Dem.
2004	3,501,007	1,961,166	Bush, George W.	1,525,849	Kerry, John	13,992	435,317 R	56.0%	43.6%	56.2%	43.8%
2000	2,911,262	1,631,163	Bush, George W.	1,257,692	Gore, Al	22,407	373,471 R	56.0%	43.2%	56.5%	43.5%
1996**	2,515,807	1,225,938	Dole, Bob	1,107,849	Clinton, Bill	182,020	118,089 R	48.7%	44.0%	52.5%	47.5%
1992**	2,611,850	1,134,661	Bush, George	1,114,042	Clinton, Bill	363,147	20,619 R	43.4%	42.7%	50.5%	49.5%
1988	2,134,370	1,237,258	Bush, George	890,167	Dukakis, Michael S.	6,945	347,091 R	58.0%	41.7%	58.2%	41.8%
1984	2,175,361	1,346,481	Reagan, Ronald	824,287	Mondale, Walter F.	4,593	522,194 R	61.9%	37.9%	62.0%	38.0%
1980**	1,855,833	915,018	Reagan, Ronald	875,635	Carter, Jimmy	65,180	39,383 R	49.3%	47.2%	51.1%	48.9%
1976	1,678,914	741,960	Ford, Gerald R.	927,365	Carter, Jimmy	9,589	185,405 D	44.2%	55.2%	44.4%	55.6%
1972	1,518,612	1,054,889	Nixon, Richard M.	438,705	McGovern, George S.	25,018	616,184 R	69.5%	28.9%	70.6%	29.4%
1968**	1,587,493	627,192	Nixon, Richard M.	464,113	Humphrey, Hubert H.	496,188	131,004 R	39.5%	29.2%	57.5%	42.5%
1964	1,424,983	624,844	Goldwater, Barry M.	800,139	Johnson, Lyndon B.		175,295 D	43.8%	56.2%	43.8%	56.2%
1960	1,368,556	655,420	Nixon, Richard M.	713,136	Kennedy, John F.		57,716 D	47.9%	52.1%	47.9%	52.1%
1956	1,165,592	575,062	Eisenhower, Dwight D.	590,530	Stevenson, Adlai E.		15,468 D	49.3%	50.7%	49.3%	50.7%
1952	1,210,910	558,107	Eisenhower, Dwight D.	652,803	Stevenson, Adlai E.		94,696 D	46.1%	53.9%	46.1%	53.9%
1948**	791,209	258,572	Dewey, Thomas E.	459,070	Truman, Harry S.	73,567	200,498 D	32.7%	58.0%	36.0%	64.0%

**In past elections, the other vote included: 1996 - 168,059 Reform (Ross Perot); 1992 - 357,864 Independent (Ross Perot); 1980 - 52,800 Independent (John Anderson); 1968 - 496,188 American Independent (George Wallace), who came in second statewide; 1948 - 69,652 States' Rights (Strom Thurmond).

NORTH CAROLINA

POSTWAR VOTE FOR GOVERNOR

Year	Total Vote	Republican Vote	Republican Candidate	Democratic Vote	Democratic Candidate	Other Vote	Rep.-Dem. Plurality	Total Vote Rep.	Total Vote Dem.	Major Vote Rep.	Major Vote Dem.
2004	3,486,688	1,495,021	Ballantine, Patrick J.	1,939,154	Easley, Michael F.	52,513	444,133 D	42.9%	55.6%	43.5%	56.5%
2000	2,942,062	1,360,960	Vinroot, Richard	1,530,324	Easley, Michael F.	50,778	169,364 D	46.3%	52.0%	47.1%	52.9%
1996	2,566,185	1,097,053	Hayes, Robin	1,436,638	Hunt, James B.	32,494	339,585 D	42.8%	56.0%	43.3%	56.7%
1992	2,595,184	1,121,955	Gardner, James C.	1,368,246	Hunt, James B.	104,983	246,291 D	43.2%	52.7%	45.1%	54.9%
1988	2,180,025	1,222,338	Martin, James G.	957,687	Jordan, Robert B.		264,651 R	56.1%	43.9%	56.1%	43.9%
1984	2,226,727	1,208,167	Martin, James G.	1,011,209	Edmisten, Rufus	7,351	196,958 R	54.3%	45.4%	54.4%	45.6%
1980	1,847,432	691,449	Lake, Beverly	1,143,145	Hunt, James B.	12,838	451,696 D	37.4%	61.9%	37.7%	62.3%
1976	1,663,824	564,102	Flaherty, David T.	1,081,293	Hunt, James B.	18,429	517,191 D	33.9%	65.0%	34.3%	65.7%
1972	1,504,785	767,470	Holshouser, James E.	729,104	Bowles, Hargrove	8,211	38,366 R	51.0%	48.5%	51.3%	48.7%
1968	1,558,308	737,075	Gardner, James C.	821,233	Scott, Robert W.		84,158 D	47.3%	52.7%	47.3%	52.7%
1964	1,396,508	606,165	Gavin, Robert L.	790,343	Moore, Dan K.		184,178 D	43.4%	56.6%	43.4%	56.6%
1960	1,350,360	613,975	Gavin, Robert L.	735,248	Sanford, Terry	1,137	121,273 D	45.5%	54.4%	45.5%	54.5%
1956	1,135,859	375,379	Hayes, Kyle	760,480	Hodges, Luther H.		385,101 D	33.0%	67.0%	33.0%	67.0%
1952	1,179,635	383,329	Seawell, H. F.	796,306	Umstead, William B.		412,977 D	32.5%	67.5%	32.5%	67.5%
1948	780,525	206,166	Pritchard, George	570,995	Scott, William Kerr	3,364	364,829 D	26.4%	73.2%	26.5%	73.5%

POSTWAR VOTE FOR SENATOR

Year	Total Vote	Republican Vote	Republican Candidate	Democratic Vote	Democratic Candidate	Other Vote	Rep.-Dem. Plurality	Total Vote Rep.	Total Vote Dem.	Major Vote Rep.	Major Vote Dem.
2004	3,472,082	1,791,450	Burr, Richard M.	1,632,527	Bowles, Erskine	48,105	158,923 R	51.6%	47.0%	52.3%	47.7%
2002	2,331,181	1,248,664	Dole, Elizabeth	1,047,983	Bowles, Erskine	34,534	200,681 R	53.6%	45.0%	54.4%	45.6%
1998	2,012,143	945,943	Faircloth, Lauch	1,029,237	Edwards, John	36,963	83,294 D	47.0%	51.2%	47.9%	52.1%
1996	2,556,456	1,345,833	Helms, Jesse	1,173,875	Gantt, Harvey B.	36,748	171,958 R	52.6%	45.9%	53.4%	46.6%
1992	2,577,891	1,297,892	Faircloth, Lauch	1,194,015	Sanford, Terry	85,984	103,877 R	50.3%	46.3%	52.1%	47.9%
1990	2,069,585	1,087,331	Helms, Jesse	981,573	Gantt, Harvy B.	681	105,758 R	52.5%	47.4%	52.6%	47.4%
1986	1,591,330	767,668	Broyhill, James T.	823,662	Sanford, Terry		55,994 D	48.2%	51.8%	48.2%	51.8%
1984	2,239,051	1,156,768	Helms, Jesse	1,070,488	Hunt, James B.	11,795	86,280 R	51.7%	47.8%	51.9%	48.1%
1980	1,797,665	898,064	East, John P.	887,653	Morgan, Robert	11,948	10,411 R	50.0%	49.4%	50.3%	49.7%
1978	1,135,814	619,151	Helms, Jesse	516,663	Ingram, John		102,488 R	54.5%	45.5%	54.5%	45.5%
1974	1,020,367	377,618	Stevens, William E.	633,775	Morgan, Robert	8,974	256,157 D	37.0%	62.1%	37.3%	62.7%
1972	1,472,541	795,248	Helms, Jesse	677,293	Galifianakis, Nick		117,955 R	54.0%	46.0%	54.0%	46.0%
1968	1,437,340	566,934	Somers, Robert V.	870,406	Ervin, Sam J.		303,472 D	39.4%	60.6%	39.4%	60.6%
1966	901,978	400,502	Shallcross, John S.	501,440	Jordan, B. Everett	36	100,938 D	44.4%	55.6%	44.4%	55.6%
1962	813,155	321,635	Greene, Claude L.	491,520	Ervin, Sam J.		169,885 D	39.6%	60.4%	39.6%	60.4%
1960	1,291,485	497,964	Hayes, Kyle	793,521	Jordan, B. Everett		295,557 D	38.6%	61.4%	38.6%	61.4%
1958S	616,469	184,977	Clarke, Richard C.	431,492	Jordan, B. Everett		246,515 D	30.0%	70.0%	30.0%	70.0%
1956	1,098,828	367,475	Johnson, Joel A.	731,353	Ervin, Sam J.		363,878 D	33.4%	66.6%	33.4%	66.6%
1954	619,634	211,322	West, Paul C.	408,312	Scott, William Kerr		196,990 D	34.1%	65.9%	34.1%	65.9%
1954S	410,574		—	410,574	Ervin, Sam J.		410,574 D		100.0%		100.0%
1950	548,276	171,804	Leavitt, Halsey B.	376,472	Hoey, Clyde R.		204,668 D	31.3%	68.7%	31.3%	68.7%
1950S	544,924	177,753	Gavin, E. L.	364,912	Smith, Willis	2,259	187,159 D	32.6%	67.0%	32.8%	67.2%
1948	764,559	220,307	Wilkinson, John A.	540,762	Broughton, J. M.	3,490	320,455 D	28.8%	70.7%	28.9%	71.1%

The 1958 election and one each of the 1954 and 1950 elections were for short terms to fill vacancies.

NORTH CAROLINA

HOUSE OF REPRESENTATIVES

CD	Year	Total Vote	Republican Vote	Republican Candidate	Democratic Vote	Democratic Candidate	Other Vote	Rep.-Dem. Plurality	Total Vote Rep.	Total Vote Dem.	Major Vote Rep.	Major Vote Dem.
1	2006	82,510		—	82,510	BUTTERFIELD, G. K.*		82,510 D		100.0%		100.0%
1	2004	215,175	77,508	DORITY, GREG	137,667	BUTTERFIELD, G. K.*		60,159 D	36.0%	64.0%	36.0%	64.0%
1	2002	146,157	50,907	DORITY, GREG	93,157	BALANCE, FRANK W. JR.	2,093	42,250 D	34.8%	63.7%	35.3%	64.7%
2	2006	129,264	43,271	MANSELL, DAN	85,993	ETHERIDGE, BOB*		42,722 D	33.5%	66.5%	33.5%	66.5%
2	2004	232,890	87,811	CREECH, BILLY J.	145,079	ETHERIDGE, BOB*		57,268 D	37.7%	62.3%	37.7%	62.3%
2	2002	153,184	50,965	ELLEN, JOSEPH L.	100,121	ETHERIDGE, BOB*	2,098	49,156 D	33.3%	65.4%	33.7%	66.3%
3	2006	144,977	99,519	JONES, WALTER B.*	45,458	WEBER, CRAIG		54,061 R	68.6%	31.4%	68.6%	31.4%
3	2004	243,090	171,863	JONES, WALTER B.*	71,227	EATON, ROGER A.		100,636 R	70.7%	29.3%	70.7%	29.3%
3	2002	144,934	131,448	JONES, WALTER B.*		—	13,486	131,448 R	90.7%		100.0%	
4	2006	195,939	68,599	ACUFF, STEVE	127,340	PRICE, DAVID E.*		58,741 D	35.0%	65.0%	35.0%	65.0%
4	2004	339,234	121,717	BATCHELOR, TODD A.	217,441	PRICE, DAVID E.*	76	95,724 D	35.9%	64.1%	35.9%	64.1%
4	2002	216,046	78,095	NGUYEN, TUAN A.	132,185	PRICE, DAVID E.*	5,766	54,090 D	36.1%	61.2%	37.1%	62.9%
5	2006	168,199	96,138	FOXX, VIRGINIA*	72,061	SHARPE, ROGER		24,077 R	57.2%	42.8%	57.2%	42.8%
5	2004	284,817	167,546	FOXX, VIRGINIA	117,271	HARRELL, JIM A. JR.		50,275 R	58.8%	41.2%	58.8%	41.2%
5	2002	196,437	137,879	BURR, RICHARD M.*	58,558	CRAWFORD, DAVID		79,321 R	70.2%	29.8%	70.2%	29.8%
6	2006	153,094	108,433	COBLE, HOWARD*	44,661	BLAKE, RORY		63,772 R	70.8%	29.2%	70.8%	29.2%
6	2004	283,623	207,470	COBLE, HOWARD*	76,153	JORDAN, WILLIAM W.		131,317 R	73.1%	26.9%	73.1%	26.9%
6	2002	167,497	151,430	COBLE, HOWARD*		—	16,067	151,430 R	90.4%		100.0%	
7	2006	139,820	38,033	DAVIS, SHIRLEY	101,787	McINTYRE, MIKE*		63,754 D	27.2%	72.8%	27.2%	72.8%
7	2004	246,466	66,084	PLONK, KEN	180,382	McINTYRE, MIKE*		114,298 D	26.8%	73.2%	26.8%	73.2%
7	2002	166,654	45,537	ADAMS, JAMES R.	118,543	McINTYRE, MIKE*	2,574	73,006 D	27.3%	71.1%	27.8%	72.2%
8	2006	121,523	60,926	HAYES, ROBIN*	60,597	KISSELL, LARRY		329 R	50.1%	49.9%	50.1%	49.9%
8	2004	225,171	125,070	HAYES, ROBIN*	100,101	TROUTMAN, BETH		24,969 R	55.5%	44.5%	55.5%	44.5%
8	2002	149,736	80,298	HAYES, ROBIN*	66,819	KOURI, CHRIS	2,619	13,479 R	53.6%	44.6%	54.6%	45.4%
9	2006	159,643	106,206	MYRICK, SUE*	53,437	GLASS, BILL		52,769 R	66.5%	33.5%	66.5%	33.5%
9	2004	300,101	210,783	MYRICK, SUE*	89,318	FLYNN, JACK		121,465 R	70.2%	29.8%	70.2%	29.8%
9	2002	193,443	140,095	MYRICK, SUE*	49,974	McGUIRE, ED	3,374	90,121 R	72.4%	25.8%	73.7%	26.3%
10	2006	152,393	94,179	McHENRY, PATRICK T.*	58,214	CARSNER, RICHARD		35,965 R	61.8%	38.2%	61.8%	38.2%
10	2004	246,117	157,884	McHENRY, PATRICK T.	88,233	FISCHER, ANNE N.		69,651 R	64.1%	35.9%	64.1%	35.9%
10	2002	173,292	102,768	BALLENGER, CASS*	65,587	DAUGHERTY, RON	4,937	37,181 R	59.3%	37.8%	61.0%	39.0%
11	2006	232,314	107,342	TAYLOR, CHARLES H.*	124,972	SHULER, HEATH		17,630 D	46.2%	53.8%	46.2%	53.8%
11	2004	290,897	159,709	TAYLOR, CHARLES H.*	131,188	KEEVER, PATSY		28,521 R	54.9%	45.1%	54.9%	45.1%
11	2002	202,260	112,335	TAYLOR, CHARLES H.*	86,664	NEILL, SAM	3,261	25,671 R	55.5%	42.8%	56.5%	43.5%
12	2006	106,472	35,127	FISHER, ADA M.	71,345	WATT, MELVIN*		36,218 D	33.0%	67.0%	33.0%	67.0%
12	2004	231,806	76,898	FISHER, ADA M.	154,908	WATT, MELVIN*		78,010 D	33.2%	66.8%	33.2%	66.8%
12	2002	151,239	49,588	KISH, JEFF	98,821	WATT, MELVIN*	2,830	49,233 D	32.8%	65.3%	33.4%	66.6%
13	2006	154,660	56,120	ROBINSON, VERNON	98,540	MILLER, BRAD*		42,420 D	36.3%	63.7%	36.3%	63.7%
13	2004	273,684	112,788	JOHNSON, VIRGINIA	160,896	MILLER, BRAD*		48,108 D	41.2%	58.8%	41.2%	58.8%
13	2002	183,270	77,688	GRANT, CAROLYN W.	100,287	MILLER, BRAD	5,295	22,599 D	42.4%	54.7%	43.7%	56.3%
TOTAL	2006	1,940,808	913,893		1,026,915			113,022 D	47.1%	52.9%	47.1%	52.9%
TOTAL	2004	3,413,071	1,743,131		1,669,864		76	73,267 R	51.1%	48.9%	51.1%	48.9%
TOTAL	2002	2,244,149	1,209,033		970,716		64,400	238,317 R	53.9%	43.3%	55.5%	44.5%

NORTH CAROLINA

GENERAL AND PRIMARY ELECTIONS

2006 GENERAL ELECTIONS

House   Other vote was:

CD 1
CD 2
CD 3
CD 4
CD 5
CD 6
CD 7
CD 8
CD 9
CD 10
CD 11
CD 12
CD 13

2006 PRIMARY ELECTIONS

Primary	May 2, 2006	**Registration** (as of April 2006)	Democratic	2,505,766
			Republican	1,893,606
			Unaffiliated	1,063,946
			TOTAL	5,463,318

Primary Type   Semi-open—Registered Democrats and Republicans could vote only in their party's primary. Unaffiliated voters could participate in the primary of either party.

NORTH CAROLINA

GENERAL AND PRIMARY ELECTIONS

Note: An asterisk (*) denotes incumbent. The names of unopposed candidates did not appear on the primary ballot; therefore, no votes were cast for these candidates. A runoff was triggered if the leading candidate received less than 40 percent of the primary vote. No runoffs were required in 2006.

	REPUBLICAN PRIMARIES			DEMOCRATIC PRIMARIES		
Congressional District 1	No Republican candidate			G. K. Butterfield*	Unopposed	
Congressional District 2	Dan Mansell	Unopposed		Bob Etheridge*	Unopposed	
Congressional District 3	Walter B. Jones*	Unopposed		Craig Weber	Unopposed	
Congressional District 4	Steve Acuff	Unopposed		David E. Price*	39,637	89.5%
				Kent Kanoy	2,768	6.2%
				Oscar Lewis	1,886	4.3%
				TOTAL	44,291	
Congressional District 5	Virginia Foxx*	Unopposed		Roger Sharpe	8,207	44.7%
				Roger N. Kirkman	4,982	27.1%
				Syndi Holmes	3,321	18.1%
				Mark Dulaney Glen	1,859	10.1%
				TOTAL	18,369	
Congressional District 6	Howard Coble*	Unopposed		Rory Blake	Unopposed	
Congressional District 7	Shirley Davis	Unopposed		Mike McIntyre*	Unopposed	
Congressional District 8	Robin Hayes*	Unopposed		Larry Kissell	13,109	53.5%
				John Autry	4,456	18.2%
				Tim Dunn	4,137	16.9%
				Mark F. Ortiz	2,822	11.5%
				TOTAL	24,524	
Congressional District 9	Sue Myrick*	Unopposed		Bill Glass	Unopposed	
Congressional District 10	Patrick T. McHenry*	Unopposed		Richard Carsner	Unopposed	
Congressional District 11	Charles H. Taylor*	27,413	80.3%	Heath Shuler	29,921	74.6%
	John C. Armor	6,746	19.7%	Michael Morgan	10,180	25.4%
	TOTAL	34,159		TOTAL	40,101	
Congressional District 12	Ada M. Fisher	Unopposed		Melvin Watt*	Unopposed	
				Kimberly "Kim" Holley	4,241	14.8%
				TOTAL	28,615	
Congressional District 13	Vernon Robinson	6,065	62.7%	Brad Miller*	Unopposed	
	Charlie Sutherland	2,417	25.0%			
	John Ross Hendrix	1,187	12.3%			
	TOTAL	9,669				

NORTH DAKOTA

One member At Large

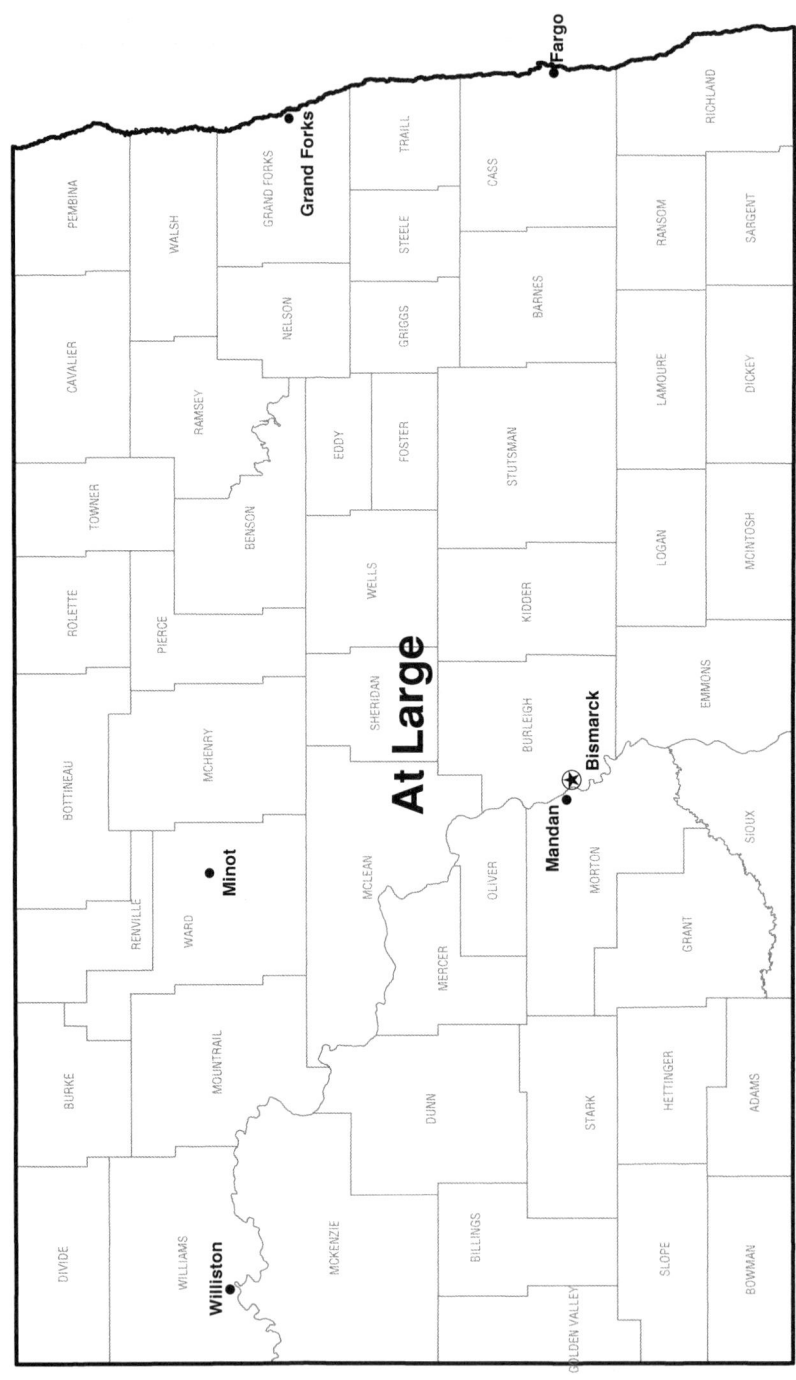

NORTH DAKOTA

GOVERNOR
John Hoeven (R). Reelected 2004 to a four-year term. Previously elected 2000.

SENATORS (2 Democrats)
Kent Conrad (D). Reelected 2006 to a six-year term. Previously elected 2000, 1994 and in a special election December 1992 to fill the remaining two years of the term vacated by the death of Senator Quentin N. Burdick (D), who died in September 1992; elected 1986 to a six-year term.

Byron L. Dorgan (D). Reelected 2004 to a six-year term. Previously elected 1998, 1992.

REPRESENTATIVES (1 Democrat)
At Large. Earl Pomeroy (D)

POSTWAR VOTE FOR PRESIDENT

Year	Total Vote	Republican Vote	Republican Candidate	Democratic Vote	Democratic Candidate	Other Vote	Plurality	Total Vote Rep.	Total Vote Dem.	Major Vote Rep.	Major Vote Dem.
2004	312,833	196,651	Bush, George W.	111,052	Kerry, John	5,130	85,599 R	62.9%	35.5%	63.9%	36.1%
2000**	288,256	174,852	Bush, George W.	95,284	Gore, Al	18,120	79,568 R	60.7%	33.1%	64.7%	35.3%
1996**	266,411	125,050	Dole, Bob	106,905	Clinton, Bill	34,456	18,145 R	46.9%	40.1%	53.9%	46.1%
1992**	308,133	136,244	Bush, George	99,168	Clinton, Bill	72,721	37,076 R	44.2%	32.2%	57.9%	42.1%
1988	297,261	166,559	Bush, George	127,739	Dukakis, Michael S.	2,963	38,820 R	56.0%	43.0%	56.6%	43.4%
1984	308,971	200,336	Reagan, Ronald	104,429	Mondale, Walter F.	4,206	95,907 R	64.8%	33.8%	65.7%	34.3%
1980**	301,545	193,695	Reagan, Ronald	79,189	Carter, Jimmy	28,661	114,506 R	64.2%	26.3%	71.0%	29.0%
1976	297,188	153,470	Ford, Gerald R.	136,078	Carter, Jimmy	7,640	17,392 R	51.6%	45.8%	53.0%	47.0%
1972	280,514	174,109	Nixon, Richard M.	100,384	McGovern, George S.	6,021	73,725 R	62.1%	35.8%	63.4%	36.6%
1968**	247,882	138,669	Nixon, Richard M.	94,769	Humphrey, Hubert H.	14,444	43,900 R	55.9%	38.2%	59.4%	40.6%
1964	258,389	108,207	Goldwater, Barry M.	149,784	Johnson, Lyndon B.	398	41,577 D	41.9%	58.0%	41.9%	58.1%
1960	278,431	154,310	Nixon, Richard M.	123,963	Kennedy, John F.	158	30,347 R	55.4%	44.5%	55.5%	44.5%
1956	253,991	156,766	Eisenhower, Dwight D.	96,742	Stevenson, Adlai E.	483	60,024 R	61.7%	38.1%	61.8%	38.2%
1952	270,127	191,712	Eisenhower, Dwight D.	76,694	Stevenson, Adlai E.	1,721	115,018 R	71.0%	28.4%	71.4%	28.6%
1948	220,716	115,139	Dewey, Thomas E.	95,812	Truman, Harry S.	9,765	19,327 R	52.2%	43.4%	54.6%	45.4%

In past elections, the other vote included: 2000 - 9,486 Green (Ralph Nader); 1996 - 32,515 Reform (Ross Perot); 1992 - 71,084 Independent (Ross Perot); 1980 - 23,640 Independent (John Anderson); 1968 - 14,244 American Independent (George Wallace).

NORTH DAKOTA

POSTWAR VOTE FOR GOVERNOR

Year	Total Vote	Republican Vote	Republican Candidate	Democratic Vote	Democratic Candidate	Other Vote	Rep.-Dem. Plurality	Total Vote Rep.	Total Vote Dem.	Major Vote Rep.	Major Vote Dem.
2004	309,873	220,803	Hoeven, John	84,877	Satrom, Joseph A.	4,193	135,926 R	71.3%	27.4%	72.2%	27.8%
2000	289,412	159,255	Hoeven, John	130,144	Heitkamp, Heidi	13	29,111 R	55.0%	45.0%	55.0%	45.0%
1996	264,298	174,937	Schafer, Edward T.	89,349	Kaldor, Lee	12	85,588 R	66.2%	33.8%	66.2%	33.8%
1992	304,861	176,398	Schafer, Edward T.	123,845	Spaeth, Nicholas	4,618	52,553 R	57.9%	40.6%	58.8%	41.2%
1988	299,080	119,986	Mallberg, Leon L.	179,094	Sinner, George		59,108 D	40.1%	59.9%	40.1%	59.9%
1984	314,382	140,460	Olson, Allen I.	173,922	Sinner, George		33,462 D	44.7%	55.3%	44.7%	55.3%
1980	302,621	162,230	Olson, Allen I.	140,391	Link, Arthur A.		21,839 R	53.6%	46.4%	53.6%	46.4%
1976	297,249	138,321	Elkin, Richard	153,309	Link, Arthur A.	5,619	14,988 D	46.5%	51.6%	47.4%	52.6%
1972	281,931	138,032	Larsen, Richard	143,899	Link, Arthur A.		5,867 D	49.0%	51.0%	49.0%	51.0%
1968	248,000	108,382	McCarney, Robert P.	135,955	Guy, William L.	3,663	27,573 D	43.7%	54.8%	44.4%	55.6%
1964**	262,661	116,247	Halcrow, Donald M.	146,414	Guy, William L.		30,167 D	44.3%	55.7%	44.3%	55.7%
1962	228,509	113,251	Andrews, Mark	115,258	Guy, William L.		2,007 D	49.6%	50.4%	49.6%	50.4%
1960	275,375	122,486	Dahl, C. P.	136,148	Guy, William L.	16,741	13,662 D	44.5%	49.4%	47.4%	52.6%
1958	210,599	111,836	Davis, John E.	98,763	Lord, John F.		13,073 R	53.1%	46.9%	53.1%	46.9%
1956	252,435	147,566	Davis, John E.	104,869	Warner, Wallace E.		42,697 R	58.5%	41.5%	58.5%	41.5%
1954	193,501	124,253	Brunsdale, C. Norman	69,248	Bymers, Cornelius		55,005 R	64.2%	35.8%	64.2%	35.8%
1952	253,934	199,944	Brunsdale, C. Norman	53,990	Johnson, Ole C.		145,954 R	78.7%	21.3%	78.7%	21.3%
1950	183,772	121,822	Brunsdale, C. Norman	61,950	Byerly, Clyde G.		59,872 R	66.3%	33.7%	66.3%	33.7%
1948	214,858	131,764	Aandahl, Fred G.	80,555	Henry, Howard	2,539	51,209 R	61.3%	37.5%	62.1%	37.9%
1946	169,391	116,672	Aandahl, Fred G.	52,719	Burdick, Quentin N.		63,953 R	68.9%	31.1%	68.9%	31.1%

**The term of office of North Dakota's governor was increased from two to four years effective with the 1964 election.

POSTWAR VOTE FOR SENATOR

Year	Total Vote	Republican Vote	Republican Candidate	Democratic Vote	Democratic Candidate	Other Vote	Rep.-Dem. Plurality	Total Vote Rep.	Total Vote Dem.	Major Vote Rep.	Major Vote Dem.
2006	218,152	64,417	Grotberg, Dwight	150,146	Conrad, Kent	3,589	85,729 D	29.5%	68.8%	30.0%	70.0%
2004	310,696	98,553	Liffrig, Mike	212,143	Dorgan, Byron L.		113,590 D	31.7%	68.3%	31.7%	68.3%
2000	287,539	111,069	Sand, Duane	176,470	Conrad, Kent		65,401 D	38.6%	61.4%	38.6%	61.4%
1998	213,358	75,013	Nalewaja, Donna	134,747	Dorgan, Byron L.	3,598	59,734 D	35.2%	63.2%	35.8%	64.2%
1994	236,547	99,390	Clayburg, Ben	137,157	Conrad, Kent		37,767 D	42.0%	58.0%	42.0%	58.0%
1992	303,957	118,162	Sydness, Steve	179,347	Dorgan, Byron L.	6,448	61,185 D	38.9%	59.0%	39.7%	60.3%
1992S	163,311	55,194	Dalrymple, Jack	103,246	Conrad, Kent	4,871	48,052 D	33.8%	63.2%	34.8%	65.2%
1988	289,170	112,937	Striden, Earl	171,899	Burdick, Quentin N.	4,334	58,962 D	39.1%	59.4%	39.6%	60.4%
1986	288,998	141,797	Andrews, Mark	143,932	Conrad, Kent	3,269	2,135 D	49.1%	49.8%	49.6%	50.4%
1982	262,465	89,304	Knorr, Gene	164,873	Burdick, Quentin N.	8,288	75,569 D	34.0%	62.8%	35.1%	64.9%
1980	299,272	210,347	Andrews, Mark	86,658	Johanneson, Kent	2,267	123,689 R	70.3%	29.0%	70.8%	29.2%
1976	283,062	103,466	Stroup, Richard	175,772	Burdick, Quentin N.	3,824	72,306 D	36.6%	62.1%	37.1%	62.9%
1974	235,661	114,117	Young, Milton R.	113,931	Guy, William L.	7,613	186 R	48.4%	48.3%	50.0%	50.0%
1970	219,560	82,996	Kleppe, Tom	134,519	Burdick, Quentin N.	2,045	51,523 D	37.8%	61.3%	38.2%	61.8%
1968	239,776	154,968	Young, Milton R.	80,815	Lashkowitz, Herschel	3,993	74,153 R	64.6%	33.7%	65.7%	34.3%
1964	258,945	109,681	Kleppe, Tom	149,264	Burdick, Quentin N.		39,583 D	42.4%	57.6%	42.4%	57.6%
1962	223,737	135,705	Young, Milton R.	88,032	Lanier, William		47,673 R	60.7%	39.3%	60.7%	39.3%
1960S	210,349	103,475	Davis, John E.	104,593	Burdick, Quentin N.	2,281	1,118 D	49.2%	49.7%	49.7%	50.3%
1958	204,635	117,070	Langer, William	84,892	Vendsel, Raymond	2,673	32,178 R	57.2%	41.5%	58.0%	42.0%
1956	244,161	155,305	Young, Milton R.	87,919	Burdick, Quentin N.	937	67,386 R	63.6%	36.0%	63.9%	36.1%
1952**	237,995	157,907	Langer, William	55,347	Morrison, Harold A.	24,741	102,560 R	66.3%	23.3%	74.0%	26.0%
1950	186,716	126,209	Young, Milton R.	60,507	O'Brien, Harry		65,702 R	67.6%	32.4%	67.6%	32.4%
1946**	165,382	88,210	Langer, William	38,368	Larson, Abner B.	38,804	49,406 R	53.3%	23.2%	69.7%	30.3%
1946S**	136,852	75,998	Young, Milton R.	37,507	Lanier, William	23,347	38,491 R	55.5%	27.4%	67.0%	33.0%

**In past elections, the other vote included: 1952 - 24,741 Independent (Fred G. Aandahl); 1946 - 38,804 Independent (Arthur E. Thompson), who finished second; 1946 Special - 20,848 Independent (Gerald P. Nye). One of the 1992 elections was for a short term to fill a vacancy and the special election was held in December. The 1960 and 1946 special elections were held in June for short terms to fill vacancies.

NORTH DAKOTA

SENATOR 2006

2000 Census Population	County	Total Vote	Republican	Democratic	Other	Rep.-Dem. Plurality	Percentage			
							Total Vote		Major Vote	
							Rep.	Dem.	Rep.	Dem.
2,593	ADAMS	970	287	661	22	374 D	29.6%	68.1%	30.3%	69.7%
11,775	BARNES	4,633	1,658	2,930	45	1,272 D	35.8%	63.2%	36.1%	63.9%
6,964	BENSON	1,842	338	1,464	40	1,126 D	18.3%	79.5%	18.8%	81.2%
888	BILLINGS	430	187	227	16	40 D	43.5%	52.8%	45.2%	54.8%
7,149	BOTTINEAU	3,265	857	2,353	55	1,496 D	26.2%	72.1%	26.7%	73.3%
3,242	BOWMAN	1,105	419	667	19	248 D	37.9%	60.4%	38.6%	61.4%
2,242	BURKE	757	225	521	11	296 D	29.7%	68.8%	30.2%	69.8%
69,416	BURLEIGH	28,631	10,457	17,662	512	7,205 D	36.5%	61.7%	37.2%	62.8%
123,138	CASS	40,271	12,167	27,598	506	15,431 D	30.2%	68.5%	30.6%	69.4%
4,831	CAVALIER	1,711	365	1,322	24	957 D	21.3%	77.3%	21.6%	78.4%
5,757	DICKEY	1,972	767	1,178	27	411 D	38.9%	59.7%	39.4%	60.6%
2,283	DIVIDE	893	197	688	8	491 D	22.1%	77.0%	22.3%	77.7%
3,600	DUNN	1,429	430	961	38	531 D	30.1%	67.2%	30.9%	69.1%
2,757	EDDY	1,134	252	865	17	613 D	22.2%	76.3%	22.6%	77.4%
4,331	EMMONS	1,570	504	1,010	56	506 D	32.1%	64.3%	33.3%	66.7%
3,759	FOSTER	1,415	354	1,029	32	675 D	25.0%	72.7%	25.6%	74.4%
1,924	GOLDEN VALLEY	766	262	481	23	219 D	34.2%	62.8%	35.3%	64.7%
66,109	GRAND FORKS	17,801	4,249	13,260	292	9,011 D	23.9%	74.5%	24.3%	75.7%
2,841	GRANT	1,100	380	689	31	309 D	34.5%	62.6%	35.5%	64.5%
2,754	GRIGGS	1,138	344	784	10	440 D	30.2%	68.9%	30.5%	69.5%
2,715	HETTINGER	1,101	356	715	30	359 D	32.3%	64.9%	33.2%	66.8%
2,753	KIDDER	1,159	368	757	34	389 D	31.8%	65.3%	32.7%	67.3%
4,701	LA MOURE	2,070	681	1,358	31	677 D	32.9%	65.6%	33.4%	66.6%
2,308	LOGAN	895	280	591	24	311 D	31.3%	66.0%	32.1%	67.9%
5,987	MCHENRY	2,259	615	1,613	31	998 D	27.2%	71.4%	27.6%	72.4%
3,390	MCINTOSH	1,481	469	975	37	506 D	31.7%	65.8%	32.5%	67.5%
5,737	MCKENZIE	2,073	687	1,346	40	659 D	33.1%	64.9%	33.8%	66.2%
9,311	MCLEAN	3,495	1,111	2,327	57	1,216 D	31.8%	66.6%	32.3%	67.7%
8,644	MERCER	3,547	1,181	2,288	78	1,107 D	33.3%	64.5%	34.0%	66.0%
25,303	MORTON	9,599	3,084	6,260	255	3,176 D	32.1%	65.2%	33.0%	67.0%
6,631	MOUNTRAIL	2,168	498	1,617	53	1,119 D	23.0%	74.6%	23.5%	76.5%
3,715	NELSON	1,487	316	1,153	18	837 D	21.3%	77.5%	21.5%	78.5%
2,065	OLIVER	906	303	581	22	278 D	33.4%	64.1%	34.3%	65.7%
8,585	PEMBINA	3,030	703	2,284	43	1,581 D	23.2%	75.4%	23.5%	76.5%
4,675	PIERCE	1,978	541	1,409	28	868 D	27.4%	71.2%	27.7%	72.3%
12,066	RAMSEY	3,845	842	2,953	50	2,111 D	21.9%	76.8%	22.2%	77.8%
5,890	RANSOM	2,105	417	1,669	19	1,252 D	19.8%	79.3%	20.0%	80.0%
2,610	RENVILLE	1,094	251	823	20	572 D	22.9%	75.2%	23.4%	76.6%
17,998	RICHLAND	5,475	1,591	3,805	79	2,214 D	29.1%	69.5%	29.5%	70.5%
13,674	ROLETTE	3,710	377	3,244	89	2,867 D	10.2%	87.4%	10.4%	89.6%
4,366	SARGENT	1,702	361	1,319	22	958 D	21.2%	77.5%	21.5%	78.5%
1,710	SHERIDAN	803	309	467	27	158 D	38.5%	58.2%	39.8%	60.2%
4,044	SIOUX	821	117	692	12	575 D	14.3%	84.3%	14.5%	85.5%
767	SLOPE	395	133	247	15	114 D	33.7%	62.5%	35.0%	65.0%
22,636	STARK	7,157	2,137	4,893	127	2,756 D	29.9%	68.4%	30.4%	69.6%
2,258	STEELE	1,043	213	826	4	613 D	20.4%	79.2%	20.5%	79.5%
21,908	STUTSMAN	7,214	2,342	4,760	112	2,418 D	32.5%	66.0%	33.0%	67.0%
2,876	TOWNER	1,288	223	1,045	20	822 D	17.3%	81.1%	17.6%	82.4%
8,477	TRAILL	2,702	725	1,949	28	1,224 D	26.8%	72.1%	27.1%	72.9%
12,389	WALSH	3,841	951	2,823	67	1,872 D	24.8%	73.5%	25.2%	74.8%
58,795	WARD	17,162	5,086	11,842	234	6,756 D	29.6%	69.0%	30.0%	70.0%
5,102	WELLS	1,957	631	1,294	32	663 D	32.2%	66.1%	32.8%	67.2%
19,761	WILLIAMS	5,757	1,819	3,871	67	2,052 D	31.6%	67.2%	32.0%	68.0%
642,200	TOTAL	218,152	64,417	150,146	3,589	85,729 D	29.5%	68.8%	30.0%	70.0%

NORTH DAKOTA

HOUSE OF REPRESENTATIVES

| CD | Year | Total Vote | Republican | | Democratic | | Other Vote | Rep.-Dem. Plurality | Percentage | | | |
| | | | Vote | Candidate | Vote | Candidate | | | Total Vote | | Major Vote | |
									Rep.	Dem.	Rep.	Dem.
AL	2006	217,621	74,687	MECHTEL, MATT	142,934	POMEROY, EARL*		68,247 D	34.3%	65.7%	34.3%	65.7%
AL	2004	310,814	125,684	SAND, DUANE	185,130	POMEROY, EARL*		59,446 D	40.4%	59.6%	40.4%	59.6%
AL	2002	231,030	109,957	CLAYBURGH, RICK	121,073	POMEROY, EARL*		11,116 D	47.6%	52.4%	47.6%	52.4%
AL	2000	285,658	127,251	DORSO, JOHN	151,173	POMEROY, EARL*	7,234	23,922 D	44.5%	52.9%	45.7%	54.3%
AL	1998	215,469	75,013	CRAMER, KEVIN	134,747	POMEROY, EARL*	5,709	59,734 D	34.8%	62.5%	35.8%	64.2%
AL	1996	263,010	113,684	CRAMER, KEVIN	144,833	POMEROY, EARL*	4,493	31,149 D	43.2%	55.1%	44.0%	56.0%
AL	1994	235,389	105,988	PORTER, GARY	123,134	POMEROY, EARL*	6,267	17,146 D	45.0%	52.3%	46.3%	53.7%
AL	1992	297,898	117,442	KORSMO, JOHN T.	169,273	POMEROY, EARL	11,183	51,831 D	39.4%	56.8%	41.0%	59.0%
AL	1990	233,979	81,443	SCHAFER, EDWARD	152,530	DORGAN, BYRON L.*	6	71,087 D	34.8%	65.2%	34.8%	65.2%
AL	1988	299,982	84,475	SYDNESS, STEVE	212,583	DORGAN, BYRON L.*	2,924	128,108 D	28.2%	70.9%	28.4%	71.6%
AL	1986	286,361	66,989	VINJE, SYVER	216,258	DORGAN, BYRON L.*	3,114	149,269 D	23.4%	75.5%	23.7%	76.3%
AL	1984	308,729	65,761	ALTENBURG, LOIS I.	242,968	DORGAN, BYRON L.*		177,207 D	21.3%	78.7%	21.3%	78.7%
AL	1982	260,499	72,241	JONES, KENT	186,534	DORGAN, BYRON L.*	1,724	114,293 D	27.7%	71.6%	27.9%	72.1%
AL	1980	293,076	124,707	SMYKOWSKI, JIM	166,437	DORGAN, BYRON L.	1,932	41,730 D	42.6%	56.8%	42.8%	57.2%
AL	1978	220,348	147,746	ANDREWS, MARK*	68,016	HAGEN, BRUCE	4,586	79,730 R	67.1%	30.9%	68.5%	31.5%
AL	1976	289,881	181,018	ANDREWS, MARK*	104,263	OMDAHL, LLOYD B.	4,600	76,755 R	62.4%	36.0%	63.5%	36.5%
AL	1974	233,688	130,184	ANDREWS, MARK*	103,504	DORGAN, BYRON L.		26,680 R	55.7%	44.3%	55.7%	44.3%
AL	1972	268,721	195,360	ANDREWS, MARK*	72,850	ISTA, RICHARD	511	122,510 R	72.7%	27.1%	72.8%	27.2%

An asterisk (*) denotes incumbent. North Dakota had two House seats before 1972.

NORTH DAKOTA

GENERAL AND PRIMARY ELECTIONS

2006 GENERAL ELECTIONS

Senator   Other vote was 2,194 Independent (Roland Riemers); 1,395 Independent (James Germalic).

House
  At Large

2006 PRIMARY ELECTIONS

Primary   June 13, 2006   **Registration**   No Formal Registration

Primary Type   Open—Any person of voting age could participate in the primary of either party. As of July 1, 2005, North Dakota's voting-age population was 500,159.

Note: An asterisk (*) denotes incumbent.

	REPUBLICAN PRIMARIES			DEMOCRATIC PRIMARIES		
Senator	Dwight Grotberg	40,647	100.0%	Kent Conrad*	58,231	100.0%
House At Large	Matt Mechtel	40,172	100.0%	Earl Pomeroy*	57,316	100.0%

OHIO

Congressional districts first established for elections held in 2002
18 members

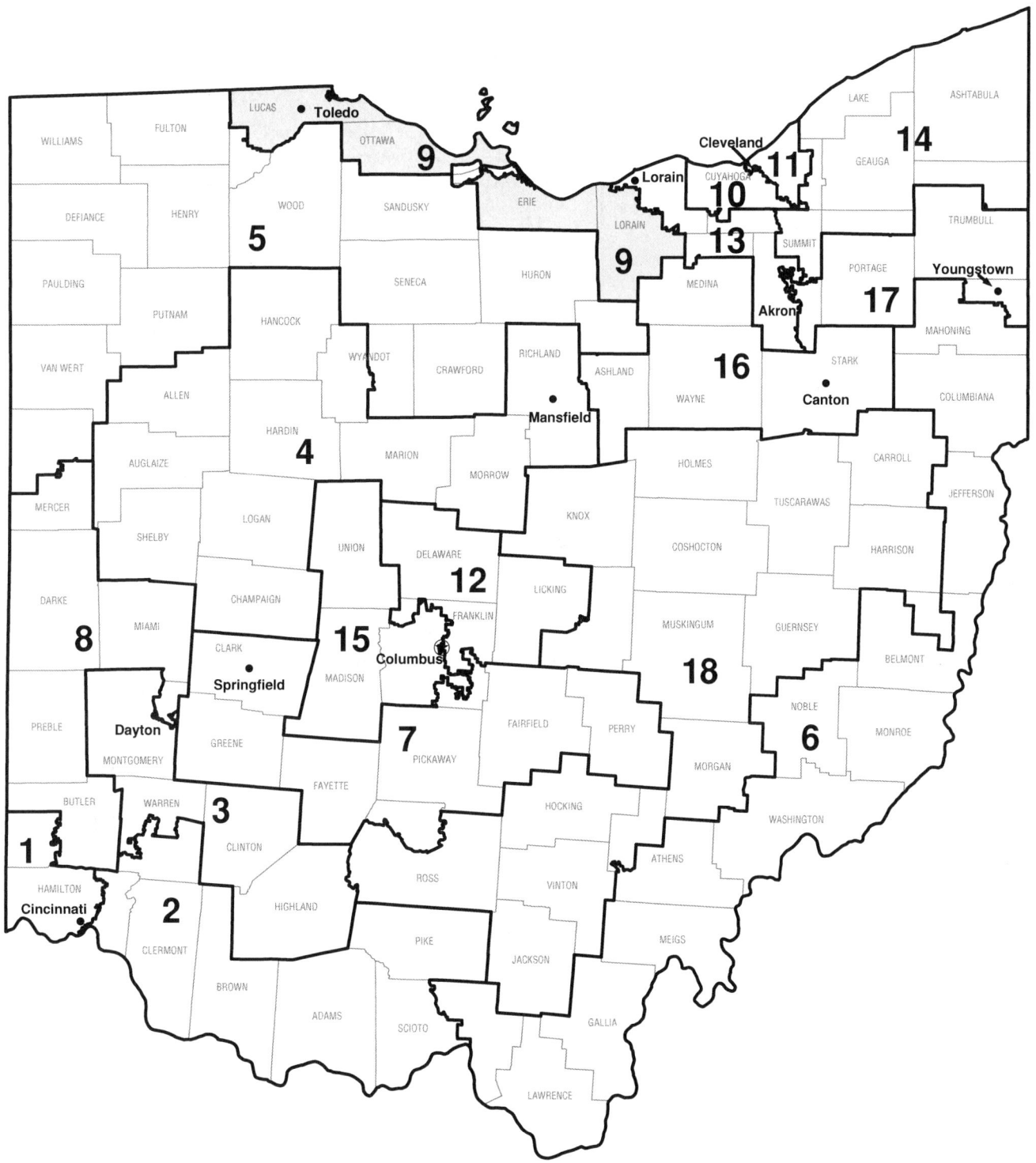

OHIO

Cleveland Area

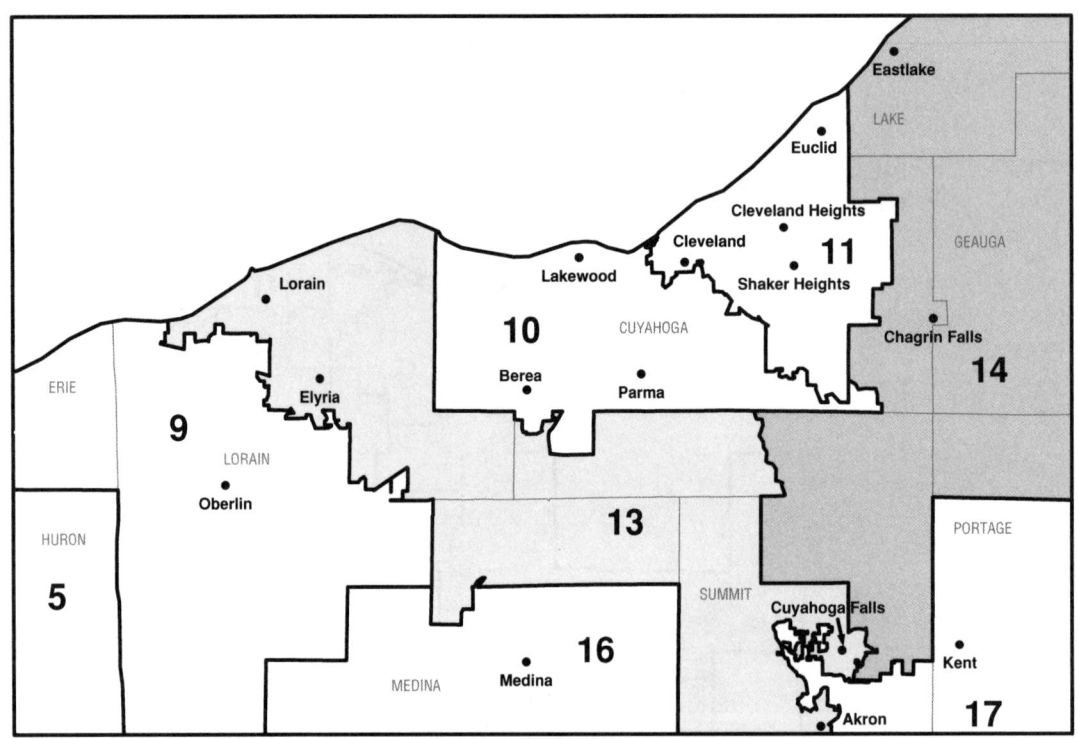

Columbus Area

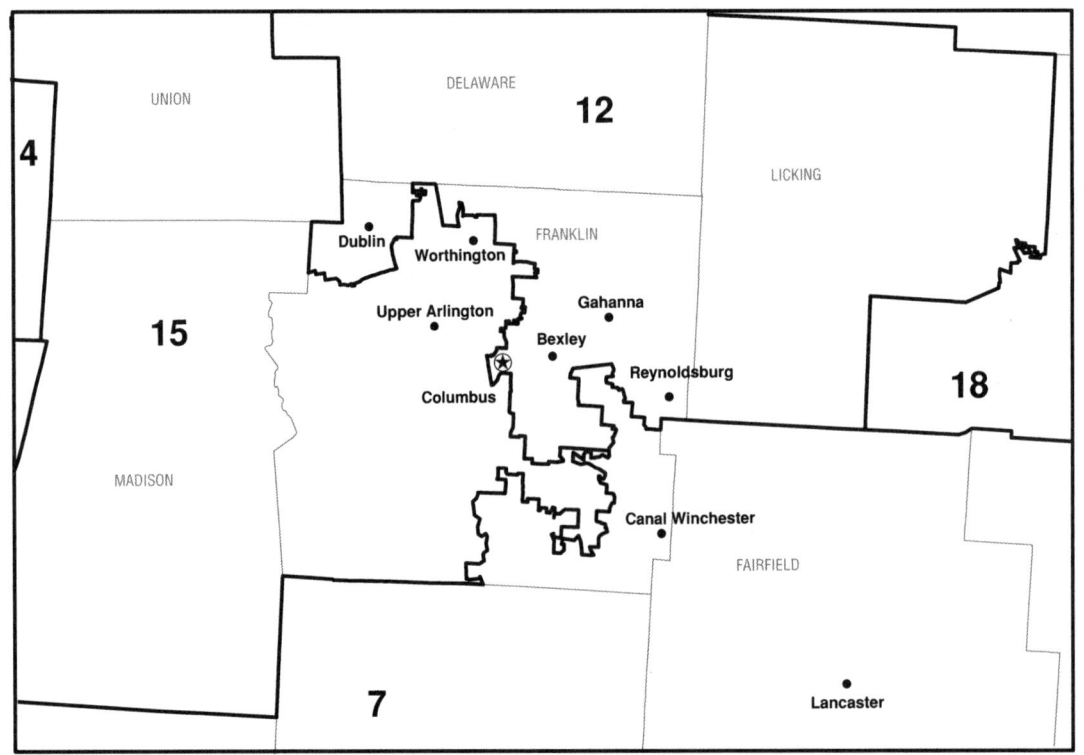

OHIO

GOVERNOR
Ted Strickland (D). Elected 2006 to a four-year term.

SENATORS (1 Democrat, 1 Republican)
Sherrod Brown (D). Elected 2006 to a six-year term.

George V. Voinovich (R). Reelected 2004 to a six-year term. Previously elected 1998.

REPRESENTATIVES (11 Republicans, 7 Democrats)

1. Steve Chabot (R)
2. Jean Schmidt (R)
3. Michael R. Turner (R)
4. Jim Jordan (R)
5. Paul E. Gillmor (R)
6. Charles A. Wilson Jr. (D)
7. David L. Hobson (R)
8. John A. Boehner (R)
9. Marcy Kaptur (D)
10. Dennis J. Kucinich (D)
11. Stephanie Tubbs Jones (D)
12. Pat Tiberi (R)
13. Betty Sutton (D)
14. Steven C. LaTourette (R)
15. Deborah Pryce (R)
16. Ralph Regula (R)
17. Tim Ryan (D)
18. Zack Space (D)

POSTWAR VOTE FOR PRESIDENT

Year	Total Vote	Republican Vote	Republican Candidate	Democratic Vote	Democratic Candidate	Other Vote	Plurality	Total Vote Rep.	Total Vote Dem.	Major Vote Rep.	Major Vote Dem.
2004	5,627,908	2,859,768	Bush, George W.	2,741,167	Kerry, John	26,973	118,601 R	50.8%	48.7%	51.1%	48.9%
2000**	4,701,998	2,350,363	Bush, George W.	2,183,628	Gore, Al	168,007	166,735 R	50.0%	46.4%	51.8%	48.2%
1996**	4,534,434	1,859,883	Dole, Bob	2,148,222	Clinton, Bill	526,329	288,339 D	41.0%	47.4%	46.4%	53.6%
1992**	4,939,967	1,894,310	Bush, George	1,984,942	Clinton, Bill	1,060,715	90,632 D	38.3%	40.2%	48.8%	51.2%
1988	4,393,699	2,416,549	Bush, George	1,939,629	Dukakis, Michael S.	37,521	476,920 R	55.0%	44.1%	55.5%	44.5%
1984	4,547,619	2,678,560	Reagan, Ronald	1,825,440	Mondale, Walter F.	43,619	853,120 R	58.9%	40.1%	59.5%	40.5%
1980**	4,283,603	2,206,545	Reagan, Ronald	1,752,414	Carter, Jimmy	324,644	454,131 R	51.5%	40.9%	55.7%	44.3%
1976	4,111,873	2,000,505	Ford, Gerald R.	2,011,621	Carter, Jimmy	99,747	11,116 D	48.7%	48.9%	49.9%	50.1%
1972	4,094,787	2,441,827	Nixon, Richard M.	1,558,889	McGovern, George S.	94,071	882,938 R	59.6%	38.1%	61.0%	39.0%
1968	3,959,698	1,791,014	Nixon, Richard M.	1,700,586	Humphrey, Hubert H.	468,098	90,428 R	45.2%	42.9%	51.3%	48.7%
1964	3,969,196	1,470,865	Goldwater, Barry M.	2,498,331	Johnson, Lyndon B.		1,027,466 D	37.1%	62.9%	37.1%	62.9%
1960	4,161,859	2,217,611	Nixon, Richard M.	1,944,248	Kennedy, John F.		273,363 R	53.3%	46.7%	53.3%	46.7%
1956	3,702,265	2,262,610	Eisenhower, Dwight D.	1,439,655	Stevenson, Adlai E.		822,955 R	61.1%	38.9%	61.1%	38.9%
1952	3,700,758	2,100,391	Eisenhower, Dwight D.	1,600,367	Stevenson, Adlai E.		500,024 R	56.8%	43.2%	56.8%	43.2%
1948	2,936,071	1,445,684	Dewey, Thomas E.	1,452,791	Truman, Harry S.	37,596	7,107 D	49.2%	49.5%	49.9%	50.1%

**In past elections, the other vote included: 2000 - 117,799 Green (Ralph Nader); 1996 - 483,207 Reform (Ross Perot); 1992 - 1,036,426 Independent (Ross Perot); 1980 - 254,472 Independent (John Anderson); 1968 - 467,495 American Independent (George Wallace).

OHIO

POSTWAR VOTE FOR GOVERNOR

Year	Total Vote	Republican Vote	Republican Candidate	Democratic Vote	Democratic Candidate	Other Vote	Rep.-Dem. Plurality	Total Vote Rep.	Total Vote Dem.	Major Vote Rep.	Major Vote Dem.
2006	4,022,754	1,474,285	Blackwell, J. Kenneth	2,435,384	Strickland, Ted	113,085	961,099 D	36.6%	60.5%	37.7%	62.3%
2002	3,228,992	1,865,007	Taft, Bob	1,236,924	Hagan, Timothy	127,061	628,083 R	57.8%	38.3%	60.1%	39.9%
1998	3,354,213	1,678,721	Taft, Bob	1,498,956	Fisher, Lee	176,536	179,765 R	50.0%	44.7%	52.8%	47.2%
1994	3,346,238	2,401,572	Voinovich, George V.	835,849	Burch, Robert L.	108,817	1,565,723 R	71.8%	25.0%	74.2%	25.8%
1990	3,477,650	1,938,103	Voinovich, George V.	1,539,416	Celebrezze, Anthony J.	131	398,687 R	55.7%	44.3%	55.7%	44.3%
1986	3,066,611	1,207,264	Rhodes, James A.	1,858,372	Celeste, Richard F.	975	651,108 D	39.4%	60.6%	39.4%	60.6%
1982	3,356,721	1,303,962	Brown, Clarence Jr.	1,981,882	Celeste, Richard F.	70,877	677,920 D	38.8%	59.0%	39.7%	60.3%
1978	2,843,351	1,402,167	Rhodes, James A.	1,354,631	Celeste, Richard F.	86,553	47,536 R	49.3%	47.6%	50.9%	49.1%
1974	3,072,010	1,493,679	Rhodes, James A.	1,482,191	Gilligan, John J.	96,140	11,488 R	48.6%	48.2%	50.2%	49.8%
1970	3,184,133	1,382,659	Cloud, Roger	1,725,560	Gilligan, John J.	75,914	342,901 D	43.4%	54.2%	44.5%	55.5%
1966	2,887,331	1,795,277	Rhodes, James A.	1,092,054	Reams, Frazier Jr.		703,223 R	62.2%	37.8%	62.2%	37.8%
1962	3,116,711	1,836,190	Rhodes, James A.	1,280,521	DiSalle, Michael V.		555,669 R	58.9%	41.1%	58.9%	41.1%
1958**	3,284,134	1,414,874	O'Neill, C. William	1,869,260	DiSalle, Michael V.		454,386 D	43.1%	56.9%	43.1%	56.9%
1956	3,542,091	1,984,988	O'Neill, C. William	1,557,103	DiSalle, Michael V.		427,885 R	56.0%	44.0%	56.0%	44.0%
1954	2,597,790	1,192,528	Rhodes, James A.	1,405,262	Lausche, Frank J.		212,734 D	45.9%	54.1%	45.9%	54.1%
1952	3,605,168	1,590,058	Taft, Charles P.	2,015,110	Lausche, Frank J.		425,052 D	44.1%	55.9%	44.1%	55.9%
1950	2,892,819	1,370,570	Ebright, Don H.	1,522,249	Lausche, Frank J.		151,679 D	47.4%	52.6%	47.4%	52.6%
1948	3,018,289	1,398,514	Herbert, Thomas J.	1,619,775	Lausche, Frank J.		221,261 D	46.3%	53.7%	46.3%	53.7%
1946	2,303,750	1,166,550	Herbert, Thomas J.	1,125,997	Lausche, Frank J.	11,203	40,553 R	50.6%	48.9%	50.9%	49.1%

**The term of office of Ohio's governor was increased from two to four years effective with the 1958 election.

POSTWAR VOTE FOR SENATOR

Year	Total Vote	Republican Vote	Republican Candidate	Democratic Vote	Democratic Candidate	Other Vote	Rep.-Dem. Plurality	Total Vote Rep.	Total Vote Dem.	Major Vote Rep.	Major Vote Dem.
2006	4,019,236	1,761,037	DeWine, Mike	2,257,369	Brown, Sherrod	830	496,332 D	43.8%	56.2%	43.8%	56.2%
2004	5,425,823	3,464,356	Voinovich, George V.	1,961,171	Fingerhut, Eric D.	296	1,503,185 R	63.8%	36.1%	63.9%	36.1%
2000	4,448,801	2,665,512	DeWine, Mike	1,595,066	Celeste, Ted	188,223	1,070,446 R	59.9%	35.9%	62.6%	37.4%
1998	3,404,351	1,922,087	Voinovich, George V.	1,482,054	Boyle, Mary O.	210	440,033 R	56.5%	43.5%	56.5%	43.5%
1994	3,436,884	1,836,556	DeWine, Mike	1,348,213	Hyatt, Joel	252,115	488,343 R	53.4%	39.2%	57.7%	42.3%
1992	4,793,953	2,028,300	DeWine, Mike	2,444,419	Glenn, John H.	321,234	416,119 D	42.3%	51.0%	45.3%	54.7%
1988	4,352,905	1,872,716	Voinovich, George V.	2,480,038	Metzenbaum, Howard	151	607,322 D	43.0%	57.0%	43.0%	57.0%
1986	3,121,189	1,171,893	Kindness, Thomas N.	1,949,208	Glenn, John H.	88	777,315 D	37.5%	62.5%	37.5%	62.5%
1982	3,395,463	1,396,790	Pfeifer, Paul E.	1,923,767	Metzenbaum, Howard	74,906	526,977 D	41.1%	56.7%	42.1%	57.9%
1980	4,027,303	1,137,695	Betts, James E.	2,770,786	Glenn, John H.	118,822	1,633,091 D	28.2%	68.8%	29.1%	70.9%
1976	3,920,613	1,823,774	Taft, Robert A. Jr.	1,941,113	Metzenbaum, Howard	155,726	117,339 D	46.5%	49.5%	48.4%	51.6%
1974	2,987,951	918,133	Perk, Ralph J.	1,930,670	Glenn, John H.	139,148	1,012,537 D	30.7%	64.6%	32.2%	67.8%
1970	3,151,274	1,565,682	Taft, Robert A. Jr.	1,495,262	Metzenbaum, Howard	90,330	70,420 R	49.7%	47.4%	51.2%	48.8%
1968	3,743,121	1,928,964	Saxbe, William B.	1,814,152	Gilligan, John J.	5	114,812 R	51.5%	48.5%	51.5%	48.5%
1964	3,830,389	1,906,781	Taft, Robert A. Jr.	1,923,608	Young, Stephen M.		16,827 D	49.8%	50.2%	49.8%	50.2%
1962	2,994,986	1,151,173	Briley, John M.	1,843,813	Lausche, Frank J.		692,640 D	38.4%	61.6%	38.4%	61.6%
1958	3,149,410	1,497,199	Bricker, John W.	1,652,211	Young, Stephen M.		155,012 D	47.5%	52.5%	47.5%	52.5%
1956	3,525,499	1,660,910	Bender, George H.	1,864,589	Lausche, Frank J.		203,679 D	47.1%	52.9%	47.1%	52.9%
1954S	2,512,778	1,257,874	Bender, George H.	1,254,904	Burke, Thomas A.		2,970 R	50.1%	49.9%	50.1%	49.9%
1952	3,442,291	1,878,961	Bricker, John W.	1,563,330	DiSalle, Michael V.		315,631 R	54.6%	45.4%	54.6%	45.4%
1950	2,860,102	1,645,643	Taft, Robert A.	1,214,459	Ferguson, Joseph T.		431,184 R	57.5%	42.5%	57.5%	42.5%
1946	2,237,269	1,275,774	Bricker, John W.	947,610	Huffman, James W.	13,885	328,164 R	57.0%	42.4%	57.4%	42.6%

The 1954 election was for a short term to fill a vacancy.

OHIO

GOVERNOR 2006

2000 Census Population	County	Total Vote	Republican	Democratic	Other	Rep.-Dem. Plurality	Percentage Total Vote Rep.	Dem.	Major Vote Rep.	Dem.
27,330	ADAMS	8,685	3,771	4,725	189	954 D	43.4%	54.4%	44.4%	55.6%
108,473	ALLEN	36,229	17,184	18,000	1,045	816 D	47.4%	49.7%	48.8%	51.2%
52,523	ASHLAND	19,355	9,154	9,492	709	338 D	47.3%	49.0%	49.1%	50.9%
102,728	ASHTABULA	33,865	10,406	22,255	1,204	11,849 D	30.7%	65.7%	31.9%	68.1%
62,223	ATHENS	19,840	3,303	16,188	349	12,885 D	16.6%	81.6%	16.9%	83.1%
46,611	AUGLAIZE	16,907	8,687	7,606	614	1,081 R	51.4%	45.0%	53.3%	46.7%
70,226	BELMONT	23,996	5,593	17,842	561	12,249 D	23.3%	74.4%	23.9%	76.1%
42,285	BROWN	14,044	5,956	7,743	345	1,787 D	42.4%	55.1%	43.5%	56.5%
332,807	BUTLER	115,895	60,018	52,365	3,512	7,653 R	51.8%	45.2%	53.4%	46.6%
28,836	CARROLL	11,152	3,753	6,903	496	3,150 D	33.7%	61.9%	35.2%	64.8%
38,890	CHAMPAIGN	14,264	6,355	7,475	434	1,120 D	44.6%	52.4%	46.0%	54.0%
144,742	CLARK	49,056	18,200	29,364	1,492	11,164 D	37.1%	59.9%	38.3%	61.7%
177,977	CLERMONT	65,010	35,687	27,307	2,016	8,380 R	54.9%	42.0%	56.7%	43.3%
40,543	CLINTON	12,646	5,947	6,342	357	395 D	47.0%	50.2%	48.4%	51.6%
112,075	COLUMBIANA	36,223	11,326	23,914	983	12,588 D	31.3%	66.0%	32.1%	67.9%
36,655	COSHOCTON	13,408	5,184	7,754	470	2,570 D	38.7%	57.8%	40.1%	59.9%
46,966	CRAWFORD	16,744	7,863	8,287	594	424 D	47.0%	49.5%	48.7%	51.3%
1,393,978	CUYAHOGA	454,100	107,234	335,306	11,560	228,072 D	23.6%	73.8%	24.2%	75.8%
53,309	DARKE	20,223	10,018	9,365	840	653 R	49.5%	46.3%	51.7%	48.3%
39,500	DEFIANCE	13,638	6,298	6,798	542	500 D	46.2%	49.8%	48.1%	51.9%
109,989	DELAWARE	64,773	30,931	32,504	1,338	1,573 D	47.8%	50.2%	48.8%	51.2%
79,551	ERIE	30,106	9,089	20,256	761	11,167 D	30.2%	67.3%	31.0%	69.0%
122,759	FAIRFIELD	54,004	22,363	30,180	1,461	7,817 D	41.4%	55.9%	42.6%	57.4%
28,433	FAYETTE	8,402	3,845	4,384	173	539 D	45.8%	52.2%	46.7%	53.3%
1,068,978	FRANKLIN	373,258	122,601	241,536	9,121	118,935 D	32.8%	64.7%	33.7%	66.3%
42,084	FULTON	16,141	7,421	8,193	527	772 D	46.0%	50.8%	47.5%	52.5%
31,069	GALLIA	10,165	3,406	6,574	185	3,168 D	33.5%	64.7%	34.1%	65.9%
90,895	GEAUGA	39,148	15,850	22,154	1,144	6,304 D	40.5%	56.6%	41.7%	58.3%
147,886	GREENE	59,113	28,713	28,612	1,788	101 R	48.6%	48.4%	50.1%	49.9%
40,792	GUERNSEY	13,375	4,601	8,350	424	3,749 D	34.4%	62.4%	35.5%	64.5%
845,303	HAMILTON	287,496	141,374	139,451	6,671	1,923 R	49.2%	48.5%	50.3%	49.7%
71,295	HANCOCK	25,675	14,007	10,934	734	3,073 R	54.6%	42.6%	56.2%	43.8%
31,945	HARDIN	9,723	4,099	5,273	351	1,174 D	42.2%	54.2%	43.7%	56.3%
15,856	HARRISON	6,095	1,661	4,238	196	2,577 D	27.3%	69.5%	28.2%	71.8%
29,210	HENRY	11,473	5,371	5,723	379	352 D	46.8%	49.9%	48.4%	51.6%
40,875	HIGHLAND	13,158	5,822	7,007	329	1,185 D	44.2%	53.3%	45.4%	54.6%
28,241	HOCKING	9,860	2,990	6,619	251	3,629 D	30.3%	67.1%	31.1%	68.9%
38,943	HOLMES	8,108	4,514	3,301	293	1,213 R	55.7%	40.7%	57.8%	42.2%
59,487	HURON	18,917	7,592	10,718	607	3,126 D	40.1%	56.7%	41.5%	58.5%
32,641	JACKSON	10,423	3,150	7,117	156	3,967 D	30.2%	68.3%	30.7%	69.3%
73,894	JEFFERSON	26,133	7,187	18,071	875	10,884 D	27.5%	69.2%	28.5%	71.5%
54,500	KNOX	20,780	9,944	10,278	558	334 D	47.9%	49.5%	49.2%	50.8%
227,511	LAKE	88,006	28,675	56,482	2,849	27,807 D	32.6%	64.2%	33.7%	66.3%
62,319	LAWRENCE	19,109	5,287	13,530	292	8,243 D	27.7%	70.8%	28.1%	71.9%
145,491	LICKING	59,051	24,740	32,455	1,856	7,715 D	41.9%	55.0%	43.3%	56.7%
46,005	LOGAN	16,080	7,941	7,611	528	330 R	49.4%	47.3%	51.1%	48.9%
284,664	LORAIN	100,632	28,342	68,783	3,507	40,441 D	28.2%	68.4%	29.2%	70.8%
455,054	LUCAS	142,784	44,307	95,118	3,359	50,811 D	31.0%	66.6%	31.8%	68.2%
40,213	MADISON	13,441	5,815	7,244	382	1,429 D	43.3%	53.9%	44.5%	55.5%
257,555	MAHONING	95,251	20,356	72,076	2,819	51,720 D	21.4%	75.7%	22.0%	78.0%
66,217	MARION	21,691	9,054	11,963	674	2,909 D	41.7%	55.2%	43.1%	56.9%
151,095	MEDINA	65,511	24,629	39,061	1,821	14,432 D	37.6%	59.6%	38.7%	61.3%
23,072	MEIGS	7,707	2,285	5,295	127	3,010 D	29.6%	68.7%	30.1%	69.9%
40,924	MERCER	15,646	9,429	5,692	525	3,737 R	60.3%	36.4%	62.4%	37.6%
98,868	MIAMI	37,054	18,395	17,263	1,396	1,132 R	49.6%	46.6%	51.6%	48.4%
15,180	MONROE	6,066	1,237	4,682	147	3,445 D	20.4%	77.2%	20.9%	79.1%
559,062	MONTGOMERY	189,201	76,189	107,593	5,419	31,404 D	40.3%	56.9%	41.5%	58.5%
14,897	MORGAN	5,516	1,876	3,468	172	1,592 D	34.0%	62.9%	35.1%	64.9%
31,628	MORROW	12,575	5,668	6,425	482	757 D	45.1%	51.1%	46.9%	53.1%
84,585	MUSKINGUM	28,719	11,073	16,733	913	5,660 D	38.6%	58.3%	39.8%	60.2%

OHIO

GOVERNOR 2006

2000 Census Population	County	Total Vote	Republican	Democratic	Other	Rep.-Dem. Plurality	Percentage			
							Total Vote		Major Vote	
							Rep.	Dem.	Rep.	Dem.
14,058	NOBLE	5,072	1,583	3,342	147	1,759 D	31.2%	65.9%	32.1%	67.9%
40,985	OTTAWA	17,207	5,809	10,858	540	5,049 D	33.8%	63.1%	34.9%	65.1%
20,293	PAULDING	7,479	3,276	3,717	486	441 D	43.8%	49.7%	46.8%	53.2%
34,078	PERRY	11,291	3,577	7,371	343	3,794 D	31.7%	65.3%	32.7%	67.3%
52,727	PICKAWAY	17,960	6,953	10,609	398	3,656 D	38.7%	59.1%	39.6%	60.4%
27,695	PIKE	9,776	2,511	7,118	147	4,607 D	25.7%	72.8%	26.1%	73.9%
152,061	PORTAGE	54,970	16,223	36,553	2,194	20,330 D	29.5%	66.5%	30.7%	69.3%
42,337	PREBLE	15,553	7,096	7,863	594	767 D	45.6%	50.6%	47.4%	52.6%
34,726	PUTNAM	14,161	7,248	6,439	474	809 R	51.2%	45.5%	53.0%	47.0%
128,852	RICHLAND	45,799	19,855	24,398	1,546	4,543 D	43.4%	53.3%	44.9%	55.1%
73,345	ROSS	23,839	7,452	15,930	457	8,478 D	31.3%	66.8%	31.9%	68.1%
61,792	SANDUSKY	22,736	8,467	13,473	796	5,006 D	37.2%	59.3%	38.6%	61.4%
79,195	SCIOTO	26,369	6,328	19,784	257	13,456 D	24.0%	75.0%	24.2%	75.8%
58,683	SENECA	20,051	8,011	11,387	653	3,376 D	40.0%	56.8%	41.3%	58.7%
47,910	SHELBY	17,029	8,358	8,061	610	297 R	49.1%	47.3%	50.9%	49.1%
378,098	STARK	139,414	45,413	89,416	4,585	44,003 D	32.6%	64.1%	33.7%	66.3%
542,899	SUMMIT	197,747	57,344	135,147	5,256	77,803 D	29.0%	68.3%	29.8%	70.2%
225,116	TRUMBULL	81,128	18,556	60,161	2,411	41,605 D	22.9%	74.2%	23.6%	76.4%
90,914	TUSCARAWAS	31,585	10,134	20,556	895	10,422 D	32.1%	65.1%	33.0%	67.0%
40,909	UNION	16,877	8,613	7,689	575	924 R	51.0%	45.6%	52.8%	47.2%
29,659	VAN WERT	10,409	5,331	4,514	564	817 R	51.2%	43.4%	54.1%	45.9%
12,806	VINTON	4,422	1,166	3,165	91	1,999 D	26.4%	71.6%	26.9%	73.1%
158,383	WARREN	68,091	39,094	27,434	1,563	11,660 R	57.4%	40.3%	58.8%	41.2%
63,251	WASHINGTON	22,788	7,412	15,037	339	7,625 D	32.5%	66.0%	33.0%	67.0%
111,564	WAYNE	38,546	17,504	19,820	1,222	2,316 D	45.4%	51.4%	46.9%	53.1%
39,188	WILLIAMS	13,033	5,853	6,696	484	843 D	44.9%	51.4%	46.6%	53.4%
121,065	WOOD	45,616	17,500	26,771	1,345	9,271 D	38.4%	58.7%	39.5%	60.5%
22,908	WYANDOT	8,160	3,852	4,097	211	245 D	47.2%	50.2%	48.5%	51.5%
11,353,140	TOTAL	4,022,754	1,474,285	2,435,384	113,085	961,099 D	36.6%	60.5%	37.7%	62.3%

OHIO

SENATOR 2006

2000 Census Population	County	Total Vote	Republican	Democratic	Other	Rep.-Dem. Plurality	Percentage			
							Total Vote		Major Vote	
							Rep.	Dem.	Rep.	Dem.
27,330	ADAMS	8,570	4,667	3,903		764 R	54.5%	45.5%	54.5%	45.5%
108,473	ALLEN	36,123	19,521	16,597	5	2,924 R	54.0%	45.9%	54.0%	46.0%
52,523	ASHLAND	19,198	10,299	8,890	9	1,409 R	53.6%	46.3%	53.7%	46.3%
102,728	ASHTABULA	34,230	13,078	21,151	1	8,073 D	38.2%	61.8%	38.2%	61.8%
62,223	ATHENS	19,827	5,839	13,988		8,149 D	29.4%	70.6%	29.4%	70.6%
46,611	AUGLAIZE	16,995	10,142	6,845	8	3,297 R	59.7%	40.3%	59.7%	40.3%
70,226	BELMONT	23,556	8,056	15,490	10	7,434 D	34.2%	65.8%	34.2%	65.8%
42,285	BROWN	14,104	7,247	6,850	7	397 R	51.4%	48.6%	51.4%	48.6%
332,807	BUTLER	115,302	65,854	49,443	5	16,411 R	57.1%	42.9%	57.1%	42.9%
28,836	CARROLL	11,053	4,908	6,143	2	1,235 D	44.4%	55.6%	44.4%	55.6%
38,890	CHAMPAIGN	14,409	7,598	6,809	2	789 R	52.7%	47.3%	52.7%	47.3%
144,742	CLARK	50,062	23,656	26,400	6	2,744 D	47.3%	52.7%	47.3%	52.7%
177,977	CLERMONT	64,955	39,588	25,333	34	14,255 R	60.9%	39.0%	61.0%	39.0%
40,543	CLINTON	12,693	7,687	5,005	1	2,682 R	60.6%	39.4%	60.6%	39.4%
112,075	COLUMBIANA	36,829	15,025	21,802	2	6,777 D	40.8%	59.2%	40.8%	59.2%

OHIO

SENATOR 2006

2000 Census Population	County	Total Vote	Republican	Democratic	Other	Rep.-Dem. Plurality	Total Vote Rep.	Total Vote Dem.	Major Vote Rep.	Major Vote Dem.
36,655	COSHOCTON	13,366	6,340	7,024	2	684 D	47.4%	52.6%	47.4%	52.6%
46,966	CRAWFORD	16,683	8,455	8,227	1	228 R	50.7%	49.3%	50.7%	49.3%
1,393,978	CUYAHOGA	452,832	133,235	319,568	29	186,333 D	29.4%	70.6%	29.4%	70.6%
53,309	DARKE	20,187	11,911	8,267	9	3,644 R	59.0%	41.0%	59.0%	41.0%
39,500	DEFIANCE	13,607	6,977	6,624	6	353 R	51.3%	48.7%	51.3%	48.7%
109,989	DELAWARE	64,750	37,624	27,109	17	10,515 R	58.1%	41.9%	58.1%	41.9%
79,551	ERIE	30,391	11,018	19,372	1	8,354 D	36.3%	63.7%	36.3%	63.7%
122,759	FAIRFIELD	53,801	28,506	25,283	12	3,223 R	53.0%	47.0%	53.0%	47.0%
28,433	FAYETTE	8,446	4,651	3,793	2	858 R	55.1%	44.9%	55.1%	44.9%
1,068,978	FRANKLIN	372,110	154,098	217,961	51	63,863 D	41.4%	58.6%	41.4%	58.6%
42,084	FULTON	16,021	8,079	7,936	6	143 R	50.4%	49.5%	50.4%	49.6%
31,069	GALLIA	10,058	5,255	4,803		452 R	52.2%	47.8%	52.2%	47.8%
90,895	GEAUGA	39,573	19,653	19,903	17	250 D	49.7%	50.3%	49.7%	50.3%
147,886	GREENE	59,288	34,797	24,415	76	10,382 R	58.7%	41.2%	58.8%	41.2%
40,792	GUERNSEY	13,239	5,905	7,334		1,429 D	44.6%	55.4%	44.6%	55.4%
845,303	HAMILTON	286,397	144,167	142,134	96	2,033 R	50.3%	49.6%	50.4%	49.6%
71,295	HANCOCK	25,622	15,121	10,498	3	4,623 R	59.0%	41.0%	59.0%	41.0%
31,945	HARDIN	9,584	4,803	4,779	2	24 R	50.1%	49.9%	50.1%	49.9%
15,856	HARRISON	5,981	2,450	3,530	1	1,080 D	41.0%	59.0%	41.0%	59.0%
29,210	HENRY	11,363	6,007	5,354	2	653 R	52.9%	47.1%	52.9%	47.1%
40,875	HIGHLAND	12,981	7,297	5,674	10	1,623 R	56.2%	43.7%	56.3%	43.7%
28,241	HOCKING	9,729	4,062	5,664	3	1,602 D	41.8%	58.2%	41.8%	58.2%
38,943	HOLMES	8,055	5,241	2,810	4	2,431 R	65.1%	34.9%	65.1%	34.9%
59,487	HURON	18,930	8,694	10,234	2	1,540 D	45.9%	54.1%	45.9%	54.1%
32,641	JACKSON	10,288	4,833	5,453	2	620 D	47.0%	53.0%	47.0%	53.0%
73,894	JEFFERSON	25,661	9,988	15,673		5,685 D	38.9%	61.1%	38.9%	61.1%
54,500	KNOX	20,678	11,036	9,641	1	1,395 R	53.4%	46.6%	53.4%	46.6%
227,511	LAKE	88,652	37,988	50,649	15	12,661 D	42.9%	57.1%	42.9%	57.1%
62,319	LAWRENCE	19,477	8,916	10,561		1,645 D	45.8%	54.2%	45.8%	54.2%
145,491	LICKING	58,923	30,312	28,599	12	1,713 R	51.4%	48.5%	51.5%	48.5%
46,005	LOGAN	16,210	9,297	6,909	4	2,388 R	57.4%	42.6%	57.4%	42.6%
284,664	LORAIN	101,563	34,129	67,429	5	33,300 D	33.6%	66.4%	33.6%	66.4%
455,054	LUCAS	142,304	47,659	94,630	15	46,971 D	33.5%	66.5%	33.5%	66.5%
40,213	MADISON	13,529	7,110	6,414	5	696 R	52.6%	47.4%	52.6%	47.4%
257,555	MAHONING	94,815	25,151	69,664		44,513 D	26.5%	73.5%	26.5%	73.5%
66,217	MARION	21,604	10,526	11,078		552 D	48.7%	51.3%	48.7%	51.3%
151,095	MEDINA	65,583	29,186	36,386	11	7,200 D	44.5%	55.5%	44.5%	55.5%
23,072	MEIGS	7,759	3,769	3,990		221 D	48.6%	51.4%	48.6%	51.4%
40,924	MERCER	15,532	10,118	5,413	1	4,705 R	65.1%	34.9%	65.1%	34.9%
98,868	MIAMI	37,039	21,299	15,734	6	5,565 R	57.5%	42.5%	57.5%	42.5%
15,180	MONROE	6,067	1,935	4,131	1	2,196 D	31.9%	68.1%	31.9%	68.1%
559,062	MONTGOMERY	188,836	88,322	100,491	23	12,169 D	46.8%	53.2%	46.8%	53.2%
14,897	MORGAN	5,484	2,523	2,955	6	432 D	46.0%	53.9%	46.1%	53.9%
31,628	MORROW	12,481	6,499	5,976	6	523 R	52.1%	47.9%	52.1%	47.9%
84,585	MUSKINGUM	28,200	12,534	15,664	2	3,130 D	44.4%	55.5%	44.4%	55.6%
14,058	NOBLE	5,170	2,559	2,611		52 D	49.5%	50.5%	49.5%	50.5%
40,985	OTTAWA	17,521	6,972	10,548	1	3,576 D	39.8%	60.2%	39.8%	60.2%
20,293	PAULDING	7,533	3,976	3,556	1	420 R	52.8%	47.2%	52.8%	47.2%
34,078	PERRY	11,189	4,555	6,627	7	2,072 D	40.7%	59.2%	40.7%	59.3%
52,727	PICKAWAY	17,917	9,059	8,858		201 R	50.6%	49.4%	50.6%	49.4%
27,695	PIKE	9,645	3,798	5,845	2	2,047 D	39.4%	60.6%	39.4%	60.6%
152,061	PORTAGE	54,685	20,075	34,576	34	14,501 D	36.7%	63.2%	36.7%	63.3%
42,337	PREBLE	15,703	8,436	7,221	46	1,215 R	53.7%	46.0%	53.9%	46.1%
34,726	PUTNAM	14,141	8,539	5,600	2	2,939 R	60.4%	39.6%	60.4%	39.6%
128,852	RICHLAND	45,889	21,451	24,431	7	2,980 D	46.7%	53.2%	46.8%	53.2%
73,345	ROSS	23,566	10,501	13,061	4	2,560 D	44.6%	55.4%	44.6%	55.4%
61,792	SANDUSKY	22,882	9,983	12,899		2,916 D	43.6%	56.4%	43.6%	56.4%
79,195	SCIOTO	26,174	10,308	15,866		5,558 D	39.4%	60.6%	39.4%	60.6%
58,683	SENECA	20,086	9,343	10,742	1	1,399 D	46.5%	53.5%	46.5%	53.5%
47,910	SHELBY	17,226	10,101	7,122	3	2,979 R	58.6%	41.3%	58.6%	41.4%

OHIO

SENATOR 2006

2000 Census Population	County	Total Vote	Republican	Democratic	Other	Rep.-Dem. Plurality		Percentage			
								Total Vote		Major Vote	
								Rep.	Dem.	Rep.	Dem.
378,098	STARK	139,264	59,353	79,900	11	20,547	D	42.6%	57.4%	42.6%	57.4%
542,899	SUMMIT	199,416	72,559	126,776	81	54,217	D	36.4%	63.6%	36.4%	63.6%
225,116	TRUMBULL	80,124	21,520	58,586	18	37,066	D	26.9%	73.1%	26.9%	73.1%
90,914	TUSCARAWAS	31,385	14,024	17,360	1	3,336	D	44.7%	55.3%	44.7%	55.3%
40,909	UNION	16,843	9,950	6,881	12	3,069	R	59.1%	40.9%	59.1%	40.9%
29,659	VAN WERT	10,420	6,239	4,177	4	2,062	R	59.9%	40.1%	59.9%	40.1%
12,806	VINTON	4,485	2,001	2,484		483	D	44.6%	55.4%	44.6%	55.4%
158,383	WARREN	68,698	43,588	25,102	8	18,486	R	63.4%	36.5%	63.5%	36.5%
63,251	WASHINGTON	22,771	11,140	11,631		491	D	48.9%	51.1%	48.9%	51.1%
111,564	WAYNE	38,293	19,985	18,299	9	1,686	R	52.2%	47.8%	52.2%	47.8%
39,188	WILLIAMS	12,988	6,543	6,438	7	105	R	50.4%	49.6%	50.4%	49.6%
121,065	WOOD	45,515	19,637	25,875	3	6,238	D	43.1%	56.8%	43.1%	56.9%
22,908	WYANDOT	8,122	4,201	3,912	9	289	R	51.7%	48.2%	51.8%	48.2%
11,353,140	TOTAL	4,019,236	1,761,037	2,257,369	830	496,332	D	43.8%	56.2%	43.8%	56.2%

OHIO

HOUSE OF REPRESENTATIVES

CD	Year	Total Vote	Republican		Democratic		Other Vote	Rep.-Dem. Plurality		Percentage			
			Vote	Candidate	Vote	Candidate				Total Vote		Major Vote	
										Rep.	Dem.	Rep.	Dem.
1	2006	202,264	105,680	CHABOT, STEVE*	96,584	CRANLEY, JOHN		9,096	R	52.2%	47.8%	52.2%	47.8%
1	2004	289,863	173,430	CHABOT, STEVE*	116,235	HARRIS, GREG	198	57,195	R	59.8%	40.1%	59.9%	40.1%
1	2002	170,928	110,760	CHABOT, STEVE*	60,168	HARRIS, GREG		50,592	R	64.8%	35.2%	64.8%	35.2%
2	2006	238,081	120,112	SCHMIDT, JEAN	117,595	WULSIN, VICTORIA	374	2,517	R	50.5%	49.4%	50.5%	49.5%
2	2004	316,760	227,102	PORTMAN, ROB*	89,598	SANDERS, CHARLES	60	137,504	R	71.7%	28.3%	71.7%	28.3%
2	2002	188,016	139,218	PORTMAN, ROB*	48,785	SANDERS, CHARLES	13	90,433	R	74.0%	25.9%	74.1%	25.9%
3	2006	218,628	127,978	TURNER, MICHAEL R.*	90,650	CHEMA, RICHARD		37,328	R	58.5%	41.5%	58.5%	41.5%
3	2004	316,738	197,290	TURNER, MICHAEL R.*	119,448	MITAKIDES, JANE		77,842	R	62.3%	37.7%	62.3%	37.7%
3	2002	189,951	111,630	TURNER, MICHAEL R.	78,307	CARNE, RICK	14	33,323	R	58.8%	41.2%	58.8%	41.2%
4	2006	216,636	129,958	JORDAN, JIM	86,678	SIFERD, RICHARD E.		43,280	R	60.0%	40.0%	60.0%	40.0%
4	2004	286,345	167,807	OXLEY, MICHAEL G.*	118,538	KONOP, BEN		49,269	R	58.6%	41.4%	58.6%	41.4%
4	2002	177,727	120,001	OXLEY, MICHAEL G.*	57,726	CLARK, JIM		62,275	R	67.5%	32.5%	67.5%	32.5%
5	2006	228,357	129,813	GILLMOR, PAUL E.*	98,544	WEIRAUCH, ROBIN		31,269	R	56.8%	43.2%	56.8%	43.2%
5	2004	293,305	196,649	GILLMOR, PAUL E.*	96,656	WEIRAUCH, ROBIN		99,993	R	67.0%	33.0%	67.0%	33.0%
5	2002	188,254	126,286	GILLMOR, PAUL E.*	51,872	ANDERSON, ROGER	10,096	74,414	R	67.1%	27.6%	70.9%	29.1%
6	2006	218,476	82,848	BLASDEL, CHUCK	135,628	WILSON, CHARLES A. JR.		52,780	D	37.9%	62.1%	37.9%	62.1%
6	2004	223,989		—	223,844	STRICKLAND, TED*	145	223,844	D		99.9%		100.0%
6	2002	191,615	77,643	HALLECK, MIKE	113,972	STRICKLAND, TED*		36,329	D	40.5%	59.5%	40.5%	59.5%
7	2006	227,478	137,899	HOBSON, DAVID L.*	89,579	CONNER, WILLIAM R.		48,320	R	60.6%	39.4%	60.6%	39.4%
7	2004	287,151	186,534	HOBSON, DAVID L.*	100,617	ANASTASIO, KARA		85,917	R	65.0%	35.0%	65.0%	35.0%
7	2002	167,632	113,252	HOBSON, DAVID L.*	45,568	ANASTASIO, KARA	8,812	67,684	R	67.6%	27.2%	71.3%	28.7%
8	2006	214,503	136,863	BOEHNER, JOHN A.*	77,640	MEIER, MORT		59,223	R	63.8%	36.2%	63.8%	36.2%
8	2004	292,249	201,675	BOEHNER, JOHN A.*	90,574	HARDENBROOK, JEFF		111,101	R	69.0%	31.0%	69.0%	31.0%
8	2002	169,391	119,947	BOEHNER, JOHN A.*	49,444	HARDENBROOK, JEFF		70,503	R	70.8%	29.2%	70.8%	29.2%
9	2006	208,999	55,119	LEAVITT, BRADLEY S.	153,880	KAPTUR, MARCY*		98,761	D	26.4%	73.6%	26.4%	73.6%
9	2004	301,132	95,983	KACZALA, LARRY A.	205,149	KAPTUR, MARCY*		109,166	D	31.9%	68.1%	31.9%	68.1%
9	2002	178,717	46,481	EMERY, ED	132,236	KAPTUR, MARCY*		85,755	D	26.0%	74.0%	26.0%	74.0%

OHIO

HOUSE OF REPRESENTATIVES

CD	Year	Total Vote	Republican Vote	Republican Candidate	Democratic Vote	Democratic Candidate	Other Vote	Rep.-Dem. Plurality	Total Vote Rep.	Total Vote Dem.	Major Vote Rep.	Major Vote Dem.
10	2006	208,389	69,996	DOVILLA, MICHAEL D.	138,393	KUCINICH, DENNIS J.*		68,397 D	33.6%	66.4%	33.6%	66.4%
10	2004	287,212	96,463	HERMAN, EDWARD FITZPATRICK	172,406	KUCINICH, DENNIS J.*	18,343	75,943 D	33.6%	60.0%	35.9%	64.1%
10	2002	175,536	41,778	HEBEN, JON	129,997	KUCINICH, DENNIS J.*	3,761	88,219 D	23.8%	74.1%	24.3%	75.7%
11	2006	175,924	29,125	STRING, LINDSEY N.	146,799	JONES, STEPHANIE TUBBS*		117,674 D	16.6%	83.4%	16.6%	83.4%
11	2004	222,371		—	222,371	JONES, STEPHANIE TUBBS*		222,371 D		100.0%		100.0%
11	2002	152,736	36,146	PAPPANO, PATRICK	116,590	JONES, STEPHANIE TUBBS*		80,444 D	23.7%	76.3%	23.7%	76.3%
12	2006	254,689	145,943	TIBERI, PAT*	108,746	SHAMANSKY, BOB		37,197 R	57.3%	42.7%	57.3%	42.7%
12	2004	321,046	198,912	TIBERI, PAT*	122,109	BROWN, EDWARD	25	76,803 R	62.0%	38.0%	62.0%	38.0%
12	2002	181,689	116,982	TIBERI, PAT*	64,707	BROWN, EDWARD		52,275 R	64.4%	35.6%	64.4%	35.6%
13	2006	221,561	85,922	FOLTIN, CRAIG	135,639	SUTTON, BETTY		49,717 D	38.8%	61.2%	38.8%	61.2%
13	2004	298,094	97,090	LUCAS, ROBERT	201,004	BROWN, SHERROD*		103,914 D	32.6%	67.4%	32.6%	67.4%
13	2002	178,382	55,357	OLIVEROS, ED	123,025	BROWN, SHERROD*		67,668 D	31.0%	69.0%	31.0%	69.0%
14	2006	250,322	144,069	LaTOURETTE, STEVEN C.*	97,753	KATZ, LEWIS R.	8,500	46,316 R	57.6%	39.1%	59.6%	40.4%
14	2004	321,366	201,652	LaTOURETTE, STEVEN C.*	119,714	CAFARO, CAPRI S.		81,938 R	62.7%	37.3%	62.7%	37.3%
14	2002	186,372	134,413	LaTOURETTE, STEVEN C.*	51,846	BLANCHARD, DALE	113	82,567 R	72.1%	27.8%	72.2%	27.8%
15	2006	220,567	110,714	PRYCE, DEBORAH*	109,659	KILROY, MARY JO	194	1,055 R	50.2%	49.7%	50.2%	49.8%
15	2004	277,435	166,520	PRYCE, DEBORAH*	110,915	BROWN, MARK		55,605 R	60.0%	40.0%	60.0%	40.0%
15	2002	162,479	108,193	PRYCE, DEBORAH*	54,286	BROWN, MARK		53,907 R	66.6%	33.4%	66.6%	33.4%
16	2006	235,122	137,167	REGULA, RALPH*	97,955	SHAW, THOMAS		39,212 R	58.3%	41.7%	58.3%	41.7%
16	2004	304,361	202,544	REGULA, RALPH*	101,817	SEEMANN, JEFF		100,727 R	66.5%	33.5%	66.5%	33.5%
16	2002	188,378	129,734	REGULA, RALPH*	58,644	RICE, JIM		71,090 R	68.9%	31.1%	68.9%	31.1%
17	2006	212,294	41,925	MANNING, DON III	170,369	RYAN, TIM*		128,444 D	19.7%	80.3%	19.7%	80.3%
17	2004	275,671	62,871	CUSIMANO, FRANK V.	212,800	RYAN, TIM*		149,929 D	22.8%	77.2%	22.8%	77.2%
17	2002	184,674	62,188	BENJAMIN, ANN WOMER	94,441	RYAN, TIM	28,045	32,253 D	33.7%	51.1%	39.7%	60.3%
18	2006	208,905	79,259	PADGETT, JOY	129,646	SPACE, ZACK		50,387 D	37.9%	62.1%	37.9%	62.1%
18	2004	268,420	177,600	NEY, BOB*	90,820	THOMAS, BRIAN R.		86,780 R	66.2%	33.8%	66.2%	33.8%
18	2002	125,546	125,546	NEY, BOB*		—		125,546 R	100.0%		100.0%	
TOTAL	2006	3,961,195	1,870,390		2,081,737		9,068	211,347 D	47.2%	52.6%	47.3%	52.7%
TOTAL	2004	5,183,508	2,650,122		2,514,615		18,771	135,507 R	51.1%	48.5%	51.3%	48.7%
TOTAL	2002	3,158,023	1,775,555		1,331,614		50,854	443,941 R	56.2%	42.2%	57.1%	42.9%

An asterisk (*) denotes incumbent.

OHIO

GENERAL AND PRIMARY ELECTION

2006 GENERAL ELECTIONS

Governor Other vote was 71,468 Non-Partisan (William S. Peirce); 40,965 Non-Partisan (Robert Fitrakis); 579 write-in (James Lundeen); 73 write-in (Larry Bays).

Senator Other vote was 830 write-in (Richard Duncan).

House Other vote was:

CD 1
CD 2   298 write-in (Nathan Noy); 76 write-in (James J. Condit Jr.).
CD 3
CD 4
CD 5
CD 6
CD 7
CD 8
CD 9
CD 10
CD 11
CD 12
CD 13
CD 14   8,500 Non-Partisan (Werner J. Lange).
CD 15   194 write-in (Bill Buckel).
CD 16
CD 17
CD 18

2006 PRIMARY ELECTIONS

| **Primary** | May 2, 2006 | **Registration** (as of May 2, 2006) | 7,685,088 | No Formal System of Party Registration |

Primary Type Open—Any registered voter can participate in the primary of either party. However, records are kept of voter participation in recent primaries, and in some counties voters who have recently cast a ballot in one party's primary can be challenged if they attempt to participate in the other party's primary. They may be asked to sign an affidavit affirming the fact that they are voting in the opposing party's primary and become identified with that party because of their primary ballot cast.

OHIO

GENERAL AND PRIMARY ELECTIONS

Note: An asterisk (*) denotes incumbent. Two special House primary elections were held to fill vacancies on the general election ballot, with 18th District Republicans voting on September 14, 2006, and 3rd District Democrats on September 15, 2006.

	REPUBLICAN PRIMARIES			DEMOCRATIC PRIMARIES		
Governor	J. Kenneth Blackwell	460,349	55.7%	Ted Strickland	634,114	79.2%
	Jim Petro	365,618	44.3%	Bryan Flannery	166,253	20.8%
	TOTAL	825,967		TOTAL	800,367	
Senator	Mike DeWine*	565,580	71.7%	Sherrod Brown	583,776	78.1%
	David R. Smith	114,186	14.5%	Merrill Samuel Keiser Jr.	163,628	21.9%
	William G. Pierce	108,978	13.8%			
	TOTAL	788,744		TOTAL	747,404	
Congressional District 1	Steve Chabot*	31,342	100%	John Cranley	17,344	100.0%
Congressional District 2	Jean Schmidt	33,938	47.7%	Victoria Wulsin	10,455	36.7%
	Bob McEwen	30,297	42.6%	Thor Jacobs	6,535	22.9%
	Deborah A. Kraus	4,433	6.2%	Jim Parker	6,376	22.4%
	James E. Constable	2,526	3.5%	Gaby Downey	3,668	12.9%
				Jeff Sinnard	1,489	5.2%
	TOTAL	71,194		TOTAL	28,523	
Congressional District 3	Michael R. Turner*	35,511	100.0%	Stephanie Studebaker	12,363	56.0%
				Charles W. Sanders	5,093	23.1%
				David J. Fierst	4,626	20.9%
				TOTAL	22,082	

Stephanie Studebaker withdrew from the race after being arrested in August on domestic violence charges. Richard Chema won a special primary election to replace her on the general election ballot.

				SPECIAL PRIMARY		
				Richard Chema	5,946	72.8%
				Charles W. Sanders	2,224	27.2%
				TOTAL	8,170	
Congressional District 4	Jim Jordan	38,017	50.6%	Richard E. Siferd	26,591	100.0%
	Frank A. Guglielmi	22,504	29.9%			
	Kevin Nestor	8,460	11.3%			
	James R. Stahl	2,596	3.5%			
	Nathan J. Martin	2,358	3.1%			
	Charles W. Weasel	1,239	1.6%			
	TOTAL	75,174				
Congressional District 5	Paul E. Gillmor*	54,168	100.0%	Robin Weirauch	28,373	100.0%
Congressional District 6	Chuck Blasdel	18,519	47.3%	Charles A. Wilson Jr. (write-in)	43,687	66.1%
	Danny Harmon	8,708	22.2%	Bob Carr	14,900	22.6%
	Tim Ginter	7,606	19.4%	John S. Luchansky	7,459	11.3%
	Richard D. Stobbs	4,315	11.0%			
	TOTAL	39,148		TOTAL	66,046	
Congressional District 7	David L. Hobson*	49,808	100.0%	William R. Conner	20,648	100.0%
Congressional District 8	John A. Boehner*	43,713	100.0%	Mort Meier	15,277	100.0%
Congressional District 9	Bradley S. Leavitt	8,625	40.2%	Marcy Kaptur*	44,234	100.0%
	Ed Emery	6,503	30.3%			
	Dirk Kubala	6,347	29.6%			
	TOTAL	21,475				
Congressional District 10	Michael D. Dovilla	15,270	65.2%	Dennis J. Kucinich*	51,485	76.4%
	Jason Werner	8,166	34.8%	Barbara Anne Ferris	15,890	23.6%
	TOTAL	23,436		TOTAL	67,375	
Congressional District 11	Lindsey N. String	7,556	100.0%	Stephanie Tubbs Jones*	55,319	100.0%

OHIO

GENERAL AND PRIMARY ELECTIONS

	REPUBLICAN PRIMARIES			DEMOCRATIC PRIMARIES		
Congressional District 12	Pat Tiberi*	76,457	100.0%	Bob Shamansky	19,387	43.3%
				Patricia J. Shaffer	13,815	30.9%
				Edward S. Brown	6,563	14.7%
				Michael Reilly	4,986	11.1%
				TOTAL	44,751	
Congressional District 13	Craig Foltin	12,088	37.5%	Betty Sutton	21,268	31.3%
	David McGrew	7,079	21.9%	Capri S. Cafaro	16,915	24.9%
	Joe Ortega III	6,536	20.3%	Thomas C. Sawyer	14,837	21.8%
	Paul S. Burtzlaff	4,261	13.2%	Gary J. Kucinich	9,891	14.6%
	C. J. DeLorean	2,306	7.1%	Bill Grace	3,537	5.2%
				Michael Lyons	1,030	1.5%
				Norbert G. Dennerll Jr.	495	0.7%
	TOTAL	32,270		TOTAL	67,973	
Congressional District 14	Steven C. LaTourette*	38,137	100.0%	Lewis R. Katz	15,401	42.5%
				Dale Virgil Blanchard	11,313	31.2%
				Palmer J. Peterson	9,534	26.3%
				TOTAL	36,248	
Congressional District 15	Deborah Pryce*	44,020	100.0%	Mary Jo Kilroy	27,895	100.0%
Congressional District 16	Ralph Regula*	32,526	58.4%	Thomas Shaw	20,508	50.8%
	Matt Miller	23,170	41.6%	Tom Mason	19,897	49.2%
	TOTAL	55,696		TOTAL	40,405	
Congressional District 17	Don Manning III (write-in)	249	100.0%	Tim Ryan*	71,532	100.0%
Congressional District 18	Bob Ney*	34,515	68.4%	Zack Space	18,251	38.7%
	James Brodbelt Harris	15,918	31.6%	Jennifer Stewart	12,071	25.6%
				Joe Sulzer	11,340	24.0%
				Ralph A. Applegate	5,514	11.7%
	TOTAL	50,433		TOTAL	47,176	

Bob Ney withdrew from the race in August, just weeks before pleading guilty to charges of conspiracy and making false statements in the Jack Abramoff influence-peddling case. Joy Padgett won a special primary election to replace Ney on the general election ballot.

SPECIAL PRIMARY

Joy Padgett	9,523	67.7%
James Brodbelt Harris	2,113	15.0%
Ray L. Feikert	1,148	8.2%
Ralph A. Applegate	781	5.6%
Jerry Firman	500	3.6%
TOTAL	14,065	

OKLAHOMA

Congressional districts first established for elections held in 2002
5 members

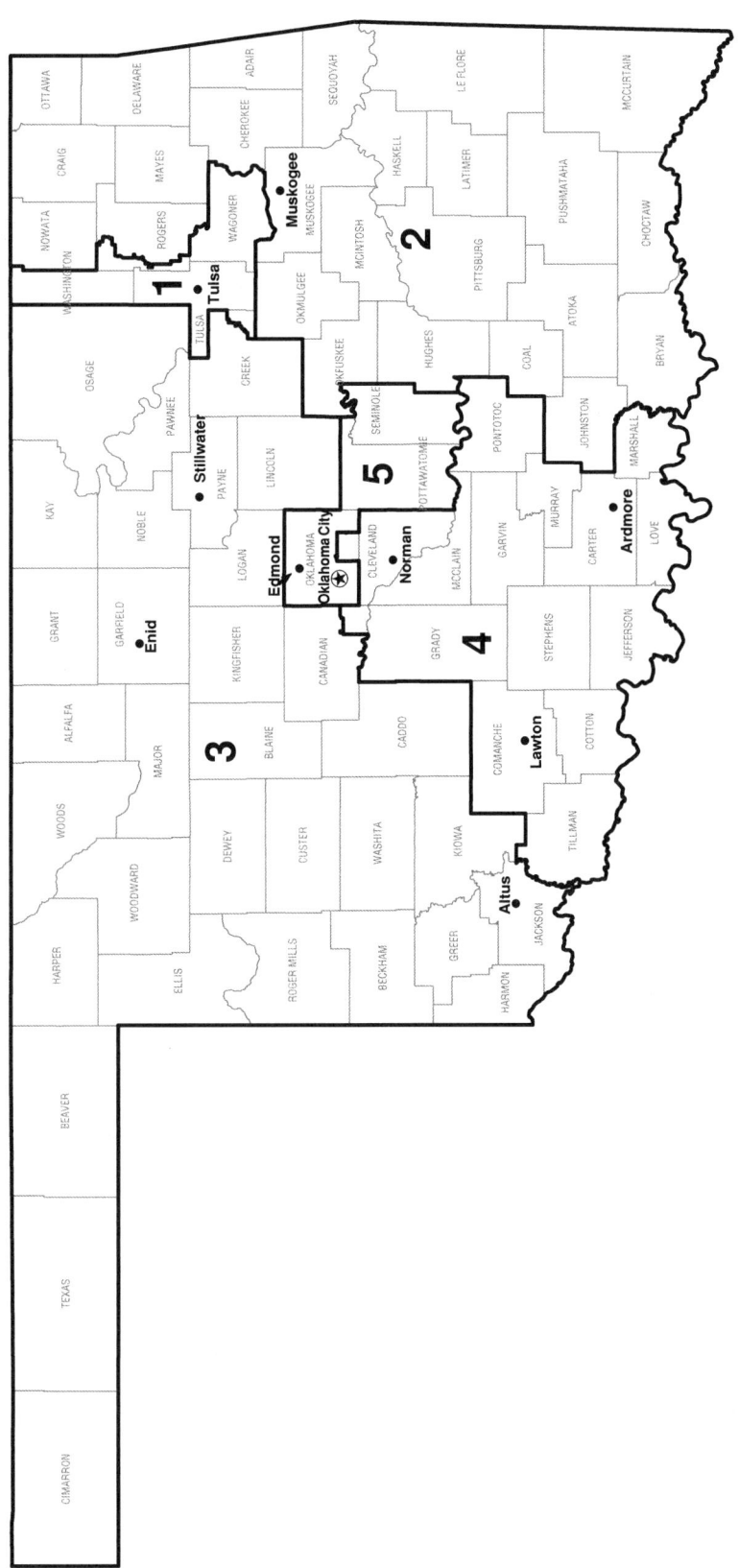

OKLAHOMA

GOVERNOR
Brad Henry (D). Reelected 2006 to a four-year term. Previously elected 2002.

SENATORS (2 Republicans)
Tom Coburn (R). Elected 2004 to a six-year term.

James M. Inhofe (R). Reelected 2002 to a six-year term. Previously elected 1996 and 1994 to fill out the remaining two years of the term vacated when David L. Boren (D) resigned to become president of the University of Oklahoma.

REPRESENTATIVES (4 Republicans, 1 Democrat)
1. John Sullivan (R)
2. Dan Boren (D)
3. Frank D. Lucas (R)
4. Tom Cole (R)
5. Mary Fallin (R)

POSTWAR VOTE FOR PRESIDENT

| | | Republican | | Democratic | | Other | | Percentage | | | |
| | | | | | | | | Total Vote | | Major Vote | |
Year	Total Vote	Vote	Candidate	Vote	Candidate	Vote	Plurality	Rep.	Dem.	Rep.	Dem.
2004	1,463,758	959,792	Bush, George W.	503,966	Kerry, John		455,826 R	65.6%	34.4%	65.6%	34.4%
2000	1,234,229	744,337	Bush, George W.	474,276	Gore, Al	15,616	270,061 R	60.3%	38.4%	61.1%	38.9%
1996**	1,206,713	582,315	Dole, Bob	488,105	Clinton, Bill	136,293	94,210 R	48.3%	40.4%	54.4%	45.6%
1992**	1,390,359	592,929	Bush, George	473,066	Clinton, Bill	324,364	119,863 R	42.6%	34.0%	55.6%	44.4%
1988	1,171,036	678,367	Bush, George	483,423	Dukakis, Michael S.	9,246	194,944 R	57.9%	41.3%	58.4%	41.6%
1984	1,255,676	861,530	Reagan, Ronald	385,080	Mondale, Walter F.	9,066	476,450 R	68.6%	30.7%	69.1%	30.9%
1980**	1,149,708	695,570	Reagan, Ronald	402,026	Carter, Jimmy	52,112	293,544 R	60.5%	35.0%	63.4%	36.6%
1976	1,092,251	545,708	Ford, Gerald R.	532,442	Carter, Jimmy	14,101	13,266 R	50.0%	48.7%	50.6%	49.4%
1972	1,029,900	759,025	Nixon, Richard M.	247,147	McGovern, George S.	23,728	511,878 R	73.7%	24.0%	75.4%	24.6%
1968**	943,086	449,697	Nixon, Richard M.	301,658	Humphrey, Hubert H.	191,731	148,039 R	47.7%	32.0%	59.9%	40.1%
1964	932,499	412,665	Goldwater, Barry M.	519,834	Johnson, Lyndon B.		107,169 D	44.3%	55.7%	44.3%	55.7%
1960	903,150	533,039	Nixon, Richard M.	370,111	Kennedy, John F.		162,928 R	59.0%	41.0%	59.0%	41.0%
1956	859,350	473,769	Eisenhower, Dwight D.	385,581	Stevenson, Adlai E.		88,188 R	55.1%	44.9%	55.1%	44.9%
1952	948,984	518,045	Eisenhower, Dwight D.	430,939	Stevenson, Adlai E.		87,106 R	54.6%	45.4%	54.6%	45.4%
1948	721,599	268,817	Dewey, Thomas E.	452,782	Truman, Harry S.		183,965 D	37.3%	62.7%	37.3%	62.7%

**In past elections, the other vote included: 1996 - 130,788 Reform (Ross Perot); 1992 - 319,878 Independent (Ross Perot); 1980 - 38,284 Independent (John Anderson); 1968 - 191,731 American Independent (George Wallace).

OKLAHOMA

POSTWAR VOTE FOR GOVERNOR

Year	Total Vote	Republican Vote	Republican Candidate	Democratic Vote	Democratic Candidate	Other Vote	Rep.-Dem. Plurality	Total Vote Rep.	Total Vote Dem.	Major Vote Rep.	Major Vote Dem.
2006	926,462	310,327	Istook, Ernest	616,135	Henry, Brad		305,808 D	33.5%	66.5%	33.5%	66.5%
2002**	1,035,620	441,277	Largent, Steve	448,143	Henry, Brad	146,200	6,866 D	42.6%	43.3%	49.6%	50.4%
1998	873,585	505,498	Keating, Frank	357,552	Boyd, Laura	10,535	147,946 R	57.9%	40.9%	58.6%	41.4%
1994**	995,012	466,740	Keating, Frank	294,936	Mildren, Jack	233,336	171,804 R	46.9%	29.6%	61.3%	38.7%
1990	911,314	297,584	Price, Bill	523,196	Walters, David	90,534	225,612 D	32.7%	57.4%	36.3%	63.7%
1986	909,925	431,762	Bellmon, Henry	405,295	Walters, David	72,868	26,467 R	47.5%	44.5%	51.6%	48.4%
1982	883,130	332,207	Daxon, Tom	548,159	Nigh, George	2,764	215,952 D	37.6%	62.1%	37.7%	62.3%
1978	777,414	367,055	Shotts, Ron	402,240	Nigh, George	8,119	35,185 D	47.2%	51.7%	47.7%	52.3%
1974	804,848	290,459	Inhofe, James M.	514,389	Boren, David L.		223,930 D	36.1%	63.9%	36.1%	63.9%
1970	698,790	336,157	Bartlett, Dewey F.	338,338	Hall, David	24,295	2,181 D	48.1%	48.4%	49.8%	50.2%
1966	677,258	377,078	Bartlett, Dewey F.	296,328	Moore, Preston J.	3,852	80,750 R	55.7%	43.8%	56.0%	44.0%
1962	709,763	392,316	Bellmon, Henry	315,357	Atkinson, W. P.	2,090	76,959 R	55.3%	44.4%	55.4%	44.6%
1958	538,839	107,495	Ferguson, Phil	399,504	Edmondson, J. Howard	31,840	292,009 D	19.9%	74.1%	21.2%	78.8%
1954	609,194	251,808	Sparks, Reuben K.	357,386	Gary, Raymond		105,578 D	41.3%	58.7%	41.3%	58.7%
1950	644,276	313,205	Ferguson, Jo O.	329,308	Murray, Johnston	1,763	16,103 D	48.6%	51.1%	48.7%	51.3%
1946	494,599	227,426	Flynn, Olney F.	259,491	Turner, Roy J.	7,682	32,065 D	46.0%	52.5%	46.7%	53.3%

**In past elections, the other vote included: 2002 - 146,200 Independent (Gary L. Richardson); 1994 - 233,336 Independent (Wes Watkins).

POSTWAR VOTE FOR SENATOR

Year	Total Vote	Republican Vote	Republican Candidate	Democratic Vote	Democratic Candidate	Other Vote	Rep.-Dem. Plurality	Total Vote Rep.	Total Vote Dem.	Major Vote Rep.	Major Vote Dem.
2004	1,446,846	763,433	Coburn, Tom	596,750	Carson, Brad	86,663	166,683 R	52.8%	41.2%	56.1%	43.9%
2002	1,018,424	583,579	Inhofe, James M.	369,789	Walters, David	65,056	213,790 R	57.3%	36.3%	61.2%	38.8%
1998	859,713	570,682	Nickles, Don	268,898	Carroll, Don E.	20,133	301,784 R	66.4%	31.3%	68.0%	32.0%
1996	1,183,150	670,610	Inhofe, James M.	474,162	Boren, Jim	38,378	196,448 R	56.7%	40.1%	58.6%	41.4%
1994S	982,430	542,390	Inhofe, James M.	392,488	McCurdy, Dave	47,552	149,902 R	55.2%	40.0%	58.0%	42.0%
1992	1,294,423	757,876	Nickles, Don	494,350	Lewis, Steve	42,197	263,526 R	58.5%	38.2%	60.5%	39.5%
1990	884,498	148,814	Jones, Stephen	735,684	Boren, David L.		586,870 D	16.8%	83.2%	16.8%	83.2%
1986	893,666	493,436	Nickles, Don	400,230	Jones, James R.		93,206 R	55.2%	44.8%	55.2%	44.8%
1984	1,197,937	280,638	Crozier, Will E.	906,131	Boren, David L.	11,168	625,493 D	23.4%	75.6%	23.6%	76.4%
1980	1,098,294	587,252	Nickles, Don	478,283	Coats, Andrew	32,759	108,969 R	53.5%	43.5%	55.1%	44.9%
1978	754,264	247,857	Kamm, Robert B.	493,953	Boren, David L.	12,454	246,096 D	32.9%	65.5%	33.4%	66.6%
1974	791,809	390,997	Bellmon, Henry	387,162	Edmondson, Ed	13,650	3,835 R	49.4%	48.9%	50.2%	49.8%
1972	1,005,148	516,934	Bartlett, Dewey F.	478,212	Edmondson, Ed	10,002	38,722 R	51.4%	47.6%	51.9%	48.1%
1968	909,119	470,120	Bellmon, Henry	419,658	Monroney, A. S. Mike	19,341	50,462 R	51.7%	46.2%	52.8%	47.2%
1966	638,742	295,585	Patterson, Pat J.	343,157	Harris, Fred R.		47,572 D	46.3%	53.7%	46.3%	53.7%
1964S	912,174	445,392	Wilkinson, Bud	466,782	Harris, Fred R.		21,390 D	48.8%	51.2%	48.8%	51.2%
1962	664,712	307,966	Crawford, B. Hayden	353,890	Monroney, A. S. Mike	2,856	45,924 D	46.3%	53.2%	46.5%	53.5%
1960	864,475	385,646	Crawford, B. Hayden	474,116	Kerr, Robert S.	4,713	88,470 D	44.6%	54.8%	44.9%	55.1%
1956	831,142	371,146	McKeever, Douglas	459,996	Monroney, A. S. Mike		88,850 D	44.7%	55.3%	44.7%	55.3%
1954	600,120	262,013	Mock, Fred M.	335,127	Kerr, Robert S.	2,980	73,114 D	43.7%	55.8%	43.9%	56.1%
1950	631,177	285,224	Alexander, W. H.	345,953	Monroney, A. S. Mike		60,729 D	45.2%	54.8%	45.2%	54.8%
1948	708,931	265,169	Rizley, Ross	441,654	Kerr, Robert S.	2,108	176,485 D	37.4%	62.3%	37.5%	62.5%

The 1994 and 1964 elections were for short terms to fill a vacancy.

OKLAHOMA

GOVERNOR 2006

2000 Census Population	County	Total Vote	Republican	Democratic	Other	Rep.-Dem. Plurality	Percentage			
							Total Vote		Major Vote	
							Rep.	Dem.	Rep.	Dem.
21,038	ADAIR	4,818	1,565	3,253		1,688 D	32.5%	67.5%	32.5%	67.5%
6,105	ALFALFA	2,072	683	1,389		706 D	33.0%	67.0%	33.0%	67.0%
13,879	ATOKA	3,178	806	2,372		1,566 D	25.4%	74.6%	25.4%	74.6%
5,857	BEAVER	1,847	990	857		133 R	53.6%	46.4%	53.6%	46.4%
19,799	BECKHAM	4,817	1,394	3,423		2,029 D	28.9%	71.1%	28.9%	71.1%
11,976	BLAINE	3,153	961	2,192		1,231 D	30.5%	69.5%	30.5%	69.5%
36,534	BRYAN	7,981	1,671	6,310		4,639 D	20.9%	79.1%	20.9%	79.1%
30,150	CADDO	6,732	1,742	4,990		3,248 D	25.9%	74.1%	25.9%	74.1%
87,697	CANADIAN	27,753	11,565	16,188		4,623 D	41.7%	58.3%	41.7%	58.3%
45,621	CARTER	10,380	3,032	7,348		4,316 D	29.2%	70.8%	29.2%	70.8%
42,521	CHEROKEE	10,398	2,495	7,903		5,408 D	24.0%	76.0%	24.0%	76.0%
15,342	CHOCTAW	3,843	704	3,139		2,435 D	18.3%	81.7%	18.3%	81.7%
3,148	CIMARRON	1,058	705	353		352 R	66.6%	33.4%	66.6%	33.4%
208,016	CLEVELAND	62,348	21,707	40,641		18,934 D	34.8%	65.2%	34.8%	65.2%
6,031	COAL	2,007	380	1,627		1,247 D	18.9%	81.1%	18.9%	81.1%
114,996	COMANCHE	20,027	5,086	14,941		9,855 D	25.4%	74.6%	25.4%	74.6%
6,614	COTTON	2,015	355	1,660		1,305 D	17.6%	82.4%	17.6%	82.4%
14,950	CRAIG	4,331	1,012	3,319		2,307 D	23.4%	76.6%	23.4%	76.6%
67,367	CREEK	19,455	6,519	12,936		6,417 D	33.5%	66.5%	33.5%	66.5%
26,142	CUSTER	6,829	2,148	4,681		2,533 D	31.5%	68.5%	31.5%	68.5%
37,077	DELAWARE	9,905	3,098	6,807		3,709 D	31.3%	68.7%	31.3%	68.7%
4,743	DEWEY	1,853	562	1,291		729 D	30.3%	69.7%	30.3%	69.7%
4,075	ELLIS	1,541	569	972		403 D	36.9%	63.1%	36.9%	63.1%
57,813	GARFIELD	16,111	5,351	10,760		5,409 D	33.2%	66.8%	33.2%	66.8%
27,210	GARVIN	8,049	2,304	5,745		3,441 D	28.6%	71.4%	28.6%	71.4%
45,516	GRADY	13,738	4,587	9,151		4,564 D	33.4%	66.6%	33.4%	66.6%
5,144	GRANT	1,891	589	1,302		713 D	31.1%	68.9%	31.1%	68.9%
6,061	GREER	1,545	460	1,085		625 D	29.8%	70.2%	29.8%	70.2%
3,283	HARMON	751	192	559		367 D	25.6%	74.4%	25.6%	74.4%
3,562	HARPER	1,156	410	746		336 D	35.5%	64.5%	35.5%	64.5%
11,792	HASKELL	3,216	790	2,426		1,636 D	24.6%	75.4%	24.6%	75.4%
14,154	HUGHES	3,329	803	2,526		1,723 D	24.1%	75.9%	24.1%	75.9%
28,439	JACKSON	5,625	1,952	3,673		1,721 D	34.7%	65.3%	34.7%	65.3%
6,818	JEFFERSON	1,745	343	1,402		1,059 D	19.7%	80.3%	19.7%	80.3%
10,513	JOHNSTON	2,768	515	2,253		1,738 D	18.6%	81.4%	18.6%	81.4%
48,080	KAY	13,150	4,096	9,054		4,958 D	31.1%	68.9%	31.1%	68.9%
13,926	KINGFISHER	4,860	1,939	2,921		982 D	39.9%	60.1%	39.9%	60.1%
10,227	KIOWA	2,778	630	2,148		1,518 D	22.7%	77.3%	22.7%	77.3%
10,692	LATIMER	2,649	630	2,019		1,389 D	23.8%	76.2%	23.8%	76.2%
48,109	LE FLORE	11,063	3,100	7,963		4,863 D	28.0%	72.0%	28.0%	72.0%
32,080	LINCOLN	10,392	3,369	7,023		3,654 D	32.4%	67.6%	32.4%	67.6%
33,924	LOGAN	10,688	4,280	6,408		2,128 D	40.0%	60.0%	40.0%	60.0%
8,831	LOVE	2,244	447	1,797		1,350 D	19.9%	80.1%	19.9%	80.1%
27,740	MCCLAIN	10,149	3,527	6,622		3,095 D	34.8%	65.2%	34.8%	65.2%
34,402	MCCURTAIN	6,411	1,926	4,485		2,559 D	30.0%	70.0%	30.0%	70.0%
19,456	MCINTOSH	6,030	1,404	4,626		3,222 D	23.3%	76.7%	23.3%	76.7%
7,545	MAJOR	2,794	1,191	1,603		412 D	42.6%	57.4%	42.6%	57.4%
13,184	MARSHALL	3,532	882	2,650		1,768 D	25.0%	75.0%	25.0%	75.0%
38,369	MAYES	11,240	2,940	8,300		5,360 D	26.2%	73.8%	26.2%	73.8%
12,623	MURRAY	3,931	916	3,015		2,099 D	23.3%	76.7%	23.3%	76.7%
69,451	MUSKOGEE	17,002	4,117	12,885		8,768 D	24.2%	75.8%	24.2%	75.8%
11,411	NOBLE	3,670	1,210	2,460		1,250 D	33.0%	67.0%	33.0%	67.0%
10,569	NOWATA	2,866	840	2,026		1,186 D	29.3%	70.7%	29.3%	70.7%
11,814	OKFUSKEE	2,873	726	2,147		1,421 D	25.3%	74.7%	25.3%	74.7%
660,448	OKLAHOMA	175,713	64,987	110,726		45,739 D	37.0%	63.0%	37.0%	63.0%
39,685	OKMULGEE	9,699	2,378	7,321		4,943 D	24.5%	75.5%	24.5%	75.5%
44,437	OSAGE	12,340	3,507	8,833		5,326 D	28.4%	71.6%	28.4%	71.6%
33,194	OTTAWA	7,140	1,929	5,211		3,282 D	27.0%	73.0%	27.0%	73.0%
16,612	PAWNEE	4,422	1,373	3,049		1,676 D	31.0%	69.0%	31.0%	69.0%
68,190	PAYNE	17,535	5,529	12,006		6,477 D	31.5%	68.5%	31.5%	68.5%

OKLAHOMA

GOVERNOR 2006

2000 Census Population	County	Total Vote	Republican	Democratic	Other	Rep.-Dem. Plurality	Percentage			
							Total Vote		Major Vote	
							Rep.	Dem.	Rep.	Dem.
43,953	PITTSBURG	10,884	2,808	8,076		5,268 D	25.8%	74.2%	25.8%	74.2%
35,143	PONTOTOC	9,905	2,592	7,313		4,721 D	26.2%	73.8%	26.2%	73.8%
65,521	POTTAWATOMIE	17,330	5,073	12,257		7,184 D	29.3%	70.7%	29.3%	70.7%
11,667	PUSHMATAHA	2,893	563	2,330		1,767 D	19.5%	80.5%	19.5%	80.5%
3,436	ROGER MILLS	1,462	479	983		504 D	32.8%	67.2%	32.8%	67.2%
70,641	ROGERS	23,952	8,278	15,674		7,396 D	34.6%	65.4%	34.6%	65.4%
24,894	SEMINOLE	6,218	1,834	4,384		2,550 D	29.5%	70.5%	29.5%	70.5%
38,972	SEQUOYAH	8,224	2,342	5,882		3,540 D	28.5%	71.5%	28.5%	71.5%
43,182	STEPHENS	13,244	4,076	9,168		5,092 D	30.8%	69.2%	30.8%	69.2%
20,107	TEXAS	3,904	2,262	1,642		620 R	57.9%	42.1%	57.9%	42.1%
9,287	TILLMAN	2,644	459	2,185		1,726 D	17.4%	82.6%	17.4%	82.6%
563,299	TULSA	147,519	57,060	90,459		33,399 D	38.7%	61.3%	38.7%	61.3%
57,491	WAGONER	17,441	6,464	10,977		4,513 D	37.1%	62.9%	37.1%	62.9%
48,996	WASHINGTON	15,260	6,265	8,995		2,730 D	41.1%	58.9%	41.1%	58.9%
11,508	WASHITA	3,874	1,108	2,766		1,658 D	28.6%	71.4%	28.6%	71.4%
9,089	WOODS	2,905	896	2,009		1,113 D	30.8%	69.2%	30.8%	69.2%
18,486	WOODWARD	5,367	1,850	3,517		1,667 D	34.5%	65.5%	34.5%	65.5%
3,450,654	TOTAL	926,462	310,327	616,135		305,808 D	33.5%	66.5%	33.5%	66.5%

OKLAHOMA

HOUSE OF REPRESENTATIVES

CD	Year	Total Vote	Republican		Democratic		Other Vote	Rep.-Dem. Plurality	Percentage			
			Vote	Candidate	Vote	Candidate			Total Vote		Major Vote	
									Rep.	Dem.	Rep.	Dem.
1	2006	183,729	116,920	SULLIVAN, JOHN*	56,724	GENTGES, ALAN	10,085	60,196 R	63.6%	30.9%	67.3%	32.7%
1	2004	310,934	187,145	SULLIVAN, JOHN*	116,731	DODD, DOUG	7,058	70,414 R	60.2%	37.5%	61.6%	38.4%
1	2002	214,955	119,566	SULLIVAN, JOHN*	90,649	DODD, DOUG	4,740	28,917 R	55.6%	42.2%	56.9%	43.1%
2	2006	168,208	45,861	MILLER, PATRICK K.	122,347	BOREN, DAN*		76,486 D	27.3%	72.7%	27.3%	72.7%
2	2004	272,542	92,963	SMALLEY, WAYLAND	179,579	BOREN, DAN		86,616 D	34.1%	65.9%	34.1%	65.9%
2	2002	197,982	51,234	PHAROAH, KENT	146,748	CARSON, BRAD*		95,514 D	25.9%	74.1%	25.9%	74.1%
3	2006	189,791	128,042	LUCAS, FRANK D.*	61,749	BARTON, SUE		66,293 R	67.5%	32.5%	67.5%	32.5%
3	2004	262,131	215,510	LUCAS, FRANK D.*		—	46,621	215,510 R	82.2%		100.0%	
3	2002	196,090	148,206	LUCAS, FRANK D.*		—	47,884	148,206 R	75.6%		100.0%	
4	2006	183,041	118,266	COLE, TOM*	64,775	SPAKE, HAL		53,491 R	64.6%	35.4%	64.6%	35.4%
4	2004	255,854	198,985	COLE, TOM*		—	56,869	198,985 R	77.8%		100.0%	
4	2002	197,774	106,452	COLE, TOM	91,322	ROBERTS, DARRYL		15,130 R	53.8%	46.2%	53.8%	46.2%
5	2006	180,425	108,936	FALLIN, MARY	67,293	HUNTER, DAVID	4,196	41,643 R	60.4%	37.3%	61.8%	38.2%
5	2004	273,149	180,430	ISTOOK, ERNEST*	92,719	SMITH, BERT		87,711 R	66.1%	33.9%	66.1%	33.9%
5	2002	195,051	121,374	ISTOOK, ERNEST*	63,208	BARLOW, LOU	10,469	58,166 R	62.2%	32.4%	65.8%	34.2%
TOTAL	2006	905,194	518,025		372,888		14,281	145,137 R	57.2%	41.2%	58.1%	41.9%
TOTAL	2004	1,374,610	875,033		389,029		110,548	486,004 R	63.7%	28.3%	69.2%	30.8%
TOTAL	2002	1,001,852	546,832		391,927		63,093	154,905 R	54.6%	39.1%	58.3%	41.7%

An asterisk (*) denotes incumbent.

OKLAHOMA

GENERAL AND PRIMARY ELECTIONS

2006 GENERAL ELECTIONS

Governor

House   Other vote was:

CD 1   10,085 Independent (Bill Wortman).
CD 2
CD 3
CD 4
CD 5   4,196 Independent (Matthew Horton Woodson).

2006 PRIMARY ELECTIONS

Primary	July 25, 2006	**Registration**	Democratic	1,029,378
Primary Runoff	August 22, 2006	(as of July 1, 2006)	Republican	786,954
			Independent	216,032
			TOTAL	2,032,364

Primary Type   Closed—Only registered Democrats and Republicans could vote in their party's primary.

OKLAHOMA

GENERAL AND PRIMARY ELECTIONS

Note: An asterisk (*) denotes incumbent. The names of unopposed candidates did not appear on the primary ballot; therefore, no votes were cast for these candidates.

	REPUBLICAN PRIMARIES			DEMOCRATIC PRIMARIES		
Governor	Ernest Istook	99,650	54.7%	Brad Henry*	226,957	85.8%
	Bob Sullivan	56,347	30.9%	Andrew W. Marr Jr.	37,510	14.2%
	James A. Williamson	17,769	9.8%			
	Jim Evanoff	8,370	4.6%			
	TOTAL	182,136		TOTAL	264,467	
Congressional District 1	John Sullivan*	38,279	83.2%	Alan Gentges	Unopposed	
	Evelyn L. Rogers	5,826	12.7%			
	Fran Moghaddam	1,895	4.1%			
	TOTAL	46,000				
Congressional District 2	Patrick K. Miller	9,941	72.2%	Dan Boren*	Unopposed	
	Raymond J. Wickson	3,829	27.8%			
	TOTAL	13,770				
Congressional District 3	Frank D. Lucas*	Unopposed		Sue Barton	24,177	53.4%
				Gregory M. Wilson	11,249	24.9%
				John Coffee Harris	9,833	21.7%
				TOTAL	45,259	
Congressional District 4	Tom Cole*	Unopposed		Hal Spake	Unopposed	48.3%
Congressional District 5	Mary Fallin	16,691	34.6%	David Hunter	24,660	63.0%
	Mick Cornett	11,718	24.3%	Bert Smith	14,455	37.0%
	Denise Bode	9,139	18.9%			
	Kevin Calvey	4,870	10.1%			
	Fred Morgan	4,493	9.3%			
	Johnny B. Roy	1,376	2.8%			
	TOTAL	48,287		TOTAL	39,115	
	PRIMARY RUNOFF					
	Mary Fallin	26,748	63.1%			
	Mick Cornett	15,669	36.9%			
	TOTAL	42,417				

294

OREGON

Congressional districts first established for elections held in 2002
5 members

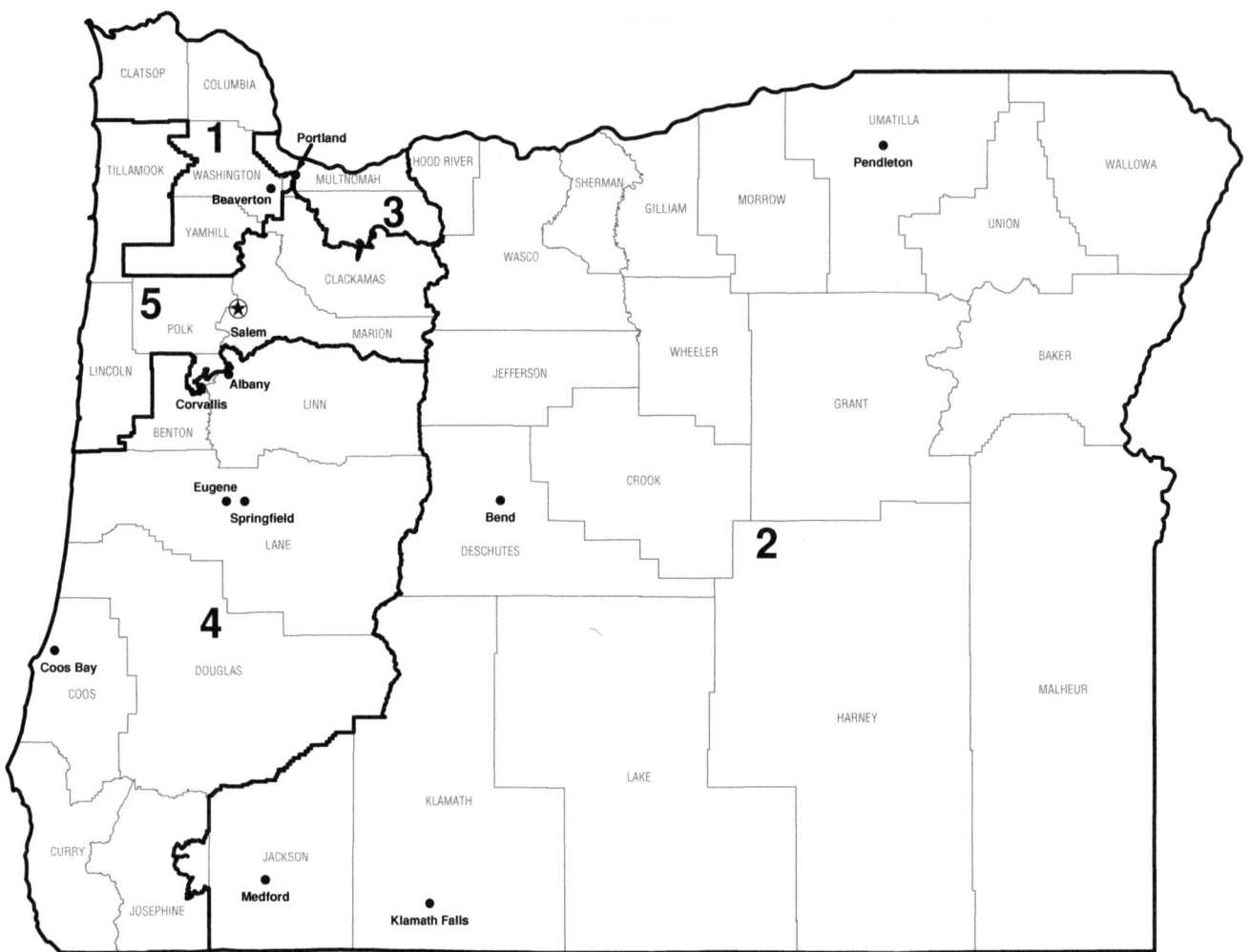

OREGON

GOVERNOR
Theodore R. Kulongoski (D). Reelected 2006 to a four-year term. Previously elected 2002.

SENATORS (1 Democrat, 1 Republican)
Ron Wyden (D). Reelected 2004 to a six-year term. Previously elected 1998 and in a special election January 30, 1996, to serve the remaining three years of the term vacated when Senator Robert W. Packwood (R) resigned.

Gordon H. Smith (R). Reelected 2002 to a six-year term. Previously elected 1996.

REPRESENTATIVES (4 Democrats, 1 Republican)
1. David Wu (D)
2. Greg Walden (R)
3. Earl Blumenauer (D)
4. Peter A. DeFazio (D)
5. Darlene Hooley (D)

POSTWAR VOTE FOR PRESIDENT

| Year | Total Vote | Republican | | Democratic | | Other Vote | Plurality | Percentage | | | |
| | | Vote | Candidate | Vote | Candidate | | | Total Vote | | Major Vote | |
								Rep.	Dem.	Rep.	Dem.
2004	1,836,782	866,831	Bush, George W.	943,163	Kerry, John	26,788	76,332 D	47.2%	51.3%	47.9%	52.1%
2000**	1,533,968	713,577	Bush, George W.	720,342	Gore, Al	100,049	6,765 D	46.5%	47.0%	49.8%	50.2%
1996**	1,377,760	538,152	Dole, Bob	649,641	Clinton, Bill	189,967	111,489 D	39.1%	47.2%	45.3%	54.7%
1992**	1,462,643	475,757	Bush, George	621,314	Clinton, Bill	365,572	145,557 D	32.5%	42.5%	43.4%	56.6%
1988	1,201,694	560,126	Bush, George	616,206	Dukakis, Michael S.	25,362	56,080 D	46.6%	51.3%	47.6%	52.4%
1984	1,226,527	685,700	Reagan, Ronald	536,479	Mondale, Walter F.	4,348	149,221 R	55.9%	43.7%	56.1%	43.9%
1980**	1,181,516	571,044	Reagan, Ronald	456,890	Carter, Jimmy	153,582	114,154 R	48.3%	38.7%	55.6%	44.4%
1976	1,029,876	492,120	Ford, Gerald R.	490,407	Carter, Jimmy	47,349	1,713 R	47.8%	47.6%	50.1%	49.9%
1972	927,946	486,686	Nixon, Richard M.	392,760	McGovern, George S.	48,500	93,926 R	52.4%	42.3%	55.3%	44.7%
1968**	819,622	408,433	Nixon, Richard M.	358,866	Humphrey, Hubert H.	52,323	49,567 R	49.8%	43.8%	53.2%	46.8%
1964	786,305	282,779	Goldwater, Barry M.	501,017	Johnson, Lyndon B.	2,509	218,238 D	36.0%	63.7%	36.1%	63.9%
1960	776,421	408,060	Nixon, Richard M.	367,402	Kennedy, John F.	959	40,658 R	52.6%	47.3%	52.6%	47.4%
1956	736,132	406,393	Eisenhower, Dwight D.	329,204	Stevenson, Adlai E.	535	77,189 R	55.2%	44.7%	55.2%	44.8%
1952	695,059	420,815	Eisenhower, Dwight D.	270,579	Stevenson, Adlai E.	3,665	150,236 R	60.5%	38.9%	60.9%	39.1%
1948	524,080	260,904	Dewey, Thomas E.	243,147	Truman, Harry S.	20,029	17,757 R	49.8%	46.4%	51.8%	48.2%

**In past elections, the other vote included: 2000 - 77,357 Green (Ralph Nader); 1996 - 121,221 Reform (Ross Perot); 1992 - 354,091 Independent (Ross Perot); 1980 - 112,389 Independent (John Anderson); 1968 - 49,683 American Independent (George Wallace).

OREGON

POSTWAR VOTE FOR GOVERNOR

Year	Total Vote	Republican Vote	Republican Candidate	Democratic Vote	Democratic Candidate	Other Vote	Rep.-Dem. Plurality	Total Vote Rep.	Total Vote Dem.	Major Vote Rep.	Major Vote Dem.
2006	1,379,475	589,748	Saxton, Ron	699,786	Kulongoski, Theodore R.	89,941	110,038 D	42.8%	50.7%	45.7%	54.3%
2002	1,260,497	581,785	Mannix, Kevin L.	618,004	Kulongoski, Theodore R.	60,708	36,219 D	46.2%	49.0%	48.5%	51.5%
1998	1,113,098	334,001	Sizemore, Bill	717,061	Kitzhaber, John	62,036	383,060 D	30.0%	64.4%	31.8%	68.2%
1994	1,221,010	517,874	Smith, Denny	622,083	Kitzhaber, John	81,053	104,209 D	42.4%	50.9%	45.4%	54.6%
1990**	1,112,847	444,646	Frohnmayer, Dave	508,749	Roberts, Barbara	159,452	64,103 D	40.0%	45.7%	46.6%	53.4%
1986	1,059,630	506,986	Paulus, Norma	549,456	Goldschmidt, Neil	3,188	42,470 D	47.8%	51.9%	48.0%	52.0%
1982	1,042,009	639,841	Atiyeh, Victor	374,316	Kulongoski, Theodore R.	27,852	265,525 R	61.4%	35.9%	63.1%	36.9%
1978	911,143	498,452	Atiyeh, Victor	409,411	Straub, Robert W.	3,280	89,041 R	54.7%	44.9%	54.9%	45.1%
1974	770,574	324,751	Atiyeh, Victor	444,812	Straub, Robert W.	1,011	120,061 D	42.1%	57.7%	42.2%	57.8%
1970	666,394	369,964	McCall, Tom	293,892	Straub, Robert W.	2,538	76,072 R	55.5%	44.1%	55.7%	44.3%
1966	682,862	377,346	McCall, Tom	305,008	Straub, Robert W.	508	72,338 R	55.3%	44.7%	55.3%	44.7%
1962	637,407	345,497	Hatfield, Mark	265,359	Thornton, Robert Y.	26,551	80,138 R	54.2%	41.6%	56.6%	43.4%
1958	599,994	331,900	Hatfield, Mark	267,934	Holmes, Robert D.	160	63,966 R	55.3%	44.7%	55.3%	44.7%
1956S	731,279	361,840	Smith, Elmo E.	369,439	Holmes, Robert D.		7,599 D	49.5%	50.5%	49.5%	50.5%
1954	566,701	322,522	Patterson, Paul	244,179	Carson, Joseph K.		78,343 R	56.9%	43.1%	56.9%	43.1%
1950	505,910	334,160	McKay, Douglas	171,750	Flegel, Austin F.		162,410 R	66.1%	33.9%	66.1%	33.9%
1948S	509,633	271,295	McKay, Douglas	226,958	Wallace, Lew	11,380	44,337 R	53.2%	44.5%	54.4%	45.6%
1946	344,155	237,681	Snell, Earl	106,474	Donaugh, Carl C.		131,207 R	69.1%	30.9%	69.1%	30.9%

**In past elections, the other vote included: 1990 - 144,062 Independent (Al Mobley). The 1956 and 1948 elections were for short terms to fill vacancies.

POSTWAR VOTE FOR SENATOR

Year	Total Vote	Republican Vote	Republican Candidate	Democratic Vote	Democratic Candidate	Other Vote	Rep.-Dem. Plurality	Total Vote Rep.	Total Vote Dem.	Major Vote Rep.	Major Vote Dem.
2004	1,780,550	565,254	King, Al	1,128,728	Wyden, Ron	86,568	563,474 D	31.7%	63.4%	33.4%	66.6%
2002	1,267,221	712,287	Smith, Gordon H.	501,898	Bradbury, Bill	53,036	210,389 R	56.2%	39.6%	58.7%	41.3%
1998	1,117,747	377,739	Lim, John	682,425	Wyden, Ron	57,583	304,686 D	33.8%	61.1%	35.6%	64.4%
1996	1,360,230	677,336	Smith, Gordon H.	624,370	Bruggere, Tom	58,524	52,966 R	49.8%	45.9%	52.0%	48.0%
1996S	1,196,608	553,519	Smith, Gordon H.	571,739	Wyden, Ron	71,350	18,220 D	46.3%	47.8%	49.2%	50.8%
1992	1,376,033	717,455	Packwood, Robert W.	639,851	AuCoin, Les	18,727	77,604 R	52.1%	46.5%	52.9%	47.1%
1990	1,099,255	590,095	Hatfield, Mark	507,743	Lonsdale, Harry	1,417	82,352 R	53.7%	46.2%	53.8%	46.2%
1986	1,042,555	656,317	Packwood, Robert W.	375,735	Bauman, Rick	10,503	280,582 R	63.0%	36.0%	63.6%	36.4%
1984	1,214,735	808,152	Hatfield, Mark	406,122	Hendriksen, Margie	461	402,030 R	66.5%	33.4%	66.6%	33.4%
1980	1,140,494	594,290	Packwood, Robert W.	501,963	Kulongoski, Theodore R.	44,241	92,327 R	52.1%	44.0%	54.2%	45.8%
1978	892,518	550,165	Hatfield, Mark	341,616	Cook, Vernon	737	208,549 R	61.6%	38.3%	61.7%	38.3%
1974	766,414	420,984	Packwood, Robert W.	338,591	Roberts, Betty	6,839	82,393 R	54.9%	44.2%	55.4%	44.6%
1972	920,833	494,671	Hatfield, Mark	425,036	Morse, Wayne L.	1,126	69,635 R	53.7%	46.2%	53.8%	46.2%
1968	814,176	408,646	Packwood, Robert W.	405,353	Morse, Wayne L.	177	3,293 R	50.2%	49.8%	50.2%	49.8%
1966	685,067	354,391	Hatfield, Mark	330,374	Duncan, Robert B.	302	24,017 R	51.7%	48.2%	51.8%	48.2%
1962	636,558	291,587	Unander, Sig	344,716	Morse, Wayne L.	255	53,129 D	45.8%	54.2%	45.8%	54.2%
1960	755,875	343,009	Smith, Elmo E.	412,757	Neuberger, Maurine	109	69,748 D	45.4%	54.6%	45.4%	54.6%
1956	732,254	335,405	McKay, Douglas	396,849	Morse, Wayne L.		61,444 D	45.8%	54.2%	45.8%	54.2%
1954	569,088	283,313	Cordon, Guy	285,775	Neuberger, Richard L.		2,462 D	49.8%	50.2%	49.8%	50.2%
1950	503,455	376,510	Morse, Wayne L.	116,780	Latourette, Howard	10,165	259,730 R	74.8%	23.2%	76.3%	23.7%
1948	498,570	299,295	Cordon, Guy	199,275	Wilson, Manley J.		100,020 R	60.0%	40.0%	60.0%	40.0%

The January 1996 election was for a short term to fill a vacancy.

OREGON

GOVERNOR 2006

2000 Census Population	County	Total Vote	Republican	Democratic	Other	Rep.-Dem. Plurality	Percentage Total Vote Rep.	Dem.	Major Vote Rep.	Dem.
16,741	BAKER	7,361	4,338	2,508	515	1,830 R	58.9%	34.1%	63.4%	36.6%
78,153	BENTON	35,205	12,736	20,661	1,808	7,925 D	36.2%	58.7%	38.1%	61.9%
338,391	CLACKAMAS	145,237	65,795	70,131	9,311	4,336 D	45.3%	48.3%	48.4%	51.6%
35,630	CLATSOP	14,940	5,886	7,936	1,118	2,050 D	39.4%	53.1%	42.6%	57.4%
43,560	COLUMBIA	19,402	8,032	9,291	2,079	1,259 D	41.4%	47.9%	46.4%	53.6%
62,779	COOS	25,152	12,103	10,977	2,072	1,126 R	48.1%	43.6%	52.4%	47.6%
19,182	CROOK	8,353	5,333	2,518	502	2,815 R	63.8%	30.1%	67.9%	32.1%
21,137	CURRY	10,130	5,332	4,162	636	1,170 R	52.6%	41.1%	56.2%	43.8%
115,367	DESCHUTES	57,843	31,256	23,631	2,956	7,625 R	54.0%	40.9%	56.9%	43.1%
100,399	DOUGLAS	42,612	24,896	15,123	2,593	9,773 R	58.4%	35.5%	62.2%	37.8%
1,915	GILLIAM	997	535	388	74	147 R	53.7%	38.9%	58.0%	42.0%
7,935	GRANT	3,367	2,401	783	183	1,618 R	71.3%	23.3%	75.4%	24.6%
7,609	HARNEY	3,007	2,186	643	178	1,543 R	72.7%	21.4%	77.3%	22.7%
20,411	HOOD RIVER	7,434	2,554	4,352	528	1,798 D	34.4%	58.5%	37.0%	63.0%
181,269	JACKSON	77,057	39,055	33,329	4,673	5,726 R	50.7%	43.3%	54.0%	46.0%
19,009	JEFFERSON	6,708	3,511	2,776	421	735 R	52.3%	41.4%	55.8%	44.2%
75,726	JOSEPHINE	32,704	18,321	11,900	2,483	6,421 R	56.0%	36.4%	60.6%	39.4%
63,775	KLAMATH	23,670	15,651	6,592	1,427	9,059 R	66.1%	27.8%	70.4%	29.6%
7,422	LAKE	3,108	2,156	723	229	1,433 R	69.4%	23.3%	74.9%	25.1%
322,959	LANE	139,847	50,290	81,550	8,007	31,260 D	36.0%	58.3%	38.1%	61.9%
44,479	LINCOLN	19,658	8,072	10,145	1,441	2,073 D	41.1%	51.6%	44.3%	55.7%
103,069	LINN	39,839	21,411	15,588	2,840	5,823 R	53.7%	39.1%	57.9%	42.1%
31,615	MALHEUR	8,101	5,296	2,357	448	2,939 R	65.4%	29.1%	69.2%	30.8%
284,834	MARION	97,126	44,474	45,304	7,348	830 D	45.8%	46.6%	49.5%	50.5%
10,995	MORROW	3,079	1,797	1,043	239	754 R	58.4%	33.9%	63.3%	36.7%
660,486	MULTNOMAH	259,804	65,488	177,797	16,519	112,309 D	25.2%	68.4%	26.9%	73.1%
62,380	POLK	27,304	12,643	12,620	2,041	23 R	46.3%	46.2%	50.0%	50.0%
1,934	SHERMAN	936	529	331	76	198 R	56.5%	35.4%	61.5%	38.5%
24,262	TILLAMOOK	10,838	4,745	5,356	737	611 D	43.8%	49.4%	47.0%	53.0%
70,548	UMATILLA	18,969	10,554	7,182	1,233	3,372 R	55.6%	37.9%	59.5%	40.5%
24,530	UNION	10,098	5,473	3,961	664	1,512 R	54.2%	39.2%	58.0%	42.0%
7,226	WALLOWA	3,798	2,335	1,253	210	1,082 R	61.5%	33.0%	65.1%	34.9%
23,791	WASCO	9,164	4,057	4,307	800	250 D	44.3%	47.0%	48.5%	51.5%
445,342	WASHINGTON	172,783	73,907	88,292	10,584	14,385 D	42.8%	51.1%	45.6%	54.4%
1,547	WHEELER	734	422	233	79	189 R	57.5%	31.7%	64.4%	35.6%
84,992	YAMHILL	33,110	16,178	14,043	2,889	2,135 R	48.9%	42.4%	53.5%	46.5%
3,421,399	TOTAL	1,379,475	589,748	699,786	89,941	110,038 D	42.8%	50.7%	45.7%	54.3%

OREGON

HOUSE OF REPRESENTATIVES

CD	Year	Total Vote	Republican Vote	Republican Candidate	Democratic Vote	Democratic Candidate	Other Vote	Rep.-Dem. Plurality		Total Vote Rep.	Total Vote Dem.	Major Vote Rep.	Major Vote Dem.
1	2006	269,627	90,904	KITTS, DERRICK	169,409	WU, DAVID*	9,314	78,505	D	33.7%	62.8%	34.9%	65.1%
1	2004	354,338	135,164	GOLI, AMERI	203,771	WU, DAVID*	15,403	68,607	D	38.1%	57.5%	39.9%	60.1%
1	2002	238,036	80,917	GREENFIELD, JIM	149,215	WU, DAVID*	7,904	68,298	D	34.0%	62.7%	35.2%	64.8%
2	2006	271,719	181,529	WALDEN, GREG*	82,484	VOISON, CAROL	7,706	99,045	R	66.8%	30.4%	68.8%	31.2%
2	2004	346,865	248,461	WALDEN, GREG*	88,914	McCOLGAN, JOHN C.	9,490	159,547	R	71.6%	25.6%	73.6%	26.4%
2	2002	252,284	181,295	WALDEN, GREG*	64,991	BUCKLEY, PETER	5,998	116,304	R	71.9%	25.8%	73.6%	26.4%
3	2006	253,610	59,529	BROUSSARD, BRUCE	186,380	BLUMENAUER, EARL*	7,701	126,851	D	23.5%	73.5%	24.2%	75.8%
3	2004	346,560	82,045	MARS, TAMI	245,559	BLUMENAUER, EARL*	18,956	163,514	D	23.7%	70.9%	25.0%	75.0%
3	2002	234,977	62,821	SEALE, SARAH	156,851	BLUMENAUER, EARL*	15,305	94,030	D	26.7%	66.8%	28.6%	71.4%
4	2006	290,244	109,105	FELDKAMP, JIM	180,607	DeFAZIO, PETER A.*	532	71,502	D	37.6%	62.2%	37.7%	62.3%
4	2004	374,909	140,882	FELDKAMP, JIM	228,611	DeFAZIO, PETER A.*	5,416	87,729	D	37.6%	61.0%	38.1%	61.9%
4	2002	263,481	90,523	VanLEEUWEN, LIZ	168,150	DeFAZIO, PETER A.*	4,808	77,627	D	34.4%	63.8%	35.0%	65.0%
5	2006	272,234	116,424	ERICKSON, MIKE	146,973	HOOLEY, DARLENE*	8,837	30,549	D	42.8%	54.0%	44.2%	55.8%
5	2004	349,634	154,993	ZUPANCIC, JIM	184,833	HOOLEY, DARLENE*	9,808	29,840	D	44.3%	52.9%	45.6%	54.4%
5	2002	251,537	113,441	BOQUIST, BRIAN J.	137,713	HOOLEY, DARLENE*	383	24,272	D	45.1%	54.7%	45.2%	54.8%
TOTAL	2006	1,357,434	557,491		765,853		34,090	208,362	D	41.1%	56.4%	42.1%	57.9%
TOTAL	2004	1,772,306	761,545		951,688		59,073	190,143	D	43.0%	53.7%	44.5%	55.5%
TOTAL	2002	1,240,315	528,997		676,920		34,398	147,923	D	42.7%	54.6%	43.9%	56.1%

An asterisk (*) denotes incumbent.

OREGON

GENERAL AND PRIMARY ELECTIONS

2006 GENERAL ELECTIONS

Governor — Other vote was 50,229 Constitution (Mary Starrett); 20,030 Pacific Green (Joe Keating); 16,798 Libertarian (Richard Morley); 2,884 scattered write-in.

House — Other vote was:

CD 1 — 4,497 Libertarian (Drake Davis); 4,370 Constitution (Dean Wolf); 447 scattered write-in.
CD 2 — 7,193 Constitution (Jack Alan Brown Jr.); 513 scattered write-in.
CD 3 — 7,003 Constitution (David Brownlow); 698 scattered write-in.
CD 4 — 532 scattered write-in.
CD 5 — 4,194 Pacific Green (Paul Aranas); 4,160 Constitution (Douglas Patterson); 483 scattered write-in.

2006 PRIMARY ELECTIONS

Primary — May 16, 2006

Registration (as of May 16, 2006)

Democratic	762,530
Republican	711,619
Others	65,398
Non-Affiliated	426,392
TOTAL	1,965,939

Primary Type — Closed—Only registered Democrats and Republicans could vote in their party's primary.

OREGON

GENERAL AND PRIMARY ELECTIONS

Note: An asterisk (*) denotes incumbent. The primary and general election were conducted entirely by mail.

		REPUBLICAN PRIMARIES		DEMOCRATIC PRIMARIES		
Governor	Ron Saxton	125,286	41.7%	Theodore R. Kulongoski*	170,944	53.6%
	Kevin Mannix	89,553	29.8%	Jim Hill	92,439	29.0%
	Jason A. Atkinson	67,057	22.3%	Pete Sorenson	51,346	16.1%
	W. Ames Curtright	7,414	2.5%	Scattered write-in	4,448	1.4%
	Gordon Leitch	3,100	1.0%			
	William E. Spidal	2,537	0.8%			
	David W. Beem	1,659	0.6%			
	Bob Leonard Forthan	841	0.3%			
	Scattered write-in	3,107	1.0%			
	TOTAL	300,554		TOTAL	319,177	
Congressional District 1	Derrick Kitts	36,565	97.9%	David Wu*	55,188	87.1%
	Scattered write-in	772	2.1%	Alexa J. Lewis	4,795	7.6%
				Shantu Shah	1,595	2.5%
				Pavel Goberman	1,582	2.5%
				Scattered write-in	234	0.4%
	TOTAL	37,337		TOTAL	63,394	
Congressional District 2	Greg Walden*	70,519	90.2%	Carol Voisin	18,982	45.3%
	Paul A. Daghlian	7,401	9.5%	Dan Davis	11,230	26.8%
	Scattered write-in	248	0.3%	Scott Silver	6,438	15.4%
				Charles H. Butcher III	4,275	10.2%
				Scattered write-in	993	2.4%
	TOTAL	78,168		TOTAL	41,918	
Congressional District 3	*No Republican candidate filed for the primary. Bruce Broussard received 353 write-in votes and appeared as the GOP candidate on the general election ballot. There were also 1,606 scattered write-in votes cast in the primary.*			Earl Blumenauer*	63,350	90.7%
				John Sweeney	6,338	9.1%
				Scattered write-in	146	0.2%
				TOTAL	69,834	
Congressional District 4	Jim Feldkamp	47,560	82.0%	Peter A. DeFazio*	66,432	99.1%
	Monica Johnson	9,757	16.8%	Scattered write-in	596	0.9%
	Scattered write-in	649	1.1%			
	TOTAL	57,966		TOTAL	67,028	
Congressional District 5	Mike Erickson	46,051	98.7%	Darlene Hooley*	54,649	98.9%
	Scattered write-in	627	1.3%	Scattered write-in	606	1.1%
	TOTAL	46,678		TOTAL	55,255	

PENNSYLVANIA

Congressional districts first established for elections held in 2004
19 members

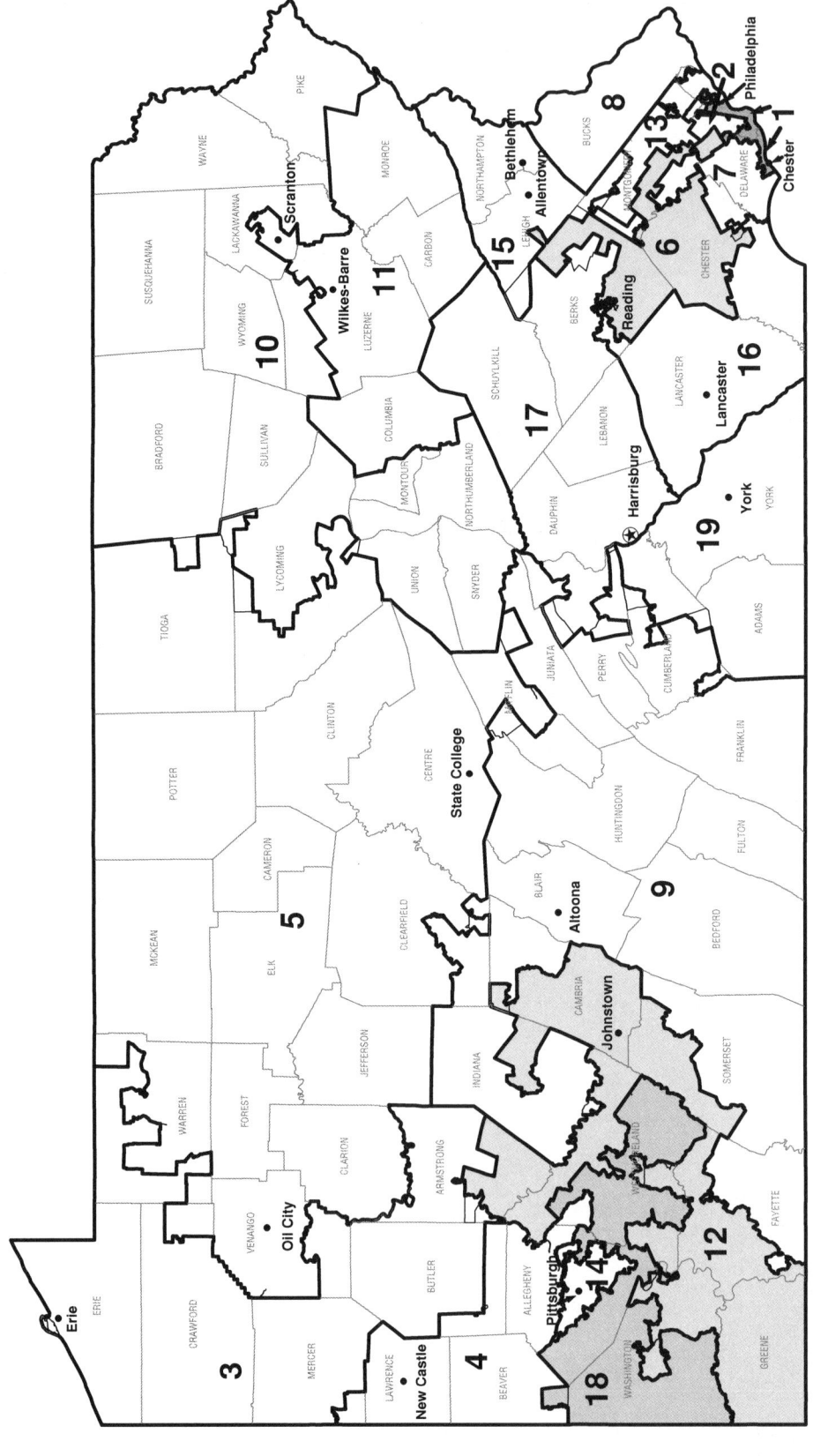

PENNSYLVANIA

Philadelphia Area

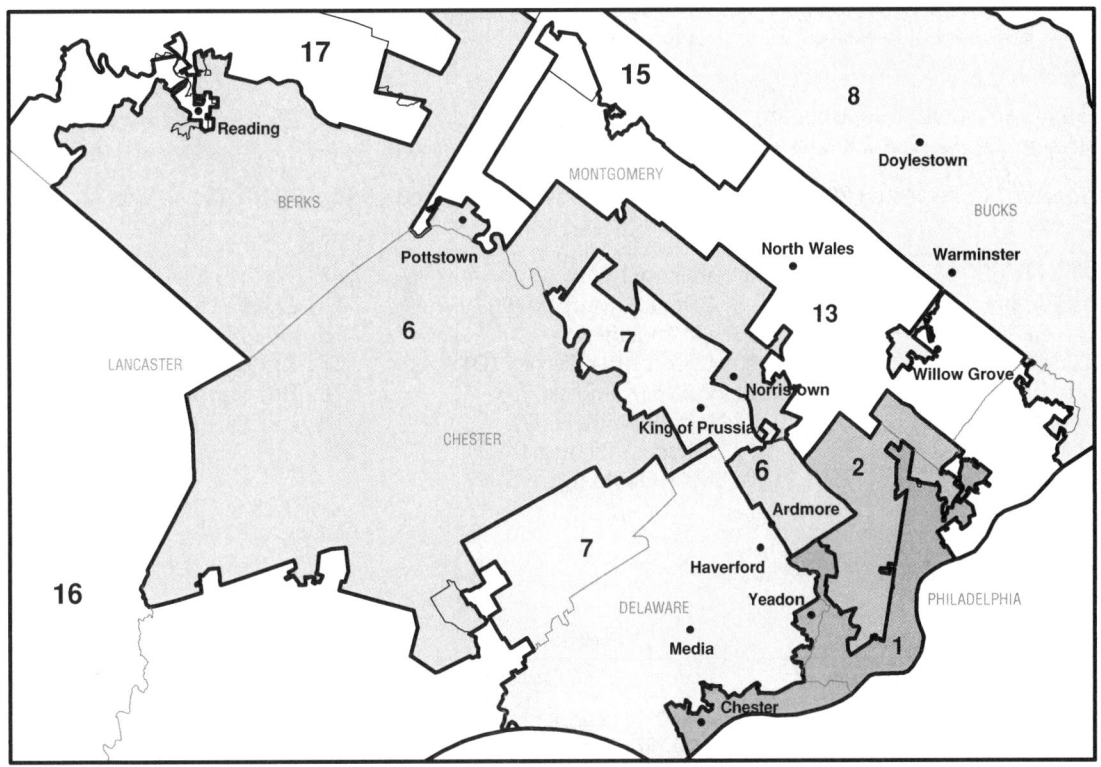

Pittsburgh Area

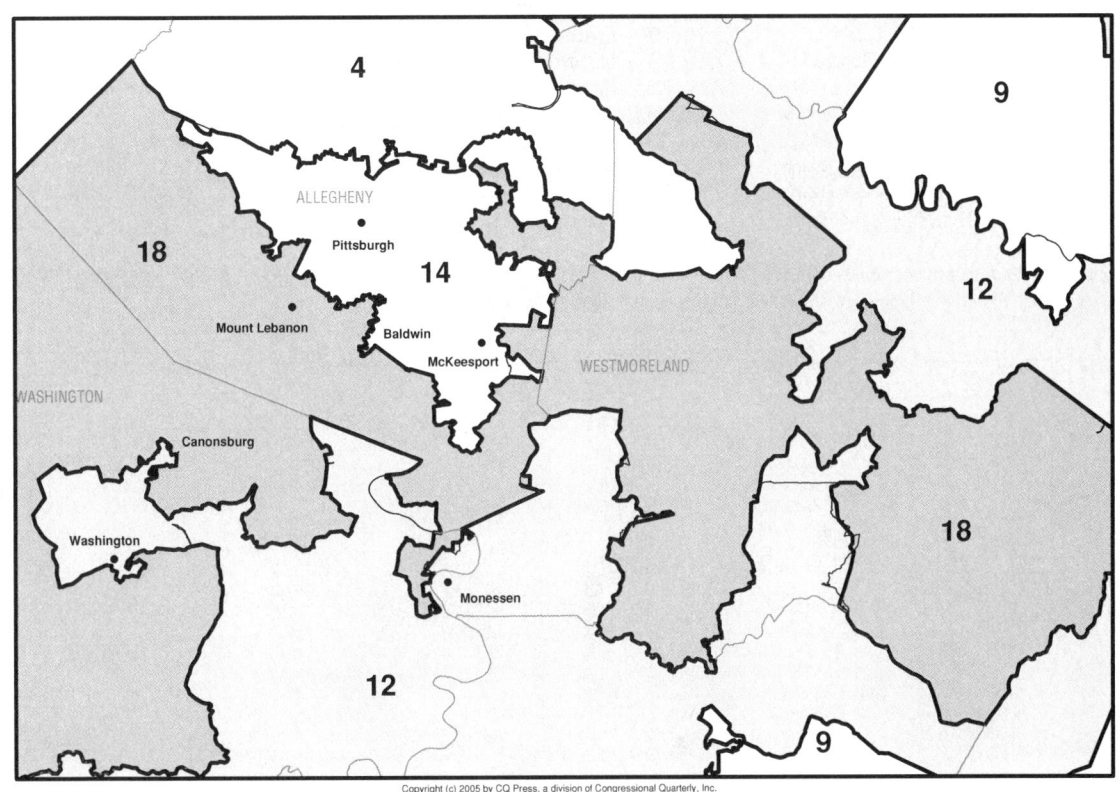

Copyright (c) 2005 by CQ Press, a division of Congressional Quarterly, Inc.

PENNSYLVANIA

GOVERNOR
Edward G. Rendell (D). Reelected 2006 to a four-year term. Previously elected 2002.

SENATORS (1 Democrat, 1 Republican)
Bob Casey Jr. (D). Elected 2006 to a six-year term.

Arlen Specter (R). Reelected 2004 to a six-year term. Previously elected 1998, 1992, 1986, 1980.

REPRESENTATIVES (11 Democrats, 8 Republicans)
1. Robert A. Brady (D)
2. Chaka Fattah (D)
3. Phil English (R)
4. Jason Altmire (D)
5. John E. Peterson (R)
6. Jim Gerlach (R)
7. Joe Sestak (D)
8. Patrick J. Murphy (D)
9. Bill Shuster (R)
10. Christopher Carney (D)
11. Paul E. Kanjorski (D)
12. John P. Murtha (D)
13. Allyson Y. Schwartz (D)
14. Mike Doyle (D)
15. Charlie Dent (R)
16. Joe Pitts (R)
17. Tim Holden (D)
18. Tim Murphy (R)
19. Todd R. Platts (R)

POSTWAR VOTE FOR PRESIDENT

| | | Republican | | Democratic | | Other | | Percentage | | | |
| | | | | | | | | Total Vote | | Major Vote | |
Year	Total Vote	Vote	Candidate	Vote	Candidate	Vote	Plurality	Rep.	Dem.	Rep.	Dem.
2004	5,769,590	2,793,847	Bush, George W.	2,938,095	Kerry, John	37,648	144,248 D	48.4%	50.9%	48.7%	51.3%
2000**	4,913,119	2,281,127	Bush, George W.	2,485,967	Gore, Al	146,025	204,840 D	46.4%	50.6%	47.9%	52.1%
1996**	4,506,118	1,801,169	Dole, Bob	2,215,819	Clinton, Bill	489,130	414,650 D	40.0%	49.2%	44.8%	55.2%
1992**	4,959,810	1,791,841	Bush, George	2,239,164	Clinton, Bill	928,805	447,323 D	36.1%	45.1%	44.5%	55.5%
1988	4,536,251	2,300,087	Bush, George	2,194,944	Dukakis, Michael S.	41,220	105,143 R	50.7%	48.4%	51.2%	48.8%
1984	4,844,903	2,584,323	Reagan, Ronald	2,228,131	Mondale, Walter F.	32,449	356,192 R	53.3%	46.0%	53.7%	46.3%
1980**	4,561,501	2,261,872	Reagan, Ronald	1,937,540	Carter, Jimmy	362,089	324,332 R	49.6%	42.5%	53.9%	46.1%
1976	4,620,787	2,205,604	Ford, Gerald R.	2,328,677	Carter, Jimmy	86,506	123,073 D	47.7%	50.4%	48.6%	51.4%
1972	4,592,106	2,714,521	Nixon, Richard M.	1,796,951	McGovern, George S.	80,634	917,570 R	59.1%	39.1%	60.2%	39.8%
1968**	4,747,928	2,090,017	Nixon, Richard M.	2,259,405	Humphrey, Hubert H.	398,506	169,388 D	44.0%	47.6%	48.1%	51.9%
1964	4,822,690	1,673,657	Goldwater, Barry M.	3,130,954	Johnson, Lyndon B.	18,079	1,457,297 D	34.7%	64.9%	34.8%	65.2%
1960	5,006,541	2,439,956	Nixon, Richard M.	2,556,282	Kennedy, John F.	10,303	116,326 D	48.7%	51.1%	48.8%	51.2%
1956	4,576,503	2,585,252	Eisenhower, Dwight D.	1,981,769	Stevenson, Adlai E.	9,482	603,483 R	56.5%	43.3%	56.6%	43.4%
1952	4,580,969	2,415,789	Eisenhower, Dwight D.	2,146,269	Stevenson, Adlai E.	18,911	269,520 R	52.7%	46.9%	53.0%	47.0%
1948	3,735,348	1,902,197	Dewey, Thomas E.	1,752,426	Truman, Harry S.	80,725	149,771 R	50.9%	46.9%	52.0%	48.0%

**In past elections, the other vote included: 2000 - 103,392 Green (Ralph Nader); 1996 - 430,984 Reform (Ross Perot); 1992 - 902,667 Independent (Ross Perot); 1980 - 292,921 Independent (John Anderson); 1968 - 378,582 American Independent (George Wallace).

PENNSYLVANIA

POSTWAR VOTE FOR GOVERNOR

Year	Total Vote	Republican Vote	Republican Candidate	Democratic Vote	Democratic Candidate	Other Vote	Rep.-Dem. Plurality	Total Vote Rep.	Total Vote Dem.	Major Vote Rep.	Major Vote Dem.
2006	4,096,077	1,622,135	Swann, Lynn	2,470,517	Rendell, Edward G.	3,425	848,382 D	39.6%	60.3%	39.6%	60.4%
2002	3,583,179	1,589,408	Fisher, Mike	1,913,235	Rendell, Edward G.	80,536	323,827 D	44.4%	53.4%	45.4%	54.6%
1998**	3,025,152	1,736,844	Ridge, Thomas J.	938,745	Itkin, Ivan	349,563	798,099 R	57.4%	31.0%	64.9%	35.1%
1994**	3,585,526	1,627,976	Ridge, Thomas J.	1,430,099	Singel, Mark S.	527,451	197,877 R	45.4%	39.9%	53.2%	46.8%
1990	3,052,760	987,516	Hafer, Barbara	2,065,244	Casey, Robert		1,077,728 D	32.3%	67.7%	32.3%	67.7%
1986	3,388,275	1,638,268	Scranton, William W. III	1,717,484	Casey, Robert	32,523	79,216 D	48.4%	50.7%	48.8%	51.2%
1982	3,683,985	1,872,784	Thornburgh, Richard L.	1,772,353	Ertel, Allen E.	38,848	100,431 R	50.8%	48.1%	51.4%	48.6%
1978	3,741,969	1,966,042	Thornburgh, Richard L.	1,737,888	Flaherty, Peter	38,039	228,154 R	52.5%	46.4%	53.1%	46.9%
1974	3,491,234	1,578,917	Lewis, Andrew L.	1,878,252	Shapp, Milton	34,065	299,335 D	45.2%	53.8%	45.7%	54.3%
1970	3,700,060	1,542,854	Broderick, Raymond	2,043,029	Shapp, Milton	114,177	500,175 D	41.7%	55.2%	43.0%	57.0%
1966	4,050,668	2,110,349	Shafer, Raymond P.	1,868,719	Shapp, Milton	71,600	241,630 R	52.1%	46.1%	53.0%	47.0%
1962	4,378,042	2,424,918	Scranton, William W.	1,938,627	Dilworth, Richardson	14,497	486,291 R	55.4%	44.3%	55.6%	44.4%
1958	3,986,918	1,948,769	McGonigle, A. T.	2,024,852	Lawrence, David	13,297	76,083 D	48.9%	50.8%	49.0%	51.0%
1954	3,720,457	1,717,070	Wood, Lloyd H.	1,996,266	Leader, George M.	7,121	279,196 D	46.2%	53.7%	46.2%	53.8%
1950	3,540,059	1,796,119	Fine, John S.	1,710,355	Dilworth, Richardson	33,585	85,764 R	50.7%	48.3%	51.2%	48.8%
1946	3,123,994	1,828,462	Duff, James H.	1,270,947	Rice, John S.	24,585	557,515 R	58.5%	40.7%	59.0%	41.0%

**In past elections, the other vote included: 1998 - 315,761 Constitutional (Peg Luksik); 1994 - 460,269 Constitutional (Luksik).

POSTWAR VOTE FOR SENATOR

Year	Total Vote	Republican Vote	Republican Candidate	Democratic Vote	Democratic Candidate	Other Vote	Rep.-Dem. Plurality	Total Vote Rep.	Total Vote Dem.	Major Vote Rep.	Major Vote Dem.
2006	4,081,043	1,684,778	Santorum, Rick	2,392,984	Casey, Bob Jr.	3,281	708,206 D	41.3%	58.6%	41.3%	58.7%
2004	5,559,105	2,925,080	Specter, Arlen	2,334,126	Hoeffel, Joseph M.	299,899	590,954 R	52.6%	42.0%	55.6%	44.4%
2000	4,735,504	2,481,962	Santorum, Rick	2,154,908	Klink, Ron	98,634	327,054 R	52.4%	45.5%	53.5%	46.5%
1998	2,957,772	1,814,180	Specter, Arlen	1,028,839	Lloyd, Bill	114,753	785,341 R	61.3%	34.8%	63.8%	36.2%
1994	3,513,361	1,735,691	Santorum, Rick	1,648,481	Wofford, Harris	129,189	87,210 R	49.4%	46.9%	51.3%	48.7%
1992	4,802,410	2,358,125	Specter, Arlen	2,224,966	Yeakel, Lynn	219,319	133,159 R	49.1%	46.3%	51.5%	48.5%
1991S	3,382,746	1,521,986	Thornburgh, Richard	1,860,760	Wofford, Harris		338,774 D	45.0%	55.0%	45.0%	55.0%
1988	4,366,598	2,901,715	Heinz, H. John	1,416,764	Vignola, Joseph C.	48,119	1,484,951 R	66.5%	32.4%	67.2%	32.8%
1986	3,378,226	1,906,537	Specter, Arlen	1,448,219	Edgar, Robert W.	23,470	458,318 R	56.4%	42.9%	56.8%	43.2%
1982	3,604,108	2,136,418	Heinz, H. John	1,412,965	Wecht, Cyril H.	54,725	723,453 R	59.3%	39.2%	60.2%	39.8%
1980	4,418,042	2,230,404	Specter, Arlen	2,122,391	Flaherty, Peter	65,247	108,013 R	50.5%	48.0%	51.2%	48.8%
1976	4,546,353	2,381,891	Heinz, H. John	2,126,977	Green, William J. III	37,485	254,914 R	52.4%	46.8%	52.8%	47.2%
1974	3,477,812	1,843,317	Schweiker, Richard S.	1,596,121	Flaherty, Peter	38,374	247,196 R	53.0%	45.9%	53.6%	46.4%
1970	3,644,305	1,874,106	Scott, Hugh	1,653,774	Sesler, William G.	116,425	220,332 R	51.4%	45.4%	53.1%	46.9%
1968	4,624,218	2,399,762	Schweiker, Richard S.	2,117,662	Clark, Joseph S.	106,794	282,100 R	51.9%	45.8%	53.1%	46.9%
1964	4,803,835	2,429,858	Scott, Hugh	2,359,223	Blatt, Genevieve	14,754	70,635 R	50.6%	49.1%	50.7%	49.3%
1962	4,383,475	2,134,649	Van Zandt, James E.	2,238,383	Clark, Joseph S.	10,443	103,734 D	48.7%	51.1%	48.8%	51.2%
1958	3,988,622	2,042,586	Scott, Hugh	1,929,821	Leader, George M.	16,215	112,765 R	51.2%	48.4%	51.4%	48.6%
1956	4,529,874	2,250,671	Duff, James H.	2,268,641	Clark, Joseph S.	10,562	17,970 D	49.7%	50.1%	49.8%	50.2%
1952	4,519,761	2,331,034	Martin, Edward	2,168,546	Bard, Guy Kurtz	20,181	162,488 R	51.6%	48.0%	51.8%	48.2%
1950	3,548,703	1,820,400	Duff, James H.	1,694,076	Myers, Francis J.	34,227	126,324 R	51.3%	47.7%	51.8%	48.2%
1946	3,127,860	1,853,458	Martin, Edward	1,245,338	Guffey, Joseph F.	29,064	608,120 R	59.3%	39.8%	59.8%	40.2%

The 1991 election was for a short term to fill a vacancy.

PENNSYLVANIA

GOVERNOR 2006

2000 Census Population	County	Total Vote	Republican	Democratic	Other	Rep.-Dem. Plurality	Total Vote Rep.	Total Vote Dem.	Major Vote Rep.	Major Vote Dem.
91,292	ADAMS	30,122	17,084	13,034	4	4,050 R	56.7%	43.3%	56.7%	43.3%
1,281,666	ALLEGHENY	459,945	184,063	275,227	655	91,164 D	40.0%	59.8%	40.1%	59.9%
72,392	ARMSTRONG	23,147	13,595	9,552		4,043 R	58.7%	41.3%	58.7%	41.3%
181,412	BEAVER	64,679	29,069	35,510	100	6,441 D	44.9%	54.9%	45.0%	55.0%
49,984	BEDFORD	16,643	10,270	6,372	1	3,898 R	61.7%	38.3%	61.7%	38.3%
373,638	BERKS	116,939	50,096	66,837	6	16,741 D	42.8%	57.2%	42.8%	57.2%
129,144	BLAIR	38,765	23,295	15,435	35	7,860 R	60.1%	39.8%	60.1%	39.9%
62,761	BRADFORD	19,181	10,670	8,485	26	2,185 R	55.6%	44.2%	55.7%	44.3%
597,635	BUCKS	233,604	69,798	163,739	67	93,941 D	29.9%	70.1%	29.9%	70.1%
174,083	BUTLER	63,629	38,613	24,936	80	13,677 R	60.7%	39.2%	60.8%	39.2%
152,598	CAMBRIA	52,362	20,506	31,856		11,350 D	39.2%	60.8%	39.2%	60.8%
5,974	CAMERON	1,782	989	793		196 R	55.5%	44.5%	55.5%	44.5%
58,802	CARBON	17,575	6,917	10,633	25	3,716 D	39.4%	60.5%	39.4%	60.6%
135,758	CENTRE	43,535	20,051	23,415	69	3,364 D	46.1%	53.8%	46.1%	53.9%
433,501	CHESTER	173,397	60,437	112,960		52,523 D	34.9%	65.1%	34.9%	65.1%
41,765	CLARION	12,959	7,505	5,451	3	2,054 R	57.9%	42.1%	57.9%	42.1%
83,382	CLEARFIELD	25,800	12,830	12,938	32	108 D	49.7%	50.1%	49.8%	50.2%
37,914	CLINTON	9,805	4,341	5,464		1,123 D	44.3%	55.7%	44.3%	55.7%
64,151	COLUMBIA	18,385	9,078	9,281	26	203 D	49.4%	50.5%	49.4%	50.6%
90,366	CRAWFORD	27,913	16,202	11,695	16	4,507 R	58.0%	41.9%	58.1%	41.9%
213,674	CUMBERLAND	79,251	46,189	32,737	325	13,452 R	58.3%	41.3%	58.5%	41.5%
251,798	DAUPHIN	87,005	47,294	39,711		7,583 R	54.4%	45.6%	54.4%	45.6%
550,864	DELAWARE	208,796	54,403	154,249	144	99,846 D	26.1%	73.9%	26.1%	73.9%
35,112	ELK	11,423	4,499	6,907	17	2,408 D	39.4%	60.5%	39.4%	60.6%
280,843	ERIE	86,179	36,059	50,042	78	13,983 D	41.8%	58.1%	41.9%	58.1%
148,644	FAYETTE	38,112	15,492	22,603	17	7,111 D	40.6%	59.3%	40.7%	59.3%
4,946	FOREST	1,989	1,059	929	1	130 R	53.2%	46.7%	53.3%	46.7%
129,313	FRANKLIN	43,058	26,043	16,945	70	9,098 R	60.5%	39.4%	60.6%	39.4%
14,261	FULTON	4,339	2,669	1,670		999 R	61.5%	38.5%	61.5%	38.5%
40,672	GREENE	12,743	5,670	7,055	18	1,385 D	44.5%	55.4%	44.6%	55.4%
45,586	HUNTINGDON	13,594	8,103	5,490	1	2,613 R	59.6%	40.4%	59.6%	40.4%
89,605	INDIANA	26,343	13,390	12,953		437 R	50.8%	49.2%	50.8%	49.2%
45,932	JEFFERSON	14,176	8,774	5,402		3,372 R	61.9%	38.1%	61.9%	38.1%
22,821	JUNIATA	7,770	4,995	2,748	27	2,247 R	64.3%	35.4%	64.5%	35.5%
213,295	LACKAWANNA	78,061	21,095	56,966		35,871 D	27.0%	73.0%	27.0%	73.0%
470,658	LANCASTER	150,842	87,668	62,934	240	24,734 R	58.1%	41.7%	58.2%	41.8%
94,643	LAWRENCE	31,886	14,329	17,557		3,228 D	44.9%	55.1%	44.9%	55.1%
120,327	LEBANON	39,653	22,775	16,813	65	5,962 R	57.4%	42.4%	57.5%	42.5%
312,090	LEHIGH	94,439	34,692	59,338	409	24,646 D	36.7%	62.8%	36.9%	63.1%
319,250	LUZERNE	95,697	31,051	64,628	18	33,577 D	32.4%	67.5%	32.5%	67.5%
120,044	LYCOMING	35,955	21,116	14,777	62	6,339 R	58.7%	41.1%	58.8%	41.2%
45,936	MCKEAN	10,940	5,890	5,044	6	846 R	53.8%	46.1%	53.9%	46.1%
120,293	MERCER	38,156	18,237	19,888	31	1,651 D	47.8%	52.1%	47.8%	52.2%
46,486	MIFFLIN	12,372	7,642	4,730		2,912 R	61.8%	38.2%	61.8%	38.2%
138,687	MONROE	35,501	14,071	21,430		7,359 D	39.6%	60.4%	39.6%	60.4%
750,097	MONTGOMERY	295,387	83,718	211,651	18	127,933 D	28.3%	71.7%	28.3%	71.7%
18,236	MONTOUR	5,830	3,059	2,764	7	295 R	52.5%	47.4%	52.5%	47.5%
267,066	NORTHAMPTON	83,101	30,081	53,007	13	22,926 D	36.2%	63.8%	36.2%	63.8%
94,556	NORTHUMBERLAND	26,610	13,140	13,470		330 D	49.4%	50.6%	49.4%	50.6%
43,602	PERRY	14,475	9,998	4,477		5,521 R	69.1%	30.9%	69.1%	30.9%
1,517,550	PHILADELPHIA	428,841	45,502	383,339		337,837 D	10.6%	89.4%	10.6%	89.4%
46,302	PIKE	13,949	6,551	7,393	5	842 D	47.0%	53.0%	47.0%	53.0%
18,080	POTTER	5,543	3,498	2,035	10	1,463 R	63.1%	36.7%	63.2%	36.8%
150,336	SCHUYLKILL	47,226	20,886	26,327	13	5,441 D	44.2%	55.7%	44.2%	55.8%
37,546	SNYDER	11,281	7,203	4,073	5	3,130 R	63.9%	36.1%	63.9%	36.1%
80,023	SOMERSET	27,562	15,028	12,499	35	2,529 R	54.5%	45.3%	54.6%	45.4%
6,556	SULLIVAN	2,539	1,275	1,264		11 R	50.2%	49.8%	50.2%	49.8%
42,238	SUSQUEHANNA	15,131	6,874	8,239	18	1,365 D	45.4%	54.5%	45.5%	54.5%
41,373	TIOGA	12,519	7,370	5,126	23	2,244 R	58.9%	40.9%	59.0%	41.0%
41,624	UNION	11,522	6,503	5,006	13	1,497 R	56.4%	43.4%	56.5%	43.5%

PENNSYLVANIA

GOVERNOR 2006

2000 Census Population	County	Total Vote	Republican	Democratic	Other	Rep.-Dem. Plurality	Percentage			
							Total Vote		Major Vote	
							Rep.	Dem.	Rep.	Dem.
57,565	VENANGO	17,661	9,742	7,906	13	1,836 R	55.2%	44.8%	55.2%	44.8%
43,863	WARREN	13,141	5,846	7,278	17	1,432 D	44.5%	55.4%	44.5%	55.5%
202,897	WASHINGTON	72,949	34,440	38,422	87	3,982 D	47.2%	52.7%	47.3%	52.7%
47,722	WAYNE	15,785	7,635	8,143	7	508 D	48.4%	51.6%	48.4%	51.6%
369,993	WESTMORELAND	130,192	69,854	60,145	193	9,709 R	53.7%	46.2%	53.7%	46.3%
28,080	WYOMING	10,265	4,726	5,518	21	792 D	46.0%	53.8%	46.1%	53.9%
381,751	YORK	126,121	70,592	55,276	253	15,316 R	56.0%	43.8%	56.1%	43.9%
12,281,054	TOTAL	4,096,077	1,622,135	2,470,517	3,425	848,382 D	39.6%	60.3%	39.6%	60.4%

PENNSYLVANIA

SENATOR 2006

2000 Census Population	County	Total Vote	Republican	Democratic	Other	Rep.-Dem. Plurality	Percentage			
							Total Vote		Major Vote	
							Rep.	Dem.	Rep.	Dem.
91,292	ADAMS	30,244	16,649	13,587	8	3,062 R	55.0%	44.9%	55.1%	44.9%
1,281,666	ALLEGHENY	459,942	161,144	298,096	702	136,952 D	35.0%	64.8%	35.1%	64.9%
72,392	ARMSTRONG	23,048	11,499	11,549		50 D	49.9%	50.1%	49.9%	50.1%
181,412	BEAVER	64,613	24,450	39,998	165	15,548 D	37.8%	61.9%	37.9%	62.1%
49,984	BEDFORD	16,598	9,703	6,895		2,808 R	58.5%	41.5%	58.5%	41.5%
373,638	BERKS	116,741	52,806	63,915	20	11,109 D	45.2%	54.7%	45.2%	54.8%
129,144	BLAIR	38,728	21,504	17,179	45	4,325 R	55.5%	44.4%	55.6%	44.4%
62,761	BRADFORD	19,102	10,804	8,277	21	2,527 R	56.6%	43.3%	56.6%	43.4%
597,635	BUCKS	232,600	96,441	136,063	96	39,622 D	41.5%	58.5%	41.5%	58.5%
174,083	BUTLER	62,169	34,253	27,818	98	6,435 R	55.1%	44.7%	55.2%	44.8%
152,598	CAMBRIA	52,129	18,928	33,196	5	14,268 D	36.3%	63.7%	36.3%	63.7%
5,974	CAMERON	1,762	914	848		66 R	51.9%	48.1%	51.9%	48.1%
58,802	CARBON	17,461	7,439	9,997	25	2,558 D	42.6%	57.3%	42.7%	57.3%
135,758	CENTRE	43,344	18,639	24,582	123	5,943 D	43.0%	56.7%	43.1%	56.9%
433,501	CHESTER	173,293	77,948	95,293	52	17,345 D	45.0%	55.0%	45.0%	55.0%
41,765	CLARION	12,883	6,801	6,081	1	720 R	52.8%	47.2%	52.8%	47.2%
83,382	CLEARFIELD	25,669	11,480	14,186	3	2,706 D	44.7%	55.3%	44.7%	55.3%
37,914	CLINTON	9,778	4,491	5,287		796 D	45.9%	54.1%	45.9%	54.1%
64,151	COLUMBIA	18,311	8,970	9,327	14	357 D	49.0%	50.9%	49.0%	51.0%
90,366	CRAWFORD	27,758	14,260	13,480	18	780 R	51.4%	48.6%	51.4%	48.6%
213,674	CUMBERLAND	79,324	42,410	36,638	276	5,772 R	53.5%	46.2%	53.7%	46.3%
251,798	DAUPHIN	87,463	40,832	46,622	9	5,790 D	46.7%	53.3%	46.7%	53.3%
550,864	DELAWARE	207,792	79,534	128,052	206	48,518 D	38.3%	61.6%	38.3%	61.7%
35,112	ELK	11,347	4,192	7,142	13	2,950 D	36.9%	62.9%	37.0%	63.0%
280,843	ERIE	85,733	34,757	50,857	119	16,100 D	40.5%	59.3%	40.6%	59.4%
148,644	FAYETTE	37,983	13,484	24,495	4	11,011 D	35.5%	64.5%	35.5%	64.5%
4,946	FOREST	1,967	938	1,029		91 D	47.7%	52.3%	47.7%	52.3%
129,313	FRANKLIN	43,296	26,524	16,710	62	9,814 R	61.3%	38.6%	61.3%	38.7%
14,261	FULTON	4,372	2,673	1,699		974 R	61.1%	38.9%	61.1%	38.9%
40,672	GREENE	12,728	4,637	8,078	13	3,441 D	36.4%	63.5%	36.5%	63.5%
45,586	HUNTINGDON	13,595	7,279	6,315	1	964 R	53.5%	46.5%	53.5%	46.5%
89,605	INDIANA	26,437	12,342	14,091	4	1,749 D	46.7%	53.3%	46.7%	53.3%
45,932	JEFFERSON	14,155	7,731	6,424		1,307 R	54.6%	45.4%	54.6%	45.4%
22,821	JUNIATA	7,808	4,557	3,236	15	1,321 R	58.4%	41.4%	58.5%	41.5%
213,295	LACKAWANNA	78,172	23,874	54,289	9	30,415 D	30.5%	69.4%	30.5%	69.5%

PENNSYLVANIA

SENATOR 2006

2000 Census Population	County	Total Vote	Republican	Democratic	Other	Rep.-Dem. Plurality	Percentage Total Vote Rep.	Total Vote Dem.	Major Vote Rep.	Major Vote Dem.
470,658	LANCASTER	150,354	87,535	62,662	157	24,873 R	58.2%	41.7%	58.3%	41.7%
94,643	LAWRENCE	31,804	13,368	18,436		5,068 D	42.0%	58.0%	42.0%	58.0%
120,327	LEBANON	39,537	21,756	17,737	44	4,019 R	55.0%	44.9%	55.1%	44.9%
312,090	LEHIGH	93,343	39,461	53,855	27	14,394 D	42.3%	57.7%	42.3%	57.7%
319,250	LUZERNE	95,558	37,648	57,868	42	20,220 D	39.4%	60.6%	39.4%	60.6%
120,044	LYCOMING	35,930	21,734	14,155	41	7,579 R	60.5%	39.4%	60.6%	39.4%
45,936	MCKEAN	10,936	5,928	5,003	5	925 R	54.2%	45.7%	54.2%	45.8%
120,293	MERCER	37,941	16,274	21,640	27	5,366 D	42.9%	57.0%	42.9%	57.1%
46,486	MIFFLIN	12,346	7,097	5,247	2	1,850 R	57.5%	42.5%	57.5%	42.5%
138,687	MONROE	35,417	15,555	19,862		4,307 D	43.9%	56.1%	43.9%	56.1%
750,097	MONTGOMERY	292,835	111,507	181,274	54	69,767 D	38.1%	61.9%	38.1%	61.9%
18,236	MONTOUR	5,820	3,110	2,704	6	406 R	53.4%	46.5%	53.5%	46.5%
267,066	NORTHAMPTON	83,078	34,644	48,419	15	13,775 D	41.7%	58.3%	41.7%	58.3%
94,556	NORTHUMBERLAND	26,444	13,304	13,140		164 R	50.3%	49.7%	50.3%	49.7%
43,602	PERRY	14,448	8,729	5,719		3,010 R	60.4%	39.6%	60.4%	39.6%
1,517,550	PHILADELPHIA	424,509	67,452	357,057		289,605 D	15.9%	84.1%	15.9%	84.1%
46,302	PIKE	13,943	7,208	6,718	17	490 R	51.7%	48.2%	51.8%	48.2%
18,080	POTTER	5,610	3,573	2,024	13	1,549 R	63.7%	36.1%	63.8%	36.2%
150,336	SCHUYLKILL	47,032	21,510	25,508	14	3,998 D	45.7%	54.2%	45.7%	54.3%
37,546	SNYDER	11,286	7,147	4,137	2	3,010 R	63.3%	36.7%	63.3%	36.7%
80,023	SOMERSET	27,489	13,391	14,054	44	663 D	48.7%	51.1%	48.8%	51.2%
6,556	SULLIVAN	2,534	1,351	1,181	2	170 R	53.3%	46.6%	53.4%	46.6%
42,238	SUSQUEHANNA	15,119	7,787	7,318	14	469 R	51.5%	48.4%	51.6%	48.4%
41,373	TIOGA	12,522	7,650	4,850	22	2,800 R	61.1%	38.7%	61.2%	38.8%
41,624	UNION	11,496	6,614	4,876	6	1,738 R	57.5%	42.4%	57.6%	42.4%
57,565	VENANGO	17,570	9,042	8,502	26	540 R	51.5%	48.4%	51.5%	48.5%
43,863	WARREN	13,032	6,325	6,677	30	352 D	48.5%	51.2%	48.6%	51.4%
202,897	WASHINGTON	72,574	29,417	43,067	90	13,650 D	40.5%	59.3%	40.6%	59.4%
47,722	WAYNE	15,709	8,400	7,294	15	1,106 R	53.5%	46.4%	53.5%	46.5%
369,993	WESTMORELAND	130,248	60,468	69,608	172	9,140 D	46.4%	53.4%	46.5%	53.5%
28,080	WYOMING	10,246	5,635	4,591	20	1,044 R	55.0%	44.8%	55.1%	44.9%
381,751	YORK	125,988	69,271	56,470	247	12,801 R	55.0%	44.8%	55.1%	44.9%
12,281,054	TOTAL	4,081,043	1,684,778	2,392,984	3,281	708,206 D	41.3%	58.6%	41.3%	58.7%

PENNSYLVANIA

HOUSE OF REPRESENTATIVES

CD	Year	Total Vote	Republican Vote	Republican Candidate	Democratic Vote	Democratic Candidate	Other Vote	Rep.-Dem. Plurality	Total Vote Rep.	Total Vote Dem.	Major Vote Rep.	Major Vote Dem.
1	2006	137,999		—	137,987	BRADY, ROBERT A.*	12	137,987 D		100.0%		100.0%
1	2004	248,587	33,266	WILLIAMS, DEBORAH L.	214,462	BRADY, ROBERT A.*	859	181,196 D	13.4%	86.3%	13.4%	86.6%
1	2002	140,090	17,444	DELANEY, MARIE G.	121,076	BRADY, ROBERT A.*	1,570	103,632 D	12.5%	86.4%	12.6%	87.4%
2	2006	187,283	17,291	GESSNER, MICHAEL	165,867	FATTAH, CHAKA*	4,125	148,576 D	9.2%	88.6%	9.4%	90.6%
2	2004	287,637	34,411	BOLNO, STEWART	253,226	FATTAH, CHAKA*		218,815 D	12.0%	88.0%	12.0%	88.0%
2	2002	171,611	20,988	DOUGHERTY, THOMAS G.	150,623	FATTAH, CHAKA*		129,635 D	12.2%	87.8%	12.2%	87.8%
3	2006	202,518	108,525	ENGLISH, PHIL*	85,110	PORTER, STEVEN	8,883	23,415 R	53.6%	42.0%	56.0%	44.0%
3	2004	277,323	166,580	ENGLISH, PHIL*	110,684	PORTER, STEVEN	59	55,896 R	60.1%	39.9%	60.1%	39.9%
3	2002	150,329	116,763	ENGLISH, PHIL*		—	33,566	116,763 R	77.7%		100.0%	
4	2006	254,084	122,049	HART, MELISSA A.*	131,847	ALTMIRE, JASON	188	9,798 D	48.0%	51.9%	48.1%	51.9%
4	2004	323,945	204,329	HART, MELISSA A.*	116303	DROBAC, STEVAN JR.	3,313	88,026 R	63.1%	35.9%	63.7%	36.3%
4	2002	202,218	130,534	HART, MELISSA A.*	71,674	DROBAC, STEVAN JR.	10	58,860 R	64.6%	35.4%	64.6%	35.4%
5	2006	191,727	115,126	PETERSON, JOHN E.*	76,456	HILLIARD, DONALD L.	145	38,670 R	60.0%	39.9%	60.1%	39.9%
5	2004	219,198	192,852	PETERSON, JOHN E.*		—	26,346	192,852 R	88.0%		100.0%	
5	2002	143,211	124,942	PETERSON, JOHN E.*		—	18,269	124,942 R	87.2%		100.0%	
6	2006	238,939	121,047	GERLACH, JIM*	117,892	MURPHY, LOIS		3,155 R	50.7%	49.3%	50.7%	49.3%
6	2004	314,386	160,348	GERLACH, JIM*	153,977	MURPHY, LOIS	61	6,371 R	51.0%	49.0%	51.0%	49.0%
6	2002	201,791	103,648	GERLACH, JIM	98,128	WOFFORD, DAN	15	5,520 R	51.4%	48.6%	51.4%	48.6%
7	2006	262,434	114,426	WELDON, CURT*	147,898	SESTAK, JOE	110	33,472 D	43.6%	56.4%	43.6%	56.4%
7	2004	334,547	196,556	WELDON, CURT*	134,932	SCOLES, PAUL	3,059	61,624 R	58.8%	40.3%	59.3%	40.7%
7	2002	221,351	146,296	WELDON, CURT*	75,055	LENNON, PETER A.		71,241 R	66.1%	33.9%	66.1%	33.9%
8	2006	249,817	124,138	FITZPATRICK, MICHAEL G.*	125,656	MURPHY, PATRICK J.	23	1,518 D	49.7%	50.3%	49.7%	50.3%
8	2004	331,276	183,229	FITZPATRICK, MICHAEL G.	143,427	SCHRADER, VIRGINIA WATERS	4,620	39,802 R	55.3%	43.3%	56.1%	43.9%
8	2002	203,687	127,475	GREENWOOD, JAMES C.*	76,178	REECE, TIMOTHY T.	34	51,297 R	62.6%	37.4%	62.6%	37.4%
9	2006	200,820	121,069	SHUSTER, BILL*	79,610	BARR, TONY	141	41,459 R	60.3%	39.6%	60.3%	39.7%
9	2004	265,272	184,320	SHUSTER, BILL*	80,787	POLITIS, PAUL I.	165	103,533 R	69.5%	30.5%	69.5%	30.5%
9	2002	174,849	124,184	SHUSTER, BILL*	50,558	HENRY, JOHN R.	107	73,626 R	71.0%	28.9%	71.1%	28.9%
10	2006	208,173	97,862	SHERWOOD, DON*	110,115	CARNEY, CHRISTOPHER	196	12,253 D	47.0%	52.9%	47.1%	52.9%
10	2004	206,839	191,967	SHERWOOD, DON*		—	14,872	191,967 R	92.8%		100.0%	
10	2002	164,159	152,017	# SHERWOOD, DON*		—	12,142	152,017 R	92.6%		100.0%	
11	2006	185,413	51,033	LEONARDI, JOSEPH F.	134,340	KANJORSKI, PAUL E.*	40	83,307 D	27.5%	72.5%	27.5%	72.5%
11	2004	181,285			171,147	KANJORSKI, PAUL E.*	10,138	171,147 D		94.4%		100.0%
11	2002	168,615	71,543	BARLETTA, LOUIS J.	93,758	KANJORSKI, PAUL E.*	3,314	22,215 D	42.4%	55.6%	43.3%	56.7%
12	2006	203,163	79,612	IREY, DIANA	123,472	MURTHA, JOHN P.*	79	43,860 D	39.2%	60.8%	39.2%	60.8%
12	2004	204,710			204,504	MURTHA, JOHN P.*	206	204,504 D		99.9%		100.0%
12	2002	169,028	44,818	CHOBY, BILL	124,201	MURTHA, JOHN P.*	9	79,383 D	26.5%	73.5%	26.5%	73.5%
13	2006	222,860	75,492	BHAKTA, RAJ PETER	147,368	SCHWARTZ, ALLYSON Y.*		71,876 D	33.9%	66.1%	33.9%	66.1%
13	2004	308,124	127,205	BROWN, MELISSA	171,763	SCHWARTZ, ALLYSON Y.	9,156	44,558 D	41.3%	55.7%	42.5%	57.5%
13	2002	211,867	100,295	BROWN, MELISSA	107,945	HOEFFEL, JOSEPH M.*	3,627	7,650 D	47.3%	50.9%	48.2%	51.8%
14	2006	179,401		—	161,075	DOYLE, MIKE*	18,326	161,075 D		89.8%		100.0%
14	2004	220,299		—	220,139	DOYLE, MIKE*	160	220,139 D		99.9%		100.0%
14	2002	123,412		—	123,323	DOYLE, MIKE*	89	123,323 D	99.9%	99.9%	100.0%	100.0%
15	2006	198,173	106,153	DENT, CHARLIE*	86,186	DERTINGER, CHARLES	5,834	19,967 R	53.6%	43.5%	55.2%	44.8%
15	2004	291,147	170,634	DENT, CHARLIE	114,646	DRISCOLL, JOE	5,867	55,988 R	58.6%	39.4%	59.8%	40.2%
15	2002	171,713	98,493	TOOMEY, PATRICK J.*	73,212	O'BRIEN, EDWARD J.	8	25,281 R	57.4%	42.6%	57.4%	42.6%
16	2006	204,669	115,741	PITTS, JOE*	80,915	HERR, LOIS K.	8,013	34,826 R	56.6%	39.5%	58.9%	41.1%
16	2004	285,313	183,620	PITTS, JOE*	98,410	HERR, LOIS K.	3,283	85,210 R	64.4%	34.5%	65.1%	34.9%
16	2002	134,597	119,046	PITTS, JOE*		—	15,551	119,046 R	88.4%	100.0%	100.0%	
17	2006	212,777	75,455	WERTZ, MATTHEW A.	137,253	HOLDEN, TIM*	69	61,798 D	35.5%	64.5%	35.5%	64.5%
17	2004	291,793	113,592	PATERNO, SCOTT	172,412	HOLDEN, TIM*	5,789	58,820 D	38.9%	59.1%	39.7%	60.3%
17	2002	201,291	97,802	GEKAS, GEORGE W.*	103,483	HOLDEN, TIM*	6	5,681 D	48.6%	51.4%	48.6%	51.4%
18	2006	250,240	144,632	MURPHY, TIM*	105,419	KLUKO, CHAD	189	39,213 R	57.8%	42.1%	57.8%	42.2%
18	2004	315,342	197,894	MURPHY, TIM*	117420	BOLES, MARK G.	28	80,474 R	62.8%	37.2%	62.8%	37.2%
18	2002	199,349	119,885	MURPHY, TIM	79,451	MACHEK, JACK	13	40,434 R	60.1%	39.9%	60.1%	39.9%
19	2006	222,898	142,512	PLATTS, TODD R.*	74,625	AVILLO, PHILIP J. JR.	5,761	67,887 R	63.9%	33.5%	65.6%	34.4%
19	2004	245,251	224,274	PLATTS, TODD R.*		—	20,977	224,274 R	91.4%		100.0%	
19	2002	157,145	143,097	PLATTS, TODD R.*		—	14,048	143,097 R	91.1%	100.0%	100.0%	
TOTAL	2006	4,013,388	1,732,163		2,229,091		52,134	496,928 D	43.2%	55.5%	43.7%	56.3%
TOTAL	2004	5,152,274	2,565,077		2,478,239		108,958	86,838 R	49.8%	48.1%	50.9%	49.1%
TOTAL	2002	3,310,313	1,859,270		1,348,665		102,378	510,605 R	56.2%	40.7%	58.0%	42.0%

An asterisk (*) denotes incumbent. A pound sign (#) indicates that the candidate had the endorsement of more than one party.

PENNSYLVANIA

GENERAL AND PRIMARY ELECTIONS

2006 GENERAL ELECTIONS

Governor   Other vote was 3,425 scattered write-in.

Senator   Other vote was 3,281 scattered write-in.

House   Other vote was:

CD 1   12 scattered write-in.
CD 2   4,125 Green (David G. Baker).
CD 3   8,706 Constitution (Timothy J. Hagberg); 177 scattered write-in.
CD 4   188 scattered write-in.
CD 5   145 scattered write-in.
CD 6
CD 7   110 scattered write-in.
CD 8   23 scattered write-in.
CD 9   141 scattered write-in.
CD 10   196 scattered write-in.
CD 11   40 scattered write-in.
CD 12   79 scattered write-in.
CD 13
CD 14   17,720 Green (Titus North); 606 scattered write-in.
CD 15   5,802 Green (Greta Browne); 32 scattered write-in.
CD 16   7,958 Independent (John A. Murphy); 55 scattered write-in.
CD 17   69 scattered write-in.
CD 18   189 scattered write-in.
CD 19   5,640 Green (Derf W. Maitland); 121 scattered write-in.

2006 PRIMARY ELECTIONS

Primary   May 16, 2006   **Registration**
(as of May 16, 2006)

Democratic	3,840,548
Republican	3,290,200
Libertarian	34,559
Green	16,813
Constitution	3,433
Other	895,034
TOTAL	8,080,587

Primary Type   Closed—Only registered Democrats and Republicans could vote in their party's primary.

Note: An asterisk (*) denotes incumbent.

	REPUBLICAN PRIMARIES			DEMOCRATIC PRIMARIES		
Governor	Lynn Swann	583,658	99.5%	Edward G. Rendell*	654,985	98.5%
	Scattered write-in	2,886	0.5%	Lynn Swann (R, write-in)	7,939	1.2%
				Scattered write-in	1,966	0.3%
	TOTAL	586,544		TOTAL	664,890	
Senator	Rick Santorum*	561,952	99.4%	Bob Casey Jr.	629,271	84.5%
	Scattered write-in	3,631	0.6%	Chuck Pennacchio	66,364	8.9%
				Alan Sandals	48,113	6.5%
				Scatterd write-in	1,114	0.1%
	TOTAL	565,583		TOTAL	744,862	
Congressional District 1	No Republican candidate			Robert A. Brady*	29,990	100.0%

PENNSYLVANIA

GENERAL AND PRIMARY ELECTIONS

	REPUBLICAN PRIMARIES			DEMOCRATIC PRIMARIES		
Congressional District 2	Michael Gessner	3,159	100.0%	Chaka Fattah*	41,566	100.0%
Congressional District 3	Phil English*	36,189	99.6%	Steven Porter	35,001	99.3%
	Scattered write-in	146	0.4%	Scattered write-in	264	0.7%
	TOTAL	36,335		TOTAL	35,265	
Congressional District 4	Melissa A. Hart*	34,559	99.1%	Jason Altmire	32,322	54.7%
	Scattered write-in	302	0.9%	Georgia Berner	26,596	45.0%
				Scattered write-in	148	0.3%
	TOTAL	34,861		TOTAL	59,066	
Congressional District 5	John E. Peterson*	44,827	99.7%	Donald L. Hilliard	28,715	99.2%
	Scattered write-in	149	0.3%	Scattered write-in	228	0.8%
	TOTAL	44,976		TOTAL	28,943	
Congressional District 6	Jim Gerlach*	30,088	100.0%	Lois Murphy	22,242	76.2%
				Mike Leibowitz	6,961	23.8%
				TOTAL	29,203	
Congressional District 7	Curt Weldon*	35,604	100.0%	Joe Sestak	17,616	100.0%
Congressional District 8	Michael G. Fitzpatrick*	22,862	99.9%	Patrick J. Murphy	17,889	64.6%
	Scattered write-in	23	0.1%	Andrew L. Warren	9,812	35.4%
				Scattered write-in	8	
	TOTAL	22,885		TOTAL	27,709	
Congressional District 9	Bill Shuster*	54,954	99.3%	Tony Barr (write-in)	1,935	78.7%
	Scattered write-in	369	0.7%	Scattered write-in	525	21.3%
	TOTAL	55,323		TOTAL	2,460	
Congressional District 10	Don Sherwood*	31,434	56.2%	Christopher Carney	26,300	99.2%
	Kathy Scott	24,396	43.6%	Scattered write-in	211	0.8%
	Scattered write-in	125	0.2%			
	TOTAL	55,955		TOTAL	26,511	
Congressional District 11	Joseph F. Leonardi	18,910	99.9%	Paul E. Kanjorski*	50,117	100.0%
	Scattered write-in	28	0.1%	Scattered write-in	23	
	TOTAL	18,938		TOTAL	50,140	
Congressional District 12	Diana Irey	21,619	99.5%	John P. Murtha*	60,376	99.5%
	Scattered write-in	115	0.5%	Scattered write-in	312	0.5%
	TOTAL	21,734		TOTAL	60,688	
Congressional District 13	Raj Peter Bhakta	17,042	100.0%	Allyson Y. Schwartz*	22,877	100.0%
Congressional District 14	No Republican candidate filed for the primary. There were 571 scattered write-in votes.			Mike Doyle*	54,213	75.8%
				Mike Issac	17,193	24.0%
				Scattered write-in	152	0.2%
				TOTAL	71,558	
Congressional District 15	Charlie Dent*	18,858	100.0%	Charles Dertinger (write-in)	4,513	77.6%
				Charlie Dent (R, write-in)	1,098	18.9%
				Scattered write-in	201	3.5%
				TOTAL	5,812	
Congressional District 16	Joe Pitts*	46,273	100.0%	Lois K. Herr	15,442	100.0%
Congressional District 17	Matthew A. Wertz	43,329	100.0%	Tim Holden*	28,720	100.0%
Congressional District 18	Tim Murphy*	33,195	99.2%	Chad Kluko	27,851	52.6%
	Scattered write-in	273	0.8%	Thomas Kovach	24,779	46.8%
				Scattered write-in	362	0.7%
	TOTAL	33,468		TOTAL	52,992	
Congressional District 19	Todd R. Platts*	43,180	100.0%	Philip J. Avillo Jr.	21,862	100.0%
	Scattered write-in	13		Scattered write-in	7	
	TOTAL	43,193		TOTAL	21,869	

RHODE ISLAND

Congressional districts first established for elections held in 2002
2 members

1

PROVIDENCE

Pawtucket

Providence

Cranston

BRISTOL

Warwick

Bristol

2

KENT

NEWPORT

1

WASHINGTON

Newport

Kingston

Westerly

2 New Shoreham

RHODE ISLAND

GOVERNOR
Donald L. Carcieri (R). Reelected 2006 to a four-year term. Previously elected 2002.

SENATORS (2 Democrats)
Sheldon Whitehouse (D). Elected 2006 to a six-year term.

Jack Reed (D). Reelected 2002 to a six-year term. Previously elected 1996.

REPRESENTATIVES (2 Democrats)
1. Patrick J. Kennedy (D) 2. Jim Langevin (D)

POSTWAR VOTE FOR PRESIDENT

Year	Total Vote	Republican Vote	Candidate	Democratic Vote	Candidate	Other Vote	Plurality	Total Vote Rep.	Dem.	Major Vote Rep.	Dem.
2004	437,134	169,046	Bush, George W.	259,760	Kerry, John	8,328	90,714 D	38.7%	59.4%	39.4%	60.6%
2000**	409,047	130,555	Bush, George W.	249,508	Gore, Al	28,984	118,953 D	31.9%	61.0%	34.4%	65.6%
1996**	390,284	104,683	Dole, Bob	233,050	Clinton, Bill	52,551	128,367 D	26.8%	59.7%	31.0%	69.0%
1992**	453,477	131,601	Bush, George	213,299	Clinton, Bill	108,577	81,698 D	29.0%	47.0%	38.2%	61.8%
1988	404,620	177,761	Bush, George	225,123	Dukakis, Michael S.	1,736	47,362 D	43.9%	55.6%	44.1%	55.9%
1984	410,492	212,080	Reagan, Ronald	197,106	Mondale, Walter F.	1,306	14,974 R	51.7%	48.0%	51.8%	48.2%
1980**	416,072	154,793	Reagan, Ronald	198,342	Carter, Jimmy	62,937	43,549 D	37.2%	47.7%	43.8%	56.2%
1976	411,170	181,249	Ford, Gerald R.	227,636	Carter, Jimmy	2,285	46,387 D	44.1%	55.4%	44.3%	55.7%
1972	415,808	220,383	Nixon, Richard M.	194,645	McGovern, George S.	780	25,738 R	53.0%	46.8%	53.1%	46.9%
1968**	385,000	122,359	Nixon, Richard M.	246,518	Humphrey, Hubert H.	16,123	124,159 D	31.8%	64.0%	33.2%	66.8%
1964	390,091	74,615	Goldwater, Barry M.	315,463	Johnson, Lyndon B.	13	240,848 D	19.1%	80.9%	19.1%	80.9%
1960	405,535	147,502	Nixon, Richard M.	258,032	Kennedy, John F.	1	110,530 D	36.4%	63.6%	36.4%	63.6%
1956	387,609	225,819	Eisenhower, Dwight D.	161,790	Stevenson, Adlai E.		64,029 R	58.3%	41.7%	58.3%	41.7%
1952	414,498	210,935	Eisenhower, Dwight D.	203,293	Stevenson, Adlai E.	270	7,642 R	50.9%	49.0%	50.9%	49.1%
1948	327,702	135,787	Dewey, Thomas E.	188,736	Truman, Harry S.	3,179	52,949 D	41.4%	57.6%	41.8%	58.2%

**In past elections, the other vote included: 2000 - 25,052 Green (Ralph Nader); 1996 - 43,723 Reform (Ross Perot); 1992 - 105,045 Independent (Ross Perot); 1980 - 59,819 Independent (John Anderson); 1968 - 15,678 American Independent (George Wallace).

RHODE ISLAND

POSTWAR VOTE FOR GOVERNOR

Year	Total Vote	Republican		Democratic		Other Vote	Rep.-Dem. Plurality	Percentage			
								Total Vote		Major Vote	
		Vote	Candidate	Vote	Candidate			Rep.	Dem.	Rep.	Dem.
2006	387,010	197,366	Carcieri, Donald L.	189,562	Fogarty, Charles J.	82	7,804 R	51.0%	49.0%	51.0%	49.0%
2002	332,655	181,827	Carcieri, Donald L.	150,229	York, Myrth	599	31,598 R	54.7%	45.2%	54.8%	45.2%
1998	306,445	156,180	Almond, Lincoln C.	129,105	York, Myrth	21,160	27,075 R	51.0%	42.1%	54.7%	45.3%
1994**	361,377	171,194	Almond, Lincoln C.	157,361	York, Myrth	32,822	13,833 R	47.4%	43.5%	52.1%	47.9%
1992	425,026	145,590	Leonard, Elizabeth Ann	261,484	Sundlun, Bruce G.	17,952	115,894 D	34.3%	61.5%	35.8%	64.2%
1990	356,672	92,177	DiPrete, Edward	264,411	Sundlun, Bruce G.	84	172,234 D	25.8%	74.1%	25.8%	74.2%
1988	400,516	203,550	DiPrete, Edward	196,936	Sundlun, Bruce G.	30	6,614 R	50.8%	49.2%	50.8%	49.2%
1986	322,724	208,822	DiPrete, Edward	104,508	Sundlun, Bruce G.	9,394	104,314 R	64.7%	32.4%	66.6%	33.4%
1984	408,375	245,059	DiPrete, Edward	163,311	Solomon, Anthony J.	5	81,748 R	60.0%	40.0%	60.0%	40.0%
1982	337,259	79,602	Marzullo, Vincent	247,208	Garrahy, J. Joseph	10,449	167,606 D	23.6%	73.3%	24.4%	75.6%
1980	405,916	106,729	Cianci, Vincent A.	299,174	Garrahy, J. Joseph	13	192,445 D	26.3%	73.7%	26.3%	73.7%
1978	314,363	96,596	Almond, Lincoln C.	197,386	Garrahy, J. Joseph	20,381	100,790 D	30.7%	62.8%	32.9%	67.1%
1976	398,683	178,254	Taft, James L.	218,561	Garrahy, J. Joseph	1,868	40,307 D	44.7%	54.8%	44.9%	55.1%
1974	321,660	69,224	Nugent, James W.	252,436	Noel, Philip W.		183,212 D	21.5%	78.5%	21.5%	78.5%
1972	412,866	194,315	DeSimone, Herbert F.	216,953	Noel, Philip W.	1,598	22,638 D	47.1%	52.5%	47.2%	52.8%
1970	346,342	171,549	DeSimone, Herbert F.	173,420	Licht, Frank	1,373	1,871 D	49.5%	50.1%	49.7%	50.3%
1968	383,725	187,958	Chafee, John H.	195,766	Licht, Frank	1	7,808 D	49.0%	51.0%	49.0%	51.0%
1966	332,064	210,202	Chafee, John H.	121,862	Hobbs, Horace E.		88,340 R	63.3%	36.7%	63.3%	36.7%
1964	391,668	239,501	Chafee, John H.	152,165	Gallogly, Edward P.	2	87,336 R	61.1%	38.9%	61.1%	38.9%
1962	327,506	163,952	Chafee, John H.	163,554	Notte, John A.		398 R	50.1%	49.9%	50.1%	49.9%
1960	401,362	174,044	Del Sesto, Christopher	227,318	Notte, John A.		53,274 D	43.4%	56.6%	43.4%	56.6%
1958	346,780	176,505	Del Sesto, Christopher	170,275	Roberts, Dennis J.		6,230 R	50.9%	49.1%	50.9%	49.1%
1956	383,919	191,604	Del Sesto, Christopher	192,315	Roberts, Dennis J.		711 D	49.9%	50.1%	49.9%	50.1%
1954	328,670	137,131	Lewis, Dean J.	189,595	Roberts, Dennis J.	1,944	52,464 D	41.7%	57.7%	42.0%	58.0%
1952	409,689	194,102	Archambault, Raoul	215,587	Roberts, Dennis J.		21,485 D	47.4%	52.6%	47.4%	52.6%
1950	296,809	120,684	Lachapelle, E. T.	176,125	Roberts, Dennis J.		55,441 D	40.7%	59.3%	40.7%	59.3%
1948	323,863	124,441	Ruerat, Albert P.	198,056	Pastore, John O.	1,366	73,615 D	38.4%	61.2%	38.6%	61.4%
1946	275,341	126,456	Murphy, John G.	148,885	Pastore, John O.		22,429 D	45.9%	54.1%	45.9%	54.1%

**The term of office of Rhode Island's governor was increased to four from two years effective with the 1994 election.

RHODE ISLAND

POSTWAR VOTE FOR SENATOR

Year	Total Vote	Republican Vote	Republican Candidate	Democratic Vote	Democratic Candidate	Other Vote	Rep.-Dem. Plurality	Total Vote Rep.	Total Vote Dem.	Major Vote Rep.	Major Vote Dem.
2006	385,451	179,001	Chafee, Lincoln	206,110	Whitehouse, Sheldon	340	27,109 D	46.4%	53.5%	46.5%	53.5%
2002	323,912	69,881	Tingle, Robert G.	253,922	Reed, Jack	109	184,041 D	21.6%	78.4%	21.6%	78.4%
2000	391,537	222,588	Chafee, Lincoln	161,023	Weygand, Bob	7,926	61,565 R	56.8%	41.1%	58.0%	42.0%
1996	363,378	127,368	Mayer, Nancy	230,676	Reed, Jack	5,334	103,308 D	35.1%	63.5%	35.6%	64.4%
1994	345,388	222,856	Chafee, John H.	122,532	Kushner, Linda J.		100,324 R	64.5%	35.5%	64.5%	35.5%
1990	364,062	138,947	Schneider, Claudine	225,105	Pell, Claiborne	10	86,158 D	38.2%	61.8%	38.2%	61.8%
1988	397,996	217,273	Chafee, John H.	180,717	Licht, Richard A.	6	36,556 R	54.6%	45.4%	54.6%	45.4%
1984	395,285	108,492	Leonard, Barbara	286,780	Pell, Claiborne	13	178,288 D	27.4%	72.6%	27.4%	72.6%
1982	342,779	175,495	Chafee, John H.	167,283	Michaelson, Julius C.	1	8,212 R	51.2%	48.8%	51.2%	48.8%
1978	305,618	76,061	Reynolds, James G.	229,557	Pell, Claiborne		153,496 D	24.9%	75.1%	24.9%	75.1%
1976	398,906	230,329	Chafee, John H.	167,665	Lorber, Richard P.	912	62,664 R	57.7%	42.0%	57.9%	42.1%
1972	413,432	188,990	Chafee, John H.	221,942	Pell, Claiborne	2,500	32,952 D	45.7%	53.7%	46.0%	54.0%
1970	341,222	107,351	McLaughlin, John	230,469	Pastore, John O.	3,402	123,118 D	31.5%	67.5%	31.8%	68.2%
1966	324,173	104,838	Briggs, Ruth M.	219,331	Pell, Claiborne	4	114,493 D	32.3%	67.7%	32.3%	67.7%
1964	386,322	66,715	Lagueux, Ronald R.	319,607	Pastore, John O.		252,892 D	17.3%	82.7%	17.3%	82.7%
1960	399,983	124,408	Archambault, Raoul	275,575	Pell, Claiborne		151,167 D	31.1%	68.9%	31.1%	68.9%
1958	344,519	122,353	Ewing, Bayard	222,166	Pastore, John O.		99,813 D	35.5%	64.5%	35.5%	64.5%
1954	326,624	132,970	Sundlun, Walter I.	193,654	Green, Theodore F.		60,684 D	40.7%	59.3%	40.7%	59.3%
1952	410,978	185,850	Ewing, Bayard	225,128	Pastore, John O.		39,278 D	45.2%	54.8%	45.2%	54.8%
1950S	297,909	114,184	Levy, Austin T.	183,725	Pastore, John O.		69,541 D	38.3%	61.7%	38.3%	61.7%
1948	320,420	130,262	Hazard, Thomas P.	190,158	Green, Theodore F.		59,896 D	40.7%	59.3%	40.7%	59.3%
1946	273,528	122,780	Dyer, W. Gurnee	150,748	McGrath, J. Howard		27,968 D	44.9%	55.1%	44.9%	55.1%

The 1950 election was for a short term to fill a vacancy.

RHODE ISLAND

GOVERNOR 2006

2000 Census Population	County	Total Vote	Republican	Democratic	Other	Rep.-Dem. Plurality	Total Vote Rep.	Total Vote Dem.	Major Vote Rep.	Major Vote Dem.
50,648	BRISTOL	21,093	12,236	8,857		3,379 R	58.0%	42.0%	58.0%	42.0%
167,090	KENT	73,018	40,503	32,515		7,988 R	55.5%	44.5%	55.5%	44.5%
85,433	NEWPORT	33,859	20,305	13,554		6,751 R	60.0%	40.0%	60.0%	40.0%
621,602	PROVIDENCE	203,224	91,623	111,601		19,978 D	45.1%	54.9%	45.1%	54.9%
123,546	WASHINGTON	55,734	32,699	23,035		9,664 R	58.7%	41.3%	58.7%	41.3%
1,048,319	TOTAL	387,010	197,366	189,562	82	7,804 R	51.0%	49.0%	51.0%	49.0%

Note: The statewide totals for "Total Vote" and "Other" include 82 scattered write-in votes that were not included in the county-by-county returns.

RHODE ISLAND

GOVERNOR 2006

2000 Census Population	City/Town	Total Vote	Republican	Democratic	Other	Rep.-Dem. Plurality		Percentage			
								Total Vote		Major Vote	
								Rep.	Dem.	Rep.	Dem.
16,819	BARRINGTON	8,358	5,470	2,888		2,582	R	65.4%	34.6%	65.4%	34.6%
22,469	BRISTOL TOWN	8,622	4,615	4,007		608	R	53.5%	46.5%	53.5%	46.5%
15,796	BURRILLVILLE	5,728	2,572	3,156		584	D	44.9%	55.1%	44.9%	55.1%
18,928	CENTRAL FALLS	2,659	696	1,963		1,267	D	26.2%	73.8%	26.2%	73.8%
7,859	CHARLESTOWN	3,821	2,185	1,636		549	R	57.2%	42.8%	57.2%	42.8%
33,668	COVENTRY	15,005	8,098	6,907		1,191	R	54.0%	46.0%	54.0%	46.0%
79,269	CRANSTON	32,343	16,944	15,399		1,545	R	52.4%	47.6%	52.4%	47.6%
31,840	CUMBERLAND	14,131	8,014	6,117		1,897	R	56.7%	43.3%	56.7%	43.3%
12,948	EAST GREENWICH	6,639	5,046	1,593		3,453	R	76.0%	24.0%	76.0%	24.0%
48,688	EAST PROVIDENCE	17,966	8,116	9,850		1,734	D	45.2%	54.8%	45.2%	54.8%
6,045	EXETER	2,822	1,698	1,124		574	R	60.2%	39.8%	60.2%	39.8%
4,274	FOSTER	2,271	1,206	1,065		141	R	53.1%	46.9%	53.1%	46.9%
9,948	GLOCESTER	4,468	1,997	2,471		474	D	44.7%	55.3%	44.7%	55.3%
7,836	HOPKINTON	3,150	1,742	1,408		334	R	55.3%	44.7%	55.3%	44.7%
5,622	JAMESTOWN	3,164	1,931	1,233		698	R	61.0%	39.0%	61.0%	39.0%
28,195	JOHNSTON	12,635	5,875	6,760		885	D	46.5%	53.5%	46.5%	53.5%
20,898	LINCOLN	9,615	5,711	3,904		1,807	R	59.4%	40.6%	59.4%	40.6%
3,593	LITTLE COMPTON	1,948	1,298	650		648	R	66.6%	33.4%	66.6%	33.4%
17,334	MIDDLETOWN	6,201	3,754	2,447		1,307	R	60.5%	39.5%	60.5%	39.5%
16,361	NARRAGANSETT	7,387	4,241	3,146		1,095	R	57.4%	42.6%	57.4%	42.6%
26,475	NEWPORT CITY	8,112	4,409	3,703		706	R	54.4%	45.6%	54.4%	45.6%
1,010	NEW SHOREHAM	926	594	332		262	R	64.1%	35.9%	64.1%	35.9%
26,326	NORTH KINGSTOWN	13,044	8,475	4,569		3,906	R	65.0%	35.0%	65.0%	35.0%
32,411	NORTH PROVIDENCE	13,941	6,039	7,902		1,863	D	43.3%	56.7%	43.3%	56.7%
10,618	NORTH SMITHFIELD	5,106	2,811	2,295		516	R	55.1%	44.9%	55.1%	44.9%
72,958	PAWTUCKET	18,644	7,092	11,552		4,460	D	38.0%	62.0%	38.0%	62.0%
17,149	PORTSMOUTH	8,132	5,467	2,665		2,802	R	67.2%	32.8%	67.2%	32.8%
173,618	PROVIDENCE CITY	39,066	12,051	27,015		14,964	D	30.8%	69.2%	30.8%	69.2%
7,222	RICHMOND	3,316	1,783	1,533		250	R	53.8%	46.2%	53.8%	46.2%
10,324	SCITUATE	5,159	3,170	1,989		1,181	R	61.4%	38.6%	61.4%	38.6%
20,613	SMITHFIELD	9,059	4,753	4,306		447	R	52.5%	47.5%	52.5%	47.5%
27,921	SOUTH KINGSTOWN	11,974	6,614	5,360		1,254	R	55.2%	44.8%	55.2%	44.8%
15,260	TIVERTON	6,302	3,446	2,856		590	R	54.7%	45.3%	54.7%	45.3%
11,360	WARREN	4,113	2,151	1,962		189	R	52.3%	47.7%	52.3%	47.7%
85,808	WARWICK	37,735	20,501	17,234		3,267	R	54.3%	45.7%	54.3%	45.7%
22,966	WESTERLY	9,294	5,367	3,927		1,440	R	57.7%	42.3%	57.7%	42.3%
5,085	WEST GREENWICH	2,583	1,534	1,049		485	R	59.4%	40.6%	59.4%	40.6%
29,581	WEST WARWICK	11,056	5,324	5,732		408	D	48.2%	51.8%	48.2%	51.8%
43,224	WOONSOCKET	10,433	4,576	5,857		1,281	D	43.9%	56.1%	43.9%	56.1%
1,048,319	TOTAL	387,010	197,366	189,562	82	7,804	R	51.0%	49.0%	51.0%	49.0%

Note: The statewide totals for "Total Vote" and "Other" include 82 scattered write-in votes that were not included in the city/town returns.

RHODE ISLAND

SENATOR 2006

2000 Census Population	County	Total Vote	Republican	Democratic	Other	Rep.-Dem. Plurality		Percentage			
								Total Vote		Major Vote	
								Rep.	Dem.	Rep.	Dem.
50,648	BRISTOL	20,989	10,554	10,435		119	R	50.3%	49.7%	50.3%	49.7%
167,090	KENT	72,719	38,370	34,349		4,021	R	52.8%	47.2%	52.8%	47.2%
85,433	NEWPORT	33,659	17,050	16,609		441	R	50.7%	49.3%	50.7%	49.3%
621,602	PROVIDENCE	202,296	82,679	119,617		36,938	D	40.9%	59.1%	40.9%	59.1%
123,546	WASHINGTON	55,446	30,348	25,098		5,250	R	54.7%	45.3%	54.7%	45.3%
	Federal Ballots	2	0	2		2	D		100.0%		100.0%
1,048,319	TOTAL	385,451	179,001	206,110	340	27,109	D	46.4%	53.5%	46.5%	53.5%

Note: The statewide totals for "Total Vote" and "Other" include 340 scattered write-in votes that were not included in the county-by-county returns.

RHODE ISLAND

SENATOR 2006

2000 Census Population	City/Town	Total Vote	Republican	Democratic	Other	Rep.-Dem. Plurality	Percentage			
							Total Vote		Major Vote	
							Rep.	Dem.	Rep.	Dem.
16,819	BARRINGTON	8,335	4,722	3,613		1,109 R	56.7%	43.3%	56.7%	43.3%
22,469	BRISTOL TOWN	8,568	3,993	4,575		582 D	46.6%	53.4%	46.6%	53.4%
15,796	BURRILLVILLE	5,658	2,660	2,998		338 D	47.0%	53.0%	47.0%	53.0%
18,928	CENTRAL FALLS	2,663	617	2,046		1,429 D	23.2%	76.8%	23.2%	76.8%
7,859	CHARLESTOWN	3,798	2,143	1,655		488 R	56.4%	43.6%	56.4%	43.6%
33,668	COVENTRY	14,941	7,356	7,585		229 D	49.2%	50.8%	49.2%	50.8%
79,269	CRANSTON	32,082	15,021	17,061		2,040 D	46.8%	53.2%	46.8%	53.2%
31,840	CUMBERLAND	14,039	6,857	7,182		325 D	48.8%	51.2%	48.8%	51.2%
12,948	EAST GREENWICH	6,574	4,305	2,269		2,036 R	65.5%	34.5%	65.5%	34.5%
48,688	EAST PROVIDENCE	17,897	7,019	10,878		3,859 D	39.2%	60.8%	39.2%	60.8%
6,045	EXETER	2,809	1,668	1,141		527 R	59.4%	40.6%	59.4%	40.6%
4,274	FOSTER	2,273	1,244	1,029		215 R	54.7%	45.3%	54.7%	45.3%
9,948	GLOCESTER	4,425	2,417	2,008		409 R	54.6%	45.4%	54.6%	45.4%
7,836	HOPKINTON	3,130	1,671	1,459		212 R	53.4%	46.6%	53.4%	46.6%
5,622	JAMESTOWN	3,161	1,672	1,489		183 R	52.9%	47.1%	52.9%	47.1%
28,195	JOHNSTON	12,564	5,150	7,414		2,264 D	41.0%	59.0%	41.0%	59.0%
20,898	LINCOLN	9,542	5,045	4,497		548 R	52.9%	47.1%	52.9%	47.1%
3,593	LITTLE COMPTON	1,938	1,097	841		256 R	56.6%	43.4%	56.6%	43.4%
17,334	MIDDLETOWN	6,150	3,005	3,145		140 D	48.9%	51.1%	48.9%	51.1%
16,361	NARRAGANSETT	7,365	3,905	3,460		445 R	53.0%	47.0%	53.0%	47.0%
26,475	NEWPORT CITY	8,066	3,679	4,387		708 D	45.6%	54.4%	45.6%	54.4%
1,010	NEW SHOREHAM	926	480	446		34 R	51.8%	48.2%	51.8%	48.2%
26,326	NORTH KINGSTOWN	12,960	7,577	5,383		2,194 R	58.5%	41.5%	58.5%	41.5%
32,411	NORTH PROVIDENCE	13,846	5,293	8,553		3,260 D	38.2%	61.8%	38.2%	61.8%
10,618	NORTH SMITHFIELD	5,064	2,580	2,484		96 R	50.9%	49.1%	50.9%	49.1%
72,958	PAWTUCKET	18,622	6,312	12,310		5,998 D	33.9%	66.1%	33.9%	66.1%
17,149	PORTSMOUTH	8,073	4,648	3,425		1,223 R	57.6%	42.4%	57.6%	42.4%
173,618	PROVIDENCE CITY	39,195	11,017	28,178		17,161 D	28.1%	71.9%	28.1%	71.9%
7,222	RICHMOND	3,301	1,819	1,482		337 R	55.1%	44.9%	55.1%	44.9%
10,324	SCITUATE	5,109	3,056	2,053		1,003 R	59.8%	40.2%	59.8%	40.2%
20,613	SMITHFIELD	8,955	4,616	4,339		277 R	51.5%	48.5%	51.5%	48.5%
27,921	SOUTH KINGSTOWN	11,959	6,406	5,553		853 R	53.6%	46.4%	53.6%	46.4%
15,260	TIVERTON	6,271	2,949	3,322		373 D	47.0%	53.0%	47.0%	53.0%
11,360	WARREN	4,086	1,839	2,247		408 D	45.0%	55.0%	45.0%	55.0%
85,808	WARWICK	37,623	20,325	17,298		3,027 R	54.0%	46.0%	54.0%	46.0%
22,966	WESTERLY	9,198	4,679	4,519		160 R	50.9%	49.1%	50.9%	49.1%
5,085	WEST GREENWICH	2,561	1,490	1,071		419 R	58.2%	41.8%	58.2%	41.8%
29,581	WEST WARWICK	11,020	4,894	6,126		1,232 D	44.4%	55.6%	44.4%	55.6%
43,224	WOONSOCKET	10,362	3,775	6,587		2,812 D	36.4%	63.6%	36.4%	63.6%
	Federal Ballots	2		2		2 D		100.0%		100.0%
1,048,319	TOTAL	385,451	179,001	206,110	340	27,109 D	46.4%	53.5%	46.5%	53.5%

Note: The statewide totals for "Total Vote" and "Other" include 340 scattered write-in votes that were not included in the city/town returns.

RHODE ISLAND

HOUSE OF REPRESENTATIVES

CD	Year	Total Vote	Republican Vote	Republican Candidate	Democratic Vote	Democratic Candidate	Other Vote	Rep.-Dem. Plurality		Total Vote Rep.	Total Vote Dem.	Major Vote Rep.	Major Vote Dem.
1	2006	180,185	41,856	SCOTT, JONATHAN P.	124,676	KENNEDY, PATRICK J.*	13,653	82,820	D	23.2%	69.2%	25.1%	74.9%
1	2004	195,010	69,819	ROGERS, DAVID W.	124,923	KENNEDY, PATRICK J.*	268	55,104	D	35.8%	64.1%	35.9%	64.1%
1	2002	159,066	59,370	ROGERS, DAVID W.	95,286	KENNEDY, PATRICK J.*	4,410	35,916	D	37.3%	59.9%	38.4%	61.6%
2	2006	193,197		—	140,352	LANGEVIN, JIM*	52,845	140,352	D		72.6%		100.0%
2	2004	207,165	43,139	BARTON, ARTHUR CHUCK III	154,392	LANGEVIN, JIM*	9,634	111,253	D	20.8%	74.5%	21.8%	78.2%
2	2002	169,580	37,767	MATSON, JOHN O.	129,390	LANGEVIN, JIM*	2,423	91,623	D	22.3%	76.3%	22.6%	77.4%
TOTAL	2006	373,382	41,856		265,028		66,498	223,172	D	11.2%	71.0%	13.6%	86.4%
TOTAL	2004	402,175	112,958		279,315		9,902	166,357	D	28.1%	69.5%	28.8%	71.2%
TOTAL	2002	328,646	97,137		224,676		6,833	127,539	D	29.6%	68.4%	30.2%	69.8%

An asterisk (*) denotes incumbent.

RHODE ISLAND

GENERAL AND PRIMARY ELECTIONS

2006 GENERAL ELECTIONS

Governor   Other vote was 82 scattered write-in.

Senator   Other vote was 340 scattered write-in.

House   Other vote was:

   CD 1   13,638 Independent (Kenneth A. Capalbo); 15 scattered write-in.
   CD 2   52,743 Independent (Rod Driver); 102 scattered write-in.

Note: Write-in votes were required to be tallied only for those who received at least five (5).

2006 PRIMARY ELECTIONS

Primary	September 12, 2006	**Registration** (as of September 12, 2006)	Democratic	263,758
			Republican	77,578
			Unaffiliated	407,318
			TOTAL	748,654

Primary Type   Semi-open—Registered Democrats and Republicans could vote only in their party's primary. Unaffiliated voters could participate in either party's primary if they were willing to become a member of that party for a period of at least 90 days.

Note: An asterisk (*) denotes incumbent.

	REPUBLICAN PRIMARIES			DEMOCRATIC PRIMARIES		
Governor	Donald L. Carcieri*	51,660	100.0%	Charles J. Fogarty	69,608	100.0%
Senator	Lincoln Chafee*	34,939	54.2%	Sheldon Whitehouse	69,301	81.5%
	Stephen P. Laffey	29,556	45.8%	Christopher F. Young	8,941	10.5%
				Carl L. Sheeler	6,758	8.0%
	TOTAL	64,495		TOTAL	85,000	
Congressional District 1	Jonathan Scott	12,407	69.2%	Patrick J. Kennedy*	38,087	100.0%
	Edmund R. Leather	5,517	30.8%			
	TOTAL	17,924				
Congressional District 2	No Republican candidate			Jim Langevin*	24,988	61.8%
				Jennifer Lawless	15,458	38.2%
				TOTAL	40,446	

SOUTH CAROLINA

Congressional districts first established for elections held in 2002
6 members

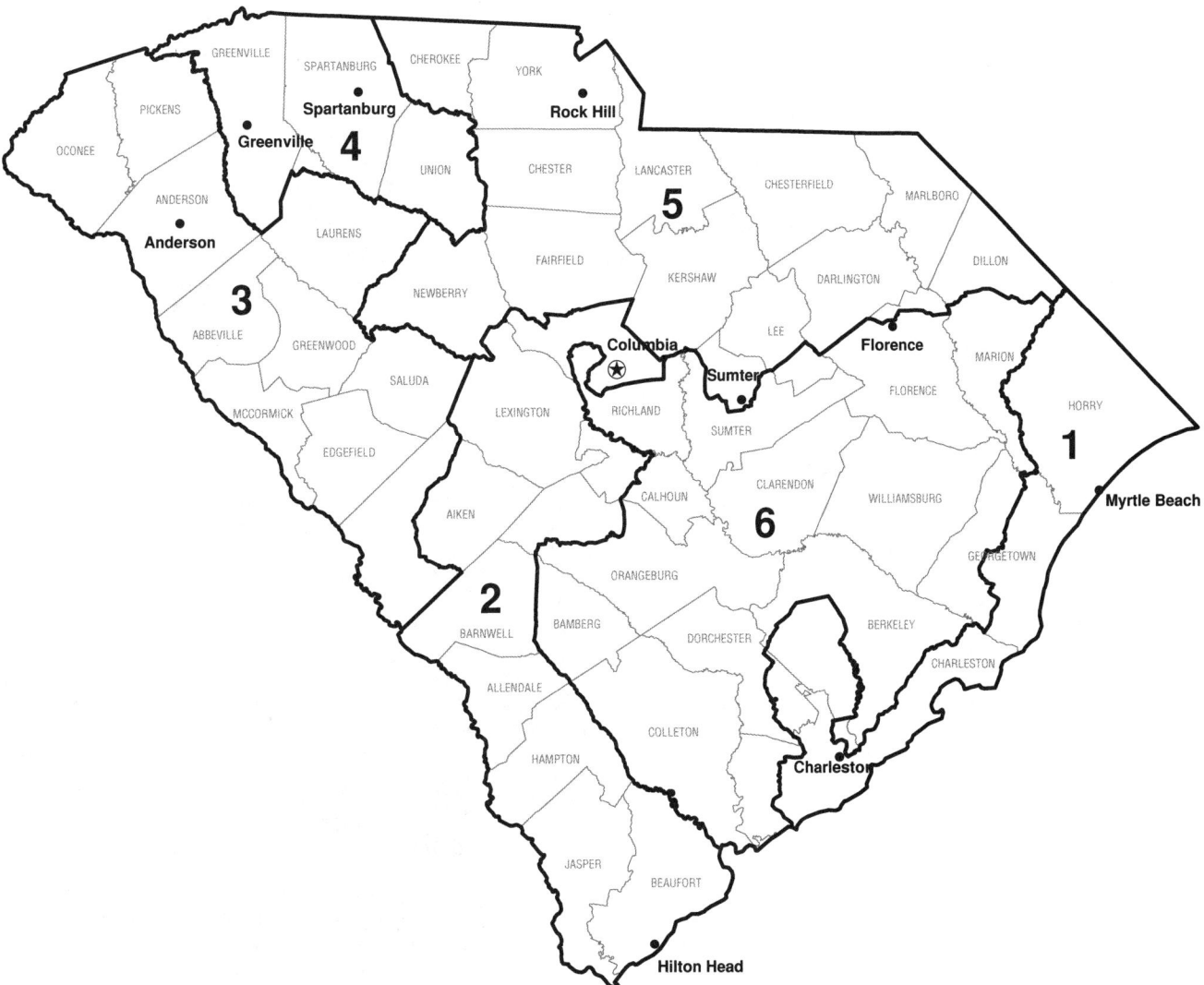

SOUTH CAROLINA

GOVERNOR
Mark Sanford (R). Reelected 2006 to a four-year term. Previously elected 2002.

SENATORS (2 Republicans)
Jim DeMint (R). Elected 2004 to a six-year term.

Lindsey Graham (R). Elected 2002 to a six-year term.

REPRESENTATIVES (4 Republicans, 2 Democrats)
1. Henry E. Brown Jr. (R)
2. Joe Wilson (R)
3. J. Gresham Barrett (R)
4. Bob Inglis (R)
5. John M. Spratt Jr. (D)
6. James E. Clyburn (D)

POSTWAR VOTE FOR PRESIDENT

Year	Total Vote	Republican Vote	Candidate	Democratic Vote	Candidate	Other Vote	Plurality		Total Vote Rep.	Dem.	Major Vote Rep.	Dem.
2004	1,617,730	937,974	Bush, George W.	661,699	Kerry, John	18,057	276,275	R	58.0%	40.9%	58.6%	41.4%
2000**	1,382,717	785,937	Bush, George W.	565,561	Gore, Al	31,219	220,376	R	56.8%	40.9%	58.2%	41.8%
1996**	1,151,689	573,458	Dole, Bob	506,283	Clinton, Bill	71,948	67,175	R	49.8%	44.0%	53.1%	46.9%
1992**	1,202,527	577,507	Bush, George	479,514	Clinton, Bill	145,506	97,993	R	48.0%	39.9%	54.6%	45.4%
1988	986,009	606,443	Bush, George	370,554	Dukakis, Michael S.	9,012	235,889	R	61.5%	37.6%	62.1%	37.9%
1984	968,529	615,539	Reagan, Ronald	344,459	Mondale, Walter F.	8,531	271,080	R	63.6%	35.6%	64.1%	35.9%
1980**	894,071	441,841	Reagan, Ronald	430,385	Carter, Jimmy	21,845	11,456	R	49.4%	48.1%	50.7%	49.3%
1976	802,583	346,149	Ford, Gerald R.	450,807	Carter, Jimmy	5,627	104,658	D	43.1%	56.2%	43.4%	56.6%
1972	673,960	477,044	Nixon, Richard M.	186,824	McGovern, George S.	10,092	290,220	R	70.8%	27.7%	71.9%	28.1%
1968**	666,978	254,062	Nixon, Richard M.	197,486	Humphrey, Hubert H.	215,430	38,632	R	38.1%	29.6%	56.3%	43.7%
1964	524,779	309,048	Goldwater, Barry M.	215,723	Johnson, Lyndon B.	8	93,325	R	58.9%	41.1%	58.9%	41.1%
1960	386,688	188,558	Nixon, Richard M.	198,129	Kennedy, John F.	1	9,571	D	48.8%	51.2%	48.8%	51.2%
1956**	300,583	75,700	Eisenhower, Dwight D.	136,372	Stevenson, Adlai E.	88,511	47,863	D	25.2%	45.4%	35.7%	64.3%
1952	341,087	168,082	Eisenhower, Dwight D.	173,004	Stevenson, Adlai E.	1	4,922	D	49.3%	50.7%	49.3%	50.7%
1948**	142,571	5,386	Dewey, Thomas E.	34,423	Truman, Harry S.	102,762	68,184	SR	3.8%	24.1%	13.5%	86.5%

**In past elections, the other vote included: 2000 - 20,200 Green (Ralph Nader); 1996 - 64,386 Reform (Ross Perot); 1992 - 138,872 Independent (Ross Perot); 1980 - 14,153 Independent (John Anderson); 1968 - 215,430 American Independent (George Wallace), which finished second in South Carolina; 1956 - 88,509 Uncommitted States' Rights electors, which placed second; 1948 - 102,607 States' Rights (Strom Thurmond), which won South Carolina with 72.0 percent of the total vote.

SOUTH CAROLINA

POSTWAR VOTE FOR GOVERNOR

Year	Total Vote	Republican Vote	Republican Candidate	Democratic Vote	Democratic Candidate	Other Vote	Rep.-Dem. Plurality	Total Vote Rep.	Total Vote Dem.	Major Vote Rep.	Major Vote Dem.
2006	1,091,952	601,868	Sanford, Mark	489,076	Moore, Tommy	1,008	112,792 R	55.1%	44.8%	55.2%	44.8%
2002	1,107,725	585,422	Sanford, Mark	521,140	Hodges, Jim	1,163	64,282 R	52.8%	47.0%	52.9%	47.1%
1998	1,070,869	484,088	Beasley, David	570,070	Hodges, Jim	16,711	85,982 D	45.2%	53.2%	45.9%	54.1%
1994	933,850	470,756	Beasley, David	447,002	Theodore, Nick A.	16,092	23,754 R	50.4%	47.9%	51.3%	48.7%
1990	760,965	528,831	Campbell, Carroll	212,034	Mitchell, Theo	20,100	316,797 R	69.5%	27.9%	71.4%	28.6%
1986	753,751	384,565	Campbell, Carroll	361,325	Daniel, Mike	7,861	23,240 R	51.0%	47.9%	51.6%	48.4%
1982	671,625	202,806	Workman, W. D.	468,819	Riley, Richard W.		266,013 D	30.2%	69.8%	30.2%	69.8%
1978	627,182	236,946	Young, Edward L.	384,898	Riley, Richard W.	5,338	147,952 D	37.8%	61.4%	38.1%	61.9%
1974	523,199	266,109	Edwards, James B.	248,938	Dorn, W. J. Bryan	8,152	17,171 R	50.9%	47.6%	51.7%	48.3%
1970	484,857	221,233	Watson, Albert W.	250,551	West, John C.	13,073	29,318 D	45.6%	51.7%	46.9%	53.1%
1966	439,942	184,088	Rogers, Joseph O.	255,854	McNair, Robert E.		71,766 D	41.8%	58.2%	41.8%	58.2%
1962	253,721		—	253,704	Russell, Donald S.	17	253,704 D		100.0%		100.0%
1958	77,740		—	77,714	Hollings, Ernest F.	26	77,714 D		100.0%		100.0%
1954	214,212		—	214,204	Timmerman, George B.	8	214,204 D		100.0%		100.0%
1950	50,642		—	50,633	Byrnes, James F.	9	50,633 D		100.0%		100.0%
1946	26,520		—	26,520	Thurmond, Strom		26,520 D		100.0%		100.0%

POSTWAR VOTE FOR SENATOR

Year	Total Vote	Republican Vote	Republican Candidate	Democratic Vote	Democratic Candidate	Other Vote	Rep.-Dem. Plurality	Total Vote Rep.	Total Vote Dem.	Major Vote Rep.	Major Vote Dem.
2004	1,597,221	857,167	DeMint, Jim	704,384	Tenenbaum, Inez	35,670	152,783 R	53.7%	44.1%	54.9%	45.1%
2002	1,102,948	600,010	Graham, Lindsey	487,359	Sanders, Alex	15,579	112,651 R	54.4%	44.2%	55.2%	44.8%
1998	1,068,367	488,132	Inglis, Bob	562,791	Hollings, Ernest F.	17,444	74,659 D	45.7%	52.7%	46.4%	53.6%
1996	1,161,372	619,859	Thurmond, Strom	510,951	Close, Elliott Springs	30,562	108,908 R	53.4%	44.0%	54.8%	45.2%
1992	1,180,438	554,175	Hartnett, Thomas F.	591,030	Hollings, Ernest F.	35,233	36,855 D	46.9%	50.1%	48.4%	51.6%
1990	750,716	482,032	Thurmond, Strom	244,112	Cunningham, Bob	24,572	237,920 R	64.2%	32.5%	66.4%	33.6%
1986	737,962	262,886	McMaster, Henry D.	465,500	Hollings, Ernest F.	9,576	202,614 D	35.6%	63.1%	36.1%	63.9%
1984	965,130	644,815	Thurmond, Strom	306,982	Purvis, Melvin	13,333	337,833 R	66.8%	31.8%	67.7%	32.3%
1980	870,594	257,946	Mays, Marshall T.	612,554	Hollings, Ernest F.	94	354,608 D	29.6%	70.4%	29.6%	70.4%
1978	632,852	351,733	Thurmond, Strom	281,119	Ravenel, Charles D.		70,614 R	55.6%	44.4%	55.6%	44.4%
1974	512,397	146,645	Bush, Gwenyfred	356,126	Hollings, Ernest F.	9,626	209,481 D	28.6%	69.5%	29.2%	70.8%
1972	672,246	426,601	Thurmond, Strom	245,457	Zeigler, Eugene N.	188	181,144 R	63.5%	36.5%	63.5%	36.5%
1968	652,855	248,780	Parker, Marshall	404,060	Hollings, Ernest F.	15	155,280 D	38.1%	61.9%	38.1%	61.9%
1966	436,252	271,297	Thurmond, Strom	164,955	Morrah, Bradley		106,342 R	62.2%	37.8%	62.2%	37.8%
1966S	435,822	212,032	Parker, Marshall	223,790	Hollings, Ernest F.		11,758 D	48.7%	51.3%	48.7%	51.3%
1962	312,647	133,930	Workman, W. D.	178,712	Johnston, Olin D.	5	44,782 D	42.8%	57.2%	42.8%	57.2%
1960	330,266			330,164	Thurmond, Strom	102	330,164 D		100.0%		100.0%
1956	279,845	49,695	Crawford, Leon P.	230,150	Johnston, Olin D.		180,455 D	17.8%	82.2%	17.8%	82.2%
1956S	251,907		—	251,907	Thurmond, Strom		251,907 D		100.0%		100.0%
1954**	227,232		—	83,525	Brown, Edgar A.	143,707	59,919 ID		36.8%		100.0%
1950	50,277		—	50,240	Johnston, Olin D.	37	50,240 D		99.9%		100.0%
1948	141,006	5,008	Gerald, J. Bates	135,998	Maybank, Burnet R.		130,990 D	3.6%	96.4%	3.6%	96.4%

**In past elections, the other vote included: 1954 - 143,444 Independent Democratic (Strom Thurmond). Thurmond ran as a write-in candidate and won with 63.1 percent of the total vote. One each of the 1966 and 1956 elections was for a short term to fill a vacancy.

SOUTH CAROLINA

GOVERNOR 2006

2000 Census Population	County	Total Vote	Republican	Democratic	Other	Rep.-Dem. Plurality		Percentage			
								Total Vote		Major Vote	
								Rep.	Dem.	Rep.	Dem.
26,167	ABBEVILLE	6,675	3,112	3,561	2	449	D	46.6%	53.3%	46.6%	53.4%
142,552	AIKEN	40,835	21,992	18,827	16	3,165	R	53.9%	46.1%	53.9%	46.1%
11,211	ALLENDALE	2,333	605	1,726	2	1,121	D	25.9%	74.0%	26.0%	74.0%
165,740	ANDERSON	44,678	26,629	18,011	38	8,618	R	59.6%	40.3%	59.7%	40.3%
16,658	BAMBERG	3,908	1,221	2,685	2	1,464	D	31.2%	68.7%	31.3%	68.7%
23,478	BARNWELL	5,845	2,474	3,367	4	893	D	42.3%	57.6%	42.4%	57.6%
120,937	BEAUFORT	39,522	24,120	15,374	28	8,746	R	61.0%	38.9%	61.1%	38.9%
142,651	BERKELEY	33,474	20,422	13,025	27	7,397	R	61.0%	38.9%	61.1%	38.9%
15,185	CALHOUN	4,436	2,156	2,275	5	119	D	48.6%	51.3%	48.7%	51.3%
309,969	CHARLESTON	91,820	52,304	39,388	128	12,916	R	57.0%	42.9%	57.0%	43.0%
52,537	CHEROKEE	13,540	7,948	5,587	5	2,361	R	58.7%	41.3%	58.7%	41.3%
34,068	CHESTER	7,627	3,591	4,031	5	440	D	47.1%	52.9%	47.1%	52.9%
42,768	CHESTERFIELD	8,521	3,811	4,708	2	897	D	44.7%	55.3%	44.7%	55.3%
32,502	CLARENDON	8,832	3,655	5,176	1	1,521	D	41.4%	58.6%	41.4%	58.6%
38,264	COLLETON	9,841	5,134	4,700	7	434	R	52.2%	47.8%	52.2%	47.8%
67,394	DARLINGTON	15,583	7,990	7,579	14	411	R	51.3%	48.6%	51.3%	48.7%
30,722	DILLON	6,136	2,617	3,515	4	898	D	42.6%	57.3%	42.7%	57.3%
96,413	DORCHESTER	28,517	18,635	9,863	19	8,772	R	65.3%	34.6%	65.4%	34.6%
24,595	EDGEFIELD	6,824	2,723	4,095	6	1,372	D	39.9%	60.0%	39.9%	60.1%
23,454	FAIRFIELD	6,610	2,529	4,073	8	1,544	D	38.3%	61.6%	38.3%	61.7%
125,761	FLORENCE	31,500	17,548	13,930	22	3,618	R	55.7%	44.2%	55.7%	44.3%
55,797	GEORGETOWN	16,533	9,167	7,359	7	1,808	R	55.4%	44.5%	55.5%	44.5%
379,616	GREENVILLE	109,714	71,854	37,777	83	34,077	R	65.5%	34.4%	65.5%	34.5%
66,271	GREENWOOD	16,827	9,191	7,616	20	1,575	R	54.6%	45.3%	54.7%	45.3%
21,386	HAMPTON	6,003	2,028	3,970	5	1,942	D	33.8%	66.1%	33.8%	66.2%
196,629	HORRY	54,911	34,599	20,253	59	14,346	R	63.0%	36.9%	63.1%	36.9%
20,678	JASPER	4,207	1,531	2,673	3	1,142	D	36.4%	63.5%	36.4%	63.6%
52,647	KERSHAW	17,672	9,678	7,983	11	1,695	R	54.8%	45.2%	54.8%	45.2%
61,351	LANCASTER	15,547	8,012	7,534	1	478	R	51.5%	48.5%	51.5%	48.5%
69,567	LAURENS	15,172	8,407	6,752	13	1,655	R	55.4%	44.5%	55.5%	44.5%
20,119	LEE	4,769	1,698	3,069	2	1,371	D	35.6%	64.4%	35.6%	64.4%
216,014	LEXINGTON	67,717	40,016	27,480	221	12,536	R	59.1%	40.6%	59.3%	40.7%
9,958	MCCORMICK	3,308	1,432	1,876		444	D	43.3%	56.7%	43.3%	56.7%
35,466	MARION	7,400	2,902	4,496	2	1,594	D	39.2%	60.8%	39.2%	60.8%
28,818	MARLBORO	5,401	1,996	3,405		1,409	D	37.0%	63.0%	37.0%	63.0%
36,108	NEWBERRY	10,009	4,789	5,214	6	425	D	47.8%	52.1%	47.9%	52.1%
66,215	OCONEE	19,594	11,980	7,607	7	4,373	R	61.1%	38.8%	61.2%	38.8%
91,582	ORANGEBURG	23,579	8,014	15,553	12	7,539	D	34.0%	66.0%	34.0%	66.0%
110,757	PICKENS	27,663	18,922	8,712	29	10,210	R	68.4%	31.5%	68.5%	31.5%
320,677	RICHLAND	89,504	36,044	53,363	97	17,319	D	40.3%	59.6%	40.3%	59.7%
19,181	SALUDA	5,561	2,658	2,902	1	244	D	47.8%	52.2%	47.8%	52.2%
253,791	SPARTANBURG	62,706	37,986	24,681	39	13,305	R	60.6%	39.4%	60.6%	39.4%
104,646	SUMTER	22,712	10,196	12,510	6	2,314	D	44.9%	55.1%	44.9%	55.1%
29,881	UNION	7,905	3,249	4,650	6	1,401	D	41.1%	58.8%	41.1%	58.9%
37,217	WILLIAMSBURG	8,825	2,869	5,949	7	3,080	D	32.5%	67.4%	32.5%	67.5%
164,614	YORK	51,656	31,434	20,196	26	11,238	R	60.9%	39.1%	60.9%	39.1%
4,012,012	TOTAL	1,091,952	601,868	489,076	1,008	112,792	R	55.1%	44.8%	55.2%	44.8%

SOUTH CAROLINA

HOUSE OF REPRESENTATIVES

			Republican			Democratic				Percentage Total Vote		Major Vote	
CD	Year	Total Vote	Vote	Candidate	Vote	Candidate	Other Vote	Rep.-Dem. Plurality		Rep.	Dem.	Rep.	Dem.
1	2006	193,375	115,766	BROWN, HENRY E. JR.*	73,218	# MAATTA, RANDY	4,391	42,548 R		59.9%	37.9%	61.3%	38.7%
1	2004	212,308	186,448	BROWN, HENRY E. JR.*		—	25,860	186,448 R		87.8%		100.0%	
1	2002	142,425	127,562	BROWN, HENRY E. JR.*		—	14,863	127,562 R		89.6%		100.0%	
2	2006	204,052	127,811	WILSON, JOE*	76,090	ELLISOR, MICHAEL R.	151	51,721 R		62.6%	37.3%	62.7%	37.3%
2	2004	279,870	181,862	WILSON, JOE*	93,249	ELLISOR, MICHAEL R.	4,759	88,613 R		65.0%	33.3%	66.1%	33.9%
2	2002	171,359	144,149	WILSON, JOE*		—	27,210	144,149 R		84.1%		100.0%	
3	2006	177,988	111,882	BARRETT, J. GRESHAM*	66,039	# BALLENGER, LEE	67	45,843 R		62.9%	37.1%	62.9%	37.1%
3	2004	191,999	191,052	BARRETT, J. GRESHAM*		—	947	191,052 R		99.5%		100.0%	
3	2002	178,195	119,644	BARRETT, J. GRESHAM	55,743	BRIGHTHARP, GEORGE L.	2,808	63,901 R		67.1%	31.3%	68.2%	31.8%
4	2006	179,931	115,553	INGLIS, BOB*	57,490	GRIFFITH, WILLIAM GRIFF	6,888	58,063 R		64.2%	32.0%	66.8%	33.2%
4	2004	270,594	188,795	INGLIS, BOB	78,376	BROWN, BRANDON P.	3,423	110,419 R		69.8%	29.0%	70.7%	29.3%
4	2002	177,417	122,422	DeMINT, JIM*	52,635	# ASHY, PETER J.	2,360	69,787 R		69.0%	29.7%	69.9%	30.1%
5	2006	175,154	75,422	NORMAN, RALPH	99,669	SPRATT, JOHN M. JR.*	63	24,247 D		43.1%	56.9%	43.1%	56.9%
5	2004	242,518	89,568	SPENCER, ALBERT F.	152,867	SPRATT, JOHN M. JR.*	83	63,299 D		36.9%	63.0%	36.9%	63.1%
5	2002	141,972		—	121,912	SPRATT, JOHN M. JR.*	20,060	121,912 D			85.9%		100.0%
6	2006	155,706	53,181	McLEOD, GARY	100,213	CLYBURN, JAMES E.*	2,312	47,032 D		34.2%	64.4%	34.7%	65.3%
6	2004	241,829	79,600	# McLEOD, GARY	161,987	CLYBURN, JAMES E.*	242	82,387 D		32.9%	67.0%	32.9%	67.1%
6	2002	174,066	55,760	McLEOD, GARY	116,586	CLYBURN, JAMES E.*	1,720	60,826 D		32.0%	67.0%	32.4%	67.6%
TOTAL	2006	1,086,206	599,615		472,719		13,872	126,896 R		55.2%	43.5%	55.9%	44.1%
TOTAL	2004	1,439,118	917,325		486,479		35,314	430,846 R		63.7%	33.8%	65.3%	34.7%
TOTAL	2002	985,434	569,537		346,876		69,021	222,661 R		57.8%	35.2%	62.1%	37.9%

A pound sign (#) indicates that candidate received votes on the ballot line of another party.

An asterisk (*) denotes incumbent.

SOUTH CAROLINA

GENERAL AND PRIMARY ELECTIONS

2006 GENERAL ELECTIONS

Governor   Other vote was 1,008 scattered write-in.

House   Other vote was:

CD 1	4,287 Green (James E. Dunn); 104 scattered write-in. (Democrat Randy Maatta received 4,875 votes on the Working Families ballot line.)
CD 2	151 scattered write-in.
CD 3	67 scattered write-in. (Democrat Lee Ballenger received 6,244 votes on the Working Families ballot line.)
CD 4	4,467 Libertarian (John Cobin); 2,336 Green (C. Faye Walters); 85 scattered write-in.
CD 5	63 scattered write-in.
CD 6	2,224 Green (Antonio Williams); 88 scattered write-in.

2006 PRIMARY ELECTIONS

Primary	June 13, 2006	**Registration** (as of June 13, 2006)	2,408,258	No Party Registration
Primary Runoff	June 27, 2006			

Primary Type   Open—Any registered voter could participate in either the Democratic or Republican primary, although any voter who participated in one party's primary could not vote in a primary runoff of the other party.

SOUTH CAROLINA

GENERAL AND PRIMARY ELECTIONS

Note: An asterisk (*) denotes incumbent. The names of unopposed candidates did not appear on the primary ballot; therefore, no votes were cast for these candidates.

	REPUBLICAN PRIMARIES			DEMOCRATIC PRIMARIES		
Governor	Mark Sanford*	160,238	64.8%	Tommy Moore	88,092	63.7%
	Oscar Fred Lovelace	87,043	35.2%	Frank Willis	42,317	30.6%
				C. Dennis Aughtry	7,934	5.7%
	TOTAL	247,281		TOTAL	138,343	
Congressional District 1	Henry E. Brown Jr.*	Unopposed		Ben Frasier	5,100	47.5%
				Randy Maatta	3,393	31.6%
				Ralph Ledford	2,236	20.8%
				TOTAL	10,729	
				PRIMARY RUNOFF		
				Randy Maatta	1,704	56.1%
				Ben Frasier	1,335	43.9%
				TOTAL	3,039	
Congressional District 2	Joe Wilson*	Unopposed		Michael R. Ellisor	11,468	58.7%
				David F. White III	8,054	41.3%
				TOTAL	19,522	
Congressional District 3	J. Gresham Barrett*	Unopposed		Lee Ballenger	9,738	67.2%
				Philip M. Cheney	4,747	32.8%
				TOTAL	14,485	
Congressional District 4	Bob Inglis*	Unopposed		William Griff Griffith	Unopposed	
Congressional District 5	Ralph Norman	Unopposed		John M. Spratt Jr.*	Unopposed	
Congressional District 6	Gary McLeod	Unopposed		James E. Clyburn*	Unopposed	

SOUTH DAKOTA

One member At Large

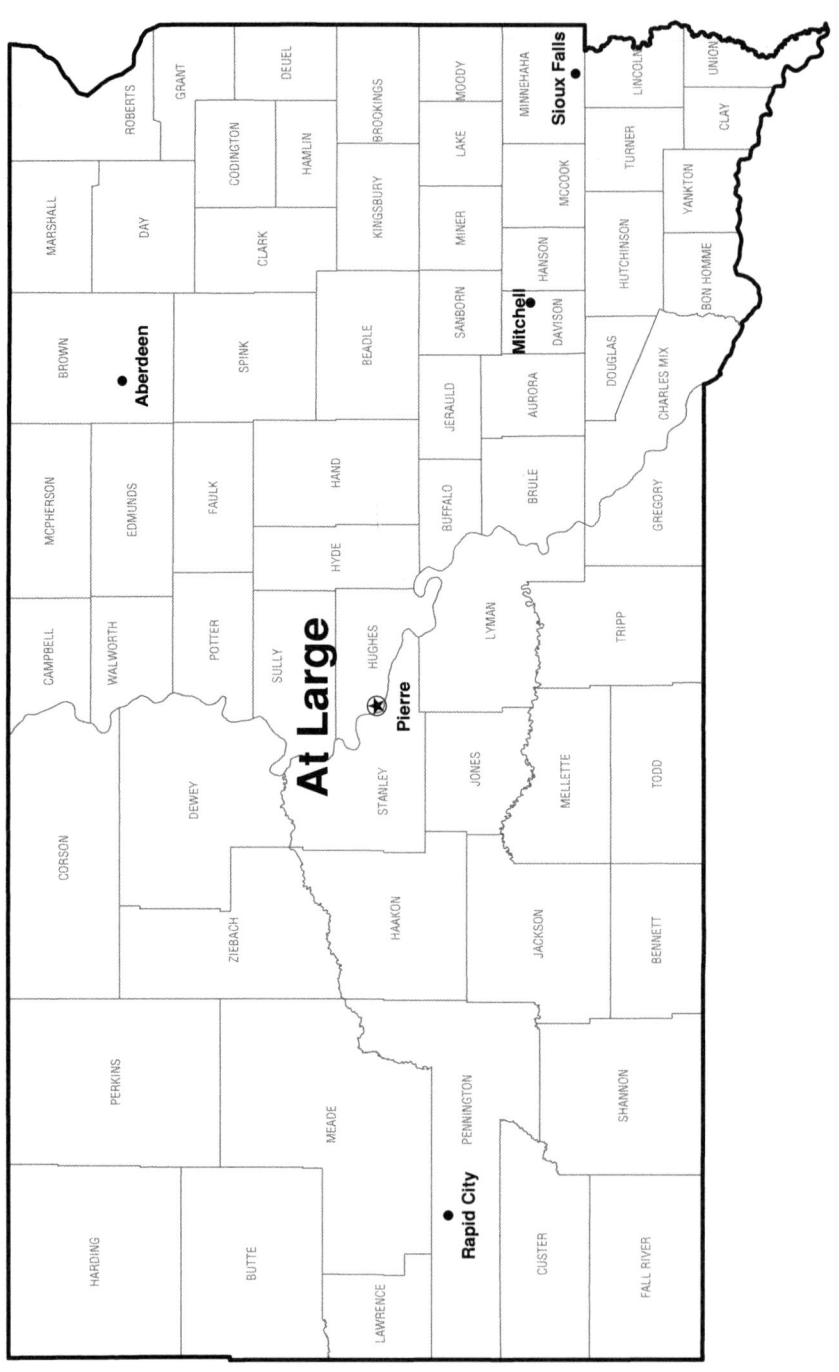

SOUTH DAKOTA

GOVERNOR
Michael Rounds (R). Reelected 2006 to a four-year term. Previously elected 2002.

SENATORS (1 Democrat, 1 Republican)
John Thune (R). Elected 2004 to a six-year term.

Tim Johnson (D). Reelected 2002 to a six-year term. Previously elected 1996.

REPRESENTATIVE (1 Democrat)
At Large. Stephanie Herseth (D)

POSTWAR VOTE FOR PRESIDENT

Year	Total Vote	Republican Vote	Candidate	Democratic Vote	Candidate	Other Vote	Plurality	Rep.	Dem.	Rep.	Dem.
2004	388,215	232,584	Bush, George W.	149,244	Kerry, John	6,387	83,340 R	59.9%	38.4%	60.9%	39.1%
2000	316,269	190,700	Bush, George W.	118,804	Gore, Al	6,765	71,896 R	60.3%	37.6%	61.6%	38.4%
1996**	323,826	150,543	Dole, Bob	139,333	Clinton, Bill	33,950	11,210 R	46.5%	43.0%	51.9%	48.1%
1992**	336,254	136,718	Bush, George	124,888	Clinton, Bill	74,648	11,830 R	40.7%	37.1%	52.3%	47.7%
1988	312,991	165,415	Bush, George	145,560	Dukakis, Michael S.	2,016	19,855 R	52.8%	46.5%	53.2%	46.8%
1984	317,867	200,267	Reagan, Ronald	116,113	Mondale, Walter F.	1,487	84,154 R	63.0%	36.5%	63.3%	36.7%
1980**	327,703	198,343	Reagan, Ronald	103,855	Carter, Jimmy	25,505	94,488 R	60.5%	31.7%	65.6%	34.4%
1976	300,678	151,505	Ford, Gerald R.	147,068	Carter, Jimmy	2,105	4,437 R	50.4%	48.9%	50.7%	49.3%
1972	307,415	166,476	Nixon, Richard M.	139,945	McGovern, George S.	994	26,531 R	54.2%	45.5%	54.3%	45.7%
1968**	281,264	149,841	Nixon, Richard M.	118,023	Humphrey, Hubert H.	13,400	31,818 R	53.3%	42.0%	55.9%	44.1%
1964	293,118	130,108	Goldwater, Barry M.	163,010	Johnson, Lyndon B.		32,902 D	44.4%	55.6%	44.4%	55.6%
1960	306,487	178,417	Nixon, Richard M.	128,070	Kennedy, John F.		50,347 R	58.2%	41.8%	58.2%	41.8%
1956	293,857	171,569	Eisenhower, Dwight D.	122,288	Stevenson, Adlai E.		49,281 R	58.4%	41.6%	58.4%	41.6%
1952	294,283	203,857	Eisenhower, Dwight D.	90,426	Stevenson, Adlai E.		113,431 R	69.3%	30.7%	69.3%	30.7%
1948	250,105	129,651	Dewey, Thomas E.	117,653	Truman, Harry S.	2,801	11,998 R	51.8%	47.0%	52.4%	47.6%

**In past elections, the other vote included: 1996 - 31,250 Reform (Ross Perot); 1992 - 73,295 Independent (Ross Perot); 1980 - 21,431 Independent (John Anderson); 1968 - 13,400 American Independent (George Wallace).

SOUTH DAKOTA

POSTWAR VOTE FOR GOVERNOR

Year	Total Vote	Republican Vote	Republican Candidate	Democratic Vote	Democratic Candidate	Other Vote	Rep.-Dem. Plurality	Total Vote Rep.	Total Vote Dem.	Major Vote Rep.	Major Vote Dem.
2006	335,508	206,990	Rounds, Michael	121,226	Billion, Jack	7,292	85,764 R	61.7%	36.1%	63.1%	36.9%
2002	334,559	189,920	Rounds, Michael	140,263	Abbott, Jim	4,376	49,657 R	56.8%	41.9%	57.5%	42.5%
1998	260,187	166,621	Janklow, Bill	85,473	Hunhoff, Bernie	8,093	81,148 R	64.0%	32.9%	66.1%	33.9%
1994	311,613	172,515	Janklow, Bill	126,273	Beddow, Jim	12,825	46,242 R	55.4%	40.5%	57.7%	42.3%
1990	256,723	151,198	Mickelson, George S.	105,525	Samuelson, Bob L.		45,673 R	58.9%	41.1%	58.9%	41.1%
1986	294,441	152,543	Mickelson, George S.	141,898	Herseth, R. Lars		10,645 R	51.8%	48.2%	51.8%	48.2%
1982	278,562	197,426	Janklow, Bill	81,136	O'Connor, Michael J.		116,290 R	70.9%	29.1%	70.9%	29.1%
1978	259,795	147,116	Janklow, Bill	112,679	McKellips, Roger		34,437 R	56.6%	43.4%	56.6%	43.4%
1974**	278,228	129,077	Olson, John E.	149,151	Kneip, Richard F.		20,074 D	46.4%	53.6%	46.4%	53.6%
1972	308,177	123,165	Thompson, Carveth	185,012	Kneip, Richard F.		61,847 D	40.0%	60.0%	40.0%	60.0%
1970	239,963	108,347	Farrar, Frank	131,616	Kneip, Richard F.		23,269 D	45.2%	54.8%	45.2%	54.8%
1968	276,906	159,646	Farrar, Frank	117,260	Chamberlin, Robert		42,386 R	57.7%	42.3%	57.7%	42.3%
1966	228,214	131,710	Boe, Nils A.	96,504	Chamberlin, Robert		35,206 R	57.7%	42.3%	57.7%	42.3%
1964	290,570	150,151	Boe, Nils A.	140,419	Lindley, John F.		9,732 R	51.7%	48.3%	51.7%	48.3%
1962	256,120	143,682	Gubbrud, Archie M.	112,438	Herseth, Ralph		31,244 R	56.1%	43.9%	56.1%	43.9%
1960	304,625	154,530	Gubbrud, Archie M.	150,095	Herseth, Ralph		4,435 R	50.7%	49.3%	50.7%	49.3%
1958	258,281	125,520	Saunders, Phil	132,761	Herseth, Ralph		7,241 D	48.6%	51.4%	48.6%	51.4%
1956	292,017	158,819	Foss, Joe J.	133,198	Herseth, Ralph		25,621 R	54.4%	45.6%	54.4%	45.6%
1954	236,255	133,878	Foss, Joe J.	102,377	Martin, Ed C.		31,501 R	56.7%	43.3%	56.7%	43.3%
1952	289,515	203,102	Anderson, Sigurd	86,413	Iverson, Sherman A.		116,689 R	70.2%	29.8%	70.2%	29.8%
1950	253,316	154,254	Anderson, Sigurd	99,062	Robbie, Joseph		55,192 R	60.9%	39.1%	60.9%	39.1%
1948	245,372	149,883	Mickelson, George	95,489	Volz, Harold J.		54,394 R	61.1%	38.9%	61.1%	38.9%
1946	162,292	108,998	Mickelson, George	53,294	Haeder, Richard		55,704 R	67.2%	32.8%	67.2%	32.8%

**The term of office of South Dakota's governor was increased to four from two years effective with the 1974 election.

POSTWAR VOTE FOR SENATOR

Year	Total Vote	Republican Vote	Republican Candidate	Democratic Vote	Democratic Candidate	Other Vote	Rep.-Dem. Plurality	Total Vote Rep.	Total Vote Dem.	Major Vote Rep.	Major Vote Dem.
2004	391,188	197,848	Thune, John	193,340	Daschle, Tom		4,508 R	50.6%	49.4%	50.6%	49.4%
2002	337,508	166,957	Thune, John	167,481	Johnson, Tim	3,070	524 D	49.5%	49.6%	49.9%	50.1%
1998	262,111	95,431	Schmidt, Ron	162,884	Daschle, Tom	3,796	67,453 D	36.4%	62.1%	36.9%	63.1%
1996	324,487	157,954	Pressler, Larry	166,533	Johnson, Tim		8,579 D	48.7%	51.3%	48.7%	51.3%
1992	334,495	108,733	Haar, Charlene	217,095	Daschle, Tom	8,667	108,362 D	32.5%	64.9%	33.4%	66.6%
1990	258,976	135,682	Pressler, Larry	116,727	Muenster, Ted	6,567	18,955 R	52.4%	45.1%	53.8%	46.2%
1986	295,830	143,173	Abdnor, James	152,657	Daschle, Tom		9,484 D	48.4%	51.6%	48.4%	51.6%
1984	315,713	235,176	Pressler, Larry	80,537	Cunningham, George V.		154,639 R	74.5%	25.5%	74.5%	25.5%
1980	327,478	190,594	Abdnor, James	129,018	McGovern, George S.	7,866	61,576 R	58.2%	39.4%	59.6%	40.4%
1978	255,599	170,832	Pressler, Larry	84,767	Barnett, Don		86,065 R	66.8%	33.2%	66.8%	33.2%
1974	278,884	130,955	Thorsness, Leo K.	147,929	McGovern, George S.		16,974 D	47.0%	53.0%	47.0%	53.0%
1972	306,386	131,613	Hirsch, Robert W.	174,773	Abourezk, James		43,160 D	43.0%	57.0%	43.0%	57.0%
1968	279,912	120,951	Gubbrud, Archie M.	158,961	McGovern, George S.		38,010 D	43.2%	56.8%	43.2%	56.8%
1966	227,080	150,517	Mundt, Karl E.	76,563	Wright, Donn H.		73,954 R	66.3%	33.7%	66.3%	33.7%
1962	254,319	126,861	Bottum, Joe H.	127,458	McGovern, George S.		597 D	49.9%	50.1%	49.9%	50.1%
1960	305,442	160,181	Mundt, Karl E.	145,261	McGovern, George S.		14,920 R	52.4%	47.6%	52.4%	47.6%
1956	290,622	147,621	Case, Francis	143,001	Holum, Kenneth		4,620 R	50.8%	49.2%	50.8%	49.2%
1954	235,745	135,071	Mundt, Karl E.	100,674	Holum, Kenneth		34,397 R	57.3%	42.7%	57.3%	42.7%
1950	251,362	160,670	Case, Francis	90,692	Engel, John A.		69,978 R	63.9%	36.1%	63.9%	36.1%
1948	242,833	144,084	Mundt, Karl E.	98,749	Engel, John A.		45,335 R	59.3%	40.7%	59.3%	40.7%

SOUTH DAKOTA

GOVERNOR 2006

2000 Census Population	County	Total Vote	Republican	Democratic	Other	Rep.-Dem. Plurality		Percentage			
								Total Vote		Major Vote	
								Rep.	Dem.	Rep.	Dem.
3,058	AURORA	1,478	903	551	24	352	R	61.1%	37.3%	62.1%	37.9%
17,023	BEADLE	7,651	5,500	2,055	96	3,445	R	71.9%	26.9%	72.8%	27.2%
3,574	BENNETT	1,173	715	422	36	293	R	61.0%	36.0%	62.9%	37.1%
7,260	BON HOMME	3,181	2,117	998	66	1,119	R	66.6%	31.4%	68.0%	32.0%
28,220	BROOKINGS	11,747	7,174	4,358	215	2,816	R	61.1%	37.1%	62.2%	37.8%
35,460	BROWN	15,850	10,092	5,460	298	4,632	R	63.7%	34.4%	64.9%	35.1%
5,364	BRULE	2,341	1,575	734	32	841	R	67.3%	31.4%	68.2%	31.8%
2,032	BUFFALO	676	305	360	11	55	D	45.1%	53.3%	45.9%	54.1%
9,094	BUTTE	3,815	2,502	1,181	132	1,321	R	65.6%	31.0%	67.9%	32.1%
1,782	CAMPBELL	822	648	162	12	486	R	78.8%	19.7%	80.0%	20.0%
9,350	CHARLES MIX	3,709	2,470	1,194	45	1,276	R	66.6%	32.2%	67.4%	32.6%
4,143	CLARK	1,932	1,226	653	53	573	R	63.5%	33.8%	65.2%	34.8%
13,537	CLAY	5,289	2,555	2,622	112	67	D	48.3%	49.6%	49.4%	50.6%
25,897	CODINGTON	10,935	7,118	3,672	145	3,446	R	65.1%	33.6%	66.0%	34.0%
4,181	CORSON	1,043	618	374	51	244	R	59.3%	35.9%	62.3%	37.7%
7,275	CUSTER	3,916	2,231	1,515	170	716	R	57.0%	38.7%	59.6%	40.4%
18,741	DAVISON	7,875	5,104	2,662	109	2,442	R	64.8%	33.8%	65.7%	34.3%
6,267	DAY	3,034	1,626	1,356	52	270	R	53.6%	44.7%	54.5%	45.5%
4,498	DEUEL	2,155	1,336	781	38	555	R	62.0%	36.2%	63.1%	36.9%
5,972	DEWEY	1,703	934	724	45	210	R	54.8%	42.5%	56.3%	43.7%
3,458	DOUGLAS	1,804	1,454	331	19	1,123	R	80.6%	18.3%	81.5%	18.5%
4,367	EDMUNDS	2,078	1,539	506	33	1,033	R	74.1%	24.4%	75.3%	24.7%
7,453	FALL RIVER	3,351	1,867	1,316	168	551	R	55.7%	39.3%	58.7%	41.3%
2,640	FAULK	1,153	867	270	16	597	R	75.2%	23.4%	76.3%	23.7%
7,847	GRANT	3,636	2,415	1,176	45	1,239	R	66.4%	32.3%	67.3%	32.7%
4,792	GREGORY	2,212	1,471	702	39	769	R	66.5%	31.7%	67.7%	32.3%
2,196	HAAKON	1,088	830	230	28	600	R	76.3%	21.1%	78.3%	21.7%
5,540	HAMLIN	2,565	1,697	822	46	875	R	66.2%	32.0%	67.4%	32.6%
3,741	HAND	2,070	1,561	484	25	1,077	R	75.4%	23.4%	76.3%	23.7%
3,139	HANSON	1,831	1,305	504	22	801	R	71.3%	27.5%	72.1%	27.9%
1,353	HARDING	672	388	223	61	165	R	57.7%	33.2%	63.5%	36.5%
16,481	HUGHES	8,133	5,675	2,325	133	3,350	R	69.8%	28.6%	70.9%	29.1%
8,075	HUTCHINSON	3,722	2,837	823	62	2,014	R	76.2%	22.1%	77.5%	22.5%
1,671	HYDE	842	645	177	20	468	R	76.6%	21.0%	78.5%	21.5%
2,930	JACKSON	999	621	332	46	289	R	62.2%	33.2%	65.2%	34.8%
2,295	JERAULD	1,086	674	396	16	278	R	62.1%	36.5%	63.0%	37.0%
1,193	JONES	652	472	165	15	307	R	72.4%	25.3%	74.1%	25.9%
5,815	KINGSBURY	2,649	1,703	917	29	786	R	64.3%	34.6%	65.0%	35.0%
11,276	LAKE	5,412	3,237	2,065	110	1,172	R	59.8%	38.2%	61.1%	38.9%
21,802	LAWRENCE	10,504	6,129	3,994	381	2,135	R	58.3%	38.0%	60.5%	39.5%
24,131	LINCOLN	16,241	10,450	5,547	244	4,903	R	64.3%	34.2%	65.3%	34.7%
3,895	LYMAN	1,541	968	545	28	423	R	62.8%	35.4%	64.0%	36.0%
5,832	MCCOOK	2,859	1,932	867	60	1,065	R	67.6%	30.3%	69.0%	31.0%
2,904	MCPHERSON	1,300	1,046	231	23	815	R	80.5%	17.8%	81.9%	18.1%
4,576	MARSHALL	1,869	1,171	672	26	499	R	62.7%	36.0%	63.5%	36.5%
24,253	MEADE	9,865	6,270	3,227	368	3,043	R	63.6%	32.7%	66.0%	34.0%
2,083	MELLETTE	724	471	220	33	251	R	65.1%	30.4%	68.2%	31.8%
2,884	MINER	1,278	812	438	28	374	R	63.5%	34.3%	65.0%	35.0%
148,281	MINNEHAHA	68,092	38,518	28,246	1,328	10,272	R	56.6%	41.5%	57.7%	42.3%
6,595	MOODY	3,111	1,716	1,347	48	369	R	55.2%	43.3%	56.0%	44.0%
88,565	PENNINGTON	38,810	22,929	14,861	1,020	8,068	R	59.1%	38.3%	60.7%	39.3%
3,363	PERKINS	1,473	981	402	90	579	R	66.6%	27.3%	70.9%	29.1%
2,693	POTTER	1,454	1,063	368	23	695	R	73.1%	25.3%	74.3%	25.7%
10,016	ROBERTS	4,263	2,396	1,785	82	611	R	56.2%	41.9%	57.3%	42.7%
2,675	SANBORN	1,239	774	438	27	336	R	62.5%	35.4%	63.9%	36.1%
12,466	SHANNON	2,360	644	1,597	119	953	D	27.3%	67.7%	28.7%	71.3%
7,454	SPINK	3,326	2,275	999	52	1,276	R	68.4%	30.0%	69.5%	30.5%
2,772	STANLEY	1,510	965	511	34	454	R	63.9%	33.8%	65.4%	34.6%
1,556	SULLY	839	620	198	21	422	R	73.9%	23.6%	75.8%	24.2%
9,050	TODD	1,824	764	980	80	216	D	41.9%	53.7%	43.8%	56.2%

SOUTH DAKOTA

GOVERNOR 2006

2000 Census Population	County	Total Vote	Republican	Democratic	Other	Rep.-Dem. Plurality	Percentage			
							Total Vote		Major Vote	
							Rep.	Dem.	Rep.	Dem.
6,430	TRIPP	2,733	1,948	739	46	1,209 R	71.3%	27.0%	72.5%	27.5%
8,849	TURNER	4,105	2,559	1,473	73	1,086 R	62.3%	35.9%	63.5%	36.5%
12,584	UNION	5,663	3,633	1,915	115	1,718 R	64.2%	33.8%	65.5%	34.5%
5,974	WALWORTH	2,444	1,805	567	72	1,238 R	73.9%	23.2%	76.1%	23.9%
21,652	YANKTON	9,044	5,765	3,114	165	2,651 R	63.7%	34.4%	64.9%	35.1%
2,519	ZIEBACH	757	379	347	31	32 R	50.1%	45.8%	52.2%	47.8%
754,844	TOTAL	335,508	206,990	121,226	7,292	85,764 R	61.7%	36.1%	63.1%	36.9%

SOUTH DAKOTA

HOUSE OF REPRESENTATIVES

CD	Year	Total Vote	Republican		Democratic		Other Vote	Rep.-Dem. Plurality	Percentage			
			Vote	Candidate	Vote	Candidate			Total Vote		Major Vote	
									Rep.	Dem.	Rep.	Dem.
AL	2006	333,562	97,864	WHALEN, BRUCE W.	230,468	HERSETH, STEPHANIE*	5,230	132,604 D	29.3%	69.1%	29.8%	70.2%
AL	2004	389,468	178,823	DIEDRICH, LARRY	207,837	HERSETH, STEPHANIE*	2,808	29,014 D	45.9%	53.4%	46.2%	53.8%
AL	2002	336,807	180,023	JANKLOW, BILL	153,656	HERSETH, STEPHANIE	3,128	26,367 R	53.4%	45.6%	54.0%	46.0%
AL	2000	314,761	231,083	THUNE, JOHN*	78,321	HOHN, CURT	5,357	152,762 R	73.4%	24.9%	74.7%	25.3%
AL	1998	258,590	194,157	THUNE, JOHN*	64,433	MOSER, JEFF		129,724 R	75.1%	24.9%	75.1%	24.9%
AL	1996	323,203	186,393	THUNE, JOHN	119,547	WEILAND, RICK	17,263	66,846 R	57.7%	37.0%	60.9%	39.1%
AL	1994	305,922	112,054	BERKHOUT, JAN	183,036	JOHNSON, TIM*	10,832	70,982 D	36.6%	59.8%	38.0%	62.0%
AL	1992	332,902	89,375	TIMMER, JOHN	230,070	JOHNSON, TIM*	13,457	140,695 D	26.8%	69.1%	28.0%	72.0%
AL	1990	257,298	83,484	FRANKENFELD, DON	173,814	JOHNSON, TIM*		90,330 D	32.4%	67.6%	32.4%	67.6%
AL	1988	311,916	88,157	VOLK, DAVID	223,759	JOHNSON, TIM*		135,602 D	28.3%	71.7%	28.3%	71.7%
AL	1986	289,723	118,261	BELL, DALE	171,462	JOHNSON, TIM		53,201 D	40.8%	59.2%	40.8%	59.2%
AL	1984	316,222	134,821	BELL, DALE	181,401	DASCHLE, TOM*		46,580 D	42.6%	57.4%	42.6%	57.4%
AL	1982	275,652	133,530	ROBERTS, CLINT	142,122	DASCHLE, TOM*		8,592 D	48.4%	51.6%	48.4%	51.6%

An asterisk (*) denotes incumbent.

SOUTH DAKOTA

GENERAL AND PRIMARY ELECTIONS

2006 GENERAL ELECTIONS

Governor   Other vote was 4,010 Constitution (Steven J. Willis); 3,282 Libertarian (Tom Gerber).

House   Other vote was:

   At Large   5,230 Libertarian (Larry Rudebusch).

SOUTH DAKOTA

GENERAL AND PRIMARY ELECTIONS

2006 PRIMARY ELECTIONS

Primary	June 6, 2006	**Registration** (active registrants as of May 22, 2006)	Republican	233,299	
			Democratic	185,768	
			Libertarian	1,092	
			Constitution	329	
			Other	68,793	
			TOTAL	489,281	

Primary Type Closed—Only registered Democrats and Republicans could vote in their party's primary. In addition to the active registered voters, there were 47,800 inactive voters at the time of the 2006 primary.

Note: An asterisk (*) denotes incumbent. The names of unopposed candidates did not appear on the primary ballot; therefore, no votes were cast for these candidates.

	REPUBLICAN PRIMARIES		DEMOCRATIC PRIMARIES		
Governor	Michael Rounds*	Unopposed	Jack Billion	22,527	61.9%
			Dennis Wiese	13,862	38.1%
			TOTAL	*36,389*	
House At Large	Bruce W. Whalen	Unopposed	Stephanie Herseth*	Unopposed	

TENNESSEE

Congressional districts first established for elections held in 2002
9 members

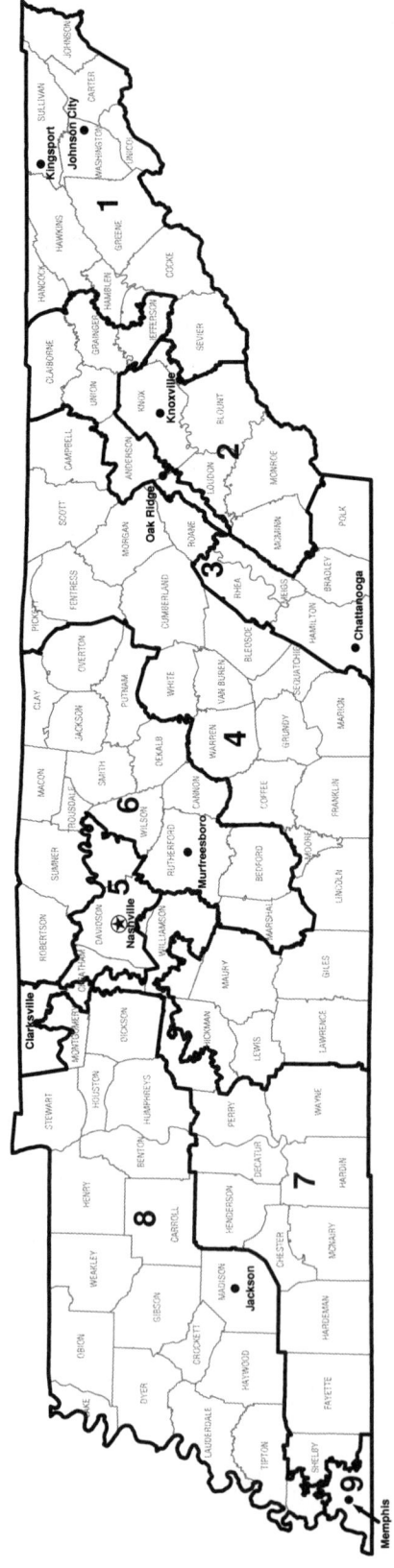

TENNESSEE

GOVERNOR
Phil Bredesen (D). Reelected 2006 to a four-year term. Previously elected 2002.

SENATORS (2 Republicans)
Bob Corker (R). Elected 2006 to a six-year term.

Lamar Alexander (R). Elected 2002 to a six-year term.

REPRESENTATIVES (5 Democrats, 4 Republicans)
1. David Davis (R)
2. John J. "Jimmy" Duncan Jr. (R)
3. Zach Wamp (R)
4. Lincoln Davis (D)
5. Jim Cooper (D)
6. Bart Gordon (D)
7. Marsha Blackburn (R)
8. John Tanner (D)
9. Steve Cohen (D)

POSTWAR VOTE FOR PRESIDENT

Year	Total Vote	Republican		Democratic		Other Vote	Plurality	Percentage			
								Total Vote		Major Vote	
		Vote	Candidate	Vote	Candidate			Rep.	Dem.	Rep.	Dem.
2004	2,437,319	1,384,375	Bush, George W.	1,036,477	Kerry, John	16,467	347,898 R	56.8%	42.5%	57.2%	42.8%
2000**	2,076,181	1,061,949	Bush, George W.	981,720	Gore, Al	32,512	80,229 R	51.1%	47.3%	52.0%	48.0%
1996**	1,894,105	863,530	Dole, Bob	909,146	Clinton, Bill	121,429	45,616 D	45.6%	48.0%	48.7%	51.3%
1992**	1,982,638	841,300	Bush, George	933,521	Clinton, Bill	207,817	92,221 D	42.4%	47.1%	47.4%	52.6%
1988	1,636,250	947,233	Bush, George	679,794	Dukakis, Michael S.	9,223	267,439 R	57.9%	41.5%	58.2%	41.8%
1984	1,711,994	990,212	Reagan, Ronald	711,714	Mondale, Walter F.	10,068	278,498 R	57.8%	41.6%	58.2%	41.8%
1980**	1,617,616	787,761	Reagan, Ronald	783,051	Carter, Jimmy	46,804	4,710 R	48.7%	48.4%	50.1%	49.9%
1976	1,476,345	633,969	Ford, Gerald R.	825,879	Carter, Jimmy	16,497	191,910 D	42.9%	55.9%	43.4%	56.6%
1972	1,201,182	813,147	Nixon, Richard M.	357,293	McGovern, George S.	30,742	455,854 R	67.7%	29.7%	69.5%	30.5%
1968**	1,248,617	472,592	Nixon, Richard M.	351,233	Humphrey, Hubert H.	424,792	47,800 R	37.8%	28.1%	57.4%	42.6%
1964	1,143,946	508,965	Goldwater, Barry M.	634,947	Johnson, Lyndon B.	34	125,982 D	44.5%	55.5%	44.5%	55.5%
1960	1,051,792	556,577	Nixon, Richard M.	481,453	Kennedy, John F.	13,762	75,124 R	52.9%	45.8%	53.6%	46.4%
1956	939,404	462,288	Eisenhower, Dwight D.	456,507	Stevenson, Adlai E.	20,609	5,781 R	49.2%	48.6%	50.3%	49.7%
1952	892,553	446,147	Eisenhower, Dwight D.	443,710	Stevenson, Adlai E.	2,696	2,437 R	50.0%	49.7%	50.1%	49.9%
1948**	550,283	202,914	Dewey, Thomas E.	270,402	Truman, Harry S.	76,967	67,488 D	36.9%	49.1%	42.9%	57.1%

**In past elections, the other vote included: 2000 - 19,781 Green (Ralph Nader); 1996 - 105,918 Reform (Ross Perot); 1992 - 199,968 Independent (Ross Perot); 1980 - 35,991 Independent (John Anderson); 1968 - 424,792 American Independent (George Wallace, who finished second); 1948 - 73,815 States' Rights (Strom Thurmond).

TENNESSEE

POSTWAR VOTE FOR GOVERNOR

| | | Republican | | Democratic | | | | Percentage | | | |
| | Total | | | | | Other | | Total Vote | | Major Vote | |
Year	Vote	Vote	Candidate	Vote	Candidate	Vote	Plurality	Rep.	Dem.	Rep.	Dem.
2006	1,818,549	540,853	Bryson, Jim	1,247,491	Bredesen, Phil	30,205	706,638 D	29.7%	68.6%	30.2%	69.8%
2002	1,653,167	786,803	Hilleary, Van	837,284	Bredesen, Phil	29,080	50,481 D	47.6%	50.6%	48.4%	51.6%
1998	976,236	669,973	Sundquist, Don	287,750	Hooker, John J.	18,513	382,223 R	68.6%	29.5%	70.0%	30.0%
1994	1,487,130	807,104	Sundquist, Don	664,252	Bredesen, Phil	15,774	142,852 R	54.3%	44.7%	54.9%	45.1%
1990	790,441	289,348	Henry, Dwight	480,885	McWherter, Ned	20,208	191,537 D	36.6%	60.8%	37.6%	62.4%
1986	1,210,339	553,449	Dunn, Winfield	656,602	McWherter, Ned	288	103,153 D	45.7%	54.2%	45.7%	54.3%
1982	1,238,927	737,963	Alexander, Lamar	500,937	Tyree, Randy	27	237,026 R	59.6%	40.4%	59.6%	40.4%
1978	1,189,695	661,959	Alexander, Lamar	523,495	Butcher, Jake	4,241	138,464 R	55.6%	44.0%	55.8%	44.2%
1974	1,040,714	455,467	Alexander, Lamar	576,833	Blanton, Ray	8,414	121,366 D	43.8%	55.4%	44.1%	55.9%
1970	1,108,247	575,777	Dunn, Winfield	509,521	Hooker, John J.	22,949	66,256 R	52.0%	46.0%	53.1%	46.9%
1966**	656,566		—	532,998	Ellington, Buford	123,568	532,998 D		81.2%		100.0%
1962**	621,064	100,190	Patty, Hubert D.	315,648	Clement, Frank G.	205,226	111,883 D	16.1%	50.8%	24.1%	75.9%
1958**	432,545	35,938	Wall, Thomas P.	248,874	Ellington, Buford	147,733	112,475 D	8.3%	57.5%	12.6%	87.4%
1954**	322,586		—	281,291	Clement, Frank G.	41,295	281,291 D		87.2%		100.0%
1952	806,771	166,377	Witt, R. Beecher	640,290	Clement, Frank G.	104	473,913 D	20.6%	79.4%	20.6%	79.4%
1950**	236,194		—	184,437	Browning, Gordon	51,757	184,437 D		78.1%		100.0%
1948	543,881	179,957	Acuff, Roy	363,903	Browning, Gordon	21	183,946 D	33.1%	66.9%	33.1%	66.9%
1946	229,456	73,222	Lowe, W. O.	149,937	McCord, Jim Nance	6,297	76,715 D	31.9%	65.3%	32.8%	67.2%

**In past elections, the other vote included: 1966 - 64,602 Independent (H. L. Crawford); 50,221 Independent (Charles Moffett); 1962 - 203,765 Independent (William R. Anderson), who finished second; 1958 - 136,399 Independent (Jim Nance McCord), who finished second; 1954 - 39,574 Independent (John R. Neal); 1950 - 51,757 Independent (Neal). In the 1958 and 1962 elections, the plurality of the winning Democratic candidate is listed over the Independent runner-up. In other elections, the plurality is the difference between the Democratic and Republican vote. The term of office of Tennessee's governor was increased from two to four years effective with the 1954 election.

POSTWAR VOTE FOR SENATOR

| | | Republican | | Democratic | | | | Percentage | | | |
| | Total | | | | | Other | Rep.-Dem. | Total Vote | | Major Vote | |
Year	Vote	Vote	Candidate	Vote	Candidate	Vote	Plurality	Rep.	Dem.	Rep.	Dem.
2006	1,833,695	929,911	Corker, Bob	879,976	Ford, Harold E. Jr.	23,808	49,935 R	50.7%	48.0%	51.4%	48.6%
2002	1,642,421	891,420	Alexander, Lamar	728,295	Clement, Bob	22,706	163,125 R	54.3%	44.3%	55.0%	45.0%
2000	1,928,613	1,255,444	Frist, Bill	621,152	Clark, Jeff	52,017	634,292 R	65.1%	32.2%	66.9%	33.1%
1996	1,778,664	1,091,554	Thompson, Fred	654,937	Gordon, Houston	32,173	436,617 R	61.4%	36.8%	62.5%	37.5%
1994	1,480,391	834,226	Frist, Bill	623,164	Sasser, James R.	23,001	211,062 R	56.4%	42.1%	57.2%	42.8%
1994S	1,465,862	885,998	Thompson, Fred	565,930	Cooper, Jim	13,934	320,068 R	60.4%	38.6%	61.0%	39.0%
1990	783,922	233,703	Hawkins, William R.	530,898	Gore, Al	19,321	297,195 D	29.8%	67.7%	30.6%	69.4%
1988	1,567,181	541,033	Anderson, Bill	1,020,061	Sasser, James R.	6,087	479,028 D	34.5%	65.1%	34.7%	65.3%
1984	1,648,064	557,016	Ashe, Victor	1,000,607	Gore, Al	90,441	443,591 D	33.8%	60.7%	35.8%	64.2%
1982	1,259,785	479,642	Beard, Robin L.	780,113	Sasser, James R.	30	300,471 D	38.1%	61.9%	38.1%	61.9%
1978	1,157,094	642,644	Baker, Howard H. Jr.	466,228	Eskind, Jane	48,222	176,416 R	55.5%	40.3%	58.0%	42.0%
1976	1,432,046	673,231	Brock, William E.	751,180	Sasser, James R.	7,635	77,949 D	47.0%	52.5%	47.3%	52.7%
1972	1,164,195	716,539	Baker, Howard H. Jr.	440,599	Blanton, Ray	7,057	275,940 R	61.5%	37.8%	61.9%	38.1%
1970	1,097,041	562,645	Brock, William E.	519,858	Gore, Albert	14,538	42,787 R	51.3%	47.4%	52.0%	48.0%
1966	866,961	483,063	Baker, Howard H. Jr.	383,843	Clement, Frank G.	55	99,220 R	55.7%	44.3%	55.7%	44.3%
1964	1,064,018	493,475	Kuykendall, Daniel H.	570,542	Gore, Albert	1	77,067 D	46.4%	53.6%	46.4%	53.6%
1964S	1,091,093	517,330	Baker, Howard H. Jr.	568,905	Bass, Ross	4,858	51,575 D	47.4%	52.1%	47.6%	52.4%
1960	828,519	234,053	Frazier, A. Bradley	594,460	Kefauver, Estes	6	360,407 D	28.2%	71.7%	28.2%	71.8%
1958	401,666	76,371	Atkins, Hobart F.	317,324	Gore, Albert	7,971	240,953 D	19.0%	79.0%	19.4%	80.6%
1954	356,094	106,971	Wall, Thomas P.	249,121	Kefauver, Estes	2	142,150 D	30.0%	70.0%	30.0%	70.0%
1952	735,219	153,479	Atkins, Hobart F.	545,432	Gore, Albert	36,308	391,953 D	20.9%	74.2%	22.0%	78.0%
1948	499,218	166,947	Reece, B. Carroll	326,142	Kefauver, Estes	6,129	159,195 D	33.4%	65.3%	33.9%	66.1%
1946	218,714	57,238	Ladd, William B.	145,654	McKellar, Kenneth	15,822	88,416 D	26.2%	66.6%	28.2%	71.8%

One each of the 1994 and 1964 elections was for a short term to fill a vacancy.

TENNESSEE

GOVERNOR 2006

2000 Census Population	County	Total Vote	Republican	Democratic	Other	Rep.-Dem. Plurality	Percentage			
							Total Vote		Major Vote	
							Rep.	Dem.	Rep.	Dem.
71,330	ANDERSON	23,316	6,049	16,881	386	10,832 D	25.9%	72.4%	26.4%	73.6%
37,586	BEDFORD	10,613	3,215	7,240	158	4,025 D	30.3%	68.2%	30.8%	69.2%
16,537	BENTON	5,519	1,273	4,128	118	2,855 D	23.1%	74.8%	23.6%	76.4%
12,367	BLEDSOE	3,935	1,560	2,274	101	714 D	39.6%	57.8%	40.7%	59.3%
105,823	BLOUNT	35,815	11,791	23,433	591	11,642 D	32.9%	65.4%	33.5%	66.5%
87,965	BRADLEY	26,259	11,401	14,492	366	3,091 D	43.4%	55.2%	44.0%	56.0%
39,854	CAMPBELL	10,061	3,073	6,793	195	3,720 D	30.5%	67.5%	31.1%	68.9%
12,826	CANNON	4,230	1,167	2,978	85	1,811 D	27.6%	70.4%	28.2%	71.8%
29,475	CARROLL	9,077	2,493	6,379	205	3,886 D	27.5%	70.3%	28.1%	71.9%
56,742	CARTER	16,266	6,686	9,211	369	2,525 D	41.1%	56.6%	42.1%	57.9%
35,912	CHEATHAM	11,499	3,824	7,506	169	3,682 D	33.3%	65.3%	33.8%	66.2%
15,540	CHESTER	4,363	1,547	2,730	86	1,183 D	35.5%	62.6%	36.2%	63.8%
29,862	CLAIBORNE	7,626	2,693	4,732	201	2,039 D	35.3%	62.1%	36.3%	63.7%
7,976	CLAY	2,482	685	1,717	80	1,032 D	27.6%	69.2%	28.5%	71.5%
33,565	COCKE	9,704	3,752	5,741	211	1,989 D	38.7%	59.2%	39.5%	60.5%
48,014	COFFEE	15,350	4,534	10,498	318	5,964 D	29.5%	68.4%	30.2%	69.8%
14,532	CROCKETT	4,460	1,090	3,299	71	2,209 D	24.4%	74.0%	24.8%	75.2%
46,802	CUMBERLAND	19,166	7,172	11,741	253	4,569 D	37.4%	61.3%	37.9%	62.1%
569,891	DAVIDSON	174,736	38,977	132,712	3,047	93,735 D	22.3%	76.0%	22.7%	77.3%
11,731	DECATUR	3,945	1,068	2,791	86	1,723 D	27.1%	70.7%	27.7%	72.3%
17,423	DE KALB	5,511	1,559	3,848	104	2,289 D	28.3%	69.8%	28.8%	71.2%
43,156	DICKSON	14,428	4,164	10,016	248	5,852 D	28.9%	69.4%	29.4%	70.6%
37,279	DYER	11,000	3,130	7,642	228	4,512 D	28.5%	69.5%	29.1%	70.9%
28,806	FAYETTE	12,467	4,599	7,701	167	3,102 D	36.9%	61.8%	37.4%	62.6%
16,625	FENTRESS	5,157	2,207	2,859	91	652 D	42.8%	55.4%	43.6%	56.4%
39,270	FRANKLIN	12,781	3,430	9,179	172	5,749 D	26.8%	71.8%	27.2%	72.8%
48,152	GIBSON	15,592	3,890	11,473	229	7,583 D	24.9%	73.6%	25.3%	74.7%
29,447	GILES	8,524	2,243	6,135	146	3,892 D	26.3%	72.0%	26.8%	73.2%
20,659	GRAINGER	5,507	2,100	3,289	118	1,189 D	38.1%	59.7%	39.0%	61.0%
62,909	GREENE	18,415	7,376	10,669	370	3,293 D	40.1%	57.9%	40.9%	59.1%
14,332	GRUNDY	3,841	1,024	2,692	125	1,668 D	26.7%	70.1%	27.6%	72.4%
58,128	HAMBLEN	16,656	6,057	10,377	222	4,320 D	36.4%	62.3%	36.9%	63.1%
307,896	HAMILTON	107,113	30,482	75,261	1,370	44,779 D	28.5%	70.3%	28.8%	71.2%
6,786	HANCOCK	1,890	880	960	50	80 D	46.6%	50.8%	47.8%	52.2%
28,105	HARDEMAN	7,798	1,740	5,895	163	4,155 D	22.3%	75.6%	22.8%	77.2%
25,578	HARDIN	7,333	2,516	4,666	151	2,150 D	34.3%	63.6%	35.0%	65.0%
53,563	HAWKINS	14,753	5,552	8,903	298	3,351 D	37.6%	60.3%	38.4%	61.6%
19,797	HAYWOOD	5,905	1,093	4,722	90	3,629 D	18.5%	80.0%	18.8%	81.2%
25,522	HENDERSON	8,573	3,072	5,293	208	2,221 D	35.8%	61.7%	36.7%	63.3%
31,115	HENRY	9,860	2,402	7,289	169	4,887 D	24.4%	73.9%	24.8%	75.2%
22,295	HICKMAN	6,688	1,844	4,714	130	2,870 D	27.6%	70.5%	28.1%	71.9%
8,088	HOUSTON	2,717	567	2,111	39	1,544 D	20.9%	77.7%	21.2%	78.8%
17,929	HUMPHREYS	6,272	1,354	4,824	94	3,470 D	21.6%	76.9%	21.9%	78.1%
10,984	JACKSON	3,914	924	2,895	95	1,971 D	23.6%	74.0%	24.2%	75.8%
44,294	JEFFERSON	13,287	4,782	8,307	198	3,525 D	36.0%	62.5%	36.5%	63.5%
17,499	JOHNSON	4,827	2,214	2,491	122	277 D	45.9%	51.6%	47.1%	52.9%
382,032	KNOX	122,504	33,266	87,537	1,701	54,271 D	27.2%	71.5%	27.5%	72.5%
7,954	LAKE	1,544	257	1,252	35	995 D	16.6%	81.1%	17.0%	83.0%
27,101	LAUDERDALE	6,859	1,567	5,146	146	3,579 D	22.8%	75.0%	23.3%	76.7%
39,926	LAWRENCE	12,458	4,399	7,843	216	3,444 D	35.3%	63.0%	35.9%	64.1%
11,367	LEWIS	3,948	1,297	2,506	145	1,209 D	32.9%	63.5%	34.1%	65.9%
31,340	LINCOLN	8,110	3,059	4,890	161	1,831 D	37.7%	60.3%	38.5%	61.5%
39,086	LOUDON	16,296	5,257	10,797	242	5,540 D	32.3%	66.3%	32.7%	67.3%
49,015	MCMINN	13,767	5,195	8,299	273	3,104 D	37.7%	60.3%	38.5%	61.5%
24,653	MCNAIRY	7,745	2,708	4,855	182	2,147 D	35.0%	62.7%	35.8%	64.2%
20,386	MACON	5,509	1,917	3,507	85	1,590 D	34.8%	63.7%	35.3%	64.7%
91,837	MADISON	30,009	7,771	21,889	349	14,118 D	25.9%	72.9%	26.2%	73.8%
27,776	MARION	8,802	2,407	6,162	233	3,755 D	27.3%	70.0%	28.1%	71.9%
26,767	MARSHALL	8,359	2,178	6,050	131	3,872 D	26.1%	72.4%	26.5%	73.5%
69,498	MAURY	23,328	6,778	16,274	276	9,496 D	29.1%	69.8%	29.4%	70.6%

TENNESSEE

GOVERNOR 2006

2000 Census Population	County	Total Vote	Republican	Democratic	Other	Rep.-Dem. Plurality	Percentage			
							Total Vote		Major Vote	
							Rep.	Dem.	Rep.	Dem.
11,086	MEIGS	3,266	1,156	2,046	64	890 D	35.4%	62.6%	36.1%	63.9%
38,961	MONROE	12,523	4,876	7,484	163	2,608 D	38.9%	59.8%	39.4%	60.6%
134,768	MONTGOMERY	35,850	9,185	25,465	1,200	16,280 D	25.6%	71.0%	26.5%	73.5%
5,740	MOORE	2,131	700	1,388	43	688 D	32.8%	65.1%	33.5%	66.5%
19,757	MORGAN	5,049	1,507	3,454	88	1,947 D	29.8%	68.4%	30.4%	69.6%
32,450	OBION	9,801	2,049	7,539	213	5,490 D	20.9%	76.9%	21.4%	78.6%
20,118	OVERTON	6,567	1,645	4,820	102	3,175 D	25.0%	73.4%	25.4%	74.6%
7,631	PERRY	2,336	600	1,673	63	1,073 D	25.7%	71.6%	26.4%	73.6%
4,945	PICKETT	2,130	890	1,205	35	315 D	41.8%	56.6%	42.5%	57.5%
16,050	POLK	5,119	1,772	3,218	129	1,446 D	34.6%	62.9%	35.5%	64.5%
62,315	PUTNAM	20,068	5,879	13,830	359	7,951 D	29.3%	68.9%	29.8%	70.2%
28,400	RHEA	8,466	3,297	5,004	165	1,707 D	38.9%	59.1%	39.7%	60.3%
51,910	ROANE	17,511	4,807	12,389	315	7,582 D	27.5%	70.7%	28.0%	72.0%
54,433	ROBERTSON	18,861	5,995	12,664	202	6,669 D	31.8%	67.1%	32.1%	67.9%
182,023	RUTHERFORD	61,371	20,535	40,034	802	19,499 D	33.5%	65.2%	33.9%	66.1%
21,127	SCOTT	5,284	1,931	3,230	123	1,299 D	36.5%	61.1%	37.4%	62.6%
11,370	SEQUATCHIE	4,215	1,351	2,761	103	1,410 D	32.1%	65.5%	32.9%	67.1%
71,170	SEVIER	22,829	9,023	13,355	451	4,332 D	39.5%	58.5%	40.3%	59.7%
897,472	SHELBY	279,666	64,593	210,470	4,603	145,877 D	23.1%	75.3%	23.5%	76.5%
17,712	SMITH	6,337	1,531	4,719	87	3,188 D	24.2%	74.5%	24.5%	75.5%
12,370	STEWART	4,394	952	3,314	128	2,362 D	21.7%	75.4%	22.3%	77.7%
153,048	SULLIVAN	45,281	17,479	27,024	778	9,545 D	38.6%	59.7%	39.3%	60.7%
130,449	SUMNER	46,146	15,938	29,713	495	13,775 D	34.5%	64.4%	34.9%	65.1%
51,271	TIPTON	16,549	5,843	10,433	273	4,590 D	35.3%	63.0%	35.9%	64.1%
7,259	TROUSDALE	2,610	557	2,000	53	1,443 D	21.3%	76.6%	21.8%	78.2%
17,667	UNICOI	5,523	2,095	3,298	130	1,203 D	37.9%	59.7%	38.8%	61.2%
17,808	UNION	4,456	1,653	2,743	60	1,090 D	37.1%	61.6%	37.6%	62.4%
5,508	VAN BUREN	1,916	533	1,347	36	814 D	27.8%	70.3%	28.4%	71.6%
38,276	WARREN	11,374	2,848	8,324	202	5,476 D	25.0%	73.2%	25.5%	74.5%
107,198	WASHINGTON	34,028	12,360	21,092	576	8,732 D	36.3%	62.0%	36.9%	63.1%
16,842	WAYNE	4,134	1,831	2,232	71	401 D	44.3%	54.0%	45.1%	54.9%
34,895	WEAKLEY	10,122	2,621	7,233	268	4,612 D	25.9%	71.5%	26.6%	73.4%
23,102	WHITE	7,590	2,140	5,231	219	3,091 D	28.2%	68.9%	29.0%	71.0%
126,638	WILLIAMSON	60,904	25,384	35,058	462	9,674 D	41.7%	57.6%	42.0%	58.0%
88,809	WILSON	35,673	11,990	23,207	476	11,217 D	33.6%	65.1%	34.1%	65.9%
5,689,283	TOTAL	1,818,549	540,853	1,247,491	30,205	706,638 D	29.7%	68.6%	30.2%	69.8%

TENNESSEE

SENATOR 2006

2000 Census Population	County	Total Vote	Republican	Democratic	Other	Rep.-Dem. Plurality	Total Vote Rep.	Total Vote Dem.	Major Vote Rep.	Major Vote Dem.
71,330	ANDERSON	23,484	12,349	10,809	326	1,540 R	52.6%	46.0%	53.3%	46.7%
37,586	BEDFORD	10,744	5,602	4,931	211	671 R	52.1%	45.9%	53.2%	46.8%
16,537	BENTON	5,517	2,176	3,232	109	1,056 D	39.4%	58.6%	40.2%	59.8%
12,367	BLEDSOE	3,953	2,210	1,692	51	518 R	55.9%	42.8%	56.6%	43.4%
105,823	BLOUNT	35,976	22,046	13,372	558	8,674 R	61.3%	37.2%	62.2%	37.8%
87,965	BRADLEY	26,587	18,161	8,057	369	10,104 R	68.3%	30.3%	69.3%	30.7%
39,854	CAMPBELL	10,087	5,051	4,896	140	155 R	50.1%	48.5%	50.8%	49.2%
12,826	CANNON	4,288	1,925	2,282	81	357 D	44.9%	53.2%	45.8%	54.2%
29,475	CARROLL	9,147	4,742	4,256	149	486 R	51.8%	46.5%	52.7%	47.3%
56,742	CARTER	16,521	10,577	5,664	280	4,913 R	64.0%	34.3%	65.1%	34.9%
35,912	CHEATHAM	11,533	6,134	5,146	253	988 R	53.2%	44.6%	54.4%	45.6%
15,540	CHESTER	4,416	2,696	1,646	74	1,050 R	61.1%	37.3%	62.1%	37.9%
29,862	CLAIBORNE	7,667	4,112	3,426	129	686 R	53.6%	44.7%	54.6%	45.4%
7,976	CLAY	2,487	1,015	1,425	47	410 D	40.8%	57.3%	41.6%	58.4%
33,565	COCKE	9,705	5,952	3,563	190	2,389 R	61.3%	36.7%	62.6%	37.4%
48,014	COFFEE	15,483	8,069	7,147	267	922 R	52.1%	46.2%	53.0%	47.0%
14,532	CROCKETT	4,511	2,212	2,246	53	34 D	49.0%	49.8%	49.6%	50.4%
46,802	CUMBERLAND	19,236	11,515	7,471	250	4,044 R	59.9%	38.8%	60.6%	39.4%
569,891	DAVIDSON	176,357	67,136	106,847	2,374	39,711 D	38.1%	60.6%	38.6%	61.4%
11,731	DECATUR	3,927	1,941	1,902	84	39 R	49.4%	48.4%	50.5%	49.5%
17,423	DE KALB	5,549	2,450	2,999	100	549 D	44.2%	54.0%	45.0%	55.0%
43,156	DICKSON	14,536	7,014	7,232	290	218 D	48.3%	49.8%	49.2%	50.8%
37,279	DYER	11,134	6,115	4,848	171	1,267 R	54.9%	43.5%	55.8%	44.2%
28,806	FAYETTE	12,666	7,296	5,275	95	2,021 R	57.6%	41.6%	58.0%	42.0%
16,625	FENTRESS	5,248	2,918	2,237	93	681 R	55.6%	42.6%	56.6%	43.4%
39,270	FRANKLIN	12,850	6,142	6,477	231	335 D	47.8%	50.4%	48.7%	51.3%
48,152	GIBSON	15,699	8,003	7,471	225	532 R	51.0%	47.6%	51.7%	48.3%
29,447	GILES	8,524	4,017	4,336	171	319 D	47.1%	50.9%	48.1%	51.9%
20,659	GRAINGER	5,507	3,198	2,211	98	987 R	58.1%	40.1%	59.1%	40.9%
62,909	GREENE	18,575	11,852	6,419	304	5,433 R	63.8%	34.6%	64.9%	35.1%
14,332	GRUNDY	3,891	1,466	2,367	58	901 D	37.7%	60.8%	38.2%	61.8%
58,128	HAMBLEN	16,813	10,186	6,366	261	3,820 R	60.6%	37.9%	61.5%	38.5%
307,896	HAMILTON	108,390	57,411	49,904	1,075	7,507 R	53.0%	46.0%	53.5%	46.5%
6,786	HANCOCK	1,895	1,130	729	36	401 R	59.6%	38.5%	60.8%	39.2%
28,105	HARDEMAN	7,931	3,367	4,484	80	1,117 D	42.5%	56.5%	42.9%	57.1%
25,578	HARDIN	7,406	4,278	3,029	99	1,249 R	57.8%	40.9%	58.5%	41.5%
53,563	HAWKINS	14,815	8,636	5,943	236	2,693 R	58.3%	40.1%	59.2%	40.8%
19,797	HAYWOOD	5,933	2,130	3,763	40	1,633 D	35.9%	63.4%	36.1%	63.9%
25,522	HENDERSON	8,620	5,360	3,126	134	2,234 R	62.2%	36.3%	63.2%	36.8%
31,115	HENRY	9,816	4,689	4,947	180	258 D	47.8%	50.4%	48.7%	51.3%
22,295	HICKMAN	6,728	2,852	3,743	133	891 D	42.4%	55.6%	43.2%	56.8%
8,088	HOUSTON	2,712	931	1,734	47	803 D	34.3%	63.9%	34.9%	65.1%
17,929	HUMPHREYS	6,271	2,236	3,915	120	1,679 D	35.7%	62.4%	36.4%	63.6%
10,984	JACKSON	3,956	1,350	2,531	75	1,181 D	34.1%	64.0%	34.8%	65.2%
44,294	JEFFERSON	13,341	8,219	4,906	216	3,313 R	61.6%	36.8%	62.6%	37.4%
17,499	JOHNSON	4,856	3,148	1,626	82	1,522 R	64.8%	33.5%	65.9%	34.1%
382,032	KNOX	123,967	69,129	53,293	1,545	15,836 R	55.8%	43.0%	56.5%	43.5%
7,954	LAKE	1,568	571	981	16	410 D	36.4%	62.6%	36.8%	63.2%
27,101	LAUDERDALE	6,987	2,953	3,954	80	1,001 D	42.3%	56.6%	42.8%	57.2%
39,926	LAWRENCE	12,496	6,715	5,550	231	1,165 R	53.7%	44.4%	54.7%	45.3%
11,367	LEWIS	3,956	1,893	1,969	94	76 D	47.9%	49.8%	49.0%	51.0%
31,340	LINCOLN	8,111	4,535	3,470	106	1,065 R	55.9%	42.8%	56.7%	43.3%
39,086	LOUDON	16,418	10,812	5,369	237	5,443 R	65.9%	32.7%	66.8%	33.2%
49,015	MCMINN	14,151	8,762	5,214	175	3,548 R	61.9%	36.8%	62.7%	37.3%
24,653	MCNAIRY	7,803	4,292	3,360	151	932 R	55.0%	43.1%	56.1%	43.9%
20,386	MACON	5,532	3,033	2,410	89	623 R	54.8%	43.6%	55.7%	44.3%
91,837	MADISON	30,183	15,367	14,549	267	818 R	50.9%	48.2%	51.4%	48.6%
27,776	MARION	8,869	3,944	4,775	150	831 D	44.5%	53.8%	45.2%	54.8%
26,767	MARSHALL	7,294	3,391	3,762	141	371 D	46.5%	51.6%	47.4%	52.6%
69,498	MAURY	23,490	11,994	11,128	368	866 R	51.1%	47.4%	51.9%	48.1%

TENNESSEE

SENATOR 2006

2000 Census Population	County	Total Vote	Republican	Democratic	Other	Rep.-Dem. Plurality		Percentage			
								Total Vote		Major Vote	
								Rep.	Dem.	Rep.	Dem.
11,086	MEIGS	3,312	1,808	1,465	39	343	R	54.6%	44.2%	55.2%	44.8%
38,961	MONROE	12,557	7,535	4,856	166	2,679	R	60.0%	38.7%	60.8%	39.2%
134,768	MONTGOMERY	35,727	17,045	17,999	683	954	D	47.7%	50.4%	48.6%	51.4%
5,740	MOORE	2,164	1,165	966	33	199	R	53.8%	44.6%	54.7%	45.3%
19,757	MORGAN	5,106	2,627	2,413	66	214	R	51.4%	47.3%	52.1%	47.9%
32,450	OBION	9,793	4,936	4,734	123	202	R	50.4%	48.3%	51.0%	49.0%
20,118	OVERTON	6,603	2,602	3,895	106	1,293	D	39.4%	59.0%	40.0%	60.0%
7,631	PERRY	2,338	964	1,326	48	362	D	41.2%	56.7%	42.1%	57.9%
4,945	PICKETT	2,140	1,124	977	39	147	R	52.5%	45.7%	53.5%	46.5%
16,050	POLK	5,139	2,655	2,412	72	243	R	51.7%	46.9%	52.4%	47.6%
62,315	PUTNAM	20,210	10,127	9,670	413	457	R	50.1%	47.8%	51.2%	48.8%
28,400	RHEA	8,532	5,146	3,278	108	1,868	R	60.3%	38.4%	61.1%	38.9%
51,910	ROANE	17,582	9,645	7,669	268	1,976	R	54.9%	43.6%	55.7%	44.3%
54,433	ROBERTSON	18,908	10,008	8,587	313	1,421	R	52.9%	45.4%	53.8%	46.2%
182,023	RUTHERFORD	61,611	33,809	26,829	973	6,980	R	54.9%	43.5%	55.8%	44.2%
21,127	SCOTT	5,366	2,798	2,504	64	294	R	52.1%	46.7%	52.8%	47.2%
11,370	SEQUATCHIE	4,270	2,227	1,986	57	241	R	52.2%	46.5%	52.9%	47.1%
71,170	SEVIER	23,042	15,361	7,326	355	8,035	R	66.7%	31.8%	67.7%	32.3%
897,472	SHELBY	284,519	103,377	179,677	1,465	76,300	D	36.3%	63.2%	36.5%	63.5%
17,712	SMITH	6,326	2,610	3,622	94	1,012	D	41.3%	57.3%	41.9%	58.1%
12,370	STEWART	4,369	1,675	2,608	86	933	D	38.3%	59.7%	39.1%	60.9%
153,048	SULLIVAN	45,318	27,872	16,814	632	11,058	R	61.5%	37.1%	62.4%	37.6%
130,449	SUMNER	46,604	26,996	18,976	632	8,020	R	57.9%	40.7%	58.7%	41.3%
51,271	TIPTON	16,689	9,717	6,775	197	2,942	R	58.2%	40.6%	58.9%	41.1%
7,259	TROUSDALE	2,605	891	1,674	40	783	D	34.2%	64.3%	34.7%	65.3%
17,667	UNICOI	5,598	3,491	2,015	92	1,476	R	62.4%	36.0%	63.4%	36.6%
17,808	UNION	4,505	2,418	2,025	62	393	R	53.7%	45.0%	54.4%	45.6%
5,508	VAN BUREN	1,919	766	1,116	37	350	D	39.9%	58.2%	40.7%	59.3%
38,276	WARREN	11,441	4,940	6,255	246	1,315	D	43.2%	54.7%	44.1%	55.9%
107,198	WASHINGTON	34,520	21,147	12,894	479	8,253	R	61.3%	37.4%	62.1%	37.9%
16,842	WAYNE	4,144	2,496	1,583	65	913	R	60.2%	38.2%	61.2%	38.8%
34,895	WEAKLEY	10,114	5,412	4,542	160	870	R	53.5%	44.9%	54.4%	45.6%
23,102	WHITE	7,680	3,601	3,894	185	293	D	46.9%	50.7%	48.0%	52.0%
126,638	WILLIAMSON	61,104	40,852	19,682	570	21,170	R	66.9%	32.2%	67.5%	32.5%
88,809	WILSON	35,727	20,662	14,520	545	6,142	R	57.8%	40.6%	58.7%	41.3%
5,689,283	TOTAL	1,833,695	929,911	879,976	23,808	49,935	R	50.7%	48.0%	51.4%	48.6%

TENNESSEE

HOUSE OF REPRESENTATIVES

CD	Year	Total Vote	Republican			Democratic		Other Vote	Rep.-Dem. Plurality	Percentage			
			Vote		Candidate	Vote	Candidate			Total Vote		Major Vote	
										Rep.	Dem.	Rep.	Dem.
1	2006	177,278	108,336		DAVIS, DAVID	65,538	TRENT, RICK	3,404	42,798 R	61.1%	37.0%	62.3%	37.7%
1	2004	233,560	172,543		JENKINS, BILL*	56,361	LEONARD, GRAHAM	4,656	116,182 R	73.9%	24.1%	75.4%	24.6%
1	2002	128,886	127,300		JENKINS, BILL*	—		1,586	127,300 R	98.8%		100.0%	
2	2006	202,120	157,095		DUNCAN, JOHN J. "JIMMY" JR.*	45,025	GREENE, JOHN		112,070 R	77.7%	22.3%	77.7%	22.3%
2	2004	272,928	215,795		DUNCAN, JOHN J. "JIMMY" JR.*	52,155	GREENE, JOHN	4,978	163,640 R	79.1%	19.1%	80.5%	19.5%
2	2002	185,981	146,887		DUNCAN, JOHN J. "JIMMY" JR.*	37,035	GREENE, JOHN	2,059	109,852 R	79.0%	19.9%	79.9%	20.1%
3	2006	199,115	130,791		WAMP, ZACH*	68,324	BENEDICT, BRENT		62,467 R	65.7%	34.3%	65.7%	34.3%
3	2004	256,636	166,154		WAMP, ZACH*	84,295	WOLFE, JOHN	6,187	81,859 R	64.7%	32.8%	66.3%	33.7%
3	2002	173,921	112,254		WAMP, ZACH*	58,824	WOLFE, JOHN	2,843	53,430 R	64.5%	33.8%	65.6%	34.4%
4	2006	186,115	62,449		MARTIN, KENNETH	123,666	DAVIS, LINCOLN*		61,217 D	33.6%	66.4%	33.6%	66.4%
4	2004	252,646	109,993		BOWLING, JANICE	138,459	DAVIS, LINCOLN*	4,194	28,466 D	43.5%	54.8%	44.3%	55.7%
4	2002	184,300	85,680		BOWLING, JANICE	95,989	DAVIS, LINCOLN	2,631	10,309 D	46.5%	52.1%	47.2%	52.8%
5	2006	178,142	49,702		KOVACH, THOMAS F.	122,919	COOPER, JIM*	5,521	73,217 D	27.9%	69.0%	28.8%	71.2%
5	2004	243,963	74,978		KNAPP, SCOTT	168,970	COOPER, JIM*	15	93,992 D	30.7%	69.3%	30.7%	69.3%
5	2002	170,886	56,825		DUVALL, ROBERT	108,903	COOPER, JIM	5,158	52,078 D	33.3%	63.7%	34.3%	65.7%
6	2006	192,380	60,392		DAVIS, DAVID R.	129,069	GORDON, BART*	2,919	68,677 D	31.4%	67.1%	31.9%	68.1%
6	2004	260,642	87,523		DEMAS, NICK	167,448	GORDON, BART*	5,671	79,925 D	33.6%	64.2%	34.3%	65.7%
6	2002	177,547	57,401		GARRISON, ROBERT L.	117,034	GORDON, BART*	3,112	59,633 D	32.3%	65.9%	32.9%	67.1%
7	2006	230,582	152,288		BLACKBURN, MARSHA*	73,369	MORRISON, BILL	4,925	78,919 R	66.0%	31.8%	67.5%	32.5%
7	2004	232,404	232,404		BLACKBURN, MARSHA*	—			232,404 R	100.0%		100.0%	
7	2002	195,558	138,314		BLACKBURN, MARSHA	51,790	BARRON, TIM	5,454	86,524 R	70.7%	26.5%	72.8%	27.2%
8	2006	177,108	47,492		FARMER, JOHN	129,610	TANNER, JOHN*	6	82,118 D	26.8%	73.2%	26.8%	73.2%
8	2004	233,567	59,853		HART, JAMES L.	173,623	TANNER, JOHN*	91	113,770 D	25.6%	74.3%	25.6%	74.4%
8	2002	167,970	45,853		McCLAIN, MAT	117,811	TANNER, JOHN*	4,306	71,958 D	27.3%	70.1%	28.0%	72.0%
9	2006	172,586	31,002		WHITE, MARK	103,341	COHEN, STEVE	38,243	72,339 D	18.0%	59.9%	23.1%	76.9%
9	2004	232,392	41,578		FORT, RUBEN M.	190,648	FORD, HAROLD E. JR.*	166	149,070 D	17.9%	82.0%	17.9%	82.1%
9	2002	144,260			—	120,904	FORD, HAROLD E. JR.*	23,356	120,904 D	0.0%	83.8%	0.0%	100.0%
TOTAL	2006	1,715,426	799,547			860,861		55,018	61,314 D	46.6%	50.2%	48.2%	51.8%
TOTAL	2004	2,218,738	1,160,821			1,031,959		25,958	128,862 R	52.3%	46.5%	52.9%	47.1%
TOTAL	2002	1,529,309	770,514			708,290		50,505	62,224 R	50.4%	46.3%	52.1%	47.9%

An asterisk (*) denotes incumbent.

TENNESSEE

GENERAL AND PRIMARY ELECTIONS

2006 GENERAL ELECTIONS

Governor	Other vote was 11,374 Independent (Carl "Twofeathers" Whitaker); 7,531 Independent (George Banks); 4,083 Independent (Charles E. Smith); 2,711 Independent (Howard M. Switzer); 2,385 Independent (David Gatchell); 2,114 Independent (Marivuana Stout Leinoff); 7 write-in (John Jay Hooker).
Senator	Other vote was 10,831 Independent (Ed Choate); 3,746 Independent (David Gatchell); 3,580 Independent (Emory "Bo" Heyward); 3,033 Independent (Gary Keplinger); 2,589 Independent (Christopher Joseph Lugo); 14 write-in (James Anthony Gray); 13 write-in (John Jay Hooker); 1 write-in (Gloria D. Reagon Price); 1 write-in (Mary Taylor-Shelby).
House	Other vote was:
CD 1	1,024 Independent (Robert N. Smith); 1,003 Independent (James W. Reeves); 966 Independent (Michael Peavler); 411 Independent (Mahmood "Michael" Sabri).
CD 2	
CD 3	
CD 4	
CD 5	3,766 Independent (Ginny Welsch); 1,755 Independent (Scott Knapp).
CD 6	2,035 Independent (Robert L. Garrison); 884 Independent (Norman R. Saliba).
CD 7	1,806 Independent (Kathleen A. Culver); 898 Independent (James B. "Mickey" White); 848 Independent (William J. Smith); 710 Independent (John L. Rimer); 663 Independent (Gayl G. Pratt).
CD 8	6 write-in (James Hart).
CD 9	38,243 Independent (Jake Ford).

Note: In Tennessee all third-party candidates were listed as Independents regardless of party affiliation.

2006 PRIMARY ELECTIONS

Primary	August 3, 2006	**Registration**	3,668,264	No Party Registration

Primary Type   Open—Any registered voter could participate in either the Democratic or Republican primary.

Note: An asterisk (*) denotes incumbent.

	REPUBLICAN PRIMARIES			DEMOCRATIC PRIMARIES		
Governor	Jim Bryson	160,786	50.0%	Phil Bredesen*	393,004	88.5%
	David M. Farmer	50,900	15.8%	John Jay Hooker	31,933	7.2%
	Joe Kirkpatrick	34,491	10.7%	Tim Sevier	11,562	2.6%
	Mark Albertini	29,184	9.1%	Walt Ward	7,555	1.7%
	Wayne Thomas Bailey	24,273	7.6%			
	Wayne Young	11,997	3.7%			
	Timothy Thomas	9,747	3.0%			
	TOTAL	321,378		TOTAL	444,054	
Senator	Bob Corker	231,541	48.1%	Harold E. Ford Jr.	333,789	79.1%
	Ed Bryant	161,189	33.5%	Gary G. Davis	41,802	9.9%
	Van Hilleary	83,078	17.3%	John Jay Hooker	27,175	6.4%
	Tate Harrison	5,309	1.1%	Charles E. Smith	14,724	3.5%
				Al Strauss	4,410	1.0%
				Jim Maynard (write-in)	96	
	TOTAL	481,117		TOTAL	421,996	

TENNESSEE

GENERAL AND PRIMARY ELECTIONS

REPUBLICAN PRIMARIES			DEMOCRATIC PRIMARIES		
Congressional District 1	David Davis	16,583	22.2%	Rick Trent	6,973	39.8%
	Richard S. Venable	16,010	21.4%	Alan Howell	4,541	25.9%
	Richard H. Roberts	13,580	18.2%	Joel Goodman	4,105	23.4%
	Phil Roe	12,864	17.2%	Dennis Dean Whaley	1,905	10.9%
	Larry Waters	7,885	10.6%			
	Vance W. Cheek Jr.	3,334	4.5%			
	Peggy Parker Barnett	1,709	2.3%			
	Dan Smith	1,087	1.5%			
	Bill F. Breeding Jr.	818	1.1%			
	Claude Cox	284	0.4%			
	Colquitt "C. P." Brackett	227	0.3%			
	John "Jay" Grose	170	0.2%			
	Douglas Heinsohn	162	0.2%			
	TOTAL	*74,713*		*TOTAL*	*17,524*	
Congressional District 2	John J. "Jimmy" Duncan Jr.*	55,295	87.4%	John Greene	9,660	54.5%
	Ralph McGill	7,994	12.6%	Robert R. Scott	8,075	45.5%
	TOTAL	*63,289*		*TOTAL*	*17,735*	
Congressional District 3	Zach Wamp*	57,569	87.3%	Brent Benedict	14,743	51.2%
	June Griffin	3,579	5.4%	Terry Stulce	14,036	48.8%
	Doug Vandagriff	3,112	4.7%			
	Charles Howard	1,702	2.6%			
	TOTAL	*65,962*		*TOTAL*	*28,779*	
Congressional District 4	Kenneth Martin	15,053	41.4%	Lincoln Davis*	56,618	86.2%
	Alan Pedigo	11,326	31.1%	Norma Cartwright	6,564	10.0%
	Don Strong	10,017	27.5%	Harvey Howard	2,511	3.8%
	TOTAL	*36,396*		*TOTAL*	*65,693*	
Congressional District 5	Thomas F. Kovach	17,113	100.0%	Jim Cooper*	38,148	91.6%
				Jason Pullias	3,518	8.4%
				TOTAL	*41,666*	
Congressional District 6	David R. Davis	27,803	100.0%	Bart Gordon*	53,916	92.3%
				J. Patrick Lyons	4,490	7.7%
				TOTAL	*58,406*	
Congressional District 7	Marsha Blackburn*	63,372	100.0%	Bill Morrison	17,080	59.6%
				Randy G. Morris	11,569	40.4%
				TOTAL	*28,649*	
Congressional District 8	John Farmer	24,753	78.8%	John Tanner*	61,764	100.0%
	Rory B. Bricco	6,661	21.2%			
	TOTAL	*31,414*				
Congressional District 9	Mark White	12,132	62.8%	Steve Cohen	23,629	30.9%
	Tom Guleff	2,949	15.3%	Nikki Tinker	19,164	25.1%
	Derrick Bennett	1,910	9.9%	Joseph S. Ford Jr.	9,334	12.2%
	Cecil Hale	1,567	8.1%	Julian T. Bolton	8,055	10.5%
	Rudolph Daniels	770	4.0%	Ed Stanton	6,927	9.1%
				Ron Redwing	2,169	2.8%
				Marvell R. Mitchell	1,804	2.4%
				Ralph White	1,700	2.2%
				Joseph B. Kyles	1,336	1.7%
				Joe Towns Jr.	675	0.9%
				Lee Harris	645	0.8%
				Jesse Blumenfeld	384	0.5%
				Bill Whitman	274	0.4%
				Tyson Pratcher	141	0.2%
				Ruben M. Fort	122	0.2%
	TOTAL	*19,328*		*TOTAL*	*76,359*	

TEXAS

Congressional districts first established for elections held in 2004
32 members

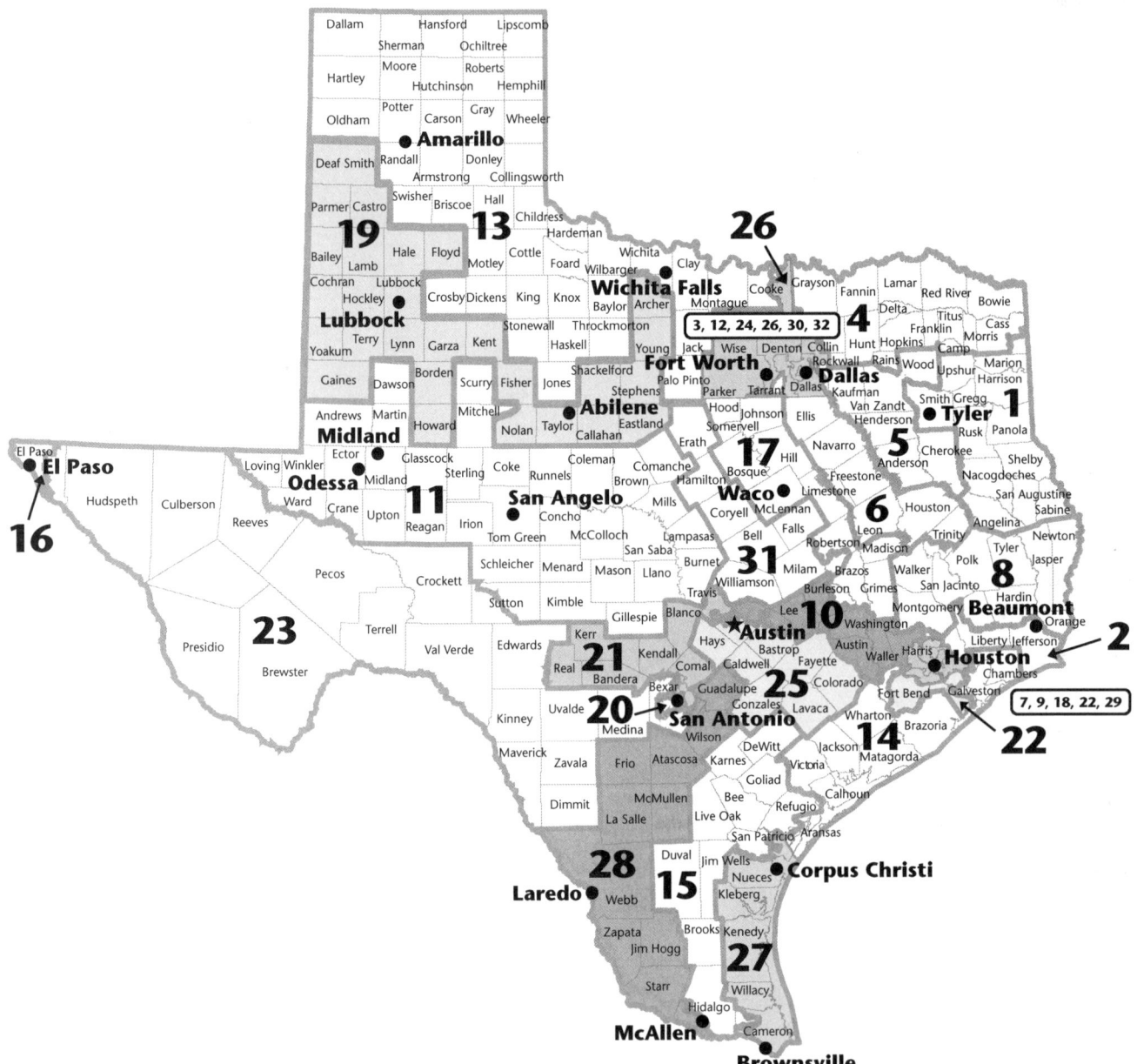

TEXAS

Houston Area

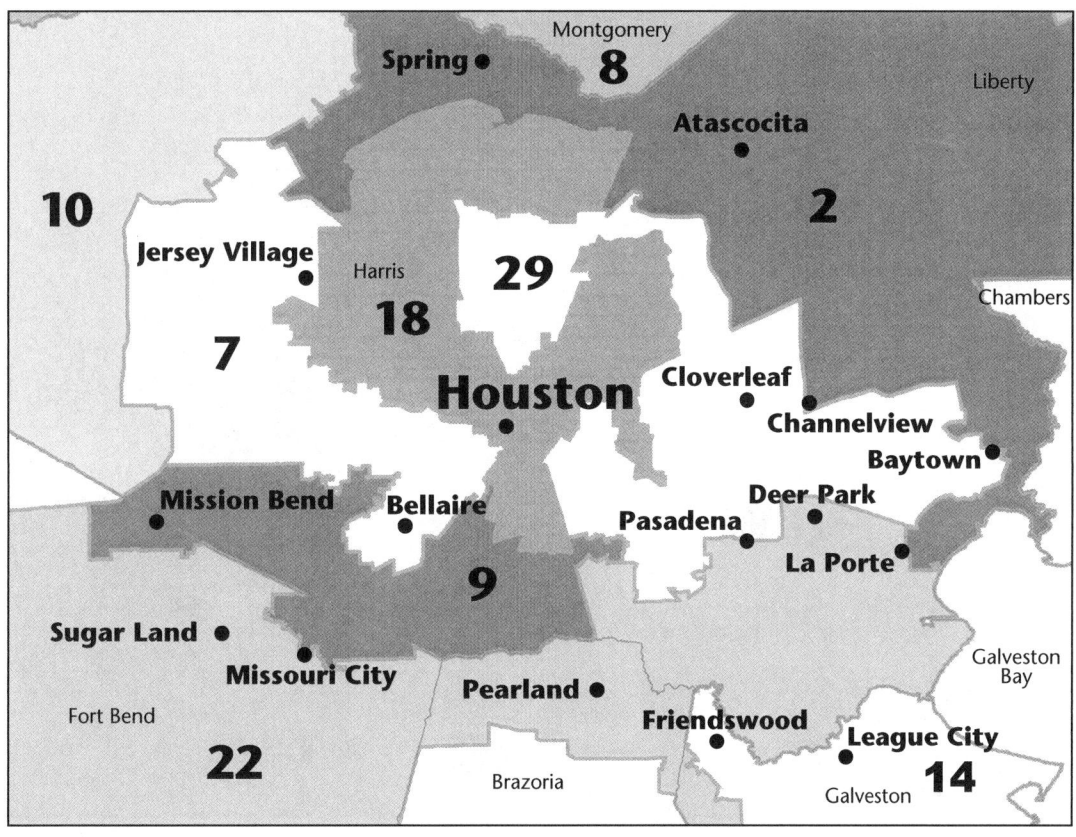

TEXAS

Dallas–Fort Worth Area

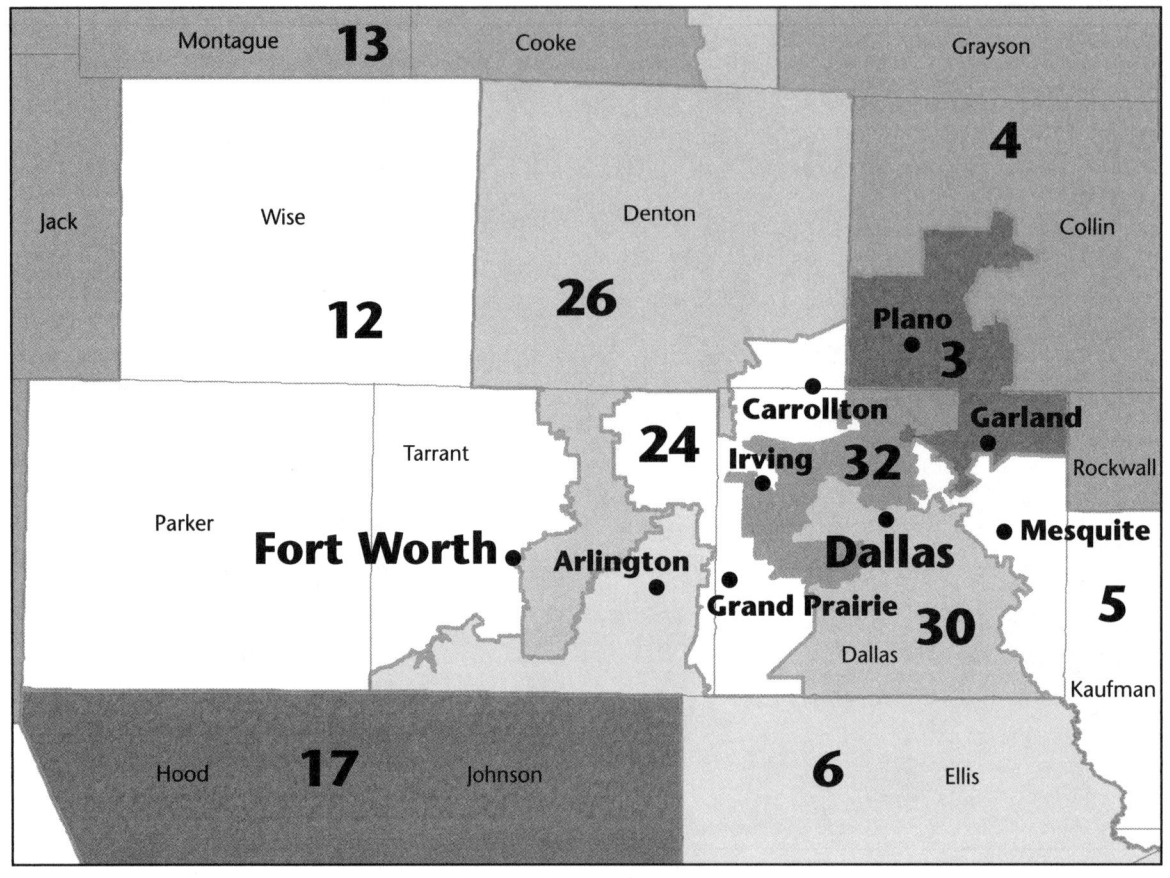

TEXAS

GOVERNOR
Rick Perry (R). Reelected 2006 to a four-year term. Previously elected 2002. Assumed office Dec. 21, 2000, following the resignation of president-elect George W. Bush.

SENATORS (2 Republicans)
Kay Bailey Hutchison (R). Reelected 2006 to a six-year term. Previously elected 2000, 1994, and in a special election June 5, 1993, to fill out the remaining year and a half of the term vacated when Senator Lloyd Bentsen (D) resigned to become Secretary of the Treasury.

John Cornyn (R). Elected 2002 to a six-year term.

REPRESENTATIVES (19 Republicans, 13 Democrats)
1. Louie Gohmert (R)
2. Ted Poe (R)
3. Sam Johnson (R)
4. Ralph M. Hall (R)
5. Jeb Hensarling (R)
6. Joe L. Barton (R)
7. John Culberson (R)
8. Kevin Brady (R)
9. Al Green (D)
10. Michael McCaul (R)
11. K. Michael Conaway (R)
12. Kay Granger (R)
13. William M. "Mac" Thornberry (R)
14. Ron Paul (R)
15. Ruben Hinojosa (D)
16. Silvestre Reyes (D)
17. Chet Edwards (D)
18. Sheila Jackson-Lee (D)
19. Randy Neugebauer (R)
20. Charlie Gonzalez (D)
21. Lamar Smith (R)
22. Nick Lampson (D)
23. Ciro D. Rodriguez (D)
24. Kenny Marchant (R)
25. Lloyd Doggett (D)
26. Michael C. Burgess (R)
27. Solomon P. Ortiz (D)
28. Henry Cuellar (D)
29. Gene Green (D)
30. Eddie Bernice Johnson (D)
31. John Carter (R)
32. Pete Sessions (R)

POSTWAR VOTE FOR PRESIDENT

		Republican		Democratic				Total Vote		Major Vote	
Year	Total Vote	Vote	Candidate	Vote	Candidate	Other Vote	Plurality	Rep.	Dem.	Rep.	Dem.
2004	7,410,765	4,526,917	Bush, George W.	2,832,704	Kerry, John	51,144	1,694,213 R	61.1%	38.2%	61.5%	38.5%
2000**	6,407,637	3,799,639	Bush, George W.	2,433,746	Gore, Al	174,252	1,365,893 R	59.3%	38.0%	61.0%	39.0%
1996**	5,611,644	2,736,167	Dole, Bob	2,459,683	Clinton, Bill	415,794	276,484 R	48.8%	43.8%	52.7%	47.3%
1992**	6,154,018	2,496,071	Bush, George	2,281,815	Clinton, Bill	1,376,132	214,256 R	40.6%	37.1%	52.2%	47.8%
1988	5,427,410	3,036,829	Bush, George	2,352,748	Dukakis, Michael S.	37,833	684,081 R	56.0%	43.3%	56.3%	43.7%
1984	5,397,571	3,433,428	Reagan, Ronald	1,949,276	Mondale, Walter F.	14,867	1,484,152 R	63.6%	36.1%	63.8%	36.2%
1980**	4,541,636	2,510,705	Reagan, Ronald	1,881,147	Carter, Jimmy	149,784	629,558 R	55.3%	41.4%	57.2%	42.8%
1976	4,071,884	1,953,300	Ford, Gerald R.	2,082,319	Carter, Jimmy	36,265	129,019 D	48.0%	51.1%	48.4%	51.6%
1972	3,471,281	2,298,896	Nixon, Richard M.	1,154,289	McGovern, George S.	18,096	1,144,607 R	66.2%	33.3%	66.6%	33.4%
1968**	3,079,216	1,227,844	Nixon, Richard M.	1,266,804	Humphrey, Hubert H.	584,568	38,960 D	39.9%	41.1%	49.2%	50.8%
1964	2,626,811	958,566	Goldwater, Barry M.	1,663,185	Johnson, Lyndon B.	5,060	704,619 D	36.5%	63.3%	36.6%	63.4%
1960	2,311,084	1,121,310	Nixon, Richard M.	1,167,567	Kennedy, John F.	22,207	46,257 D	48.5%	50.5%	49.0%	51.0%
1956	1,955,168	1,080,619	Eisenhower, Dwight D.	859,958	Stevenson, Adlai E.	14,591	220,661 R	55.3%	44.0%	55.7%	44.3%
1952	2,075,946	1,102,878	Eisenhower, Dwight D.	969,228	Stevenson, Adlai E.	3,840	133,650 R	53.1%	46.7%	53.2%	46.8%
1948**	1,249,577	303,467	Dewey, Thomas E.	824,235	Truman, Harry S.	121,875	520,768 D	24.3%	66.0%	26.9%	73.1%

**In past elections, the other vote included: 2000 - 137,994 Green (Ralph Nader); 1996 - 378,537 Reform (Ross Perot); 1992 - 1,354,781 Independent (Ross Perot); 1980 - 111,613 Independent (John Anderson); 1968 - 584,269 American Independent (George Wallace); 1948 - 113,920 States' Rights (Strom Thurmond).

TEXAS

POSTWAR VOTE FOR GOVERNOR

Year	Total Vote	Republican Vote	Candidate	Democratic Vote	Candidate	Other Vote	Rep.-Dem. Plurality	Total Vote Rep.	Total Vote Dem.	Major Vote Rep.	Major Vote Dem.
2006**	4,399,116	1,716,792	Perry, Rick	1,310,337	Bell, Chris	1,371,987	406,455 R	39.0%	29.8%	56.7%	43.3%
2002	4,553,987	2,632,591	Perry, Rick	1,819,798	Sanchez, Tony	101,598	812,793 R	57.8%	40.0%	59.1%	40.9%
1998	3,738,483	2,551,454	Bush, George W.	1,165,444	Mauro, Garry	21,585	1,386,010 R	68.2%	31.2%	68.6%	31.4%
1994	4,396,242	2,350,994	Bush, George W.	2,016,928	Richards, Ann	28,320	334,066 R	53.5%	45.9%	53.8%	46.2%
1990	3,892,746	1,826,431	Williams, Clayton	1,925,670	Richards, Ann	140,645	99,239 D	46.9%	49.5%	48.7%	51.3%
1986	3,441,460	1,813,779	Clements, William P.	1,584,515	White, Mark	43,166	229,264 R	52.7%	46.0%	53.4%	46.6%
1982	3,191,091	1,465,937	Clements, William P.	1,697,870	White, Mark	27,284	231,933 D	45.9%	53.2%	46.3%	53.7%
1978	2,369,764	1,183,839	Clements, William P.	1,166,979	Hill, John	18,946	16,860 R	50.0%	49.2%	50.4%	49.6%
1974**	1,654,984	514,725	Granberry, Jim	1,016,334	Briscoe, Dolph	123,925	501,609 D	31.1%	61.4%	33.6%	66.4%
1972	3,410,128	1,534,060	Grover, Henry C.	1,633,970	Briscoe, Dolph	242,098	99,910 D	45.0%	47.9%	48.4%	51.6%
1970	2,235,847	1,037,723	Eggers, Paul W.	1,197,726	Smith, Preston	398	160,003 D	46.4%	53.6%	46.4%	53.6%
1968	2,916,509	1,254,333	Eggers, Paul W.	1,662,019	Smith, Preston	157	407,686 D	43.0%	57.0%	43.0%	57.0%
1966	1,425,861	368,025	Kennerly, T. E.	1,037,517	Connally, John B.	20,319	669,492 D	25.8%	72.8%	26.2%	73.8%
1964	2,544,753	661,675	Crichton, Jack	1,877,793	Connally, John B.	5,285	1,216,118 D	26.0%	73.8%	26.1%	73.9%
1962	1,569,181	715,025	Cox, Jack	847,036	Connally, John B.	7,120	132,011 D	45.6%	54.0%	45.8%	54.2%
1960	2,250,718	612,963	Steger, William M.	1,637,755	Daniel, Price		1,024,792 D	27.2%	72.8%	27.2%	72.8%
1958	789,133	94,098	Mayer, Edwin S.	695,035	Daniel, Price		600,937 D	11.9%	88.1%	11.9%	88.1%
1956	1,828,161	271,088	Bryant, William R.	1,433,051	Daniel, Price	124,022	1,161,963 D	14.8%	78.4%	15.9%	84.1%
1954	636,892	66,154	Adams, Tod R.	569,533	Shivers, Allan	1,205	503,379 D	10.4%	89.4%	10.4%	89.6%
1952	1,881,202		—	1,844,530	Shivers, Allan	36,672	1,844,530 D		98.1%		100.0%
1950	394,747	39,737	Currie, Ralph W.	355,010	Shivers, Allan		315,273 D	10.1%	89.9%	10.1%	89.9%
1948	1,208,860	177,399	Lane, Alvin H.	1,024,160	Jester, Beauford	7,301	846,761 D	14.7%	84.7%	14.8%	85.2%
1946	378,744	33,231	Nolte, Eugene	345,513	Jester, Beauford		312,282 D	8.8%	91.2%	8.8%	91.2%

**In past elections, the other vote included: 2006 - 796,851 Independent (Carole Keeton Strayhorn); 547,674 Independent (Richard "Kinky" Friedman). The term of office of Texas' governor was increased to four from two years effective with the 1974 election.

TEXAS

POSTWAR VOTE FOR SENATOR

Year	Total Vote	Republican		Democratic		Other Vote	Rep.-Dem. Plurality	Percentage			
								Total Vote		Major Vote	
		Vote	Candidate	Vote	Candidate			Rep.	Dem.	Rep.	Dem.
2006	4,314,663	2,661,789	Hutchison, Kay Bailey	1,555,202	Radnofsky, Barbara Ann	97,672	1,106,587 R	61.7%	36.0%	63.1%	36.9%
2002	4,514,012	2,496,243	Cornyn, John	1,955,758	Kirk, Ron	62,011	540,485 R	55.3%	43.3%	56.1%	43.9%
2000	6,276,652	4,082,091	Hutchison, Kay Bailey	2,030,315	Kelly, Gene	164,246	2,051,776 R	65.0%	32.3%	66.8%	33.2%
1996	5,527,441	3,027,680	Gramm, Phil	2,428,776	Morales, Victor M.	70,985	598,904 R	54.8%	43.9%	55.5%	44.5%
1994	4,279,940	2,604,218	Hutchison, Kay Bailey	1,639,615	Fisher, Richard	36,107	964,603 R	60.8%	38.3%	61.4%	38.6%
1993S	1,765,254	1,188,716	Hutchison, Kay Bailey	576,538	Krueger, Robert		612,178 R	67.3%	32.7%	67.3%	32.7%
1990	3,822,157	2,302,357	Gramm, Phil	1,429,986	Parmer, Hugh	89,814	872,371 R	60.2%	37.4%	61.7%	38.3%
1988	5,323,606	2,129,228	Boulter, Beau	3,149,806	Bentsen, Lloyd	44,572	1,020,578 D	40.0%	59.2%	40.3%	59.7%
1984	5,319,178	3,116,348	Gramm, Phil	2,202,557	Doggett, Lloyd	273	913,791 R	58.6%	41.4%	58.6%	41.4%
1982	3,103,167	1,256,759	Collins, James M.	1,818,223	Bentsen, Lloyd	28,185	561,464 D	40.5%	58.6%	40.9%	59.1%
1978	2,312,540	1,151,376	Tower, John G.	1,139,149	Krueger, Robert	22,015	12,227 R	49.8%	49.3%	50.3%	49.7%
1976	3,874,516	1,636,370	Steelman, Alan	2,199,956	Bentsen, Lloyd	38,190	563,586 D	42.2%	56.8%	42.7%	57.3%
1972	3,413,903	1,822,877	Tower, John G.	1,511,985	Sanders, Barefoot	79,041	310,892 R	53.4%	44.3%	54.7%	45.3%
1970	2,231,671	1,035,794	Bush, George	1,194,069	Bentsen, Lloyd	1,808	158,275 D	46.4%	53.5%	46.5%	53.5%
1966	1,493,182	842,501	Tower, John G.	643,855	Carr, Waggoner	6,826	198,646 R	56.4%	43.1%	56.7%	43.3%
1964	2,603,856	1,134,337	Bush, George	1,463,958	Yarborough, Ralph	5,561	329,621 D	43.6%	56.2%	43.7%	56.3%
1961S	886,091	448,217	Tower, John G.	437,874	Blakley, William A.		10,343 R	50.6%	49.4%	50.6%	49.4%
1960	2,253,784	926,653	Tower, John G.	1,306,625	Johnson, Lyndon B.	20,506	379,972 D	41.1%	58.0%	41.5%	58.5%
1958	787,128	185,926	Whittenburg, Roy	587,030	Yarborough, Ralph	14,172	401,104 D	23.6%	74.6%	24.1%	75.9%
1957S	957,298		[See note below]				D				
1954	636,475	94,131	Watson, Carlos G.	539,319	Johnson, Lyndon B.	3,025	445,188 D	14.8%	84.7%	14.9%	85.1%
1952	1,895,192		—	1,895,192	Daniel, Price		1,895,192 D		100.0%		100.0%
1948	1,061,563	349,665	Porter, Jack	702,985	Johnson, Lyndon B.	8,913	353,320 D	32.9%	66.2%	33.2%	66.8%
1946	380,681	43,750	Sells, Murray C.	336,931	Connally, Tom		293,181 D	11.5%	88.5%	11.5%	88.5%

The June 1993 election was for a short term to fill a vacancy; the vote above was for the special election runoff. The May 1961 and April 1957 elections were also for short terms to fill vacancies. Although neither vote was held with official party designations, the 1961 vote above was a runoff contest between unofficial party candidates. In 1957 there was a single ballot without a runoff and Democrat Ralph Yarborough polled 364,605 votes (38.1% of the total vote) and won the election with a 73,802-vote plurality over Democrat Martin Dies.

TEXAS

GOVERNOR 2006

2000 Census Population	County	Total Vote	Republican	Democratic	Independent (Friedman)	Independent (Strayhorn)	Other	Plurality	Rep.	Dem.	Ind. (Friedman)	Ind. (Strayhorn)
55,109	ANDERSON	10,641	4,305	2,496	1,035	2,751	54	1,554 R	40.5%	23.5%	9.7%	25.9%
13,004	ANDREWS	2,611	1,282	352	284	685	8	597 R	49.1%	13.5%	10.9%	26.2%
80,130	ANGELINA	21,939	8,788	6,618	2,228	4,170	135	2,170 R	40.1%	30.2%	10.2%	19.0%
22,497	ARANSAS	6,799	3,051	1,349	1,223	1,140	36	1,702 R	44.9%	19.8%	18.0%	16.8%
8,854	ARCHER	2,932	1,335	419	315	853	10	482 R	45.5%	14.3%	10.7%	29.1%
2,148	ARMSTRONG	683	324	71	151	132	5	173 R	47.4%	10.4%	22.1%	19.3%
38,628	ATASCOSA	7,752	2,423	2,040	1,314	1,934	41	383 R	31.3%	26.3%	17.0%	24.9%
23,590	AUSTIN	7,961	2,908	1,377	1,354	2,284	38	624 R	36.5%	17.3%	17.0%	28.7%
6,594	BAILEY	1,523	692	284	202	331	14	361 R	45.4%	18.6%	13.3%	21.7%
17,645	BANDERA	6,576	2,595	881	1,853	1,192	55	742 R	39.5%	13.4%	28.2%	18.1%
57,733	BASTROP	17,102	5,216	5,709	3,057	2,962	158	493 D	30.5%	33.4%	17.9%	17.3%
4,093	BAYLOR	982	396	202	98	283	3	113 R	40.3%	20.6%	10.0%	28.8%
32,359	BEE	7,030	2,300	2,489	774	1,430	37	189 D	32.7%	35.4%	11.0%	20.3%
237,974	BELL	43,299	17,633	10,404	4,276	10,717	269	6,916 R	40.7%	24.0%	9.9%	24.8%
1,392,931	BEXAR	274,081	92,387	86,906	35,596	57,150	2,042	5,481 R	33.7%	31.7%	13.0%	20.9%
8,418	BLANCO	3,352	1,411	709	612	598	22	702 R	42.1%	21.2%	18.3%	17.8%
729	BORDEN	256	118	48	34	56		62 R	46.1%	18.8%	13.3%	21.9%
17,204	BOSQUE	5,645	2,099	1,162	810	1,559	15	540 R	37.2%	20.6%	14.3%	27.6%
89,306	BOWIE	18,404	7,936	5,851	1,529	3,019	69	2,085 R	43.1%	31.8%	8.3%	16.4%
241,767	BRAZORIA	58,441	22,543	13,661	11,250	10,650	337	8,882 R	38.6%	23.4%	19.3%	18.2%
152,415	BRAZOS	30,388	15,590	6,449	3,772	4,325	252	9,141 R	51.3%	21.2%	12.4%	14.2%
8,866	BREWSTER	2,439	749	722	559	385	24	27 R	30.7%	29.6%	22.9%	15.8%
1,790	BRISCOE	560	220	130	74	133	3	87 R	39.3%	23.2%	13.2%	23.8%
7,976	BROOKS	1,162	224	662	93	181	2	438 D	19.3%	57.0%	8.0%	15.6%
37,674	BROWN	8,871	4,147	1,647	1,118	1,896	63	2,251 R	46.7%	18.6%	12.6%	21.4%
16,470	BURLESON	4,498	1,837	1,178	544	912	27	659 R	40.8%	26.2%	12.1%	20.3%
34,147	BURNET	11,233	5,246	2,330	1,537	2,013	107	2,916 R	46.7%	20.7%	13.7%	17.9%
32,194	CALDWELL	7,779	2,502	2,478	1,207	1,520	72	24 R	32.2%	31.9%	15.5%	19.5%
20,647	CALHOUN	4,413	1,435	1,496	505	958	19	61 D	32.5%	33.9%	11.4%	21.7%
12,905	CALLAHAN	3,299	1,385	574	900	420	20	485 R	42.0%	17.4%	27.3%	12.7%
335,227	CAMERON	41,051	14,407	14,327	2,581	9,433	303	80 R	35.1%	34.9%	6.3%	23.0%
11,549	CAMP	3,030	1,254	953	256	561	6	301 R	41.4%	31.5%	8.4%	18.5%
6,516	CARSON	2,049	965	287	327	463	7	502 R	47.1%	14.0%	16.0%	22.6%
30,438	CASS	7,455	2,758	2,544	575	1,550	28	214 R	37.0%	34.1%	7.7%	20.8%
8,285	CASTRO	1,775	723	471	274	302	5	252 R	40.7%	26.5%	15.4%	17.0%
26,031	CHAMBERS	7,773	3,142	1,577	1,587	1,427	40	1,555 R	40.4%	20.3%	20.4%	18.4%
46,659	CHEROKEE	11,214	4,847	2,436	1,061	2,823	47	2,024 R	43.2%	21.7%	9.5%	25.2%
7,688	CHILDRESS	1,210	533	249	170	253	5	280 R	44.0%	20.6%	14.0%	20.9%
11,006	CLAY	3,532	1,530	613	438	939	12	591 R	43.3%	17.4%	12.4%	26.6%
3,730	COCHRAN	897	356	174	137	220	10	136 R	39.7%	19.4%	15.3%	24.5%
3,864	COKE	1,138	522	182	163	260	11	262 R	45.9%	16.0%	14.3%	22.8%
9,235	COLEMAN	2,306	939	430	324	598	15	341 R	40.7%	18.6%	14.1%	25.9%
491,675	COLLIN	138,088	67,813	32,457	15,340	21,467	1,011	35,356 R	49.1%	23.5%	11.1%	15.5%
3,206	COLLINGSWORTH	1,075	486	201	121	261	6	225 R	45.2%	18.7%	11.3%	24.3%
20,390	COLORADO	5,615	1,803	1,213	832	1,743	24	60 R	32.1%	21.6%	14.8%	31.0%
78,021	COMAL	28,477	13,551	4,616	4,570	5,491	249	8,060 R	47.6%	16.2%	16.0%	19.3%
14,026	COMANCHE	3,555	1,408	1,000	458	668	21	408 R	39.6%	28.1%	12.9%	18.8%
3,966	CONCHO	835	373	169	167	124	2	204 R	44.7%	20.2%	20.0%	14.9%
36,363	COOKE	10,047	3,297	1,817	977	3,908	48	611 S	32.8%	18.1%	9.7%	38.9%
74,978	CORYELL	9,702	4,279	2,030	1,096	2,243	54	2,036 R	44.1%	20.9%	11.3%	23.1%
1,904	COTTLE	636	209	166	126	129	6	43 R	32.9%	26.1%	19.8%	20.3%
3,996	CRANE	1,089	488	182	123	286	10	202 R	44.8%	16.7%	11.3%	26.3%
4,099	CROCKETT	1,045	502	220	173	143	7	282 R	48.0%	21.1%	16.6%	13.7%
7,072	CROSBY	1,395	447	467	178	294	9	20 D	32.0%	33.5%	12.8%	21.1%
2,975	CULBERSON	427	170	122	68	63	4	48 R	39.8%	28.6%	15.9%	14.8%
6,222	DALLAM	866	439	97	177	152	1	262 R	50.7%	11.2%	20.4%	17.6%
2,218,899	DALLAS	406,211	143,132	161,886	41,330	57,581	2,282	18,754 D	35.2%	39.9%	10.2%	14.2%
14,985	DAWSON	3,178	1,397	767	362	625	27	630 R	44.0%	24.1%	11.4%	19.7%
18,561	DEAF SMITH	2,730	1,237	525	327	635	6	602 R	45.3%	19.2%	12.0%	23.3%
5,327	DELTA	1,527	577	433	176	335	6	144 R	37.8%	28.4%	11.5%	21.9%

TEXAS

GOVERNOR 2006

2000 Census Population	County	Total Vote	Republican	Democratic	Independent (Friedman)	Independent (Strayhorn)	Other	Plurality	Percentage			
									Rep.	Dem.	Ind. (Friedman)	Ind. (Strayhorn)
432,976	DENTON	108,513	50,888	25,156	13,536	18,300	633	25,732 R	46.9%	23.2%	12.5%	16.9%
20,013	DE WITT	4,082	1,449	795	580	1,243	15	206 R	35.5%	19.5%	14.2%	30.5%
2,762	DICKENS	611	230	151	96	128	6	79 R	37.6%	24.7%	15.7%	20.9%
10,248	DIMMIT	1,835	443	900	158	324	10	457 D	24.1%	49.0%	8.6%	17.7%
3,828	DONLEY	1,262	538	170	258	292	4	246 R	42.6%	13.5%	20.4%	23.1%
13,120	DUVAL	3,242	526	2,087	395	221	13	1,561 D	16.2%	64.4%	12.2%	6.8%
18,297	EASTLAND	4,704	2,073	898	481	1,230	22	843 R	44.1%	19.1%	10.2%	26.1%
121,123	ECTOR	17,720	8,843	2,748	2,031	4,003	95	4,840 R	49.9%	15.5%	11.5%	22.6%
2,162	EDWARDS	742	346	116	100	173	7	173 R	46.6%	15.6%	13.5%	23.3%
111,360	ELLIS	29,342	12,738	5,833	3,810	6,799	162	5,939 R	43.4%	19.9%	13.0%	23.2%
679,622	EL PASO	90,723	29,989	32,854	9,386	17,973	521	2,865 D	33.1%	36.2%	10.3%	19.8%
33,001	ERATH	7,746	3,372	1,676	892	1,762	44	1,610 R	43.5%	21.6%	11.5%	22.7%
18,576	FALLS	3,661	853	982	299	1,508	19	526 S	23.3%	26.8%	8.2%	41.2%
31,242	FANNIN	7,517	2,819	2,261	862	1,531	44	558 R	37.5%	30.1%	11.5%	20.4%
21,804	FAYETTE	7,787	2,492	1,801	1,212	2,242	40	250 R	32.0%	23.1%	15.6%	28.8%
4,344	FISHER	1,199	317	455	93	331	3	124 D	26.4%	37.9%	7.8%	27.6%
7,771	FLOYD	2,088	877	530	217	455	9	347 R	42.0%	25.4%	10.4%	21.8%
1,622	FOARD	380	87	166	28	97	2	69 D	22.9%	43.7%	7.4%	25.5%
354,452	FORT BEND	98,427	39,819	33,241	10,414	14,454	499	6,578 R	40.5%	33.8%	10.6%	14.7%
9,458	FRANKLIN	3,129	1,447	649	312	700	21	747 R	46.2%	20.7%	10.0%	22.4%
17,867	FREESTONE	4,415	1,933	976	429	1,054	23	879 R	43.8%	22.1%	9.7%	23.9%
16,252	FRIO	2,111	530	729	255	587	10	142 D	25.1%	34.5%	12.1%	27.8%
14,467	GAINES	2,468	1,202	475	306	472	13	727 R	48.7%	19.2%	12.4%	19.1%
250,158	GALVESTON	65,241	21,072	19,926	13,522	10,417	304	1,146 R	32.3%	30.5%	20.7%	16.0%
4,872	GARZA	1,162	522	200	153	277	10	245 R	44.9%	17.2%	13.2%	23.8%
20,814	GILLESPIE	8,403	4,375	1,170	1,404	1,385	69	2,971 R	52.1%	13.9%	16.7%	16.5%
1,406	GLASSCOCK	332	169	27	50	86		83 R	50.9%	8.1%	15.1%	25.9%
6,928	GOLIAD	2,398	657	659	396	678	8	19 S	27.4%	27.5%	16.5%	28.3%
18,628	GONZALES	4,186	1,494	899	531	1,246	16	248 R	35.7%	21.5%	12.7%	29.8%
22,744	GRAY	5,382	3,104	550	709	998	21	2,106 R	57.7%	10.2%	13.2%	18.5%
110,595	GRAYSON	26,116	11,945	6,852	2,865	4,304	150	5,093 R	45.7%	26.2%	11.0%	16.5%
111,379	GREGG	22,530	10,834	4,851	1,404	5,349	92	5,485 R	48.1%	21.5%	6.2%	23.7%
23,552	GRIMES	5,419	1,766	1,361	903	1,345	44	405 R	32.6%	25.1%	16.7%	24.8%
89,023	GUADALUPE	24,847	10,324	5,094	3,561	5,658	210	4,666 R	41.6%	20.5%	14.3%	22.8%
36,602	HALE	6,325	2,678	1,674	678	1,267	28	1,004 R	42.3%	26.5%	10.7%	20.0%
3,782	HALL	927	335	227	158	204	3	108 R	36.1%	24.5%	17.0%	22.0%
8,229	HAMILTON	2,852	1,093	636	427	688	8	405 R	38.3%	22.3%	15.0%	24.1%
5,369	HANSFORD	1,433	782	125	221	292	13	490 R	54.6%	8.7%	15.4%	20.4%
4,724	HARDEMAN	1,428	553	325	194	345	11	208 R	38.7%	22.8%	13.6%	24.2%
48,073	HARDIN	10,319	5,244	2,100	1,283	1,659	33	3,144 R	50.8%	20.4%	12.4%	16.1%
3,400,578	HARRIS	589,348	215,150	203,102	80,808	86,890	3,398	12,048 R	36.5%	34.5%	13.7%	14.7%
62,110	HARRISON	14,987	6,244	3,857	912	3,928	46	2,316 R	41.7%	25.7%	6.1%	26.2%
5,537	HARTLEY	1,257	665	161	217	213	1	448 R	52.9%	12.8%	17.3%	16.9%
6,093	HASKELL	1,732	539	572	150	465	6	33 D	31.1%	33.0%	8.7%	26.8%
97,589	HAYS	31,244	10,591	9,845	5,457	4,955	396	746 R	33.9%	31.5%	17.5%	15.9%
3,351	HEMPHILL	1,184	532	131	227	289	5	243 R	44.9%	11.1%	19.2%	24.4%
73,277	HENDERSON	18,170	7,715	3,942	2,332	4,118	63	3,597 R	42.5%	21.7%	12.8%	22.7%
569,463	HIDALGO	47,821	16,029	20,404	2,644	8,403	341	4,375 D	33.5%	42.7%	5.5%	17.6%
32,321	HILL	9,246	3,192	2,130	1,101	2,767	56	425 R	34.5%	23.0%	11.9%	29.9%
22,716	HOCKLEY	4,608	2,081	871	710	920	26	1,161 R	45.2%	18.9%	15.4%	20.0%
41,100	HOOD	14,063	6,770	2,988	1,670	2,564	71	3,782 R	48.1%	21.2%	11.9%	18.2%
31,960	HOPKINS	8,468	3,379	2,361	939	1,764	25	1,018 R	39.9%	27.9%	11.1%	20.8%
23,185	HOUSTON	5,962	2,650	1,452	573	1,264	23	1,198 R	44.4%	24.4%	9.6%	21.2%
33,627	HOWARD	6,790	2,652	1,424	650	2,009	55	643 R	39.1%	21.0%	9.6%	29.6%
3,344	HUDSPETH	567	269	83	100	109	6	160 R	47.4%	14.6%	17.6%	19.2%
76,596	HUNT	17,707	7,731	3,899	2,228	3,781	68	3,832 R	43.7%	22.0%	12.6%	21.4%
23,857	HUTCHINSON	5,460	2,904	730	745	1,047	34	1,857 R	53.2%	13.4%	13.6%	19.2%
1,771	IRION	520	240	105	109	62	4	131 R	46.2%	20.2%	21.0%	11.9%
8,763	JACK	2,187	979	378	244	571	15	408 R	44.8%	17.3%	11.2%	26.1%
14,391	JACKSON	3,360	1,058	862	405	1,016	19	42 R	31.5%	25.7%	12.1%	30.2%

TEXAS

GOVERNOR 2006

2000 Census Population	County	Total Vote	Republican	Democratic	Independent (Friedman)	Independent (Strayhorn)	Other	Plurality		Percentage Rep.	Dem.	Ind. (Friedman)	Ind. (Strayhorn)
35,604	JASPER	7,496	3,341	2,147	666	1,317	25	1,194	R	44.6%	28.6%	8.9%	17.6%
2,207	JEFF DAVIS	1,067	378	293	208	178	10	85	R	35.4%	27.5%	19.5%	16.7%
252,051	JEFFERSON	46,775	17,110	18,519	4,373	6,600	173	1,409	D	36.6%	39.6%	9.3%	14.1%
5,281	JIM HOGG	939	310	466	46	111	6	156	D	33.0%	49.6%	4.9%	11.8%
39,326	JIM WELLS	7,532	2,122	3,705	605	1,072	28	1,583	D	28.2%	49.2%	8.0%	14.2%
126,811	JOHNSON	30,014	12,989	6,399	4,038	6,450	138	6,539	R	43.3%	21.3%	13.5%	21.5%
20,785	JONES	3,817	1,298	964	398	1,126	31	172	R	34.0%	25.3%	10.4%	29.5%
15,446	KARNES	3,192	1,013	851	482	818	28	162	R	31.7%	26.7%	15.1%	25.6%
71,313	KAUFMAN	19,055	7,910	4,375	2,342	4,344	84	3,535	R	41.5%	23.0%	12.3%	22.8%
23,743	KENDALL	10,350	5,120	1,346	1,827	1,966	91	3,154	R	49.5%	13.0%	17.7%	19.0%
414	KENEDY	144	68	42	8	25	1	26	R	47.2%	29.2%	5.6%	17.4%
859	KENT	291	105	85	50	51		20	R	36.1%	29.2%	17.2%	17.5%
43,653	KERR	15,596	7,711	2,325	3,035	2,437	88	4,676	R	49.4%	14.9%	19.5%	15.6%
4,468	KIMBLE	1,373	647	222	243	256	5	391	R	47.1%	16.2%	17.7%	18.6%
356	KING	85	38	12	13	22		16	R	44.7%	14.1%	15.3%	25.9%
3,379	KINNEY	1,096	441	279	172	197	7	162	R	40.2%	25.5%	15.7%	18.0%
31,549	KLEBERG	4,987	1,806	1,674	539	948	20	132	R	36.2%	33.6%	10.8%	19.0%
4,253	KNOX	900	336	237	113	212	2	99	R	37.3%	26.3%	12.6%	23.6%
48,499	LAMAR	11,544	4,600	3,498	1,140	2,259	47	1,102	R	39.8%	30.3%	9.9%	19.6%
14,709	LAMB	2,728	1,179	610	330	598	11	569	R	43.2%	22.4%	12.1%	21.9%
17,762	LAMPASAS	5,048	2,490	905	575	1,042	36	1,448	R	49.3%	17.9%	11.4%	20.6%
5,866	LA SALLE	1,199	304	433	134	323	5	110	D	25.4%	36.1%	11.2%	26.9%
19,210	LAVACA	5,021	1,864	1,118	775	1,228	36	636	R	37.1%	22.3%	15.4%	24.5%
15,657	LEE	4,260	1,380	1,316	599	933	32	64	R	32.4%	30.9%	14.1%	21.9%
15,335	LEON	4,345	2,279	771	431	836	28	1,443	R	52.5%	17.7%	9.9%	19.2%
70,154	LIBERTY	14,609	5,134	3,306	3,037	3,085	47	1,828	R	35.1%	22.6%	20.8%	21.1%
22,051	LIMESTONE	5,382	1,994	1,503	1,347	510	28	491	R	37.0%	27.9%	25.0%	9.5%
3,057	LIPSCOMB	759	401	103	74	178	3	223	R	52.8%	13.6%	9.7%	23.5%
12,309	LIVE OAK	2,822	1,210	538	476	573	25	637	R	42.9%	19.1%	16.9%	20.3%
17,044	LLANO	7,185	3,489	1,303	933	1,414	46	2,075	R	48.6%	18.1%	13.0%	19.7%
67	LOVING	90	45	9	11	22	3	23	R	50.0%	10.0%	12.2%	24.4%
242,628	LUBBOCK	53,564	24,030	11,484	7,963	9,778	309	12,546	R	44.9%	21.4%	14.9%	18.3%
6,550	LYNN	1,449	530	394	219	303	3	136	R	36.6%	27.2%	15.1%	20.9%
8,205	MCCULLOCH	2,066	924	392	273	465	12	459	R	44.7%	19.0%	13.2%	22.5%
213,517	MCLENNAN	53,154	19,451	14,577	4,644	14,283	199	4,874	R	36.6%	27.4%	8.7%	26.9%
851	MCMULLEN	431	142	55	109	120	5	22	R	32.9%	12.8%	25.3%	27.8%
12,940	MADISON	2,888	1,267	704	290	610	17	563	R	43.9%	24.4%	10.0%	21.1%
10,941	MARION	2,281	759	794	206	507	15	35	D	33.3%	34.8%	9.0%	22.2%
4,746	MARTIN	968	394	115	118	337	4	57	R	40.7%	11.9%	12.2%	34.8%
3,738	MASON	1,340	589	269	164	299	19	290	R	44.0%	20.1%	12.2%	22.3%
37,957	MATAGORDA	7,848	2,637	2,083	1,253	1,841	34	554	R	33.6%	26.5%	16.0%	23.5%
47,297	MAVERICK	3,956	1,109	1,888	244	690	25	779	D	28.0%	47.7%	6.2%	17.4%
39,304	MEDINA	9,847	3,895	1,908	1,515	2,464	65	1,431	R	39.6%	19.4%	15.4%	25.0%
2,360	MENARD	891	422	148	181	120	20	241	R	47.4%	16.6%	20.3%	13.5%
116,009	MIDLAND	25,448	14,394	2,922	2,773	5,184	175	9,210	R	56.6%	11.5%	10.9%	20.4%
24,238	MILAM	5,550	1,707	1,646	685	1,477	35	61	R	30.8%	29.7%	12.3%	26.6%
5,151	MILLS	1,492	593	331	177	381	10	212	R	39.7%	22.2%	11.9%	25.5%
9,698	MITCHELL	1,427	499	290	137	493	8	6	R	35.0%	20.3%	9.6%	34.5%
19,117	MONTAGUE	5,325	2,353	1,036	663	1,238	35	1,115	R	44.2%	19.5%	12.5%	23.2%
293,768	MONTGOMERY	80,822	41,066	11,700	13,805	13,786	465	27,261	R	50.8%	14.5%	17.1%	17.1%
20,121	MOORE	3,058	1,698	402	440	504	14	1,194	R	55.5%	13.1%	14.4%	16.5%
13,048	MORRIS	2,893	886	1,181	174	637	15	295	D	30.6%	40.8%	6.0%	22.0%
1,426	MOTLEY	403	205	75	46	71	6	130	R	50.9%	18.6%	11.4%	17.6%
59,203	NACOGDOCHES	12,506	5,425	3,109	1,703	2,219	50	2,316	R	43.4%	24.9%	13.6%	17.7%
45,124	NAVARRO	11,051	4,296	2,794	1,340	2,571	50	1,502	R	38.9%	25.3%	12.1%	23.3%
15,072	NEWTON	2,897	1,072	1,153	253	409	10	81	D	37.0%	39.8%	8.7%	14.1%
15,802	NOLAN	3,176	981	731	378	1,078	8	97	S	30.9%	23.0%	11.9%	33.9%
313,645	NUECES	67,623	25,066	20,931	9,423	11,870	333	4,135	R	37.1%	31.0%	13.9%	17.6%
9,006	OCHILTREE	1,713	1,114	114	221	253	11	861	R	65.0%	6.7%	12.9%	14.8%
2,185	OLDHAM	547	269	62	97	118	1	151	R	49.2%	11.3%	17.7%	21.6%

TEXAS

GOVERNOR 2006

2000 Census Population	County	Total Vote	Republican	Democratic	Independent (Friedman)	Independent (Strayhorn)	Other	Plurality		Percentage Rep.	Dem.	Ind. (Friedman)	Ind. (Strayhorn)
84,966	ORANGE	17,310	7,377	5,484	1,744	2,658	47	1,893	R	42.6%	31.7%	10.1%	15.4%
27,026	PALO PINTO	6,456	2,432	1,577	1,000	1,410	37	855	R	37.7%	24.4%	15.5%	21.8%
22,756	PANOLA	5,831	2,586	1,497	283	1,449	16	1,089	R	44.3%	25.7%	4.9%	24.8%
88,495	PARKER	27,013	12,877	5,178	3,344	5,483	131	7,394	R	47.7%	19.2%	12.4%	20.3%
10,016	PARMER	1,817	944	251	209	400	13	544	R	52.0%	13.8%	11.5%	22.0%
16,809	PECOS	3,202	1,288	833	291	766	24	455	R	40.2%	26.0%	9.1%	23.9%
41,133	POLK	11,979	4,653	2,938	2,075	2,238	75	1,715	R	38.8%	24.5%	17.3%	18.7%
113,546	POTTER	17,272	7,326	3,395	3,044	3,367	140	3,931	R	42.4%	19.7%	17.6%	19.5%
7,304	PRESIDIO	945	209	419	147	163	7	210	D	22.1%	44.3%	15.6%	17.2%
9,139	RAINS	2,854	1,128	627	396	699	4	429	R	39.5%	22.0%	13.9%	24.5%
104,312	RANDALL	31,118	15,486	4,232	4,552	6,687	161	8,799	R	49.8%	13.6%	14.6%	21.5%
3,326	REAGAN	636	254	107	103	168	4	86	R	39.9%	16.8%	16.2%	26.4%
3,047	REAL	1,110	534	168	191	212	5	322	R	48.1%	15.1%	17.2%	19.1%
14,314	RED RIVER	3,353	1,145	1,198	291	705	14	53	D	34.1%	35.7%	8.7%	21.0%
13,137	REEVES	2,119	712	737	166	487	17	25	D	33.6%	34.8%	7.8%	23.0%
7,828	REFUGIO	1,964	705	522	305	424	8	183	R	35.9%	26.6%	15.5%	21.6%
887	ROBERTS	307	173	12	61	60	1	112	R	56.4%	3.9%	19.9%	19.5%
16,000	ROBERTSON	4,990	1,791	1,778	406	982	33	13	R	35.9%	35.6%	8.1%	19.7%
43,080	ROCKWALL	15,633	8,390	2,757	1,631	2,782	73	5,608	R	53.7%	17.6%	10.4%	17.8%
11,495	RUNNELS	2,425	1,016	408	388	601	12	415	R	41.9%	16.8%	16.0%	24.8%
47,372	RUSK	11,880	5,555	2,536	978	2,741	70	2,814	R	46.8%	21.3%	8.2%	23.1%
10,469	SABINE	3,037	1,323	763	331	602	18	560	R	43.6%	25.1%	10.9%	19.8%
8,946	SAN AUGUSTINE	2,435	929	871	216	401	18	58	R	38.2%	35.8%	8.9%	16.5%
22,246	SAN JACINTO	6,506	2,246	1,742	1,141	1,345	32	504	R	34.5%	26.8%	17.5%	20.7%
67,138	SAN PATRICIO	13,103	5,057	4,208	1,565	2,217	56	849	R	38.6%	32.1%	11.9%	16.9%
6,186	SAN SABA	1,521	757	265	159	333	7	424	R	49.8%	17.4%	10.5%	21.9%
2,935	SCHLEICHER	698	336	171	97	91	3	165	R	48.1%	24.5%	13.9%	13.0%
16,361	SCURRY	2,798	1,331	494	290	659	24	672	R	47.6%	17.7%	10.4%	23.6%
3,302	SHACKELFORD	946	451	133	115	243	4	208	R	47.7%	14.1%	12.2%	25.7%
25,224	SHELBY	5,945	2,783	1,563	452	1,132	15	1,220	R	46.8%	26.3%	7.6%	19.0%
3,186	SHERMAN	619	294	72	99	151	3	143	R	47.5%	11.6%	16.0%	24.4%
174,706	SMITH	43,289	23,701	8,477	3,966	6,973	172	15,224	R	54.8%	19.6%	9.2%	16.1%
6,809	SOMERVELL	2,532	1,067	536	364	553	12	514	R	42.1%	21.2%	14.4%	21.8%
53,597	STARR	6,382	1,283	4,215	216	611	57	2,932	D	20.1%	66.0%	3.4%	9.6%
9,674	STEPHENS	2,109	897	408	248	547	9	350	R	42.5%	19.3%	11.8%	25.9%
1,393	STERLING	305	158	42	45	60		98	R	51.8%	13.8%	14.8%	19.7%
1,693	STONEWALL	540	136	192	62	149	1	43	D	25.2%	35.6%	11.5%	27.6%
4,077	SUTTON	1,111	537	264	150	153	7	273	R	48.3%	23.8%	13.5%	13.8%
8,378	SWISHER	1,661	463	520	279	383	16	57	D	27.9%	31.3%	16.8%	23.1%
1,446,219	TARRANT	326,337	130,513	101,402	36,770	56,084	1,568	29,111	R	40.0%	31.1%	11.3%	17.2%
126,555	TAYLOR	28,335	12,280	5,127	2,793	7,989	146	4,291	R	43.3%	18.1%	9.9%	28.2%
1,081	TERRELL	517	186	179	74	70	8	7	R	36.0%	34.6%	14.3%	13.5%
12,761	TERRY	2,497	1,015	681	338	446	17	334	R	40.6%	27.3%	13.5%	17.9%
1,850	THROCKMORTON	492	187	87	63	154	1	33	R	38.0%	17.7%	12.8%	31.3%
28,118	TITUS	5,838	2,242	1,851	484	1,235	26	391	R	38.4%	31.7%	8.3%	21.2%
104,010	TOM GREEN	21,576	10,987	4,296	3,423	2,740	130	6,691	R	50.9%	19.9%	15.9%	12.7%
812,280	TRAVIS	226,176	59,794	101,989	30,519	31,090	2,784	42,195	D	26.4%	45.1%	13.5%	13.7%
13,779	TRINITY	4,288	1,296	1,259	681	1,031	21	37	R	30.2%	29.4%	15.9%	24.0%
20,871	TYLER	5,248	2,043	1,494	634	1,053	24	549	R	38.9%	28.5%	12.1%	20.1%
35,291	UPSHUR	9,531	4,221	2,230	938	2,102	40	1,991	R	44.3%	23.4%	9.8%	22.1%
3,404	UPTON	635	292	94	63	185	1	107	R	46.0%	14.8%	9.9%	29.1%
25,926	UVALDE	5,418	1,981	1,582	846	984	25	399	R	36.6%	29.2%	15.6%	18.2%
44,856	VAL VERDE	7,273	2,651	2,736	661	1,184	41	85	D	36.4%	37.6%	9.1%	16.3%
48,140	VAN ZANDT	12,404	5,695	2,525	1,513	2,629	42	3,066	R	45.9%	20.4%	12.2%	21.2%
84,088	VICTORIA	18,750	7,757	4,743	1,942	4,152	156	3,014	R	41.4%	25.3%	10.4%	22.1%
61,758	WALKER	11,096	4,012	2,600	1,882	2,520	82	1,412	R	36.2%	23.4%	17.0%	22.7%
32,663	WALLER	8,099	2,389	2,161	1,129	2,382	38	7	R	29.5%	26.7%	13.9%	29.4%
10,909	WARD	2,091	828	361	205	685	12	143	R	39.6%	17.3%	9.8%	32.8%
30,373	WASHINGTON	9,407	3,867	1,774	1,831	1,882	53	1,985	R	41.1%	18.9%	19.5%	20.0%
193,117	WEBB	18,391	4,641	9,254	1,222	3,172	102	4,613	D	25.2%	50.3%	6.6%	17.2%

TEXAS

GOVERNOR 2006

2000 Census Population	County	Total Vote	Republican	Democratic	Independent (Friedman)	Independent (Strayhorn)	Other	Plurality		Rep.	Dem.	Ind. (Friedman)	Ind. (Strayhorn)
41,188	WHARTON	8,769	2,278	2,396	1,256	2,797	42	401	S	26.0%	27.3%	14.3%	31.9%
5,284	WHEELER	1,312	671	194	201	239	7	477	R	51.1%	14.8%	15.3%	18.2%
131,664	WICHITA	27,476	12,475	5,211	2,820	6,824	146	5,651	R	45.4%	19.0%	10.3%	24.8%
14,676	WILBARGER	3,400	1,405	663	438	873	21	532	R	41.3%	19.5%	12.9%	25.7%
20,082	WILLACY	2,056	713	759	131	442	11	46	D	34.7%	36.9%	6.4%	21.5%
249,967	WILLIAMSON	84,028	35,956	23,072	9,561	14,242	1,197	12,884	R	42.8%	27.5%	11.4%	16.9%
32,408	WILSON	10,938	2,989	2,702	1,726	3,456	65	467	S	27.3%	24.7%	15.8%	31.6%
7,173	WINKLER	1,498	641	277	168	401	11	240	R	42.8%	18.5%	11.2%	26.8%
48,793	WISE	12,345	5,299	2,610	1,669	2,705	62	2,594	R	42.9%	21.1%	13.5%	21.9%
36,752	WOOD	11,279	5,641	2,017	1,249	2,321	51	3,320	R	50.0%	17.9%	11.1%	20.6%
7,322	YOAKUM	1,577	743	275	194	354	11	389	R	47.1%	17.4%	12.3%	22.4%
17,943	YOUNG	4,748	2,393	851	521	958	25	1,435	R	50.4%	17.9%	11.0%	20.2%
12,182	ZAPATA	1,204	385	648	77	88	6	263	D	32.0%	53.8%	6.4%	7.3%
11,600	ZAVALA	1,757	322	1,078	110	232	15	756	D	18.3%	61.4%	6.3%	13.2%
20,851,820	TOTAL	4,399,116	1,716,792	1,310,337	547,674	796,851	27,462	406,455	R	39.0%	29.8%	12.4%	18.1%

Note: The plurality is based on the margin of victory by the winner over the runner-up. "S" indicates that the county was carried by Carole Keeton Strayhorn, an independent candidate. The other major independent candidate, Richard "Kinky" Friedman, failed to carry a single county.

TEXAS

SENATOR 2006

2000 Census Population	County	Total Vote	Republican	Democratic	Other	Rep.-Dem. Plurality		Total Vote		Major Vote	
								Rep.	Dem.	Rep.	Dem.
55,109	ANDERSON	10,588	7,242	3,130	216	4,112	R	68.4%	29.6%	69.8%	30.2%
13,004	ANDREWS	2,584	2,107	446	31	1,661	R	81.5%	17.3%	82.5%	17.5%
80,130	ANGELINA	21,592	14,099	7,115	378	6,984	R	65.3%	33.0%	66.5%	33.5%
22,497	ARANSAS	6,688	4,686	1,835	167	2,851	R	70.1%	27.4%	71.9%	28.1%
8,854	ARCHER	2,859	2,204	612	43	1,592	R	77.1%	21.4%	78.3%	21.7%
2,148	ARMSTRONG	672	549	107	16	442	R	81.7%	15.9%	83.7%	16.3%
38,628	ATASCOSA	7,549	4,677	2,701	171	1,976	R	62.0%	35.8%	63.4%	36.6%
23,590	AUSTIN	7,905	5,940	1,814	151	4,126	R	75.1%	22.9%	76.6%	23.4%
6,594	BAILEY	1,496	1,181	281	34	900	R	78.9%	18.8%	80.8%	19.2%
17,645	BANDERA	6,355	4,807	1,317	231	3,490	R	75.6%	20.7%	78.5%	21.5%
57,733	BASTROP	16,956	9,275	7,011	670	2,264	R	54.7%	41.3%	57.0%	43.0%
4,093	BAYLOR	966	660	289	17	371	R	68.3%	29.9%	69.5%	30.5%
32,359	BEE	6,810	3,786	2,911	113	875	R	55.6%	42.7%	56.5%	43.5%
237,974	BELL	43,001	28,434	13,713	854	14,721	R	66.1%	31.9%	67.5%	32.5%
1,392,931	BEXAR	269,735	150,315	112,981	6,439	37,334	R	55.7%	41.9%	57.1%	42.9%
8,418	BLANCO	3,250	2,206	938	106	1,268	R	67.9%	28.9%	70.2%	29.8%
729	BORDEN	250	197	52	1	145	R	78.8%	20.8%	79.1%	20.9%
17,204	BOSQUE	5,574	4,041	1,427	106	2,614	R	72.5%	25.6%	73.9%	26.1%
89,306	BOWIE	18,324	11,654	6,385	285	5,269	R	63.6%	34.8%	64.6%	35.4%
241,767	BRAZORIA	57,144	38,045	17,461	1638	20,584	R	66.6%	30.6%	68.5%	31.5%
152,415	BRAZOS	29,786	20,760	8,270	756	12,490	R	69.7%	27.8%	71.5%	28.5%
8,866	BREWSTER	2,337	1,211	1,025	101	186	R	51.8%	43.9%	54.2%	45.8%
1,790	BRISCOE	537	398	128	11	270	R	74.1%	23.8%	75.7%	24.3%
7,976	BROOKS	1,123	336	773	14	437	D	29.9%	68.8%	30.3%	69.7%
37,674	BROWN	8,830	6,587	2,029	214	4,558	R	74.6%	23.0%	76.5%	23.5%

TEXAS
SENATOR 2006

2000 Census Population	County	Total Vote	Republican	Democratic	Other	Rep.-Dem. Plurality	Percentage			
							Total Vote		Major Vote	
							Rep.	Dem.	Rep.	Dem.
16,470	BURLESON	4,355	2,805	1,451	99	1,354 R	64.4%	33.3%	65.9%	34.1%
34,147	BURNET	10,983	7,795	2,819	369	4,976 R	71.0%	25.7%	73.4%	26.6%
32,194	CALDWELL	7,538	4,328	2,969	241	1,359 R	57.4%	39.4%	59.3%	40.7%
20,647	CALHOUN	4,372	2,470	1,826	76	644 R	56.5%	41.8%	57.5%	42.5%
12,905	CALLAHAN	3,213	2,498	661	54	1,837 R	77.7%	20.6%	79.1%	20.9%
335,227	CAMERON	38,902	19,178	18,885	839	293 R	49.3%	48.5%	50.4%	49.6%
11,549	CAMP	2,994	1,804	1,151	39	653 R	60.3%	38.4%	61.0%	39.0%
6,516	CARSON	2,026	1,605	384	37	1,221 R	79.2%	19.0%	80.7%	19.3%
30,438	CASS	7,213	4,215	2,895	103	1,320 R	58.4%	40.1%	59.3%	40.7%
8,285	CASTRO	1,729	1,175	533	21	642 R	68.0%	30.8%	68.8%	31.2%
26,031	CHAMBERS	7,501	5,314	1,957	230	3,357 R	70.8%	26.1%	73.1%	26.9%
46,659	CHEROKEE	10,796	7,580	3,029	187	4,551 R	70.2%	28.1%	71.4%	28.6%
7,688	CHILDRESS	1,146	853	280	13	573 R	74.4%	24.4%	75.3%	24.7%
11,006	CLAY	3,499	2,503	929	67	1,574 R	71.5%	26.6%	72.9%	27.1%
3,730	COCHRAN	871	633	216	22	417 R	72.7%	24.8%	74.6%	25.4%
3,864	COKE	1,113	893	200	20	693 R	80.2%	18.0%	81.7%	18.3%
9,235	COLEMAN	2,200	1,659	491	50	1,168 R	75.4%	22.3%	77.2%	22.8%
491,675	COLLIN	136,874	97,055	36,670	3,149	60,385 R	70.9%	26.8%	72.6%	27.4%
3,206	COLLINGSWORTH	1,028	784	223	21	561 R	76.3%	21.7%	77.9%	22.1%
20,390	COLORADO	5,363	3,810	1,430	123	2,380 R	71.0%	26.7%	72.7%	27.3%
78,021	COMAL	27,767	20,699	6,265	803	14,434 R	74.5%	22.6%	76.8%	23.2%
14,026	COMANCHE	3,493	2,314	1,106	73	1,208 R	66.2%	31.7%	67.7%	32.3%
3,966	CONCHO	814	602	197	15	405 R	74.0%	24.2%	75.3%	24.7%
36,363	COOKE	9,946	7,302	2,383	261	4,919 R	73.4%	24.0%	75.4%	24.6%
74,978	CORYELL	9,477	6,648	2,632	197	4,016 R	70.1%	27.8%	71.6%	28.4%
1,904	COTTLE	640	400	218	22	182 R	62.5%	34.1%	64.7%	35.3%
3,996	CRANE	1,016	741	249	26	492 R	72.9%	24.5%	74.8%	25.2%
4,099	CROCKETT	991	694	276	21	418 R	70.0%	27.9%	71.5%	28.5%
7,072	CROSBY	1,349	878	452	19	426 R	65.1%	33.5%	66.0%	34.0%
2,975	CULBERSON	397	218	173	6	45 R	54.9%	43.6%	55.8%	44.2%
6,222	DALLAM	858	667	163	28	504 R	77.7%	19.0%	80.4%	19.6%
2,218,899	DALLAS	400,541	213,215	179,781	7,545	33,434 R	53.2%	44.9%	54.3%	45.7%
14,985	DAWSON	2,996	2,110	825	61	1,285 R	70.4%	27.5%	71.9%	28.1%
18,561	DEAF SMITH	2,691	2,073	588	30	1,485 R	77.0%	21.9%	77.9%	22.1%
5,327	DELTA	1,490	1,038	435	17	603 R	69.7%	29.2%	70.5%	29.5%
432,976	DENTON	107,670	74,977	30,198	2,495	44,779 R	69.6%	28.0%	71.3%	28.7%
20,013	DE WITT	3,939	2,941	930	68	2,011 R	74.7%	23.6%	76.0%	24.0%
2,762	DICKENS	593	416	157	20	259 R	70.2%	26.5%	72.6%	27.4%
10,248	DIMMIT	1,716	641	1,051	24	410 D	37.4%	61.2%	37.9%	62.1%
3,828	DONLEY	1,230	966	244	20	722 R	78.5%	19.8%	79.8%	20.2%
13,120	DUVAL	3,066	672	2,363	31	1,691 D	21.9%	77.1%	22.1%	77.9%
18,297	EASTLAND	4,488	3,271	1,101	116	2,170 R	72.9%	24.5%	74.8%	25.2%
121,123	ECTOR	17,197	12,830	3,977	390	8,853 R	74.6%	23.1%	76.3%	23.7%
2,162	EDWARDS	680	548	118	14	430 R	80.6%	17.4%	82.3%	17.7%
111,360	ELLIS	29,191	21,309	7,175	707	14,134 R	73.0%	24.6%	74.8%	25.2%
679,622	EL PASO	89,756	43,012	44,927	1,817	1,915 D	47.9%	50.1%	48.9%	51.1%
33,001	ERATH	7,577	5,611	1,825	141	3,786 R	74.1%	24.1%	75.5%	24.5%
18,576	FALLS	3,506	2,117	1,327	62	790 R	60.4%	37.8%	61.5%	38.5%
31,242	FANNIN	7,345	4,640	2,574	131	2,066 R	63.2%	35.0%	64.3%	35.7%
21,804	FAYETTE	7,650	5,474	2,019	157	3,455 R	71.6%	26.4%	73.1%	26.9%
4,344	FISHER	1,192	623	555	14	68 R	52.3%	46.6%	52.9%	47.1%
7,771	FLOYD	2,015	1,514	479	22	1,035 R	75.1%	23.8%	76.0%	24.0%
1,622	FOARD	365	180	178	7	2 R	49.3%	48.8%	50.3%	49.7%
354,452	FORT BEND	96,748	57,530	37,594	1,624	19,936 R	59.5%	38.9%	60.5%	39.5%
9,458	FRANKLIN	3,066	2,212	805	49	1,407 R	72.1%	26.3%	73.3%	26.7%
17,867	FREESTONE	4,339	3,024	1,242	73	1,782 R	69.7%	28.6%	70.9%	29.1%
16,252	FRIO	2,008	1,076	900	32	176 R	53.6%	44.8%	54.5%	45.5%
14,467	GAINES	2,389	1,884	455	50	1,429 R	78.9%	19.0%	80.5%	19.5%
250,158	GALVESTON	63,466	36,551	25,173	1,742	11,378 R	57.6%	39.7%	59.2%	40.8%
4,872	GARZA	1,125	895	202	28	693 R	79.6%	18.0%	81.6%	18.4%

TEXAS
SENATOR 2006

2000 Census Population	County	Total Vote	Republican	Democratic	Other	Rep.-Dem. Plurality	Percentage Total Vote Rep.	Dem.	Major Vote Rep.	Dem.
20,814	GILLESPIE	8,344	6,564	1,531	249	5,033 R	78.7%	18.3%	81.1%	18.9%
1,406	GLASSCOCK	331	294	35	2	259 R	88.8%	10.6%	89.4%	10.6%
6,928	GOLIAD	2,298	1,426	815	57	611 R	62.1%	35.5%	63.6%	36.4%
18,628	GONZALES	4,000	2,784	1,138	78	1,646 R	69.6%	28.5%	71.0%	29.0%
22,744	GRAY	5,258	4,425	724	109	3,701 R	84.2%	13.8%	85.9%	14.1%
110,595	GRAYSON	25,656	17,111	8,016	529	9,095 R	66.7%	31.2%	68.1%	31.9%
111,379	GREGG	22,084	16,065	5,704	315	10,361 R	72.7%	25.8%	73.8%	26.2%
23,552	GRIMES	5,210	3,387	1,686	137	1,701 R	65.0%	32.4%	66.8%	33.2%
89,023	GUADALUPE	24,538	17,216	6,661	661	10,555 R	70.2%	27.1%	72.1%	27.9%
36,602	HALE	6,234	4,618	1,544	72	3,074 R	74.1%	24.8%	74.9%	25.1%
3,782	HALL	883	600	266	17	334 R	68.0%	30.1%	69.3%	30.7%
8,229	HAMILTON	2,822	2,017	748	57	1,269 R	71.5%	26.5%	72.9%	27.1%
5,369	HANSFORD	1,414	1,254	131	29	1,123 R	88.7%	9.3%	90.5%	9.5%
4,724	HARDEMAN	1,410	935	439	36	496 R	66.3%	31.1%	68.0%	32.0%
48,073	HARDIN	10,040	7,079	2,763	198	4,316 R	70.5%	27.5%	71.9%	28.1%
3,400,578	HARRIS	572,031	323,004	236,007	13,020	86,997 R	56.5%	41.3%	57.8%	42.2%
62,110	HARRISON	14,412	9,309	4,870	233	4,439 R	64.6%	33.8%	65.7%	34.3%
5,537	HARTLEY	1,253	1,000	227	26	773 R	79.8%	18.1%	81.5%	18.5%
6,093	HASKELL	1,694	1,046	627	21	419 R	61.7%	37.0%	62.5%	37.5%
97,589	HAYS	30,018	17,172	11,602	1,244	5,570 R	57.2%	38.7%	59.7%	40.3%
3,351	HEMPHILL	1,165	943	209	13	734 R	80.9%	17.9%	81.9%	18.1%
73,277	HENDERSON	17,627	12,267	4,960	400	7,307 R	69.6%	28.1%	71.2%	28.8%
569,463	HIDALGO	46,401	20,274	25,214	913	4,940 D	43.7%	54.3%	44.6%	55.4%
32,321	HILL	9,045	6,342	2,550	153	3,792 R	70.1%	28.2%	71.3%	28.7%
22,716	HOCKLEY	4,604	3,609	905	90	2,704 R	78.4%	19.7%	80.0%	20.0%
41,100	HOOD	13,877	10,322	3,286	269	7,036 R	74.4%	23.7%	75.9%	24.1%
31,960	HOPKINS	8,153	5,566	2,466	121	3,100 R	68.3%	30.2%	69.3%	30.7%
23,185	HOUSTON	5,873	4,094	1,704	75	2,390 R	69.7%	29.0%	70.6%	29.4%
33,627	HOWARD	6,666	4,767	1,748	151	3,019 R	71.5%	26.2%	73.2%	26.8%
3,344	HUDSPETH	511	373	118	20	255 R	73.0%	23.1%	76.0%	24.0%
76,596	HUNT	17,343	12,152	4,771	420	7,381 R	70.1%	27.5%	71.8%	28.2%
23,857	HUTCHINSON	5,400	4,370	918	112	3,452 R	80.9%	17.0%	82.6%	17.4%
1,771	IRION	492	384	100	8	284 R	78.0%	20.3%	79.3%	20.7%
8,763	JACK	2,109	1,638	429	42	1,209 R	77.7%	20.3%	79.2%	20.8%
14,391	JACKSON	3,231	2,289	872	70	1,417 R	70.8%	27.0%	72.4%	27.6%
35,604	JASPER	7,405	4,699	2,569	137	2,130 R	63.5%	34.7%	64.7%	35.3%
2,207	JEFF DAVIS	1,034	609	378	47	231 R	58.9%	36.6%	61.7%	38.3%
252,051	JEFFERSON	45,520	23,901	21,098	521	2,803 R	52.5%	46.3%	53.1%	46.9%
5,281	JIM HOGG	856	292	561	3	269 D	34.1%	65.5%	34.2%	65.8%
39,326	JIM WELLS	7,294	2,936	4,258	100	1,322 D	40.3%	58.4%	40.8%	59.2%
126,811	JOHNSON	29,844	21,596	7,570	678	14,026 R	72.4%	25.4%	74.0%	26.0%
20,785	JONES	3,750	2,552	1,117	81	1,435 R	68.1%	29.8%	69.6%	30.4%
15,446	KARNES	3,063	2,036	963	64	1,073 R	66.5%	31.4%	67.9%	32.1%
71,313	KAUFMAN	18,637	12,970	5,275	392	7,695 R	69.6%	28.3%	71.1%	28.9%
23,743	KENDALL	10,109	7,901	1,932	276	5,969 R	78.2%	19.1%	80.4%	19.6%
414	KENEDY	138	83	54	1	29 R	60.1%	39.1%	60.6%	39.4%
859	KENT	280	175	96	9	79 R	62.5%	34.3%	64.6%	35.4%
43,653	KERR	15,431	11,718	3,344	369	8,374 R	75.9%	21.7%	77.8%	22.2%
4,468	KIMBLE	1,336	1,065	244	27	821 R	79.7%	18.3%	81.4%	18.6%
356	KING	80	61	15	4	46 R	76.3%	18.8%	80.3%	19.7%
3,379	KINNEY	1,051	682	344	25	338 R	64.9%	32.7%	66.5%	33.5%
31,549	KLEBERG	4,931	2,701	2,152	78	549 R	54.8%	43.6%	55.7%	44.3%
4,253	KNOX	868	600	251	17	349 R	69.1%	28.9%	70.5%	29.5%
48,499	LAMAR	11,454	7,404	3,847	203	3,557 R	64.6%	33.6%	65.8%	34.2%
14,709	LAMB	2,616	1,975	583	58	1,392 R	75.5%	22.3%	77.2%	22.8%
17,762	LAMPASAS	4,887	3,678	1,101	108	2,577 R	75.3%	22.5%	77.0%	23.0%
5,866	LA SALLE	1,006	509	478	19	31 R	50.6%	47.5%	51.6%	48.4%
19,210	LAVACA	4,912	3,402	1,406	104	1,996 R	69.3%	28.6%	70.8%	29.2%
15,657	LEE	4,156	2,712	1,349	95	1,363 R	65.3%	32.5%	66.8%	33.2%
15,335	LEON	4,239	3,180	984	75	2,196 R	75.0%	23.2%	76.4%	23.6%

TEXAS

SENATOR 2006

2000 Census Population	County	Total Vote	Republican	Democratic	Other	Rep.-Dem. Plurality	Percentage Total Vote Rep.	Dem.	Major Vote Rep.	Dem.
70,154	LIBERTY	13,990	9,180	4,410	400	4,770 R	65.6%	31.5%	67.5%	32.5%
22,051	LIMESTONE	5,260	3,379	1,808	73	1,571 R	64.2%	34.4%	65.1%	34.9%
3,057	LIPSCOMB	735	605	119	11	486 R	82.3%	16.2%	83.6%	16.4%
12,309	LIVE OAK	2,721	1,990	667	64	1,323 R	73.1%	24.5%	74.9%	25.1%
17,044	LLANO	7,032	5,292	1,548	192	3,744 R	75.3%	22.0%	77.4%	22.6%
67	LOVING	85	66	11	8	55 R	77.6%	12.9%	85.7%	14.3%
242,628	LUBBOCK	53,064	39,100	12,849	1,115	26,251 R	73.7%	24.2%	75.3%	24.7%
6,550	LYNN	1,430	991	418	21	573 R	69.3%	29.2%	70.3%	29.7%
8,205	MCCULLOCH	1,993	1,476	478	39	998 R	74.1%	24.0%	75.5%	24.5%
213,517	MCLENNAN	52,176	34,889	16,540	747	18,349 R	66.9%	31.7%	67.8%	32.2%
851	MCMULLEN	393	324	61	8	263 R	82.4%	15.5%	84.2%	15.8%
12,940	MADISON	2,799	1,918	836	45	1,082 R	68.5%	29.9%	69.6%	30.4%
10,941	MARION	2,209	1,162	995	52	167 R	52.6%	45.0%	53.9%	46.1%
4,746	MARTIN	925	770	143	12	627 R	83.2%	15.5%	84.3%	15.7%
3,738	MASON	1,333	993	293	47	700 R	74.5%	22.0%	77.2%	22.8%
37,957	MATAGORDA	7,708	4,963	2,588	157	2,375 R	64.4%	33.6%	65.7%	34.3%
47,297	MAVERICK	3,729	1,424	2,243	62	819 D	38.2%	60.2%	38.8%	61.2%
39,304	MEDINA	9,683	6,955	2,509	219	4,446 R	71.8%	25.9%	73.5%	26.5%
2,360	MENARD	827	584	202	41	382 R	70.6%	24.4%	74.3%	25.7%
116,009	MIDLAND	24,658	20,032	4,148	478	15,884 R	81.2%	16.8%	82.8%	17.2%
24,238	MILAM	5,437	3,181	2,163	93	1,018 R	58.5%	39.8%	59.5%	40.5%
5,151	MILLS	1,445	1,055	363	27	692 R	73.0%	25.1%	74.4%	25.6%
9,698	MITCHELL	1,412	994	383	35	611 R	70.4%	27.1%	72.2%	27.8%
19,117	MONTAGUE	5,137	3,676	1,335	126	2,341 R	71.6%	26.0%	73.4%	26.6%
293,768	MONTGOMERY	79,600	60,593	16,916	2,091	43,677 R	76.1%	21.3%	78.2%	21.8%
20,121	MOORE	3,000	2,389	551	60	1,838 R	79.6%	18.4%	81.3%	18.7%
13,048	MORRIS	2,853	1,416	1,393	44	23 R	49.6%	48.8%	50.4%	49.6%
1,426	MOTLEY	383	302	73	8	229 R	78.9%	19.1%	80.5%	19.5%
59,203	NACOGDOCHES	12,104	8,452	3,432	220	5,020 R	69.8%	28.4%	71.1%	28.9%
45,124	NAVARRO	10,716	7,368	3,147	201	4,221 R	68.8%	29.4%	70.1%	29.9%
15,072	NEWTON	2,878	1,503	1,326	49	177 R	52.2%	46.1%	53.1%	46.9%
15,802	NOLAN	3,126	2,097	960	69	1,137 R	67.1%	30.7%	68.6%	31.4%
313,645	NUECES	65,853	39,223	25,181	1,449	14,042 R	59.6%	38.2%	60.9%	39.1%
9,006	OCHILTREE	1,705	1,546	131	28	1,415 R	90.7%	7.7%	92.2%	7.8%
2,185	OLDHAM	541	451	77	13	374 R	83.4%	14.2%	85.4%	14.6%
84,966	ORANGE	17,211	10,437	6,490	284	3,947 R	60.6%	37.7%	61.7%	38.3%
27,026	PALO PINTO	6,256	4,310	1,807	139	2,503 R	68.9%	28.9%	70.5%	29.5%
22,756	PANOLA	5,799	3,921	1,791	87	2,130 R	67.6%	30.9%	68.6%	31.4%
88,495	PARKER	26,383	20,045	5,753	585	14,292 R	76.0%	21.8%	77.7%	22.3%
10,016	PARMER	1,786	1,471	284	31	1,187 R	82.4%	15.9%	83.8%	16.2%
16,809	PECOS	3,033	1,879	1,091	63	788 R	62.0%	36.0%	63.3%	36.7%
41,133	POLK	11,689	7,488	3,899	302	3,589 R	64.1%	33.4%	65.8%	34.2%
113,546	POTTER	16,816	11,762	4,600	454	7,162 R	69.9%	27.4%	71.9%	28.1%
7,304	PRESIDIO	896	332	544	20	212 D	37.1%	60.7%	37.9%	62.1%
9,139	RAINS	2,743	1,873	799	71	1,074 R	68.3%	29.1%	70.1%	29.9%
104,312	RANDALL	30,425	24,556	5,241	628	19,315 R	80.7%	17.2%	82.4%	17.6%
3,326	REAGAN	612	510	88	14	422 R	83.3%	14.4%	85.3%	14.7%
3,047	REAL	1,046	797	207	42	590 R	76.2%	19.8%	79.4%	20.6%
14,314	RED RIVER	3,123	1,826	1,244	53	582 R	58.5%	39.8%	59.5%	40.5%
13,137	REEVES	1,977	943	996	38	53 D	47.7%	50.4%	48.6%	51.4%
7,828	REFUGIO	1,886	1,245	605	36	640 R	66.0%	32.1%	67.3%	32.7%
887	ROBERTS	295	267	25	3	242 R	90.5%	8.5%	91.4%	8.6%
16,000	ROBERTSON	4,921	2,579	2,277	65	302 R	52.4%	46.3%	53.1%	46.9%
43,080	ROCKWALL	15,480	12,054	3,159	267	8,895 R	77.9%	20.4%	79.2%	20.8%
11,495	RUNNELS	2,365	1,839	475	51	1,364 R	77.8%	20.1%	79.5%	20.5%
47,372	RUSK	11,483	8,281	2,980	222	5,301 R	72.1%	26.0%	73.5%	26.5%
10,469	SABINE	3,002	1,942	1,006	54	936 R	64.7%	33.5%	65.9%	34.1%
8,946	SAN AUGUSTINE	2,396	1,361	994	41	367 R	56.8%	41.5%	57.8%	42.2%
22,246	SAN JACINTO	6,423	4,006	2,254	163	1,752 R	62.4%	35.1%	64.0%	36.0%
67,138	SAN PATRICIO	12,635	7,488	4,920	227	2,568 R	59.3%	38.9%	60.3%	39.7%

TEXAS

SENATOR 2006

2000 Census Population	County	Total Vote	Republican	Democratic	Other	Rep.-Dem. Plurality	Percentage Total Vote Rep.	Dem.	Major Vote Rep.	Dem.
6,186	SAN SABA	1,504	1,139	332	33	807 R	75.7%	22.1%	77.4%	22.6%
2,935	SCHLEICHER	683	481	190	12	291 R	70.4%	27.8%	71.7%	28.3%
16,361	SCURRY	2,732	2,090	580	62	1,510 R	76.5%	21.2%	78.3%	21.7%
3,302	SHACKELFORD	911	738	156	17	582 R	81.0%	17.1%	82.6%	17.4%
25,224	SHELBY	5,884	3,901	1,902	81	1,999 R	66.3%	32.3%	67.2%	32.8%
3,186	SHERMAN	599	509	79	11	430 R	85.0%	13.2%	86.6%	13.4%
174,706	SMITH	42,525	31,499	10,359	667	21,140 R	74.1%	24.4%	75.3%	24.7%
6,809	SOMERVELL	2,487	1,853	577	57	1,276 R	74.5%	23.2%	76.3%	23.7%
53,597	STARR	6,027	1,235	4,717	75	3,482 D	20.5%	78.3%	20.7%	79.3%
9,674	STEPHENS	2,080	1,559	486	35	1,073 R	75.0%	23.4%	76.2%	23.8%
1,393	STERLING	310	270	39	1	231 R	87.1%	12.6%	87.4%	12.6%
1,693	STONEWALL	533	298	225	10	73 R	55.9%	42.2%	57.0%	43.0%
4,077	SUTTON	1,086	791	281	14	510 R	72.8%	25.9%	73.8%	26.2%
8,378	SWISHER	1,625	955	634	36	321 R	58.8%	39.0%	60.1%	39.9%
1,446,219	TARRANT	322,760	203,994	112,324	6,442	91,670 R	63.2%	34.8%	64.5%	35.5%
126,555	TAYLOR	27,859	21,917	5,411	531	16,506 R	78.7%	19.4%	80.2%	19.8%
1,081	TERRELL	488	283	191	14	92 R	58.0%	39.1%	59.7%	40.3%
12,761	TERRY	2,476	1,770	675	31	1,095 R	71.5%	27.3%	72.4%	27.6%
1,850	THROCKMORTON	452	315	128	9	187 R	69.7%	28.3%	71.1%	28.9%
28,118	TITUS	5,775	3,489	2,180	106	1,309 R	60.4%	37.7%	61.5%	38.5%
104,010	TOM GREEN	21,223	15,864	4,887	472	10,977 R	74.7%	23.0%	76.4%	23.6%
812,280	TRAVIS	223,750	95,754	119,087	8,909	23,333 D	42.8%	53.2%	44.6%	55.4%
13,779	TRINITY	4,217	2,496	1,635	86	861 R	59.2%	38.8%	60.4%	39.6%
20,871	TYLER	5,175	3,159	1,892	124	1,267 R	61.0%	36.6%	62.5%	37.5%
35,291	UPSHUR	9,414	6,490	2,746	178	3,744 R	68.9%	29.2%	70.3%	29.7%
3,404	UPTON	606	491	107	8	384 R	81.0%	17.7%	82.1%	17.9%
25,926	UVALDE	5,272	3,387	1,780	105	1,607 R	64.2%	33.8%	65.6%	34.4%
44,856	VAL VERDE	7,016	3,718	3,161	137	557 R	53.0%	45.1%	54.0%	46.0%
48,140	VAN ZANDT	12,303	8,868	3,189	246	5,679 R	72.1%	25.9%	73.6%	26.4%
84,088	VICTORIA	18,435	12,829	5,286	320	7,543 R	69.6%	28.7%	70.8%	29.2%
61,758	WALKER	10,983	7,356	3,337	290	4,019 R	67.0%	30.4%	68.8%	31.2%
32,663	WALLER	7,900	5,119	2,609	172	2,510 R	64.8%	33.0%	66.2%	33.8%
10,909	WARD	2,008	1,411	539	58	872 R	70.3%	26.8%	72.4%	27.6%
30,373	WASHINGTON	9,337	6,928	2,150	259	4,778 R	74.2%	23.0%	76.3%	23.7%
193,117	WEBB	17,894	7,117	10,522	255	3,405 D	39.8%	58.8%	40.3%	59.7%
41,188	WHARTON	8,646	5,710	2,794	142	2,916 R	66.0%	32.3%	67.1%	32.9%
5,284	WHEELER	1,264	996	235	33	761 R	78.8%	18.6%	80.9%	19.1%
131,664	WICHITA	26,894	18,884	7,465	545	11,419 R	70.2%	27.8%	71.7%	28.3%
14,676	WILBARGER	3,320	2,392	863	65	1,529 R	72.0%	26.0%	73.5%	26.5%
20,082	WILLACY	1,946	932	976	38	44 D	47.9%	50.2%	48.8%	51.2%
249,967	WILLIAMSON	83,437	53,215	27,289	2,933	25,926 R	63.8%	32.7%	66.1%	33.9%
32,408	WILSON	10,709	7,190	3,275	244	3,915 R	67.1%	30.6%	68.7%	31.3%
7,173	WINKLER	1,462	1,075	353	34	722 R	73.5%	24.1%	75.3%	24.7%
48,793	WISE	12,161	8,908	2,995	258	5,913 R	73.3%	24.6%	74.8%	25.2%
36,752	WOOD	11,205	8,256	2,739	210	5,517 R	73.7%	24.4%	75.1%	24.9%
7,322	YOAKUM	1,563	1,257	282	24	975 R	80.4%	18.0%	81.7%	18.3%
17,943	YOUNG	4,596	3,496	1,026	74	2,470 R	76.1%	22.3%	77.3%	22.7%
12,182	ZAPATA	1,136	409	703	24	294 D	36.0%	61.9%	36.8%	63.2%
11,600	ZAVALA	1,640	445	1,173	22	728 D	27.1%	71.5%	27.5%	72.5%
20,851,820	TOTAL	4,314,663	2,661,789	1,555,202	97,672	1,106,587 R	61.7%	36.0%	63.1%	36.9%

TEXAS

HOUSE OF REPRESENTATIVES

| | | | Republican | | Democratic | | Other | | Percentage | | | |
| | | Total | | | | | | | Total Vote | | Major Vote | |
CD	Year	Vote	Vote	Candidate	Vote	Candidate	Vote	Plurality	Rep.	Dem.	Rep.	Dem.
1	2006	153,070	104,099	GOHMERT, LOUIE*	46,303	OWEN, ROGER L.	2,668	57,796 R	68.0%	30.2%	69.2%	30.8%
1	2004	255,507	157,068	GOHMERT, LOUIE	96,281	SANDLIN, MAX*	2,158	60,787 R	61.5%	37.7%	62.0%	38.0%
2	2006	137,865	90,490	POE, TED*	45,080	BINDERIM, GARY E.	2,295	45,410 R	65.6%	32.7%	66.7%	33.3%
2	2004	252,038	139,951	POE, TED	108,156	LAMPSON, NICK*	3,931	31,795 R	55.5%	42.9%	56.4%	43.6%
3	2006	141,881	88,690	JOHNSON, SAM*	49,529	DODD, DAN	3,662	39,161 R	62.5%	34.9%	64.2%	35.8%
3	2004	210,352	180,099	JOHNSON, SAM*		—	30,253	180,099 R	85.6%		100.0%	
4	2006	165,269	106,495	HALL, RALPH M.*	55,278	MELANCON, GLENN	3,496	51,217 R	64.4%	33.4%	65.8%	34.2%
4	2004	267,942	182,866	HALL, RALPH M.*	81,585	NICKERSON, JIM	3,491	101,281 R	68.2%	30.4%	69.1%	30.9%
5	2006	143,252	88,478	HENSARLING, JEB*	50,983	THOMPSON, CHARLIE	3,791	37,495 R	61.8%	35.6%	63.4%	36.6%
5	2004	230,845	148,816	HENSARLING, JEB*	75,911	BERNSTEIN, BILL	6,118	72,905 R	64.5%	32.9%	66.2%	33.8%
6	2006	152,036	91,927	BARTON, JOE L.*	56,369	HARRIS, DAVID T.	3,740	35,558 R	60.5%	37.1%	62.0%	38.0%
6	2004	255,627	168,767	BARTON, JOE L.*	83,609	MEYER, MORRIS	3,251	85,158 R	66.0%	32.7%	66.9%	33.1%
7	2006	167,785	99,318	CULBERSON, JOHN*	64,514	HENLEY, JIM	3,953	34,804 R	59.2%	38.5%	60.6%	39.4%
7	2004	273,651	175,440	CULBERSON, JOHN*	91,126	MARTINEZ, JOHN	7,085	84,314 R	64.1%	33.3%	65.8%	34.2%
8	2006	157,058	105,665	BRADY, KEVIN*	51,393	WRIGHT, JAMES "JIM"		54,272 R	67.3%	32.7%	67.3%	32.7%
8	2004	260,628	179,599	BRADY, KEVIN*	77,324	WRIGHT, JAMES "JIM"	3,705	102,275 R	68.9%	29.7%	69.9%	30.1%
9	2006	60,253		—	60,253	GREEN, AL*		60,253 D		100.0%		100.0%
9	2004	158,566	42,132	MOLINA, ARLETTE	114,462	GREEN, AL	1,972	72,330 D	26.6%	72.2%	26.9%	73.1%
10	2006	176,755	97,726	McCAUL, MICHAEL*	71,415	ANKRUM, TED	7,614	26,311 R	55.3%	40.4%	57.8%	42.2%
10	2004	231,643	182,113	McCAUL, MICHAEL		—	49,530	182,113 R	78.6%		100.0%	
11	2006	107,268	107,268	CONAWAY, K. MICHAEL*		—		107,268 R	100.0%		100.0%	
11	2004	230,977	177,291	CONAWAY, K. MICHAEL	50,339	RAASCH, WAYNE	3,347	126,952 R	76.8%	21.8%	77.9%	22.1%
12	2006	146,935	98,371	GRANGER, KAY*	45,676	MORRIS, JOHN R.	2,888	52,695 R	66.9%	31.1%	68.3%	31.7%
12	2004	239,538	173,222	GRANGER, KAY*	66,316	ALVARADO, FELIX		106,906 R	72.3%	27.7%	72.3%	27.7%
13	2004	145,396	108,107	THORNBERRY, WILLIAM M. "MAC"*	33,460	WAUN, ROGER J.	3,829	74,647 R	74.4%	23.0%	76.4%	23.6%
13	2004	205,241	189,448	THORNBERRY, WILLIAM M. "MAC"*		—	15,793	189,448 R	92.3%		100.0%	
14	2006	156,809	94,380	PAUL, RON*	62,429	SKLAR, SHANE		31,951 R	60.2%	39.8%	60.2%	39.8%
14	2004	173,668	173,668	PAUL, RON*		—		173,668 R	100.0%		100.0%	
15	2006	69,987	26,751	HARING/ZAMORA	43,236	HINOJOSA, RUBEN*		26,635 D	38.2%	61.8%	38.2%	61.8%
16	2006	77,688		—	61,116	REYES, SILVESTRE*	16,572	61,116 D		78.7%		100.0%
16	2004	160,773	49,972	BRIGHAM, DAVID	108,577	REYES, SILVESTRE*	2,224	58,605 D	31.1%	67.5%	31.5%	68.5%
17	2006	159,124	64,142	TAYLOR, VAN	92,478	EDWARDS, CHET*	2,504	28,336 D	40.3%	58.1%	41.0%	59.0%
17	2004	244,748	116,049	WOHLGEMUTH, ARLENE	125,309	EDWARDS, CHET*	3,390	9,260 D	47.4%	51.2%	48.1%	51.9%
18	2006	86,051	16,448	HASSAN, AHMAD	65,936	JACKSON-LEE, SHEILA*	3,667	49,488 D	19.1%	76.6%	20.0%	80.0%
18	2004	152,988		—	136,018	JACKSON-LEE, SHEILA*	16,970	136,018 D		88.9%		100.0%
19	2006	140,007	94,785	NEUGEBAUER, RANDY*	41,676	RICKETTS, ROBERT	3,546	53,109 R	67.7%	29.8%	69.5%	30.5%
19	2004	233,514	136,459	NEUGEBAUER, RANDY*	93,531	STENHOLM, CHARLES W.*	3,524	42,928 R	58.4%	40.1%	59.3%	40.7%
20	2006	78,245		—	68,348	GONZALEZ, CHARLIE*	9,897	68,348 D		87.4%		100.0%
20	2004	171,804	54,976	SCOTT, ROGER	112,480	GONZALEZ, CHARLIE*	4,348	57,504 D	32.0%	65.5%	32.8%	67.2%
21	2006	203,782	122,486	SMITH, LAMAR*	68,312	COURAGE/KELLY	12,984	72,529 R	60.1%	33.5%	64.2%	35.8%

TEXAS

HOUSE OF REPRESENTATIVES

		Total	Republican		Democratic		Other		Percentage			
									Total Vote		Major Vote	
CD	Year	Vote	Vote	Candidate	Vote	Candidate	Vote	Plurality	Rep.	Dem.	Rep.	Dem.
22	2006	148,239	61,938	GIBBS, SHELLEY SEKULA	76,775	LAMPSON, NICK	9,526	14,837 D	41.8%	51.8%	44.7%	55.3%
22	2004	272,620	150,386	DeLAY, TOM*	112,034	MORRISON, RICHARD R.	10,200	38,352 R	55.2%	41.1%	57.3%	42.7%
23	2006	70,473	32,217	BONILLA, HENRY*	38,256	RODRIGUEZ, CIRO D.		6,039 D	45.7%	54.3%	45.7%	54.3%
24	2006	140,138	83,835	MARCHANT, KENNY*	52,075	PAGE, GARY R.	4,228	31,760 R	59.8%	37.2%	61.7%	38.3%
24	2004	241,374	154,435	MARCHANT, KENNY	82,599	PAGE, GARY R.	4,340	71,836 R	64.0%	34.2%	65.2%	34.8%
25	2006	163,424	42,975	ROSTIG, GRANT	109,911	DOGGETT, LLOYD*	10,538	66,936 D	26.3%	67.3%	28.1%	71.9%
26	2006	156,483	94,219	BURGESS, MICHAEL C.*	58,271	BARNWELL, TIM	3,993	35,948 R	60.2%	37.2%	61.8%	38.2%
26	2004	274,539	180,519	BURGESS, MICHAEL C.*	89,809	REYES, LICO	4,211	90,710 R	65.8%	32.7%	66.8%	33.2%
27	2006	109,314	42,538	VADEN, WILLIAM "WILLIE"	62,058	ORTIZ, SOLOMON P.*	4,718	19,520 D	38.9%	56.8%	40.7%	59.3%
27	2004	177,536	61,955	VADEN, WILLIAM "WILLIE"	112,081	ORTIZ, SOLOMON P.*	3,500	50,126 D	34.9%	63.1%	35.6%	64.4%
28	2006	77,755		—	68,372	CUELLAR*/ENRIQUEZ	9,383	36,776 D		87.9%		100.0%
29	2006	50,550	12,347	STORY, ERIC	37,174	GREEN, GENE*	1,029	24,827 D	24.4%	73.5%	24.9%	75.1%
29	2004	83,124		—	78,256	GREEN, GENE*	4,868	78,256 D		94.1%		100.0%
30	2006	101,448	17,850	AURBACH, WILSON	81,348	JOHNSON, EDDIE BERNICE*	2,250	63,498 D	17.6%	80.2%	18.0%	82.0%
30	2004	155,334		—	144,513	JOHNSON, EDDIE BERNICE*	10,821	144,513 D		93.0%		100.0%
31	2006	155,383	90,869	CARTER, JOHN*	60,293	HARRELL, MARY BETH	4,221	30,576 R	58.5%	38.8%	60.1%	39.9%
31	2004	247,427	160,247	CARTER, JOHN*	80,292	PORTER, JON	6,888	79,955 R	64.8%	32.5%	66.6%	33.4%
32	2006	126,652	71,461	SESSIONS, PETE*	52,269	PRYOR, WILL	2,922	19,192 R	56.4%	41.3%	57.8%	42.2%
32	2004	202,236	109,859	SESSIONS, PETE*	89,030	FROST, MARTIN*	3,347	20,829 R	54.3%	44.0%	55.2%	44.8%
TOTAL	2006	4,179,701	2,183,833		1,852,613		143,255	331,220 R	52.2%	44.3%	54.1%	45.9%
TOTAL	2004	6,958,603	4,012,534		2,713,968		232,101	1,298,566 R	57.7%	39.0%	59.7%	40.3%
TOTAL	2002	4,295,210	2,290,723		1,885,178		119,309	405,545 R	53.3%	43.9%	54.9%	45.1%

An asterisk (*) denotes incumbent. The designated Republican candidate in the 22nd District in 2006 was a write-in candidate, Shelley Sekula Gibbs.

Note: Congressional district lines in Texas were redrawn between the elections of 2002 and 2004, and for Districts 15, 21, 23, 25, and 28 between the 2006 primary and general elections. In each of these five districts, candidates of all parties ran together in a special election on the November ballot, with the plurality measured as the difference between the vote for the winner and the vote for the runner-up, regardless of party. In other districts, the plurality is the difference between the Democratic and Republican vote. The results listed for the 23rd District are from a December runoff, required when no candidate won a majority of the vote in November voting. The statewide vote totals represent the aggregate vote for all House candidates of each party in the November balloting. The results from 2002, and a map of the Texas congressional district lines that year, can be found in *America Votes 25*, p. 454. The results from 2004, and a map of the Texas congressional district lines that year, can be found in *America Votes 26*, p. 418.

TEXAS

GENERAL AND PRIMARY ELECTIONS

2006 GENERAL ELECTIONS

Governor   Other vote was 26,749 Libertarian (James Werner); 713 write-in (James "Patriot" Dillon). (Carole Keeton Strayhorn, an independent candidate, received 796,851 votes, 18.1 percent of the total vote. Richard "Kinky" Friedman, another independent candidate, received 547,674 votes, 12.4 percent. The vote for both independents are listed in the county table for the 2006 gubernatorial election in Texas.)

Senator   Other vote was 97,672 Libertarian (Scott Lanier Jameson).

House   Other vote was:

CD 1   2,668 Libertarian (Donald Perkison).
CD 2   2,295 Libertarian (Justo J. Perez).
CD 3   3,662 Libertarian (Christopher J. Claytor).
CD 4   3,496 Libertarian (Kurt G. Helm).
CD 5   3,791 Libertarian (Mike Nelson).
CD 6   3,740 Libertarian (Carl Nulsen).
CD 7   3,953 Libertarian (Drew Parks).
CD 8
CD 9
CD 10   7,614 Libertarian (Michael Badnarik).
CD 11
CD 12   2,888 Libertarian (Gardner Osborne).
CD 13   3,829 Libertarian (Jim Thompson).
CD 14
CD 15   The district was reconfigured between the primary and general elections, forcing candidates of all parties to run together on the November ballot. There were two Republicans: Paul B. Haring received 16,601 votes, 23.7 percent of the total vote; Eddie Zamora received 10,150 votes, 14.5 percent.
CD 16   16,572 Libertarian (Gordon R. Strickland).
CD 17   2,504 Libertarian (Guillermo Acosta).
CD 18   3,667 Libertarian (Patrick Warren).
CD 19   3,349 Libertarian (Fred C. Jones); 197 write-in (Mike Sadler).
CD 20   9,897 Libertarian (Michael Idrogo).
CD 21   The district was reconfigured between the primary and general elections, forcing candidates of all parties to run together on the November ballot. There were two Democrats: John Courage received 49,957 votes, 24.5 percent of the total vote; Gene Kelly received 18,355 votes, 9.0 percent. The following third-party and independent candidates also received votes: 5,280 Independent (Tommy Calvert); 4,076 Libertarian (James Arthur Strohm); 2,189 Independent (James Lyle Peterson); 1,439 Independent (Mark J. Rossano).
CD 22   9,009 Libertarian (Bob Smither); 428 write-in (Don Richardson); 89 write-in (Joe Reasbeck). (The designated Republican candidate, Shelley Sekula Gibbs, also ran as a write-in.)
CD 23   The district was reconfigured between the primary and general elections, forcing candidates of all parties to run together on the November ballot. Incumbent Henry Bonilla was the only Republican in the race and received 60,175 votes, 48.6 percent of the total vote. There were six Democrats listed: Ciro D. Rodriguez received 24,594 votes, 19.9 percent of the total vote; Albert Uresti received 14,552 votes, 11.8 percent; Lukin Gilliland received 13,728 votes, 11.1 percent; August G. "Augie" Beltran received 2,647 votes, 2.1 percent; Rick Bolanos received 2,564 votes, 2.1 percent; Adrian DeLeon received 2,198 votes, 1.8 percent. Also on the ballot: 3,341 Independent (Craig T. Stephens). Since no candidate received a majority of the vote in the November balloting, a runoff was held December 12, 2006. The results of that contest are listed in the House of Representatives table.
CD 24   4,228 Libertarian (Mark Frohman).
CD 25   The district was reconfigured between the primary and general elections, forcing candidates of all parties to run together on the November ballot. The following third-party and independent candidates received votes: 6,942 Libertarian (Barbara Cunningham); 3,596 Independent (Brian Parrett).
CD 26   3,993 Libertarian (Rick Haas).
CD 27   4,718 Libertarian (Robert Powell).

TEXAS

GENERAL AND PRIMARY ELECTIONS

CD 28   The district was reconfigured between the primary and general elections, forcing candidates of all parties to run together on the November ballot. There were two Democrats: Incumbent Henry Cuellar received 52,574 votes, 67.6 percent of the total vote; Frank Enriquez received 15,798 votes, 20.3 percent. Also on the ballot: 9,383 Constitution (Ron Avery).

CD 29   1,029 Libertarian (Clifford Lee Messina).

CD 30   2,250 Libertarian (Ken Ashby).

CD 31   4,221 Libertarian (Matt McAdoo).

CD 32   2,922 Libertarian (John B. Hawley).

2006 PRIMARY ELECTIONS

Primary	March 7, 2006	**Registration** (as of March 7, 2006)	12,722,671	No Party Registration

Primary Runoff   April 11, 2006

Primary Type   Open—Any registered voter could participate in the Democratic or Republican primary, although if they voted in the primary of one party they could not vote in the runoff of the other party.

Note: An asterisk (*) denotes incumbent. Texas underwent court-ordered redistricting between the 2006 primary and general elections. Districts 15, 21, 23, 25, and 28 were redrawn, followed by an open filing period that resulted in candidates from all parties running together in each of these districts in a special election that was held as part of the November general election. Those candidates that received a majority of the vote were elected outright. A runoff was required in District 23 and was held on December 12, 2006.

	REPUBLICAN PRIMARIES			**DEMOCRATIC PRIMARIES**		
Governor	Rick Perry*	552,545	84.2%	Chris Bell	324,869	63.9%
	Larry Kilgore	50,119	7.6%	Bob Gammage	145,081	28.5%
	Rhett R. Smith	30,225	4.6%	Rashad Jafer	38,652	7.6%
	Star Locke	23,030	3.5%			
	TOTAL	*655,919*		*TOTAL*	*508,602*	
Senator	Kay Bailey Hutchison*	627,163	100.0%	Barbara Ann Radnofsky	215,776	43.1%
				Gene Kelly	191,400	38.2%
				Darrel Reece Hunter	93,609	18.7%
				TOTAL	*500,785*	
				PRIMARY RUNOFF		
				Barbara Ann Radnofsky	124,663	60.2%
				Gene Kelly	82,589	39.8%
				TOTAL	*207,252*	
Congressional District 1	Louie Gohmert*	35,267	100.0%	Roger L. Owen	10,121	53.3%
				Duane Shaw	8,851	46.7%
				TOTAL	*18,972*	
Congressional District 2	Ted Poe*	16,723	100.0%	Gary E. Binderim	18,491	100.0%
Congressional District 3	Sam Johnson*	13,348	85.3%	Dan Dodd	2,478	100.0%
	Bob Johnson	2,292	14.7%			
	TOTAL	*15,640*				
Congressional District 4	Ralph M. Hall*	24,409	100.0%	Glenn Melancon	15,696	100.0%
Congressional District 5	Jeb Hensarling*	24,793	100.0%	Charlie Thompson	7,516	100.0%
Congressional District 6	Joe L. Barton*	23,222	100.0%	David T. Harris	8,538	100.0%

TEXAS

GENERAL AND PRIMARY ELECTIONS

REPUBLICAN PRIMARIES			DEMOCRATIC PRIMARIES		
Congressional District 7	John Culberson*	27,788	100.0%	Jim Henley	3,950	67.5%
				David Murff	1,902	32.5%
				TOTAL	*5,852*	
Congressional District 8	Kevin Brady*	24,727	100.0%	James "Jim" Wright	19,881	100.0%
Congressional District 9	No Republican candidate			Al Green*	10,549	100.0%
Congressional District 10	Michael McCaul*	22,901	100.0%	Ted Ankrum	3,703	36.7%
				Paul Foreman	3,610	35.8%
				Sid Smith	1,475	14.6%
				Pat Mynatt	1,291	12.8%
				TOTAL	*10,079*	
				PRIMARY RUNOFF		
				Ted Ankrum	2,611	70.8%
				Paul Foreman	1,078	29.2%
				TOTAL	*3,689*	
Congressional District 11	K. Michael Conaway*	37,391	100.0%	No Democratic candidate		
Congressional District 12	Kay Granger*	20,426	100.0%	John R. Morris	4,846	100.0%
Congressional District 13	William M. "Mac" Thornberry*	36,477	100.0%	Roger J. Waun	10,651	100.0%
Congressional District 14	Ron Paul*	24,086	77.6%	Shane Sklar	13,244	100.0%
	Cynthia Sinatra	6,935	22.4%			
	TOTAL	*31,021*				
Congressional District 15	Paul B. Haring	5,552	70.9%	Ruben Hinojosa*	39,094	100.0%
	Eddie Zamora	2,278	29.1%			
	TOTAL	*7,830*				
Congressional District 16	No Republican candidate			Silvestre Reyes*	28,931	100.0%
Congressional District 17	Van Taylor	17,291	54.0%	Chet Edwards*	11,913	100.0%
	Tucker Anderson	14,712	46.0%			
	TOTAL	*32,003*				
Congressional District 18	Ahmad Hassan	2,753	100.0%	Sheila Jackson-Lee*	9,512	100.0%
Congressional District 19	Randy Neugebauer*	37,038	100.0%	Robert Ricketts	9,656	100.0%
Congressional District 20	No Republican candidate			Charlie Gonzalez*	16,398	100.0%
Congressional District 21	Lamar Smith*	27,166	100.0%	John Courage	11,264	100.0%
Congressional District 22	Tom DeLay*	20,563	62.0%	Nick Lampson	7,993	100.0%
	Tom Campbell	9,941	30.0%			
	Mike Fjetland	1,550	4.7%			
	Pat Baig	1,115	3.4%			
	TOTAL	*33,169*				

Under indictment for alleged campaign finance violations and doubting his electability, Tom DeLay quit the race after the primary. But Republicans were not allowed to fill the vacancy on the general election ballot. Their designated candidate, Shelley Sekula Gibbs, ran as a write-in.

REPUBLICAN PRIMARIES			DEMOCRATIC PRIMARIES		
Congressional District 23	Henry Bonilla*	17,929	100.0%	Rick Bolanos	30,164	100.0%
Congressional District 24	Kenny Marchant*	9,716	100.0%	Gary R. Page	3,089	100.0%

TEXAS

GENERAL AND PRIMARY ELECTIONS

REPUBLICAN PRIMARIES				DEMOCRATIC PRIMARIES		
Congressional District 25	*No Republican candidate filed for the primary. But with redistricting, Republican Grant Rostig was able to file for the November election.*			Lloyd Doggett*	29,919	100.0%
Congressional District 26	Michael C. Burgess*	17,964	100.0%	Tim Barnwell	5,157	100.0%
Congressional District 27	William "Willie" Vaden	7,207	100.0%	Solomon P. Ortiz*	31,563	100.0%
Congressional District 28	No Republican candidate			Henry Cuellar* Ciro D. Rodriguez Victor Morales *TOTAL*	24,256 18,484 2,943 *45,683*	53.1% 40.5% 6.4%
Congressional District 29	Eric Story	2,113	100.0%	Gene Green*	4,538	100.0%
Congressional District 30	Wilson Aurbach Amir Omar Fred A. Wood *TOTAL* PRIMARY RUNOFF Wilson Aurbach Amir Omar *TOTAL*	1,614 1,308 704 *3,626* 1,129 727 *1,856*	44.5% 36.1% 19.4% 60.8% 39.2%	Eddie Bernice Johnson*	17,490	100.0%
Congressional District 31	John Carter*	23,438	100.0%	Mary Beth Harrell	7,023	100.0%
Congressional District 32	Pete Sessions*	13,210	100.0%	Will Pryor	3,622	100.0%

UTAH

Congressional districts first established for elections held in 2002
3 members

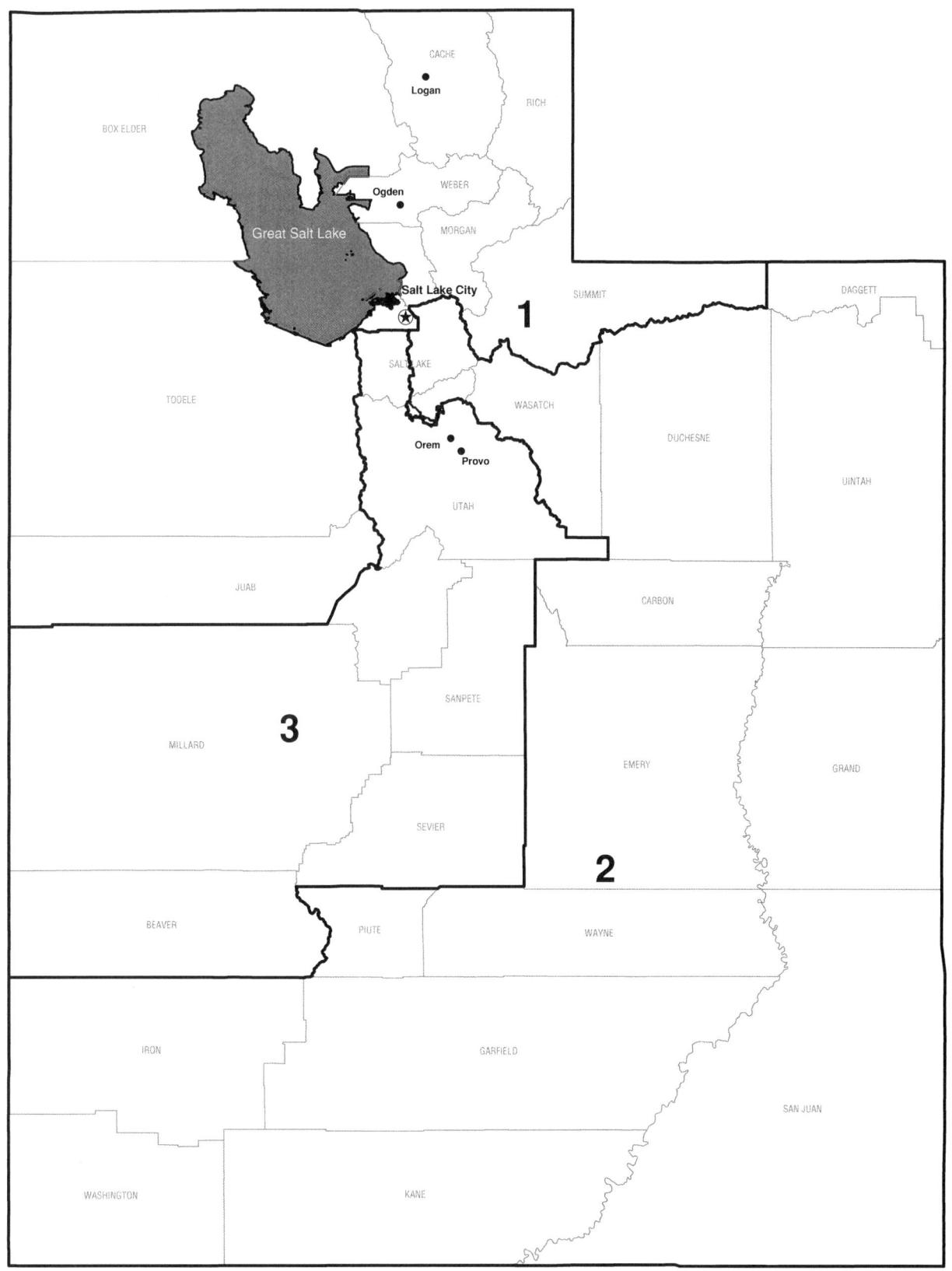

UTAH

GOVERNOR
Jon Huntsman Jr. (R). Elected 2004 to a four-year term.

SENATORS (2 Republicans)
Orrin G. Hatch (R). Reelected 2006 to a six-year term. Previously elected 2000, 1994, 1988, 1982, 1976.

Robert F. Bennett (R). Reelected 2004 to a six-year term. Previously elected 1998, 1992.

REPRESENTATIVES (2 Republicans, 1 Democrat)
1. Rob Bishop (R)   2. Jim Matheson (D)   3. Chris Cannon (R)

POSTWAR VOTE FOR PRESIDENT

| Year | Total Vote | Republican | | Democratic | | Other Vote | Plurality | Percentage | | | |
| | | Vote | Candidate | Vote | Candidate | | | Total Vote | | Major Vote | |
								Rep.	Dem.	Rep.	Dem.
2004	927,844	663,742	Bush, George W.	241,199	Kerry, John	22,903	422,543 R	71.5%	26.0%	73.3%	26.7%
2000**	770,754	515,096	Bush, George W.	203,053	Gore, Al	52,605	312,043 R	66.8%	26.3%	71.7%	28.3%
1996**	665,629	361,911	Dole, Bob	221,633	Clinton, Bill	82,085	140,278 R	54.4%	33.3%	62.0%	38.0%
1992**	743,999	322,632	Bush, George	183,429	Clinton, Bill	237,938	119,232 R	43.4%	24.7%	63.8%	36.2%
1988	647,008	428,442	Bush, George	207,343	Dukakis, Michael S.	11,223	221,099 R	66.2%	32.0%	67.4%	32.6%
1984	629,656	469,105	Reagan, Ronald	155,369	Mondale, Walter F.	5,182	313,736 R	74.5%	24.7%	75.1%	24.9%
1980**	604,222	439,687	Reagan, Ronald	124,266	Carter, Jimmy	40,269	315,421 R	72.8%	20.6%	78.0%	22.0%
1976	541,198	337,908	Ford, Gerald R.	182,110	Carter, Jimmy	21,180	155,798 R	62.4%	33.6%	65.0%	35.0%
1972	478,476	323,643	Nixon, Richard M.	126,284	McGovern, George S.	28,549	197,359 R	67.6%	26.4%	71.9%	28.1%
1968**	422,568	238,728	Nixon, Richard M.	156,665	Humphrey, Hubert H.	27,175	82,063 R	56.5%	37.1%	60.4%	39.6%
1964	401,413	181,785	Goldwater, Barry M.	219,628	Johnson, Lyndon B.		37,843 D	45.3%	54.7%	45.3%	54.7%
1960	374,709	205,361	Nixon, Richard M.	169,248	Kennedy, John F.	100	36,113 R	54.8%	45.2%	54.8%	45.2%
1956	333,995	215,631	Eisenhower, Dwight D.	118,364	Stevenson, Adlai E.		97,267 R	64.6%	35.4%	64.6%	35.4%
1952	329,554	194,190	Eisenhower, Dwight D.	135,364	Stevenson, Adlai E.		58,826 R	58.9%	41.1%	58.9%	41.1%
1948	276,306	124,402	Dewey, Thomas E.	149,151	Truman, Harry S.	2,753	24,749 D	45.0%	54.0%	45.5%	54.5%

**In past elections, the other vote included: 2000 - 35,850 Green (Ralph Nader); 1996 - 66,461 Reform (Ross Perot); 1992 - 203,400 Independent (Ross Perot), who finished second statewide; 1980 - 30,284 Independent (John Anderson); 1968 - 26,906 American Independent (George Wallace).

UTAH

POSTWAR VOTE FOR GOVERNOR

Year	Total Vote	Republican		Democratic		Other Vote	Rep.-Dem. Plurality	Percentage			
								Total Vote		Major Vote	
		Vote	Candidate	Vote	Candidate			Rep.	Dem.	Rep.	Dem.
2004	919,960	531,190	Huntsman, Jon Jr.	380,359	Matheson, Scott M. Jr.	8,411	150,831 R	57.7%	41.3%	58.3%	41.7%
2000	761,806	424,837	Leavitt, Michael O.	321,979	Orton, Bill	14,990	102,858 R	55.8%	42.3%	56.9%	43.1%
1996	671,879	503,693	Leavitt, Michael O.	156,616	Bradley, Jim	11,570	347,077 R	75.0%	23.3%	76.3%	23.7%
1992**	762,549	321,713	Leavitt, Michael O.	177,181	Hanson, Stewart	263,655	65,960 R	42.2%	23.2%	64.5%	35.5%
1988**	649,114	260,462	Bangerter, Norman H.	249,321	Wilson, Ted	139,331	11,141 R	40.1%	38.4%	51.1%	48.9%
1984	629,619	351,792	Bangerter, Norman H.	275,669	Owens, Wayne	2,158	76,123 R	55.9%	43.8%	56.1%	43.9%
1980	600,019	266,578	Wright, Bob	330,974	Matheson, Scott M.	2,467	64,396 D	44.4%	55.2%	44.6%	55.4%
1976	539,649	248,027	Romney, Vernon B.	280,706	Matheson, Scott M.	10,916	32,679 D	46.0%	52.0%	46.9%	53.1%
1972	476,447	144,449	Strike, Nicholas L.	331,998	Rampton, Calvin L.		187,549 D	30.3%	69.7%	30.3%	69.7%
1968	421,012	131,729	Buehner, Carl W.	289,283	Rampton, Calvin L.		157,554 D	31.3%	68.7%	31.3%	68.7%
1964	398,256	171,300	Melich, Mitchell	226,956	Rampton, Calvin L.		55,656 D	43.0%	57.0%	43.0%	57.0%
1960	371,489	195,634	Clyde, George D.	175,855	Barlocker, W. A.		19,779 R	52.7%	47.3%	52.7%	47.3%
1956**	332,889	127,164	Clyde, George D.	111,297	Romney, L. C.	94,428	15,867 R	38.2%	33.4%	53.3%	46.7%
1952	327,704	180,516	Lee, J. Bracken	147,188	Glade, Earl J.		33,328 R	55.1%	44.9%	55.1%	44.9%
1948	275,067	151,253	Lee, J. Bracken	123,814	Maw, Herbert B.		27,439 R	55.0%	45.0%	55.0%	45.0%

**In past elections, the other vote included: 1992 - 255,753 Independent (Merrill Cook), who finished second; 1988 - 136,651 Independent (Cook); 1956 - 94,428 Independent (J. Bracken Lee).

POSTWAR VOTE FOR SENATOR

Year	Total Vote	Republican		Democratic		Other Vote	Rep.-Dem. Plurality	Percentage			
								Total Vote		Major Vote	
		Vote	Candidate	Vote	Candidate			Rep.	Dem.	Rep.	Dem.
2006	571,252	356,238	Hatch, Orrin G.	177,459	Ashdown, Pete	37,555	178,779 R	62.4%	31.1%	66.7%	33.3%
2004	911,726	626,640	Bennett, Robert F.	258,955	Van Dam, R. Paul	26,131	367,685 R	68.7%	28.4%	70.8%	29.2%
2000	769,704	504,803	Hatch, Orrin G.	242,569	Howell, Scott N.	22,332	262,234 R	65.6%	31.5%	67.5%	32.5%
1998	494,909	316,652	Bennett, Robert F.	163,172	Leckman, Scott	15,085	153,480 R	64.0%	33.0%	66.0%	34.0%
1994	519,323	357,297	Hatch, Orrin G.	146,938	Shea, Patrick A.	15,088	210,359 R	68.8%	28.3%	70.9%	29.1%
1992	758,479	420,069	Bennett, Robert F.	301,228	Owens, Wayne	37,182	118,841 R	55.4%	39.7%	58.2%	41.8%
1988	640,702	430,089	Hatch, Orrin G.	203,364	Moss, Brian H.	7,249	226,725 R	67.1%	31.7%	67.9%	32.1%
1986	435,111	314,608	Garn, E. J.	115,523	Oliver, Craig	4,980	199,085 R	72.3%	26.6%	73.1%	26.9%
1982	530,802	309,332	Hatch, Orrin G.	219,482	Wilson, Ted	1,988	89,850 R	58.3%	41.3%	58.5%	41.5%
1980	594,298	437,675	Garn, E. J.	151,454	Berman, Dan	5,169	286,221 R	73.6%	25.5%	74.3%	25.7%
1976	540,108	290,221	Hatch, Orrin G.	241,948	Moss, Frank E.	7,939	48,273 R	53.7%	44.8%	54.5%	45.5%
1974	420,642	210,299	Garn, E. J.	185,377	Owens, Wayne	24,966	24,922 R	50.0%	44.1%	53.1%	46.9%
1970	374,303	159,004	Burton, Laurence J.	210,207	Moss, Frank E.	5,092	51,203 D	42.5%	56.2%	43.1%	56.9%
1968	419,262	225,075	Bennett, Wallace F.	192,168	Weilenmann, Milton	2,019	32,907 R	53.7%	45.8%	53.9%	46.1%
1964	397,384	169,562	Wilkinson, Ernest L.	227,822	Moss, Frank E.		58,260 D	42.7%	57.3%	42.7%	57.3%
1962	318,411	166,755	Bennett, Wallace F.	151,656	King, David S.		15,099 R	52.4%	47.6%	52.4%	47.6%
1958**	291,311	101,471	Watkins, Arthur V.	112,827	Moss, Frank E.	77,013	11,356 D	34.8%	38.7%	47.4%	52.6%
1956	330,381	178,261	Bennett, Wallace F.	152,120	Hopkin, Alonzo F.		26,141 R	54.0%	46.0%	54.0%	46.0%
1952	327,033	177,435	Watkins, Arthur V.	149,598	Granger, Walter K.		27,837 R	54.3%	45.7%	54.3%	45.7%
1950	264,440	142,427	Bennett, Wallace F.	121,198	Thomas, Elbert D.	815	21,229 R	53.9%	45.8%	54.0%	46.0%
1946	197,399	101,142	Watkins, Arthur V.	96,257	Murdock, Abe		4,885 R	51.2%	48.8%	51.2%	48.8%

**In past elections, the other vote included: 1958 - 77,013 Independent (J. Bracken Lee).

UTAH

SENATOR 2006

2000 Census Population	County	Total Vote	Republican	Democratic	Other	Rep.-Dem. Plurality	Percentage Total Vote Rep.	Dem.	Major Vote Rep.	Dem.
6,005	BEAVER	2,293	1,688	435	170	1,253 R	73.6%	19.0%	79.5%	20.5%
42,745	BOX ELDER	12,761	9,422	2,374	965	7,048 R	73.8%	18.6%	79.9%	20.1%
91,391	CACHE	21,195	14,611	4,412	2,172	10,199 R	68.9%	20.8%	76.8%	23.2%
20,422	CARBON	4,875	2,408	2,255	212	153 R	49.4%	46.3%	51.6%	48.4%
921	DAGGETT	558	402	127	29	275 R	72.0%	22.8%	76.0%	24.0%
238,994	DAVIS	61,009	43,023	14,632	3,354	28,391 R	70.5%	24.0%	74.6%	25.4%
14,371	DUCHESNE	3,962	3,098	574	290	2,524 R	78.2%	14.5%	84.4%	15.6%
10,860	EMERY	3,805	2,764	780	261	1,984 R	72.6%	20.5%	78.0%	22.0%
4,735	GARFIELD	1,658	1,324	253	81	1,071 R	79.9%	15.3%	84.0%	16.0%
8,485	GRAND	2,921	1,425	1,272	224	153 R	48.8%	43.5%	52.8%	47.2%
33,779	IRON	9,858	7,274	1,701	883	5,573 R	73.8%	17.3%	81.0%	19.0%
8,238	JUAB	3,260	2,200	729	331	1,471 R	67.5%	22.4%	75.1%	24.9%
6,046	KANE	2,353	1,701	518	134	1,183 R	72.3%	22.0%	76.7%	23.3%
12,405	MILLARD	3,887	2,667	626	594	2,041 R	68.6%	16.1%	81.0%	19.0%
7,129	MORGAN	3,403	2,558	577	268	1,981 R	75.2%	17.0%	81.6%	18.4%
1,435	PIUTE	734	595	99	40	496 R	81.1%	13.5%	85.7%	14.3%
1,961	RICH	835	702	86	47	616 R	84.1%	10.3%	89.1%	10.9%
898,387	SALT LAKE	222,823	113,359	96,779	12,685	16,580 R	50.9%	43.4%	53.9%	46.1%
14,413	SAN JUAN	3,977	2,529	1,220	228	1,309 R	63.6%	30.7%	67.5%	32.5%
22,763	SANPETE	6,567	4,726	1,094	747	3,632 R	72.0%	16.7%	81.2%	18.8%
18,842	SEVIER	5,719	4,324	830	565	3,494 R	75.6%	14.5%	83.9%	16.1%
29,736	SUMMIT	11,043	4,980	5,322	741	342 D	45.1%	48.2%	48.3%	51.7%
40,735	TOOELE	12,178	7,794	3,438	946	4,356 R	64.0%	28.2%	69.4%	30.6%
25,224	UINTAH	5,975	4,690	815	470	3,875 R	78.5%	13.6%	85.2%	14.8%
368,536	UTAH	85,843	65,413	14,464	5,966	50,949 R	76.2%	16.8%	81.9%	18.1%
15,215	WASATCH	6,006	4,062	1,587	357	2,475 R	67.6%	26.4%	71.9%	28.1%
90,354	WASHINGTON	28,978	20,746	6,220	2,012	14,526 R	71.6%	21.5%	76.9%	23.1%
2,509	WAYNE	1,167	890	210	67	680 R	76.3%	18.0%	80.9%	19.1%
196,533	WEBER	41,609	24,863	14,030	2,716	10,833 R	59.8%	33.7%	63.9%	36.1%
2,233,169	TOTAL	571,252	356,238	177,459	37,555	178,779 R	62.4%	31.1%	66.7%	33.3%

UTAH

HOUSE OF REPRESENTATIVES

CD	Year	Total Vote	Republican Vote	Candidate	Democratic Vote	Candidate	Other Vote	Rep.-Dem. Plurality	Percentage Total Vote Rep.	Dem.	Major Vote Rep.	Dem.
1	2006	178,474	112,546	BISHOP, ROB*	57,922	OLSEN, STEVEN	8,006	54,624 R	63.1%	32.5%	66.0%	34.0%
1	2004	293,961	199,615	BISHOP, ROB*	85,630	THOMPSON, STEVEN	8,716	113,985 R	67.9%	29.1%	70.0%	30.0%
1	2002	179,412	109,265	BISHOP, ROB	66,104	THOMAS, DAVE	4,043	43,161 R	60.9%	36.8%	62.3%	37.7%
2	2006	225,818	84,234	CHRISTENSEN, LAVAR	133,231	MATHESON, JIM*	8,353	48,997 D	37.3%	59.0%	38.7%	61.3%
2	2004	341,968	147,778	SWALLOW, JOHN	187,250	MATHESON, JIM*	6,940	39,472 D	43.2%	54.8%	44.1%	55.9%
2	2002	224,098	109,123	SWALLOW, JOHN	110,764	MATHESON, JIM*	4,211	1,641 D	48.7%	49.4%	49.6%	50.4%
3	2006	165,398	95,455	CANNON, CHRIS*	53,330	BURRIDGE, CHRISTIAN	16,613	42,125 R	57.7%	32.2%	64.2%	35.8%
3	2004	272,928	173,010	CANNON, CHRIS*	88,748	BABKA, BEAU	11,170	84,262 R	63.4%	32.5%	66.1%	33.9%
3	2002	153,643	103,598	CANNON, CHRIS*	44,533	WOODSIDE, NANCY JANE	5,512	59,065 R	67.4%	29.0%	69.9%	30.1%
TOTAL	2006	569,690	292,235		244,483		32,972	47,752 R	51.3%	42.9%	54.4%	45.6%
TOTAL	2004	908,857	520,403		361,628		26,826	158,775 R	57.3%	39.8%	59.0%	41.0%
TOTAL	2002	557,153	321,986		221,401		13,766	100,585 R	57.8%	39.7%	59.3%	40.7%

An asterisk (*) denotes incumbent.

UTAH

GENERAL AND PRIMARY ELECTIONS

2006 GENERAL ELECTIONS

Senator   Other vote was 21,526 Constitution (Scott N. Bradley); 9,089 Personal Choice (Roger I. Price); 4,428 Libertarian (Dave Seely); 2,512 Desert Greens (Julian Hatch).

House   Other vote was:

CD 1   5,539 Constitution (Mark Hudson); 2,467 Libertarian (Lynn Badler).
CD 2   3,395 Constitution (W. David Perry); 3,338 Green (Bob Brister); 1,620 Libertarian (Austin Sherwood Lett).
CD 3   14,533 Constitution (Jim Noorlander); 2,080 Libertarian (Philip Lear Hallman).

2006 PRIMARY ELECTIONS

Primary	June 27, 2006	**Registration** (as of June 27, 2006)	1,286,694	In process of instituting registration by party

Note: Rich County did not have a primary in June 2006 and is not included in the statewide registration total.

Primary Type   Any registered voter could participate in the Democratic primary. Only registered Republicans could vote in the Republican primary. (As of May 2007, there were 531,104 registered Republicans in Utah and 121,507 registered Democrats.)

Note: An asterisk (*) denotes incumbent. Candidates in Utah are usually nominated by convention. It is up to each party to determine the percentage of the convention vote that is needed to force a primary.

	REPUBLICAN PRIMARIES			**DEMOCRATIC PRIMARIES**	
Senator	Orrin G. Hatch*	Nominated by convention		Pete Ashdown	Nominated by convention
Congressional District 1	Rob Bishop*	Nominated by convention		Steven Olsen	Nominated by convention
Congressional District 2	Lavar Christensen	Nominated by convention		Jim Matheson*	Nominated by convention
Congressional District 3	Chris Cannon*	32,881	55.7%	Christian Burridge	Nominated by convention
	John D. Jacob	26,143	44.3%		
	TOTAL	59,024			

VERMONT

One member At Large

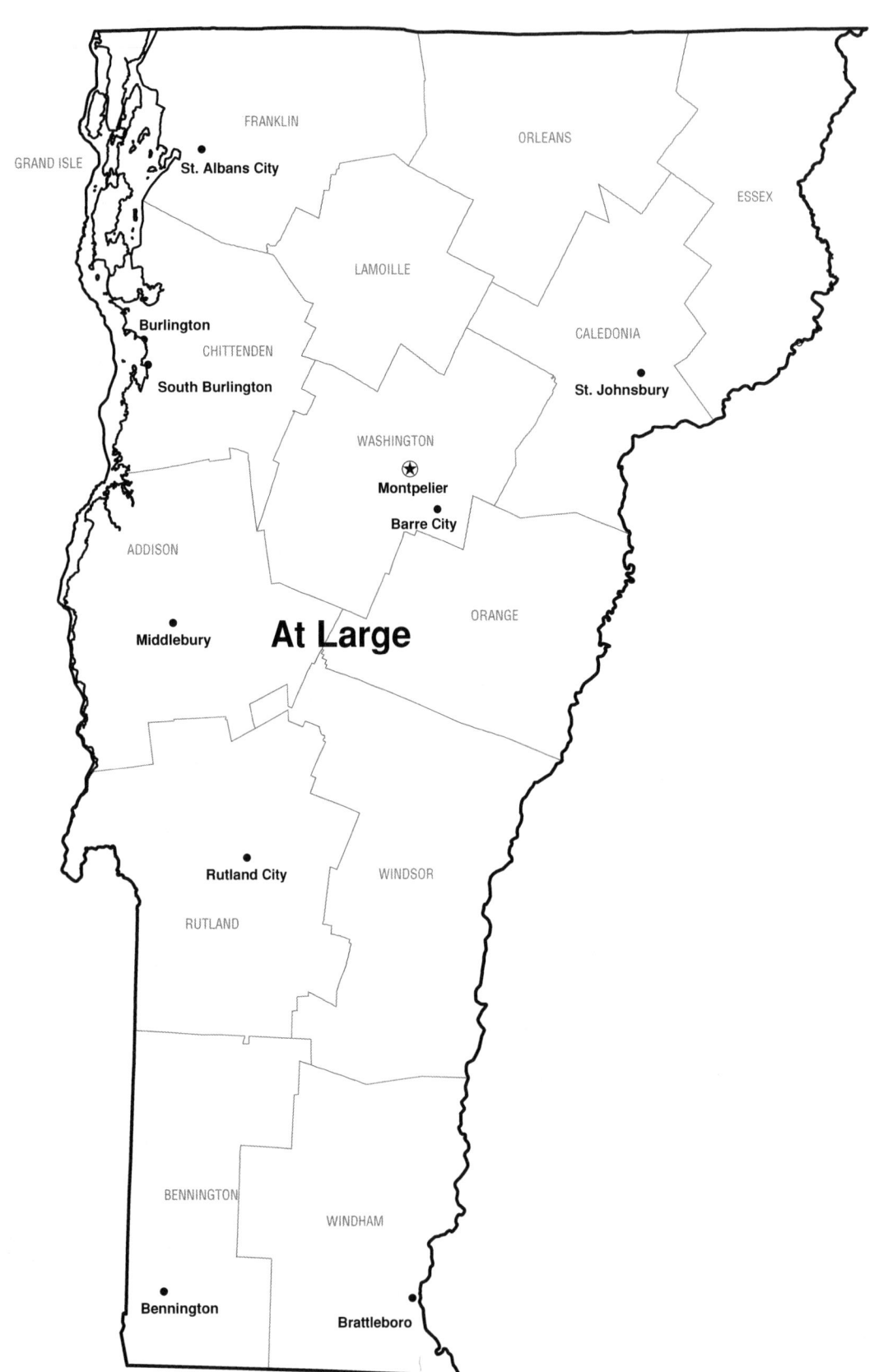

VERMONT

GOVERNOR
Jim Douglas (R). Reelected 2006 to a two-year term. Previously elected 2004 and January 2003 by the State Legislature. Douglas had finished first in the 2002 general election but failed to win a majority of the vote as required by Vermont law.

SENATORS (1 Democrat, 1 Independent)
Bernard Sanders (I). Elected 2006 to a six-year term.

Patrick J. Leahy (D). Reelected 2004 to a six-year term. Previously elected 1998, 1992, 1986, 1980, 1974.

REPRESENTATIVES (1 Democrat)
At Large. Peter Welch (D)

POSTWAR VOTE FOR PRESIDENT

Year	Total Vote	Republican		Democratic		Other Vote	Plurality	Percentage			
								Total Vote		Major Vote	
		Vote	Candidate	Vote	Candidate			Rep.	Dem.	Rep.	Dem.
2004	312,309	121,180	Bush, George W.	184,067	Kerry, John	7,062	62,887 D	38.8%	58.9%	39.7%	60.3%
2000**	294,308	119,775	Bush, George W.	149,022	Gore, Al	25,511	29,247 D	40.7%	50.6%	44.6%	55.4%
1996**	258,449	80,352	Dole, Bob	137,894	Clinton, Bill	40,203	57,542 D	31.1%	53.4%	36.8%	63.2%
1992**	289,701	88,122	Bush, George	133,592	Clinton, Bill	67,987	45,470 D	30.4%	46.1%	39.7%	60.3%
1988	243,328	124,331	Bush, George	115,775	Dukakis, Michael S.	3,222	8,556 R	51.1%	47.6%	51.8%	48.2%
1984	234,561	135,865	Reagan, Ronald	95,730	Mondale, Walter F.	2,966	40,135 R	57.9%	40.8%	58.7%	41.3%
1980**	213,299	94,628	Reagan, Ronald	81,952	Carter, Jimmy	36,719	12,676 R	44.4%	38.4%	53.6%	46.4%
1976	187,765	102,085	Ford, Gerald R.	80,954	Carter, Jimmy	4,726	21,131 R	54.4%	43.1%	55.8%	44.2%
1972	186,947	117,149	Nixon, Richard M.	68,174	McGovern, George S.	1,624	48,975 R	62.7%	36.5%	63.2%	36.8%
1968**	161,404	85,142	Nixon, Richard M.	70,255	Humphrey, Hubert H.	6,007	14,887 R	52.8%	43.5%	54.8%	45.2%
1964	163,089	54,942	Goldwater, Barry M.	108,127	Johnson, Lyndon B.	20	53,185 D	33.7%	66.3%	33.7%	66.3%
1960	167,324	98,131	Nixon, Richard M.	69,186	Kennedy, John F.	7	28,945 R	58.6%	41.3%	58.6%	41.4%
1956	152,978	110,390	Eisenhower, Dwight D.	42,549	Stevenson, Adlai E.	39	67,841 R	72.2%	27.8%	72.2%	27.8%
1952	153,557	109,717	Eisenhower, Dwight D.	43,355	Stevenson, Adlai E.	485	66,362 R	71.5%	28.2%	71.7%	28.3%
1948	123,382	75,926	Dewey, Thomas E.	45,557	Truman, Harry S.	1,899	30,369 R	61.5%	36.9%	62.5%	37.5%

**In past elections, the other vote included: 2000 - 20,374 Green (Ralph Nader); 1996 - 31,024 Reform (Ross Perot); 1992 - 65,991 Independent (Ross Perot); 1980 - 31,761 Independent (John Anderson); 1968 - 5,104 American Independent (George Wallace).

VERMONT

POSTWAR VOTE FOR GOVERNOR

Year	Total Vote	Republican		Democratic		Other Vote	Rep.-Dem. Plurality	Percentage			
								Total Vote		Major Vote	
		Vote	Candidate	Vote	Candidate			Rep.	Dem.	Rep.	Dem.
2006	262,524	148,014	Douglas, Jim	108,090	Parker, Scudder	6,420	39,924 R	56.4%	41.2%	57.8%	42.2%
2004	309,285	181,540	Douglas, Jim	117,327	Clavelle, Peter	10,418	64,213 R	58.7%	37.9%	60.7%	39.3%
2002**	230,161	103,436	Douglas, Jim	97,565	Racine, Doug	29,160	5,871 R	44.9%	42.4%	51.5%	48.5%
2000	293,473	111,359	Dwyer, Ruth	148,059	Dean, Howard B.	34,055	36,700 D	37.9%	50.5%	42.9%	57.1%
1998	218,120	89,726	Dwyer, Ruth	121,425	Dean, Howard B.	6,969	31,699 D	41.1%	55.7%	42.5%	57.5%
1996	254,648	57,161	Gropper, John L.	179,544	Dean, Howard B.	17,943	122,383 D	22.4%	70.5%	24.1%	75.9%
1994	212,046	40,292	Kelley, David F.	145,661	Dean, Howard B.	26,093	105,369 D	19.0%	68.7%	21.7%	78.3%
1992	285,728	65,837	McClaughry, John	213,523	Dean, Howard B.	6,368	147,686 D	23.0%	74.7%	23.6%	76.4%
1990	211,422	109,540	Snelling, Richard A.	97,321	Welch, Peter	4,561	12,219 R	51.8%	46.0%	53.0%	47.0%
1988	243,130	105,319	Bernhardt, Michael	134,594	Kunin, Madeleine M.	3,253	29,275 D	43.3%	55.4%	43.9%	56.1%
1986**	196,716	75,162	Smith, Peter	92,379	Kunin, Madeleine M.	29,175	17,217 D	38.2%	47.0%	44.9%	55.1%
1984	233,753	113,264	Easton, John J.	116,938	Kunin, Madeleine M.	3,551	3,674 D	48.5%	50.0%	49.2%	50.8%
1982	169,251	93,111	Snelling, Richard A.	74,394	Kunin, Madeleine M.	1,746	18,717 R	55.0%	44.0%	55.6%	44.4%
1980	210,381	123,229	Snelling, Richard A.	77,363	Diamond, J. Jerome	9,789	45,866 R	58.6%	36.8%	61.4%	38.6%
1978	124,482	78,181	Snelling, Richard A.	42,482	Granai, Edwin C.	3,819	35,699 R	62.8%	34.1%	64.8%	35.2%
1976	185,929	99,268	Snelling, Richard A.	75,262	Hackel, Stella B.	11,399	24,006 R	53.4%	40.5%	56.9%	43.1%
1974	141,156	53,672	Kennedy, Walter L.	79,842	Salmon, Thomas P.	7,642	26,170 D	38.0%	56.6%	40.2%	59.8%
1972	189,237	82,491	Hackett, Luther F.	104,533	Salmon, Thomas P.	2,213	22,042 D	43.6%	55.2%	44.1%	55.9%
1970	153,528	87,458	Davis, Deane C.	66,028	O'Brien, Leo	42	21,430 R	57.0%	43.0%	57.0%	43.0%
1968	161,089	89,387	Davis, Deane C.	71,656	Daley, John J.	46	17,731 R	55.5%	44.5%	55.5%	44.5%
1966	136,262	57,577	Snelling, Richard A.	78,669	Hoff, Philip H.	16	21,092 D	42.3%	57.7%	42.3%	57.7%
1964	164,199	57,576	Foote, Ralph A.	106,611	Hoff, Philip H.	12	49,035 D	35.1%	64.9%	35.1%	64.9%
1962	121,422	60,035	Keyser, F. Ray	61,383	Hoff, Philip H.	4	1,348 D	49.4%	50.6%	49.4%	50.6%
1960	164,632	92,861	Keyser, F. Ray	71,755	Niquette, Russell F.	16	21,106 R	56.4%	43.6%	56.4%	43.6%
1958	123,728	62,222	Stafford, Robert T.	61,503	Leddy, Bernard J.	3	719 R	50.3%	49.7%	50.3%	49.7%
1956	153,809	88,379	Johnson, Joseph B.	65,420	Branon, E. Frank	10	22,959 R	57.5%	42.5%	57.5%	42.5%
1954	114,360	59,778	Johnson, Joseph B.	54,554	Branon, E. Frank	28	5,224 R	52.3%	47.7%	52.3%	47.7%
1952	150,862	78,338	Emerson, Lee E.	60,051	Larrow, Robert W.	12,473	18,287 R	51.9%	39.8%	56.6%	43.4%
1950	87,155	64,915	Emerson, Lee E.	22,227	Moran, J. Edward	13	42,688 R	74.5%	25.5%	74.5%	25.5%
1948	120,183	86,394	Gibson, Ernest W. Jr.	33,588	Ryan, Charles F.	201	52,806 R	71.9%	27.9%	72.0%	28.0%
1946	72,044	57,849	Gibson, Ernest W. Jr.	14,096	Coburn, Berthold	99	43,753 R	80.3%	19.6%	80.4%	19.6%

**In past elections, the other vote included: 1986 - 28,430 Independent (Bernard Sanders). In 2002 and 1986, in the absence of a majority for any candidate, the state legislature elected the governor — Republican Jim Douglas in January 2003, Democrat Madeleine M. Kunin in January 1987.

VERMONT

POSTWAR VOTE FOR SENATOR

Year	Total Vote	Republican		Democratic		Other Vote	Plurality	Percentage			
								Total Vote		Major Vote	
		Vote	Candidate	Vote	Candidate			Rep.	Dem.	Rep.	Dem.
2006**	262,419	84,924	Tarrant, Rich		—	177,495	86,714 I	32.4%		100.0%	
2004	307,208	75,398	McMullen, Jack	216,972	Leahy, Patrick J.	14,838	141,574 D	24.5%	70.6%	25.8%	74.2%
2000	288,500	189,133	Jeffords, James M.	73,352	Flanagan, Ed	26,015	115,781 R	65.6%	25.4%	72.1%	27.9%
1998	214,036	48,051	Tuttle, Fred H.	154,567	Leahy, Patrick J.	11,418	106,516 D	22.4%	72.2%	23.7%	76.3%
1994	211,672	106,505	Jeffords, James M.	85,868	Backus, Jan	19,299	20,637 R	50.3%	40.6%	55.4%	44.6%
1992	285,739	123,854	Douglas, Jim	154,762	Leahy, Patrick J.	7,123	30,908 D	43.3%	54.2%	44.5%	55.5%
1988	240,111	163,203	Jeffords, James M.	71,469	Gray, William	5,439	91,736 R	68.0%	29.8%	69.5%	30.5%
1986	196,532	67,798	Snelling, Richard A.	124,123	Leahy, Patrick J.	4,611	56,325 D	34.5%	63.2%	35.3%	64.7%
1982	168,003	84,450	Stafford, Robert T.	79,340	Guest, James A.	4,213	5,110 R	50.3%	47.2%	51.6%	48.4%
1980	209,124	101,421	Ledbetter, Stewart M.	104,176	Leahy, Patrick J.	3,527	2,755 D	48.5%	49.8%	49.3%	50.7%
1976	189,060	94,481	Stafford, Robert T.	85,682	Salmon, Thomas P.	8,897	8,799 R	50.0%	45.3%	52.4%	47.6%
1974	142,772	66,223	Mallary, Richard W.	70,629	Leahy, Patrick J.	5,920	4,406 D	46.4%	49.5%	48.4%	51.6%
1972S	71,348	45,888	Stafford, Robert T.	23,842	Major, Randolph T.	1,618	22,046 R	64.3%	33.4%	65.8%	34.2%
1970	154,899	91,198	Prouty, Winston L.	62,271	Hoff, Philip H.	1,430	28,927 R	58.9%	40.2%	59.4%	40.6%
1968**	157,375	157,154	Aiken, George D.		—	221	157,154 R	99.9%		100.0%	
1964	164,350	87,879	Prouty, Winston L.	76,457	Fayette, Frederick J.	14	11,422 R	53.5%	46.5%	53.5%	46.5%
1962	121,571	81,241	Aiken, George D.	40,134	Johnson, W. Robert	196	41,107 R	66.8%	33.0%	66.9%	33.1%
1958	124,442	64,900	Prouty, Winston L.	59,536	Fayette, Frederick J.	6	5,364 R	52.2%	47.8%	52.2%	47.8%
1956	155,289	103,101	Aiken, George D.	52,184	O'Shea, Bernard G.	4	50,917 R	66.4%	33.6%	66.4%	33.6%
1952	154,052	111,406	Flanders, Ralph E.	42,630	Johnston, Allan R.	16	68,776 R	72.3%	27.7%	72.3%	27.7%
1950	89,171	69,543	Aiken, George D.	19,608	Bigelow, James E.	20	49,935 R	78.0%	22.0%	78.0%	22.0%
1946	73,340	54,729	Flanders, Ralph E.	18,594	McDevitt, Charles P.	17	36,135 R	74.6%	25.4%	74.6%	25.4%

**In past elections, the other vote included: 2006 - 171,638 Independent (Bernard Sanders). Sanders received 65.4 percent of the total vote and won the election with a 86,714 vote plurality. The January 1972 election was for a short term to fill a vacancy. In 1968 the Republican candidate won both major party nominations.

VERMONT

GOVERNOR 2006

2000 Census Population	County	Total Vote	Republican	Democratic	Other	Rep.-Dem. Plurality	Percentage			
							Total Vote		Major Vote	
							Rep.	Dem.	Rep.	Dem.
35,974	ADDISON	16,349	9,336	6,780	233	2,556 R	57.1%	41.5%	57.9%	42.1%
36,994	BENNINGTON	14,443	7,492	6,434	517	1,058 R	51.9%	44.5%	53.8%	46.2%
29,702	CALEDONIA	12,188	7,611	4,276	301	3,335 R	62.4%	35.1%	64.0%	36.0%
146,571	CHITTENDEN	66,226	37,097	27,982	1147	9,115 R	56.0%	42.3%	57.0%	43.0%
6,459	ESSEX	2,542	1,696	729	117	967 R	66.7%	28.7%	69.9%	30.1%
45,417	FRANKLIN	17,554	12,056	5,145	353	6,911 R	68.7%	29.3%	70.1%	29.9%
6,901	GRAND ISLE	3,667	2,350	1,229	88	1,121 R	64.1%	33.5%	65.7%	34.3%
23,233	LAMOILLE	10,457	5,970	4,233	254	1,737 R	57.1%	40.5%	58.5%	41.5%
28,226	ORANGE	12,473	6,900	5,262	311	1,638 R	55.3%	42.2%	56.7%	43.3%
26,277	ORLEANS	10,383	6,566	3,531	286	3,035 R	63.2%	34.0%	65.0%	35.0%
63,400	RUTLAND	25,521	16,298	8,534	689	7,764 R	63.9%	33.4%	65.6%	34.4%
58,039	WASHINGTON	27,268	14,003	12,688	577	1,315 R	51.4%	46.5%	52.5%	47.5%
44,216	WINDHAM	18,563	7,204	10,666	693	3,462 D	38.8%	57.5%	40.3%	59.7%
57,418	WINDSOR	24,890	13,435	10,601	854	2,834 R	54.0%	42.6%	55.9%	44.1%
608,827	TOTAL	262,524	148,014	108,090	6,420	39,924 R	56.4%	41.2%	57.8%	42.2%

Note: Bernard Sanders won the Senate election running as an independent. There was no Democratic candidate. The plurality represents the difference in the vote for Sanders and the Republican candidate. In the percentage columns, Sanders' share of the total vote and of the Sanders–Republican vote is featured.

	City/Town									
9,291	BARRE CITY	3,265	1,939	1,267	59	672 R	59.4%	38.8%	60.5%	39.5%
7,602	BARRE TOWN	3,673	2,573	1,052	48	1,521 R	70.1%	28.6%	71.0%	29.0%
15,737	BENNINGTON	5,157	2,437	2,542	178	105 D	47.3%	49.3%	48.9%	51.1%
12,005	BRATTLEBORO	4,721	1,442	3,155	124	1,713 D	30.5%	66.8%	31.4%	68.6%
38,889	BURLINGTON	14,909	5,744	8,721	444	2,977 D	38.5%	58.5%	39.7%	60.3%
16,986	COLCHESTER	6,476	4,328	2,034	114	2,294 R	66.8%	31.4%	68.0%	32.0%
4,604	DERBY	1,816	1,228	552	36	676 R	67.6%	30.4%	69.0%	31.0%
18,626	ESSEX	8,996	5,991	2,876	129	3,115 R	66.6%	32.0%	67.6%	32.4%
10,367	HARTFORD	3,766	2,119	1,548	99	571 R	56.3%	41.1%	57.8%	42.2%
5,015	JERICHO	2,702	1,570	1,096	36	474 R	58.1%	40.6%	58.9%	41.1%
5,448	LYNDON	1,890	1,304	542	44	762 R	69.0%	28.7%	70.6%	29.4%
4,180	MANCHESTER	1,829	1,124	661	44	463 R	61.5%	36.1%	63.0%	37.0%
8,183	MIDDLEBURY	2,836	1,400	1,402	34	2 D	49.4%	49.4%	50.0%	50.0%
9,479	MILTON	3,912	2,845	1,018	49	1,827 R	72.7%	26.0%	73.6%	26.4%
8,035	MONTPELIER	4,093	1,457	2,559	77	1,102 D	35.6%	62.5%	36.3%	63.7%
5,139	MORRISTOWN	2,220	1,276	889	55	387 R	57.5%	40.0%	58.9%	41.1%
5,791	NORTHFIELD	2,026	1,316	670	40	646 R	65.0%	33.1%	66.3%	33.7%
4,853	RANDOLPH	2,028	1,158	843	27	315 R	57.1%	41.6%	57.9%	42.1%
4,090	RICHMOND	2,156	1,144	987	25	157 R	53.1%	45.8%	53.7%	46.3%
5,309	ROCKINGHAM	1,894	770	1,029	95	259 D	40.7%	54.3%	42.8%	57.2%
17,292	RUTLAND CITY	6,067	3,804	2,118	145	1,686 R	62.7%	34.9%	64.2%	35.8%
4,038	RUTLAND TOWN	2,111	1,531	534	46	997 R	72.5%	25.3%	74.1%	25.9%
6,944	SHELBURNE	3,962	2,272	1,653	37	619 R	57.3%	41.7%	57.9%	42.1%
15,814	SOUTH BURLINGTON	7,958	4,719	3,152	87	1,567 R	59.3%	39.6%	60.0%	40.0%
9,078	SPRINGFIELD	3,511	1,983	1,365	163	618 R	56.5%	38.9%	59.2%	40.8%
7,650	ST. ALBANS CITY	2,273	1,503	730	40	773 R	66.1%	32.1%	67.3%	32.7%
5,086	ST. ALBANS TOWN	2,385	1,770	580	35	1,190 R	74.2%	24.3%	75.3%	24.7%
7,571	ST. JOHNSBURY	2,592	1,660	879	53	781 R	64.0%	33.9%	65.4%	34.6%
2,548	SWANTON	2,280	1,661	583	36	1,078 R	72.9%	25.6%	74.0%	26.0%
4,915	WATERBURY	2,371	1,280	1,053	38	227 R	54.0%	44.4%	54.9%	45.1%
7,650	WILLISTON	4,422	2,881	1,501	40	1,380 R	65.2%	33.9%	65.7%	34.3%
6,561	WINOOSKI	2,074	1,097	912	65	185 R	52.9%	44.0%	54.6%	45.4%
3,232	WOODSTOCK	1,676	905	736	35	169 R	54.0%	43.9%	55.1%	44.9%

VERMONT

SENATOR 2006

2000 Census Population	County	Total Vote	Republican	Democratic	Independent (Sanders)	Other	Plurality	Percentage Total Vote Rep.	Ind.	Sanders/Rep. Vote Rep.	Ind.
35,974	ADDISON	16,335	4,834		11,257	244	6,423 I	29.6%	68.9%	30.0%	70.0%
36,994	BENNINGTON	14,398	4,844		8,865	689	4,021 I	33.6%	61.6%	35.3%	64.7%
29,702	CALEDONIA	12,165	4,472		7,414	279	2,942 I	36.8%	60.9%	37.6%	62.4%
146,571	CHITTENDEN	66,306	22,603		42,861	842	20,258 I	34.1%	64.6%	34.5%	65.5%
6,459	ESSEX	2,523	925		1,480	118	555 I	36.7%	58.7%	38.5%	61.5%
45,417	FRANKLIN	17,524	6,406		10,830	288	4,424 I	36.6%	61.8%	37.2%	62.8%
6,901	GRAND ISLE	3,665	1,423		2,174	68	751 I	38.8%	59.3%	39.6%	60.4%
23,233	LAMOILLE	10,468	3,106		7,183	179	4,077 I	29.7%	68.6%	30.2%	69.8%
28,226	ORANGE	12,410	3,667		8,426	317	4,759 I	29.5%	67.9%	30.3%	69.7%
26,277	ORLEANS	10,383	3,690		6,456	237	2,766 I	35.5%	62.2%	36.4%	63.6%
63,400	RUTLAND	25,533	9,282		15,629	622	6,347 I	36.4%	61.2%	37.3%	62.7%
58,039	WASHINGTON	27,216	7,934		18,760	522	10,826 I	29.2%	68.9%	29.7%	70.3%
44,216	WINDHAM	18,584	4,613		13,245	726	8,632 I	24.8%	71.3%	25.8%	74.2%
57,418	WINDSOR	24,909	7,125		17,058	726	9,933 I	28.6%	68.5%	29.5%	70.5%
608,827	TOTAL	262,419	84,924		171,638	5,857	86,714 I	32.4%	65.4%	33.1%	66.9%
	City/Town										
9,291	BARRE CITY	3,260	1,081		2,107	72	1,026 I	33.2%	64.6%	33.9%	66.1%
7,602	BARRE TOWN	3,662	1,565		2,042	55	477 I	42.7%	55.8%	43.4%	56.6%
15,737	BENNINGTON	5,133	1,492		3,400	241	1,908 I	29.1%	66.2%	30.5%	69.5%
12,005	BRATTLEBORO	4,730	868		3,728	134	2,860 I	18.4%	78.8%	18.9%	81.1%
38,889	BURLINGTON	14,977	3,258		11,498	221	8,240 I	21.8%	76.8%	22.1%	77.9%
16,986	COLCHESTER	6,492	2,724		3,693	75	969 I	42.0%	56.9%	42.4%	57.6%
4,604	DERBY	1,823	747		1,036	40	289 I	41.0%	56.8%	41.9%	58.1%
18,626	ESSEX	8,999	3,656		5,233	110	1,577 I	40.6%	58.2%	41.1%	58.9%
10,367	HARTFORD	3,762	1,085		2,567	110	1,482 I	28.8%	68.2%	29.7%	70.3%
5,015	JERICHO	2,701	964		1,698	39	734 I	35.7%	62.9%	36.2%	63.8%
5,448	LYNDON	1,887	768		1,087	32	319 I	40.7%	57.6%	41.4%	58.6%
4,180	MANCHESTER	1,826	771		982	73	211 I	42.2%	53.8%	44.0%	56.0%
8,183	MIDDLEBURY	2,841	637		2,159	45	1,522 I	22.4%	76.0%	22.8%	77.2%
9,479	MILTON	3,908	1,600		2,257	51	657 I	40.9%	57.8%	41.5%	58.5%
8,035	MONTPELIER	4,082	876		3,146	60	2,270 I	21.5%	77.1%	21.8%	78.2%
5,139	MORRISTOWN	2,218	599		1,573	46	974 I	27.0%	70.9%	27.6%	72.4%
5,791	NORTHFIELD	2,022	649		1,333	40	684 I	32.1%	65.9%	32.7%	67.3%
4,853	RANDOLPH	2,024	599		1,375	50	776 I	29.6%	67.9%	30.3%	69.7%
4,090	RICHMOND	2,157	653		1,477	27	824 I	30.3%	68.5%	30.7%	69.3%
5,309	ROCKINGHAM	1,900	403		1,408	89	1,005 I	21.2%	74.1%	22.3%	77.7%
17,292	RUTLAND CITY	6,068	2,140		3,787	141	1,647 I	35.3%	62.4%	36.1%	63.9%
4,038	RUTLAND TOWN	2,105	953		1,121	31	168 I	45.3%	53.3%	45.9%	54.1%
6,944	SHELBURNE	3,959	1,551		2,354	54	803 I	39.2%	59.5%	39.7%	60.3%
15,814	SOUTH BURLINGTON	7,945	3,095		4,760	90	1,665 I	39.0%	59.9%	39.4%	60.6%
9,078	SPRINGFIELD	3,518	1,031		2,336	151	1,305 I	29.3%	66.4%	30.6%	69.4%
7,650	ST. ALBANS CITY	2,271	791		1,435	45	644 I	34.8%	63.2%	35.5%	64.5%
5,086	ST. ALBANS TOWN	2,383	1,030		1,320	33	290 I	43.2%	55.4%	43.8%	56.2%
7,571	ST. JOHNSBURY	2,579	985		1,534	60	549 I	38.2%	59.5%	39.1%	60.9%
2,548	SWANTON	2,267	859		1,381	27	522 I	37.9%	60.9%	38.3%	61.7%
4,915	WATERBURY	2,368	677		1,657	34	980 I	28.6%	70.0%	29.0%	71.0%
7,650	WILLISTON	4,419	1,811		2,562	46	751 I	41.0%	58.0%	41.4%	58.6%
6,561	WINOOSKI	2,082	600		1,453	29	853 I	28.8%	69.8%	29.2%	70.8%
3,232	WOODSTOCK	1,680	531		1,115	34	584 I	31.6%	66.4%	32.3%	67.7%

VERMONT

HOUSE OF REPRESENTATIVES

			Republican		Democratic		Other		Percentage Total Vote		Major Vote	
CD	Year	Total Vote	Vote	Candidate	Vote	Candidate	Vote	Plurality**	Rep.	Dem.	Rep.	Dem.
AL	2006	262,726	117,023	RAINVILLE, MARTHA	139,815	WELCH, PETER	5,888	22,792 D	44.5%	53.2%	45.6%	54.4%
AL	2004	305,008	74,271	PARKE, GREG	21,684	DROWN, LARRY	209,053	131,503 I	24.4%	67.5% (I)		
AL	2002	225,476	72,813	MEUB, WILLIAM "BILL"	—		152,663	72,067 I	32.3%	64.3% (I)		
AL	2000	283,366	51,977	KERIN, KAREN ANN	14,918	# DIAMONDSTONE, PETE	216,471	144,141 I	18.3%	69.2% (I)		
AL	1998	215,133	70,740	CANDON, MARK	—		144,393	65,663 I	32.9%	63.4% (I)		
AL	1996	254,706	83,021	SWEETSER, SUSAN W.	23,830	LONG, JACK	147,855	57,657 I	32.6%	55.2% (I)		
AL	1994	211,449	98,523	CARROLL, JOHN	—		112,926	6,979 I	46.6%	49.9% (I)		
AL	1992	281,626	86,901	PHILBIN, TIMOTHY	22,279	YOUNG, LEWIS E.	172,446	75,823 I	30.9%	57.8% (I)		
AL	1990	209,856	82,938	SMITH, PETER*	6,315	SANDOVAL, DOLORES	120,603	34,584 I	39.5%	56.0% (I)		
AL	1988	240,131	98,937	SMITH, PETER	45,330	POIRIER, PAUL N.	95,864	53,607 R	41.2%	18.9%	68.6%	31.4%
AL	1986	188,954	168,403	# JEFFORDS, JAMES M.*	—		20,551	168,403 R	89.1%		100.0%	
AL	1984	226,297	148,025	JEFFORDS, JAMES M.*	60,360	POLLINA, ANTHONY	17,912	87,665 R	65.4%	26.7%	71.0%	29.0%
AL	1982	164,951	114,191	JEFFORDS, JAMES M.*	38,296	KAPLAN, MARK A.	12,464	75,895 R	69.2%	23.2%	74.9%	25.1%
AL	1980	194,697	154,274	JEFFORDS, JAMES M.*	—		40,423	154,274 R	79.2%		100.0%	
AL	1978	120,502	90,688	JEFFORDS, JAMES M.*	23,228	DIETZ, S. MARIE	6,586	67,460 R	75.3%	19.3%	79.6%	20.4%
AL	1976	184,783	124,458	JEFFORDS, JAMES M.*	60,202	# BURGESS, JOHN A.	123	64,256 R	67.4%	32.6%	67.4%	32.6%
AL	1974	140,899	74,561	JEFFORDS, JAMES M.	56,342	# CAIN, FRANCIS J.	9,996	18,219 R	52.9%	40.0%	57.0%	43.0%
AL	1972	186,028	120,924	MALLARY, RICHARD W.	65,062	MEYER, WILLIAM H.	42	55,862 R	65.0%	35.0%	65.0%	35.0%
AL	1970	152,557	103,806	STAFFORD, ROBERT T.*	44,415	O'SHEA, BERNARD G.	4,336	59,391 R	68.0%	29.1%	70.0%	30.0%
AL	1968	157,133	156,956	# STAFFORD, ROBERT T.*	—		177	156,956 R	99.9%		100.0%	
AL	1966	135,748	89,097	STAFFORD, ROBERT T.*	46,643	RYAN, WILLIAM J.	8	42,454 R	65.6%	34.4%	65.6%	34.4%
AL	1964	163,452	92,252	STAFFORD, ROBERT T.*	71,193	O'SHEA, BERNARD G.	7	21,059 R	56.4%	43.6%	56.4%	43.6%
AL	1962	121,381	68,822	STAFFORD, ROBERT T.*	52,535	RAYNOLDS, HAROLD	24	16,287 R	56.7%	43.3%	56.7%	43.3%
AL	1960	166,035	94,905	STAFFORD, ROBERT T.	71,111	MEYER, WILLIAM H.	19	23,794 R	57.2%	42.8%	57.2%	42.8%
AL	1958	122,702	59,536	ARTHUR, HAROLD J.	63,131	MEYER, WILLIAM H.	35	3,595 D	48.5%	51.5%	48.5%	51.5%
AL	1956	154,536	103,736	PROUTY, WINSTON L.*	50,797	ST. AMOUR, CAMILLE	3	52,939 R	67.1%	32.9%	67.1%	32.9%
AL	1954	114,289	70,143	PROUTY, WINSTON L.*	44,141	BAYLAN, JOHN J.	5	26,002 R	61.4%	38.6%	61.4%	38.6%
AL	1952	153,060	109,871	PROUTY, WINSTON L.*	43,187	COMINGS, HERBERT B.	2	66,684 R	71.8%	28.2%	71.8%	28.2%
AL	1950	88,851	65,248	PROUTY, WINSTON L.	22,709	COMINGS, HERBERT B.	894	42,539 R	73.4%	25.6%	74.2%	25.8%
AL	1948	121,968	74,076	PLUMLEY, CHARLES A.*	47,767	READY, ROBERT W.	125	26,309 R	60.7%	39.2%	60.8%	39.2%
AL	1946	73,066	46,985	PLUMLEY, CHARLES A.*	26,056	CALDBECK, MATTHEW J.	25	20,929 R	64.3%	35.7%	64.3%	35.7%

An asterisk (*) denotes incumbent. Seat was won in 1990, 1992, 1994, 1996, 1998, 2000, 2002, and 2004 by Bernard Sanders, an Independent. Other Vote for those years includes the total for Sanders and other independent and minor party candidates. A double asterisk (**) indicates the plurality and percentage of total vote figures from 1990 through 2004 compare the Republican candidate and Sanders. For other years, the comparison is between the Republican and Democratic candidates. A pound sign (#) indicates that a candidate received votes from another party.

Democratic candidates from 1990 through 2004 received the following shares of the total vote: 2004 - Larry Drown, 7.1 percent; 2000 - Pete Diamondstone, 5.3 percent; 1996 - Jack Long, 9.4 percent; 1992 - Lewis E. Young, 7.9 percent; 1990 - Dolores Sandoval, 3.0 percent.

VERMONT

GENERAL AND PRIMARY ELECTIONS

2006 GENERAL ELECTIONS

Governor   Other vote was 2,477 Independent (Cris Ericson); 1,936 Vermont Green (Jim Hogue); 1,216 Vermont Localist (Benjamin Clarke); 638 Liberty Union (Bob Skold); 153 scattered write-in.

Senator   Other vote was 1,735 Independent (Cris Ericson); 1,536 Vermont Green (Craig Hill); 1,518 Anti-Bushist Candidate (Peter Moss); 801 Liberty Union (Pete Diamondstone); 267 scattered write-in. (Bernard Sanders ran and won as an independent.)

House   Other vote was:

    At Large   1,390 Impeach Bush Now (Dennis Morrisseau); 1,013 Independent (Jerry Trudell); 994 Vermont Green (Bruce R. Marshall); 963 Independent (Keith Stern); 721 Liberty Union (Jane Newton); 599 We the People (Chris Karr); 208 scattered write-in.

VERMONT

GENERAL AND PRIMARY ELECTIONS

2006 PRIMARY ELECTIONS

Primary September 12, 2006 **Registration** 431,477 No Party Registration
(as of September 12, 2006)

Note: The registration total is inflated due to a statutorily mandated delay in removing names of persons who moved to another voting district, but who had not notified the clerk in writing of the change.

Primary Type Open—Any registered voter could participate in the primary of any recognized party.

Note: An asterisk (*) denotes incumbent.

	REPUBLICAN PRIMARIES			DEMOCRATIC PRIMARIES		
Governor	Jim Douglas*	33,645	98.1%	Scudder Parker	31,048	94.8%
	Scattered write-in	635	1.9%	Scattered write-in	1,702	5.2%
	TOTAL	34,280		TOTAL	32,750	
Senator	Rich Tarrant	22,008	61.8%	Bernard Sanders	35,954	94.2%
	Greg Parke	10,479	29.4%	Louis W. Thabault	585	1.5%
	Cris Ericson	1,722	4.8%	Craig Hill	504	1.3%
	Scattered write-in	1,382	3.9%	Larry Drown	403	1.1%
				Peter D. Moss	385	1.0%
				Scattered write-in	355	0.9%
	TOTAL	35,591		TOTAL	38,186	

Shortly after winning the primary, Bernard Sanders declined the Democratic nomination in order to run as an independent in the general election. There was no Democratic candidate in the general election.

	REPUBLICAN PRIMARIES			DEMOCRATIC PRIMARIES		
House At Large	Martha Rainville	26,199	71.3%	Peter Welch	34,706	97.1%
	Mark Shepard	10,285	28.0%	Scattered write-in	1,033	2.9%
	Scattered write-in	258	0.7%			
	TOTAL	36,742		TOTAL	35,739	

VIRGINIA

Congressional districts first established for elections held in 2002
11 members

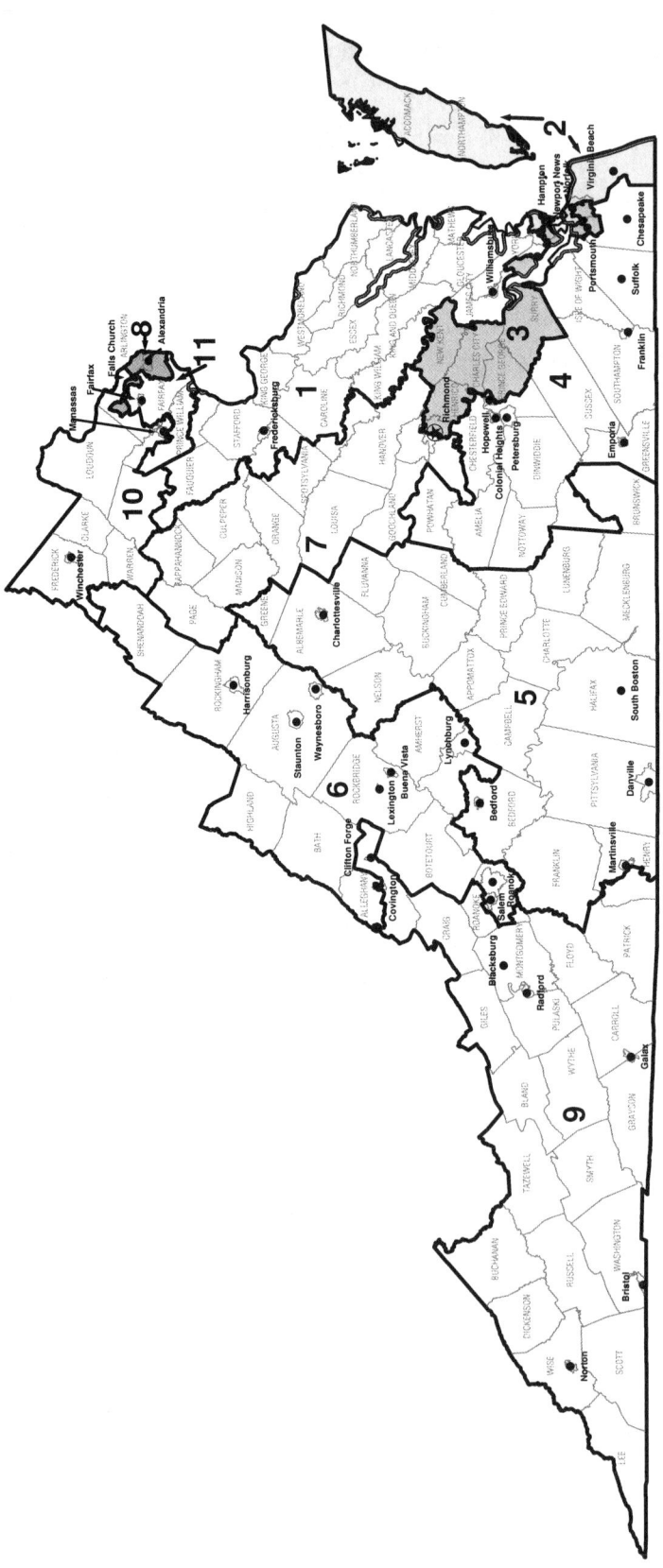

VIRGINIA

Northern Virginia Area

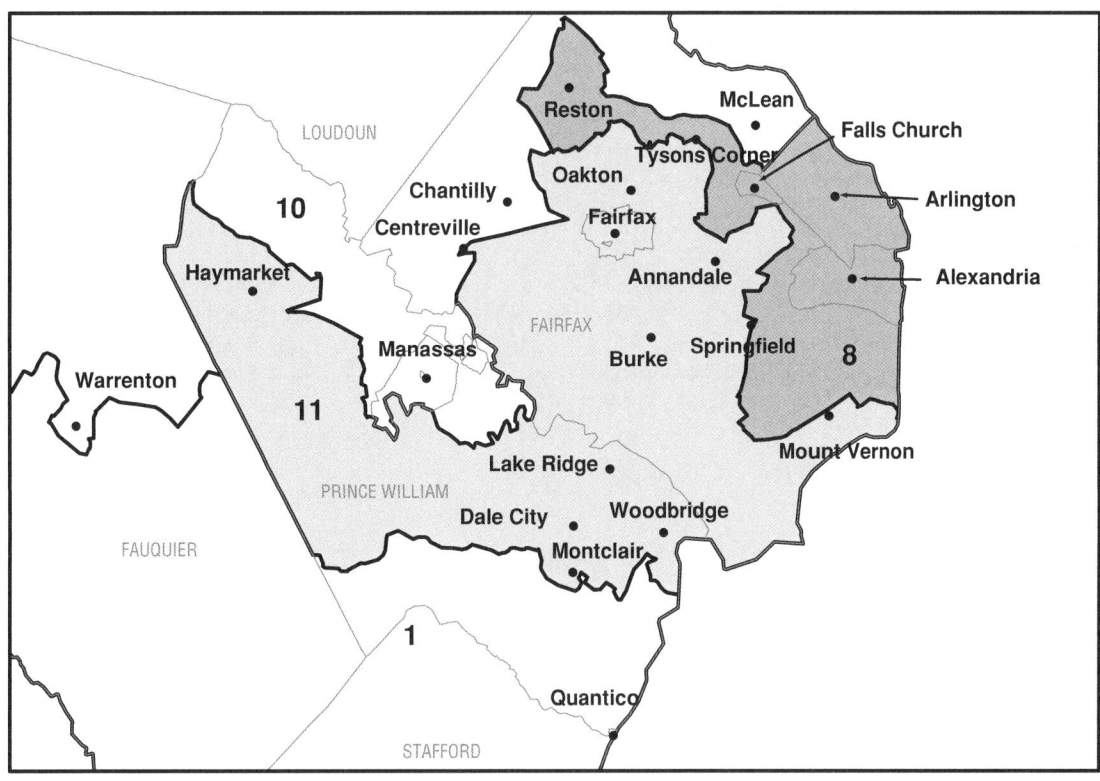

Hampton Roads, Virginia Beach Area

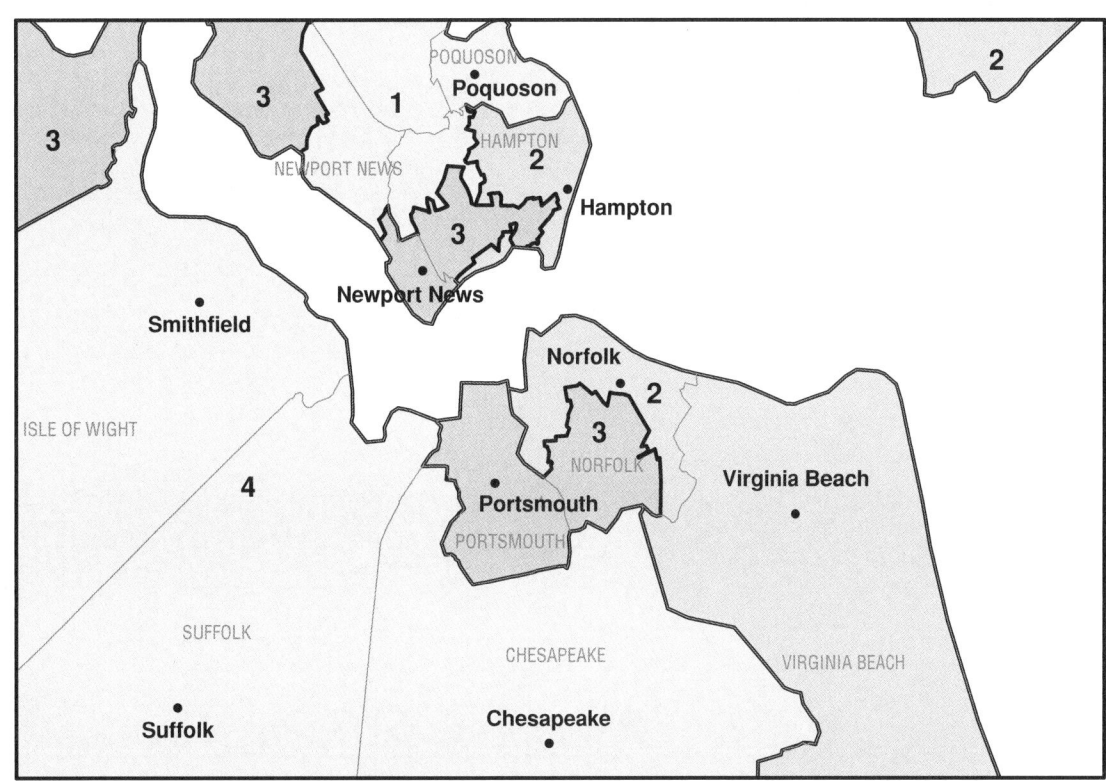

VIRGINIA

GOVERNOR
Timothy M. Kaine (D). Elected 2005 to a four-year term.

SENATORS (1 Democrat, 1 Republican)
James Webb (R). Elected 2006 to a six-year term.

John W. Warner (R). Reelected 2002 to a six-year term. Previously elected 1996, 1990, 1984, 1978.

REPRESENTATIVES (8 Republicans, 3 Democrats)
1. Jo Ann Davis (R)
2. Thelma Drake (R)
3. Robert C. Scott (D)
4. J. Randy Forbes (R)
5. Virgil H. Goode Jr. (R)
6. Robert W. Goodlatte (R)
7. Eric Cantor (R)
8. James P. Moran (D)
9. Rick Boucher (D)
10. Frank R. Wolf (R)
11. Thomas M. Davis III (R)

POSTWAR VOTE FOR PRESIDENT

| | | Republican | | Democratic | | | | Percentage | | | |
| | Total | | | | | Other | | Total Vote | | Major Vote | |
Year	Vote	Vote	Candidate	Vote	Candidate	Vote	Plurality	Rep.	Dem.	Rep.	Dem.
2004	3,198,367	1,716,959	Bush, George W.	1,454,742	Kerry, John	26,666	262,217 R	53.7%	45.5%	54.1%	45.9%
2000**	2,739,447	1,437,490	Bush, George W.	1,217,290	Gore, Al	84,667	220,200 R	52.5%	44.4%	54.1%	45.9%
1996**	2,416,642	1,138,350	Dole, Bob	1,091,060	Clinton, Bill	187,232	47,290 R	47.1%	45.1%	51.1%	48.9%
1992**	2,558,665	1,150,517	Bush, George	1,038,650	Clinton, Bill	369,498	111,867 R	45.0%	40.6%	52.6%	47.4%
1988	2,191,609	1,309,162	Bush, George	859,799	Dukakis, Michael S.	22,648	449,363 R	59.7%	39.2%	60.4%	39.6%
1984	2,146,635	1,337,078	Reagan, Ronald	796,250	Mondale, Walter F.	13,307	540,828 R	62.3%	37.1%	62.7%	37.3%
1980**	1,866,032	989,609	Reagan, Ronald	752,174	Carter, Jimmy	124,249	237,435 R	53.0%	40.3%	56.8%	43.2%
1976	1,697,094	836,554	Ford, Gerald R.	813,896	Carter, Jimmy	46,644	22,658 R	49.3%	48.0%	50.7%	49.3%
1972	1,457,019	988,493	Nixon, Richard M.	438,887	McGovern, George S.	29,639	549,606 R	67.8%	30.1%	69.3%	30.7%
1968**	1,361,491	590,319	Nixon, Richard M.	442,387	Humphrey, Hubert H.	328,785	147,932 R	43.4%	32.5%	57.2%	42.8%
1964	1,042,267	481,334	Goldwater, Barry M.	558,038	Johnson, Lyndon B.	2,895	76,704 D	46.2%	53.5%	46.3%	53.7%
1960	771,449	404,521	Nixon, Richard M.	362,327	Kennedy, John F.	4,601	42,194 R	52.4%	47.0%	52.8%	47.2%
1956	697,978	386,459	Eisenhower, Dwight D.	267,760	Stevenson, Adlai E.	43,759	118,699 R	55.4%	38.4%	59.1%	40.9%
1952	619,689	349,037	Eisenhower, Dwight D.	268,677	Stevenson, Adlai E.	1,975	80,360 R	56.3%	43.4%	56.5%	43.5%
1948**	419,256	172,070	Dewey, Thomas E.	200,786	Truman, Harry S.	46,400	28,716 D	41.0%	47.9%	46.1%	53.9%

**In past elections, the other vote included: 2000 - 59,398 Green (Ralph Nader); 1996 - 159,861 Reform (Ross Perot); 1992 - 348,639 Independent (Ross Perot); 1980 - 95,418 Independent (John Anderson); 1968 - 321,833 American Independent (George Wallace); 1948 - 43,393 States' Rights (Strom Thurmond).

VIRGINIA

POSTWAR VOTE FOR GOVERNOR

Year	Total Vote	Republican		Democratic		Other Vote	Plurality	Percentage			
								Total Vote		Major Vote	
		Vote	Candidate	Vote	Candidate			Rep.	Dem.	Rep.	Dem.
2005	1,983,778	912,327	Kilgore, Jerry W.	1,025,942	Kaine, Timothy M.	45,509	113,615 D	46.0%	51.7%	47.1%	52.9%
2001	1,886,721	887,234	Earley, Mark L.	984,177	Warner, Mark	15,310	96,943 D	47.0%	52.2%	47.4%	52.6%
1997	1,736,314	969,062	Gilmore, James S. III	738,971	Beyer, Donald S. Jr.	28,281	230,091 R	55.8%	42.6%	56.7%	43.3%
1993	1,793,916	1,045,319	Allen, George	733,527	Terry, Mary Sue	15,070	311,792 R	58.3%	40.9%	58.8%	41.2%
1989	1,789,078	890,195	Coleman, J. Marshall	896,936	Wilder, L. Douglas	1,947	6,741 D	49.8%	50.1%	49.8%	50.2%
1985	1,343,243	601,652	Durrette, Wyatt B.	741,438	Baliles, Gerald L.	153	139,786 D	44.8%	55.2%	44.8%	55.2%
1981	1,420,611	659,398	Coleman, J. Marshall	760,357	Robb, Charles S.	856	100,959 D	46.4%	53.5%	46.4%	53.6%
1977	1,250,940	699,302	Dalton, John	541,319	Howell, Henry	10,319	157,983 R	55.9%	43.3%	56.4%	43.6%
1973**	1,035,495	525,075	Godwin, Mills E.	—		510,420	14,972 R	50.7%		100.0%	
1969	915,764	480,869	Holton, Linwood	415,695	Battle, William C.	19,200	65,174 R	52.5%	45.4%	53.6%	46.4%
1965**	562,789	212,207	Holton, Linwood	269,526	Godwin, Mills E.	81,056	57,319 D	37.7%	47.9%	44.1%	55.9%
1961	394,490	142,567	Pearson, H. Clyde	251,861	Harrison, Albertis	62	109,294 D	36.1%	63.8%	36.1%	63.9%
1957	517,655	188,628	Dalton, Ted	326,921	Almond, J. Lindsay	2,106	138,293 D	36.4%	63.2%	36.6%	63.4%
1953	414,025	183,328	Dalton, Ted	226,998	Stanley, Thomas B.	3,699	43,670 D	44.3%	54.8%	44.7%	55.3%
1949	262,350	71,991	Johnson, Walter	184,772	Battle, John S.	5,587	112,781 D	27.4%	70.4%	28.0%	72.0%
1945	168,783	52,386	Landreth, S. Floyd	112,355	Tuck, William M.	4,042	59,969 D	31.0%	66.6%	31.8%	68.2%

**In past elections, the other vote included: 1973 - 510,103 Independent (Henry Howell); 1965 - 75,307 Conservative (William J. Story Jr.). In the 1973 election, the plurality reflects the difference in the vote for the Republican candidate and Howell. In other elections, the plurality is the difference between the Republican and Democratic vote.

POSTWAR VOTE FOR SENATOR

Year	Total Vote	Republican		Democratic		Other Vote	Plurality	Percentage			
								Total Vote		Major Vote	
		Vote	Candidate	Vote	Candidate			Rep.	Dem.	Rep.	Dem.
2006	2,370,445	1,166,277	Allen, George	1,175,606	Webb, James	28,562	9,329 D	49.2%	49.6%	49.8%	50.2%
2002	1,489,422	1,229,894	Warner, John W.	—		259,528	1,229,894 R	82.6%		100.0%	
2000	2,718,301	1,420,460	Allen, George	1,296,093	Robb, Charles S.	1,748	124,367 R	52.3%	47.7%	52.3%	47.7%
1996	2,354,715	1,235,744	Warner, John W.	1,115,982	Warner, Mark R.	2,989	119,762 R	52.5%	47.4%	52.5%	47.5%
1994**	2,057,463	882,213	North, Oliver L.	938,376	Robb, Charles S.	236,874	56,163 D	42.9%	45.6%	48.5%	51.5%
1990	1,083,690	876,782	Warner, John W.	—		206,908	876,782 R	80.9%		100.0%	
1988	2,068,897	593,652	Dawkins, Maurice A.	1,474,086	Robb, Charles S.	1,159	880,434 D	28.7%	71.2%	28.7%	71.3%
1984	2,007,487	1,406,194	Warner, John W.	601,142	Harrison, Edythe C.	151	805,052 R	70.0%	29.9%	70.1%	29.9%
1982	1,415,622	724,571	Trible, Paul	690,839	Davis, Richard	212	33,732 R	51.2%	48.8%	51.2%	48.8%
1978	1,222,256	613,232	Warner, John W.	608,511	Miller, Andrew P.	513	4,721 R	50.2%	49.8%	50.2%	49.8%
1976**	1,557,500	—		596,009	Zumwalt, Elmo R.	961,491	294,769 I		38.3%		100.0%
1972	1,396,268	718,337	Scott, William L.	643,963	Spong, William B.	33,968	74,374 R	51.4%	46.1%	52.7%	47.3%
1970**	946,751	145,031	Garland, Ray	295,057	Rawlings, George C.	506,663	211,576 I	15.3%	31.2%	33.0%	67.0%
1966	733,879	245,681	Ould, James P.	429,855	Spong, William B.	58,343	184,174 D	33.5%	58.6%	36.4%	63.6%
1966S	729,839	272,804	Traylor, Lawrence M.	389,028	Byrd, Harry Flood Jr.	68,007	116,224 D	37.4%	53.3%	41.2%	58.8%
1964**	928,363	176,624	May, Richard A.	592,260	Byrd, Harry Flood	159,479	415,636 D	19.0%	63.8%	23.0%	77.0%
1960	622,820	—		506,169	Robertson, A. Willis	116,651	506,169 D		81.3%		100.0%
1958	457,640	—		317,221	Byrd, Harry Flood	140,419	317,221 D		69.3%		100.0%
1954	306,510	—		244,844	Robertson, A. Willis	61,666	244,844 D		79.9%		100.0%
1952	543,516	—		398,677	Byrd, Harry Flood	144,839	398,677 D		73.4%		100.0%
1948	386,178	118,546	Woods, Robert	253,865	Robertson, A. Willis	13,767	135,319 D	30.7%	65.7%	31.8%	68.2%
1946	252,863	77,005	Parsons, Lester S.	163,960	Byrd, Harry Flood	11,898	86,955 D	30.5%	64.8%	32.0%	68.0%
1946S	248,962	72,253	Woods, Robert	169,680	Robertson, A. Willis	7,029	97,427 D	29.0%	68.2%	29.9%	70.1%

**In past elections, the other vote included: 1994 - 235,324 Independent (J. Marshall Coleman); 1976 - 890,778 Independent (Harry Flood Byrd Jr.), who won the election with 57.2 percent of the total vote; 1970 - 506,633 Independent (Harry Flood Byrd Jr.), who won the election with 53.5 percent of the total vote; 1964 - 95,526 Independent (James W. Respess). In the 1970 and 1976 elections Byrd's plurality is listed over the Democratic candidate, who in each case finished second. In other elections the plurality is the difference between the Republican and Democratic vote. One each of the 1966 and 1946 elections was for a short term to fill a vacancy.

VIRGINIA

GOVERNOR 2005

2000 Census Population	County	Total Vote	Republican	Democratic	Other	Rep.-Dem. Plurality	Percentage Total Vote Rep.	Dem.	Major Vote Rep.	Dem.
38,305	ACCOMACK	7,745	3,754	3,860	131	106 D	48.5%	49.8%	49.3%	50.7%
79,236	ALBEMARLE	30,174	10,994	18,455	725	7,461 D	36.4%	61.2%	37.3%	62.7%
17,215	ALLEGHANY	5,397	2,373	2,907	117	534 D	44.0%	53.9%	44.9%	55.1%
11,400	AMELIA	3,696	2,251	1,368	77	883 R	60.9%	37.0%	62.2%	37.8%
31,894	AMHERST	8,205	4,450	3,576	179	874 R	54.2%	43.6%	55.4%	44.6%
13,705	APPOMATTOX	4,570	2,663	1,804	103	859 R	58.3%	39.5%	59.6%	40.4%
189,453	ARLINGTON	56,989	13,631	42,319	1,039	28,688 D	23.9%	74.3%	24.4%	75.6%
65,615	AUGUSTA	19,325	12,197	6,395	733	5,802 R	63.1%	33.1%	65.6%	34.4%
5,048	BATH	1,617	860	729	28	131 R	53.2%	45.1%	54.1%	45.9%
60,371	BEDFORD COUNTY	20,288	12,330	7,524	434	4,806 R	60.8%	37.1%	62.1%	37.9%
6,871	BLAND	1,916	1,176	706	34	470 R	61.4%	36.8%	62.5%	37.5%
30,496	BOTETOURT	10,373	6,053	4,083	237	1,970 R	58.4%	39.4%	59.7%	40.3%
18,419	BRUNSWICK	4,466	1,742	2,691	33	949 D	39.0%	60.3%	39.3%	60.7%
26,978	BUCHANAN	6,077	2,875	3,171	31	296 D	47.3%	52.2%	47.6%	52.4%
15,623	BUCKINGHAM	3,801	1,899	1,822	80	77 R	50.0%	47.9%	51.0%	49.0%
51,078	CAMPBELL	14,462	8,864	5,319	279	3,545 R	61.3%	36.8%	62.5%	37.5%
22,121	CAROLINE	6,325	2,786	3,396	143	610 D	44.0%	53.7%	45.1%	54.9%
29,245	CARROLL	7,571	4,485	2,942	144	1,543 R	59.2%	38.9%	60.4%	39.6%
6,926	CHARLES CITY	2,265	671	1,565	29	894 D	29.6%	69.1%	30.0%	70.0%
12,472	CHARLOTTE	3,786	2,078	1,637	71	441 R	54.9%	43.2%	55.9%	44.1%
259,903	CHESTERFIELD	89,811	48,112	40,134	1,565	7,978 R	53.6%	44.7%	54.5%	45.5%
12,652	CLARKE	4,942	2,350	2,225	367	125 R	47.6%	45.0%	51.4%	48.6%
5,091	CRAIG	1,780	975	754	51	221 R	54.8%	42.4%	56.4%	43.6%
34,262	CULPEPER	9,698	5,762	3,689	247	2,073 R	59.4%	38.0%	61.0%	39.0%
9,017	CUMBERLAND	2,614	1,420	1,144	50	276 R	54.3%	43.8%	55.4%	44.6%
16,395	DICKENSON	4,957	2,559	2,377	21	182 R	51.6%	48.0%	51.8%	48.2%
24,533	DINWIDDIE	6,826	3,523	3,168	135	355 R	51.6%	46.4%	52.7%	47.3%
9,989	ESSEX	3,078	1,533	1,500	45	33 R	49.8%	48.7%	50.5%	49.5%
969,749	FAIRFAX COUNTY	272,100	103,285	163,667	5,148	60,382 D	38.0%	60.1%	38.7%	61.3%
55,139	FAUQUIER	17,847	9,505	7,746	596	1,759 R	53.3%	43.4%	55.1%	44.9%
13,874	FLOYD	4,412	2,324	1,959	129	365 R	52.7%	44.4%	54.3%	45.7%
20,047	FLUVANNA	7,227	3,456	3,592	179	136 D	47.8%	49.7%	49.0%	51.0%
47,286	FRANKLIN COUNTY	15,618	8,157	7,017	444	1,140 R	52.2%	44.9%	53.8%	46.2%
59,209	FREDERICK	17,876	10,698	6,027	1,151	4,671 R	59.8%	33.7%	64.0%	36.0%
16,657	GILES	5,214	2,507	2,570	137	63 D	48.1%	49.3%	49.4%	50.6%
34,780	GLOUCESTER	10,058	5,688	3,985	385	1,703 R	56.6%	39.6%	58.8%	41.2%
16,863	GOOCHLAND	7,756	4,313	3,292	151	1,021 R	55.6%	42.4%	56.7%	43.3%
17,917	GRAYSON	4,651	2,710	1,875	66	835 R	58.3%	40.3%	59.1%	40.9%
15,244	GREENE	4,488	2,526	1,846	116	680 R	56.3%	41.1%	57.8%	42.2%
11,560	GREENSVILLE	3,283	1,424	1,833	26	409 D	43.4%	55.8%	43.7%	56.3%
37,355	HALIFAX	8,972	4,887	3,931	154	956 R	54.5%	43.8%	55.4%	44.6%
86,320	HANOVER	35,210	21,637	12,784	789	8,853 R	61.5%	36.3%	62.9%	37.1%
262,300	HENRICO	92,359	41,619	49,170	1,570	7,551 D	45.1%	53.2%	45.8%	54.2%
57,930	HENRY	14,659	7,004	7,454	201	450 D	47.8%	50.8%	48.4%	51.6%
2,536	HIGHLAND	1,211	700	478	33	222 R	57.8%	39.5%	59.4%	40.6%
29,728	ISLE OF WIGHT	10,215	5,262	4,664	289	598 R	51.5%	45.7%	53.0%	47.0%
48,102	JAMES CITY	21,029	10,104	10,205	720	101 D	48.0%	48.5%	49.8%	50.2%
6,630	KING AND QUEEN	2,051	896	1,114	41	218 D	43.7%	54.3%	44.6%	55.4%
16,803	KING GEORGE	4,749	2,569	2,042	138	527 R	54.1%	43.0%	55.7%	44.3%
13,146	KING WILLIAM	4,570	2,509	1,951	110	558 R	54.9%	42.7%	56.3%	43.7%
11,567	LANCASTER	4,625	2,463	2,043	119	420 R	53.3%	44.2%	54.7%	45.3%
23,589	LEE	7,135	4,640	2,453	42	2,187 R	65.0%	34.4%	65.4%	34.6%
169,599	LOUDOUN	60,179	27,539	31,074	1,566	3,535 D	45.8%	51.6%	47.0%	53.0%
25,627	LOUISA	8,090	4,179	3,716	195	463 R	51.7%	45.9%	52.9%	47.1%
13,146	LUNENBURG	3,289	1,749	1,490	50	259 R	53.2%	45.3%	54.0%	46.0%
12,520	MADISON	3,871	2,105	1,672	94	433 R	54.4%	43.2%	55.7%	44.3%
9,207	MATHEWS	3,568	1,946	1,452	170	494 R	54.5%	40.7%	57.3%	42.7%
32,380	MECKLENBURG	6,981	3,864	2,986	131	878 R	55.4%	42.8%	56.4%	43.6%
9,932	MIDDLESEX	3,802	2,167	1,530	105	637 R	57.0%	40.2%	58.6%	41.4%
83,629	MONTGOMERY	20,758	8,670	11,509	579	2,839 D	41.8%	55.4%	43.0%	57.0%

VIRGINIA

GOVERNOR 2005

2000 Census Population	County	Total Vote	Republican	Democratic	Other	Rep.-Dem. Plurality	Percentage Total Vote Rep.	Dem.	Major Vote Rep.	Dem.
14,445	NELSON	4,972	2,113	2,755	104	642 D	42.5%	55.4%	43.4%	56.6%
13,462	NEW KENT	5,549	3,179	2,241	129	938 R	57.3%	40.4%	58.7%	41.3%
13,093	NORTHAMPTON	3,387	1,256	2,058	73	802 D	37.1%	60.8%	37.9%	62.1%
12,259	NORTHUMBERLAND	4,753	2,548	2,104	101	444 R	53.6%	44.3%	54.8%	45.2%
15,725	NOTTOWAY	3,994	1,942	1,993	59	51 D	48.6%	49.9%	49.4%	50.6%
25,881	ORANGE	8,551	4,481	3,888	182	593 R	52.4%	45.5%	53.5%	46.5%
23,177	PAGE	6,165	3,591	2,385	189	1,206 R	58.2%	38.7%	60.1%	39.9%
19,407	PATRICK	5,061	2,853	2,111	97	742 R	56.4%	41.7%	57.5%	42.5%
61,745	PITTSYLVANIA	16,871	10,252	6,363	256	3,889 R	60.8%	37.7%	61.7%	38.3%
22,377	POWHATAN	8,500	5,580	2,744	176	2,836 R	65.6%	32.3%	67.0%	33.0%
19,720	PRINCE EDWARD	4,891	2,259	2,546	86	287 D	46.2%	52.1%	47.0%	53.0%
33,047	PRINCE GEORGE	8,266	4,751	3,382	133	1,369 R	57.5%	40.9%	58.4%	41.6%
280,813	PRINCE WILLIAM	66,797	32,178	33,364	1,255	1,186 D	48.2%	49.9%	49.1%	50.9%
35,127	PULASKI	9,527	4,901	4,427	199	474 R	51.4%	46.5%	52.5%	47.5%
6,983	RAPPAHANNOCK	2,732	1,283	1,397	52	114 D	47.0%	51.1%	47.9%	52.1%
8,809	RICHMOND COUNTY	2,198	1,293	863	42	430 R	58.8%	39.3%	60.0%	40.0%
85,778	ROANOKE COUNTY	31,595	16,686	14,125	784	2,561 R	52.8%	44.7%	54.2%	45.8%
20,808	ROCKBRIDGE	6,494	3,354	2,993	147	361 R	51.6%	46.1%	52.8%	47.2%
67,725	ROCKINGHAM	20,245	13,262	6,560	423	6,702 R	65.5%	32.4%	66.9%	33.1%
30,308	RUSSELL	7,814	4,314	3,431	69	883 R	55.2%	43.9%	55.7%	44.3%
23,403	SCOTT	8,215	6,016	2,156	43	3,860 R	73.2%	26.2%	73.6%	26.4%
35,075	SHENANDOAH	12,320	7,874	3,996	450	3,878 R	63.9%	32.4%	66.3%	33.7%
33,081	SMYTH	8,135	5,053	2,989	93	2,064 R	62.1%	36.7%	62.8%	37.2%
17,482	SOUTHAMPTON	4,907	2,354	2,442	111	88 D	48.0%	49.8%	49.1%	50.9%
90,395	SPOTSYLVANIA	25,267	13,635	11,061	571	2,574 R	54.0%	43.8%	55.2%	44.8%
92,446	STAFFORD	25,075	13,559	10,924	592	2,635 R	54.1%	43.6%	55.4%	44.6%
6,829	SURRY	2,439	919	1,480	40	561 D	37.7%	60.7%	38.3%	61.7%
12,504	SUSSEX	3,188	1,401	1,739	48	338 D	43.9%	54.5%	44.6%	55.4%
44,598	TAZEWELL	10,274	5,970	4,194	110	1,776 R	58.1%	40.8%	58.7%	41.3%
31,584	WARREN	8,451	4,705	3,408	338	1,297 R	55.7%	40.3%	58.0%	42.0%
51,103	WASHINGTON	15,310	10,009	5,188	113	4,821 R	65.4%	33.9%	65.9%	34.1%
16,718	WESTMORELAND	4,239	1,924	2,219	96	295 D	45.4%	52.3%	46.4%	53.6%
40,123	WISE	10,122	6,190	3,871	61	2,319 R	61.2%	38.2%	61.5%	38.5%
27,599	WYTHE	8,269	4,954	3,125	190	1,829 R	59.9%	37.8%	61.3%	38.7%
56,297	YORK	18,343	9,565	8,142	636	1,423 R	52.1%	44.4%	54.0%	46.0%
	City/Town									
128,283	ALEXANDRIA	34,864	9,173	25,061	630	15,888 D	26.3%	71.9%	26.8%	73.2%
6,299	BEDFORD CITY	1,818	877	892	49	15 D	48.2%	49.1%	49.6%	50.4%
17,367	BRISTOL	4,091	2,515	1,548	28	967 R	61.5%	37.8%	61.9%	38.1%
6,349	BUENA VISTA	1,540	713	799	28	86 D	46.3%	51.9%	47.2%	52.8%
45,049	CHARLOTTESVILLE	10,104	1,870	8,018	216	6,148 D	18.5%	79.4%	18.9%	81.1%
199,184	CHESAPEAKE	52,888	24,885	26,612	1,391	1,727 D	47.1%	50.3%	48.3%	51.7%
16,897	COLONIAL HEIGHTS	6,038	4,116	1,777	145	2,339 R	68.2%	29.4%	69.8%	30.2%
6,303	COVINGTON	1,662	587	1,022	53	435 D	35.3%	61.5%	36.5%	63.5%
48,411	DANVILLE	11,350	5,177	6,052	121	875 D	45.6%	53.3%	46.1%	53.9%
5,665	EMPORIA	1,637	815	796	26	19 R	49.8%	48.6%	50.6%	49.4%
21,498	FAIRFAX CITY	6,756	2,750	3,865	141	1,115 D	40.7%	57.2%	41.6%	58.4%
10,377	FALLS CHURCH	4,327	1,102	3,138	87	2,036 D	25.5%	72.5%	26.0%	74.0%
8,346	FRANKLIN CITY	2,423	988	1,394	41	406 D	40.8%	57.5%	41.5%	58.5%
19,279	FREDERICKSBURG	4,294	1,561	2,611	122	1,050 D	36.4%	60.8%	37.4%	62.6%
6,837	GALAX	1,459	693	730	36	37 D	47.5%	50.0%	48.7%	51.3%
146,437	HAMPTON	32,878	11,078	20,961	839	9,883 D	33.7%	63.8%	34.6%	65.4%
40,468	HARRISONBURG	6,940	3,251	3,539	150	288 D	46.8%	51.0%	47.9%	52.1%
22,354	HOPEWELL	5,099	2,705	2,300	94	405 R	53.0%	45.1%	54.0%	46.0%
6,867	LEXINGTON	1,697	567	1,097	33	530 D	33.4%	64.6%	34.1%	65.9%
65,269	LYNCHBURG	16,372	7,708	8,329	335	621 D	47.1%	50.9%	48.1%	51.9%
35,135	MANASSAS	6,850	3,532	3,167	151	365 R	51.6%	46.2%	52.7%	47.3%
10,290	MANASSAS PARK	1,423	751	650	22	101 R	52.8%	45.7%	53.6%	46.4%
15,416	MARTINSVILLE	3,788	1,380	2,363	45	983 D	36.4%	62.4%	36.9%	63.1%
180,150	NEWPORT NEWS	37,872	15,095	21,743	1,034	6,648 D	39.9%	57.4%	41.0%	59.0%
234,403	NORFOLK	42,030	12,899	27,791	1,340	14,892 D	30.7%	66.1%	31.7%	68.3%

VIRGINIA

GOVERNOR 2005

2000 Census Population	City/Town	Total Vote	Republican	Democratic	Other	Rep.-Dem. Plurality		Percentage			
								Total Vote		Major Vote	
								Rep.	Dem.	Rep.	Dem.
3,904	NORTON	999	539	449	11	90	R	54.0%	44.9%	54.6%	45.4%
33,740	PETERSBURG	7,330	1,274	5,995	61	4,721	D	17.4%	81.8%	17.5%	82.5%
11,566	POQUOSON	4,044	2,515	1,383	146	1,132	R	62.2%	34.2%	64.5%	35.5%
100,565	PORTSMOUTH	24,817	7,926	16,314	577	8,388	D	31.9%	65.7%	32.7%	67.3%
15,859	RADFORD	3,558	1,534	1,928	96	394	D	43.1%	54.2%	44.3%	55.7%
197,790	RICHMOND CITY	51,238	11,529	38,900	809	27,371	D	22.5%	75.9%	22.9%	77.1%
94,911	ROANOKE CITY	22,972	8,239	14,207	526	5,968	D	35.9%	61.8%	36.7%	63.3%
24,747	SALEM	8,035	3,993	3,788	254	205	R	49.7%	47.1%	51.3%	48.7%
23,853	STAUNTON	6,769	3,112	3,384	273	272	D	46.0%	50.0%	47.9%	52.1%
63,677	SUFFOLK	19,509	8,561	10,480	468	1,919	D	43.9%	53.7%	45.0%	55.0%
425,257	VIRGINIA BEACH	96,889	46,471	47,120	3,298	649	D	48.0%	48.6%	49.7%	50.3%
19,520	WAYNESBORO	5,000	2,596	2,223	181	373	R	51.9%	44.5%	53.9%	46.1%
11,998	WILLIAMSBURG	2,944	1,081	1,782	81	701	D	36.7%	60.5%	37.8%	62.2%
23,585	WINCHESTER	5,951	2,497	2,683	771	186	D	42.0%	45.1%	48.2%	51.8%
7,078,515	TOTAL	1,983,778	912,327	1,025,942	45,509	113,615	D	46.0%	51.7%	47.1%	52.9%

VIRGINIA

SENATOR 2006

2000 Census Population	County	Total Vote	Republican	Democratic	Other	Rep.-Dem. Plurality		Percentage			
								Total Vote		Major Vote	
								Rep.	Dem.	Rep.	Dem.
38,305	ACCOMACK	9,901	5,059	4,704	138	355	R	51.1%	47.5%	51.8%	48.2%
79,236	ALBEMARLE	36,198	15,048	20,821	329	5,773	D	41.6%	57.5%	42.0%	58.0%
17,215	ALLEGHANY	5,466	2,578	2,818	70	240	D	47.2%	51.6%	47.8%	52.2%
11,400	AMELIA	4,131	2,668	1,425	38	1,243	R	64.6%	34.5%	65.2%	34.8%
31,894	AMHERST	9,825	5,732	3,974	119	1,758	R	58.3%	40.4%	59.1%	40.9%
13,705	APPOMATTOX	5,029	3,256	1,717	56	1,539	R	64.7%	34.1%	65.5%	34.5%
189,453	ARLINGTON	73,069	19,200	53,021	848	33,821	D	26.3%	72.6%	26.6%	73.4%
65,615	AUGUSTA	23,411	16,084	7,086	241	8,998	R	68.7%	30.3%	69.4%	30.6%
5,048	BATH	1,748	1,025	698	25	327	R	58.6%	39.9%	59.5%	40.5%
60,371	BEDFORD COUNTY	25,122	16,769	8,056	297	8,713	R	66.8%	32.1%	67.5%	32.5%
6,871	BLAND	2,105	1,318	760	27	558	R	62.6%	36.1%	63.4%	36.6%
30,496	BOTETOURT	12,788	8,187	4,438	163	3,749	R	64.0%	34.7%	64.8%	35.2%
18,419	BRUNSWICK	4,761	2,046	2,676	39	630	D	43.0%	56.2%	43.3%	56.7%
26,978	BUCHANAN	7,089	3,094	3,943	52	849	D	43.6%	55.6%	44.0%	56.0%
15,623	BUCKINGHAM	4,408	2,360	1,995	53	365	R	53.5%	45.3%	54.2%	45.8%
51,078	CAMPBELL	17,495	11,802	5,497	196	6,305	R	67.5%	31.4%	68.2%	31.8%
22,121	CAROLINE	7,448	3,580	3,771	97	191	D	48.1%	50.6%	48.7%	51.3%
29,245	CARROLL	9,129	5,549	3,442	138	2,107	R	60.8%	37.7%	61.7%	38.3%
6,926	CHARLES CITY	2,482	941	1,514	27	573	D	37.9%	61.0%	38.3%	61.7%
12,472	CHARLOTTE	3,995	2,393	1,548	54	845	R	59.9%	38.7%	60.7%	39.3%
259,903	CHESTERFIELD	104,371	60,987	42,025	1,359	18,962	R	58.4%	40.3%	59.2%	40.8%
12,652	CLARKE	5,222	2,700	2,463	59	237	R	51.7%	47.2%	52.3%	47.7%
5,091	CRAIG	2,016	1,182	799	35	383	R	58.6%	39.6%	59.7%	40.3%
34,262	CULPEPER	11,372	6,796	4,428	148	2,368	R	59.8%	38.9%	60.5%	39.5%
9,017	CUMBERLAND	3,045	1,757	1,252	36	505	R	57.7%	41.1%	58.4%	41.6%
16,395	DICKENSON	5,417	2,417	2,960	40	543	D	44.6%	54.6%	45.0%	55.0%
24,533	DINWIDDIE	7,860	4,495	3,256	109	1,239	R	57.2%	41.4%	58.0%	42.0%
9,989	ESSEX	3,154	1,674	1,444	36	230	R	53.1%	45.8%	53.7%	46.3%
969,749	FAIRFAX COUNTY	342,998	137,313	202,036	3,649	64,723	D	40.0%	58.9%	40.5%	59.5%
55,139	FAUQUIER	22,310	12,777	9,260	273	3,517	R	57.3%	41.5%	58.0%	42.0%

VIRGINIA

SENATOR 2006

2000 Census Population	County	Total Vote	Republican	Democratic	Other	Rep.-Dem. Plurality		Percentage			
								Total Vote		Major Vote	
								Rep.	Dem.	Rep.	Dem.
13,874	FLOYD	5,429	3,106	2,239	84	867	R	57.2%	41.2%	58.1%	41.9%
20,047	FLUVANNA	8,435	4,514	3,837	84	677	R	53.5%	45.5%	54.1%	45.9%
47,286	FRANKLIN COUNTY	17,953	10,898	6,786	269	4,112	R	60.7%	37.8%	61.6%	38.4%
59,209	FREDERICK	21,444	13,363	7,807	274	5,556	R	62.3%	36.4%	63.1%	36.9%
16,657	GILES	5,731	3,070	2,592	69	478	R	53.6%	45.2%	54.2%	45.8%
34,780	GLOUCESTER	11,905	7,129	4,583	193	2,546	R	59.9%	38.5%	60.9%	39.1%
16,863	GOOCHLAND	8,892	5,393	3,390	109	2,003	R	60.7%	38.1%	61.4%	38.6%
17,917	GRAYSON	5,609	3,318	2,208	83	1,110	R	59.2%	39.4%	60.0%	40.0%
15,244	GREENE	5,323	3,310	1,955	58	1,355	R	62.2%	36.7%	62.9%	37.1%
11,560	GREENSVILLE	3,078	1,323	1,735	20	412	D	43.0%	56.4%	43.3%	56.7%
37,355	HALIFAX	10,258	6,053	4,078	127	1,975	R	59.0%	39.8%	59.7%	40.3%
86,320	HANOVER	39,347	26,449	12,534	364	13,915	R	67.2%	31.9%	67.8%	32.2%
262,300	HENRICO	101,017	50,165	49,603	1,249	562	R	49.7%	49.1%	50.3%	49.7%
57,930	HENRY	16,588	9,100	7,319	169	1,781	R	54.9%	44.1%	55.4%	44.6%
2,536	HIGHLAND	1,208	762	429	17	333	R	63.1%	35.5%	64.0%	36.0%
29,728	ISLE OF WIGHT	12,396	7,105	5,126	165	1,979	R	57.3%	41.4%	58.1%	41.9%
48,102	JAMES CITY	25,961	13,832	11,860	269	1,972	R	53.3%	45.7%	53.8%	46.2%
6,630	KING AND QUEEN	2,283	1,213	1,049	21	164	R	53.1%	45.9%	53.6%	46.4%
16,803	KING GEORGE	6,079	3,577	2,419	83	1,158	R	58.8%	39.8%	59.7%	40.3%
13,146	KING WILLIAM	5,418	3,350	2,022	46	1,328	R	61.8%	37.3%	62.4%	37.6%
11,567	LANCASTER	5,132	2,928	2,141	63	787	R	57.1%	41.7%	57.8%	42.2%
23,589	LEE	6,721	3,731	2,928	62	803	R	55.5%	43.6%	56.0%	44.0%
169,599	LOUDOUN	80,649	39,249	40,381	1,019	1,132	D	48.7%	50.1%	49.3%	50.7%
25,627	LOUISA	9,731	5,444	4,133	154	1,311	R	55.9%	42.5%	56.8%	43.2%
13,146	LUNENBURG	3,630	2,047	1,543	40	504	R	56.4%	42.5%	57.0%	43.0%
12,520	MADISON	4,525	2,607	1,864	54	743	R	57.6%	41.2%	58.3%	41.7%
9,207	MATHEWS	3,966	2,364	1,564	38	800	R	59.6%	39.4%	60.2%	39.8%
32,380	MECKLENBURG	8,369	4,941	3,351	77	1,590	R	59.0%	40.0%	59.6%	40.4%
9,932	MIDDLESEX	4,330	2,556	1,724	50	832	R	59.0%	39.8%	59.7%	40.3%
83,629	MONTGOMERY	24,435	11,598	12,485	352	887	D	47.5%	51.1%	48.2%	51.8%
14,445	NELSON	5,874	2,722	3,101	51	379	D	46.3%	52.8%	46.7%	53.3%
13,462	NEW KENT	6,617	4,210	2,308	99	1,902	R	63.6%	34.9%	64.6%	35.4%
13,093	NORTHAMPTON	4,213	1,860	2,302	51	442	D	44.1%	54.6%	44.7%	55.3%
12,259	NORTHUMBERLAND	5,289	3,096	2,149	44	947	R	58.5%	40.6%	59.0%	41.0%
15,725	NOTTOWAY	4,520	2,457	2,008	55	449	R	54.4%	44.4%	55.0%	45.0%
25,881	ORANGE	10,136	5,738	4,294	104	1,444	R	56.6%	42.4%	57.2%	42.8%
23,177	PAGE	7,270	4,358	2,813	99	1,545	R	59.9%	38.7%	60.8%	39.2%
19,407	PATRICK	5,675	3,310	2,270	95	1,040	R	58.3%	40.0%	59.3%	40.7%
61,745	PITTSYLVANIA	19,660	12,813	6,645	202	6,168	R	65.2%	33.8%	65.8%	34.2%
22,377	POWHATAN	9,892	7,047	2,727	118	4,320	R	71.2%	27.6%	72.1%	27.9%
19,720	PRINCE EDWARD	5,351	2,771	2,519	61	252	R	51.8%	47.1%	52.4%	47.6%
33,047	PRINCE GEORGE	9,778	5,923	3,755	100	2,168	R	60.6%	38.4%	61.2%	38.8%
280,813	PRINCE WILLIAM	88,111	42,409	44,503	1,199	2,094	D	48.1%	50.5%	48.8%	51.2%
35,127	PULASKI	11,075	6,277	4,616	182	1,661	R	56.7%	41.7%	57.6%	42.4%
6,983	RAPPAHANNOCK	3,372	1,593	1,741	38	148	D	47.2%	51.6%	47.8%	52.2%
8,809	RICHMOND COUNTY	2,545	1,578	940	27	638	R	62.0%	36.9%	62.7%	37.3%
85,778	ROANOKE COUNTY	36,729	21,520	14,745	464	6,775	R	58.6%	40.1%	59.3%	40.7%
20,808	ROCKBRIDGE	7,307	4,005	3,202	100	803	R	54.8%	43.8%	55.6%	44.4%
67,725	ROCKINGHAM	23,708	16,525	6,917	266	9,608	R	69.7%	29.2%	70.5%	29.5%
30,308	RUSSELL	8,593	4,193	4,364	36	171	D	48.8%	50.8%	49.0%	51.0%
23,403	SCOTT	7,354	4,527	2,785	42	1,742	R	61.6%	37.9%	61.9%	38.1%
35,075	SHENANDOAH	13,839	8,753	4,867	219	3,886	R	63.2%	35.2%	64.3%	35.7%
33,081	SMYTH	9,306	5,692	3,540	74	2,152	R	61.2%	38.0%	61.7%	38.3%
17,482	SOUTHAMPTON	5,437	2,805	2,569	63	236	R	51.6%	47.3%	52.2%	47.8%
90,395	SPOTSYLVANIA	31,567	17,938	13,208	421	4,730	R	56.8%	41.8%	57.6%	42.4%
92,446	STAFFORD	32,448	17,885	13,982	581	3,903	R	55.1%	43.1%	56.1%	43.9%
6,829	SURRY	2,722	1,162	1,534	26	372	D	42.7%	56.4%	43.1%	56.9%
12,504	SUSSEX	3,181	1,504	1,623	54	119	D	47.3%	51.0%	48.1%	51.9%
44,598	TAZEWELL	11,900	6,614	5,194	92	1,420	R	55.6%	43.6%	56.0%	44.0%
31,584	WARREN	10,164	5,684	4,362	118	1,322	R	55.9%	42.9%	56.6%	43.4%

VIRGINIA

SENATOR 2006

2000 Census Population	County	Total Vote	Republican	Democratic	Other	Rep.-Dem. Plurality		Percentage			
								Total Vote		Major Vote	
								Rep.	Dem.	Rep.	Dem.
51,103	WASHINGTON	17,448	10,815	6,499	134	4,316	R	62.0%	37.2%	62.5%	37.5%
16,718	WESTMORELAND	4,898	2,405	2,421	72	16	D	49.1%	49.4%	49.8%	50.2%
40,123	WISE	9,846	5,224	4,558	64	666	R	53.1%	46.3%	53.4%	46.6%
27,599	WYTHE	9,043	5,690	3,199	154	2,491	R	62.9%	35.4%	64.0%	36.0%
56,297	YORK	22,865	13,222	9,370	273	3,852	R	57.8%	41.0%	58.5%	41.5%
	City/Town										
128,283	ALEXANDRIA	44,789	12,659	31,638	492	18,979	D	28.3%	70.6%	28.6%	71.4%
6,299	BEDFORD CITY	1,940	1,048	868	24	180	R	54.0%	44.7%	54.7%	45.3%
17,367	BRISTOL	4,859	2,933	1,894	32	1,039	R	60.4%	39.0%	60.8%	39.2%
6,349	BUENA VISTA	1,748	946	777	25	169	R	54.1%	44.5%	54.9%	45.1%
45,049	CHARLOTTESVILLE	11,852	2,575	9,159	118	6,584	D	21.7%	77.3%	21.9%	78.1%
199,184	CHESAPEAKE	65,329	33,772	30,761	796	3,011	R	51.7%	47.1%	52.3%	47.7%
16,897	COLONIAL HEIGHTS	5,925	4,290	1,544	91	2,746	R	72.4%	26.1%	73.5%	26.5%
6,303	COVINGTON	1,617	650	936	31	286	D	40.2%	57.9%	41.0%	59.0%
48,411	DANVILLE	12,484	6,271	6,086	127	185	R	50.2%	48.8%	50.7%	49.3%
5,665	EMPORIA	1,571	729	820	22	91	D	46.4%	52.2%	47.1%	52.9%
21,498	FAIRFAX CITY	8,096	3,451	4,541	104	1,090	D	42.6%	56.1%	43.2%	56.8%
10,377	FALLS CHURCH	5,006	1,424	3,532	50	2,108	D	28.4%	70.6%	28.7%	71.3%
8,346	FRANKLIN CITY	2,457	1,131	1,300	26	169	D	46.0%	52.9%	46.5%	53.5%
19,279	FREDERICKSBURG	5,321	2,129	3,109	83	980	D	40.0%	58.4%	40.6%	59.4%
6,837	GALAX	1,809	937	853	19	84	R	51.8%	47.2%	52.3%	47.7%
146,437	HAMPTON	39,422	14,541	24,325	556	9,784	D	36.9%	61.7%	37.4%	62.6%
40,468	HARRISONBURG	8,061	4,018	3,947	96	71	R	49.8%	49.0%	50.4%	49.6%
22,354	HOPEWELL	5,363	2,943	2,349	71	594	R	54.9%	43.8%	55.6%	44.4%
6,867	LEXINGTON	1,807	651	1,128	28	477	D	36.0%	62.4%	36.6%	63.4%
65,269	LYNCHBURG	19,935	10,369	9,364	202	1,005	R	52.0%	47.0%	52.5%	47.5%
35,135	MANASSAS	8,415	4,301	4,003	111	298	R	51.1%	47.6%	51.8%	48.2%
10,290	MANASSAS PARK	1,973	995	948	30	47	R	50.4%	48.0%	51.2%	48.8%
15,416	MARTINSVILLE	3,929	1,680	2,211	38	531	D	42.8%	56.3%	43.2%	56.8%
180,150	NEWPORT NEWS	45,739	19,851	25,242	646	5,391	D	43.4%	55.2%	44.0%	56.0%
234,403	NORFOLK	49,487	16,879	31,909	699	15,030	D	34.1%	64.5%	34.6%	65.4%
3,904	NORTON	1,056	504	546	6	42	D	47.7%	51.7%	48.0%	52.0%
33,740	PETERSBURG	7,531	1,488	5,944	99	4,456	D	19.8%	78.9%	20.0%	80.0%
11,566	POQUOSON	5,270	3,640	1,569	61	2,071	R	69.1%	29.8%	69.9%	30.1%
100,565	PORTSMOUTH	27,341	9,527	17,453	361	7,926	D	34.8%	63.8%	35.3%	64.7%
15,859	RADFORD	3,564	1,637	1,882	45	245	D	45.9%	52.8%	46.5%	53.5%
197,790	RICHMOND CITY	53,769	14,478	38,527	764	24,049	D	26.9%	71.7%	27.3%	72.7%
94,911	ROANOKE CITY	25,923	10,768	14,816	339	4,048	D	41.5%	57.2%	42.1%	57.9%
24,747	SALEM	8,764	5,007	3,648	109	1,359	R	57.1%	41.6%	57.9%	42.1%
23,853	STAUNTON	7,474	3,858	3,526	90	332	R	51.6%	47.2%	52.2%	47.8%
63,677	SUFFOLK	23,692	11,638	11,810	244	172	D	49.1%	49.8%	49.6%	50.4%
425,257	VIRGINIA BEACH	124,050	64,852	57,657	1,541	7,195	R	52.3%	46.5%	52.9%	47.1%
19,520	WAYNESBORO	5,995	3,374	2,546	75	828	R	56.3%	42.5%	57.0%	43.0%
11,998	WILLIAMSBURG	3,481	1,375	2,066	40	691	D	39.5%	59.4%	40.0%	60.0%
23,585	WINCHESTER	6,661	3,351	3,230	80	121	R	50.3%	48.5%	50.9%	49.1%
7,078,515	TOTAL	2,370,445	1,166,277	1,175,606	28,562	9,329	D	49.2%	49.6%	49.8%	50.2%

VIRGINIA

HOUSE OF REPRESENTATIVES

CD	Year	Total Vote	Republican Vote	Republican Candidate	Democratic Vote	Democratic Candidate	Other Vote	Rep.-Dem. Plurality	Total Vote Rep.	Total Vote Dem.	Major Vote Rep.	Major Vote Dem.
1	2006	228,534	143,889	DAVIS, JO ANN*	81,083	O'DONNELL, SHAWN M.	3,562	62,806 R	63.0%	35.5%	64.0%	36.0%
1	2004	286,534	225,071	DAVIS, JO ANN*	—		61,463	225,071 R	78.5%		100.0%	
1	2002	117,997	113,168	DAVIS, JO ANN*	—		4,829	113,168 R	95.9%		100.0%	
2	2006	173,159	88,777	DRAKE, THELMA*	83,901	KELLAM, PHILIP J.	481	4,876 R	51.3%	48.5%	51.4%	48.6%
2	2004	241,380	132,946	DRAKE, THELMA	108,180	ASHE, DAVID B.	254	24,766 R	55.1%	44.8%	55.1%	44.9%
2	2002	124,846	103,807	SCHROCK, ED*	—		21,039	103,807 R	83.1%		100.0%	
3	2006	138,994		—	133,546	SCOTT, ROBERT C.*	5,448	133,546 D		96.1%		100.0%
3	2004	229,892	70,194	SEARS, WINSOME E.	159,373	SCOTT, ROBERT C.*	325	89,179 D	30.5%	69.3%	30.6%	69.4%
3	2002	91,073		—	87,521	SCOTT, ROBERT C.*	3,552	87,521 D		96.1%		100.0%
4	2006	198,340	150,967	FORBES, J. RANDY*	—		47,373	150,967 R	76.1%		100.0%	
4	2004	283,027	182,444	FORBES, J. RANDY*	100,413	MENEFEE, JONATHAN R.	170	82,031 R	64.5%	35.5%	64.5%	35.5%
4	2002	111,041	108,733	FORBES, J. RANDY*	—		2,308	108,733 R	97.9%		100.0%	
5	2006	212,079	125,370	GOODE, VIRGIL H. JR.*	84,682	WEED, AL C. II	2,027	40,688 R	59.1%	39.9%	59.7%	40.3%
5	2004	270,758	172,431	GOODE, VIRGIL H. JR.*	98,237	WEED, AL C. II	90	74,194 R	63.7%	36.3%	63.7%	36.3%
5	2002	150,233	95,360	GOODE, VIRGIL H. JR.*	54,805	RICHARDS, MEREDITH M.	68	40,555 R	63.5%	36.5%	63.5%	36.5%
6	2006	203,995	153,187	GOODLATTE, ROBERT W.*	—		50,808	153,187 R	75.1%		100.0%	
6	2004	213,648	206,560	GOODLATTE, ROBERT W.*	—		7,088	206,560 R	96.7%		100.0%	
6	2002	108,732	105,530	GOODLATTE, ROBERT W.*	—		3,202	105,530 R	97.1%		100.0%	
7	2006	256,397	163,706	CANTOR, ERIC*	88,206	NACHMAN, JAMES M.	4,485	75,500 R	63.8%	34.4%	65.0%	35.0%
7	2004	305,658	230,765	CANTOR, ERIC*	—		74,893	230,765 R	75.5%		100.0%	
7	2002	163,665	113,658	CANTOR, ERIC*	49,854	JONES, BEN L. "COOTER"	153	63,804 R	69.4%	30.5%	69.5%	30.5%
8	2006	217,909	66,639	O'DONOGHUE, TOM M.	144,700	MORAN, JAMES P.*	6,570	78,061 D	30.6%	66.4%	31.5%	68.5%
8	2004	287,919	106,231	CHENEY, LISA MARIE	171,986	MORAN, JAMES P.*	9,702	65,755 D	36.9%	59.7%	38.2%	61.8%
8	2002	171,799	64,121	TATE, SCOTT C.	102,759	MORAN, JAMES P.*	4,919	38,638 D	37.3%	59.8%	38.4%	61.6%
9	2006	191,415	61,574	CARRICO, C. W. "BILL"	129,705	BOUCHER, RICK*	136	68,131 D	32.2%	67.8%	32.2%	67.8%
9	2004	252,947	98,499	TRIPLETT, KEVIN R.	150,039	BOUCHER, RICK*	4,409	51,540 D	38.9%	59.3%	39.6%	60.4%
9	2002	152,183	52,076	KATZEN, JAY K.	100,075	BOUCHER, RICK*	32	47,999 D	34.2%	65.8%	34.2%	65.8%
10	2006	241,134	138,213	WOLF, FRANK R.*	98,769	FEDER, JUDY M.	4,152	39,444 R	57.3%	41.0%	58.3%	41.7%
10	2004	323,011	205,982	WOLF, FRANK R.*	116,654	SOCAS, JAMES R.	375	89,328 R	63.8%	36.1%	63.8%	36.2%
10	2002	161,615	115,917	WOLF, FRANK R.*	45,464	STEVENS, JOHN B. JR.	234	70,453 R	71.7%	28.1%	71.8%	28.2%
11	2006	235,280	130,468	DAVIS, THOMAS M. III*	102,511	HURST, ANDREW L.	2,301	27,957 R	55.5%	43.6%	56.0%	44.0%
11	2004	309,233	186,299	DAVIS, THOMAS M. III*	118,305	LONGMYER, KEN	4,629	67,994 R	60.2%	38.3%	61.2%	38.8%
11	2002	163,298	135,379	DAVIS, THOMAS M. III*	—		27,919	135,379 R	82.9%		100.0%	
TOTAL	2006	2,297,236	1,222,790		947,103		127,343	275,687 R	53.2%	41.2%	56.4%	43.6%
TOTAL	2004	3,004,007	1,817,422		1,023,187		163,398	794,235 R	60.5%	34.1%	64.0%	36.0%
TOTAL	2002	1,516,482	1,007,749		440,478		68,255	567,271 R	66.5%	29.0%	69.6%	30.4%

An asterisk (*) denotes incumbent.

VIRGINIA

GENERAL AND PRIMARY ELECTIONS

2006 GENERAL ELECTIONS

Governor Other vote was 43,953 Independent (H. Russ Potts Jr.); 1,556 scattered write-in.

Senator Other vote was 26,102 Independent Green (Glenda Gail Parker); 2,460 scattered write-in.

House Other vote was:

VIRGINIA

GENERAL AND PRIMARY ELECTIONS

CD 1	3,236 Independent (Marvin F. Pixton III); 326 scattered write-in.
CD 2	481 scattered write-in.
CD 3	5,448 scattered write-in.
CD 4	46,487 Independent Green (Albert P. Burckard Jr.); 886 scattered write-in.
CD 5	1,928 Independent Green (Joseph P. Oddo); 99 scattered write-in.
CD 6	25,129 Independent (Barbara Jean Pryor); 24,731 Independent (Andre D. Peery); 948 scattered write-in.
CD 7	4,213 Independent (W. Brad Blanton); 272 scattered write-in.
CD 8	6,094 Independent (James T. "Jim" Hurysz); 476 scattered write-in.
CD 9	136 scattered write-in.
CD 10	2,107 Libertarian (Wilbur N. Wood III); 1,851 Independent (Neeraj C. Nigam); 194 scattered write-in.
CD 11	2,042 Independent Green (Ferdinando C. Greco); 259 scattered write-in.

2006 PRIMARY ELECTIONS

Primary	June 14, 2005 (Governor) June 13, 2006 (Congress)	Registration (active registrants as of June 1, 2006 —also 202,291 inactive registrants and 2,431 overseas voters)	4,310,841	No Party Registration

Primary Type   Open—Any registered voter could participate in the primary of either party.

Note: An asterisk (*) denotes incumbent. The state parties and local party committees traditionally have the option of holding a primary or nominating candidates by convention or committee. If a primary was called and only one candidate filed to run in it, then no primary was held.

	REPUBLICAN PRIMARIES			DEMOCRATIC PRIMARIES		
Governor (2005)	Jerry W. Kilgore George Fitch TOTAL	145,002 30,168 175,170	82.8% 17.2%	Timothy M. Kaine	Unopposed	
Senator	George Allen*	Unopposed		James Webb Harris Miller TOTAL	83,298 72,486 155,784	53.5% 46.5%
Congressional District 1	Jo Ann Davis*	Unopposed		Shawn M. O'Donnell	Nominated by other method	
Congressional District 2	Thelma Drake*	Unopposed		Philip J. Kellam	Unopposed	
Congressional District 3	No Republican candidate			Robert C. Scott*	Nominated by other method	
Congressional District 4	J. Randy Forbes*	Unopposed		No Democratic candidate		
Congressional District 5	Virgil H. Goode Jr.*	Unopposed		Al C. Weed II	Nominated by other method	
Congressional District 6	Robert W. Goodlatte*	Unopposed		No Democratic candidate		
Congressional District 7	Eric Cantor*	Unopposed		James M. Nachman	Nominated by other method	
Congressional District 8	Tom M. O'Donoghue M. W. Ellmore TOTAL	3,064 1,345 4,409	69.5% 30.5%	James P. Moran*	Unopposed	
Congressional District 9	C. W. "Bill" Carrico	Nominated by other method		Rick Boucher*	Nominated by other method	
Congressional District 10	Frank R. Wolf*	Unopposed		Judy M. Feder	Unopposed	
Congressional District 11	Thomas M. Davis III*	Unopposed		Andrew L. Hurst Ken Longmyer TOTAL	10,831 8,818 19,649	55.1% 44.9%

WASHINGTON

Congressional districts first established for elections held in 2002
9 members

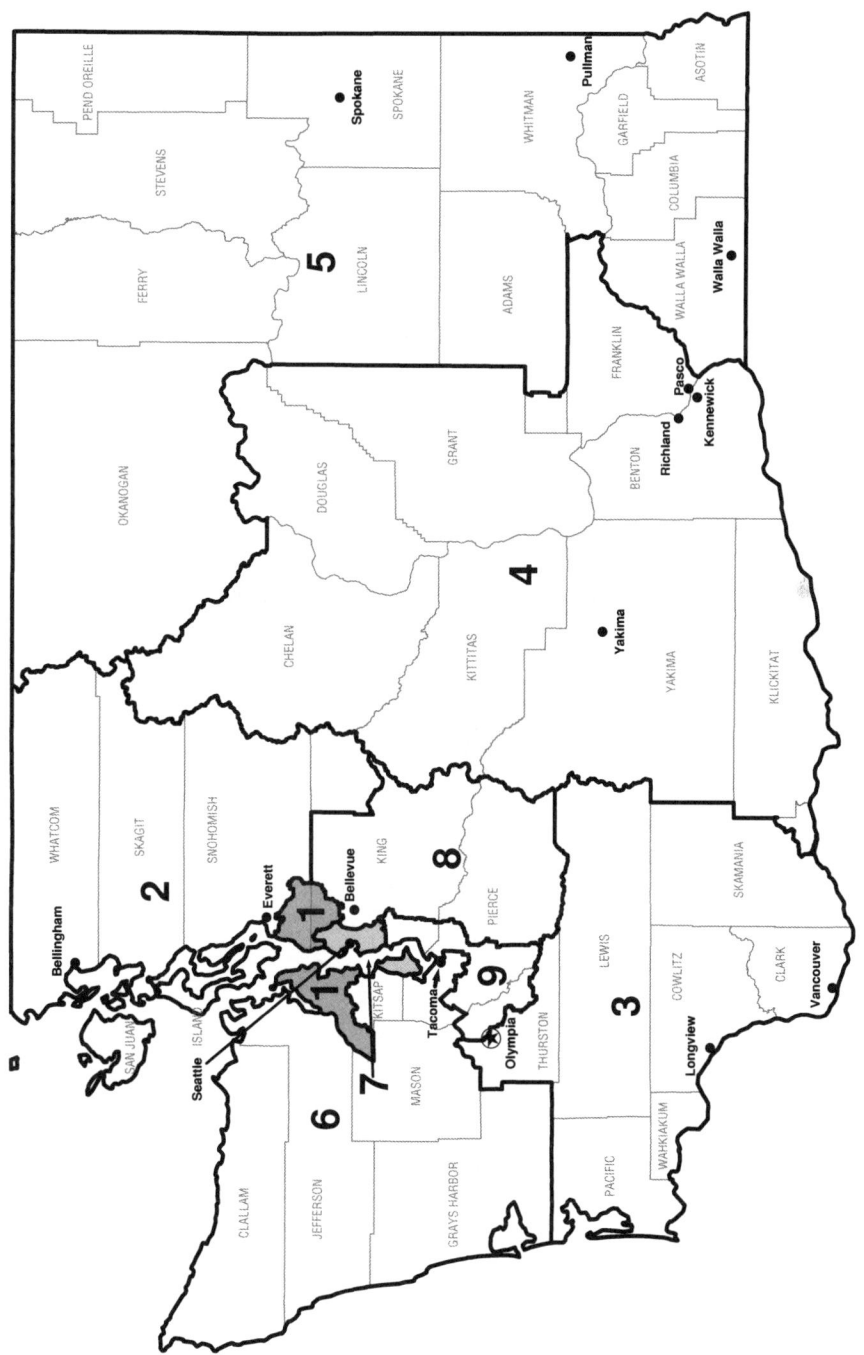

WASHINGTON

Seattle, Puget Sound Area

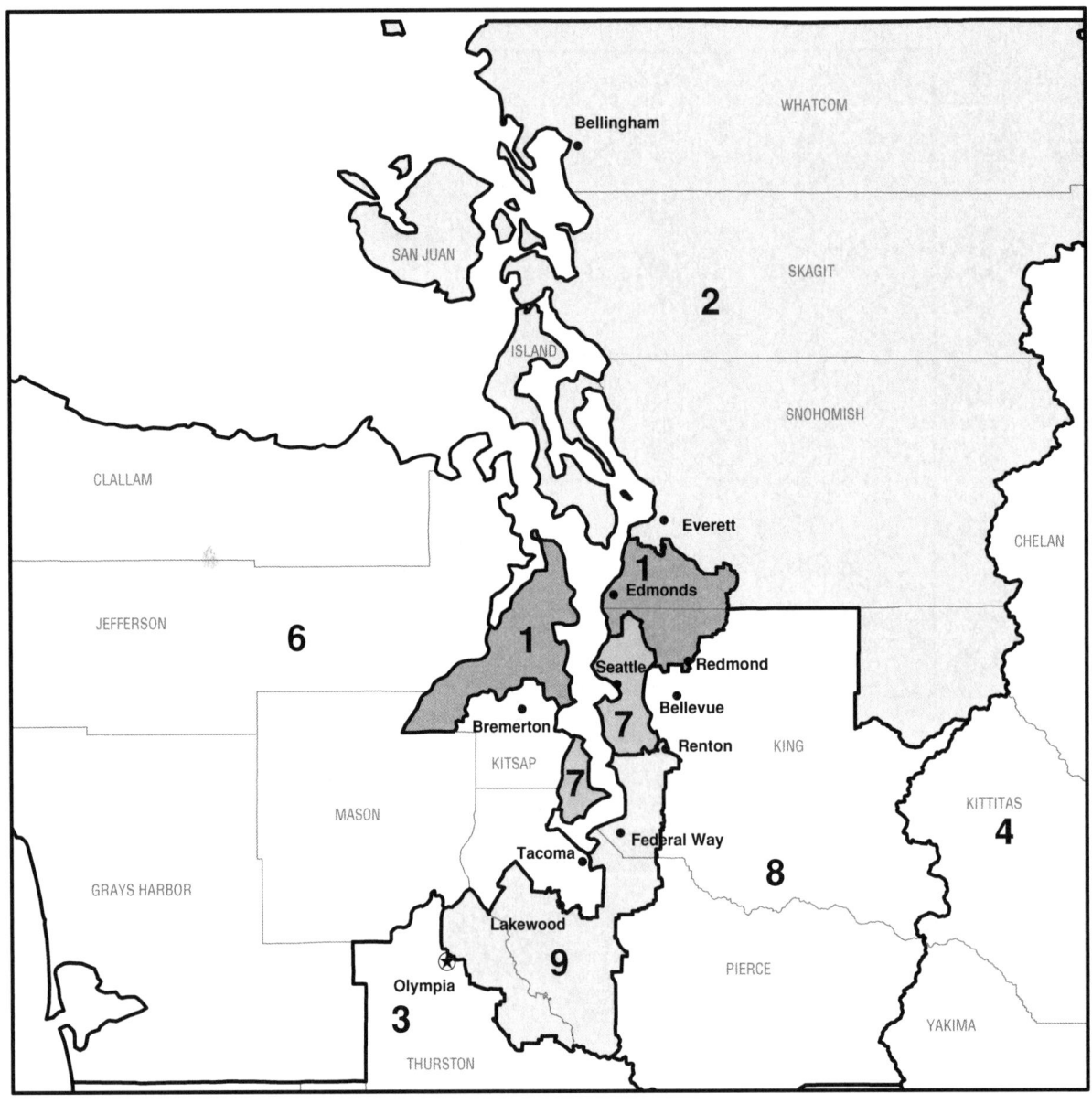

WASHINGTON

GOVERNOR
Christine Gregoire (D). Elected 2004 to a four-year term.

SENATORS (2 Democrats)
Maria Cantwell (D). Reelected 2006 to a six-year term. Previously elected 2000.

Patty Murray (D). Reelected 2004 to a six-year term. Previously elected 1998, 1992.

REPRESENTATIVES (6 Democrats, 3 Republicans)
1. Jay Inslee (D)
2. Rick Larsen (D)
3. Brian Baird (D)
4. Doc Hastings (R)
5. Cathy McMorris (R)
6. Norm Dicks (D)
7. Jim McDermott (D)
8. Dave Reichert (R)
9. Adam Smith (D)

POSTWAR VOTE FOR PRESIDENT

Year	Total Vote	Republican		Democratic		Other Vote	Plurality	Percentage			
								Total Vote		Major Vote	
		Vote	Candidate	Vote	Candidate			Rep.	Dem.	Rep.	Dem.
2004	2,859,084	1,304,894	Bush, George W.	1,510,201	Kerry, John	43,989	205,307 D	45.6%	52.8%	46.4%	53.6%
2000**	2,487,433	1,108,864	Bush, George W.	1,247,652	Gore, Al	130,917	138,788 D	44.6%	50.2%	47.1%	52.9%
1996**	2,253,837	840,712	Dole, Bob	1,123,323	Clinton, Bill	289,802	282,611 D	37.3%	49.8%	42.8%	57.2%
1992**	2,288,230	731,234	Bush, George	993,037	Clinton, Bill	563,959	261,803 D	32.0%	43.4%	42.4%	57.6%
1988	1,865,253	903,835	Bush, George	933,516	Dukakis, Michael S.	27,902	29,681 D	48.5%	50.0%	49.2%	50.8%
1984	1,883,910	1,051,670	Reagan, Ronald	807,352	Mondale, Walter F.	24,888	244,318 R	55.8%	42.9%	56.6%	43.4%
1980**	1,742,394	865,244	Reagan, Ronald	650,193	Carter, Jimmy	226,957	215,051 R	49.7%	37.3%	57.1%	42.9%
1976	1,555,534	777,732	Ford, Gerald R.	717,323	Carter, Jimmy	60,479	60,409 R	50.0%	46.1%	52.0%	48.0%
1972	1,470,847	837,135	Nixon, Richard M.	568,334	McGovern, George S.	65,378	268,801 R	56.9%	38.6%	59.6%	40.4%
1968**	1,304,281	588,510	Nixon, Richard M.	616,037	Humphrey, Hubert H.	99,734	27,527 D	45.1%	47.2%	48.9%	51.1%
1964	1,258,556	470,366	Goldwater, Barry M.	779,881	Johnson, Lyndon B.	8,309	309,515 D	37.4%	62.0%	37.6%	62.4%
1960	1,241,572	629,273	Nixon, Richard M.	599,298	Kennedy, John F.	13,001	29,975 R	50.7%	48.3%	51.2%	48.8%
1956	1,150,889	620,430	Eisenhower, Dwight D.	523,002	Stevenson, Adlai E.	7,457	97,428 R	53.9%	45.4%	54.3%	45.7%
1952	1,102,708	599,107	Eisenhower, Dwight D.	492,845	Stevenson, Adlai E.	10,756	106,262 R	54.3%	44.7%	54.9%	45.1%
1948	905,058	386,314	Dewey, Thomas E.	476,165	Truman, Harry S.	42,579	89,851 D	42.7%	52.6%	44.8%	55.2%

**In past elections, the other vote included: 2000 - 103,002 Green (Ralph Nader); 1996 - 201,003 Reform (Ross Perot); 1992 - 541,780 Independent (Ross Perot); 1980 - 185,073 Independent (John Anderson); 1968 - 96,990 American Independent (George Wallace).

WASHINGTON

POSTWAR VOTE FOR GOVERNOR

Year	Total Vote	Republican Vote	Republican Candidate	Democratic Vote	Democratic Candidate	Other Vote	Rep.-Dem. Plurality	Percentage Total Vote Rep.	Total Vote Dem.	Major Vote Rep.	Major Vote Dem.
2004**	2,810,058	1,373,232	Rossi, Dino	1,373,361	Gregoire, Christine	63,465	129 D	48.9%	48.9%	50.0%	50.0%
2000	2,469,852	980,060	Carlson, John	1,441,973	Locke, Gary	47,819	461,913 D	39.7%	58.4%	40.5%	59.5%
1996	2,237,030	940,538	Craswell, Ellen	1,296,492	Locke, Gary		355,954 D	42.0%	58.0%	42.0%	58.0%
1992	2,270,826	1,086,216	Eikenberry, Ken	1,184,315	Lowry, Mike	295	98,099 D	47.8%	52.2%	47.8%	52.2%
1988	1,874,929	708,481	Williams, Bob	1,166,448	Gardner, Booth		457,967 D	37.8%	62.2%	37.8%	62.2%
1984	1,888,987	881,994	Spellman, John D.	1,006,993	Gardner, Booth		124,999 D	46.7%	53.3%	46.7%	53.3%
1980	1,730,896	981,083	Spellman, John D.	749,813	McDermott, James A.		231,270 R	56.7%	43.3%	56.7%	43.3%
1976	1,546,382	687,039	Spellman, John D.	821,797	Ray, Dixy Lee	37,546	134,758 D	44.4%	53.1%	45.5%	54.5%
1972	1,472,542	747,825	Evans, Daniel J.	630,613	Rosellini, Albert D.	94,104	117,212 R	50.8%	42.8%	54.3%	45.7%
1968	1,265,355	692,378	Evans, Daniel J.	560,262	O'Connell, John J.	12,715	132,116 R	54.7%	44.3%	55.3%	44.7%
1964	1,250,274	697,256	Evans, Daniel J.	548,692	Rosellini, Albert D.	4,326	148,564 R	55.8%	43.9%	56.0%	44.0%
1960	1,215,748	594,122	Andrews, Lloyd J.	611,987	Rosellini, Albert D.	9,639	17,865 D	48.9%	50.3%	49.3%	50.7%
1956	1,128,977	508,041	Anderson, Emmett T.	616,773	Rosellini, Albert D.	4,163	108,732 D	45.0%	54.6%	45.2%	54.8%
1952	1,078,497	567,822	Langlie, Arthur B.	510,675	Mitchell, Hugh B.		57,147 R	52.6%	47.4%	52.6%	47.4%
1948	883,141	445,958	Langlie, Arthur B.	417,035	Wallgren, Mon C.	20,148	28,923 R	50.5%	47.2%	51.7%	48.3%

**In 2004, the initial official vote count put Republican Dino Rossi ahead by 261 votes. A machine recount reduced Rossi's margin to 42 votes. A subsequent manual recount gave Democrat Christine Gregoire the election by a margin of 129 votes (see above), and she was inaugurated governor.

POSTWAR VOTE FOR SENATOR

Year	Total Vote	Republican Vote	Republican Candidate	Democratic Vote	Democratic Candidate	Other Vote	Rep.-Dem. Plurality	Percentage Total Vote Rep.	Total Vote Dem.	Major Vote Rep.	Major Vote Dem.
2006	2,083,734	832,106	McGavick, Mike	1,184,659	Cantwell, Maria	66,969	352,553 D	39.9%	56.9%	41.3%	58.7%
2004	2,818,651	1,204,584	Nethercutt, George	1,549,708	Murray, Patty	64,359	345,124 D	42.7%	55.0%	43.7%	56.3%
2000	2,461,379	1,197,208	Gorton, Slade	1,199,437	Cantwell, Maria	64,734	2,229 D	48.6%	48.7%	50.0%	50.0%
1998	1,888,561	785,377	Smith, Linda	1,103,184	Murray, Patty		317,807 D	41.6%	58.4%	41.6%	58.4%
1994	1,700,173	947,821	Gorton, Slade	752,352	Sims, Ron		195,469 R	55.7%	44.3%	55.7%	44.3%
1992	2,219,162	1,020,829	Chandler, Rod	1,197,973	Murray, Patty	360	177,144 D	46.0%	54.0%	46.0%	54.0%
1988	1,848,542	944,359	Gorton, Slade	904,183	Lowry, Mike		40,176 R	51.1%	48.9%	51.1%	48.9%
1986	1,337,367	650,931	Gorton, Slade	677,471	Adams, Brock	8,965	26,540 D	48.7%	50.7%	49.0%	51.0%
1983S	1,213,307	672,326	Evans, Daniel J.	540,981	Lowry, Mike		131,345 R	55.4%	44.6%	55.4%	44.6%
1982	1,368,476	332,273	Jewett, Doug	943,655	Jackson, Henry M.	92,548	611,382 D	24.3%	69.0%	26.0%	74.0%
1980	1,728,369	936,317	Gorton, Slade	792,052	Magnuson, Warren G.		144,265 R	54.2%	45.8%	54.2%	45.8%
1976	1,491,111	361,546	Brown, George M.	1,071,219	Jackson, Henry M.	58,346	709,673 D	24.2%	71.8%	25.2%	74.8%
1974	1,007,847	363,626	Metcalf, Jack	611,811	Magnuson, Warren G.	32,410	248,185 D	36.1%	60.7%	37.3%	62.7%
1970	1,066,807	170,790	Elicker, Charles W.	879,385	Jackson, Henry M.	16,632	708,595 D	16.0%	82.4%	16.3%	83.7%
1968	1,236,063	435,894	Metcalf, Jack	796,183	Magnuson, Warren G.	3,986	360,289 D	35.3%	64.4%	35.4%	64.6%
1964	1,213,088	337,138	Andrews, Lloyd J.	875,950	Jackson, Henry M.		538,812 D	27.8%	72.2%	27.8%	72.2%
1962	943,229	446,204	Christensen, Richard G.	491,365	Magnuson, Warren G.	5,660	45,161 D	47.3%	52.1%	47.6%	52.4%
1958	886,822	278,271	Bantz, William B.	597,040	Jackson, Henry M.	11,511	318,769 D	31.4%	67.3%	31.8%	68.2%
1956	1,122,217	436,652	Langlie, Arthur B.	685,565	Magnuson, Warren G.		248,913 D	38.9%	61.1%	38.9%	61.1%
1952	1,058,735	460,884	Cain, Harry P.	595,288	Jackson, Henry M.	2,563	134,404 D	43.5%	56.2%	43.6%	56.4%
1950	744,783	342,464	Williams, Walter	397,719	Magnuson, Warren G.	4,600	55,255 D	46.0%	53.4%	46.3%	53.7%
1946	660,342	358,847	Cain, Harry P.	298,683	Mitchell, Hugh B.	2,812	60,164 R	54.3%	45.2%	54.6%	45.4%

The 1983 election was for a short term to fill a vacancy.

WASHINGTON

SENATOR 2006

2000 Census Population	County	Total Vote	Republican	Democratic	Other	Rep.-Dem. Plurality		Percentage			
								Total Vote		Major Vote	
								Rep.	Dem.	Rep.	Dem.
16,428	ADAMS	3,644	2,215	1,355	74	860	R	60.8%	37.2%	62.0%	38.0%
20,551	ASOTIN	7,357	3,393	3,730	234	337	D	46.1%	50.7%	47.6%	52.4%
142,475	BENTON	49,623	27,369	21,099	1,155	6,270	R	55.2%	42.5%	56.5%	43.5%
66,616	CHELAN	23,132	13,024	9,527	581	3,497	R	56.3%	41.2%	57.8%	42.2%
64,525	CLALLAM	30,419	13,699	15,730	990	2,031	D	45.0%	51.7%	46.5%	53.5%
345,238	CLARK	114,910	51,254	60,525	3,131	9,271	D	44.6%	52.7%	45.9%	54.1%
4,064	COLUMBIA	1,921	1,125	754	42	371	R	58.6%	39.3%	59.9%	40.1%
92,948	COWLITZ	31,108	12,569	17,390	1,149	4,821	D	40.4%	55.9%	42.0%	58.0%
32,603	DOUGLAS	11,148	6,621	4,273	254	2,348	R	59.4%	38.3%	60.8%	39.2%
7,260	FERRY	2,806	1,544	1,174	88	370	R	55.0%	41.8%	56.8%	43.2%
49,347	FRANKLIN	12,903	7,208	5,438	257	1,770	R	55.9%	42.1%	57.0%	43.0%
2,397	GARFIELD	1,193	659	502	32	157	R	55.2%	42.1%	56.8%	43.2%
74,698	GRANT	19,793	11,830	7,314	649	4,516	R	59.8%	37.0%	61.8%	38.2%
67,194	GRAYS HARBOR	22,008	8,517	12,739	752	4,222	D	38.7%	57.9%	40.1%	59.9%
71,558	ISLAND	29,985	12,977	16,289	719	3,312	D	43.3%	54.3%	44.3%	55.7%
25,953	JEFFERSON	16,094	5,212	10,164	718	4,952	D	32.4%	63.2%	33.9%	66.1%
1,737,034	KING	630,726	190,678	419,898	20,150	229,220	D	30.2%	66.6%	31.2%	68.8%
231,969	KITSAP	89,925	35,932	50,939	3,054	15,007	D	40.0%	56.6%	41.4%	58.6%
33,362	KITTITAS	12,342	6,419	5,567	356	852	R	52.0%	45.1%	53.6%	46.4%
19,161	KLICKITAT	7,373	3,439	3,670	264	231	D	46.6%	49.8%	48.4%	51.6%
68,600	LEWIS	25,233	14,517	9,898	818	4,619	R	57.5%	39.2%	59.5%	40.5%
10,184	LINCOLN	4,775	2,735	1,911	129	824	R	57.3%	40.0%	58.9%	41.1%
49,405	MASON	21,222	8,736	11,747	739	3,011	D	41.2%	55.4%	42.7%	57.3%
39,564	OKANOGAN	12,892	6,555	5,841	496	714	R	50.8%	45.3%	52.9%	47.1%
20,984	PACIFIC	8,722	3,239	5,175	308	1,936	D	37.1%	59.3%	38.5%	61.5%
11,732	PEND OREILLE	5,168	2,564	2,346	258	218	R	49.6%	45.4%	52.2%	47.8%
700,820	PIERCE	214,685	88,219	120,050	6,416	31,831	D	41.1%	55.9%	42.4%	57.6%
14,077	SAN JUAN	8,228	2,483	5,323	422	2,840	D	30.2%	64.7%	31.8%	68.2%
102,979	SKAGIT	41,069	18,094	21,612	1,363	3,518	D	44.1%	52.6%	45.6%	54.4%
9,872	SKAMANIA	4,031	1,738	2,134	159	396	D	43.1%	52.9%	44.9%	55.1%
606,024	SNOHOMISH	206,178	81,992	118,170	6,016	36,178	D	39.8%	57.3%	41.0%	59.0%
417,939	SPOKANE	155,142	72,209	77,295	5,638	5,086	D	46.5%	49.8%	48.3%	51.7%
40,066	STEVENS	17,061	9,378	7,042	641	2,336	R	55.0%	41.3%	57.1%	42.9%
207,355	THURSTON	84,136	30,683	49,529	3,924	18,846	D	36.5%	58.9%	38.3%	61.7%
3,824	WAHKIAKUM	1,815	733	1,010	72	277	D	40.4%	55.6%	42.1%	57.9%
55,180	WALLA WALLA	17,999	9,059	8,463	477	596	R	50.3%	47.0%	51.7%	48.3%
166,814	WHATCOM	69,200	28,267	38,219	2,714	9,952	D	40.8%	55.2%	42.5%	57.5%
40,740	WHITMAN	13,004	6,115	6,425	464	310	D	47.0%	49.4%	48.8%	51.2%
222,581	YAKIMA	54,764	29,106	24,392	1,266	4,714	R	53.1%	44.5%	54.4%	45.6%
5,894,121	TOTAL	2,083,734	832,106	1,184,659	66,969	352,553	D	39.9%	56.9%	41.3%	58.7%

WASHINGTON

HOUSE OF REPRESENTATIVES

CD	Year	Total Vote	Republican Vote	Republican Candidate	Democratic Vote	Democratic Candidate	Other Vote	Rep.-Dem. Plurality	Total Vote Rep.	Total Vote Dem.	Major Vote Rep.	Major Vote Dem.
1	2006	241,937	78,105	ISHMAEL, LARRY W.	163,832	INSLEE, JAY*		85,727 D	32.3%	67.7%	32.3%	67.7%
1	2004	327,769	117,850	EASTWOOD, RANDY	204,121	INSLEE, JAY*	5,798	86,271 D	36.0%	62.3%	36.6%	63.4%
1	2002	205,034	84,696	MARINE, JOE	114,087	INSLEE, JAY*	6,251	29,391 D	41.3%	55.6%	42.6%	57.4%
2	2006	244,794	87,730	ROULSTONE, DOUG	157,064	LARSEN, RICK*		69,334 D	35.8%	64.2%	35.8%	64.2%
2	2004	316,682	106,333	SINCLAIR, SUZANNE	202,383	LARSEN, RICK*	7,966	96,050 D	33.6%	63.9%	34.4%	65.6%
2	2002	202,150	92,528	SMITH, NORMA	101,219	LARSEN, RICK*	8,403	8,691 D	45.8%	50.1%	47.8%	52.2%
3	2006	232,980	85,915	MESSMORE, MICHAEL	147,065	BAIRD, BRIAN*		61,150 D	36.9%	63.1%	36.9%	63.1%
3	2004	312,653	119,027	CROWSON, THOMAS A.	193,626	BAIRD, BRIAN*		74,599 D	38.1%	61.9%	38.1%	61.9%
3	2002	193,329	74,065	ZARELLI, JOSEPH	119,264	BAIRD, BRIAN*		45,199 D	38.3%	61.7%	38.3%	61.7%
4	2006	192,300	115,246	HASTINGS, DOC*	77,054	WRIGHT, RICHARD		38,192 R	59.9%	40.1%	59.9%	40.1%
4	2004	247,113	154,627	HASTINGS, DOC*	92,486	MATHESON, SANDY		62,141 R	62.6%	37.4%	62.6%	37.4%
4	2002	161,829	108,257	HASTINGS, DOC*	53,572	MASON, CRAIG		54,685 R	66.9%	33.1%	66.9%	33.1%
5	2006	239,324	134,967	McMORRIS, CATHY*	104,357	GOLDMARK, PETER J.		30,610 R	56.4%	43.6%	56.4%	43.6%
5	2004	300,933	179,600	McMORRIS, CATHY	121,333	BARBIERI, DON		58,267 R	59.7%	40.3%	59.7%	40.3%
5	2002	202,282	126,757	NETHERCUTT, GEORGE*	65,146	HAGGIN, BART	10,379	61,611 R	62.7%	32.2%	66.1%	33.9%
6	2006	224,085	65,883	CLOUD, DOUG	158,202	DICKS, NORM*		92,319 D	29.4%	70.6%	29.4%	70.6%
6	2004	294,147	91,228	CLOUD, DOUG	202,919	DICKS, NORM*		111,691 D	31.0%	69.0%	31.0%	69.0%
6	2002	196,444	61,584	LAWRENCE, BOB	126,116	DICKS, NORM*	8,744	64,532 D	31.3%	64.2%	32.8%	67.2%
7	2006	246,133	38,715	BEREN, STEVE	195,462	McDERMOTT, JIM*	11,956	156,747 D	15.7%	79.4%	16.5%	83.5%
7	2004	337,528	65,226	CASSADY, CAROL	272,302	McDERMOTT, JIM*		207,076 D	19.3%	80.7%	19.3%	80.7%
7	2002	211,003	46,256	CASSADY, CAROL	156,300	McDERMOTT, JIM*	8,447	110,044 D	21.9%	74.1%	22.8%	77.2%
8	2006	251,383	129,362	REICHERT, DAVE*	122,021	BURNER, DARCY		7,341 R	51.5%	48.5%	51.5%	48.5%
8	2004	336,499	173,298	REICHERT, DAVE	157,148	ROSS, DAVE	6,053	16,150 R	51.5%	46.7%	52.4%	47.6%
8	2002	203,335	121,633	DUNN, JENNIFER*	75,931	BEHRENS-BENEDICT, HEIDI	5,771	45,702 R	59.8%	37.3%	61.6%	38.4%
9	2006	181,120	62,082	COFCHIN, STEVEN C.	119,038	SMITH, ADAM*		56,956 D	34.3%	65.7%	34.3%	65.7%
9	2004	256,671	88,304	LORD, PAUL J.	162,433	SMITH, ADAM*	5,934	74,129 D	34.4%	63.3%	35.2%	64.8%
9	2002	163,710	63,146	CASADA, SARAH	95,805	SMITH, ADAM*	4,759	32,659 D	38.6%	58.5%	39.7%	60.3%
TOTAL	2006	2,054,056	798,005		1,244,095		11,956	446,090 D	38.9%	60.6%	39.1%	60.9%
TOTAL	2004	2,729,995	1,095,493		1,608,751		25,751	513,258 D	40.1%	58.9%	40.5%	59.5%
TOTAL	2002	1,739,116	778,922		907,440		52,754	128,518 D	44.8%	52.2%	46.2%	53.8%

An asterisk (*) denotes incumbent.

WASHINGTON

GENERAL AND PRIMARY ELECTIONS

2006 GENERAL ELECTIONS

Senator	Other vote was 29,331 Libertarian (Bruce Guthrie); 21,254 Green (Aaron Dixon); 16,384 Independent (Robin Adair).
House	Other vote was:
CD 1	
CD 2	
CD 3	
CD 4	
CD 5	
CD 6	
CD 7	11,956 Independent (Linnea S. Noreen).
CD 8	
CD 9	

2006 PRIMARY ELECTIONS

Primary	September 19, 2006	**Registration** (as of September 19, 2006)	3,250,216	No Party Registration

Primary Type   Open—Any registered voter could participate in the primary of their choice, but were limited to the ballot of one party.

Note: An asterisk (*) denotes incumbent.

	REPUBLICAN PRIMARIES			DEMOCRATIC PRIMARIES		
Senator	Mike McGavick	397,524	85.9%	Maria Cantwell*	570,677	90.8%
	Brad Klippert	32,213	7.0%	Hong Tran	33,124	5.3%
	Warren E. Hanson	17,881	3.9%	Mike the Mover	11,274	1.8%
	B. Barry Massoudi	6,410	1.4%	Michael Goodspaceguy Nelson	9,454	1.5%
	Gordon Allen Pross	5,196	1.1%	Mohammad H. Said	4,222	0.7%
	William Edward Chovil	3,670	0.8%			
	TOTAL	462,894		TOTAL	628,751	
Congressional District 1	Larry W. Ishmael	39,592	100.0%	Jay Inslee*	75,644	100.0%
Congressional District 2	Doug Roulstone	39,761	77.6%	Rick Larsen*	70,662	100.0%
	Teri Moats	11,487	22.4%			
	TOTAL	51,248				
Congressional District 3	Michael Messmore	29,289	67.1%	Brian Baird*	66,618	100.0%
	Daniel R. Miller	14,341	32.9%			
	TOTAL	43,630				
Congressional District 4	Doc Hastings*	54,968	76.7%	Richard Wright	22,145	85.1%
	Claude L. Oliver	16,661	23.3%	Lewis Picton	3,875	14.9%
	TOTAL	71,629		TOTAL	26,020	
Congressional District 5	Cathy McMorris*	73,902	100.0%	Peter J. Goldmark	50,866	100.0%
Congressional District 6	Doug Cloud	37,088	100.0%	Norm Dicks*	76,210	100.0%
Congressional District 7	Steve Beren	15,205	100.0%	Jim McDermott*	95,065	91.0%
				Donovan Rivers	4,837	4.6%
				Joshua Smith	4,526	4.3%
				TOTAL	104,428	
Congressional District 8	Dave Reichert*	52,598	100.0%	Darcy Burner	54,776	100.0%
Congressional District 9	Steven C. Cofchin	31,700	100.0%	Adam Smith*	52,428	100.0%

392

WEST VIRGINIA

Congressional districts first established for elections held in 2002
3 members

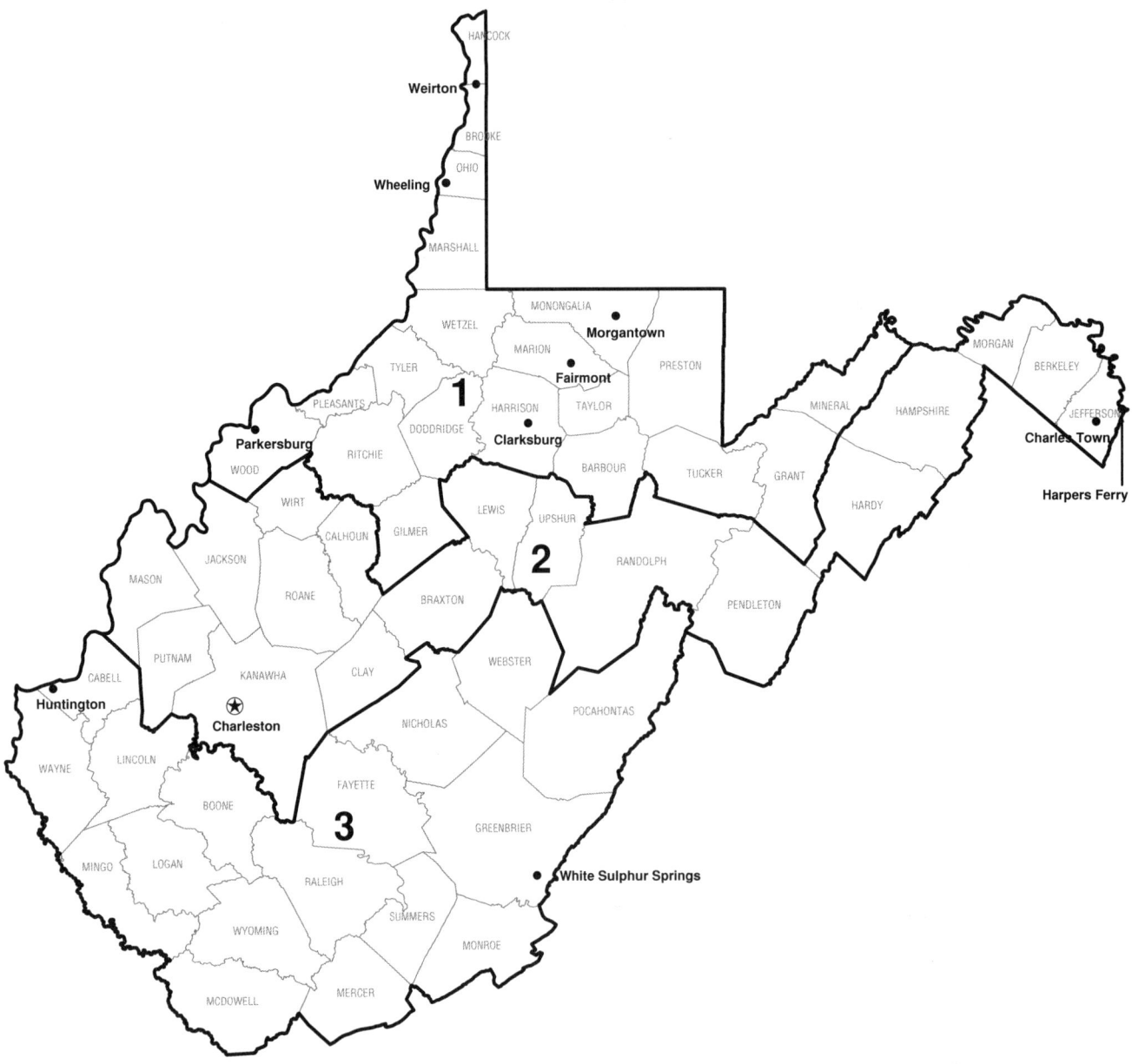

WEST VIRGINIA

GOVERNOR
Joe Manchin III (D). Elected 2004 to a four-year term.

SENATORS (2 Democrats)
Robert C. Byrd (D). Reelected 2006 to a six-year term. Previously elected 2000, 1994, 1988, 1982, 1976, 1970, 1964, 1958.

John D. Rockefeller IV (D). Reelected 2002 to a six-year term. Previously elected 1996, 1990, 1984.

REPRESENTATIVES (2 Democrats, 1 Republican)
1. Alan B. Mollohan (D)   2. Shelley Moore Capito (R)   3. Nick J. Rahall II (D)

POSTWAR VOTE FOR PRESIDENT

| | | Republican | | Democratic | | Other | | Percentage | | | |
| | | | | | | | | Total Vote | | Major Vote | |
Year	Total Vote	Vote	Candidate	Vote	Candidate	Vote	Plurality	Rep.	Dem.	Rep.	Dem.
2004	755,887	423,778	Bush, George W.	326,541	Kerry, John	5,568	97,237 R	56.1%	43.2%	56.5%	43.5%
2000**	648,124	336,475	Bush, George W.	295,497	Gore, Al	16,152	40,978 R	51.9%	45.6%	53.2%	46.8%
1996**	636,459	233,946	Dole, Bob	327,812	Clinton, Bill	74,701	93,866 D	36.8%	51.5%	41.6%	58.4%
1992**	683,762	241,974	Bush, George	331,001	Clinton, Bill	110,787	89,027 D	35.4%	48.4%	42.2%	57.8%
1988	653,311	310,065	Bush, George	341,016	Dukakis, Michael S.	2,230	30,951 D	47.5%	52.2%	47.6%	52.4%
1984	735,742	405,483	Reagan, Ronald	328,125	Mondale, Walter F.	2,134	77,358 R	55.1%	44.6%	55.3%	44.7%
1980**	737,715	334,206	Reagan, Ronald	367,462	Carter, Jimmy	36,047	33,256 D	45.3%	49.8%	47.6%	52.4%
1976	750,964	314,760	Ford, Gerald R.	435,914	Carter, Jimmy	290	121,154 D	41.9%	58.0%	41.9%	58.1%
1972	762,399	484,964	Nixon, Richard M.	277,435	McGovern, George S.		207,529 R	63.6%	36.4%	63.6%	36.4%
1968**	754,206	307,555	Nixon, Richard M.	374,091	Humphrey, Hubert H.	72,560	66,536 D	40.8%	49.6%	45.1%	54.9%
1964	792,040	253,953	Goldwater, Barry M.	538,087	Johnson, Lyndon B.		284,134 D	32.1%	67.9%	32.1%	67.9%
1960	837,781	395,995	Nixon, Richard M.	441,786	Kennedy, John F.		45,791 D	47.3%	52.7%	47.3%	52.7%
1956	830,831	449,297	Eisenhower, Dwight D.	381,534	Stevenson, Adlai E.		67,763 R	54.1%	45.9%	54.1%	45.9%
1952	873,548	419,970	Eisenhower, Dwight D.	453,578	Stevenson, Adlai E.		33,608 D	48.1%	51.9%	48.1%	51.9%
1948	748,750	316,251	Dewey, Thomas E.	429,188	Truman, Harry S.	3,311	112,937 D	42.2%	57.3%	42.4%	57.6%

**In past elections, the other vote included: 2000 - 10,680 Green (Ralph Nader); 1996 - 71,639 Reform (Ross Perot); 1992 - 108,829 Independent (Ross Perot); 1980 - 31,691 Independent (John Anderson); 1968 - 72,560 American Independent (George Wallace).

WEST VIRGINIA

POSTWAR VOTE FOR GOVERNOR

Year	Total Vote	Republican Vote	Republican Candidate	Democratic Vote	Democratic Candidate	Other Vote	Rep.-Dem. Plurality	Total Vote Rep.	Total Vote Dem.	Major Vote Rep.	Major Vote Dem.
2004	744,433	253,131	Warner, Monty	472,758	Manchin, Joe III	18,544	219,627 D	34.0%	63.5%	34.9%	65.1%
2000	648,047	305,926	Underwood, Cecil H.	324,822	Wise, Bob	17,299	18,896 D	47.2%	50.1%	48.5%	51.5%
1996	628,559	324,518	Underwood, Cecil H.	287,870	Pritt, Charlotte	16,171	36,648 R	51.6%	45.8%	53.0%	47.0%
1992	657,193	240,390	Benedict, Cleveland K.	368,302	Caperton, Gaston	48,501	127,912 D	36.6%	56.0%	39.5%	60.5%
1988	649,593	267,172	Moore, Arch A.	382,421	Caperton, Gaston		115,249 D	41.1%	58.9%	41.1%	58.9%
1984	741,502	394,937	Moore, Arch A.	346,565	See, Clyde M.		48,372 R	53.3%	46.7%	53.3%	46.7%
1980	742,150	337,240	Moore, Arch A.	401,863	Rockefeller, John D. IV	3,047	64,623 D	45.4%	54.1%	45.6%	54.4%
1976	749,270	253,420	Underwood, Cecil H.	495,661	Rockefeller, John D. IV	189	242,241 D	33.8%	66.2%	33.8%	66.2%
1972	774,279	423,817	Moore, Arch A.	350,462	Rockefeller, John D. IV		73,355 R	54.7%	45.3%	54.7%	45.3%
1968	743,845	378,315	Moore, Arch A.	365,530	Sprouse, James M.		12,785 R	50.9%	49.1%	50.9%	49.1%
1964	788,582	355,559	Underwood, Cecil H.	433,023	Smith, Hulett C.		77,464 D	45.1%	54.9%	45.1%	54.9%
1960	827,420	380,665	Neely, Harold E.	446,755	Barron, W. W.		66,090 D	46.0%	54.0%	46.0%	54.0%
1956	817,623	440,502	Underwood, Cecil H.	377,121	Mollohan, Robert H.		63,381 R	53.9%	46.1%	53.9%	46.1%
1952	882,527	427,629	Holt, Rush D.	454,898	Marland, William C.		27,269 D	48.5%	51.5%	48.5%	51.5%
1948	768,061	329,309	Boreman, Herbert	438,752	Patteson, Okey L.		109,443 D	42.9%	57.1%	42.9%	57.1%

POSTWAR VOTE FOR SENATOR

Year	Total Vote	Republican Vote	Republican Candidate	Democratic Vote	Democratic Candidate	Other Vote	Rep.-Dem. Plurality	Total Vote Rep.	Total Vote Dem.	Major Vote Rep.	Major Vote Dem.
2006	459,884	155,043	Raese, John R.	296,276	Byrd, Robert C.	8,565	141,233 D	33.7%	64.4%	34.4%	65.6%
2002	436,183	160,902	Wolfe, Jay	275,281	Rockefeller, John D. IV		114,379 D	36.9%	63.1%	36.9%	63.1%
2000	603,477	121,635	Gallaher, David T.	469,215	Byrd, Robert C.	12,627	347,580 D	20.2%	77.8%	20.6%	79.4%
1996	595,614	139,088	Burks, Betty A.	456,526	Rockefeller, John D. IV		317,438 D	23.4%	76.6%	23.4%	76.6%
1994	420,936	130,441	Klos, Stan	290,495	Byrd, Robert C.		160,054 D	31.0%	69.0%	31.0%	69.0%
1990	404,305	128,071	Yoder, John	276,234	Rockefeller, John D. IV		148,163 D	31.7%	68.3%	31.7%	68.3%
1988	634,547	223,564	Wolfe, M. Jay	410,983	Byrd, Robert C.		187,419 D	35.2%	64.8%	35.2%	64.8%
1984	722,212	344,680	Raese, John R.	374,233	Rockefeller, John D. IV	3,299	29,553 D	47.7%	51.8%	47.9%	52.1%
1982	565,314	173,910	Benedict, Cleveland K.	387,170	Byrd, Robert C.	4,234	213,260 D	30.8%	68.5%	31.0%	69.0%
1978	493,351	244,317	Moore, Arch A.	249,034	Randolph, Jennings		4,717 D	49.5%	50.5%	49.5%	50.5%
1976	566,790		—	566,423	Byrd, Robert C.	367	566,423 D		99.9%		100.0%
1972	731,841	245,531	Leonard, Louise	486,310	Randolph, Jennings		240,779 D	33.5%	66.5%	33.5%	66.5%
1970	445,623	99,658	Dodson, Elmer H.	345,965	Byrd, Robert C.		246,307 D	22.4%	77.6%	22.4%	77.6%
1966	491,216	198,891	Love, Francis J.	292,325	Randolph, Jennings		93,434 D	40.5%	59.5%	40.5%	59.5%
1964	761,087	246,072	Benedict, Cooper P.	515,015	Byrd, Robert C.		268,943 D	32.3%	67.7%	32.3%	67.7%
1960	828,292	369,935	Underwood, Cecil H.	458,355	Randolph, Jennings	2	88,420 D	44.7%	55.3%	44.7%	55.3%
1958	644,917	263,172	Revercomb, Chapman	381,745	Byrd, Robert C.		118,573 D	40.8%	59.2%	40.8%	59.2%
1958S	630,677	256,510	Hoblitzell, John D.	374,167	Randolph, Jennings		117,657 D	40.7%	59.3%	40.7%	59.3%
1956S	805,174	432,123	Revercomb, Chapman	373,051	Marland, William C.		59,072 R	53.7%	46.3%	53.7%	46.3%
1954	593,329	268,066	Sweeney, Tom	325,263	Neely, Matthew M.		57,197 D	45.2%	54.8%	45.2%	54.8%
1952	876,573	406,554	Revercomb, Chapman	470,019	Kilgore, Harley M.		63,465 D	46.4%	53.6%	46.4%	53.6%
1948	763,888	328,534	Revercomb, Chapman	435,354	Neely, Matthew M.		106,820 D	43.0%	57.0%	43.0%	57.0%
1946	542,768	269,617	Sweeney, Tom	273,151	Kilgore, Harley M.		3,534 D	49.7%	50.3%	49.7%	50.3%

One of the 1958 elections and the 1956 election were for short terms to fill vacancies.

WEST VIRGINIA

SENATOR 2006

2000 Census Population	County	Total Vote	Republican	Democratic	Other	Rep.-Dem. Plurality	Percentage Total Vote Rep.	Dem.	Major Vote Rep.	Dem.
15,557	BARBOUR	4,324	1,407	2,845	72	1,438 D	32.5%	65.8%	33.1%	66.9%
75,905	BERKELEY	19,652	8,206	11,133	313	2,927 D	41.8%	56.7%	42.4%	57.6%
25,535	BOONE	6,031	1,085	4,850	96	3,765 D	18.0%	80.4%	18.3%	81.7%
14,702	BRAXTON	3,780	974	2,747	59	1,773 D	25.8%	72.7%	26.2%	73.8%
25,447	BROOKE	6,137	1,747	4,300	90	2,553 D	28.5%	70.1%	28.9%	71.1%
96,784	CABELL	23,665	8,580	14,644	441	6,064 D	36.3%	61.9%	36.9%	63.1%
7,582	CALHOUN	1,666	612	991	63	379 D	36.7%	59.5%	38.2%	61.8%
10,330	CLAY	2,294	642	1,589	63	947 D	28.0%	69.3%	28.8%	71.2%
7,403	DODDRIDGE	1,716	890	795	31	95 R	51.9%	46.3%	52.8%	47.2%
47,579	FAYETTE	9,525	2,244	7,084	197	4,840 D	23.6%	74.4%	24.1%	75.9%
7,160	GILMER	1,785	512	1,202	71	690 D	28.7%	67.3%	29.9%	70.1%
11,299	GRANT	2,919	1,359	1,525	35	166 D	46.6%	52.2%	47.1%	52.9%
34,453	GREENBRIER	8,630	2,848	5,524	258	2,676 D	33.0%	64.0%	34.0%	66.0%
20,203	HAMPSHIRE	5,213	2,216	2,894	103	678 D	42.5%	55.5%	43.4%	56.6%
32,667	HANCOCK	8,166	2,931	5,056	179	2,125 D	35.9%	61.9%	36.7%	63.3%
12,669	HARDY	3,279	939	2,273	67	1,334 D	28.6%	69.3%	29.2%	70.8%
68,652	HARRISON	18,603	5,744	12,587	272	6,843 D	30.9%	67.7%	31.3%	68.7%
28,000	JACKSON	9,479	3,752	5,532	195	1,780 D	39.6%	58.4%	40.4%	59.6%
42,190	JEFFERSON	12,628	4,129	8,301	198	4,172 D	32.7%	65.7%	33.2%	66.8%
200,073	KANAWHA	53,884	17,715	34,998	1,171	17,283 D	32.9%	65.0%	33.6%	66.4%
16,919	LEWIS	4,659	1,639	2,925	95	1,286 D	35.2%	62.8%	35.9%	64.1%
22,108	LINCOLN	5,483	1,476	3,884	123	2,408 D	26.9%	70.8%	27.5%	72.5%
37,710	LOGAN	7,519	1,323	6,071	125	4,748 D	17.6%	80.7%	17.9%	82.1%
27,329	MCDOWELL	3,856	563	3,199	94	2,636 D	14.6%	83.0%	15.0%	85.0%
56,598	MARION	15,637	4,337	11,056	244	6,719 D	27.7%	70.7%	28.2%	71.8%
35,519	MARSHALL	10,441	3,514	6,716	211	3,202 D	33.7%	64.3%	34.3%	65.7%
25,957	MASON	7,192	2,370	4,687	135	2,317 D	33.0%	65.2%	33.6%	66.4%
62,980	MERCER	12,681	4,855	7,557	269	2,702 D	38.3%	59.6%	39.1%	60.9%
27,078	MINERAL	7,294	2,429	4,801	64	2,372 D	33.3%	65.8%	33.6%	66.4%
28,253	MINGO	5,679	878	4,748	53	3,870 D	15.5%	83.6%	15.6%	84.4%
81,866	MONONGALIA	21,212	6,715	14,078	419	7,363 D	31.7%	66.4%	32.3%	67.7%
14,583	MONROE	3,869	1,312	2,474	83	1,162 D	33.9%	63.9%	34.7%	65.3%
14,943	MORGAN	4,291	1,890	2,313	88	423 D	44.0%	53.9%	45.0%	55.0%
26,562	NICHOLAS	6,653	1,940	4,612	101	2,672 D	29.2%	69.3%	29.6%	70.4%
47,427	OHIO	13,070	4,558	8,321	191	3,763 D	34.9%	63.7%	35.4%	64.6%
8,196	PENDLETON	2,156	663	1,465	28	802 D	30.8%	67.9%	31.2%	68.8%
7,514	PLEASANTS	1,966	719	1,206	41	487 D	36.6%	61.3%	37.4%	62.6%
9,131	POCAHONTAS	2,501	762	1,662	77	900 D	30.5%	66.5%	31.4%	68.6%
29,334	PRESTON	8,464	3,606	4,710	148	1,104 D	42.6%	55.6%	43.4%	56.6%
51,589	PUTNAM	15,792	6,822	8,639	331	1,817 D	43.2%	54.7%	44.1%	55.9%
79,220	RALEIGH	17,218	5,934	10,981	303	5,047 D	34.5%	63.8%	35.1%	64.9%
28,262	RANDOLPH	7,654	2,219	5,317	118	3,098 D	29.0%	69.5%	29.4%	70.6%
10,343	RITCHIE	2,506	1,215	1,237	54	22 D	48.5%	49.4%	49.6%	50.4%
15,446	ROANE	3,775	1,447	2,237	91	790 D	38.3%	59.3%	39.3%	60.7%
12,999	SUMMERS	3,213	980	2,152	81	1,172 D	30.5%	67.0%	31.3%	68.7%
16,089	TAYLOR	4,296	1,354	2,888	54	1,534 D	31.5%	67.2%	31.9%	68.1%
7,321	TUCKER	2,609	867	1,712	30	845 D	33.2%	65.6%	33.6%	66.4%
9,592	TYLER	2,444	1,030	1,370	44	340 D	42.1%	56.1%	42.9%	57.1%
23,404	UPSHUR	5,905	2,261	3,534	110	1,273 D	38.3%	59.8%	39.0%	61.0%
42,903	WAYNE	10,863	3,616	7,070	177	3,454 D	33.3%	65.1%	33.8%	66.2%
9,719	WEBSTER	2,399	509	1,848	42	1,339 D	21.2%	77.0%	21.6%	78.4%
17,693	WETZEL	4,422	1,353	3,005	64	1,652 D	30.6%	68.0%	31.0%	69.0%
5,873	WIRT	1,326	547	748	31	201 D	41.3%	56.4%	42.2%	57.8%
87,986	WOOD	22,356	9,570	12,377	409	2,807 D	42.8%	55.4%	43.6%	56.4%
25,708	WYOMING	5,107	1,238	3,806	63	2,568 D	24.2%	74.5%	24.5%	75.5%
1,808,344	TOTAL	459,884	155,043	296,276	8,565	141,233 D	33.7%	64.4%	34.4%	65.6%

WEST VIRGINIA

HOUSE OF REPRESENTATIVES

CD	Year	Total Vote	Republican Vote	Republican Candidate	Democratic Vote	Democratic Candidate	Other Vote	Rep.-Dem. Plurality	Total Vote Rep.	Total Vote Dem.	Major Vote Rep.	Major Vote Dem.
1	2006	157,000	55,963	WAKIM, CHRIS	100,939	MOLLOHAN, ALAN B.*	98	44,976 D	35.6%	64.3%	35.7%	64.3%
1	2004	245,779	79,196	PARKS, ALAN LEE	166,583	MOLLOHAN, ALAN B.*		87,387 D	32.2%	67.8%	32.2%	67.8%
1	2002	111,261		—	110,941	MOLLOHAN, ALAN B.*	320	110,941 D		99.7%		100.0%
2	2006	164,580	94,110	CAPITO, SHELLEY MOORE*	70,470	CALLAGHAN, MIKE		23,640 R	57.2%	42.8%	57.2%	42.8%
2	2004	257,025	147,676	CAPITO, SHELLEY MOORE*	106,131	WELLS, ERIK	3,218	41,545 R	57.5%	41.3%	58.2%	41.8%
2	2002	163,676	98,276	CAPITO, SHELLEY MOORE*	65,400	HUMPHREYS, JIM		32,876 R	60.0%	40.0%	60.0%	40.0%
3	2006	133,233	40,820	WOLFE, KIM	92,413	RAHALL, NICK J. II*		51,593 D	30.6%	69.4%	30.6%	69.4%
3	2004	218,852	76,170	SNUFFER, RICK	142,682	RAHALL, NICK J. II*		66,512 D	34.8%	65.2%	34.8%	65.2%
3	2002	125,012	37,229	CHAPMAN, PAUL E.	87,783	RAHALL, NICK J. II*		50,554 D	29.8%	70.2%	29.8%	70.2%
TOTAL	2006	454,813	190,893		263,822		98	72,929 D	42.0%	58.0%	42.0%	58.0%
TOTAL	2004	721,656	303,042		415,396		3,218	112,354 D	42.0%	57.6%	42.2%	57.8%
TOTAL	2002	399,949	135,505		264,124		320	128,619 D	33.9%	66.0%	33.9%	66.1%

An asterisk (*) denotes incumbent.

WEST VIRGINIA

GENERAL AND PRIMARY ELECTIONS

2006 GENERAL ELECTIONS

Senator   Other vote was 8,565 Mountain (Jesse Johnson).

House   Other vote was:

CD 1   69 write-in (David Moran); 29 write-in (Bennie Kyle).
CD 2
CD 3

2006 PRIMARY ELECTIONS

Primary   May 9, 2006   **Registration**
(as of May 9, 2006)

Democratic	648,106
Republican	340,760
Mountain	747
Other Parties	11,083
No Party	129,312
TOTAL	1,130,008

Primary Type   Only registered Democrats could vote in the Democratic primary. Registered Republicans and those with no party registration could vote in the Republican primary.

WEST VIRGINIA

GENERAL AND PRIMARY ELECTIONS

Note: An asterisk (*) denotes incumbent.

	REPUBLICAN PRIMARIES			DEMOCRATIC PRIMARIES		
Senator	John R. Raese	47,408	58.3%	Robert C. Byrd*	159,154	85.7%
	Hiram Lewis	18,496	22.7%	Billy Hendricks Jr.	26,609	14.3%
	Rick Snuffer	4,870	6.0%			
	Charles G. "Bud" Railey	4,364	5.4%			
	Paul J. Brown	3,464	4.3%			
	Zane Lawhorn	2,723	3.3%			
	TOTAL	81,325		TOTAL	185,763	
Congressional District 1	Chris Wakim	21,197	100.0%	Alan B. Mollohan*	46,143	100.0%
Congressional District 2	Shelley Moore Capito*	29,031	100.0%	Mike Callaghan	19,155	37.1%
				Mark Hunt	16,906	32.8%
				Richie Robb	15,543	30.1%
				TOTAL	51,604	
Congressional District 3	Kim Wolfe	8,975	57.9%	Nick J. Rahall II*	60,396	100.0%
	Marty Gearheart	6,529	42.1%			
	TOTAL	15,504				

WISCONSIN

Congressional districts first established for elections held in 2002
8 members

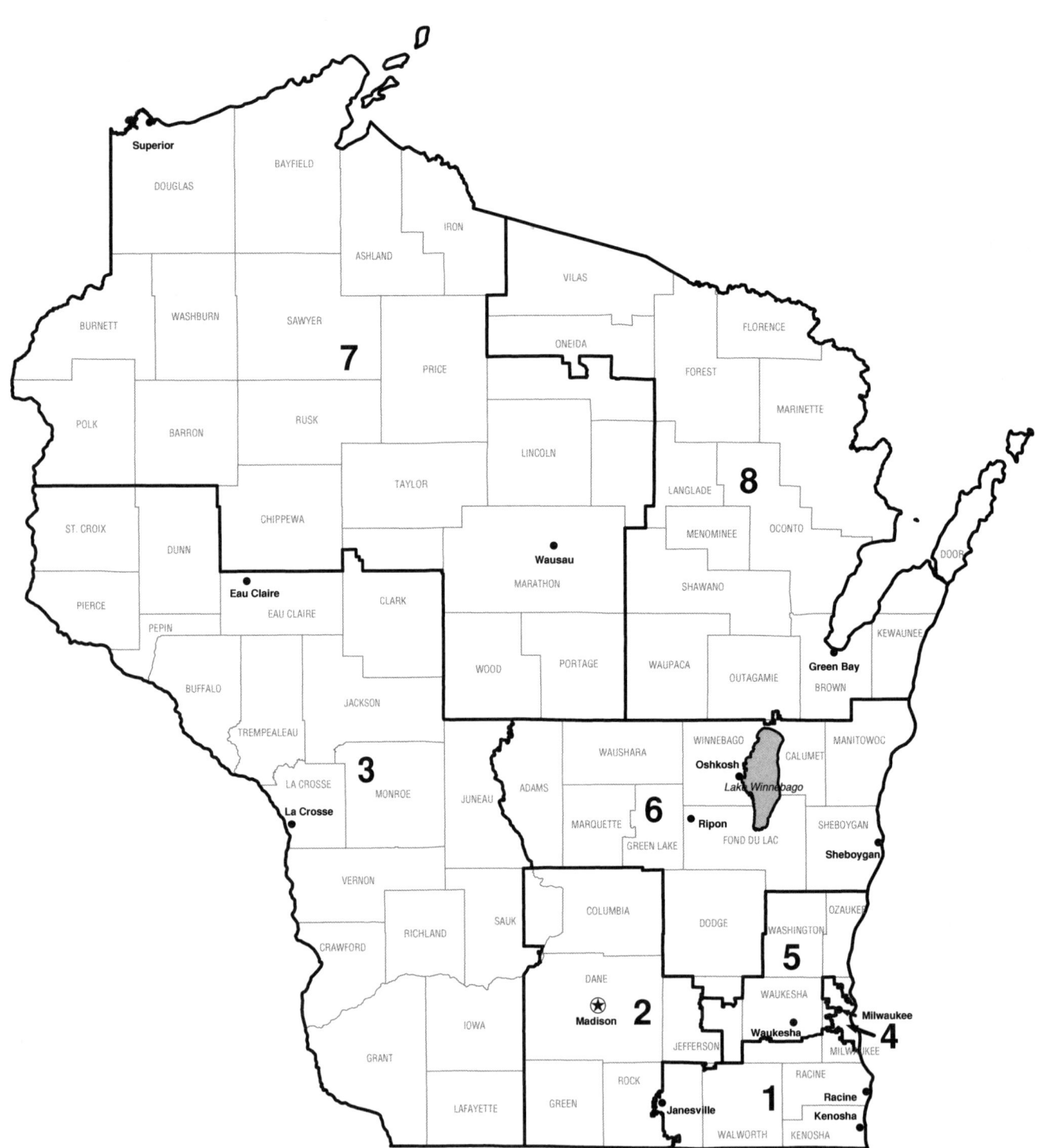

WISCONSIN

GOVERNOR

James E. Doyle (D). Reelected 2006 to a four-year term. Previously elected 2002.

SENATORS (2 Democrats)

Herb Kohl (D). Reelected 2006 to a six-year term. Previously elected 2000, 1994, 1988.

Russell D. Feingold (D). Reelected 2004 to a six-year term. Previously elected 1998, 1992.

REPRESENTATIVES (5 Democrats, 3 Republicans)

1. Paul D. Ryan (R)
2. Tammy Baldwin (D)
3. Ron Kind (D)
4. Gwen Moore (D)
5. F. James Sensenbrenner Jr. (R)
6. Tom Petri (R)
7. David R. Obey (D)
8. Steven L. Kagen (D)

POSTWAR VOTE FOR PRESIDENT

Year	Total Vote	Republican Vote	Republican Candidate	Democratic Vote	Democratic Candidate	Other Vote	Plurality	Total Vote Rep.	Total Vote Dem.	Major Vote Rep.	Major Vote Dem.
2004	2,997,007	1,478,120	Bush, George W.	1,489,504	Kerry, John	29,383	11,384 D	49.3%	49.7%	49.8%	50.2%
2000**	2,598,607	1,237,279	Bush, George W.	1,242,987	Gore, Al	118,341	5,708 D	47.6%	47.8%	49.9%	50.1%
1996**	2,196,169	845,029	Dole, Bob	1,071,971	Clinton, Bill	279,169	226,942 D	38.5%	48.8%	44.1%	55.9%
1992**	2,531,114	930,855	Bush, George	1,041,066	Clinton, Bill	559,193	110,211 D	36.8%	41.1%	47.2%	52.8%
1988	2,191,608	1,047,499	Bush, George	1,126,794	Dukakis, Michael S.	17,315	79,295 D	47.8%	51.4%	48.2%	51.8%
1984	2,211,689	1,198,584	Reagan, Ronald	995,740	Mondale, Walter F.	17,365	202,844 R	54.2%	45.0%	54.6%	45.4%
1980**	2,273,221	1,088,845	Reagan, Ronald	981,584	Carter, Jimmy	202,792	107,261 R	47.9%	43.2%	52.6%	47.4%
1976	2,104,175	1,004,987	Ford, Gerald R.	1,040,232	Carter, Jimmy	58,956	35,245 D	47.8%	49.4%	49.1%	50.9%
1972	1,852,890	989,430	Nixon, Richard M.	810,174	McGovern, George S.	53,286	179,256 R	53.4%	43.7%	55.0%	45.0%
1968**	1,691,538	809,997	Nixon, Richard M.	748,804	Humphrey, Hubert H.	132,737	61,193 R	47.9%	44.3%	52.0%	48.0%
1964	1,691,815	638,495	Goldwater, Barry M.	1,050,424	Johnson, Lyndon B.	2,896	411,929 D	37.7%	62.1%	37.8%	62.2%
1960	1,729,082	895,175	Nixon, Richard M.	830,805	Kennedy, John F.	3,102	64,370 R	51.8%	48.0%	51.9%	48.1%
1956	1,550,558	954,844	Eisenhower, Dwight D.	586,768	Stevenson, Adlai E.	8,946	368,076 R	61.6%	37.8%	61.9%	38.1%
1952	1,607,370	979,744	Eisenhower, Dwight D.	622,175	Stevenson, Adlai E.	5,451	357,569 R	61.0%	38.7%	61.2%	38.8%
1948	1,276,800	590,959	Dewey, Thomas E.	647,310	Truman, Harry S.	38,531	56,351 D	46.3%	50.7%	47.7%	52.3%

**In past elections, the other vote included: 2000 - 94,070 Green (Ralph Nader); 1996 - 227,339 Reform (Ross Perot); 1992 - 544,479 Independent (Ross Perot); 1980 - 160,657 Independent (John Anderson); 1968 - 127,835 American Independent (George Wallace).

WISCONSIN

POSTWAR VOTE FOR GOVERNOR

Year	Total Vote	Republican Vote	Republican Candidate	Democratic Vote	Democratic Candidate	Other Vote	Rep.-Dem. Plurality	Percentage Total Vote Rep.	Percentage Total Vote Dem.	Percentage Major Vote Rep.	Percentage Major Vote Dem.
2006	2,161,700	979,427	Green, Mark	1,139,115	Doyle, James E.	43,158	159,688 D	45.3%	52.7%	46.2%	53.8%
2002**	1,775,349	734,779	McCallum, Scott	800,515	Doyle, James E.	240,055	65,736 D	41.4%	45.1%	47.9%	52.1%
1998	1,756,014	1,047,716	Thompson, Tommy G.	679,553	Garvey, Edward R.	28,745	368,163 R	59.7%	38.7%	60.7%	39.3%
1994	1,563,835	1,051,326	Thompson, Tommy G.	482,850	Chvala, Chuck	29,659	568,476 R	67.2%	30.9%	68.5%	31.5%
1990	1,379,727	802,321	Thompson, Tommy G.	576,280	Loftus, Thomas	1,126	226,041 R	58.2%	41.8%	58.2%	41.8%
1986	1,526,960	805,090	Thompson, Tommy G.	705,578	Earl, Anthony S.	16,292	99,512 R	52.7%	46.2%	53.3%	46.7%
1982	1,580,344	662,838	Kohler, Terry J.	896,812	Earl, Anthony S.	20,694	233,974 D	41.9%	56.7%	42.5%	57.5%
1978	1,500,996	816,056	Dreyfus, Lee S.	673,813	Schreiber, Martin J.	11,127	142,243 R	54.4%	44.9%	54.8%	45.2%
1974	1,181,976	497,195	Dyke, William D.	628,639	Lucey, Patrick J.	56,142	131,444 D	42.1%	53.2%	44.2%	55.8%
1970**	1,343,160	602,617	Olson, Jack B.	728,403	Lucey, Patrick J.	12,140	125,786 D	44.9%	54.2%	45.3%	54.7%
1968	1,689,738	893,463	Knowles, Warren P.	791,100	LaFollette, Bronson C.	5,175	102,363 R	52.9%	46.8%	53.0%	47.0%
1966	1,170,173	626,041	Knowles, Warren P.	539,258	Lucey, Patrick J.	4,874	86,783 R	53.5%	46.1%	53.7%	46.3%
1964	1,694,887	856,779	Knowles, Warren P.	837,901	Reynolds, John W.	207	18,878 R	50.6%	49.4%	50.6%	49.4%
1962	1,265,900	625,536	Kuehn, Philip G.	637,491	Reynolds, John W.	2,873	11,955 D	49.4%	50.4%	49.5%	50.5%
1960	1,728,009	837,123	Kuehn, Philip G.	890,868	Nelson, Gaylord A.	18	53,745 D	48.4%	51.6%	48.4%	51.6%
1958	1,202,219	556,391	Thomson, Vernon W.	644,296	Nelson, Gaylord A.	1,532	87,905 D	46.3%	53.6%	46.3%	53.7%
1956	1,557,788	808,273	Thomson, Vernon W.	749,421	Proxmire, William	94	58,852 R	51.9%	48.1%	51.9%	48.1%
1954	1,158,666	596,158	Kohler, Walter J.	560,747	Proxmire, William	1,761	35,411 R	51.5%	48.4%	51.5%	48.5%
1952	1,615,214	1,009,171	Kohler, Walter J.	601,844	Proxmire, William	4,199	407,327 R	62.5%	37.3%	62.6%	37.4%
1950	1,138,148	605,649	Kohler, Walter J.	525,319	Thompson, Carl W.	7,180	80,330 R	53.2%	46.2%	53.6%	46.4%
1948	1,266,139	684,839	Rennebohm, Oscar	558,497	Thompson, Carl W.	22,803	126,342 R	54.1%	44.1%	55.1%	44.9%
1946	1,040,444	621,970	Goodland, Walter	406,499	Hoan, Daniel W.	11,975	215,471 R	59.8%	39.1%	60.5%	39.5%

**In past elections, the other vote included: 2002 - 185,455 Libertarian (Ed Thompson). The term of office of Wisconsin's governor was increased from two to four years effective with the 1970 election.

POSTWAR VOTE FOR SENATOR

Year	Total Vote	Republican Vote	Republican Candidate	Democratic Vote	Democratic Candidate	Other Vote	Rep.-Dem. Plurality	Percentage Total Vote Rep.	Percentage Total Vote Dem.	Percentage Major Vote Rep.	Percentage Major Vote Dem.
2006	2,138,297	630,299	Lorge, Robert Gerald	1,439,214	Kohl, Herb	68,784	808,915 D	29.5%	67.3%	30.5%	69.5%
2004	2,949,743	1,301,183	Michels, Tim	1,632,697	Feingold, Russell D.	15,863	331,514 D	44.1%	55.4%	44.4%	55.6%
2000	2,540,083	940,744	Gillespie, John	1,563,238	Kohl, Herb	36,101	622,494 D	37.0%	61.5%	37.6%	62.4%
1998	1,760,836	852,272	Neumann, Mark W.	890,059	Feingold, Russell D.	18,505	37,787 D	48.4%	50.5%	48.9%	51.1%
1994	1,565,628	636,989	Welch, Robert T.	912,662	Kohl, Herb	15,977	175,673 D	40.7%	58.3%	41.1%	58.9%
1992	2,455,124	1,129,599	Kasten, Robert W.	1,290,662	Feingold, Russell D.	34,863	161,063 D	46.0%	52.6%	46.7%	53.3%
1988	2,168,190	1,030,440	Engeleiter, Susan	1,128,625	Kohl, Herb	9,125	98,185 D	47.5%	52.1%	47.7%	52.3%
1986	1,483,174	754,573	Kasten, Robert W.	702,963	Garvey, Edward R.	25,638	51,610 R	50.9%	47.4%	51.8%	48.2%
1982	1,544,981	527,355	McCallum, Scott	983,311	Proxmire, William	34,315	455,956 D	34.1%	63.6%	34.9%	65.1%
1980	2,204,202	1,106,311	Kasten, Robert W.	1,065,487	Nelson, Gaylord A.	32,404	40,824 R	50.2%	48.3%	50.9%	49.1%
1976	1,935,183	521,902	York, Stanley	1,396,970	Proxmire, William	16,311	875,068 D	27.0%	72.2%	27.2%	72.8%
1974	1,199,495	429,327	Petri, Tom	740,700	Nelson, Gaylord A.	29,468	311,373 D	35.8%	61.8%	36.7%	63.3%
1970	1,338,967	381,297	Erickson, John E.	948,445	Proxmire, William	9,225	567,148 D	28.5%	70.8%	28.7%	71.3%
1968	1,654,861	633,910	Leonard, Jerris	1,020,931	Nelson, Gaylord A.	20	387,021 D	38.3%	61.7%	38.3%	61.7%
1964	1,673,776	780,116	Renk, Wilbur N.	892,013	Proxmire, William	1,647	111,897 D	46.6%	53.3%	46.7%	53.3%
1962	1,260,168	594,846	Wiley, Alexander	662,342	Nelson, Gaylord A.	2,980	67,496 D	47.2%	52.6%	47.3%	52.7%
1958	1,194,678	510,398	Steinle, Roland J.	682,440	Proxmire, William	1,840	172,042 D	42.7%	57.1%	42.8%	57.2%
1957S	772,620	312,931	Kohler, Walter J.	435,985	Proxmire, William	23,704	123,054 D	40.5%	56.4%	41.8%	58.2%
1956	1,523,356	892,473	Wiley, Alexander	627,903	Maier, Henry W.	2,980	264,570 R	58.6%	41.2%	58.7%	41.3%
1952	1,605,228	870,444	McCarthy, Joseph R.	731,402	Fairchild, Thomas E.	3,382	139,042 R	54.2%	45.6%	54.3%	45.7%
1950	1,116,135	595,283	Wiley, Alexander	515,539	Fairchild, Thomas E.	5,313	79,744 R	53.3%	46.2%	53.6%	46.4%
1946	1,014,594	620,430	McCarthy, Joseph R.	378,772	McMurray, Howard J.	15,392	241,658 R	61.2%	37.3%	62.1%	37.9%

The August 1957 election was for a short term to fill a vacancy.

WISCONSIN

GOVERNOR 2006

2000 Census Population	County	Total Vote	Republican	Democratic	Other	Rep.-Dem. Plurality	Percentage Total Vote Rep.	Dem.	Major Vote Rep.	Dem.
18,643	ADAMS	7,899	3,324	4,416	159	1,092 D	42.1%	55.9%	42.9%	57.1%
16,866	ASHLAND	6,258	1,902	4,118	238	2,216 D	30.4%	65.8%	31.6%	68.4%
44,963	BARRON	16,333	7,920	8,136	277	216 D	48.5%	49.8%	49.3%	50.7%
15,013	BAYFIELD	7,253	2,468	4,653	132	2,185 D	34.0%	64.2%	34.7%	65.3%
226,778	BROWN	93,635	46,989	45,046	1,600	1,943 R	50.2%	48.1%	51.1%	48.9%
13,804	BUFFALO	5,362	2,196	3,078	88	882 D	41.0%	57.4%	41.6%	58.4%
15,674	BURNETT	6,184	2,900	3,225	59	325 D	46.9%	52.2%	47.3%	52.7%
40,631	CALUMET	19,382	9,995	9,059	328	936 R	51.6%	46.7%	52.5%	47.5%
55,195	CHIPPEWA	21,818	9,839	11,467	512	1,628 D	45.1%	52.6%	46.2%	53.8%
33,557	CLARK	11,240	5,152	5,758	330	606 D	45.8%	51.2%	47.2%	52.8%
52,468	COLUMBIA	22,164	9,936	11,662	566	1,726 D	44.8%	52.6%	46.0%	54.0%
17,243	CRAWFORD	6,331	2,439	3,751	141	1,312 D	38.5%	59.2%	39.4%	60.6%
426,526	DANE	213,940	58,302	149,661	5,977	91,359 D	27.3%	70.0%	28.0%	72.0%
85,897	DODGE	31,049	17,302	13,137	610	4,165 R	55.7%	42.3%	56.8%	43.2%
27,961	DOOR	14,393	6,479	7,592	322	1,113 D	45.0%	52.7%	46.0%	54.0%
43,287	DOUGLAS	16,284	5,233	10,670	381	5,437 D	32.1%	65.5%	32.9%	67.1%
39,858	DUNN	14,608	6,208	8,070	330	1,862 D	42.5%	55.2%	43.5%	56.5%
93,142	EAU CLAIRE	38,911	15,733	22,240	938	6,507 D	40.4%	57.2%	41.4%	58.6%
5,088	FLORENCE	1,963	1,079	865	19	214 R	55.0%	44.1%	55.5%	44.5%
97,296	FOND DU LAC	38,226	21,515	16,073	638	5,442 R	56.3%	42.0%	57.2%	42.8%
10,024	FOREST	3,614	1,712	1,853	49	141 D	47.4%	51.3%	48.0%	52.0%
49,597	GRANT	16,952	7,427	9,242	283	1,815 D	43.8%	54.5%	44.6%	55.4%
33,647	GREEN	13,241	5,149	7,769	323	2,620 D	38.9%	58.7%	39.9%	60.1%
19,105	GREEN LAKE	7,986	4,714	3,122	150	1,592 R	59.0%	39.1%	60.2%	39.8%
22,780	IOWA	9,047	3,267	5,630	150	2,363 D	36.1%	62.2%	36.7%	63.3%
6,861	IRON	2,782	1,189	1,560	33	371 D	42.7%	56.1%	43.3%	56.7%
19,100	JACKSON	6,938	2,931	3,858	149	927 D	42.2%	55.6%	43.2%	56.8%
74,021	JEFFERSON	30,965	16,038	14,247	680	1,791 R	51.8%	46.0%	53.0%	47.0%
24,316	JUNEAU	8,289	4,101	3,969	219	132 R	49.5%	47.9%	50.8%	49.2%
149,577	KENOSHA	51,071	21,737	28,338	996	6,601 D	42.6%	55.5%	43.4%	56.6%
20,187	KEWAUNEE	9,045	4,479	4,354	212	125 R	49.5%	48.1%	50.7%	49.3%
107,120	LA CROSSE	43,010	17,235	24,663	1,112	7,428 D	40.1%	57.3%	41.1%	58.9%
16,137	LAFAYETTE	5,846	2,405	3,344	97	939 D	41.1%	57.2%	41.8%	58.2%
20,740	LANGLADE	8,591	4,276	4,184	131	92 R	49.8%	48.7%	50.5%	49.5%
29,641	LINCOLN	11,083	4,713	6,019	351	1,306 D	42.5%	54.3%	43.9%	56.1%
82,887	MANITOWOC	32,463	16,154	15,736	573	418 R	49.8%	48.5%	50.7%	49.3%
125,834	MARATHON	49,152	22,186	25,836	1,130	3,650 D	45.1%	52.6%	46.2%	53.8%
43,384	MARINETTE	17,037	8,455	8,408	174	47 R	49.6%	49.4%	50.1%	49.9%
15,832	MARQUETTE	6,108	3,095	2,879	134	216 R	50.7%	47.1%	51.8%	48.2%
4,562	MENOMINEE	1,073	180	886	7	706 D	16.8%	82.6%	16.9%	83.1%
940,164	MILWAUKEE	324,068	118,949	199,536	5,583	80,587 D	36.7%	61.6%	37.3%	62.7%
40,899	MONROE	13,446	6,517	6,556	373	39 D	48.5%	48.8%	49.9%	50.1%
35,634	OCONTO	14,378	7,497	6,639	242	858 R	52.1%	46.2%	53.0%	47.0%
36,776	ONEIDA	16,203	7,425	8,372	406	947 D	45.8%	51.7%	47.0%	53.0%
160,971	OUTAGAMIE	69,737	33,511	34,901	1,325	1,390 D	48.1%	50.0%	49.0%	51.0%
82,317	OZAUKEE	41,274	25,460	15,229	585	10,231 R	61.7%	36.9%	62.6%	37.4%
7,213	PEPIN	2,921	1,256	1,627	38	371 D	43.0%	55.7%	43.6%	56.4%
36,804	PIERCE	14,157	6,034	7,829	294	1,795 D	42.6%	55.3%	43.5%	56.5%
41,319	POLK	15,529	7,103	8,128	298	1,025 D	45.7%	52.3%	46.6%	53.4%
67,182	PORTAGE	28,845	10,206	17,754	885	7,548 D	35.4%	61.5%	36.5%	63.5%
15,822	PRICE	6,412	2,737	3,581	94	844 D	42.7%	55.8%	43.3%	56.7%
188,831	RACINE	71,368	35,286	34,968	1,114	318 R	49.4%	49.0%	50.2%	49.8%
17,924	RICHLAND	6,413	2,814	3,489	110	675 D	43.9%	54.4%	44.6%	55.4%
152,307	ROCK	55,129	20,156	33,774	1,199	13,618 D	36.6%	61.3%	37.4%	62.6%
15,347	RUSK	5,743	2,622	2,968	153	346 D	45.7%	51.7%	46.9%	53.1%
63,155	ST. CROIX	26,896	13,117	13,392	387	275 D	48.8%	49.8%	49.5%	50.5%
55,225	SAUK	21,938	9,148	12,232	558	3,084 D	41.7%	55.8%	42.8%	57.2%
16,196	SAWYER	6,283	2,965	3,218	100	253 D	47.2%	51.2%	48.0%	52.0%
40,664	SHAWANO	15,677	8,227	7,236	214	991 R	52.5%	46.2%	53.2%	46.8%
112,646	SHEBOYGAN	47,397	25,257	21,388	752	3,869 R	53.3%	45.1%	54.1%	45.9%

WISCONSIN

GOVERNOR 2006

2000 Census Population	County	Total Vote	Republican	Democratic	Other	Rep.-Dem. Plurality	Percentage			
							Total Vote		Major Vote	
							Rep.	Dem.	Rep.	Dem.
19,680	TAYLOR	7,258	3,551	3,506	201	45 R	48.9%	48.3%	50.3%	49.7%
27,010	TREMPEALEAU	9,488	3,725	5,557	206	1,832 D	39.3%	58.6%	40.1%	59.9%
28,056	VERNON	10,523	4,240	6,034	249	1,794 D	40.3%	57.3%	41.3%	58.7%
21,033	VILAS	10,630	5,623	4,799	208	824 R	52.9%	45.1%	54.0%	46.0%
93,759	WALWORTH	33,714	18,781	14,154	779	4,627 R	55.7%	42.0%	57.0%	43.0%
16,036	WASHBURN	6,551	3,135	3,323	93	188 D	47.9%	50.7%	48.5%	51.5%
117,493	WASHINGTON	53,325	35,262	17,219	844	18,043 R	66.1%	32.3%	67.2%	32.8%
360,767	WAUKESHA	176,114	112,243	61,402	2,469	50,841 R	63.7%	34.9%	64.6%	35.4%
51,731	WAUPACA	19,380	10,296	8,767	317	1,529 R	53.1%	45.2%	54.0%	46.0%
23,154	WAUSHARA	8,926	4,590	4,155	181	435 R	51.4%	46.5%	52.5%	47.5%
156,763	WINNEBAGO	64,892	30,629	32,765	1,498	2,136 D	47.2%	50.5%	48.3%	51.7%
75,555	WOOD	29,559	12,711	16,043	805	3,332 D	43.0%	54.3%	44.2%	55.8%
5,363,675	TOTAL	2,161,700	979,427	1,139,115	43,158	159,688 D	45.3%	52.7%	46.2%	53.8%

WISCONSIN

SENATOR 2006

2000 Census Population	County	Total Vote	Republican	Democratic	Other	Rep.-Dem. Plurality	Percentage			
							Total Vote		Major Vote	
							Rep.	Dem.	Rep.	Dem.
18,643	ADAMS	7,762	1,979	5,635	148	3,656 D	25.5%	72.6%	26.0%	74.0%
16,866	ASHLAND	6,128	1,327	4,579	222	3,252 D	21.7%	74.7%	22.5%	77.5%
44,963	BARRON	16,180	5,120	10,467	593	5,347 D	31.6%	64.7%	32.8%	67.2%
15,013	BAYFIELD	7,180	1,778	5,113	289	3,335 D	24.8%	71.2%	25.8%	74.2%
226,778	BROWN	92,664	26,742	63,614	2,308	36,872 D	28.9%	68.7%	29.6%	70.4%
13,804	BUFFALO	5,233	1,277	3,848	108	2,571 D	24.4%	73.5%	24.9%	75.1%
15,674	BURNETT	6,037	2,356	3,543	138	1,187 D	39.0%	58.7%	39.9%	60.1%
40,631	CALUMET	19,228	6,170	12,599	459	6,429 D	32.1%	65.5%	32.9%	67.1%
55,195	CHIPPEWA	21,727	5,762	15,305	660	9,543 D	26.5%	70.4%	27.4%	72.6%
33,557	CLARK	11,235	2,981	7,940	314	4,959 D	26.5%	70.7%	27.3%	72.7%
52,468	COLUMBIA	21,998	6,119	15,206	673	9,087 D	27.8%	69.1%	28.7%	71.3%
17,243	CRAWFORD	6,177	1,355	4,658	164	3,303 D	21.9%	75.4%	22.5%	77.5%
426,526	DANE	212,294	36,047	163,151	13,096	127,104 D	17.0%	76.9%	18.1%	81.9%
85,897	DODGE	30,843	11,604	18,323	916	6,719 D	37.6%	59.4%	38.8%	61.2%
27,961	DOOR	14,264	3,728	10,009	527	6,281 D	26.1%	70.2%	27.1%	72.9%
43,287	DOUGLAS	16,187	3,876	11,736	575	7,860 D	23.9%	72.5%	24.8%	75.2%
39,858	DUNN	14,508	4,235	9,783	490	5,548 D	29.2%	67.4%	30.2%	69.8%
93,142	EAU CLAIRE	38,612	9,912	27,553	1,147	17,641 D	25.7%	71.4%	26.5%	73.5%
5,088	FLORENCE	1,853	776	1,053	24	277 D	41.9%	56.8%	42.4%	57.6%
97,296	FOND DU LAC	37,807	13,863	22,952	992	9,089 D	36.7%	60.7%	37.7%	62.3%
10,024	FOREST	3,460	846	2,574	40	1,728 D	24.5%	74.4%	24.7%	75.3%
49,597	GRANT	16,583	4,540	11,622	421	7,082 D	27.4%	70.1%	28.1%	71.9%
33,647	GREEN	13,188	3,020	9,698	470	6,678 D	22.9%	73.5%	23.7%	76.3%
19,105	GREEN LAKE	7,889	2,956	4,710	223	1,754 D	37.5%	59.7%	38.6%	61.4%
22,780	IOWA	8,872	1,795	6,870	207	5,075 D	20.2%	77.4%	20.7%	79.3%
6,861	IRON	2,725	828	1,855	42	1,027 D	30.4%	68.1%	30.9%	69.1%
19,100	JACKSON	6,854	1,557	5,172	125	3,615 D	22.7%	75.5%	23.1%	76.9%
74,021	JEFFERSON	30,732	11,161	18,511	1,060	7,350 D	36.3%	60.2%	37.6%	62.4%
24,316	JUNEAU	8,124	2,649	5,293	182	2,644 D	32.6%	65.2%	33.4%	66.6%
149,577	KENOSHA	50,312	13,399	35,072	1,841	21,673 D	26.6%	69.7%	27.6%	72.4%
20,187	KEWAUNEE	8,972	2,087	6,558	327	4,471 D	23.3%	73.1%	24.1%	75.9%
107,120	LA CROSSE	42,752	11,151	30,331	1,270	19,180 D	26.1%	70.9%	26.9%	73.1%
16,137	LAFAYETTE	5,792	1,414	4,275	103	2,861 D	24.4%	73.8%	24.9%	75.1%
20,740	LANGLADE	8,446	2,305	6,008	133	3,703 D	27.3%	71.1%	27.7%	72.3%
29,641	LINCOLN	11,014	2,785	7,882	347	5,097 D	25.3%	71.6%	26.1%	73.9%

WISCONSIN

SENATOR 2006

2000 Census Population	County	Total Vote	Republican	Democratic	Other	Rep.-Dem. Plurality	Percentage Total Vote Rep.	Dem.	Major Vote Rep.	Dem.
82,887	MANITOWOC	31,939	8,809	22,357	773	13,548 D	27.6%	70.0%	28.3%	71.7%
125,834	MARATHON	48,999	13,727	33,856	1,416	20,129 D	28.0%	69.1%	28.8%	71.2%
43,384	MARINETTE	16,666	5,338	11,078	250	5,740 D	32.0%	66.5%	32.5%	67.5%
15,832	MARQUETTE	6,014	2,022	3,860	132	1,838 D	33.6%	64.2%	34.4%	65.6%
4,562	MENOMINEE	1,039	85	939	15	854 D	8.2%	90.4%	8.3%	91.7%
940,164	MILWAUKEE	318,885	70,997	238,034	9,854	167,037 D	22.3%	74.6%	23.0%	77.0%
40,899	MONROE	13,380	4,182	8,836	362	4,654 D	31.3%	66.0%	32.1%	67.9%
35,634	OCONTO	14,396	4,535	9,552	309	5,017 D	31.5%	66.4%	32.2%	67.8%
36,776	ONEIDA	15,917	4,492	10,997	428	6,505 D	28.2%	69.1%	29.0%	71.0%
160,971	OUTAGAMIE	69,061	21,529	45,696	1,836	24,167 D	31.2%	66.2%	32.0%	68.0%
82,317	OZAUKEE	40,887	18,467	21,239	1,181	2,772 D	45.2%	51.9%	46.5%	53.5%
7,213	PEPIN	2,891	754	2,087	50	1,333 D	26.1%	72.2%	26.5%	73.5%
36,804	PIERCE	14,016	4,634	8,911	471	4,277 D	33.1%	63.6%	34.2%	65.8%
41,319	POLK	15,236	5,647	9,107	482	3,460 D	37.1%	59.8%	38.3%	61.7%
67,182	PORTAGE	28,504	6,323	21,116	1,065	14,793 D	22.2%	74.1%	23.0%	77.0%
15,822	PRICE	6,294	1,697	4,512	85	2,815 D	27.0%	71.7%	27.3%	72.7%
188,831	RACINE	70,686	22,971	45,817	1,898	22,846 D	32.5%	64.8%	33.4%	66.6%
17,924	RICHLAND	6,209	1,867	4,217	125	2,350 D	30.1%	67.9%	30.7%	69.3%
152,307	ROCK	54,879	12,712	40,727	1,440	28,015 D	23.2%	74.2%	23.8%	76.2%
15,347	RUSK	5,670	1,440	4,062	168	2,622 D	25.4%	71.6%	26.2%	73.8%
63,155	ST. CROIX	26,561	10,526	15,102	933	4,576 D	39.6%	56.9%	41.1%	58.9%
55,225	SAUK	21,826	5,318	15,689	819	10,371 D	24.4%	71.9%	25.3%	74.7%
16,196	SAWYER	6,181	2,347	3,693	141	1,346 D	38.0%	59.7%	38.9%	61.1%
40,664	SHAWANO	15,500	5,219	10,002	279	4,783 D	33.7%	64.5%	34.3%	65.7%
112,646	SHEBOYGAN	46,961	16,038	29,789	1,134	13,751 D	34.2%	63.4%	35.0%	65.0%
19,680	TAYLOR	7,256	1,832	5,195	229	3,363 D	25.2%	71.6%	26.1%	73.9%
27,010	TREMPEALEAU	9,371	1,963	7,191	217	5,228 D	20.9%	76.7%	21.4%	78.6%
28,056	VERNON	10,215	2,870	6,999	346	4,129 D	28.1%	68.5%	29.1%	70.9%
21,033	VILAS	10,572	3,711	6,570	291	2,859 D	35.1%	62.1%	36.1%	63.9%
93,759	WALWORTH	33,397	13,101	18,992	1,304	5,891 D	39.2%	56.9%	40.8%	59.2%
16,036	WASHBURN	6,436	2,383	3,912	141	1,529 D	37.0%	60.8%	37.9%	62.1%
117,493	WASHINGTON	52,810	25,013	26,198	1,599	1,185 D	47.4%	49.6%	48.8%	51.2%
360,767	WAUKESHA	174,246	80,807	88,680	4,759	7,873 D	46.4%	50.9%	47.7%	52.3%
51,731	WAUPACA	19,191	6,907	11,802	482	4,895 D	36.0%	61.5%	36.9%	63.1%
23,154	WAUSHARA	8,836	2,991	5,608	237	2,617 D	33.9%	63.5%	34.8%	65.2%
156,763	WINNEBAGO	64,345	19,996	42,266	2,083	22,270 D	31.1%	65.7%	32.1%	67.9%
75,555	WOOD	29,393	7,549	21,028	816	13,479 D	25.7%	71.5%	26.4%	73.6%
5,363,675	TOTAL	2,138,297	630,299	1,439,214	68,784	808,915 D	29.5%	67.3%	30.5%	69.5%

WISCONSIN

HOUSE OF REPRESENTATIVES

CD	Year	Total Vote	Republican		Democratic		Other Vote	Rep.-Dem. Plurality	Percentage			
			Vote	Candidate	Vote	Candidate			Total Vote		Major Vote	
									Rep.	Dem.	Rep.	Dem.
1	2006	257,596	161,320	RYAN, PAUL D.*	95,761	THOMAS, JEFFREY C.	515	65,559 R	62.6%	37.2%	62.8%	37.2%
1	2004	356,976	233,372	RYAN, PAUL D.*	116,250	THOMAS, JEFFREY C.	7,354	117,122 R	65.4%	32.6%	66.7%	33.3%
1	2002	208,613	140,176	RYAN, PAUL D.*	63,895	THOMAS, JEFFREY C.	4,542	76,281 R	67.2%	30.6%	68.7%	31.3%
2	2006	304,688	113,015	MAGNUM, DAVE	191,414	BALDWIN, TAMMY*	259	78,399 D	37.1%	62.8%	37.1%	62.9%
2	2004	397,724	145,810	MAGNUM, DAVE	251,637	BALDWIN, TAMMY*	277	105,827 D	36.7%	63.3%	36.7%	63.3%
2	2002	247,410	83,694	GREER, RON	163,313	BALDWIN, TAMMY*	403	79,619 D	33.8%	66.0%	33.9%	66.1%
3	2006	252,087	88,523	NELSON, PAUL R.	163,322	KIND, RON*	242	74,799 D	35.1%	64.8%	35.1%	64.9%
3	2004	363,008	157,866	SCHULTZ, DALE W.	204,856	KIND, RON*	286	46,990 D	43.5%	56.4%	43.5%	56.5%
3	2002	208,581	69,955	ARNDT, BILL	131,038	KIND, RON*	7,588	61,083 D	33.5%	62.8%	34.8%	65.2%
4	2006	191,742	54,486	RIVERA, PERFECTO	136,735	MOORE, GWEN*	521	82,249 D	28.4%	71.3%	28.5%	71.5%
4	2004	305,142	85,928	BOYLE, GERALD H.	212,382	MOORE, GWEN	6,832	126,454 D	28.2%	69.6%	28.8%	71.2%
4	2002	141,367		—	122,031	KLECZKA, GERALD D.*	19,336	122,031 D		86.3%		100.0%
5	2006	315,180	194,669	SENSENBRENNER, F. JAMES JR.*	112,451	KENNEDY, BRYAN	8,060	82,218 R	61.8%	35.7%	63.4%	36.6%
5	2004	407,291	271,153	SENSENBRENNER, F. JAMES JR.*	129,384	KENNEDY, BRYAN	6,754	141,769 R	66.6%	31.8%	67.7%	32.3%
5	2002	222,012	191,224	SENSENBRENNER, F. JAMES JR.*		—	30,788	191,224 R	86.1%		100.0%	
6	2006	203,557	201,367	PETRI, TOM*		—	2,190	201,367 R	98.9%		100.0%	
6	2004	355,995	238,620	PETRI, TOM*	107,209	HALL, JEF	10,166	131,411 R	67.0%	30.1%	69.0%	31.0%
6	2002	171,161	169,834	PETRI, TOM*		—	1,327	169,834 R	99.2%		100.0%	
7	2006	260,428	91,069	REID, NICK	161,903	OBEY, DAVID R.*	7,456	70,834 D	35.0%	62.2%	36.0%	64.0%
7	2004	281,752		—	241,306	OBEY, DAVID R.*	40,446	241,306 D		85.6%		100.0%
7	2002	227,955	81,518	ROTHBAUER, JOE	146,364	OBEY, DAVID R.*	73	64,846 D	35.8%	64.2%	35.8%	64.2%
8	2006	278,135	135,622	GARD, JOHN	141,570	KAGEN, STEVEN L.	943	5,948 D	48.8%	50.9%	48.9%	51.1%
8	2004	353,725	248,070	GREEN, MARK*	105,513	LE CLAIR, DOTTIE	142	142,557 R	70.1%	29.8%	70.2%	29.8%
8	2002	210,447	152,745	GREEN, MARK*	50,284	BECKER, ANDREW M.	7,418	102,461 R	72.6%	23.9%	75.2%	24.8%
TOTAL	2006	2,063,413	1,040,071		1,003,156		20,186	36,915 R	50.4%	48.6%	50.9%	49.1%
TOTAL	2004	2,821,613	1,380,819		1,368,537		72,257	12,282 R	48.9%	48.5%	50.2%	49.8%
TOTAL	2002	1,637,546	889,146		676,925		71,475	212,221 R	54.3%	41.3%	56.8%	43.2%

An asterisk (*) denotes incumbent.

WISCONSIN

GENERAL AND PRIMARY ELECTIONS

2006 GENERAL ELECTIONS

Governor   Other vote was 40,709 Wisconsin Green (Nelson Eisman); 2,449 scattered write-in.

Senator   Other vote was 42,434 Wisconsin Green (Rae Vogeler); 25,096 Independent (Ben J. Glatzel); 1,254 scattered write-in.

House   Other vote was:

CD 1   515 scattered write-in.
CD 2   259 scattered write-in.
CD 3   242 scattered write-in.
CD 4   521 scattered write-in.
CD 5   4,432 Wisconsin Green (Bob Levis); 3,525 Independent (Robert R. Raymond); 103 scattered write-in.
CD 6   2,190 scattered write-in.
CD 7   7,391 Wisconsin Green (Mike Miles); 65 scattered write-in.
CD 8   943 scattered write-in.

WISCONSIN

GENERAL AND PRIMARY ELECTIONS

2006 PRIMARY ELECTIONS

Primary   September 12, 2006

Note: Wisconsin began introducing statewide voter registration in 2006, but no total was readily available at the time of the September primary.

Primary Type   Open—Any registered voter could participate in the primary of their choice.

Note: An asterisk (*) denotes incumbent.

	REPUBLICAN PRIMARIES			DEMOCRATIC PRIMARIES		
Governor	Mark Green	233,216	99.7%	James E. Doyle*	318,523	99.3%
	Scattered write-in	804	0.3%	Scattered write-in	2,259	0.7%
	TOTAL	*234,020*		*TOTAL*	*320,782*	
Senator	Robert Gerald Lorge	194,633	99.7%	Herb Kohl*	308,178	85.7%
	Scattered write-in	530	0.3%	Ben Masel	51,245	14.2%
				Scattered write-in	335	0.1%
	TOTAL	*195,163*		*TOTAL*	*359,758*	
Congressional District 1	Paul D. Ryan*	22,734	99.9%	Jeffrey C. Thomas	7,111	25.2%
	Scattered write-in	33	0.1%	Mike Hebert	6,206	22.0%
				Ruth Santa Cruz Bradley	5,277	18.7%
				Steven Herr	5,205	18.5%
				Don Hall	4,306	15.3%
				Scattered write-in	79	0.3%
	TOTAL	*22,767*		*TOTAL*	*28,184*	
Congressional District 2	Dave Magnum	19,219	99.8%	Tammy Baldwin*	53,656	99.6%
	Scattered write-in	32	0.2%	Scattered write-in	209	0.4%
	TOTAL	*19,251*		*TOTAL*	*53,865*	
Congressional District 3	Paul R. Nelson	22,170	99.9%	Ron Kind*	39,765	83.7%
	Scattered write-in	19	0.1%	Chip De Nure	7,744	16.3%
				Scattered write-in	20	
	TOTAL	*22,189*		*TOTAL*	*47,529*	
Congressional District 4	Perfecto Rivera	5,614	99.2%	Gwen Moore*	31,042	97.4%
	Scattered write-in	46	0.8%	Scattered write-in	823	2.6%
	TOTAL	*5,660*		*TOTAL*	*31,865*	
Congressional District 5	F. James Sensenbrenner Jr.*	46,686	99.8%	Bryan Kennedy	26,178	99.7%
	Scattered write-in	92	0.2%	Scattered write-in	86	0.3%
	TOTAL	*46,778*		*TOTAL*	*26,264*	
Congressional District 6	Tom Petri*	34,527	99.8%	*No Democratic candidate filed for the primary. There were 170 scattered write-in votes.*		
	Scattered write-in	80	0.2%			
	TOTAL	*34,607*				
Congressional District 7	Nick Reid	12,742	58.8%	David R. Obey*	45,887	99.7%
	Jeff Tyberg	8,901	41.1%	Scattered write-in	130	0.3%
	Scattered write-in	9				
	TOTAL	*21,652*		*TOTAL*	*46,017*	
Congressional District 8	John Gard	39,451	68.2%	Steven L. Kagen	25,623	47.6%
	Terri McCormick	18,424	31.8%	Jamie Wall	15,427	28.7%
	Scattered write-in	12		Nancy Nusbaum	12,731	23.7%
				Scattered write-in	16	
	TOTAL	*57,887*		*TOTAL*	*53,797*	

WYOMING

One member At Large

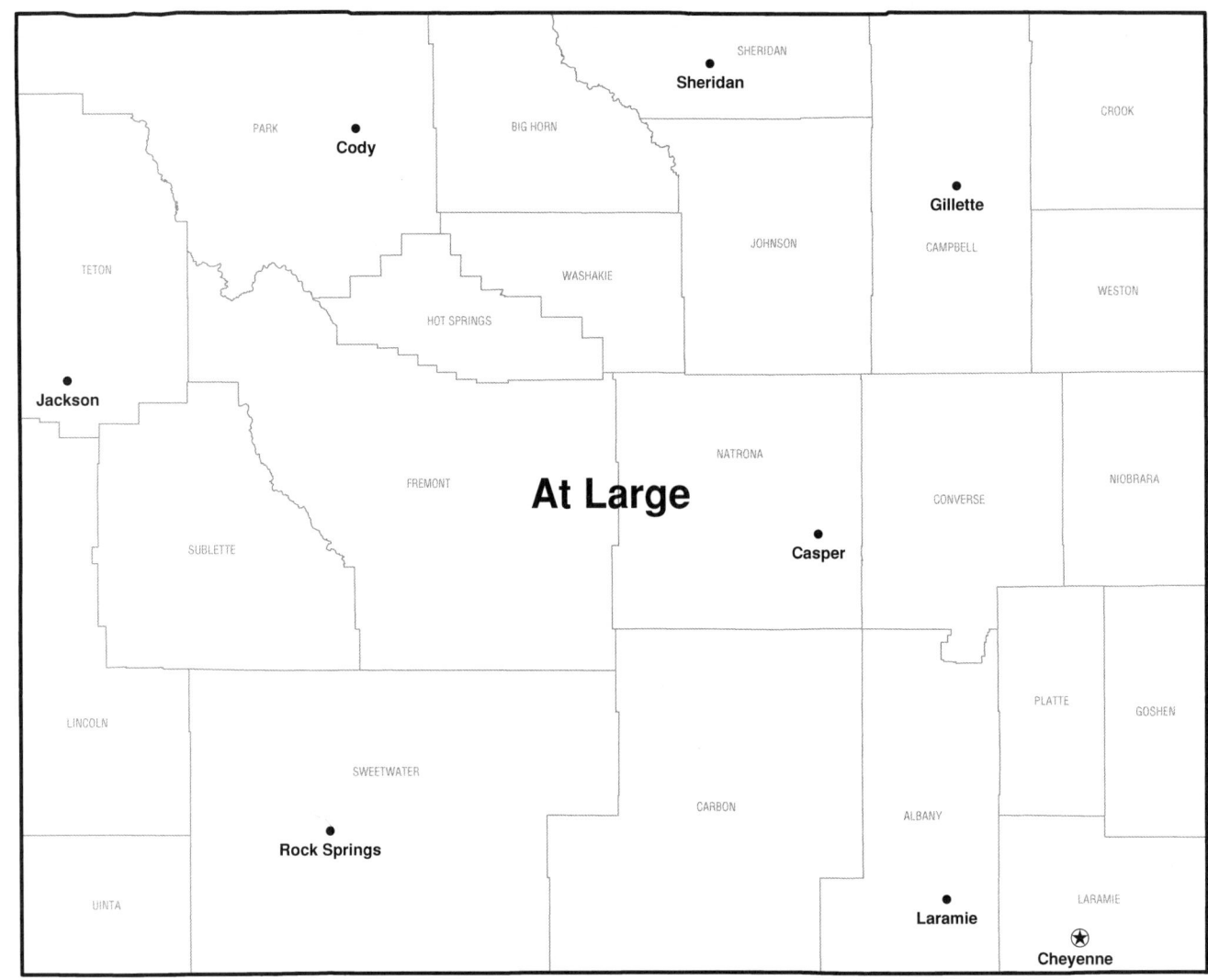

WYOMING

GOVERNOR
Dave Freudenthal (D). Reelected 2006 to a four-year term. Previously elected 2002.

SENATORS (1 Republican, 1 Vacancy)
John Barrasso (R). Appointed on June 22, 2007, to fill the vacancy created by the death of Craig Thomas (R) on June 4, 2007. Barrasso was sworn into office on June 23, 2007. Craig Thomas (R) died June 4, 2007. He had been reelected in 2006 to a six-year term after first winning the seat in 1994.

Michael B. Enzi (R). Reelected 2002 to a six-year term. Previously elected 1996.

REPRESENTATIVE (1 Republican)
At Large. Barbara Cubin (R)

POSTWAR VOTE FOR PRESIDENT

Year	Total Vote	Republican Vote	Republican Candidate	Democratic Vote	Democratic Candidate	Other Vote	Plurality	Total Vote Rep.	Total Vote Dem.	Major Vote Rep.	Major Vote Dem.
2004	243,428	167,629	Bush, George W.	70,776	Kerry, John	5,023	96,853 R	68.9%	29.1%	70.3%	29.7%
2000**	218,351	147,947	Bush, George W.	60,481	Gore, Al	9,923	87,466 R	67.8%	27.7%	71.0%	29.0%
1996**	211,571	105,388	Dole, Bob	77,934	Clinton, Bill	28,249	27,454 R	49.8%	36.8%	57.5%	42.5%
1992**	200,598	79,347	Bush, George	68,160	Clinton, Bill	53,091	11,187 R	39.6%	34.0%	53.8%	46.2%
1988	176,551	106,867	Bush, George	67,113	Dukakis, Michael S.	2,571	39,754 R	60.5%	38.0%	61.4%	38.6%
1984	188,968	133,241	Reagan, Ronald	53,370	Mondale, Walter F.	2,357	79,871 R	70.5%	28.2%	71.4%	28.6%
1980**	176,713	110,700	Reagan, Ronald	49,427	Carter, Jimmy	16,586	61,273 R	62.6%	28.0%	69.1%	30.9%
1976	156,343	92,717	Ford, Gerald R.	62,239	Carter, Jimmy	1,387	30,478 R	59.3%	39.8%	59.8%	40.2%
1972	145,570	100,464	Nixon, Richard M.	44,358	McGovern, George S.	748	56,106 R	69.0%	30.5%	69.4%	30.6%
1968**	127,205	70,927	Nixon, Richard M.	45,173	Humphrey, Hubert H.	11,105	25,754 R	55.8%	35.5%	61.1%	38.9%
1964	142,716	61,998	Goldwater, Barry M.	80,718	Johnson, Lyndon B.		18,720 D	43.4%	56.6%	43.4%	56.6%
1960	140,782	77,451	Nixon, Richard M.	63,331	Kennedy, John F.		14,120 R	55.0%	45.0%	55.0%	45.0%
1956	124,127	74,573	Eisenhower, Dwight D.	49,554	Stevenson, Adlai E.		25,019 R	60.1%	39.9%	60.1%	39.9%
1952	129,253	81,049	Eisenhower, Dwight D.	47,934	Stevenson, Adlai E.	270	33,115 R	62.7%	37.1%	62.8%	37.2%
1948	101,425	47,947	Dewey, Thomas E.	52,354	Truman, Harry S.	1,124	4,407 D	47.3%	51.6%	47.8%	52.2%

**In past elections, the other vote included: 2000 - 4,625 Green (Ralph Nader); 1996 - 25,928 Reform (Ross Perot); 1992 - 51,263 Independent (Ross Perot); 1980 - 12,072 Independent (John Anderson); 1968 - 11,105 American Independent (George Wallace).

WYOMING

POSTWAR VOTE FOR GOVERNOR

Year	Total Vote	Republican Vote	Republican Candidate	Democratic Vote	Democratic Candidate	Other Vote	Rep.-Dem. Plurality	Total Vote Rep.	Total Vote Dem.	Major Vote Rep.	Major Vote Dem.
2006	193,892	58,100	Hunkins, Ray	135,516	Freudenthal, Dave	276	77,416 D	30.0%	69.9%	30.0%	70.0%
2002	185,459	88,873	Bebout, Eli	92,662	Freudenthal, Dave	3,924	3,789 D	47.9%	50.0%	49.0%	51.0%
1998	174,888	97,235	Geringer, Jim	70,754	Vinich, John P.	6,899	26,481 R	55.6%	40.5%	57.9%	42.1%
1994	200,990	118,016	Geringer, Jim	80,747	Karpan, Kathy	2,227	37,269 R	58.7%	40.2%	59.4%	40.6%
1990	160,109	55,471	Mead, Mary	104,638	Sullivan, Mike		49,167 D	34.6%	65.4%	34.6%	65.4%
1986	164,720	75,841	Simpson, Peter	88,879	Sullivan, Mike		13,038 D	46.0%	54.0%	46.0%	54.0%
1982	168,555	62,128	Morton, Warren A.	106,427	Herschler, Ed		44,299 D	36.9%	63.1%	36.9%	63.1%
1978	137,567	67,595	Ostlund, John C.	69,972	Herschler, Ed		2,377 D	49.1%	50.9%	49.1%	50.9%
1974	128,386	56,645	Jones, Dick	71,741	Herschler, Ed		15,096 D	44.1%	55.9%	44.1%	55.9%
1970	118,257	74,249	Hathaway, Stan	44,008	Rooney, John J.		30,241 R	62.8%	37.2%	62.8%	37.2%
1966	120,873	65,624	Hathaway, Stan	55,249	Wilkerson, Ernest		10,375 R	54.3%	45.7%	54.3%	45.7%
1962	119,268	64,970	Hansen, Clifford P.	54,298	Gage, Jack R.		10,672 R	54.5%	45.5%	54.5%	45.5%
1958	112,537	52,488	Simpson, Milward L.	55,070	Hickey, J. J.	4,979	2,582 D	46.6%	48.9%	48.8%	51.2%
1954	111,438	56,275	Simpson, Milward L.	55,163	Jack, William		1,112 R	50.5%	49.5%	50.5%	49.5%
1950	96,959	54,441	Barrett, Frank A.	42,518	McIntyre, John J.		11,923 R	56.1%	43.9%	56.1%	43.9%
1946	81,353	38,333	Wright, Earl	43,020	Hunt, Lester C.		4,687 D	47.1%	52.9%	47.1%	52.9%

POSTWAR VOTE FOR SENATOR

Year	Total Vote	Republican Vote	Republican Candidate	Democratic Vote	Democratic Candidate	Other Vote	Rep.-Dem. Plurality	Total Vote Rep.	Total Vote Dem.	Major Vote Rep.	Major Vote Dem.
2006	193,136	135,174	Thomas, Craig	57,671	Groutage, Dale	291	77,503 R	70.0%	29.9%	70.1%	29.9%
2002	183,280	133,710	Enzi, Michael B.	49,570	Corcoran, Joyce Jansa		84,140 R	73.0%	27.0%	73.0%	27.0%
2000	213,659	157,622	Thomas, Craig	47,087	Logan, Mel	8,950	110,535 R	73.8%	22.0%	77.0%	23.0%
1996	211,077	114,116	Enzi, Michael B.	89,103	Karpan, Kathy	7,858	25,013 R	54.1%	42.2%	56.2%	43.8%
1994	201,710	118,754	Thomas, Craig	79,287	Sullivan, Mike	3,669	39,467 R	58.9%	39.3%	60.0%	40.0%
1990	157,632	100,784	Simpson, Alan K.	56,848	Helling, Kathy		43,936 R	63.9%	36.1%	63.9%	36.1%
1988	180,964	91,143	Wallop, Malcolm	89,821	Vinich, John P.		1,322 R	50.4%	49.6%	50.4%	49.6%
1984	186,898	146,373	Simpson, Alan K.	40,525	Ryan, Victor A.		105,848 R	78.3%	21.7%	78.3%	21.7%
1982	167,191	94,725	Wallop, Malcolm	72,466	McDaniel, Rodger		22,259 R	56.7%	43.3%	56.7%	43.3%
1978	133,364	82,908	Simpson, Alan K.	50,456	Whitaker, Raymond B.		32,452 R	62.2%	37.8%	62.2%	37.8%
1976	155,368	84,810	Wallop, Malcolm	70,558	McGee, Gale		14,252 R	54.6%	45.4%	54.6%	45.4%
1972	142,067	101,314	Hansen, Clifford P.	40,753	Vinich, Mike		60,561 R	71.3%	28.7%	71.3%	28.7%
1970	120,486	53,279	Wold, John S.	67,207	McGee, Gale		13,928 D	44.2%	55.8%	44.2%	55.8%
1966	122,689	63,548	Hansen, Clifford P.	59,141	Roncalio, Teno		4,407 R	51.8%	48.2%	51.8%	48.2%
1964	141,670	65,185	Wold, John S.	76,485	McGee, Gale		11,300 D	46.0%	54.0%	46.0%	54.0%
1962S	119,372	69,043	Simpson, Milward L.	50,329	Hickey, J. J.		18,714 R	57.8%	42.2%	57.8%	42.2%
1960	138,550	78,103	Thomson, E. Keith	60,447	Whitaker, Ray		17,656 R	56.4%	43.6%	56.4%	43.6%
1958	114,157	56,122	Barrett, Frank A.	58,035	McGee, Gale		1,913 D	49.2%	50.8%	49.2%	50.8%
1954	112,252	54,407	Harrison, William H.	57,845	O'Mahoney, Joseph C.		3,438 D	48.5%	51.5%	48.5%	51.5%
1952	130,097	67,176	Barrett, Frank A.	62,921	O'Mahoney, Joseph C.		4,255 R	51.6%	48.4%	51.6%	48.4%
1948	101,480	43,527	Robertson, Edward V.	57,953	Hunt, Lester C.		14,426 D	42.9%	57.1%	42.9%	57.1%
1946	81,557	35,714	Henderson, Harry B.	45,843	O'Mahoney, Joseph C.		10,129 D	43.8%	56.2%	43.8%	56.2%

The 1962 election was for a short term to fill a vacancy.

WYOMING

GOVERNOR 2006

2000 Census Population	County	Total Vote	Republican	Democratic	Other	Rep.-Dem. Plurality	Percentage Total Vote Rep.	Dem.	Major Vote Rep.	Dem.
32,014	ALBANY	11,925	2,425	9,472	28	7,047 D	20.3%	79.4%	20.4%	79.6%
11,461	BIG HORN	4,557	1,695	2,860	2	1,165 D	37.2%	62.8%	37.2%	62.8%
33,698	CAMPBELL	10,923	3,985	6,926	12	2,941 D	36.5%	63.4%	36.5%	63.5%
15,639	CARBON	5,733	1,921	3,803	9	1,882 D	33.5%	66.3%	33.6%	66.4%
12,052	CONVERSE	5,068	1,756	3,307	5	1,551 D	34.6%	65.3%	34.7%	65.3%
5,887	CROOK	2,906	1,207	1,694	5	487 D	41.5%	58.3%	41.6%	58.4%
35,804	FREMONT	13,791	4,246	9,523	22	5,277 D	30.8%	69.1%	30.8%	69.2%
12,538	GOSHEN	4,836	1,592	3,242	2	1,650 D	32.9%	67.0%	32.9%	67.1%
4,882	HOT SPRINGS	2,299	558	1,738	3	1,180 D	24.3%	75.6%	24.3%	75.7%
7,075	JOHNSON	3,416	1,159	2,256	1	1,097 D	33.9%	66.0%	33.9%	66.1%
81,607	LARAMIE	31,357	8,300	23,001	56	14,701 D	26.5%	73.4%	26.5%	73.5%
14,573	LINCOLN	6,171	2,819	3,348	4	529 D	45.7%	54.3%	45.7%	54.3%
66,533	NATRONA	25,599	6,667	18,894	38	12,227 D	26.0%	73.8%	26.1%	73.9%
2,407	NIOBRARA	1,058	458	596	4	138 D	43.3%	56.3%	43.5%	56.5%
25,786	PARK	11,721	4,212	7,482	27	3,270 D	35.9%	63.8%	36.0%	64.0%
8,807	PLATTE	3,977	1,362	2,607	8	1,245 D	34.2%	65.6%	34.3%	65.7%
26,560	SHERIDAN	11,525	3,530	7,981	14	4,451 D	30.6%	69.2%	30.7%	69.3%
5,920	SUBLETTE	2,877	1,143	1,733	1	590 D	39.7%	60.2%	39.7%	60.3%
37,613	SWEETWATER	12,784	3,045	9,730	9	6,685 D	23.8%	76.1%	23.8%	76.2%
18,251	TETON	8,984	1,730	7,247	7	5,517 D	19.3%	80.7%	19.3%	80.7%
19,742	UINTA	6,283	2,317	3,959	7	1,642 D	36.9%	63.0%	36.9%	63.1%
8,289	WASHAKIE	3,436	945	2,482	9	1,537 D	27.5%	72.2%	27.6%	72.4%
6,644	WESTON	2,666	1,028	1,635	3	607 D	38.6%	61.3%	38.6%	61.4%
493,782	TOTAL	193,892	58,100	135,516	276	77,416 D	30.0%	69.9%	30.0%	70.0%

SENATOR 2006

2000 Census Population	County	Total Vote	Republican	Democratic	Other	Rep.-Dem. Plurality	Percentage Total Vote Rep.	Dem.	Major Vote Rep.	Dem.
32,014	ALBANY	11,827	6,934	4,841	52	2,093 R	58.6%	40.9%	58.9%	41.1%
11,461	BIG HORN	4,552	3,714	831	7	2,883 R	81.6%	18.3%	81.7%	18.3%
33,698	CAMPBELL	10,916	8,775	2,139	2	6,636 R	80.4%	19.6%	80.4%	19.6%
15,639	CARBON	5,730	3,831	1,892	7	1,939 R	66.9%	33.0%	66.9%	33.1%
12,052	CONVERSE	5,051	3,954	1,093	4	2,861 R	78.3%	21.6%	78.3%	21.7%
5,887	CROOK	2,900	2,372	524	4	1,848 R	81.8%	18.1%	81.9%	18.1%
35,804	FREMONT	13,779	8,945	4,811	23	4,134 R	64.9%	34.9%	65.0%	35.0%
12,538	GOSHEN	4,812	3,717	1,094	1	2,623 R	77.2%	22.7%	77.3%	22.7%
4,882	HOT SPRINGS	2,280	1,679	597	4	1,082 R	73.6%	26.2%	73.8%	26.2%
7,075	JOHNSON	3,395	2,766	624	5	2,142 R	81.5%	18.4%	81.6%	18.4%
81,607	LARAMIE	31,242	20,504	10,699	39	9,805 R	65.6%	34.2%	65.7%	34.3%
14,573	LINCOLN	6,169	4,595	1,567	7	3,028 R	74.5%	25.4%	74.6%	25.4%
66,533	NATRONA	25,522	17,888	7,594	40	10,294 R	70.1%	29.8%	70.2%	29.8%
2,407	NIOBRARA	1,055	874	179	2	695 R	82.8%	17.0%	83.0%	17.0%
25,786	PARK	11,644	9,325	2,293	26	7,032 R	80.1%	19.7%	80.3%	19.7%
8,807	PLATTE	3,963	2,852	1,108	3	1,744 R	72.0%	28.0%	72.0%	28.0%
26,560	SHERIDAN	11,457	8,013	3,425	19	4,588 R	69.9%	29.9%	70.1%	29.9%
5,920	SUBLETTE	2,877	2,272	603	2	1,669 R	79.0%	21.0%	79.0%	21.0%
37,613	SWEETWATER	12,774	8,004	4,759	11	3,245 R	62.7%	37.3%	62.7%	37.3%
18,251	TETON	8,822	4,943	3,863	16	1,080 R	56.0%	43.8%	56.1%	43.9%
19,742	UINTA	6,285	4,459	1,821	5	2,638 R	70.9%	29.0%	71.0%	29.0%
8,289	WASHAKIE	3,427	2,613	806	8	1,807 R	76.2%	23.5%	76.4%	23.6%
6,644	WESTON	2,657	2,145	508	4	1,637 R	80.7%	19.1%	80.9%	19.1%
493,782	TOTAL	193,136	135,174	57,671	291	77,503 R	70.0%	29.9%	70.1%	29.9%

WYOMING

HOUSE OF REPRESENTATIVES

| | | | Republican | | Democratic | | | | Percentage | | | |
| | | Total | | | | | Other | Rep.-Dem. | Total Vote | | Major Vote | |
CD	Year	Vote	Vote	Candidate	Vote	Candidate	Vote	Plurality	Rep.	Dem.	Rep.	Dem.
AL	2006	193,369	93,336	CUBIN, BARBARA*	92,324	TRAUNER, GARY	7,709	1,012 R	48.3%	47.7%	50.3%	49.7%
AL	2004	239,034	132,107	CUBIN, BARBARA*	99,989	LADD, TED	6,938	32,118 R	55.3%	41.8%	56.9%	43.1%
AL	2002	182,152	110,229	CUBIN, BARBARA*	65,961	AKIN, RON	5,962	44,268 R	60.5%	36.2%	62.6%	37.4%
AL	2000	212,312	141,848	CUBIN, BARBARA*	60,638	GREEN, MICHAEL ALLEN	9,826	81,210 R	66.8%	28.6%	70.1%	29.9%
AL	1998	174,219	100,687	CUBIN, BARBARA*	67,399	FARRIS, SCOTT	6,133	33,288 R	57.8%	38.7%	59.9%	40.1%
AL	1996	209,983	116,004	CUBIN, BARBARA*	85,724	MAXFIELD, PETE	8,255	30,280 R	55.2%	40.8%	57.5%	42.5%
AL	1994	196,197	104,426	CUBIN, BARBARA	81,022	SCHUSTER, BOB	10,749	23,404 R	53.2%	41.3%	56.3%	43.7%
AL	1992	196,977	113,882	THOMAS, CRAIG*	77,418	HERSCHLER, JON	5,677	36,464 R	57.8%	39.3%	59.5%	40.5%
AL	1990	158,055	87,078	THOMAS, CRAIG*	70,977	MAXFIELD, PETE		16,101 R	55.1%	44.9%	55.1%	44.9%
AL	1988	177,651	118,350	CHENEY, RICHARD*	56,527	SHARRATT, BRYAN	2,774	61,823 R	66.6%	31.8%	67.7%	32.3%
AL	1986	159,787	111,007	CHENEY, RICHARD*	48,780	GILMORE, RICK		62,227 R	69.5%	30.5%	69.5%	30.5%
AL	1984	187,904	138,234	CHENEY, RICHARD*	45,857	MCFADDEN, HUGH B.	3,813	92,377 R	73.6%	24.4%	75.1%	24.9%
AL	1982	159,277	113,236	CHENEY, RICHARD*	46,041	HOMMEL, THEODORE H.		67,195 R	71.1%	28.9%	71.1%	28.9%
AL	1980	169,699	116,361	CHENEY, RICHARD*	53,338	ROGERS, JIM		63,023 R	68.6%	31.4%	68.6%	31.4%
AL	1978	129,377	75,855	CHENEY, RICHARD	53,522	BAGLEY, BILL		22,333 R	58.6%	41.4%	58.6%	41.4%
AL	1976	151,868	66,147	HART, LARRY	85,721	RONCALIO, TENO*		19,574 D	43.6%	56.4%	43.6%	56.4%
AL	1974	126,933	57,499	STROOK, TOM	69,434	RONCALIO, TENO*		11,935 D	45.3%	54.7%	45.3%	54.7%
AL	1972	146,299	70,667	KIDD, WILLIAM	75,632	RONCALIO, TENO*		4,965 D	48.3%	51.7%	48.3%	51.7%
AL	1970	116,304	57,848	ROBERTS, HARRY	58,456	RONCALIO, TENO		608 D	49.7%	50.3%	49.7%	50.3%
AL	1968	123,313	77,363	WOLD, JOHN S.	45,950	LINFORD, VELMA		31,413 R	62.7%	37.3%	62.7%	37.3%
AL	1966	119,426	62,984	HARRISON, WILLIAM H.	56,442	CHRISTIAN, AL		6,542 R	52.7%	47.3%	52.7%	47.3%
AL	1964	139,175	68,482	HARRISON, WILLIAM H.*	70,693	RONCALIO, TENO		2,211 D	49.2%	50.8%	49.2%	50.8%
AL	1962	116,474	71,489	HARRISON, WILLIAM H.*	44,985	MANKUS, LOUIS A.		26,504 R	61.4%	38.6%	61.4%	38.6%
AL	1960	134,331	70,241	HARRISON, WILLIAM H.	64,090	ARMSTRONG, H. T.		6,151 R	52.3%	47.7%	52.3%	47.7%
AL	1958	111,780	59,894	THOMSON, E. KEITH*	51,886	WHITAKER, RAY		8,008 R	53.6%	46.4%	53.6%	46.4%
AL	1956	120,128	69,903	THOMSON, E. KEITH*	50,225	O'CALLAGHAN, JERRY		19,678 R	58.2%	41.8%	58.2%	41.8%
AL	1954	108,771	61,111	THOMSON, E. KEITH	47,660	TULLY, SAM		13,451 R	56.2%	43.8%	56.2%	43.8%
AL	1952	126,720	76,161	HARRISON, WILLIAM H.*	50,559	ROSE, ROBERT R.		25,602 R	60.1%	39.9%	60.1%	39.9%
AL	1950	93,348	50,865	HARRISON, WILLIAM H.	42,483	CLARK, JOHN B.		8,382 R	54.5%	45.5%	54.5%	45.5%
AL	1948	97,464	50,218	BARRETT, FRANK A.*	47,246	FLANNERY, L. G.		2,972 R	51.5%	48.5%	51.5%	48.5%
AL	1946	79,438	44,482	BARRETT, FRANK A.*	34,956	MCINTYRE, JOHN J.		9,526 R	56.0%	44.0%	56.0%	44.0%

An asterisk (*) denotes incumbent.

WYOMING

GENERAL AND PRIMARY ELECTIONS

2006 GENERAL ELECTIONS

Governor Other vote was 276 scattered write-in.

Senator Other vote was 291 scattered write-in.

House Other vote was:

At Large 7,481 Libertarian (Thomas R. Rankin); 228 scattered write-in.

2006 PRIMARY ELECTIONS

Primary August 22, 2006 **Registration**
(as of August 21, 2006)

Republican	157,936
Democratic	65,837
Libertarian	434
Other	33,508
TOTAL	257,715

WYOMING

GENERAL AND PRIMARY ELECTIONS

Primary Type   Only registered Democrats and Republicans could vote in their party's primary, although on primary day any new voter could register with the party of their choice and any previously registered voter could participate in another party's primary by changing their registration to that party.

Note: An asterisk (*) denotes incumbent.

	REPUBLICAN PRIMARIES			DEMOCRATIC PRIMARIES		
Governor	Ray Hunkins	51,803	74.6%	Dave Freudenthal*	26,550	89.7%
	John H. Self	17,598	25.4%	Al Hamburg	3,062	10.3%
	TOTAL	69,401		TOTAL	29,612	
Senator	Craig Thomas*	78,211	100.0%	Dale Groutage	24,924	100.0%
House At Large	Barbara Cubin*	50,004	60.0%	Gary Trauner	25,914	100.0%
	Bill Winney	33,287	40.0%			
	TOTAL	83,291